The Handbook of Internet Studies

Handbooks in Communication and Media

This series aims to provide theoretically ambitious but accessible volumes devoted to the major fields and subfields within communication and media studies. Each volume sets out to ground and orientate the student through a broad range of specially commissioned chapters, while also providing the more experienced scholar and teacher with a convenient and comprehensive overview of the latest trends and critical directions.

The Handbook of Children, Media, and Development, *edited by Sandra L. Calvert and Barbara J. Wilson*

The Handbook of Crisis Communication, *edited by W. Timothy Coombs and Sherry J. Holladay*

The Handbook of Internet Studies, *edited by Mia Consalvo and Charles Ess*

The Handbook of Rhetoric and Public Address, *edited by Shawn J. Parry-Giles and J. Michael Hogan*

The Handbook of Critical Intercultural Communication, *edited by Thomas K. Nakayama and Rona Tamiko Halualani*

The Handbook of Global Communication and Media Ethics, *edited by Robert S. Fortner and P. Mark Fackler*

The Handbook of Communication and Corporate Social Responsibility, *edited by Øyvind Ihlen, Jennifer Bartlett, and Steve May*

The Handbook of Gender, Sex, and Media, *edited by Karen Ross*

The Handbook of Global Health Communication, *edited by Rafael Obregon and Silvio Waisbord*

The Handbook of Global Media Research, *edited by Ingrid Volkmer*

The Handbook of Global Online Journalism, *edited by Eugenia Siapera and Andreas Veglis*

The Handbook of Communication and Corporate Reputation, *edited by Craig E. Carroll*

Forthcoming

The Handbook of International Advertising Research, *edited by Hong Cheng*

The Handbook of Internet Studies

Edited by

Mia Consalvo and Charles Ess

A John Wiley & Sons, Ltd., Publication

This paperback edition first published 2013
© 2013 Blackwell Publishing Ltd

Edition history: Blackwell Publishing Ltd (hardback, 2011)

Blackwell Publishing was acquired by John Wiley & Sons in February 2007. Blackwell's publishing program has been merged with Wiley's global Scientific, Technical, and Medical business to form Wiley-Blackwell.

Registered Office
John Wiley & Sons Ltd, The Atrium, Southern Gate, Chichester, West Sussex, PO19 8SQ, UK

Editorial Offices
350 Main Street, Malden, MA 02148-5020, USA
9600 Garsington Road, Oxford, OX4 2DQ, UK
The Atrium, Southern Gate, Chichester, West Sussex, PO19 8SQ, UK

For details of our global editorial offices, for customer services, and for information about how to apply for permission to reuse the copyright material in this book please see our website at www.wiley.com/wiley-blackwell.

The right of Mia Consalvo and Charles Ess to be identified as the authors of the editorial material in this work has been asserted in accordance with the UK Copyright, Designs and Patents Act 1988.

Library of Congress Cataloging-in-Publication Data

The handbook of internet studies / edited by Mia Consalvo and Charles Ess.
   p. cm. — (Handbooks in communication and media)
  Includes bibliographical references and index.
  ISBN 978-1-1184-0007-4 (pbk. : alk. paper)
  1. Internet—Social aspects.   I. Consalvo, Mia, 1969–   II. Ess, Charles, 1951–

  HM1017.H36 2010
  303.48′34—dc22

                                                    2009032170

A catalogue record for this book is available from the British Library.

Cover image: Junction of the M25 and M11 Motorways at Night. © Jason Hawkes/Corbis
Cover design by Simon Levy

Set in 10/13pt Galliard by Graphicraft Limited, Hong Kong
Printed and bound in Malaysia by Vivar Printing Sdn Bhd

1   2013

Contents

Notes on Editors and Contributors

Mia Consalvo is Associate Professor in the School of Media Arts and Studies at Ohio University. She is the author of *Cheating: Gaining Advantage in Videogames* (MIT Press, 2007) and was executive editor of the Research Annual series, produced by the Association of Internet Researchers. Her research focuses on the hybrid character of the global games industry, as well as gender and sexuality as related to digital gameplay.

Charles Ess is Professor of Philosophy and Religion and Distinguished Professor of Interdisciplinary Studies at Drury University (Springfield, Missouri). He is Professor with special responsibilities in the Information and Media Studies Department, Aarhus University (Denmark, 2009–2012). He has published extensively in computer-mediated communication and cross-cultural approaches to information and computing ethics.

Maria Bakardjieva is Professor at the Faculty of Communication and Culture, University of Calgary, Canada. She is the author of *Internet Society: The Internet in Everyday Life* (Sage, 2005) and co-editor of *How Canadians Communicate* (University of Calgary Press, 2004, 2007). Her research examines Internet use practices across different social and cultural contexts, focusing on the ways users appropriate new media communication possibilities in their daily projects.

Naomi S. Baron is Professor of Linguistics at American University in Washington, DC. A specialist in electronically mediated communication, she is the author of *Alphabet to Email* (Routledge, 2000) and *Always On: Language in an Online and Mobile World* (Oxford, 2008). Her current research is a cross-cultural study of mobile-phone use in Sweden, the US, Italy, Japan, and Korea.

Nancy K. Baym is Associate Professor of Communication Studies, University of Kansas. She teaches about communication technology, interpersonal communication, and qualitative research methods. Her books include *Tune In, Log On:*

Soaps, Fandom and Online Community (Sage, 2000) and, co-edited with Annette Markham, *Internet Inquiry: Conversation about Method* (Sage, 2009). She was a co-founder of the Association of Internet Researchers, co-organized its first conference, and served as its President.

Sandra Braman has studied the macro-level effects of digital technologies and their policy implications since the early 1980s. Her recent work includes *Change of State: Information, Policy, And Power* (MIT Press, 2007), and the edited volumes *The Emergent Global Information Policy Regime* (Palgrave Macmillan, 2004), *Biotechnology and Communication: The Meta-Technologies of Information* (Lawrence Erlbaum, 2004), among others.

Janne Bromseth is working with cultural analysis, in particular queer perspectives, on new media, education and lgbtq subcultures (i.e. lesbian, gay, bisexual, transgender, and queer subcultures). She has long focused on Scandinavian mailing lists, studying constructions of group norms, gender and sexuality, and the intersection of online/offline in creating local (sub)cultural mediated community. At present she works as a researcher at the Centre for Gender Research, Uppsala University, Sweden.

Niels Brügger is Associate Professor at the Centre for Internet Research (CIR), University of Aarhus, Denmark. His primary research interest is website history, including his current work on the Danish Broadcasting Corporation's website, *The History of dr.dk, 1996–2006*, and the volume *Web History* (Peter Lang, 2009). He has published a number of articles, monographs, and edited books, including *Archiving Websites: General Considerations and Strategies* (CIR, 2005).

Elizabeth A. Buchanan is Associate Professor and Director of the Center for Information Policy Research, School of Information Studies, University of Wisconsin-Milwaukee. She specializes in the areas of information and research ethics, information policy, and intellectual freedom, including a current project funded by the National Science Foundation (US). Most recently, she co-authored with Kathrine Henderson *Case Studies in Library and Information Science Ethics* (2008, McFarland Press).

Heidi Campbell is Assistant Professor of Communication at Texas A&M University. She teaches Media Studies. For over a decade she has studied the impact of the Internet on religious communities and culture as well as the sociology of technology. Her work has appeared in a variety of publications including *New Media & Society*, *The Information Society*, and the *Journal of Computer-Mediated Communication*. She is the author of *Exploring Religious Community Online* (Peter Lang, 2005).

Laurel Dyson is a senior lecturer in Information Technology at the University of Technology, Sydney, Australia. She has published many articles on the adoption of information and communication technologies by Indigenous people. She has also published the book *Information Technology and Indigenous People*

(Information Science Publishing, 2007), and a report for UNESCO evaluating their Indigenous ICT4ID Project. The focus of her current research is on the use of mobile technology by Indigenous Australians.

Lorna Heaton is Associate Professor at the Department of Communications, University of Montreal. She is author of *The Computerization of Work* (Sage, 2001) and a number of articles in journals such as *Management Communication Quarterly* and the *Journal of the American Society for Information Science and Technology*. Her research focuses on organizational and inter-organizational issues in the implementation and use of information and communication technologies.

Klaus Bruhn Jensen is Professor at the University of Copenhagen, Denmark. Publications include *A Handbook of Media and Communication Research* (Routledge, 2002) and contributions to the *International Encyclopedia of Communication* (12 vols., Blackwell, 2008), for which he served as Area Editor of Communication Theory and Philosophy. His current research interests are Internet studies, mobile media, and communication theory.

Steve Jones is UIC Distinguished Professor, Professor of Communication, and Research Associate in the Electronic Visualization Laboratory at the University of Illinois at Chicago. He is author and editor of numerous books, including *Society Online, CyberSociety, Virtual Culture, Doing Internet Research, CyberSociety 2.0,* the *Encyclopedia of New Media,* and *Afterlife as Afterimage.* He founded the Association of Internet Researchers and is co-editor of *New Media & Society.*

Lori Kendall is Associate Professor in the Graduate School of Library and Information Science, University of Illinois, Urbana-Champaign, and researches in the areas of online community and culture. Her publications include "Beyond Media Producers and Consumers" (on online videos, in *Information, Communication and Society*) and her most recent of several chapters on online research in *Internet Inquiry* (Annette Markham and Nancy Baym, eds.).

Sonia Livingstone is Professor in the Department of Media and Communications, London School of Economics and Political Science. Her research interests center on media audiences, children and the Internet, domestic contexts of media use and media literacy. Books include *The Handbook of New Media* (Leah Lievrouw, co-editor, Sage, 2006), *The International Handbook of Children, Media and Culture* (Kirsten Drotner, co-editor, Sage, 2008), and *Children and the Internet* (Polity, 2009).

Marika Lüders is Research scientist at SINTEF ICT (the Foundation for Industrial and Technical Research), Oslo. She studies emerging uses of personal and social media, particularly with a focus on young people. She is a co-editor of the Norwegian anthology, *Personlige medier: Livet mellom skjermene* [*Personal Media: Life between Screens*] (Gyldendal Akademiske, 2007), and her work has been published in Norwegian and international anthologies and journals.

P. David Marshall is Professor and Chair of New Media, Communication, and Cultural Studies at Deakin University, and head of the School of Communication and Creative Media. His publications include *New Media Cultures* (Edward Arnold/Oxford, 2004), *The Celebrity Culture Reader* (Routledge, 2006), and many articles on the media, new media, and popular culture. He has two principal research areas: the study of the public personality and the study of new media forms.

Susanna Paasonen is Research Fellow at the Helsinki Collegium for Advanced Studies, University of Helsinki, with interests in Internet research, feminist theory, affect, and pornography. She is the author of *Figures of Fantasy* (Peter Lang, 2005), and co-editor of *Women and Everyday Uses of the Internet* (Peter Lang, 2002), *Pornification: Sex and Sexuality in Media Culture* (Macmillan, 2007), as well as the forthcoming *Working with Affect in Feminist Readings: Disturbing Differences* (Routledge).

Jennifer Stromer-Galley is Assistant Professor in the Department of Communication, University at Albany, State University of New York. Her research interests include: the uses of communication technology and its implications for democratic practice; mediated political campaign communication; and, deliberative democracy. Her research has appeared in the *Journal of Communication*, *Javnost/The Public*, the *Journal of Computer-Mediated Communication*, and the *Journal of Public Deliberation*.

Jenny Sundén is Assistant Professor in the Department of Media Technology, Royal Institute of Technology (KTH), Stockholm, with interests in new media studies, queer/feminist theory, and games. She is the author of *Material Virtualities: Approaching Online Textual Embodiment* (Peter Lang, 2003), and co-editor of *Cyberfeminism in Northern Lights: Gender and Digital Media in a Nordic Context* (Cambridge Scholars Publishing, 2007) and *Second Nature: Origins and Originality in Art, Science and New Media* (forthcoming).

T. L. Taylor is Associate Professor at the Center for Computer Games Research, IT University of Copenhagen. She has published on values in design, avatars and online embodiment, play and experience in online worlds, gender and gaming, and pervasive gaming, including her book, *Play Between Worlds: Exploring Online Game Culture* (MIT Press, 2006), which uses her multi-year ethnography of *EverQuest*. She is currently at work on a book about professional computer gaming.

Barry Wellman directs NetLab, Department of Sociology, at the University of Toronto, a team studying the intersection of online and offline networks – social, communication, and computer – in communities and at work. He is currently writing *Networked* with Lee Rainie. Wellman has (co-)written more than 200 papers with more than 80 co-authors, including *The Internet in Everyday Life* (2002). Wellman is a Fellow of the Royal Society of Canada.

Deborah L. Wheeler is Assistant Professor in Political Science at the United States Naval Academy. Her areas of research include information technology diffusion and impact in the Arab world; Gender and international development; and the Palestinian–Israeli conflict. Her extensive publications include *The Internet in the Middle East: Global Expectations and Local Imaginations in Kuwait* (State University of New York Press, 2006).

Alexis Wichowski is a doctoral candidate in Information Science at the University at Albany, State University of New York. Her research interests include computer-mediated communication, incidental information encountering, Internet studies, and the evolution of information environments.

Acknowledgments

We begin with our contributors: you have each researched and authored what we take to be watershed chapters – and you have further worked with us patiently and cooperatively throughout the course of developing this volume. We cannot thank you enough.

We are further very grateful indeed for the Association of Internet Researchers (AoIR) that in innumerable ways has served as the inspiration, incubator, and scholarly "sandbox" of this volume – i.e., the place where we can freely explore and play with both new and old ideas in a supportive but still appropriately critical milieu. In particular, we hope that the mix here between younger and more senior scholars and researchers faithfully reflects one of AoIR's distinctive characteristics – namely, recognizing that some of the best work in Internet studies comes precisely from the fresh eyes and minds of those at the beginnings of their scholarly careers, especially as this work is fostered and enhanced through mutual dialogue with their more experienced peers.

We wish also to thank Elizabeth Swayze at Wiley-Blackwell, who first invited us to develop this *Handbook*. It has always been a pleasure to work with Elizabeth, Margot Morse, Jayne Fargnoli, and their other colleagues at Wiley-Blackwell, who could be counted on for unfailing support, advice, and encouragement.

Mia would like to thank Ohio University and the Massachusetts Institute of Technology for providing wonderful environments to engage in this work. Likewise she would like to thank students in her classes on new media, who have sharpened her thinking on many of these topics, as they have challenged her to consider (and then explore) multiple aspects of life online that she had not yet studied.

Charles thanks Drury University for leaves of absence and a sabbatical year; and the Institute for Information and Media Studies (IMV), Aarhus University, for correlative guest professorships. The IMV secretaries, librarians, colleagues, and head of department Steffen Ejnar Brandorff, were consistently generous with their resources, insight, and perhaps most importantly, warm hospitality, all of which created an ideal environment in which much of this *Handbook* took shape.

Last, but certainly not least, we are deeply grateful to our families and friends. You know all too well how we were compelled on more than one occasion to ask for your forgiveness and patience as we struggled to sort out yet one more snarl or meet still one more deadline. As only friends and family would do, you have lovingly supported this work in manifold ways. As one says – but only rarely – in Danish, *tusind tak!* (a thousand thanks!), and in New England, that the publication of this volume represents a "Finestkind" of day.

Introduction: What is "Internet Studies"?

Charles Ess and Mia Consalvo

The project of saying what something *is* may helpfully begin by saying what it is *not*. In our case, "Internet studies" as used here is *not* primarily a study of the technologies constituting the ever-growing, ever-changing networks of computers (including mobile devices such as Internet-enabled mobile phones, netbooks, and other devices) linked together by a single TCP/IP protocol. Certainly, Internet studies in this sense is relevant – in part historically, as these technologies required two decades of development before they became so widely diffused as to justify and compel serious academic attention. That is, we can trace the origins of the Internet to the first efforts in 1973 by Vincent Cerf and Robert E. Kahn to develop the internetworking protocol that later evolved into TCP/IP (cf. Abbate, 2000, pp. 127–33). By contrast, we and our colleagues seek to study the distinctive sorts of human communication and interaction facilitated by the Internet. These begin to emerge on a large scale only in the late 1980s and early 1990s as within the US, ARPANET and its successor, NSFNET (an academic, research-oriented network sponsored by the United States National Science Foundation) opened up to proprietary networks such as *CompuServe* and others (Abbate, 2000, pp. 191–209). NSFNET simultaneously fostered connections with networks outside the US built up in the 1970s and 1980s: 250 such networks were connected to NSFNET by January 1990, "more than 20 percent of the total number of networks" – and then doubled (to more than 40 percent) by 1995 (Abbate, 2000, p. 210). Following close behind the resulting explosion of Internet access, as Barry Wellman details in our opening chapter, Internet studies may be traced to the early 1990s.

As Susan Herring reminds us, prior to this activity there were computers, networks, and networked communication – studied as computer-mediated communication (CMC), beginning in the late 1970s with Hiltz and Turoff's *The Network Nation* (1978: Herring, 2008, p. xxxv). Nonetheless, if we define Internet studies to include CMC as facilitated through the Internet, Internet studies is still barely two decades old. On the one hand, the rapid pace of technological development and the rapid global diffusion of these technologies (at the time of this writing, over 26 percent of the world's population have access to the Internet in one form or another [Internet World Stats, 2010]) would suggest that two decades is a very long time. On the other hand, scholars, researchers, and others interested in what happens as human beings (and, eventually, automated agents) learn how to communicate and interact with one another via the Internet are not simply faced with the challenge of pinpointing a rapidly changing and moving target. Our task is further complicated by complexities that almost always require approaches drawn from the methodologies and theoretical frameworks of many disciplines – a multi-disciplinarity or interdisciplinarity that is itself constantly in flux. Moreover, as the Internet grew beyond the US in the late 1990s,[1] it became clear that cultur-ally variable dimensions, including communicative preferences and foundational norms, values, practices, and beliefs, further complicated pictures we might develop of the diverse interactions facilitated through the Internet (e.g., Ess, 2001, 2007; Ess & Sudweeks, 2005). Finally, while initial activity on the Internet was mostly text-based, we now navigate a sea of images, videos, games, sound, and graphics online, often all at once. Given these complexities, two decades to build a new academic field is not much time at all.

Nonetheless, when we began work on this volume in 2007, we were convinced that Internet studies had emerged as a relatively stable field of academic study – one constituted by an extensive body of research that defines and depends upon multiple methodologies and approaches that have demonstrated their usefulness in distilling the multiple interactions made possible via the Internet. These know-ledges[2] appear in many now well-established journals (in many languages), includ-ing *New Media & Society* (established 1990), the *Journal of Computer-Mediated Communication* (1995), and *Information, Communication, & Society* (1998). Such activity is fostered by both individual scholars and researchers across the range of academic disciplines (humanities, social sciences, and computer science), as well as diverse centers and institutes around the globe.

The first purpose of our *Handbook*, then, is to provide both new students and seasoned scholars with an initial orientation to many (though not all) of the most significant foci and *topoi* that define and constitute this field. To begin with, our contributors were charged with providing a comprehensive overview of relevant scholarship in their specific domains, conjoined with their best understandings of important future directions for research. Each chapter thus stands as a snapshot of the state of scholarship and research within a specific domain. To be sure, no one would claim finality, in light of the constantly changing technologies in play. Nonetheless, each chapter provides one of the most authoritative and compre-hensive accounts of a given aspect of Internet studies as can be asked for – and thereby our contributors demarcate and document in fine detail many of the most significant domains or subfields of Internet studies.

Internet Studies: Emerging Domains, Terrains, Commonalities

We originally organized our chapters into three parts. These constitute a general structure that offers an initial taxonomy and orientation. Part I collects historical overviews of Internet studies, including web archiving, methodologies, and ethics, that serve as a primer for Internet studies *per se* and as the introduction to the following sections. The chapters constituting Part II examine eight distinctive domains: language, policy, democratization and political discourse, international development, health services, religion, indigenous peoples, and sexuality. Part III approaches "culture" in terms of online community, virtual worlds, the cultures of children and young people, games, social networking sites (SNSs), media most broadly, pornography, music, and the social life of teenagers online.

Moreover, we found that our contributors, independently of one another, contributed to a larger picture – one of shared insights and conceptual coherencies that add substantial structure and content to the map of Internet studies initially demarcated by these three parts.

One of the first commonalities to emerge is an interesting agreement between sociologist Barry Wellman and religion scholar Heidi Campbell. For Wellman, we are in the third age of Internet studies; Campbell similarly characterizes studies of religion and the Internet as now in their third wave. Wellman describes two distinct trends of this third age. First, Internet research is increasingly incorporated into "the mainstream conferences and journals" of given disciplines, so as to bring "the more developed theories, methods, and substantive lore of the disciplines into play" (this volume, chapter 1). Second is "the development of 'Internet studies' as a field in its own right, bringing together scholars from the social sciences, humanities, and computer sciences" (ibid.). For Wellman, a key focus of this third age is *community*, specifically as "community ties . . . [are] thriving, with online connectivity intertwined with offline relationships" (ibid.). In parallel, Campbell notes that the third wave of Internet research is marked by a shift towards "more collaborative, longitudinal, and interdisciplinary explorations of religion online," along with the development of increasingly sophisticated theoretical frameworks for examining online religious communities (this volume, chapter 11).

Where Are We Now – And Where Are We Going?

Our contributors highlight two further commonalities that articulate a significant current perspective of Internet studies, and point towards an important direction for research in Internet studies.

First, several contributors note that Internet studies are no longer constrained by certain dualisms prevailing in the 1990s – specifically, strong dichotomies presumed to hold between such *relata*[3] as the offline and the online in parallel with "the real" and "the virtual," and, most fundamentally from a philosophical perspective, between a material body and a radically distinct, disembodied mind. These dualisms appear in the highly influential science-fiction novel *Neuromancer* (Gibson, 1984). The resulting emphasis on opposition between these *relata* is at work in the central literatures of hypermedia and hypertext, much of the early (pre-1995) work on virtual communities, postmodernist celebrations of identity play and exploration in (early) MUDs and MOOs (most famously Turkle, 1995), and influential punditry regarding "liberation in cyberspace" for disembodied minds radically freed from "meatspace" (e.g., Barlow, 1996). Of course, such dualisms were questioned as early as 1991 by Allucquére Roseanne Stone (1991) and more forcefully into the 1990s. In 1996, for example, Susan Herring demonstrated that, *contra* postmodernist dreams, our gender is hard to disguise online in even exclusively text-based CMC. By 1999, Katherine Hayles could characterize "the post-human" as involving the clear rejection of such dualism in favor of notions of embodiment that rather emphasize the inextricable interconnections between body and self/identity (p. 288; cf. Ess, in press).

The shift away from such dualisms is consistently documented by our contributors, including Nancy Baym, whose early studies of fan communities highlighted important ways that offline identities and practices were interwoven with online interactions (1995; this volume, chapter 18). Similarly, Janne Bromseth and Jenny Sundén point to the work of Beth Kolko and Elizabeth Reid (1998), which highlights the importance of a coherent and reasonably accurate self-representation in online communities (cited in Bromseth and Sundén, this volume, chapter 13). In a volume appropriately titled *The Internet in Everyday Life*, by 2002, Barry Wellman and Caroline Haythornthwaite could document how "networked individuals" seamlessly interweave their online and offline lives. That same year, Lori Kendall reiterated Herring's findings in her study of the BlueSky online community (2002; see Kendall, this volume, chapter 14).

Barring some important exceptions (e.g., venues dedicated explicitly to exploration of multiple and otherwise marginalized sexualities or identities, etc.), the earlier distinctions between the real and the virtual, the offline and the online no longer seem accurate or analytically useful. This means that the character of research is likewise changing. As Kendall observes, "In recent research on community and the Internet, the emphasis is shifting from ethnographic studies of virtual communities, to studies of people's blending of offline and online contacts" (this volume, chapter 14). More broadly, Klaus Bruhn Jensen makes the point that, *contra* 1990s' celebrations of the imminent death of the book, "Old media rarely die, and humans remain the reference point and prototype for technologically mediated communication" (this volume, chapter 3).

Second, several of our contributors point towards a shared set of issues emerging alongside this shift. As Maria Bakardjieva observes, Internet studies has long involved what she characterizes as "the critical stream of studies," defined by the central question: "Is the Internet helping users achieve higher degrees of emancipation and equity, build capacity, and take control over their lives as individuals and citizens?" (this volume, chapter 4). While some of our contributors can provide positive examples and responses to this question (e.g., Lorna Heaton and Laurel Dyson), all caution us not to fall (back) into the cyber-utopianism characteristic of the previous decade. So, Deborah Wheeler summarizes her review of Internet-based development projects this way: "some development challenges are too big for the Internet. When people need food, safe drinking-water, medicine, and shelter, Internet connectivity does little to provide for these basic necessities" (this volume, chapter 9).

Others raise similar concerns. Janne Bromseth and Jenny Sundén note that the restoration of the embodied person – in contrast with an ostensibly disembodied mind divorced from an embodied person and identity – means that such a user "brings to the table of his/her interactions the whole world of interrelations that body means with larger communities, environments, their histories, cultures, traditions, practices, beliefs, etc." (this volume, chapter 13). But this implicates in turn central matters of gender, sexuality, and *power*: "Online communities are embedded in larger sociopolitical structures and cultural hegemonies, with a growing amount of empirical research slowly dissolving the image of a power-free and democratic Internet" (ibid.). Bromseth and Sundén refer to the work of Leslie Regan Shade (2004) who called attention to the commercial roots and foci of these powers: *"online communities are today deeply embedded in a commercialized Internet culture, creating specific frames for how community, gender, and – we will add – sexuality are constructed on the Internet* (ibid.; our emphasis, MC, CE).

This commercialized culture, Marika Lüders points out, has long been recognized as problematic: "online content and service providers have developed a commercial logic where they offer their material for free in return for users giving away personal information (Shapiro, 1999)" (Lüders, this volume, chapter 22). But especially for young people in the now seemingly ubiquitous and ever-growing SNSs such as Facebook, as Sonia Livingstone explains, their emerging and/or shifting identities are increasingly shaped by a culture of consumerism built around sites offering targeted advertising and marketing. In these venues,

> the development of "taste" and lifestyle is shaped significantly by powerful commercial interests in the fashion and music industries online as offline. [. . .] the user is encouraged to define their identity through consumer preferences (music, movies, fandom). Indeed, the user is themselves commodified insofar as a social networking profile in particular can be neatly managed, exchanged, or organized in various ways by others precisely because it is fixed, formatted, and context-free. (Livingstone, this volume, chapter 16)

But finally, these concerns are compelling not only for those seeking to explore alternative understandings and sensibilities regarding gender and sexuality, nor simply for young people. Rather, SNSs increasingly attract the participation and engagement of ever-more diverse demographics – leading to Nancy Baym's eloquent appeal for further research and critical analysis:

> *What are the practical and ethical implications of the move from socializing in not-for-profit spaces to proprietary profit-driven environments?* [. . .] *As SNSs become practical necessities for many in sustaining their social lives, we become increasingly beholden to corporate entities whose primary responsibility is to their shareholders, not their users.* Their incentive is not to help us foster meaningful and rewarding personal connections, but to deliver eyeballs to advertisers and influence purchasing decisions. [. . .] *Questions are also raised about the lines between just reward for the content users provide and exploitation of users through free labor.* (Baym, this volume, chapter 18; our emphasis, MC, CE)

No one is arguing that we are witnessing an inevitable slide into an inescapable, *Matrix*-like reality driven by greed and little regard for human beings as anything other than commodified cogs in a consumer machine. Echoing Stromer-Galley and Wichowski's cautious optimism (chapter 8) regarding deliberative democracy online, Baym continues here:

> At the same time, users are not without influence. When Facebook implemented their Beacon system tracking user purchases and other activities across the Internet and announcing them to their friends, a user backlash forced them to change their plans. The power struggles between owners/staffs and users are complex and thus far all but ignored in scholarship. (Ibid.)

Certainly, one way to foster the critical attention and research Baym calls for here is to endorse the call made by Bromseth and Sundén, who point out that "During the mid-1990s, the Internet was central for theoretical debates in feminist theory. Today, Internet studies needs to reconnect with central debates concerning the relationship between gender and sexuality, as well as between feminist and queer theory" (this volume, chapter 13). Joining these two large commonalities together: as the Internet and its multitude of communication and interaction possibilities continue to expand and interweave with our everyday lives, these concerns promise to become all the more extensive – and thereby, critical research and reflection on their impacts and meanings for our lives, not simply as users and consumers, but as human beings and citizens, become all the more important to pursue.

Postlude

As editors, we have been privileged to discover how the individual chapters constituting this *Handbook* only become richer and more fruitful with each return visit. In addition, as we hope these examples of larger commonalities make clear, careful and repeated reading in this *Handbook* will unveil still other important insights and conceptual coherencies across diverse chapters – thereby further articulating and demarcating the maps and guides to Internet studies offered here.

Notes

1   As late as 1998, ca. 84% of all users of the Internet were located in North America (GVU, 1998). As of this writing, North American users constitute 14.4% of users worldwide (Internet World Stats, 2010).
2   "Knowledges," a literal translation of the German *Erkenntnisse*, is used to denote the plurality of ways of knowing and shaping knowledge defining both the diverse academic disciplines represented in this volume, along with non-academic modalities of knowing that are legitimate and significant in their own right. Cf. van der Velden, 2010.

3 "*Relata*" is the plural Latin term referring to the two (or more) components that stand in some form of relationship with one another, whether oppositional, complementary, analogical, etc. It thus serves as a shorthand term to refer to virtual/real, online/offline, mind/body, and other *relata* without having to repeatedly name each of these.

References

Abbate, J. (2000). *Inventing the Internet*. Cambridge, MA: MIT Press.

Barlow, J. P. (1996). A declaration of the independence of cyberspace. Retrieved July 7, 2010, from http://w2.eff.org/Censorship/Internet_censorship_bills/barlow_0296.declaration.

Baym, N. (1995). The emergence of community in computer-mediated communication. In S. G. Jones (ed.), *CyberSociety: Computer-Mediated Communication and Community* (pp. 138–63). Thousand Oaks, CA: Sage.

Ess, C. (2001). *Culture, Technology, Communication: Towards an Intercultural Global Village*. Albany, NY: State University of New York Press.

Ess, C. (in press). Self, community, and ethics in digital mediatized worlds. In C. Ess & M. Thorseth (eds.), *Trust and Virtual Worlds: Contemporary Perspectives*. London: Peter Lang.

Ess, C., with Kawabata, A., & Kurosaki, H. (2007). Cross-cultural perspectives on religion and computer-mediated communication. *Journal of Computer-Mediated Communication*, 12(3), April 2007. http://jcmc.indiana.edu/vol12/issue3/.

Ess, C., & Sudweeks, F. (2005). Culture and computer-mediated communication: Toward new understandings. Theme issue, *Journal of Computer-Mediated Communication*, 11(1), October 2005. http://jcmc.indiana.edu/vol11/issue1/ess.html/.

Gibson, W. (1984). *Neuromancer*. New York: Ace Books.

GVU (Graphic, Visualization, and Usability Center, Georgia Technological University). (1998). GVU's 10th WWW user survey. Retrieved July 7, 2010, from http://www-static.cc.gatech.edu/gvu/user_surveys/survey-1998-10/graphs/general/q50.htm.

Hayles, K. (1999). *How We Became Posthuman: Virtual Bodies in Cybernetics, Literature, And Informatics*. Chicago: University of Chicago Press.

Herring, S. (1996) Posting in a different voice: Gender and ethics in computer-mediated communication. In C. Ess (ed.), *Philosophical Perspectives on Computer-Mediated Communication* (pp. 115–45). Albany, NY: SUNY Press.

Herring, S. (2008). Foreword. In S. Kelsey & K. St Amant (eds.), *Handbook of Research on Computer Mediated Communication*, vol. 1 (pp. xxxv–xxxvi). Hershey, PA: Information Science Reference.

Hiltz, R., & Turoff, M. (1978). *The Network Nation*. Reading, MA: Addison-Wellesley.

Internet World Stats. (2010). Retrieved July 7, 2010, from http://www.internetworldstats.com/stats.htm.

Kendall, L. (2002). *Hanging Out in the Virtual Pub: Masculinities and Relationships Online*. Berkeley: University of California Press.

Kolko, B., & Reid, E. (1998). Dissolution and fragmentation: Problems in online communities. In S. Jones (ed.), *Cybersociety 2.0* (pp. 212–31). Thousand Oaks, CA: Sage.

Shade, L. R. (2004). Bending gender into the net. In P. N. Howard & S. Jones (eds.), *Society Online. The Internet in Context* (pp. 57–71). Thousand Oaks, CA, London, New Delhi: Sage.

Shapiro, A. L. (1999). *The Control Revolution: How the Internet is Putting Individuals in Charge and Changing the World We Know*. New York: Public Affairs.

Stone, A. R. (1991). Will the real body please stand up? Boundary stories about virtual cultures. In M. Benedikt (ed.), *Cyberspace: First Steps* (pp. 81–118). Cambridge, MA: MIT Press.

Turkle, S. (1995). *Life on the Screen: Identity in the Age of the Internet*. New York: Simon & Schuster.

Van der Velden, M. (2010). Design for the contact zone: Knowledge management software and the structures of indigenous knowledges. In F. Sudweeks, H. Hrachovec & C. Ess (eds.), *Proceedings Cultural Attitudes Towards Communication and Technology 2010* (pp. 1–18). Murdoch, WA: Murdoch University.

Wellman, B., & Haythornthwaite, C. (2002). *The Internet in Everyday Life*. Oxford, Malden, MA: Blackwell.

Part I

Beyond the Great Divides?
A Primer on Internet Histories,
Methods, and Ethics

Introduction to Part I

Charles Ess

Part I provides an initial orientation – to Internet studies *per se*, and thereby to the subsequent work gathered in parts II and III. The first chapter is a brief history of Internet studies by Barry Wellman. This history is particularly important as it clears away a series of dichotomies – what Klaus Bruhn Jensen in his contribution aptly calls "the Great Divides" – that dominated 1990s approaches to computer-mediated communication (CMC) and the Internet. Overcoming these divides is crucial for a number of reasons, as we will see. First of all, these divides included an emphasis on the Internet as utterly novel and thereby revolutionary – hence making all previous history and insight irrelevant. At the same time, however, the Internet is undoubtedly marked by novelty in important ways. So in his chapter, Niels Brügger will highlight how the Internet requires new approaches in terms of archiving and our understanding of archived materials. Similarly, Elizabeth Buchanan argues that in some ways, the ethical challenges to Internet researchers evoked especially by what we call Web 2.0 may require novel approaches, alongside more traditional ones. But we will further see in the contributions by Klaus Bruhn Jensen and Maria Bakardjieva the point emphasized by Wellman: in contrast with such 1990s divides, more contemporary approaches focus on an Internet that is embedded in our everyday lives (at least in the developed world). This means that more traditional methods – quantitative, qualitative, and, for Bakardjieva, qualitative methods conjoined with critical theory of a specific sort – remain fruitful. Buchanan's introduction to Internet research ethics likewise makes this point with regard to a number of important examples and watershed cases.

Introducing the Chapters

We begin with Barry Wellman's "Studying the Internet Through the Ages." As a self-described "tribal elder," Wellman provides a history that is at once personal and comprehensive. His own engagement with CMC through a sociological lens begins in 1990, just prior to what he identifies as the "first age of Internet studies" – an age he aptly captures as dominated more by punditry than by empirical research and data. The pundits, in turn, swing between a strikingly ahistorical utopianism and a darker (but not necessarily better informed) dystopianism. Both tended to assume a sharp (what I and others have called a Cartesian) dichotomy between real and virtual worlds and lives – an assumption that Wellman's own research (along with others such as Nancy Baym, 1995, 2002) directly challenged. The "second age of Internet studies" begins for Wellman in 1998, as a turn towards more extensive empirical work. As is now well recognized, these more recent studies undermine any sharp diremption between real and virtual: correlatively, neither the best nor worst possibilities of the early pundits have been realized. The current "third age" focuses on an Internet that, in the developed world at least, has become "the utility of the masses" – simply part of everyday life. And, if the question posed by the first age was "utopia or dystopia?" – research in the third age increasingly answers "yes." That is, both the darker and brighter sides of the Internet are explored with increasing nuance and sophistication – e.g., social stratification and possible loss of community, on the one hand, countered by recognition of how "networked individuals" utilize the Internet in all its capacities to increase their communicative interactions and relationships with others.

Along the way, Internet studies have likewise evolved – to the point that now, on Wellman's showing, they move in two different but complementary directions. Exemplified in the annual conferences of the Association of Internet Researchers (AoIR), Internet studies now stands as a – highly interdisciplinary – field in its own right. Simultaneously, Internet research is increasingly incorporated within more disciplinary conferences and publications.

Wellman's account thus serves as a succinct roadmap – not only for Internet studies in a broad sense, but also for the project of this volume. To be sure, there are additional elements and more fine-grained twists and turns along the way that this initial map does not fully capture. But no map ever does, of course – which is why, to use Wellman's metaphor of what was once Internet *incognita*, we continue with a journey initially demarcated through our first maps.

Niels Brügger's chapter, "Web Archiving – Between Past, Present, and Future" reminds us that the objects of our study can be profoundly ephemeral; hence, stabilizing the objects of our study by way of archiving practices that follow carefully developed guidelines becomes a foundational component of Internet studies. But this further means that archiving methods and guidelines in turn require the critical attention of Internet researchers more broadly. Brügger argues first that the Internet is characterized by a dynamic, ephemeral, and changing medium: since it is therefore fundamentally different from any other known media type, it must be approached in new ways in our efforts to archive it. Second, when Internet material is archived, it is also fundamentally different from well-known media types, and again we have to approach it in new ways. Brügger then provides a comprehensive overview of both important web archiving methods and significant web archives and archiving projects. He further offers guidelines

for "web philology," for how web scholars may critically evaluate and interpret archived materials vis-à-vis originals that may no longer be accessible. He
concludes by sketching out the future research agenda for web archiving, an agenda
that, not surprisingly, involves not only Internet researchers specifically interested in web archiving, but, more broadly, the Internet researchers' community
at large. Brügger's chapter is critical as it calls our attention to a dimension of
Internet research that, while essential, has received comparatively little attention
or reflection.

In Chapter 3, "New Media, Old Methods – Internet Methodologies and the
Online/Offline Divide," Klaus Bruhn Jensen recalls what we have now seen to
be a thematic 1990s utopian/dystopian dichotomy as challenging researchers to
assess whether the Internet entraps or empowers its users. Referring to a second
1990s dichotomy, Jensen reiterates that while the initial emphasis on a radical
distinction between the online and the offline may have been necessary, "it has
become increasingly counterproductive in methodological terms." Likewise – and
again, consonant with others in this volume who foreground the importance of
embodiment, despite its temporary banishment during celebrations in the 1990s
of the virtual self and virtual communities – Jensen points out that *contra* early
rhetoric of a revolution in cyberspace, "Old media rarely die, and humans remain
the reference point and prototype for technologically mediated communication."
This means that old methods retain much of their salience in contemporary Internet
studies. Jensen first distinguishes among three media types in order to sharpen
our focus on the Internet, not so much as a distinctive (much less, revolutionary) technology, but as one among many "constituents of layered social and
technological networks." This view moves us past, in his phrase, "the great divides"
of the 1990s (e.g. offline/online, etc.) and serves as the basis for a six-celled schema
of possible research methods. In discussing additional considerations that might
guide researchers' choices, Jensen highlights Giddens' notion of "double hermeneutics" (1979): that is, researchers' work, as a specific interpretation of and
hermeneutical framework for understanding the Internet, can thereby reshape a
broader understanding and use of the Internet – especially as the much-celebrated
interactivity of Web 2.0 highlights users' abilities to modify and reshape both web
content and web form.

Maria Bakardjieva's chapter, "The Internet in Everyday Life" carries us forward
from Jensen's essay on method by providing a fine-grained look at the multiple
dimensions of Internet use – where, as emphasized by Jensen and Wellman, we
are now dealing with an Internet that is *embedded* in our everyday lives, not somehow radically divorced from them. Again, this means that the Internet is no longer
solely a technological *unicum*, demanding utterly new methodologies for its study
– however much it requires new methods for its archiving and interpretations of
those archives. Rather, as normalized in these ways, the Internet can thus be
approached through a wide range of familiar and established methodologies and
disciplines – thereby helping us further contextualize this technology with similar research and analyses of "familiar media and communication phenomena."

Bakardjieva offers her own schema for understanding diverse approaches – approaches clustered first of all around different understandings of what "the everyday" means: statistical, interpretive/constructivist, and critical. What follows is a comprehensive survey of the significant studies and findings within each of these three approaches. In her conclusion, Bakardjieva highlights some of the most significant outcomes of this work, showing how each approach and set of findings complements the others to constitute a comprehensive but also very fine-grained understanding of the Internet and its interactions in our everyday lives.

We conclude Part I with Elizabeth A. Buchanan's "Internet Research Ethics: Past, Present, and Future." Buchanan provides here the definitive history and overview of Internet research ethics (IRE), first of all establishing its background and broad context in the emergence of human subjects protections and concomitant research ethics evoked by the disasters of the Tuskegee studies and the atrocities committed in the name of research on prisoners during World War Two. Buchanan interweaves this important history with the specific ethical norms and principles that come to be articulated through the various reports and legislative acts that gradually establish the background and precedents for what became an explicit focus on IRE in the 1990s. Buchanan then follows out the development and growing literature of IRE as such – but again, with a view towards thereby highlighting the substantive considerations of research ethics, especially as these are interwoven with specific methodologies. These lead to her detailed discussion of "ethical considerations" – in effect, a primer on IRE that summarizes the most important guidelines and reflections articulated in the rapidly growing literature of IRE. Finally, Buchanan sketches out some of the contemporary issues and possible future concerns of IRE. As with others in this volume (e.g., Baym, Jensen), Buchanan notes that the advent of Web 2.0 signals a new range of ethical challenges and concerns that, in part at least, have yet to be fully addressed. Building on the participatory "open source" approach of the AoIR guidelines (2002), Buchanan urges Internet researchers to engage in the ongoing development of IRE as an interdisciplinary and cross-cultural enterprise – one essential to the further development of Internet studies as such.

Taken together, these chapters thus provide an initial orientation to the history of Internet studies and to central questions of methods and approaches, including crucial attention to Internet research ethics. We find here as well an initial overview of what historical and contemporary research tells us about the Internet. Finally, these chapters foreground several important thematics for contemporary research, beginning with the everydayness of an Internet that is embedded in our lives. These more contemporary emphases thus shift us from a 1990s fascination with novelty and revolution, and thereby, a "user" who was often presumed to be radically disembodied and thereby disconnected from her larger communities and histories, and oftentimes relatively passive vis-à-vis the technologies envisioned to somehow inevitably carry us all along in their deterministic sweep. By contrast, more contemporary methods and approaches presume not only the activity of the persons taking up these technologies and applications (and their interactivity, as emphasized by the rubric of Web 2.0); they further bring into play the central importance of *embodiment* as crucial to our understanding of the persons who design and take up the Internet and its multiple applications.

This embeddedness, embodiment, and engagement, finally, extends not only to what Wellman calls "networked selves" – but to Internet researchers themselves, especially as our contributors here call us to engage not only in our research and reflection on the methods of that research, but also in reflection and construction of our archiving methods and research ethics.

In all these ways, these chapters thus orient our readers to what follows – and demarcate a broad agenda for Internet researchers at large, as we move forward with this most ephemeral but most central medium.

References

Association of Internet Researchers (AoIR) and Ess. C. (2002). *Ethical Decision Making and Internet Research.* <www.aoir.org/reports/ethics.pdf> Accessed 3 November 2008

Baym, Nancy K. (1995). The Emergence of Community in Computer-Mediated Communication. In *CyberSociety: Computer-Mediated Communication and Community*, Steven G. Jones (ed.), 138–163. Thousand Oaks, CA: Sage.

Baym, Nancy K. Interpersonal Life Online (2002). In L. Lievrouw & S. Livingstone (eds.), *Handbook of New Media*, pp. 62–76. Thousand Oaks: Sage.

Giddens, A. (1979). *Central problems in social theory.* London: Macmillan

1

Studying the Internet Through the Ages

Barry Wellman

Pre-History

As a tribal elder, I often think back to the state of Internet and society scholarship before the dawning of the Internet. Although sociologist Roxanne Hiltz and computer scientist Murray Turoff had published their prophetic *Network Nation* in 1978, linking social science with computerized communication, the word "Internet" hadn't been invented.

As one of the first social scientists to be involved in research studying how people communicate online, I started going in 1990 to biannual gatherings of the then-tribe: CSCW (computer supported cooperative work) conferences that were dominated by computer scientists writing "groupware" applications. Lotus Notes applications were in vogue. Lab studies were the predominant research method of choice, summarized in Lee Sproull and Sara Kiesler's *Connections* (1991).

But all that people wanted to deal with were small closed groups. I remember standing lonely and forlorn at the microphone during a comments period at the CSCW 1992 conference. Feeling extremely frustrated (and now prophetic), I exclaimed:

> You don't understand! The future is not in writing stand-alone applications for small groups. It is in understanding that computer networks support the kinds of social networks in which people usually live and often work. These social networks are not the densely-knit, isolated small groups that groupware tries to support. They are sparsely-knit, far-reaching networks, in which people relate to shifting relationships and communities. Moreover, people don't just relate to each other online, they incorporate their computer mediated communication into their full range of interaction: in-person, phone, fax, and even writing.

I pleaded for paying more attention to how people actually communicate in real life. But this approach was disparagingly referred to as "user studies," much less exciting to computer geeks than writing new applications. Conference participants listened politely and went back to developing applications for small groups. I helped develop one too, for it was exciting and fun to collaborate with computer scientists and be one of the few sociologists who actually built stuff. Maybe, we'd get rich and famous. Our Cavecat/Telepresence desktop videoconferencing systems were stand-alone groupware at their then-finest (Mantei et al., 1991; Buxton, 1992). But, they never got out of the laboratory as our grant ran out and they were expensive to hardwire in those pre-Internet days. Little did we realize that Cisco would appropriate our Telepresence name as a trademark 15 years later, without so much as a hand-wave.

The First Age of Internet Studies: Punditry Rides Rampant

Economic forces were already fueling the turn away from stand-alone groupware towards applications that supported social networks. This was the proliferation of the Internet as it became more than an academic chat room. Unlike groupware, the Internet was open-ended, far-flung, and seemingly infinite in scope. The Internet became dot.com'ed, and the boom was on by the mid-1990s.

The Internet was seen as a bright light shining above everyday concerns. It was a technological marvel, thought to be bringing a new Enlightenment to transform the world. Communication dominated the Internet, by asynchronous email and discussion lists and by synchronous instant messaging and chat groups. All were supposedly connected to all, without boundaries of time and space. As John Perry Barlow, a leader of the Electric Frontier Foundation, wrote in 1995:

> With the development of the Internet, and with the increasing pervasiveness of communication between networked computers, we are in the middle of the most transforming technological event since the capture of fire. I used to think that it was just the biggest thing since Gutenberg, but now I think you have to go back farther (p. 56).

In their euphoria, many analysts lost their perspective and succumbed to presentism and parochialism. Like Barlow, they thought that the world had started anew with the Internet (*presentism*). They had gone beyond groupware, and realized that computer-mediated communication – in the guise of the Internet – fostered widespread connectivity. But like the groupware folks, they looked at online phenomena in isolation (*parochialism*). They assumed that only things that happened on the Internet were relevant to understanding the Internet. Their initial analyses of the impact of the Internet were often unsullied by data and informed only by conjecture and anecdotal evidence: travelers' tales from Internet *incognita*. The analyses were often utopian: extolling the Internet as egalitarian and globe-spanning, and ignoring how differences in power and status might affect interactions on and offline. The dystopians had their say too, worrying that "while all this razzle-dazzle connects us electronically, it disconnects us from each other, having us 'interfacing' more with computers and TV screens than looking in the face of our fellow human beings" (Texas broadcaster Jim Hightower, quoted in Fox, 1995, p. 12).

Pundits and computer scientists alike were still trying to get a handle on what was happening without taking much account of social science knowledge. In my frustration, I began to issue manifestos in the guise of scholarly articles. Two presented my case, based on my 30-plus years of experience as a social network analyst and community analyst. "An Electronic Group is Virtually a Social Network" (1997) contrasted groups and groupware with social networks and social networkware. It asserted that the Internet was best seen as a computer-supported social network, in fact the world's largest component (a network in which all points are ultimately connected, directly or indirectly). The second paper, "Net Surfers Don't Ride Alone" (with Milena Gulia, 1999) took aim at the vogue for calling every interaction online a "community." It argued that the Internet was not the coming of the new millennium, despite the gospel of *Wired* magazine (then the *Vogue* magazine of the Internet), but was a new technology following the path of other promoters of transportation and communication connectivity, such as the telegraph, railroad, telephone, automobile, and airplane. It showed how community dynamics continued to operate on the Internet – this was not a totally new world – and how intertwined offline relationships were with online relationships.

The Second Age of Internet Studies: Systematic Documentation of Users and Uses

The second age of Internet studies began about 1998 when government policy-makers, commercial interests, and academics started to want systematic accounts of the Internet. They realized that if the Internet boom were to continue, it would be good to describe it rather than just to praise it and coast on it. But the flames of Internet euphoria dimmed with the collapse of the dot.com boom early in 2000. The pages of *Wired* magazine shrank 25 percent from 240 pages in September 1996 to 180 pages in September 2001, and then shrank another 17 percent to 148 pages in September 2003: a decline of 38 percent since 1996.

Moreover, the uses of the Internet kept expanding and democratizing. The initial killer applications of communication – variants of email and instant mes-saging – were joined by information, via the Netscape/Internet Explorer enabled World Wide Web. Search engines, such as Alta Vista and then Google moved web exploring beyond a cognoscenti's game of memorizing arcane URLs and IP addresses. What exactly was going on, besides the hype of Internet promotion by the mass media, governments, NGOs, entrepreneurs, and academics going for suddenly available grants?

The Internet opened our field up way beyond small-group studies. The second age of Internet studies was devoted to documenting this proliferation of Internet users and uses. It was based on large-scale surveys, originally done by marketing-oriented firms (and with some bias towards hyping use), but increasingly done by governments, academics, and long-term enterprises such as the Pew Internet and American Life Study (www.pewinternet.org) and the World Internet Project (www.worldinternetproject.net). These studies counted the number of Internet users, compared demographic differences, and learned what basic things people have been doing on the Internet. For example, we came to know that a majority of adults in many developed countries have used the Internet, and women were rapidly increasing their presence. However, we discovered that the socioeconomic gap persists in most countries even with increasing use, because poorer folks are not increasing their rate of use as much as wealthier, better-educated ones (Chen & Wellman, 2005).

Neither the utopian hopes of Barlow nor the dystopian fears of Hightower have been borne out. Despite Barlow's hopes, the Internet has not brought a utopia of widespread global communication and democracy. Despite Hightower's fears, high levels of Internet use have not lured people away from in-person contact. To the contrary, it seems as if the more people use the Internet, the more they see each other in person (distance permitting) and talk on the telephone (see the studies in Wellman & Haythornthwaite, 2002). This may be because the Internet helps arrange in-person meetings and helps maintain relationships in between meetings (Haythornthwaite & Wellman, 1998). It may also mean that gregarious, extroverted people will seize on all media available to communicate (Kraut et al., 2002).

To the surprise of some, the purportedly global village of the Internet has not even destroyed in-person neighboring. In "Netville," a suburb near Toronto, the two-thirds of the residents who had always-on, super-fast Internet access knew the names of three times as many neighbors as their unwired counterparts, spoke with twice as many, and visited in the homes of 1.5 as many (Hampton & Wellman, 2003). Given opportunities to organize, people will often connect with those who live nearby, online as well as offline (Hampton, 2007).

Yet, the globe-spanning properties of the Internet are obviously real, nowhere more so than in the electronic diasporas that connect émigrés to their homeland. In so doing, they enable diasporas to aggregate and transmit reliable, informal news back to often-censored countries (Miller & Slater, 2000; Mitra, 2003; Mok, Wellman, & Carrasco, 2009).

The Third Age: From Documentation to Analysis

The use of the Internet has kept growing. But, its proliferation has meant that it no longer stands alone, if it ever did. It has become embedded in everyday life. The ethereal light that dazzled from above has become part of everyday things. We have moved from a world of Internet wizards to a world of ordinary people routinely using the Internet. The Internet has become an important thing, but it is not a special thing. It has become the utility of the masses, rather than the plaything of computer scientists. Rather than explosive growth, the number of Internet users has become steady state in North America, although the types of Internet use have proliferated. Yet, the burgeoning of diverse Web 2.0 applications, from Facebook social-networking software to YouTube home videos, has increased desires to know about which applications to use. Reflecting the routinization of the Internet, *Wired* has moved from its *Vogue*-ish origins to become more of a how-to-do-it magazine. Its length of 160 pages in September 2008 is an 8 percent increase from September 2003, although I wonder how it will withstand the new global recession.

How do scholars engage with the Internet in this third age? The first two ages of Internet studies were easy. In the first age, little large-scale data were used, just eloquent euphoria or despair. In the second age, researchers grabbed low-hanging fruit using standard social scientific methods – surveys and fieldwork – to document the nature of the Internet.

Two opposing – but complementary – trends are now apparent in the third age. One trend is the development of "Internet studies" as a field in its own right, bringing together scholars from the social sciences, humanities, and computer sciences. The annual conference of the Association of Internet Researchers (AoIR) started in 2000, and has become institutionalized in the last few years, so much so that many participants do not realize what a shoestring, hope-filled gathering the first meeting was at the University of Kansas. AoIR quickly became international, with conferences in the Netherlands, Australia, Canada, and Denmark attracting many hundreds. Its AIR list serve is even bigger. For vacation-minded researchers, the Hawaii International Conference on System Science offers a congenial venue. Many journals, often backed by major publishers, focus on the Internet and society, including *Computers in Human Behavior, Information, Communication and Society* (which puts out an annual AoIR conference issue), *The Information Society*, the online-only *Journal of Computer Mediated Communication, New Media and Society*, and the *Social Science Computing Review*.

The second trend is the incorporation of Internet research into the mainstream conferences and journals of their disciplines, with projects driven by ongoing issues. This brings the more developed theories, methods, and substantive lore of the disciplines into play, although sometimes at the cost of the adventurous innovativeness of interdisciplinary Internet research. I take two examples from my own discipline of sociology.

One phenomenon is the incorporation of the longstanding concern about the "digital divide" into the study of stratification. Moving beyond the second-age counting of which kinds of people are on – or off – line, Eszter Hargittai (2004) has shown the differential distribution of skills – and not just access – in the American population. It is not just getting connected; it is getting usably connected. Put another way, there are non-economic factors of social inequality – linked to skill and cultural capital – that strongly affect the structure of increasingly computerized societies and the life chances of their members (DiMaggio et al., 2004).

A second continuing debate has been about the loss of community first discussed more than a century ago, by Ferdinand Tönnies in 1887. Instead of the former debate about whether industrialization and urbanization had withered community, research now turned to television (Putnam, 2000) and the Internet (Kraut et al., 1998, 2002). Systematic field research showed that community ties were thriving, with online connectivity intertwined with offline relationships (Wellman & Haythornthwaite, 2002; Boase et al., 2006; Wellman et al., 2006; Wang & Wellman, 2010). For example, our NetLab is currently looking at what kinds of relationships the Internet does (and does not) foster. As an overarching thought, our NetLab believes that the evolving personalization, portability, ubiquitous connectivity, and wireless mobility of the Internet are facilitating a move towards individualized networks (Kennedy et al., 2008). The Internet is helping each person to become a communication and information switchboard, between persons, networks, and institutions.

What of groupware, where I started nearly 20 years ago? It has been transmuted from supporting small closed groups into social-network software that connects dispersed, complex networks of friends and colleagues and helps to connect the hitherto unconnected.

I am not standing alone any more. Groups have clearly become networked individuals: on the Internet and off it (Wellman, 2001, 2002). The person has become the portal.

Note

This is a revised version of an article originally published in *New Media & Society*, 6 (2004), 108–14.

Acknowledgements: My thanks to Cavecat/Telepresence colleagues who first involved me in this area: Ronald Baecker, Bill Buxton, Janet Salaff, and Marilyn Mantei Tremaine. Bernie Hogan and Phuoc Tran are among the NetLab members who have provided useful comments along the way. Intel Research's People and Practices, the Social Science and Humanities Research Council of Canada, and Bell Canada have been the principal supporters of our NetLab research.

References

Barlow, J. P. (1995). Is there a there in cyberspace? *Utne Reader*, March–April, 50–56.

Boase, J., Horrigan, J., Wellman, B., & Rainie, L. (2006). *The Strength of Internet Ties*. Washington: Pew Internet and American Life Project. www.pewinternet.org.

Buxton, B. (1992). Telepresence: Integrating shared task and person spaces. Paper presented at the Proceedings of Graphics Interface, May, Vancouver.

Chen, W., & Wellman, B. (2005). Charting digital divides within and between countries. In W. Dutton, B, Kahin, R. O'Callaghan, & A. Wyckoff (eds.), *Transforming Enterprise* (pp. 467–97). Cambridge, MA: MIT Press.

DiMaggio, P., Hargittai, E., Celeste, C., & Shafter, S. (2004). From unequal access to differentiated use: A literature review and agenda for research on digital inequality. In K. Neckerman (ed.), *Social Inequality*. New York: Russell Sage Foundation.

Fox, R. (1995). Newstrack. *Communications of the ACM*, 38 (8), 11–12.

Hampton, K. (2007). Neighbors in the network society: The e-neighbors study. *Information, Communication, and Society*, 10 (5), 714–48.

Hampton, K., & Wellman, B. (2003). Neighboring in Netville: How the Internet supports community and social capital in a wired suburb. *City & Community*, 2 (3), 277–311.

Hargittai, E. (2004). Internet use and access in context. *New Media & Society*, 6, 137–43.

Haythornthwaite, C., & Wellman, B. (1998). Work, friendship and media use for information exchange in a networked organization. *Journal of the American Society for Information Science*, 49 (12), 1101–14.

Hiltz, S. R., & Turoff, M. (1978). *The Network Nation*. Reading, MA: Addison-Wesley.

Kennedy, T., Smith, A., Wells, A. T., & Wellman, B. (2008). Networked families. Pew Internet and American Life Project, October. http://www.pewinternet.org/PPF/r/266/report_display.asp.

Kraut, R., Kiesler, S., Boneva, B., Cummings, J., Helgeson, V., & Crawford, A. (2002). Internet paradox revisited. *Journal of Social Issues*, 58 (1), 49–74.

Kraut, R., Patterson, M., Lundmark, V., Kiesler, S., Mukhopadhyay, T., & Scherlis, W. (1998). Internet paradox: A social technology that reduces social involvement and psychological well-being? *American Psychologist*, 53 (9), 1017–31.

Mantei, M., Baecker, R., Sellen, A., Buxton, W., Milligan, T., & Wellman, B. (1991). Experiences in the use of a media space: Reaching through technology. *Proceedings of the CHI '91 Conference* (pp. 203–8). Reading, MA: Addison-Wesley.

Miller, D., & Slater, D. (2000). *The Internet: An Ethnographic Approach*. Oxford: Berg.

Mitra, A. (2003). Online communities, diasporic. *Encyclopedia of Community*, vol. 3 (pp. 1019–20). Thousand Oaks, CA: Sage.

Mok, D., Wellman, B., & Carrasco, J-A. (2009). Does distance still matter in the age of the Internet? *Urban Studies*, forthcoming.

Putnam, R. (2000). *Bowling Alone*. New York: Simon & Schuster.

Sproull, L., & Kiesler, S. (1991). *Connections*. Cambridge, MA: MIT Press.

Wang, H. H., & Wellman, B. (2010). Social connectivity in America. *American Behavioral Scientist*, Forthcoming, 53.

Wellman, B. (1997). An electronic group is virtually a social network. In S. Kiesler (ed.), *Culture of the Internet* (pp. 179–205). Mahwah, NJ: Lawrence Erlbaum.

Wellman, B. (2001). Physical place and cyberspace: The rise of personalized networks. *International Urban and Regional Research*, 25 (2), 227–52.

Wellman, B. (2002). Little boxes, glocalization, and networked individualism. In M. Tanabe, Peter van den Besselaar, & T. Ishida (eds.), *Digital Cities II: Computational and Sociological Approaches* (pp. 10–25). Berlin: Springer.

Wellman, B., & Gulia, M. (1999). Net surfers don't ride alone: Virtual communities as communities. In B. Wellman (ed.), *Networks in the Global Village* (pp. 331–66). Boulder, CO: Westview.

Wellman, B., & Haythornthwaite, C. (eds.) (2002). *The Internet in Everyday Life*. Oxford: Blackwell.

Wellman, B., & Hogan, B., with Berg, K., Boase, B., Carrasco, J-A., Côté, R., Kayahara, J., Kennedy, T., and Tran, P. (2006). Connected lives: The project. In P. Purcell (ed.), *Networked Neighbourhoods: The Online Community in Context* (pp. 157–211). Guildford, UK: Springer.

2

Web Archiving – Between Past, Present, and Future

Niels Brügger

This chapter argues that one of the most important issues for Internet scholars in the future is to get a hold on the Internet of the past – and the Internet of the present. There are two reasons for this. First, the archiving of the web enables us to write web *history*, which is a necessary condition for the understanding of the Internet of the present as well as of new, emerging Internet forms. Second, it enables us to document our findings when we study *today's* web, since in practice most web studies preserve the web in order to have a stable object to study and refer to when the analysis is to be documented (except for studies of the live web). Therefore, the problems related to web archiving as well as the special characteristics of the archived web document are not only important to web historians; they are also of relevance for any web scholar studying, for example, online communities, online games, news websites, etc.

This chapter aims at putting the general discussion of web archiving on the research agenda. The focus is on the consequences of the archiving process for the Internet scholar, and not on the archiving process itself. Hence, the point of view is that of the Internet researcher, and the archived web is basically discussed as a medium and a text.[1]

The Internet scholar who intends to make use of archived web material, no matter how it has been created, and in which archive it is found, faces two fundamental questions that will also serve as guides in the chapter: (1) is the archived web document a new kind of document? – and if "yes," then, (2) must this document be treated in new ways when used as an object of study? Both questions revolve around "the new" and whether new media necessarily call for new methods and new theories. I will argue in this chapter that, in general, new media are not necessarily new (different) just because they are new (newcomers). And if they are not different from existing media in any significant way, we do not have to approach them with new methods or seek new explanations by the use of new theories. Therefore, the advent of "new" media only implies that we question, on the one hand, their possible differences from existing media and, on the other hand, our well-known theories in the light of the existence of the new media. We will find, however, that the archiving of the Internet in fact entails new methods. First, the Internet as a type of medium is characterized by being dynamic, ephemeral, changing, etc., in other words – in relation to archiving – it is fundamentally different from any other known media type, and therefore it must be approached in different ways than we are used to when we archive; second, when it is archived, it is also fundamentally different from well-known media types, and again we have to approach it in new ways.

We will see this, however, only following a careful discussion of the two questions above. And for this discussion, it must first be determined what we mean by web archiving. In exploring this matter, I further present a brief history of web archiving.

Web Archiving and Archiving Strategies

In order to avoid limiting the field of web archiving to the understanding that has been predominant for the last 10–12 years, I would suggest the following broad definition of web archiving: Any form of deliberate and purposive preserving of web material. This definition will be elaborated by explaining each of its constituents in more detail.

Micro- and macro-archiving

Regardless of the form, the purpose, and the kind of web material preserved, a distinction may be drawn between micro- and macro-archiving. Micro-archiving means archiving carried out on a small scale by "amateurs" on the basis of an immediate, here-and-now need to preserve an object of study. In contrast, macro-archiving is carried out on a large scale by institutions with professional technical expertise at their disposal, in order to archive, for instance, cultural heritage in general (cf. Brügger, 2005, pp. 10–11; cf. also Masanès, 2006, pp. 213–14). Micro-archiving is, for instance, what an Internet researcher does when she uses her own PC to archive the Internet newspapers to be studied, while macro-archiving is performed by, for instance, national libraries who use a complex setup of computers and software with a view to securing the Internet activity related to a nation-state for the years to come.

Web material

Web material has two general characteristics: It is digital and it is present on the Internet. It can therefore be considered a sub-set of, on the one hand, digital media (e.g. e-print, e-books, computer game consoles, CD-ROM/DVDs, etc.), and, on the other hand, the Internet (an infrastructure with a variety of protocols, software types, etc. – Usenet, Gopher, Internet relay chat, email, etc.). Thus, web material is the specific part of digital media and of the Internet that is related to the use of protocols and markup languages originating from the world wide web in the broadest sense.

However, "web material" is still a very broad term that needs to be clarified further. A framework for doing this is to identify some of the main analytical levels on which we can talk about web material as a delimited signifying unity (cf. Brügger, 2009). At one end of a five-level scale we have all the material that is present on the *web as a whole*, and at the other end of the scale an *individual web element* on a webpage, such as an image. And in between, we can focus on different analytical clusters of web material, of which the most significant are: the *web sphere*, which is "a set of dynamically defined digital resources spanning multiple Web sites deemed relevant or related to a central event, concept, or theme" (Schneider & Foot, 2006, p. 20); the *website*, which is a coherent unity of web pages; and the individual *webpage*. Following this five-level stratification, the preserved web material can thus be anything from the web as a whole to a web sphere, a website, a webpage or a single web element on a webpage, and these five strata are mutually each other's context.

One last distinction has to be made. Normally web material must have been made public on the web. But, in fact, material that does not meet this criterion might also deserve to be archived. At least the following three types should be taken into consideration: (1) non- or semi-public material: i.e. web material kept on an intranet, where it is only accessible to a limited and known number of people; (2) pre-public material: i.e. design outlines, dummies, beta versions, etc.; (3) public material that has been published in other media types, for instance in printed media (newspapers, magazines, books, journals) or television (commercials, TV spots, etc.). Especially with regard to the early period of web history, the only preserved sources are these indirect, non-digital pieces of evidence (this last category is thus the exception to the above-mentioned point that all web material is digital). With this last addition in mind, web material can therefore also be material that has not been made public on the web for one reason or another, or material that stems from the web but that we only can access in other types of media.

Deliberate and purposive preserving

That web archiving is considered a deliberate and purposive act means that one has to be conscious, first, *that* one is preserving the material at all, and, second, *why* the web material is being preserved. The simple act of putting an html-file on a web server that is connected to the Internet in order to publish it is, in fact, a way of preserving the file. Still, it is not done deliberately with a view to archiving the file, but simply as an "unconscious" and integrated part of making the file public (although the result is the same, as long as the file is not removed or the web server is not closed).

And in order to be designated as web archiving, the casual storing of web material is not sufficient. In addition, the act of preserving must be accompanied by some degree of reflection on why the archiving is carried out – be that for fun;

with a view to preserving the old family home page; in order to document how a certain webpage looked at a certain point in time; with a research project in mind; or with a view to preserving the cultural heritage of a nation or a culture.

Forms of web preserving

By far the most widespread way of web preserving is *web harvesting*, which in short means that a web crawler downloads files from a web server by following links from a given starting point URL. Web harvesting has been the predominant approach to web archiving in all major (inter)national archiving projects, just as it has been setting the agenda for most of the literature (e.g. Masanès, 2006; Brown, 2006).

However, two other forms of web preserving have to be mentioned in order to complete the picture, although their use is not yet very widespread, at least not among larger archiving institutions. The first can be distinguished from web harvesting by the fact that it transforms the html text into *images*. One of the simplest ways of preserving web material is to capture what is present on the screen or in a browser window by saving it either as a static image or in the form of moving images by recording a screen movie.[2]

Delivery is another way of getting web material archived. In contrast to web harvesting, where the web material is retrieved from the "outside" by contacting the web server, the material can be delivered from the "inside," that is directly from the producer. From the point of view of the archive, one can distinguish between proactive and reactive delivery: proactive delivery being based on some kind of prior agreement with the producer and made from a certain point in time and onwards, while reactive delivery is random delivery of old material that the producer, a researcher, or the like delivers to an archive without prior agreement.[3]

Each of these three forms of web archiving has advantages as well as disadvantages. In short: web harvesting is very useful with large amounts of web material, and it can to a great extent be automated, though far from completely; indeed, the more automated, the more deficient is the archived material as to missing elements and functions, and some types of elements can only be harvested with great difficulty. In addition it is possible to keep the link structure intact to some extent, and harvested material is easier to use afterwards since it is searchable; it looks much like the live web (but as we shall see this is far from the case, cf. the section below, *The Archived Web Document*), and it can be treated automatically as a digital corpus, which is why it is well suited for use in research projects where these demands have to be met, such as projects involving content analysis, link and network analysis, sociological analysis, or ethnographical analysis.

Screen capture is very useful for smaller amounts of web material. The capture of static images can to a certain extent be automated, whereas the capture of screen movies requires the active presence of an individual. Both types of screen capture have the advantage that all textual elements on the individual webpage are preserved, and screen movies have the further advantage of being capable of preserving some of the web forms that web harvesting has great difficulty in archiving, e.g. streaming media, computer games, user interaction, personalized websites, etc. It is also possible to preserve working links, with the disadvantage, however, for the screen movie that a later user has to follow the movements made by the individual who made the recording. Screen capture is very useful when one wishes to study style and design, carry out rhetorical or textual analysis, or in general carry out studies where access to the html code is not important.

The overall advantage of delivered web material is that it can provide access to web material that has not yet been archived, and makes it possible to complete existing web archives. The disadvantage is that delivered material is often very heterogeneous and it can be difficult to reconstruct it meaningfully, or to integrate it in an already existing archival structure: this is a serious problem with proactive delivery and even more so for reactive delivery.

Archiving strategies

As indicated by this brief presentation of the constituents in the definition of web archiving, a complete web archiving that preserves web material exactly as it was on the live web is very much an exception. To a great extent, archiving involves deciding to what extent we can accept omissions in our archived web document, and this fundamental condition forces us to formulate and choose between different archiving strategies, each focusing on specific web material, purposes, and forms of archiving, and each with their gain and loss. The following three strategies have been used by larger web archives that all base their collections on web harvesting. (For examples of each strategy see below, the section headed *The dynamic web in (trans)national web archives*).[4]

The *snapshot* strategy intends to take a snapshot of a certain portion of the web at a certain point in time. This strategy is often used for the harvest of a large number of websites, where either no specific websites have been selected prior to the archiving, or a very general selection has been made, based on, for instance, domain names (e.g. country codes such as .uk, .fr). In general, archiving using the snapshot strategy is not very deep, and normally it is not accompanied by a subsequent quality control and an eventual supplementary archiving, which is why the result is often of erratic quality – the price to pay for the large number of websites. Although this strategy is called "snapshot," it can take up to several months to archive something like a national domain, which is why it cannot be used for rapidly updated websites.

The *selective* strategy sets out to archive a limited number of websites that have been selected individually prior to archiving, because they are considered important, because they are supposedly updated with short intervals, because one wants to carry out a deep archiving, or a combination of these reasons; it is often accompanied by a quality control and an eventual supplementary archiving, which is why this type of material is in general of good quality, but for a limited number of websites. The selective strategy is normally used for harvests with very short intervals (hours, days), meaning that this strategy has a more continuous form.

The *event* strategy aims at archiving web activity in relation to an event in the broadest sense of the word, for instance, general elections, sports events, catastrophes, etc.; in other words planned as well as unplanned events. It can be considered a combination of the two above-mentioned, since the intention is to archive a larger number of websites than the selective strategy, and with a higher frequency than the snapshot strategy.

A Brief History of Web Archiving

Three main phases can be distinguished in the brief history of web archiving. However, the history of web archiving is so short – 10–12 years – that it can be difficult to draw clear lines, which is why the phases in many cases persist side by side with various degrees of overlaps. In addition there are great national differences.[5]

The pre-history of web archiving

In the very first years of the existence of the web, individuals, families, organizations, and institutions from time to time felt a need to preserve what they had created or what they met on their way through what was once called "cyberspace," mostly preserved as either a number of html-files or screenshots. In this amateur era, archiving was random and based on here-and-now needs, just as the act of preserving was not accompanied by reflections as to what was done in terms of archiving and it was not considered part of a greater, systematic effort with a view to preserving the cultural heritage.

There exists no systematic overview of the existence of this kind of material, but a lot of it is presumably either in the possession of the people who created it, or scattered all over today's web. Famous examples are Tim Berners-Lee's first browser screenshot from 1990 and the least recently modified webpage (1990).[6] These amateur archivings are in many cases the only existing evidence of the early web (together with the above-mentioned non-digital media types), and this early approach to web archiving lives on in the many forms of micro-archiving.

Static web publications in national libraries

In the same period a few of the major national libraries begin to preserve material that has been published on the web. Thus, an increased professionalism as well as a clearly formulated intention of preserving the national digital cultural heritage emerge. However, since these initiatives are carried out by libraries, the overall approach is very much that of print culture. Focus is on the nexus between legal deposit law[7] and a conventional understanding of publishing

(delivery by or download from publishing houses), on well-known library infrastructures (cataloguing, organizing), and based on a conception of web material
as primarily static documents, like books or periodicals that just happen to be
published on the web.

The first example of this approach is the Electronic Publications Pilot Project
(EPPP) conducted by the National Library of Canada in 1994 (EPPP, 1996,
pp. 3–4). Here the mindset of traditional libraries is applied to the web, at least
in this early pilot project: primarily static web material that looks like printed
publications is archived (journals, articles, etc.) just as the archived material is
catalogued. However, later on, web documents such as websites and blogs are
also archived by the National Library of Canada, based on a selective strategy and
on submission of the publication from the publisher. The traditional librarian
approach with focus on static web publications continues parallel to the third phase,
namely different forms of web harvesting.

The dynamic web in (trans)national web archives

As a spin-off of search engine technology, web crawlers were developed, and what
proved to be the most important phase in the brief history of web archiving was
born. In this phase, the number of archiving initiatives increases dramatically. The
professional approach and the ambition of preserving the digital cultural heritage
are still predominant, but the libraries are no longer the only archiving institutions, and their manner of conceptualizing the material worthy of being preserved
is being challenged. In this period the idea of archiving virtually anything that
can be found on the web is formulated, with regard for neither the kind of web
document in question nor who has made it public – not only material that looks
like printed publications from publishers is to be archived, but also dynamic
web material.

However, in terms of strategy, there are substantial differences among the major
initiatives as to how this overall aim is pursued. The following four examples
illustrate this, each being the first of its kind.

The Internet Archive was created in 1996 as a non-profit organization, located
in The Presidio of San Francisco, and with the purpose of preserving historical
collections that exist in digital format, among others the web. The web collection is built on web crawls done by the for-profit company Alexa Internet, and
crawls are done according to link data and usage trails – what is crawled is where
the links point and where the users go, which is why the Internet Archive is transnational by nature (cf. Kimpton & Ubois, 2006, pp. 202–4). The main archiving
strategy is the *snapshot* approach, where all the web material that the web crawler
encounters is archived every eight weeks. The material is not catalogued in a library
sense, but is organized much as it looked on the web. However, the Internet
Archive actually started its collection by making an *event*-based collection of
the websites of all the 1996 Presidential candidates, but this event harvest is not
conceptualized as such; it was done for more strategic reasons, in order to

demonstrate the potential value of preserving webpages at a point in time where this value was not self-evident to everyone (cf. Kimpton & Ubois, 2006, p. 202).

The Swedish web archiving project Kulturarw3 was initiated by the Royal Library (national library of Sweden); it was inaugurated in 1996 and made its first harvests in the summer of 1997 (Arvidson, 2001, pp. 101–2). It is also based on a *snapshot* strategy, but in contrast to the Internet Archive, it is the first snapshot-based archive that delimits the archive by the borders of a nation state, since the main objective is to archive everything Swedish on the web (for a definition of "Swedish," see Arvidson, 2001, p. 101).

The Pandora archive was created in 1996 by the National Library of Australia, and uses the *selective* strategy with a view to preserving "significant Australian web sites and web-based on-line publications" (Cathro et al., 2001, p. 107). On the one hand, a limited number of websites are selected, archived, and catalogued, in which Pandora resembles the first library-inspired collections (like the Canadian EPPP project). But on the other hand, the archive is similar to the two above-mentioned inasmuch as entire websites are also archived from the very beginning (from 2005 the National Library of Australia has also used the snapshot strategy).

The Danish Internet archive Netarchive.dk is a joint venture between the State and University Library and The Royal Library, the two Danish national libraries, and was created in 2005, when a new legal deposit law came into force (from 1997, only static web publications were to be submitted to the national libraries). Although Netarchive.dk was not created until almost 10 years after the above mentioned, it was nevertheless the first web archive to formulate an overall strategy combining all three strategies, which means making four annual snapshots of the Danish portion of the web, selective harvests of 80 websites (on a daily basis), and two or three annual event harvests (Jacobsen, 2007, pp. 1–4).

With the Internet Archive as the exception with its transnational scope, each of these first national initiatives has been taken up by several other countries. In addition, several small-scale special archives and collections have been created (some of which are organized in national consortiums), in the same way as archiving on a commercial basis and aimed at both companies and scholars has appeared.[8]

Concurrently with the growing number of web archives, still more formalized forums and institutionalized professional forms of cooperation emerge, especially among the primary players, i.e., technicians and librarians. In 1994, the Commission on Preservation and Access and the Research Libraries Group created the Task Force on Digital Archiving, which in 1996 completed the report *Preserving Digital Information.* In 1997 the Nordic national libraries founded the working group the Nordic Web Archive, and in 1998 the European initiative Networked European Deposit Library (Nedlib) was created by eight European national libraries, a national archive, ICT organizations, and publishers. In 2003 11 major national libraries and the Internet Archive joined forces in the creation of the International Internet Preservation Consortium, and finally in 2004 the European Archive was created, based on partnerships with libraries, museums, and other collection bodies. In addition, the field of web archiving has for some years now had its annual conferences, email lists, websites, monographs, edited volumes, etc.[9]

Gradually members of the Internet research community that might be expected to use the archived material are beginning to show interest in being more closely involved in the discussions of web archiving. Some of the first examples of collaboration between scholars and web-archiving institutions are the Dutch project Archipol (2000), the conference "Preserving the Present for the Future" (2001) and webarchivist.org (2001).[10]

The Archived Web Document

No matter how an archived web document has been created, and no matter in what archive it is found, the Internet scholar cannot expect it to be an identical copy on a 1:1 scale of what was actually on the live web at a given time. In this respect the archived website differs significantly from other known archived media types. This point can be clarified by focusing on two interrelated clusters of characteristics of the archived web document: on the one hand, it is an *actively created and subjective reconstruction*; on the other hand, it is almost always *deficient*.[11]

An actively created and subjective reconstruction

Archived web material has one fundamental characteristic, regardless of the type of web material in question and regardless of the form and strategy of the archiving process: it is an actively created subjective reconstruction. First, the simple fact that a choice has to be made between different archiving forms and strategies, both in general and in detail, implies that the archived web document is based on a subjective decision by either an individual or an institution. For instance, it has to be decided which form of archiving has to be used, where the archiving should start, how far from the start-URL the crawl is to continue, whether specific file-types are to be included/excluded (e.g. images, sounds, flash), whether material is to be collected from other servers, how the material is to be preserved, both here-and-now and in a long-term perspective, etc.[12] Second, the archived web document is a reconstruction, in the sense that it is re-created on the basis of a variety of web elements that stem from either the live web or the producer, and that are reassembled and recombined in the archive.

Thus, the archived web document is the result of an active process that takes place at the nexus of the "raw material" present on the web, and a number of choices with regard to selecting and recombining the bits and pieces at hand. In this sense the archived web document does not exist prior to the act of archiving; it is only created in a stable form through the archiving process. In this respect the archived web document stands apart from other media types. When archiving newspapers, film, radio, and television, the main choices are related to the selection of the material, while the archiving process itself *grosso modo* consists of taking a copy out of circulation and storing it; no matter who stacks the newspapers or presses the record button on the video recorder, the archived copies are identical to what was once in circulation, just as all copies are identical. In contrast, with web material, choices have to be made in relation to both selecting and archiving, and we always do more than just remove the web material from circulation; the material is never totally unchanged.

Deficiencies

The other cluster of characteristics of the archived web document is that it is almost always deficient when compared to what was on the live web. Apart from the deficiencies caused by deliberate omissions, two other sources of deficiencies can be singled out: those related to time, and those caused by technological problems during the process of archiving.

One of the major reasons for deficiencies in relation to time is what could be called the dynamics of updating, that is the fact that the web content might have changed during the process of archiving, and we do not know if, where, and when this happens (cf. Schneider & Foot, 2004, p. 115; Brügger, 2005, pp. 21–27; Masanès, 2006, pp. 12–16). A brief example can illustrate this:

> During the Olympics in Sydney in 2000, I wanted to save the website of the Danish newspaper *JyllandsPosten*. I began at the first level, the front page, on which I could read that the Danish badminton player Camilla Martin would play in the finals a half hour later. My computer took about an hour to save this first level, after which time I wanted to download the second level, "Olympics 2000." But on the front page of this section, I could already read the result of the badminton finals (she lost). The website was – as a whole – not the same as when I had started; it had changed in the time it took to archive it, and I could now read the result on the front page, where the match was previously only announced. (Brügger, 2005, pp. 22–3)

As this example illustrates, it is obvious that the archived web document is deficient, since it is incomplete compared to what was once on the live web – something is lost in the process of archiving, due to the asynchrony between updating and archiving. But it is also deficient in another and less obvious way: since the archived web document is not only incomplete, it is also "too complete" – something that was not on the live web at the same time, the content on two webpages or website sections, is now combined in the archive, and it is difficult to determine what the website actually looked like at a given point in time on the basis of these two. The consequence is that the archived web document is in danger of being subject to the following paradoxical double inconsistency: "on the one hand, the archive is not exactly as the website *really* was in the past (we have lost something), but on the other, the archive may be exactly as the Internet *never* was in the past (we get something different)" (Brügger, 2005, p. 23). And we have great difficulty in determining which of these two is actually the case, if either. In this fundamental way we cannot rely on archived web documents to be identical to what was once on the live web. On the one hand, this problem is minimized the smaller the web material in question and the longer the intervals between the updating; on the other, the problem remains latent, and even worse, we do not know if there is in fact a problem or not.

If the archived web document has been created on the basis of web material delivered from the producer instead of harvested material, we are confronted with other problems related to time, and thereby to other kinds of deficiencies. Delivered material is often complex and fragmented, and it can be almost impossible to reconstruct a meaningful and datable entity out of, for instance, a collection of graphic files, the database of a Content Management System, or the like. The temporally based deficiencies in relation to delivered material are not caused by an asynchrony between two archived elements from different points in time, but rather by the impossibility of assigning more fragments to one fixed point in time at all (cf. Brügger, 2008a, p. 156).

Apart from the possible deficiencies caused by the dynamics of updating or the possible fragmented character of delivered material, the archived web document is also very likely to be deficient due to more technical reasons (software or hardware). For instance, words, images/graphics, sounds, moving images can be missing, or some of the possibilities of interaction can be non-functional in the archived web document.[13]

In summary, it can be argued that since the actual act of preserving web material in almost all cases changes the material that was on the web in a number of ways, the process of archiving creates a unique *version* and not a copy. Two consequences follow from this.

The first is the very obvious but often neglected fact that if several archived versions of, for instance, a given website exist from the same date they will probably differ from one another. Although this consequence might seem obvious, it has not so far attracted much attention in the literature on web archiving. However, a test conducted as part of the research project "The History of www.dr.dk, 1996–2006" clearly shows that versions of the same website that had been archived on the same date by different archives showed great differences in all respects (cf. Brügger, 2008b).

The second consequence is that the archived web document is a version of an original that we can never expect to find in the form it actually took on the live web; neither can we find an original among the different versions, nor can we reconstruct an original based on the different versions.

Web Philology and the Use of Archived Web Material

As it has been shown, the archived web document is a new kind of document, since it differs significantly from other types of archived documents in a number of ways. Taking these new conditions into account, must the web scholar then treat the archived web document in new ways compared to well-known media types and material on the live web? As shall be argued below, the answer to this question is "yes."[14]

Web philology

Since we are always dealing with a version, the major problem is to determine how close each version is to what was actually on the live web at a specific point in time (day, hour). Still, we must be aware that this can only be determined with various degrees of probability, not with certainty. One of the best ways of increasing the probability is to compare several existing versions that are as close as possible to each other in terms of time of archiving; but in doing this we can only base our comparisons on a study of the differences and similarities between existing versions, and not between an original and the versions. In this task we are in many ways close to the textual criticism of the philology of manuscripts (manuscript books as well as draft manuscripts) where a variant is also compared to a variant, without any authoritative original at hand. Some of the basic approaches of classical textual philology are probably of relevance to what could be called web philology; however, they must be brought into line with the media material specificity of the archived web document.

In short, the task of the manuscript scholar is to examine, on the one hand, the differences and similarities between a variety of ancient manuscripts with a view to determining whether one or more of them constitutes a source text, and on the other hand to clarify the relations between variants succeeding in time in the past, i.e. their provenance and affiliation backwards in time. (See Figure 2.1. The arrows indicate the direction of examination.)

Since the Internet scholar takes up another type of document based on a different media materiality than written or printed text on parchment or paper, she is confronted with other kinds of problems. First, she cannot set out to examine the differences and similarities between existing versions with a view to establishing

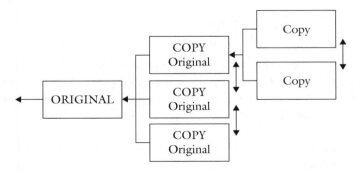

Figure 2.1 The Examination of Manuscripts

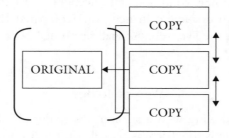

Figure 2.2 The Examination of Archived Websites

one of them as a source text, since none of them is likely to be identical to what was once on the live web. Second, she is examining versions that might have been created at almost the same point of time, which is why she has to trace differences and similarities in simultaneity rather than backwards in time. Third, and as a consequence of the first two points, she can only take one step back in time, inso-far as she can be said to examine things backwards in time at all. (See Figure 2.2.)

Apart from these three points, the archived web document has a number of constraints and possibilities that make its examination different from that of the written manuscript, due to the media materiality of digital writing (cf. Finnemann, 1999, pp. 142–8; Brügger, 2002, p. 21). First, the archived web document is a multi-leveled text, in the sense that it can be examined on levels ranging from the immediately perceptible text (the signifying units that we see/hear) to the variety of underlying textual levels that are not immediately perceptible (the source code (HTML, XML, etc.), as well as the layers of the Internet (the TCP/IP model, the OSI model or the like). Second, digital writing makes it possible that the archived web document might have been continuously rewritten in another sense than we know it from manuscripts, since the continuous rewriting can take place after the act of archiving, for instance in relation to long-term preservation, migration to other data formats, etc. Third, digital writing makes it possible to automatically compare archived web documents, at least to some extent. And fourth, exactly identical versions of the same web material can actually exist in different archives (most likely small, non-complicated websites that are rarely updated).

Rules and recommendations

Thus, the web scholar has to make comparisons that differ substantially from those of the classical philologist, and she must therefore proceed in other ways when she sets out to make a consistent statement about how close a given version is to what was on the live web. The following methods and rules might guide the web scholar in this task.[15]

First of all, anyone who uses an archived website must be critical as to his sources. He must be conscious that the version used is not necessarily the only existing one, and that he should therefore try to trace other versions in order to be on more solid ground when determining how close a version is to what was once on the live web.

He also must be prepared for the fact that due to the faulty and deficient character of the archived web document it often has to be navigated differently and examined more closely and by other means than normal on the live web.[16]

And finally, when evaluating the probabilities of what a given web document actually looked like on the live web by comparing different versions, the nature of these comparisons can follow a set of basic rules and procedures. The following six points constitute an attempt to formulate such a set of rules in more detail.[17]

1   The least deficient version as original: one way of getting as close to having an "original" for the comparisons as possible is to use the least deficient version as original. By "original" is not meant "as it was on the web" but just the most complete of the available versions. This "original" could be termed original*.[18]

2   Proximity in time and space: the closer the versions compared are to each other in terms of time (from same version to same day to earlier/later day) and space (same version, same archive, another archive) the greater the possibility of rendering probable what a given textual element actually looked like on the live web.

3   Speed of change: the more stable an element is, the greater the increase in the possibility of rendering probable what it actually looked like on the live web.[19]

4   Types of texts: as we move from the global paratexts of the website via the regional and local paratexts to the text itself, we also move from stable to presumably very frequently changing textual elements, thus decreasing the possibility of rendering probable what the element actually looked like on the live web.[20]

5   Genre characteristics: a given textual element is less likely to have been changed if it is found on a website or sub-site that is supposedly relatively stable in terms of genre.

6   Characteristics typical of the period: it can be relevant to involve knowledge of typical websites from the period of time in question.

These rules provide a set of indicators as to what a given textual element looked like on the live web. Moreover, it can be maintained that the indicators interact by forming a constellation of indicators. One might say that the probability is relatively high that an element actually appeared on the live web as it is in the archive if, for instance, the same element is present at the same position in several versions from the same day in the same archive, and if it is a supposedly stable type of text on a supposedly stable sub-site genre, and if this is supported by knowledge of typical websites from the period. However, in many cases we will supposedly be confronted with constellations of indicators that are neither clearly high nor clearly low in terms of probability, but constitute more conflicting intermediate forms where the indicators point in different directions, thus blurring the picture. In conclusion the following general rule can be formulated: the more indicators that point towards a high probability, the higher the probability becomes in general, and vice versa (cf. Brügger, 2008a, pp. 165–6).

The Future of Web Archiving

As the brief history of web archiving shows, Internet researchers are much better off today than they were five or ten years ago in terms of obtaining access to archived web material. Extensive national and international web archives have been established, and the number of archives, as well as the international knowledge infrastructure (working groups, conferences, email lists, etc.) in the field is rapidly increasing. However, there are still challenges to be dealt with from the point of view of the Internet researcher. A research agenda for the next few years could focus on two main areas: The interplay between web archives and Internet researchers, and the Internet researchers' community itself.

Web archives and Internet researchers

In general, it is important to expand the cooperation between web-archiving institutions and Internet research communities (or to establish such cooperation where it does not yet exist). The most compelling argument for this is that the processes of research and archiving are more closely connected than is the case with other types of media, since the research questions that a researcher intends to examine must to a certain degree be anticipated at the time of archiving. With collaboration, the web researcher has a better chance of getting a useful object of study, while the web archives get users who can actually use what has been archived.

Collaborations can take place in a number of ways, of which the following three seem most obvious. First, collaborations can be an integrated part of the day-to-day operations of the web archive, for instance by associating an advisory board of Internet researchers and other users with the archive. Second, collaborations could be occasional, in relation either to specific research projects or to event archivings, for instance by researchers cooperating with the archiving institutions already in the planning of a research project and not after the funding has been found or the project is halfway through. Third, these two types of collaborations could take place on a global scale in relation to transnational research projects, for instance in relation to events with a (nearly) global impact: wars, catastrophes, sports events such as the Olympic Games, etc.[21]

As regards the interplay between web archives and Internet researchers, three other future challenges should be mentioned. First, a targeted tracing and preservation of the heterogeneous web material that has not been made public on the web should be initiated, possibly in collaboration with other memory institutions such as museums. Second, the web archiving institutions should start to experiment more systematically with the two other forms of web archiving mentioned above, i.e. screen capture and delivery. Both tasks have a view to preserving as much as possible of the cultural heritage of relevance for the history of the web; and just to get an overview of these presumably important areas would be a huge step forward.[22] Third, discussions should be initiated regarding the extent to which the analytical software that is used on the live web can be applied to archived web material, with the specific composition of this material in mind.

The Internet researchers' community

In general, efforts should be made to increase Internet researchers' awareness of the problems related to web archiving. This includes, among others, an increased methodological consciousness – by whom, why, and how has an archived web document been created? – as well as an increased awareness of source criticism, since we are basically dealing with versions.

Methodological developments are also needed, partly in relation to micro-archiving, partly as regards web philology, a task that could be carried out in collaboration with archiving institutions as well as with philologists.

Furthermore, it is important to initiate discussions within the research communities about the specific legal and research-ethical issues related to the use of *archived* web documents, in contrast with Internet material in general. A start would be to map the specific problems of archiving, selecting, access, and subsequent use of the material, as well as the national differences (legal deposit laws, archiving based on prior agreement, crawling ethics, acceptance of robots.txt, copyright, privacy, open/restricted access, etc.).

Since the number of archived web sources in web archives is now gradually increasing, the time might seem right to encourage more Internet researchers to begin making historical studies of the web. As maintained at the beginning of this chapter, historical research is the basis for the understanding of the Internet of yesterday, today, and tomorrow.

And finally, the Internet researchers' community has to confront the challenge of diffusing knowledge of web archiving, both to other disciplines within the social sciences and the humanities (political science, sociology, linguistics, literature, arts, media studies, history, etc.) and to memory institutions in general (museums, archives, etc.). The argument for this is that for some years now the Internet has been an integral part of the communicational infrastructure of our societies. This means that there are phenomena that cannot be analyzed and explained exhaustively if the Internet is not part of the analysis, for instance political movements (the extreme right, non-governmental organizations like Attac, international terrorism), youth culture, artworks, and all kinds of existing media (newspapers, film, radio, and television). In as far as these phenomena are entangled in the Internet in various degrees, an in-depth explanation of these involves the Internet, and therefore the Internet has to be archived. Thus, Internet researchers should make an effort to enter into a dialogue with other research communities about their common interest in preserving the Internet of the past, the present, and the future.

Notes

1   Most of the existing literature brings the process of archiving into focus in either a technical or a librarian sense (questions about what hardware and software to use and how, selection, cataloguing, organizing, etc.), e.g. Masanès (2006) and Brown (2006).

2   For a short discussion of archiving by image capture, see Brügger (2005), pp. 47–53.

3   Masanès talks about server-side archiving (2006), p. 27. However, he discusses neither the delivery of old material nor reactive delivery.

4   For strategies in relation to micro-archiving, see Brügger (2005), pp. 33–60, and in relation to delivery see Brügger (2008b).

5   A comprehensive and systematic history of web archiving that does more than just mention the various archives still needs to be written; the following is only a rough sketch.

6   Cf. http://www.w3.org/History/1994/WWW/Journals/CACM/screensnap2_24c.gif, http://www.w3.org/History/19921103-hypertext/hypertext/WWW/Link.html.

7   Legal deposit law is a law which states that a person who publishes a work is obliged to deliver a copy of it to a deposit institution (normally national libraries). The first legal deposit laws came into force in the seventeenth century, which is why "work" was understood as printed work on paper or the like (book, newspaper, poster, etc). Later, several countries have stretched the law out to include audiovisual media (radio, television), and now the Internet.

8   For an overview of the many different archiving initiatives, see Brown (2006), pp. 8–18; Masanès (2006), pp. 40–45. An updated overview can be found at www.nla.gov.au/padi.

9   Examples are the International Web Archiving Workshop (IWAW, since 2001), the email list web-archive (http://listes.cru.fr/wws/info/web-archive, since 2002), the website Preserving Access to Digital Information (PADI, www.nla.gov.au/padi, since 1996), and the books Brügger (2005), Brown (2006), and Masanès (2006).

10 Archipol is a collaboration between historians from the Documentation Centre for Dutch Political Parties (DNPP) and the University Library Groningen (cf. Hollander & Voerman and www.archipol.nl). The international conference "Preserving the Present for the Future – Strategies for the Internet" (Copenhagen 2001) brought together a variety of members of the user community and persons with technical and library knowledge (cf. Preserving the Present for the Future 2001). Webarchivist.org is a collaborative project at the University of Washington and the SUNY Institute of Technology where researchers since 2001 have worked together with archiving institutions (cf. Schneider 2004 and webarchivist.org).

11 This section presents a short version of the insights in Brügger (2005) and Brügger (2008a).

12 Cf. Brügger (2005), pp. 15–19, 30–31, 61–2; cf. also Schneider & Foot (2004), p. 115; Masanès (2006), pp. 17–18, 76.

13 Cf. the test of the quality of archived web documents in different archives in Brügger (2008b); cf. also the discussion of quality and completeness in Masanès (2006), pp. 38–40, and of the technical problems related to reading and integrating delivered material into an existing archive in Andersen (2007).

14 The considerations on web philology in this section are an abridged version of Brügger (2008a).

15 The methods and rules outlined are produced as part of a work in progress, and have therefore to be tested and discussed further (cf. Brügger 2008a, 2008b). It should

also be stressed that they might not all be relevant in relation to all types of archived web material.

16   A deficient link structure often forces us to navigate, for instance by using a sitemap, by making detours, by clicking on something, etc.; and missing textual elements or functions compel us to make use of the visual marks in the archived document showing that something is missing (mouse-over etc.) or to use the source code to reveal what should have been displayed, etc., cf. Brügger (2008a), pp. 161–2.

17   The six rules are quoted almost *verbatim* from Brügger (2008a), pp. 163–5 where each of them is also elaborated.

18   We owe this convention to Grodzinsky, Miller, & Wolf (2008).

19   This rule is based upon a distinction between stability and high-frequency changes; by "stable" is meant that the same textual element is present at the same position on more than one of the webpages of a website.

20   This rule is based on the assumption that a website is composed of different types of textual elements, respectively texts and paratexts, the latter being the small pieces of text that serve as thresholds to the text itself (menu item, headline, footer, "bread crumbs," etc.) and that make the website coherent on either a local, regional, or global scale. Cf. Brügger (2007a), pp. 75, 84–5 for a definition of "textual element" and pp. 86–7 for a brief discussion of paratexts in relation to the website.

21   There are isolated examples of these three types of collaboration. The Danish web archive Netarchive.dk has an advisory board. Webarchivist.org has collaborated with archiving institutions in relation to both research projects and event harvests. And finally, "The Internet and Elections" was a transnational research initiative (cf. http://oase.uci.kun.nl/~jankow/elections).

22   There are examples of initiatives in these directions. The Danish Web Museum – a national web museum that builds curated exhibitions of websites – has based parts of its collections on web material from other media types (print media, TV spots), just as some of the first web-designer companies have donated material (the museum is hosted by the Danish Museum of Art and Design). And the research project "The History of www.dr.dk, 1996–2006" has traced valuable unpublished as well as older published web material at the producer (both kinds of material have been delivered to an existing archive, see Andersen 2007, Brügger 2008b).

References

Andersen, B. (2007). Integration of non-harvested web data into an existing web archive. Retrieved November 2007 from http://netarkivet.dk/publikationer/IntegrationOfDeliveredData.pdf.

Arvidson, A. (2001). Kulturarw3. In *Preserving the Present for the Future. Conference on Strategies for the Internet. Proceedings.* Copenhagen: Danish National Library Authority. Retrieved February 2008 from http://www.deflink.dk/arkiv/dokumenter2.asp?id=695.

Brown, A. (2006). *Archiving Websites. A Practical Guide for Information Management Professionals.* London: Facet Publishing.

Brügger, N. (2002). Does the materiality of the Internet matter? In N. Brügger & H. Bødker (eds.), *The Internet and Society? Questioning Answers and Answering Questions* (pp. 13–22). Papers from The Centre for Internet Research no. 5. Aarhus: Centre for Internet Research.

Brügger, N. (2005). *Archiving Websites. General Considerations and Strategies.* Aarhus: Centre for Internet Research.

Brügger, N. (2007). The website as unit of analysis? Bolter and Manovich revisited. In A. Fetveit & G. B. Stald (eds.), *Digital Aesthetics and Communication* (pp. 75–88). Northern Lights: Film and Media Studies Yearbook, vol. 5. Bristol: Intellect.

Brügger, N. (2008a). The archived website and website philology – a new type of historical document? *Nordicom Review,* 29(2), 151–71.

Brügger, N. (2008b). *Archived Websites Between Copies And Versions: Test of Versions In Existing Web Archives.* Papers from the Centre for Internet Research. Aarhus: Centre for Internet Research.

Brügger, N. (2009). Website history and the website as an object of study. *New Media & Society,* 11(1–2), 115–32.

Cathro, W., Webb, C., & Whiting, J. (2001). Archiving the web: The PANDORA archive at the National Library of Australia. In *Preserving the Present for the Future. Conference on strategies for the Internet. Proceedings.* Copenhagen: Danish National Library Authority. Retrieved February 2008 from http://www.deflink.dk/arkiv/dokumenter2.asp?id=695.

EPPP (1996). *Summary of the Final Report.* National Library of Canada, May. Retrieved February 2008 from http://epe.lac-bac.gc.ca/100/200/301/nlc-bnc/eppp_summary-e/ereport.htm.

Finnemann, N. O. (1999). Modernity modernised: The cultural impact of computerisation. In P. A. Mayer (ed.), *Computer, Media and Communication* (pp. 141–59). Oxford: Oxford University Press.

Grodzinsky, F., Miller, K. W., & Wolf, M. J. (2008). The ethics of designing artificial agents. *Ethics and Information Technology,* 10, 115–21.

Hollander, F. den, & Voerman, G. (eds.) (2003). *Het Web Gevangen. Het Archiveren van de Websites van de Nederlandse Politieke Partijen.* Groningen: Universiteitsbibliotheek Groningen/Documentatiecentrum Nederlandse Politieke Partijen.

Jacobsen, G. (2007). Harvesting the Danish Internet: The first two years. May. Retrieved March 2008 from http://netarkivet.dk/publikationer/CollectingTheDanishInternet_2007.pdf.

Kimpton, M., & Ubois, J. (2006). Year-by-year: From an archive of the Internet to an archive on the Internet. In J. Masanès (ed.), *Web Archiving* (pp. 201–12). Berlin: Springer.

Masanès, J. (ed.) (2006). *Web Archiving.* Berlin: Springer.

Preserving the Present for the Future. Conference on strategies for the Internet. Proceedings (2001). Copenhagen: Danish National Library Authority, 2001. Retrieved February 2008 from http://www.deflink.dk/arkiv/dokumenter2.asp?id=695.

Schneider, S. M. (2004). *Library of Congress. Election 2002 Web Archive Project. Final Project Report.* Research Foundation of the State University of New York/SUNY Institute of Technology/WebArchivist.org. Retrieved February 2008 from http://www.webarchivist.org/911-final-report.pdf.

Schneider, S. M., & Foot, K. A. (2004). The web as an object of study. *New Media & Society,* 6(1), 114–22.

Schneider, S. M., & Foot, K. A. (2006). *Web Campaigning.* Cambridge, MA: MIT Press.

3

New Media, Old Methods – Internet Methodologies and the Online/Offline Divide

Klaus Bruhn Jensen

Introduction

In an imagined conversation between two of the key profiles of twentieth-century American social science – C. Wright Mills and Paul F. Lazarsfeld – Stein (1964) summarized an issue that has remained key to research methodologies concerning communication and culture. The fantasy has Mills reading aloud the first sentence of *The Sociological Imagination* (Mills, 1959): "Nowadays men often feel that their private lives are a series of traps." "Lazarsfeld" replies: "How many men, which men, how long have they felt this way, which aspects of their private lives bother them, do their public lives bother them, when do they feel free rather than trapped, what kinds of traps do they experience, etc., etc., etc." (Stein, 1964, p. 215) (discussed in Gitlin, 1978, p. 223).

Whereas "Lazarsfeld's" quantitative formulations remain subject to debate, and while the vocabulary of how "men" feel belongs to Mills' "nowadays," it is still true today that grand theoretical assertions call for concrete empirical investigation. The many utopian as well as dystopian conceptions of the Internet during its first two decades as a public medium are a case in point, challenging research to assess recurring claims that the Internet may be either entrapping or empowering its users. In a future perspective, the new medium of the Internet will grow old, enabling research to review early projections of its likely consequences and implications (Marvin, 1988). And other new media, perhaps an "Internet of things" (ITU, 2005) that further embeds media within common objects and everyday settings, will follow. The role of research is not to predict future media, but to prepare the resources for studying them. What the philosopher Søren Kierkegaard said about life as such applies to the study of new media: "Life can only be understood backwards; but it must be lived forwards" ([1843] 2008).

In this chapter, I outline some of the opportunities for studies that approach the Internet as one constituent of a historically evolving media environment. My first premise is that while the early emphasis on a divide between offline and online practices and worlds – cyberspaces and virtual realities – may have been a necessary step for theory development of the 1990s, it has become increasingly counter-productive in methodological terms (see also Slater, 2002). My second premise is that the common notions of convergence and mediatization – that previously separate media are joined into similar formats and shared platforms, and that the sum of media is displacing embodied interaction – are, at best, partial accounts of contemporary culture. Old media rarely die, and humans remain the reference point and prototype for technologically mediated communication. In this vein, I suggest that research on present as well as future incarnations of the Internet still has much to gain from a range of old methods that have examined how people communicate through analog as well as embodied media. Communicative practices crisscross bodies and technologies.

The first section situates the Internet in the current media environment. I refer to a configuration of media of three degrees, including humans as media. The second section briefly considers the variety of methods that have served Internet studies so far. Here, I reemphasize the distinction between methods and method-ologies – concrete research instruments and theoretically informed research designs. Before asking which particular methods may serve to sample the requi-site empirical data from and about the Internet, it is important to ask, in the first place, what are the relevant questions and purposes of Internet studies. The third section discusses some of the ways in which the Internet and other digital tech-nologies are replacing or complementing traditional methods of data collection. In certain respects, new media remediate old methods.

In the fourth and final section, I return to the sort of grand questions that Mills and Lazarsfeld posed, specifically the issue of how people exercise their agency vis-à-vis the Internet, and how these practices can be tapped by research. Compared to previous media forms, the Internet holds a potential for more widely dispersed and differentiated forms of social and cultural innovation. Scholarship is a specialized case of human inquiry; Internet studies rely, in part, on the sociological imagination of ordinary users. Through the perspectives of different constituencies of informants, research is in a position to ask both what is, and what could be. Even though scholarship has few grounds for predicting the future of the Internet, the people using and developing the Internet day by day are import-ant sources of insight into what it might become.

Media of Three Degrees

The coming of digital media has served to question the long-standing dichotomies of mass versus interpersonal and mediated versus non-mediated communication. For one thing, computer-mediated communication resembles face-to-face inter-action in important respects, more so than mass communication. For another thing, everyday conversations, while non-mediated by technologies, are mediated by aural-oral modalities and by non-verbal expressions. The very idea of communication has been informed over time by the available media. In fact, communication only came to be thought of as a general category of human activity following the rise of electronic media from the last half of the nineteenth century, beginning with the telegraph. These media encouraged researchers and other commentators to think of diverse practices of social interaction – in the flesh, through wires, and over the air – in terms of their family resemblances. In John Durham Peters' (1999, p. 6) words, "mass communication came first." Responding to yet another generation of technologies, research today rarely speaks of "mass communication" or "mass media." The question is, What comes after mass media? To address this question, I refer to media of three degrees (Jensen, 2008b).

Media of the first degree are the biologically based, socially formed resources that enable human beings to articulate an understanding of reality, and to engage in communication about it with others. The central example is verbal language, or speech; additional examples include song, dance, drama, painting, and creative arts generally, often incorporating mechanical techniques such as musical instruments and writing utensils. *Media of the second degree* are what Walter Benjamin ([1936] 1977) defined as the media of technical reproduction, enabling the mass distribution of artworks and other representations, while undermining their quality of aura or uniqueness. Whereas Benjamin was commenting on photography, film, and radio, in the present context media of the second degree include printed books and newspapers as well as television and video. *Media of the third degree* are the digitally processed forms of representation and interaction, recombining media of the first and second degree on a single platform – the computer is a meta-medium (Kay & Goldberg, [1977] 1999). The central current examples of how the principles of computing allow for a recombination of previously separate print and electronic media are networked personal computers and smartphones, although these interfaces are likely to change substantially in future developments of the Internet.

It is the place of the Internet in the total configuration of media that is of particular interest in this chapter. The terminology of degrees refers to the fact that different media offer distinctive and ascending degrees of programmability, not just in the familiar technological sense, but also in terms of their flexible modalities of expression and institutional arrangements. Various media afford diverse means of expression that are extremely, if variably, adaptable – programmable – for different purposes and contexts of human interaction; media are institutions that facilitate the reorganization of society on a grand scale across time and space. At the same time, each new type and degree of medium recycles the forms and contents of old media in a process of *remediation* (Bolter & Grusin, 1999). Over time, this process involves a reconfiguration of the old as well as the new: traditions of typography and printing, not surprisingly, came to inform web design; television adopted an aesthetics of overlapping windows from the graphic computer interface. Even more important, old and new media enter into a shifting social division of labor in getting the many jobs of communication done. For example, email, text messaging, phone calls, and face-to-face contact are acquiring culturally consensual profiles as well as more varied patterns of use – for instance among different age groups (Kim et al., 2007). Being able to choose the right medium and genre for the occasion is to have been socialized and acculturated within a particular historical and social context of communication.

Whereas it is easy, as always, to exaggerate the implications of a new medium, the Internet has taken center stage over the past two decades, in two interrelated respects. First, it now constitutes a common global *infrastructure* for the distribution of one-to-one, one-to-many, and many-to-many communications. This is in spite of the many outstanding issues concerning diffusion and access in different regions and cultures of the world. Also, viable business models and legal frameworks for both one-to-many and many-to-many communication are still taking shape. Second, at least in the industrialized West, the Internet has been taking over the role of being the most widely shared *cultural forum* (Newcomb & Hirsch, 1984), in which public issues can be articulated and negotiated. Twenty-five years ago, this was the role of television, notably in the context of those nation-states that had previously taken shape as imagined communities through the press and other print media (Anderson, 1991). Despite technological and institutional differences, the Internet has come to constitute the sort of information reference and communicative resource for everyday political and cultural interactions that television had provided from the 1950s to the 1980s, affording themes, frames, and agendas of public discourse in local, national, and global arenas. This is not to say that television was the primary originator or controller of public communication in the decades following World War Two, nor that the Internet is approaching the status of a unified equivalent. In network terminology, however, television served as a key node in the flow of cultural forms across print and audiovisual media. As the field of media and communication research took shape during those same decades, the flow lent itself to studies of *intermediality* and *intertextuality*, that is, the interconnectedness of media, with each other and with various social institutions, as discourses and organizational structures (for overviews, see Jensen, 2008a, 2008c).

Such perspectives, focusing on media not as discrete entities, but as constituents of layered social and technological networks, translate well into Internet studies. A relational approach to media and texts helps to bring out some of the distinctive features of the Internet, not just as a source of information and representations, but as a resource for action. With digital media, action, interaction, and *interactivity* have acquired new prominence as aspects of media use, even if research has been struggling to arrive at a workable definition of interactivity (Kiousis, 2002). For methodological purposes, interactivity can be conceptualized and operationalized, not only as a matter of the users' selectivity at the interface, but also as a repertoire of actions reaching beyond the interface – to significant others at a distance and into the impersonal institutions of politics, economy, and culture (Neuman, 2008). To take full advantage of the lessons of previous communication studies, and of the research opportunities presented by the Internet, the research agenda should include those intermedial, intertextual, and interactive relations

– across media types – that enter into the ongoing structuration of modern societies (Giddens, 1984).

After the Great Divides

Following early and widely popular notions of the Internet as an extraordinary cyberspace (Benedikt, 1991) – a place apart in which identity experiments, avant-garde artworks, and innovative business models might find an outlet – the Internet has been going through a process of becoming ordinary. Likewise, Internet studies have been maturing as well as diversifying. The Internet can now be recognized as one more resource for communicating about and co-constructing a shared reality of social ends and means. During the heyday of *mass* communication studies, Andreas Huyssen (1986) commented that the pervasiveness of popular cultural forms had made the presumed great divide between elite and mass culture increasingly untenable. For a brief moment, Internet studies have been facing another great divide – that between online and offline communication. At present, research is in a position to move beyond the latter divide and perhaps, in time, to revisit the former, as well.

Fifty years ago, Elihu Katz introduced a motto for media studies that may also serve Internet studies, arguing that research should ask, not only what media do to people, but also what people do with media (Katz, 1959). In a later study, appropriately entitled, "On the Use of Mass Media for Important Things," Katz and his co-authors explored the comparative relevance of different media for the public, asking in what respects newspapers, cinema, television, etc., might replace or complement one another (Katz et al., 1973). The question today is how online and offline media, and media of different degrees, complement each other for important things that people do.

Methodologies versus Methods

In response to its public breakthrough since the mid-1990s, the Internet predictably has invited a wealth of research approaches. In overview, the approaches can be characterized with reference to methods – the concrete instruments for collecting and analyzing data, traditionally divided into qualitative and quantitative groupings. Table 3.1 lays out six basic forms of research evidence, with typical examples from and about the Internet in each cell.

The various data types can be thought of, in communicative terms, as vehicles of information that allow for inferences about the contents, forms, and contexts of communication which are enabled by the Internet. First, verbal evidence is a mainstay of social-scientific and humanistic inquiry into culture and communication. As noted commonsensically by Bower (1973, p. vi) "the best way to find out what the people think about something is to ask them" – although the

Table 3.1 Basic Methods in Internet Studies

	Quantitative	*Qualitative*
Discourse/speech/writing	Survey interviewing (offline and online)	In-depth individual and focus-group interviewing (offline and online)
Behavior/action	Experiment (e.g., web usability studies)	Participating observation (e.g., digital ethnographies)
Texts/documents/artifacts	Content analysis (e.g., of political information resources and search engines as meta-information)	Discourse analysis; historical and aesthetic criticism (e.g., of "netspeak" and digital artworks)

inference from what people say, in either surveys or focus groups, to what they think, is fraught with methodological and epistemological difficulties. Second, human actions are meaningful, as established both by social actors themselves and by scholars and others observing them. In the words of Clifford Geertz (1983, p. 58), much research on human culture and communication seeks to determine "what the devil they think they are up to." Third, the records that individuals, organizations, and historical epochs leave behind, again, bear witness to what people may have been up to, or what they may have thought about. Historical sources, of course, amount to one-way communication. Luckily, several sources may lend themselves to comparison. And, like different media, different research approaches complement each other.

Methods handbooks of the day habitually state that the "how" of research depends on "what" and "why" – that the approaches should fit the purpose and the domain of inquiry – in contrast to past calls for a unitary "scientific method" (cited in Jankowski & Wester, 1991, p. 46). The difficulty is how, specifically, to link theoretical conceptions of the Internet, and the public issues it raises, to particular empirical instruments, data sets, and analytical procedures. Studies *about* the Internet do not necessarily entail a focus on samples or specimens *of* the Internet in any concrete technological, organizational, or demographic sense. In order to elaborate on the options for Internet studies, it is useful to revisit some basic levels of planning, conducting, documenting, and interpreting research projects, which may too often be taken for granted. Figure 3.1 distinguishes six levels of doing empirical research (Jensen, 2002, p. 258).

Each of the levels can be addressed, again, in terms of the discourses or symbolic vehicles through which research is constituted as an intersubjective, social practice – language, mathematical symbols, graphical representations, and other meaningful signs:

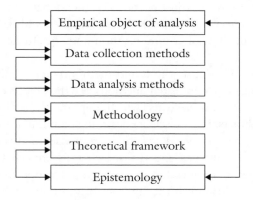

Figure 3.1   Six Levels of Empirical Research

- The empirical *objects of analysis* include discourses arising from or addressing the Internet (from websites and chat sequences, to policy documents and user-test responses), but also discourses with different origins for comparative purposes. In order to know what the Internet is, it can be important to ask what it is not, or what it might become.
- *Data collection methods* – from content sampling frames to interview guides – delineate that small portion of reality from which inferences and interpretations will be made. I return below to the distinction between data that are "found" (e.g., archives of debate forums), and data that are "made" (e.g., interviews with moderators), which has taken on new salience in digital media.
- *Data analysis methods* cover diverse operations of segmenting, categorizing, and interpreting evidence. In addition, empirical projects typically include a meta-analytical component in the form of statistical tests for significance or an "audit trail" (Lincoln & Guba, 1985) documenting the steps of qualitative inquiry.
- *Methodology* is a theoretically informed plan of action in relation to a particular empirical field. It is at this level that the status of the data that *methods* produce, and their relevance for "the Internet," is explicated. If methods are techniques, methodologies amount to technologies of research, mapping theoretical frameworks onto empirical domains.
- *Theoretical frameworks* lend meaning to the given configuration of empirical findings, linking a highly selective empirical microcosm with a conceptual macrocosm. Theories can be thought of as frames (Goffman, 1974; Lakoff & Johnson, 1980), which enable certain interpretations, while discouraging others.
- Whereas theoretical frameworks tend to apply to particular substantive domains – nature or culture, society or the human psyche – such a partitioning of reality is supported by more general, meta-theoretical, or *epistemological* arguments and assumptions. In the practice of research, epistemology provides

preliminary definitions and justifications of the "what" and "why" of empirical research, its object and purpose. The Internet should be studied as, among other things, a medium of communication and social interaction.

In this general perspective, methods and methodologies represent two sides of an interface – the Janus face of research: methods face the objects of analysis; methodologies spring from human subjectivity, which, importantly, is not a source of noise, but a resource for scholarship, as disciplined through communication within research communities. Methods only yield insight in response to theoretically informed questions and plans to answer them. In order to discern what are the appropriate methods and methodologies for Internet research, one overarching research question is what may distinguish the Internet from other media forms as a social infrastructure of information and communication, and as a common cultural forum.

Availability, Accessibility, and Performativity

Media are vehicles of *information*; they are channels of *communication*; and they serve as means of both interpersonal and macro-social *action*. As part of social interaction, the three aspects of media translate into relations of availability, accessibility, and performativity: What is known – in particular historical and cultural contexts? Who knows what – compared to whom? And, who says and does what – in relation to whom?

Despite continuing debates about the epochal significance of computing and the Internet, it is commonly recognized that information has taken on a specific structural and strategic role over recent decades in economic production and social governance (Porat, 1977). The proliferating *availability* of different kinds of information for everyday living and social coordination is, to a significant extent, a product of digitalization. Current institutions of information and communication, to be sure, stand on the shoulders of the "control revolution" of 1880–1930 (Beniger, 1986), which refers to the emergence of an entire sector of opinion polling, advertising, and organizational bureaucracies that would facilitate social self-regulation. In comparison, however, digitalization promotes the availability of information on a different order of magnitude, for example, about the individual social actor. Today, people habitually provide, more or less willingly and knowingly, and into operational systems, the sorts of information about themselves that previously had to be sampled and documented for distinct purposes. A radical example of the more general phenomenon is Gordon Bell's MyLifeBits project of documenting each and every aspect of his interactions with the world around him (Bell & Gemmell, 2007). In response to the rather different kind of documentation that authorities and marketers accumulate about citizens and consumers, it is relevant to begin to think in terms of "the right not to be identified" (Woo, 2006). And yet, there can be a trade-off between protecting one's privacy and practicing personalized search and communication, which users appear to consider more important than their privacy (Kobsa, 2007). These issues might be addressed in future research under a heading of *reverse copyrights* – rights not to be linked to certain items of information or acts of communication. Such a project is one example of studies that require several different kinds of methods and interdisciplinary competences to lay out popular attitudes, legal degrees of freedom, and technological models of implementation.

The question of *accessibility* involves access to information, but also to other people seeking information and engaging in interactions, as part of the growing centrality of pull modes of communication (Negroponte, 1995, p. 170). In advertising jargon, people are accessible as "eyeballs" in front of computer and television screens; they also make themselves accessible in chat rooms and gaming environments. The Internet has contributed to a greater differentiation of the ways in which information entities and communicative events become accessible. Moreover, given interactivity, reciprocal forms of accessibility come to the fore. For example, pulling a later push of information through an RSS feed, forwarding a web news story to a friend via an embedded email service, and meta-tagging a blog entry, all amount to instances of communication, making information accessible to oneself or others. In theoretical terms, this configuration of interactions calls for a better understanding with reference to what Gregory Bateson (1972, pp. 150–66) termed meta-information and meta-communication: by meta-informing about the meaning of message elements, and by meta-communicating about why and how they would like to communicate, people establish social contexts for themselves. In empirical terms, Bateson worked from face-to-face encounters, whose interrelations with, for example, mobile-phone interactions call for much further research: The micro-coordination of everyday routines by phone (Ling, 2004) can be considered meta-communication that anticipates a great deal of our face-to-face professional and family contacts.

Performativity, finally, reemphasizes the close links that exist between communication and action – in several respects. First of all, any instance of communication can be considered a form of action, occurring in a context and for a purpose. Speech-act theory (Austin, 1962; Searle, 1969) has helped to displace the understanding of communication as, first and foremost, a representation of reality. Furthermore, actions similarly constitute communications in their own right. As Bateson's student, Paul Watzlawick put it, "one cannot *not* communicate" in the presence of others (Watzlawick et al., 1967, p. 49). Most important, communication anticipates action – it allows for doubt, delay, and deliberation before undertaking actions that will make a practical difference. In all three respects, the Internet has contributed to a new kind of communicative infrastructure: emails are actions; surfing the mobile web on the subway is a way of communicating distance to fellow travelers. And, the Internet supports all manner of discussion and socially coordinated action – from political debate and activism, to e-banking and peer production. Again, it is not so much that we go online into a different political system or economic market, but rather that politics and markets exist online as well.

Remediated Methods

In most research fields, the Internet is primarily an instrument for sharing data and findings as well as debating and deliberating on their implications. In Internet studies, it is emphatically both a tool and an object of analysis. Throughout this chapter, I have suggested that Internet *methodologies* require data about other things than the Internet and *methods* that compare communications across media. At the same time, the Internet is a special kind of analytical object which, in part, generates its own data.

The issue of data of, about, and around the Internet highlights the common distinction between research evidence that is either "found" or "made." In one sense, all the evidence needed for Internet studies is already there, documented in and of the system, with a little help from network administrators and service providers. In this sense, the system *is* the method. In another sense, hardly anything is documented in advance, given the radically dispersed nature of the Internet and the local embedding of its communications. Joining the two extremes of auto-generated and highly contextualized evidence poses one of the main challenges for future Internet research.

Returning to the six prototypical methods of Table 3.1, one could say that the two lower cells – content analysis and discourse studies – have been coming back in style with the Internet. A wealth of online information lends itself to study as texts and documents, including the meta-information that situates this information in relation to its contexts of communication – the origin of the information, its interrelations with other items, their interdependent trajectories, the users accessing the information and perhaps adding meta-information, etc. Not just the contents, but the forms and some of the contexts of communication are available for analysis, depending on the formal conditions of access, ethical considerations, and the ability of the researcher to anticipate information of interest to be auto-generated. Lessig (2006) has argued persuasively that, at the juncture of technological, political, and legal practices, code is law; also for Internet studies, code is one of the enabling and constraining conditions of empirical research.

For other prototypical methods, as well, the line between what is made and what is found, has been shifting. The most obvious case is digital or virtual ethnographies (Hine, 2000), in which the archives of, for instance, virtual worlds or social network sites present themselves as "contents" and "discourses" for analysis. In comparison with the traditional written and, later, electronic records of anthropological fieldwork, such archives provide a measure of real-time details, to be complemented by other sources of evidence on the intersections of online and offline interactions. Internet applications, further, give rise to natural experiments, akin to studies of how the introduction of television affected the social life of communities (Gunter, 2002, p. 226; Williams, 1986). For surveys as well as qualitative interviews (Mann & Stewart, 2000), the Internet provides not just a research tool that complements, for instance, telephone interviewing, but also a diverse repository of data on the public's lifestyle preferences and everyday activities. Amid legal and ethical concerns, data-mining (Han & Kamber, 2006) has become a standard approach to examining what people say or think they are up to. With pervasive and ubiquitous forms of computing (Lyytinen & Yoo, 2002), the research opportunities as well as the ethical and political stakes are raised (see Buchanan, this volume, chapter 5).

A corresponding challenge comes from the complex embedding of the Internet in everyday contexts of use. How does the Internet enable users to exercise their agency in different types of social contexts? In what respects does the Internet enter into reproducing or readjusting the embedding structure of political, economic, and cultural institutions? And, to what extent does the Internet replace or complement other media with regard to either agency or structure? Auto-generated evidence on the Internet is an instance of what Webb and colleagues (Webb et al., 2000) referred to, in 1966, as *unobtrusive measures*, which avoid the direct elicitation of input from research subjects. Since then, the resurgence of qualitative approaches to social and cultural research (Denzin & Lincoln, 2005) has brought new attention to the relative merits of obtrusive and unobtrusive, experimental and naturalistic research. Also the everyday contexts of Internet use lend themselves to unobtrusive and naturalistic methods. Like most other fields, Internet studies are constantly engaged in balancing what evidence can be found, and what must be made. The thing for Internet researchers to remind themselves, from time to time, is that both kinds of evidence exist on both sides of the online/offline divide.

The Double Hermeneutics of the Internet

The Internet constitutes a historically unique configuration of informational and communicative resources, being the digital marriage of a massive information archive with high-speed communications, accessible and applicable, in principle, anywhere and anytime. Most distinctively perhaps, the Internet enables its users to interact, not just with each other and with major social institutions and imagined communities, but with the system of communication itself, in ways that may significantly reshape the system (Finnemann, 2005). This was brought home on a grand scale by Tim Berners-Lee's public posting in 1991 of the protocols and principles that came to support the World Wide Web (http://groups.google.com/group/alt.hypertext/msg/395f282a67a1916c, accessed March 29, 2008). The ongoing process of reproducing and reinventing the Internet, partly through contributions from research, can be specified with reference to the concept of double hermeneutics.

Hermeneutics refers to the long tradition in the history of ideas that has examined principles and procedures for interpreting texts, originally within religion and law, but increasingly with reference to texts of any kind and, indeed, to human experience as such, understood as a text. The particular terminology of a double hermeneutics was advanced by Giddens (1979), who was summarizing widespread criticisms of the predominant natural-scientific conceptions of social science after 1945. In contrast to natural sciences, the social sciences encounter a world that is pre-interpreted by its participants. And, when research feeds *its* interpretations of *their* interpretations back into society, it reshapes the object of study. Examples range from the mundane opinion poll that may affect the course of an electoral process, to paradigmatic shifts in the understanding of what is an economic transaction or an ego, which may have global consequences. Marx's works reshaped twentieth-century history in decisive ways; Freud's ideas introduced a realm of the unconscious into common parlance and everyday dealings.

Studies of the Internet, and of media as such, are a distinctive instance of a double-hermeneutic practice. Media and communication studies examine the basic processes by which social reality is reinterpreted and reconstructed on a daily basis (Berger & Luckmann, 1966). Double hermeneutics underscores, first, that such processes occur in everyday conversation as well as in dedicated institutions, from schools and universities, to news media and museums. Second, the concept places special emphasis on the nexus between domains of practice and of reflection. New media suggest new agendas to academic research; the social context of research further contributes to the dominant conceptual repertoires by which new media will be understood and examined.

In the case of the Internet, the hermeneutic process could be said to take on an added dimension. Because ordinary users can reprogram, to some degree, the Internet as they find it, they may be in a position to change, not just interpretations of themselves and their social context, but the very medium through which they perform their interpretations. The double hermeneutics of the Internet thus involves both form and content. Again, it is easy to exaggerate the distinctive and empowering aspects of the Internet and the implications for the users' performativity vis-à-vis the Internet or their conditions of life. As a research strategy for exploring what the Internet might become, however, double hermeneutics holds potential.

The interpretive capacities of users have been tapped for some time under headings of user-driven innovation and social or peer production (Von Hippel, 2005) – as exemplified by Wikipedia and the wider Web 2.0 phenomenon. The Internet has been part of a reconfiguration of the relationship between business, consumers, and civil society, and of a changing role for states and governments in administering rights of information and communication. In critical social theory, as well, an extended notion of immaterial production, deriving from Marx, has been associated with the Internet to suggest avenues of cultural resistance and social change. The dynamic of capitalism has contributed to the emergence of a general intellect, which may contain the seeds of the system's own destruction (Dyer-Witheford, 1999). Regardless of the ideological inferences, there is an opportunity for Internet studies to tap such mass intellectuality, as recognized in business as well as civil-society settings (Benkler, 2006), in order to explore what the Internet is, and what it could be.

In doing so, it is timely for Internet studies to return to and extend Katz's (1959) motto, asking not just what users and (other) developers do with existing media, but how they may be seeking to change them, to do something different with them. The Internet is a moving target for developers, users, and researchers alike. In a methodological sense, this returns Internet studies to a classic distinction between *emic* and *etic* perspectives on social reality – the internal perspectives of community members and native speakers, as opposed to the external, general, theoretical perspectives of an academic discipline (Pike, 1967). A central task for research is to translate between the discursive and conceptual repertoires of the two perspectives. In the case of the Internet, the emic perspectives that users may be willing to act on, are of special interest, because they outline future forms of the Internet. As such, users themselves participate in the translation of local, emic views into general, etic plans of action, which in time may become code and law.

Conclusion

In addition to the temptation to commit prediction, Internet studies may have had an inclination to exaggerate the novelty and specificity of its object of study. In this essay, I have argued that the Internet should be studied in the context of the composite media environment of which it is a part. The media of three degrees provide a framework in which to reflect on its current configuration. Specifically, the online/offline divide has long been a guiding metaphor for substantial portions of Internet research, and its dismantling will require further research on theoretical alternatives and on the multiple empirical interrelations of MySpace and my space. Toward this end, I have suggested that more explicit distinctions be made between the different levels and stages of empirical research, particularly regarding the methods for sampling the Internet *and* other relevant objects of analysis, and the methodologies informing why we do Internet studies in the first place. On the one hand, the Internet in and of itself is, in part, self-documenting; on the other hand, the embedding of the Internet in social structures and human agency means that it can never be self-analyzing or self-explanatory. Instead, Internet studies have an opportunity to revisit the full range of social-scientific and humanistic research approaches, across emic/etic, obtrusive/unobtrusive, experimental/naturalistic, and online/offline divides. In doing so, Internet studies can neither predict nor shape the future of the Internet, but they inevitably participate in the exercise of a sociological imagination, as users and developers articulate the present and future of the Internet.

It is still the early days of Internet studies. In certain respects, the field today is comparable to anthropology in the early twentieth century, when Bronislaw Malinowski (1922) was charting the western Pacific, equally trying to come to terms with several interrelated realities. Malinowski commented on the danger of having "preconceived ideas" about one's object of study. He added, however, that it is important to recognize "foreshadowed problems" in the field, which he took to be the role of theory. By explicating the relationship between field and theory in methodological terms, and by encountering the field both online and offline, Internet studies may contribute to a better understanding of how humans feel about their mediated lives nowadays.

References

Anderson, B. (1991). *Imagined Communities: Reflections on The Origin and Spread of Nationalism* (2nd edn.). London: Verso.

Austin, J. L. (1962). *How to Do Things with Words.* Oxford: Oxford University Press.

Bateson, G. (1972). *Steps to an Ecology of Mind.* London: Granada.

Bell, G., & Gemmell, J. (2007). A digital life. Retrieved February 21, 2007, from http://www.sciam.com/article.cfm?id=a-digital-life.

Benedikt, M. (ed.) (1991). *Cyberspace: First Steps.* Cambridge, MA: MIT Press.

Beniger, J. (1986). *The Control Revolution.* Cambridge, MA: Harvard University Press.

Benjamin, W. ([1936] 1977). The work of art in the age of mechanical reproduction. In J. Curran, M. Gurevitch, & J. Woollacott (eds.), *Mass Communication and Society.* London: Edward Arnold.

Benkler, Y. (2006). *The Wealth of Networks: How Social Production Transforms Markets and Freedom.* New Haven, CT: Yale University Press.

Berger, P. L., & Luckmann, T. (1966). *The Social Construction of Reality.* London: Allen Lane.

Bolter, J. D., & Grusin, R. (1999). *Remediation: Understanding New Media.* Cambridge, MA: MIT Press.

Bower, R. T. (1973). *Television and the Public.* New York: Holt, Rinehart, & Winston.

Denzin, N. K., & Lincoln, Y. S. (eds.) (2005). *The Sage Handbook of Qualitative Research* (3rd edn.). Thousand Oaks, CA: Sage.

Dyer-Witheford, N. (1999). *Cyber-Marx: Cycles and Circuits of Struggle in High-Technology Capitalism.* Urbana, IL: University of Illinois Press.

Finnemann, N. O. (2005). The cultural grammar of the Internet. In K. B. Jensen (ed.), *Interface://culture – The World Wide Web as Political Resource and Aesthetic Form.* Copenhagen: Samfundslitteratur/Nordicom.

Geertz, C. (1983). *Local Knowledge.* New York: Basic Books.

Giddens, A. (1979). *Central Problems in Social Theory.* London: Macmillan.

Giddens, A. (1984). *The Constitution of Society.* Berkeley, CA: University of California Press.

Gitlin, T. (1978). Media sociology: The dominant paradigm. *Theory and Society,* 6, 205–53.

Goffman, E. (1974). *Frame Analysis.* Cambridge, MA: Harvard University Press.

Gunter, B. (2002). The quantitative research process. In K. B. Jensen (ed.), *A Handbook of Media and Communication Research: Qualitative and Quantitative Methodologies.* London: Routledge.

Han, J., & Kamber, M. (2006). *Data Mining: Concepts and Techniques* (2nd edn.). Boston: Elsevier.

Hine, C. (2000). *Virtual Ethnography.* London: Sage.

Huyssen, A. (1986). *After the Great Divide: Modernism, Mass Culture, and Postmodernism.* London: Macmillan.

ITU (International Telecommunication Union) (2005). The Internet of things: Executive summary. Retrieved March 28, 2008, from http://www.itu.int/dms_pub/itu-s/opb/pol/S-POL-IR.IT-2005-SUM-PDF-E.pdf.

Jankowski, N. W., & Wester, F. (1991). The qualitative tradition in social science inquiry: Contributions to mass communication research. In K. B. Jensen & N. W. Jankowski (eds.), *A Handbook of Qualitative Methodologies for Mass Communication Research*. London: Routledge.

Jensen, K. B. (2002). The complementarity of qualitative and quantitative methodologies in media and communication research. In K. B. Jensen (ed.), *A Handbook of Media and Communication Research: Qualitative and Quantitative Methodologies*. London: Routledge.

Jensen, K. B. (2008a). Intermediality. In W. Donsbach (ed.), *International Encyclopedia of Communication*. Malden, MA: Blackwell.

Jensen, K. B. (2008b). Media. In W. Donsbach (ed.), *International Encyclopedia of Communication*. Malden, MA: Blackwell.

Jensen, K. B. (2008c). Text and intertextuality. In W. Donsbach (ed.), *International Encyclopedia of Communication*. Malden, MA: Blackwell.

Katz, E. (1959). Mass communication research and the study of popular culture: An editorial note on a possible future for this journal. *Studies in Public Communication*, 2, 1–6.

Katz, E., Gurevitch, M., & Haas, H. (1973). On the use of mass media for important things. *American Sociological Review*, 38(2), 164–81.

Kay, A., & Goldberg, A. ([1977] 1999). Personal dynamic media. In P. A. Mayer (ed.), *Computer Media and Communication: A Reader*. Oxford: Oxford University Press.

Kierkegaard, S. ([1843] 2008). Entry 167, Journalen, JJ (1842–1846), Søren Kierkegaards Skrifter, Elektronisk udgave [Electronic edition] 1.3. Retrieved November 18, 2008, from http://sks.dk/JJ/txt_167.htm.

Kim, H., Kim, G. J., Park, H. W., & Rice, R. E. (2007). Configurations of relationships in different media. *Journal of Computer-Mediated Communication*, 12(4). http://jcmc.indiana.edu/vol12/issue4/kim.html.

Kiousis, S. (2002). Interactivity: A concept explication. *New Media & Society*, 4(3), 355–83.

Kobsa, A. (2007). Privacy-enhanced personalization. *Communications of the ACM*, 50(8), 24–33.

Lakoff, G., & Johnson, M. (1980). *Metaphors We Live By*. Chicago: University of Chicago Press.

Lessig, L. (2006). *Code Version 2.0*. New York: Basic Books.

Lincoln, Y. S., & Guba, E. G. (1985). *Naturalistic Inquiry*. London: Sage.

Ling, R. (2004). *The Mobile Connection: The Cell Phone's Impact on Society*. Amsterdam: Elsevier.

Lyytinen, K., & Yoo, Y. (2002). Issues and challenges in ubiquitous computing. *Communications of the ACM*, 45(12), 63–5.

Malinowski, B. (1922). *Argonauts of the Western Pacific*. London: Routledge.

Mann, C., & Stewart, F. (2000). *Internet Communication and Qualitative Research: A Handbook for Researching Online*. London: Sage.

Marvin, C. (1988). *When Old Technologies Were New: Thinking About Electric Communication in The Late-Nineteenth Century*. New York: Oxford University Press.

Mills, C. W. (1959). *The Sociological Imagination*. London: Oxford University Press.

Negroponte, N. (1995). *Being Digital.* London: Hodder and Stoughton.

Neuman, W. R. (2008). Interactivity. In W. Donsbach (ed.), *International Encyclopedia of Communication.* Malden, MA: Blackwell.

Newcomb, H., & Hirsch, P. (1984). Television as a cultural forum: Implications for research. In W. D. Rowland & B. Watkins (eds.), *Interpreting Television.* Beverly Hills, CA: Sage.

Peters, J. D. (1999). *Speaking Into The Air: A History of The Idea of Communication.* Chicago: University of Chicago Press.

Pike, K. L. (1967). *Language in Relation to a Unified Theory of the Structure of Human Behavior* (2nd edn.). The Hague: Mouton.

Porat, M. (1977). *The Information Economy: Definition and Measurement.* Washington, DC: Government Printing Office.

Searle, J. R. (1969). *Speech Acts.* London: Cambridge University Press.

Slater, D. (2002). Social relationships and identity online and offline. In L. Lievrouw & S. Livingstone (eds.), *Handbook of New Media: Social Shaping and Consequences of ICTs.* London: Sage.

Stein, M. (1964). The eclipse of community: Some glances at the education of a sociologist. In A. Vidich, J. Bensman & M. Stein (eds.), *Reflections of Community Power.* New York: Wiley.

Von Hippel, E. (2005). *Democratizing Innovation.* Cambridge, MA: MIT Press.

Watzlawick, P., Beavin, J. H., & Jackson, D. D. (1967). *Pragmatics of Human Communication: A Study of Interactional Patterns, Pathologies, and Paradoxes.* New York: Norton.

Webb, E. J., Campbell, D. T., Schwartz, R. D., & Sechrest, L. (2000). *Unobtrusive Measures* (rev. edn.). Thousand Oaks, CA: Sage.

Williams, T. M. (ed.) (1986). *The Impact of Television: A Natural Experiment in Three Communities.* New York: Academic Press.

Woo, J. (2006). The right not to be identified: Privacy and anonymity in the interactive media environment. *New Media & Society*, 8(6), 949–67.

4

The Internet in Everyday Life: Exploring the Tenets and Contributions of Diverse Approaches

Maria Bakardjieva

Introduction

The Internet in everyday life is a newly emergent continent on the map of Internet research that has not been properly explored and charted yet. At the same time, its contours and substantive make-up seem distinct enough to warrant a special designation. The elements that distinguish the Internet in everyday life from its boisterous Internet research kin can be captured by several key words: use, users, offline context and embeddedness. First and foremost, this means that researchers in this area manifest avid interest in Internet use performed by ordinary people as one among their many different activities and related to the broader horizons of their lives. Secondly, this means attention to the social and cultural environment in which Internet use takes place with its different levels and variations: personal, domestic, organizational, national, etc. In other words, the user is not perceived exclusively as an online persona involved in different pursuits in cyberspace, but as a physical actor who sits in a chair and stares at a screen for a variety of time stretches and purposes. Thirdly, the interconnectedness between Internet use and numerous other practices and relations is emphasized in this approach. For some authors (Haythornthwaite & Wellman, 2002; Ward, 2005) looking at the Internet as part of everyday life is a marker of the second age of the medium or of a second-generation research that breaks away from the early euphoria surrounding everything "cyber" and the effervescent speculations about how the Internet will transform society as we know it.

Indeed, to insist on talking about the Internet in everyday life is to deny the medium its extraordinary status, to see it as ordinary, but in no case as unimportant. There are some decisive advantages to be gained from redefining the glorious new communication medium in this way. Among them is the sobering realization that conceptual frameworks, methodologies, trends, and patterns established in other areas of social and cultural studies may be applicable to the Internet. All of a sudden, neither the Internet nor its study are so special and exclusive any more – quite a disappointment to some. Yet at the same time, and to the great excitement of others, many tested and true tools and familiar paradigms can be put into use for the exploration of the new object. Thus research on the Internet in everyday life has been able to draw on models and methods tried in other areas and to examine the Internet in relation and comparison to familiar media and communication phenomena.

Common ground notwithstanding, there is also significant epistemological and methodological diversity among Internet in everyday life approaches themselves. These differences flow from the ambiguity of the concept of everyday life and its multiple interpretations. At first glance, the commonsense notion of everyday life refers to the ordinary and routine activities of people in various social areas. It signifies the repetitive, the unglamorous, and the typical. Taken at that level, the first type of research on the Internet in everyday life to be discussed here has sought to map out the trends emerging when the daily dealings of multiple users with and on the Internet are carefully surveyed. This approach, as a rule, has produced large-scale quantitative studies painting the big picture of Internet use and its relation to a broad gamut of mundane activities such as shopping, banking, traveling, studying, and socializing, to name just a few. To this approach we owe the discernment of differences in access, opportunity, and preference that cut across socioeconomic, demographic, educational, ethnic, and cultural categories of people. A central question for many studies carried out in this vein has been that of the Internet's impact on daily life. Is the new medium supporting new forms of relationships and behavior, or is it reproducing existing patterns (see Haythornthwaite & Wellman, 2002)? As opposed to the early speculative forecasts concerning the Internet's transformative powers, this type of research has stayed firmly grounded in the replies of actual users asked to account for their Internet-related activities. It has sought to identify the relationships between and among variables that reflect the changes brought about by the Internet in the ways people perform their daily activities and associate with others. In short, this type of study has used large-scale statistics to describe the patterns of an everyday life affected by the presence of the Internet.

Along with the immediate commonsense meaning of the phrase "everyday life," there exists a depth of theoretical work that has imbued the notion with complex cultural and critical overtones. In its career as a "second order" concept (Giddens, 1984, p. 284) invented and employed by social and cultural theorists, the concept of everyday life has opened dimensions of inquiry suggested by an epistemology very different from that driving the quantitative approach. Applied to the Internet, this second-order concept has called for two further types of investigation characterized by an interpretative and a critical orientation respectively. It has posed questions concerning the agency of users in making meanings and choices with regard to the Internet. How do users understand the medium and why do they decide to adopt or reject it? How do different kinds and styles of usage emerge from the contexts and situations characterizing users' lives? What are the impacts of users and usage on the Internet? And important for the

Table 4.1 Different Types of Approach to the Internet in Everyday Life

	Statistical approach	*Interpretative approach*	*Critical approach*
Epistemology	Positivistic/ objectivist	Interpretative/ constructivist	Interpretative plus normative
Types of questions asked	Who is online? What do they do online? How much time do they spend online? What is the impact?	Why do people go online? How do they make the Internet their own? What does it mean to them? How does it restructure their lifeworlds?	Is Internet use empowering or oppressing people? Is Internet use leading to more equality and opportunity for people? Does it alienate and exploit people?
Key issues	Trends Factors Impacts	Meaning Agency Appropriation Domestication Negotiation	Empowerment Emancipation Alienation Exploitation
Methodologies	Quantitative	Qualitative	Qualitative plus critical

critical stream of studies: Is the Internet helping users achieve higher degrees of emancipation and equity, build capacity, and take control over their lives as individuals and citizens?

Table 4.1 summarizes the different types of approach to the Internet in everyday life sketched so far. I will discuss each of them in more detail in the following sections of this chapter.

What is Everyday Life?

Before I move on to examine the different approaches to the Internet in everyday life and their achievements, I will linger for a while on the deeper meaning of the concept of everyday life that I alluded to and will briefly examine its intellectual history. Behind the obvious and quantifiable meaning of the everyday as the most-repeated actions, the most-traveled journeys, and the most-inhabited spaces, Highmore (2002) points out, creeps another: "the everyday as value and quality – everydayness" (p. 1). This quality can be defined by boredom and oppressive routine, but it can also be seen as marked by authenticity and vitality, an unobtrusive, but always present potential for growth and change. In the metaphoric formulation of Lefebvre (1991, quoted in Gardiner, 2000) the everyday can be construed as the "fertile humus, which is the source of life-enhancing power as we walk over it unnoticed" (p. 2). The everyday also harbors those elementary relations and actions that form the flow of social life and give the culture that we inhabit its distinctive characteristics.

Speaking more precisely, the concept of everyday life has been central to two traditions of social theory: the phenomenological and the critical, as well as to a range of contributions that span the space between the two. In the phenomeno-logical tradition, the preferred notion is the "everyday life-world" (Schutz & Luckmann, 1973) which refers to the realm of the immediately experienced world. This is, Schutz says, the "fundamental and paramount reality" to which we wake up every morning. It is "the region of reality in which man [*sic*] can engage himself and which he can change while he operates in it by means of his animate organism" (Schutz and Luckmann, 1973, p. 3). In this region the person experiences other people with whom she constructs a shared world. Hence, Schutz states: "The problems of action and choice must, therefore, have a central place in the analysis of the life-world" (Schutz and Luckmann, 1973, p. 18). Importantly, the lifeworld is a reality which we modify through our acts and which also shapes our actions. In that sense, the everyday lifeworld is where we can exercise our agency as thinking human beings. The everyday lifeworld represents a mosaic of situations through which we move, driven by our pragmatic interest. Many of these situations are routine and unproblematic and we apply to them pre-given concepts and action recipes that we have been taught by our culture. Occasionally however, due to various constellations of social and biographical circumstances, we encounter problematic situations which necessitate the generation of new concepts and definitions as well as the crafting of novel courses of action. Thus the fundamental taken-for-grantedness of the everyday lifeworld can be disrupted, and the habitual models can prove inefficient in guiding our actions. When that happens, we face the need to creatively "deliberate," or in other words to come up with new ways of seeing a particular sector of our lifeworld and acting within it. Once objectified or acted out in a particular fashion, such novel courses of action can be picked up and applied by other people in similar situations. In this process, the culturally shared "stock of knowledge" grows in response to new conditions and historical developments. Notably also in this process, individuals, in cooperation and negotiation with their "fellow-men," can actively contribute to the change of the cultural stock of knowledge.

Schutz's system of thought offers an elaborate set of concepts that describe the organization of the lifeworld as it is experienced by humans. In that system, the experiences of space, time, and social entities represent three of the central dimensions. Depending on the combination of spatial, temporal, and social parameters characterizing different situations, individuals perceive certain actions as relevant and practicable. Based on this conception, it can be expected that significant changes in the way space, time, and the social landscape are experienced by subjects would fundamentally transform their everyday lifeworlds and the activities considered possible within them.

While Schutz's model of the everyday lifeworld is centered in the experiencing subject and aims to capture the mental picture that he or she has of their surrounding world, Henri Lefebvre's (1971, 1991) take on everyday life is categorically anchored in the material and structural realities of modern society. For Lefebvre, modernity fragments and separates distinct areas of social reproduction – work and leisure, individual and community, public and private – into highly rationalized and tightly controlled institutions that impoverish human existence. Everyday life, in contrast, brings all human thoughts and activities, and ultimately the whole person, back together. Lefebvre further characterizes it as follows:

> Everyday life is profoundly related to all activities, and encompasses them with all their differences and their conflicts; it is their meeting place, their bond, their common ground. And it is in everyday life that the sum of total relations which make the human – and every human being – a whole takes its shape and its form. (1991, p. 97)

As a result, everyday life is riven by contradictions. It is steeped in boredom, drudgery, and alienation, and yet at the same time, staggering creative forces lay dormant at its core. In contrast to descriptive historians and ethnographers, the stated goal of Lefebvre's investigation of everyday life was to develop a transformative *critique*. That critique would be a method for evaluation of social and individual practices against ideals such as fulfillment, liberation, and equality, and a search for directions and sources for change.

In this project, Lefebvre has not remained alone, as Gardiner (2000) and Highmore (2002) have demonstrated. His work is one among several streams forming a critical tradition in the study of everyday life which includes schools of thought such as Dada, surrealism, the Bakhtin circle, the Situationist International, Michel de Certeau (1984), and Dorothy Smith's institutional ethnography (1984, 1999), to name just a few. Following Gardiner (2000), the common features shared by the representatives of this tradition can be summarized as follows: All these authors seek to problematize everyday life, to expose its contradictions and to unearth its hidden potentialities. They insist on relating everyday life to wider socio-historical developments as opposed to simply describing it as an insulated container of ordinary social practices and modes of consciousness. In so doing, they place asymmetrical power relations at the focus of their inquiry into the dynamic of everyday activities and cognitive constructs. This inquiry for its part is aimed at fostering "radical reflexivity" (Pollner, 1991), or critical consciousness that would enable the actors of everyday life to understand their conditions within a larger social and political context and to undertake concerted action toward challenging and transforming oppressive relations. In short, this brand of everyday life theorist openly espouses an ethico-political stance, which places it in sharp contrast to the interpretative school of microsociology exemplified by Schutz and his followers. At the same time, it differs significantly from the Frankfurt School style of critical theory by virtue of its recognition of the potentialities for resistance and emancipation contained within everyday life itself. It is in the nature of everyday life to be punctuated by the eruption of creative energies, by transformative possibilities that challenge the routine and taken-for-granted behavioral and relational order. Because instrumental rationalization, commodification, and bureaucratic power cannot fully suppress the impulses of human desire, sociability, hope and creativity, everyday life will always harbor "the buds and shoots of new potentialities" (Bakhtin, 1984, p. 73, quoted in Gardiner, 2000, p. 20). How these contradictory sides of everyday life, or in Lefbvre's (1991) words, its misery and power, blend with and shape Internet use is a central question of the critical strand of inquiry.

In my own work (Bakardjieva, 2005a) I have argued that both the interpretative and the critical perspectives are necessary for understanding the complex role of the Internet in everyday life. Closely examining users' experiences with the Internet through the phenomenological approach has made it possible to discover how the new medium is construed as an element of subjects' everyday lifeworlds as well as to map out the transformations in the structures of users' everyday lifeworlds brought about in this process. Lefebvre's (1971, 1991) critical method, on the other hand, directs attention to the characteristic alienations to which Internet users are exposed. Taken together, the two approaches bring to the fore the productive work performed by users through and around the Internet. In the course of this work users create new meanings, spaces, and social relations. They express their human potential in new ways and contribute to the shaping of the Internet as a medium of social communication. This kind of user agency in the social construction of the Internet far precedes the more obvious and also more problematic forms of involvement accentuated by Web 2.0. The results of this interaction between medium and users are certainly contradictory. Both alienation and empowerment can be detected in the daily practices of Internet use. By throwing into relief the emancipatory as well as the oppressive aspects of these practices, research on the Internet in everyday life is poised to offer a basis for critical reflexivity and conscious-raising among users and a solid basis for reflexive design and democratic policymaking. Such research would not only register the typical and the recurrent, but would be able to pinpoint versions of the possible discovered and implemented by users as they follow their creative impulses and desire for self-emancipation.

The Surface Everyday: Measuring Trends and Impacts

Arguably, one of the first concerted attempts to force the Internet to descend from the firmament (to use Haythornthwaite & Wellman's (2002) metaphor), and to take its proper place as an object of systematic social investigation was represented by the HomeNet study at Carnegie Mellon University in the mid-1990s. It was designed and implemented at the critical point of Internet diffusion when it was becoming clear that the home rather than the office would be the most likely site of user engagement with the new medium and that the Internet user population would grow far beyond the early professional adopters and hobbyists. The HomeNet study team wanted to take a glimpse into that impending future by inducing some of its developments in an experimental setting. Thus, the team set up a field experiment of domestic Internet use, initially recruiting 48 families (157 individuals and note that this number grew at the later stages of the project) of a diverse socio-demographic make-up from the Pittsburgh area who were given free computers, Internet service subscription, and technical help with getting online. In exchange, participants agreed to be subjected to intensive examination with respect to multiple parameters of their emergent Internet use, as well as to testing and interviewing regarding selected aspects of their lifestyle and well-being. Going over one of the first HomeNet reports (Kraut et al., 1996) today feels like tarot reading because the seeds of so many uses of the Internet now considered typical can be noticed in the inventory of activities that those experimental subjects immediately jumped into: popular culture, sports, sex, movie times, and bus schedules didn't take much time to come on top of the usage trends registered by the researchers. Teenagers led Internet adoption and quickly turned themselves into the domestic Internet gurus. Participants diverged widely in terms of the websites and newsgroups they accessed, but their practices came together around an important discovery – the discovery of communication:

> According to their pretrial questionnaires, participants didn't see computers as particularly useful for interpersonal communication. They thought computers were valuable for doing school work, for learning, and for performing household chores. Yet like people discovering the telephone at the turn of the century, chit-chat quickly became the dominant use of the Internet, and especially so for teenagers. (Kraut et al. 1996, n.p.)

Emails, Internet relay chat sessions, and MUDs (text-based multi-user dungeons), all the available Internet communication tools at the time were recruited by users to make that chit-chat possible. The first HomeNet report had also its shred of romantic spice: it noted the case of a teenage girl who had never dated before, but started dating a boy she met over a chat service. In sum, the preliminary 1996 paper from the HomeNet study reads like a futuristic thriller putting its finger on many of the exciting experiences that the Internet was poised to bring into the homes and everyday lives of the unsuspecting still-unwired public.

But the ambitions of the HomeNet team went far beyond the descriptive statistics of the Internet uses proliferating among their study participants. They set out on a search for predictors of Internet adoption and use which they expected to find in particular demographic features, psychological dispositions, and existing media-use habits. Furthermore, the cornerstone of their endeavor became the search for impacts: How will the Internet affect the lives of users? Following some of the early pointers and research performed on the effects of television, the study hypothesized that a major effect of the medium could be expected to manifest itself in the area of social interaction. Thus, they focused part of their inquiry on the relationships between Internet use and social involvement. The outcome of this particular investigation was the now famous article in the *American Psychologist* that declared the Internet to be a "social technology that reduces social involvement and psychological well-being" (Kraut et al., 1998). The researchers measured participants' degree of social involvement through their communication with other family members and the size of their local social networks. On both counts, they found that greater Internet use was associated with, and possibly led to, a decline in involvement. Also negatively affected by Internet use was participants' feeling of loneliness, a psychological state associated with social involvement. Weak ties of a lower quality and intensity maintained through Internet communication, the argument went, were displacing strong ties of a deeper and more substantive nature. These findings reverberated across popular media and helped whip up a measurable wave of moral panic at a moment when Internet adoption was growing exponentially and social pundits as well as ordinary users were feeling uncertain as to where the Internet bandwagon was headed.

After several years and a lot of critical questioning by the research community, some of the original "Internet paradox" authors conducted a successor study involving a panel of former HomeNet participants and a newly recruited sample of Americans who used the Internet in 1998–9 (Kraut et al., 2002). The original disturbing results were not replicated. Instead, the new research found that Internet effects on social involvement would be better reflected by what they called "rich get richer" model. According to that model, those Internet users who were extroverts and had stronger social support networks enjoyed positive social effects of Internet use, while the introverts and the isolated suffered some degree of decline in social involvement and psychological well-being. Compelled to reflect on the inconsistency between the results from the two studies, the researchers recognized that the pursuit of generalizable and unequivocal Internet effects on users' lives had turned out to be a shaky undertaking. The likelihood was high that different stages of use, different types of users, and different ways of using, as well as changing technical and functional features of the Internet and the different combinations thereof, would bring about widely divergent consequences. Note also that the effects projected so far originated from exclusively American research sites and developments. Was the rest of the world of Internet users going to follow the same path? It was clear that the "impact approach" to studying the Internet in everyday life needed to undergo a significant philosophical, conceptual, and methodological rethinking.

Many larger- and smaller-scale projects conducted in this vein have left and continue to make their mark on the area. Employing methodologies such as the social survey, interviewing, time-use diaries, cross-sectional and longitudinal designs in combination with sophisticated statistics, researchers have been able to significantly advance the understanding of the ways in which Internet use interacts with other habitual everyday activities. Does the Internet substitute for previous technologies in the performance of customary practices such as reading the news and entertainment? Does it bring about new dynamics in interpersonal communication? Where does the time that goes into using the Internet come from? After all, something has to give. What about social, community, and civic involvement? Interesting takes on these questions have emerged from various research corners with international and cross-national comparisons and contrasts becoming more readily available (see World Internet Project; PEW Internet and American Life Project; Wellman & Haythornthwaite, 2002; Katz & Rice, 2002; Anderson, Brynin, & Raban, 2007).

Kraut and colleagues (2006), for example, took a careful and detail-oriented approach to the effects of Internet use on television viewing. They compared results from cross-sectional and longitudinal surveys with the goal to "differentiate among users of the Internet in a richer way and to identify uses that lead to changes in other media use" (p. 72). Their findings revealed that over time, television viewing increased among non-users, but declined among heavy Internet users. In addition, they showed that the way in which people used the Internet makes a difference with respect to their television viewing. Users who went online for entertainment and news did not see a significant decline in television viewing, while people who sought new social relationships and participated in groups on the Internet watched less television. These outcomes limit the validity of the widely adopted "functional displacement hypothesis" which postulates that a new medium will take away from an old one the satisfaction of a particular need, especially when it is able to offer new opportunities or reduces costs. On the contrary, a functional enhancement effect seemed to manifest itself: people who were interested in a particular type of content or kind of medium use were likely to employ both the old and the new medium to meet their needs.

Focused attention on specific user categories, such as teenagers, has uncovered various mutual displacements and enhancement among new and old media. Teens enthusiastically take up chat and instant messaging applications, which displaces their avid use of the telephone, and at the same time makes new modes of communication possible (Boneva et al., 2006). More frequent chatting with representatives of the opposite gender and with several friends at the same time represent new opportunities embraced by teenagers. It also gives them a sense of belonging to a group and more leverage in crafting their own social networks. It fits into the structural conditions determining their offline lives such as limited mobility and scarce time free of adult supervision. With the benefit of hindsight it can be observed that these uses anticipate the current explosion of social networking applications.

Participation in local community is another activity that is affected by the Internet in complex and differential ways. A longitudinal study on patterns of participation in the Blacksburg Electronic Village, a community network connecting the town of Blacksburg, Virginia, reported by Carroll et al. (2006), points to a model that by analogy with the Kraut et al. (2002) finding introduced earlier can be called "the active get more active." People who used the Internet for civic purposes tended to become more actively involved in their community, while those who used the Internet heavily but for other purposes remained relatively discon-nected from community activities. The researchers concluded that Internet use mediated between an existing disposition to be civically engaged and the enact-ment of this disposition by making involvement easier.

Hampton and Wellman (2003), for their part, found that belonging to the local mailing list of Netville, a wired neighbourhood near Toronto, increased the number of neighbours with whom residents had established weak ties. Strong ties, on the other hand, were influenced by the number of years people had lived in the neighbourhood and did not depend on electronic communication. Wired residents knew people who lived farther away in the neighbourhood compared to residents not connected to the network who only knew their next-door neighbours. The mailing list was also used by residents to organize local events and undertake collective action to protect their interests when those were at stake. The Netville developer, for example, was caught by surprise when he found that residents of the wired suburb were capable of organizing a protest at unprecedented speed. Consequently, Netville inhabitants received much better than usual customer service and many of their actions against unpopular decisions of the developer were successful. Ultimately, Hampton and Wellman concluded that the presence of high-speed Internet in the community did not weaken or radically transform neigh-bouring ties. It added another layer to the communicative opportunities existing in the suburb with subtle but important consequences for residents' quality of life.

In a recent review of approaches to studying the social impacts of information and communication technologies, Brynin and Kraut (2006) identify four levels at which such impacts are conceptualized by researchers. The first level is the one at which new technologies are perceived as tools allowing people to perform familiar activities in new ways, possibly with increased efficiency. These could be the cases of functional displacement and enhancement. The second level of social impact of technologies refers to the cases in which the use of technologies leads to qualitative changes in daily life. Here, people employ the technology to accomplish new goals, that is, new functions emerge that have no equivalents in the preceding state of affairs. The third level of social impacts discerned by researchers looks for the ways in which new forms of behaviour made possible by techno-logy result in changes in people's more general well-being – psychological health, social capital, educational achievements, life opportunities, etc. At the fourth level, researchers are interested in consequences that extend beyond the specific activ-ities enabled by technologies and affect the organization of society at large. The examination of the trajectory of research in the social impact vein suggests that results have been convincing and corroborated mostly at the first two levels. Attempts to identify impacts at the level of general well-being and social organization at large have run into great difficulties and have not been widely accepted. In the conclusions of their study of the impacts of the Internet on the way time is spent in UK households, Anderson and Tracey (2001) introduce the possibility that the impact approach as such may not be the most promising route toward under-standing the role of the Internet in the everyday lives of users. Instead, these authors propose, attention should be directed to lifestyle and life stage as setting the context in which the Internet itself is construed and mobilized by users in a variety of ways. What is needed, they argue, is a "deeper understanding of the triggers for the processes of the medium's domestication, and a more detailed examination of how individuals and households are making sense of and integrating its applications and services into their lives" (p. 471). A statement like this signals a major philosophical turn in the course of the inquiry and its premises. Instead of the search for impacts of an invariable technology or communication medium on users' lives as a receiving end, recognition of the active and complex role of users in fitting and adapting the medium to their lives takes center stage. With this comes an acknowledgement of the fact that the Internet, with its various applications, emerges out of a process of continuous social shaping and that its ostensible impacts cannot be treated as a force external to the social fabric. Thus the question becomes: What do users do to the medium and why as it presents itself to them in the midst of their everyday lives? The next approach to the study of Internet in everyday life that I will discuss takes this question to heart.

The Deeper Everyday: Interpretation and Critique

Researchers who espouse the interpretative approach do not see the everyday as an objective flow of routine events by which human beings are swept passively along. Neither do they look at the Internet as an external agent that brings about changes in the everyday by virtue of its own logic and momentum. Theirs is an effort to capture and understand the Internet as it is perceived and made sense of by reflexive actors who perform conscious and consequential choices as they look for the place of the medium in their daily lives. Actor's choices are conscious, especially in the instance of their early encounter with the technological novelty. That novelty creates a problematic situation, in Schutz' terms, and hence has to be given meaning, value, and practical application by drawing on cultural and personal experiences and resources. Actor's choices are consequential because their decisions to employ the Internet in one or another specific way that makes sense within their situation contribute to the shaping of the medium itself. This way of viewing the process aligns interpretative research on the Internet in everyday life with the social construction of technology perspective (Pinch and Bijker, 1984; Bijker, 1995; Bijker and Law, 1992; Bijker, 2001) which traces the origins and evolution of technical devices to the choices made by various groups of social actors. The examination of the Internet in everyday life from that point of view opens the door for serious consideration of the role of ordinary users in the social construction of technology. After all, users are the ultimate decision-makers with respect to the success or failure of technical devices and applications. Their daily tinkering with devices and applications adds new and sometimes unexpected layers to the social understanding and, directly or indirectly, to the functionality of technologies. Yet at the same time, the social construction of technology is a two-way process; that is why many authors talk about the co-construction between users and technologies (Oudshoorn and Pinch, 2003). This means that the everyday lifeworlds into which new technologies are drawn do not remain unchanged. New elements and dimensions are added to the spatial, temporal, practical, and social arrangements of these worlds. The user of the Internet wakes up into a daily world of a different make-up compared to the world that preceded the medium's arrival. What then are the experiences defining that change? Are they important? What happens to the culture inhabited by Internet users when these new experiences are intersubjectively shared and sedimented into the social stock of knowledge?

One of the traditions that researchers of this persuasion naturally turned to for help when they endeavoured to design their projects conceptually and methodologically was the domestication of media technologies (Haddon, 2004; Berker et al., 2005). The domestication approach was first articulated in relation to studies of television use in households (Silverstone, Hirsh, & Morley, 1992; Silverstone, 1994; Silverstone & Haddon, 1996). These authors were interested in the ways in which television, a system of technologies and messages produced in the public world, is appropriated and blended into the private life of the family and, more specifically, into what they called "the moral economy" of the household. Throughout the qualitative studies (ethnographic observations and in-depth interviews) that they carried out looking closely at the practices of a diverse range of domestic users, a model of television's appropriation eventually took shape. Thus Silverstone, Hirsh, and Morley (1992), and later Silverstone and Haddon (1996), isolated four intersecting processes that constituted television's domestication: appropriation, incorporation, objectification, and conversion. Objectification refers to the physical placement or inscription of the technical object, a commodity bought in the market and hence initially alien to the domestic fabric. The physical placement of material artifacts into a particular domestic environment, Silverstone and colleagues (1992) argue, objectifies the moral, aesthetic, and cognitive universe of those feeling comfortable with them. It also reveals the "pattern of spatial differentiation (private, shared, contested; adult, child; male, female, etc.) that provides the basis for the geography of the home" (p. 23). As it became clear in the social history of television, new technologies do not descend on the household along with a precise description of their appropriate place and surrounding. Women, men, and children living alone or together had to make more or less conscious decisions about where the novelty belonged. Thus, even if users of new technologies do not literally write and publicize their own definitions of artifacts' meanings, they objectify these meanings by inscribing artifacts into an already meaningful structure of objects. Incorporation, for its part, focuses on temporalities (p. 24). While Silverstone and his colleagues apply the term broadly to cover "ways in which objects, especially technologies, are used" (p. 24), it can be interpreted as a caption for the temporal arrangements and patterns of activity that arise around a new domestic technology. The organization of time-sharing of the artifact among family members and the way in which its use fits into the overall structure of the daily course of events represent another measure of social and cultural significance. Finally, conversion captures the current of activities that take the meanings constructed within the household outside of its walls through exchanges and conversations with family, friends, and commercial and public organizations.

This model, clearly, reflects well the appropriation of the Internet as a new technical commodity and communication channel into the everyday life spaces and rhythms of home-based users. Notably, as is characteristic of the interpretative approach, the meanings and values as well as the routine practices that household members as individuals and groups attach to the Internet are taken as the point of departure. The notion of domestication has sometimes burst out of the confines of the home and has been applied to the ways larger social entities such as local communities and organizations make the Internet their own. In some instances appropriation of the medium by individuals has been found to occur at sites other than the home – computer clubs, IT-literacy courses, and others (see the studies reported in Berker et al., 2005). These cases have proven that it is beneficial to conceive of domestication not as a process strictly related to the setting of the private home, but more broadly to the everyday lives of new users as they move through different sites of activity.

This broader idea of domestication as a process of making the Internet ones' own on the part of individual and social and cultural groups has inspired numerous researchers to investigate the detailed workings of the process. In her theoretically sophisticated and empirically meticulous research, Lally (2002) has traced the fascinating twists and turns of the penetration of computers into Australian households in the mid-1990s. Internet communication had not been part of the machine's definition at the beginning of Lally's data collection, but eventually became an important aspect of it. Employing concepts such as objectification and the extended self, Lally uncovers the painstaking reflexive efforts that people go through in order to take ownership of their computers in the true cultural sense of the term. Users perform hard signifying work not only while they assign the computer its proper place in the living room or basement, but also as they make decisions about the "proper" use of computer time and reconstitute family relationships and personal identities around it. Household values and projections for the future, gender dynamics as well as temporal rhythms and stages of family life represent the background as well as the outcome of this appropriation process. (For a similarly rich description of media use in Welsh households see Mackay & Ivey, 2004).

In her ethnographic study of the role of the Internet in the everyday life of a small community north of Dublin, Ireland, that she names "Coastal Town," Katie Ward (2003) raises questions concerning the relationships between the public and private spheres, the local and global contexts, and "new" and "old" media as they are reconfigured by the arrival of the Internet. Her analysis offers a nuanced understanding of the anxieties and struggles that accompany the appropriation process. Parents, she demonstrates, are thrown into a tension field between exalted promises and murky threats from within which they have to erect the regulatory order of Internet use in their homes. Typically, they turn for help to the trusted old media, expecting them to offer a higher-level understanding of the proper ways for employing the new one. Local institutions, as exemplified by the school, the club, and the civic group studied by Ward, tend to tread timidly into the field of opportunities for education and community involvement offered by the Internet. Shyly and cautiously, they extend their existing practices into the new media environment, putting off the implementation of new forms of connectivity and interaction for the indefinite future. Ward does not register significant shifts in the patterns of participation of Internet users in local community life. When questioned about that, respondents expressed satisfaction with and preference for the traditional media of print and public meetings as adequate for handling local issues. However, a number of people had discovered the novel possibilities for involvement in communication about public issues stretching beyond Coastal Town. These informants shared that they would rather use the Internet to participate in national or global political movements.

Ward's work is a component of the European Media Technology and Everyday Life Network that was constituted in the beginning of the 2000s with the objective of carrying out cutting-edge research oriented toward creating a user-friendly information society. Many of the projects undertaken under the auspices of the network adopted the interpretative approach in their efforts to elucidate the role the Internet was taking on in the everyday life of Europeans. As a result, rich accounts emerged of the Internet-related daily practices of different categories of users across a range of European countries. Berker (2005), for example, examined the process through which the Internet was being appropriated in the lives of migrant researchers in Norway and Germany. He demonstrated how a novel life-form characterized by "extreme flexibility" was emerging from the combination of employment opportunities available to this group and the functionalities of the new medium. Hartmann (2005) studied the attitudes and practices of young adults in Belgium and went on to challenge the myths circulated by the "web-generation discourse" (p. 141). She was able to show that while the young adults she followed and interviewed in depth felt at ease with Internet technologies, they consciously resisted the prospect of online interactions and preoccupations taking up too big a part of their lives. Those young people jealously guarded their existing patterns of relationships and ways of doing things and allowed the Internet in only to a measured extent.

Starting from a different theoretical basis, not directly related to the domestication approach and yet in accord with its ethnographic tenets, Miller and Slater (2000) launched a forceful appeal intended to dispel researchers' fixation on the idea of cyberspace as a disembedded "placeless place" (p. 4). In their ethnographic study of the take-up of the Internet in Trinidad, they demonstrated the profound degree to which Trini users were crafting an Internet inseparable from their national culture and everyday life. From home users in poor and middle-class settlements though youth-frequented chat rooms to governmental offices and business websites, Trini culture, sense of identity, and pride permeated the Internet-related practices that Miller and Slater found in that country through and through. Playful cultural rituals had vigorously migrated online. Citizens of the country were embracing online communication affordances eagerly in their desire to stay closer to the large and spread-out Trinidadian diaspora. Miller and Slater drew on their observations to propose a number of concepts that usefully frame the understanding of the role of the Internet in the lives of Trinidadians and are certainly applicable to other cultural contexts. Their notion of "expansive realization" (p. 10) refers to the dynamic between identity and the Internet that allowed users to pursue on the terrain of the Internet visions of themselves which were previously unfeasible: an ingenious entrepreneur, a caring distant parent, etc. The second dynamic, that of "expansive potential" (p. 11) enables users to catch glimpses of novel versions of themselves never imagined before. These dynamics exemplify the changing horizons of users' lifeworlds in which the experience of reach and what Schutz has called "the province of the practicable" (Schutz & Luckmann, 1973, p. 50) has shifted far beyond its pre-Internet boundaries. Miller and Slater's (2000) research on the Internet in Trinidad highlights also the important role macro-factors such as the economy, communication infrastructure, governmental policy, and business culture played in shaping everyday Internet use practices in that society.

In my own research on the trajectory of "becoming an Internet user in Bulgaria" (Bakardjieva, 2005b), I discovered similarly embedded, albeit substantively different, developments occurring in the Bulgarian context where low average income and the absence of effective government programs had led potential users to break their own unconventional paths into the online world. Numerous devious practices at both the individual and business levels proliferated in the country, all aimed at making the most of limited resources. Users shared Internet subscriptions, which begot wires dangling across the open spaces between apartment buildings, or creeping from one apartment into another. Internet service providers offered pirate content through illegal servers in their effort to entice customers to invest in pricy computer equipment and to buy subscriptions. Neighborhood Internet cafes were turning into hotbeds of software pirating and computer training. Professional users were cramming screens and wires into their tiny bedrooms and kitchens driven by the dynamics of expansive realization and potential. Many of them wanted to be players on a larger scene where they could prove their entrepreneurship and professional skills.

While these are important representative examples, it would be too ambitious a task to try to present a comprehensive account of the work undertaken in the interpretative stream of research on the Internet in everyday life. It will suffice to point out that its main achievements lie in the conceptual framing of the process of Internet appropriation by users and the introduction of new analytical categories. Miller's and Slater's notions of expansive realization and expansive potential coined on the basis of their ethnographic data from Trinidad represent a good example. So does Berker's definition of the lifestyle of "extreme flexibility."

Petersen (2007) identifies patterns of what he dubs "mundane cyborg practice" in the activities of his informants whose emergent daily routines weave the computer and the Internet into a web of material interconnections with books, refrigerators, and the meal prepared for dinner. My research on members of the first wave of home-based ordinary (i.e. non-professional or commercial) users of the Internet led me to formulate the concept of the "warm expert" (Bakardjieva, 2005a). This is a close friend or relative who possesses relatively advanced knowledge of computer networks and personal familiarity with the novice user's situation and interests. On that basis, the warm expert is able to reveal to the new user the personal relevance that the Internet can have for him or her. In my study I noticed also the tight connection between the kinds of uses that people invented for the medium and their own social and biographical situations. This finding resonates with the importance of lifestyles and life stages discussed by Anderson and Tracey (2001), but is focused on more concrete and complex micro-phenomena (see also Sewlyn et al., 2005). I opted to talk about the specific configurations of Internet-related practices I observed across a variety of individual cases as "use genres." These genres, I argued, arise in typical situations in which people find themselves at different junctions of life in contemporary society. Thus use genres are personally molded and yet significantly widespread.

With the help of these and other analytical categories, interpretative research on the Internet in everyday life has been able to offer a detailed conceptual map of the adoption and appropriation of the Internet by users across personal, social, and cultural contexts paying due attention to those contexts themselves (for example, Haddon, 1999; Lelong & Thomas, 2001). It has also cast light on the intricate changes in daily practices that have been brought about by the affordances of the Internet. Finally, the qualitative restructuring of the everyday lifeworlds of Internet users in terms of their spatial, temporal, practical, and social dimensions has been closely scrutinized to determine its individual and social implications (see Haddon, 2004, for an overview of findings).

While the interpretative studies discussed so far have demonstrated the agency of users in taking up, adapting, and fine-tuning internet applications to their situations and daily needs, the question remains to what extent they have addressed the dynamics of Internet use critically. Users, these studies have proven beyond reasonable doubt, are not technological dopes swept along by the digital imperative (Wyatt, 2008). Users engage in active sense-making and put up resistance to any such imperatives that threaten to undermine their individual and familial moral economies. They take up the functionalities of the new medium carefully and critically and work to create arrangements that will allow them to remain in control of their daily activities in the presence of the powerful new technical system. The efforts at micro-regulation registered across numerous studies, be it on the part of parents, young adults, or seniors, offer clear evidence of that. Does this mean however, that we should not worry about possible oppressive, exploitative, or alienating aspects of Internet use? And further: Have the empowering possibilities that many commentators have read into the Internet been realized?

Regarding the first question, it would be helpful to keep in mind that while the richness of everyday life in its life-enhancing capacity and the space for agency it offers to its practitioners is indisputable, as critical theorists have warned, the quotidian remains a site infested by numerous oppressive powers. In the words of Gardiner (2000):

> Social agents are not "cultural dopes," but nor are their thoughts and actions fully transparent to them. As Bourdieu cogently notes, whilst people's everyday interpretation of their social world has considerable validity that must be recognized and accorded legitimacy, at the same time we should not succumb to "the illusion of immediate knowledge" (Bourdieu et al., 1991, p. 250; also Watier, 1989). Critical reason and structural analysis therefore have a critical role to play in exposing such patterns of ideological determination and enhancing what Melvin Pollner (1991) has called "radical reflexivity," whereby people can develop a heightened understanding of their circumstances and use this comprehension as the basis of conscious action designed to alter repressive social conditions. (pp. 7–8)

As Internet infrastructure as well as the cultural content of cyberspace become more and more subject to corporate domination (McChesney, 2000; Dahlberg, 2005), there are more reasons to scrutinize everyday use practices with a critical eye. A number of red flags have been raised by feminist scholars who have drawn attention to the "gendering of Internet use" (Van Zoonen, 2002; Wyatt et al., 2005) and the "feminization of the Internet" (Shade, 2002, p. 107; see also Consalvo & Paasonen, 2002). According to Shade, over the years, digital capitalism has turned luring women to the Internet in the capacity of mindless shoppers into a major enterprise. Contrary to early expectations that the Internet would become a vehicle for feminist mobilization and organizing, the lavish offerings of fashion, gossip, diet, and shopping-oriented sites have worked to constrict women to the role of nothing more than avid online consumers. Children and young people, for their part, have become attractive and responsive targets of digital consumerism. An early report by the US Center for Media Education (Montgomery and Pasnik, 1996; see also Montgomery, 2007) drew attention to the numerous deceptive techniques that online marketers were devising with the aim of capturing children. In a detailed investigation of British children's Internet use, Livingstone and Bober (2003) observed that their young respondents embraced the commercial and entertainment opportunities of the online world much more readily and frequently than the creative and the civic ones (see also Livingstone, 2006; Seiter, 2005). Grimes and Feenberg (forthcoming) have analyzed online games in terms of both design and user involvement, showing that games create a controlled world in which users' imagination and relationships are harshly determined by designers' aesthetics and ideology.

Thus, research has signaled the possibility of users being exposed to a whole new system of ideological and manipulative influences. The pressure to get connected to the Internet exerted by cyberspace discourses has only grown recently with the transformation of the Internet into a social space inseparably entwined with each and every institution and practice existing in the offline world. Peer pressure has joined marketing strategies in forcing selected commercially profitable applications upon various categories of users. Eliciting and subsequently data-mining user-generated information has become a common trick of the trade for both market and political strategists (Lyon, 2007). With all the excitement spurred by participatory (popular) culture and Web 2.0 applications, critical reflection on the invasive new avenues that these applications open up for the market to encroach (in the Habermasian sense) on the lifeworld of peer interaction is urgently needed. Therefore, the first important goal of critical research should be to distinguish the everyday use practices that succumb to these diverse alienating tendencies from the life-enhancing possibilities as Lefebvre (1991) advocated. It is not enough to demonstrate that users make mindful choices when they interact with and in the online environment. The oppressive forces prying on users and working behind their backs have to be brought to light and raised to consciousness. But neither is it enough to demonstrate corporate domination in the large infra-structural, political, and economic cyberscapes towering over users' heads. Alienation has to be spotted and laid bare in the nooks and crannies of everyday life where it may thrive under the mask of convenience, popularity, or pleasure. Its impov-erishing effects on the lives of users need to be exposed in concrete and person-ally meaningful ways. Equipped with "radical reflexivity" (Pollner, 1991) borne from critical research like that, users would be able to navigate the Internet both tactically and strategically in ways that defy oppression and advance emancipation.

The second goal for critical research, one that counters the common percep-tion of critics as crabby and pessimistic, is to identify the "the buds and shoots of new potentialities" (Bakhtin, 1984, p. 73, quoted in Gardiner, 2000, p. 20), or the concrete shapes and instances in which "the possible" (Lefebvre, 1991), the life-enhancing opportunities, present themselves in daily Internet use practice. For its part, this approach sets out to go beyond the registration of the typical in terms of, first, repetitive patterns and routines of use, and, second, the disturb-ing realization that the economic and ideological powers reigning in the offline world will inevitably muscle Internet development into the forms most beneficial to them. (See Feenberg, 1999, for an articulation of a critical theory of techno-logy elaborating such an approach). Unlike the purely speculative optimistic projections made by pundits, studies in this vein have sought to isolate eman-cipatory possibilities by carefully inspecting users' actual practices. Feenberg and Bakardjieva (2004), for example, have interpreted users' participation in virtual communities as opening possibilities for collective meaning-making and mobilization around interests and issues that may not be directly political, but are important to people's self-realization and well-being. Through such mobilization, ordinary users find means of dealing with difficulties and pursuing causes that may not be available otherwise. Orgad (2005a, 2005b) has examined carefully the exchanges among women participants in online breast cancer groups. She has demonstrated that these forums offer breast-cancer sufferers and survivors the opportunity to express and share their personal experiences and redefine their condition themselves as opposed to leaving those definitions to be provided by the medical establishment or the media. At the same time, Orgad (2005b) argues, the personal has stopped short of becoming political in these conversations because breast cancer has been understood as a personal problem and responsibility rather than as a condition embedded in broader configurations of material conditions and cultural practices. Moreover, participants' online articulations of the personal and the private have remained constrained in their safe group communicative spaces and have not influenced the understanding of breast cancer in the wider culture.

Franklin (2004) has offered a more heartening account of everyday practices in online spaces created by Samoans and Pacific Islanders who have come together to debate and independently articulate the political, economic, and sociocultural crosscurrents shaping their postcolonial subjectivities. Discussing the meaning of gender, race, and ethnicity in a postcolonial context these participants have practiced democracy in their own terms and for their own needs. In their online texts, the personal and the political are inextricably linked, Franklin insists. Bringing together offline and online research methods, Olsson (2006, 2007) has looked at the practices of young Swedish activists with a view to the specific ways the Internet is drawn into their civic or political projects. Boler's (2008; see also www.meganboler.net) studies of the motivations of Internet users who produce viral political videos, remix, satirical art, and political blogs have demonstrated that such practices foster offline activism as well. Her analysis of the surveys and interviews conducted with such user-producers suggests that web-based communities sparked by political commentary like *The Daily Show* are vibrant and translating into action. Drawing on my data from interviews with home-based users in Canada, I have attempted to trace the small gestures of what I call "subactivism:" civic engagement deeply immersed into everyday life. I have found that the Internet is implicated in many of the activities that make such engagement possible and communicable to other people in respondents' close personal networks as well as in the larger society (Bakardjieva, forthcoming).

This current of Internet in everyday life research is conspicuously sparse and understated. It has had to deal with the common methodological challenges regarding objectivity and representativeness because it speaks about occurrences and instances that stray from the most frequently registered behaviors of user populations. It also has to fend off accusations that, like abstract cyber-optimism, it looks at developments through pink glasses and extols Internet life-enhancing or democratic potential beyond the limits of the realistic. It has to be noted, however, that researchers working in this stream make the conscious choice to look for the "extraordinary" and indeed the "buds and shoots" of new possibilities across a terrain that is clearly colonized by a different kind of vegetation. In contrast to sheer speculation and cheerful technological determinism, however, they do not make up the "buds and shoots" that constitute the object of their interest out of thin air or hypothetical techno-logic. They *find* them in the garden of everyday life and then attempt to understand their origin, conditions, and properties. The ultimate hope of this project is that its findings will be translated into practical strategies *by and for* users, as well as for civic and political actors, which would lead to the conscious nurturing and proliferation of emancipatory possibilities.

Conclusion

Studies of the Internet in everyday life comprise a broad field of inquiry animated by diverse philosophies, interests, and objectives. In this chapter I have analytically isolated three distinct currents shaping the landscape of this field, although in multiple studies, at least two of these approaches can be found going hand in hand (e.g. Sewlyn et al., 2005). All three of them share the commitment to understanding the Internet as part of a broader social context of situations, relations, and activities in which users engage in the course of everyday life. The Internet is one among many ways in which people connect to each other, Wellman and Gulia (1999) have argued, and this straightforward observation represents one of the shared tenets of the everyday life approach. The Internet is one among many other ways in which people flirt, gossip, learn, shop, organize, etc. Hence Internet use has to be studied not exclusively by the traces that it leaves in cyberspace, but as it meshes with other common activities and projects comprising the common ground of people's daily lives. As I have shown, different schools of thought have chosen their own philosophical and methodological paths for dealing with this challenge. Each one of them represents a distinct scholarly paradigm and the respective culture that has spun around it. Despite their different and sometimes even conflicting philosophical tenets, they have all contributed valuable insights to the understanding of the role of the Internet in society. As a goal for future research, one would wish that work associated with these different paradigms becomes more equitably represented. Considering their contributions alongside each other, what becomes increasingly clear is that all these perspectives and research strategies are needed, if the objective is to assemble a comprehensive, thorough, and practically useful account of the Internet phenomenon. This is not a tale of blind men and an elephant. This could and should be an exercise in mutually respectful and productive intellectual multiculturalism.

References

Anderson, B., & Tracey, K. (2001). Digital living: the impact or otherwise of the Internet on everyday life. *American Behavioral Scientist*, 45(3), pp. 456–75.

Anderson, B., Brynin, B., & Raban, Y. (2007) *Information and Communication Technologies in Society: E-living in a Digital Europe*. London: Routledge.

Bakardjieva, M. (2005a). *Internet Society: The Internet in Everyday Life*. London, Thousand Oaks, New Delhi: Sage.

Bakardjieva, M. (2005b). Becoming an Internet user in Bulgaria: notes on a tangled journey. *Media Studies/Studia Medioznawcze*, 3(22), pp. 103–17.

Bakardjieva, M. (2009). Subactivism: Lifeworld and politics in the age of the Internet. *The Information Society*, 25, 91–104.

Bakhtin, M. (1984). *Rabelais and His World*. Bloomington: Indiana University Press.

Bakhtin, M. (1986). *Speech Genres and Other Late Essays*. Trans. V. W. McGee. Texas: University of Texas Press.

Berker, T., Hartmann, M., Punie, Y., & Ward, K. (2005). *Domestication of Media and Technology*. New York: Open University Press.

Berker, T. (2005). The everyday of extreme flexibility: The case of migrant researchers' use of new information and communication technologies. In R. Silverstone (ed.), *Media, Technology, and Everyday Life in Europe: From Information to Communication* (pp. 125–40). Aldershot and Burlington: Ahgate.

Bijker, W. (1995). *Of Bicycles, Bakelites, and Bulbs: Toward a Theory of Sociotechnical Change*. Cambridge, MA: MIT Press.

Bijker, W. (2001). Technology, social construction of. In Neil J. Smelser & P. Baltes (eds.), *International Encyclopedia of the Social and Behavioral Sciences* (1st edn.) Amsterdam, New York: Elsevier.

Bijker, W., & Law, J. (eds.) (1992). *Shaping Technology/Building Society: Studies in Socio-Technical Change*. Cambridge, MA: MIT Press.

Boler, M. (2008). Highlight on current research: Rethinking media, democracy, and citizenship. http://www.meganboler.net/.

Boler, M. Introduction. In *Digital Media and Democracy: Tactics in Hard Times* (pp. 1–50). Cambridge, MA: MIT Press.

Boneva, B., Quinn, A., Kraut, R., Kiesler, S., & Shklovski, I. (2006). Teenage communication in the Internet messaging era. In Kraut, R., Kiesler, S., & Brynin, M. (eds.), *Computers, Phones, and The Internet: Domesticating Information Technology* (pp. 201–18). Oxford: Oxford University Press.

Bourdieu, P., Chamboredon, J-C., & Passerson, J-C. (1991). Meanwhile I have come to know all the diseases of sociological understanding: an interview. In Kreis, B. (ed.), *The Craft of Sociology: Epistemological Preliminaries* (pp. 247–59). New York: Walter de Gruyer.

Brynin, M., & Kraut, R. (2006). Social studies of domestic information and communication technologies. In Kraut, R., Kiesler, S., & Brynin, M. (eds.), *Computers, Phones, and The Internet: Domesticating Information Technology* (pp. 3–20). Oxford: Oxford University Press.

Carrol, J., Rosson, M., Kavanaugh, A., et al. (2006). Social and civic participation in a community network. In Kraut, R., Kiesler, S., & Brynin, M. (eds.), *Computers, Phones, and The Internet: Domesticating Information Technology* (pp. 168–81). Oxford: Oxford University Press.

Certeau, M. de (1984). *The Practice of Everyday Life*. Berkley and Los Angeles: University of California Press.

Consalvo, M., & Paasonen, S. (2002). *Women and Everyday Uses of the Internet: Agency and Identity*. New York: Peter Lang.

Dahlberg, L. (2005). The corporate colonization of online attention and the marginalization of critical communication. *Journal of Communication Inquiry*, 29(2), 160–80.

Feenberg, Andrew (1999). *Questioning Technology*. London: Routledge.

Feenberg, A., & Bakardjieva, M. (2004). Consumers or citizens? The online community debate. In A. Feenberg & D. Barney (eds.), *Community in the Digital Age: Philosophy and Practice* (pp. 1–30). Lanham, MD: Rowan & Littlefield.

Franklin, M. I. (2004). *Postcolonial Politics, the Internet, and Everyday Life: Pacific Traversals Online*. London and New York: Routledge.

Gardiner, M. (2000). *Critiques of Everyday Life*. London: Routledge.

Giddens, Anthony (1984). *The Constitution of Society: Outline of the Theory of Structuration*. Berkeley and Los Angeles: University of California Press.

Grimes, S., & Feenberg, A. (2009). Rationalizing play: a critical theory of digital gaming. *The Information Society*, 25, 105–18.

Haddon, L. (1999). European perceptions and use of the Internet. Paper presented at Usages and Services in Telecommunications, June 7–9, Arcachon, France.

Haddon, L. (2004). *Information and Communication Technologies in Everyday Life: A Concise Introduction and Research Guide*. Oxford: Berg.

Hampton, K., & Wellman, B. (2003). Neighboring in Netville: how the Internet supports community and social capital in a wired suburb. *City and Community*, 2(4), 277–311.

Hartmann, M. (2005). The discourse of the perfect future: young people and new technologies. In R. Silverstone (ed.), *Media, Technology, and Everyday Life in Europe: From Information to Communication* (pp. 141–158). Aldershot and Burlington: Ahgate.

Haythornthwaite, C., & Wellman, B. (2002). The Internet in everyday life: An introduction. In B. Wellman, & C. Haythornthwaite (eds.), *The Internet in Everyday Life* (3–44). Oxford, Malden, MA: Blackwell.

Highmore, B. (2002). *Everyday Life and Cultural Theory: An Introduction*. London: Routledge.

Katz, J., & Rice, R. (2002). *Social Consequences of Internet Use: Access, Involvement and Interaction*. Cambridge, MA: MIT Press.

Kraut, R., Scherlis, W., Mukhopadhyay, T., Manning, J., & Kiesler, S. (1996). HomeNet: A field trial of residential internet services. *Proceedings of the CHI '96 Conference* (pp. 284–91). New York: Association for Computing Machinery. http://www.sigchi.org/chi96/proceedings/papers/Kraut/rek_txt.htm.

Kraut, R., Patterson, M., Lundmark, V., Kiesler, S., Mukophadhyay, T., & Scherlis, W. (1998). Internet paradox: A social technology that reduces social involvement and psychological well-being? *American Psychologist*, 53(9), 1017–31.

Kraut, R., Kiesler, S., Boneva, B., Cummings, J., Helgeson, V., & Crawford, A. (2002). Internet paradox revisited. *Journal of Social Issues*, 58, 49–74.

Kraut, R., Kiesler, S., Boneva, B., & Shklovski, I. (2006). Examining the effect of Internet use on television viewing: details make a difference. In R. Kraut, S. Kiesler, & M. Brynin (eds.), *Computers, Phones, and The Internet: Domesticating Information Technology* (pp. 70–83). Oxford: Oxford University Press.

Lally, E. (2002). *At Home with Computers*. Oxford, New York: Berg.

Lelong, B., & Thomas, F. (2001). L'Apprentissage de l'Internaute: Socialization et autonomisation. Paper presented at *e-Usages*, June 12–14, Paris.

Lyon, D. (2007). Surveillance, power and everyday life. In R. Mansell, C. Avgerou, D. Quah, & R. Silverstone (eds.). The *Oxford Handbook of Information and Communication Technologies*. Oxford: Oxford University Press.

Lefebvre, H. (1971). Everyday Life in the Modern World. New York, Evanston, San Francisco, London: Harper & Row.

Lefebvre, H. (1991). *Critique of Everyday Life*. Vol. 1, *Introduction*. London, New York: Verso.

Livingstone, S. (2006). Drawing conclusions from new media research: Reflections and puzzles regarding children's experience of the Internet. *The Information Society*, 22, 219–30.

Livingstone, S., & Bober, M. (2003). UK children go online: Listening to young people's experiences. London: London School of Economics and Political Science.

Mackay, H., & Ivey, D. (2004). *Modern Media in the Home: An Ethnographic Study*. Rome: John Libbey Publishing.

McChesney, R. (2000). So much for the magic of technology and the free markets: The world wide web and the global corporate order. In A. Herman & T. Swiss (eds.), *The World Wide Web and Contemporary Cultural Theory: Metaphor, Magic, and Power* (pp. 5–35). New York and London: Routledge.

Miller, D., & Slater, D. (2000). *The Internet: An Ethnographic Approach*. Oxford, New York: Berg.

Montgomery, K. (2007). *Generation Digital: Politics, Commerce, and Childhood in the Age of the Internet*. Cambridge, MA: MIT Press.

Montgomery, K., & Pasnik, S. (1996). *Web of Deception*. Center for Media Education. http://www.soc.american.edu/docs/deception.pdf.

Orgad, S. (2005a). *Storytelling Online: Talking Breast Cancer on the Internet*. New York: Peter Lang.

Orgad, S. (2005b). The transformative potential of online communication: The case of breast cancer patients' Internet spaces. *Feminist Media Studies*, 5(2), 141–61.

Petersen, S. (2007). Mundane cyborg practice material aspects of broadband internet use. *Convergence: The International Journal of Research into New Media Technologies*, 13(1), 79–91.

Pinch, T., & Bijker, W. (1987). The social construction of facts and artifacts. In W. Bijker, T. Huges, & T. Pinch (eds.), *The Social Construction of Technological Systems* (pp. 17–50). Cambridge, MA: MIT Press.

Olsson, T. (2006). Active and calculated media use among young citizens: Empirical examples from a Swedish study. In D. Buckingham & R. Willett (eds.), *Digital Generations: Children, Young People, and New Media* (pp. 115–30). London: Routledge.

Olsson, T. (2007). A tripartite analysis of a civic website: understanding reklamsabotage.org. In N. Carpentier et al. (eds.), *Democracy in an Enlarged Europe: The Intellectual Work of the 2007 European Media and Communication Doctoral Summer School* (pp. 153–70). Tartu: Tartu University Press.

Oudshoorn, N., & Pinch, T. (2003). *How Users Matter: The Co-Construction of Users and Technology*. Cambridge, MA: MIT Press.

PEW Internet & American Life Project. http://www.pewinternet.org/.

Pollner, M. (1991). Left of ethnomethodology: the rise and fall of radical reflexivity. *American Sociological Review*, 56, 370–80.

Schutz, A., & Luckmann, T. (1973). *The Structures of the Life-world*. Evanston, IL: North-Western University Press.

Seiter, E. (2005). *The Internet Playground: Children's Access, Entertainment and Mis-Education*. New York: Peter Lang.

Selwyn, N., Gorard, S., & Furlong, J. (2005). Whose Internet is it anyway? Exploring adults' (non)use of the Internet in everyday life. *European Journal of Communication*, 20(1), 5–26.

Shade, L. (2002). *Gender and Community in the Social Construction of the Internet*. New York: Peter Lang.

Silverstone, Roger (1994). *Television and Everyday Life*. London and New York: Routledge.

Silverstone, R., & Haddon, L. (1996). Design and the domestication of information and communication technologies: technical change and everyday life. In R. Mansell

& R. Silverstone (eds.), *Communication by Design: The Politics of Information and Communication Technologies* (pp. 44–74). Oxford, New York: Oxford University Press.

Silverstone, R., Hirsch, E., & Morley, D. (1992). Information and communication technologies and the moral economy of the household. In R. Silverstone & E. Hirsch (eds.), *Consuming Technologies: Media and Information in Domestic Spaces* (pp. 15–31). London: Routledge.

Smith, D. (1987). *The Everyday World as Problematic: A Feminist Sociology.* Toronto: University of Toronto Press.

Smith, D. (1999). *Writing the Social.* Toronto, Buffalo, London: University of Toronto Press.

Van Zoonen, L. (2002). Gendering the Internet: claims, controversies and cultures. *European Journal of Communication*, 17(1), 5–23.

Ward, K. (2003). An ethnographic study of Internet consumption in Ireland: Between domesticity and the public participation. http://www.lse.ac.uk/collections/EMTEL/reports/ward_2003_emtel.pdf.

Ward, K. (2005). Internet consumption in Ireland – towards a connected domestic life. In R. Silverstone (ed.), *Media, Technology, and Everyday Life in Europe: From Information to Communication* (pp. 107–24). Aldershot and Burlington: Ahgate.

Watier, P. (1989). Understanding and everyday life. *Current Sociology*, 37(1), 71–81.

Wellman, B., & Haythornthwaite, C. (2002). *The Internet in Everyday Life.* Oxford, Malden, MA: Blackwell.

Wellman, B., & Gulia, M. (1999). Net-surfers don't ride alone: virtual communities as communities. In B. Wellman (ed.), *Networks in the Global Village: Life in Contemporary Communities* (pp. 331–66). Boulder, CO, Oxford: Westview Press.

World Internet Project. http://www.worldinternetproject.net/.

Wyatt, S. (2008). Challenging the digital imperative. Inaugural lecture presented upon the acceptance of the Royal Netherlands Academy of Arts and Sciences (KNAW) Extraordinary Chair in Digital Cultures in Development, March 28, 2008, Maastricht University.

Wyatt, S., Henwood, F., Hart, A., & Smith, J. (2005). The digital divide, health information and everyday life. *New Media & Society*, 7(2), 199–218.

5

Internet Research Ethics: Past, Present, and Future

Elizabeth A. Buchanan

Introduction and Background

What would the early visionaries of the Internet, or its earlier manifestations, who saw these virtual networks as a participatory goldmine for research collaboration and conduct, say today about Internet-based research? Would they have imagined such diversity, such potential, such debate, as has emerged around the forms of online datasets, knowledge reuse databases, virtual communities, listservs, blogs, social networking sites, and any of the yet to be determined technologies, tools, or venues? And, would they themselves be surprised with the depth and breadth of ethical conundrums, debates, and conflicts that have emerged from the use of the Internet as a vehicle for, or site of, research activities? Would they explain to the writers of, for instance, *The Belmont Report*, that the Internet was not conceived as a field of human subjects research? Or, would they suggest that this "thing," the Internet, has the potential to change human subjects research as we have known it for some time, and across locales, embraced, formalized, codified, and regulated it? And, let's ask how the users of these networks imagine themselves in this research debate. As the lines, the boundaries between and among participants, subjects, objects, creators, owners, borrowers, voyeurs, and researchers are disrupted, potentially becoming unrecognizable, (how) are research and research ethics changing? Ultimately, the Internet, broadly conceived, has the potential to fundamentally disturb extant models of human subjects research. Given that ethical guidelines for Internet research have been articulated, and established (e.g., AoIR, 2002; NESH, 2003), there indeed may be a "research ethics" 2.0 emerging. This concept, research ethics 2.0, allows us to think holistically and evolutionarily about the meeting of research methods, ethics, and technologies in general, and Internet, or online, technologies in particular, which will be the focus of this chapter.

In order to get to the current dialogue of Internet research ethics, it is important to contextualize the discussion in the larger framework of research ethics, which, as a strict discipline, has a relatively brief history. The modern traditions of codified, formalized research ethics stem from the Nuremburg Code, released in 1947 as a response to atrocities committed in the name of research during World War Two ([1947] 1949). From the Code, the concept of informed consent of subjects or participants emerged as a basic premise of medical or biomedical research. The World Medical Association's Declaration of Helsinki (first adopted in 1964), which followed the Code, included the concept of informed consent along with broader notions of human dignity and safety. Both the Nuremburg Code and the Declaration of Helsinki were strongly grounded in the medical/biomedical perspectives, while the 1948 United Nations Declaration of Human Rights spoke to a range of basic rights beyond research specificity. Nevertheless, the UN Declaration shares in common with codified research ethics a commitment to basic rights of autonomy, protection, safety, and knowledge.

In the United States, research violations of human rights of dignity and autonomy became well known through the Tuskegee experiments, which began in 1930 and lasted for 42 years. Such ethical issues as deception, respect for persons, and disclosure were raised along research lines. One major debate that emerged specifically out of the Tuskegee experiments is the balance between individual harms and greater scientific knowledge, the latter of which was used as a rationale for the conduct of the research. This debate between the greater good of the individual versus the societal underscores the diverse consequentialist and non-consequentialist ethical approaches to research ethics. As Israel and Hay (2006) describe them,

> consequentialist approaches see the judgement of acts as ethical or not on the basis of the consequences of those acts. Deontological approaches suggest that our evaluation of moral behaviour requires consideration of matters other than the ends produced by people's actions and behaviours . . . Consequentialism exhorts us to promote the good; the latter to exemplify it. (2006, p. 16)

The United States issued formal regulations protecting human subjects in medical and biomedical research in 1974 in the National Research Act; the creation of institutional review boards (IRBs) ensued, and the highly influential National Commission for the Protection of Human Subjects of Biomedical and Behavioral Research was formed. In 1979, *The Belmont Report* was released, and as a policy statement to this day remains the single most important document to use as an ethical base for subject research. It identified three basic ethical principles on which research must be reviewed: respect for persons, beneficence, and justice. Respect for persons is articulated through the informed consent process, and

> incorporates at least two ethical convictions: first, that individuals should be treated as autonomous agents, and second, that persons with diminished autonomy are entitled to protection. The principle of respect for persons thus divides into two separate moral requirements: the requirement to acknowledge autonomy and the requirement to protect those with diminished autonomy. (n.p.)

Beneficence entails the concept that

> Persons are treated in an ethical manner not only by respecting their decisions and protecting them from harm, but also by making efforts to secure their well-being. Such treatment falls under the principle of beneficence. The term "beneficence" is often understood to cover acts of kindness or charity that go beyond strict obligation. In this document, beneficence is understood in a stronger sense, as an obligation. Two general rules have been formulated as complementary expressions of beneficent actions in this sense: (1) do no harm and (2) maximize possible benefits and minimize possible harms. (n.p.)

Justice, the third basic principle, plays out in research ethics in terms of participation and the fair distribution of risks and benefits. Moreover, using certain selected groups as subjects of research raises questions about justice; specific populations are designated as "vulnerable," and include, for example, children, prisoners, mentally ill or challenged, and pregnant women. Increasingly, students (over the age of 18) are being considered by some boards to fall into this realm as well to avoid higher education researchers tapping into their classes too often and, potentially, inappropriately. Ultimately, as *The Report* asserts,

> An injustice occurs when some benefit to which a person is entitled is denied without good reason or when some burden is imposed unduly . . . There are several widely accepted formulations of just ways to distribute burdens and benefits. Each formulation mentions some relevant property on the basis of which burdens and benefits should be distributed. These formulations are (1) to each person an equal share, (2) to each person according to individual need, (3) to each person according to individual effort, (4) to each person according to societal contribution, and (5) to each person according to merit. (n.p.)

Similar statements, using analogous principles of respect for persons, beneficence, and justice, emerged out of Canada in the late 1970s, policies which since 1994 are embedded under the Tri-Council Policy Statement's *Ethical Conduct for Research Involving Humans*. Various European Union directives, as well as individual nations' policies, ground human subjects work, including the EU Data Privacy Protection Acts (Directive 95/46/EC, 1995, Directive 2006/24/EC, 2006), the Norwegian research codes (NESH, 2003), and the UK's NHS National Research Ethics Service and the Research Ethics Framework of the Economic and Social Research Council (ESRC) General Guidelines. Since the 1960s, Australian research ethics programs are governed under the National Health and Medical Research Council's *Statement on Human Experimentation*, with social and behavioral research added to the policy statement in 1986 (NHMRC, 2007). Research ethics committees (RECs) in African countries have a varied existence. In South Africa, for example, RECs date to 1966, at the University of the Witwatersrand (Moodely & Myer, 2007), while other African countries are still working on training and development of formal programs. India adopted its set of medical ethics guidelines in 1980, in its "Indian Council of Medical Research," recently revised and updated in 2000. Also, in 1998, there was a great push for greater ethical awareness and codification of ethics principles for social sciences. In January 2000, the Forum for Ethical Review Committees in Asia and the Western Pacific (FERCAP) was established. While these examples do not constitute a comprehensive review, we can see that formalized research ethics programs range in maturity across the globe.

Indeed, the application of strict medical or biomedical principles to social and behavioral research is itself more recent. In their seminal work, Tom Beauchamp and James Childress (1982) provided a thorough discussion of the applicability of medical/biomedical principles in social science research, and, from then on, researchers from disparate non-medical disciplines have done everything from critiquing, lamenting, grudgingly embracing, to outright rejecting such models. For example, Joan Siebert, Stuart Plattner, and Philip Rubin describe the situation as it has played out in the United States:

> The biomedical focus of the regulations has always posed problems for social scientists since biomedical (especially clinical) research requires standards that are often inappropriate for social and behavioral research. Although these problems existed in the 1970s through the 1990s, it seems that more flexibility prevailed during these years. IRBs tended to interpret the regulations in ways that were not unduly restrictive of social and behavioral research. (2002, p. 2)

And, moreover, in 2005, in light of ethics reviews of social and behavioral research, some have suggested that ethics boards are suffering from "mission creep," extending reviews into unnecessary terrains:

> We recommend focusing on those areas of research that pose the greatest risk, such as biomedical research, while removing or reducing scrutiny of many fields within the social sciences and humanities that pose minimal risk. Some fields, such as journalism and ethnography, and methods, such as oral history, have their own, well-established sets of ethical guidelines and appeal procedures. In addition, they pose virtually no risk to the subjects. (Center for Advanced Study, 2005, n.p.)

Such mission creep became a very public scholarly and policy discussion, as the American Historical Association (AHA) and the Oral History Association (OHA) worked to remove IRB review of oral history research, citing the profession's "long and unhappy experience with the way these policies have been implemented," and concluding "that IRB oversight is in conflict with the essential canons of our practice" (AHA, 2008, n.p). A major issue revolved around the Office for Human Research Protections (OHRP) definition of "human subjects," and the AHA and OHA argued clearly and soundly why oral history as a method *and* practice failed to meet the conditions of OHRP's definition. In consideration of the oral history decision, it is important to recall what an ethics board's functions are. Research ethics are operationalized by their institutional committees, known in various acronyms as IRBs, ERBs (Ethics Review Boards), or RECs (Research Ethics Committees). Based on their defining guidelines and principles, such review boards are charged with three primary tasks:

1 To ensure that adequate informed consent is in place within all research protocols, in order to educate potential subjects about the nature of the proposed research, their rights as research subjects, and the potential risks in order to further respect autonomy and free choice as a research subject.
2 To ensure that the risks of research are minimized to the extent possible, and are justified relative to the value of the knowledge to be gained from research. Related to this, the IRB should ensure that the proposed research has scientific merit, so that potential subjects are not exposed to risk for no valuable purpose.
3 To ensure that the proposed research is consistent with principles of justice, so that particular segments of the population are not selected to bear the burdens of research while other segments reap the benefits; and conversely, that particular segments of the population are not unjustifiably excluded from participation in research (see, for more discussion, Gallin & Ognibene, 2007).

To those ends, which are indeed appropriate and fair when executed properly, and transnationally, ethics review boards function quite similarly, though their philosophical perspectives will differ. For instance, Buchanan and Ess (2008, p. 276) discuss the differences between Anglo-American-oriented ethics reviews and other EU models:

US (and UK) codes characteristically justify research on the basis of its anticipated outcomes – i.e., as these promise to benefit society at large in some way – thereby requiring researchers only to *minimize, not eliminate, risks to research subjects* . . . Moreover, the research ethics of countries such as Norway can be accurately characterized as deontological, as they emphasize that the rights of human subjects must never be compromised, no matter the potential benefits (NESH, 2003, 2006). Indeed, this contrast between more utilitarian Anglo-American approaches and more deontological European approaches has been noted by earlier researchers.

While ethics boards worldwide will find common ground within the traditional discourse of research ethics, as articulated in the three aforementioned principles (respect for persons, beneficence, and justice), even in the face of disparate research methods, disciplinary perspectives and norms, and professional codes of ethics, they now face another set of methodological, and thus ethical, challenges: Internet-based research, which at once contests methodologies, ethics, and the application of "rules" to researchers and researched. The concept of ethical pluralism, described below, is emerging as a core framework and philosophical approach from which to conceptualize Internet research ethics. First used as a framework for the Association of Internet Researchers (AoIR) *Ethical Decision Making* document (2002), it stresses the importance of shared ethical norms coexisting alongside distinct cultural (and methodological) difference (see Ess, 2007).

Enter the Internets

Research has been long been conducted on or about early "populations" of Internet users – for example, Usenet studies and early studies of computer-mediated communication – though these were often not considered "human subjects" research. But, there have been a few "notorious" examples of early online research ethics, or violations thereof, which will help us to discuss the field today: first, a telling incident from Carnegie Mellon's infamous Rimm study in the mid-1990s, followed by Dibble's account of "rape in cyberspace" (1993), and Van Gelder's (1985) report of deception of physically handicapped women online and the psychologist who pretended to be one of them. Countless other examples could be included, from the many researchers who were first members of online communities prior to their research role and the subsequent reactions to their presences (eg, Walstrom, 2004; Baker, 2009) to discussions by Stern (2004) and Bober (2004) of online research with minors and the emotional, and methodological, tolls such research can exert, to AOL's mass data dump (Barbaro & Zeller, 2006), to "special" online populations and issues, such as pro-anorexic/pro-eating-disorder websites, which pose unique ethical quandaries (eg, Dias, 2003; Walstrom, 2004), research on medical conditions (eg, Clark & Sharf, 2007; Dyer, 2001), sexual relationships (eg, Mustanski, 2001; Whitty, Baker, & Inman, 2007), and so on. Ultimately, the field of online research ethics is continually redefined by *and defining* the ethical challenges researchers experience daily vis-à-vis Internet environments and technologies. Regularly, ethics boards, researchers, and online participants experience highly challenging ethical dilemmas as we see in the following.

Setting the stage

Martin Rimm, an undergraduate student, used the "information superhighway" to investigate access to various types of pornographic images, creating a typology of porn and its viewers. At its core, the case was about research ethics as much as pornography, though it became widely known for the latter. Research misconduct was found, while the university's report of the research included the following statements:

> The nature of this research has made this inquiry complex. The research pertained to human sexuality, a topic that is emotionally and politically explosive. As a result of the human, social and political implications of the work, it would be given special scrutiny and held to high standards of scientific integrity. At the same time, the *research concerned interactions on computer networks, a relatively new domain where research standards and university policy have not been fully discussed and debated.* (They should be.) Because of this context, and although a few of the problems are easily categorized as "serious" or "not serious," many of the allegations fall into a gray area. (CMU, 1995, emphasis added)

Ultimately, this case showed a growing uncertainty around human subjects models and Internet research. According to the Carnegie Mellon report, the research included a database

> which showed the log files from 1994 of one BBS [bulletin board system] porno-graphic service. The fields included name, telephone number, address, driver's license, age, dates and times which pictures had been downloaded . . . In addition to that dataset, Martin Rimm also obtained another set of log files from a different BBS operator, described by Martin Rimm as a friend. This friend obtained further log files of customer-level information from friends who were in the same business. (CMU, 1995)

This one case raises issues of consent, access, privacy, anonymity and identifica-tion, researcher integrity, misuse of data by researchers, representation, limits of "public" and "private" data, and ownership of data. Moreover, while this case allows us to think directly about discrete research ethics issues, it forces us to consider the parameters of human subjects research in these emergent, Internet-based realities.

While the Rimm study raised questions of online *researcher* ethics, we can look to another incident from 1993, the well-known "rape in cyberspace," as Julian Dibble reported it, as a case of online *participant* ethics. The virtual assault, taking place in a MUD (multi-user dungeon), *LambdaMoo*, resulted in online outrage, but, more than that, it showed how emotion, harms, victimization, and harassment were indeed experienced in and by online communities. Far from being detached, the experiential power of online speech as it impacts participants gave researchers much to think about in terms of methods and ethics; far from being only a representation, this was a reality, with direct human implications, and the effects of the event showed that words and dialogue online could not be separated from real-world harms. As such, this incident was seminal in pushing the bound-aries of online experiences into human subjects research: as online/offline realities are diminished as more of our everyday lives exist in some interconnected fashion between or across the two, this case forces us to delve beyond the simplistic dyad of online versus offline and into a more fluid sphere. Within the developed world, at least, the concepts of "being online" and "being offline" are anachronistic as we embrace the ultraconnectivity of our present technological existences, and thus blur research boundaries and binaries. Dibble's subsequent writing on the incident pushed researchers to reconsider the narratives emerging from online research – how are identities represented, retold? And, what should researchers do to pro-tect identities in online research? Thus, from the rape incident, the "annihilation" of an online character emphasized to researchers the great importance of online identities, an issue which has continued to garner attention and debate among scholars (see, for example, Lawson, 2004; Reid, 1996; Roberts, Smith, & Pollock, 2004, St Amant, 2004).

Finally, there was Van Gelder's account, originally published in 1985, of Alex/Joan, a male psychologist who, posing as a woman, befriended handicapped women in a Compuserve BBS. Using a form of deception research, Alex posed as Joan, who shared in the trials and tribulations of an online community. Deep friendships were made, trust built, until the online realities presented by Joan were questioned (p. 534).

> Thus it was a huge shock early this year when, through a complicated series of events, Joan was revealed as being not disabled at all. More to the point, in fact, Joan was not a woman. She was really a man we'll call Alex – a prominent New York psychiatrist in his early fifties who was engaged in a bizarre, all-consuming experiment to see what it felt like to be female, and to experience the intimacy of female friendship.
>
> Even those who barely knew Joan felt implicated – and somehow betrayed – by Alex's deception. Many of us online like to believe that we're a utopian community of the future, and Alex's experiment proved to us that technology is no shield against deceit. We lost our innocence, if not our faith.

Joan, like Mr Bungle as described by Dibble, was "outed" by the online community: Van Gelder's account, like Dibble's, raised serious issues of identity, pseudonymity, truth, and rights of participants, as we explore below, while it pushed the normative questions of what researchers *should* do as researchers in online environments, including, and in particular, in forms of deception research. Interestingly, many years later, despite the unique challenges of using deception in online environments, Skitka and Sargis (2006) found that the methodology is actually a common occurrence across psychological research online. (For a fascinating reinterpretation of the Milgram experiment, which brought deception research out very publically, see Slater and colleagues (2006), in which humans interact with onscreen avatars, inflicting "shocks" to examine how the infamous experiment unfolds in light of virtual reality. Among other significant results, this virtual experiment suggested that while the participants certainly comprehended the distinctions of "real" humans versus avatars, there was a significant feeling of ethical sensitivity for the avatars.)

Using these incidents as examples, we can explore how researchers from diverse disciplines think through media and methods, and, as such, think through ethics (or, in the Rimm and Van Gelder cases, *fail* to think through ethics). Historically, then, we can situate the emergence of this sub-discipline of research ethics, Internet research ethics (IRE), in the early 1990s. IRE is defined as the analysis of ethical issues and application of research ethics principles as they pertain to research conducted on and in the Internet. Internet-based research, broadly defined, is research which utilizes the Internet to collect information through an online tool, such as an online survey; studies about how people use the Internet, e.g., through collecting data and/or examining activities in or on any online environments; and/or, uses of online datasets or databases.

If Rimm was infamous for ignoring the ethical issues raised in and by research conducted online, Dibble's *Rape in Cyberspace*, Turkle's *Life on the Screen* (1995) and Markham's *Life Online* (1998), showed the potential for deeper engagement with the realities of conducting – and participating in – Internet-based research, as they brought the "human" aspect, and more specifically, the reality of human harm, to the fore of online realities, including, and especially in, research activities. The "virtual field" was exposed, and its inhabitants became "subjects." There was much to explore, and many methodological ways of doing so. This was confirmed in 1996, in a watershed issue of *The Information Society*, when a range of international and cross-disciplinary scholars addressed directly the meeting of ethics and online research, calling into question the applicability and appropriateness of extant ethical guidelines, notably, human subjects protections models as articulated in the US in particular, for emerging forms of online research. Scholarly interest was piqued, and subsequent work followed in the landmark meeting and report of the American Association for the Advancement of Science (AAAS); Frankel and Siang asserted in 1999 in order to "both protect human subjects and promote innovative and scientifically sound research, it is important to consider the ethical, legal, and technical issues associated with this burgeoning area of research" (p. 2). Frankel and Siang based their approach on traditional research ethics principles of respect for persons, beneficence, and justice. Following Frankel and Siang, in 2000, the AoIR formed an Ethics Working Group, which put together a foundational set of ethical guidelines for online research (AoIR, 2002). Theirs was the first international and interdisciplinary framework to emerge, and articulated disparate ethical traditions and the ways such traditions inform researchers. It built on the aforementioned long-standing human subjects models, while considering a host of disciplines and new media that challenge any direct application of such models to online environments; the rationale behind the guidelines is stated:

> The Internet has opened up a wide range of new ways to examine human inter/ actions in new contexts, and from a variety of disciplinary and interdisciplinary approaches. As in its offline counterpart, online research also raises critical issues of risk and safety to the human subject. Hence, online researchers may encounter conflicts between the requirements of research and its possible benefits, on the one hand, and human subjects' rights to and *expectations* of autonomy, privacy, informed consent, etc. (AoIR, 2002)

Importantly, the AoIR document stresses the plurality of ways in which ethical decisions can be made, depending on the approaches or traditions used to frame and analyze an issue, and, it emphasizes cultural difference in human subjects models and approaches to how research ethics are to be regulated (if at all).

Following in 2003 and 2004, three major books (Buchanan, 2004; Johns, Chen, & Hall 2004; Thorseth, 2003) were published on Internet research ethics, and each delved deeper into the array of ethical issues outlined by Frankel and Siang, and AoIR, and built on the development of IRE as a discrete field, with its own evolving research base. While those texts were inter- and cross-disciplinary perspectives on IRE, the discipline-specific guidelines of the American Psychological

Association's report from the Board of Scientific Affairs' Advisory Group on the Conduct of Research on the Internet were also released in 2004. Kraut et al. argued that while Internet research is not inherently more risky than traditional forms of research, the risks and safeguards will be different for psychological research. Then, two Internet-research specific journals appeared: 2006 saw the first publication of the *International Journal of Internet Science*, which emphasizes "empirical findings, methodology, and theory of social and behavioral science concerning the Internet and its implications for individuals, social groups, organizations, and society" (*International Journal of Internet Science*, 2006); and in 2008, the *International Journal of Internet Research Ethics* was released, dedicated to exploring "cross-disciplinary, cross-cultural research on Internet Research Ethics. All disciplinary perspectives, from those in the arts and humanities, to the social, behavioral, and biomedical sciences, are reflected" (*International Journal of Internet Research Ethics*, 2008).

Thus, scholarly interest in the Internet has become clearly evident, with the research base around "Internet studies" bridging disciplines and locales. Methodological diversity – and with it, ethical pluralism, what AoIR (2002) and Ess (2006) describe as an acceptance of more than one judgment regarding the interpretation and application of a shared ethical norm – abounds in Internet studies. A continuum of online research is emerging, where on one extreme, the "human" in the human subjects aspect of the research, is not at any risk, and the research is, perhaps, not human subjects based at all, as is the case in discourse or content analyses of Internet materials, to authentic human subjects work, where lives can be affected, risks and benefits must be calculated, and individual identities must be strongly protected. Specific research methods range widely along a continuum. At one extreme we have analyses of datasets, aggregated and decontextualized, merely representing some facet of experience, devoid of connection with individual people (though the 2008 Facebook dataset release and subsequent identification reveals that researchers must exercise great caution when making datasets and code books publically available; see, for example, Zimmer, 2008a). Further along the continuum there is the use of online surveys, in which a range of ethical issues can be found, sometimes to the surprise of the researcher and researched, for instance, where individuals may or may not be readily identifiable, and where data may or may not be in the full control of the researcher, depending on the tool (see Buchanan & Hvizdak, 2009). Toward the other end of the continuum we have participant observations of lists and the people who inhabit them, and complex, in-depth ethnographies of people and their communities online, with the potential to harm individuals if their real-life (or onscreen-life) identities were exposed (see Baker, 2009; Walstrom, 2004).

Researchers from all disciplines may find themselves along this continuum: Methodological choices inform and are informed by ethical issues, as Annette Markham (1998, 2006) has long argued convincingly, while the topics of research themselves vary from non-sensitive (entertainment, for example) to highly sensitive (eating disorders, health), thereby adding another dimension to the ethical complexity of research online. Thus, we must consider the ethics of the methodological choices as well as the ethics of research questions and/or problems in determining how we evaluate and respond to the myriad ethical issues in online research. These issues abound, ranging from questions around privacy, consent, representation, attribution, authorship, plagiarism, redefinitions of personal and public, to legal issues, including copyright, libel, defamation, and harms. All of these have been explored extensively across the literature in descriptive ways, and normative discussions have emerged across disciplines (see, for example, the IRE bibliographies at the Internet Research Ethics Clearinghouse, 2008).

Academic disciplines from arts and humanities, to social sciences, to medical and health-related disciplines are all represented in the IRE literature, though Buchanan and Ess (2008) have found that in the US, ethics boards review online research primarily from the social sciences, followed by medical/health. Moreover, bibliometric counts of scholarly articles reveal increasing numbers of articles addressing Internet ethics issues across all disciplines (Buchanan & Hvizdak, in progress), while IRBs in the United States are reporting increasing interest and/or concern around Internet-based research protocols in general (Buchanan & Ess, 2008). To some extent, varying disciplines, in their own methodological fashion, engage with these and other potential ethical issues on their own unique disciplinary terms; with methods guiding ethics, these disparate issues are often challenging to define in absolute terms. In short, when dealing with Internet research ethics debates, definitive "answers" are often elusive. Ethics boards in particular must make *judgments* around research ethics issues, and there is a large degree of subjectivity involved when the issue or problem in question is not well "codified." Bringing the ethics review process to a highly transparent level holds potential for much richer dialogues around ethical issues, and removes a great deal of the confusions which emerge around research review. Especially because Internet research changes amazingly quickly, codification of general principles and their application to specific issues is quite difficult. This means that judgment concerning a given set of issues or contexts – specifically as ethical pluralism enables such judgments to vary in ways appropriate to local contexts and specific details – becomes an especially crucial component of our approach to IRE.

To this end, we will discuss discrete research ethics issues as they exist across Internet venues. This range of venues is expansive. In 2002, Ess and AoIR identified such venues as homepages, blogs, search engine searches, email (personal email exchanges), listservs (exchanges and archives), Usenet newsgroups, ICQ/IM (text-based), iChat, CUSeeMe and other audio-video exchanges, chat rooms including Internet relay chat (IRC), multiple-user domains (MUDs) and object-oriented MUDs (MOOs), gaming, images and other forms of multimedia presentation (webcams, etc.), and (some forms of) computer-supported cooperative work systems. Since the AoIR *Ethical Decision Making* document, Web 2.0 has produced more interactive forums, such as social networking sites and hyper-blogging, which are producing their own emergent normative zones of research ethics. This chapter will conclude with a discussion around those issues.

Ethical Considerations

Public/private

Traditionally, the IRE literature has been highly concerned with privacy issues, as it is a prominent concern for ethics boards, and, as our examples earlier revealed, the relationship between public and private online plays out in complex ways. Sveningsson (2004) provides some clarity, by suggesting that

> if the medium is public and the information shared is not sensitive, we might conclude that it is acceptable to make exceptions as for ethical requirements. If, on the other hand, the medium is public and the information is sensitive, we might have to be more careful when making our decisions. (p. 55)

Thus, how researchers protect the privacy of their subjects or participants dictates the extent of interactions with them. And if the venue has a specific notice to researchers, stating its site policy about expectations, researchers should first review those. In this way, the "rules" surrounding what is public and what is private come from the participants or "gatekeepers" of a site, and a researcher should convey this information to an ethics board for consideration. For instance, there may be a statement notifying users that the site is public, and open to/for researchers, or, it may have an explanation of expectations of privacy in specific areas or domains. There may be a statement affiliated with the venue indicating whether discussion, postings, etc., are ephemeral, logged for a specific time, and/or archived in a private and/or publicly accessible location such as a website. For example, the AoIR list states:

> air-l is a public forum and . . . your words will be available to everyone subscribed to the list and placed in a public archive. Messages sent via email can easily be reproduced and circulated beyond their originally intended audience, and neither the list manager, the association's officers, nor the server's host are responsible for consequences arising from list messages being re-distributed.

Moreover, researchers can look to see if there are mechanisms that participants or users may choose to employ to indicate that their exchanges should be regarded as private, for instance, "moving" to a private chat room, using specific encryption software, or conversing through a dedicated email or instant message account. Ethics boards may suggest that researchers inform participants that online communications are not necessarily secure, and that electronic communication is subject to tracking, permanence and thus long-term use beyond the scope of the intended research, and other online abuses. The prevailing interest in databanks or shared data hubs, and the emerging policies from ethics boards on banking hold potential for ethical debate as well. Informing the participants of these risks allows them to assess the extent of possible harms from engaging in an online research project. An interesting example of potential risk involves research on illegal activities online. Consider an ethics board in the US which received a protocol from a researcher who was interested in studying sexual minorities (homosexuality) in India through chat rooms. In India, homosexuality itself is not "illegal," but the act of, or the solicitation of, same-sex relations are grouped under illegal sexual activity. Thus, if a chat room participant solicits same-sex relations in a chat room, it would be construed under Indian law as illegal activity. Risk to subjects becomes much higher in this instance, and, thus, increased informed-consent processes are critical.

As we are seeing, misuses of online activities in the forms of pre-interview screening on social networking sites by potential employers, irresponsible representations by military recruiters, privacy violations by insurance industries, among others (see, for example, Elefant, 2008; Olsen, 2006; Gallagher, 2008), raise concerns for researchers who do intend to protect against risk of privacy violations. We hope that researchers are not seen as yet another entity trolling for information, and that ethics boards can play a proactive role in facilitating research, not inhibiting the kinds of online research taking place, by working to understand and mediate the complexities of Internet research ethics. And, moreover, researchers and boards which begin from a point of protecting basic participant rights from the outset will avoid such reputational and/or professional damage to the research enterprise. With this, "research creep," the use of research data to inappropriate and/or unethical ends, can hopefully be avoided.

Determining the extent of public and private is also meshed within methodological choice. For instance, Dias (2003, p. 33) describes her own methodological, and thus ethical, choices in her research of pro-anorexia (pro-ana) websites:

> Because many on-line sites are openly accessible to the public, the obtaining of informed consent is often not done . . . However, care needs to be taken to exercise the "fair use" of contributions to public forums that respects participants' privacy and protects them from harm. My ongoing research is a feminist poststructuralist discourse analysis of the data I have collected from various pro-ana websites since September 2001 . . . In order to guarantee participants' confidentiality, I have removed all names and pseudonyms from the narratives I present. I have only accessed publicly available information from pro-ana websites; that is, I have not accessed any forums or chat rooms that required a password, pseudonym or my participation. I have not asked participants any direct questions, nor have I directly interacted with them in any way. Though most of the links to the websites I am referencing are no longer active . . . I have chosen not to provide any links in referencing my sources in order to further protect the women's privacy. Instead, I have referenced them as "Anonymous."

Notably, a common assumption holds that the greater the acknowledged publicity of the venue, the less obligation there may be to protect individual privacy, confidentiality, and rights to informed consent. Dias, despite using "public" sites, chose to maximize privacy concerns, due to the sensitive nature of her research. Ess (2007), among others, has called this "good Samaritan ethics," the response to go above and beyond the letter of the law and push towards "harmony and resonance" (p. 3).

Other interesting venues from which to consider the public/private debate are blogs. Technorati's "State of the Blogosphere 2008" reveals there is variation in the actual numbers of blogs but reports on data suggesting that there were 94.1 million US blog readers in 2007 (50 percent of Internet users), 22.6 million US bloggers in 2007 (12 percent), 84 million worldwide have started a blog, with 26.4 million in the US, and 346 million worldwide read blogs, with 60.3 million in the US. Of course, the range of topics is exhaustive, and online researchers have found fertile ground in blogs. From a research ethics perspective, in the US, research conducted using a blog as a data source would not be reviewable by an IRB. For instance, if a researcher used only text from a blog, as part of an analysis, and did not interact with the blog author through, e.g., interviews or surveys, no IRB review or approval would be needed, as it is not considered "human subjects" under the federal definition (45cfr46.102f): "Human subject means a living individual about whom an investigator (whether professional or student) conducting research obtains (1) Data through intervention or interaction with the individual, or (2) Identifiable private information." "Identifiable private information" is "information about behavior that occurs in a context in which an individual can reasonably expect that no observation or recording is taking place, and information which has been provided for specific purposes by an individual and which the individual can reasonably expect will not be made public (for example, a medical record)." Therefore, if a researcher is getting data from a blog that is public, then it would not meet the criteria for review as set forth in the US regulatory documents. Still, using a blog as a data source in research raises significant ethical issues. These issues revolve around identities and consent, and ownership.

Identities and consent

Dias's choice to anonymize the sites in her research speaks directly to the issue of identification, anonymization, and pseudonymization across online research. Roberts, Smith, and Pollock (2004) suggest a range of considerations for researchers using pseudonyms in their reports, as online pseudonyms are often identifiable. Indeed, online posturing and reputation must be considered, and in order to address this, Bruckman (2002, n.p.) found "Disguising subjects in written accounts is not a binary (yes/no) decision, but a continuum," while Sixsmith and Murray (2001) recommended removing all references to pseudonyms, names of sites, and so on. This, of course, raises methodological concerns, as ethnographers, for instance, rely on such details to weave the realities of their narratives. Bruckman also suggested that "the better you protect your subjects, the more you may reduce the accuracy and replicability of your study," and "if it is not possible to fully disguise your subjects, you may need to omit sensitive information from published results, even if this diminishes the quality of the research" (2002, n.p.). We can see how decisions researchers make around participant contextualization and identification simultaneously raise ethical and methodological complexities.

And, the issue of identification is ultimately interrelated with the process of consent. Lawson (2004) provided a well-crafted array of options for consenting to research and its products. Notably, Lawson calls informed consent a "negotiation," which allows researchers to think of it in less rigid, static ways than the traditional research ethics models suggest. Consent is a process, from which participants can select a range of options:

1. consent to having their nickname and communicative text used for data analysis only (no publication of name or text);
2. consent to having either their nickname or text published in an academic work, but never together (i.e., no identifiers);
3. consent to having either their nickname or text published in an academic work, but never together (i.e., no identifiers) and providing they get to see the "write up" prior to publication;
4. consent to having both their nickname and text published in academic work, thereby being credited as the authors of their own words; or
5. consent to having both their nickname and text published in academic work, thereby being credited as the authors of their own words, providing they get to see the "write up" prior to publication. (Lawson, 2004, p. 93)

Lawson's suggestions push us as online researchers to embrace a more fluid interaction with participants, but, beyond that, she calls into question the concept of ownership of words and data in online research, an issue that becomes more complex in online research.

The issue of consent is confounded greatly in the use of databanks and data repositories. As more funding bodies and institutions require, or highly encourage, some form of "data deposit" from researchers, including such products as field notes, code books, instruments, and results, how consent applies must be considered. Consent typically covers strict parameters of participation. A research subject understands the context in which his or her participation will take place: she understands, in theory, how the data will be used. Once a reuse database or databank removes the original context, questions of risk, intentionality, and ownership immediately rise. A participant – and a researcher – may lose the control and ownership once assumed with one's data. An interplay of complex methodological and ethical integrity, disciplinary difference, and disagreements around "data" face an array of stakeholders. Growing interest in the construction of databanks and reuse repositories stems from a sense of data as a public good, that research data can increase in value for society (a utilitarian model) when multiple researchers have access to them. Hesitation on the part of researchers to deposit such data stems from multiple points: a long-standing model of the ownership of one's data; certain disciplinary beliefs around revealing one's method or "trade secrets:" lack of incentive and lack of support to do the "work" to actually deposit the data sources; and ethical review models which restrict or delimit the terms of research data. The ethics of reuse databanks has been confronted by medical boards, who typically require participants/subjects to consent to banking of data for a future use. Social science boards will indeed now need to consider the implications of banking of such artifacts as video, audio, and text, as each media raises unique ethical quandaries (see Carusi & Jirotka, 2008). The relationship among researchers, researched, ethics boards, and funders in light of data repositories promises to be fascinating, and should be the subject of future considerations.

Ownership

The concept of ownership of data in traditional research is fairly straightforward. The researcher and his/her institution typically own the data that is collected – participants consent to that implicitly. Researchers have the paper copies of surveys, the audio recordings, the field notes. In the US, these documents or recordings are protected under copyright law, while international treaties such as the World Intellectual Property Organization (WIPO) Copyright Treaty, as well as individual data laws worldwide protect such expressions (for detailed discussions of information law, see Lipinski, 2008; Burk, Allen, & Ess, 2008). Online research activities, whether in the form of an online survey (to be described hereafter), or list activities, or blog postings, for example, experience different forms of ownership, and it is less clear who is the sole, or shared, owner. Venues may express specifically what the terms of ownership may be. Recently, Hvizdak (2008) found in her analysis of 138 blogs authored by women that 38 percent of the blogs expressed some type of copyright-protected status, indicating that creators in the digital realm seek to contribute to cultural production while at the same time retaining authorial credit. This was made especially evident through a high rate of requests for attribution in future uses of the bloggers' works. Thus, a researcher may not need an ethics board review to use a blog, but the blog author him or herself may dictate the terms of use, ownership, and attribution, perhaps through Creative Commons licenses or other self-designated attribution models. Participant-observation as a methodology can contribute to a very fuzzy notion of ownership, as a researcher is at once contributing and taking, in a dyadic or dialogical relationship. The onus falls on the researcher and the community/venue to assure his/her parameters around the ownership of the data, and how s/he portrays these data is notably, and intricately, connected with identity and representation. A researcher can easily alienate the community being studied by wrongfully representing their words, images, and ideologies, and claiming them as his/her own "research data." International boundaries – or lack thereof – confound ownership, as databanks, datasets, servers, find their homes across borders. Transborder data flow became a well-known issue in light of Refworks, an online research management tool. Its servers were housed in the US, and data stored there were therefore subject to release under the auspices of the Patriot Act (CBC News, 2006). Finally, researchers' misuse or misappropriation of online data raises other legal issues, such as harm and negligence, which Lipinski (2008) has recently detailed. Lipinski's focus on the legal issues of researchers using listserv, discussion board, blog, chat room and other sorts of web or Internet-based postings uses a legal framework for considering risks and benefits in researcher activity and subsequent reporting. His work does not include a discussion of online survey tools, to which we now turn, as another major venue for online research.

Online surveys

Few can argue that online survey products, such as Zoomerang, SurveyMonkey, and QuestionPro have emerged over the last few years as the most convenient online research tools available. They have been embraced by an array of disciplines and professions, as *the* way to conduct both formal scientific research as well as informal surveys, such as customer or employee satisfaction. We will consider these tools now, given their predominance in Internet-based research, and because the literature surrounding the use of online survey tools points to a number of ethical areas for consideration.

Convenience is often cited as the reason for adopting any of the many free, or inexpensive, tools available, as users can generate surveys, send a link to their respondents, and have their data automatically compiled and analyzed without the wear and tear of mailings, data entry, and subsequent data analysis. Recent data collected by Buchanan and Ess (2008) reveal that in the US, the most frequently reviewed type of online research by IRBs is the online survey. But, only roughly half of responding IRBs review the privacy policies or user agreements that go along with these commercial tools, while even fewer (one third) of those have their own institutional tools to assist researchers in developing survey tools which are built around ethical or value-sensitive design considerations.

Yet, if a researcher uses a tool such as QuestionPro or SurveyMonkey, issues of privacy, ownership, and data security emerge that do not necessarily arise with traditional paper-based surveys. Tracking IP addresses, third-party access, auto-fill-ins, public Internet terminals, and ownership of the data contribute to a situation where research subject/participants can be identified. In traditional research settings, the researcher assumes responsibility for protecting the participants' identities, but in online research, he or she may not be solely responsible. The risks increase when certain types of sensitive data are being collected, such as medical information, and thus participants deserve greater protections (Svengingsson, 2004). Recent debates in the EU have shed light on the differences in opinion around personal privacy and IP addresses. While, for instance, Google's Gmail strips IP addresses from users' mail on the view that even dynamic IP addresses can be used to determine a sender's identity, the EU data privacy provisions specifically consider IPs as personal information and thus subject to regulation.

The literature around online surveys is growing, as researchers are considering the methodological *and* ethical components of online survey tools. Cho and LaRose (1999) and Nancarrow, Bruce, and Pallister (2001) discuss ethical and most notably privacy issues in their examinations of web survey methodology. Cho and LaRose list physical, informational, psychological, and interactional as those types of privacy that invitation recipients and respondents are most likely to feel are being invaded. As computers become extensions of ourselves and are used outside of the home, an unsolicited invitation to participate might be seen as an invasion of physical privacy. The authors, however, name the most serious privacy violations as psychological and informational. Psychological privacy violations include a concern that researchers have observed certain emotional states while trolling chat rooms for participants, less perceived control over information online and so less trust in the researchers, the demarcated boundary between researcher and respondent. Informational privacy violations involve questions of how a researcher collects data, what he or she collects, and how it is used and disposed of; matching responses with data obtained while trolling; false identity of the researcher; cookies, IP addresses, and linking personal data to web use.

In their discussion of the use of web and specifically email surveys for health research, Scriven and Smith-Ferrier (2003) mention privacy, confidentiality, and anonymity concerns of respondents, the perception of survey invitations as spam or as containing a virus, and the level of data security as all having a possible impact on data quality and response rates. The authors note that such measures as encryption should be taken to protect data. Simsek and Veiga (2001) also note that in order to increase both response rates and quality of data (such as responses to sensitive questions), researchers must establish trust with the respondents and provide an explanation of the purpose of the study, how a respondent is selected, how data will be used, and who will have access to it. The authors argue that this should all be done in the introduction to the survey. These recommendations are in keeping with traditional components of an informational document and informed-consent process in research protocols. Moreover, Cho and LaRose (2001) assert that a respondent's concerns about informational privacy leads to decreased response rates. Im, Chee, Tsai, Bender, and Lim (2007) have examined the feasibility of contacting members of Internet communities for participation in survey research. Interestingly, while this method raises serious, and obvious, privacy concerns such as trolling and unannounced chat room observation as a means of collecting participant data, this paper did not discuss these issues. Spam and trust building were addressed, but only as related to increasing response rate, and informed consent was obtained by having respondents click an "I agree to participate" button. Participants were assured that data was confidential "unless a participant appeared at risk for harm." Kaye and Johnson (1999) retrieved email addresses from newsgroups, chat rooms, and listservs in their use of a survey to examine the use of the web for political information, stating that "Response rates also might be influenced by a general mistrust of online surveys and a reluctance to share opinions and preferences in a nontraditional environment" (p. 334), and also that invitations might be perceived as spam. The authors used IP addresses in their study to crosscheck against a list of emails for duplication, which raises questions about IP addresses and privacy.

Some of the literature around online surveys centers on discussions of privacy (including privacy policies), confidentiality, informed consent, and security, with a focus on the suggested steps one should take in carrying out online surveys. Evan's (2005) overview of the strengths and weaknesses of online surveys states that "clear, visible, respondent-friendly privacy policies are imperative;" further, security concerns can be lessened by having respondents "visit secure websites rather than e-mailing surveys as attachments" (p. 211). Eysenbach and Wyatt (2002, p. e13) give respondent, survey, and investigator features that are suitable and unsuitable for web surveys, stating "under no circumstances should a researcher blindly spam" to attain survey respondents. "Informed consent may also play a role when researchers report aggregate (collated and hence anonymous) data on usage patterns . . . crucial here is an appropriate privacy statement," stating how and why cookies will be used, and asking communities and individuals if they agree to be quoted in a retrievable archive. Further, informed consent can be obtained by stating the study's purpose, who is involved, that privacy will be assured, how data will be reported, and who it will be shared with "before participants complete the questionnaire (p. e13)." Gunn (2002) notes security and privacy as a concern of web survey respondents, but also interestingly points out that data collected without the respondents' knowledge – time of survey, browser used, IP address – can be a "double-edged sword" (n.p.). Respondent data can be beneficial to the researcher in discovering statistics related to the respondents, and can also be used to demonstrate that respondents act differently when taking web surveys. It is suggested that researchers be concerned about data privacy and security and allow for an alternate mode of response (mail, phone) if the respondents have these concerns.

Of relevance to this discussion of online surveys is transaction log analysis, which is typically not considered reviewable research by ethics boards, as it is not human subjects research. Transaction log analysis, as a form of research, has been used since the 1960s, and is a systematic analysis of searches, or user queries, and outputs. While once contained within closed (non-networked) systems, transaction logs of Internet searching are widely used by researchers. While in the United States IP addresses typically fall outside of the definition of "personal information," and thus some deny the identifiable connection between an IP address and a "person," others have raised privacy and identity concerns. As we have seen above, EU data laws define IPs as personal information – Peter Scharr, Germany's data protection commissioner, caused strong reaction among such search engines as Google and Yahoo with his statement in early 2008 that an IP address "has to be regarded as personal data" (2008, p. D01). In the US specifically, public awareness of transaction log methodology hit home in 2006 when AOL released a huge dataset of some 650,000 users' searches, under the presumption that the data were anonymous. This was quickly proven untrue, as individuals could indeed be identified, when the *New York Times* crosschecked this "anonymous" data with other publicly available data (Barbaro & Zeller, 2006). A similar incident occurred the following year with NetFlix, when two Texas-based researchers de-anonymized some of the Netflix data by comparing rankings and timestamps with public information in the Internet Movie Database (IMDb) (Narayanan & Shmatikov, 2005; see also, Schneier, 2007).

As online survey use continues, ethics boards and researchers must consider the implications of their use – as we have accepted throughout, methodological choices are indeed ethical choices (Markham, 2006), and, as such, the choice of an online survey should be made with reason and attention to integrity and responsibility, not only with an eye to convenience and possible research outcomes, including possible benefits of such research for both the researcher and others.

Future Directions and Future Research: Research Ethics 2.0?

The emergence, or acceptance, of Web 2.0 allows us to think through research ethics and methods in a dyadic or dialogical fashion. It is strongly likely that 2.0 technologies *and* ideologies will amplify the process of community decision-making, precisely as it blurs the boundaries that are essential to more dichotomous models of research ethics. For instance, Michael Zimmer (2008b, n.p.) has recently suggested that

> Web 2.0 represents a blurring of the boundaries between Web users and producers, consumption and participation, authority and amateurism, play and work, data and the network, reality and virtuality. The rhetoric surrounding Web 2.0 infrastructures presents certain cultural claims about media, identity, and technology. It suggests that everyone can and should use new Internet technologies to organize and share information, to interact within communities, and to express oneself. It promises to empower creativity, to democratize media production, and to celebrate the individual while also relishing the power of collaboration and social networks.

For instance, Web 2.0 could seem to reinforce the importance of procedural (Habermasian/feminist/communitarian) approaches that emphasize the importance of fostering the ethical as it emerges "from the ground up," that is, from within the communities in question, rather than from the top down, as ethics boards typically function as enforcers of law or policy. The technologies of Web 2.0 themselves dictate authorship and the types of content created, thus imposing a predetermined structure (or anti-structure) which makes determining authorship, the role of subject and object, researcher and researched, more complicated. User guidelines and agreements set the parameters of what a user can do and say, thus there is a set of rules that override what an ethics board may actually consider. And beyond that, normative zones are also self- and community-generated. Thus, ethical norms are being imposed from hierarchical powers (i.e., user guidelines/terms of agreements), the users themselves (who can, for example, determine the levels of access they individually allow to others), *and* research ethics boards who then determine how a researcher can interact in this process. As social networking, hyper-blogging, folksonomies, Wikis, etc., continue to change social interaction, research itself and thus research ethics *must* change. E-research is growing, across disciplines, and with it research ethics boundaries are morphing. Ess (2003) and Berry (2004) used the concept of "open-source ethics" to describe a vision of participatory ethical models. This vision holds great promise for the future relationship between and among researchers, policymakers and enforcers, and the "researched." This "open-source" or participatory model is not unique to, or owned by Web 2.0, of course. As noted, the AoIR guidelines grew out of this framework, and transcend Web 1.0, 2.0, and beyond, as they provide the essential pluralistic judgment described earlier. Moreover, as a framework or foundation from which to make decisions and assert judgment, this model can be found in Aristotle's work and his emphasis on *praxis* as the domain against which theory must always be tested and out of which theory will be revised (Ess, 2008). Ultimately, through this particular moment in research, Web 2.0 holds the potential, as a ubiquitous medium that encourages the collapse of binary models, to push stakeholders in the research process to creatively – and productively – disrupt research itself. The concept of transformative research is at stake – and research itself cannot be transformative if the models that govern it remain static. Research ethics itself must be transformative.

The Internet and its various technologies, tools, platforms, and venues have provided novel research grounds for decades, and there is no sign of stopping. What has changed is the dynamic raised between researchers and researched. Feenberg, Bakardjieva, and Goldie (2004) asked directly, "what do the subjects get out of it anyway?" and this question continues to give us pause, as the boundaries between subjects and objects lessen more and more. Ethics boards across the world have specific and distinctive legal and ethical responsibilities, and since their inception, their approach has been a top-down, regulatory design, for practical, institutional reasons. Their philosophical approaches may favor rights or duties over consequences; they may operate as rule-based over relationship-based, given their cultural specificity; they may be less "strict" with social sciences over medical reviews; they may exempt oral histories. But, fundamentally, they have been static, while research around them changes. Institutions benefit, economically, socially, ideologically, politically, from certain models and modes of research. Yet, they stand to learn from the community-based, emergent forms of ethics that are coming from such guidelines as AoIR's, and from the many self-generated models and modes of ethical decision-making abounding on the Internet. Researchers should not turn away from their ethics boards; instead, they should work in tandem to forge the next generation of research ethics, one that still embraces core principles while creating new opportunities for important research endeavors. A time of intercultural research ethics (borrowing from Capurro's 2008 concept of intercultural information ethics) is upon us, in the guise of Internet research ethics. It is in all of our interests, as researchers across disciplines and across cultural boundaries, to embrace the potential of Internet research ethics 2.0 and beyond.

References

American Association for the Advancement of Science (AAAS) (1999). Ethical and legal aspects of human subjects research on the Internet. Washington, DC: American Association for the Advancement of Science. Retrieved December 10, 2008, from http://www.aaas.org/spp/sfrl/projects/intres/main.htm.

American Historical Association (AHA) (2008). AHA Statement on IRBs and oral history research. Retrieved December 10, 2008, from http://www.historians.org/perspectives/issues/2008/0802/0802aha1.cfm.

American Psychological Association (APA) (2004). Report from the board of scientific affairs' advisory group on the conduct of research on the Internet.

Association of Internet Researchers (AoIR) & Ess, C. (2002). Ethical decision making and Internet research. Retrieved November 3, 2008, from www.aoir.org/reports/ethics.pdf.

Baker, A. (2009). Media, ethics, and research subjects: Rockin' out in the NY Times. *International Journal of Internet Research*, (2)1.

Barbaro, M., & Zeller, T., Jr (2006). A face is exposed for AOL searcher no. 4417749. *New York Times*, August 9. Retrieved October 1, 2008, from http://www.nytimes.com/2006/08/09/technology/09aol.html?ex=1312776000.

Beauchamp, T., & Childress, J. (1982). *Principles of Biomedical Ethics*. Oxford: Oxford University Press.

Berry, D. (2004). Internet research: Privacy, ethics and alienation: An open source approach. *Internet Research*, 14(4), 323–32.

Bober, M. (2004). Virtual youth research: An exploration of methodological and ethical dilemmas from a British perspective. In E. Buchanan (ed.), *Readings in Virtual Research Ethics: Issues and controversies* (pp. 288–316). Hershey: Idea Group.

Bruckman, A. (2002). Studying the amateur artist: A perspective on disguising data collected in human subjects research on the Internet. *Ethics and Information Technology*, 4(3), 217–31.

Buchanan, E. (ed.) (2004). *Readings in Virtual Research Ethics: Issues and Controversies*. Hershey, PA: Idea Group.

Buchanan, E., & Ess, C. (2008). Internet research ethics: The field and its critical issues. In K. Himma & H. Tavani (eds.), *The Handbook of Computer and Information Ethics* (pp. 272–92). Boston: Wiley.

Buchanan, E., & Hvizdak, E. (2009). Online survey tools: Ethical and methodological concerns of human research ethics committees. *Journal of Empirical Research on Human Research Ethics* (JERHRE) 4(2), 37–48.

Buchanan, E., & Hvizdak, E. (in progress). Bibliometric counts of Internet research ethics.

Burk, D., Allen, G., & Ess, C. (2008). Ethical approaches to robotic data gathering in academic research. *International Journal of Internet Research Ethics*, 1(1), 9. Retrieved October 1 2008 from www.ijire.uwm.edu/burk.pdf.

Canadian Broadcasting Corporation News (2006). Patriot Act fears prompt universities to patriate computers. *CBC News*, October 31. Retrieved April 5, 2008, from http://www.cbc.ca/technology/story/2006/10/31/patriot-act.html.

Canadian Institutes of Health Research, Natural Sciences and Engineering Research Council of Canada, Social Sciences and Humanities Research Council of Canada (1998). *Tri-Council Policy Statement: Ethical Conduct for Research Involving Humans*, (with 2000, 2002, 2005 amendments). Ottawa: Interagency Secretariat on Research Ethics.

Capurro, R. (2008). Intercultural information ethics. In E. Buchanan & K. Henderson (eds.), *Cases in Library and Information Science Ethics* (pp. 118–36). Jefferson: McFarland.

Carnegie Mellon University. (1995). Internal memorandum. Pittsburgh, PA: Carnegie Mellon University. Retrieved December 10, 2008, from http://venus.soci.niu.edu/~cudigest/rimm/cmu.report.

Carusi, A., & Jirotka, M. (forthcoming). From data archives to ethical labyrinths. *Qualitative Research*.

Cathcart, R., & Gumpert, G. (1983). Mediated interpersonal communication: Toward a new typology. *Quarterly Journal of Speech*, 69, 267–77.

Center for Advanced Study (2005). Improving the system for protecting human subjects: Counteracting IRB mission creep, November 5. Champaign, IL: University of Illinois. Retrieved December 10, 2008, from http://www.law.uiuc.edu/conferences/whitepaper/summary.html.

Cho, H., & LaRose, R. (1999). Privacy issues in Internet surveys. *Social Science Computer Review*, 17(4), 421–34.

Clark, M., & Sharf, B. (2007). The dark side of truth(s): Ethical dilemmas in researching the personal. *Qualitative Inquiry*, 13(3), 399–416.

Dias, K. (2003). The Ana Sanctuary: Women's Pro-Anorexia Narratives in Cyberspace. *Journal of International Women's Studies*, 4(2), 31–45.

Dibble, J. (1993). A rape in cyberspace or how an evil clown, a Haitian trickster spirit, two wizards, and a cast of dozens turned a database into a society. *The Village Voice*, December 21, 36–42.

Dyer, K. (2001). Ethical Challenges of Medicine and Research on the Internet. *Journal of Medical Internet Research*, 3(2), e23.

Elefant, C. (2008). Do employers using Facebook for background checks face legal risks? Legal BlogWatch, March 11. Retrieved December 10, 2008, from http://legalblogwatch.typepad.com/legal_blog_watch/2008/03/do-employers-us.html.

Ess, C. (2003). The Cathedral or the Bazaar? The AoIR document on Internet research ethics as an exercise in open source ethics. In M. Consalvo et al. (eds.), *Internet Research Annual Volume 1: Selected Papers from the Association of Internet Researchers Conferences 2000–2002*, 95–103. New York: Peter Lang.

Ess, C. (2006). Ethical pluralism and global information ethics. *Ethics and Information Technology*, 8(4), 215–26.

Ess, C. (2007). Universal information ethics? Ethical pluralism and social justice. In E. Rooksby & J. Weckert (eds.), *Information Technology and Social Justice* (pp. 69–92). Hershey, PA: Idea Group.

European Union Data Privacy Protection Acts (1995). Directive 95/46/EC.

European Union Data Privacy Protection Acts (2006). Directive 2006/24/EC.

Evans, J., & Mathur, A. (2005). The value of online surveys. *Internet Research*, 15(2), 195–219.

Eysenbach, G., & Wyatt, J. (2002). Using the Internet for surveys and health research. *Journal of Medical Internet Research*, 4(2). http://www.jmir.org/2002/2/e13/.

Feenberg, A., Bakardjieva M., & Goldie, J. (2004). User-centered Internet research: The ethical challenge. In E. Buchanan (ed.), *Readings in Virtual Research Ethics: Issues and Controversies* (pp. 338–50). Hershey, PA: Idea Group.

Frankel, M., & Siang, S. (1999). *Ethical and Legal Aspects of Human Subjects Research on the Internet*. Washington, DC: American Association for the Advancement of Science.

Gallager, M. P. (2008). MySpace, Facebook pages called key to dispute over insurance coverage for eating disorders. Retrieved December 10, 2008, from http://www.law.com/jsp/article.jsp?id=1201779829458.

Gallin, J., & Ognibene, F. (2007). *Principles and Practices of Clinical Research*. Boston: Academic Press.

Gunn, H. (2002). Web-based surveys: changing the survey process. *First Monday*, 7(12). Retrieved July 17, 2008, from http://www.firstmonday.org/issues/issue7_12/gunn/.

Hvizdak, E. (2008). Creating a web of attribution in feminist blogs. *International Journal of Internet Research Ethics*, 1(1). Retrieved December 10, 2008, from www.ijire.uwm.edu/hvizdak.pdf.

Im, E., Chee, W., Tsai, H., Bender, M., & Lin, H. (2007). Internet communities for recruitment of cancer patients into an internet survey: A discussion paper. *International Journal of Nursing Studies*, 44(7), 1261–9.

Israel, M., & Hay, I., (2006). *Research Ethics for Social Scientists*. London: Sage.

Kaye, B. K., & Johnson, T. J. (1999). Taming the cyber frontier: Techniques for improving online surveys. *Social Science Computer Review*, 17, 323–37.

Kraut, R. et al. (2004). Psychological research online: Report of board of scientific affairs' advisory group on the conduct of research on the Internet. *American Psychologist*, 59(2), 105–17.

Lawson, D. (2004). Blurring the Boundaries: Ethical Considerations for Online Research Using Synchronous CMC Forums. In Buchanan, E. (ed.), *Readings in Virtual Research Ethics: Issues and Controversies* (pp. 80–100). Hershey, PA: Idea Group.

Lipinski, T. (2008). Emerging legal issues in the collection and dissemination of Internet-sourced research data: Part I, basic tort law issues and negligence. *International Journal of Internet Research Ethics*, 1(1), 92–114. Retrieved December 10, 2008, from http://www.uwm.edu/Dept/SOIS/cipr/ijire/ijire_1.1_lipinski.pdf.

Markham, A. (1998). *Life Online*. Walnut Creek, CA: Alta Mira Press.

Markham, A. (2006). Method as ethic, ethic as method. *Journal of Information Ethics*, 15(2), 37–54.

Moodely, K., & Myer, L. (2007). Health research ethics committees in South Africa 12 years into democracy. *BMC Med Ethics*, 8(1). http://ukpmc.ac.uk/articlerender.cgi?artid=887112.

Mustanski, B. S. (2001). Getting wired: exploiting the Internet for the collection of valid sexuality data. *The Journal of Sex Research*. The Free Library (November, 1). Retrieved December 4, 2008, from http://www.thefreelibrary.com/.

Nancarrow, C., Pallister, J., & Brace, I. (2001). A new research medium, new research populations and seven deadly sins for Internet researchers. *Qualitative Market Research*, 4(3), 136–49.

Narayanan, A., & Shmatikov, V. (2005). Obfuscated databases and group privacy. In Proceedings of the 12th ACM Conference on Computer and Communications Security, November 7–11, Alexandria, VA. http://doi.acm.org/10.1145/1102120.1102135.

National Commission for the Protection of Human Subjects of Biomedical and Behavioral Research (1979). *The Belmont Report: Ethical Principles and Guidelines for the Protection of Human Subjects of Research*. Washington, DC.

National Committees for Research Ethics in the Sciences and the Humanities (NESH), Norway (2003). *Research Ethics Guidelines for Internet Research*. Retrieved December 10, 2008, from http://www.etikkom.no/English/Publications/internet03/view_publikasjon.

National Health and Research Council, Australia (2007). History of ethics and ethical review of human research in Australia. Retrieved December 10, 2008, from http://www.nhmrc.gov.au/health_ethics/history.htm.

National Health Service, United Kingdom (1999). National research ethics service and the research ethics framework (REF) of the ESRC (Economic and Social Research Council) general guidelines. Retrieved December 10, 2008, from http://www.esrc.ac.uk/ESRCInfoCentre/Images/ESRC_Re_Ethics_Frame_tcm6-11291.pdf.

Nuremburg Code ([1947] 1949). In A. Mitscherlich & F. Mielke (eds.), *Doctors of Infamy: The Story of the Nazi Medical Crimes* (pp. xxiii–xxv). New York: Schuman.

Olsen, S. (2006). Military recruiters are newest MySpace buddy. Retrieved December 10, 2008, from http://news.cnet.com/8301-10784_3-6097875-7.html.

Reid, E. (1996). Informed consent in the study of online communities: A reflection on the effects of computer-mediated social research. *Information Society*, 12(2), 169–74.

Roberts, L., Smith, L., & Pollock, C. (2004). Conducting ethical research online: Respect for individuals, identities, and the ownership of words. In E. Buchanan (ed.), *Readings in Virtual Research Ethics: Issues and Controversies* (pp. 156–73). Hershey, PA: Idea Group.

St Amant, K. (2004). International digital studies: A research approach for examining international online interactions. In E. Buchanan (ed.), *Readings in Virtual Research Ethics: Issues and Controversies* (pp. 317–37). Hershey, PA: Idea Group.

Schneier, B. (2007). Anonymity and the Netflix dataset. Schneier on security blog. Retrieved December 10, 2008, from http://www.schneier.com/blog/archives/2007/12/anonymity_and_t_2.html.

Scriven, A., & Smith-Ferrier, S. (2003). The application of online surveys for workplace health research. *Journal Of The Royal Society Of Health*, 123(2), 95–101.

Siebert, J., Plattner, S., & Rubin, P. (2002). How (not) to regulate social and behavioral research. *Professional Ethics Report*, 15(2), 1–3.

Simsek, Z., & Veiga, J. F. (2001). A primer on Internet organizational surveys. *Organizational Research Methods*, 4, 218–35.

Sixsmith J. A., & Murray C. D. (2001). Ethical Issues in the documentary data analysis of Internet posts and archives? *Qualitative Health Research*, 11(3), 424–32.

Skitka, L., & Sargis, E. (2006). The Internet as psychological laboratory. *Annual Review of Psychology*, 57, 529–55.

Slater M., Antley A., Davison A., Swapp D., et al. (2006). A virtual reprise of the Stanley Milgram obedience experiments. *PLoS ONE* 1(1), e39. doi:10.1371/journal.pone.0000039.

Stern, S. (2004). Studying adolescents online: A consideration of ethical issues. In E. Buchanan (ed.), *Readings in Virtual Research Ethics: Issues and Controversies* (pp. 274–87). Hershey, PA: Idea Group.

Sveningsson, M. (2004). Ethics in internet ethnography. In E. Buchanan (ed.), *Readings in Virtual Research Ethics: Issues and Controversies* (pp. 45–61). Hershey, PA: Idea Group.

Technorati. (2007). State of the blogosphere 2008. Retrieved December 10, 2008, from http://www.technorati.com/blogging/state-of-the-blogosphere/.

Thorseth, M. (2003). *Applied Ethics in Internet Research*. Trondheim: Programme for Applied Ethics, Norwegian University of Science and Technology.

Turkle, S. (1995). *Life on the Screen: Identity in the Age of the Internet*. New York: Touchstone.

United Nations (1948). *Universal Declaration of Human Rights*, G.A. res. 217A (III), U.N. Doc A/810 at 71.

Van Gelder, L. (1985). The strange case of the electronic lover. In C. Dunlop & R. Kling (eds.), *Computerization and Controversy* (pp. 364–375). San Diego: Academic Press.

Walstrom, M. (2004). Ethics and engagement in communication scholarship: Analyzing public online support groups as researcher/participant-experiencer. In Buchanan, E. (ed.), *Readings in Virtual Research Ethics: Issues and Controversies* (pp. 174–202). Hershey, PA: Idea Group.

Whitty, M., Baker, A., & Inman, J. (eds.) (2007). *Online Matchmaking*. New York: Palgrave Macmillan.

World Medical Association. (1964). Declaration of Helsinki: Ethical principles for medical research involving human subjects. Retrieved December 10, 2008, from http://www.wma.net/e/policy/b3.htm.

Zimmer, M. (2008a). On the "anonymity" of the Facebook data set. Retrieved October 2, 2008, from http://michaelzimmer.org/2008/09/30/on-the-anonymity-of-the-facebook-dataset/.

Zimmer, M. (2008b). Preface: critical perspectives on Web 2.0 *First Monday*, 13(3). Retrieved December 10, 2008, from http://www.uic.edu/htbin/cgiwrap/bin/ojs/index.php/fm/article/view/2137/1943.

Part II

Shaping Daily Life: The Internet and Society

Introduction to Part II

Mia Consalvo

The Internet's impact on society is fundamental. How we seek information, how we transact daily business, how we communicate with each other, how all of those activities are regulated and controlled – all are being changed by the choices we make in regard to the code, hardware, and governance surrounding the Internet. Such shifts in the fabric of social life may come slowly, incrementally, and in everyday, banal ways as well as through dramatic changes. But the quiet changes are no less profound for a lack of attention or excitement surrounding them.

Part II examines the multiple roles the Internet has played in contemporary society. In doing so, we study how the Internet mediates and transforms specific societal elements such as politics, religion, and language, as well as healthcare and advancement of developing nations and indigenous groups. But before introducing the individual chapters that tackle those topics in more depth, we should mention common elements that cut across the chapters, and important questions that Part II raises for future studies of the Internet.

There's a common tendency when studying or even talking about the Internet to make it seem that it is fundamentally new in terms of a communications technology, that its role in the transformation of our world is unprecedented, that it is so new and different, past models cannot apply. Yet as several of the authors in Part II point out, the Internet is only one in a growing line of transformative technological developments. Equally if not more important were technologies such as writing, the printing press, and the telegraph. Likewise, fears and hopes surround the introduction of each new technology. Optimists promise how inherent aspects of the medium will restore or instantiate democracy, or level hierarchies, or give us increased access to information and thus knowledge. Pessimists bemoan the losses of traditional cultures and ways of life, growing commercialization of public space, and troubling losses of privacy. Yet as the chapters in this section show, the Internet's effects and potentials lie somewhere in between the hyperbole and promises, both positive and negative.

The following chapters illustrate how the Internet has indeed changed society in fundamental ways, most notably in its integration into everyday life practices (see Chapter 4 for more on that topic). More specifically, individuals and groups have used the Internet to transform as well as supplement religious and spiritual activities, political discussion, international development, and health communication. Likewise, it has given a voice to indigenous peoples globally, at the same time that it has reified particular gendered positions. The Internet is also transforming our corpus of laws and policy, from the most local instances to the widest global changes; just as it contributes to certain changes in our language.

While each contributor takes a slightly different approach to their topic, Heidi Campbell's identification of "waves" of Internet research is particularly helpful in understanding how research has progressed over the past decade. While each area of inquiry is different, it is fair to say that much work has progressed from early descriptive accounts to more nuanced, interpretive, theory-related work. That work has also drawn upon familiar as well as new methods and theories, as researchers have attempted both to draw linkages with other bodies of work and past technologies, and to figure out how to best study something so seemingly new, particularly in relation to its interactivity, its multiple forms (blogs, websites, email, chat, games, transfer protocols, and so on), and its growing reach globally.

Another point of convergence among the chapters is the insistence that online/offline distinctions are difficult, if not impossible, to draw. While policy must address how the Internet functions as a medium or technology that is different from broadcast or other media, policy must also distinguish which issues are truly medium-related, and which are simply old issues in a new form. And as we move away from policy to topics such as health communication or political discussions, we can see how the Internet gives us new opportunities to communicate or create communities of interest, but also how those activities inevitably tie back to daily lives and decisions. Likewise, chapters that discuss the role of the Internet for women, or indigenous peoples, or international development, demonstrate the challenges of seeing Internet activities as cut off or separate from daily lived activities. One way to gauge that problematic is in the increasing discomfort that researchers have with terms such as "virtual/real" or "online/offline," as there is little that is fundamentally in one or the other category. Likewise, the loadedness of particular terms such as "real" and the wrongness of a simple binary designation, suggest that we need as a field to find better ways of expressing those differences, which cannot be so easily contained now, if they ever were in the past.

Introducing the Chapters

Part II begins with Naomi S. Baron's chapter "Assessing the Internet's Impact on Language." Baron explores the somewhat hyperbolic claim that online and mobile language are influencing essential mechanics of grammar. She highlights popular fears that abbreviations and lack of proper grammar usage are widespread and changing how we communicate. Her survey of literature includes both large-scale and small-scale studies, documenting not only types of changes and their actual prevalence, but also their relation to the wider history of language use in societies. She concludes that while we have not witnessed the significant changes to our language that some alarmists have claimed, we must still consider the role of online and mobile technologies in shaping language, calling for studies which meaningfully assess "the full range of potential influences that EMC [electronically mediated communication] may be having on language, not just at the surface phenomena such as abbreviations and acronyms."

Moving from language to regulation, Sandra Braman provides a comprehensive overview of the topic in Chapter 7, "Internet Policy." Explaining that the Internet is "simultaneously a general use tool, communication medium, set of material objects, and factor of economic production," Braman helps us see the range of issues critical to Internet policymakers, and those who advise them. Taking us from local topics such as community wi-fi access to challenges facing the future of global governing bodies, Braman argues for four "big issues" that must be confronted in terms of making future Internet policy – access to the Internet, access to content, property rights, and privacy.

Jennifer Stromer-Galley and Alexis Wichowski ask who is talking about politics and why in Chapter 8, "Political Discussion Online." In their review of research spanning North America, Europe, and parts of Asia, Stromer-Galley and Wichowski seek to counter a claim that online political conversation is "sophomoric" and "an insult to democracy." Their chapter details who is talking about politics online, and why they seek to do so, finding that while some talk can indeed be limited, more structured opportunities for collaborative discussion have produced better outcomes. They conclude that while high-quality discussions may not always predominate, political conversations of any type can offer useful – even critical – functions, particularly for citizens in non-democratic countries.

Deborah L. Wheeler explores other avenues for change in non-democratic and developing nations in Chapter 9, "Does the Internet Empower? A Look at the Internet and International Development." Taking an interdisciplinary, multi-regional case-study approach, her chapter "analyzes several projects which illustrate facets of a complex development dance" to ask how the Internet can help to create a more equitable world. Ultimately she argues that while some problems are simply too big for the Internet – such as food and safe drinking-water – Internet connectivity can empower some people and their communities, providing them access to information, capital, and economic development.

Lorna Heaton analyses the changes in health care communication resulting from Internet use in Chapter 10, "Internet and Health Communication." Covering a wide terrain including the accessing of health information now online, assessments and systems built to assess the quality of that information, patient online communities, health interventions, and electronic health records, Heaton writes that quality-control measures and privacy concerns remain paramount, even as new technological possibilities emerge. Her survey and analysis of the literature leads her to conclude that "the human and social side of the health communication and Internet equation is developing more slowly than its technical possibilities," but still, some of the most interesting and inventive uses of the Internet center on patient-driven communities, a fundamentally social use of the technology.

In Chapter 11, "Internet and Religion" Heidi Campbell takes us through three waves of research concerning religion and spirituality online. She describes the metaphor of the wave as implying a process, where "each wave or phase of research moves forward with a distinctive approach informed by a certain set of cultural and social perceptions about the research topic it is studying . . . the knowledge gained creates new momentum and gives birth to another wave which is pushed forward by a new set of questions and refined approaches." Her analysis of those waves in religious studies encompasses descriptive studies of practices, more refined research that explores the integration of online and offline religious practices, and emerging work that is more collaborative, interdisciplinary, and longitudinal than what has come before. She argues in her conclusion that such new research should focus on a multitude of areas, including greater attention to Asian religions and better study of the nature and quality of people's experiences when doing religious tasks online.

Taking on the task of engaging in global research, Laurel Dyson helps us understand research about "Indigenous Peoples on the Internet" (Chapter 12). Focusing on Internet practices and products created *by* indigenous peoples, rather than those created for or about them, Dyson explores the tensions surrounding the deployment of what some see as a "foreign" or "Western" technology which could also bring benefits or advances to one's life or community. Surveying challenges to access and misappropriation of identities, Dyson also details how specific Internet uses can reaffirm indigenous identity, reconnect diasporic communities, and promote particular forms of activism. And she reminds us that the Internet is still relatively new, and therefore "it has the power to be shaped by those who choose to use it."

Finally, in Chapter 13, Janne Bromseth and Jenny Sundén close the section with "Queering Internet Studies: Intersections of Gender and Sexuality." Moving between careful synthesis of the literature and stories and accounts that highlight their themes, Bromseth and Sundén argue persuasively that we cannot study aspects of identity in isolation from each other. Gender, in particular, has critical links to sexuality and indeed their co-construction must not be ignored. Tracing a history of study of the Internet from early utopian cyberfeminist accounts to more recent work on massively multiplayer games, the authors explore how notions of play and identity have likewise evolved, and call for more queer critiques of the Internet.

Final Questions

Before commencing with the individual chapters, it's also useful to consider a few questions that contributors ask which draw across the specific issues and areas discussed. First to consider is the global impact of the Internet. Most chapters draw from international studies, and likewise show the importance of the local in understanding particular practices. How might that continue, as the Internet diffuses even more deeply across the globe? Will common standards or uses emerge, or will there always be divergence in how local users take up, understand, and reconfigure the Internet?

Likewise, what are the best practices and methods involved in studying such changes and activities? While traditional methodological approaches can continue to give us reliable ways to study the Internet, we will need new and innovative ways to study emerging forms, as well as scale upward in greater levels of complexity. Understanding broad social trends is just as important as studying deeper local practices, and we will need methods equal to both tasks.

Finally, contributors in this section question where research is going, and make arguments for what is needed next. We have clearly moved beyond the broad brush strokes of early descriptive work, we have deconstructed the idea that we radically change when we "go online." For most of us, the online is a mixture of the banal and the extraordinary, helping with the everyday, as well as redefining what communication in our lives might mean. Researchers need to be up to the task of following those changes, being careful to interpret that activity in the context of the social.

6

Assessing the Internet's Impact on Language

Naomi S. Baron

When the printing press was introduced into Western Europe in the mid-fifteenth century, skeptics bemoaned the demise of the handwritten book. A German bishop named Trithemius, writing in 1492, worried that printed works were inferior to manuscripts in a host of ways: Parchment would outlast paper; many printed books would not be easily available or affordable; and perhaps most importantly of all, the scribe could be more accurate than the printer:

> Printed books will never be the equivalent of handwritten codices, especially since printed books are often deficient in spelling and appearance. The simple reason is that copying by hand involves more diligence and industry. (Trithemius, [1492] 1974, p. 65)

New language technologies have long been met with a blend of enthusiasm and disdain. Computer-mediated communication is no exception. Early email brought the mixed blessing of convenient written exchange between colleagues and not-so-collegial flaming. Instant messaging (IM) on computers and now text messaging on mobile phones render communication instantaneous and portable, but language purists (along with many parents and teachers) worry that such technologies are undermining language.

The aim of this chapter is to evaluate the language we produce using online and mobile devices, especially computers and mobile phones. Is language created and consumed via these technologies affecting traditional language, especially writing? While the answer is itself empirically interesting to students of the Internet (and of mobile communication), the outcome has broader implications for educational policy, literacy, and social interaction.

Chapter Overview

The first half of the chapter considers whether online and mobile language are influencing the essential "mechanics" through which we construct sentences, including spelling, punctuation, word choice, and use of abbreviations or acronyms. We survey relevant empirical research on IM and text messaging, focusing on English sources. These findings are then examined in the context of language use and change more generally, including a growing move towards informality and nonchalance regarding linguistic rules.

The remainder of the chapter is devoted to less obvious effects of information and communication technologies (ICTs) on language. We begin by considering the impact online language (particularly via computer) is having upon written culture. We then examine the potential of ICTs (both computers and mobile phones) to empower people to manipulate access to one another. Our ability to multitask while engaging in communication is increasingly part of this story.

The chapter closes by summarizing linguistic and social implications of communicating through online and mobile devices. We also suggest future research directions.

A Note on Terminology

Initially, studies of new media language all involved computer-based communication, some of which predated the arrival of the Internet in 1983. Both email and computer conferencing debuted in 1971. MUDs (multi-user dungeons) appeared in 1980, followed a year later by newsgroups, which resided on USENET. Familiar platforms such as IRC (Internet relay chat), developed in 1988, make special reference to the Internet, but the fact that today's email and IM travel across the Internet is coincidental for our purposes. What has mattered is that such messages are composed at and read from a computer (Baron, 2003).

By the mid-1990s, it became increasingly common to speak of "computer-mediated communication" or CMC. The online *Journal of Computer-Mediated Communication* was launched in 1995, and Susan Herring's edited collection *Computer-Mediated Communication: Linguistic, Social, and Cross-Cultural Perspectives* was published the year after. Although text messaging on mobile phones was available in Europe via the GSM (global system for mobile communications) by 1993, substantial language-based research did not appear until the early 2000s. Moreover, since text messaging in the United States lagged nearly a decade behind Europe, American interest in the linguistic nature (and potential impact) of text messaging was also slow to develop.

Mobile phones and computers began as markedly distinct devices: phones were for spoken conversation; computers were for written discourse. Over the years, with the explosion of text messaging on mobile phones and the growing availability of voice (as well as video) on computers, lines between the technologies have continued to blur. Further confounding the distinction is the growing availability of computer-based programs on mobile phones and vice versa (e.g., text messaging on computers, blogging on mobile phones). Yet there remain two fundamental differences between these ICTs, which potentially result in different sorts of language being produced. The first issue is portability, and the second is keyboard size. Computers remain heavier to carry around than mobile phones. And while computer keyboards have one key for each letter and number, standard phone keypads are compressed in both size and functionality. Several characters appear on the same physical key, and multiple taps are necessary to input most letters or punctuation marks.

Since phones are not computers, some researchers have questioned the appropriateness of referring to messaging constructed on mobile phones as "computer-mediated communication." In July 2006, contributors to the listserv of the Association of Internet Researchers actively debated the issue.[1] Some urged incorporating the study of mobile messaging under the rubric of computer-mediated communication, while others proposed alternative terminology. I favor the umbrella term "electronically mediated communication" (EMC) to encompass language used with any online or mobile device, though the term CMC is more broadly used, at least in referring to language actually composed on a computer.

Direct Effects: Is EMC Harming the Language?

Popular discussion of EMC has often celebrated its potential for linguistic innovation. Yet at the same time, the media have warned that EMC is damaging language. Crispin Thurlow (2006) surveyed the English-language press to assess concern over the effects of EMC. Among his citations:

> Texting is penmanship for illiterates. (*Sunday Telegraph*, July 11, 2004)

> [T]ext chats are starting to bleed over into other aspects of life. (*National Post*, January 4, 2005)

Even more apocalyptic,

> [T]he changes we see taking place today in the language will be a prelude to the dying use of good English. (*The Sun*, April 24, 2001)

In thinking about possible effects of EMC on language, we must be careful to distinguish between negative judgments and the more fundamental notion of linguistic evolution. One defining property of human languages is that they continually change. In the words of the British philologist Ernest Weekley, "Stability in language is synonymous with *rigor mortis*" (Weekley, 1952, p. 21). As we will see, linguistic innovation that was at one time frowned upon may later be accepted as standard usage.

There are empirical questions to deal with as well. Discussion of whether changes originating through online or mobile devices are having deleterious effects upon language presupposes first, that such technology-driven language is actually distinct from everyday writing (or speech) and second, that if such distinctions exist, they are impacting offline language. We need to examine both premises.

The mechanics of IM and text messaging

Whether the popular press depicts online and mobile language as creative or degenerate, our first task is to assess the linguistic guts of such language. There have been a number of insightful discussions of both IM and text messaging. (For discussions of IM see, for example, Boneva et al., 2006; Grinter & Paylen, 2002; Lenhart, Rainie, & Lewis, 2001; Tagliamonte & Denis, 2008. For discussions of text messaging see, for example, Döring, 2002; Grinter & Eldridge, 2001; Hård af Segerstad, 2002; Harper, Paylen, & Taylor, 2005; Ito, Okabe, & Matsuda, 2005; Lasen & Hamill, 2005; Lenhart, Madden, & Hitlin, 2005; Ling, 2004, 2005; Traugott, Joo, Ling, & Qian, 2006). However, relatively few have involved quantitative analysis of corpora.

Statistical counts are important because they measure the prevalence of linguistic phenomena. We know, for example, that EMC is commonly described as being filled with abbreviations, acronyms, and emoticons. But unless we know how frequently such forms are used, we cannot gauge their potential impact on the broader language.

Analyses of the sentence mechanics of IM conversations (Baron, 2004) and text messages (Ling & Baron, 2007) constructed by college students in the US suggest that the occurrence of "special" language is infrequent. Empirical studies have their sampling limitations, e.g. with respect to language, culture, age group, ethnicity, or socioeconomic status. We therefore need to exercise caution in generalizing findings to all users of EMC. Nonetheless, data from one population are likely to be suggestive of more widespread patterns.

The IM study analyzed 11,718 words of text from 23 IM conversations. While many aspects of the conversations were examined (including words per message, number of messages per conversation, length of conversational closings, spelling errors, and self-corrections in subsequent messages), we focus here on abbreviations, acronyms, and emoticons. *Note*: In tallying abbreviations and acronyms, we only included forms that appear to be distinctive to mobile or online language. Lexical shortenings commonly appearing in offline writing (such as *hrs* = *hours*) or representing spoken language (*cuz* = *because*) were excluded.

In the IM corpus, there were 31 abbreviations (e.g., *cya* = *see you*), 90 acronyms (e.g., *lol* = *laughing out loud*), and 49 emoticons (e.g., ☺ = smiley face). Taken together (170 instances) they constituted barely 1 percent of the text. In fact, if we remove the 76 instances of *lol* and the 31 smileys, we are left with only 63 examples of "other" EMC language – that is, 0.5 percent of the word total. For this sample, it is difficult to argue that college-aged Americans have adopted a distinctive computer-based writing style. Tagliamonte and Denis (2008) reported similar findings for Canadian teens.

The text messaging study was based upon a corpus of 1,473 words that appeared in the text messages of 23 females, over a period of 24 hours. While the sample is small, trends paralleled those reported by Thurlow (2003) in a study of text messages sent by mostly British female college students in Wales.

In the Ling and Baron study, there were 47 clear uses of EMC abbreviations, including 26 instances of *U* (for *you*) and 9 cases of *R* (for *are*). Four other abbreviated forms appeared (e.g., *latr* for *later*), though it is hard to know whether they represent intentional lexical shortenings or typing mistakes. There were 8 acronyms, of which 5 were cases of *lol*. Collectively, texting abbreviations, acronyms, and emotions totaled 57, which represents 3.9 percent of the total corpus. Although this statistic for texting is higher than in the case of IM, it is still hardly overwhelming. Thurlow reported that nearly 19 percent of the words in his sample constituted abbreviations, though his criteria for inclusion were looser than those of Ling and Baron. Nonetheless, even at 19 percent, Thurlow concluded that his findings appear "to run counter to popular ideas about the unintelligible, highly abbreviated 'code' of young people's text-messaging."

Distinguishing between language registers

Beyond the issue of the frequency with which abbreviations, acronyms, and emoticons appear in IM and text messages, we need to probe whether such forms are creeping into non-Internet written language. In his examples from the English-language press, Thurlow (2006) includes this sample from the UK:

> Appalled teachers are now presented with essays written not in standard English but in the compressed, minimalist language of mobile phone text messaging. (*The Scotsman*, March 4, 2003)

American faculties anecdotally report students inserting a smiley face or a *btw* (*by the way*) into what was supposed to be a formal essay. The question, however, is how frequently such intrusions occur.

In talking about varieties of language use, linguists speak of distinct "registers," that is, styles of speaking (or writing) that are appropriate to particular circumstances. As part of our linguistic socialization, we learn, for example, to speak one way to a monarch ("Your Royal Highness") and another to the neighborhood barber ("Hey, Phil"). Similarly, schools are charged with teaching children differences between spoken and written registers, along with distinctions within each (e.g., a note to a friend is not written the same way as a job application).

Are children and young adults who use abbreviations, acronyms, and such in their IMs and text messages also employing this language in venues that call for more formal style? Answers have tended to be anecdotal, though empirical research is beginning to appear.

Ylva Hård af Segerstad and Sylvana Sofkova Hashemi (2006) compared language that Swedish schoolchildren between ages 10 and 15 produced (during leisure time) online and on mobile phones against language used in school assignments. The authors found evidence, particularly among the older children, of awareness that certain kinds of linguistic adaptations (including abbreviations and emotions) were suitable in EMC but not for school work. Similarly, in the UK, Beverly Plester and her colleagues report that 10 to 11-year-old children who were frequent users of text messaging were also high scorers on standard spelling tests, and suggest that the playfulness inherent in texting may facilitate conventional literacy skills (Plester, Wood, & Bell, 2008).

It is, however, premature to assume that nothing from EMC will be incorporated into standard language. Historically, there are ample cases in which language judged to be somehow improper – ungrammatical, a regionalism rather than standard usage, or not deemed suitable for polite society – works its way into everyday speech and writing. One famous case is the word *hello*, which traditionally was a call to the hounds ("Halloo!"), and not to be uttered in the presence of ladies. In 1877, Thomas Edison suggested a caller should shout "Hello!" into a telephone to summon the person being called. (Telephones originally had no ringers.) Eventually, *hello* became not just an acceptable word to initiate a telephone conversation but even a rather formal way to greet people face-to-face (Grimes, 1992).

Given their relatively high frequency in contemporary EMC, a few elements (such as *U* for *you*, *lol*, *brb* for *be right back*, or the smiley face) might eventually make their way into more standard usage. (Note that *U* long predates computers – think of the truck rental company U-Haul – though EMC could strengthen its traction.) However, given the empirical paucity of such "special" language in the EMC of at least college students in the US, there is little evidence that online and mobile devices will be radically reshaping offline language any time soon.

Yet change in language is not always so overt. Here are three tangible – though non-obvious – ways in which computer-mediated communication may be influencing writing:

Uncertainty over what constitutes a word. One challenge in learning to spell (especially in English) is determining what constitutes a single word, a hyphenated word, or two words. Sometimes the rules change from one era to the next. According to the *Oxford English Dictionary*, what began in 1898 as *tea bag* (two words) became *tea-bag* (hyphenated) by 1936 and then *teabag* (one word) by 1977.[2] Within the computer world, as new words enter the language, there is often disagreement over how to parse them: Is it *online* or *on-line*? *homepage* or *home page*?

The Internet itself may be coaxing language towards increased confusion regarding compounding. URLs commonly compress together words that normally stand apart, as when the Fresh Fields Bakery & Cafe (in Stillwater, Montana) becomes www.freshfieldsbakery.com – not to be confused with the international law firm of Freshfields Bruckhaus Deringer at www.freshfields.com. The more we have to deal with words that are sometimes separated, sometimes compressed, the harder it becomes to keep track of when words in ordinary language are distinct or contracted: Is it "a part" or "apart"? "any one" or "anyone"?

General nonchalance about spelling. Such nonchalance regarding what constitutes a word seems to be extending to spelling more generally. Increasingly, we put our faith in ever-smarter versions of spell-check, which promptly correct our errors even before we press the space bar. As a result, our motivation to focus on spelling is understandably diminished. We also seem to forget sometimes that spell-check cannot save us from confusing words such as *affect* and *effect*, or from needing to distinguish between *it's* and *its*.

Nonchalance about apostrophes. Knowledge of punctuation – when to capitalize a word, when to use a comma, when an apostrophe is needed – has undergone a slow decline in recent decades, as the emphasis in writing instruction (at least in the US) has shifted from formal structures to content and style (Baron, 2000, Chapter 5). Contemporary students often enter college having little knowledge of punctuation rules. At the same time, having been raised on spell-check, this generation commonly relies upon it to handle punctuation. Anecdotally, some students indicate they no longer bother to type apostrophes in contractions, since spell-check will automatically insert them into words such as *couldn't* and *don't*. Unfortunately, the strategy fails with strings of letters such as "c-a-n-t" and "w-o-n-t." The problem is exacerbated by the fact that URLs and email addresses cannot include the apostrophe, so Martha's Table, a non-profit organization in Washington, DC, appears on the web as www.marthastable.org – which, to the unknowing, looks like "Martha Stable."

Even more subtle than adjustments in vocabulary or sentence mechanics are changes in the attitudes that speakers and listeners, writers and readers have towards their language and the way they use it to interact with one another. Elsewhere I have argued (Baron, 2000, 2008) that the most powerful effects of EMC are to magnify broader shifts in language usage that were already afoot. Here we address three such shifts: a move towards linguistic informality and relativism, a shift in attitudes towards written culture, and increased tendencies to manipulate our terms of linguistic engagement with one another.

Increased Linguistic Informality and "Whatever-ism"

Language change is often a valuable mirror on social transformation. Over the second half of the twentieth century, the US witnessed a progressive shift in attitudes regarding formality. Offices introduced "dress-down Fridays;" churches introduced "alternative" services (with less pomp and circumstance); and class-rooms dismantled serried rows of desks in favor of circles or small clusters. This move had important linguistic correlates.

The most obvious shift was in terms of address: "M'am" and "Sir" gave way to "Juanita" or "David," and "Hello" yielded to "Hi" or now even "Hey." Ending sentences with prepositions no longer felt like a venal sin. Increasingly, people stopped apologizing for using *who* in places where grammar books called for *whom* ("Who did you call yesterday?").

It is one thing to note that language is in the process of changing, e.g., that the distinction between *affect* and *effect* (or between *it's* and *its*) is being obliterated. However, an even more profound transformation is what I refer to as linguistic "whatever-ism" (Baron, 2008, Chapter 8). The primary manifestation of this "whatever" attitude is an indifference to the need for consistency in linguistic usage.

The issue is not whether to use *affect* or *effect* but whether the choice matters. Seen in more formal linguistic terms, this attitude challenges a fundamental principle of linguistic theory by which human language is defined as rule-governed behavior. To be a native speaker of a language is to "know" the rules (e.g., how to form new words, how to combine words into sentences, how to pronounce things). Noam Chomsky's theory of transformational grammar refers to knowledge of such rules as "linguistic competence" (Chomsky, 1965). Traditionally, speakers (and writers) have been sensitive to grammatical conventions (e.g., *it's* versus *its*) and known what language register is appropriate for a given situation ("Hello" versus "Hey"), even if they err in actual usage. What is new is a growing sense of uncertainty as to what the rules are, along with an attitude that the decisions are of little consequence.

The sources of a "whatever" stance towards language use are largely identifiable. The first is education. Since World War Two, American education has become increasingly informal, student-centered, and non-normative. As we have already noted, writing instruction has de-emphasized sentence mechanics (such as grammar and spelling), with the predictable consequence that Americans have diminished interest (first as students, and later as adults in the professional world) in the fine points of orthography, punctuation, and even grammatical number agreement (e.g., "Every Democrat [singular] needs to cast their [plural]vote").

A second important shift has been in social agenda. Regardless of actual practice, the majority of Americans generally espouse tolerance of divergent peoples and customs, a position that became codified under the national rhetoric of multiculturalism. The diversity agenda has linguistic implications. If we teach children not to pass judgment on regional dialects or non-native speakers of English, we reduce the importance of notions such as linguistic correctness and consistency.

Finally, current language patterns (especially in writing) reflect the haste with which "finished" writing is now often produced. As we will see later in this chapter, the growing tendency to live "on the clock" (fast food, express lanes in grocery stores and on highways) is a shift long in the making, with speedy writing being just part of a larger picture.

Moves towards informal language and away from a focus on linguistic consistency have been shaping American linguistic attitudes for several decades. Since Internet-based communication is the relative newcomer, we cannot blame the Internet for linguistic trends already in progress before networked language arrived.

At the same time, we cannot dismiss online and mobile language as irrelevant to the change process. Even when we are using computers as word processors (rather than connected via the Internet), the writing habits we develop for online communication naturally seep into other writing we are doing on the same keyboard-as-typewriter (and vice versa). The fact that so much of the communication we used to do face-to-face or via (voice) telephone has now shifted to online or mobile written text is also likely to reinforce our notions of writing as an informal, casually structured medium. Not all speech is informal, but much is. As ICTs increasingly assume many prior spoken-language functions, computer-based and mobile phone written communication may well be magnifying trends earlier in place.

Effects on Written Culture

Shifting attitudes towards language formality and the relevance of rule-based usage is one domain in which online and mobile usage may be subtly contributing to language change. A second arena involves literacy habits, and how they affect our notion of written culture.

What is a written culture?

For roughly the past 300 years, the English-speaking world has functioned in terms of what has been called a written or print culture (e.g., Chartier, 1989). Expanded use of the printing press, a rise in literacy rates (along with growing social mobility), and the spread of Bible-reading through Protestantism were some of the forces contributing to the establishment of written culture. Among the attributes of written culture are:

- Having access to the tools of production (e.g., pens and paper, computers) and knowing how to use them;
- Having means of disseminating written texts (e.g., printing presses for duplicating copies, highways for transporting letters and newspapers, affordable postage rates);
- Providing opportunities for the general public to become literate;
- Developing the modern notion of an author, who has long-term ownership over his or her text, and the right to profit from it financially;
- Developing specific conventions (in vocabulary, grammar, and punctuation) that distinguish writing from speech (e.g., no contractions in formal writing);
- Caring about writing mechanics (including spelling);
- Revering tangible written volumes (e.g., first editions, elegant bindings);
- Viewing reading and writing as contemplative activities.

(For more discussion of written culture, see Baron, 2005.)

Today, written culture is being challenged in a number of ways, some of which involve the general shift towards linguistic informality and the "whatever" attitude we have described. Other challenges are linked to computers and the

Internet. One issue involves reading on a computer screen rather than from a printed book: Is it the same cognitive experience? Another question is the viability of copyright conventions in the age of open access and our ability to cut and paste other people's written words without acknowledgment.

We will look at four less obvious dimensions of online or mobile language that potentially alter our understanding of written culture. I refer to these domains as: text in the fast lane, flooding the scriptorium, snippet literacy, and vapor text.

Text in the fast lane

Written language has long been subject to two contravening forces. One leads us to slow down when we read and write; the other, to speed up.

In analyzing the intellectual and social consequences of writing in sixth and fifth century (BC) Greece, Jack Goody and Ian Watt argue that the kind of philosophical inquiry we see in philosophers such as Plato and later Aristotle – inquiry that challenged received truths; inquiry that probed relationships between ideas – was made possible by the physical ability to scrutinize historical accounts and propositions in a written form, coupled with opportunity to reflect upon what was recorded (Goody & Watt, 1963). Alphabetic writing did not develop in Greece until the eighth and seventh centuries BC, and it has been suggested that the alphabet enabled Greeks to lay out their thoughts unambiguously (Havelock, 1963). Looking at a much later historical period, Elizabeth Eisenstein (1979) maintains that print technology in early modern Europe encouraged readers to reflect upon (and critique) other people's arguments. Because printing enabled many libraries to own copies of the same text, scholars could now compare a variety of different works at the same time, rather than needing to travel from one library to another (as happened in the medieval world) to view manuscripts seriatim.

All these discussions suggest that reading and writing are activities involving contemplation – and ample time. But for at least two millennia, the written word has also been hastened along by a variety of forces. The motivation: savings in time, money, or both.

Shorthand systems date back at least to the time of Cicero. Abbreviations were used both in Roman and in medieval manuscripts to reduce copying time – and the number of pages needed to complete a manuscript. Cursive scripts helped speed up the writing process (scribes did not need to lift their hand between letters). And in the heyday of telegrams (which were priced by the word), paring down text sometimes rose to an art form (Baron, 2002).

Alongside these language-specific trends, the introduction of timekeeping in the West (initially to alert Christian monks when it was time to pray) set the stage for modern life on the clock (Landes, 1983). With the coming of the industrial revolution and the railroad in the eighteenth and nineteenth centuries, life in general speeded up, and people became obsessed with time. Lewis Carroll's White Rabbit (from *Alice's Adventures in Wonderland*, published in 1865) rushed past Alice and declared, "Oh dear! Oh dear! I shall be too late" as he reached into his waistcoat pocket to check his large watch. In the early twentieth century, the American engineer Frederick W. Taylor demonstrated to Henry Ford how manufacturing processes could be broken down into distinct, timed, tasks – and Ford's auto assembly line was born.

Feeling the drive to do everything faster and having enabling tools available (in the case of writing, tools ranging from shorthand, abbreviations, and cursive script to electric typewriters and then stand-alone computers) set the backdrop for today's online writing. Not only do we compose quickly on computers, but, increasingly, we write an enormous amount. Our next question is whether the volume we are producing is affecting the quality of our prose.

Flooding the scriptorium

New writing technologies enable us to generate text more quickly – and to generate more of it. A century ago, studies documented how schoolchildren wrote more words with typewriters than when composing by hand (Haefner, 1932). Similar increases in text production have been noted since the early days of word processing on stand-alone computers (Stoddard, 1985).

The Internet enhances writing opportunities. Email replaces not only most traditional letter writing but also many phone calls and face-to-face conversations. Chat, IM, and text messaging share some of these one-to-one functions, while blogs, web diaries, and social networking sites encourage writing for broader audiences. We sometimes hear Internet aficionados speak of an "epistolary renaissance," in which we are rediscovering the joy of writing (Day, 2001). If the Internet has facilitated our own writing, it has also multiplied text available to us as readers. The Internet invites us to access vast amounts of written material: emails from friends, articles from obscure newspapers, the complete works of Charles Dickens.

But can there be too much of a good thing? I have come to describe the profusion of our own online and mobile compositions, along with the vast quantities of written works literally at our fingertips, as "flooding the scriptorium." With our own compositions, can we any longer afford to pay careful attention to the words and sentences we produce? The proliferation of writing, often done in haste, may be diminishing opportunity and motivation for crafting carefully honed text. In the words of the Norwegian sociologist Thomas Eriksen,

> if [email] more or less entirely replaced the old-fashioned letter, the culture as a whole will end up with a deficit; it will have lost in quality whatever it has gained in quantity. (Eriksen, 2001, p. 59)

Using terminology from this chapter, the "whatever" attitude towards the written word may be the inexorable consequence.

Similarly, does the abundance of online works diminish reverence for tangible written volumes? Text is increasingly seen as fungible. Many university courses post online readings, which students often print out. Given that Plato, Wordsworth, and the New Testament are all in the public domain, why ask students to buy printed copies, since they can run off their own for the cost of paper and ink? When the assignment has been turned in or the examination taken, the pages are generally trashed.

What if pages are never printed in the first place? Traditional forms of learning typically involved marking up books, taking notes, and re-reading – either for testing purposes or, more significantly, for pleasure or deeper understanding. While printouts discourage annotation, contemplation, and re-reading, online alternatives are even less hospitable. It remains to be seen if e-books such as Amazon's Kindle successfully overcome these obstacles (Stross, 2008).

Snippet literacy

A third challenge to written culture derives from the very tools that make the Internet so convenient to use. I call the problem "snippet literacy."

In recent years, university faculties have increasingly found students balking at lengthy reading assignments. In the words of Katherine Hayles (professor of literature at UCLA), "I can't get my students to read whole books anymore."[3] However much we temporize that the current generation of students learn "differently" (from visual imagery rather than from text; collaboratively rather than individually), responsibility also lies with the educational establishment. We have heavily invested in computing infrastructures. Faculties are urged to assign reading materials that students can access online, and because of copyright laws, readings are increasingly limited to journal articles and book chapters, rather than entire books.

Equally problematic is the effect that search engines in general and the "Find" function in particular are having upon the way we read. Suppose I ask my class to write papers on child labor in the nineteenth century. Perhaps I forbid them from citing Wikipedia and further insist that all references be to published books. A web-savvy student mining just Google Book – which reveals but one page at a time, and allows neither copying nor printing – could make considerable inroads on the assignment without ever cracking an actual volume.

In my own teaching, I have discovered that the "Find" function is often used to avoid reading online material I have assigned. When the reading in question comes from a website or from a journal to which my library has an online subscription, nearly everyone manages to contribute something to class debate or online discussion. However, when the article or book chapter has been physically scanned before being mounted on electronic reserves, students balk: The "Find" function does not work on a scanned document, meaning they may need to peruse the entire document. More than once, students have requested I replace the scanned version with a "real" online document, meaning one amenable to online searching.

Snippet literacy hardly originated with the Internet. Readers have been leafing through written texts (rather than reading them from cover to cover) for centuries. What is new is the technological ease with which we can zero in on just those few lines that we assume are relevant for our purposes, effectively ignoring the context that gives those lines meaning.

Vapor text

The fourth challenge to written culture deriving from Internet practices is what I call "vapor text." At issue is not just the ephemeral nature of online texts but our resulting understanding of what constitutes a written work.

Our idea of a "finished" written work has evolved historically. In the middle ages, manuscripts of the "same" text typically revealed some disparity. The causes were varied: scribal error, differences in the scribes' dialectal provenance, attempts at correcting the original model, introduction of the scribe's own perspective. With the coming of the printing press in the mid-fifteenth century, circumstances were ripe for "enclosing" a text – preserving it from these earlier sorts of variations (Bruns, 1980).

The emergence of written culture over the next two centuries ushered in a growing assumption that copies of the "same" printed text were, indeed, the same, down to the last capital letter or comma. Yet we have also found it worthwhile to analyze – and preserve – revisions to written works. Scholars compare the first quarto versus the first folio edition of the "same" Shakespearean play. The early drafts of manuscripts by novelists, poets, or short story writers are collected by libraries, encouraging scholars to trace authors' literary journeys.

With the coming of word processing, writers of all ilk – from college sophomores to government bureaucrats or Pulitzer Prize-winners – often simply revise the same document file as they work on a manuscript, leaving no trace of earlier drafts. If a prior version turns out to have been superior, it is often irretrievable.

The problem becomes compounded with the introduction of online text. If, for example, an online news source runs a story with inaccurate information, the error can be corrected online, leaving no trace of the earlier faux pas. If the initial version happened to be personally embarrassing or even libelous, lack of a tangible record makes it difficult to build a case, even though we are dealing with written, not spoken language. Similarly, consider hard-copy newspapers that also have online editions. If the two have different versions of the "same" story (e.g., an error from the early-morning print edition is then corrected online), which becomes the documentary record? Since most of us only have access to the online version (especially a few days following publication), is the value of traditional newspapers therefore diminished?

The "whatever" attitude towards linguistic consistency, a flooded scriptorium, a "snippet" approach to reading, and the growing ease with which unwanted text disappears all challenge a cultural stance towards the written word that characterized the English-speaking world for roughly three centuries. While the Internet (and computers more generally) were often not the only forces of change at work, online technology has reinforced earlier trends. A similar magnifying effect is at work in our final topic of discussion: the ways in which online and mobile language enable us to exert control over our terms of linguistic engagement with others.

Controlling the Volume and Multitasking

Consider three scenarios:

- A woman has just had an argument with her boyfriend. Her mobile phone rings, and his number appears on the screen. Still angry, she ignores the call.
- A job applicant tries to telephone a potential employer but cannot get past the secretary. He therefore Googles the man, finds his email address, and contacts him online.
- A high-school girl agrees to Skype her father while he is away on business for the month. Before leaving, he installs webcams on both computers so they can see one another. She, however, refuses to use the video function. As she explains to her disappointed father, this way she can IM her friends and talk with him simultaneously without appearing rude.

Each example illustrates a phenomenon I call "controlling the volume" on interpersonal interaction. The metaphor derives from the audio volume control on radios, televisions, and music devices. We turn up the communication "volume" when we forward emails to people for whom they were not intended, secretly put an interlocutor on speaker phone, or exchange rapid-fire volleys of text messages with friends on our mobile phones. We turn down the "volume" when we block Buddies or Friends on IM or Facebook, monitor caller-ID before answering the phone, or ignore an email. The volume control image here refers less to physical noise level than to the amount and type of access.

People were controlling the volume on interpersonal communication long before the advent of mobile phones or the Internet. We crossed the street to avoid talking with a particular individual or shared communiqués with their authors' enemies. We wrote letters rather than delivering messages face-to-face, and refused to answer the knock on our door.

Contemporary language technologies ratchet up the control we can exercise. While caller-ID has been an "extra" feature for which you paid your (landline) telephone company, the function comes automatically with mobile phone subscriptions. Email grants access to people we never could have contacted – or thought of contacting – through face-to-face encounters, the telephone, or traditional letters. Social networking sites such as Facebook offer detailed privacy settings, allowing us to manipulate which groups of people (or even specific individuals) can see particular kinds of information about us – or if they can find us at all.

Beyond these specific tools for manipulating whom we can access – and who can access us – the Internet affords users another powerful form of communication control: the ability to multitask. You can talk on the phone while checking email, conduct simultaneous IM conversations, Skype your parents while purchasing (online) a plane ticket for Spring Break. To rephrase Peter Steiner's famous 1993 *New Yorker* cartoon ("On the Internet, nobody knows you're a dog"), while using the Internet, nobody needs to know you are multitasking.

Multitasking is common enough in everyday life. We chat with family members while preparing dinner. Organists simultaneously control the movements of their left and right hands, and of their feet. Many teenagers watch television or listen to music while doing their homework. What is new about the Internet is the extent to which it enables us to multitask while engaging in social interaction (what elsewhere I have called "social multitasking" – Baron, 2008).

In 2004–5, my students and I examined multitasking on an American college campus.[4] In our first study, out of 158 subjects (half male, half female), 98 percent were engaged in at least one other computer-based or offline behavior while using IM:

Computer-based activities	
Web-based activities:	70%
Computer-based media player:	48%
Word processing:	39%
Offline activities	
Face-to-face conversation:	41%
Eating or drinking:	37%
Watching television:	29%
Talking on the telephone:	22%

Subjects often participated in multiple examples of the same activity (such as having three web applications open or being involved in more than one IM conversation).

Students in this first study averaged 2.7 "simultaneous" IM conversations, with a range from 1 to 12. Since IM entails typing, people cannot literally participate in multiple conversations simultaneously. Subsequent focus groups revealed that many students used IM both synchronously and asynchronously, that is, turning the volume up or down on particular conversations. Decisions depended upon such factors as "how good the gossip is" in a conversation, how serious the conversation is, and individual communication habits.

We used both the focus groups and a second study (with 51 subjects) to probe why students multitask while using a computer. Most respondents mentioned time pressures, though a number also cited boredom. Boredom sometimes resulted from having to wait for the person with whom they were IM-ing to respond. Others spoke of "get[ing] bored with just one activity" or "having too short an attention span to only do one thing at a time."

Focus-group members observed that with IM, people are in control of how dynamic a given IM conversation is. With lengthy IM dialogues, users may go through spurts of communication interlaced with periods of inactivity. One student aptly described IM as "language under the radar," meaning it resides in the background of other online or offline endeavors. Users control whether to make a particular conversation active (synchronous) or let it lie dormant (asynchronous), without formally closing the exchange.

We asked a series of free-response questions regarding multitasking behaviors that the students felt were appropriate. A typical response was "IM-ing, listening to music, browsing the web. Those are all things that do not interfere with one another." Of the 50 students responding to this question, 86 percent specifically mentioned IM or email – both forms of interpersonal communication – or indicated that any type of multitasking behavior is acceptable.

When we inquired about non-computer activities for which multitasking was not appropriate, 59 percent of the 44 respondents singled out face-to-face or telephone conversations. This number stands in stark contrast to the 86 percent who felt that conducting an IM conversation or doing email while using the computer for other functions was appropriate.

Students offered various explanations for avoiding multitasking while speaking face-to-face or by phone. The most prevalent answer was that such behavior was simply wrong, e.g., "because the person on the other phone line usually feels left out or unattended to." Similar feelings of personal abandonment were reported in a study conducted by Sprint in 2004. Half of the respondents said they felt unimportant when a friend or colleague interrupted a face-to-face conversation with them to answer a mobile phone (Sprint, 2004). In 2005, Hewlett-Packard reported that almost 90 percent of office workers judged that colleagues who responded to emails or text messages during a face-to-face meeting were being rude.

To what degree do college undergraduates use computer-based language technologies to multitask while engaging in face-to-face or telephone conversations? Researchers at the University of Kansas found that 74 percent of their nearly 500 subjects reported multitasking with a computer while in face-to-face conversation (Baym, Zhang, & Lin, 2004). Of the 158 students in our initial multitasking study, 41 percent were engaged in at least one computer activity while talking face-to-face, and 22 percent were simultaneously on the computer and on the phone. Clearly, many American college students control the volume on their face-to-face and telephone conversations through computer-based multitasking.

Conclusions

Our goal in this chapter has been to assess the impact of the Internet (and, more broadly, of computers and mobile phones) on language. The press often demonizes language technologies, though it also celebrates their creativity. As we have seen, the actual effects are at once more limited and more far-reaching. Moreover, the influence of online and mobile language is best understood in light of broader linguistic and social processes, rather than as a stand-alone phenomenon.

The most obvious face of networked communication is linguistic forms that deviate from standard language, such as abbreviations or emoticons. Empirical evidence from IM conversations of young adults in the US indicates that such forms are infrequent (at least in this demographic cohort), thereby offering limited potential for influence. Equally importantly, the informal – and often unedited – nature of online and mobile messages reflects a prior tendency for people to adopt a "whatever" perspective on language.

We also considered four subtle – and perhaps more significant – arenas in which computer, Internet, and mobile language use may be affecting modern written culture. The first of these – text in the fast lane – illustrates the power of electronic devices to rapidly create and dispatch the written word, reinforcing a trend long at work in the Western world. The other three phenomena – flooding the scriptorium, snippet literacy, and vapor text – exemplify the power of technology to create vast quantities of text, to zero in on selected passages while ignoring context, and to challenge the importance of having "finished" texts (or authoritative versions of them).

Finally, we looked at ways in which online and mobile technologies heighten our ability to control the volume on social interaction. In the case of IM, we charted how young adults exercise such control through multitasking.

As with any linguistic change, it is difficult to establish direct causation. A famous example in the history of English illustrates the challenge. Between about 800 AD and 1600 AD, English lost the majority of its inflections at the ends of words. While Old English looked rather similar to modern German (for example, with endings on nouns that identified not just number but also gender and grammatical case), modern English nouns only retain the distinction between singular and plural. During that 800-year period, a number of linguistic and social forces were at work: variation across geographic dialects, the Viking invasions (introducing another Germanic language, Old Norse, which had different grammatical inflections), influences from Norman French, the Black Death (which killed much of the educated population), the emergence of London as a melting pot of sorts. Which specific event – or set of events – was the prime cause remains an issue for scholars to debate, but perhaps never resolve.

Online and mobile technologies are still in their relative infancies. It may be premature to judge their impact upon language, even if we could successfully distinguish between the primary role these technologies play and the extent to which they magnify change already in evidence. Nonetheless, it is important to study mediated language change in process for several reasons.

First, as we showed in the cases of IM and text messaging by college students, actual usage patterns may have little in common with media caricatures. To further contextualize the findings reviewed here, we need to apply quantitative analysis to a broader range of data, including from a variety of age groups, cultures, and languages.

Second, we need to design meaningful assessments of the direct effects of electronic communication upon offline writing done in the classroom, the workplace, or the written culture at large. In school settings, we should undertake more comparisons of writing submitted for school assignments versus text produced by the same individuals in their online communiqués. These comparisons should be supplemented by qualitative analyses of student and teacher perceptions of the appropriateness of different language registers. In the workplace – as well as in the general world of print – scholars should be looking at both linguistic productions and user attitudes, comparing young adults who grew up on IM and text messaging with older users (especially those having more limited experience with EMC).

In all of these investigations, it will be important to look at the full range of potential influences that EMC may be having on language, not just at surface phenomena such as abbreviations and acronyms. Human language does more than chain together sounds and words to convey meanings. Rather, it helps shape the way we forge both our culture and our relationships with one another. Given the increasing role that online and mobile technologies are playing in the way we construct and exchange linguistic messages, it is especially timely that we study EMC to understand its effects – direct and indirect – upon us.

Notes

1   http://listserv.aoir.org/htdig.cgi/air-l-aoir.org/2006-July/010219.html.
2   The example is from Cook (2004).
3   Address at the Phi Beta Kappa 41st Triennial Council Meeting, October 25–29, 2006, Atlanta, GA.
4   Tim Clem and Brian Rabinovitz played key roles in the multitasking project.

References

Baron, N. S. (2000). *Alphabet to Email: How Written English Evolved and Where It's Heading*. London: Routledge.

Baron, N. S. (2002). Who sets email style: Prescriptivism, coping strategies, and democratizing communication access. *The Information Society*, 18, 403–13.

Baron, N. S. (2003). Language of the Internet. In A. Farghali (ed.), *The Stanford Handbook for Language Engineers* (pp. 59–127). Stanford, CA: CSLI Publications (Stanford Center for the Study of Language and Information). Distributed by the University of Chicago Press.

Baron, N. S. (2004). "See you online": Gender issues in college student use of instant messaging. *Journal of Language and Social Psychology*, 23(4), 397–423.

Baron, N. S. (2005). The future of written culture. *Ibérica*, 9, 7–31.

Baron, N. S. (2008). *Always On: Language in an Online and Mobile World*. New York: Oxford.

Baym, N. K., Zhang, Y. B., & Lin, M.-C. (2004). Social interactions across media: Interpersonal communication on the Internet, face-to-face, and the telephone. *New Media & Society*, 6, 299–318.

Boneva, B., Quinn, A., Kraut, R., Kiesler, S., & Shklovski, I. (2006). Teenage communication in the instant messaging era. In R. Kraut & S. Kiesler (eds.), *Computers, Phones, and the Internet* (pp. 201–18). Oxford: Oxford University Press.

Bruns, G. (1980). The originality of texts in a manuscript culture. *Comparative Literature*, 32, 113–29.

Chartier, R. (ed.) (1989). *The Culture of Print: Power and the Uses of Print in Early Modern Europe*, trans. L.G. Cochrane. Princeton, NJ: Princeton University Press.

Chomsky, N. (1965). *Aspects of the Theory of Syntax*. Cambridge, MA: MIT Press.

Cook, V. (2004). *The English Writing System*. London: Arnold.

Day, M. (2001). A meshing of minds: The future of online research for print and electronic publication. In J. Barber & D. Grigar (eds.), *New Worlds, New Words: Exploring Pathways for Writing about and in Electronic Environments* (pp. 251–77). Cresskill, NJ: Hampton Press.

Döring, N. (2002). "Kurzm. wird gesendet" – Abkürzungen und Akronyme in der SMS-Kommunikation. *Muttersprache. Vierteljahresschrift für deustche Sprache*, 2.

Eisenstein, E. (1979). *The Printing Press as an Agent of Change*. Cambridge: Cambridge University Press.

Eriksen, T. H. (2001). *Tyranny of the Moment: Fast and Slow Time in the Information Age*. London: Pluto Press.

Goody, J., & Watt, I. (1963). The consequences of literacy. *Comparative Studies in Society and History*, 5(3), 304–45.

Grimes, W. (1992). Great "hello" mystery is solved. *New York Times*, March 5, p. C1.

Grinter, R., & Eldridge, M. (2001). y do tngrs luv 2 txt msg? *Proceedings of the Seventh European Conference on Computer Supported Cooperative Work* (ECSCW '01) (pp. 219–38). Bonn, Dordrecht: Kluwer.

Grinter, R., & Palen, L. (2002). Instant messaging in teen life. *Proceedings of the ACM Conference on Computer Supported Cooperative Work* (CSCW '02) (pp. 21–30). New York: ACM Press.

Haefner, R. (1932). *The Typewriter in the Primary and Intermediate Grades: A Basic Educational Instrument for Younger Children*. New York: Macmillan.

Harper, R., Paylen, L., & Taylor, A. (eds.) (2005). *The Inside Text: Social, Cultural, and Design Perspectives on SMS*. Dordrecht: Springer.

Havelock, E. (1963). *Preface to Plato*. Cambridge, MA: Harvard University Press.

Herring, S. (ed.) (1996). *Computer-Mediated Communication: Linguistic, Social, and Cross-Cultural Perspectives*. Amsterdam: John Benjamins.

Hewlett-Packard (2005). Abuse of technology can reduce UK workers' intelligence. *Small & Medium Business*, press release, April 22.

Hård af Segerstad, Y. (2002). *Use and Adaptation of Written Language to the Conditions of Computer-Mediated Communication*. Department of Linguistics, Göteborg, Sweden: Göteborg University.

Hård af Segerstad, Y., & Hashemi, S. S. (2006). Learning to write in the information age: A case study of schoolchildren's writing in Sweden. In L. van Waes, M. Leijten, & C. Neuwirth (eds.), *Writing and Digital Media* (pp. 49–64). Amsterdam: Elsevier.

Ito, M., Okabe, D., & Matsuda, M. (eds.) (2005). *Personal, Portable, Pedestrian: Mobile Phones in Japanese Life*. Cambridge, MA: MIT Press.

Landes, D. (1983). *Revolution in Time: Clocks and The Making of the Modern World*. Cambridge, MA: Harvard University Press.

Lasen, A., & Hamill, L. (eds.) (2005). *Mobile World: Past, Present, and Future*. London: Springer.

Lenhart, A., Madden, M., & Hitlin, P. (2005). Teens and technology. Pew Internet & American Life Project, July 27. Retrieved February 17, 2008, from http://www.pewInternet.org/pdfs/PIP_Teens_Tech_July2005web.pdf.

Lenhart, A., Rainie, L., & Lewis, O. (2001). Teenage life online: The rise of the instant-message generation and the Internet's impact on friendships and family relationships. Pew Internet & American Life Project, June 21. Retrieved February 17, 2008, from http://www.pewInternet.org/pdfs/PIP_Teens_Report.pdf.

Ling, R. (2004). *The Mobile Connection: The Cell Phone's Impact on Society.* San Francisco, CA: Morgan Kaufmann.

Ling, R. (2005). The socio-linguistics of SMS: An analysis of SMS use by a random sample of Norwegians. In R. Ling & P. Pedersen (eds.), *Mobile Communications: Re-Negotiation of the Social Sphere* (pp. 335–49). London: Springer.

Ling, R., & Baron, N. S. (2007). Text messaging and IM: A linguistic comparison of American college data. *Journal of Language and Social Psychology*, 26(3), 291–8.

Plester, B., Wood, C., & Bell, V. (2008). Txt msg in school literacy: Does mobile phone use adversely affect children's written language attainment? *Literacy*, 42(3), 137–44.

Sprint (2004). Sprint survey finds nearly two-thirds of Americans are uncomfortable over-hearing wireless conversations in public, press release, July 7. Retrieved February 17, 2008, from http://www2.sprint.com/mr/news_dtl.do?id=2073.

Stoddard, P. (1985). The effects of the WANDAH program on the writing productivity of high school students. Paper presented at the UCLA Conference on Computers and Writing, May 4–5, Los Angeles, CA.

Stross, R. (2008). Freed from the page, but a book nonetheless. *New York Times*, January 27.

Tagliamonte, S., & Denis, D. (2008). Linguistic ruin? LOL! Instant messaging and teen language. *American Speech*, 83(1), 3–34. Paper presented at the Linguistic Association of Canada and the United States (LACUS), July 31–August 4, Toronto.

Thurlow, C. (2006). From statistical panic to moral panic: The metadiscursive construction and popular exaggeration of new media language in the print media. *Journal of Computer-Mediated Communication*, 11(3). Retrieved February 17, 2008, from http://jcmc.indiana.edu/vol11/issue3/thurlow.html.

Thurlow, C., with Brown, A. (2003). Generation txt? The sociolinguistics of young people's text-messaging. *Discourse Analysis Online*. Retrieved February 17, 2008, from http://extra.shu.ac.uk/daol/articles/v1/n1/a3/thurlow2002003-paper.html.

Traugott, M., Joos, S.-H., Ling, R., & Qian, Y. (2006). *On the Move: The Role of Cellular Communication in American Life.* Pohs Report on Mobile Communication. Ann Arbor: University of Michigan.

Trithemius, J. ([1492] 1974). *In Praise of Scribes, De Laude Scriptorum*, ed. K. Arnold, trans. R. Behrendt. Lawrence, KS: Coronado Press.

Weekley, E. (1952). *The English Language.* New York: British Book Centre.

7

Internet Policy

Sandra Braman

The Internet is simultaneously a general use tool, communication medium, set of material objects, idea, and factor of economic production. Thus any discussion of Internet policy must begin by looking at what it is, and what it is not. Internet policy is made at every level, from the global to the most local, involving private-sector entities and personal practices as well as governments. The Internet raises a myriad of legal problems, but the "Big Four" – access to the Internet, access to content, property rights, and privacy – stand out because policies in these areas create the conditions under which all Internet activity takes place. This chapter addresses the foundational questions: What is policy? What is Internet policy? Where is Internet policy made? What are the most important issues?

What is Policy?

The word "policy" has many faces. It can refer to general legal principles as articulated in constitutions or constitution-like documents, such as freedom of expression. A policy can be a proposed law still being debated, or a program to implement a law once passed. Organizations, communities, and families create policies that don't apply outside of those contexts but that serve as regulation within them. Policy can be public (governmental) or private (corporate, personal, or generated by civil society groups), and it can be formal or informal. Here the focus is on formal laws and regulations of governments, with the important exception of the Internet Corporation for Assigned Names and Numbers (ICANN). This section introduces the elements of the policy world,[1] critical distinctions among types of policies, and policy convergence.

The policy world

Policymakers hold power in decision-making entities. The *audience* for each law includes those who are affected; for an Internet law or regulation the audience may be specialized (e.g., those who gamble), but often it is society-wide. A policy *issue* is the social problem that the law is asked to address (privacy, or equity), and political scientists group related issues into *issue areas*. Policy *tools* are the legal mechanisms used to achieve given goals. The *target* of a law is the entity to which a law applies; antitrust (competition) law, for example, targets corporations. *Citizens* influence policy through traditional political means such as the vote and work as policy advocates and activists. Because so much Internet policy is still emerging, often appearing in areas in which there are lacunae in the law or in which traditional perspectives must be reconsidered, citizens also play important roles by developing norms and practices that affect, inspire, or actually generate legal innovations.[2]

These various law–society relations are often mixed in policy analysis, and sometimes confused and/or conflated, so an example may be helpful. For copyright in the US, members of Congress and the World Intellectual Property Organization (WIPO) are the policymakers; the audience is society but the nature of the interest can differ (concerns of the music industry are not those of music students); the issue is how to balance motivations for content production with society's need for access to content; tools include education, lawsuits, and digital rights management (DRM) systems; and targets include individual and corporate content users as well as Internet service providers (ISPs) and ISP-like entities such as universities. Citizens affect decision-making and practice in each of these.

Latent versus manifest policy

Whether or not any given policy affects the Internet may not be evident on the surface. We can refer to laws and regulations that clearly and directly affect the Internet and how we use it as "manifest," and those for which the influence is indirect and not necessarily evident "latent." It is easy to identify manifest Internet policy issues, such as privacy. Discerning latent policies can be more difficult, as exemplified by antitrust. In the early 1980s, the US government began to relax antitrust restrictions on the high-speed computer chip industry in response to assertions that closer collaboration among corporations was needed to retain international competitiveness, a matter of deep concern not only economically but also from a military perspective. This was justified publicly by arguing that such chips were needed for high-definition television, a technology that also requires a broadband network like the Internet. Thus changes in antitrust law that on the surface had little to do with the Internet have influenced its development.

Public versus private law

Public law is the law made by geopolitically recognized entities that include states (France, Singapore, Egypt) and legally effective regional bodies (the European Commission). It affects everyone and every entity within its jurisdiction. Private law is created through contractual agreements between individuals and individual entities, such as corporations, with each contract applying only to signatories. Historically, public law created the environment for private law, but today increasingly the reverse is true. The audience of private contracts can go far beyond signatories, as when environmental damage occurs; these effects are called "externalities." Privatization of former government functions also contributes to the rising importance of private law. In the many areas in which networked digital technologies have presented issues not previously the subject of national or international law, private contracts have set precedent for public law. ICANN, the global organization that manages the Internet, has set up a parallel legal world through a flow-down contract system derived from control over domain names (Mueller, 1999).

Criminal versus civil law

Most countries distinguish between criminal and civil law, though there are national differences in the definitions of each and interactions between the two. In the US, it is a matter of criminal law when an explicit law or regulation has been broken, an action understood to be an attack on society as well as on the victim; Internet examples include sexual predation against children, libel, and some invasions of privacy. Civil law, on the other hand, involves conflicts or harms that do not involve a specific law; these are considered to harm the victim, but not society at large, and are called torts. Providing false information is an example of Internet behavior that might be tortious. Legal systems can expand by turning torts into crimes through new laws and regulations. Criminalizing even unintentional damage to computer systems that costs $5,000 or more to fix (under the USA PATRIOT Act) is an Internet policy example of this process.

Policy convergence

The Internet was made possible by the convergence of computing and communication technologies, and Internet content displays a convergence among genres. In the same way, coping with the Internet has made us aware of at least four forms of convergence processes among previously distinct categories of law.

First, Internet policy appears across silos of the law that have been separated from each other in the past. Internet interfaces – what one attaches to the network in order to use the net, also known as customer premises equipment (CPE) – provide one example of why this makes a difference. In the US, historically two very different bodies of law applied. In constitutional law, interpreted by the courts, the postal provision governs privately owned interfaces with the public message distribution system with an emphasis on equity and ubiquity of access to the system. In administrative law, managed by the Federal Communications Commission (FCC), telecommunications regulation dealt with CPE for the telecommunications network with an emphasis on network efficiency. Extensive discussions about such interfaces have appeared in both environments, and both approaches must be taken into account for the Internet, but in the past these discussions never referenced each other.

Second, though typically legal practice and scholarship treat legal issues as if each exists in isolation, this is never the case. Anonymous use of the Internet, for example, simultaneously involves privacy, authenticity, free speech, surveillance, and access. Internet policy analysis must thus include attention to "policy precession," interactions between the effects of two or more laws and regulations.

Third, technological convergence has made it impossible to keep previously distinct systems for regulating communication separate. In a highly influential work of enduring value, political scientist Ithiel de Sola Pool (1983) pointed out that the separate frameworks for regulating broadcasting, telecommunications, and expression would themselves converge into a single legal system. His prescient warning that the result would most likely use the most restrictive elements of each approach is worth heeding today.

Fourth, the global nature of the Internet has given it a role in both requiring and facilitating what political scientists and legal scholars refer to as legal "harmonization," the convergence of laws and regulations across states so that they conform with each other. Harmonization comes about through a variety of processes of policy transfer and coordination that have received very little attention from scholars of Internet policy (Braman, 2009).

What Is Internet Policy?

Over the 50-year history of what we currently refer to as the Internet, perceptions of the boundaries of the domain of pertinent law have mutated, and are likely to continue to do so. Here, Internet policy is defined as those laws and regulations that are either specific to Internet infrastructure and its uses (e.g., domain names, or trying to control spam) or apply to long-standing legal issues that have so qualitatively changed in nature in the digital environment that significant changes are required of the legal system (e.g., privacy and copyright). Some of the legal tools in play to regulate the Internet and its uses are familiar from earlier communication law; others are innovations specific to the Internet.

A short history

Since the time of the reinvention of the printing press in Western Europe in the fifteenth century, each new information or communication technology has been followed by changes to the legal system. From the mid-nineteenth century on, governments responded to the telegraph, telephone, and radio with new regulatory systems. Technological innovation was ongoing, triggering essentially constant reconsideration by governments of how those communication systems should operate.[3]

By the mid-1990s, three stages of thinking about what we now refer to as Internet policy were already discernible.[4] The first involved forecasts of legal problems that would result from digitization such as warnings by cyberneticist Norbert Wiener, detailed analyses of growing threats to privacy by Alan Westin, and inquiries into the regulatory status of new technologies by numerous legal scholars. Government explorations of the legal consequences of digitization in the late 1970s included, notably, the French Nora/Minc report and the Swedish Tengelin report. During the second, sometimes overlapping, stage, attention focused on consequences of the convergence of computing and communication technologies that had taken place during World War II and was quickly diffusing throughout the commercial world. In some cases, regulatory agencies took the lead; in the United States, the FCC, which had responsibilities for both telecommunications and broadcasting, explored the legal status of new forms of communication with characteristics of both in a series of "Computer Inquiries" from the mid-1960s to the mid-1980s. Communication scholars such as Cees Hamelink, Marjorie Ferguson, and Larry Gross began to look ahead. Attorneys at influential law firms often took the lead role in developing new legal approaches to communications in the digital environment.[5]

The third stage saw such an explosion of detailed analyses of very specific legal issues that it rather quickly led to efforts to conceptualize a single umbrella for Internet policy as a distinct legal domain. In the 1990s, Internet-specific courses began to appear in law schools.[6] By the first decade of the twenty-first century, courses, books, and journal articles all take the concept of Internet policy as a given and both the scholarly literature and the legal problems themselves continue to explode in number. But there is still no consensus about what exactly the domain includes. Now that there are Internet dimensions of every area of human activity, it is likely that this period of treating Internet-related legal problems as a special class will, in its turn, also pass.

When it does, distinctions among legal issues specific to the Internet, those that are traditional and appear in traditional forms on the Internet, and those that are traditional but appear in qualitatively new forms on the Internet will be important. Those in the first category, such as treatment of denial of service (DNS) attacks or the theft of wi-fi signals, will clearly fall within the domain of Internet policy. Those in the second category, such as most forms of fraud that use the Internet as a tool and pornography, may well fold back into their originary legal frames.

Those in the third category, traditional legal problems that are experienced as qualitatively new in the Internet environment, will remain particularly problematic. For these issues, the change in scale and relative ease of socially troublesome activity made possible by networked digital technologies completely shift the experience and the perception of the legality of particular practices. In most democratic societies, for example, we have long had the right to access many types of the personal data of others, such as date of birth, license plate number, and legal records. In the analog environment, however, gathering all of this information about a person required physical travel to diverse locations, working with numerous organizations and individuals to locate the data, and steep costs in money and time. Today, the work can be done within minutes for minimal cost on the

Internet, with the result that it is done so much more frequently that many people believe the information has become publicly available for the first time. As a consequence, laws in this area are undergoing deep reconsideration.

Digitization, expansion of the global information infrastructure, and continuous technological innovation are not the only factors affecting the contours of the domain of Internet policy. Other profound changes in the nature of the law and in law–society–state relations have also been important.[7] These include the privatization, liberalization, and deregulation of communication networks by governments around the world that began in the late 1970s; oligopolization of most communication and information industries and the concomitant growth in size of dominant corporations; and the transition from an industrial to an information economy. The fact that very few policymakers understand the technologies they are regulating, or know anything about their uses and the effects of those uses, is particularly problematic.

The policy subject

Differences in operational definitions of the Internet, whether implicit or explicit, often underlie contradictory legal positions from different venues treating the same problem. When the Internet is seen as a marketing and distribution mechanism, for example, differentially pricing access to various websites (which undermines network neutrality) can seem appropriate. When the Internet is seen as a medium for political and other forms of free speech, however, backing away from network neutrality is highly inappropriate. Several pre-digital distinctions among ways of conceptualizing communications media for legal purposes remain important to Internet policy, though often with a twist. Here we look at two types of technologically driven differences as well as at the distinction between content and conduit (message versus medium) and the variety of issue areas involved.

Wired versus wireless Though digitization has made transitions between wired and wireless communications relatively easy for service providers and seamless for users, in the analog environment the difference between transmission of messages by wire (using the telegraph, and then the telephone, for telecommunications) and through the air, wirelessly (in radio and television broadcasting) was crucial to regulators. In most countries both types of systems were managed under the same regulatory roof, though usually in different work units and with different sets of regulations.

It is possible that techniques for communicating across the wired/wireless border would have developed more quickly had there not also been antitrust (competition law) concerns about organizations that engaged in both types of activities. In the US, the Kingsbury Commitment of 1913 forced corporations to choose one or the other, leaving AT&T with wired communications (and voice) and Western Electric with wireless (and data). Even so, from at least the 1920s on, broadcasters regularly leased telecommunications circuits to transmit program content from one geographically based station to another. In the digital environment messages and data regularly flow across the wired/wireless divide, but the distinction retains regulatory importance in areas such as network security.

Broadcasting versus telecommunications versus speech There is a wide variety of approaches to regulating communications across states, but even within single societies several different legal frameworks can simultaneously apply to digital technologies even though the rights and responsibilities of each may conflict. In the US, three quite different approaches to regulating communications developed, each put in place to manage a different technology. (1) The First Amendment protects free speech and press, the right of association, and the right to ask for changes in the government. It developed in a print environment and is a matter of constitutional law. (2) Telecommunications regulation, managed by the FCC, was created to deal first with telegraphy, and then with telephony. (3) Broadcasting regulation, which applied first to radio and then to television, is also handled by the FCC, but under a second set of regulations.

Each of these systems started from a different regulatory assumption. For print, the fundamental principle was maximizing the free flow of information. For broadcast, the original approach treated those relatively few speakers with licenses as "trustees" with responsibilities to represent all speakers that justified constraints not applied to print. For telecommunications, the governing principle was common carriage with its two basic rules: service must be provided to all who desire it, and content should be transmitted untouched.

These three approaches yield significant legal differences, as exemplified by treatment of editorial control. Those who publish in print have complete editorial control over the content that is produced. In broadcasting, however, there are some editorial constraints because of trustee responsibilities. In telecommunications, there should be no editorial control at all. On the Internet, a single network provider almost inevitably carries all three types of content, yielding regulatory confusion.

The medium versus the message Since the first decades of the twentieth century, the law has distinguished between medium (the technologies that produce and carry communications) and message (the content of the communications) or, in an alternative phrasing, between conduit and content. Two different types of regulatory tools – structural regulation and content regulation – replicated this distinction in the law. Additional dimensions appear with the Internet.

Traditionally, the medium was managed through structural regulation dealing with matters such as network structure, pricing issues, interconnection, and rules for customer premises equipment. Technical standard setting (detailed specifications for technologies) was largely carried out by the private sector, even when this was accomplished under cover of international organizations. It was assumed that network architecture mapped onto organizational structure; each changed, if at all, slowly and in response to the actions of a relatively small set of players. In the digital environment, however, network structure is also a matter of software that can change frequently and market entry is achieved through the contractual relations of ICANN's domain-name system. Many more players – potentially all Internet users – are involved in structural issues. Thus there is much greater awareness of the political importance of standard setting and network design as forms of regulation, strengthened by theories of and research on socio-technical development. On the content side, differences of scale rather than kind are so extreme that they qualitatively change the nature of regulated activities as well as the previously discussed perceptions of appropriate legal positions. As a consequence, governments are reconsidering when content regulation should be acceptable for the Internet.

In most countries, communication policy has long been used to regulate behavior, but this motive was rarely at the center of attention and affected relatively few people. Websites, however, often combine speech and action, so that regulation of speech is often a technique for regulating behavior. It is still important not to conflate the two; a gambling website involves both a contract for the website's domain name and, separately, legal permission for the gambling activity. Both types of legal arrangements are necessary, but they involve different processes, each under its own rules, and they can be carried out in different legal jurisdictions.

A final medium/message complexity is that in the digital environment it is often possible to choose whether or not a given set of material should be considered content or conduit. Software, for example, can be treated as a text, covered by copyright and replaceable by other programs in a computer or network. It can also, however, be hardwired into a machine, in which case it would be covered by patent instead of copyright, and it would not be replaceable by other programs in a given computer or network. As text, the program is content, or message; as technology, it is conduit or medium. Competitive factors often influence which form any given program will take.

One way of summarizing the medium/message distinction in the Internet environment, then, is to say that there are three processes through which the Internet is governed. Technical decision-making is conducted through a relatively informal "requests for comments" (RFC) process (http://www.ietf.org/rfc.html), open to anyone anywhere in the world, whether public or private, and through ultimate standard-setting processes that are more formal. ICANN (http://www.icann.org) manages the operations of the Internet. National and regional governments and international organizations make laws and regulations to govern uses of the Internet and the content that flows through it. It is the last subject that is the central focus of this chapter, though it is impossible to completely segregate laws and regulations from the contract system of ICANN and from technical decision-making.

Issue area   Governments have always approached communication policy through the lenses of multiple issue areas. While military concerns provided the initial impetus for funding to create the distributed communications network we refer to as the Internet, other issue areas of importance for further Internet development included European concerns about vulnerabilities deriving from over-dependence on US-based computing capacity and networks, Middle Eastern government desires to attract business to the region, US interest in a network to support scientific research, and African-country eagerness to bring rural areas into the capital-based economy. Corporations believed there were profits to be had in new forms of content distribution and efficiencies to be gained through Internet-based coordination of activities, and civil society groups recognized possibilities for diversifying public discourse and engaging in participatory democracy. Today, support comes from governments that see the Internet as critical for economic viability, international competitiveness, research and development, the delivery of government services, and national-security-related surveillance. Corporations use the Internet for internal operational purposes as well as external marketing and production input functions. Individual and community users perceive the net as an entertainment medium, a means of interpersonal communication, a political tool, and a tool for scanning the environment.

This diversity of issue areas matters because each frames legal issues in its own way. As a result, problems that may be singular from a sociological perspective are often the subject of laws or regulations generated by numerous different entities that put in place mutually exclusive rights and responsibilities. Internet speech involving the sexuality of children, for example, can be seen as an issue of criminal behavior of primary concern to the those in law enforcement; as critical educational content of interest to those in education; as a matter of free speech – whether by corporate producers of such content or by individual communicators – of primary concern from a constitutional law perspective; as an economic issue to vendors concerned about their ability to deliver services across jurisdictions, to be viewed through the lenses of commercial regulation; or as a matter of privacy, also a constitutional matter in the United States. No one of these should stand alone in analysis of the legal issue, as all concerns are legitimate. Rather, the range of interests needs to be taken into account and evaluations made regarding the value hierarchy that should dominate in resolution of any given issue.

Traditional Internet policy tools

Many legal tools available are considered inappropriate for communications because of the intimacy, social functions, and political valence of much content. A number of traditional communication policy tools, however, remain useful for the Internet.

Content regulation Content regulation constrains or forbids communications on the basis of message content. The kinds of content regulated vary across time, from country to country, and in response to shifts in the political, social, and cultural environments. In many countries there is a bias against content regulation because it impedes the free flow of information, but there is no country that absolutely protects free speech. Content that is commonly not protected includes that which is treasonous, libelous, or involves criminal activity. Many governments outlaw hate speech. In Thailand, it is forbidden to criticize the monarchy. In most

Islamic countries, criticism or parody of the Koran is illegal. Aside from these exceptions, policy must, in the language of US law, be "content neutral" – applicable irrespective of message content. Anti-terrorism laws are currently expanding the domains of restricted content in many countries around the world. In 2008, the European Commission criminalized content that suggests intention to promote or commit a terrorist act. Because these are very broad rules, and because they are vague and susceptible to multiple interpretations, it is unclear how far this will go. There have been several efforts in the US to claim that any expression of concern about damage to civil liberties is itself a form of support for the enemy.

Structural regulation   When a policy intervenes in how a market, industry, or organization operates, it is referred to as structural regulation. For networks, technological design of the infrastructure is a form of structural regulation. Spectrum allocation – licensing specific types of communications to certain bands of the radio-magnetic spectrum – is an area of structural regulation over which there are intense struggles in the early twenty-first century because service providers would like to use the "white space" between portions of the spectrum given to analog broadcasting in order to expand wi-fi offerings. Antitrust law, regularly used against Microsoft, tries to prevent a single or a few corporations from inappropriately dominating the market. Policy precession in structural regulation can multiply its effects. Changing to a spectrum auction system in the US made it easier for large corporations to dominate the market in a way not traditionally the subject of examination on antitrust grounds. ICANN has put in place a parallel world of global structural regulation specific to the Internet with its division of the world into geographic and top-level-domain material and virtual spaces.

Time, place, and manner regulation   Time, place, and manner regulation restricts communication under specific circumstances in a content-neutral way. Laws criminalizing disruption of networks are examples of Internet time, place, and manner regulation.

Contracts as regulation   Contractual agreements among private parties can restrict content, legally (Braman & Lynch, 2003). ISPs typically do so in the end-user licensing terms everyone must agree to in order to gain access to the Internet. Sometimes users experience the results as direct censorship, as when even US-based ISPs refuse to transmit messages that take particular political positions. In other cases, those with an interest in civil liberties approve of ISP constraints on content such as hate speech. We are just beginning to see the complexities of where this can lead: provider claims that content must be "throttled" in order to meet service provision commitments that are also contractually based are one technique being used to undermine network neutrality.

Self-regulation   Self-regulation takes place when an organization or association of organizations sets up rules regarding content some consider harmful to society.

(This can be a defensive measure undertaken to prevent government intervention.) Self-regulation can involve informal agreements not to distribute certain types of content, as when American newspaper editors agreed in the 1970s not to publish news of terrorist activity because it was understood that doing so stimulated further aggression. It can also involve setting up rating systems to help users or audience members avoid content to which they do not wish to be exposed, as the film and videogame industries have done. The Entertainment Software Rating Board is a self-regulatory organization that provides ratings, advertising guidelines, and online privacy principles for electronic games and other forms of online entertainment.

Balancing   It is rare – perhaps never – that a particular legal issue involves only a single constitutional right or regulatory principle. Rather, balancing is an important legal practice that can be considered an Internet policy tool. At least three types of balancing are of concern for Internet law and policy. A content producer's right to property may come into conflict with an artist's right to free speech if the former believes that the latter has used content inappropriately, and these two rights must be balanced against each other. Historically, the First Amendment has been considered to have an acceptably heavy thumb on the balancing scale relative to other constitutional rights because of its importance to democratic practice, but in the twenty-first century national security concerns so far have the heavier thumb. Second, different stakeholders may come into conflict with each other on the basis of the same legal principle; conflicts over which corporation has the right to a particular patent can fall into this category, particularly when resolution of the conflict requires a conceptual distinction rather than matter of fact. Third, the same stakeholder may find him- or herself on different sides of the same issue at different times; university professors have an interest both in expanding fair use so that they can take advantage of the materials of others in the classroom and for research purposes, and an interest in strengthening intellectual property rights, to maximize the benefit from their own work.

Designation as critical infrastructure   Defining the Internet as critical infrastructure has justified numerous interventions into network structure, content, and uses. This has a very long history; government uses of the network are always privileged, though often the impact on regulation and practice is not widely perceived. Today, this is at the center of public debate and political struggles over the Internet because of its utility for surveillance and concerns about information warfare.

New Internet policy tools

It should not be surprising that with each innovation, new ways of infusing practice, organizational form, and the material environment with techniques for enforcing the law should become available. Certainly with the Internet this has been so.

Deputization of private sector entities   Because of their gateway functions, ISPs and ISP-like entities such as universities and public libraries are under an enormous amount of pressure to essentially serve as policing arms of the government. In the US, the first dramatic example of this came with the statutory requirement that ISPs should cut off users accused of copyright infringement from service. A particularly disturbing feature of this policy tool is that it reverses the assumption of innocence until proven guilty. Under the governing legislation (the Digital Millennium Copyright Act), the mere charge that someone is infringing is all that is required to cut someone off from the net, *before* legal evaluation of the validity of the charge takes place.

Technology design and network architecture   Because technology design and network architecture are not only forms of social policy themselves, design features can also serve as policy tools. While those involved in Internet design often took privacy, security, and other policy issues into account, in the past this was often done outside of governmental frameworks and without legal oversight. Today there is deliberate use of such techniques by policymakers for a variety of purposes, including protection of privacy and facilitating use of the Internet for surveillance. One contentious example is the use of digital rights management (DRM) systems to embed particular interpretations of copyright law into technology design so that content cannot be viewed in what vendors believe to be an infringing manner.

Evidence as regulator   One of the most fascinating developments in law–society relations has been driven by electronic discovery, subjecting electronic communications and files to the demands of the evidence-gathering process attorneys use to prepare for court cases. Working papers – documents produced in the course of work that are ephemeral in nature, emphasizing speculative, exploratory, partial, and/or intermediary stages of work processes – are typically exempt even when final work products must be produced. However, in most places corporate email is now subject to discovery, whether or not documents being circulated are working papers, final work products, or other types of communication. This has vastly expanded the amount of material subject to discovery, stimulating savvy organizations to redesign knowledge management and communication systems in order to maximize legal protection should a problem ever arise. This procedural matter, too, then, has effectively become a form of structural Internet policy.

What Internet policy is *not*

As the short history of Internet policy above suggests, the range of issues perceived to fall within Internet policy has been steadily expanding. Indeed, given that the Internet is involved in all social processes today, this could lead to an equation of Internet policy with all law. At that point the concept would have no utility. Thus it is worth marking boundaries as well.

Internet policy is not laws and regulations that apply to all digital technologies. Digital manufacturing technologies, for example, do not fall within the domain of Internet policy even if networked among themselves to facilitate interoperability. Ambient, or ubiquitous embedded, computing which fills our material and organic environments with communicating sensors and computational devices, would not fall within the domain. And the Internet is a sub-set of – not identical with – the global information infrastructure. There remain many uses of the global telecommunications network that do not involve the publicly available Internet, so Internet policy is not the same thing as telecommunications policy.

Where is Internet Policy Made?

Internet policy is made in numerous venues. This section looks at the jurisdictional problem, briefly introduces sources of Internet policy, and looks at the different types of Internet policymaking by governments.

The jurisdiction problem

Internet law and policy is made at every level of the legal structure, from the most local to the global. A legal jurisdiction is the geographic space within which laws and regulations of a specific government are in force; since the Internet is global, Internet-based activities always involve multiple jurisdictions.[8]

There are many areas of communication law in which multiple jurisdictions have long been possible or probable. Libel law, for example, is a matter of state (provincial) law in the US, so libel cases involving national publications always have a choice of jurisdiction within which to press a case. Satellite broadcasting caused many tensions between national governments over differences in content regulation and treatment of commercial content. Jurisdiction is thus another area in which the problem is not new with the Internet, but our experience of it has changed in the Internet environment because it is now endemic.

This presents several challenges. Interactions across levels of the legal structure can yield differences from one place to another in the legal context for a specific type of Internet-based activity or communication. It is also possible for differences in the stage of the information production chain – the distinction between content creation, processing, flows, and use – to affect the legality of any particular content or activity within a jurisdiction. The prohibition on Nazi content in Germany illustrates both of these. For a long while, Nazi content was being produced in the US (where hate speech is considered a protected form of political expression) and made available over the Internet to German receivers. When the German government turned its attention to a large-scale Internet service provider through whose services the content was being distributed within German territory, the private corporation elected to ban all such content everywhere it operated rather than be subject to the legal process in Germany. Ultimately, the European Court of Justice determined that the German law could not be upheld in the Internet environment. A recent South African domain-name case presented a different example of how jurisdictional differences affect Internet policy. When the South African government felt that its intellectual property was being infringed by a corporation, it took the case to a US court for resolution, believing – correctly, as it turned out – that this choice would be favorable to its case.

Internet policy across levels of the legal infrastructure

Internet policy is inherently global since it is a global information infrastructure, a network of networks. But the global is experienced only under local conditions; Internet policy is also, therefore, made at the level of municipality as well as within organizations and homes. In this section we look briefly at all of the sources of Internet policy other than those of national governments, the subject of the next section.

Global The desire for a global communications network has long been an important spur to the development of new forms of regulation that cross state borders. It was the telegraph that inspired the formation of the first international organization in the 1860s – what we now know as the International Telecommunications Union (ITU, http://www.itu.org). Similarly, the Internet has lead to the formation of the first global organization, ICANN (http://www.icann.org). An international organization is comprised of representatives of geopolitically recognized governmental entities (states), but in global organizations civil society entities such as non-governmental organizations (NGOs) and corporations also have a voice in decision-making.

ICANN was born in a decision by the US Department of Commerce in 1998 to establish an entity at arm's length from the government. The result was a private not-for-profit organization incorporated under California law. Decision-makers came from the private sector, and decision-making took place in secret until pressure from civil society groups concerned about the public interest succeeded in achieving greater transparency. ICANN has operated under the over-sight of the US government, in recent years under terms that made it possible to completely privatize the organization should certain conditions be met. At the time of writing, it is still unclear what form ICANN will ultimately take. Some argue that the time for complete privatization has come, but others claim that the organization has failed to serve the public interest and needs to remain under governmental oversight. Options involving the public sector include remaining under US control, putting the organization under the rubric of the ITU, itself a part of the United Nations (UN) system. Recently, an ITU-sponsored multi-year process – the World Summit on the Information Society (WSIS) – concluded with the creation of a new forum for multi-stakeholder policy discussions, the Internet Governance Forum (IGF), a venue for policy discussions that has no actual author-ity. Another option is to allow other countries besides the US – Brazil and China have pursued this with particular eagerness – to become active in ICANN governance mechanisms. Whichever way it goes, many extremely important issues will remain, particularly in the areas of public accountability and democratic representation of the interests of all in decision-making.

Effects of current ICANN rules include constraints on free speech via the end-user licensing agreements (EULAs) contractually required in order to access the Internet by Internet service providers (ISPs) and ISP-like entities; intersections between domain names and other forms of intellectual property rights; and invasions of privacy enabled by the domain-name system. Many believe that the constitutional or constitution-like principles underlying the law in most countries should also apply to ICANN's decisions, particularly in the area of civil liberties (Froomkin, 2000). EULAs give ISPs the rights to prevent users from accessing the system, censor content, or use content for otherwise unauthorized commercial purposes in ways that would be considered unconstitutionally vague and overbroad under US constitutional law. One can legally choose to sign away one's rights by contract, but historically that has been available in contexts in which one can also choose *not* to do so because other types of contractual arrangements are available. EULAs are becoming more and more like each other in content, and more and more restrictive, with the consequence that it is essentially impossible to choose a means of accessing the Internet through an access provider that provides the full range of speech and related protections available in all other communicative contexts under the US Constitution.

International   Several international organizations make Internet policy directly and indirectly. Treaties are the basis of these activities, whether multilateral (obligatory for all participants, or members, of the organization), plurilateral (binding only a sub-set of the members of an alliance), or bilateral (two-party).

Long-standing responsibilities of the ITU for technical standard-setting remain key. The ITU is also involved in development activities through efforts such as those of the Applications and Cybersecurity Division, which works with developing countries to improve infrastructure capacity and security; and work in areas such as e-government, Internet multilingualism, and uses of the Internet for healthcare. Regional meetings within the ITU framework provide support for other national- and regional-level Internet policymaking.

The World Trade Organization (WTO) was created in 1995 as a managerial home for the international trade system first created after World War II and significantly changed in the 1990s. Formation of the WTO was very much a product of the transition to an information economy, driven by the need to expand the trade system to cover not only goods (via the General Agreement on Tariffs and Trade, or GATT, in place since the late 1940s) but also information processing and related services (via the General Agreement on Trade in Services, or GATS), and to treat more systematically the trade dimensions of intellectual property rights (via the Trade Related Aspects of Intellectual Property Rights, or TRIPS, agreement). Each country develops its own package of proposals for consideration by the WTO. These packages include multiple policies, distinguished by industrial sector, type of economic or social vulnerability, and the techniques used to constrain trade. Within each of these areas, there are agreements specific to each service or product. Telecommunications agreements, for example, have an impact on rates that in turn affect the cost of network access to the Internet, and agreements that cover trade in computing and networking equipment affect the cost of equipment used to use the Internet.

Regional   When multilateral treaties cover a broad purview they effectively create an additional layer of legal infrastructure between the international and state levels. The most comprehensive of such regional legal entities is, of course, the European Commission (EC). Other regional entities created by multilateral treaties with such features include those of the North American Free Trade Agreement (NAFTA) and the Association of South East Asian Nations (ASEAN). Within the ICANN system, regional groups also establish policies that differ from each other in areas such as which elements of the Internet are deemed to be critical infrastructure. Other regional groups focus more broadly on networking issues. Civil society groups actively contribute to the regionalization of Internet policy efforts. Two examples of regional groups that make Internet policy are briefly introduced here.

The European Commission (EC) has laws and regulations that affect the Internet in three ways. In the area of regulating the market, EC network policies attempt to reduce levels of spam and cybercrime, manage the spectrum, and prevent negative health-related effects of electromagnetic fields. Policies dealing with copyright, web accessibility, and regulation of the audiovisual industry affect Internet content. EC policies that stimulate Internet development include those dealing with taxation of Internet service and e-commerce, research and development, and use of the net to pursue social goals such as improving the quality of healthcare and education. The i2010 Initiative brings many of these policies together under a single rubric, and international dimensions of what the EC is doing in this area are a part of its international relations program.

In 2003, ASEAN brought together diverse regulations dealing with Internet-related matters in the Singapore Declaration, an action agenda devoted to using ICTs to promote digital opportunities within ASEAN countries and enhancing their competitiveness. Issues such as network interoperability and interconnectivity, security, and data integrity are key. Harmonization of Internet-related laws across ASEAN countries, reduction in tariffs on trade in the technologies involved, and collaboration on cyber-security issues are seen as major ways of improving the environment for users. Stated goals include reducing the digital divide within ASEAN countries as well as improving the infrastructure.

Sub-state policy   In most countries, there are several layers of additional decision-making about Internet-related matters below the level of the national government. In many cases, laws and regulations dealing with a specific subject may exist at multiple levels of government and governance within a single state. The provincial, municipal, organizational, and domestic environments are of particular importance.

Most countries have laws and regulations at the provincial level that pertain to the Internet. In Canada, for example, provinces have data protection laws in addition to those of the federal government. In Germany, the Länder (states) are responsible for the research and development that results in innovations in Internet technologies. In some cases these are laws that are put in place only at the provincial level, while in others the same laws can be found at the national level as well. Access to government information laws, for example, are found at both the state and national levels in the US.

Municipalities (legally defined urban areas) are sources of Internet policy in multiple ways. Municipalities have regulations (in the US these are called ordinances) regarding protection of personal data about citizens and their activities, access to information, and other e-government issues. In many countries, municipalities support public libraries through which citizens can gain Internet access. The municipal issue currently receiving the most attention is the establishment of community-wide free public access to the Internet through a wireless network.

Community wi-fi access provides a good example of ways in which contemporary debates over Internet policy often repeat battles that have come before and from which we can learn, as municipal wi-fi struggles echo those over municipal control over cable networks of several decades ago. In the case of cable, municipalities had a deep interest because putting in the network involved changes to existing infrastructure – streets had to be dug up and new equipment was installed on existing buildings themselves subject to zoning and other regulation. For the same infrastructure reason, it was long argued – as it had been with telephony and telegraphy – that cable was a "natural" monopoly, and licensing cable systems was a source of revenue for municipal governments. Challenges to municipally governed cable networks came from vendors who saw themselves as possible competitors to licensees but who were forbidden market entry in monopolistic city environments. First Amendment challenges were pressed against municipal limitations on access to television content and the inevitable sole-sourcing of televised government proceedings that was a concomitant of the public service channel requirements of municipal cable franchises. Ultimately, the municipal cable issue was made moot by the appearance of competition from satellite television and, with digitization, the ability to transmit cable content via the telecommunications network rather than a second, cable-specific network.

Given the technical nature of wireless networking, infrastructure issues remain important, but in a different way. Nothing needs to be dug up, but a system of transmitters does need to be put in place, and concerns over such matters as the health impact of these transmitters (10 percent of the population is extremely sensitive to the wavelengths involved) also suggest that municipal regulation remains important. The larger issue at the center of debate, however, is again the competitive matter. Opposition from telecommunications providers who see in free or low-cost municipal wi-fi a loss of ISP subscribers has so emphasized the cost of building such networks that decision-makers in many cities have become shy of the process. Institutions such as universities that consider offering community-wide access are often scared away by attendant legal responsibilities for uses and content. Meanwhile many businesses see offering free or low-cost access to wireless networking as a competitive attraction, community groups sometimes make access available in service to other aspects of their mission, and many individuals are happy to leave their personal wireless transmitters unprotected so that others can take advantage of the signal. After a period of widespread enthusiasm, and a shorter one of dismay and reluctance, it is still too early to know the extent to which we will see municipal wireless networks in future.

National governments and Internet policy

Within each country there are many different ways in which laws are made, ranging from executive fiat at one extreme to votes of the entire population in plebiscites at the other. Within the US, the four most important ways of making law each bring a different type of knowledge, decision-making process, and perspective into the legal system.

Constitutional law   Fundamental policy principles are put forward in constitutions, or constitution-like documents. These go under many different names. In Germany, for example, it is the Basic Law, interpreted by the Federal Constitutional Court in response to petitions from federal bodies, government officials, or citizens. In Britain there is no written constitution *per se*, but an unwritten constitution is comprised of fundamental principles of enduring importance and consensual acknowledgment.

Law at the constitutional level is based on philosophy, social theory, and beliefs about the nature of society and of democracy. While other types of law deal with existing social categories and relations within and between them, it is the job at the level of constitutional law to define the very categories through which we will relate to each other and to establish the constraints and responsibilities for just how those relationships unfold. Because communication law creates the conditions under which all other types of decision-making take place, it can be argued that all Internet policy is of constitutional status.

The US Constitution includes 20 principles that should underlie Internet policy (see Table 7.1). Constitutional law changes via court interpretations of the law (in the US, any court can deal with constitutional issues, though in many other countries this can only be done in special constitutional courts), and through amendments to the Constitution. The First Amendment to the US Constitution, which provides the foundation for freedom of expression in that country, requires "state action" – governmental responsibility for laws, regulations, or activities affecting freedom of expression. If the government is not involved in a particular activity or restriction, the First Amendment provides no protections.

Table 7.1 Internet Policy Principles in the US Constitution

Principle	*Location*
Information collection by the government	Art. 1, sec. 2
Open government	Art. 1, sec. 5; art. 2, sec. 3
Free speech within government	Art. 1, sec. 6
Federal government control over currency	Art. 1, sec. 8
Universal access to an information distribution system	Art. 1, sec. 8, cl. 7
Intellectual property rights	Art. 1, sec. 8, cl. 8
Restriction of civil liberties during time of war	Art. 1, sec. 9, cl. 2
Treason	Art. 3, sec. 3
Freedom of opinion	1st Amend.
Freedom of speech	1st Amend.
Freedom of the press	1st Amend.
Freedom of assembly and association	1st Amend.
Freedom to petition the government for change	1st Amend.
Privacy	1st Amend.; 4th Amend.
Right to receive information	Art. 1, sec. 8, cl. 7; 1st Amend.
Protection against unlawful search	4th Amend.
Protection against self-incrimination	5th Amend.
Due process	5th Amend.
Rights beyond those enumerated	9th Amend.
Incorporation of federal constitution into state constitutions	14th Amend.

Statutory law Statutory law translates general constitutional principles into laws, or statutes. Statutory law is created by parliamentary entities such as the US Congress (the Senate and the House of Representatives, at the federal level) and by legislatures (at the state level) or, in Germany, the Bundestag (representatives of the people) and Bundesrat (representatives of states). Statutory law is considered the product of representative democracy because it is created by representatives who have been elected to serve as lawmakers, though of course many forces in addition to popular opinion influence statutes. Statutory law changes through amendments to existing laws, replacements of existing laws, addition of new laws, development of programs or institutions through which to implement the law, or as a result of interpretations of the law made by judges in court cases. The USA PATRIOT Act, passed after the terrorist attacks of September 11, 2001, is an example of statutory law that has had enormous impact on Internet policy. There are many other recent examples of statutory Internet policy, including those that are manifest (such as the spam-fighting CAN-SPAM Act of 2003) and those that are latent (such as the Central America Free Trade Agreement, which requires countries to bring their laws into line with US laws requiring ISPs to withdraw Internet access from those accused by rights holders of infringing copyright).

Regulatory, or administrative, law   When decision-making in a particular area requires detailed technical knowledge and must be made over and over again, Congress uses statutory law to set up a regulatory, or administrative, agency to put in place regulations that have the force of law. Regulatory law brings technical expertise into the legal system. These agencies bridge all three branches of government, for they report to the White House and those in conflict submit to decisions by courts, if resolution cannot be reached through internal agency processes. When very large issues appear – such as in the current debate over media concentration – Congress can step in and assert its will.

A number of agencies regulate certain kinds of content; the Food and Drug Administration (FDA), for example, requires publication of specific information about things we take into or put onto our bodies, and has rules for how such things are described in the media. The FCC has already been mentioned. Other administrative agencies in the US key to Internet policy include the Securities and Exchange Commission (SEC), which regulates financial information of publicly held corporations (corporations that sell their stock to the public); and the Federal Trade Commission (FTC), which regulates advertising and marketing practices.

Common, or case, law   Common law is the history of decisions made by judges when legal issues cannot be resolved outside of a courtroom. The impact of decisions in lawsuits extends beyond parties to the case because court opinions provide precedent that must be taken into account in future when conflicts involving related issues arise. Case law has been extremely important to the protection of civil liberties in the Internet environment, and in recent years has been key to pushing back against unconstitutional repressive statutes. Public interest non-profit organizations concerned about Internet policy, such as the Electronic Frontier Foundation (EFF, www.eff.org) and the Electronic Privacy Information Center (EPIC, www.epic.org), devote a great deal of their energy to participating in such lawsuits.[9]

The "Big Four" Issues

A few policy issues deserve special attention because they create the conditions for all Internet activity and must be addressed by every country. Because these are such complex issues, each can be framed in many different ways and is addressed by numerous policymaking entities. All affect freedom of expression and access to information.

Access to the Internet

The phrase "digital divide" refers to problems generated by unequal access to the Internet; the divide appears both within and across societies. This metaphor involves one dimension of what sociologists have for many decades referred to as the "knowledge gap," the mutual reinforcement among lack of access to knowledge, lack of political efficacy, and low socioeconomic status.[10] The dimensions of access are multiple; in most countries separate laws and regulations are needed to address each facet separately.

Physical access Physical access involves access both to the network itself and to the interface through which one accesses the Internet. This is often an economic issue as well as a geographic one.

Access to network infrastructure falls under the purview of governments and/or of large-scale corporate vendors as they operate within the regulatory parameters of governments. "Reach" is the extent to which the network is available across space, and "penetration" is the extent to which the population in an area in which the network is available actually does access it. Where the network is under government control, both can be accomplished with particular effectiveness, as in South Korea. Under the more common competitive conditions, governments intervene to encourage widespread diffusion of geographic access to the network through techniques such as establishing conditions for a license, pricing mechanisms, and laws requiring public access at the community level.

Governments and vendors are also involved in access to network interfaces, but because such interfaces may be available at the community or household level as well as the individual level, other types of groups can also have an impact. In both developed societies and developing societies governments support community-level access, whether through libraries, schools, or "tele-centers," to ensure that those who do not have personal access can still use the Internet. Many different kinds of technologies can serve as the Internet interface. In Italy, for example, use of the Internet did not become widespread until it was available through cell phones and that technology itself had become fashionable. "One laptop per child" initiatives seek to expand access to the network interface in developing societies by producing very inexpensive laptop computers, with governments signing contracts to purchase these in large numbers for their schoolchildren.

Those with physical disabilities face additional access barriers. Internet policies to address this problem include establishing usability standards for websites and support for research and development to create technologies that serve those with specific disabilities.

Education Several types of literacy are also key to Internet access. *Traditional literacy* is the ability to make sense out of messages communicated and to create meaningful messages. Because the concept of literacy arose in the print era, it historically referred to reading and writing. Today, however, the importance of images is also acknowledged, leading to *media literacy* as a distinct category. *Information literacy* is the ability to locate, evaluate, and use information in diverse forms, and to create and communicate valid and reliable information. And *technology literacy* is the ability to use technologies to achieve one's goals, including learning how to do new things with those technologies. All of these are necessary for full use of the Internet.

Historically we have distinguished various levels of traditional literacy. Functional literacy – the ability to read and write as necessary to get through the activities of daily life, including reading signs, locating items one needs to buy, and filling out employment and government forms – is one end of a spectrum. At the other, *avant garde* writers have such mastery that they push language and narrative form forward into new realms. The functional end of the media literacy spectrum involves being able to not only understand mass media programming, but also to discern motives behind such messages and their political economic implications. At the most sophisticated end of the media literacy spectrum are those who produce content that achieves a mass audience, though increasingly the ability to produce at least simple media content is being defined as necessary for all. At one end of the spectrum of information literacy is the ability to locate and evaluate information, and to manage information of importance to oneself; at the other end of this spectrum are those who design and manage large-scale information architectures for large populations and multiple uses. In the world of technological literacy, the functional end of the spectrum would include being able to engage in basic functions such as word processing, surfing the web, and managing email, while at the other end of the spectrum are those who are writing their own code for specific purposes.

All these forms of literacy become the subjects of Internet policy when standards for at least functional levels of mastery are included in education systems and training is provided at government-supported public access centers. Traditional literacy has long been the focus of primary, secondary, and tertiary education, but today media, information, and technology literacy are also increasingly taught at all three levels. Technology transfer programs can serve this Internet policy goal as well when they include knowledge transfer elements.

Cultural access   Cultural preferences can generate barriers to Internet use that, in many societies, become the subject of Internet policy. It is a complex area for Internet policy, because regulations intended to break down one barrier can raise others. In South Africa, for example, the government required two managers for each publicly supported tele-center, one of whom had to be a woman, but in many tribal areas gender differentiation is so powerful that the presence of a woman prevented men from using the tele-centers. Successful examples of government policies to reduce cultural barriers to access include support for the creation of web content from marginalized communities, ensuring that culturally based geographic isolation does not prevent access, and efforts to make it easier to use the Internet across languages and alphabets.

Access to content

Once access to the Internet has been achieved, access to content becomes important. Conditions of access, the issue currently popularly labeled "network neutrality," and censorship are key Internet policy issues in this area.

Conditions of access   Governments place a variety of types of constraints on the conditions of access in pursuit of diverse goals, beginning with the limits to freedom of expression in any medium discussed above. Some constraints are Internet-specific; China, for example, limits the amount of time one can spend online per day in an attempt to fight Internet addiction. Organizational and public sites for access to the Internet can forbid certain types of activity (e.g., gambling) or access to particular categories of content (e.g., pornography). Parents may insist on devotion of a certain percentage of time on the Internet to educational activities.

While these are all highly variable, conditions of access established by the terms of service, acceptable use, and licensing agreements now collectively referred to as end-user licensing agreements (EULAs) are ubiquitous and contain many features that are uniform across countries and access sites. The conditions of access these put in place, discussed in more detail above in the description of ICANN's law-like impact, can run directly counter to national law and constitutional principles. These, too, are slowly being tested in the courts, with transnational courts playing particularly important roles.

Network neutrality   Basic common carriage principles, combined with the value to the network of expanding the network itself, have up until this point ensured that all websites could be reached with the same ease and speed whether they were associated with the world's largest corporation, a retail store, a non-profit organization, or an individual artist or political activist. The phrase "network neutrality" is used to describe this situation.[11] While everyone has experienced delays in reaching certain sites, or at times found them unavailable, these time differentials have resulted from technical difficulties. There can be too much traffic on the network, or a portion of it, slowing everyone down, or the server hosting a particular website may be down.

In the US, however, there is currently a very tense debate over legislation proposing an end to network neutrality. Network providers are seeking the right to slow down your access to websites that have not paid special fees to ensure favorable treatment. There are fears that in some cases ISPs might make it altogether impossible to reach certain websites. If network neutrality is lost, ISPs in essence have the legal right to censor Internet content. The extraordinary diversity of voices and information available – the most important characteristic of the Internet for many – will have been destroyed. Even when it may still be possible to access websites of small, independent, or politically marginal groups more slowly than other websites, research on surfing habits suggests that the time difference is experienced as a difference in ease by users and it is likely that traffic to those websites would go down. There are already numerous well-documented reports of these types of activities by ISPs in countries around the world, including the US; often these ISPs admit to such activities when they are made public, either explicitly or implicitly by stopping the practices about which complaints have been received.

Users set up their own conditions of access to content when they use filtering software to prevent access to categories of websites considered undesirable. Most such software programs base their decision-making rules on computerized analysis of texts, leading to the problem that perfectly safe – even highly desirable proactive content – may also become unavailable. Software that tries to prevent access to pornographic websites, for example, may also bar access to sites dealing with adult education or support for those with breast cancer. Some filtering software uses decision rules put in place by individuals who examine sites for their acceptability from a particular perspective such as those of specific religions.

Property rights

One of the most fascinating Internet developments has been the creation of entirely new forms of property that expand the boundaries of the economy itself. The transition from an industrial to an information economy has also brought very old forms of intellectual property rights to the center of the economic system and stimulated transformations in how those rights are managed. This issue is so important that it is worth separately thinking about expansion of these rights and about current efforts to correspondingly restrict them through fair use when doing so serves other social goals. A third set of changes to property rights occurs where intensification and expansion of interest in previously existing non-intellectual forms of property has altered how such property is conceptualized and treated.

Expansion of the property system   This is not the first time in history that new forms of property have appeared, but the process is relatively rare and always accompanies significant change in the nature of society. Two examples of this with import for Internet policy are the domain-name system and property in virtual worlds.

We don't buy the street addresses for our homes and businesses, but the domain names that are the addresses for our sites in cyberspace are bought and sold. Creation of the domain-name system managed by ICANN generated billions of dollars, and the amount is still growing. Numerous policy issues have arisen in association with domain names. Those resolved by ICANN include identifying which organizations within regions and countries will be allowed to generate funds through domain-name related transactions. Domain-name issues resolved in national courts include struggles over the use of trademarks in domain names and efforts to stop cybersquatting, the practice of purchasing domain names incorporating the names of others with the hope of then reselling the domains at a profit.

Complex interactions between virtual property, capital within virtual games and worlds, and capital in the offline world raise a number of legal issues that governments have yet to resolve. Should national laws and regulations regarding financial matters be applied to operations within virtual worlds? How is offline income generated through virtual-world activity to be treated for taxation purposes? Should employment laws be applied to those who engage in virtual-world activity to generate either in-world or offline capital for their employers? Should the law intervene in the industry of cheating in electronic games?

Transformations of intellectual property rights　There are four types of intellectual property rights – copyright, patent, trademark, and trade secrets – and all four have undergone changes. Copyright establishes a bundle of separable property rights in symbolic expressions such as texts and images; this bundle includes the rights to reproduce the work, to prepare derivative works based upon the original, to distribute the work, to perform the work publicly, and to display the work publicly. In recent years the duration of copyright has greatly lengthened; in the US, instead of the original 17 years owners can now control uses of copyrighted materials for almost 100 years. Techniques for enforcing copyright have become embedded in digital rights management (DRM) technologies, and it is relatively easy to track who is downloading what content over the Internet. Associations of copyright owners, such as the Recording Industry Association of America (RIAA) have become extremely aggressive about pursuing those whom they believe are infringing copyright. All of these are Internet policy issues because they affect what we can access over the Internet, and what we can do with material once we find it.

Patents establish property rights in three categories, two of which are pertinent to the Internet: utility patents protect processes, machines, articles of manufacture, compositions of matter, and genetic manipulations of animals; and design patents protect the ornamental appearance of objects. Internet technologies each involve numerous patents, almost always under the control of different corporations. Disputes over patents, some claim, slow innovation, and we are increasingly seeing corporations trying to assert that entire classes of activity such as one-click shopping have been patented. Many believe that software underlying ways of conducting business or communicating with each other should not be patentable, but under current law this is possible. The number of patents sought, the lack of pertinent expertise within patent offices, and massive confusion over whether or not there is "prior art" – previously existing patents on aspects of products or services being presented as new – have lead to calls for reform of the patent system altogether. Meanwhile, the open-source software movement has inspired experimentation with public opportunities to contribute to evaluation of whether or not there is prior art for any given new product or service.

Trademarks protect the name or image associated with the product to which they are attached; service marks do the same for services. Legal issues involving trademarks arise in the Internet environment when trademarks are incorporated into domain names or used for avatars or other creations within virtual worlds.

Trade secrets are types of information owners try to prevent others from using through non-disclosure practices. Historically corporations have had the legal right to try to protect trade secrets, but today's electronic discovery practices make it much more difficult to do so.

Fair use　Fair use is the concept that there are limits to the extent to which owners can prevent others from using their intellectual property when, under certain conditions, the use of that property serves social goals of particular importance.

Historically, fair use has been central to copyright law, though today there is also discussion of developing fair use principles for patents. In the US, to qualify, uses of copyrighted material must actively transform the material, serve social goals such as education or promoting public discourse about political affairs via the news, and not damage the market for the copyrighted work. Because it is often difficult to determine whether many of the new Internet-based genres and communicative practices meet these criteria, currently there are efforts underway to establish consensual norms among communities of practice to serve as guidelines for courts.

Privacy

Privacy laws have always been sensitive to technological innovation, with each stage of the development of new information and communication technologies triggering evolution in pertinent regulation. Privacy is considered a fundamental human right because it is essential to many of our most profoundly human activities as well as to our ability to exercise many other rights, including free speech, association with others, and property ownership. In many countries legal protections for various forms of privacy are spread across many different laws and regulations in addition to appreciation of privacy torts. Both governments and private sector entities (most often, corporations) threaten privacy on the Internet. Among the many forms of privacy, those involving communications, anonymity, and data protections are particularly important for Internet policy.

Communications privacy   Communications privacy involves the right to protect interpersonal communications from being accessed by people who are not intended parties to the conversation. Historically, democratic countries have protected the privacy of face-to-face conversations in the home and other places in which there is a legitimate expectation of privacy; in letters and phone calls; and in conversations with professional advisors such as physicians, religious confessors, and attorneys. When governments have felt the need to access such communications to pursue criminal activity or behavior that threatens national security, evidence of probable cause – sufficient evidence-supported reasons to suspect the individuals involved – was required in order to gain permission to access such interpersonal communications. Repressive governments, on the other hand, used techniques such as opening mail, listening to telephone conversations, and encouraging citizen reports on the conversations of others as a means of invading communications privacy. In many countries, citizens were even required to register their typewriters, each of which produces a uniquely identifiable text, making it impossible to communicate interpersonally in an anonymous manner. (Today unique identifiers for digital printers can serve this function.)

The digitized and networked information flows of the Internet make it much easier than ever before not only to access interpersonal communications efficiently, but also to analyze them for the appearance of particular words, phrases, concepts, and interpersonal relationship networks. While in the past interpersonal communications were targeted for governmental surveillance only after an individual's behavior raised suspicion, in the Internet environment the reverse is the case: it is possible to collect all communications and identify individuals of interest through data analysis rather than behavior. Despite the ease with which such activities can be undertaken, the law stood in the way of massive surveillance of interpersonal web-based communications until 2001, when anti-terrorism concerns came to the fore. As is always the case in any country, national security concerns can be used by governments to reduce the scope of civil liberties as a means of defense. Though civil libertarians continue to push back against this development, at the time of writing in 2009 anti-terrorism laws support government surveillance of email and other forms of web-based communication. Policy tools used to accomplish this include such techniques as requiring ISPs to keep all traffic that flows through them for periods of six months to two years and dropping any requirement that specific permission should be needed to surveil the communications of any specific individual or group.

Corporations are also interested in reducing the scope of communications privacy because information about what people are saying to each other has marketing value. Emails are a medium for "viral" marketing, reveal clusters of consumption preferences, alert marketers to social networks of demographic importance, and enable the refinement of niche marketing. Interpersonal communications also provide ISPs with salable content, since end-user licensing agreements can give ISPs the right to use content of anything sent through their systems, including personal emails, for commercial purposes. One of the first examples of this was a website charging for access to salacious emails sent by a particular ISP's users.

Anonymity   Anonymity protects the privacy of a communicator's identity. In the United States, anonymity is constitutionally protected because it is believed necessary for free and open discourse about political issues that may include strong critique. It is also considered necessary to protect "whistleblowers," individuals who want to report wrongdoing by either public or private sector entities the activities of which are damaging to society.

The Internet has created new types of pressures to forbid anonymity, including most importantly the need to authenticate identity for e-commerce and e-government purposes, and to identify those involved in criminal activity using the net. Internet users actively give up anonymity when they sign into their ISP accounts, and passively when the network acquires the "IP address," an address for the computer being used to access the Internet, in order to complete a connection. Cookies, which gather user data – including personal data entered into website forms – that is often shared across websites, also reduce anonymity unwittingly. The political and whistleblowing arguments for permitting anonymity remain, however. The ease with which web-surfing habits can be observed has added another – people should be free to learn about issues such as mental illness and sexually transmitted diseases without suggesting to authorities that they themselves have such problems or are engaged in activities that might lead to them.

There are both legal and technological approaches to protecting anonymity online. Techniques such as encrypting your email and directing your web traffic through anonymizing websites, search engines, or software are available to the average user and can increase anonymity. Legally, debates over whether or not all Internet communication, or at minimum communication of particular types, should be permitted to be anonymous, continue. Legal and technical approaches to anonymity come together in the development of networking technologies that create trust relationships, authenticate identity when necessary, and permit anonymous communication in all other circumstances.

Data privacy   The phrase "data privacy" refers to information about individuals, whether that is data about finances, health, transactions, or reading and surfing habits. The EU has lead the way in developing umbrella data privacy directives that cover all types of personal data; at the other extreme, in the US there are different data privacy regulations for each type of personal information. Invasions of data privacy may merely be embarrassing, but they can also have far-ranging consequences. Access to the personal data of others facilitates identity theft and a variety of types of fraud. Misuse or falsification of personal data may make it impossible for the victim to buy a home, get credit, graduate college, or take a particular job. The ability to identify groups of people with particular medical problems makes it possible to "redline," or refuse to offer services of specific types to those perceived to have raised risk levels. Illegal access to personal data can have free speech implications when surveillance agencies treat as suspect anyone who reads particular texts or websites. Corporate access to personal data can target victims as subjects of marketing campaigns that may be unwelcome.

Data privacy is an area in which organizational, community, and personal practice are particularly important. Sometimes data privacy is invaded deliberately, but often it happens accidentally, through loss of a laptop or memory stick, mistakes in hardware and software system design, and inadequate training on the part of users. Responsibility for implementing practices to protect data privacy is incumbent upon every individual and organization.

Conclusions

Today it is hard to imagine an activity, social process, or type of communicative content that does not involve the Internet, so from one perspective the domain of Internet policy is co-extensive with the entire legal system. More practicably, we can define Internet policy as those laws and regulations that are either specific to Internet infrastructure and its uses or apply to long-standing legal issues that have so qualitatively changed in nature in the digital environment that significant changes are required of the legal system.

The impact of the Internet on the law is enormous and profound. It is an important stimulus to and facilitator of changes in law–society–state relations so fundamental that many legal scholars and political scientists believe a complete transformation is underway. More immediately, the functions of particular elements of the legal system are changing places. The subjects of regulation (technologies) are now being used as policy tools. The digitization of possible evidence that might be considered in the resolution of legal disputes has reoriented organizations away from the front end (laws themselves) and towards the back end (dispute resolution) of the legal process in terms of design of practices and information systems. Private sector entities such as ISPs are being deputized to serve law enforcement functions. And private law, through the flow-down contract system of ICANN, now provides precedent for and the vessel within which public law around the world operates and is evolving.

The multiplicity and variety of decision-making venues of importance present enormous challenges to those who seek to protect civil liberties and human rights in the Internet environment. For many issues, long-standing practices of participatory democracy are irrelevant at worst, or ineffective at best. One of the points of greatest leverage in these areas may be including an understanding of the basics of Internet policy in information/media/technology literacy courses that should be required of all students.

Still, there are key battles to be fought at the state level through familiar political processes. The "Big Four" Internet policy issues – those that shape the context for all other pertinent activity and policymaking – are access to the Internet itself, access to content and activities on the Internet, intellectual property rights, and surveillance and privacy.

Notes

1 For an excellent introduction to the range of types of policy analysis, from cost-benefit calculations to examination of discourse frames, see Schön and Rein (1994).
2 *Command Lines: The Emergence of Governance in Global Cyberspace* (Braman & Malaby, 2006) examines some of the ways in which practices within virtual worlds interact with and affect the law.
3 For the history of this process in the United States, and discussion of the various ways in which the boundaries of the domain of communications policy have been conceptualized, see Braman (2004).
4 For detailed discussion of the pre-history and early years of Internet policy, see Braman (1995).
5 For a well-written, accessible, rich, and still useful discussion of the various regulatory frameworks under consideration for digital networks by countries around the world during the 1980s, written by attorneys who were particularly influential, see Bruce, Cunard, & Director (1986).
6 The first book with "Internet law" in its title was Chissick's *Internet Law: A Practical Guide for Business* (1997). Most of the first wave of such books was, like this one,

aimed at business users. The second wave of books with the phrase in the title was comprised of coursebooks for continuing legal education seminars. The first casebook for law schools with the phrase in the title was Chris Reed's *Internet Law: Text and Materials* (2000). Internet issues, however, appeared in casebooks on topics such as telecommunications regulation and freedom of expression much earlier as units dealing with "electronic media," "new media," and "new technologies," and casebooks appeared earlier dealing with electronic commerce, software, etc. Influential contemporary casebooks on Internet law and policy include Radin, Rothchild, & Silverman (2006); Lemley, Merges, Samuelson, & Menell (2006); and Maggs, Soma, & Sprowl (2005). For legal analyses from the perspective of mutual interactions between law and society, see Berman (2007).

7   Robert Horwitz's *The Irony of Regulatory Reform* (1989) provides the essential history of network regulation in the United States that is the context within which Internet policy has developed. Historians of technology Mowery and Simcoe (2002) explain why US law has been particularly important even though technical development of the Internet began in the UK and many innovations critical to its success have come from and continue to be developed in other countries.

8   A succinct introduction to jurisdictional issues can be found in Zittrain (2005).

9   The websites of these and other non-profit organizations are particularly valuable sources of information on Internet policy issues – what they are about, what arguments are being put forward, what the technological foundations of these issues are, etc.

10 A good introduction to the knowledge gap literature can be found in Vishwanath & Finnegan (1996) and Kwak (1999).

11 Legal scholar Timothy Wu, who coined the phrase "network neutrality," has a particularly useful webpage that explains the basics of the issue and provides links to a selection of scholarly articles presenting diverse perspectives about it, on his website at http://www.timwu.org/network_neutrality.ht.

References

Berman, P. S. (ed.) (2007). *Law and Society Approaches to Cyberspace*. Aldershot, UK: Ashgate.

Braman, S. (2009). Globalizing media law and policy. In D. Thussu (ed.), *Internationalizing Media Studies* (93–115). New York: Routledge.

Braman, S. (2004). Where has media policy gone? Defining the field in the twenty-first century. *Communication Law and Policy*, 9(2), 153–82.

Braman, S. (1995). Policy for the net and the Internet. *Annual Review of Information Science and Technology*, 30, 5–75.

Braman, S., & Lynch, S. (2003). Advantage ISP: Terms of service as media law. *New Media & Society*, 5(3), 422–48.

Braman, S., & Malaby, T. (eds.) (2006). *Command Lines: The Emergence of Governance in Global Cyberspace, First Monday*, special issue no. 7, http://firstmonday.org/htbin/cgiwrap/bin/ojs/index.phph/fm/issue/view/223.

Bruce, R. R., Cunard, J. P., & Director, M. D. (1986). *From Telecommunications to Information Services: A Global Spectrum of Definitions, Boundary Lines, and Structures*. London: Butterworths.

Chissick, M. (1997). *Internet Law: A Practical Guide for Business*. London: Financial Times Media and Telecoms.

Froomkin, M. (2000). Wrong turn in cyberspace: Using ICANN to route around the APA and the Constitution. *Duke Law Journal*, 50, 17–184.

Horwitz, R. (1989). *The Irony of Regulatory Reform*. New York: Oxford University Press.

Kwak, N. (1999). Revisiting the knowledge gap hypothesis. *Communication Research*, 26(4), 385–413.

Lemley, M., Merges, R., Samuelson, P., & Menell, P. (2006). *Software and Internet Law*. Gaithersburg, MD: Aspen Law & Business.

Maggs, P. B., Soma, J. T., & Sprowl, J. A. (2005). *Internet and Computer Law: Cases, Comments, Questions*, 2nd edn. St Paul, MN: Thomson West.

Mowery, D. C., & Simcoe, T. (2002). Is the Internet a US Invention? An Economic and Technological History of Computer Networking. *Research Policy*, 31(8–9), 1369–87.

Mueller, M. (1999). *Ruling the Root*. Cambridge, MA: MIT Press.

Pool, I. de Sola (1983). *Technologies of Freedom*. Cambridge, MA: Belknap Press.

Radin, M. J., Rothchild, J. A., & Silverman, G. M. (2006). *Internet Commerce: The Emerging Legal Framework*, 2nd edn. New York: Foundation Press.

Reed, C. (2000). *Internet Law: Text and Materials*. London: Butterworths.

Schön, D. A., & Rein, M. (1994). *Frame Reflection*. New York: Basic Books.

Vishwanath, K., & Finnegan, J. R. (1996). The knowledge gap hypothesis: 25 years later. *Communication Yearbook*, 19, 187–227.

Zittrain, J. L. (2005). *Jurisdiction*. St Paul, MN: Thomson West.

8

Political Discussion Online

Jennifer Stromer-Galley and Alexis Wichowski

In 2002, soon after the US and its allies went to war in Iraq, Nicholas Thompson wrote an opinion column for the *Boston Globe* on the then current state of online political conversation. The headline of Thompson's article spoke volumes about his opinion of online talk: "Freedom to Flame. Online Political Chat is an Insult to Democracy." He argued that online political conversation is "sophomoric," ranting, full of insults, and "an insult to democracy."

Thompson's views likely resonate with many who have spent time engaged in online discussions of a political, social, or policy issue. In the US, as in Europe, it is a common view that online talk is far from the ideals of what political conversation should be. Instead of carefully thought out and reasonably argued positions, we see hastily written, irrational, or poorly argued posts. Instead of a willingness to hear the other side, we see a willingness to attack the other side.

Why then do academics bother studying online political conversation? In the early days of Internet studies, as the Internet was diffusing, there was great optimism about what this new communication technology could offer. Specifically, the channel characteristics of the Internet – the ability to bridge vast distances, to connect diverse people together, to bring together the like-minded, and to do so quickly and relatively easy – seemed to promise a new means for people to hash through the tough problems facing communities, nation-states, and the globe.

The reality, as is usually the case, is starkly different from the hope and the hype. Several studies have been conducted over the years, including some from the first author of this chapter, to help paint a picture of who spends time talking politics online, why they do it, and whether or not such conversations are any good for those who participate and for their societies. The studies provide a complex portrait of people, motives, and quality of conversation. Sometimes it looks exactly as Thompson described in his editorial piece. Sometimes, though, it is better.

This chapter details that research and its significance. Before that, however, it is necessary to step back and consider why scholars should even contemplate online political conversation in the first place, and, specifically, why political talk in general is thought to be good for society. After providing that explanation, this chapter turns to a discussion of the Internet and its channel characteristics, which provide both affordances and challenges for political conversations. This discussion of the technology and its implications sets the stage for a thorough discussion of what we currently know about people who do and do not talk, and about the qualities of that talk in democratic countries as well as authoritarian regimes. Along the way attention will be paid to where more research is needed to get fuller understanding of the phenomenon of political conversations channeled over the Internet.

Why Political Discourse Matters for Democracy

Writing in 1939, John Dewey declared American democracy to be in a state of crisis. Americans mistakenly viewed democracy as passive, he suggested, "something that perpetuated itself automatically" (Dewey et al., 1993, p. 241). Dewey declared that the only remedy for this crisis was for citizens to rethink democracy, not simply as a mass of government institutions, but rather as a way of life. One remedy was for people to form heterogeneous associations, to interact with and talk to others, for in so doing a public sphere would be created (Dewey, 1946).

This notion of the public sphere has resonated strongly in Western political thought, and perhaps found its strongest voice in Jürgen Habermas's ([1962] 1989) *The Structural Transformation of the Public Sphere.* This work advanced the idea that educated elites of society, collectively formed into a civil society, should engage in rational-critical debate over issues of public concern thereby creating a public sphere. Critical discussions, firmly grounded in information and reason, would enhance public opinion such that it would influence and create a check on the policies and actions of elected officials. Habermas's conceptualizations of the public sphere and of rational-critical debate situated informed discussion as the cornerstone for democratic participation. Benjamin Barber (1984) advanced the ideas of Dewey and Habermas, proposing the notion of "strong democracies": democratic societies in which citizens are active, capable agents influencing change not only to occasionally serve self-interests but also as a function of daily life. Unlike Habermas, Barber's conceptualization of democracy requires participation beyond educated elites, to include all members of democratic societies. Through the very practice of participating in politics, individuals learn how to be effective members of the citizenry, regardless of their prior education or expertise.

These theories of democracy designate political conversation as essential to democratically organized societies. It is through political conversations that members of society come to clarify their own views, learn about the opinions of others, and discover what major problems face the collective. Through such conversations, political participation is made possible, enabling citizens to affect the practices and policies of their elected leaders and ultimately ensuring a democratic process of governance.

In the modern era of mass media, especially television, much concern had been raised about the state of affairs of political participation in the West, particularly the US. Putnam's (2000) _Bowling Alone_, Verba, Schlozman, and Brady's (1995) _Voice and Equality_, and Delli Carpini and Keeter's (1996) _What Americans Know About Politics and Why it Matters_, suggested a general decline in organizing, participating, learning, and talking about political and social matters. These authors, especially Putnam, placed the problem squarely on television, citing the powerful relationship between the increase in television viewing and the decline of civic associations specifically and political participation generally in the US. Television, and other mass media, seemed to turn people off politics. Then, along came the Internet.

The Internet, as a channeler-of-channels, offers a number of characteristics that invite the possibility for increased political participation generally, and political conversation specifically. The unique characteristics of the Internet enable citizens to produce, comment on, edit, remove, and recommend portions of a global dialogue. This has set it apart as a medium with the potential to transform the democratic landscape at large and expand the public sphere.

Internet and Discourse Online: Features and Challenges

Several scholars have noted the channel characteristics that are important when considering online political conversation. Among the most frequently researched channel characteristics are: interactivity, which permits genuine dialogue between Internet users; the possibility of bridging physical distances between people, which in turn allows people to find both homogenous and heterogeneous groups; the potential for anonymity, which permits expressions without fear of recrimination; and reduced feelings of social presence in online discussions, which both increases the willingness to speak on political subjects, but also increases the chances for anti-social behavior, such as flaming. These characteristics and their implications are taken up next.

Interactivity

Conversation online is made possible by one of the defining characteristics of Internet-channeled technologies: interactivity. The ability for moderately computer-savvy individuals to create content, to comment on the content created by others, and to converse with individuals in both asynchronous and real-time forums is arguably the most distinctive and revolutionary characteristic of the Internet as a communication medium. Interactivity is heavily cited as one of the most promising aspects of the Internet in promoting democratic society (McMillan & Hwang, 2002; Stromer-Galley & Foot, 2002; Stromer-Galley, 2004; Sundar et al., 2003; Endres & Warnick, 2004; Warnick et al., 2005; Stromer-Galley &

Baker, 2006; Heeter, 1989), in part because it allows for both horizontal communication between citizens and vertical communication between citizens and elites (Hacker, 1996).

Interactivity online has been variously characterized, with definitions that span to include interaction with the technology itself, interaction with other people, and interaction as existing in the perceptions of the users. Characterizing interactivity as a function of involvement between users and the technology or between discussants generally refers to the degree and type of reciprocity present in an exchange. In a study by this chapter's first author (Stromer-Galley, 2000), such reciprocity was conceptualized as being either with the technology or with other people, what she termed "media interaction" and "computer-mediated human interaction" respectively. Media interaction was a common characteristic of political campaign websites in the early days of the World Wide Web as it allowed campaigns to retain a high degree of control, such as online polls and email signups. Equally important, interactive technologies enable distant others to come together (Stromer-Galley & Foot, 2002), allowing diverse demographics of people to interact in ways that may be impossible in the physical environment.

Bridging the distance: homophily and heterogeneity

Yet, for all the ways that Internet technologies permit interaction of diverse peoples, researchers are concerned that heterogeneous discourse online may not be happening. Although one of the great appeals for many users is the ability to find others online who share similar interests both politically and personally in online arenas (Davis, 2005; Stromer-Galley, 2002a), some theorists have expressed concern that this ability to find like others will result in a fragmentation of online users into interest and issue publics (Sunstein, 2000; Doheny-Farina, 1996). Research both supports and contradicts this assertion. A study by Postmes, Spears & Lea (1998) found that some of the very characteristics that may attract some users to interacting online, such as anonymity and the ability to find groups with like interests, may result in strengthening of conformation to group norms, which may in turn lead to increased discrimination against those who are different, thereby reinforcing a desire to interact only with those of like minds. Conversely, the first author (Stromer-Galley, 2002a) conducted a series of interviews with participants in online political discussion spaces and found that people both sought out and enjoyed the diversity of opinions that they encountered. The issue of who is talking to whom, if people are only seeking out homogenous groups or venturing into heterogeneous discussions, is addressed in greater detail further on in this chapter.

Free to speak freely

Just as there is a tension between the benefits and drawbacks of finding issue, interest, or hobby groups of like-minded others online, Internet technologies also produce a tension between the benefits of affording users a forum to speak freely and the drawbacks of opening the gate for negative or hostile verbal attacks. The ability to express one's opinion anonymously is often noted as of essential importance to democratic discourse, as anonymous speech permits the expression of unpopular sentiments or statements by disadvantaged peoples without fear of recrimination (Lee, 1996). The option to be anonymous may also permit expression by marginalized or isolated members of a community (McKenna & Bargh, 1998). Kling and colleagues (1999) identify that there is a need, however, to strike a balance between the benefits to be gained by users who perceive anonymity as necessary for free expression and the potential threats to the traditional norms that govern communications, such as personal accountability, which may be lost in anonymous speech. They characterize anonymity as both a "shield" and a "sword" – those who require protection can benefit from the option to talk anonymously, but this can also empower others to use anonymous expressions as a means to attack from a distance. Anonymous talk online is also attractive for less lofty but arguably equally valuable reasons, such as attracting notice and advocating beliefs (Donath & boyd, 2004), permitting catharsis (Davis, 2005), and as a venue for self-presentation (Trammell & Keshelashvili, 2005; Wynn & Katz, 1997).

The dark side of anonymous discussion online, however, is substantial in its effect. *Flaming* – verbal attacks or insults in online discourse – and *trolling* – posts in online community forums meant to disrupt or disparage conversation – are two common phenomena in online discussion forums that may repel many otherwise interested people from participating in the discussion. Unsurprisingly, flaming is found more often in certain interest groups than others. For example, online discussions that are moderated by a neutral party or hosted by government officials or agencies exhibit fewer personal attacks than organic, citizen-hosted discussions (Coleman, 2004). As well, research suggests that more flaming occurs in groups with homogeneous than heterogeneous participants (Douglas & McGarty, 2001). Yet some researchers have, if not defended, begun to make attempts to contextualize flaming in certain circumstances. Wang and Hong (1995) argue that in academic discussion lists, for instance, flaming helps to promote effective communication by social sanctioning and enforcing group behavior norms. Others have claimed that flaming has been unfairly attacked due to studies that focus too highly on content rather than considering the context and strategic choice in language chosen based on those contexts (Vrooman, 2002). The harmful effects of trolls are less contested, as studies have indicated that trolls are more likely to seek out traditionally underrepresented or non-mainstream groups, such as feminist discussion spaces (Herring et al., 2002).

Technologies for Political Discourse Online

Before discussing the research about online political discussion, it is important to step back and clarify what we mean by political conversation online. The concept has been defined in various ways and has included or excluded particular channels of communication. Political conversation can be as broad as any exchange between any set of people on a social, political, or current event, or as narrow as an organized and moderated deliberation on a key issue facing a group of people. For the purposes of this review, we cast our net broadly to incorporate organic conversations started and maintained by ordinary citizens as well as moderated deliberations with recruited or invited participants hosted by organizations or governments.

As well, the channels are many through which such conversation occur on the Internet. In the 1980s, users of the Internet had available to them Internet relay chat (IRC), MUDs (text-based multi-user domains), message boards, and email lists. In the 1990s, with the development and diffusion of the World Wide Web, conversation spaces expanded to include web-hosted message boards and forums, such as E-thepeople.org, and synchronous chat spaces, such as Yahoo! chat, as well as community-generated news sites, such as Slashdot.com. In the 2000s the technology has expanded further to include weblogs (blogs), and social networking sites such as Facebook and MySpace. For this review, we have included all channels except websites that do not include a forum or message board or comment component. We recognize that the content from citizen, activist, news, and government websites contribute to political discourse online, but the lack of interactivity on such sites excludes them from this analysis.

Who Talks

Over the past two decades, the portrait of who engages in political discourse online has been fairly consistent. For instance, Davis's (2005) research surveying people who used the Internet in the late 1990s in the US found that those who reported talking about social or political issues online were generally well-educated, more affluent, younger, and less likely to be married. They also were more likely to follow politics and vote than those who do not talk politics online. A more recent study of weblog users suggests a similar profile. According to Johnson et al. (2007) blog users are more likely to be white, affluent, well-educated, male, and more interested and knowledgeable about politics.

Indeed, over two decades of studies suggest a consistent and large gender gap in online political discussion. Research in the 1980s by Garramone and colleagues (1986) studied politically oriented message boards in a university context in the US and found that the majority of users were men. Similar findings were born out in research in the 1990s (Hill & Hughes, 1998; Savicki et al., 1996; Davis, 1999). These results were not surprising given that a gender gap in general Internet users existed until the late 1990s in the US. Research since then, however, continues to identify a gender gap in political talk online (Stromer-Galley, 2002c; Stromer-Galley, 2002a; Harp & Tremayne, 2006; Trammell & Keshelashvili, 2005).[1] A gap also exists in European countries, including Germany (Albrecht, 2006), the Netherlands (Hagemann, 2002; Jankowski & van Selm, 2000), and Denmark (Jensen, 2003a).

The reasons for this gender gap are understudied. In the first author's dissertation research (Stromer-Galley, 2002d), she found that of 69 people interviewed who talk politics online, only nine were women. That research suggested three reasons for such a small number, including that female participants likely receive unwanted sexual attention that leads them either to hide their gender by using gender-neutral or male handles when posting or to leave the discussion altogether. An interview with one of the nine women who used synchronous chat to talk politics indicated that she felt that she was outnumbered ten to one, and that she believed many women did not sustain participation in political chat rooms, because women tend to take disagreements to heart. She said that some of the attacks she received as a participant made her cry, but she loved politics enough to keep participating. She also changed her handle to one that is more masculine so that men would take her seriously. Only one study has systematically investigated why women are not co-equal participants in the online discussion arena of blogs. Harp and Tremayne (2006) found that women were less likely to be top political bloggers in the US, in part because male bloggers do not link or draw attention to female political bloggers, unless they are also engaging in sexualized talk. These two studies suggest a "boy's club" exists online making it difficult for women to join in the conversation; When they do, they are belittled, attacked, and sexualized. As well, Davis (2005) found that the topics of political discussions online are those that not only do not mirror the concerns facing the US, but also do not include typically "female" issues, such as childcare, education, and healthcare. A lack of "female" topics likely also means that women are less drawn to participating in the conversation.

As the dynamic of gender has been understudied, so too has race. Survey-driven studies include race as a demographic "control" variable, and the results are mixed as to whether race is a factor in political conversations. If we grant that racial identity still matters online (Burkhalter, 1999), then more research is needed that looks specifically at the dynamics of race in online political discussion. One such study by Byrne (2007) investigated African-American political discussion on the social networking site BlackPlanet.com. Her research suggested that few opportunities exist online for African-Americans to network in black-only spaces, but that in the spaces that do exist, conversations that were race-focused were more likely to draw attention and additional conversation than posts that were race-neutral. Studies such as these draw attention to the need for further research not only on broader issues of access and the digital divide, but also what spaces and opportunities exist for underrepresented populations once they get online and what type of activities they engage in once there.

Although race and gender have been understudied, youth engagement has been given greater attention. Heightened attention has occurred for a couple of reasons. First, there is much interest in political socialization and political participation among youth – those who are presumably the next generation of political actors in democratic societies. Second, a pervasive assumption exists that new communication technologies, which tend to be adopted by younger members of society quickly, might bring more youth into the political process. Indeed, the research suggests that those who populate online discussion spaces tend to be younger than the population at large in the US (Davis, 2005), Italy (Calenda & Mosca, 2007), and Germany. Albrecht's (2006) analysis of online discussions in Hamburg, Germany, found that young people were overrepresented in the discussions as compared with the overall population. He wrote: "Seemingly, the Internet has a positive effect on the participation of young people" (p. 72). Bers and Chau (2006) observed that a specially designed 3-D environment could foster civic values and engagement among youth. As children of the Internet era come of age, researchers will undoubtedly keep a careful eye on the ways that technology as part of life does or does not translate to civic participation.

Alongside questions of who talks is whether there is a relationship between online and offline political conversation. The first author (Stromer-Galley, 2002c), for example, theorized that the Internet's channel characteristics, including anonymity and the ability to choose discussion partners, might draw people to talk politics online who would not do so face-to-face. Survey analysis suggests that of 87 percent of those who reported talking politics online "in the past year" reported talking politics with friends and family. That number, however, dropped when the question shifted to political talk with acquaintances. Only 51 percent of those who reported talking online reported talking with acquaintances, which she takes as a sign that the technology may be affording opportunities for political conversation that are avoided face-to-face.

If we grant that there are people using the Internet to talk with others who are less likely to do so face-to-face, especially with acquaintances like co-workers or community members, are these users as well as those who will talk anywhere actively participating online? The answer seems to be no. Of those who visit online discussion spaces, generally only a small percentage actually contribute comments. The rest engage in what has been perhaps unfairly termed "lurking," merely reading the discussions. Davis (2005), for example, found in a 1999 survey of US citizens that "lurkers" make up as much as three quarters of the people who visit online discussion spaces. These results hold for other countries as well (Albrecht, 2006; Robinson, 2005; Hagemann, 2002; Jankowski & van Selm, 2000; Jankowski & van Os, 2004; Tsaliki, 2002). There is concern that those who participate dominate the conversation, but Hagemann (2002) found that frequent contributors to an email list discussion about two Dutch political parties did not monopolize the discussion. Albrecht's (2006) observations of the Hamburg forum were similar, suggesting that frequent contributors did not dominate the discussions with their own views, but instead "behaved as 'old hands,'" by helping facilitate the discussion (p. 72). Others, such as Davis (1999) and Robinson (2005), suggest that the frequent contributors dominated the discussions they analyzed.

Lack of active participation in online discussions is of particular concern to researchers as it is often interpreted as yet another instance of diminished civic engagement. Yet the picture of participation online may be more complex than this. The online environment affords people the opportunity to visit, or "listen in" on, a wide array of ongoing conversations generated by both mainstream news media and unknown others. Yet if they do not post comments, they are considered to be non-participating, or worse "lurking," a term that connotes socially deviant behavior. If citizens were to attend political deliberations in an offline environment, such as those hosted by Study Circles or the National Issues Forum, as audience members, it seems unlikely that this would elicit the same concern. Rather than handily dismissing non-commenting visitors of online discussion sites as disengaged, research is needed to determine what effect this type of activity actually has. If being audience to the diverse points of view that arise from group conversations contributes to political knowledge in offline environments, it is possible that online audiences stand to gain from such exposure as well.

As mentioned in an earlier section, there also is deep concern that people online fragment into like-minded interest or issue groups (Doheny-Farina, 1996; Sunstein, 2001). The question then is who is talking to whom? Are people online talking with people like themselves or people different from themselves? The answer is both. There is little doubt that people gather into like-minded discussion groups. There is also evidence, however, that people participate and talk with diverse others. Kelly et al. (2005) analyzed political Usenet newsgroups to ascertain if people of similar political ideologies were primarily talking amongst themselves. Their research suggests a high degree of cross-talk, or conversations between people of differing ideologies. In the blogosphere, research of linking patterns on political blogs suggests that as many as 60 percent of links to other news and blog sites are not of the political ideology of the author or authors of the blog site (Reese et al., 2007).

Now that we have a picture of who talks, it needs to be considered why they do it. Few studies have investigated why people talk politics online, although there is a growing number of studies that have researched motives for Internet use more generally (Papacharissi & Rubin, 2000) and for political information seeking (Kaye & Johnson, 2002). This question of why people talk politics online has been the focus of the first author's research (Stromer-Galley, 2002a, 2002b, 2002c, 2002d). If, as is popular wisdom, online political conversation is "an insult to democracy," what draws people to engage in it? Interviews conducted with 69 people who participate in online political discussions suggested a range of motives, including the ability to seek a diverse range of perspectives, to learn about political topics, and to learn more about one's own views in the process. They participate in online conversations so that they can "vent" about what frustrates them about politics, to observe the views of those with whom they disagree, to gain information outside the mainstream media context, to find others with similar perspectives, and to pick on or attack others just for the fun of it. This range of motives reflects the range of behaviors that are seen in online discussions, the behaviors which lead us back to the question of the quality of the discussions. Does the prevailing notion that online discussions are "an insult democracy" bear out in the research? Perhaps it is unsurprising that a large number of studies have been conducted that focus specifically on this question. These are detailed next.

The Quality of Online Deliberation

Several studies have attempted to measure how deliberative online discussions are. These studies rely on Habermasian notions of deliberative democracy, including the requirements of equality of participation, reciprocity – which is defined in many ways, but generally means the degree to which there is genuine exchange between discussants – and rational argument.

Studies have been conducted both in the US and in Europe that investigate whether online discussions meet Habermasian ideals. In a European context, Hagemann (2002) analyzed the discussion on two Dutch political party email lists and found that there was a fairly high degree of reciprocity and interaction between participants, but that discussion was of limited rationality. He concludes that the email lists were not deliberative in the Habermasian sense. Jankowski and van Os (2004) analyzed the online discussions established by the city of Hoogeveen, Netherlands, to facilitate greater information exchange between residents and political elites. Their results suggested a "gloomy picture" (p. 190). They found a low level of reciprocity and a general lack of mutual understanding of others' perspectives. In the US, several studies have analyzed the deliberativeness of online discussions, with similar results. Wilhelm (1998), for example, content analyzed a random sample of Usenet posts and found that for the most part people were talking with like-minded others on political topics and that only one fifth of messages were responding to others. On the question of rationality, he found that three quarters of the messages provided reasons for opinions expressed, but that the conversations were not sustained or the topics deeply engaged by the discussants. Similar results have been found by Davis (1999) Hill and Hughes (1998), and Schneider (1996).

Yet these studies offer different definitions of deliberativeness, making it difficult to compare results. Others make general claims based on thin observations without clearly defining, operationalizing, and then measuring the elements that signal a deliberative discussion (Davis, 2005). Two studies have addressed that shortcoming. A coding scheme developed by Graham and Witschge (2003) offers a complex coding system for measuring arguments and counter-arguments of messages in an online discussion in an effort to capture "rationality," an essential component of deliberation. The primary shortcoming is that Graham and Witschge's coding scheme did not meet standards of systematic content analysis (established by Krippendorf, 2004; Neuendorf, 2002; and others). By not having multiple people apply the coding to a set of discussions to see if they can achieve a satisfactory level of intercoder agreement, they failed to ensure that their coding scheme was valid and reliable. The first author (Stromer-Galley, 2007) created a simpler coding system to measure deliberative discussion, using research from deliberation, small group discussions, and discourse analysis to define and operationalize the categories. She achieved a satisfactory level of intercoder agreement on the content categories in a study of online deliberation that used teleconferencing software. It remains to be seen, however, whether others can adapt and use the coding scheme.

One of the reasons that so many scholars have looked to Internet-channeled discussions for deliberation is because the channel characteristics of the technology seem to invite such a possibility. Dalhberg (2001a), for example, identified several characteristics of the Internet that he believes permit democratic discourse in Western societies. These include the autonomy of individuals to freely express opinions, the ability and opportunity to criticize claims, and the degree of reflexivity of those expressing opinions. This, however, may be true for certain channels for interaction, but not others. Specifically, email lists, message boards, and blogs may enable reflexive, thoughtful, and rational messages, in part because people have time to contemplate a message, find evidence to support it, and consider how it might be responded to before posting. However, synchronous chat may invite problems for genuinely deliberative interactions, given the shorter messages, faster responses, and incoherence of multiple conversations occurring near simultaneously without clear indication of who is speaking to whom. Weger and Aakhus (2003) studied online political chat and found that the quality of the arguments was low, as exhibited by underdeveloped arguments, because people opt for short, catchy messages rather than thoughtful and well-crafted positions. The first author's research on this topic (Stromer-Galley & Martinson, 2005), by contrast, found that political chat was more coherent and the interactions sustained longer than those on other topics in a chat, like cancer support. Moreover, experiments such as that by Price and Cappella (2002) have successfully used synchronous chat for political deliberation, further suggesting that synchronous chat may not be inherently problematic for hosting political conversations.

What this body of research suggests is that the quality of online discussion rests, in part, on the design of the discussion space (Beierle, 2004; Noveck, 2004; Wright, 2006). Wright and Street (2007) argue that "how discussion is organized within the medium of communication helps to determine whether or not the result will be deliberation or cacophony" (p. 850). They argue that the way that discussion spaces are designed matters greatly to whether one sees high- or low-quality discussion. Replicating the study conducted by Wilhelm (1998), but focusing on the European Union's online discussion forum, Futurum, Wright and Street found an overall higher-quality discussion than Wilhelm found of Usenet. They credit the positive results to the design of Futurum, including the recruiting of people who were likely interested in the topics for discussion, the threaded message board, which promoted reciprocity, and the connection to the European Union parliament and hence the possibility that conversations would be heard by policymakers. Other research projects that have studied online discussions that co-mingled citizens and politicians found similar, positive results (Jensen, 2003b; Coleman, 2004).

Such studies, however, also identified problems that arise when citizens and politicians come together. Coleman's (2004) research examined two online forums hosted by the British parliament on the topics of domestic abuse and communications legislation. Coleman found that participants in the forum about domestic violence in the UK were satisfied with their experiences, engaged in a high degree of interaction with each other, but did not feel that the parliamentarians who participated really cared about what they had to say. By contrast, the analysis of the forum on communications legislation suggested that participants did not interact much, but felt that parliamentarians cared about what they had to say – even though there were fewer members of parliament (MPs). As well, interviews with the MPs indicated the challenges of getting political leaders to participate. MPs were enthusiastic but had difficulty devoting the time to the discussions. In a study of a Danish online discussion between politicians and citizens, Jensen (2003b) found that politicians dominated the debate. They represented slightly more than half the total number of participants and they contributed three times the number of posts. Moreover, citizens and politicians primarily talked with each other; there was little citizen-to-citizen interaction. Jankowski and van Selm (2000) found similar results in a forum that brought together senior citizens, political candidates, and representatives of organizations. Candidates and organizations primarily talked to each other, ignoring citizens who directed comments at them. This research suggests benefits and challenges when citizens and politicians come together in a shared online discussion.

Another component of deliberation that merits consideration is the absence or presence of a moderator. Albrecht (2006), for example, found that citizens in a discussion about land use in the city of Hamburg, Germany, produced a high-quality discussion. He attributes this to the existence of professional moderators who helped guide the discussion and helped establish "mutual respect and rational orientation" (p. 73). Research by Trenel (2004) on the role of moderators in "Listening to the City" dialogues focused on lower Manhattan's redevelopment after the terrorist attacks of September 11, 2001, found that moderators had a positive effect on those who actively participated in the online discussion, particularly "advanced moderation," which entailed trained facilitators who kept participants focused on the discussion, intervened if interpersonal conflicts arose, created a respectful climate, balanced the discussion by offering alternative perspectives, and summarized the discussions. Women and minorities were less likely than white men to participate overall in the deliberations, but in the advanced moderation condition they were more likely to actively participate than those in a "basic moderation" condition, where moderators only helped keep the discussion moving forward. These studies indicate that the presence of a moderator can have beneficial effects. More research, particularly experiments with different levels and types of moderation, is needed to further investigate what benefit a moderator might provide for the quality of online discussion.

It should be noted that there is one area quite lacking in online discussion research: that which focuses on political discussions occurring on sites not specifically designated as political. Just as many people talk about politics casually, informally, and as a part of everyday life (Wyatt et al., 2000), it stands to reason that political talk arises amidst conversations about sports, religion, business, or entertainment. Research into this area may provide insight into the quality and nature of discussions that occur in places not designated as "political," as well as how to design discussion spaces that capitalize on the ways that people naturally and voluntarily engage in political discussions online.

In sum, online discussions, created by and for citizens and left to their own devices tend not to produce high-quality discussions. Better discussions seem to occur when there is moderation of the discussions, well-designed software to promote reciprocity and contemplation, and co-mingling of citizens and political elites.[2] More research, however, is needed to systematically and carefully identify what elements seem to provide the greatest benefits for quality online discussion.

Nation-Based Influences of Online Discussion

As noted earlier, most of the research of online political discussion focuses on discourse in the West, yet there is a growing body of research that has analyzed political discourse online in countries with authoritarian governments. Researchers analyzing political conversation online in China focus on the difficulty of public, political conversations in a context where censorship and government oversight is ever present. Fung (2002) analyzed a chat room on a newspaper website in Hong Kong in order to study the tensions in the government, economic, and civic structures between China and Hong Kong after China assumed governance of Hong Kong from Britain. Fung found that there were two types of posters: ordinary citizens and professional writers. The professional writers appeared on the forums as average citizens, but their use of a distinctively Chinese way of writing coupled with phrases common in China but unknown in Hong Kong suggested that they were members of the Chinese government sent to marginalize and silence those opposing or critiquing China. The Hong Kong citizens, by contrast, were not well coordinated and were unable to mount effective arguments against those advocating for China. Nevertheless, Fung argues, there were counter-arguments to the pro-China positions, which he notes would not occur in online discussions on mainland China, due either to government censorship or to self-censorship. He also found other protest strategies, including simply ignoring the pro-China arguments. Fung explained "The silence became effective opposition" (p. 89). Another study of online discussion in authoritarian regimes by Kulikova and Perlmutter (2007) analyzed the role that citizen-written blogs played in the Kyrgyzstan revolution in 2005. Kyrgyzstan was a nation with an authoritarian government and state-controlled media, similar to China. The researchers investigated whether citizen-controlled blogs effectively disseminated unofficial information to citizens, and what role such blogs played in the revolution. They found that they contributed greatly in providing information to people outside of the state-run media and played an important role in the revolution. Studies like these provide important insight into the use of information and communication technologies for resistance and to support revolutions against authoritarian governments. More research is needed, especially of countries where the Internet is still diffusing, such as those in Africa.

As is true of Internet studies generally, there is a lack of comparative research focusing on political discussions online. Robinson (2005) provided one of the few studies that look across multiple countries to see how culture shapes the discussion. She studied three countries, the US, Brazil, and France, and the online message boards hosted on prominent newspapers in each country for two weeks – one week immediately following the September 11, 2001, terrorist attacks in the US, and one week at the end of October 2001. Her research found that the conversations in all three countries quickly divided along ideological lines, and generally into three camps: pro-American, anti-American, and anti-anti-American. She found distinct differences in how the discussants interacted in the three forums. Brazilians adopted formal address to the people with whom they argued, writing notably long messages as compared with discussions in the US and France. She found that French and Americans used humor, mockery, sarcasm, and *ad hominem* attacks in response to posts with which they disagreed. She concluded that differences in the discussions could be attributed to cultural differences: "The 'intimacy' strategies of the Americans and the French, for example, were not shared by the Brazilians, who relied upon 'distancing' strategies that exacerbated the pre-existing ideological antagonisms" (Robinson, 2005, "Conclusion," paragraph 2). More studies of this sort are needed to understand what role culture plays in the quality and kind of political discussions seen online.

Conclusions

When Thompson wrote his article in 2002 on political discussion, he concluded that online conversation is "an insult to democracy." What we aim to show in this chapter is a picture that partly confirms and partly rejects Thompson's conclusion. In order to have high-quality discussion, there must be people willing to participate, and willing to abide by the high expectations of political conversation at its best: a willingness to hear other perspectives, to rationally argue for one's own opinions while grounding those opinions in sound evidence, to aim for identifying problems and solutions that will benefit the greater good (Dahlberg, 2001). None of the research studies reviewed in this chapter suggests that political conversations online meet such lofty ideals, especially those that are organically created by citizens for citizens. This suggests that even if the technology makes online political discussion *possible*, that does not mean people will necessarily use the technology in those ways.

Having said that, why should we think there is any benefit to online discussion? There are at least three reasons. First, for those who use various online discussion channels to talk politics, they derive not only pleasure but also benefits from such participation (Stromer-Galley, 2002a, 2002b). It would be a mistake to minimize the experiences of those who use these forums, simply because they fail to engage in the kind of discussions theorists hold as an unattainable ideal. Second, for those in non-democratically organized societies, online discussion forums can serve as places for resistance (Fung, 2002; Hill & Sen, 2000; Kulikova & Perlmutter, 2007). In such contexts, online forums are not an "insult" to democracy but rather *enable* it. Third, such online discussions, particularly when they are hosted by government agencies or policymakers, enact democracy by situating citizens as agents within the policymaking process. This has benefits not only for citizens but also for government policymaking and for governmental bodies as institutions *of* democracy (for an example see Stanley et al., 2004).

Although there are benefits, we believe more research is needed to identify those benefits. Specifically: What effects do online political conversations have on those who participate both in the short term and in the long term? By effects, we need to know more about whether and what people learn about political actors, events, and institutions through their conversations. We need to know whether they are more likely to get involved in other political activities as a result of their online conversations. We need to know whether they develop a more sophisticated opinion on the topic and whether they develop greater understanding of those who hold contrary opinions. Research exists from deliberation experiments that suggest that there are such benefits (Price et al., 2002), but further investigation is needed of online deliberations that are naturally occurring and not created as part of an academic experiment. We also need more research that compares online and offline political discussions (for one example of such a comparison see Min, 2007). There is a prevailing assumption in much of the online political discussion literature that face-to-face casual political discussion and more structured political deliberation are gold standards which online discussions must meet. Yet we do not have a clear understanding of the quality of face-to-face discussions.

Research also is needed to investigate the larger social impact of online political discussions. For example, how does online political conversation affect social capital? Much of the research on social capital focuses on Internet use generally, rather than discussion specifically. People who go online for entertainment purposes are not found to be producing social capital as much as information-seekers (Norris & Jones, 1998; Shah et al., 2001). Yet participation online generally provides a broader sense of community (Norris, 2002) and increased offline and face-to-face social interaction (Matei, 2004; Wellman et al., 2001; Parks & Floyd, 1996). Participation in online political discussions may increase social capital (Jensen, 2006), but more research is needed to know for certain.

Finally, in our estimation, it is not enough to create online deliberation spaces with advanced technological features that offer no true interaction between citizens and politicians, or to host unmoderated discussion forums that scare off otherwise interested discussants due to the vitriol of the few. Encouraging participation in political discussion online, as offline, will not happen *en masse* until it is perceived to be useful, beneficial, normal, or as Dewey (1993) suggested, a way of life. To this end, more work needs to be done to design forums to promote good discussion. Such work will likely need to be done by good government groups, advocacy organizations, and governments themselves, in an effort to bring citizens into the political conversation, for their own benefit and for the common good.

Notes

1   For an exception see Beierle (2004).
2   See Noveck (2004) for a discussion and example of "Unchat," a software system designed for quality political discussion.

References

Albrecht, S. (2006). Whose voice is heard in online deliberation? A study of participation and representation in political debates on the Internet. *Information, Communication & Society*, 9, 62–82.

Barber, B. (1984). *Strong Democracy: Participatory Politics for a New Age*. Berkeley, CA: University of California Press.

Beierle, T. C. (2004). Digital deliberation: Engaging the public through online policy dialogues. In P. M. Shane (ed.), *Democracy Online: The Prospects for Political Renewal through the Internet* (pp. 155–66). New York: Routledge.

Bers, M. U., & Chau, C. (2006). Fostering civic engagement by building a virtual city. *Journal of Computer-Medicated Communication* 11. http://jcmc.indiana.edu/vol11/issue3/bers.html.

Burkhalter, B. (1999). Reading race online: Discovering racial identity in Usenet discussions. In M. A. Smith & P. Kollock (eds.), *Communities in Cyberspace* (pp. 60–75). London: Routledge.

Byrne, D. N. (2007). Public discourse, community concerns, and civic engagement: Exploring Black social networking traditions on BlackPlanet.com. *Journal of Computer-Medicated Communication*, 13. http://jcmc.indiana.edu/vol13/issue1/byrne.html.

Calenda, D., & Mosca, L. (2007). The political use of the Internet: Some insights from two surveys of Italian students. *Information, Communication, & Society*, 10, 29–47.

Coleman, S. (2004). Connecting parliament to the public via the Internet. *Information, Communication & Society*, 7, 1–22.

Dahlberg, L. (2001). The Internet and democratic discourse: Exploring the prospects of online deliberative forums extending the public sphere. *Information, Communication and Society*, 4, 615–33.

Davis, R. (1999). *The Web of Politics: The Internet's Impact on the American Political System*. New York: Oxford University Press.

Davis, R. (2005). *Politics Online: Blogs, Chatrooms, and Discussion Groups in American Democracy*. New York: Routledge.

Delli Carpini, M. X., & Keeter, S. (1996). *What Americans Know about Politics and Why It Matters*. New Haven, CT: Yale University Press.

Dewey, J. (1946). *The Public and Its Problems: An Essay on Political Inquiry*. Chicago: Gateway Books.

Dewey, J., Morris, D., & Shapiro, I. (1993). *The Political Writings*. Indianapolis: Hackett.

Doheny-Farina, S. (1996). *The Wired Neighborhood*. New Haven, CT: Yale University Press.

Donath, J., & boyd, d. (2004). Public displays of connection. *BT Technology Journal*, 22, 71.

Douglas, K. M., & McGarty, C. (2001). Identifiability and self-presentation: Computer-mediated communication and intergroup interaction. *British Journal of Social Psychology*, 40, 399–416.

Endres, D., & Warnick, B. (2004). Text-based interactivity in candidate campaign web sites: A case study from the 2002 elections. *Western Journal of Communication*, 68, 322–43.

Fung, A. (2002). One city, two systems: Democracy in an electronic chat room in Hong Kong. *Javnost/The Public*, 9, 77–94.

Garramone, G. M., Harris, A. C., & Anderson, R. (1986). Uses of political computer bulletin boards. *Journal of Broadcasting & Electronic Media*, 30, 325–39.

Graham, T., & Witschge, T. (2003). In search of online deliberation: Towards a new method for examining the quality of online discussions. *Communications*, 28, 173–204.

Habermas, J. ([1962] 1989). *The Structural Transformation of the Public Sphere*. Cambridge, MA: MIT Press.

Hacker, K. L. (1996). Missing links in the evolution of electronic democratization. *Media, Culture & Society*, 18, 213–32.

Hagemann, C. (2002). Participation in and contents of two Dutch political party discussion lists on the internet. *Javnost/The Public*, 9, 61–76.

Harp, D., & Tremayne, M. (2006). The gendered blogosphere: Examining inequality using network and feminist theory. *Journalism & Mass Communication Quarterly*, 83, 247–64.

Heeter, C. (1989). Implications of new interactive technologies for conceptualizing communication. In J. L. Salvaggio & J. Bryant (ed.), *Media Use in the Information Age: Emerging Patterns of Adoption and Consumer Use* (pp. 217–35). Hillsdale, NJ: Lawrence Erlbaum.

Herring, S., Job-Sluder, K., Scheckler, R., & Barab, S. (2002). Searching for safety online: Managing "trolling" in a feminist forum. *The Information Society*, 18, 371–84.

Hill, D. T., & Sen, K. (2000). The Internet in Indonesia's new democracy. In P. Ferdinand (ed.), *The Internet, Democracy And Democratization* (pp. 119–136). London: Frank Cass Publishers.

Hill, K. A., & Hughes, J. E. (1998). *Cyberpolitics: Citizen Activism in the Age of the Internet*. Lanham, MD: Rowman & Littlefield.

Jankowski, N., & van Os, R. (2004). Internet-based political discourse: A case study of electronic democracy in Hoogeveen. In P. M. Shane (ed.), *Democracy Online: The Prospects for Political Renewal through the Internet* (pp. 181–93). New York: Routledge.

Jankowski, N., & van Selm, M. (2000). The promise and practice of public debate in cyberspace. In K. T. Hacker & J. van Dijk (ed.), *Digital Democracy: Issues of Theory and Practice* (pp. 149–65). Thousand Oaks, CA: Sage.

Jensen, J. L. (2003a). Public spheres on the Internet: Anarchic or government-sponsored – A comparison. *Scandinavian Political Studies*, 26, 349–74.

Jensen, J. L. (2003b). Virtual democratic dialogue? Bringing together citizens and politicians. *Information Polity*, 8, 29–47.

Jensen, J. L. (2006). The Minnesota e-democracy project: Mobilising the mobilised? In S. Oates, D. Owen, & R. K. Gibson (eds.), *The Internet and Politics: Citizens, Voters and Activists* (pp. 39–58). London: Routledge.

Johnson, T. J., Kaye, B. K., Bichard, S. L., & Wong, W. J. (2007). Every blog has its day: Politically-interested Internet users' perceptions of blog credibility. *Journal of Computer-Medicated Communication*, 13. http://jcmc.indiana.edu/vol13/issue1/johnson.html.

Kaye, B. K., & Johnson, T. J. (2002). Online and in the know: Uses and gratifications of the web for political information. *Journal of Broadcasting and Electronic Media*, 46, 54–71.

Kelly, J., Fisher, D., & Smith, M. (2005). Debate, division, and diversity: Political discourse networks in Usenet newsgroups. Paper presented at the Stanford Online Deliberation Conference, Stanford University, Palo Alto, California.

Krippendorff, K. (2004). *Content Analysis: An Introduction to its Methodology*. New York: Sage.

Kulikova, S. V., & Perlmutter, D. D. (2007). Blogging down the dictator? The Kyrgyz revolution and Samizdat websites. *International Communication Gazette*, 69, 29–50.

Matei, S. (2004). The impact of state-level social capital on the emergence of virtual communities. *Journal of Broadcasting & Electronic Media*, 48, 23–41.

McKenna, K. Y. A., & Bargh, J. A. (1998). Coming out in the age of the Internet: Identity "demarginalization" through virtual group participation. *Journal of Personality and Social Psychology*, 75, 681–94.

McMillan, S. J., & Hwang, J. S. (2002). Measures of perceived interactivity: An exploration of the role of direction of communication, user control, and time in shaping perceptions of interactivity. *Journal of Advertising*, 31, 29–43.

Min, S. (2007). Online vs. face-to-face deliberation: Effects on civic engagements. *Journal of Computer-Medicated Communication*, 12. http://jcmc.indiana.edu/vol12/issue4/.

Neuendorf, K. A. (2002). *The Content Analysis Guidebook*. Thousand Oaks, CA: Sage.

Norris, P. (2002). The bridging and bonding role of online communities. *Press/Politics*, 7, 3–13.

Norris, P., & Jones, D. (1998). Virtual democracy. *Harvard International Journal of Press/Politics*, 3, 1–4.

Noveck, B. S. (2004). Unchat: democratic solution for a wired world. In P. M. Shane (ed.), *Democracy Online: The Prospects for Political Renewal through the Internet* (pp. 21–34). New York: Routledge.

Papacharissi, Z., & Rubin, A. M. (2000). Predictors of Internet use. *Journal of Broadcasting & Electronic Media*, 44, 175–96.

Parks, M. R., & Floyd, K. (1996). Making friends in cyberspace. *Journal of Computer-Mediated Communication*, 1. http://jcmc.indiana.edu/vol1/issue4/parks.html.

Price, V., & Cappella, J. N. (2002). Online deliberation and its influence: the electronic dialogue project in campaign 2000. *IT & Society*, 1, 303–29.

Price, V., Cappella, J. N., & Nir, L. (2002). Does disagreement contribute to more deliberative opinion? *Political Communication*, 19, 95–112.

Putnam, R. D. (2000). *Bowling Alone: The Collapse and Revival of American Community*. New York: Simon & Schuster.

Reese, S. D., Rutigliano, L., Hyun, K., & Jeong, J. (2007). Mapping the blogosphere: Professional and citizen-based media in the global news arena. *Journalism*, 8, 235–61.

Robinson, L. (2005). Debating the events of September 11th: Discursive and interactional dynamics in three online fora. *Journal of Computer-Medicated Communication*, 10, http://jcmc.indiana.edu/vol10/issue4/robinson.html.

Savicki, V., Lingenfelter, D., & Kelley, M. (1996). Gender language style and group composition in Internet discussion groups. *Journal of Computer-Mediated Communication*, 2. http://jcmc.huji.ac.il/vol2/issue3/savicki.html.

Schneider, S. M. (1996). Creating a democratic public sphere through political discussion: A case study of abortion conversation on the Internet. *Social Science Computer Review*, 14, 373–93.

Shah, D. V., Kwak, N., & Holbert, R. L. (2001). "Connecting" and "disconnecting" with civic life: Patterns of Internet use and the production of social capital. *Political Communication*, 18, 141–62.

Stanley, J. W., Weare, C., & Musso, J. (2004). Participation, deliberative democracy, and the Internet: Lessons from a National Forum on Commercial Vehicle Safety. In P. M. Shane (ed.), *Democracy Online: The Prospects for Political Renewal through the Internet* (pp. 167–79). New York: Routledge.

Stromer-Galley, J. (2000). On-line interaction and why candidates avoid it. *Journal of Communication*, 50, 111–32.

Stromer-Galley, J. (2002a). Diversity and political conversations on the Internet: Users' perspectives. *Journal of Computer-Mediated Communication*, 8. http://jcmc.indiana.edu/vol8/issue3/stromergalley.html.

Stromer-Galley, J. (2002b). Motives for political talk online: Implications for political conversations and deliberation. Paper presented at the National Communication Association Annual Convention, New Orleans, LA.

Stromer-Galley, J. (2002c). New voices in the public sphere: A comparative analysis of interpersonal and online political talk. *Javnost/The Public*, 9, 23–42.

Stromer-Galley, J. (2002d). *New Voices in the Public Sphere: Political Conversation in the Age of the Internet*. Doctoral dissertation. Annenberg School for Communication, University of Pennsylvania, Philadelphia.

Stromer-Galley, J. (2004). Interactivity-as-product and interactivity-as-process. *The Information Society*, 20, 391–4.

Stromer-Galley, J. (2007). Measuring deliberation's content: A coding scheme. *Journal of Public Deliberation*, 3. http://services.bepress.com/jpd/vol3/iss1/art12.

Stromer-Galley, J., & Baker, A. B. (2006). Joy and sorrow of interactivity on the campaign trail: Blogs in the primary campaign of Howard Dean. In A. P. Williams & J. C. Tedesco (eds.), *The Internet Election: Perspectives on the Web in Campaign 2004* (pp. 111–131). Landham, MD: Rowman & Littelfield.

Stromer-Galley, J., & Foot, K. A. (2002). Citizens' perceptions of online interactivity and implications for political campaign communication. *Journal of Computer-Mediated Communication*, 8. http://jcmc.indiana.edu/vol8/issue1/stromerandfoot.html.

Stromer-Galley, J., & Martinson, A. (2005). Conceptualizing and measuring coherence in online chat. Paper presented at the International Communication Association Annual Meeting, May, New York, NY.

Sundar, S. S., Kalyanaraman, S., & Brown, J. (2003). Explicating web site interactivity: Impression formation effects in political campaign sites. *Communication Research*, 30, 30–59.

Sunstein, C. R. (2001). *republic.com*. Princeton, NJ: Princeton University Press.

Thompson, N. (2002). Freedom to flame. Online political chat is an insult to democracy. Can it be fixed? *The Boston Globe*, p. D1.

Trammell, K. D., & Keshelashvili, A. (2005). Examining the new influencers: A self-presentation study of A-list blogs. *Journalism & Mass Communication Quarterly*, 82, 968–82.

Trenel, M. (2004). Facilitating deliberation online: What difference does it make? Paper presented at the second Deliberation Online Conference, May, Palo Alto, CA.

Tsaliki, L. (2002). Online forums and the enlargement of public space: Research findings from a European project. *Javnost/The Public*, 9, 95–112.

Verba, S., Schlozman, K. L., & Brady, H. E. (1995). *Voice and Equality: Civic Voluntarism in American Politics.* Cambridge, MA: Harvard University Press.

Vrooman, S. S. (2002). The art of invective. *New Media & Society*, 4, 51–70.

Wang, H. (1996). Flaming: More than a necessary evil for academic mailing lists. *Electronic Journal of Communication*, 6, http://p7979–shadow.cios.org.libproxy.albany.edu/journals%5CEJC%5C006%5C1%5C00612.html.

Warnick, B., Xenos, M., Endres, D., & Gastil, J. (2005). Effects of campaign-to-user and text-based interactivity in political candidate campaign web sites. *Journal of Computer-Mediated Communication*, 10. http://jcmc.indiana.edu/vol10/issue3/warnick.html.

Weger, H. J., & Aakhus, M. (2003). Arguing in Internet chat rooms: Argumentative adaptations to chat room design and some consequences for public deliberation at a distance. *Argumentation and Advocacy*, 40, 23–38.

Wellman, B., Haase, A. Q., Witte, J., & Hampton, K. (2001). Does the Internet increase, decrease, or supplement social capital? Social networks, participation, and community commitment. *American Behavioral Scientist*, 45, 437–65.

Wilhelm, A. G. (1998). Virtual sounding boards: How deliberative is on-line political discussion? *Information, Communication & Society*, 1, 313–38.

Wright, S. (2006). Design matters: The political efficacy of government-run discussion boards. In S. Oates, D. Owen, & R. K. Gibson (eds.), *The Internet and Politics: Citizens, Voters and Activists* (pp. 80–99). London: Routledge.

Wright, S., & Street, J. (2007). Democracy, deliberation and design: The case of online discussion forums. *New Media & Society*, 9, 849–69.

Wyatt, R. O., Katz, E., & Kim, J. (2000). Bridging the spheres: Political and personal conversation in public and private spaces. *Journal of Communication*, 50, 71–92.

Wynn, E., & Katz, J. E. (1997). Hyperbole over cyberspace: Self-presentation and social boundaries in Internet home pages and discourse. *The Information Society*, 13, 297–327.

9

Does the Internet Empower?
A Look at the Internet and
International Development

Deborah L. Wheeler

There is no way to compare the Arab world before or after the net, of course it has made a huge difference, especially for the younger generations. The internet is a door to the outside world. If we cannot have the chance to travel and live abroad, at least through the net people have access to get in touch with the world through chat discussions. These discussions are making people in the Arab world more open minded. (Interview with Internet café manager in Zamalek, Cairo, May 2004)

Over 1 billion people subsist on less than a dollar a day, and nearly half the world's population on less than $2 a day. Twenty-seven percent of children under age five in the developing world are malnourished, and 20 million people have died of AIDS since 1986. If the Internet has a role to play in meeting those challenges, it needs to be elaborated. At the same time, if there are limits to that role, they need to be clarified as well. (Charles Kenny, 2006, p. viii.)

This new [communications] technology greatly facilitates the acquisition and absorption of knowledge, offering developing countries unprecedented opportunities to enhance educational systems, improve policy formation and execution, and widen the range of opportunities for business and the poor. One of the greatest hardships endured by the poor, and by many others, who live in the poorest countries, is their sense of isolation. The new communication technologies promise to reduce that sense of isolation, and to open access to knowledge in ways unimaginable not long ago. (World Development Report, 1998/9, p. 9)

Left unchecked, the digital divide will increasingly add to the knowledge divide, the skill divide, the opportunity divide, the income divide, and the power divide. (Yunus, 2007, p. 193)

The quotes above provide a nutshell view of the challenges of international development and the place of the Internet within it. The Cairo Internet café manager and the World Development Report echo the optimism of the information age. Scholars and policymakers who argue that the Internet provides a path towards hope have imagined an Internet-enabled world without poverty; a world where networked communications erase social status issues like race, gender, class; a world where change makes it possible for the marginal to have a voice. These images of equality, empowerment, and mobility are all facets of the perceived positive impacts of the Internet. On the more pessimistic side of the scholarly and policy spectrum, skeptics, as represented by Kenny's and Yunus' observations above, illuminate the contextual challenges in which Internet users, and potential Internet users, are mired. The un-level playing field into which the Internet is introduced creates the possibilities of a world where the gap between rich and poor ever widens; a world where cosmopolitan elites network, sharing business, education, and cultural opportunities, while the majority of the world's citizens can't even make a phone call; a world where the global economy offers new opportunities for already developed economies, while placing further at risk those countries at the bottom of the global economic pyramid. The pessimistic narratives of the Internet and its potential contribution to international development challenge the technology's cheerleaders with realities from the global community, as explored more completely below.

Aspects of the promises and the perils of the information age are present throughout the interdisciplinary literature on the Internet and development. Moreover, practitioners from heads of state to aid workers, corporate executives to community organizers, are interpreting and shaping the global information revolution and its meanings for international development. This chapter gives an overview of the major theories and agents of Internet-led development. Several key questions are at the core of this analysis: (1) Does the Internet empower? If so, whom, what, when, where, and how? (2) What is the digital divide, and what practices seem to be the best at narrowing it? (3) Is the Internet contributing to development – e.g. "making the lives of ordinary people better" (Collier, 2007, p. 12) and "closing the hope gap" (Queen Rania, speech at Intel Computer Clubhouse Opening, Hashem al-Shemali neighborhood, Amman Jordan, November 2004).

This chapter adopts an interdisciplinary, multi-regional case-study approach to the Internet and development. In the process it draws upon theories constructed by academics and practitioners who are working to make the future one less fractured by poverty and lack of opportunity. After providing an overview of theories of Internet-led development, this chapter analyzes several projects which illustrate facets of a complex development dance, including the Leland Initiative, a multimillion dollar effort by the United States Agency for International Development (USAID) to bridge the digital divide in Africa; Kiva, a global micro-financing scheme to channel individually contributed development dollars to people at the grassroots; and the Cisco Least Developed Countries Initiative, which aims to use global training through the Cisco Networking Academies to empower youth for the global economy. These projects were selected in order to illustrate global partnerships for development. The Leland Initiative illustrates a project constructed and implemented by one of the world's largest international aid organizations. Kiva represents the role of non-governmental organizations (NGOs), both global and local, in using micro-finance to alleviate poverty. This organization especially demonstrates the phenomenal power of the Internet to foster people-to-people networks leveraged to promote the global good. The Cisco Least Developed Countries Initiative represents the private sector and public–private partnerships at work trying to leverage the knowledge economy into creating economic growth.

The ultimate conclusion of this analysis is that the Internet can be a tool for "creating an enabling environment for [some] people to enjoy long, healthy and creative lives." (UNDP, 1999, p. 1). The process through which this happens and for whom (and how many) is not automatic, nor transparent. Without the right context, agency, access, imagination, and bit of luck, poverty and lack of opportunity persist. One should also not be misled into thinking that empowerment means closing the gap between rich and poor, which, as indicators illustrate, continues to widen. As the United Nations Development Program (UNDP) observes, "the new rules of globalization – and the players writing them – focus on integrating global markets, neglecting the needs of people that markets cannot meet. The process is concentrating power and marginalizing the poor, both countries and people" (UNDP, 1999, p. 30). Nobel Peace Prize-winner Muhammad Yunus, banker to the poor, translates these inequalities into numbers when he observes that globalization has concentrated wealth in the hands of the few to the degree that "94 percent of world income goes to 40 percent of the people, while the other 60 percent must live on only 6 percent of world income" (Yunus, 2007, p. 3). Can the Internet help to craft a more equitable world? Ultimately, it is this question which those who practice Internet studies and development need to answer. This chapter seeks to provide at least an initial response.

Theories of Information Technology (IT) for Development – a Cross-Disciplinary Global Narrative

At least since the first critical reflections on the meaning of the invention of fire, thinkers have attempted to interpret the impact of new technologies on society. The community of scholars trying to make sense out of the Internet are thus preceded and superseded by a long chain of thoughts on the ways in which our tools shape our lives, and our lives shape our tools. This chapter limits itself to a concern with the meaning and implication of the Internet for international development. When first conceived as a tool for global change, the most common shorthand for the Internet and development was "global information infrastructure" (GII). The ideas behind this GII and its implications for the world community were presented by Vice President Albert Gore in 1994 at the International Telecommunications Union (ITU) meeting on international development in Brazil:

we now have at hand the technological breakthroughs and economic means to bring all the communities of the world together. We now can at last create a planetary information network that transmits messages and images with the speed of light from the largest city to the smallest village on every continent.

I am very proud to have the opportunity to address the first development conference of the ITU because the President of the United States and I believe that an essential prerequisite to sustainable development, for all members of the human family, is the creation of this network of networks . . .

. . . From these connections we will derive robust and sustainable economic progress, strong democracies, better solutions to global and local environmental challenges, improved health care, and – ultimately – a greater sense of shared stewardship of our small planet . . .

. . . The GII will not only be a metaphor for a functioning democracy, it will in fact promote the functioning of democracy by greatly enhancing the participation of citizens in decision-making. (Gore, 1994, pp. 1–2)

These bold promises were what drew me to the study of the Internet's global diffusion and impact. As a scholar of the politics of the developing world, and the Middle Eastern and North African portions of it in particular, I was curious to see if Gore's techno-deterministic outlook would prove prophetic. I had a sense that as Landes observed, "If we learn anything from the history of economic development, it is that culture makes all the difference" (Landes, 1999, p. 48). Put another way, "every society achieves a pattern to its politics, technology and culture" (Jordan, 1999, p. 2). Especially Gore's promise of Athenian-style democracy taking root worldwide, delivered and nurtured by global Internet connections, peaked my curiosity. Would authoritarian states, many of whom defend themselves with secret police and proactive ministries of information, wither away, only to be replaced by civically engaged citizens, armed with new media tools, defining their own visions of politics and empowerment? If given the freedom to decide on their own forms of accountable government, would Middle Easterners choose Athenian-style democracy? If the Internet diffused relatively evenly throughout the world (a big "if"), would the technology create sustainable livelihoods for the marginalized? For the past 10 years these questions have been my focus (Wheeler, 1998, 2000, 2001, 2002, 2003, 2004, 2005, 2008).

Optimistic theories of the Internet and development assume that changing the way we communicate has the potential to change the way we live, politically, economically, and socially. Al Gore's speech outlines an approach to these three types of development. He tells us that in political terms the Internet will spread democracy, and it will make cooperation between nations more likely. In terms of economic development, Gore tells us that the Internet will be a key element in promoting growth in both national and international economies. Socially, Gore explains that the network of networks will enable us to connect as a "human family" which will breed an enhanced sense of shared stewardship for our small planet, and for each other. Each of these three promises forms a litmus test for the Internet and development, as explored more completely below.

Politics of Internet and development

As a political scientist, the alpha and omega of my interest in the Internet as a tool for development is the following question, "does the Internet alter individual or institutional agency, and if so, how does this opportunity shape the power relations of any given context?" Typically, political scientists focus upon the state and its relationship with society, and studies of the Internet by political scientists are no exception. For example, Andrew Chadwick in his book *Internet Politics* observes, "The overriding question driving my account is this: is the Internet, by reconfiguring the relations between states and between citizens and states, causing fundamental shifts in patterns of governance?" (Chadwick, 2006, p. 1.) Chadwick also argues that in Western political contexts, "the Internet is now more heavily politicized than at any time in its short history" (Chadwick, p. 2). In the developing world, where the technology was slower to diffuse, and where most regimes police Internet traffic for signs of opposition, the main focus of studies on the Internet and political development "is on issues to effect democratic transition or secure rights and freedoms" for citizens (Abbott, 2001, p. 101).

Questions about whether or not the Internet will enhance individual agency or the powers of the state are particularly relevant in the developing world, since in most of these societies, political activism is stunted by the coercive capacities of the authoritarian state. Moreover, development specialists have stressed that economic growth is not likely without good governance. Thus scholars of the Internet and development in the global south have often focused upon the impact of the Internet on the politics of participation and inclusiveness, as well as upon issues of transparency and the rule of law. If good governance can be encouraged, then the likelihood of economic growth is also enhanced. The key question remains, "What role will the Internet play in this process?"

The United Nations Economic and Social Commission for Asia and the Pacific defines "good governance" as "participatory, consensus oriented, accountable, transparent, responsive, effective and efficient, equitable and inclusive and follows the rule of law" (UNESCAP, n.d., p. 1).

Providing a linkage between good governance and development, Paula Dobriansky, then US Undersecretary of State for Global Affairs, observed in 2003 that:

> Practicing these principles of good and just governance results in a free and open society where people can pursue their hopes and dreams. This will facilitate the creation of robust and open economies, which are trusted by investors and financial institutions. (Dobriansky, 2003, p. 1)

Scholars and practitioners who study the Middle East have seen the Internet as a tool for promoting good governance and thus contributing to the development process. For example, Augustus Richard Norton observes that new media channels in Egypt mean "that growing civic pluralism in the Muslim world will result increasingly in organized demands for equitable treatment by the government"

(Norton, 1999, p. 27). Similarly, Marlyn Tadros claims, "the Internet has shifted power to access and present information from governments to people, which has given rise to hope, and fuel to the claim, that it is indeed a possible democratizing force" (Tadros, 2005, p. 175). In Saudi Arabia, according to Mamun Fandy,

> New technologies and new means of communication have provided opposition groups as well as the state with an intermediate space and a new means of disseminating information in a "virtual space" beyond their limited conceptual and physical spaces. But more for the opposition than for the state, the Internet and other media, such as fax machines, cellular phones, satellite dishes, and cassette tapes, provide a new space for airing grievances with minimal risk. (Fandy, 1999, p. 127)

In my own work on the Internet and political development in the Arab world, I have written about how the technology is enabling a new culture of discursive openness and an unprecedented degree of global engagement, at the same time that institutional arrangements in the Arab world have allowed relatively few opportunities for free and open political participation and expression. For example, in a study of 250 Internet café users in Cairo and Amman, I found the following illustrations of Internet users taking advantage of the potential democratizing capabilities of the Internet: engaging a global cyber-public in political debate; building networks of influence and opportunity beyond one's structural position (defined by nation, tribe, religion, class, gender); becoming accustomed to having opinions and wanting to share their ideas publicly; growing accustomed to exercising agency to create change in their circumstances; and openly challenging social norms online and offline, especially those which govern gender relations. All of these forms of experimentation illustrate ways in which the Internet precipitates civic engagement (Wheeler, 2006, 2007, 2008b). But the question remains, will the state be forced (or encouraged) to retreat? Or will it lash out, violently and repressively, to maintain the status quo? As Norton observes, "the post-independence Muslim state has proven remarkably durable and resistant to reform" (Norton, p. 21). I characterize this situation of Internet-emboldened public expression, continued state recalcitrance, and enhanced repression as "information without revolution."

A handful of scholars have asked about how the Internet will affect citizens' political life in East Asia (Huang, 1999; Abbott, 2001; Harwit & Clark, 2001; Hill, 2002; Lim, 2003; Hundley et al., 2003). For example, Merlyna Lim, writing about the development and impact of the Internet in Indonesia, observes,

> The ability of the Internet to facilitate communication and distribution of information has caused many to identify it as the "new technology of democracy" – as the principal means to enable the expansion of a newly emerging public sphere of political discourse and decision-making actively involving civil society. Yet despite the utopian perspectives on the impact of the Internet upon global society, the Internet, as a technology originating in the US but now existing all over the world is always localized. Its democratic potential is thus indeterminate and must be worked out in the context of local constellations of power. (Lim, 2003, p. 113)

Several scholars have offered more contextualized views of the political development potential of the Internet in Asia. David T. Hill, also writing on Indonesia, explains that the Internet "is proving [to be] a new medium for separatist and minority ethnic groups within the archipelago seeking self-determination or international recognition for their aspirations" (Hill, p. 26). Throughout his study, Hill shows how the Internet provides individuals "new strategic possibilities" and "how these new technological possibilities could exert international political leverage" (Hill, p. 26). Writing on the impact of the Internet in China, Xiguang Li, Qin Xuan and Randolph Kluver illustrate how the use of chat rooms "increases the ability of Chinese to bypass the traditional mechanisms of news selection on the part of the authorities, thus increasing their ability to think politically outside the parameters endorsed by the state" (Li, Xuan, & Kluver, 2003, p. 143). While these new capabilities awarded to IT-savvy citizens are important, studies have shown how the Internet is also an effective tool for surveillance (Lyon, p. 67). Prominent arrests of Chinese and Burmese dissidents for online opposition, for example, remind development specialists and local citizens that the Internet is open to multiple levels of empowerment, including strengthening the hand of the authoritarian state.

Claire Mercer's work is representative of a collective of scholars interested in political development and the Internet in Africa (Hundley et al., 2003; Mercer, 2004; Ibahrine, 2005; Muiruri, 2007; Wilson, 2007). Mercer examines the gap between the international development community's expectations for Internet-enabled democratic change and realities on the ground in Tanzania. She observes, "The international development community has recently focused attention on the potential role of ICTs [information and communication technologies] in promoting democratic development" (Mercer, 2004, p. 49). Aid specialists base their claims on the view that "ICTs will strengthen civil society by giving voice to the poor and marginalized, widening popular participation, and encouraging information-sharing and alliance-building" (Mercer, 2004, p. 49). Using case studies of NGO use of the Internet in Dar es Salaam and Arusha, however, Mercer claims that donor expectations for a democratic ICT effect are "likely to result in a case of misplaced optimism" (Mercer, 2004, p. 49). Her case studies reveal that ICT use by NGOs in Tanzania "has simply widened the gap between Tanzania's elite urbane NGO sector which engages in the debates of international development discourse, and the majority of small rural NGOs . . . which do not" (Mercer, 2004, p. 62). She notes, "this seems a somewhat ironic outcome, given the rhetoric of inclusivity and participation currently associated with ICTs" (Mercer, 2004, p. 62).

There are important parallels between Mercer's study of Internet-led development in Africa, and Lim's study of Indonesia. Lim argues that the Internet in Indonesia has undoubtedly "contributed a new space enabling the rise of civil society" (Lim, 2003, p. 125). But, talk is one thing, and action is another. Thus Lim probes further: "will these cyber-communities help create the civil institutions that constitute a more democratic political reality in Indonesia? Will resistance identities emerging from these spaces become identity projects that lead Indonesia towards democratization?" (p. 125.) Her article ends with these questions, saying that an affirmative answer will require future evidence that cyber-activism actually "contributes to the . . . material and social support for a better future of the country" and its population (p. 126).

One of the few texts to provide comprehensive global perspectives on the relationships between the Internet and political development in authoritarian contexts is the work of Shanthi Kalathil and Taylor C. Boas (2003; see also Kedzie, 1997; Franda 2002). In their book *Open Networks, Closed Regimes*, Kalathil and Boas challenge the assumed link between the Internet and political development towards democracy. They challenge the notion that "ending authoritarian rule is simply a matter of wiring enough people" (Kalathil & Boas, 2003, p. 150). Instead, Kalathil and Boas argue that "the Internet is only a set of connections between computers" and as such, "it can have no impact apart from its use by human beings" (Kalathil & Boas, 2003, p. 2). Moreover, "assertions about the technology's political effects are usually made without consideration of the full national context in which the Internet operates in any given country. Hence, they fail to weigh politically challenging uses of the Internet against those that might reinforce authoritarian rule" (Kalathil & Boas, 2003, p. 2).

As the examples above illustrate, from East Asia to West Asia, and across Africa, the development community's expectations for an Internet-enabled democratic effect must be contextualized and balanced by the power relationships and institutions of any given context. Both power arrangements and institutions can act as a powerful buffer to technologically enhanced agency. Moreover, as the discussion of economic development below suggests, countries in Asia have shown that economic growth is possible without democratization. Especially Middle Eastern states have found this possibility encouraging. The governments of both Jordan and Egypt have looked to Asia, especially China and Singapore, for models of economic growth which do not require democratization. But, one of the key reasons for a more inclusive definition of development beyond just economic growth is that well-being is not about eliminating poverty alone. This is because human development and "the elimination of global poverty can never truly take place until the poor take their rightful place as fully empowered citizens of free societies" (Yunus, p. 199). Moreover, there is still convincing evidence that economic growth and human development are most common in democracies. According to one observer, "the proof is in the numbers: 42 of the 49 high human development countries on the UN Development Index are democracies. With just two exceptions, all of the world's richest countries have the world's most democratic regimes" (Dobriansky, 2003, p. 1). Regardless of whether or not the Internet helps to build democracy and economic growth worldwide, most scholars agree that the Internet "is expanding access to politically relevant information and offering citizens new possibilities for political learning and action world wide" (Bimber, 1998, p. 133).

Economics of Internet and development

In 1998 President Bill Clinton observed that "democracies are the outgrowth of democratic freedom and the creation of a middle class," and that "without the free flow of information, democracies simply cannot be built" (quoted in Kapstein & Marten, 1998, p. 8). We have seen in the section above how in the developing world, Internet access and freer flows of information do not necessarily build democracy. But what about the middle-class part of the argument? Will the Internet facilitate the economic empowerment of citizens in the developing world thus creating the conditions for their more active participation in political development? It has become common to talk of the twenty-first century as a time of "information revolution" and surely those living through this time, especially those living in advanced knowledge economies, have been fundamentally transformed. What is less well understood, according to Muhammad Yunus, "is the enormous potential of the new IT for transforming the status of the poorest people in the world" where Internet access is relatively new (Yunus, 2007, 187).

The narratives on the Internet and economic development are divided into two main camps, one optimistic and the other pessimistic. IT-led economic growth from the optimistic perspective is best characterized by the Okinawa consensus.

> The Okinawa consensus . . . can be summarized as follows: the Internet and related technologies present a significant opportunity for developing countries to improve their growth prospects. Indeed, the Internet may be a leapfrog technology – one that creates an opportunity for developing countries to catch up economically with the industrial world. (Kenny, 2006, p. 5)

Stated another way, from the optimist's perspective,

> The twenty-first century can be a century of shared prosperity . . . The global economy can be marked by a narrowing of the income gap between rich and poor countries, not because of a decline in incomes in the richer societies but because of a rapid catch-up by the poor. Shared prosperity would not only mean the end of massive and unnecessary suffering among those who are now trapped in extreme poverty but would also mean a safer and more democratic world as well. (Sachs, 2008, p. 205)

In this way, the Internet is said to speed processes of development because "leapfrogging" made possible by the technology "helps developing countries accelerate their pace of development or skip stages of development" (Singh, 1999, p. 17).

From the pessimists' point of view, the information revolution creates another layer of marginalization for the poor economies of the world. Muhammad Yunus summarizes the main points of this perspective when he observes,

With the emergence of new economic forces driven by IT and their ever-increasing strength in the world economy, nations that were small, weak, and poor under the old dispensation will be further marginalized, making it even more difficult for them to compete. Under this scenario, IT will make the current rush towards uncontrolled globalization even stronger and more unstoppable. Global corporations will dictate terms to the weak economies, which will have no choice but to submit. Their role in the new information-driven economy – if any – will be to provide the most menial services and the cheapest, least-differentiated products, while the lion's share of the economic rewards will go to their better-educated, richer, more advanced, and more powerful counterparts to the north. (Yunus, 2007, p. 188)

While Yunus above maps how IT can exacerbate uneven development in the global community, he does not end his argument on a sour note. Instead, he argues that "when IT enters a poor economy, it creates wider choices and new relationships, replacing the traditional uni-directional relationship between rich and poor with a set of multi-dimensional and global relationships in which the poor have an equal footing" (Yunus, 2007, p. 190). We must keep in mind, however, that an equally convincing body of literature highlights that "although a steady stream of optimists see ubiquitous communications as the salvation of rural and remote areas, the growth of new [communications] technologies does not automatically result in the decentralization of economic activity" (Malecki, 2002, p. 419). The case study of the Kiva organization as profiled below illustrates how economic empowerment of the poor can happen when social networking and micro-financing diffuse capital where it is needed most.

Social theories of the Internet and development

A more "comprehensive" definition of development has brought into focus political as well as social capabilities within society as development indicators. For example, the World Bank "has argued for widening our [development] goals beyond the traditional macroeconomic objectives, such as national income, fiscal health, and stability in the balance of payments, to encompass 'societal development' including basic human rights, access to a legal system, literacy, and good health" (Basu, 2001, p. 65). What role might the Internet play in social development?

Scholars who study the social impact of the Internet have noted that "through email, listservs, and news groups, the Internet is seen to have created a network of activists" (Johnston & Laxer, 2003, p. 52). These networks represent "a shift from traditional politics centered on political parties and states, to movement politics focused on global networks opposing [for example] transnational corporate power" (Johnston & Laxer, 2003, p. 59). Some of the key issues upon which these Internet-supported social movements are based include "democracy, popular sovereignty, control over natural resources, human rights, and the environment" (Johnston & Laxer, 2003, p. 62). The Internet has also been seen as a tool that "facilitates civil society activities by offering new possibilities for citizen participation" (Yang, 2003, p. 406). But as Guobin Yang observes, "technology is used by members of society; its diffusion and use depend on social conditions. The conditions of society, in other words, shape technological development" (Yang, 2003, p. 405). Recognizing that social givens shape the diffusion and meaning of Internet use, a handful of scholars have studied the impact of culture and context on social development and the Internet. For example, Yang has looked at the Internet and civil society in China (Yang, 2003). Wheeler has examined the impact of the Internet on gender relationships, youths, and civil society in the Arab world (Wheeler, 2001, 2005, 2006, 2008a, 2008b). Several scholars have examined the ways in which culture and structural conditions in Africa shape the meaning and use of the Internet (Mercer, 2004; Powell, 2001; Wilson & Wong, 2007).

The most comprehensive social theory of the Internet was developed by Manuel Castells, who observes that the Internet creates "a new social form, the network society" (Castells, 2001, p. 275). Castells' idea of the rise of the network society has significance for the study of the Internet and development because as Castells observes, "the ability or inability of societies to master technology" (in this case, information technology) "largely shapes their destiny, to the point where we could say that while technology *per se* does not determine historical evolution and social change, technology (or the lack of it) embodies the capacity of societies to transform themselves" (Castells, 2000, p. 7).

The global rise of the network society has been uneven. Those countries and communities that are slow to transition to this new "network-based social structure" that is characterized by a "highly dynamic open system susceptible to innovating, without threatening its balance" (Castells, 2000, p. 502) are said to be caught in the digital divide. The digital divide is defined by "inequalities in access to the Internet, extent of use, knowledge of search strategies, quality of technical connections and social support, ability to evaluate the quality of information, and diversity of uses" (DiMaggio, Hargittai, Newman, & Robinson, 2001, p. 310). These technological capabilities are fundamental to participation in the new network society. As well, as explored above, "the actual social uses of ICTs are to a large extent guided by the political-institutional arrangements within which they are embedded" (Hamelink, 2000, p. 27). Perhaps the key role of political institutions in shaping the diffusion, use, and impact of the Internet explains why democratic societies are among the first to benefit from new information technologies and countries like Myanmar, for example, are among the last. Capital also influences access to and use of new technologies. Thus in 1999, the UNDP observed that "the network society is creating parallel communication systems: one for those with income, education and – literally – connections, giving plentiful information at low cost and high speed; the other for those without connections, blocked by high barriers of time, cost, and uncertainty and dependent on outdated information" (UNDP, 1999, p. 63, quoted in Hamelink, 2000, p. 81). While as Hamelink explains "when new technologies are introduced in societies the chances to benefit from them are always unequally distributed," scholars and policymakers are concerned to respond to evidence that the rise of the global network society is resulting in a situation where "the global gap between haves and have-nots, between know and know-nots, is widening" (UNDP, 1999, p. 57). Three examples of projects to bridge the digital divide and to more equitably share the promises and opportunities of the information age are examined below.

IT and Development in Practice

Bridging the digital divide: the Leland Initiative and wiring Africa

Jeffrey Sachs argues that there are eight ways in which information technology can contribute to sustainable development: "connectivity, division of labor, scale, replication, accountability, matching, building communities of interest, and education" (Sachs, 2008, p. 225). Before these IT-enabled processes of sustainable development can take place, an IT infrastructure must exist. Sachs observes that in Africa, "the difficulties of geography, fiscal distress, and governance come together to create the epicenter of the world's development challenge" (Sachs, 2008, p. 225). Africa is also the least wired continent in the global community. Understanding these development challenges and the role of IT in ameliorating or exacerbating them, the World Bank in 1995 argued that "the information revolution offers Africa a dramatic opportunity to leapfrog into the future, breaking out of decades of stagnation or decline." But, "Africa must seize this opportunity quickly. If African countries cannot take advantage of the information revolution and surf this great wave of technological change, they may be crushed by it" (World Bank, 1995, quoted in Royce, 2001, p. 1). The Leland Initiative was among the first comprehensive development projects to build IT infrastructure in Africa as a step towards sustainable development. The following case study explores what the Leland Initiative is, and how it used the Internet to create sustainable development in Africa.

The Leland Initiative, also known as the African Global Information Infrastructure Gateway Project, was created in 1996 by USAID to honor Congressman Mickey Leland who died in 1989 in a plane crash while working on famine relief in Ethiopia (USAID, "Leland Initiative: End of Project Report" 2001, p. 3). The project budget was 15 million dollars, and it was designed to provide full Internet connectivity and training to 20 African nations,[1] over a five-year period (USAID, "Leland Initiative End-User Applications," p. 1).

In order to build an IT infrastructure in Africa, the Leland Initiative worked to "encourage states to adopt Internet enabling policies in exchange for assistance in the form of equipment and training" (Wilson & Wong, 2007, p. 166). The main goal of the Leland Initiative was to introduce "cost-based tariff structures to stimulate private sector competition, the introduction or enhancement of full national Internet connectivity through the provision of requisite technologies, and the achievement of broad-based utilization of the Internet and other ICTs for sustainable development" (Wilson & Wong, 2007, p. 166). In terms of the motivations behind the project, Ed Royce, Chairman of the Africa Subcommittee of the US House of Representatives, testified that "the concern is that without IT tools, Africa will be unable to expand, or even maintain, its already very low level of engagement with the world marketplace. Africa also risks forgoing the advantages IT brings to confronting educational, health, governance and other challenges" (Royce, 2001, p. 1).

The Leland Initiative operated on the basis of three broad strategic objectives:

1 To create an "enabling policy environment in project countries to facilitate elec-tronic networking and access to global information infrastructure technologies."
2 To "strengthen local telecommunications infrastructure to facilitate Internet access and support a local ISP [Internet service provider] industry."
3 To "achieve broad-based utilization of information and global information technologies among USAID's development partners to promote sustainable development." (USAID, "Leland Initiative: End of Project Report," 2001, p. 3)

In Africa in 1995, only 1000 Internet users outside of South Africa existed, and only 6 out of 53 African nations had access to the Internet (including South Africa, Namibia, Ghana, Uganda, and Zambia). Moreover, Internet access cost about $80 a month for five hours of service in 1995 (USAID, "Leland Initiative: End of Project Report," 2001, p. 2). By 1998, the number of African countries connected to the Internet rose to 47. The Leland Initiative played a significant role in bring-ing African nations online and in reducing the costs of IT services by introduc-ing market-based competition in the ISP realm, which meant more people in Africa could afford Internet access (Burmeister, 1998, p. 1).

The first step of the Leland Initiative's effort to foster sustainable development via IT diffusion is an individual country assessment and plan of action. The assess-ments address three main issues: "national and regional policies and regulations concerning telecommunications and information access and use, the present con-dition of the national telecommunications infrastructure, and the current condi-tion of and potential demand for Internet access in the public and private sectors" (USAID, "Leland Initiative End-User Applications," p. 1).

The second step is to identify potential partners for implementing USAID's IT diffusion and use projects. In addition, analyses of the "barriers to Internet access and effective use" are constructed (USAID, "Leland Initiative End-User Applications," p. 2). The barriers identified by the Leland Initiative include in-effective national telecommunications policies, low-quality telecommunications service, lack of computer technology, lack of adequately trained IT professionals, lack of a competitive ISP market, and costly ISP services, lack of public aware-ness and demand for the Internet, and lack of training on strategic uses of the Internet (USAID, "Leland Initiative End-User Applications," p. 2). The Memorandum of Understanding signed between the participant country and USAID represents an agreement between the two parties to build an IT infrastructure, reform information policy environments, and train locals to implement, maintain, and diffuse IT access and knowledge throughout the host society. The desired end result is an increase in public demand for IT, a more equitably distributed network of access to IT, and a heightened awareness of the ways in which the government and the public can use the technology to promote sustainable development. At the root of this project is the view that:

> The Internet is emerging as a low cost pathway that allows information to be more accessible, transferable and manageable; ready access to information is becoming the catalyst that transforms economic and social structures around the world and supports fast-paced sustainable development. (USAID, "Leland Initiative: Africa GII Gateway Project – Project Description and Frequently Asked Questions," pp. 1–2)

According to Wilson and Wong, the Leland Initiative achieved its greatest success in Mali, and limited success in Benin, Guinea, Guinea-Bissau, Cote d'Ivoire, Eritrea, Ghana, Kenya, Lesotho, Madagascar, Malawi, Mozambique, Rwanda, Senegal, and Uganda. The Leland Initiative was not successful in Gambia, Mauritania, Nigeria, and Swaziland, because these countries refused to participate in the initiative's "conditional assistance" (Wilson & Wong, 2007, pp. 167–8). Lane Smith, manager of the Leland Initiative, explains how these conditions for participation work:

> We were only willing to help those countries that wanted to adopt modern, Internet "friendly" policies. We offered to help them reach out to the private sector to implement these policies, and we offered to provide them with the equipment necessary to establish their national Internet infrastructure, and the training on how to use it. We noted that we would not help those who insisted on doing business the old-fashioned, state monopoly way. (Smith, quoted in Wilson & Wong, 2007, p. 167)

USAID's Leland Initiative highlights the following projects as evidence of the Internet's contribution to sustainable development in Africa:

USAID Community Learning Center Program

> Leland Initiative sponsored Ghanaian Community Learning Centers (CLCs) provide public access to the wealth of information on the Internet. Each CLC will be equipped with a local area network of multimedia personal computers and shared high-speed access to the Internet. In addition to Internet access, each CLC will contain a library of supporting print materials. A training room will allow the CLC to conduct classes for the public to improve computer literacy and awareness of resources available through the Internet. Skilled support staff will be available to help visitors learn to use the Internet effectively. CLC's will be operated on a cost-recovery basis by local NGOs and will employ local staff. (USAID, "Innovative Programs Utilizing Information Technology: Case Studies," p. 1)

USAID Decentralization Project-ARDnet   USAID Leland Initiative sponsored Africa Regional Dialogue in Decentralization Network (ARDnet) promotes a

> sustainable network of decision makers and stakeholders in decentralization in West Africa. The first four member states, Benin, Cote d'Ivorie, Guinea, and Mali have agreed to: establish national mechanisms for dialogue to support a decentralization reform process, assure responsiveness to citizens needs in local electoral procedures, improve resource mobilization by increasing public participation in such processes, elect municipal teams to better respond to citizen needs. (USAID, "Innovative Programs Utilizing Information Technology: Case Studies," p. 2)

USAID Global Trade Network Program   USAID Leland Initiative funded Global Trade Network (USGTN) assists "African and US business communities in finding current business opportunities in Africa and facilitating trade and investment between the US and Africa" (USAID, "Innovative Programs Utilizing Information Technology: Case Studies," p. 2).

Lane Smith provides a retrospective on the lessons learned from it. First of all, he estimates that the Leland Initiative is responsible for providing Internet access to at least 2 million Africans. Moreover, it built Internet gateways and national connections to the web for 10 African countries. Through the Leland Initiative, USAID provided 16 additional countries Internet access via universities, parliaments, and private sector groups (Smith, 2003, pp. 12f). According to Smith, the main impact of the Leland Initiative is a "more vibrant [IT] market, better [IT] access and lower prices" (Smith, 2003, p. 13). Moreover, as a result of the Leland Initiative "private companies have invested capital, established businesses, built infrastructure, and aggressively pursued new business opportunities" (Smith, 2003, p. 13). In terms of sustainable development, we see the Leland Initiative's contribution when a furniture-maker in Guinea uses his new Internet access provided by the initiative "to keep up with the latest woodworking technology" (Inter@ctive Week, 1999, p. 42). Similarly, Internet connectivity in Madagascar "transformed the business climate" in that producers of "vanilla and coffee" can now trade "with companies world wide" thus cutting out middle men and increasing their profits (Inter@ctive Week, 1999, p. 42).

Micro-finance: Kiva leverages the people-to-people power of the net

In Jordan when I was working as an international consultant for the UNDP in Amman, repeatedly the problem of aspiring (but poor) entrepreneurs was not lack of imagination or initiative, but rather lack of access to capital for investment in growing their business ideas. Micro-finance changes all of this by providing the missing link in many people's quest to exit the poverty trap. While loans provided via micro-credit are not large enough for buying real estate, for example, they are key to global economic development among the poor. This is because small loans are provided without the need for collateral, and repayment plans are manageable so that a borrower can start a business, grow a business, and support themselves and their families at the same time that they pay back their loans with interest. Micro-finance has gained global attention, especially after 2006, the year in which Muhammad Yunus won the Nobel Peace Prize for his Grameen Bank, a micro-finance company established in the 1980s to provide loans to Bangladesh's poor.

One micro-finance initiative in particular is leveraging notably the full power of the Internet to promote development worldwide. Kiva is a non-profit micro-finance company founded in 2005 by Matthew and Jessica Flannery, a husband and wife team, both with degrees from Stanford University. Kiva means "unity" or "agreement" in Swahili, and Kiva is uniting poor entrepreneurs in the global south with charitable individuals in the global north. The Internet provides the link, allowing those wanting loans to ask for funds directly from a global community of donors who individually contribute $25 loans, which when pooled to meet an entrepreneur's loan request, add up to significant opportunities for empowerment for the poor. Kiva partners with "field partners," local micro-finance companies in the developing world who "charge borrowers interest, take responsibility for identifying responsible entrepreneurs, disbursing the loan, collecting repayments and giving lenders periodic updates on how the business is going" (Duffy, 2007, p. 33). On Kiva's website, potential donors can screen poor business men and women seeking loans and learn more about local field partners. For example, a recent scan of loan requests made on the Kiva website by poor Lebanese entrepreneurs revealed the following:

> Khaled Amhaz is a 32-year-old male businessman who owns a mobile phone store. He has had five loans from Kiva, all of which he has paid back in full. He uses the loans to buy new merchandise and to sustain and develop his business. (www.kiva.org)

> Khalil Sharkaoui is a 31-year-old businessman who lives and works in Tyre, Lebanon. He sells and fixes mobile phones. He has two loans from Kiva one of which he has paid back in full. He uses the loans to buy merchandise and to sustain and develop his business. (www.kiva.org)

> Issam is a 48-year-old man who lives with his family in South Lebanon in Tyre. He has three children and owns an Internet café. He is asking for a loan from Kiva to buy more computers. Issam started with one computer and is always striving to develop his business, which is in high demand in the area. This will be his first loan with Kiva. (www.kiva.org)

> Zenab al-Abedallah is a 20-year-old woman living in Beirut. She is paying her university tuition with revenue from her DVD rental and sales business. She requested a loan from Kiva with which to purchase new movies and to sustain and develop her business. (www.kiva.org)

A link on the Kiva website illustrates who has contributed to fund each of these entrepreneurs. In Issam's case, funding has come from Australia, across the US, the UK, France, Denmark, and Canada. In Zenab's case, donors come from Canada, across the US, and Singapore.

Although loan increments are small ($25 for individuals wishing to donate), collectively, a global community meets all demands eventually. In fact, in September of 2007, the website had to announce that "due to a recent surge in support ignited by viewers of the Oprah Winfrey Show, the Today Show, and readers of President Clinton's newly released book *Giving*, there is currently a shortage of businesses in need of loans" (Duffy, 2007, p. 33). It takes on average less than a day for each loan posted on the site to be funded (*Sunday Telegraph*, 2008, p. 2). Moreover, Kiva has a less than 1 percent default rate on its loans (*Sunday Telegraph*, 2008, p. 2).

What makes Kiva special is that "with a few clicks you can help someone on the other side of the world and play a part in solving the problems of global inequality which so often seem insurmountable" (Walker, 2008, p. 22). Another observer states that "with a few clicks of the mouse, most everyone can become a microfinancer" (Narang, 2006, p. 84). The World Bank estimates that only one in three working-age people in the developing world who need access to credit actually get it (Brown, 2007, p. 1). Organizations like Kiva attempt to solve this roadblock to economic development for the world's poor and underfinanced. The most transformative aspect of Kiva is that "it personalizes aid" by "allowing an individual in the West to choose who they will help in the developing world via its website" (Brown, 2007, p. 1). Kiva also solves one of the biggest challenges of development – giving someone fish fills their belly for a day; teaching someone to fish means their full belly will be sustainable. One observer notes that with Kiva aid, "what they are being offered is a loan rather than a handout. Simply giving aid assumes people in the developing world are helpless and robs them of their self-respect. A loan is a business arrangement – borrowers are trusted to pay it back. It helps people to help themselves" (Brown, 2007, p. 1).

In the first two years of operation, Kiva "enabled 90,000 people to lend nearly $10,000,000 to 15,000 entrepreneurs across the developing world" (Brown, 2007, p. 1). By 2008, Kiva had distributed 22 million dollars across 40 countries (O'Brian, 2008, p. 18). Kiva success stories include the following:

> A brick manufacturer in Kenya used a $150 loan to rent a brick press which allowed him to double his production over night, and greatly increase his profit. The growth of his business also enabled him to hire 5 additional staff members. (Brown, 2007, p. 1)

> Abdul Satar in Kabul owned a bakery. He used a Kiva loan to open a second bakery and to add 4 employees to run the new business. Now Abdul Satar "benefits from economies of scale when he buys flour and firewood for his oven." He says that over the next 10 years he plans to have 6 or more bakeries. (Kristof, 2007, p. 19)

Abdul Saboor runs a small TV repair shop in Afghanistan. He used a Kiva loan to "open a second shop, employing two people and to increase his inventory of spare parts." He notes that he used to "go to the market every day to buy parts." The Kiva loan allowed him to reduce the two and a half hour daily trip to the market to once every two weeks, saving him significant money and time. (Kristof, 2007, p. 19)

Jeffrey Sachs prescribes eight steps we can take as individuals to build "a world of peace and sustainable development" (Sachs, 2008, p. 336). Number five on the list is to "promote sustainable development through social networking sites, which deploy the most popular and advanced tools of the Internet for the spread and support of social activism" (Sachs, 2008, p. 338). This is the Kiva spirit, blending social networking and micro-finance strategies to solve poverty one person-to-person network at a time. Kiva epitomizes the ways in which the Internet "boosts our capacity for effective global cooperation" making us, in Al Gore's words, more clearly "members of the human family" (Sachs, 2008, p. 307; Gore, 1994, p. 1).

Least Developed Countries Initiative

Cisco Network Academies

The Least Developed Countries Initiative was launched in July 2000 at the G-8 Summit meeting in Okinawa, Japan. The initiative partners include Cisco Systems, the world's leading Internet networking company, the UN, and USAID. The goal of the project is to set up Cisco Networking Academies in the UNDP-designated 49 least developed countries (LDCs), in order to "train students for the Internet economy" (Park, 2001, p. 61). Students who enroll in a Cisco Networking Academy program receive "a comprehensive 560 hour course designed to provide students with conceptual and practical skills that will enable them to design, build and maintain computer networks" (Park, 2001, p. 61).[2] At the end of the course, students take the Cisco Certified Networking Associate examination (Park, 2001 p. 61).

In the first year of operation, the Least Developed Countries Initiative succeeded in setting up training academies in more than half of the LDCs, and trained a total of 1,100 students, of which 22 percent were women (Park, 2001 p. 61). By June of 2004, after four years of operation, 10,000 Cisco Networking Academies existed in 149 countries (Selinger, 2004, p. 224). Programs were established beyond LDCs, but tended to be placed in countries suffering from "poverty, as well as from weak human resources and economic institutions" (Park, 2001 p. 61). By 2004, these 10,000 academies had an enrollment of nearly 300,000 students. Moreover, by 2004, "more than 123,000 students had graduated from the program" (Selinger, 2004 p. 224). By 2007, the number of students trained in Cisco Networking Academies rose to 2 million (GCR, 2007, p. 3).

One of the goals of the Least Developed Countries Initiative is to bridge the gendered nature of the digital divide. This is achieved by "proactively promoting greater participation of women in information technology through the Net-working Academies," specifically by designing special courses for women only (Park, 2001, p. 62). Other gender-sensitive strategies include reduced tuition for women students and recruiting female instructors (Park, 2001 p. 62). In 2005, University of Maryland's IRIS Center completed an impact assessment of Cisco Networking Academy's Gender Initiative in Bangladesh (IRIS, 2005, p. 1). The findings of this study in a nutshell were that "the program has made great inroads in offering quality information technology education. Yet there remain significant challenges facing women as IT professionals in Bangladesh, and many of these are the result of deep-rooted cultural attitudes and a broad expanse of societal problems that exist beyond the scope of the program" (IRIS, 2005, p. i). One of the most pressing concerns with regard to this program is that many gradu-ates of Cisco Networking Academies in Bangladesh, both male and female, "express difficulty with finding a job upon graduation" (IRIS, 2005, p. 6). This phenomenon led IRIS analysts to recommend the establishment of a job place-ment organization that can link recent graduates with businesses and organiza-tions seeking employees. This organization could offer recent graduates assistance with searching for a job, enhance their skills at interviewing, and help them with their résumé (IRIS, 2005, p. 10).

In terms of best practices, the IRIS study highlights the following success stories.

Rubaiyat Koli provided private tutoring in her home to raise enough money to attend the Cisco Networking Academy. After graduating and passing the certification exams, she got a job with Bangladesh's largest telecommunications company, Grameen Phone (IRIS, 2005, p. 11).

Rawnak Anjuman received a partial scholarship to attend the Cisco Networking Academy. After completing the program and gaining her certificate, Rawnak was hired by the Ministry of Science and ICT to work on a program entitled "Establishment of Technology Dissemination Cell." The program was designed to "bring the Ministry under full network coverage and establish e-governance" in this and other ministries (IRIS, 2005, p. 12).

In June 2007, GCR Custom Research conducted an impact assessment on the Cisco Least Developed Countries Initiative in Africa. As of 2007, 40,000 students were trained in academies throughout the continent (GCR, 2007, p. 5). Of those trained, 30 percent of them were female (GCR, 2007, p. 5). The study found that "The Cisco Networking Academy is having a strong positive impact on indi-viduals, communities and economies across" Africa (GCR, 2007, p. 19). One of the recommendations of this study is to provide increased "assistance with gaining employment" (GCR, 2007, p. 20). This observation resonates with the experiences of Bangladeshis participating in the program. At the same time, the GRC study found that nearly two thirds of students surveyed had found employ-ment (GRC, 2007, p. 21). Most of the students who are employed after gradu-ation hold positions in the IT field, illustrating a clear link between training and employability in the IT field (GCR, 2007, p. 30). Of those graduates finding jobs, two thirds of them go to work in the private sector (GCR, 2007, p. 33).

The public–private partnership represented by the Cisco Networking Academy project illustrates "how businesses, international organizations and governments can work together to contribute to the advancement of the world's underserved communities" (USAID, 2008, p. 1). Collectively, the Cisco Networking Academies worldwide have "positively transformed lives and communities, giving people the skills necessary to find employment and make a better life for themselves and their families in the world's least developed countries" (GCR, 2007, p. 5). In general, students who graduate from a Cisco Networking Academy contribute to sustainable development by raising the knowledge level and job skills of their communities (GCR, 2007, p. 45).

Conclusions – The Persistence of Development Challenges, in Spite of Web Diffusion

As this chapter draws to a close, headline news provides a disturbing picture of the inequalities and development challenges which characterize our global community, many of which are seemingly beyond human control. The Chinese province of Sichuan is reeling from strong aftershocks following a massive earthquake, which has killed nearly 70,000 and left 5 million people homeless. Twenty-three thousand people are still missing (Barboza, 2008, pp. A5, A7). Cyclone Nargis has killed at least 134,000 people, while the Myanmar government is resisting international aid because of conditions imposed by donors wanting direct access to hardest hit areas. (*New York Times*, 2008, p. 1A). Food riots have broken out across Bangladesh, beginning what locals call "the Rice Revolution" (Wax, 2008, pp. A1, A14). In Egypt, bread riots are an increasingly common feature, as rising commodity prices have led to "a growing crisis over primary foodstuffs" (Knickmeyer, 2008, p. A1). Egypt's economy is increasingly characterized by "rising prices, depressed salaries" and "an unprecedented gap between rich and the poor" (Slackman, 2008, p. A6). The same rise in prices that is leading to bread and rice riots in Egypt and Bangladesh is producing record waves of growth across the developing world. For example, Ghana, a country rich in gold and cocoa, has "joined a long list of developing countries in Africa and beyond enjoying record periods of growth" (Faiola, 2008, p. 1).

In terms of IT and development, headline news paints a positive picture. For example, the USAID Last Mile Initiative has provided Internet access, computer training, and improved job skills for the rural inhabitants of the Gorongosa District of Mozambique. In the words of Jose Nhamitambo, one of the computer-station users, having computer and Internet access is "very important." With access, "I write documents, I go on the Internet, I write to people who live far from here. Everyone is excited about the computers" (Hanes, 2008, p. 14). Similarly encouraging is the role that IT is playing in the Egyptian public's demand for increasing government accountability. In Egypt, public protests are increasingly enabled "by technology, especially cell phones, [which] are used to spread the word" (Slackman, 2008, p. A6). In April 2008, a workers' strike spread through-out the country by word of mouth and mobile phone. People took to the streets and "mass messages circulated, listing 'demands' that included increased security, no more inflation, housing aid for young couples and an end to torture in police stations" (Slackman, 2008, p. A6).

This chapter began with a question, "can the Internet help to create a more equitable world?" The snapshot provided above of the state of our world suggests that some development challenges are too big for the Internet. When people need food, safe drinking-water, medicine, and shelter, Internet connectivity does little to provide for these basic necessities except for potentially ending one of the root causes of extreme poverty, namely, "isolation" (Brown, 2000, quoted in Kenny 2006, p. 4). The three case studies analyzed above, the Leland Initiative, the Kiva movement, and the Cisco Least Developed Countries Initiative, all illustrate that Internet connectivity can empower some people and communities. The success stories provided show that while it is important not to "oversell the web" at the same time, one must not underestimate its potential either (Kenny, 2006).

Notes

1 For a list of participating African countries see www.usaid.gov/leland/countries.htm.
2 According to Michelle Selinger, of Cisco Systems, UK office, the training course is only 280 hours.

References

Abbott, J. P. (2001). Democracy@internet.asia? The challenges to the emancipatory potential of the net: Lessons from China and Malaysia. *Third World Quarterly*, 22(1), 99–114.

Barboza, D. (2008). China pleads for aid to help millions made homeless by earthquake. *New York Times*, May 26, pp. A5, A7.

Basu, K. (2001). On the goals of development. In G. M. Meier & J. E. Stiglitz (eds.), *Frontiers of Development Economics: The Future in Perspective* (pp. 61–86). Oxford: Oxford University Press.

Bimber, B. (1998). The Internet and political transformation: Populism, community, and the accelerated pluralism. *Polity*, 31(1), 133–160.

Brown, G. (2007). Micro-finance gives developing world a chance to ease poverty. *The Business*, September, 8, p. 1.

Burmeister, T. (1998). Internet arrives in Africa, Deutsche Presse-Agentur, November 13, p. 1.

Castells, M. (2000). *The Rise of the Network Society*, vol. 1, *The Information Age: Economy Society and Culture* (2nd edn.). Oxford: Blackwell.

Castells, M. (2001). *The Internet Galaxy: Reflections on the Internet, Business and Society*. Oxford: Oxford University Press.

Chen, W., Boase, J., & Wellman, B. (2002). The global villagers: Comparing Internet users and uses around the world. In B. Wellman & C. Haythornthwaite (eds.), *The Internet and Everyday Life* (pp. 74–113). Oxford: Blackwell.

Collier, P. (2007). *The Bottom Billion: Why the Poorest Countries Are Failing and What Can Be Done About It.* Oxford: Oxford University Press.

De Sola Pool, I. (1998). *Politics in Wired Nations: Selected Writings of Ithiel de Sola Pool,* ed. L. S. Etheredge. New York: Transaction Books.

Duffy, M. (2007). Harnessing the power of the net to support third world businesses. *Sydney Morning Herald,* September 29, p. 33.

Faiola, A. (2008). As global wealth spreads, the IMF recedes. *Washington Post,* May 24, pp. A1, A15.

Fandy, M. (1999). Cyber resistance: Saudi opposition between globalization and localization. *Comparative Studies in Society and History,* 41(1), 124–47.

Franda, M. (2002). *Launching into Cyberspace: Internet Development and Politics in Five World Regions.* Boulder: Lynne Rienner Press.

GCR (2007). *Africa Least Developed Countries Initiative Independent Impact Assessment: Final Report,* June. Washington, DC: USAID.

Hamelink, C. J. (2000). *The Ethics of Cyberspace.* London: Sage.

Hanes, S. (2008). African park bridges the "last mile" of the digital divide. *Christian Science Monitor,* May 22, pp. 15–16.

Harwit, E., & Clark, D. (2001). Shaping the Internet in China: Evolution of political control over network infrastructure and content. *Asian Survey,* 41(3), 377–408.

Henkin, J. (2007). *Matrimony.* New York: Pantheon.

Hill, D. T. (2002). East Timor and the Internet: Global political leverage in/on Indonesia. *Indonesia,* 73, 25–51.

Huang, E. (1999). Flying freely but in the cage: An empirical study of using Internet for democratic development in China. *Information Technology for Development,* 8(3), 145–62.

Inkeles, A., & Smith, D. H. (1974). *Becoming Modern: Individual Change in Six Developing Countries.* Cambridge, MA: Harvard University Press.

Inter@ctive Week (1999). USAID's African initiative: Tiny program with a big kick, November 29, p. 42.

IRIS (2005). *Community Impact Assessment of Cisco Networking Academy Program's Gender Initiative in Bangladesh.* College Park: University Research Corporation.

Johnston, J., & Laxer, G. (2003). Solidarity in the age of globalization: Lessons from the anti-MAI and Zapatista struggles. *Theory and Society,* 32(1), 39–91.

Jordan, T. (1999). *Cyberpower: The Culture and Politics of Cyberspace and the Internet.* London: Routledge.

Kalathil, S., & Boas, T. (2003). *Open Networks, Closed Regimes: The Impact of the Internet on Authoritarian Rule.* Washington, DC: Carnegie Endowment for International Peace.

Kapstein, E., & Marten, T. (1998). Africa is missing out on a revolution. *International Herald Tribune,* September 24, p. 8.

Knickmeyer, E. (2008). In Egypt, upper crust gets the bread. *Washington Post,* April 5, pp. A1, A10.

Kristof, N. (2007). You, too, can be a banker to the poor. *New York Times,* March 27, p. A19.

Landes, D. (1999). *The Wealth and Poverty of Nations.* New York: W. W. Norton.

Lim, M. (2003). From real to virtual (and back again): Civil society, public sphere, and the Internet in Indonesia. In K. C. Ho, R. Kluver, & C. C. Yang (eds.), *Asia.com: Asia Encounters the Internet* (pp. 113–128). London: Routledge/Curzon.

Malecki, E. J. (2002). The economic geography of the Internet's infrastructure. In *Economic Geography* 78(4), 399–424.

Mercer, C. (2004). Engineering civil society: ICT in Tanzania. *Review of African Political Economy*, 99, 49–64.

Narang, S. (2006). Web based microfinancing. *New York Times Magazine, 6th Annual Year in Ideas*, December 10, p. 84.

New York Times (2008). Weeks after cyclone in Myanmar, survivors wait for food, May 26, pp. A1, A6.

Nissenbaum, H., & Monroe E. P. (eds.) (2004). *Academy and the Internet*. New York: Peter Lang.

Norris, P. (2001). *Digital Divide: Civic Engagement, Information Poverty, and the Internet Worldwide*. Cambridge: Cambridge University Press.

Norton, A. R. (1999). The new media, civic pluralism, and the slowly retreating state. In D. F. Eickelman & J. W. Anderson (eds.), *New Media in the Muslim World: The Emerging Public Sphere* (pp. 19–28). Bloomington: Indiana University Press.

O'Brian, J. M. (2008). The only nonprofit that matters. *Fortune*, 157(4), 17–20.

Park, K. E.-M. (2001). Central to the mission of UNDP: Networking with Cisco Systems. *UN Chronicle*, 4, 61–2.

Powell, M. (2001). Knowledge, culture and the Internet in Africa: A challenge for political economists. *Review of African Political Economy*, 28(88), 241–60.

Royce, E. (2001). Bridging the information technology divide. US House of Representatives Subcommittee on Africa Information Technology Hearing, May 16.

Sachs, J. (2008). *Common Wealth: Economics for a Crowded Planet*. New York: Penguin Press.

Selinger, M. (2004). Cultural and pedagogical implications of a global e-learning programme. *Cambridge Journal of Education*, 34(2), pp. 223–39.

Singh, J. P. (1999). *Leapfrogging Development: The Political Economy of Telecommunications Restructuring*. Albany: SUNY.

Slackman, M. (2008). In Egypt, technology helps spread discontent of workers. *New York Times*, April 7, p. A6.

Smith, L. (2003). Bringing Africa online. http://pdf.usaid.gov/pdf_docs/PCAAB300.pdf.

Sunday Telegraph (Australia) (2008). Money Matters. January 13, p. 2.

Tadros, M. (2005). Knowing the promises, facing the challenges: The role of the Internet in development and human rights campaigns and movements in the Arab Middle East. In J. Leatherman & J. A. Webber (eds.), *Charting Transnational Democracy: Beyond Global Arrogance* (pp. 173–93). New York: Palgrave MacMillan.

UNDP (1999). *Human Development Report 1999*. Oxford: Oxford University Press.

UNESCAP (n.d.) What is good governance? United Nations Economic and Social Commission for Asia and the Pacific. Retrieved April 5, 2008, from http://www.unescap.org/pdd/prs/ProjectActivities/Ongoing/gg/governance.asp.

USAID. Innovative programs utilizing information technology: Case studies. http://www.usaid.gov/leland/casestudies.htm.

USAID. Leland Initiative: Africa GII Gateway Project, project description and frequently asked questions. http://www.usaid.gov/leland/project.htm.

USAID. Leland Initiative End-User Applications. www.usaid.gov/leland/enduser.htm.

USAID (2001). *African Global Information Infrastructure Gateway Project: End of Project Report and Evaluation Summary.* Washington, DC: USAID, Academy for Educational Development.

USAID (2008). USAID, Cisco extend international development partnership. Press release, February 5, p. 1. www.usaid.gov/press/releases/2008/pr080205_2.html.

Walker, R. (2008). Extra helping. *New York Times Sunday Magazine,* January 27, p. 22.

Wax, E. (2008). Food costs push Bangladesh to brink of unrest. *Washington Post,* May 24, pp. A1, A14.

Wheeler, D. (1998). Global culture or culture clash? New communications technologies and the Islamic world – a view from Kuwait. *Communication Research* 25(4), 359–76.

Wheeler, D. (2000). New media, globalization and Kuwaiti national identity. *Middle East Journal,* Summer, 432–44.

Wheeler, D. (2001). New technologies, old culture: A look at women, gender and the Internet in Kuwait. In C. Ess & Fay S. (eds.), *Culture, Technology, Communication: Towards an Intercultural Global Village* (pp. 187–212). New York: SUNY.

Wheeler, D. (2002). Islam, community and the Internet: New possibilities in the digital age. *Berglund Center for Internet Studies Journal,* March. http://bcis.pacificu.edu/journal/2002/03/islam.php.

Wheeler, D. (2003). Building and information society for international development: A look at the Egyptian experiment. *Review of African Political Economy,* December 2003.

Wheeler, D. (2004). Blessings and curses: Women and the Internet revolution in the Arab world. In N. Sakr (ed.), *Women and the Media in the Middle East* (pp. 138–161). London: IB Taurus.

Wheeler, D. (2005). *The Internet in the Middle East: Global Expectations, Local Imaginations in Kuwait.* Albany: State University of New York.

Wheeler, D. (2006). Empowering publics: Information technology and democratization in the Arab world: Lessons from Internet cafes and beyond. OII Research Report No. 11. www.oii.ox.ac.uk/research/publications/RR11.pdf.

Wheeler, D. (2007). Digital governance and democratization in the Arab world. *Encyclopedia of Digital Governance.* Hershey: IGI Global.

Wheeler, D. (2008a). Empowerment zones? Women, Internet cafés and life transformations in Egypt. *Information Technologies and International Development.* http://itidjournal.org/itid/article/viewArticle/257.

Wheeler, D. (2008b). Working around the state: Internet use and political identity in the Arab world. In A. Chadwick & P. N. Howard (eds.), *Handbook of Internet Politics.* London: Routledge.

Wilson, E. J. III, & Kelvin, R. W. (2007). *Negotiating the Net in Africa: The Politics of Internet Diffusion.* Boulder: Lynne Rienner Press.

World Bank. *World Development Report 1998/99.* Oxford: Oxford University Press.

Yang, G. (2003). The co-evolution of the Internet and civil society in China. *Asian Survey,* 43(3), 405–22.

10

Internet and Health Communication

Lorna Heaton

With the popularity of the Internet, more and more people are turning to their computers for health information, advice, support, and services. This chapter provides an analysis of the changes in healthcare communication resulting from the Internet revolution. It provides a variety of examples, including information about health websites and portals, online patient communities, Internet pharmacies, and web-enabled hospitals.

The chapter's general structure is from the most simple uses to the more complex, from information retrieval and use, through situations where information is exchanged, either between patients and physicians or in patient online communities. Health interventions using the Internet are next. These consultations, promotion programs, and clinical applications involve actual medical treatment. Since the more complex health-related uses of the Internet rely heavily on infrastructure, we conclude with a discussion of computerized physician order entry (CPOE) and electronic health records. Each section concludes with a discussion of issues, implications, and challenges. Throughout, we have maintained a focus on how the Internet is affecting health *communication*. Economic, technical, and regulatory aspects of changes in healthcare are addressed only secondarily.

Information

Online health information

Perhaps the most widely felt impact of the Internet on communication in healthcare is in the widespread availability of, and interest for, health information on the web. A 2005 Harris Interactive poll of 1000 Americans suggested that approximately 75 percent of US adults have gone online to look for health or medical information. What is more, the frequency of searching is impressive: almost 60 percent reported that they had looked "often"(25 percent) or "sometimes"(33 percent), whereas the percentage saying that they rarely searched for health information fell to 14 percent, down from 24 percent the previous year. Some 85 percent of those who had looked for health information had done so in the previous month. On average, respondents reported searching for health information seven times a month (up from three times per month in 2001). A large majority (89 percent) were successful in their searches, and nine out of ten believed that the health information they found online was reliable (37 percent very reliable and 53 percent somewhat reliable).

The World Wide Web offers an environment that provides free access to a global repository of information on a large variety of topics. It has become easy to search for and consult information on health or lifestyle matters. Widespread availability of information may ultimately lead to better quality healthcare, since decisions can be based on a larger pool of evidence. This rise of the Internet health consumer[1] has the potential to increase awareness of the variety of medical choices available. This may result in a number of changes in the healthcare relationship, with well-informed patients potentially more active participants in managing or directing their care. This shift is not automatic, however. It takes work to become an informed patient. For example, in assessing web-based health information, users must be able to conduct a search and find the "right" sites. They must also be able to judge the quality of information provided and synthesize that information into a useful form for their particular purpose.

By far the most studied aspect of health information on the Internet has been the problem of how to determine and guarantee its quality. Fears that Internet health information is inaccurate, unreliable, biased, unsanctioned, and unrefereed are widespread. Obviously this is an important issue, since faulty health information can have disastrous consequences. Based on a thematic review of a random sampling of 200 abstracts in the area of Internet and consumer health information, Powell, Lowe, Griffiths, and Thorogood (2005) identified what they term as an obsession with the quality of health information on the Internet. Over 80 percent of the articles reviewed described evaluations of the quality of information consumers might find in an Internet search. Despite this concern, Powell and colleagues found that most of the studies were small and failed to address shortcomings that had been identified in an earlier review, concluding that, at most, the studies demonstrate that the quality of information available online is variable and that health professionals are concerned about the results of misinformation.

Are these concerns justified? There is, as yet, limited literature on why health consumers go online, what they actually look for, or how they use the information they find. It is extremely difficult to associate health outcomes with consumer use of the Internet for health information.

A counterpoint to the literature about the questionable reliability of health-related websites is the problem of too much information. The sheer volume of information may represent a significant obstacle to health consumers. How can lay people sift through, digest, interpret, and evaluate the significance or relevance of the health information they find?

Clearly, as the Internet grows in popularity, so does the need for evaluating information quality and appropriateness. A number of initiatives and approaches have developed to help health consumers find accurate and relevant information on reliable sites. Increasingly, consumers are offered access to sites that propose pre-selected information as well as guidelines for patients to use in checking the characteristics of the information they find (author, date, sources, site sponsorship, etc.) Health consumers can use government-provided links or portals, click on pre-approved seals of approval or trustmarks provided by non-profit or non-governmental organizations, follow checklists created by professionals or health educators, and download special toolbars, all of which will help them find and evaluate information on the web.

Many governments support portals of carefully selected and freely available consumer health information. For example, the US Department of Health and Human Services provides a portal with contact information for organizations (www.healthfinder.gov) and the National Library of Medicine provides a portal with health content from the National Institute of Health (www.medlineplus.gov). Outside the US, the United Kingdom's National Library for Health (NLH) and its associated web-based programs offer a mix of freely available and password-protected subscription access to a wide range of information sources. In Canada, the Public Health Agency offers a good public service that does not reproduce already existing health information but provides links to more than 12, 000 web-based resources that have been rigorously evaluated for quality. Similarly, within Europe the focus has been on networks and on managing access and quality rather than creating content. The Catalog and Index of French Language Health Internet Resources (CISMeF) project in France describes and indexes the principal French-language health resources, while the primary website for health information in Germany is Medizin-Forum AG. Finally, this type of pre-selection and filtering initiative is not limited to national governments. The Health on the Net Foundation (HON), an independent foundation based in Switzerland, provides medical information, while the World Health Organization (WHO) provides an online list of recommended websites for information.

Another approach to ensuring quality and reliability of health information is third-party certification. Most popular, the quality label Health On the Net's (HON) logo graces over 3000 sites, signifying conformity with HON's eight principles: authority, complementarity, confidentiality, attribution, justifiability, transparency (authorship), transparency of sponsorship, and honesty (www.hon.ch). The Utilization Review Accreditation Program (URAC) is an increasingly popular independent third-party certifying organization. Launched in 2001, with the goal of patient empowerment and consumer education and safety, URAC's accreditation is voluntary and indicates adhesion to a series of ethical and quality standards that address several issues, including privacy protection, security, and the process used for developing content (http://www.urac.org). These approaches rely essentially on the structural characteristics of the sites they evaluate, however. They are proxy measures and address the comprehensiveness, currency, and accuracy of information contained on the sites only indirectly. The challenge of developing criteria to evaluate content is enormous, especially since health information changes rapidly.

An alternative approach is to use a user-rating tool, such as the Health Information Technology Institute Information Quality Tool developed by the Health Summit Working Group. Reviewers fill in a questionnaire based on the information they can find on a given site and submit it. A report is returned with a review of answers, a score, and information on what is missing in the site. The overall purpose is to educate health consumers. Here again, the list of criteria is a mixture of standard information quality measures, security and privacy concerns, and web content management issues, but it may do little to help consumers assess the actual medical information contained in a given site.

Finally, filtering using web technologies is an emerging approach. Search tools accept or reject entire sites based on preset criteria (i.e. they may accept only online journal articles or those from professional associations). For example, the MedCIRCLE concept uses the semantic web to evaluate a combination of quality assurance systems, strictly managed metadata or tags, and third-party ratings.

All these measures rest on assumptions that lay people cannot adequately assess the reliability of Internet health information. Adams, de Bont, and Berg (2006) is one of few empirical studies to examine how lay people actually assess the value of health-related information they find on the web. The authors found that, while patients did not utilize special user tools (checklists, seals, portals) to assist in searching for and evaluating information, they did develop explicit strategies for checking information within their established patterns of searching, such as on- and offline triangulation of information and checking the information provider and dates. More research of this type is required to develop a better idea of how patients assess information and then how these assessments influence subsequent actions.

It is extremely difficult to try to apply a regulatory approach to authorizing sites that deliver health information, and this problem will only grow as the web develops. As filtering technologies become more sophisticated, they may offer a way to filter out either substandard medical information or sites that do not meet quality standards. In addition, it is vital that users be able to apply their own quality standards.

Health information for professionals

Just as patients look up information on the Internet, health professionals are also accessing Internet information to support healthcare in various ways. Most recent surveys suggest that the percentage of clinicians and other health professionals using the Internet is increasing steadily. The American Medical Association's 2002 study on "Physician Use of the World Wide Web" reported that 78 percent of physicians went online in their practice and that more than two thirds of this group used the web daily. According to the study, about half felt that the Internet has had a major impact on the way they practice medicine.

A 2004 update of the study reported that most physicians "believe it is important for patient care."

For the most part, it appears that the Internet tends to be used as an additional
resource to complement or to replace libraries and other formal, printed sources
of information. A 2002 study from Harris Interactive (2003) revealed that
increasing numbers of physicians are using the Internet to research clinical information (90 percent compared to 19 percent in 2001) and to search for medical
journal articles (74 percent). Online databases, combined with instruments such
as BlackBerries and PDAs, enable easy access to timely information, best practices,
and decision chains. The trend to evidence-based medicine is strongly supported
by Internet technologies.

Some national government also provide portals for their health professionals,
linking to major resources such as the National Library of Medicine's PubMed
site or the UK National Health Service's Bandolier. In the US, for example, the
PubMed website (www.ncbi.nih.gov) currently attracts over 30 million searchers
per month. Highly specialized databases give practicing physicians easy access to
information that was previously too difficult to follow consistently, given its specificity.
For instance, the National Library maintains a database of trials of alternative
and complementary medicines. Similarly, the UK's National Cancer Research
Institute hosts an international information exchange for cancer research. Finally,
the Online Database of Unknown Clinical Cases provides an environment for
collecting knowledge about rare pathologies that are difficult to classify and potentially life-threatening.

The problem with online databases is the work and resources required to
maintain their currency. Given the volume and rapidly changing nature of health
information, only major international and collaborative initiatives can reasonably
target sustainability.

Exchange

Online support for patients

The Internet is not just a repository of information. It has also given rise to new
forms of interaction and new groupings, or communities, that can bring together
people across geographical space and time in all spheres of life. In the field of
health, patient advocacy sites and online social support, such as that found in chat
rooms and discussion lists, have been established by major research groups, foundations, and voluntary patient-driven groups. Such sites typically target chronic
conditions, critical illness, or caregivers. They usually offer a mix of informational
support (information, advice, feedback), tangible support (direct forms of aid),
and social and emotional support. They vary widely in size, from less than a hundred participants to tens of thousands.

One such mega community, the Association of Cancer Online Resources (ACOR,
www.acor.org) has thousands of active participants and hundreds of thousands of

registered but silent readers. The heart of ACOR is a large collection of cancer-related Internet mailing lists, which deliver over 1.5 million email messages weekly to subscribers across the globe. In addition to supporting the mailing lists, ACOR develops and hosts Internet-based knowledge systems that allow the public to find and use credible information relevant to their illness. ACOR also hosts several Wikis and a blog. As it notes on its website, "ACOR is also invested in researching medical online communities and has helped to produce some of the most important and groundbreaking projects designed to understand how the Internet helps people to become informed patients, able to maximize the quality of medical care they receive." In this, they are at the forefront of using the participatory web (or Web 2.0) in the field of health.

Research on online social support for health conditions typically falls into one of two categories: analysis of interactions in various communities or identification of reasons for using online social support. Compared with the information-use literature, this literature tends to be more qualitative in nature.

Josefsson (2005) argues that the specific driving forces and dynamics of patients' online communities (POC) differ from those in other online communities of shared interests. These communities are initiated and maintained because people's lives are changed, sometimes drastically and overnight, by illness. One of the major coping strategies of patients is to get more information, both medical and on how to manage in daily life. The goal is to acquire an in-depth understanding of the condition and also to be able to discuss it knowledgeably with the doctor. Patients and caregivers dealing with only one condition have time and energy necessary to explore and evaluate resources thoroughly. They may make important contributions to the identification and dissemination of high-quality health information for both patients and health professionals.

A central component of a POC is usually one or more online discussion spaces for synchronous (chats) or asynchronous (forums or distribution lists) exchange. Such spaces provide a communication channel for interaction between people facing the same or a similar situation. Several research studies report the benefits of such social support (Reeves, 2000; Eysenbach et al., 2004) that can complement or even replace traditional patient support groups. Participants share technical information about new treatments, discuss their experiences, and encourage each other. A considerable body of experiences is created as different patients describe how they discovered the disease, how they were diagnosed, and how they have experienced various treatments. In addition, these informative practices are accompanied by interpretive practices, when fellow patients help each other interpret what physicians and their health professionals are saying about test results, examinations, and so on. The possibility of sharing experiences creates a sense of belonging. Uncertainties and anxieties can be dealt with as they arise, not only in the doctor's office.

Participation in POCs may be more or less active, and participants may tailor their participation to support their individual needs for information and social support. "Lurking" (listening without contributing) is described as a good way of becoming informed as well as of confirming personal experience (Josefsson, 2005). Writing about health problems and formulating disclosure of personal concerns have been shown to be therapeutic in and of themselves (Wright & Bell, 2003). In addition, POCs allow patients to help others, another important coping strategy. For instance, in a study of HIV-positive individuals, Reeves (2000) found that the opportunity to help others was a central motivation for participating in online discussions and it was judged the most rewarding.

When compared with other online communities or face-to-face patient support groups, the therapeutic value of POCs is evaluated very positively by their members. POCs also demonstrate higher levels of expressed emotional support, empathy, and self-disclosure than face-to-face self-help groups. Josefsson (2005) suggests that the maintenance of behavioral norms is extremely important since participants are particularly vulnerable and the subject matter is close to them. The reduction of social-status clues brought about by being online supports anonymity, disclosure, and more heterogeneous supportive relationships.

Potential problems of POCs include concerns about privacy and the inappropriate use of information that is posted by participants. As everywhere, there is a risk of unreliable information and the difficulty of sifting through masses of information to find what is most appropriate. For example, reading about the advanced stages of a disease or all potential complications of a treatment may be devastating for an individual who has just been diagnosed and is not ready for that information.

POCs often include an extensive mixture of translated, rewritten, and combined medical information together with personal experiences and beliefs about a given disease. This collection of lay and professional information empowers e-health consumers to become producers of medical information. More importantly, this mix plays a central role in meeting patients' requirements for specific experience and knowledge about a certain condition. Finally, the possibility of influencing public opinion may be an explicit goal of some POCs. They may seek to increase awareness of some lesser-known diseases – among patients as well as in the population in general, or even lobby for governmental policy changes. The spaces may also provide a field for recruiting for clinical trials and collecting data on heredity patterns and rare diseases.

Online support for clinicians

While Internet-based information is increasingly substituted for libraries and other formal, printed sources of information, it does not replace colleagues and specialists, who remain physicians' preferred sources of information for reasons of credibility, availability, and applicability. A consulting physician can tailor his or her answer to a question so that it is concise and sufficiently complete, with explanations and process information that will allow the requesting physician to implement any suggestion with the appropriate level of confidence. Berg (2004) reports that half of information demands in clinical practice are met by colleagues rather than document sources. He also notes that about 60 percent of clinician time is devoted to talk.

The Internet is providing opportunities here, too. A 2002 Harris Interactive study reported that 63 percent of physicians were communicating with colleagues on the Internet. Email is the most obvious connection but online mailing lists and discussion forums also offer the opportunity to discuss emerging scientific issues and trends with peers, often in real time. This is a growing phenomenon in medical associations in several countries. Professionals are connected with each other so that they can share knowledge and support each other in their work.

Hara and Hew (2007) report on knowledge sharing across organizations by an online community of nurses. They detail the activities and types of knowledge shared in a large (1300 members) online listserv involving professional nurses in critical care. This decade-old community was well established. Members interviewed noted that participation enabled them to connect with other nurses (to ask questions or seek pertinent knowledge), and that the listserv was a means of compensating for isolation due to job function and geographic location. Through participating the nurses also strengthened their identity as advanced care nurses, either explicitly through discussions about nurses' roles and responsibilities, or indirectly through the sharing of their everyday practices which, taken as a whole, provides a detailed portrait of what it means to be an advanced nurse. Content analysis of the activities on the listserv revealed that knowledge sharing was most common (51 percent), followed by solicitation, i.e. asking for information or advice (33 percent). In sharp contrast with patients' online communities, emotional communication such as compliments, statements of appreciation, or empathy was minimal. The authors suggest that this type of communication was likely directed off-list through individual emails. Finally, approximately half of all knowledge shared was information on institutional practices, i.e. how do you do it where you work. Clearly, this listserv fulfills an important function in keeping the nurses involved informed of best practices in their field and in allowing them to communicate with a large number of individuals with similar experiences.

The Heart Health project is another example of an online community for health professionals. Cardiac nurses from hospitals, health centers, and heart-care institutes in three Canadian provinces came together over a six-month period to discuss problems affecting the cardiac patient population. They moved through brainstorming and knowledge sharing in discussions and eventually to the production of a co-authored document, the Heart Health Kit (Campos, 2007). The toolkit was later produced as a resource to help community groups plan and deliver heart health workshops with the support of public health nurses.

As in other spheres, Internet technologies are finding their way into the classrooms of medical students and enabling new forms of learning – through online discussions, blogs, etc. Computer technologies also enable students to practice their skills virtually, but a discussion of this aspect is beyond scope of this chapter.

To maintain certification, many health professionals must accumulate a certain number of credit hours. This ensures that they are up to date on developments in their field. The Internet has become a very popular, medium for delivering continuing professional education (CPE). The ability to transcend distance produces a larger population base and thus enables providers to offer a wider variety of subjects. Sometimes CPE courses also integrate a videoconferencing component, which can increasingly be conducted with webcams. Delivering CPE courses over the web enables professionals who have trouble attending live sessions due to time or budgetary restrictions to continue to learn. In Nunavut (northern Canada), for example, nurses can attend virtual sessions from their communities, whereas previously they had to find replacements in order to leave the community, a difficult undertaking in a context of chronic understaffing.

The changing practitioner–patient relationship

The rise of the Internet health consumer suggests a shifting of power within the healthcare relationship. An informed patient is potentially a more active participant in his or her care. This may have consequences for the physician–patient relationship. When patients arrive at a medical encounter "empowered" with information, blind trust in medical expertise may yield to "informed trust." Physicians who are more accustomed to an authoritative or expert role may have difficulty collaborating rather than directing. Informed patients may be perceived as a challenge to medical authority. While the issue of the changing nature of relationships with health professionals has been raised, there has been little empirical work on the question, however.

A Harris Interactive poll in 2005 suggested that around half (53 percent) of patients sometimes discuss information found online with their physician, while 70 percent had gone to the Internet for additional information following discussions with their doctors. Several studies of physicians' use of the Internet investigate how physicians deal with the increasing trend of patients to bring information from the Internet to a consultation. In two separate studies, one in Switzerland and the other in New Zealand, around 90 percent of physicians reported this behavior, but not from a substantial proportion of their patients in either study. Murray, Lo, Pollack, Donelan, Catania, Lee, Zapert and Turner's (2003) report of a random US survey of physicians found that, if physicians felt that the information was accurate and relevant, they judged it to be beneficial, but inaccurate or irrelevant information was felt to harm health outcomes. A substantial minority (38 percent) believed that patients bringing in information made the visit less efficient in terms of time, and some admitted to acquiescing to what, in their view, were inappropriate clinical requests by their patients either to save time or to avoid damaging the physician–patient relationship.

Despite concerns about unfiltered, unreliable information and the need to interpret and evaluate this in context, physicians generally welcome patients taking an interest in their own care and their efforts to participate and become more knowledgeable. The advantages of a well-informed patient are higher likelihood of compliance to treatment and improved health outcomes. Similarly, Rice and

Katz's (2006) review of physician–patient interaction suggests that "despite physicians' concern over web quality, and lack of confidence in their patients' ability to accurately judge and use such information, . . . the literature overwhelmingly describes the favorable impact of patient-found Internet information on doctor–patient communication" (pp. 157–8). They conclude that there is little foundation for fears of challenges to authority and that the research literature overwhelmingly indicates that patients would much rather discuss Internet information with their doctors than use it to replace them. This is borne out by Umefjord, Hamberg, Malker and Petersson (2006).

Treatment

Online medical consultations

For more than a decade, studies have consistently shown that some members of the public want access to Internet-based communication with healthcare providers, with preference estimates for online patient–provider communication ranging from 40 percent to 83 percent (Burke Beckjord et al., 2007). Surveys of the general American public in 2005 and 2006 (Harris Interactive, 2007) suggest that they would like to receive online reminders to visit their doctors (77 percent), communicate with their doctors by email (74 percent), schedule appointments online (75 percent) and receive test results by email (67 percent). Online patient–provider communication remains relatively uncommon, however. Estimates vary widely, with commercial survey estimates generally between 20 percent and 40 percent. More systematic, larger-scale studies such as the Pew Internet and American Life Project and the Health Information National Trends Survey (HINTS), which surveyed over 3000 respondents, put these figures much lower, with only 7 percent (in 2003), 10 percent (in 2005) or 11 percent (2006) of adult Internet users having communicated with their physician using the Internet (Burke Beckjord et al., 2007; Kolbasuk McGee, 2007).

Ferguson (2001) proposes a distinction between two types of physician–patient relationship in online consultations. A Type 1 relationship is one in which a patient contacts a health provider with whom he or she has no previous relationship. This type of relationship is patient-driven and may be likened to a coach–consultant relationship in which the physician typically answers questions, recommends other information sources, and offers an informal second opinion. There is typically no diagnosis, treatment, or prescription involved. In contrast, Ferguson's Type 2 relationship is one where the patient has a pre-existing clinical relationship and where the physician assumes some form of contractual responsibility for ongoing care.

Free services, supported by government agencies or charitable medical foundations, are a common model of online "Ask the Doctor" services. For example, Sweden's Karolinska Institutet, Europe's largest medical university, runs a portal listing several hundred Ask the Doctor and Second Opinion services. This extensive site has an online medical encyclopedia and covers medical topics in depth. Users' questions are answered briefly by a physician, who may direct the user to other online sources. Another model is a subscription-based site such as WebMD which offers information services, personalized advice and chat rooms in which physicians may sometimes participate. Concerns about liability and insurance costs constrain the offer and activities of this type of site. In the past, there have been online services offering treatment or prescriptions, but we could not find any at the time of writing.

There is little research on what may incite patients to seek online consultations with strangers. Umefjord and colleagues (2006) reported on a survey of over 3500 users of a Swedish Ask the Doctor service. Convenience and anonymity were reported as the major reasons for recourse to such a service, with frustration with previous doctors' visits also cited as a reason. Approximately a third of patients wanted a preliminary diagnosis of symptoms, and another third a more complete information or explanation, while lesser numbers were interested in a second opinion or alternative treatment options. Following their session, about half reported that they had found what they needed, while about a quarter said they would return to their previous physician. The appreciation of the service was generally positive and many respondents endorsed the service as a valuable complement to regular healthcare.

Despite over a decade of research and the availability of guidelines for use of Internet-based communication by healthcare providers (Kane & Sands, 1998), online patient–provider communication remains a marginal practice. Its use is increasing but at a much slower pace than Internet use in general. User satisfaction and impacts on healthcare have been generally favorable among both healthcare consumers and healthcare providers (Burke Beckjord et al., 2007). It seems likely that systemic factors and policies (for example, concerns with being paid for time spent online) rather than attitudes may be at issue here (Weiss, 2004). Increased availability and integration of electronic health records will likely affect the prevalence of online patient–provider communication, as will policies promoting the use of health information technology.

Health promotion and interventions

Increasingly, the Internet is being used as a channel for delivering health education and promotion programs as well as chronic disease management tools. Programs exist in a variety of fields such as smoking cessation, obesity and physical activity, diabetes, cardiac health, HIV/AIDS, eating disorders, and mental health. Cognitive behavior therapy is also being given over the Internet for conditions such as tinnitus, migraine, and panic disorders. A number of constants emerge across this wide variety of fields. Most programs aim to take advantage of technological features of the Internet: the ability to reach large populations, easy storage of large volumes of information, quick updating of information, and the ability to provide personalized feedback (Griffiths, Lindenmayer, Powell, Lowe, & Thorogood, 2006).

A major motivation for designing programs for delivery over the Internet involves reducing costs and increasing convenience for users – saving time, and allowing access anytime anywhere. This mode of delivery is also seen as a way of reducing costs and increasing accessibility. Limited numbers of a target group in a given area, such as rural women with chronic disease or diabetes, may make program delivery over the Internet a viable, cost-effective solution. In other cases, isolation may be the result of a lack of mobility or physical restrictions, for example care-givers who find it difficult to leave their homes, people living with HIV/AIDS, or children with cystic fibrosis.

In certain cases, the anonymity of Internet delivery can be used to advantage, for instance in cases where their condition may cause participants embarrassment or stigmatization. Griffiths et al. (2006) offer a number of examples, such as inter-ventions targeting obesity if people are feeling embarrassed about failure to lose weight, programs for young women with eating disorders, and breast cancer patients.

Many developers of health interventions on the Internet suggest that users can tailor the information they receive to meet their own needs or go through the program at their own pace. This enhances their sense of control and empower-ment. The depersonalization afforded by the Internet may make it an ideal channel for the delivery of carefully structured, step-by-step self-help programs, particularly if they are supplemented with individualized email feedback.

Despite the enormous potential and interest in Internet delivery of health education and promotion, there have been few direct comparisons between Internet and face-to-face delivery. Griffiths and colleagues (2006) call for such studies in order to evaluate possible unintended consequences, such as reduced availability of face-to-face interventions or reducing the visibility of certain groups or issues outside the anonymity of the Internet.

Telehealth

We define telehealth as the use of information and communication technologies to deliver clinical services at a distance. Increasingly, telehealth is being delivered using the Internet, often in combination with other technologies, such as videoconferencing using webcams or with mobile telephones. It may involve patient–provider consultation, including physical exams using peripheral equip-ment. There are two basic models of telehealth: real time and "store and forward." In real-time telehealth, the parties are online together. For example, a telehealth session may involve a consultation with an ophthalmologist in one location and a patient and health professional in another. The health professional manipulates an ophthalmological scope and the image it produces is transmitted to the spe-cialist, who can see inside the patient's eye and advise on diagnosis and treatment.

The term "store and forward" refers to the concept that data (such as images, video and sound clips, and other patient information) can be transmitted between computers, stored electronically, and retrieved at a later time (often at a distant location) by another health professional. If bandwidth is sufficient and both ends have compatible software, patient information can travel using an Internet protocol over standard channels. Security measures integrated in the software ensure the confidentiality of patient information. The Alaska Federal Healthcare Access Network (AFHCAN, www.afhcan.org) is a good example of store-and-forward telemedicine. Begun in 2000 to provide healthcare to 248 villages and military installations across Alaska, AFHCAN integrates web-based technologies and satellite links. Essentially, the software stores all user input in a server until a case is sent. If a system crashes, a real possibility in low- or fragile-connectivity environments, that information is still available the next time the user logs in from a different machine. Using a combination of small transmission packets and multiple retry attempts, it is even possible to send cases over satellite connectivity that is too poor to permit phone, fax, or email connections.

Telehealth also encompasses consultations between professionals and the transfer of medical data. Monitoring at a distance is also a major telehealth application. For example, patients with renal disease may be discharged from hospital on the condition that they do their own dialysis and hook themselves up to a monitor that automatically takes and transmits the appropriate data. Other monitors, such as those for patients with cardiovascular disease, may be worn continuously and automatically send data to the local hospital. Since this type of application involves less communication between persons, we will not discuss it here. Whatever the application, telehealth depends heavily on appropriate infrastructure.

Infrastructure

Computerization and the easy, secure exchange of information are at the heart of modern healthcare. There are a number of issues to be addressed, among them system interoperability, data security, and economics. Ideally, all data would be interchangeable and it would only go to those who need it; duplicate entries would be eliminated and the entire process would be streamlined, leading to better healthcare and lower costs. Although there is still a long way to go to reach this ideal, concrete steps are being taken. We will discuss two such initiatives: computerized physician order entry and the electronic health record.

Computerized physician order entry (CPOE)

Computerized physician order entry (CPOE), or e-prescribing, refers to the process of sending prescriptions directly from the physician's office to the pharmacy. Gone is the little white slip of paper with often illegible writing. CPOE systems facilitate the process of entering prescriptions into the computer. They are often linked to electronic health records (EHRs) and incorporate clinical decision support algorithms. A CPOE system will typically suggest optimal choices, often proposing generic drug equivalents, and provide alerts to potential adverse reactions, contraindications, or incorrect dosages. All of this relies heavily on infrastructure.

By proposing generic equivalents and reducing prescription errors or duplications, including prescription fraud or abuse, CPOE generates cost savings that have been estimated at $29 billion yearly in the US alone (Hopkins Tanne, 2004).

CPOE systems can also track compliance (physicians may receive alerts when their patients refill prescriptions), thus enabling better follow-up and standard of care. At another level, widespread use could make CPOEs invaluable public health tools. They could be used to monitor abnormal prescription patterns in real time – for example, increased prescriptions for upper respiratory infections, which could indicate the arrival of a strain of flu virus.

In addition to physician e-prescribing, patients are able to directly access online pharmacies. Online pharmacies may be grouped into three general categories: independent, Internet-only sites; online branches of established pharmacy chains; and sites that represent partnerships among neighborhood pharmacies. Potential benefits of online pharmacies are increased access, lower transaction and production costs, and greater anonymity. However, different standards of practice have resulted in vast differences in the quality of online pharmacies. The nature of the Internet and the difficulty of controlling e-commerce in general make online pharmacies difficult to regulate. There are concerns about the ease with which patients may obtain drugs, sometimes without valid prescription. For example, if patients do not fully disclose symptoms to a "cyberdoctor," they may expose themselves to dangerous drug interactions and/or adverse effects. The importation of prescription medicines is another area of concern. Although the importation of unapproved, misbranded, or adulterated drugs is unlawful in the US, some sites may dispense expired, sub-potent, contaminated, or counterfeit products (Fung, Woo, & Asch, 2004). Cross-border traffic is a complicated regulatory, jurisdictional, ethical, and commercial issue. In Canada, for example, there has been concern that online sales of drugs to the US, estimated at $1 billion per year, could threaten domestic supply and drive lower Canadian prices up.

Electronic health record (EHR)

Also known as digital medical records, an electronic health record is essentially a longitudinal collection of electronic health information about an individual. Data are generally entered in EHRs by different groups of healthcare professionals, although patients may sometimes enter data that is later validated. EHRs may include some or all of the following components: daily charting, medication administration, physical assessment, admission nursing note, nursing care plan, referral, present complaint (e.g. symptoms), past medical history, lifestyle, physical examination, diagnoses, tests, procedures, treatment, medication, discharge, history, diaries, problems, findings, and immunization. The extent of file sharing also varies widely, from files compiled within single departments or practices to sharing across institutions in primary, secondary, and tertiary care (Häyrinen, Saranto, & Nykänen, 2007).

The changing role of the general physician, shifting power of insurance companies, and the role of the patient are all bound up with the introduction and development of the EHR. The need for a closer link between medical (patient record) and financial (hospital bill) information is a major incentive for introducing the EHR. In addition to its obvious cost-saving advantages, several studies suggest that an EHR is conducive to more complete and accurate documentation by health-care professionals. Electronic record systems can help reduce medical error, eliminate handwritten notes, enable error-reducing technologies, increase consistency in records, and provide data for research. They also speed up transfer of information between healthcare professionals and institutions. For example, a digital x-ray can be sent from the radiology department to the physician's desktop, or test results from a clinic to the general practitioner and a consulting specialist.

The extent of actual use of EHRs varies widely according to the context of each country. In Scandinavian countries, which have a long tradition of computerization and e-health infrastructure, penetration is high. For example, in Sweden about 90 percent of patients have an EHR.

Unlike the healthcare systems of many Western countries, the US system is composed of private, independent individual and group providers, hospitals, ambulatory, and long-term care centers that compete with one another. The system is decentralized with multi-payers. This climate of competition offers few incentives for information sharing and consolidation. In the US, although 70 percent of hospitals had full or partial EHR systems, penetration of integrated records was estimated at about 4 percent in 2006.

Somewhere between these to extremes, is the UK National Health Service (NHS) Connecting for Health program. It provides an example of what the future face of healthcare may look like. Begun in 2000, Connecting for Health aims to link all 30,000 NHS professionals and 300 hospitals, creating an active EHR for each citizen, and implementing nationwide booking and electronic prescription services. The NHS Care Records Service contains two types of records: detailed records (held locally) and the summary care record (held nationally). Detailed records can be securely shared between different parts of the local NHS, such as the physician's office and the hospital. Patients will be able to access their summary care record, a summary of their important health information, using a secure website and make it available to authorized NHS staff throughout England. There is also a service for direct, secure transfer of files between physicians (GP2GP) and a PACS (Picture Archiving and Communication System) that stores images such as x-rays and scans electronically, creating a near filmless process and improved diagnostic methods. Doctors and other health professionals in any hospital in England can access and compare images at the touch of a button. England's national electronic referral service, Choose and Book, gives patients a choice of place, date, and time for their first outpatient appointment in a hospital or clinic. Patients can choose their hospital or clinic, and then book their appointment to see a specialist with a member of the practice team at the general practitioner's surgery, or at home by telephone or over the internet at a time more convenient to them. As of March 2008, Choose and Book was being used for around 50 percent of NHS referral activity, and over 85 percent of practices were participating. The system also incorporates an electronic prescription service that enables prescribers to send prescriptions to a dispenser of the patient's choice. EPS was being used for over 17 percent of daily prescription messages in 2008. All of these possibilities rest on the underlying network, N3 (National Network for the NHS), a secure broadband virtual private network (VPN). In addition to transmitting digital images, it also has a voiceover IP component that enables health professionals to talk to each other over the Internet.

Despite the explosion of EHR initiatives in the Western world starting in the 1990s, the technical, social, and organizational complexity of widespread implementation has become increasingly apparent. Most initiatives have been only marginally successful or have evaporated quickly. They have proved to be extremely costly and difficult to maintain, with important privacy and security questions. Clearly, data must be interoperable and travel over secure channels. Who should have access to the information contained in an EHR? If access extends from primary-care physician and patient to health insurance companies, boundaries between medical and financial issues may become blurred. For example, could insurance coverage be denied or premiums increased because of some information contained in an individual's health record? In a 2003 Connecting for Health (UK) survey of online users, nearly all (91 percent) were "very concerned" about privacy and health information security.

In the US, the most notable legislation relevant to EHRs is the Health Insurance Portability and Accountability Act (HIPAA), which is designed to ensure the integrity of patient information as it travels between healthcare providers, insurers, and data clearing-houses. Since 2000, HIPAA has required healthcare organizations to inform patients about how their health information is collected and used, how its security is guaranteed, and how they may access their medical records, correct errors, and control most disclosure of their information to people outside the healthcare system.

While the advantages of EHRs are increasingly recognized, the problems of integration and interdependency, not to mention lingering security questions, have led to a less ambitious, more gradual approach in the twenty-first century. The emphasis is shifting to certain elements, particularly order entry and decision support as means to reduce errors and ensure more streamlined, legible, and traceable actions.

Studies focusing on the content of EHRs are needed, especially studies of nursing documentation or patient self-documentation. The challenge for ongoing national health record projects around the world is to take into account all the different types of EHRs and the needs and requirements of different healthcare professionals and consumers in the development of EHRs.

Theoretical Approaches to Health and the Internet

Current research in the field of health communication and the Internet tends to be problem driven. When theories are evoked, they tend to focus on functions of media use. Uses and gratifications theory – how media are used and the effects they produce – has been widely applied to new communication technologies for various purposes, including health. A number of key concepts underpin this theoretical framework: communication behavior is goal-directed; individuals select and use communication channels to satisfy perceived needs; individual communication behavior is moderated by a multitude of social and psychological factors; and media compete amongst each other and with other forms of communication, such as discussion with friends and family. People's goals shape the media types they selected and their subsequent processing of media content. This approach typically emphasizes the active audience, a concept that is particularly important in considering the Internet, and increasingly the participative web (Web 2.0). Uses and gratifications theory is also used to explain why people adhere to online patient communities.

In particular, theories that seek to explain why people seek information and how they use it are well represented in research on health information on the Internet. A number of models exist, but most come back to the idea of motivation. Selective processing refers to the idea that individuals orient to specific stimuli in the environment that are consistent with existing beliefs and attitudes and avoid information that might require them to rethink or re-evaluate their frames of reference. For example, Dutta-Bergman (2004) has demonstrated that individuals who are highly engaged in health-related issues are more likely to seek out health-specialized media content than individuals who are not particularly health-conscious. Compared to traditional mass media, the interactivity of the Internet facilitates selective processing of information: a visit to a particular Internet site is likely based on the interest of that user in the information content of the site.

Motivation is also an important factor in studies about health promotion and intervention campaigns since these initiatives seek to understand engagement in health behaviors, particularly what makes people change their behavior. The heath belief model suggests that motivation is based on an individual's perception of consequences, benefits, justifiable costs, and cues to action (such as an enticing incentive or a brush with illness). Social cognitive theory views people as reasonable, rational decision-makers who make decisions based on the interplay of internal factors, such as knowledge, skills, emotions, etc., and environmental factors such as social approval, physical environment, or institutional rules. Particularly interesting for health campaigns on the Internet is the transtheoretical model, which suggests that people may not proceed directly from thinking about a problem to changing their behavior. Change typically involves five stages: pre-contemplation (not aware of the problem), contemplation, preparation (deciding to take action), action, and maintenance (Prochaska, DiClemente, & Norcross, 1992). The implication is that people may react differently to health-promotion efforts depending on the stage they are in. Therefore, information alone is not sufficient to change behavior. This theory is especially important for Internet campaigns since the medium allows for personalization. Once an individual's readiness is assessed, subsequent messages may target specifically the stage of the person receiving them.

Future Directions

The Internet provides a global repository of information of all kinds, including health information at various levels of specialization. It also offers people a way to connect with each other, minimizing distance and time constraints. Whether we use it for looking up information, for exchanging with others, for medical consultations, or for largely invisible applications such as streamlining medical records, the Internet has become an integral tool for communication in healthcare.

Special-purpose systems and dedicated health networks continue to exist but are increasingly interfaced with the larger Internet. As information infrastructures develop, this interconnection will likely intensify. In first-world countries the Internet health revolution is well underway, but it is also gaining momentum in developing nations. The Internet's ability to telescope distance makes it an invaluable aid in making health information and expertise available even in areas where physicians, nurses, and medical libraries are scarce. Future developments, particularly with secure transmission and wireless technologies, should further propel the use of the Internet in healthcare.

The human and social side of the health communication and Internet equation is developing more slowly than its technical possibilities. It takes time for people to adjust their practices to new realities and possibilities. The Internet is not likely to replace patient–provider interaction, although it may shape it in new ways as expectations evolve. Telehealth provides one more option for service delivery but is unlikely to replace most face-to-face consultations. Most interestingly, people are inventing new ways of using the Internet to advantage. Health education and promotion campaigns are now routinely using the Internet as a channel for program delivery, and are finding new ways to take advantage of its unique characteristics to personalize feedback and reach dispersed groups. Perhaps the best example of invention is the development of online, patient-driven communities that provide resources and social support on a scale that would have been unthinkable before the widespread diffusion of the Internet. In the future, we are likely to see many more initiatives of this type, as the web moves toward enabling participation and user-generated content – the famous Web 2.0, or participatory web.

Note

1 Discussions about empowering patients and the role of web-based information have led to the semantic challenge of properly naming non-medically trained individuals who search for information online. For example, the term patient does not include those persons who search for information about the health situation of a friend or family member. Throughout this article, we have tried to use the term health rather than medical, because it is more inclusive, and we have dealt with the problem of user initiative differently according to the context. For example, although "health-information consumer" has its own connotations, we have used this term when users appear primarily

to be finding and using information without transforming it. In other situations we have used the word "patient" as appropriate.

References

Adams, S., de Bont, A., & Berg, M. (2006). Looking for answers, constructing reliability: An exploration into how Dutch patients check web-based medical information. *International Journal of Medical Informatics*, 75(1), 66–72.

Burke Beckjord, E., Finney Rutten, L. J., & Squiers, L., et al. (2007). Use of the Internet to communicate with healthcare providers in the United States: Estimates from the 2003 and 2005 Health Information National Trends Surveys (HINTS). *Journal of Medical Internet Research*, 9(3), e20. Retrieved February 21, 2008, from http://www.jmir.org/2007/3/e20.

Campos, M. (2007). Communication as argumentation: The use of scaffolding tools by a networked nursing community. *Canadian Journal of Communication*, 32(3), 457–74.

Dutta-Bergman, M. (2004). Primary sources of health information: Comparison in the domain of health attitudes, health cognitions, and health behaviors. *Health Communication*, 16, 273–88.

Eysenbach, G., Powell, J., Englesakis, M., Rizo, C., & Stern, A. (2004). Health related virtual communities and electronic support groups: Systematic review of the effects of online peer to peer interactions. *British Medical Journal*, 328(7449), 1166.

Ferguson, T. (2001). Type 1 vs. type 2 provider–patient relationships. *Ferguson Report, no. 7*. Retrieved April 21, 2008, from http://www.fergusonreport.com/archives/idx007.htm.

Fox, S., & Fallows, D. (2003). Internet Health Resources. Washington, DC: Pew Internet and American Life Project. Retrieved February 21, 2008, from http://www.pewinternet.org/PPF/r/95/report_display.asp.

Fox, S. (2005). Digital Divisions. Washington, DC: Pew Internet and American Life Project. Retrieved February 21, 2008, from http://www.pewinternet.org/pdfs/PIP_Digital_Divisions_Oct_5_2005.pdf.

Fung, C., Woo, H., & Asch, S. (2004). Controversies and legal issues of prescribing and dispensing medication using the Internet. *Mayo Clinic Proceedings*, 79, 188–94.

Griffiths, F., Lindenmeyer, A., Powell, J., Lowe, P., & Thorogood, M. (2006). Why are health interventions delivered over the Internet? A systematic review of the published literature. *Journal of Medical Internet Research*, 8(2), e10. Retrieved February 21, 2008, from http://www.jmir.org/2006/2/e10.

Harris Interactive (2005). Number of "cyberchondriacs" – US adults who go online for health information – increases to 117 million. *Healthcare News*, 5(8), 1–7. Retrieved April 21, 2008, from http://www.harisinteractive.com/news/newsletters_healthcare.asp.

Harris Interactive (2003). eHealth's influence continues to grow as usage of the Internet by physicians and patients increases. *Healthcare News*, 3(6), 1–7. Retrieved April 21, 2008, from http://www.harisinteractive.com/news/newsletters_healthcare.asp.

Häyrinen, K., Saranto, K., & Nykänen, P. (2007). Definition, structure, content, use and impacts of electronic health records: A review of the research literature. *International Journal of Medical Informatics*, 76, 66–72.

Hara, N., & Hew, K. F. (2007). Knowledge-sharing in an online community of health professionals. *Information Technology and People*, 20(3), 235–61.

Hopkins Tanne, J. (2004). Electronic prescribing could save at least $29 billion. *British Medical Journal*, 328, 1145–6.

Josefsson, U. (2005). Coping with Illness online: The case of patients' online communities. *The Information Society*, 21(2), 143–53.

Kane, B., & Sands, D. Z. (1998). Guidelines for the clinical use of electronic mail with patients. The AMIA Internet Working Group, task force on guidelines for the use of clinic–patient electronic mail. *Journal of the American Medical Informatics Association*, 5(1), 104–11. Retrieved February 21, 2008, from http://www.pubmedcentral.nih.gov/articlerender.fcgi?tool=pubmed&pubmedid=9452989.

Kolbasuk McGee, M. (2007). Americans use Internet to manage their health, but most doctors are slow to use tech tools, says survey. *InformationWeek*, February 27, 2007. Retrieved February 21, 2008, from www.informationweek.com/story/showArticle.jhtml?articleID=197009125.

Murray, E., Lo, B., & Pollack, L., et al. (2003). The impact of health information on the Internet on healthcare and the physician–patient relationship: National US survey among 1,050 physicians. *Journal of Medical Internet Research*, 5(3), e17. Retrieved February 21, 2008, from http://www.jmir.org/2003/3/e17.

Murero, M., & Rice, R. E. (eds.) (2006). *The Internet and Healthcare: Theory, Research, Practice*. Mahwah, NJ: Lawrence Erlbaum.

Pew Internet and American Life Project. *Internet Activities*. Washington, DC: Pew Internet and American Life Project, June 22, 2007. Retrieved February 21, 2008, from http://www.pewinternet.org/trends/Internet_Activities_7.19.06.htm.

Powell, J. A., Lowe, P., Griffiths, F. E., & Thorogood, M. (2005). A critical analysis of the literature on the Internet and consumer health information. *Journal of Telemedicine and Telecare*, 11, suppl. 1, 41–3.

Prochaska, J. O., DiClemente, C., & Norcross, J. (1992). In search of how people change: Applications to addictive behaviors. *American Psychologist*, 47, 1102–14.

Reeves, P. (2000). Coping in cyberspace: The impact of internet use on the ability of HIV-positive individuals to deal with their illness. *Journal of Health Communication*, 5, 47–59.

Rice, R. E., & Katz., J. (eds.) (2001). *The Internet and Health Communication: Experiences and Expectations*. Thousand Oaks, CA: Sage.

Rice, R. E., & Katz., J. (2006). Internet use in physician practice and patient interaction. In M. Murero & R. Rice (eds.), *The Internet and Healthcare: Theory, Research, Practice* (pp. 149–76). Mahwah, NJ: Lawrence Erlbaum.

Umefjord, G., Hamberg, K., Malker, H., & Petersson, G. (2006). The use of an Internet-based Ask the Doctor service involving family physicians: Evaluation by a web survey. *Family Practice*, 23, 259–66.

Weiss, N. (2004). E-mail consultation: Clinical, financial, legal, and ethical implications. *Surgical Neurology*, 61(5), 455–9.

Wright, K., & Bell, S. (2003). Health-related support groups on the Internet: Linking empirical findings to social support and computer-mediated communication theory. *Journal of Health Psychology*, 8(1), 39–54.

11

Internet and Religion

Heidi Campbell

Since the 1980s, there has been a steady rise in the performance and practice of religion within online environments. Starting with the formation of religious sub-groups on Usenet and email-based religious communities, a diversity of forms of religious engagement began to emerge and catch the attention of the media and academic world. Some examples include the creation of virtual temples or churches and sites of online spiritual pilgrimage (for a detailed review see Campbell, 2006). By the mid-1990s, scholars began to take serious notice and explore the development of these unique social-spiritual practices related to the Internet, and to speculate on the potential impact of importing offline religious beliefs and practices online. In the past decade, we have seen even more innovative and novel examples of religion spring up online from "godcasting" (religious podcasting) to religious versions of popular mainstream websites, such as Godtube.com to online worship spaces in *Second Life* for Christians, Muslims, and Jews. This chapter provides a critical review of the study of religion online, emphasizing how research on religion and the Internet has become an interdisciplinary area of study. It synthesizes previous research on religion and the Internet, and highlights one particular area at the focus of my own work: online religious communities. By focusing on how the study of religious community online has developed since the 1990s, this chapter demonstrates a progressive refinement of research themes, methods, and questions related to religion online. Furthermore, the chapter suggests how future studies of religion online may need to develop.

The development of this research area can be seen in terms of maturing research questions and methods that can be framed in terms of three phases or "waves" of research. This provides a framework for understanding how religious community has been studied online in the past decade, advancing along with the further discoveries and developments in the field of Internet research. In each wave of research, the common themes and implications of these findings related to the study of religious community online are highlighted. Finally, this chapter addresses areas that have been neglected in research, and suggests issues and questions that would be fruitful for further exploration in relation to religion online.

Mapping Three Waves of Research

While a growing body of literature is accumulating around religion and Internet studies, the interdisciplinary focus within studies of religion and the Internet has meant in some respects this area remains a disparate collection of ideas and approaches. O'Leary & Brasher's (1996) article, "The Unknown God of the Internet," provided a foundational overview of how religion began to be influenced and manifested in online environments. This was followed by the landmark article, "Cyberspace as sacred space" (1996), where O'Leary, details the emergence of religion online by identifying how online rituals perform an important function, enabling users to import their religious sensibilities online. These articles marked the starting point for serious academic inquiry into religious engagement on the Internet and led to a decade of diverse research. These ranged from focused studies investigating the connections between online and offline religious practice, such as a study of prayer in a multi-user virtual reality environment by Schroeder and colleagues (1998), to large-scale studies of user behavior patterns such as those undertaken by the Pew Internet and American Life Project *Wired Churches, Wired Temples* (Larsen, 2000) and *CyberFaith* (Larsen, 2001), which provided empirical evidence about the religious use of the Internet. A decade after the publication of *Cybersociety* (Jones, 1995), that earmarked the birth of Internet studies, Baym in a special issue of *The Information Society* (2005) highlights the fact that religion online has become a valid part of the emerging field and a dimension in need of more attention (Campbell, 2005c).

Since 2000, three key edited collections on religion online have been produced which highlight the diversity of research topics and approaches related to new expressions of religious practice seen in networked computer technologies. The first edited collection was *Religion on the Internet – Research Prospects and Promise* (Cowan & Hadden, 2000), bringing together early studies of researchers in the above-mentioned disciplines in an attempt to mark out the Internet's new sphere for studying religion. In this volume, Dawson stated "sociology of cyberspace, let alone religion on-line, is still in its infancy" (2000, p. 49). This links the research of religion online to similar struggles being faced by those taking an interdisciplinary approach to study of life online in the mid-1990s. In many respects, the study of religion online followed a similar path to Internet studies, beginning with simple research topics and basic questions which attempted simply to describe what was happening online. These approaches likewise had to be refined over time as the research matured. Dawson and Cowan (2004), in the second edited collection, state that the first studies on religion in cyberspace veered towards "utopian and dystopian extremes," mirroring the speculative nature of many of the first works published on the social impact of the Internet. As Internet studies began to come into its own field in the late 1990s with substantial empirical studies emerging, religion too began to receive more serious reflection. Yet in Dawson and Cowan's assessment the study of "how religion is being practiced online is only just beginning." They emphasize a need to "understand developments online in the context of wider social and cultural conditions changing life in later-modern societies" (p. 9).

In the most recent of these collections, Hojsgaard & Warburg (2005) provide a helpful but brief typology which identifies three waves of research related to the academic study of religion on the Internet (pp. 8–9). The imagery of a wave is used to show how particular research questions and foci moved scholars in a particular direction, and eventually gave rise to new areas of focus. This development also illustrates how the study of religious communities online has correlated with the overall growth of Internet studies, with progressive changes occurring in the questions asked, methods used, and topics pursued.

Hojsgaard and Warburg describe the first wave of research on religion online as focusing on the new and extraordinary aspects of cyberspace, where religion "could (and probably would) do almost anything" (p. 8). The Internet is seen as a tool and symbol for religious and social transformation. Initial interest in many studies was in how this new technology created possibilities for new religions, or at least provided practitioners the possibility of reinventing traditional religious practices online. As Brasher states, the Internet "reconfigures the content of what we do and redefines who we are" (2001, p. 4). First-wave studies in the 1990s were often overly utopian or dystopian in their views; the Internet was seen as either building religious solidarity or potentially destroying traditional religiosity. Many of these early studies were focused on a single case study – a specific online community, website, or other online environment – and were highly descriptive, seeking to simply define the range of religious practices and phenomena online (Hennerby & Dawson, 1999; Davis, 1998).

The second wave, as Hojsgaard & Warburg describe it, was built on early descriptive studies but moved towards a "more realistic perspective" by seeking to more concretely define and compare different forms of online religious phenomena. Researchers began to understand that it was not simply the technology, but rather people who were generating these new forms of religious expression online. Researchers began to put their findings on topics such as online community and identity construction within a broader and more critical perspective, thus drawing on sociological, political, and philosophical debates and research related to community and identity in general. An important contribution in this area was Helland's (2000) popular distinction between religion-online (importing traditional forms of religion and religious practice online) and online-religion (adapting religion to create new and interactive forms of networked spirituality). This distinction has been employed by many researchers seeking to distinguish forms of religion in online environments. There is also a marked movement in the second-wave studies to try to link findings related to online religion with offline developments in religious structures and identification. For example, a special symposium issue of *Religion* (2002), describing itself as "a second wave of academic studies" on religion online, and building on the work of Brasher and O'Leary (1996), Wertheim (1999), and Zaleski (1996), sought to categorize and begin to theorize about the changing shape of religion in a wired world, as well to inaugurate "a new-sub-field of religious studies" (MacWilliams, 2002, p. 277).

As research questions and methodologies have begun to further mature, Hojsgaard and Warburg surmise that a third wave of research "may be just around the corner" (p. 9). They describe this research as a "bricolage of scholarship coming from different backgrounds with diverse methodological preference" (p. 9). Third-wave research thus will be marked by more collaborative, longitudinal, and interdisciplinary explorations of religion online. One example of this is Laney's (2005) study of application of uses and gratifications theory in order to determine the relationship between personal motive or desires and Christian website usage. This is also exemplified by the work of the University of Colorado's Center for Mass Media and Religion, which has taken a lead in investigating how the Internet acts as "symbolic or meaning resource" used by spiritual seekers in contemporary society for religious orientation and formation practices (Hoover & Park, 2004). If newer studies such as these of religion online are indicative of what is to come, we can expect to see a sharper turn towards theoretical and interpretive scholarship. We will see individual, focused studies seeking to relate their findings to other research in an effort to further analyze the implications of life online for wider society, and to provide grounds constructing theoretical frameworks to aid in these interpretations. Third-wave studies will also seek to demonstrate how studies of religion online add unique insights and help contribute to the overall understanding of life in a global information society.

Hojsgaard and Warburg's description of the "state of the field" in terms of waves of research illustrates how religion and the Internet can be seen as an evolving area of study, and one in need of continued mapping. It is important to note that these waves imply a process. Each wave or phase of research moves forward with a distinctive approach informed by a certain set of cultural and social perceptions about the research topic it is studying (i.e. how the Internet is perceived and under-stood at that moment). As knowledge is gained so is impetus; the research wave gathers information until a critical mass moves it towards a peak and then a break-point. At the breakpoint, some questions fall away and insufficient approaches or methods fall aside. Yet instead of the wave completely disappearing, the know-ledge gained creates new momentum and gives birth to another wave which is pushed forward by a new set of questions and refined approaches. One wave of research gives rise to the next. Yet this is not to say that researchers not involved in the initial waves of research of religion online are excluded from future explora-tion. Rather, this is a helpful image to show how the area has moved forward from focus on the descriptive and definitional, to developing typologies and comparisons, to entering a phase focused on theory and interpretation. As new technologies and religious trends emerge online, it is likely that this will require further waves or phases of research to emerge in order to map, contextualize, and analyze the implication of these occurrences.

Using the image of a wave provides a helpful attempt to describe in more detail how different questions and approaches have arisen and been carried forward in the past decade of research on religion and the Internet. This sets the stage to investigate how one key area within studies of religion and the Internet community has been approached. Focusing on the study of religious community online allows us to highlight the questions that have been addressed and those still unanswered that relate to the study of religion online.

"First-Wave" Research on Religion and the Internet

As stated above, first-wave studies of religion and the Internet were highly descriptive and focused on identifying and defining the latest religious practices online. Like ethnographers investigating unexplored and newly discovered territories, these researchers often launched themselves into the exotic world of cyberspace and traveled alongside these new religious netizens. They sought to describe the practices of life online and the blurring boundaries of online culture. These studies of religion online were similar to those found in early computer-mediated communications (CMC) research, as scholars attempted to describe in detail online social practices surfacing on the Internet. This ranges from Mnookin's (1996) discussion of the rise of legal boundaries in the multi-user dimension of *LambdaMOO* to Dibble's (1993) exploration of how anti-social behavior of online users in a text-based environment resulted in "virtual rape" of other community members, fueling an interesting discussion of what is "virtual" in a virtual community. First-wave Internet studies focused on questions related to the who, what, where, and when of life online. Of particular interest were questions of who is going online, what they are doing, and how this influences users at individual and group levels. In general, many first-wave researchers focused on key questions such as: What is happening online? How might these social aggregations be seen as communities? What effect does life online have on individual and group identities? Similarly, researchers interested in religion online attempted to pinpoint, conceptualize, and explain the rise of online community and issues related to the identity of those on the other side of the screen.

First-wave: defining online community

Online community has arguably been one of the most popular research topics within Internet studies. Beginning with Rheingold (1993), who presented the first study of how an online discussion forum might be conceptualized as a "virtual community," researchers have taken a particular interest in observing how life online was being experienced in terms of community. Through the 1990s and onward, numerous case studies seeking to describe online communities emerged, from studies of bulletin-board-based fan communities (Baym, 1995) to group interactions in textually or visually oriented multi-user fantasy environments (Reid, 1995). Such studies attempted to define community in a digital age.

Since the 1980s, religious groups have used computers to facilitate new forms of meeting and building "community" online. This is illustrated by Lochead's (1997, p. 53) early study of the emergence of Christian discussion groups; he states online religious groups began to form "a sense of identity as a community that existed independently of whatever service they chose for their electronic communication." A central concern for researchers in first-wave studies was trying to characterize and describe "virtual communities" as a new phenomenon representing the emerging Internet culture. Researchers focused attention on identifying the technologies and methods people use to congregate online and the type of discussions and practice that became the focal point of these groups. Studies of religious "virtual community" often highlighted certain traits that might serve as markers for defining online community.

These studies were highly descriptive and often used an ethnographic methodological approach in order to provide an in-depth picture of an online community. For example, in Fernback's (2002) study of a neopagan online community, she highlighted how the Internet allows groups to constitute and define themselves as a community through creating distinct conversation patterns and putting into place communal religious ritual practices. In my early work, I offered a picture of how one online Charismatic-Pentecostal community could be described as the "congregation of the disembodied" (Campbell, 2003b). This suggested that the mere transporting of traditional religious community online might help widen Christians' perception and understanding of global Christian community by allowing them to interact with "brothers and sisters in Christ from all over the world" (Campbell, 2003b, p. 197). Similarly, Herring's work (2005), which combined online ethnography with contextual theology, outlined how a newsgroup could be defined as a religious community and formulate a distinctive theological method or praxis through its online activities.

Other first-wave studies sought to uncover how online conversations create the basis for online community formation. Howard's (2000) ethnography of Christian fundamentalist websites showed how online conversations might emerge and create a common voice around a specific set of topics or shared religious conviction. In this way, a shared discourse from different online participants could create an online community, which may "facilitate multilateral communication between disparate individuals" (Howard, 2000, p. 242).

Still other first-wave studies approached the idea of online community as an overarching concept rather than identifying a single online community or a series of online communities. This allowed researchers to connect different expressions of religious practice online arising from a single religious tradition as being an "online community." This is illustrated by Bunt's work in *Virtually Islamic* (2000) which describes the online Islamic community in terms of various artifacts from online *fatwas* to online discussion forums such as "Ask the Iman," yet links them as simply diverse manifestations of the worldwide Muslim community. Bunt's understanding of a religious community online emerges through identifying specific forms of religious practice online that can be connected to the greater religious community of a specific religious tradition. Similarly, Lawrence (2002) offered insight into different expressions of Islam online, demonstrating how different online groups frequently seek to reinforce global religious structures by employing dominant metaphors found in Islam online. Taylor's (2003) study of Buddhist community online centered on the phenomena of cybersanghas where he argued that monasteries in Thailand are losing their place of centrality with populations shifting to urban centers. Yet in cyberspace, the cybersangha (*sangha* referring to a Buddhist monastic order) reconstitutes a new central connection-point for both monks and lay practitioners. He states, "Thai religion is changing to conform to new imagining (or mental religio-scapes) of this abstracted space" (p. 302). These first-wave studies offered detailed descriptions of both unique examples of religious community that were emerging in different online contexts and discussion of how online practice (or rituals) could be characterized as creating an online version of an offline faith community or tradition. Overall, first-wave studies focused on descriptive analysis of specific religious online communities, either by providing a detailed analysis of a single community or by considering how online religious community was emerging in relation to a specific religious tradition.

"Second-Wave" Studies of Religion Online

There is no clear date or marker to indicate when studies of online research began to make the transition from predominantly descriptive and definitional to more focused exploration of common trends within online culture. However, by the late 1990s we began to see researchers involved in the first-wave of Internet research starting to shift in their work from the descriptive to more definitional explorations. This can be seen in Jones's shift in approach to the question "how do we study computer-mediated community?" The shift occurs between his *Cybersociety*, where he focuses on the challenges of defining online aggregations as communities (1995, p. 11), and *Cybersociety 2.0* in which he considers more critically what kind of community is an online community (1998, p. 4). Second-wave studies are marked by questions related to the how and why of life online; they further consider how themes such as community and identity function online, and why this challenges or relates to offline manifestations of the same. Another key question is: How might online community reshape definitions of religious community and culture? Thus, second-wave studies can be described as focusing on mapping typologies and comparative studies of forms of online community.

Second-wave: contextualizing community online

Second-wave studies of online community moved from focusing on detailing patterns of group interaction and definitions of community to providing more concrete reflection on how members go about constructing and living these out in relation to their sense of online community. Researchers began to tease out the details of different roles and structures within online communities as a way to explain how these often influenced the extent to which members became involved in that community, as well as demonstrated varying levels of attachment to the community (Blanchard & Markus, 2004). Commonalities between studies emerged, as researchers began to note that members of online communities often identified similar characteristics or valued traits as part of their lived experiences of online groups (Kollock & Smith, 1994; Curtis, 1997). This work also led to investigating the direct connections between online and offline community patterns and behaviors. Research showed that online communities are unique in that they "are not tied to a particular place or time, but still serve common interest in social, cultural and mental reality ranging from general to special interest or activities" (van Dijk, 1998, p. 40).

In the second-wave studies of online religious community, attention shifted from primarily describing the form and function of online religious community to asking more refined questions related to members' practices. Researchers began to explore not just members' motivation for joining and investing in online communities, but also how online participation might begin to affect offline religion and community. This meant critically investigating how online community members were transforming traditional understandings of community through their online participation. A key question was: How might new forms of congregating online reshape community and religious culture? A forerunner of this line of questioning is Anderson's study (1999) of the emergence of new communities of interpreters in Islam created through conversations supported by CMC. He identifies three new groups of interpreters of Islam online: "creole" pioneers, activist interpreters, and "officializing" interpreters. These new classes of interpreters online highlight an important factor of religious online community formation: the possibilities for technology to facilitate new religious identities outside traditional structures. Thus, online community may be a new source of authority and influence, potentially challenging traditional religious communities. Another example of second-wave research is Kim's work on Chollian Buddhist online community in Korea. His study draws out specific characteristics and functions of online community seen through the ways members interacted together. By looking at the complexity of one individual Buddhist community and its members, he "makes a plea for the development of a new ideal-typical construct that takes into account the diverse functions of contemporary religious organizations – interpretive, interactive, integrative and instrumental" (Kim, 2005, p. 147). This shows how studying one religious community in detail can provide clues that point to a more refined understanding of community online, as well as shifts within contemporary religious communities and organizations at large.

Within second-wave studies, an important question has been the connection between online and offline religious community. For example, Young's study (2004) applies Helland's online-religion/religion-online distinction to Christian websites as a way to explain different expressions of "Internet Christianity" surfacing. He shows that whether it is providing traditional religious information online or new mediated forms of Christian practice/ritual, Internet Christianity is not unconnected to offline Christianity. There is evidence that online religious communities consciously import traditional religious ritual into online contexts, even if these practices must be modified in some form in order for them to be online. These claims are supported by my in-depth study of the challenges online religious community pose to offline religious community (Campbell, 2004a). Here I identify some of the key fears expressed by religious practitioners and organizations: that the online religious community is in some way inauthentic, impoverished, and deceptive, and has the seductive potential power to lead people out of the pew and away from face-to-face community interaction. The study found online religious community is not a substitute for offline community participation; it merely serves as a supplement to extend these relationships and communication in unique and novel ways (Campbell, 2004b). Second-wave studies have focused on "the question of community" by highlighting how characteristics of membership practice and motivations for online community involvement point to larger shifts in understanding of the concept of community as a whole.

Second-wave studies turned their attention to inquiries of members' practices and how their interactions and beliefs influenced conceptions and forms of online community. Here, how online communities relate to or challenge their offline counterparts has become an interesting and important question. These studies provide insight into the defining characteristics of online religious community as well as highlighting unique roles and forms of practice online that may lead to redefinition of people's conception of community.

"Third-Wave" Research

Over the past ten years, Internet research has moved from exploratory and definitional investigations to mapping dominant typologies and trends, which are being compared across contexts. We have also seen a turn towards an interpretative focus in research, as the growing body of knowledge about life online provides resources for making more substantive claims about dominant practices and influences of social interactions online. The current or "third wave" of research can be described as moving towards more theoretical, interpretive, and integrative work. Within CMC studies we see this move exemplified in the April 2007 issue of the *Journal of Computer Mediated Communication* (http://jcmc.indiana.edu/vol12/issue3/), where Internet researchers utilize theories of cultural variation, social capital, organizational identity, and interactivity in new media as tools to assess how the Internet both influences and reflects trends within the larger social sphere. In the study of community online, we see the progression to questions such as: How do the conditions of online community reflect or influence offline community? How do offline community patterns and discourse determine online use and beliefs? Thus, third-wave research moves towards opening up the investigation from just mapping life online to considering how online–offline interaction and integration point towards findings about life in an information-dominated culture.

Third-wave: current research on online religious community

Twenty-first century work on study of online community has emphasized that online social practices are closely linked to online social patterns; indeed researchers continue to emphasize that the Internet is "embedded" in everyday life (Wellman & Haythornwaite, 2002). Over and over, studies have found Internet users conceptually and practically connect their online and offline social practices as part of their social lives, rather than these being separate or disconnected spheres. Central to these investigations is considering how online groups point to the reshaping of traditional concepts of community, and point to larger social shifts within society about the very nature of community in contemporary society. As Katz and Rice's (2002) *Synoptia Project* found, being an Internet user was positively associated with also being a member of a community, cultural, or religious organization, with users being slightly more likely than non-users to belong to more religious organizations (2002, p. 155). Findings such as these demonstrate that involvement in offline (including religious) organizations seems unaffected by Internet usage, neither encouraging nor distracting from participation in these groups (2002, p. 160). Katz and Rice also found that the Internet "does not supplant communication forms, but rather supplements them" as they found no reduction in overall levels of communication amongst Internet users (2002, p. 329). Their research, along with Kavanagh and Patterson's (2002) work on the intersection of the Internet with voluntary organizations, seems to suggest that the net encourages and stimulates social interaction. This indicates that the Internet does not reduce overall social involvement, as many early pundits of online community feared. The connection between online and offline social involvement is echoed in recent studies of online religious community where it was found that community online served as a "supplement, not substitute" for offline church involvement (Campbell, 2003a, 2005a). Members joined and stayed involved in an online community in order to meet specific relational needs. Yet this participation could not fully meet religious members' desire for face-to-face interaction and a shared embodied worship experience. Therefore, online religious activities represent simply one part of an individual's overall religious involvement.

In general, studies of online religious community have evolved from broad to more refined questions. These studies began with attempts to define new forms of online interaction, such as looking at a specific online religious community as a way to explore new forms of social construction taking place online (Fernback, 2002), or by focusing on how online discourses may provide shape for new forms of religious community connection (Howard, 2000). This gave rise to general questions of why religious users go online, which helped document the many new forms of religious expression online as well as the variety of adaptations of traditional religious practices within religious communities online (Dawson & Cowan,

2004). This moved researchers toward mapping typologies of online community and other forms of spiritual experience or rituals online (Campbell, 2005b). Studies have begun to focus on questions about the extent to which offline religious communities and structures can influence online expressions of religious community (Livio & Tennebaum, 2004; Campbell, 2005a). Other studies are investigating the new forms of practice and social construction occurring within online religious communities (Krogh & Pillifant, 2004; Cowan, 2005). A key question within this third wave is how authority and power relations are constituted and challenged in online religious communities (Barker, 2005; Barzalai-Nahon & Barzalai, 2005; Campbell, 2007a; Campbell & Caulderon, 2007), and how online religious community can elucidate the ritual aspect of online community life (Krueger, 2005).

Research comparing online and offline participation has laid the ground for a current or emerging third wave of research within online religious community studies. Attention is moving towards developing theoretical frameworks for interpreting the conditions and functions of online religious communities. One way this is being done is through applying theories of the social construction of technology (SCOT) such as domestication (Silverstone, Hirsch, & Morley, 1992), which investigates religious communities as a distinctive user community of technology (Zimmerman-Umble, 1992). This is grounded in a social-shaping approach to technology, where engagement with technology is seen as a social process, informed by community values and beliefs that guide choices about technology. An example of this approach is the work of Barzilai-Nahon and Barzilai's (2005) study of how female religious users in fundamentalist religious communities utilize the Internet and are influenced by communal discourse related to authority. Users describe and conceive of the Internet in terms of needs. The Internet is valued for meeting particular needs within the community, enabling women to work at home. This study led to a change in official views about the technology, yet this also required the technology to be reshaped to fit within the boundaries and beliefs of the community's culture. Similarly, my work on the Jewish Ultra Orthodox negotiation with the cell phone to create the "kosher cell phone" demonstrates how religious users employ shared narratives and beliefs to frame and reconstruct new media technologies (2006). These studies open up interesting theoretical questions of how religious groups may "culture a technology" (see Barzilai-Nahon & Barzilai, 2005), such as the Internet, so that it can be incorporated into the community and provide opportunities for group- or self-expression within these boundaries. It also shows how studies of online religious community are moving towards broader interpretive frameworks to help explain the conditions and practices of religious community online. Third-wave studies build upon previous work and seek to develop a more refined theoretical understanding of the motivations and social functions of online religious community.

The rise of third-wave studies does not negate or diminish the work that has gone on before; instead, it highlights the progressive building of knowledge about online culture. Each wave has provided the details essential for asking deeper and more focused questions about topics such as community and identity formation online. As new technologies and phenomena arise, or are discovered, research will need to transition through each of these waves of research in order to define, map, and interpret these new areas. This process is essential in order to contextualize them with the growing interdisciplinary area of Internet studies. This framing also suggests that more waves of research and questioning are still ahead of us.

Future of Research on Religion Online

From the previous review, we see can see a profile forming of the past 12 years of research. Religion online research has focused on several key areas, most notably definitional and typology work on religious community, identity, ritual, and ethics online. Primarily qualitative methods have been employed, such as ethnographic studies involving online participant observation and/or interviews or content/discourse analysis. It is also evident that many researchers have focused predominantly on studying dominant religions from their geographical context – especially Christianity – and those seen as new or novel, such as Paganism and the new religious movements.

The Internet provides an important space to explore how community and other important elements such as identity and ritual are formed and negotiated within late modernity. While the study of religion typically falls within the bounds of religious studies and theology, we can see that studies of religion and the Internet bring together scholars from a wide variety of fields, which has contributed to the methodological and theoretical developments of current work. As has been shown above, the Internet is being used for a variety of religious purposes as Internet users continue to import traditional religious practices online and experiment with new representations of sacred and religious narratives. These religious uses of the Internet demonstrate that individuals continue to use media and technology to mediate meaning and negotiate the malleable character of identity and community in postmodern society (Hoover, 2006).

Yet, even after more than a decade of work, in some respects researchers have only begun to raise the necessary questions about when, how, and for whom the Internet can provide spaces where people can explore the meaning of religion and its function in their lives. Clearly there is need for more studies of community in religious contexts online, as well other themes, such as religious identity formation and presentation online (see Lövheim, 2004, 2006), in order to more fully develop our understanding of how the Internet is transforming religion. In light of this, I wish to suggest a potential agenda for the emerging and future waves of research on religion online. Some of these suggestions have been noted by Dawson and Cowan (2004, pp. 10–11) related to the future of the social-scientific study of religion online. Here, I spotlight six areas where studies of religion and the Internet would benefit from further input and exploration.

First, there is a need investigate why religious individuals are using the Internet and what specific groups they represent. Many current studies base their claims on a single case study. There is need for more large-scale and long-term studies of religious Internet users to see how patterns of religious life emerge online. This is exemplified by the work of the Pew American and Internet Life Project and their studies such as *Faith Online* that have sought to track trends on religious Internet use in the US. Here, researchers within the interdisciplinary study of media, religion, and culture have played an important role in formulating research survey tools that help reach correlations between religiosity and media use (see Hoover et al., 2004). Yet in order to map trends within a global information society, more studies are needed of different cultural and religious groups such as recent work on global Catholic Internet users (Cantoni & Zyga, 2007) and a national survey on Swedish teens' Internet use for religious purposes (Lövheim, 2008).

A second area that has been neglected has been attention to the types of groups investigated in studies of religion online. While some religious groups (namely Christianity and Paganism) and geographic contexts (North America) have received significant study, others, namely Asian traditions such as Hinduism and Buddhism, have received little attention. Researchers focused on Asia have noted this lack and have begun to respond to it. This response is exemplified by a large-scale study of how religious leaders in Singapore have made use of the Internet – a study that demonstrates a need for other national studies of how religion influences Internet use and perception (Kluver & Cheong, 2007; Kluver et al., forthcoming). Scholars working on religion within diaspora communities have also noted that the Internet is playing an important role by helping displaced believers connect to holy sites and centers in their countries of origin (Helland, 2007; Helland, 2008). Also, much of the focus has been on studies of youth and mainstream groups. There is a need for studies that focus on other areas such as how issues of age, ethnicity, culture, and gender might influence religious Internet use.

Thirdly, studies of the nature and quality of people's experience when doing religious tasks online are needed. This will involve studies utilizing a combination of methodologies, including surveys and interviews of religious users. As stated above, early studies were often weak or limited in their methodological development of studying the phenomenon of religion online. Researchers could contribute to this area by providing methodological input on qualitative and quantitative research techniques through collaborative studies of religion online, as illustrated in more recent multiple method studies (Hashim et al., 2007). Also, future research should address and seek to further interpret previous claims from studies focused on a single case study.

Fourthly, there is a further need within future studies to review previous methods of study used in ethnographies and online content analysis to see which approaches have yielded the most detailed and reliable results. Identifying the most fruitful methods are important so that a common or even standardized format for study might be suggested.

Fifthly, as third-wave studies move towards interpreting the relationship between people's online and offline religious activities, more theoretical framing and interpretation are needed. As new methodologies are often driven by new theoretical understandings, and vice versa, the connection between theory and method needs to be more carefully explored within studies of religion online. Researchers could especially offer input based on their experience studying media use and effects that might aid interpretation of the findings of these studies. The application and development of theoretical frameworks is especially important in order to consider the role media technologies play in audience/user responses, such as how religious authority is formed or negotiated online and its influence on offline faith communities. An example of this is my current work applying SCOT-based approaches to interpret how religious communities negotiate their use of new media (Campbell, 2007b). Also, more work needs to be done in applying existing theoretical frameworks to determine patterns of Internet usage, such as how the theory of planned behavior might determine norms of religious Internet usage (Ho, Lee, & Hameed, 2007). Studying how Internet user-practice correlates with offline behavior requires not just relying on user self-reports and observations: researchers further need to draw more explicitly on studies that consider how mass media mediates behavior, and historic studies of media use within religious communities.

Sixth and finally, there is a need for studies that uncover what features of technology are being utilized in the service of religious ends and what consequences result. As new forms of religious use of the Internet and other new media emerge, more studies will be needed to address the impact of these technologies on religious culture and belief (see Fukamizu, 2007). Recent developments, such as religious blogging, podcasting, and online worship in *Second Life*, are creating new forms of religious outreach and reception. These developments are trends in need of detailed exploration.

This chapter has argued that the study of religion online has been an inter-disciplinary venture. As studies of religion and the Internet move forward, it will be important to continue to draw in new discussion partners who bring with them expertise and interpretive tools that are currently missing in attempts to understand this growing area of technology use. Scholars from area studies, organizational communication, and media studies should be especially encouraged to join this conversation. Work on the global impact of religion online will benefit from input from political science or rhetoric; studies of gender and religion online should engage with scholars of gender and women's studies in such a discussion. While over a decade of research on religion and the Internet has accumulated, providing interesting insights into religious transformation and adaptation to the online context, much work still lies ahead in order to answer the question of where the Internet is taking religion. As the Internet is still an emerging technology, we have many years of research ahead of us to fully understand its complexities and its impact on religion. This provides a challenge and fertile opportunity for a variety of scholars who seek to become involved with the study of how religion is being altered in an age of information.

References

Anderson, J. (1999). The Internet and Islam's new interpreters. In D. F. Eickleman (ed.), *New Media in the Muslim World: The Emerging Public Sphere* (pp. 41–55). Bloomington, IN: Indiana University Press.

Barker, E. (2005). Crossing the boundary: New challenges to religious authority and control as a consequence of access to the Internet. In M. Hojsgaard & M. Warburg (eds.), *Religion and Cyberspace* (pp. 207–24). Routledge, London.

Barzilai-Nahon, K., & Barzilai, G. (2005). Cultured technology: Internet and religious fundamentalism. *The Information Society*, 21(1). Retrieved May 26, 2006, from http://www.indiana.edu/~tisj/21/1/ab-barzilai.html.

Baym, N. (1995). The emergence of community in computer-mediated communication. In S. Jones (ed.), *Cybersociety* (pp. 138–63). Thousand Oaks, CA: Sage.

Baym, N. (2005). ICT research and disciplinary boundaries: Is Internet research a virtual field, a proto-discipline, or something else? *The Information Society*, special issue, 21(4).

Brasher, B. (2001). *Give Me That Online Religion*. San Francisco: Jossey-Bass.

Blanchard, A., & Markus, M. L. (2004). The experienced "sense" of a virtual community: characteristics and processes. *ACM. SIGMIS Database*, 35(1), 64–79.

Bunt, G. (2000). *Virtually Islamic: Computer-Mediated Communication and Cyber Islamic Environments*. Lampeter, Wales: University of Wales Press.

Campbell, H. (2003a). A review of religious computer-mediated communication research. In S. Marriage & J. Mitchell (eds.), *Mediating Religion: Conversations in Media, Culture and Religion* (pp. 213–28). Edinburgh: T & T Clark/Continuum.

Campbell, H. (2003b) congregation of the disembodied. A look at religious community on the Internet. In M. Wolf (ed.), *Virtual Morality: Morals, Ethics and New Media* (pp. 179–99). New York: Peter Lang Publishing.

Campbell, H. (2004a). Challenges created by online religious networks. *Journal of Media and Religion*, 3(2), 81–99.

Campbell, H. (2004b). This is my church. Seeing the Internet and club culture as spiritual spaces. In L. Dawson & D. Cowan (eds.), *Religion Online: Finding Faith on the Internet* (pp. 107–23). New York: Routledge.

Campbell, H. (2005a). *Exploring Religious Community Online: We are One in the Network*. New York: Peter Lang Publishing.

Campbell, H. (2005b). Spiritualising the Internet: Uncovering discourse and narrative of religious Internet usage. *Heidelberg Journal of Religion on the Internet*, 1(1). Retrieved March 12, 2008, from http://www.ub.uni-heidelberg.de/archiv/5824.

Campbell, H. (2005c). Making space for religion in Internet studies. *The Information Society*, 21(4), 309–15.

Campbell, H. (2005d). Considering spiritual dimensions within computer-mediated communication studies. *New Media & Society*, 7(1), 111–35.

Campbell, H. (2006). Religion and the Internet. *Communication Research Trends*, 26(1), 3–24.

Campbell, H. (2007a). Who's got the power? Religious authority and the Internet. *Journal of Computer-Mediated Communication*, 12(3), article 14. http://jcmc.indiana.edu/vol12/issue3/campbell.html.

Campbell, H. (2007b). What hath God wrought: Considering how religious communities culture (or kosher) the cell phone. *Continuum: Journal of Media and Cultural Studies*, 21(2), 191–203.

Campbell, H., & Calderon, P. (2007). The question of Christian community online. *Studies in World Christianity*, 13(3), 261–77.

Cantoni, L. & Zyga, S. (2007). The use of Internet communication by Catholic congregations: A quantitative study. *Journal of Media and Religion*, 6(4), 291–309.

Curtis, P. (1997). Mudding: Social phenomena in text-based virtual realities. In S. Kiesler (ed.), *Culture of the Internet*. Mahwah, NJ: Lawrence Erlbaum.

Cobb, J. (1998). *Cybergrace: The Search for God in the Digital World*. New York: Crown Publishers.

Cowan, D. (2005). *Cyberhenge: Modern Pagans on the Internet*. New York: Routledge.

Davis, E. (1998). *TechGnosis: Myth, Magic, and Mysticism in the Age of Information*. New York: Random House.

Dawson, L. (2000). Researching religion in cyberspace: Issues and strategies. In Hadden, J. K. & Cowan, D. E. (eds.), *Religion on the Internet: Research Prospects and Promises*, (pp. 25–54). Amsterdam, London and New York: JAI Press.

Dawson, L. & Cowan, D. (eds.) (2004). *Religion Online: Finding Faith on the Internet*. New York: Routledge.

Dawson, L., & Cowan, D. (2004). Introduction. In L. Dawson & D. Cowan (eds.), *Religion Online: Finding Faith on the Internet* (pp. 1–16). New York: Routledge.

Dibble, J. (1993). A rape in cyberspace or how an evil clown, a Haitian trickster spirit, two wizards, and a cast of dozens turned a database into a society. *The Village Voice*, December 21, 36–42.

Dixon, P. (1997). *Cyberchurch, Christianity and the Internet*. Eastborne, UK: Kingsway Publications.

Fernback, J. (2002). Internet ritual: A case of the construction of computer-mediated neopagan religious meaning. In S. Hoover & L. S. Clark (eds.), *Practicing Religion in the Age of Media* (pp. 254–75). New York: Columbia University Press.

Fukamizu, K. (2007). Internet use among religious followers: Religious postmodernism in Japanese Buddhism. *Journal of Computer-Mediated Communication*, 12(3), article 11. http://jcmc.indiana.edu/vol12/issue3/fukamizu.html.

Hadden, J. K., & Cowan, D. E. (2000). *Religion on the Internet: Research Prospects and Promises*. Amsterdam, London, New York: JAI Press.

Hashim, N. H., Murphy, J., & Hashim, N. M. (2007). Islam and online imagery on Malaysian tourist destination websites. *Journal of Computer-Mediated Communication*, 12(3), article 16. http://jcmc.indiana.edu/vol12/issue3/hashim.html.

Helland, C. (2000). Online-religion/religion-online and virtual communitas. In J. K. Hadden & D. E. Cowan (eds.), *Religion on the Internet: Research Prospects and Promises* (pp. 205–23). New York: JAI Press.

Helland, C. (2007). Diaspora on the electronic frontier: Developing virtual connections with sacred homelands. *Journal of Computer-Mediated Communication*, 12(3), article 10. http://jcmc.indiana.edu/vol12/issue3/helland.html.

Helland, C. (2008). Canadian religious diversity online: A network of possibilities. In P. Beyer & L. Beaman (eds.), *Religion and Diversity in Canada*. Boston: Brill Academic Publishers.

Hennerby, J., & Dawson, L. (1999). New religions and the Internet: Recruiting in a new public sphere. *Journal of Contemporary Religions*, 14, 17–39.

Herring, D. (2005). Virtual as contextual: A net news theology. In M. Hojsgaard & M. Warburg (eds.), *Religion and Cyberspace* (pp. 149–65). London: Routledge.

Hojsgaard, M., & Warburg, M. (2005). Introduction: Waves of research. In Hojsgaard, M. & Warburg, M. (eds.), *Religion and Cyberspace* (pp. 1–11). London: Routledge.

Howard, R. G. (2000). Online ethnography of dispensationalist discourse: Revealed verses negotiated truth. In J. K. Hadden & D. E. Cowan (eds.), *Religion on the Internet: Research Prospects and Promises* (pp. 225–46). New York: JAI Press.

Ho, S. H., Lee, W., & Hameed, S. S. (2007). Muslim surfers on the Internet: Using the theory of planned behaviour to examine the factors influencing engagement in online religious activities. *New Media & Society*, 10(1), 93–113.

Hoover, S. (2006). *Religion in the Media Age*. Oxford, New York: Routledge.

Hoover, S., Clark, L. S., & Rainie, L. (2004). Faith online: 64% of wired Americans have used the Internet for spiritual or religious information. Pew Internet and American Life Project. Retrieved May 26, 2006, from http://www.pewinternet.org/reports/toc.asp?Report=119.

Hoover, S., & Park, J. K. (2004). Religious meaning in the digital age: Field research on Internet/web religion. In P. Horsfield, M. Hess, & A. M. Medrano (eds.), *Belief in Media: Cultural Perspective on Media and Christianity* (pp. 121–36). Aldershot, UK: Ashgate.

Houston, G. (1998). *Virtual Morality*. Leicester: Apollos.

Jones, S. (ed.) (1995). *CyberSociety*. Thousand Oaks, CA: Sage.

Jones, S. (ed.) (1998). *CyberSociety 2.0*. Thousand Oaks, CA: Sage.

Katz, J., & Rice, R. (2002). *Social Consequences of Internet Use: Access Involvement and Interaction*. Cambridge, MA: MIT Press.

Kavanagh, A., & Patterson, S. (2002). The impact of community computer networks on social capital and community involvement in Blacksburg. In B. Wellman & C. Haythornthwaite (eds.), *The Internet in Everyday Life* (pp. 325–44). Oxford: Blackwell.

Kim, M. C. (2005). Online Buddhist community: An alternative organization in the information age. In M. Hojsgaard & M. Warburg (eds.), *Religion and Cyberspace* (pp. 138–48). London: Routledge.

Kluver, R., & Cheong, P. H. (2007). Technological modernization, the Internet, and religion in Singapore. *Journal of Computer-Mediated Communication*, 12(3), article 18. http://jcmc.indiana.edu/vol12/issue3/kluver.html.

Kluver, R., Cheong, P. H., Detenber, B., Peng, L.W., Hameed, S. B. S., & Yanli, C. (forthcoming). Religious diversity in Singapore. In L. A. Eng (ed.), *Beyond Rituals and Riots: Ethnic Relations and Social Cohesion at a Time of Uncertainty*. Singapore: Institute of Southeast Asian Studies Publishing.

Kollock, P., & Smith, M. (1994). Managing the virtual commons: Cooperation and conflict in computer communities. In S. Herring (ed.), *Computer-Mediated Communication*. Amsterdam: John Benjamins. Retrieved May 26, 2006, from http://www.sscnet.ucla.edu/soc/faculty/kollock/papers/vcommons.htm.

Krogh, M. C., & Pillfant, B. A. (2004). The house of Netjer: A new religious community online. In L. Dawson and D. Cowan (eds.), *Religion Online: Finding Faith on the Internet* (pp. 107–21). New York: Routledge.

Kruger, O. (2005). Discovering the invisible Internet: Methodological aspects of searching religion on the Internet. *Heidelberg Journal of Religion on the Internet* 1(1). Retrieved May 26, 2006, from http://www.ub.uni-heidelberg.de/archiv/5828.

Laney, M. (2005). Christian web sites: Usage and desires. In L. Dawson & D. Cowan (eds.), *Religion Online: Finding Faith on the Internet* (pp. 166–79). London: Routledge.

Larsen, E. (2000). Wired churches, wired temples: Taking congregations and missions into cyberspace. Pew Internet and American Life Project, December 20. Retrieved March 2, 2008, from http://www.pewinternet.org/reports/toc.asp?Report=28.

Larsen, E. (2001). CyberFaith: How Americans pursue religion online. Pew Internet and American Life Project, December 23. Retrieved March 2, 2008, from http://www.pewinternet.org/reports/toc.asp?Report=53.

Lawrence, B. F. (2002). Allah on-line: The practice of global Islam in the information Age. In S. Hoover & L. S. Clark (eds.), *Practicing Religion in the Age of Media* (pp. 237–53). New York: Columbia University Press.

Livio, O., & Tenenboim, K. (2004). Discursive legitimation of a controversial technology: Ultra-Orthodox Jewish women in Israel and the Internet. Paper presented at AoIR 5.0, University of Sussex, UK.

Lövheim, M. (2004). *Intersecting Identities: Young People, Religion and Interaction on the Internet.* Uppsala: Uppsala University.

Lövheim, M. (2006). A space set apart? Young people exploring the sacred on the Internet. In J. Sumiala-Seppänen, K. Lundby, & R. Salokangas (eds.), *Implications of the Sacred in (Post)Modern Media* (pp. 255–72). Göteborg: Nordicom.

Lövheim, M. (2008). Rethinking cyberreligion? Teens, religion and the Internet in Sweden. *Nordicom Review,* 29(2), pp. 205–16.

MacWilliams, M. (2002). Introduction to the symposium. *Religion,* 32, 277–78.

Mnookin, J. (1996). Virtual(ly) law: The emergence of law in LamdaMOO. *Journal of Computer-Mediated Communication,* 2(1). Retrieved May 26, 2006, from http://www.ascusc.org/jcmc/vol2/issue1/lambda.html.

O'Leary, S. (1996). Cyberspace as sacred space. Communicating religion on computer networks. *Journal of the American Academy of Religion,* 4, 781–808.

O'Leary, S., & Brasher, B. (1996). The unknown God of the Internet. In C. Ess (ed.), *Philosophical Perspectives on Computer-Mediated Communication.* Albany, NY: State University of New York Press.

Reid, E. (1995). Virtual worlds: Culture and imagination. In S. Jones (ed.), *Cybersociety* (pp. 164–83). Thousands, CA: Sage.

Rheingold, H. (1993). *The Virtual Community.* New York: HarperPerennial.

Schroeder, R., Heather, N., & Lee, R. M. (1998). The sacred and the virtual: Religion in multi-user virtual reality. *Journal of Computer Mediated Communication,* 4. http://www.ascusc.org/jcmc/vol4/issue2/schroeder.html#LANGUAGE.

Silverstone, R., Hirsch, E., & Morley, D. (1992). Information and communication technologies and the moral economy of the household. In R. Silverstone & E. Hirsch (eds.), *Consuming Technologies: Media and Information in Domestic Spaces* (pp. 15–29). London: Routledge.

Spears, R., & Lea, M. (1992). Social influence and the influence of the "social" in computer-mediated communication. In M. Lea (ed.), *Contexts of Computer-Mediated Communication* (pp. 30–65). London: Wheatsheaf/Harvester.

Taylor, J. (2003). Cyber-Buddhism and the changing urban space in Thailand. *Space and Culture,* 6(3), 292–308.

Van Dijk, J. (1998). The reality of virtual communities. *Trends in Communication* 1(1), 39–63.

Wellman, B., & Haythornwaite, C. (2002). The Internet in everyday life: An introduction. In B. Wellman & C. Haythornwaite, (eds.), *The Internet in Everyday Life* (pp. 3–44). Oxford: Blackwell.

Wertheim, M. (1999). *The Pearly Gates of Cyberspace.* London: Virago.

Wilson, W. (2000). *The Internet Church.* Nashville: Word Publishing.

Wolf, M. (ed.) (2003). *Virtual Morality: Morals, Ethics and New Media*. New York: Peter Lang Publishing.

Young, G. (2004). Reading and praying online: The continuity in religion online and online religion in Internet Christianity. In L. Dawson & D. Cowan (eds.), *Religion Online: Finding Faith on the Internet* (pp. 93–106). New York: Routledge.

Zaleski, J. (1997). *The Soul of Cyberspace: How Technology is Changing our Spiritual Lives*. San Francisco: HarperSanFranciso.

Zimmerman-Umble, D. (1992). The Amish and the telephone: Resistance and reconstruction. In R. Silverstone & E. Hirsch (eds.), *Consuming Technologies: Media and Information in Domestic Spaces* (pp. 183–94). London: Routledge.

12

Indigenous Peoples on the Internet

Laurel Dyson

Introduction

Increasingly since the mid-1990s Indigenous peoples around the world have been establishing a presence on the Internet. Nathan (2000, p. 39) notes that they were early participants and that their involvement has been "vigorous and successful."

Here the term "Indigenous" is used to refer to those who "having a historical continuity with pre-invasion and pre-colonial societies that developed on their territories, consider themselves distinct from other sectors of the societies now prevailing in those territories" (UNESCO, 2004). The term embraces Native Americans of the US and Latin America; First Nations, Inuit, and Métis peoples of Canada; Aboriginal people and Torres Strait Islanders in Australia; various tribal peoples throughout Asia; Indigenous minorities in Africa; and the Sami of northern Europe. In addition, the Polynesian, Melanesian, and Micronesian nations of the Pacific identify as Indigenous, even if some, like the Tongans, were never colonized and so do not strictly fit the UNESCO definition. In total, there are an estimated 350 million Indigenous people living in over 70 countries round the world, comprising 4 percent of humanity (UNESCO, 2006). They represent over 5,000 language and cultural groups.

As a result Indigenous websites and uses of the Internet are remarkably diverse. Websites include many established by Indigenous communities, Indigenous organizations, as well as individuals. Mitten (2003) and Dyson and Underwood (2006) attempt to summarize some of the major categories of Indigenous sites. Mitten (2003), who studied 120 Native American sites, describes portals, websites of tribes and Native American organizations, educational sites, Native media sites, e-commerce, music sites, and websites for promoting Native languages. She further notes that the diversity of Native American websites is such that there are almost unlimited categories in addition to those she examined. For example, there are websites for health, the military, powwows, legal issues, Native authors and artists, genealogy, Indigenous museum collections, and digital libraries of history and anthropology. Dyson and Underwood (2006), describing Indigenous-controlled sites around the world, list additional categories of e-government, cultural management, political activism, Native title, treaty, intercultural dialogue, reconnection and community rebuilding, youth support, and sport.

These two studies reveal a huge variety of websites. Some fulfill comparable roles to websites run by non-Indigenous people, for example the e-commerce and sport sites. In addition, Indigenous uses of the Internet often coincide with the everyday practice of non-Indigenous people, for example searching for information, downloading music and movies, and using email for their work (Gaidan, 2007). However, there are also interests of special concern to Indigenous people. These particular applications will be the focus of this chapter and include the employment of the Internet to reaffirm Indigenous identity and rebuild shattered communities, as a tool to achieve self-determination, and as a medium of communication in Indigenous languages.

Despite Indigenous peoples' active engagement with the Internet, there still remain many challenges. There have been concerns expressed by some authors over whether the Internet will act as a tool of further colonization and continue the process of Western enculturation of Indigenous peoples begun in the colonial era (McConaghy, 2000). Indigenous spokespeople have voiced dismay over the power of misrepresentation offered by the Internet (Iseke-Barnes & Danard, 2007), and the misappropriation of Indigenous knowledge and culture (Radoll, 2004). There have been questions raised regarding the ownership of many websites which purport to offer an Indigenous worldview and the likely audience for Indigenous websites when most Indigenous people remain unconnected to the Internet. Any consideration of the Indigenous presence on the Internet must be evaluated in the light of concerns such as these, given the entitlement of all peoples to maintain their cultural identity as part of their universal human rights (UNESCO, 2002). A careful examination not only of how Indigenous people are using the Internet but also how they might be negatively affected is needed.

I will begin by a consideration of the strength of the Indigenous presence on the Internet both historically and today. This will be followed by an examination of the main challenges to Indigenous participation. Finally, an analysis of four major and distinctive uses of the Internet by Indigenous people will be presented and discussed in the light of the challenges to full inclusion.

The Strength of the Indigenous Internet Presence

There are many Indigenous Internet users and many Indigenous websites, chat rooms, and online forums around the world. NativeNet was probably the first bulletin board and listserv to foster discussions about Indigenous identity and culture, established in the US in 1989–90 by Hispanic-American Gary Trujillo (Zimmerman, Zimmerman, & Bruguier, 2000). Similarly, the first Indigenous websites were initiated in the US: Paula Giese, a Native American, began publishing on the web in 1993 and launched her Native American Indian Resources website in 1994 (Strom, 2000); while the Oneida nation inaugurated the first tribal website the same year (Polly, 1998). In 1995 the first conference paper on Indigenous self-determination using the Internet was delivered by Hawaiian cyberactivist Kekula Bray-Crawford (2000), who was also responsible in 1996 for the first real-time Internet broadcast of a UN formal session – on the draft Declaration on the Rights of Indigenous Peoples. In 1998 NativeWeb, a portal dedicated to resources and websites from and about Native American and other Indigenous people, had links to 2,000 websites (Caraveo, 1998). In 2001 Hobson (2001) counted over 400 websites in Australia alone. By 2003 in the US Anderson (2003) identified 132 tribes with their own website, that is, roughly 25 percent of all federally recognized tribes, not including sites run by other Indigenous organizations and individuals.

Entering "Indigenous people," "Aboriginal people," "Native American," or similar keywords into a search engine today will bring up millions of hits. These give some sense of the "virtual face of indigeneity," to quote a phrase from Landzelius (2006, p. 4). However, when considering the strength of the Indigenous presence on the Internet, we must also ask questions regarding the authenticity of many of these websites, given the misrepresentation of Indigenous cultures from colonial times down to the present. Authenticity may be gauged by attempting to answer two questions, "*By* whom is the site run?" and "*For* whom is it run?" If a site is not managed by Indigenous people, or at least run by others in the interests of Indigenous people, we must question whether it can truly be regarded as an Indigenous website even if it purports to deal with Indigenous topics or culture, or sells Indigenous artifacts.

For many Indigenous people, governance is the key issue. When websites are managed by or have input from Indigenous people, they tend to offer a view which is free from racist stereotyping. On the other hand, when run by non-Indigenous people, they are more likely to reflect the dominant discourse. This can happen through the commodification of Indigenous culture, the decontextualization and distancing of Indigenous knowledge from the people who created it, and by non-Indigenous people assuming control over how Indigenous people are represented. Iseke-Barnes and Danard (2007) give examples of these phenomena. They note the commodification of traditional Indigenous crafts and images on the Internet to sell products which have no connection to Indigenous culture (e.g., Indian motorcycles, and LandOLakes butter with its "Indian maiden" image), and remark on how Indigenous artisans are often completely removed from the manufacturing cycle (many of the dream catchers and moccasins for sale online are not made by Indigenous people). They also discuss issues concerning Indigenous artifacts exhibited on museum websites, where often non-Indigenous staff maintain control over how the objects are represented and as a result sometimes misinterpret them. Carlos Efraín Peréz Rojas, a Native American film-maker and video-activist from Mexico, highlights the difference between Indigenous self-representation and non-Indigenous representation:

> It's important to say that there's more than just hunger, pain and poverty in Native communities. Solutions are also being offered. . . . I've noticed that views from outside tend to show indigenous peoples as victims, the gaze is attracted to the sandals, the hungry people, the dirty child. . . . When Native people represent themselves they show more dignity. . . . Of course I talk about the problems that exist, but I will also offer a message that brings hope. (quoted in Zamorano, 2005)

The worst cases of Indigenous misrepresentation on the Internet are websites purporting to be Indigenous but actually produced by imposters, protected from exposure by the anonymity of the net. There are many "professional Indians" online exploiting Native culture for their own profit (Anderson, 2003, p. 451). One sign of a fake website is where detailed religious descriptions are provided. A famous case was a chat room called Blue Snake's Lodge in which a software consultant adopted a fraudulent persona, teaching his version of Native American healing and spirituality, and inducting visitors to the site into honorary membership of the "Evening Sky Clan." In 1993 Native Americans closed the chat room down, affirming the "sacred, proprietary – and indeed, exclusionary" nature of their religious rituals (Martin, 1995).

It is difficult to say exactly how many websites are under Indigenous control. Hobson (2001) concluded that most of the Australian sites he located were governed by non-Indigenous people: their use of the pronoun "they" showed that they were *about* rather than *by* Indigenous people. The dominance of the English language on websites offering Indigenous information and views (Niezen, 2005) might suggest that many are, indeed, in the charge of outsiders, particularly where the website originates in a non-English-speaking country. However, if we consider that the majority of Indigenous people establishing websites would be "a formally educated . . . elite with the linguistic and technological skills to use the Internet as a tool of global networking, lobbying, and self-expression" (Niezen, 2005, p. 534), and furthermore that many Indigenous people were discouraged from passing on their own language to their children through assimilatory practices, then we cannot take language as a firm indicator of authorship. Many English-language websites would be *by* Indigenous people, or at least involve collaborative efforts. One thing that is clear is that Indigenous people from certain English-speaking countries – particularly the US, Canada, Australia, and Aotearoa (New Zealand) – have been more active in establishing websites than, for example, their Spanish-speaking counterparts. Part of this is no doubt a matter of economic differences, but it is also due to the fact that in those countries Indigenous groups received a great deal of technical support from collaborators based in universities, which was rare in Latin America (Becker & Delgado-P., 1998). For example, NativeWeb, which now has a majority of Native American and First Nations people on its board of directors, received its start from hosting at universities in Kansas and New York.

Even if websites are not under Indigenous control, they can be valid expressions of indigeneity if established and maintained to further the aspirations of Indigenous people. Again, the use of English or other major European languages is not a definitive indicator since there is usually an assumption by web designers that Indigenous people using the Internet will be able to operate in the dominant language. For example, in the African context Osborn (2006) points out that there is not a great audience at present for websites in Indigenous African languages because most Indigenous users are wealthier, educated people who are quite at home in their country's official language, usually English or French. There are many websites and webpages established around the world by governments, non-governmental organizations (NGOs), educational, and other institutions which are providing useful and necessary services for Indigenous people. Many of these focus on online services and information in the basic areas of health (e.g., Indigenous health centers, prevention of diseases common in Indigenous communities), education (Indigenous scholarships and educational programs), legal issues (Indigenous rights, land rights, and legal services), housing, family programs, employment and development schemes, and cultural heritage. Most of these may be considered authentic Indigenous uses of the Internet even if not created or controlled by the Indigenous people themselves. However, Dyson and Underwood (2006) compared a selection of these websites and concluded that probably those which were most effective in reaching Indigenous people were still those that had Indigenous involvement, either through collaborations with Indigenous communities or through Indigenous staff members employed by the organization. For example, the website of Te Papa Tongarewa, the Museum of New Zealand, is bilingual in Maori and English, with photographs of woodcarvers and weavers presenting their art as a living tradition, and offers training and collaborations with Maori organizations. Maori people have obviously been involved in the creation and ongoing maintenance of this website.

In conclusion, it is impossible to state precisely how many Indigenous websites, blogs, chat rooms, etc. there are today. Certainly no one has attempted the enormous task of evaluating and counting them all. However, we can say that the number is considerable but not as great as a search engine will appear to reveal. The cyber-surfer will always need to use their judgment based on the "by whom and for whom" test, or as Métis scholar Carol Leclair states, "who" and "how useful":

> Web sites, which claim to offer native knowledge, are scrutinized through some of the basic concepts embedded in oral tradition. I check for clear statements of who is writing, identifying self, family, place, of how you come to know from your own experience, or who has passed on the information and how this person has demonstrated knowledge in the past. . . . I use my intellect and my intuition (another word for wisdom or experience) to assess the usefulness of the site. (Leclair & Warren, 2007, p. 5)

Challenges to Indigenous Participation on the Internet

Despite the strength of the Indigenous cyber presence, the Internet also poses a number of real and potential challenges. It is fair to say that some of these are similar to barriers facing any community with low socioeconomic status and there-fore living on the other side of the digital divide, lacking access to the Internet and the skills to use it effectively. Moreover, some of Indigenous peoples' fears of unethical behavior in cyberspace, such as the exposure of their children to pedophiles and pornography, coincide with those of non-Indigenous parents, even if exacerbated in this group by a certain naivety about information and com-munication technology (ICT) (Latu & Dyson, 2006).

However, if we are seeking to understand the distinctive features of Indigenous engagement with the Internet, we must also add the weight of historic and present-day abuse perpetrated through colonization and postcolonialism. The deep mistrust born of this experience has led some Indigenous communities and researchers to extend their suspicion to the Internet, seeing it as potentially another tool of Indigenous disempowerment.

Internet access

The most obvious challenge to Indigenous peoples' full participation on the Internet is access. Difficulties of access faced by Indigenous populations are the result of a complex of socioeconomic factors, geographical location, and language issues. In this respect, their situation is distinct from those groups who experience the digital divide for largely socioeconomic reasons, for example poorer people from the dominant ethnic groups living in Europe, the Americas, or Australasia.

Generally, poverty combined with the high cost of ICT means that Indigenous people have low computer ownership, low ICT literacy, and low connectivity to the Internet. An exacerbating factor is the remoteness of many Indigenous com-munities, which are often located in regions where connectivity is difficult. In remote regions, too, costs escalate: Internet connections via satellite are more expensive than standard telephone-line or cable connections in the cities, and maintenance and repair services are likewise more costly and prone to long delays because people have to be brought in from outside since there is a lack of trained Indigenous ICT technicians to provide maintenance locally (Dyson, 2005). In addition, sup-porting infrastructure, such as electricity, is often absent or intermittent.

Access issues are normally defined purely in terms of technology provision, but Osborn (2006) directs our attention to the linguistic dimension of the digital divide. Low literacy, particularly in English, the main computer language, does not help Indigenous people to get online (Secretariat of the UN, 2003). The multiplicity of Indigenous languages and complexities in handling their scripts offer major chal-lenges (Osborn, 2006). Indigenous people require localized versions of browsers and search engines with displays written in their own language as well as ortho-graphical support to type the letters and accents necessary for communication. For those who cannot read text – or cannot read well – multimedia support is necessary by way of graphical interfaces and audio files.

Access, or lack of it, is not evenly distributed across Indigenous communities. Shorter (2006) clearly illustrates the gap between two Yoeme communities, one rich and living in a first-world country, one poor and located in a developing nation: while the Yoeme community in the US had daily access to the Internet, the Yoeme on the Mexican side of the border did not even have access at their schools, let alone in their homes. Taylor (2007), writing in the context of northern Scandinavia, points out that it is mainly urbanized Sami youth who are using the Internet, not Sami living on the land.

Successful programs to increase Internet access have generally employed technologies which are cost effective in remote regions, for example wireless and satellite networks (Cullen 2005), and access models which share costs across the community, thus improving affordability. Indigenous communities in many parts of the world have found that the way to improve Internet access and skills is via computer labs in schools and libraries as well as community technology centers (also referred to as community multimedia centers or telecenters) owned by the whole community (Daly, 2007; Meer, 2003; Hughes, 2004).

Sustainability of Indigenous websites

Poverty impacts not only on access but also on the sustainability of many Indigenous communities' websites. Money for updates is sometimes lacking, resulting in dead links and dated content (Taylor, 2007; Delgado-P., 2002).

E-commerce offers one way of funding both websites and Indigenous business. However, Salazar (2007), while quoting several e-commerce ventures in Peru, Ecuador, and Bolivia, notes that commercial uses of the Internet have so far failed to turn a profit for Indigenous entrepreneurs and community enterprises.

Misappropriation of Indigenous knowledge and culture

The Internet represents a particular challenge to Indigenous communities wishing to place traditional knowledge or culture online. There is a widespread perception by many web users that the Internet is the way of the free and there is a lack of understanding that material is covered by copyright laws. Indigenous people risk losing income from illegal downloads and risk misappropriation of cultural artifacts by their incorporation into the works or products of others without permission (Radoll, 2004). Protection by existing copyright is itself problematical, as it is usually based on notions of individual authorship and economic rights, whereas Indigenous cultural ownership is more diffuse and communally based, with rights centered on ideas of spiritual obligations and custodianship (ICIPTF, 1999).

Further, Indigenous people have concerns over who has the right to knowledge: they do not wish unauthorized members of even their own community, let alone outsiders, to gain access to knowledge that is seen as sacred or secret, viewable only by the initiated or by people of a certain gender (Dyson & Underwood, 2006). These restrictions need to be managed dynamically by Indigenous communities since restrictions are to some extent fluid and change over time. For example, Aboriginal Australians ban the naming, viewing of images, or playing of recordings of dead people for varying periods of time after death, depending on a range of factors (Anderson, 2005). So references to the deceased need to be taken down from websites or have warnings prominently displayed.

The attitude towards placing knowledge online may well be different depending on whether Indigenous communities are situated within wealthy countries and have better access to ICT and other resources, or within the third world with few opportunities for dialogue with the outside. Shorter (2006) reported a marked distinction between the two Yoeme communities living on opposite sides of the US–Mexico border: the Mexican Yoeme were eager to have cultural tapes and documents placed on a website by a collaborating ethnographer, while the much richer US community tried to stop this.

Concerns over misappropriation of knowledge are not insuperable and a number of communities have developed approaches to managing this issue while still taking advantage of Internet technology. The Wangka Maya Pilbara Aboriginal Language Centre in Western Australia, for example, decided that access to cultural materials and language resources could best be delivered via the web, given the scattering of small communities across a wide area of the Pilbara region (Injie & Haintz, 2004). Individuals who are not able to visit head office can search lists of items online and order copies on CD-ROM. To maintain absolute security and to avoid misuse of intellectual property, items cannot be directly downloaded from the website. Online requests can be vetted so that outsiders pay for copyright material and do not gain access to culturally sensitive material or private stories.

Western enculturation

There have been concerns expressed by some commentators about the potential of the Internet to seriously impact Indigenous culture (McConaghy, 2000). These fears of the Internet as a tool for assimilating Indigenous people into Western society come from an acknowledgement that no technology is completely neutral and that all come embedded with the values of the civilization that produced them. Certainly Indigenous representatives at the first World Summit on the Information Society sponsored by the United Nations in 2003 expressed worries that Western influences brought to them on the information superhighway might overwhelm their own cultures. Some feared change and the impact on their traditional knowledge and way of life (Secretariat of the UN, 2003).

However, other researchers have discredited this idea of the Internet as a tool of assimilation (Becker & Delgado-P., 1998; Dyson, 2003). Schoenhoff is one author who notes the adaptability of the new technologies:

> The computer is a unique tool because its purpose is constantly being reinvented by its users. Its power consists in the fact that it is a symbol machine, and its symbols and their interpretations can be altered. (1993, p. 76)

Nathan (2000) sees the catalyst for Indigenous engagement with the Internet as lying in the inherent nature of the medium: the challenge it poses to standard ideas of literacy, its interconnectivity, and the fact that it is still "soft" and can be molded by those who engage with it. The "breakout of the visual" on the Internet through graphic interfaces, photographs, animation, and video (Bolter, 2001, p. 72) has a particular appeal to the visual strengths of Indigenous users, most of whom come from cultures with strong artistic traditions. In addition, the sound files which have become increasingly available, such as online music, language recordings, and podcasts, speak to the oral cultures of Indigenous people. The active participation of Indigenous people on the Internet and the wide range of uses for which they have established websites support this notion of the Internet as a highly adaptive technology which can be used by Indigenous peoples for whatever objectives they choose.

Reaffirmation of Indigenous Identity

In contrast with the concerns of the technological determinists, Indigenous peoples are using the Internet as a tool to revitalize and rebuild their cultures. It must be said that all authentic Indigenous websites are reaffirmations of Indigenous identity and assertions of the right of Indigenous peoples to survive. Ironically, the greatest tool of globalization is helping small communities to reinforce their culture and sense of connection to place. Landzelius (2006) distinguishes two different orientations of online Indigenous identity: those aimed at "inreach" (building community and creating a virtual space for shared meanings within an Indigenous people) and those aimed at outreach (connecting with people from outside). Many websites do both at the same time, offering a public face but sometimes excluding outsiders from private spaces and protected knowledge on the site through a variety of mechanisms, such as log-ins and the use of Indigenous languages only spoken by members of the community.

Kitalong and Kitalong (2000) describe the role of the Internet in articulating a postcolonial identity for the Pacific island nation of Palau. Palauans have used the Internet to teach themselves and outsiders about their culture, language, people, and current community concerns, and from this knowledge to achieve positive social outcomes, such as the ban on prostitution by the parliament that was instigated in 1998 through an e-petition signed by residents and expatriates. Community is created in various ways: via Palauan language, proverbs and sayings, Palauan music and images, and guestbooks in which visitors can leave their email addresses in order to keep in contact. Kitalong and Kitalong note how many Palauan websites create a sense of Palauanness but without specifically excluding the outsider, for example by the use of vernacular and insider expressions, and of uncaptioned images that would only be totally understandable by people who have grown up in Palau.

A major reason why Indigenous websites often focus on reaching out beyond the community is the desire to create intercultural dialogue with the outside world in order to correct false representations and stereotypes. The Karen website is one that is designed specifically as a "Cultural Exchange and a Communication

Centre," obviously intended for the outside world since its chosen language is English (Dyson & Underwood, 2006). The site presents images and information about the Karen people in the Burma-Thailand region including traditional stories, songs, news items, personal pages, FAQs (frequently asked questions), and links. It avoids stereotyping by presenting a profile of a Karen IT professional, modern and historical political issues, as well as traditional culture. The message board and chat facility transform the site from purely information-provider to a tool of communication and interaction between educated Karen and the outside.

Indigenous e-tourism is another form of outreach. It can generate income as well as enhance respect for the people and their way of life. Arnold and Plymire (2000) contrast the official homepages of the Eastern and Western bands of the Cherokee. Whereas that of the Western band is largely for Cherokee users, the website of the Eastern Cherokee is mainly for non-Native visitors. Its purpose is to expand tourism through providing information about tourist attractions. However, the website also provides links to the Cherokee elementary-school site, with its recordings of Cherokee elders relating traditional legends and its fifth-graders' homepages. Arnold and Plymire see this backdrop to the tourism website as a deliberate encouragement for outside visitors to recognize the connection between their purchasing of tourism products and both the financing of community projects (like the computer labs and school) and the rebuilding of culture through the children's learning from their elders. The tourism site is thus realizing the potential of the Internet to simultaneously generate income and control the outsider view of Cherokee identity.

Reconnecting the Indigenous Diaspora

One powerful way in which Indigenous peoples are redefining their identities is through reunification via the Internet. In the past and present Indigenous peoples have often been forced from their territories to make way for colonization or development, or to seek jobs. Sioui (2007) describes how the Wendat/Wyandotte nation were dispersed from their original home in Ontario, Canada, to four localities, some as far away as Oklahoma, beginning in 1649. Following the first reunion on their ancestral lands 350 years after the dispersal, the Internet is being used for daily communications and to rebuild the Wendat Confederacy. Several discussion groups have been established on Yahoo. Members of the "Wendat Culture" group talk about a range of topics from identity, culture, and language, to planned gatherings and cultural groups, to reacquisition of their ancestral territory. The "Wendat Longhouse" arrives at decisions about sensitive topics, while the "Longhouse Women" work towards rebuilding the role of women in what was once a matrifocal society. The Internet is crucial in helping them re-establish a sense of community.

Indigenous Mexican residents of Teotitlán del Valle participated in the creation of community webpages to link with the transborder diaspora of immigrant workers in the US. Zapotec members of 13 cooperatives and the community museum created the webpages as "a form of digital border crossing that involves dialogue – usually at multiple levels – around cultural memory and contested ideas about shared heritage and tradition" (Stephen, 2007, p. 282). Three elements were prominent in the pages: the residents claim to being the first Zapotec settlement in the region; an emphasis on the cultural continuity of language and pre-colonial weaving and dying techniques; and connections between Zapotec identity and wider Indigenous groupings. In common with many Indigenous websites, the Zapotec pages reflected the importance of the landscape and how "place-based and literally 'in the land' " cultural memory is for this community, far from the nightmare of cultural homogenization and globalization predicted by some for Indigenous people in the Internet age (Stephen, 2007, p. 289).

For the Sami people in northern Europe, the Internet has been instrumental in restoring – at least virtually – a borderless territory. In the nineteenth century the borders between Norway, Sweden, and Finland were closed, forcing Sami reindeer herders to choose in which country they were to register (Blind, 2005). The establishment of SameNet in 1997 created a digital meeting-place for all Sami and so allowed the people to overcome, at least virtually, the divisions which had been imposed on them.

Indigenous Cyberactivism

Far from a colonizing force, ICT has become a powerful weapon for fighting colonization and the postcolonial forces that continue to oppress Indigenous peoples. There have been many studies conducted on Indigenous cyberactivism. It represents a highly targeted form of intercultural dialogue and affirmation of identity for political ends. Most cases come from Latin America, where particularly repressive regimes have been in place, but online battles for Indigenous rights are also common in other regions. Land rights, the right to self-determination and native sovereignty, self-government, treaty, legal issues, the right to economic resources, environmental issues and protection of the land and waterways usually form the focus of these online campaigns.

In Chile the Mapuche have been at the forefront of waging an online debate on issues which impact them historically and today, such as assimilation, logging, planting of exotic timbers, construction of highways bisecting Mapuche lands, and forced relocations when dams are built (Dyson & Underwood, 2006). For them, the Internet has challenged and replaced traditional media and channels of communication: despite the fact that Mapuche make up 10 percent of the population of Chile, they have almost no access to mainstream media, which is largely controlled by the political establishment, military, and church (Paillan, quoted in Dyson & Underwood, 2006). Mapuche organizations and individuals, residing in Chile and overseas, have established 25 or more websites used primarily for two functions. Firstly, they provide a means of communication and mobilization of Mapuche people. Secondly, they have been successful as a tool for "building a counter-hegemonic discourse that has started to impact the national public sphere" (Salazar, 2007, p. 23).

Websites to support treaties and land rights are one form of political activism which lies at the heart of Indigenous cultures, given their traditional links with the land and the dishonoring of many treaties historically. The Agreements Treaties and Negotiated Settlements (ATNS) database is an online resource of agreements struck between Indigenous people in Australia and governments, mining companies, or other parties. With over 20,000 visits per month, it is assisting Aboriginal and Torres Strait Islander communities to arrive at recognition of their rights and entitlements with respect to land use, resource management, heritage protection, etc. (Langton, Mazel, & Palmer, 2007).

The Internet has been instrumental in forging new Indigenous identities beyond those of individual nations. Its ability to connect people over vast geographic distances has allowed the creation of regionally based and international pan-Indigenous movements and organizations which would not have been possible before. These allow collective action based on the commonality of Indigenous peoples' struggles for human rights. Niezen (2005) argues that the term "Indigenous peoples" is a relatively new one, a product of the mid-twentieth century. He notes that most sites associated with the word "Indigenous" are devoted to legal and political goals, and that almost all are ultimately associated with collective claims of self-determination. He attributes to the influence of the Internet the extension of the word "Indigenous" beyond the Americas, Australia, Aotearoa (New Zealand), Oceania and northern Europe to now include tribal minorities in Africa and Asia.

Language Online

One of the most significant manifestations of Indigenous identity on the Internet is the use of language. With many languages no longer spoken and others known by a mere handful of living speakers the Internet is providing a way for language revitalization and cultural reaffirmation.

It is not known how many websites there are in Indigenous languages. Crystal (2006) guesses that probably more than a quarter of the world's 6,000 languages have some sort of Internet presence. He states that it is not hard to find minority languages in cyberspace, particularly in the more technologically advanced countries like the US, Canada, and Australia. The Internet is "the ideal medium for minority languages, given the relative cheapness and ease of creating a web page, compared with the cost and difficulty of obtaining a newspaper page, or a programme or advertisement on radio or television" (Crystal, 2006, p. 234).

Many Indigenous languages are represented on the Internet, in the form of dictionaries, word lists, grammars, stories in text or on audio recording, translations, etc., but most are not used as media of communication (Osborn, 2006). The sites are generally *about* Indigenous languages: they form linguistic and educational resources for those wishing to learn or teach the language or acquire background information about the language. Some of these are controlled by Indigenous organizations, but more often they are authored by non-Indigenous linguists and made available by public organizations such as libraries, universities, or other institutions, or language projects such as LINGUIST List, the Endangered Language Fund, SIL International, the Archive of the Indigenous Languages of Latin America (AILLA), the Society for the Study of the Indigenous Languages of the Americas (SSILA), and the Hans Rausing Endangered Languages Project (HRELP).

There are many challenges to establishing a web presence for an Indigenous language and developing an active online community of users, even where that language is still in daily use. Sustainability is a major impediment when the number of speakers who have an Internet connection is very small: for the Sami people, media websites publish news in North Sami, the major dialect, but only give limited coverage in Inari and Skolt Sami, and completely ignore the two rarest dialects (Taylor, 2007). Moreover, many Indigenous communities are not large enough to make viable the development of specialized keyboards suitable for typing their languages and voice recognition software for translating oral input into written text (Crystal, 2006).

The physical representation of Indigenous languages in email, in discussion forums or on websites can be difficult. In Africa, with over 2,000 languages, Osborn (2006) notes that for some languages there is no standardized method of spelling; sometimes variations in spelling occur when languages cross national borders; and for the less widely spoken languages there is perhaps no system of writing them down at all. There are enormous difficulties in representing languages which require specialized fonts or characters. Even with the development of the Unicode system, which expands the old ASCII character-set hugely and so makes many more characters possible, Osborne claims that it is not widely understood in Africa by ICT professionals and therefore not widely applied.

Notwithstanding these challenges – and those outlined earlier, such as fears over possible misappropriation of stories and other language materials placed online – there have been many Internet success stories with regard to Indigenous languages. In Australia there is a great interest in using ICT, such as the Internet, CD-ROMs, touch-screen systems, etc., to revitalize Indigenous languages. Nathan, who maintains the Aboriginal Languages of Australia portal to resources for 80 languages, claims that only 20 remain strong, out of an estimated 600 before colonization. One of the most ambitious projects is to revive Arwarbukarl, an Aboriginal language from the Hunter Valley district north of Sydney. This language has long since been regarded as extinct apart from a written grammar, vocabulary, and translations of prayers and St Luke's Gospel made in the 1830s by missionary Rev. Threlkeld in collaboration with Biraban, the then leader of the clan. In 2005 there were 20 members of the community learning the language for the first time in well over a century, using a language database delivered over the Internet or distributed to language centers on CD-ROM (McKenny, Hughes, & Arposio, 2007).

Of longer duration and more wide-ranging have been the language programs in Hawai'i. Almost a century after the banning of Hawaiian as the language of instruction, concerns over the small number of children who could speak their native language caused a major change of direction in the school system in the 1980s (Warschauer, 1998). Hawaiian immersion schools were established and university programs in Hawaiian language and culture launched. A major challenge was how to connect small, isolated communities of learners strung across the Hawaiian Islands and provide opportunities for them to converse with each other. The founding in 1992 of the Leokï ("Powerful Voice") Bulletin Board – the first such system completely in an Indigenous language – allowed collaborative learning and support through email, chat, discussion forums, and file sharing. The interactive communication technologies of the Internet and its multimedia capabilities allowed learning to take place in a culturally appropriate way, fitting with the cooperative nature of Hawaiian culture and its strengths in oral and graphical media. However, this was not achieved easily. All menus, error messages, and other linguistic features of the screen display had to be translated into Hawaiian (Donaghy, 1998). Methods had to be devised for displaying the diacritical marks of the Hawaiian language correctly both on the website and in communications. A customized keyboard was developed to allow easy typing in Hawaiian. A database of new terms to describe aspects of modern life was devised, as well as teaching materials for learning Hawaiian. Students created new multimedia Hawaiian language materials and published these on the web to extend the resources available to their peers.

Lee (2006) examines a somewhat different aspect of Indigenous language use online: the participation of Indigenous adults in discussion forums and chat rooms. Just as with the language revitalization projects, these too are a scene of reaffirmation of collective identity, although here there is also an interrogation of what that identity means in a globalized world. The heightened sense of contestation arises because most of the Tongan participants she studied were expatriates, members of the diaspora looking for a better life in wealthier countries. They were the ones who had access to the Internet, unlike many of their compatriots back home who would not have been able to take part in forums such as these. Lee found that the discussion forums allowed expatriates to return to an older sense of self and a shared sense of Tongan values, rooted in their cultural homeland. Yet it also meant that younger Tongans could query issues they would not have been allowed to raise normally in the more conservative society in Tonga.

Central to the issue of the identity of the Tongan online community was language, most poignantly fought out when children of immigrants, who enjoyed varying levels of fluency in Tongan, sought inclusion. For many of these younger people, forums conducted at least partially in Tongan provided an ideal opportunity to learn more language. However, there was some dismay when their language skills did not allow them to participate fully and they were forced to include "Tonglish" as they mixed the few words of Tongan they knew with their dominant language English. A dilemma arose in the discussions: to insist on Tongan as the sole medium of communication and so exclude many migrant offspring, or to conduct the forums in English and thus shut out older Tongans. From her study over several years Lee concluded that language is central to the debate on cultural identity since it is a direct expression of culture and the ultimate means of retaining identity in the face of globalization.

Most Indigenous peoples would agree with this position, seeing language as "the root and heart of our culture" (quoted in Hennessy & Moore, 2007). However, it does raise the issue of how Indigenous people who no longer speak their language can achieve and reaffirm their identity. Indeed, Lee found that, for Tongans of the diaspora, identity can be asserted in other ways without a knowledge of the native language.

Conclusion

Indigenous peoples around the world have appropriated the medium of the Internet for their own purposes. As has been shown, they have been extremely proactive in establishing their own websites from as early as 1994 when many others in the non-Indigenous community had not even considered it (Polly, 1998). They have been eager to use the Internet to re-establish lines of communication long since broken, revitalize languages so often endangered, reaffirm their identity once again, and mobilize their communities to fight for their right to exist in the twenty-first century.

It should not be surprising that Indigenous people have so effectively engaged with this new medium. Cullen (2005) sees this engagement in terms of "adapting a foreign invention and making it their own." The Internet is relatively new. It has the power to be shaped by those who choose to use it. Its lack of any defined hierarchy, its absence of a centralized hub, and its laterally spreading network of links represent a propensity towards democracy (Delgado-P., 2002). This paves the way for the inclusion of minority groups, such as Indigenous people, who have previously been excluded or underrepresented in conventional media.

However, despite the success of Indigenous peoples' appropriation of the Internet, there are still many challenges. Probably the greatest challenge and the most persistent is the lack of Internet access for most Indigenous people due to poor connectivity, the cost of technology, and their lack of computer skills, exacerbated by the remote locations where they often live. Given the low numbers of Indigenous people connected to the Internet, one must question who their websites are really for. The relatively few websites in Indigenous languages confirm that many are probably aimed more at an outside audience. This would be the case particularly where the language chosen for the site is the major international language of English in regions where this is not the normal means of communication, such as Latin America and Asia.

Much more work will have to be done, and is being done, on a national and global scale. Community owned and run computer-technology centers have been the most effective means of improving access and are now widespread in the developed world as well as increasingly in many developing countries, often financed by governments or NGOs. Some issues, such as protecting intellectual property and traditional knowledge and culture have to some extent been solved by password protection or by keeping sensitive information off the Internet, but there are also new technical solutions in the pipeline, such as the use of rights markup languages to restrict access and enforce protection (Hunter, 2002). Measures such as these will ensure that Indigenous people continue to expand their presence on the Internet.

References

Anderson, C. G. (2003). American Indian tribal web sites: A review and comparison. *The Electronic Library*, 21, suppl. 5, 450–55.

Anderson, J. (2005). Access and control of Indigenous knowledge in libraries and archives: Ownership and future use. American Library Association and the MacArthur Foundation, Columbia University, May 5–7, New York.

Arnold, E. L., & Plymire, D. C. (2000). The Cherokee Indians and the Internet. In D. Gauntlett (ed.), *Web Studies: Rewiring Media Studies for the Digital Age* (pp. 186–93). London: Arnold.

Becker, M., & Delgado-P. G. (1998). Latin America: The Internet and Indigenous texts. *Cultural Survival Quarterly*, 21, suppl. 4. http://www.culturalsurvival.org/ourpublications/csq/article/latin-america-the-internet-and-indigenous-texts.

Blind, H. (2005). SameNet – digital meeting place for Sami, trans. F. Mena. Swedish Institute. Retrieved March 29, 2008, from www.sweden.se/templates/cs/Article_11094.aspx.

Bolter, J. D. (2001). *Writing Space: Computers, Hypertext, and the Remediation of Print*, 2nd edn. Mahwah, NJ: Lawrence Erlbaum.

Bray-Crawford, K. P. (1999). The Ho'okele netwarriors in the liquid continent. In W. Harcourt (ed.) *Women@Internet: Creating New Cultures in Cyberspace* (pp. 162–72). London and New York: Zed Books.

Caraveo, S. (1998). We have links to over 2000 web sites that contain information important to Indigenous cultures. *Zum Thema*, 24 (December).

Crystal, D. (2006). *Language and the Internet*, 2nd edn. Cambridge: Cambridge University Press.

Cullen, T. T. (2005). Sovereignty unplugged: Wireless technology and self-governance in the Navajo nation. *Cultural Survival Quarterly*, 29, suppl. 2.

Daly, A. (2007). The diffusion of new technologies: Community online access centres in Indigenous communities in Australia. In L. E. Dyson, M. Hendriks, & S. Grant (eds.), *Information Technology and Indigenous People* (pp. 272–85). Hershey, PA: Information Science Publishing.

Delgado-P., G. (2002). Solidarity in cyberspace: Indigenous peoples online. *NACLA Report on the Americas*, 35, suppl. 5, 49–51.

Donaghy, K. (1998). 'Olelo Hawai'i: A rich oral history, a bright digital future. *Cultural Survival Quarterly*, 21, suppl. 4.

Dyson, L. E. (2003). Indigenous Australians in the information age: Exploring issues of neutrality in information technology. In C. Ciborra, R. Mercurio, M. de Marco, M. Martinez, & A. Carignani (eds.), *New Paradigms in Organizations, Markets and Society: Proceedings of the 11th European Conference on Information Systems (ECIS)* (pp. 1–12). June 19–21, Naples.

Dyson, L. E. (2006). Remote Indigenous Australian communities and ICT. In S. Marshall, W. Taylor, & X.-H. Yu (eds.), *Encyclopedia of Developing Regional Communities with Information and Communication Technology* (pp. 608–13). Hershey, PA: Idea Group Reference.

Dyson, L. E., & Underwood, J. (2006). Indigenous people on the web. *Journal of Theoretical and Applied Electronic Commerce Research*, 1, suppl. 1, 65–76.

Gaidan, B. (2007). My life with computers on a remote island. In L. E. Dyson, M. Hendriks, & S. Grant (eds.), *Information Technology and Indigenous People* (pp. 58–60). Hershey, PA: Information Science Publishing.

Hennessy, K., & Moore, P. J. (2007). Language, identity and community control: The Taglish first voices project. In L. E. Dyson, M. Hendriks, & S. Grant (eds.), *Information Technology and Indigenous People* (pp. 189–91). Hershey, PA: Information Science Publishing, Hershey.

Hobson, J. (2001). Growing the Indigenous Australian Internet. European Network for Indigenous Australian Rights. Retrieved May 16, 2004, from http://eniar.org/news/net1.html.

Hughes, S. (2004). CMC Scale-Up – Opportunities and Challenges. UNESCO. Retrieved April 12, 2008, from http://portal.unesco.org/ci/en/ev.php-url_id=16968&url_do=do_printpage &url_section=201.html.

Hunter, J. (2002). Rights markup extensions for the protection of Indigenous knowledge. In *Proceedings of Global Communities Track, WWW2002*, Honolulu, USA. Retrieved January 29, 2004, from www202.org/CDROM/alternate/748.

ICIPTF (Indigenous Cultural and Intellectual Property Task Force) (1999). The 1989 UNESCO recommendation and Aboriginal and Torres Strait Islander Peoples' intellectual property rights. *A Global Assessment of the 1989 Recommendation on the Safeguarding of Traditional Culture and Folklore: Local Empowerment and International Co-operation* (pp. 1–12). UNESCO/Smithsonian Conference, June 27–30, Washington, DC.

Injie, L., & Haintz, F. (2004). The natural development of Wangka Maya into the direction of a knowledge centre. Indigenous studies – sharing the cultural and theoretical space. AIATSIS Conference. Canberra, Australia.

Iseke-Barnes, J., & Danard, D. (2007). Indigenous knowledges and worldview: Representations and the Internet. In L. E. Dyson, M. Hendriks, & S. Grant (eds.), *Information Technology and Indigenous People* (pp. 27–37). Hershey, PA: Information Science Publishing.

Kitalong, K. S., & Kitalong, T. (2000). Complicating the tourist gaze: Literacy and the Internet as catalysts for articulating a postcolonial Palauan identity. In G. E. Hawisher & C. L. Selfe (eds.), *Global Literacies and the World-Wide Web* (pp. 95–113). London and New York: Routledge.

Landzelius, K. (ed.) (2006). *Native on the Net: Indigenous and Diasporic Peoples In The Virtual Age*. Milton Park: Routledge.

Langton, M., Mazel, O., & Palmer, L. (2007). Agreements treaties and negotiated settlements database. In L. E. Dyson, M. Hendriks, & S. Grant (eds.), *Information*

Technology and Indigenous People (pp. 266–70). Hershey, PA: Information Science Publishing.

Latu, S., & Dyson, L. E. (2006). ICT – The perception of the Tongan minority in New Zealand. In F. Sudweeks, H. Hrachovec, & C. Ess (eds.), *Proceedings of the Fifth International Conference on Cultural Attitudes towards Technology and Communication (CATaC)* (pp. 360–71), Tartu. Murdoch, Australia: Murdoch University.

Leclair, C., & Warren, S. (2007). Portals and Potlatch. In L. E. Dyson, M. Hendriks, & S. Grant (eds.), *Information Technology and Indigenous People* (pp. 1–13). Hershey, PA: Information Science Publishing.

Lee, H. (2006). Debating language and identity online: Tongans on the net. In K. Landzelius (ed.) *Native on the Net: Indigenous and Diasporic Peoples in the Virtual Age* (pp. 152–68). Milton Park: Routledge.

Martin, G. (1995). Internet Indian wars. *Wired*, 3, suppl. 12.

McConaghy, C. (2000). The web and today's colonialism. *Australian Aboriginal Studies*, 1 & 2, 48–54.

McKenny, D., Hughes, B., & Arposio, A. (2007). Towards an Indigenous language knowledge base: Tools and techniques from the Arwarbukarl community. In L. E. Dyson, M. Hendriks, & S. Grant (eds.), *Information Technology and Indigenous People* (pp. 192–9). Hershey, PA: Information Science Publishing.

Meer, J. (2003). Getting on the Net: The struggle for digital inclusion of the Navajo. *IEEE Technology and Society Magazine*, Spring, 53–8.

Mitten, L. (2003). Indians on the Internet – selected Native American web sites. *Electronic Library*, 21, suppl. 5, 443–9.

Nathan, D. (2000). Plugging in Indigenous knowledge: Connections and innovations. *Australian Aboriginal Studies*, 1 & 2, 39–47.

Osborn, D. Z. (2006). African languages and information and communication technologies: Literacy, access, and the future. In J. Mugane, J. P. Hutchison, & D. A. Woman (eds.), *Selected Proceedings of the 35th Annual Conference on African Linguistics* (pp. 86–93), Cascadilla. Sommerville, MA: Proceedings Project.

Polly, J. A. (1998). Standing stones in cyberspace: The Oneida Indian Nation's territory on the Web. *Cultural Survival Quarterly*, 21, suppl. 4.

Radoll, P. J. (2004). Protecting copyrights on the Internet: A cultural perspective from Indigenous Australia. In F. Sudweeks & C. Ess (eds.), *Proceedings of the Fourth International Conference on Cultural Attitudes towards Technology and Communication (CATaC)* (pp. 339–48), Karlstad. Murdoch, Australia: Murdoch University.

Salazar, J. F. (2007). Indigenous peoples and the cultural construction of information and communication technology (ICT) in Latin America. In L. E. Dyson, M. Hendriks, & S. Grant (eds.), *Information Technology and Indigenous People* (pp. 14–26). Hershey, PA: Information Science Publishing.

Schoenhoff, D. (1993). *The Barefoot Expert: The Interface of Computerized Knowledge Systems and Indigenous Knowledge Systems*. Westport, CT: Greenwood Press.

Secretariat of the United Nations Permanent Forum on Indigenous Issues (2003). *The Report of the Global Forum of Indigenous Peoples and the Information Society* (pp. 1–34). Geneva: World Summit on the Information Society.

Shorter, D. D. (2006). "How do you say 'search engine' in your language?": translating Indigenous world view into digital ethnographies. *Journal of World Anthropology Network*, 1, suppl. 2, 109–13.

Sioui, L. (2007). Reunification of the Wendat/Wyandotte Nation at a time of globalization. In L. E. Dyson, M. Hendriks, & S. Grant (eds.), *Information Technology and Indigenous People* (pp. 310–15). Hershey, PA: Information Science Publishing.

Stephen, L. (2007). *Transborder Lives: Indigenous Oaxacans in Mexico, California and Oregon.* Durham, NC, and London: Duke University Press.

Strom, K. (2000). Paula's website lives! Retrieved April, 15, 2008, from www.kstrom.net/isk/Paula.html.

Taylor, J. (2007). Indigenous Internet representation among the Nordic Sámi. In C. Montgomerie & J. Seale (eds.), *Proceedings of the World Conference on Educational Multimedia, Hypermedia and Telecommunications* (pp. 1071–83). Chesapeake, VA: Association for the Advancement of Computing in Education.

UNESCO (2002). *UNESCO Universal Declaration on Cultural Diversity.* Adopted by the 31st Session of the General Conference of UNESCO, November 2, 2001. Paris: UNESCO.

UNESCO (2004). About Indigenous Peoples, March 15. Retrieved August 19, 2008, from http://portal.unesco.org/ci/en/ev.php-url_id=14205&url_do=do_topic&url_section=201.html.

UNESCO (2006). ICT4ID, October 18. Retrieved August 19, 2008, from http://portal.unesco.org/ci/en/ev.php-url_id=14203&url_do=do_topic&url_section=201.html.

Warschauer, M. (1998). Technology and Indigenous language revitalization: Analysing the experience of Hawai'i. Retrieved April 21, 2004, from http://www.gse.uci.edu/markw/revitalization.html.

Zamorano, G. (2005). Community video and self-representation: Interview with Carlos Efraín Pérez Rojas. *Native Networks*, April.

Zimmerman, L. J., Zimmerman, K. P., & Bruguier, L. R. (2000). Cyberspace smoke signals: New technologies and Native American ethnicity. In C. Smith, & G. K. Ward (eds.), *Indigenous Cultures in an Interconnected World* (pp. 69–86). Vancouver: UBC Press.

13

Queering Internet Studies: Intersections of Gender and Sexuality

Janne Bromseth and Jenny Sundén

It appears nearly impossible to speak of the recent history of gender, sexuality, and the Internet without the seemingly mandatory etymological trace-back of the concept "cyberspace" to the cyberpunk writer William Gibson who coined the term (1984). For Gibson, the story of his console cowboys who "jacked in" to "the Matrix," their bodies left behind as obsolete "meat," was a dark, twisted tale of a future of no future. Ironically, the sinister Gibsonian image of cyberspace as disembodied was turned on its head and transformed into a utopian possibility of freedom from the flesh by early 1990s' cybercultural theorists. They pictured cyberspace as a free, democratic, placeless space, unlimited by biology, geography, and matter (Benedikt, 1991; Lanier & Biocca, 1992). This line of thinking had resonance in early cyberfeminism, as exemplified in the writing of Sadie Plant (1997). Cyberspace was imagined to be a place unbound by physical bodies, where users could create and recreate themselves, endlessly, in experimental and liberating ways (Wiley, 1999). Amy Bruckman (1993) talked about such experiences and experiments as "gender swapping," and Sandy Stone (1995) wrote, seductively, on the queer, transgendered body as a possible point of departure in virtual worlds.

Parallel to the cyberfeminist discussion of the hopes of new media technologies were feminist studies of the material/discursive intersection of gender and technology. One recurring feature of this debate was the consistent critique of the naturalized link between masculinity and technology, between men and their machines, boys and their toys.[1] The analysis, typically, was fairly pessimistic. There seemed to be little way around the modes in which masculinity appeared to be hardwired into the machinery itself, which efficiently positioned femininity (collapsed into the category of biological women) as incommensurable with technology. Within the discourses of information and communication technologies (ICTs) of the 1980s and the early 1990s, women were routinely positioned as non-users and computer illiterates. But with the explosive growth of the web and of computer use in general, these discourses have come to focus on more specific practices, such as the distinction between production and consumption of technologies.

Expert skills, such as hacking, programming, and design, are arguably still highly masculinized domains in the West (Corneliussen, 2002; Gansmo et al., 2003; Lagesen, 2005; Nordli, 2003). Gender and technology are co-constructed, the discussion goes, but what is coded as masculine versus feminine, and how, changes over time and across cultures.[2]

The cyberfeminist movements of the 1990s in the fields of art, theory, and activism were, partly, a reaction against the perceived pessimism of the 1980s feminist studies of gender and technology. Cyberfeminists attempted to find alternative strategies in the struggle against the ways sexism, homophobia, and racism seemed to be hardcoded into the very interfaces of new media technologies. They did not boycott the seemingly "masculine" technology, but attempted to master it and make it an ally for their own feminist purposes and pleasures. Like Donna Haraway's (1991) emblematic cyborg figure, notoriously unfaithful to its founding fathers,[3] cyberfeminists made themselves available for the most inappropriate and promiscuous couplings with technologies. In their *Cyberfeminist Manifesto for the 21st Century* from 1991, the Australian artists' group VNS Matrix made quite literal efforts to contaminate technology with sexuality. Sentences like "The clitoris is a direct line to the matrix," from their manifesto, have not only been interpreted as bad girls talking dirty, but can also be seen as female appropriation of computer technologies. At the same time, feminist philosopher Rosi Braidotti (1996) argued for a "cyberfeminism with a difference" and pointed to the risks for women in buying into the notion of cyberspace as merely a place for subversive identity performances, freed from the limitations of the physical body. According to Braidotti, rather than liberate women this would repeat the Cartesian fallacy of separating mind from body. The dream of getting rid of the body reflects the understanding of masculinity as abstraction, she argued, of men as physically disconnected and independent, remapped onto cyberspace discourses.

The notion of cyberspace as disembodied utopia – or as playground for unlimited gender play – was soon criticized by a growing number of Internet scholars for being merely theoretically speculative and wishful thinking. In response, researchers set out to systematically study virtual worlds and venues, to find out what people "actually did" when they went online. Kira Hall (1996), in her now-classic article "Cyberfeminism," argues for "concrete studies" of computer-mediated communication. The field of online ethnography, or "virtual ethnography" to use a term from Christine Hine (2000), began to take shape. The pictures of life online provided by ethnographers and others with an interest in empirically sound explorations were quite different from those of the more utopian thinkers. No longer depicted as a coherent, unambiguous whole, "cyberspace" was rather revealed to consist of a wide range of particular cultures and contexts, each with its own flavor and each with its own rules. The idea of cyberspace as placeless was countered by studies of the very locations in which cyberspaces are always produced and consumed. If the focus originally had been on "readings"of interface cultures, the focus shifted toward the ways in which onscreen performances are always embedded in everyday practices, as well as part of larger politico-economic structures (Wakeford, 1997). The understanding of cyberspace as disembodied was taken apart by findings according to which the body was consistently reintroduced, represented, even on demand in virtual worlds (Sundén, 2003). It also soon became clear that even if the act of "swapping gender" was only a few keystrokes away, the modes and codes surrounding gender performances online were often quite restrictive. "Are you male or female?" seemed to be the question most frequently asked (Kendall, 1998), as a counterstrategy to online gender ambiguity.

The theoretical perspectives in the early days of feminist Internet studies both reflected and contributed to the general discussions within women's studies and gender studies, being in a phase of profound changes whose consequences we are just now starting to understand. Moving from a rather singular understanding of women and men, as well as from structuralist power analysis and patriarchal theories, core concepts have been challenged and questioned; of power, and of gender, and other social identities (Richardson et al., 2007). Women's studies became gender studies, gender and other differences were understood as socially constructed and flexible phenomena, and postcolonial and queer theoretical perspectives sought to challenge the white, Western, and heterosexual norms within feminist theory.[4] Interestingly, the Internet as a cultural phenomenon was entangled with the discussion of poststructuralism and queer theory in ways that had consequences for Internet studies and queer/feminist studies alike. The "ideal cybersubject" and "the ideal queer subject" seem to overlap noticeably, with significance for ideas of self, body, and their interrelations (O'Riordan, 2007). The possibilities of playfulness, passing, and identity experimentation in online contexts became the archetypical example of gender and sexuality as situated, flexible performances and of subjectivity as multiple and incoherent. Then again, as with the idea of gender flexibility in online contexts, the level of technological possibility cannot easily be conflated with that of queer politics. Even if the options of being fluid and flexible seem to come with the technology, that does not automatically lead to online performances along such lines.

If early Internet studies were primarily tied to the level of online representations and issues of identity, playfulness, and deception, where are we today? And what is the status of sexuality as an analytical concept in a field that has been dominated by discussions of (heteronormative) gender? These are questions that have guided the writing of this chapter, and our ambition is to place this discussion within the very interplay between Internet culture, theoretical development, and technological development. We both came of age, academically, at the time of the 1990s discussion of cyberspace as possible feminist utopia (and dystopia). In response, we have both formulated our research agendas as clearly critical, yet hopeful, of the ways in which the Internet can be used for queer, feminist purposes. Our research backgrounds in the field of new media, gender, and sexuality are different, but not without overlaps: Bromseth (2001, 2006a, 2006b, 2007) has primarily focused on mailing lists and web-based queer communities, whereas Sundén (2001, 2003, 2008; Sveningsson Elm, & Sundén, 2007) started out with text-based MUDs (multi-user dungeons) and MOOs (object-oriented MUDs), and then – via studies of hypertext fiction and new media art – moved into game studies.[5]

This chapter is a collaborative effort. The writing "we" stands for the voices of us both, blended together. This "we" is repeatedly disrupted by a succession of what we have called "scenes" based on more personal reflections. Each scene evokes an image through which certain key concepts are discussed. The "I" of the scenes belongs to only one of us – and to whom will be made clear in each case. The chapter starts out with a discussion of the seriousness of play and the power of imagination in shifting Internet cultures. Secondly, it moves on to contextualize more clearly the notion of play as serious in looking at questions of credibility, accountability, and genre. Central to this line of argument is research in the connectiveness between physical bodies and their onscreen representations. Thirdly, our attempt is to make explicit the inter-linkages between gender and sexuality in understanding body politics in online contexts. This is a debate that has, largely, been absent from Internet research. Fourthly, we look at some of the implications of making explicit intersections of gender and sexuality in understanding sub-cultural communities online. Finally, we touch upon research on questions of body, spatiality, and affect to bring into view a possible queer feminist politics of the sensorial. In an Internet era which appears to privilege visual cultures and ways of seeing, it is important not to forget about other modes of sensing and knowing online spaces. The chapter ends with a summary of the key points of the discussion.

Serious Play and Shifting Internet Cultures

Scene 1, Jenny: The entrance at street level is not easy to detect. It looks like a drive-way. The innocent by-passer might, if she is attentive, discover a discreet sign on the door. And if in the right mood, and with the appropriate attire, she may even decide, bravely, to enter. A harsh looking woman in skintight leather greets her, as she descends a steep staircase. The room is dark, winding, sparsely lit by candles, and holds a group of women, circulating, all in black; leather, rubber, plastic, silk. Strict buttoned-up shirts, ties and pants for some, even full uniforms with cleverly cut jackets, and caps shadowing wandering eyes. Dropping necklines, tightly laced-up corsets, dresses hugging the body as a second skin on others. Glimpses of bare skin in between where the dress ends and the stockings begin. Black jeans with black tops at a minimum. All ages, all sizes. Heavy baselines resonate through bodies and make them vibrate, if ever so slightly. A tight-fitted leather necklace around someone's neck attached to a chain, a steady grip in some-one else's hair. Whips. The mandatory wooden cross, situated in a more secluded area, not immediately visible from the main room. The perfect setting for a night of play with bodies, and with power, in which the roles may seem fixed once and for all (What is your inclination? To dominate or be dominated?). But these are nights that may hold surprising flexibility for those willing to experiment and push the boundaries – of bodies and minds. Welcome to the dungeon.

Where is this place located? It could be a chat room straight out of the novel *Nearly Roadkill: An Infobahn Erotic Adventure* by Caitlin Sullivan and Kate Bornstein (1996), which was an early attempt to fictionalize points of intersection between same-sex desire and new media technologies. It could also be a scene from one of the more experimental MOOs (purely text-based virtual worlds) of the early1990s. Or is it an event from Linden Lab's *Second Life* of the Web 2.0 era? Either way, it is a scene belonging to one of those velvety yet rough places of the urban, lesbian underworld. It could be computer-coded, or coded directly into the flesh. Most likely, it is both of these things simultaneously.

The research story of gender and sexuality in Internet cultures can be told in many ways, but one question that seems to be recurring – and which still holds relevance – is that of the significance of play. Play and playfulness have been discussed as key features in online cultures. Brenda Danet and her colleagues (Danet, 1998; Danet, Ruedenberg, & Rosenbaum-Tamari, 1998) did some early accounts of the meaning of playful performances in text-based online worlds. But, as Donna Haraway (1991, p. 161) has made clear, "we are living through a movement from an organic, industrial society to a polymorphous, information system – from all work to all play, a deadly game." Play, rather than being innocent or insignificant, can be dead serious. Since the advent of the web in 1994, the stages on which play can be performed have shifted significantly. Grassroots-driven communities of the text-based Internet are at the margins of ultra-commercial visual interfaces of portals, communities, and games. Queer political sites and zines (online magazines), discussion groups, mailing lists, and blogs coexist, but tend to be overshadowed by – or embedded in – significantly larger structures of social networking sites with ready-made identity menus and pre-coded profiles. Cybercultures have always been about participation, but the participatory cultures of Web 2.0 are fairly different, both symbolically and ideologically, from those of its predecessor Web 1.0. Lisa Nakamura (2007) formulates this shift in online ethos and alter egos as a movement from "avatar 1.0" to "avatar 2.0." The former provided the kind of therapeutic self-work of cycling through layers of windows and worlds as pictured by Sherry Turkle (1995) in *Life on the Screen*, along with the relative freedom of textuality and possibilities of "passing." In contrast, Nakamura argues that the latter is rather an instantiation of a "culture of profiling," distinguished by behavior and choices in the circuits of capital, labor, and profit.

A culture of profiling is one of point-and-click menus and ready-made identity options, of a coming together of mediated identities across scales, scores, and ratings. It distinguishes itself from previous perhaps more subtle modes of self-making by spelling it all out in high-resolution graphics and sound. In this shift from text-based interfaces to those based on images, it is possible to, anew, trace a desire for the authentic and the sincere. If the inhabitants of MUDs and MOOs of the 1990s asked for a simple logic which linked specific gendered performances to sexually specific bodies ("Are you male or female?"), in certain cultures of profiling, there is a similar and possibly even more distinct demand for realism and authenticity now. For example, on Swedish Qruiser – a social networking site catering for local, queer interests – one of the most recent features is called "verification." This is a function that lets other members "verify" that you actually are who you claim to be. A question that immediately comes to mind is what such verification entails. Is it to verify that I look like myself in my pictures (and not better than myself)? Is it to verify the truthfulness in my written statements about myself in my profile?

In this particular culture of profiling, the body of the typist is not only called into being by the question "are you male or female," but interrogated by a process of regulated identification and confirmation. Such profiling cultures appear to provide mediations which bring material bodies closer to each other. This closeness, or nakedness even, is created through the attempt to minimize the room for playfulness and deception, and to make more critical than ever questions of trust and authenticity. Access to online communities has become all the more widespread, and the intertwining of community interfaces and off-screen encounters face-to-face – or, we should perhaps say body-to-body in the example of Qruiser – all the more pronounced. But whereas we know quite a lot about the meaning and matter of avatar 1.0, the sexual politics of avatar 2.0 remain yet to be seen.

Thinking online embodiment through notions of play and performance is thinking through the many ways in which the body is created, recreated, and evoked in online worlds through image, text, and sound. It is, simultaneously, thinking through the corporeal situatedness of users. Perhaps more intriguingly, issues of embodiment online highlight the many connections – and possible disconnections – between the body performing (at the keyboard) and the body being performed (onscreen). The introductory scene raises questions of power, play, and sexuality. It raises questions of the location and direction of bodies and desires. What in one moment may look like a recreation of a steamy online encounter typed up by warm hands, hearts pounding, may in the next moment come forth as an everyday-like description of a particular queer/lesbian subculture "offline." And in reality, the two are usually interlocked in ways which render terms such as "online" and "offline," if not obsolete, then at least increasingly complicated.

Play can also have significant feminist political implications. In the rear-view mirror, it seems like research with an interest in the politics of the body online had to make a choice between imagination and reality, theoretical inventiveness and empirical proof, the radically new and business as usual. This divide was sometimes disciplinary, inserting a distinction between humanist discussions of textuality and social-science-oriented approaches to the everyday and the situatedness of Internet practices. Our own research positions echo what Silver and Massanari (2006) name "critical cyberculture studies." A critical approach to Internet practices refuses to take sides. It remains empirically sound, carefully situated, and context specific, yet open to what the medium might bring. In the name of queer/feminist politics, it seems as important as ever to discuss how online bodies are disconnected neither from dominating discourses of gender and sexuality, nor from the material specificity of bodies. At the same time, it seems equally important for strategic, political reasons to not completely discard early research on cyberculture, but to insist on the transgressive, perhaps even rebellious, potential of Internet media. Utopian thinking in/of cyberspace is not merely far-fetched and illusory, but holds real feminist promise in its way of imagining things differently. Such imaginative power should not be underestimated.

Genre, Accountability, and Credible Selves

Scene 2, Janne:

> Is it really a man who has continuously written "undercover" of four women – as aggressive ListBitch, angry radical feminist with strong opinions and as "smart academic feminist" with great knowledge of feminist theory? It's almost too good to be true!!! This is the "Joan-story" from Stone!! In my material!! (Field diary notes, December 3, 2003).[6]

In the middle of the fieldwork of a mailing-list community for lesbian and bisexual women, Sapfo, which had the option of anonymous self-presentations, I was introduced to some ethical dilemmas of creating selves online. Over a period of three years, one man had successfully passed as at least four different female personae on the list, slowly building images of credible lesbian or bisexual women. He'd convinced us all through showing knowledge of lesbian subculture and of feminist positions in the local political debates offline, and by creating images of situated lesbian and bisexual women through creative life-stories. When suspicion grew that the bodies did not have a corresponding gendered corporeality offline, the "real body was asked to stand up"[7] and account for its existence in the woman-only group. But the male body typing had the wrong materiality to be a valid list-member, the majority concluded. His female online characters were not granted continued existence status either, as they lacked the flesh of a woman and names in the phonebook. Thus, the vivid participants Malin, Nicole, Flisan, and Anna were left like masks without life on the floor, while their male author ran naked through the backdoor followed by the angry cries from the former lesbian sisters.

Competing understandings of identity, gender, and body, but also the question of accountability, were central to the ethical dilemmas that arose in the group following the "revelation" of the multiple-personality cross-dresser – in line with other mediated communities. Who is responsible for fictional bodies online, and when can the concept of multiple bodies be an ethical problem for building community online? What happens to accountability when singular conceptions of identity are challenged?

Identity deception in different forms, when an online character is created with the purpose of making others believe that it is "real," is one of the phenomena that have fascinated – and worried – many people since the early days of the Internet. The term stretches beyond spam-fraud and fishing for victims of sexual abuse. Long-term gender-bending/cross-dressing online is often understood as deceit. The episode referred above is strikingly similar to the famous tale of the handicapped woman Joan,[8] a popular participant in one of the early commercial text-based inter-active spaces in the days before the World Wide Web, who in the end was revealed to be a male psychologist (Turkle, 1995; Stone, 1995).[9] The online world was confronted with the offline, where the online character did not have an existing offline equivalent. Both Turkle and Stone argued at the time that the reactions were strong because this happened in the early days of the Internet, and that when people were more experienced with using the Internet, they would be aware that events like these could take place. Stone in particular predicted that online com-munication would eventually change our perceptions of identity, gender, and sexuality in a more poststructuralist direction, where identity is understood as unstable, multiple, and contradictory. However, 20 years later, empirical studies have repeatedly shown how self-presentations that deviate severely between online character and embodied typist are still often interpreted as deceptions and betrayals (Bromseth, 2006a; Kendall, 2002; Sundén, 2003). In the multi-medial Web 2.0, verified identities increase participants' credibility, for example through publishing a photo on net-dating sites (Sommer, 2003). The more "trust cues," the less the feelings of social risk, which creates better conditions for social inter-action, Bødker and Christensen conclude (2003).

Thus, the basic question remains the same: What is at stake when boundaries of credible selves are challenged, when images of bodies online are confronted with deviant material realities? As Jodi O'Brien writes (1999), these expectations can be related to Western modernist understanding of what a "self" is, where multiple selves in social-realistic contexts obviously fall outside the border of a normal/healthy self. Also, it can be related to the importance of gender as a central resource for how we make sense of reality; how we interpret and relate to other people. In physical contexts, the body is used as a central resource in this interpretative interactional work. To be culturally intelligible online, it is even more crucial to give a coherent gendered self-presentation in creating credible selves, Kolko and Reid (1998) argue in their article "Dissolution and Fragmentation: Problems in Online Communities." In offline contexts our performances are still anchored in a material representation of our selves, allowing flexibility in beha-viors and subjectivity, because we can still be recognized visually. There is some-one physically accountable for our actions, something that is not the case in anonymous spaces online, when the mediated self is not merged with the embodied self. Because of the possibility of not being physically present at the same place, options of creating images of an embodied persona that do not match with the typist in social interaction have increased with new ICTs. These possibilities and practices have caused many discussions about implications and consequences that include several important dimensions, theoretically as well as ethically.[10] As in other offline contexts, what is *possible* to do online is not necessarily socially accepted or even desirable. Establishing online selves is also always a situated process and dependent on genre as well as the social frame created within a group, as Judith Donath argues:

New ways of establishing and of hiding identity are evolving in the virtual world. There is no formula that works best in all forums: balancing privacy and account- ability, reliability and self-expression, security and accessibility requires a series of compromises and tradeoffs whose value is very dependent on the goals of the group and of the individuals that comprise it. (1999, p. 56)

The situations and conflicts that have emerged from what is considered accountable behavior have nevertheless been interesting ways of looking at the boundary practices that have arisen, because it is here that cultural phenomena are negotiated (Bromseth, 2001; Donath, 1999; Kolko & Reid, 1998; Kollock & Smith, 1999). What are encouraged and devalued practices in various Internet- mediated communication contexts, and why? How are they related to gender, sexuality, identity and embodiment? As Donath argues, these are questions with many answers, depending on the frames of a group and its social purposes. Conflicts often arise when frames are not made explicit, and the discursive concepts of identity, body, and gender are often an invisible part of social frames, visible only when they are broken, such as with the Scandinavian mailing-list community Sapfo referred to above. Only when the multiple cross-dresser is revealed, the norma- tive identity concept is made visible, causing strong emotional reactions among list members, and the death of the vivid group (Bromseth, 2006a). It will surely not be the last time, because our discourses of subjectivity still do not encourage bodies without organs outside the world of fiction, and thus we expect online bodies in non-fictional spaces to be authentic representations of one gendered body.

Online multiplicity and cross-dressing events are related to Western ideas of subjectivity and identity. They are also related to different cultural scripts of social genres (Bromseth, 2006a). When it comes to social-realistic versus fic- tional genres, the social frames create different sets of rules for how we should behave and how we interpret others in social interaction (Goffman, 1974). These frames operate in spite of poststructuralist challenges to understanding identity, Jodi O'Brien argues (1999), based upon a late modernity conception of identity; presuming that each individual has one authentic body and one identity. This implies that to pass as a credible human being, the one body should not have more than one personality – whereas the contrast is described as a mental personality disorder. Since gender is considered as being an important part of our selves, this also excludes the option of having more than one gendered identity:

The existing cultural scripts that provide a repertoire for handling multiplicity render it either as pathological disorder or allowable as fiction. . . . [W]e have only one body, therefore we have only one "true" gendered self of which we can be "hon- estly" aware. To represent this self as something other than that which is consistent with physical form is acceptable only if the performance conforms to mutually under- stood rules of "fiction." (O'Brien, 1999, p. 96)

Multiple selves, then, have problems with being accepted as valid ways of performing identity within online genres that are not associated with "fiction," such as discussion groups. The need for locating authentic bodies behind the screen is alive even in online environments designated for play and fantasy-games, several studies have shown (Sundén, 2003; Kendall, 2002; Danet, 1998). As Sundén (2003) points out, bodies not only become text; to pass as a credible self is itself turned into a textual practice. Cyberselves are created within a range of different social contexts. What is rarely the case, as O'Brien (1999) shows, is a social-realistic frame where selves are not expected to be predictable, unified, stable or singular; or where fiction is accepted, where a poststructuralist understanding of identity makes out the rules for a credible participant in social interaction.

However, the narrative of the fragmented self in mediated communities and its connection to material bodies, needs to be problematized in relation to account-ability and community, Kolko and Reid (1998) argue. Being critical of the pos-sibilities of multiple identities in the online realm has easily been interpreted as being stuck in modernist and essentialized ways of understanding identity. This is however not in opposition to having a social constructivist/postmodern view of identity: "Perhaps we might draw on the works of Donna Haraway . . . and other postmodern feminists to explain how embodiment does not equal modernism, and how accountability does not negate the idea of play" (p. 224).

As socially embodied individuals in face-to-face settings, we are never one and the same in our human everyday relations, but act according to the social situation, and in contradictory ways. Diversity exists within the self, according to postmodern theories of identity, and we change over time, across situations and within long-term relations. At the same time, our bodies hold us accountable for our actions, in the sense that they are our physical representations of selves. Kolko and Reid (1998) address the question: In which ways is fragmentation problem-atic in relation to creating stable and democratic online communities over time? And, we would add, how is fragmentation related to gender and sexuality? They refer to the problem of conflicts and conflict solving, where the accountable body can easily be replaced by a new online character, while the typist remains invis-ible, but materially the same. In these processes, it is crucial to differentiate between different techno-cultural spaces and their social functions and purposes. All social networks and groups that meet regularly for a specific purpose need to establish and develop ways to interact that meet basic criteria that strengthen their goals. Most online communities reproduce traditional concepts of gender, sexuality, and identity as part of their norms – without reflecting upon it. This implies that members identify as either male or female, and that their body signs and gender identity should indeed match – including feminist and lesbian communities, as we will exemplify later (Kendall, 1998; Hall, 1996).

The development of trust and predictability through social responsibility are central for these processes, as communities are collective, not individual, entities. In relation to community then, making accountability possible is very much a question of stating the obvious in constructing its frame, Bromseth argues (2006a). Should we allow more than one voice per body, and what would that imply? What would be beneficial and what could be problematic? Negotiating social frames actively makes it possible to influence them, asking the questions that are never asked, where answers are usually taken for granted. To make visible norms of specific social practices has also been crucial in gender research, as we will look into next.

Intersections of Gender and Sexuality

Scene 3, Jenny: A female figure is kneeling in the sand, right by the water's edge. The wind ruffles her already tangled green hair. Her pointy ears flutter. The soothing sounds of sea and waves are blended with the drums of the Darkspear trolls at a distance. Right next to her, an abandoned wooden rowboat lies safely, and further along the beach, a female troll stands fishing, posture straight. The sun makes the waves glitter, temptingly. She stands up and starts to undress. First, the tall boots and the long, thick gloves, reaching well above the elbow. Then, the heavy cape, the shoulder pads, the beautiful harness protecting her chest along with the fitted shirt. She unzips the sturdy leather pants, and peels them off. Left are only her grass-like underwear and a couple of piercings, shimmering against blue skin. Left are also two long knives, deadly sharp, tied around her waist, and a big gun strapped across her back. One can never be too careful. She steps out into the water, takes a few strokes, dives deeply and lets her body almost brush against the bottom of the sea, soon forced to surface to fill her lungs with air. This is the Zoram Strand, or, more specifically, the Horde outpost of Zoram'gar. Further up on land, right where Andruk the Wind Rider Master offers flights to and from the beach, a visitor has just arrived. Across the dunes, a muscular orc woman comes riding on a big, black wolf. The troll girl quickly slips out of the water to greet her guest. When her orc friend descends from her wolf, the creature is transformed into a white tiger. Or so it seems. She watches them come running and jumping towards her, the sand spurting from under foot and paw. Her heart skips a beat. Or is it mine? Or both? Does it matter? Time to quest.

This scene could be a narrated account of an event in the MMOG (massively multiplayer online game) *World of Warcraft*. It could also be expanded field notes from an all-the-more-common form of "doing ethnography" in mediated spaces, such as game worlds. Our aim here is to illustrate the vivacity and interconnectedness of bodies online. There are certainly many differences between, for example, the lives of social networking profiles on the one hand, and of game avatars on the other, but participation in online worlds and communities more often than not has something to do with the body, and with bodily differentiation. The privileged difference in the field of feminist studies of Internet cultures is gender, but to critically discuss the concept gender within a feminist political framework is rarely enough. As feminist theorists have made explicit for decades, there are several differences – and forms of oppression – which intersect, overlap, collide with and reinforce each other in a myriad of ways.[11] Gender has fragmented into multiple differences, such as sexuality, ethnicity, class, and age. What difference would it make for the understanding of "gender online" if Internet scholars more consistently explored the ways in which gender intersects with sexuality? How would an intersectional project of looking at how gender and sexuality co-construct one another in multiple ways change our knowledge of online embodiment?

Queer theory has primarily been preoccupied with queer subjectivities and queer lives. Writing on cyber-queer has gained ground during the last decade (Bromseth, 2006a; Bryson, 2004; Case, 1996; Stone, 1995; Wakeford, 1997). The discussion of the many couplings between cyber and queer is alive and well in recent volumes, such as Kate O'Riordan and David Phillips (2007) *Queer Online: Media Technology and Sexuality*. One challenge, it seems, is to make the necessary connections between cyber/queer and cyber/gender in ways that dissect not only the explicitly queer, but also more mainstreamed, heterosexually framed interfaces. Another challenge is to make the necessary connections and coalitions between feminist and queer theory in Internet studies, and to place the discussion of sexuality at the heart of discussions of gender (cf. Karl, 2007).

There have been numerous readings of Judith Butler's (1990, 1993) theory of gender performativity in cyberspatial contexts. These readings, typically, take from Butler the idea of gender as being something which is performed, but completely disconnect this figuration from the ways in which gender performances are played out as part of the regulatory fiction of "compulsory heterosexuality" (Rich, 1980). A typical (heteronormative) gender analysis of the troll in the opening scene would give a multilayered, yet limited image of in-game femininity. Her war equipment would be coded typically "masculine," whereas the act in which she takes her gear off a conventionally "feminine" strip performance (and probably, as such, demeaning). Female sexuality in research on gender and games appears to, primarily, be something problematic in need of a cover-up. The feminist critique of representations of femininity in games often engages with how female avatars, from Lara Croft in *Tomb Raider* and onwards, tend to be designed along the lines of a hyped-up, "stereotypical" sexuality (see, for example, Jenson & de Castell, 2005; Kerr, 2003; Graner Ray, 2004).[12] The arrival of the orc woman would be read as the arrival of a friend, nothing else. No attention would be paid to her heart beating faster. Or, if this fact were acknowledged, it would be recognized as excitement for the upcoming battle. At best, these two female characters getting ready to quest would be understood as taking part in activities that possibly widen the space in which femininities can be performed – through the ways in which these activities are played out within a masculine domain of war machines and computer technologies. If a heteronormative gender analysis merely operates on a feminine/masculine scale, on which the former often maps pretty straightforwardly onto a biological female body and the latter onto a biological male body, that which is not feminine/female can then only be masculine/male. Even if a range of possible femininities and masculinities are considered, the foundational dichotomous figure remains.

If, instead, the reading is played out in a queer feminist framework, the picture will shift. An analysis with queer sensibilities and intersectional awareness could still view the female troll ready to battle as masculine, but this time with rather "butch" implications. Female masculinity is certainly a type of masculinity, but disconnected from the male body and read (primarily) across a female body within a framework of same sex desire (Halberstam, 1998). At the point where the straight gender analysis tips femininity into masculinity, a queer reading sticks with the multiple and contradictory meanings of femininity itself in ways which involve the sexual specificity and potential queerness of bodies and their relationships. Her heart skipping a beat once the orc woman comes into view would be acknowledged as a possible sign of sexual attraction and desire. And even if the reading stays at the level of friendship, the two players/avatars setting out to quest is in itself a rather queer act. The research on gender and games seems to be heavily populated by boyfriends, brothers, and other men as the ones who introduce women to gaming, and who also moderate and monitor their behavior (see Bryce & Rutter, 2007; Lin, 2005; Schott & Horrell, 2000). But there are other stories to be told according to which female game bodies and players introduce and protect each other, and where their guilds carry names such as "bad girls" (cf. Kennedy, 2006).

There is nothing wrong with studying "gender online," as long as there is an awareness of how the seemingly unproblematic, non-sexual bipolarity of "masculinity" and "femininity" is most concretely part of the hetero*sexual* matrix.[13] Discussions of gender online often come into play by deceivingly universal terms of all-encompassing masculinity and femininity in ways that overshadow how these terms become intelligible primarily within a heteronormalized context. A lack of awareness of how gender has everything to do with sexuality makes invisible other ways of shaping and understanding gendered bodies. If gender is bipolar, how can we then understand, for example, female masculinity? Or high femme (i.e. femininity taken to its extreme, performed with a twist for a female, lesbian gaze)? And what about the gendered positions of transsexual/transgender women (and men)? In what follows, we will take a look at how such distinctions and intersections of gender and sexuality have come to form the boundaries of online communities.

Bodies as Borders of Community

Scene 4, Janne: Do you think they're family? My girlfriend bends over the restaurant table and whispers half loud while she throws a quick glance at the two middle-aged women sitting a couple of tables from us. I study them discreetly, counting signs, clothing, jewelry, haircut, and the positions of their bodies in relation to each other. Thumb rings or little-finger rings, piercings or earrings in one ear? Short hair? Holding hands? It's all over in a couple of seconds before we conclude positively to ourselves, giggling over our little game that we play whenever we're in the public sphere. We don't really want to know though, if they are or not — and most probably, if we started talking and they were indeed a couple, we might not feel familiar with them at all. Like last summer, when we spent our holidays at Lesvos, the place crowded with dykes of all ages and types; from the Greek femmes and butches to the Scandinavian sport dykes, and the "dolphins;" new-age lesbians from the good old times. We were of course having a ball with categorizing them all. All family, as defined from the minimum communal element: that element being, we all desire women. And yet, a part of me is constantly distancing myself from others, negotiating the grounds for who's a part of my community. We're having dinner with another couple, and my neighbor has a constant need of creating an "us" from how she perceives "lesbians" – in rather stereotyping ways. I discover that I find it disturbing, being forced into a "we" just because I live with and love another woman. "I'm not like you, I don't believe in the homo-hetero us and them, I'm a queer dyke," my inner voice replies while I am flashing a polite smile. Actually it feels quite similar to being normatively included in the "us women" in the heterosexual feminist community after I started dating women, forever complicating feelings of feminist sisterhood. Even if I keep on loving women.

With Benedict Anderson (1991), we might ask, how do we negotiate borders for our imagined and lived communities? And how do we negotiate our selves in relation to communities in a never-ending co-dependent dialectics? Our experienced communities, and the discourses structuring them, are not static, but change throughout life and time. Boundaries are created, negotiating the grounds for community, defining who and what is considered to be part of "us," in response to other positions and identities. Sometimes resulting in irreparable splits, as inclusion and exclusion are two sides of the same coin. Sometimes we change our perspectives and the others do not, as with the (hetero-) feminist community mentioned above. And sometimes what once created the grounds for community dissolve along the way, leaving an empty space. Ideas of identity, gender, and sexuality create borders and battlefields, solidarity and oppression, hand in hand.

Constructing difference through marking specific bodies is tightly connected to power, and thus also to resistance, since power and resistance can be understood as reflecting each other (Foucault, [1974] 2002). These differentiating processes that structure society and social life also have consequences for and contribute to shaping online community on several levels. The deviant is always already marked linguistically, separating women, queers, blacks, and people with disabilities from the invisible norm, organizing social spaces. Critical researchers have shown how race, gender, and sexuality both structurally organize online community as well as being (re)produced through cultural representations in social interaction online (Alexander, 2002; Herring, 1996; Nakamura, 2002; Wakeford, 1996, 1997; Gajjala, 2004; O'Riordan & Philips, 2007; Ward, 1999).[14] Some paths appear as more natural and desirable within the built-in designs of online communities, which create and reinforce navigable social landscapes.

Online communities are embedded in larger sociopolitical structures and cultural hegemonies, with a growing amount of empirical research slowly dissolving the image of a power-free and democratic Internet. Organizing community on the basis of non-normative, and anti-normative, identity positions online has been met with resistance from owners of certain servers and sites. Even if it seems long ago since the first groups for non-heterosexuals were denied access by owners of leading servers at the beginning of the 1980s (Wakeford, 1997), homophobia, transphobia, racism, and sexism continue online structurally as well as through interactional practices (Alexander, 2002; Bernhardtz et al., 2005; Ward, 1999; Hall, 1996).[15] For example, the administrators of *World of Warcraft* have responded negatively to a player's announcement of a "gay-friendly guild" in the game's open chat channel. Wedding webpages are, as in most cultures, structured with the heterosexual couple as norm in their log-in menus and design. And did you ever see an identity option on an ordinary net-dating club exceeding the dichotomy of male/female, including trans-identities? In the heteronormative world of pre-profiled online communities, people identifying outside of gender and sexuality norms are not encouraged to take part in (dating) communities (even if they usually are not actively discouraged either). Reality bites, shapes, and forms, standard size fits all. Maintaining sexual difference through separating norm from Other(s), for example through the structuring of online social spaces, makes possible the continued privileging of specific gendered bodies, sexualities, and ways of living, and the othering of the marked deviant (Butler, 1993).

Critical and feminist online researchers have, from different theoretical/analytical perspectives, studied how community borders are negotiated through the phenomena of gender and sexuality, and their consequences.[16] As Shade (2004) notes, online communities are today deeply embedded in a commercialized Internet culture, creating specific frames for how community, gender, and – we will add – sexuality are constructed on the Internet. In addition to studies of (gender-) mainstream communities (see, for example, Consalvo & Paasonen, 2002; Consalvo, 2003; Sveningsson Elm, 2007; Sundén, 2003)[17] there is a growing corpus of research on constructions of gender, sexuality, and identity in explicitly feminist and lgbti/queer[18] communities (Alexander, 2002; Berry & Martin, 2000; Blair & Takayoshi, 1999; Harcourt, 1999; O'Riordan & Philips, 2007; Shade, 2002; Wakeford, 1997).

Communities created on the grounds of non-normative identities, aiming at political change and personal empowerment, can work as important counter-discursive places and spaces. Internet-mediated spaces have strengthened opportunities for making resistance possible globally as well as locally, and increased marginalized groups' access to the traditionally restricted public sphere (Harcourt, 1999; Mitra, 2001; Mele, 1999; Shade, 2002). Countercultural Internet-mediated groups have appeared to represent unique arenas for creating networks, solidarity, and community (Wakeford, 1996; Corell, 1995; Nip, 2004). For many people, experiencing recognition and community on non-normative grounds is not possible in their local community offline. Internet-mediated lgbti/queer communities have "revolutionized the experience of growing up gay," as Egan (2000, p. 113) claims enthusiastically.[19] Simultaneously, studies of queer community online have made visible how conceptions of both community and identity among queers are challenged and altered by Internet communications due to the intensified local–global intersections (Alexander, 2002, p. 82). Several studies of local queer online communities show how localized identities "take part in, support, negotiate and resist more globalized identities." (Heinz et al., 2002), and there are also various intersections between local queer community online and offline. For example, Nip (2004) describes the close relations of online and offline discourses of gender, sexuality, and identity in a local Hong Kong group online, and its community-strengthening functions offline.

At the same time, minority-based communities are also arenas reproducing hegemonies – for example, white-normativity and heteronormativity in feminist spaces, or sexism in queer groups – which calls for a more intersectional analytical approach to studying them (Gajjala, 2004; Wakeford, 1997; O'Riordan, 2007). Problematic sides of identity-based communities have been addressed by feminist researchers, looking critically at the grounds for community in line with the general queer/postmodern critiques of identity (O'Brien, 1999; Munt et al., 2002; Consalvo & Paasonen, 2002). Feminist scholars also critique the mainstreaming and commercializing of online queer community, creating the consuming, white, middle-class gay male as cultural norm (O'Riordan, 2007). These spaces contribute to confirming heteronormative structures, rather than challenging the normative grounds producing them. They are often referred to as "liberal queer": fighting for civil rights such as "gay marriage," but reproducing the values and social inequalities of the neo-liberal economy (Duggan, 2003; Halberstam, 2005).

Another dimension of the relations between community and embodiment that empirical studies of feminist and queer communities have shown is a range of tensions between "cybersubjects" and their embodied authors, and their consequences for community grounds. They can be related to both the fear of losing the "authentic" gendered body as an anchor for separatist feminist community, and the confrontations between radical and liberal/queer feminism, which has been a conflicting issue online as well as off (Bromseth, 2007; O'Riordan, 2007; Hall, 1996; Richardson et al., 2007). This has been expressed through a policing of the borders of the categories "woman" and "lesbian," and by trying to regulate the group boundaries through a strict discursive femininity. For example, some feminist and lesbian communities have been characterized by hostility towards male-to-female transgendered and transsexual persons and towards bisexuals (Hall, 1996; Bromseth, 2006a), legitimized by understandings of gender and sexual identity within a patriarchal and socio-essentialist framework (Aragón, 2006). A new paradigm is challenging the old though, at least on the surface; leading to more diverse and inclusive feminist and lgbti/queer-communities, where the ideas of a unified concept of Women or authentic gay and lesbians are not dominant. In practice, conflicting ideas and presentations of selves are living more or less peacefully side by side; where lesbian authenticity as a subcultural ideal is both reproduced and problematized, at its best, as in the study by Munt and colleagues of Gaygirls.com (2002). At its worst, conflicting views end up in frustrated and destructive debates leading to exclusion and harassment of male-to-female transsexual and transgendered participants (Bromseth, 2007). Both Nip (2004) and Bromseth (2007) have shown how ideological differences have affected the sense of community within lesbian/queer groups, where understandings of gender, identity, and sexuality have been important boundary objects. Who are part of the "us" and who are part of the "them" is certainly a constant negotiation where discourses and ideas of gender, sexuality, and embodiment contribute to shaping the grounds for community and the frames for interpreting social practices, as the introductory scene suggests. Instead of reproducing group identity on the basis of bodily and sexual difference, it would be more fruitful to problematize how such categorical differences remain important and with which consequences.

Queer Movements and Emotions

Scene 5, Jenny: Coffee and wireless. The location is Café Paradiso on the campus of Peking University – or Beida – in Beijing. I am the only blonde person in the room, and also the only woman with short hair. Most women here have long hair, unless they are lalas, lesbians. In lesbian bars, I repeatedly get the question: "Are you T or P?" which roughly translates as "Are you butch or femme?" in Western queer vocabularies (cf. Chou, 1999). During my stay, I've only seen a couple of women who, in my view, can be read as butch. The rest of the Ts are tomboys, at least to me. "T or P?" I hesitate. "I am both," I tell them, and they disappear. You cannot be "both" here, I know, but I refuse to take sides. Chinese lesbian online communities seem to be thriving. This is how women meet, I am told. The web has provided lalas with powerful means of connectivity. At the same time, it is important to bear in mind that to be gay in China, let alone queer, is for most people merely a possibility that figures as a double life on the margins of straight life. It is a life that with very few exceptions is lived as the hidden underside of the regulatory display of heterosexual family making. Beijing's lala scene makes me think a lot about how desire is figured culturally, and figured differently across time and space. These bars have surprisingly little to do with the body (at least not to me), which is not surprising in a place where the sexually explicit has been long repressed. Physical attraction may instead be coded at a much more subtle level, one that I am not yet able to decode. Desire lost in translation. Or is it that ways of desiring are not nearly as flexible as we may imagine them to be?

In *The Cultural Politics of Emotion*, Sara Ahmed (2004) explores the ways in which emotions shape bodies by circulating between them, how they may stick to some, and slide over others. She suggests that it is through emotions and how we relate to others that the very boundaries and surfaces of bodies take shape. Emotions involve relations of "towardness" or "awayness":

> Compulsory heterosexuality shapes bodies by the assumption that the body "must" orient itself toward some objects and not others, objects that are secured as ideal through the fantasy of difference. . . . Hence, the failure to orient oneself "towards" the ideal sexual object affects how we live in the world, an effect that is readable as a failure to reproduce, and as a threat to the social ordering of life itself." (p. 145)

Ahmed discusses the comfort of heteronormative life for those who can live by its rules. She puts forth how social spaces presume certain bodies, shapes, directions, desires, and movements in ways which make the distinction between bodies and objects unclear. The relation between the two is one of comfort, and being comfortable is a state of not having to recognize what conditions the perfect fit. What happens, then, when bodies fail to fit, "a failure that we can describe as a 'queering' of space" (p. 152)? Discomfort – the feeling of being out of place, or of being in the wrong place – makes visible the premises and promises of the (hetero-)normative, and as such makes the safety of heterosexuality slightly less safe.

What bearing does this line of argument have on contemporary Internet studies? How, for example, do corporeal desires and belongings map onto game worlds? How do emotions circulate in and through games? Could certain game spaces or moments of play be termed "queer"? The multifaceted domain of "gender and games" or "women and/in games" (the notion of gender interestingly but not surprisingly collapsing into the category woman) is expanding steadily (Bryce et al., 2006; Casell & Jenkins, 1998; Royse et al., 2007), but feminist game studies scholars are still few and far between. Feminist game scholars such as Diane Carr (2002, 2006a, 2006b) and Helen Kennedy (2002, 2006) have explored the pleasures of gaming; Mia Consalvo (2003) has researched the much overlooked area of sexuality and games; Mary Flanagan (2005) has engaged with alternative game design; and T. L. Taylor (2006) has made important contributions to the area of embodiment and gaming. But surprisingly little has been done in the intersection of, for example, queer theory and games.

With (perhaps unexpected) affinity with the play and performances of the subcultural lesbian scene in Beijing, computer games too are spaces for affective circulation. One strand in Western games studies that deserves closer attention – and which has a resonance within queer/feminist theory – is the emerging discussion of game spatiality and affect. Certain game studies scholars with an interest in geography and navigational practices argue that computer games are, primarily, occupied with notions of space and spatiality, with ways of moving through, exploring, and controlling game territories (see Flynn, 2003; Jenkins, 2002; Manovich, 2001). Game researcher Diane Carr (2006c) takes this argument one step further by looking at how different ways of moving in games seem to support different affects in the player, more clearly linking issues of embodiment to the fields of game design and game play. A horror game may use a fairly strict, linear, labyrinthine mode of moving to create a claustrophobic feeling and frighten the player. A fantasy game may instead develop through a more open-ended, rhizomatic structure that encourages exploration and reflection. A different – but not unrelated – tendency in game studies is research focusing on the importance of particular spaces for game experiences, emphasizing the importance of "where" gaming takes place. Typically, the picture painted in this research is one of arcades and game cafés as an extension of the boy's room, whereas young women rather play at home – if and when the game technologies are not occupied by their brothers or boyfriends (Bryce and Rutter, 2007; Lin, 2005). While depicting the female gamer as straight by default, situated in nuclear family-like households in which housework competes with game time, these discussions are productive in emphasizing how the materiality of place makes a difference to game experiences.

To Ahmed (2004), it is through the circulation of emotions and ways of orienting oneself that bodies take shape, or materialize. This way of thinking about contact, emotional intensity, and the creation of bodies and boundaries has important consequences for her politics of emotion, and in particular for queer bodies and emotions (cf. Ahmed, 2006). In Internet cultures with relational interfaces and emotional charge, such as online games, it becomes clear that bodies of avatars and players alike can be understood as taking shape by ways of sensing and moving. In the case of *World of Warcraft*, moving through the spaces of Azeroth is in many ways a journey through a heteronormative landscape (cf. Corneliussen, 2008). Even if Blizzard Entertainment (the company producing *World of Warcraft*) has made sure that, for example, male and female avatars are equally powerful as vehicles in the game world (i.e. male bodies are not stronger or better by default), different bodies may generate different player experiences.[20] In interviews that Sundén is doing with queer female players, it becomes clear that female characters of highly popular races, such as humans and night elves, regularly become objects of sexual attention, whereas for example female orcs and the undead appear to move through the game with greater ease in ways which might suggest a "queering" of space. Female orcs have a strong, muscular build and can have their heads shaven, and the undead have a slouching posture with their bones ripping through the skin. Or, as one informant formulated this matter in relation to her female orc: "She's clearly not a babe." In not being a "babe," the orc woman fails to fit the hetero-norm. But instead of primarily producing a disorienting feeling, this failure appears to generate a certain free-dom of movement. Moreover, there seem to be important ways in which female game bodies, even in the midst of heteronormative game interfaces, appear to be sexing these spaces in ways that are intriguingly queer. Even if the number of female players of online games is constantly growing, the ideas and ideals of hegemonic straight femininity seem to collide frequently with how gaming is habitually coded as a masculine activity. An appropriation of game technologies can thus be a quite powerful activity, transgressive in its challenging of the tech-nological masculine. Female players could in this sense be understood as engaging in non-normative, or even anti-normative ways of doing femininity through their culturally illegitimate couplings with straight masculinity, technology, and power (Kennedy, 2006).

At the same time, following Ahmed (2004), there also seems to be a move-ment in reverse through which playing bodies take shape through game play, by the very contacts they have with others (objects as well as subjects). *World of Warcraft* players give evidence of a fairly complex connection between one spatial, embodied mode and another. In particular through the ways in which the bodies of players come to act as interfaces between different ways of moving and sensing. Players talk a lot about how they duck their own head when their avatar approaches a low-sitting roof joist, how they flinch just before making the avatar come to an abrupt halt at a steep slope, and lean closer to the screen, so that they can cautiously look over the edge. But again, there also seems to be a movement in reverse in the sense that the many ways of moving around in Azeroth leave traces in, or shape, the body of the player itself (cf. Colman, 2008). Internet studies have, in our view, a lot to gain from more clearly addressing the intimately corporeal, yet political dimensions of online spaces. Inhabiting or moving through onscreen venues is as much a full-body experience as it is a visual one (Lahti, 2003). The exploration of ways of sensing and knowing movement through Internet spaces affectively has only just begun.

Future Challenges of Internet Studies, Gender, and Sexuality

In this chapter, we have delivered an overview of certain strands in the research on gender, sexuality, and Internet technologies. Against the backdrop of changes in mediation and ownership from Web 1.0 to Web 2.0, as well as the impact of poststructuralist and queer theories of embodiment, gender, and sexuality, we have discussed what we identify as the pressing questions today. If text-based online worlds and communities were the flavor of the day when we started out in the mid-1990s, the focus has shifted significantly since, primarily due to the rapid expansion of blogs, social networking sites, and online game worlds. Another important shift that has highly influenced media use is the commercialization of the Internet. Given the speed of technological development, changing user demographics and patterns of use, writing about Internet phenomena is in a sense always media history in the making. Then again, looking back at the rich body of research on text-based online locations, it is clear that this work still holds a lot of value for research on Internet-mediated social interaction and cultural representations. In spite of the fantasy of the ideal cyber/queer subject, and regardless of rapid technological change, hegemonic heteronormative understandings of gender and sexuality remain, or are not so easily altered. These mutually shaping intersections – of the technological, economic, and social developments of the Internet on one hand, and of the discourses on gender and sexuality on the other – need to be explored further in a historical perspective.

What represents other future challenges of studying gender and sexuality in Internet studies? This is certainly a question with many answers. If we compare the current situation with that of some 15 years ago, a number of lines of development emerge that need to be considered. Production and consumption of the Internet – such as the web – is becoming more and more widespread, globally – but English remains the dominant language (Internet World Stats, 2008).[21] At the same time, internet-mediated practices appear to be increasingly integrated in people's everyday lives (cf. Berry & Martin, 2000). Alongside transnational websites, a growing number of more clearly localized online spaces are emerging (Halavais, 2000). Here, the social interactions and community practices build on material and discursive intersections between online and offline locations, influencing each other in diverse ways (Mueller, 2003).[22] The distinction previously made between online and offline contexts is increasingly contested and blurred, as social interactions overlap between mediated and offline local spaces.[23] Thus, the body accountable online is to a larger degree connected to a material representation offline, creating other conditions for constructing and negotiating gendered selves as situated processes.

Throughout the chapter, we have delivered a queer critique of the study of gender, sexuality, and the Internet. In so doing, we have argued for tighter linkages between feminist and queer theory, primarily for two reasons. First, it is important to make explicit how gender intersects with sexuality, to not repeat the "straight" gender fallacy, which understands gender as disconnected from (hetero)sexuality. Second, we have emphasized the significance of opening up the field of possible queer feminist interventions. Not only to let queer theory analyze that which is most evidently queer, but to also use queer theoretical strategies to make manifest the heterosexual modes and codes of "mainstream" media. This also includes investigating the co-productions of "heteronormality" and techno-cultural spaces as related to neo-liberal discourses and global structures, and how heteronormal gender and sexuality necessarily contributes to support these very structures (Halberstam, 2005). What gets to be included in the "normal," in the "charming circle" of good sex (Rubin, [1984] 1993)? What is repeatedly questioned and othered – in heteronormative as well as homonormative mediated contexts?

It has been beyond the scope of this chapter to look at other differences and power relations that are significant in the coming together of cybersubjects, such as race and ability. Nevertheless, it is important to keep making room for transdisciplinary interrogations of multiple intersections and ways of thinking the body as intrinsically enmeshed in multiple and complex webs of power. During the mid-1990s, the Internet was central for theoretical debates in feminist theory. Today, Internet studies needs to reconnect with central debates concerning the relationship between gender and sexuality, as well as between feminist and queer theory.

Notes

1 On the close connection between masculinity and science and technology, see, for example, Cockburn, 1983 and 1985; Oldenziel, 1999; Wajcman, 1991 and 1995.

2 For example, Corneliussen (2002) shows how doing informatics is in the Western world still seen as "naturally linked" to men and not to women, giving men a privileged discursive access to an exclusive area of ICT use. In Malaysia, however, computer science is not gendered in this way, and the number of women and men in the profession is about the same (Lagesen, 2005).

3 Haraway (1991, p. 151) acknowledges that "a cyborg body is not innocent; it was not born in a garden" gesturing at the unnaturalness of cyborg origins. It does not

come from the (supposedly natural) Garden of Eden, but is in troubling ways "the illegitimate offspring of militarism and patriarchal capitalism" (p. 151). Transposing this argument onto Internet cyborg bodies (Haraway's argument covers a much wider terrain of information- and biotechnologies), it becomes clear that the building blocks, the very materiality of virtual bodies, are far from neutral, let alone natural. The matter with which bodies online are built (ranging from the zeros and ones of machine code combined by acts of programming, to the more ready-made codes and protocols of various interfaces) is marked in multiple ways by the worldviews and cultural assumptions of designers and developers. Then again, illegitimate offspring, as Haraway observes, "are often exceedingly unfaithful to their origins. Their fathers, after all, are inessential" (p. 151). Like everything technological, the cyborg has multiple possibilities, both of promises and of dangers. Their beginnings do not dictate their outcomes and uses. There is always the possibility of infidelity as political strategy.

4   Of course, the criticisms of feminist theory as normatively white and heterosexual were also raised before the 1990s (cf. Hooks, 1981; Wittig, 1980), contributing to challenge norms within feminist theorizing. But the major influential breakthrough on feminist theories came with poststructuralist ideas of subjectivity, queer theory, black feminism, and postcolonial theory during the 1990s.

5   The Swedish Research Council (Vetenskapsrådet) has given its financial support to the research project "Gender Play: Intersectionality in Computer Game Culture," which Sundén is doing together with Dr Malin Sveningsson Elm.

6   From an ethnography of a Scandinavian mailing list for lesbian/bisexual women, Sapfo. Quoted from Bromseth, 2006a, p. 166.

7   Playing with the rhetorical title of Stone's (1991) article "Will the Real Body Please Stand Up? Boundary Stories of Virtual Cultures."

8   Joan is the name that Sherry Turkle (1995) uses, while Sandy Stone (1995) called her Julie.

9   According to Stone (1995, p. 65), the episode took place on a chat space owned by CompuServe, one of the first commercial companies offering a range of services online, who also developed several chat channels.

10   See, for example Ess and The Association of Internet researchers (2002) and Thorseth, (2003).

11   If first-wave feminism in the nineteenth and early twentieth century, with figures such as Mary Wollstonecraft, relied on Enlightenment liberal ideas based on "sameness" to protest against the subordination of women, second wave-feminism of the 1960s and 1970s primarily turned the identity-as-sameness discussion on its head and instead worked to reclaim the "feminine." Then again, much US-based second-wave feminism was also premised on the liberal, "we are all the same" model. One variant was cultural feminism which sought to valorize difference, but it was not a primary strand, especially not by groups like the National Organization for Women and those advocating for the Equal Rights Amendment. Women's liberation as formulated by the second wave grew out of the declaration of women's difference (from men), rather than their search for (illusory) equality. Third-wave feminism, which gained significant influence in the 1990s, is primarily a critical response to the political exclusions and biases of the second wave, disclosed as merely having included white Western middle-class straight women under the seemingly unifying category "women." The third wave, entwined with poststructuralism, postmodernism, queer theory, black feminism, and postcolonial theory, is a multifaceted acknowledgement of the many

differences and power hierarchies that position women in relation to men, and that position women in relation to one another.

12   This argument presumes that excessive female sexuality is a problem, since it turns women's bodies into objects of a (particular, yet culturally dominating straight) male gaze. Why this particular type of sexuality is problematic is rarely addressed, nor is its reliance on a heterosexual framework through which it becomes intelligible. Moreover, the discussion often appears to depart from an understanding of the relationship between player and avatar as one of identification, inserting an alienating distance between the female body as object in mainstream game design and the female players (Graner Ray, 2004). Then again, such understanding puts aside other notions of game play, game context, and other ways of making sense of and thinking the relationships between player and avatar. For alternative readings of this relationship in the case of Lara Croft, see Carr, 2002; Flanagan, 1999; Kennedy, 2002. These analyses take into account how Lara's body is not merely a visual object, but also a powerful and pleasurable subject, a vehicle, and a finely tuned machinery of game play.

13   Adrienne Rich (1980) draws on the term "compulsory heterosexuality" as a feminist critique of those powers that force women to devote themselves sexually to the model of reproductive heterosexuality. Butler (1990), in turn, uses the concept "heterosexual matrix," partly as a continuation of Rich's term to "designate that grid of cultural intelligibility through which bodies, genders, and desires are naturalized . . . that assumes that for bodies to cohere and make sense there must be a stable sex expressed through a stable gender (masculine expresses male, feminine expresses female) that is oppositional and hierarchically defined through the compulsory practice of hetero-sexuality" (p. 151).

14   In line with social life in general, the group having the position of the hegemonic masculine is typically never marked explicitly in online social organizing either, even if there are a lot of white heterosexual men doing things together. Mailing lists or online communities explicitly reserved for "white heterosexual middle-class Western men" are a rare sight.

15   For example, the number of webpages with explicitly homophobic content is growing, a recent study shows (Bernhardtz et al., 2005).

16   The theoretical approaches and analytical foci vary from sociolinguistic feminist ana-lysis of gender differences in participation and domination on public mailing lists (Herring, 1996, 2000) to how (hetero-)gender is constructed in social interaction, to queer the-oretical analysis of how gender and sexual identity categories themselves are made into boundary objects in creating mainstream and subcultural feminist and queer communities (Munt et al., 2002). The fundamental differences in theoretical points of departure in Internet studies of gender and sexuality, and how they affect the knowledge claims produced, are however surprisingly rarely problematized, in our opinion.

17   It is obviously a difficult task to give credit to all the studies done in relation to gender, community, and the Internet, and we have in this part of the chapter chosen to look at gender and sexuality in relation to queer/lgbti and feminist communities.

18   Lgbti stands for lesbian, gay, bisexual, transgender/transsexual, intersexual.

19   Cited from Alexander (2002, p. 80).

20   To game scholar Espen Aarseth (2004, p. 48), "a differently-looking body would not make me play differently . . . When I play, I don't even see [the] body, but see through it and past it." But as Dovey and Kennedy (2006, pp. 92–3) argue, while it is true

that a different-looking body does not affect the underlying game mechanic, it most certainly has an impact on game experiences and affects.

21 See also Halavais (2000), who looks critically into the idea of a "global" use of the Internet. From a selection of 4000 webpages Halavais found that webpages are more likely to link to another site hosted in the same country than to cross national borders, and if they do cross borders, they are more likely to lead to pages hosted in the United States than to anywhere else in the world.

22 See also Berry and Martin, 2002; Nip, 2004; Bromseth, 2006a, who all look at communities targeting a queer audience in national cultural contexts. Other examples include national net-dating sites in Western countries (see Sommer, 2003). There are also many studies of communities targeting a North American audience that are not interpreted as "local" but as "global/international," and the specific cultural context not considered as such, or its meaning for online–offline intersections (Sveningsson Elm & Sundén, 2007). This is a general pattern that needs to be corrected.

23 Social communities such as Facebook, for example, obviously create community across online and offline spaces as do a range of other targeted communities for youth, queers, feminists etc., where local discourses and languages condition online interaction. Vice versa, online social practices can also be important resources for developing local community offline (Mueller, 2002).

References

Aarseth, E. (2004). Genre trouble: Narrativism and the art of simulation. In P. Harrington & N. Wardrip-Fruin (eds.), *First Person: New Media as Story, Performance, and Game* (pp. 45–56). Cambridge, MA: MIT Press.

Ahmed, S. (2004). *The Cultural Politics of Emotion*. Edinburgh: Edinburgh University Press.

Ahmed, S. (2006). *Queer Phenomenology: Orientations, Objects, Others*. Durham, NC, and London: Duke University Press.

Alexander, J. (2002). Queer webs: Representations of LGBT people and communities on the World Wide Web. *International Journal of Sexuality and Gender Studies*, 7(2/3), 77–84.

Aragón, A. P. (2006). *Challenging Lesbian Norms. Intersex, Transgender, Intersectional and Queer Perspectives*. New York: Harrington Park Press.

Benedikt, M. (1991). Cyberspace: First steps. In M. Benedikt (ed.), *Cyberspace: First Steps*. Cambridge, MA: MIT Press.

Bernhardtz, V., Dalsbro, A., & Lagerlöf, D. (2005). *Det homosexuella hotet mot den vita rasen – nazistisk och rasistisk homofobi på Internet. En rapport från RFSL och Expo om nazistisk och rasistiska gruppers homofobiska propaganda på Internet*. RFSL and Expo. Retrieved February 1, 2006, from http://www.rfsl.se/?p=2835.

Berry, C., & Martin, F. (2000). Queer 'n' Asian on – and off – the net: The role of cyberspace in queer Taiwan and Korea. In D. Gauntlett (ed.), *Web.Studies: Rewiring Media Studies for the Digital Age* (pp. 65–80). London: Arnold.

Blair, K., & Takayoshi, P. (1999). *Feminist Cyberscapes: Mapping Gendered Academic Spaces*. Ablex, CT: Greenwood.

Bødker, M., & Christensen, M. S. (2003). Trust in the network society. Paper presented at the Association of Internet Researchers fourth annual conference, Internet Research 4.0: Broadening the Band, October 16–19, Toronto, Canada.

Braidotti, R. (1996). Cyberfeminism with a difference. *New Formations*, 29 (Fall) 9–25.

Bromseth, J. (2001). The Internet as arena for public debate: Constructions and negotiations of interactional norms on two male dominated discussion lists in Norway. *NORA*, 2(2), 1–9.

Bromseth, J. (2006a). Genre trouble and the body that mattered. Negotiations of gender, sexuality and identity in a Scandinavian mailing list community for lesbian and bisexual women. Doctoral dissertation. The STS report 76/2006, Department of Interdisciplinary Studies of Culture. Norwegian University of Technology and Science, Trondheim.

Bromseth, J. (2006b). Researcher/woman/lesbian? Finding a voice in creating a researcher position, trust and credibility as a participant researcher in a mediated mailing-list environment for lesbian and bisexual women in a time of conflict. In P. Liamputtong (ed.), *Health Research in Cyberspace* (pp. 85–104). Hauppauge, NY: Nova Publishers.

Bromseth, J. (2007). Nordic feminism in a cyberlight? In M. Sveningsson Elm & J. Sundén (eds.), *Cyberfeminism in Northern Lights: Digital Media and Gender in a Nordic Context* (pp. 73–104). Newcastle upon Tyne: Cambridge Scholars Press.

Bruckman, A. (1993). Gender swapping on the Internet. *Proceedings of INET '93*. Reston, VA: The Internet Society. Retrieved June 10, 2002, from http://www.cc.gatech.edu/fac/Amy.Bruckman/papers/index.html#INET.

Bryce, J., Rutter, J., & Sullivan, C. (2006). Digital games and gender. In J. Rutter & J. Bryce (eds.), *Understanding Digital Games* (pp. 185–204). London: Sage.

Bryce, J., & Rutter, J. (2007). Gender dynamics and the social and spatial organization of computer gaming. *Leisure Studies*, 22(1), 1–15.

Bryson, M. (2004). When Jill jacks in: Queer women and the net. *Feminist Media Studies*, 4(3), 239–54.

Butler, J. (1990). *Gender Trouble: Feminism and the Subversion of Identity*. New York and London: Routledge.

Butler, J. (1993). *Bodies that Matter: On the Discursive Limits of "Sex."* New York and London: Routledge.

Carr, D. (2002). Playing with Lara. In G. King & T. Kryzwinska (eds.), *Screenplay: Cinema/Videogames/Interfaces* (pp. 178–80). London: Wallflower Press.

Carr, D. (2006a). Contexts, gaming pleasures, and gendered preferences. *Simulation & Gaming*, 36(4), 464–82.

Carr, D. (2006b). Games and gender. In D. Carr, D. Buckingham, A. Burn, & G. Scott (eds.), *Computer Games: Text, Narrative and Play* (pp. 162–78). Cambridge and Malden, MA: Polity.

Carr, D. (2006c). Space, navigation and affect. In D. Carr, D. Buckingham, A. Burn, & G. Scott (eds.), *Computer Games: Text, Narrative and Play* (pp. 59–71). Cambridge, Malden, MA: Polity.

Case, S-E. (1996). *The Domain-Matrix: Performing Lesbian at the End of Print Culture*. Bloomington: Indiana University Press.

Casell, J., & Jenkins, H. (eds.) (1998). *From Barbie to Mortal Combat: Gender and Computer Games*. Cambridge, MA: MIT Press.

Chou, Y. A. (1999). Performing like a p'o and acting as a big sister: Reculturating into the indigenous lesbian circle in Taiwan. In F. Markowitz & M. Ashkenazi (eds.), *Sex, Sexuality and the Anthropologist* (pp. 128–44). Urbana: University of Illinois Press.

Cockburn, C. (1983). *Brothers: Male Dominance and Technological Change*. London: Pluto.

Cockburn, C. (1985). *Machinery of Dominance: Women, Men, and Technical Know-How.* London: Pluto.

Colman, F. (2008). Affective game topologies: Any-space-whatevers. *Refractory: A Journal of Entertainment Media,* 13. Retrieved June 29, 2008, from http://blogs.arts.unimelb. edu.au/refractory/2008/05/25/games-and-metamateriality/.

Consalvo, M. (2003). It's a queer world after all: Studying *The Sims* and sexuality. GLAAD Centre for the Study of Media and Society. Retrieved April 1, 2008, from http://www.glaad.org/documents/csms/The_Sims.pdf.

Consalvo, M., & Paasonen, S. (eds.) (2002). *Women and Everyday Uses of the Internet: Agency and Identity.* New York: Peter Lang.

Corneliussen, H. (2002). Diskursen makt – Individets frihet. Kjönnede posisjoner I diskursen om data [The power of discourse – The freedom of the individual. Gendered positions in the discourse about computing]. Doctoral dissertation. Faculty of Humanities, University of Bergen.

Corneliussen, H. (2008). *World of Warcraft* as playground for feminism. In H. Corneliussen & J. Walker Rettberg (eds.), *Digital Culture, Play and Identity: A World of Warcraft Reader* (pp. 63–86). Cambridge, MA: MIT Press.

Correll, S. (1995). The ethnography of an electronic bar. The lesbian café. *Journal of Contemporary Ethnography,* 24(3), pp. 270–98.

Danet, B. (1998). Text as mask: Gender, play, and performance on the Internet. In S. Jones (ed.), *Cybersociety 2.0* (pp. 129–59). Thousand Oaks, CA, London, New Delhi: Sage.

Danet, B., Ruedenberg, L., & Rosenbaum-Tamari, Y. (1998). Hmmm . . . where is that smoke coming from? Writing, play and performance on Internet relay chat. In F. Sudweeks, M. McLaughlin, & S. Rafaeli (eds.), *Network and Netplay: Virtual Groups on the Internet* (pp. 41–76). Menlo Park, CA: AAAI Press.

Donath, J. (1999). Identity and deception in the virtual community. In P. Kollock & M. A. Smith (eds.), *Communities in Cyberspace* (pp. 29–60). London and New York: Routledge.

Dovey, J., & Kennedy, H. (eds.) (2006). *Game Cultures: Computer Games as New Media.* Berkshire: Open University Press.

Duggan, L. (2003). *The Twilight of Equality: Neo-Liberalism, Cultural Politics and the Attack on Democracy.* Boston: Beacon Press.

Egan, J. (2000). Lonely gay teen seeking same. *New York Times,* December 10, 2000.

Ess, C., & The Association of Internet Researchers (2002). Ethical decision-making and Internet research recommendations from the AOIR ethics working committee. Approved by the AoIR membership, November 27, 2002. Retrieved August 20, 2008, from http://www.aoir.org/?q=node/30.

Flanagan, M. (1999). Mobile identities, digital stars and post-cinematic selves. *Wide Angle,* 21(1), 76–93.

Flanagan, M. (2005). Troubling "games for girls": Notes from the edge of game design. Proceedings of DiGRA 2005 Conference: Changing Views – Worlds in Play, June 16–20, 2005. Retrieved August 21, 2007, from http://www.digra.org/dl/db/06278.14520.pdf.

Flynn, B. (2003). Languages of navigation within computer games. Proceedings from Melbourne DAC, the fifth International Digital Arts and Culture Conference, May 19–23. Retrieved September 25, 2005, from hypertext.rmit.edu.au/dac/papers/Flynn.pdf.

Foucault, M. ([1974] 2002). *Sexualitetens historia. Viljan att veta.* Göteborg: Daidalos.

Gajjala, R. (2004). *Cyberselves. Feminist Ethnographies of South Asian Women.* Walnut Creek, CA: AltaMira Press.

Gansmo, H., Lagesen, V., & Sørensen, K. H. (2003) Out of the boy's room? A critical analysis of the understanding of gender and ICT in Norway. *NORA Nordic Journal of Women's Studies,* 11(3), 130–39.

Gibson, W. (1984). *Neuromancer.* New York: Ace Books.

Goffman, E. (1974). *Frame Analysis.* New York: Harper & Row.

Graner Ray, S. (2004). *Gender Inclusive Game Design: Expanding the Market.* Hingham, MA: Charles River Media.

Halavais, A. (2000). National borders on the World Wide Web. *New Media & Society,* 1(3), 7–28.

Halberstam, J. (1998). *Female Masculinity.* Durham, NC: Duke University Press.

Halberstam, J. (2005). *In a Queer Time and Place. Transgender Bodies, Subcultural Lives.* London & New York: New York University Press.

Hall, K. (1996). Cyberfeminism. In S. Herring (ed.), *Computer-Mediated Communication: Linguistic, Social and Cross-Cultural Perspectives* (pp. 147–73). Amsterdam: John Benjamins.

Haraway, D. (1991). A Cyborg manifesto: Science, technology, and socialist-feminism in the late twentieth century. In D. Haraway, *Simians, Cyborgs and Women: The Reinvention of Nature.* New York: Routledge.

Harcourt, W. (1999). *Women@Internet.* New York: St Martin's Press.

Heinz, B., Gu, L., Inuzuka, A., & Zender, R. (2002). Under the rainbow flag: Webbing global gay identities. *International Journal of Sexuality and Gender Studies,* 7(2/3), 107–24.

Herring, S. (1996). Two variants of an electronic message schema. In S. Herring (ed.), *Computer-Mediated Communication: Linguistic, Social and Cross-Cultural Perspectives* (pp. 81–109). Amsterdam: John Benjamins.

Herring, S. (2000). Gender differences in CMC. Findings and implications. *CPRS Newsletter* 18(1). Retrieved March 31, 2008, from http://www.cpsr.org/prevsite/publications/newsletters/issues/2000/Winter2000/herring.html.

Hine, C. (2000). *Virtual Ethnography.* London: Sage.

Hooks, B. (1981). *Ain't I a Woman?* New York: South End Press.

Internet World Statistics (2008). Usage and population statistics. Retrieved June 30, 2008, from http://www.internetworldstats.com/stats.htm.

Jenkins, H. (2002). Game design as narrative architecture. In P. Harrington & N. Wardrip-Fruin (eds.), *First Person: New Media as Story, Performance, and Game* (pp. 118–30). Cambridge, MA: MIT Press.

Jenson, J., & de Castell, S. (2005). Her own boss: Gender and the pursuit of incompetent play. Proceedings of DiGRA 2005 Conference: Changing Views – Worlds in Play, June. Retrieved August 21, 2007, from http://www.digra.org/dl/db/06278.14520.pdf.

Karl, I. (2007). On-/offline: Gender, sexuality, and the techno-politics of everyday life. In K. O'Riordan & D. Phillips (eds.), *Queer Online: Media Technology and Sexuality* (pp. 45–66). New York: Peter Lang.

Kendall, L. (1998). "Are you male or female?" Gender performances on MUDs. In J. O'Brien & J. A. Howard (eds.), *Everyday Inequalities: Critical Inquiries* (pp. 131–53). Malden, MA, Oxford: Blackwell.

Kendall, L. (2002). *Hanging Out in the Virtual Pub*. Berkeley: University of California Press.

Kennedy, H. (2002). Lara Croft: Feminist icon or cyberbimbo? On the limits of textual analysis. *Game Studies* 2(2). Retrieved August 21, 2007, from http://gamestudies.org.

Kennedy, H. (2006). Illegitimate, monstrous and out there: Female "quake" players and inappropriate pleasures. In J. Hollows & R. Moseley (eds.), *Feminism in Popular Culture* (pp. 183–202). Oxford: Berg.

Kerr, A. (2003). Girls/women just want to have fun: A study of adult female players of digital games. Paper presented at DiGRA: Level Up, November. Retrieved August 5, 2008, from http://www.digra.org/dl/db/05163.29339.pdf.

Kolko, B., & Reid, E. (1998). Dissolution and fragmentation problems in online communities. In S. Jones (ed.), *Cybersociety 2.0* (pp. 212–31). Thousand Oaks, CA: Sage.

Kollock, P., & Smith, M. A. (eds.) (1999). *Communities in Cyberspace*. London and New York: Routledge.

Lagesen, V. A. B. (2005). Extreme make-over? The making of gender and computer science. Doctoral dissertation. Faculty of Arts, Norwegian University of Technology and Science, Trondheim.

Lahti, M. (2003). As we become machines: Corporealized pleasures in video games. In M. J. P. Wolf & B. Perron (eds.), *The Video Game Theory Reader* (pp. 157–70). London: Routledge.

Lanier, J., & Biocca, F. (1992). An insider's view of the future of virtual reality. *Journal of Communication*, 42(4), 150–72.

Lin, H. (2005). Gendered gaming experience in social space: From home to Internet café. Proceedings of DiGRA 2005 Conference: Changing Views – Worlds in Play, June. Retrieved August 21, 2007, from http://www.digra.org/dl/db/06278.14520.pdf.

Manovich, L. (2001). *The Language of New Media*. Cambridge, MA: MIT Press.

Mele, C. (1999). Cyberspace and disadvantaged communities: The Internet as tool for collective action. In P. Kollock & M. A. Smith (eds.), *Communities in Cyberspace* (pp. 290–311). London and New York: Routledge.

Mitra, A. (2001). Marginal voices in cyberspace. *New Media & Society*, 3(1), 29–48.

Mueller, C. (2002). Online communities in a "glocal" context. Paper presented at the Association of Internet Researcher's third annual conference, Internet Research 3.0: Net/Work/Theory, October 13–16, Maastricht.

Munt, S., Bassett, E. H., & O'Riordan, K. (2002). Virtually belonging: Risk, connectivity and coming out on-line. *International Journal of Sexuality and Gender Studies*, 7(2/3), 125–37.

Nakamura, L. (2002). *Cybertypes. Race, Ethnicity and Identity on the Internet*. London and New York: Routledge.

Nakamura, L. (2007). Virtual economies of race and embodiment: The case of Asian farmers in MMORGs. Internet Research 8.0 – Let's Play, October 17–20, Vancouver.

Nip, J. (2004). The Queer Sisters and its electronic bulletin board. *Media, Culture & Society*, 26(3), 409–28.

Nordli, H. (2003). The net is not enough. Searching for the female hacker. Doctoral dissertation, Faculty of Arts, Norwegian University of Technology and Science, Trondheim.

O'Brien, J. (1999). Writing in the body: Gender (re)production in online interaction. In P. Kollock & M. A. Smith (eds.), *Communities in Cyberspace* (pp. 76–107). London and New York: Routledge.

Oldenziel, R. (1999). *Making Technology Masculine: Men, Women and Modern Machines in America, 1870–1945*. Amsterdam: Amsterdam University Press.

O'Riordan, K. (2007). Queer theories and cybersubjects: Intersecting figures. In K. O'Riordan & D. Phillips (eds.), *Queer Online: Media Technology and Sexuality* (pp. 13–30). New York: Peter Lang.

O'Riordan, K., & Phillips, D. (eds.) (2007). *Queer Online: Media Technology and Sexuality*. New York: Peter Lang.

Plant, S. (1997). *Zeros + Ones: Digital Women + The New Technoculture*. New York: Doubleday.

Rich, A. (1980). Compulsory heterosexuality and lesbian existence. *Signs*, 5(4), 631–60.

Richardson, D., McLaughlin, J., & Casey, M. E. (eds.) (2007). *Intersections between Feminist and Queer Theory*. London: Palgrave Macmillan.

Royse, P., Lee, J., Undrahbuyan, B., Hopson, M., & Consalvo, M. (2007). Women and games: Technologies of the gendered self. *New Media & Society*, 9(4), 555–76.

Rubin, G. ([1984] 1993). Thinking sex: Notes for a radical theory of the politics of sexuality. In H. Abelove, M. A. Barale, & D. M. Halperin (eds.), *The Lesbian and Gay Studies Reader* (pp. 3–44). New York and London: Routledge.

Schott, G., & Horrell, K. (2000). Girl gamers and their relationship with gaming culture. *Convergence*, 6(4), 36–53.

Shade, L. R. (2002). *Gender and Community in the Social Construction of the Internet*. New York: Peter Lang.

Shade, L. R. (2004). Bending gender into the net. In P. N. Howard & S. Jones (eds.), *Society Online. The Internet in Context* (pp. 57–71). Thousand Oaks, CA, London, New Delhi: Sage.

Silver, D., & Massanari, A. (eds.) (2006). *Critical Cyberculture Studies*. New York: New York University Press.

Sommer, I. (2003). Skjermede kropper. En analyse av kroppen på IRC-chat. Master's dissertation, Institutt for sosiologi og samfunnsgeografi, University of Oslo.

Stone, A. R. (1991). Will the real body please stand up? Boundary stories about virtual cultures. In M. Benedikt (ed.), *Cyberspace: First Steps* (pp. 81–118). Cambridge, MA: MIT Press.

Stone, A. R. (1992). Virtual systems. In J. Crary & K. Sandford (eds.), *Incorporations* (pp. 608–25). New York: Zone.

Stone, A. R. (1995). *The War of Desire and Technology at the Close of the Mechanical Age*. Cambridge, MA: MIT Press.

Sullivan, C., & Bornstein, K. (1996). *Nearly Roadkill: An Infobahn Erotic Adventure*. New York: High Risk/Serpent's Tail.

Sundén, J. (2001). What happened to difference in cyberspace? The (re)turn of the she-cyborg. *Feminist Media Studies*, 1(2), 215–32.

Sundén, J. (2003). *Material Virtualities: Approaching Online Textual Embodiment*. New York: Peter Lang.

Sundén, J. (2008). What if Frankenstein('s monster) was a girl? Reproduction and subjectivity in the digital age. In A. Smelik & N. Lykke (eds.), *Bits of Life: Feminism at the Intersections of Media, Bioscience, and Technology* (pp. 147–62). Seattle: Washington University Press.

Sveningsson Elm, M., & Sundén, J. (eds.) (2007). *Cyberfeminism in Northern Lights: Digital Media and Gender in a Nordic Context*. Newcastle upon Tyne: Cambridge Scholars Press.

Taylor, T. L. (2006). *Play Between Worlds: Exploring Online Game Culture*. Cambridge, MA: MIT Press.

Thorseth, M. (2003). *Applied Ethics in Internet Research*. Program for Applied Ethics, publication series no. 1, Norwegian University of Science and Technology, Trondheim. NTNU University Press, Trondheim, Norway.

Turkle, S. (1995). *Life on the Screen: Identity in the Age of the Internet*. New York: Simon and Schuster.

Vance, C. F. (ed.) (1984). *Pleasure and Danger. Exploring Female Sexuality*. London: Routledge & Paul Keagan.

VNS Matrix (1991). Cyberfeminist manifesto for the 21st century. Retrieved September 5, 2006, from http://www.sysx.org/gashgirl/VNS/TEXT/PINKMANI.HTM.

Wajcman, J. (1991). *Feminism Confronts Technology*. Cambridge: Polity.

Wajcman, J. (1995). Feminist theories of technology. In S. Jasanoff (ed.), *Handbook of Science and Technology Studies* (pp. 189–204). Thousand Oaks, CA: Sage.

Wakeford, N. (1996). Sexualized bodies in cyberspace. In W. Chernaik, M. Deegan, & A. Gibson (eds.), *Beyond the Book. Theory, Culture, and the Politics of Cyberspace* (pp. 9–105). Office for Humanities Communication Publications 7. Centre for English Studies, University of London, Oxford.

Wakeford, N. (1997). Cyberqueer. In A. Medhurst & S. Munt (eds.), *Lesbian and Gay Studies: A Critical Introduction* (pp. 20–39). London: Cassell.

Ward, K. (1999). The cyber-ethnographic (re)construction of two feminist online communities. *Sociological Research Online*, 4(4). Retrieved August 20, 2008, from http://www.socresonline.org.uk/4/1/ward.html.

Wiley, J. (1999). NO BODY is "doing it": Cybersexuality. In J. Price & M. Shildrick (eds.), *Feminist Theory and the Body* (pp. 134–40). New York: Routledge.

Wittig, M. (1980). The straight mind. *Feminist Issues*, 1(1), 103–11.

Part III

Internet and Culture

Introduction to Part III

Mia Consalvo

In considering what culture is relative to the Internet, there are two useful if perhaps oppositional touchstones to consider. One is from Matthew Arnold: that culture comprises "the best that has been thought and said in the world" (2003). The second is from Raymond Williams, who in defining culture claimed that it comprised "a whole way of life" in addition to "the special processes of discovery and creative efforts" (Williams & Higgins, 2001, p. 11). There's a wide gulf separating those two definitions, and many battles have been fought over what should "count" as culture. Yet if we take a dialectic approach and see these two definitions as boundary poles, a place emerges for what culture might mean, and, here, for what it means applied to the Internet.

Arnold's definition, although considered elitist by some, reminds us that culture is something that we should celebrate, and look to as exemplary work, being inspirational, thought-provoking, and perhaps challenging to more pedestrian thoughts and activities. On the other hand, Williams encompasses a much broader circuit, arguing that we must envision culture as a set of activities, practices, beliefs, and artifacts of a people or society. Williams is more inclusive, discarding value judgments, instead believing that societies become cultures when their beliefs, practices, and ideas evolve and become distinct from those of others.

Both definitions can be useful in thinking through how "culture" intersects with the Internet and activities found online. There are practices, artifacts, and elements we can celebrate, and that can challenge us. And increasingly, we find practices, beliefs, and activities that are distinct from physical counterparts found in daily life. Both systems need to be explored, documented, and theorized. We will see our contributors do just that with particular attention to how diverse components of culture have emerged on the Internet.

Introducing the Chapters

Lori Kendall begins Part III by examining one of the central topics in the field of Internet studies in her chapter, "Community and the Internet." She explores scholarly work on the topic, taking us through the rise of the (concept of the) virtual community, debates about whether online communities count (or should count) as real communities, and how identity plays a key role in mediating our experiences with community. In doing so she points to several key advances in this area – the acknowledgment that most communities span online and offline life, and that we are struggling between twin desires to be the central node in a network over which we have control, and to experience genuine ties of sociality with others. Kendall closes by arguing that we need better studies of how such communities fit into the larger life activities of users (over time as well as geography), and what such communities could do to materially improve our daily lives.

Next, Mia Consalvo explores a particular type of space or place on the Internet in Chapter 15, "MOOs to MMOs: The Internet and Virtual Worlds." Chronicling both the history of virtual worlds and scholarship about them, she points to key areas of research done so far, including discussion of the (often hidden implications of the) spatial aspect of virtual worlds, the role and importance of avatars, as well as how ideas about community and identity are central to what happens in such spaces. She also argues that we need to expand our repertoire as scholars, going beyond studying a few well-known virtual worlds, as well as to begin investigating the business and economics of creating such worlds, which are built in particular cultures and contexts which can and do shape assumptions about their design and use.

The particularities of studying "Internet, Children, and Youth" is tackled in a chapter by Sonia Livingstone. Countering myths that all children are Internet-savvy millennials, prolifically creating and posting media online as well as questioning authority, Livingstone instead asserts that although some children may indeed find the Internet to be a rich and engaging part of their lives, for others "it remains a narrow and relatively unengaging if occasionally useful resource." In her extensive studies of youth and the Internet, Livingstone paints a more nuanced portrait of youth online, suggesting that while children and young adults do use the Internet for communicating, learning, playing, connecting and so on, we must also consider the contexts that both constrain and enable that use, and continue to be cognizant of the risks as well as benefits that await them online.

In her chapter on "Internet and Games," T. L. Taylor provides a much-needed overview of the history of games' relationship with the Internet, taking us back to games played via bulletin board systems as well as early text adventures. Indeed, Taylor demonstrates the centrality of games to the Internet's developing history, as well as showing how research about online games is central to our understandings of Internet use at large. She touches on familiar themes in games research such as identity and community, yet also points to important work done focusing on the "digital play industry," and argues following Kendall that we need to continue to study crossovers between online and offline activities, as these mutually construct one another. Finally, she calls for research in this area to expand its reach to the global, as games have players around the world, yet research touches on only a few countries and cultures.

One key area of recent interest in Internet studies has been the rapid rise in popularity of social network sites, which Nancy Baym addresses in her chapter "Social Networks 2.0." To contextualize this topic, she points out that media hype surrounding the development of "Web 2.0" and social networking fails to recognize that prior to the development of the World Wide Web, "all of the content was generated by the people, for the people." Thus, we have not so much a new activity, but new attention to that activity, although this time orchestrated by for-profit enterprises such as Facebook. In her exploration of research on social network sites, she finds that much of the work focuses on a few major sites (including Facebook and MySpace), with more work needed studying how users might travel across various networks, and how use occurs beyond such groups as college and high-school students. Finally, she makes a plea for the study of ethics in this space, arguing that the investment of so many individuals' time and effort in what are privately controlled domains demands more careful accounting and study, as well as critical scrutiny of the corporations that build such sites.

Focusing more specifically on such for-profit organizations, P. David Marshall explores the intersections of media writ large and the Internet in "Newly Mediated Media: Understanding the Changing Internet Landscape of the Media Industries." To make sense of such a large task, he focuses on five central concerns and research about them: how the Internet is used to *promote* other media forms (such as the foundational campaign surrounding *The Blair Witch Project* film); the extent to which an online source is a *copy or replica* of a traditional media form; how the Internet has changed *income* expectations for media firms and caused them to explore new revenue models; changing forms and the extent of new *alliances* that media firms are engendering due to the Internet; and finally the role of the Internet in *replacing* other forms of media. Marshall concludes by suggesting that while the Internet is indeed changing how traditional media operate, it is also true that "past models are still working – perhaps not as strongly, but still quite well," and likewise that we still have much to learn about how consumers of traditional media have translated their interests to online possibilities and offerings.

Susanna Paasonen tackles a subject largely overlooked in the field despite its overwhelming global popularity in her chapter, "Online Pornography: Ubiquitous and Effaced." She argues that "there is little doubt as to the centrality of pornography in terms of Internet history, its technical development, uses, business models, or legislation" yet it remains "one of the more understudied areas of Internet research." In bringing attention to work that has been done, Paasonen highlights the challenges involved in how to study porn online, including how to define it and access it, as well as how to recognize what the bounds of a research project might be, given how little we know about its actual use and availability. She points to work being done in relation to alternative porn as well as amateur porn online (among other areas), demonstrating the value of the work as well as the potential to learn from areas still mostly unexplored. She concludes that although pornographic content production may not be the most popular example of user-created content, it must be studied to give us a more representative picture of how the Internet is being used by everyday citizens.

Tackling a somewhat less controversial topic (at least for consumers), Steve Jones explores "Music and the Internet" in the next chapter. As he points out, for most people the obvious connection between music and the Internet is Napster and illegal downloading. Yet there is much more to take into account beyond repercussions for the music industry, particularly how the Internet has changed the role and identities, as well as practices, of musicians themselves as well as music fans. And as Jones concludes, "the debates about music and the Internet are ultimately about commerce and art, and are thus extraordinarily complicated and, perhaps, irresolvable." While certainly true in relation to music and the Internet, such a statement also is relevant in regards to many other practices we now see online.

In the last chapter of the volume, Marika Lüders explores "Why and How Online Sociability Became Part and Parcel of Teenage Life." In doing so, she argues that it is now impossible to research the social life of teenagers without studying their activities online. Furthermore, there are important ramifications that such activity can have on their development, both psychologically as well as culturally. She argues, much as Livingstone has in her chapter, that the Internet offers young people increasing opportunities as well as potential dangers to experiment with identity and create and manage social ties, although we do have to look beyond simplistic media panics to understand the actual constraints or problems that teens face online.

Future Questions

Overall, the chapters included here provide excellent insight into emerging as well as more established phenomena resulting from Internet use, as that use impacts culture. The contributors also point to important questions to consider as more research is done, and as we consider how we *want* to see the Internet impacting daily life. One central question concerns who controls these activities, as well as shapes how we participate in them. As we develop more broadly in our Introduction, little in the way of critical study of the ownership and business practices surrounding Internet-related activities has been done, and we need more detailed study of how individual companies, sites such as Silicon Valley, and cultural factors shape and constrain what is built, and what is not built. Likewise, we need to consider how individuals are faring through the entire life course, now that it is being lived more and more online. How are the rhythms of daily life as well as generational changes impacting people's activities online? How do people move around and through diverse social network sites, virtual worlds, games, religious sites, and perhaps even porn sites? We have some very good studies of individual aspects of use, but little that can tell us about how people actually use the Internet – not as discrete bounded spaces but as overlapping, contradictory, simple-to-complex places for meaning making. Finally, how are the methods we use adapting to acknowledge the complexity, diversity, and scope of online activity? There are text, sound, images, video, and interactivity to explore, on devices that include desktops, laptops, netbooks, mobile phones, and other emerging technologies. We are not place-bound as we use the Internet, nor do we often do only one thing at a time. How can we best study all of that activity, particularly as it is embedded in everyday life? These are only a few questions to ponder, as we consider the future of Internet studies.

References

Arnold, M. (2003). *Culture and Anarchy*. Available online at http://www.gutenberg.org/etext/4212.

Williams, R., & Higgins, J. (2001). *The Raymond Williams Reader*. Oxford: Wiley-Blackwell.

14

Community and the Internet

Lori Kendall

Defining the Undefinable

Even prior to research on Internet communities, the concept of "community" posed a problem for scholars. Rather than objectively describing a type of human group or association, it carries significant emotional baggage. Imagine trying to use it as an epithet. One might spit out the word "community" sarcastically to call into question the legitimacy of a *particular* group, but it is hard to imagine using the term to provide a straightforward negative evaluation. Community evokes empathy, affection, support, interdependence, consensus, shared values, and proximity. Real communities (however those might be defined) of course may contain all of these, as well as all of their opposites. This contradiction has had several effects on the study of communities, especially the study of online communities and other communities that intersect the Internet.

Community's feel-good fuzziness requires that scholars first grapple with its definition. The scope of community definitions ranges from the extremely minimalist to more elaborate lists of facets. For instance, the definition of "virtual community" offered on Wikipedia includes only two simple elements: (1) "a group of people," who (2) "interact via communication media" (Wikipedia, 2008). Porter's (2004) similarly simple definition of virtual community adds one more element: (1) "an aggregation of individuals," who (2) "interact" around a (3) "shared interest" (p. 3). While these definitions strip the word community of most of its usually understood meaning, they accord with conceptions of the term in the business world. This was especially true during the dot.com boom in the late 1990s, when many businesses became excited about online communities as potential marketing tools, and conceived of such communities as little more than groups of consumers who would gather and enthuse about specific products.

More recently, articles about online community oriented towards business interests address more than just marketing applications of virtual communities. However, definitions of community in those articles continue to emphasize communication as the central component of community. Ridings and Gefen (2006), who discuss virtual communities as "crucial to organizations that want to tap into their enormous information potential," provide a three-part definition, that includes: (1) "shared interests or goals," (2) a "sense of permanence," and (3) some sufficient degree of "frequency" of interaction (p. 2).

Scholars who, on the other hand, seek to identify the potential of the Internet for facilitating deeper human connections tend to emphasize relationships and values rather than communication and shared interests. Amitai Etzioni (2004) states that communities have "two elements": (1) "a web of affect-laden relationships" that are interconnected, and (2) "commitment to a set of shared values, norms, and meanings, and a shared history and identity" (p. 225). Strictly speaking, this sneaks in a good deal more than two elements, since having a shared history and identity is rather a different thing than having shared meanings, let alone shared values. In any case, Etzioni, a central figure in the communitarian movement, provides a definition of community with much more emotional heft. His focus on tightly woven webs of relationships that "crisscross and reinforce one another" (p. 225) follows a long tradition of conceiving of communities as tightly-knit and cooperative. This dates back at least to Tönnies' concept of *Gemeinschaft*, or community, conceived of in distinction to the more atomistic and anonymous experience of *Gesellschaft*, or society (Tönnies, [1887] 1979, as cited in Borgmann, 2004).

A third theme in scholarly writing on Internet communities concerns the design of online forums that could facilitate virtual community. When defining community, authors with this focus generally find it necessary to more explicitly list numerous facets of community in order to determine what aspects of system design correspond with those facets. Feenberg and Bakardjieva (2004) list five attributes of community, derived from sociology and philosophy: "(1) identification with symbols and ritual practices; (2) acceptance of common rules; (3) mutual aid; (4) mutual respect; [and] (5) authentic communication" (p. 5).

But with the emphasis on systems design, an exact definition of community itself fades in importance in favor of lists of requirements for the systems that would support community. After their discussion of the definition of community, Feenberg and Bakardjieva (2004) quote Mynatt and colleagues' (1998) list of five "affordances" that "span the various technologies used in Internet-based communities": persistence, periodicity, boundaries, engagement, and authoring (pp. 130–32). Similarly, Porter (2004) suggests a typology of virtual communities that includes five "attributes": (1) "purpose (content)," (2) "place (extent of mediation)," (3) "platform" (system design), (4) "population interaction structure (pattern of interaction)," and (5) "profit model" (p. 8). While seemingly abandoning the difficult philosophical task of defining communities in order to get to the important practical work of designing them, these lists of affordances or attributes nevertheless contain important assumptions about what communities are for. Porter's model, for instance, assumes that understanding virtual communities requires determining whether or not they "create tangible economic value" (p. 7). Mynatt and colleagues' list of affordances emphasizes the quasi-physical construction of the virtual place as a communication space.

Some researchers suggest abandoning the term community entirely. This again is not a new strategy, as at least one urban sociologist suggested in the 1970s that community sociologists (somewhat paradoxically) should abandon the term that defined their subdiscipline (personal conversation with Lyn Lofland). Fernback (2007) similarly asserts that the "concept of online community . . . has become increasingly hollow as it evolves into a pastiche of elements that ostensibly 'signify' community" (p. 53). Rather than defining community *a priori*, Fernback takes a symbolic interactionist approach by interviewing participants about their own conceptions of their online group interactions. She finds that "participants in online groups possess incongruous understandings of the character of online social relations" (p. 57). While her respondents employ the term community to express the sense of "unity and support" (p. 62) they experience in their online groups, Fernback suggests that a more important, and elusive aspect is that of commitment.

Community versus Networked Individualism

Fernback found that online participants still use the term community, albeit idiosyncratically, to describe their online groups. However, Barry Wellman (2002) suggests that people, at least in developed nations, are abandoning communities in favor of "networked individualism." He asserts that this process pre-dates, but has been facilitated by, the Internet. In the condition of networked individualism, "[p]eople remain connected, but as individuals rather than being rooted in the home bases of work unit and household. Individuals switch rapidly between their social networks. Each person separately operates his networks to obtain information, collaboration, orders, support, sociability, and a sense of belonging" (p. 5). Rather than identifying with a single, close-knit community, each networked individual sits at the center of a set of personal networks. This analysis stems in part from Wellman's methodological approach, in which he uses social network analysis to study individuals, networks, and groups.

As is clear from its name, Wellman's concept "is highly individualistic in nature," lacking "the sense of collectivity" found in earlier conceptions of community (Fernback, 2007, p. 54). Gurstein (2007), however, argues that this conception of individuals paradoxically strips them of any agency. "Within Wellman's model of 'networked individualism,' the only ontological mover (independent agent or source of independent action/agency) is the network itself" (p. 19). Gurstein further views networks as susceptible to centralized control and asserts that communities, as independent ontologies, continue to provide a basis for group action in opposition to networked control.

Gochenour (2006) provides a view of individual online participants similar to Wellman's, but derived from the completely different theoretical perspectives of cognitive science and systems theory. He wishes to "shift thinking about 'online communities' away from specific [virtual] places and practices, and toward thinking about 'distributed communities' as arising from nodes . . . connected by a communications infrastructure" (p. 47). He presents a view of the self as coming "into being only through the field of social relations" (p. 39). In short, the networks create the nodes. Despite this, Gochenour sees these networks as "nonetheless communities that give members the ability to work together in taking action" (p. 46), but only as long as they continue to have Internet access.

Postill (2008), on the other hand, advocates abandoning both "community" and "networked individualism" as analytical terms. Like Fernback, he finds community useful only "as a polymorphous folk notion," rather than as an analytical concept (p. 416). Following Bourdieu, Postill suggests that social network analysis relies too much on "interaction as the basis of human life," failing to take account of "the invisible network of objective relations" (p. 418). Postill recommends a grounded "social field" analysis, open to different forms of sociality.

Whatever the implications of networked individualism for personal agency and group action, there is some empirical evidence in support of Wellman's characterization, at least with regard to online interactions. Both Hodkinson (2007) and Kendall (2007) find that LiveJournal users, with their interlinked personal diary-style blogs, follow more individualistic patterns of interaction than participants in previous online communities on forums such as newsgroups and MUDs (multi-user dungeons/domains). Hodkinson studied members of a Goth subculture who moved from discussion forums to LiveJournal. He suggests that "the use of interactive online journals can be expected to encourage patterns of interaction that are significantly more individually-centered than has been observed in the case of many discussion forums" (p. 646). Previously, interactions amongst this group had occurred in an online forum in which shared norms were adopted and policed. However, once the group moved to LiveJournal, "rather than occurring in the context of shared space in which behaviour and content is governed primarily by group norms, the majority of interactions take place on the personal territory of one individual and are initiated, centred around and regulated by that individual" (p. 632).

Kendall (2007) similarly found that the existence of each LiveJournal as a single participant's own personal space suppressed dialogue among participants, despite their expressed desire to use LiveJournal to increase their social interaction. "LiveJournal participants seek connection with others. LiveJournal theoretically provides several tools that facilitate such connections. But its structure as a linked set of individually controlled journals mitigates against the kinds of connection and feedback people seek" (p. 20). LiveJournal users express two contradictory desires. On the one hand, they seek the networked individual's autonomous control of their own nodal space. On the other hand, they still desire meaningful interpersonal connections, which can only come from autonomous others, freely contributing to a group dialogue. In a fully networked individualistic world, it is unclear where this dialogue could occur.

Real Communities versus Pseudocommunities

Debates about the definition or usefulness of the term "community" concern the central questions of the kinds of bonds we form, and the ways those bonds change as we blend our offline lives with online interactions. Discussions of online communities or of the effects of the Internet on both online and offline communities, rest on a long history of concerns with the fate of communities. Wellman (1979) identifies three strands in these discussions: "community lost," "community saved," and "community liberated." As he discusses, works based on Tönnies' distinctions between *Gesellschaft* and *Gemeinschaft* imply that community is being lost to the inexorable progression of modernity, leaving us isolated and anonymous. In reaction, many urban scholars developed the "community saved," argument through documenting vibrant urban communities. Wellman argues, however, that these studies fail to capture the important ties that people maintain outside of the densely local groups studied by the "saved" researchers. In his "community liberated" argument, he makes the case for a social network approach to the study of community in order to capture people's densely knit sets of strong ties as well as their more far-flung networks of weak ties.

The considerable body of research that documents new and vibrant forms of community and connections has failed to dispel the popularity of the "community lost" argument. Both academic and popular discourse abound with nostalgic claims concerning the kinds of connections we used to have, and the dire consequences of their loss. This leads to two responses among Internet community researchers and chroniclers. Some suggest that the Internet will restore to us the community we have lost. Rheingold (1993), for instance, describes a "hunger for community," created by the disappearance of informal public spaces, that drives people to create virtual communities (p. 6).

Others insist that the Internet merely continues previous processes of increasing isolation and anomie, or perhaps even makes them worse. Barney (2004) argues that "digital technology impoverishes rather than enriches our shared reality . . . so far as the concrete material foundations of community are concerned" (p. 32). Similarly, Borgmann (2004) claims that the Internet cannot foster what he calls "final communities" – "communities [that] are ends rather than means" . . . and "groups of people where one finds or works out one's reason for living" (p. 63). This is so because "the Internet is culturally commodifying by its nature," reducing people to "glamorous and attractive personae" (p. 64).

Borgmann's argument resonates with popular conceptions of Internet interactions as not truly social. Cultural biases against online socializing persist, despite the continually increasing numbers of people who participate in online interactions. People with active online lives nevertheless "appear ardent to distance themselves from what they may perceive to be the stereotype of the introverted internet user" (Fernback, 2007, p. 60). Researchers are also mindful of the possibility that, even offline, not everything that looks like a community necessarily is one. Jones (1995) discusses the concept of pseudocommunity, as defined by a lack of sincerity and commitment. Similar work by the sociologist Bellah and colleagues (1985) distinguishes between communities and "lifestyle enclaves," in which individuals are united by shared leisure interests rather than complex interdependencies.

These issues result in a tendency, especially in the early research on Internet communities, to focus on the question of whether or not online communities are "real" communities. Much of this research is valuable in that it details the richness of online interactions. However, it has led to a certain degree of wheel-spinning as researchers over and over feel it necessary to assert that online communities are indeed possible.

Virtual Communities

The earliest researchers of virtual communities came from several different academic disciplines, including anthropology, communication, linguistics, media studies, and sociology. But they shared in common the experience of being among the first within their discipline to explore the online world, often in the face of skeptical mentors and colleagues. Not surprisingly, most began their research on the online world as graduate students. Junior scholars were more likely to be drawn to the new world of online socializing, and most able to turn their scholarly careers toward the job of explaining that world. (Indeed, one of the earliest, and most-cited, treatises on online community, Elizabeth Reid's 1991 "Electropolis: Communication and Community on Internet Relay Chat," is an undergraduate honors thesis.)

Some of these early researchers had no experience with online interaction prior to being drawn there by research interests (Kendall, 2002). Others, in the ethnographic tradition of "starting where you are" (Lofland & Lofland, 1995), conducted their research on virtual groups in which they already participated (Cherny, 1999; Baym, 2000). Yet others created online communities to facilitate professional goals and interests, while incidentally also furthering a research agenda (Bruckman & Resnick, 1995; Bruckman & Jensen, 2002). The work of these early virtual community researchers focused on asynchronous forums like Usenet and The WELL, and on near-synchronous forums of MUDs and chat. These venues reflect the conditions of the time (the mid-1990s to early 2000s), when almost all communication over the Internet was text-based. Taken as a whole, research on virtual communities focuses on several key issues. These include the formation and demise of virtual communities; conflict, cooperation, and social control; and identity, including both the possibility for online identity deception, and the connection between offline social identities and online interactions.

Community Lifecycles

As a relatively new phenomenon, online communities don't have histories extending back for generations. Virtual community researchers frequently talk to still-active community founders. Current participants have vivid memories of formative events; events with clear connections to current policies, activities, and conflicts. Such events provide insight into the ways communities form and cohere, and point to issues of interest to others hoping to form similar communities.

Cherny (1999) describes the history of *ElseMOO* and its relationship to the earlier *LambdaMOO* community. Founded by several people who had been active *LambdaMOO* participants, *ElseMOO* established many of its norms and practices through specifically differentiating itself from *LambdaMOO*. For instance, at the time *ElseMOO* began, *LambdaMOO* was in the early stages of building a democratic system of government heavily reliant on a petition process. *ElseMOO*, a much smaller group, was run more like a private club. Through the course of its life, *ElseMOO* continued to acquire members from *LambdaMOO*, especially older participants who felt that *LambdaMOO* had too many "newbies."

Kendall (2002) similarly describes the growth of *BlueSky* from several previous groups, and explains its continued relationship to other outgrowths of these groups, including *ElseMOO*. *BlueSky* participants characterized themselves as "crusty dinos," recognizing their relatively long-term participation in online communities, as well as their somewhat cantankerous interactional style. In keeping with this self-description, *BlueSky* participants tended to be critical of other communities, especially those they deemed silly. These included *LambdaMOO* and *FurryMUCK*, two other long-standing online communities. *BlueSky* participants considered *LambdaMOO* to be too full of clueless newbies and disdained the *FurryMUCK* practice of role-playing as anthropomorphic animals.

Communities thus often form in reaction to other available communities, with participants distinguishing their own identity and values from those of others. However, internal events can also be crucial to members' sense of themselves as constituting a community. Some of the earliest examples of this appear in the journalistic accounts of virtual communities by Rheingold (1993) and Dibbell (1993, 1998). Rheingold (1993) describes how events such as the suicide and funeral of a WELL participant brought other members together and highlighted for them the growing strength of their bonds. Dibbell's (1993) famous account of a "rape in cyberspace" demonstrates how negative events – in this case the abuse by a *LambdaMOO* participant of several other participants – force community members to consider issues of governance and conflict resolution. This can lead to a stronger feeling of community.

Relatively few accounts exist of the demise of virtual communities. Gatson and Zweerink's (2004) account of *The Bronze*, an online group of fans of the television series *Buffy the Vampire Slayer*, notes that communities fostered and controlled by corporate entities exist at the whim of those corporations. Cherny (1999) similarly describes a period when *ElseMOO* was shut down by one of its founders. Virtual communities require non-virtual hardware and software resources, and those resources may be controlled by one or a few members (as in the *ElseMOO* case), or by persons or groups completely outside of the community (as in the case of *The Bronze*). This can make virtual communities more vulnerable to disruption or dissolution than their offline counterparts.

Bruckman and Jensen (2002) provide one of the few detailed analyses of the demise of a virtual community. Bruckman and others founded *MediaMOO* in 1993 "to enhance professional community among media researchers" (Bruckman & Resnick, 1995, p. 1). For several years, it grew and successfully functioned as a site for collaboration and networking. However, by 1999 it was all but completely dead. Bruckman and Jensen identify several key contributing factors.

The *MediaMOO* founders originally assumed that community members would continue their participation indefinitely. But in Bruckman and Jensen's analysis, *MediaMOO* provided greater benefits to new scholars than to established researchers. *MediaMOO* also successfully fostered several groups that later split off to form separate communities. The resulting losses in membership from these two factors were not adequately compensated by the addition of new members. Bruckman and Jensen felt that encouraging new members would require more active participation by leadership, especially in acclimating new members and making them feel welcome.

Conflict, Cooperation, and Control

Depending on how it is managed, conflict can destroy communities. Virtual communities are particularly vulnerable to disruption by miscreant outsiders or disgruntled insiders. Yet, as described by Rheingold and Dibbell, conflicts can also foster community. Conflict can promote reflection and a growth in community identity. This can involve more explicitly spelling out norms and rules for behavior. Conflicts can also generate new mechanisms for social control. For these reasons, conflicts provide researchers with information about community values.

Stone (1992), describes the difficulties experienced by *CommuniTree*, a virtual community created on a bulletin-board system in 1978 (and thus predating most of the Internet-based virtual communities described here). In 1982, *CommuniTree* suffered from an influx of boys who jammed the system "with obscene and scatological messages," and found ways to "'crash' the system by discovering bugs in the system commands" (p. 91). These problems were exacerbated by privacy policies which prevented administrators from viewing messages as they came in. Within months, *CommuniTree* became unusable. "Thus, in practice, surveillance and control proved necessary adjuncts to maintaining order in the virtual community" (p. 91).

Quittner (1994) recounts a similar incident when rec.pets.cats, a Usenet newsgroup, was invaded by participants on other newsgroups, including alt.tasteless and alt.bigfoot. In that case, participants were unable to access software in ways that threatened the continuation of the community. However, by spamming the list with disruptive and objectionable messages, they rendered normal conversations among participants impossible. The conflict also escalated to include threats to specific individual participants. Rec.pets.cats eventually recovered, in part through the use of technical features allowing users to block objectionable messages.

In her discussion of "conflict management in virtual communities," Smith (1999) describes numerous conflicts on *MicroMUSE*. *MicroMUSE* was an online community constructed for the purpose of science education for children, but allowed public visitors as well. Smith recounts several instances in which participants who committed severe transgressions were banned from the community – the ultimate sanction available in virtual communities. As in the case of *CommuniTree*, the actions of these transgressors threatened the continued operation of the software that allowed the community to exist, as well as disrupting the work of others. But, though banned, the transgressors were able to return through the exploitation of technical loopholes in the software.

Smith argues that virtual communities "must include diversity and find some way to integrate it if they are to thrive" (1999, p. 160), but diversity results in conflict. She notes that "to survive, virtual communities must protect their primary resources" (p. 143), and must therefore find ways to manage conflict before it escalates such that it harms the community as a whole. However, the imposition of sanctions is complicated by the inability to confront transgressors face-to-face, and the difficulty in keeping specific transgressors out, while still enabling the influx of new participants.

Not all conflicts originate from malicious outsiders. Communities can also suffer conflicts among members. Kendall (2002) recounts a disagreement among several *BlueSky* participants that resulted in one participant permanently leaving the group. This caused some soul-searching amongst the remaining participants. "[A]ny departure, especially a rancorous one, disturbs the harmony of the group and reminds people of the fragility of online relationships. . . . The rehashings and evaluations of the event helped people repair the breach in the group and reassure themselves of the group's continuation" (p. 177).

Such internal conflicts often stem from power differences among members. On *ElseMOO*, conflicts emerged from a complicated mix of factors. Contributing was the fact that only some participants had the ability to contribute to the creation of the community environment through programming its software. Participants who could program, including the founding members of the community, could dispense that ability to others. However, they tended to do so sparingly and somewhat arbitrarily. This fostered feelings of exclusion among non-programming participants. Another factor leading to conflict was the fact that some of the earliest *ElseMOO* participants lived in close proximity and were able to conduct their relationships face-to-face as well as on *ElseMOO*, leaving other participants feeling left out.

No one engaged in malicious hacking, or bombarded the others with offensive messages. However, ill-will and arguments increased to the point that the founder – and, importantly, the person upon whose computer the community existed – felt it necessary to temporarily shut the community down. It returned later with a reorganization that attempted to share power among a wider group of users. This reorganization was only partly successful in mitigating the interpersonal tensions on *ElseMOO*. Cherny notes that "if it's ultimately the community itself that deserves protection, it is never clear just who the community is . . . Boundaries are continually being negotiated, expressed in dynamic symbolic language and evolving community policies" (Cherny, 1999, p. 273).

Not all virtual communities experience these kinds of conflicts, and conflict is not necessarily required for the formation of close community bonds. In her description of rec.arts.tv.soaps (r.a.t.s.), Baym (2000) describes the ways in which r.a.t.s. participants actively construct r.a.t.s. as a community in which friendliness is a core value and expected behavior. They do this through several conversational strategies, including (1) qualifying their expression of points of disagreement, (2) aligning themselves with other participants through partial agreement, and (3) moving conversations away from disagreement and back to the core activity of the group: the interpretation of soap operas.

Identity

Communities do not exist without some sense of community identity among participants. As Anderson (1991) notes in his study of nationalism, "all communities . . . are imagined" (p. 6). Community exists through people's imagined bonds to others whom they identify as members of the same community. Thus community confers identity, and participant identities also play an important part in the formation and continuation of communities. In studies of virtual communities, scholars have discussed identity in several different ways. One concerns the greater ability of virtual community participants to mask their identity. Another concerns the intersection of various facets of social identities – especially race and gender – with norms and values of virtual communities.

Donath (1999) points out that "knowing the identity of those with whom you communicate is essential for understanding and evaluating an interaction" (p. 29). But in both text-based and graphical virtual worlds, much more than in face-to-face encounters, it is possible to mask identity, or to present a deliberately deceptive identity. (Since online identities are by definition mediated, people may also present identities they feel represent their true selves, but that would not be so evaluated by their interlocutors.) Early research was particularly caught up with this aspect of online life. Some lauded the ability to masquerade online as leading to a postmodern understanding of the self as multiple and socially constructed (Turkle, 1995). Others worried about the potential harm to virtual communities (Donath, 1999).

Tales of identity deception have taken on an almost mythical quality in writings about the Internet. The same stories are told over and over as cautionary tales to inoculate the unwary. One such tale is that of "Julie," a "totally disabled older woman" who turned out to be "a middle-aged male psychiatrist" who wanted to engage in conversations with other women as a woman (Stone, 1992, pp. 82–3). In the early MUD communities, participants warned each other about men who represented themselves as women online, engaged in netsex with other men, and then humiliated them by posting logs of the encounters on public forums.

Donath (1999) discusses a slightly different form of deception, that of trolling. Trolls represent themselves as serious members of the community, but then attempt to disrupt the community by baiting participants. The rec.pets.cats "invasion" described above occurred in the form of such trolling. As discussed both in Donath and in Herring and colleagues (2002), trolling harms communities in two ways: (1) causing community members to engage in fruitless and frustrating arguments, and (2) creating a loss of trust. Kendall (2002) and Herring and colleagues (2002) also point out the gendered nature of trolling, in which the trolls are often male and the victims most often female.

The extent of online identity deceptions is impossible to gauge, but researchers of online community find that in most long-standing communities, deception is minimized. The formation of community depends upon consistent identities. Participants come to know each other, even if only through pseudonyms, and often seek to connect offline as well as online. Kendall (2002) presents several examples of *BlueSky* participants who abandoned their initial identity masquerades, either because they wanted to meet people face-to-face, or because they tired of the deception. Borgmann (2004) suggests that "in the end and deep down . . . we crave recognition, the acknowledgement of who we are in fact" (p. 59).

However, not all online identity ambiguity is intentionally produced. The communication limitations of online forums can make it difficult to be sure of the identities of all participants. As Baym (1995) says about participation on newsgroups, "people never know who all the readers of their messages are" (p. 145). Kendall (2002) reports incidents in which people were confused by "robots" (characters run by computer programs rather than people), or encountered people they knew in other forums under other names. This sometimes leads people to attempt to pin down others' identities. On *BlueSky*, where people could log in anonymously as "guests," participants harassed guests who were deemed overly cagey about their identity (Kendall, 2002, pp. 129–35).

Despite these difficulties, most people in virtual communities wish to represent themselves in consistent and realistic ways. People do manage to perform consistent identities online. Among other things, this means that the aspects of identity that some hoped would become insignificant online – such as race, class, and gender – remain salient. Burkhalter (1999) details the ways in which Usenet participants perform racial identities, and evaluate – and dispute – the racial representations of others. Nakamura (2002) analyzes the phenomenon of "identity tourism," in which virtual community participants reinforce racial stereotypes through taking on the identity of exoticized others.

Although not focusing specifically on the issue of community, Susan Herring's work has been among the most influential in addressing the issue of gender identity online. She and her associates have analyzed many different aspects of gendered communication online, including: men's language online (Herring, 1992), gender differences in values leading to different online conversational styles (Herring, 1996), men's expectations about and reaction to women's online participation (Herring et al., 1995), and harassment of women online (Herring, 1999).

Her meticulous, prodigious, and early work in this area make it clear that gender does not disappear online simply because people communicating through text cannot see each other's bodies.

Later work on gender in online communities confirms Herring's findings. Kendall (2002) found that *BlueSky* participants brought their offline understandings and expectations about gender to their online interactions. As in people's offline relationships and communities, *BlueSky* participants enacted and constructed gender identities through their online interactions, asserting gendered identities, and, in some cases, arguing about what gender means.

With commercial interests added to the mix, gender becomes an important aspect of the creation and marketing of virtual community. Cooks, Paredes, and Scharrer (2002) analyze women's participation on "O Place," an online community on Oprah.com. While they find that the site does provide a forum in which women can connect with each other for mutual support and community, this occurs "within the topical confines of the talk show and the magazine" (p. 155). Advertisers can thus be assured of a particular demographic to target. This makes the meaning of community in this case ambiguous, and calls into question the ability of the site to better the lives of women in general, beyond providing a supportive space for individual women.

How commercial entities structure their sites has important ramifications for the possible emergence of community. Gustafson (2002) examined three different online sites geared towards women, and found that these sites provided only "a simulation of community" (p. 183). Through discursive framing, and various strategies for social control of users, each of the sites she analyzed "firmly frames women in the traditionally feminine role of consumer" (p. 183). While the sites bring people together, they merely masquerade as communities. Through hierarchical control by people who are not themselves members, they hold out the promise of community in order to gather information about members for marketing purposes.

Community On- and Offline

Most communities connected through the Internet involve both online and offline components. Even in virtual communities that primarily exist online, participants often seek to meet one another face-to-face. Meanwhile, many offline groups seek to enhance their communities through online participation. In recent research on community and the Internet, the emphasis is shifting from ethnographic studies of virtual communities, to studies of people's blending of offline and online contacts.

A key question in this research has been whether online participation helps or harms offline communities. In the face of what some have analyzed as a general decline in community participation (Putnam, 1995), researchers have attempted to determine what role the Internet plays in this. Following Putnam's analysis, much of this research has concerned increase or decrease in "social capital."

For instance, Quan-Haase and colleagues (2002) used data from a National Geographic survey of website visitors to measure the effects of Internet participation on social capital. They used questions on the survey as indicators of three forms of social capital: (1) network capital (contact with friends, relatives, and co-workers), (2) civic engagement (participation in voluntary organizations and political activities), and (3) sense of community (a sense of community belonging). In general, their findings do not indicate that Internet interactions have much of an effect, either positive or negative, on these types of social capital. Internet interactions do not significantly decrease other forms of contact, and active Internet users report more positive feelings about *online* community. But participation on the Internet does not increase civic engagement or a sense of belonging to *offline* communities.

Kavanaugh and Patterson (2002) report similar results from their study of the Blacksburg Electronic Village. Like many offline communities, the town of Blacksburg, Virginia, sought to provide Internet access to its citizens and to encourage civic connections through the Internet. While the town's efforts did increase Internet access, as well as the use of the Internet for activities building social capital, these activities did not seem to increase community involvement or attachment.

In contrast to these reports, Hampton and Wellman (2002) found that Internet access and participation increased neighborhood connections for the residents of Netville, a newly constructed Canadian suburb in which some residents' homes came equipped with broadband network connections. Wired residents knew and communicated with more of their neighbors than non-wired residents. They even used these contacts to support collective action, although the actions observed were limited to very local concerns, including housing deficiencies and a dispute concerning the Internet access itself.

If community is in general decreasing, these reports suggest that growing Internet participation provides no solution. On the other hand, they also do not support the idea that the Internet itself is a force destructive of community. Online communities, however defined, seem to be thriving. If, as Borgmann (2004) argues, such communities are not "final communities," and thus can never really fulfill our need for community, this is not necessarily good news. But as Borgmann points out, "there is no good social science evidence about the emotional effects of prolonged socializing in cyberspace" (p. 65). We don't have longitudinal studies of online communities, and there are only a few studies that look at very long-term users, except to determine if they engage in different kinds of online activities than less experienced users.

Future Directions

Future studies of Internet and community need to close the gap Borgmann identifies and analyze people's Internet participation over time. Are they, as Wellman (2002) argues, turning from communities to networked individualism? We need to investigate further whether, as Wellman claims, this is an inevitable progression, as well as the advantages and disadvantages of the growing phenomenon of networked individualism. Hodkinson's (2007) and Kendall's (2007) studies suggest that system design also has an impact on the level of individualism in online groups, and the extent to which this interferes with interpersonal bonds. We need to look not just at how to design systems to foster community, but at the community definitions embedded in those designs as well as the ramifications these definitions have for use.

System design also figures in the question of control versus connection that I noted in my work on LiveJournal (Kendall, 2007). There is a fundamental contradiction contained in our needs and desires that cannot ever be fully resolved, but that is definitely affected by what technologies we employ and how we use them. Each of us wants to be able to control how others perceive us and to control how and when we communicate with them. But the more control we exert, the less we are likely to receive the kind of close and spontaneous connections that we also desire. LiveJournal participants want to receive more comments in their journals, but are reluctant to leave comments in journals controlled by others. I have seen these same issues arise in interviews recently conducted with college students (for research in progress) about their cell phone use. Students often screen calls but are unhappy when they suspect their calls are being screened by others. The degree and type of control that different communications systems afford can affect the balance between these competing desires for control and connection and thereby directly impact the ability to form or enhance communities.

Good work continues to be done on how people perform particular identities online, on what these identities mean, and on what these performances tell us about identity (gender, race, age, etc.) in general. There is room for more of this kind of research. However, we also need studies that push beyond such questions as, for instance, whether gender matters online (of course it does), and whether online gender performances reify or call into question existing hegemonic conceptions of gender. (Some do one, some the other, but why? And in what circumstances?) We also need studies that take a broader look at how the Internet and related media technologies intersect with our conceptions of identity and our very sense of self. Are, for instance, changes occurring in how we conceive of gender, of what gender means in society, and of the gendered balance of power? If so, what role do new media play? If not, why do the new forms of sociality afforded by new media *not* effect such changes?

This approach applies to community as well as identity. Fernback (2007) argues that participants' own conceptions of the meaning of community are so contradictory that analyzing online participation in terms of community no longer makes sense. This introduces the question of how to determine the boundaries of research into community and the Internet. If participants themselves present contradictory notions of community, it might or might not make sense to limit a study to the boundaries of a specific group. This is particularly so since individuals may participate in numerous "communities," both online and offline. Yet adopting a strictly social network analysis approach risks reifying or even valorizing individualism. (For further discussion of the boundaries of research projects, see "Question One," in Markham & Baym, 2009.)

Wellman is right to caution against a nostalgic view of community that fosters the assumption that modern life is increasingly depriving us of strong interpersonal bonds. But we need more studies of the kinds of commitments and connections people form and the ways these relationships intersect communications technologies. These investigations need to go beyond the already difficult-to-answer questions of increases or decreases in social capital and community involvement. We need a better sense of (1) how people function in modern society, (2) whether some forms of social organization foster better, more fulfilling, lives than others, and (3) how we might intervene to create such forms of social organization. The answers to these questions concern what makes us human. At issue are our identities, relationships, commitments, and obligations, our personal and social needs and our sense of support and belonging.

References

Anderson, B. (1991). *Imagined Communities*. London: Verso.

Barney, D. (2004). The vanishing table, or community in a world that is no world. In A. Feenberg & D. Barney (eds.), *Community in the Digital Age* (pp. 31–51). Lanham: Rowman & Littlefield.

Baym, N. (1995). The emergence of community in computer-mediated communication. In S. Jones (ed.), *Cybersociety: Computer-mediated communication and community* (pp. 138–63). Thousand Oaks, CA: Sage.

Baym, N. (2000). *Tune In, Log On*. Thousand Oaks, CA: Sage.

Bellah, R. N., Madsen, R., Sullivan, W. M., Swidler, A., & Tipton, S. M. (1985). *Habits of the Heart: Individualism and commitment in American life*. New York: Harper & Row.

Borgmann, A. (2004). Is the Internet the solution to the problem of community? In A. Feenberg & D. Barney (eds.), *Community in the Digital Age* (pp. 53–67). Lanham: Rowman & Littlefield.

Bruckman, A., & Jensen, C. (2002). The mystery of the death of *MediaMOO*, seven years of evolution of an online community. In A. Renninger & W. Shumar (eds.), *Building Virtual Communities* (pp. 21–33). Cambridge: Cambridge University Press.

Bruckman, A., & Resnick, M. (1995). The *MediaMOO* Project: Constructionism and Professional Community. *Convergence*, 1(1), 94–109.

Burkhalter, B. (1999). Reading race online: discovering racial identity in Usenet discussions. In M. A. Smith & P. Kollock (eds.), *Communities in Cyberspace* (pp. 60–75). London: Routledge.

Cherny, L. (1999). *Conversation and Community: Chat in a Virtual World*. Stanford: CSLI Publications.

Cooks, L., Paredes, M. C., & Scharrer, E. (2002). "There's 'O Place' Like Home": Searching for community on Oprah.com. In M. Consalvo & S. Paasonen (eds.), *Women and Everyday Uses of the Internet* (pp. 139–67). New York: Peter Lang.

Dibbell, J. (1993). A rape in cyberspace. Retrieved September 15, 2008, from http://www.juliandibbell.com/texts/bungle_vv.html. (Originally published in *The Village Voice*, December 23, 1993.)

Dibbell, J. (1998). *My Tinylife: Crime and Passion in a Virtual World.* New York: Henry Holt.

Donath, J. (1999). Identity and deception in the virtual community. In M. A. Smith & P. Kollock (eds.), *Communities in Cyberspace* (pp. 29–59). London: Routledge.

Etzioni, A. (2004). On virtual, democratic communities. In A. Feenberg & D. Barney (eds.), *Community in the Digital Age* (pp. 225–38). Lanham: Rowman & Littlefield.

Feenberg, A., & Barney, D. (eds.) (2004). *Community in the Digital Age.* Lanham: Rowman & Littlefield.

Feenberg, A., & Makardjieva, M. (2004). Consumers or citizens? The online community debate. In A. Feenberg & D. Barney (eds.), *Community in the Digital Age* (pp. 1–28). Lanham: Rowman & Littlefield.

Fernback, J. (2007). Beyond the diluted community concept: A symbolic interactionist perspective on online social relations. *New Media & Society*, 9(1), 49–69.

Gatson, S., & Zweerink, A. (2004). *Interpersonal Culture on the Internet – Television, the Internet, and the Making of a Community*, Studies in Sociology Series, no. 40. Lewiston, NY: Edwin Mellen Press.

Gochenour, P. H. (2006). Distributed communities and nodal subjects. *New Media & Society*, 8(1), 33–51.

Gurstein, M. (2007). *What is Community Informatics and Why Does it Matter?* Milan: Polimetrica.

Gustafson, K. (2002). Join now, membership is free: Women's web sites and the coding of community. In M. Consalvo & S. Paasonen (eds.), *Women and Everyday Uses of the Internet* (pp. 168–90). New York: Peter Lang.

Hampton, K. N., & Wellman, B. (2002). The not so global village of Netville. In B. Wellman & C. Haythornthwaite (eds.), *The Internet in Everyday Life* (pp. 325–44). Oxford: Blackwell.

Herring, S. (1992). Men's language: A study of the discourse of the LINGUIST list. In A. Crochetière, J-C. Boulanger, & C. Ouellon (eds.), *Les Langues Menacées: Actes du XVe Congrès International des Linguistes* (vol. 3, pp. 347–50). Québec: Les Presses de l'Université Laval.

Herring, S. (1996). Posting in a different voice: Gender and ethics in computer-mediated communication. In C. Ess (ed.), *Philosophical Perspectives on Computer-Mediated Communication* (pp. 115–45). Albany: SUNY Press.

Herring, S. (1999). The rhetorical dynamics of gender harassment on-line. *The Information Society*, 15(3), 151–67.

Herring, S., Johnson, D. A., & DiBenedetto, T. (1995). "This discussion is going too far!" Male resistance to female participation on the Internet. In M. Bucholtz & K. Hall (eds.), *Gender Articulated: Language and the Socially Constructed Self* (pp. 67–96). New York: Routledge.

Herring, S., Job-Sluder, K., Scheckler, R., & Barab, S. (2002). Searching for safety online: Managing "trolling" in a feminist forum. *The Information Society*, 18(5), 371–84.

Hodkinson, P. (2007). Interactive online journals and individualization. *New Media & Society*, 9(4), 625–50.

Jones, S. G. (1995). Understanding Community in the Information Age. In S. G. Jones (ed.), *Cybersociety* (pp. 10–35). Thousand Oaks, CA: Sage.

Kavanaugh, A., & Patterson, S. (2002). The impact of community computer networks on social capital and community involvement in Blacksburg. In B. Wellman & C. Haythornthwaite (eds.), *The Internet in Everyday Life* (pp. 325–44). Oxford: Blackwell.

Kendall, L. (2002). *Hanging Out in the Virtual Pub.* Berkeley: University of California Press.

Kendall, L. (2007). "Shout into the wind, and it shouts back": Identity and interactional tensions on LiveJournal. *First Monday*, 12(9). Retrieved September 8, 2008, from http://firstmonday.org/issues/issue12_9/kendall/index.html.

Lofland, J., & Lofland, L. (1995). *Analyzing Social Settings.* Belmont, CA: Wadsworth.

Markham, A., & Baym, N. (2009). *Internet Inquiry: Conversations about Method.* Los Angeles: Sage.

Mynatt, E., O'Day, V. L., Adler, A., & Ito, M. (1998). Network communities: Something old, something new, something borrowed. . . . *Computer-Supported Cooperative Work*, 7, 123–56.

Nakamura, L. (2002). *Cybertypes: Race, Ethnicity, and Identity on the Internet.* New York: Routledge.

Porter, E. (2004). A typology of virtual communities: A multi-disciplinary foundation for future research. *Journal of Computer-Mediated Communication*, 10(1), article 3.

Postill, J. (2008). Localizing the internet beyond communities and networks. *New Media & Society*, 10(3), 413–31.

Putnam, R. (1995). Bowling alone: America's declining social capital. *Journal of Democracy*, 6(1), 65–78.

Quan-Haase, A., Wellman, B., Witte, J., & Hampton, K. (2002). Capitalizing on the net: Social contact, civic engagement, and sense of community. In B. Wellman & C. Haythornthwaite (eds.), *The Internet in Everyday Life* (pp. 291–324). Oxford: Blackwell.

Quittner, J. (1994). The war between alt.tasteless and rec.pets.cats. *Wired Magazine*, 2.05, May. http://www.wired.com/wired/archive/2.05/alt.tasteless_pr.html.

Rheingold, H. (1993). *The Virtual Community.* Reading, MA: Addison-Wesley.

Smith, A. D. (1999). Problems of conflict management in virtual communities. In M. A. Smith & P. Kollock (eds.), *Communities in Cyberspace* (pp. 134–63). London: Routledge.

Stone, A. R. (1992). Will the real body please stand up? Boundary stories about virtual cultures. In M. Benedikt (ed.), *Cyberspace: First Steps* (pp. 81–118). Cambridge, MA: MIT Press.

Turkle, S. (1995). *Life on the Screen.* New York: Simon & Schuster.

Wellman, B. (1979). The community question: The intimate networks of East Yorkers. *American Journal of Sociology*, 84(5), 1201–30.

Wellman, B. (2002). Little boxes, glocalization, and networked individualismin. In M. Tanabe, P. van den Besselaar, & T. Ishida (eds.), *Digital Cities II: Computational and Sociological Approaches* (pp. 10–25). Berlin: Springer.

Wikipedia (2008). Virtual Community. Retrieved September 23, 2008, from http://en.wikipedia.org/wiki/Virtual_community.

15

MOOs to MMOs: The Internet and Virtual Worlds

Mia Consalvo

The virtual worlds *World of Warcraft* and *Habbo Hotel* claim 11 million and 7.5 million users respectively, from North America, Europe, and Asia. *Second Life*'s LindeX market reported more than 59 million LindeX dollars traded on October 10, 2008. The educationally themed *Whyville* has 60,000 new registrations each month. Clearly, virtual worlds are popular, and becoming big business. And just as virtual worlds themselves are exploding in popularity, so too is research about them. In this chapter I seek to carve a path through existing literature about such spaces, offering a history of virtual worlds, and synthesizing the growing body of scholarly work about them. In doing so, I will try to disentangle work that has been done relative to online games (covered more extensively in Chapter 17, "Internet and Games," by T. L. Taylor) from work on virtual communities, while at the same time highlighting important overlaps.

It's important to acknowledge "we have, in a sense, created virtual worlds since the invention of writing" (Jones, 1995, p. 7). Jäkälä and Pekkola point out that throughout history, immersion in different worlds and alternate roles "has been provided by literature, theatre, drama and games" (2007, p. 12).

But before exploring a piece of that history, we should define what we mean by "virtual world." Most definitions include the concept of a shared space that allows a number of people to come together from different locations to interact (Croon Fors & Jakobsson, 2002, p. 41). Users should also be able to perform a variety of actions (Bellman & Landauer, 2000, p. 98), and increasingly such worlds are conceptualized as synchronous and persistent, although some early research did refer to asynchronous sites such as The WELL as virtual worlds (as well as virtual communities: see Rheingold, 1993).

Some form of embodiment is also required for participants to interact in a virtual world. Early researchers of MUDs (multi-user dungeons) and MOOs (MUD object-oriented) believed that a textual form of embodiment was either sufficient or superior to graphical depictions; rather than having avatars, users had characters consisting of a name and a textual description of a body, rather than a visual image of one (Bellman & Landauer, 2000; Jacobson, 2001). As virtual worlds have developed, more recent definitions of embodiment have moved away from text-based bodies to some form of graphical avatar (Taylor, 1999; Webb, 2001). Yet even the term "avatar" is ambiguous in how it has been used. Early forms of avatars in virtual worlds consisted of static, digitally modified pictures used in spaces like *The Palace*, while contemporary virtual worlds feature a range of avatar possibilities, inclusive of the 2D faces of *Whyville*, the 2.5D menu-driven options in *Gaia Online*, and the 3D fully customizable human and non-human creations found in *Second Life*.

As with the multiplicity of types of avatars that might constitute embodiment in virtual worlds, researchers and popular writers also group together persistent worlds that do and do not have specific goals – particularly game-like goals. In using the term "virtual worlds" in the 1990s, early researchers and journalists often drew connections between game-based and non-game-based (often socially or educationally based) environments. Socially based worlds allowed for a greater number of individuals who might not have been interested in fantasy worlds, where dungeons, elves, and killing for treasure were the principle attractions. Instead, socially based virtual worlds allowed users themselves to determine their own goals, be they socializing, world-building, or perhaps simple virtual tourism.

Many contemporary scholars and journalists continue to conflate such different spaces, either under the traditional moniker of "virtual worlds" or under the newer term "massively multiplayer online role-playing games" (MMORPGs, or MMOGs), replacing MOOs and MUDS with the world-builder *Second Life* and the fantasy role-playing game *World of Warcraft*. However, those environments have very different experiences for users, different structures, and divergent user bases. The practice of conflating these very different spaces continues today, as for example, in a highly cited article on law in virtual worlds, Lastowka and Hunter (2003) use *The Sims Online* as their first example of a virtual world, and then continue with a history of virtual worlds that intertwines the game-based worlds *Ultima Online* and *EverQuest*, along with non-game-based worlds such as *There*, *LambdaMOO*, and *Project Entropia*. They also tie in a history of literary virtual worlds, offline games, and the development of electronic games (2003).

Current industry activities also blur the line between game-based and socially based worlds. The group Virtual Worlds Management, for example, reports on financing and development of both types of virtual worlds, and the professional conference Worlds in Motion likewise does little to draw hard and fast distinctions between types of worlds, although in both cases the default assumption is that such spaces are commercial and revenue-focused. Some cracks in this edifice are beginning to show, however, as groups like the Virtual Policy Network in the UK have begun to advocate for distinctions to be made in policymaking between different types of virtual worlds, to distinguish between worlds that allow for the creation of user-created content and worlds that do not (Reynolds, 2008).

And as mentioned above, with the advent of corporate investment in such spaces, there is growing commercialization of virtual worlds, even as educators and other groups still work to maintain their own worlds, or build on sites such as the islands of *Second Life*. During the first quarter of 2008, for example, over $184 million was invested in 23 virtual-worlds-related companies, and during that same time period, over 60 virtual worlds targeted towards children under 18 were live, with more than 50 additional such spaces under development (Virtual Worlds Management, 2008). Of course non-commercial virtual worlds will continue to be built, but due to the high costs of building and maintaining such worlds, they are likely to become fewer and farther between, at least if they are very broad in scope or ambition.

To sum up and offer a definition of virtual worlds that is inclusive and somewhat timeless, I define virtual worlds as either text- or graphics-based environments that allow multiple users to come together, socialize, and interact. Virtual worlds employ some sort of spatial metaphor, and offer affordances and constraints based on the technologies and ideologies constructing the space. The goals of the world are based mostly on the interests of the users, but there may be some input from world developers. Interaction occurs online, and is persistent. Within the world, individuals are distinguished from each other based on a form of representation suitable for the built environment, which may be commercially or non-commercially based.

A Short History of Virtual Worlds

In 1978, multi-user dungeon, (or MUD1), the first networked, persistent multi-player space, came into being. Developed by Roy Trubshaw and Richard Bartle and drawing from the fantasy themes of role-playing games, the space was "filled with characters, treasures, and adventures to be shared and explored by multiple players" (Miller, 2003, p. 440). Once distributed, the game spawned many copies, and other developers began tinkering with the technology. In the late 1980s and early 1990s less competitive environments such as *TinyMUD* and *LambdaMOO* were built, with the added benefit that users themselves could now build some of the objects within the world (Jones, 2007).

Chip Morningstar and Randy Farmer developed the first graphical virtual world – *Habitat* – in 1985. Users could control and customize avatars while interacting with other users in the persistent world known as *Populus* (Morningstar & Farmer, 1990). A version of the space ran for several years, and a later version was introduced in Japan in 1990, sponsored by Fujitsu (Koster, 2002). Through *Habitat*, both developers and users learned the importance of rules (and especially code as rule) in virtual worlds, as some users started to engage in anti-social activities, including attacking other players, attempting to hack code, and exploiting bugs found in the space's code (Morningstar & Farmer, 1990).

Following *Habitat*, other virtual worlds began to emerge, including *Furry-MUCK* in 1990, which allowed users to create characters that were anthropomorphic animals; *MediaMOO* in 1993, a space designed for educators; and *The*

Palace in 1998, a social world with graphical avatars (Koster, 2002). Such spaces were more and less successful, but all offered users a space that did not have predefined goals, apart from a particular theme that might attract likeminded individuals, such as an interest in using new media for educational purposes. Such worlds were revolutionary in their time for being able to gather geographically dispersed groups and allow individuals to communicate with each other, be creative in some way, and perhaps build a community. (For an excellent discussion of the ambiguities and debates about definitions of virtual or online communities and their perceived presence or absence, see Chapter 14 in this volume, Lori Kendall's "Community and the Internet.")

MOOs in particular allowed creative individuals to build their own objects and spaces within the confines of the world, often rivaling developers in their expertise and creativity. That element of user-created content would go on to become one of the most well-known features of Web 2.0 where, along with social networks, individuals are seen as the keys to creating content that attracts other users, rather than relying solely on professional world-builders to do so.

Intertwined with that history of socially based worlds was the parallel development of game-based virtual worlds, including *Meridian 59* in 1996, *Ultima Online* in 1997, and *EverQuest* in 1999. During that early phase, nearly all such worlds were fantasy-based, following in the footsteps of their text-based predecessors. They did move from private networks to the open Internet, and began charging subscription fees for participation. And they began billing themselves as "massively multiplayer," even though at the time that meant a concurrent load of about 250 players (Kent, 2003).

Game-based virtual worlds differed from the social worlds of the time in two key aspects. First, as previously mentioned, they had clearly defined goals – to play and advance in a game atmosphere (kill or be killed, by monsters, other players, or both). Second, they generally did not permit the same type of world-building by players that the social spaces allowed. Such an approach made sense, as players intent on advancing or leveling up a character might then easily build themselves all-powerful weapons that could dispatch the toughest enemies with a single blow. Instead, developers of game-based worlds carefully controlled what individuals in those worlds might be able to do, or how they could achieve their goals. Players who enjoyed such worlds thrived under the game-based rules and constraints, and likewise socialized and perhaps engaged in non-game activities within the worlds, such as exploring or experimenting with the boundaries of code.

Development of graphically based virtual worlds has primarily come from commercial endeavors, due to their high costs and extensive resource demands. Yet text-based non-commercial worlds continue to proliferate, simply flying below the radar of popular media attention. Marketing and advertising has made commercial spaces known to a wider audience, and now estimates are that tens of millions of people are enjoying interactions in some form of virtual world globally (Reynolds, 2008).

The contemporary landscape of virtual worlds is shifting constantly, as new entrants emerge and others shut down their servers. Spaces such as *Active Worlds* and *Second Life* receive a great share of popular media attention, primarily due to their multiple uses as educational, healthcare and social spaces, as well as their extensive world-building opportunities. Other spaces have gained visibility due to their marketing to very young users, including Disney's *Club Penguin*, Sulake's *Habbo Hotel*, and the Korean-based Nexon's *Maple Story*, all with more than 5 million registered users (Reynolds, 2008).

Overall, the future of virtual worlds looks quite bright. There is still a range of worlds to be found online, and they are used for an array of purposes, as individuals and groups continue investigating their affordances and constraints. While graphical virtual worlds and game-based worlds capture most of the popular attention, non-commercial and textual spaces are still operating, and offering users opportunities to create, socialize, learn, and have fun. Along each step of this history, virtual-world researchers have investigated how individuals and groups use those places, and how they approximate to or deviate from offline life. Their areas of focus and key findings are examined next.

Research on Virtual Worlds

Virtual worlds and space

One of the key elements of virtual worlds is the "worldness" or spaces they create for participants. More than webpages, email text, or photo albums, virtual worlds attempt to create geographies, lands, or experiential spaces for us to explore and populate. Whether it has been via text, or 2D or 3D graphics, virtual worlds have been most memorable for how they construct space, and how we co-construct it via our imaginations. As Flanagan argues, "one cannot seem to avoid using metaphors of space to describe computer activities" (2000, p. 74). Thus it is critical that we keep aware of our discourse, and how we choose the words, descriptions, and metaphors that seem to "fit" our new experiences.

And our imaginations have had priming in envisioning such spaces, primarily through early discourses related to cyberspace and virtual reality. The work of cyberpunk authors such as William Gibson and Neil Stephenson has shaped our understandings of what virtual worlds might entail, if we dared to imagine worlds decoupled from our bodies. In *Neuromancer*, for example, Gibson coined the term "cyberspace" and painted it as a matrix of colored lights that console cowboys "jack in" to, where data was conceptualized as "city lights, receding." By leaving the body or flesh behind, Gibson's vision re-inscribed a Cartesian dualism of mind–body split, and with most console cowboys being male, the privilege of abandoning the body and becoming "pure mind" was acceded to men (Consalvo, 2000).

Stephenson's conception of a Metaverse in his 1992 novel *Snow Crash* was likewise influential, as it offered a vision of not only an imaginary world, but also one where we could employ avatars that expertly simulated human facial expressions, giving the space enough bandwidth so that it could be a space for pleasure, business, and almost anything else. His vision has been instrumental in encouraging the creation of graphical virtual worlds, most explicitly *Second Life*, which is referred to in many places as the realization of the Metaverse.

Mary Flanagan and others have agreed that such early discourses began the process of gendering our ideas about the virtual, where "the mythos of cyberspace as a place begins by being depicted as a permeable, 'feminine place' that must be categorized, controlled, and conquered" (Flanagan, 2000, p. 77). She also believes the interface is a prime site for how we come to understand our place within virtual worlds, and that our current interfaces also reflect a masculine bias in their privileging of usefulness, information and status, as well as constructing a subject that is unified and individual, in control of all he surveys (p. 79).

Scholars also suggest that the idea of a computer being conceptualized as a space pre-dates virtual worlds, going back to Douglas Englebart's early work developing computer screens that could visualize information, drawn from his work with radar systems in World War Two (Bardini, 2000), as well as his 1968 invention of the mouse, which "transformed the computer screen into a new three-dimensional 'informationscape'" (Berland, 2000, p. 253). Johnson elaborates that because of that invention, "for the first time, a machine was imagined not as an attachment to our bodies, but as an environment, a space to be explored" (1997, p. 24). Thus, because of the mouse, the conceptual logics that computers made possible were transformed into potential spaces, spaces that awaited construction and definition by developers and users.

Early virtual worlds were limited to text, yet that constraint did not diminish creativity or users' sense of presence or interest in interacting in such spaces. Researchers investigating the first MUDs and MOOs found places that were fantastical, as well as places that sought to replicate the familiar. For example, upon entering the popular *LambdaMOO*, visitors found themselves within a coat closet, and after exiting the closet encountered the living room of a large and comfy (yet expanding) house, which formed a hub for much social interaction in the world (Dibbell, 1993). Reid found that such entry points were common and useful in orienting individuals to virtual worlds, as "MUD anterooms typically contain pointers to helpful information and rules" (Reid, 1995, p. 168).

Likewise, MOOs allow users to build spaces of their own choosing. In documenting various examples, Bellman and Landauer write of one small girl who "built a 30-room mansion with garden and pools" (2000, p. 101). Such creations speak to users' desires to build the familiar as well as the novel, and, overall, to the importance of locating the self within some sort of landscape, in order to be able to make sense of an experience. As Reid concludes, "physical context is a dimension of social context – place and time are as much loaded with cultural meaning as are dress and gesture" (1995, p. 169).

Seeking to understand how written text could create such dynamic systems, Bellman and Landauer argue, "text-based MUDs allow people the freedom and richness of word pictures, something that we can't imitate with graphical environments. Text-based MUDs have a much richer and more dynamic visual imagery than, say, movies or games, because it is customized to each player's imagination" (2000, p. 101). Other scholars have agreed with that formulation, choosing to highlight the superior qualities of text-based worlds (McRae, 1996). But Reid suggests a way of thinking of virtual worlds and their construction that supersedes any particular technological form, to instead focus on how users actually engage with a world, writing "virtual worlds exist not in the technology used to represent them nor purely in the mind of the user, but in the relationship between internal mental constructs and technologically generated representations of these constructs" (1995, p. 166). Thus, it is the relationships formed between the world and its users that are key.

But inevitably, graphical virtual worlds appeared, and scholars and users found them equally – if not more – rich in possibilities Steven Johnson wrote that *The Palace* interface added an entirely new dimension to the experience of being in virtual worlds, suggestive of "the more visual, improvised theater of town squares and urban parks, pickup softball games and water cooler banter" (1997, p. 67). He felt that the visuality of such a space lent itself to approximating "the thrill, the unpredictability, of casual encounters in a more textured space, shaped by the physical presence of those around you" (pp. 67–8). Yet at the same time he also acknowledged that "you don't really see a community in these exchanges" and that for *The Palace* at least, at that moment, there were limits to how much of a community or world it might be. Further development of graphics and graphical systems led to the belief that virtual worlds could be "enablers of or tools for simulation, visualization, or rehearsing unique circumstances" (Jäkälä & Pekkola, 2007, p. 12). And the ability to more concretely simulate both real and fantasy worlds kept developers constantly creating advanced versions of virtual worlds.

However, the terminology used to discuss activities within the spaces of virtual worlds often evokes discourses of colonization, which have a fraught history. In the mid-1990s, Laura Miller examined the metaphor of the Internet as a "wild west" or "frontier" space that needed law and order to settle it and thus make it safe for women (1995). I added to that examination, arguing that although such frontier and wild-west rhetorics seemed to imply the necessity of law and order to protect women, that protection was actually needed to create a safe space for business and commerce – women in this case were a valuable purchasing group, so it was easy to couch rhetorics of safety as being about them (2002).

And frontiers and lawless spaces also articulate with colonization and the settling of new lands. As Flanagan reports, such spatial rhetorics often are accompanied by imperialist overtones, as "worlds are gridded and parceled out to users in a system reminiscent of activities during a nineteenth-century land rush" (2000, p. 72). Taking the critique another step further, Gunkel and Gunkel (2009) demonstrate how virtual-world researchers have themselves imbued ideas about such spaces with a colonization rhetoric, one which either intentionally or unintentionally "forgets" past histories of colonization, where already-present native peoples were often forcibly removed. While they remind us that there are no "real people" to be displaced in the newly developed virtual worlds, there are those who will never get the chance to "settle" in such lands, those for whom such opportunities are either beyond their reach, or may come as part of work-related activities such as gold-farming in an MMOG.

Space is a vital element in virtual worlds, and researchers have examined its import-ance, and how it comes to matter, in textual as well as graphical virtual environ-ments. That space signifies so much cannot be over-emphasized, as it provides a framework, literally structuring all the encounters that take place.

Community in virtual spaces

Due to being public spaces, early virtual worlds were populated by various groups, and so researchers perhaps logically began to search for evidence of community. One of the best-known popular accounts investigated the role of community in users' responses to a virtual crime – a "rape" in cyberspace (Dibbell, 1993). In *LambdaMOO*, Julian Dibbell reported that one user (Mr Bungle) had virtually assaulted another through the use of a voodoo doll used to broadcast lewd acts performed on the other player, without her consent. After much discussion among residents, an administrator ended up "toading" (permanently deleting) Mr Bungle and his account, an action that led to a system of demo-cracy being installed in the MOO, where residents debated and enacted the rules that would govern subsequent interactions. The case is important to the history of virtual worlds and the development of communities within them for acknow-ledging the importance of self-governance, and the role that individual inhabit-ants could play in running virtual worlds. It is also important as an indicator of the turn away from early techno-utopian libertarianism that was so prevalent even in early business discourses. Sadly, that sort of system has remained only within non-commercial virtual worlds, as commercial ones give inhabitants few if any "rights" to governance or rule making.

Howard Rheingold furthered the investigation of virtual communities, writing about San Francisco's Whole Earth 'Lectronic Link (WELL). Rheingold's early spaces did seem at the time to be "spaces apart" where individuals could come together in much the same way that users of virtual worlds do today. While Dibbell's work dealt with what seemed the seamier side of virtual world life, Rheingold's work normalized the activity of going online to socialize, and suggested that more could be done online than slaying dragons for treasure in a virtual dungeon, or worrying about evil clowns with voodoo dolls and rape on their minds.

While researchers working in this area were often interested in studying community formation online, that work led to speculation and debate over how to actually define the term "community." Some writers drew sharp lines between online and offline communities, and as Wellman explains, "they insisted on looking at online phenomena in isolation. They assumed that only things that happened on the Internet were relevant to understanding the Internet" (2004, p. 124). In contrast, Wellman pointed to successful experiments such as Netville outside of Toronto, where Internet users were *more* likely to know their neighbors' name than non-users (2004).

Beyond Dibbell, early research on persistent virtual worlds did not take community or democracy as a central focus. But Tari Lin Fanderclai, writing on the media education space *MediaMOO*, did report that the attraction of the place was the conversation it afforded with likeminded others, and that "like the informal settings and interactions of those real-life hallways and coffee shops, MUDs provide a sense of belonging to a community and encourage collaboration among participants, closing geographical distances among potential colleagues and collaborators" (1996, p. 229).

Virtual worlds and identity

An important aspect of virtual worlds is the ability to craft a persona with which to navigate the world – an avatar or textual description of the self that can persist over time. That persona could represent one aspect of a person's identity, be it a faithful reproduction, or be it an alternate self, and it could also build a reputation that could be altered over the avatar's history. The emergence of such personas led to research concerning them, and that work was often tied to matters of identity, including how individuals related their real-life identities to their created identities.

Just as some early studies of virtual communities often tried to draw lines between online and offline, so too did investigators of virtual identity. Here research was usually more focused on persistent synchronous spaces. Two of the most influential theorists of the period were Allucquere Roseanne Stone and Sherry Turkle, who were both fascinated with how individuals engaged in often radical identity play online. That preoccupation had later consequences for future study, as I will explain shortly.

Stone's interest centered on how the Internet provided spaces for individuals to either create or express multiple personas or "selves." This went beyond gender-bending, to questioning the assemblage of a unitary self residing in one body. She popularized the idea that selves and bodies were not necessarily bound together in a one-to-one correspondence, and virtual worlds might be spaces where individuals could experiment with multiple aspects of the self, writing that "the technosocial space of virtual systems, with its irruptive ludic quality and its potential for experimentation and emergence, is a domain of nontraumatic multiplicity" (1995, pp. 59–60). She also felt that such identity play would become more common online (with positive and negative consequences), and perhaps become the norm as people got used to the (seeming) fluidity of identity in virtual worlds. Turkle (1995) also investigated individuals and identity work online, but from a psychological perspective. She studied users of virtual worlds who created characters who were different from their real-life personas, in order to experiment with or work through new, troublesome, or unexplored aspects of their identity.

Both Stone's and Turkle's work suggested not only that the Internet could be a space conducive to identity play, but also that identity play was becoming a norm in life online. As Lüders points out however, such analyses "were largely connected to the specific situation of the early 1990s, when people with no prior offline relations connected online and communicated in an environment where identity cues were less visible, and . . . where one of the main points was in fact to role-play" (Lüders, 2007, p. 10). Thus, early discourses suggested a space where individuals were perhaps much more radical in their activity than they really were, at least compared to mainstream users as they began to come online. Yet, they did popularize and legitimize the study of identity in virtual worlds, and established it as a mainstream avenue of research.

Other virtual-world researchers have looked at more specific aspects of identity including gender and race. Kendall examined gender in the MUD *BlueSky*, suggesting that identity could be central to feeling included (or excluded) in virtual worlds, because "on some MUDs, portrayals of females as sexual objects become part of ritual-like interactions. These rituals are important because they demonstrate belonging to, and shared history with, the group" (1996, p. 210). And such a gendering of identity was often a requisite for participation, as "all MUDs allow, and some insist, that players set their "gender flag," which controls which set of pronouns are used by the MUD program in referring to the player" (Reid, 1995, p. 179). While some MUDs and MOOs offered multiple genders (including *LambdaMOO*'s famous "spivak" gender), as virtual worlds have developed, most now have a default of two genders, and users must choose one, permanently affixing a gender to their activities in those worlds.

While gender may be a central component of identity in virtual worlds, such spaces do allow for the gender play that Turkle initially popularized, or at least, early spaces did. Researchers who took such studies a step further included Suler, who explored the activity of gender switching in *The Palace*, and Taylor, who investigated individuals' use of multiple (and multiply gendered) avatars in *EverQuest* (Suler, 1999; Taylor, 1999).

While early research promoted virtual worlds as places for active gender identity play, the same could not be said for another aspect of identity – that of race. In particular, Nakamura explored how race and "cybertypes" played a role in spaces such as *The Palace* and *LambdaMOO*, a role not very positive or liberating (2002). Nakamura detailed how individuals' choices of avatars that drew on limited images of Asians such as ninjas, samurai and geishas, was a form of "identity tourism" that was hardly transgressive or to be lauded. Instead, the reductive and stereotypical avatars encouraged "the enactment of cybertyped notions of the oriental" (p. 43). Thus, playing with identity was not always a positive or progressive activity.

Many other aspects of identity as expressed in virtual worlds have been explored, including sexuality, which is also given much more thorough treatment, along with gender, in Chapter 13 in this volume, "Queering Internet Studies: Intersections of Gender and Sexuality," by Janne Bromseth and Jenny Sundén. What makes virtual worlds important or different in regards to sexuality is that they allow individuals and groups to build spaces and craft personas to engage in real-time interactions online, and create some sort of persistence and history for those representations. Because individuals with alternate sexualities often have difficulties in establishing publicly visible spaces in the physical world, the opportunity to do so in a virtual space is important.

Several scholars have examined those spaces, such as Woodland's study of the gay space Weaveworld within *LambdaMOO* (2000) and Jones's investigation of gay spaces in *Second Life* (2007). In Weaveworld users exploring the space would find cottages and tree houses "inhabited overwhelmingly by male characters – with a preponderance of strapping young men with artistic sensibilities" (Woodland, 2000, p. 422). Jones's exploration of gay spaces in *Second Life* also notes a preponderance of such spaces as markers of identity (2007). Thus, even as identity is often focused on avatars as a site for experimentation and marking, sites can also serve to construct identity, particularly spaces that are tied to identity struggles, or particular symbols or markers of identity.

Work that focuses on identity in virtual worlds is growing, yet increasingly refined. While some reports still talk of gender swapping in virtual worlds, we now know that such activities are not always the deeply motivated actions of individuals intent on exploring hidden aspects of the self, or expressing one of their many selves, but instead more mundane uses of multiple identities, for aesthetic, strategic, as well as possibly experimental reasons.

Avatars in virtual worlds: text made flesh

There has been additional work done on avatars separate from a focus on identity, and as graphical virtual worlds become the standard, understanding how avatars function within them for users is a critical focus. While avatars might not allow us to actually transcend our particular subject positions, they have allowed users to take different and multiple forms, across and within various virtual worlds. Taylor found that early virtual world users often created multiple avatars, and would use them strategically, writing "on several occasions, a person hinted at knowing me in some other form, but preferred to keep that interaction separate" (1999, p. 439). Different avatars allowed individuals to interact with others in various ways, to check on the reputation of a particular avatar, or to simply play with different forms. Such multiples have also been employed in game-based virtual worlds, as users often create a "main" avatar and then a series of alternates (or "alts"), which may or may not be publicly linked to each other (Consalvo, 2007).

Researchers have also documented how individuals learn to use their avatars to achieve whatever in-world goals they may have. Croon Fors and Jakobsson found that among new users in particular, the first question asked was "where am I?" but the question masked a larger intent, asking "where and what is my 'I,'" as users struggled to resolve their point of view in the world and to differentiate their body/avatar from others around them (2001, p. 43). Yet users often adapt quickly, and Webb writes that participants in at least some virtual worlds then "use the medium to market their avatar character as a means of obtaining prestige, status and influence" (2001, p. 587). They also, of course, move their avatars around, and have been found to geographically arrange themselves in ways that mirror real-life proxemics. Webb described 2D avatars in chat-focused virtual worlds as spread out in relation to each other, maintaining a specific proximity (2001, p. 587).

More recent research confirms that we tend to carry real-life conventions into our virtual worlds, as "the rules that govern our physical bodies in the real world have come to govern our embodied identities in the virtual world" (Yee et al., 2007, p. 120). Such findings suggest that while we cannot easily "break free" of our embodied selves, conversely, we can use virtual worlds to help us better function in the real world. In research using *Second Life*, Yee and Bailenson found that "participants using attractive avatars became more intimate and friendly with strangers" (2007, p. 286). They conclude, "although avatars are usually construed as something of our own choosing – a one-way process – the fact is that our avatars come to change how we behave" (p. 287). Thus, we can use avatars to maintain or experiment with various versions of ourselves, as well as potentially use our avatars to better live our real-world lives.

Of course, many of those avatars are not far from normative real-life bodies, as research has consistently shown. Webb's virtual-world chatters were "heavily stereotyped along lines of gender and ethnicity" (2001, p. 563), just as Nakamura found in *The Palace* several years later (2002). Jones sees users of *Second Life* creating similarly normed avatars, as even queer users "adhere to stereotypical 'types,' such as the 'leather daddy' or the 'club kid' that are identifiable as such to other queer people" (2007, p. 59). This suggests that the pleasures we may take in avatars map back to our visions of real life, such that the avatar "reflects an ideal of beauty that the user desires within himself or herself" (p. 60). So although we may not be experimenting that deeply with different avatar forms, we are engaging in a form of self-expression that may reflect positively in our interactions across worlds, or at least bring us pleasure in the act of creation.

Virtual worlds and surveillance, privacy, and control

Part of thinking about virtual worlds encompasses its control, which brings up concerns about privacy and surveillance. Early work in such areas mostly documented how virtual worlds were dealing with the systems they had set up, many of which were designed to be open and allow users great amounts of privacy and freedom. Scholars discussed how such systems dealt with the inevitable abuses that occurred, and how such activities helped formulate current notions about privacy, control, and surveillance.

One of the earliest cases was Stone's examination of the CommuniTree project in San Francisco in the late 1970s. In efforts to promote community and openness, the developers of the system allowed users to post anonymously, and in initial versions of the software had created no easy way for system administrators to delete postings or block the activities of troublesome posters. Such efforts to encourage widespread, communal, and non-controlled discourse quickly led to the Tree's downfall. As Stone documents, "after only a few months of nearly continual assault that the system operators were powerless to prevent, the Tree expired, choked to death by a kind of teenage mutant kudzu vine, a circumstance that one participant saw as 'the consequences of unbridled freedom of expression'" (1995, p. 116).

Having learned their lesson, administrators created a second version of the Tree software, which ushered in "the age of surveillance and social control" (p. 117). Such changes spread slowly, however, as early MUD and MOO administrators gave users a certain level of anonymity in their activities. Such freedom offered individuals opportunities for greater exploration and play, as they were decoupled from real-life identities and attendant controls on their behavior. Yet for all the benefits this might offer, it also encouraged deviant behaviors, which were then difficult or impossible to track. The case of Mr Bungle in *LambdaMOO*, discussed earlier, is a prime example. Without being able to physically locate the offender, the MOO was left only with the option of deleting the offender's account. That would not, of course, stop the individual from creating a new account under a different name, which is what Dibbell believed happened (1993). But although Mr Bungle seemed to have either learned from his experience or moved on, other disruptive individuals do not always do so readily.

In assessing another incident with a disruptive individual, Bellman and Landauer report that one MUD's community decided to shun the offending individual, rather than do something radical such as restrict character creation in some way (such as tying character creation to real-life identities), which the residents felt would be "worse than the original problem" (2000, p. 108). Yet other system operators did not share that view, and some virtual worlds began keeping closer track of the ties between online and offline identities. In *Habitat*, for example, administrators known as Oracles were "able to observe both the official records of who has signed up for *Habitat* and also who is inside the simulation" (Stone, 1995, p. 119). And the designers of the system, writing of their experiences, warned new world creators "you can't trust anyone" (Morningstar & Farmer, 1990).

Such problems led to activities such as warranting (the attempt to verify the authenticity of real bodies behind an online character) and the creation of what have been termed location technologies, as the battle for control of systems continued (Stone, 1995; Tetzlaff, 2000). System operators needed to keep worlds not only operational but also satisfying for all users, and so they started to better track and control movements in virtual worlds, via the addition of new code. Operators learned that the early freedom that users had in virtual worlds came at too steep a price: without the ability to locate and punish egregious offenders, virtual worlds could lose the communities they had so carefully built. A balance had to be created between freedom for users, and surveillance and control of potentially troublesome individuals.

More recently, my own work on cheating in MMOGs has pointed to the difficulties of permanently ascribing identities to activities that are usually fleeting and harmless, such as the use of walkthroughs or cheat codes in multiplayer games (Consalvo, 2007). Individuals may experiment with cheating in virtual worlds, but attempts to track users often rely on computer and hardware identifiers rather than individuals, providing an imperfect system at best for finding offenders. What seems more promising is giving other residents of virtual worlds the opportunity to call out and perhaps punish offenders, through blacklists, in game patrolling, and reports to the game administrators. Thus control and surveillance can become a dynamic, shared enterprise between developers and users, rather than a top-down system that implies little or no trust in users (Consalvo, 2007).

Additional strands of interest and research related to control have also emerged, investigating areas such as the control of virtual items, virtual property, and users' rights within the spaces of virtual worlds. Particularly as more virtual worlds have become commercial ventures, it has become necessary to identify where the rights of users begin and end, relative to world creators. So with the affixing of a "real" identity to an avatar or character, users and developers have begun to wrestle with concerns about what those users own or control within virtual worlds, and how policies deciding such things are made.

The roots of studies of virtual property and ownership also began back in the era of MUDs. William Mitchell argued in 1999 that "as pioneering MUDs and MOOs quickly discovered, there have to be some concepts of property and ownership, some conventions governing who has control of what, and some ways of enforcing the conventions" (p. 126). Yet as other scholars pointed out, such ownership had consequences not only for the status quo in virtual worlds, but for contemporary society, which increasingly recognizes "virtual" items (such as digital versions of films, and credit cards) as real. David Tetzlaff explains, "the postmodern economy depends on the ability of capital to make the virtual act like the real, to make information, ideas, strings of ones and zeroes function as material commodities" (2000, pp. 117–18).

Thus it was only a matter of time before legal scholars became interested in how to regulate as well as to understand ownership in virtual worlds. In one of the earliest pieces to address the subject, Lastowka and Hunter argue that virtual property must be taken seriously as a legal issue, along with the "enforceable moral and legal rights" of avatars (2003, p. 2). Drawing from the work of Castronova, who studied the economy of *EverQuest* and found it equal to several developing nations (2001), they believe that "virtual assets can be characterized as property for the purposes of real world law" (Lastowka & Hunter, 2003, p. 96). They also believe that while traditional legal approaches will work, the issue must be addressed soon to redress the imbalance of power between the creators and users of virtual worlds, because "if corporate gods own every part of our lives, it cannot be too long before courts decide that property interests can be asserted against those corporations without deferring to the contract we signed to enter our (avatar) lives" (p. 96).

That approach led to a flood of interest in the legal world in addressing issues relative to virtual worlds, including virtual property generally (Hunt, 2007), the role of contracts (Fairfield, 2007), copyright (Miller, 2003), intellectual property (Herman, Coombe, & Kaye, 2006), end-user license agreements (Glushko, 2007; Miller, 2003), and taxation (Camp, 2007). Lastowka's and Hunter's call for avatar rights has likewise led to debate, with some developers (Bartle, 2007) calling for very limited versions of rights, and others (Koster, 2007) famously advocating for an "avatar bill of rights."

A particular challenge for legal studies of virtual worlds is the variety of virtual worlds themselves, including variations in what rights they assign to users and how virtual worlds differ. A major challenge to total control of intellectual property (IP) rights by world developers came in 2003 when Linden Lab announced that it would allow all users of its virtual world *Second Life* to keep IP rights for items they created in the world (Ondrejka, 2004). Most other virtual worlds maintain strict end-user license agreements (EULAs) asserting that anything users create "in world" is the property of the world creators, and further attempt to limit practices such as real-money trade that make in-game assets convertible into real currencies. Again, Linden Lab takes a different approach, operating its own exchange market (the LindeX). Scholars are currently attempting to tease out the distinctions between different kinds of virtual worlds, and to make the best arguments for how real-world laws should intersect with virtual worlds and their legal and economic systems.

To help policymakers get informed on such issues and keep track of rapid developments in research and study, specialized groups are forming. In 2007, a "Declaration of Virtual World Policy" was posted to the virtual worlds blog Terra Nova by Thomas Malaby, following a conference at Indiana University where participants debated the importance of issues relative to governing and running virtual worlds (Malaby, 2007). A year later, Ren Reynolds formed the international Virtual Policy Network as a thinktank "established to explore the policy implications of virtual worlds" (Reynolds, 2008). Such groups and activities have attempted to explore and differentiate between different types of virtual worlds, the competing interests of owners and users, and how various legal bodies (national, international, regional) can make reasoned and intelligent decisions on how to regulate such spaces.

Virtual worlds applications and their study

Many virtual worlds are game-based, and studies of their inhabitants are well documented in Chapter 17. However, socially based virtual worlds often developed purposes and uses going far beyond the merely social. Such activities often centered around education, therapy, and healthcare, with researchers documenting as well as evaluating those practices, which are highlighted in this section. Systematic psychological study actually began with early virtual reality systems and then migrated to persistent virtual worlds, as therapists began to use them for behavior modification, treating individuals with phobias of heights, spiders, and other phenomena (Anderson, Rothbaum, & Hodges, 2000; Taylor, 1997). And, in education, many professors saw promise in early MOO systems for teaching a variety of topics, including writing, foreign languages, group dynamics, and programming (Banks, 1994; Fanderclai, 1996).

The history of virtual worlds' use for serious purposes has of course been tied to other new media developments, as for example healthcare providers and patients began to experiment with Internet-based communities, employing mailing lists, websites for information, chat forums, as well as virtual worlds; attempting to see what would work best, across a variety of contexts for diverse individuals and their needs. Yet the specificity of virtual worlds offered particular affordances for such groups, and as graphics have advanced and more individuals have access to high-speed Internet connections and more powerful computers, virtual worlds have become increasingly important sites for education and healthcare.

Research documenting the development of such activities has often been summative, providing post-mortems of singular activities such as one college course or the work of one health-related education group (Elliott, 2007; Watson et al., 2008). Overarching analyses of the large-scale effectiveness of such activities are rare (Jäkälä & Pekkola, 2007) and needed. Yet such experiments and projects are proliferating, with researchers taking varied approaches to using virtual worlds. But although schools and universities are busily constructing virtual campuses, these practices don't necessarily take advantage of the unique properties of virtual worlds.

Innovative researchers have used virtual worlds in a couple of different ways. First, they have used the building of such spaces as itself an educational activity, attempting to demonstrate that "conceptual understanding and contextualized activity are fundamentally interrelated and mutually constitutive" (Barab et al., 2001, p. 86). Thus, learning is not divorced from doing, and in the case of Barab et al., students learn about some phenomenon, such as astronomy, through the building of 3D interactive models of galaxies. Likewise, Croon Fors & Jakobsson (2002) had students construct a virtual world based on the early *Active Worlds* software that was supposed to be used for a meeting place, but they found that the structure was "better understood through the notion of the unfinished," as the space came to center on exploration and construction possibilities, rather than as a simple conference area (p. 50).

The second approach has focused on using the capacities of virtual worlds to transform education. The work of many educators in the *Second Life* Educators Group is illustrative of this, as they re-envision how we learn in a networked environment, and how to best take advantage of that (Kemp, 2008). Robbins, for example, has not only explored how we can use virtual worlds to create new sorts of learning experiences, but also argues that universities and formal learning institutions must adopt approaches that mirror how individuals learn through online social networks, as the gate-keeping function that formal learning institutions have held over traditional knowledge could soon disappear (2008).

In healthcare, individuals and groups have been active in creating spaces to learn, to support one another, and to build community. Many healthcare institutions such as the American Cancer Society and the US Centers for Disease Control are active in spaces such as *Second Life*, and more healthcare providers are seeing the possibilities of virtual worlds (Watson et al., 2008). Medical researchers have begun to document the positive as well as negative implications of virtual worlds on individuals with disabilities such as paralysis (Ford, 2001). While advantages are often easy to imagine (such as the creation of communities, and more opportunities to educate individuals), drawbacks include the further erasure of the visibility of certain disabilities, and a related lack of agency in overcoming problems associated with life outside of virtual worlds (Ford, 2001). Yet there are still many positive outcomes and experiences, as such spaces give individuals with disabilities the chance to interact with others without the stigmas attached to their disabilities (Ford, 2001). Other uses have included the modeling of certain disability experiences such as schizophrenia to increase empathy in others (Elliott, 2007), and the possibilities for virtual worlds to help diabetes patients better manage their illness (Watson et al., 2008).

Future research directions

Virtual worlds are a constantly moving target, as new worlds are regularly being built and older ones are quietly shutting down. But beyond simply studying worlds themselves, there are key overarching areas that deserve further investigation by virtual-worlds researchers. First, there is little scholarly work done on how children are interacting in commercially based, entertainment-focused virtual worlds, or how such spaces might differ from worlds targeted at older users. Sara Grimes investigates regulation and ethical issues surrounding online games created for kids (2008), and Deborah Fields and Yasmin Kafai have studied kids' use of semi-educational spaces such as *Whyville* (2007), but more attention in this area is clearly needed. More than 100 virtual worlds devoted to children are either online or in development (Virtual World News, 2008), and high-profile sites draw massive numbers of users. The Finnish world *Habbo Hotel* draws 7.5 million unique users per month globally, mostly in the 13–16-year-old range, yet we know little about the game other than what the developers have found through their own studies (Nutt, 2007). Likewise, news that Disney paid $350 million in cash to acquire *Club Penguin*, which has 700,000 paid subscribers (Arrington, 2007), and that the virtual world *Barbie Girls* had 3 million users sign up in the first 60 days after launch (Riley, 2007) suggest that virtual worlds for kids are mainstream, and are desperately in need of study.

Another area in need of attention relates to the role of business in virtual worlds. We need more critical analyses of how businesses are operating in virtual worlds, as they have set up their own worlds and spaces within other worlds in increasing numbers. Spaces such as *Second Life* have seen influxes of corporations as such institutions try to take advantage of new ways to reach potential consumers, yet often without knowing how best to do so. But beyond attention to in-game economies or potential business models (Castronova, 2001; MacInnes & Hu, 2007; Mennecke, McNeil, Roche et al., 2008), we need to understand the implications of businesses within worlds, their impacts, and the long-term effects of their activities. Do branding and corporate sponsorship mean different types of virtual worlds, or changes to their character? How does the spread of consumerism and capitalism shape the design and user space of virtual worlds, especially given the early roots of the industry in libertarian and utopian possibilities? Right now we don't have answers to such questions. Likewise, we need political economic analyses of virtual worlds. Who is making virtual worlds, and what are their agendas? If we are encouraged to spend great amounts of time (as well as money) in such spaces, what are the limits of our abilities to speak, act, or control our virtual property? Beyond legal studies, we must scrutinize the corporations that are building worlds, and the design decisions they are making. Who is actively cultivated as a user base, and who is excluded or marginalized? If online worlds are increasingly important places for individuals to gather and socialize, we must have a better idea of who is in control of those spaces, and how they are defining rules for participation (Steinkuehler & Williams, 2006).

Finally, virtual worlds are global. Although many operators limit their user base through language options or regionally based servers, users are increasingly moving across spaces regardless of such limitations (Nutt, 2007). Some game-based virtual worlds make a point of bringing together users from around the world (such as *EVE Online* and *Final Fantasy XI*), and socially based spaces such as *Second Life* have user bases ranging across North America, Europe, and Asia. But we don't have much research yet addressing how disparate user groups might interact with each other, if they are interacting at all. Some research suggests that some North American game players in *FFXI* enjoy interactions with Japanese players, particularly if they are already interested in Japanese popular culture and are learning Japanese (Consalvo, 2008). But we need to know how users might be crossing language and cultural barriers to communicate, and what they take from those interactions. We also need to know if they are *not* crossing language and cultural barriers – if separate worlds within worlds are actually being created, as users self-segregate for reasons related to built-in technological affordances for certain communicative preferences or cultural values, or for reasons we have yet to discover. Finally, if users are coming from around the globe, how does that affect matters of law and policy? The Internet already challenges many traditional approaches to policy and law formation (see Chapter 7 in this volume, "Internet Policy" by Sandra Braman, for a more detailed discussion), yet virtual worlds have their own particular needs. We need more attention paid to the global base of virtual worlds, and what players are doing in those spaces that might be unique or different from more regionally based virtual worlds.

Conclusions

Writing about the technological boom of the late 1990s, Berland described how discourse about new media often employed a metaphor of evolution, describing developments as natural or inevitable, the result, apparently, of some kind of natural selection. She argued such approaches ignored the materiality of the body, and led to calls that were non-critical and did not engage with new media in ways other than being celebratory or automatically accepted. It would be well for us to similarly engage with virtual worlds in critical ways. Such spaces are no more inevitable than any other technology. Every day, developers, users, businesses, and regulatory bodies choose to make them matter, to call them into being, in particular ways. And the ways that we talk about such worlds likewise forms them, and shapes how we understand them. Clearly they are not free and liberating spaces, nor are they all mindless consumerist shopping malls in disguise. Our building of them and use of them must be careful and considered. We must likewise avoid the easy rhetoric of the brave new virtual world, lest we forget our past histories with worlds and spaces, and what happens when we don't carefully consider the possible ramifications of what we are doing. Virtual worlds have great potential, but research on them is only really beginning. We must continue to critically investigate them, asking thoughtful questions and using careful methods, to best arrive at an understanding of what virtual worlds are and can be.

References

Anderson, P., Rothbaum, B., & Hodges, L. (2001). Virtual reality: Using the virtual world to improve quality of life in the real world. *Bulletin of the Menninger Clinic*, 65(1), 78–91.

Arrington, M. (2007). Extremely happy feet: Disney acquires *Club Penguin* for up to $700 million. *TechCrunch*. http://www.techcrunch.com/2007/08/01/disney-acquires-club-penguin/.

Banks, D. (1994). Education MOOs. http://tecfa.unige.ch/edu-comp/DUJVRE/vol1/no1/education_MOOs.text.

Barab, S., Hay, K., Barnett, M., & Squire, K. (2001). Constructing virtual worlds: Tracing the historical development of learning practices. *Cognition and Instruction*, 19(1), 47–94.

Bardini, T. (2000). *Bootstrapping: Douglas Englebart, Coevolution, and the Origins of Personal Computing*. Stanford: Stanford University Press.

Bartle, R. (2007). Virtual worldliness. In J. Balkin & B. S. Noveck (eds.), *The State of Play: Laws, Games and Virtual worlds* (pp. 31–54). New York: New York University Press.

Bellman, K., & Landauer, C. (2000). Playing in the MUD: Virtual worlds are real places. *Applied Artificial Intelligence*, 14, 93–123.

Berland, J. (2000). Cultural technologies and the "evolution" of technological cultures. In A. Herman & T. Swiss (eds.), *The World Wide Web and Contemporary Cultural Theory* (pp. 235–58). New York: Routledge.

Camp, B. (2007). The play's the thing: A theory of taxing virtual worlds. *Hastings Law Journal*, 59(1). http://papers.ssrn.com/sol3/papers.cfm?abstract_id=980693.

Castronova, E. (2001). Virtual worlds: A first-hand account of market and society on the cyberian frontier. *CESifo Working Paper Series*, no. 618. http://papers.ssrn.com/sol3/papers.cfm?abstract_id=294828.

Consalvo, M. (2000). From razor girls to bionic women: Extraordinary cyborg women in popular culture. In B. Miedema, J. M. Stoppard, & V. Anderson (eds.), *Women's Bodies/Women's Lives: The Material and the Social.* Toronto: Sumach Press.

Consalvo, M. (2002). Selling the Internet to women: The early years. In M. Consalvo & S. Paasonen (eds.), *Women and Everyday Uses of the Internet: Agency and Identity.* New York: Peter Lang.

Consalvo, M. (2007). *Cheating: Gaining Advantage in Videogames.* Cambridge, MA: MIT Press.

Consalvo, M. (2008). Translating Vana' diel: Japanese and North American game players creating a hybrid culture. Paper presented at the Global Media Research Center, Southern Illinois University at Carbondale, April.

Croon Fors, A., & Jakobsson, M. (2002). Beyond use and design: The dialectics of being in virtual worlds. *Digital Creativity*, 13(1), 39–52.

Dibbell, J. (1993). A rape in cyberspace. http://www.juliandibbell.com/texts/bungle_vv.html.

Elliot, J. (2007). What it's like to have schizophrenia. *BBC News.* http://news.bbc.co.uk/2/hi/health/6453241.stm.

Fairfield, J. (2007). Anti-social contracts: The contractual governance of online communities. Indiana Legal Research Studies Paper, no. 89. http://papers.ssrn.com/sol3/papers.cfm?abstract_id=1002997&rec=1&srcabs=1097392.

Fanderclai, T. L. (1996). Like magic, only real. In L. Cherny & E. R. Weise (eds.), *Wired Women: Gender and New Realities in Cyberspace* (pp. 224–41). Seattle: Seal Press.

Fields, D., & Kafai, Y. (2007). Stealing from Grandma or generating cultural knowledge? Contestations and effects of cheats in a teen virtual world. Paper presented at the Digital Games Research Association conference, September, Tokyo, Japan.

Flanagan, M. (2000). Navigating the narrative in space: Gender and spatiality in virtual worlds. *Art Journal*, Fall, 74–85.

Ford, P. (2001). Paralysis lost: Impacts of virtual worlds on those with paralysis. *Social Theory and Practice*, 27(4), 661–80.

Gibson, W. (1984). *Neuromancer.* New York: Ace Books.

Glushko, B. (2007). Tales of the (virtual) city: Governing property disputes in virtual worlds. *Berkeley Technology Law Journal*, 22, 507–32.

Grimes, S. M. (2008). Kids' ad play: Regulating children's advergames in the converging media context. *International Journal of Communications Law and Policy*, 8(12), 162–78. http://www.ijclp.net/

Gunkel, D., & Gunkel, A. (2009). Terra Nova 2.0 – The New World of MMORPGs. *Critical Studies in Media Communication*, 26(2), 104–27.

Herman, A., Coombe, R., & Kaye, L. (2006). Your *Second Life*? Goodwill and the performativity of intellectual property in online digital gaming. *Cultural Studies*, 20(2–3), 184–210.

Hunt, K. (2007). This land is not your land: *Second Life*, copybot, and the looming question of virtual property rights. *Texas Review of Entertainment and Sports Law*, 9, 141–73.

Jacobson, D. (2001). Presence revisited: Imagination, competence, and activity in text-based virtual worlds. *Cyberpsychology & Behavior*, 4(6), 653–71.

Jäkälä, M., & Pekkola, S. (2007). From technology engineering to social engineering: 15 years of research on virtual worlds. *The Data Base for Advances in Information Systems*, 38(4), 11–16.

Johnson, S. (1997). *Interface Culture: How New Technology Transforms the Way we Create and Communicate*. San Francisco: Pantheon.

Jones, S. (1995). Introduction: From where to who knows? In S. Jones (ed.), *Cybersociety: Computer-Mediated Communication and Community* (pp. 10–35). Thousand Oaks, CA: Sage.

Jones, D. (2007). Queered virtuality: The claiming and making of queer spaces and bodies in the user-constructed synthetic world of *Second Life*. Master's thesis, Georgetown University.

Kemp, J. (2008). SimTeach: Information and community for educators using MUVEs. http://www.simteach.com/.

Kendall, L. (1996). MUDder? I hardly know 'er! Adventures of a feminist MUDder. In L. Cherny & E. R. Weise (eds.), *Wired Women: Gender and New Realities in Cyberspace* (pp. 207–23). Seattle: Seal Press.

Kent, S. (2003). Alternate reality: The history of massively multiplayer online games. *Gamespy.com*. http://archive.gamespy.com/amdmmog/week1/.

Koster, R. (2002). Online world timeline. http://www.raphkoster.com/gaming/mudtimeline.shtml.

Koster, R. (2007). Declaring the rights of players. In J. Balkin & B. S. Noveck (eds.), *The State of Play: Laws, Games and Virtual Worlds* (pp. 55–67). New York: New York University Press.

Lastowka, G., & Hunter, D. (2003). The laws of the virtual worlds. *Social Science Research Network*. http://papers.ssrn.com/sol3/papers.cfm?abstract_id=402860.

Lüders, M. (2007). *Being in Mediated Spaces: An Enquiry into Personal Media Practices*. Doctoral thesis, University of Oslo.

MacInnes, I., & Hu, L. (2007). Business models and operational issues in the Chinese online game industry. *Telematics and Informatics*, 24, 130–44.

Malaby, T. (2006). Virtual world bill of rights, TerraNova blog.

McRae, S. (1996). Coming apart at the seams: Sex, text and the virtual body. In L. Cherny & E. R. Weise (eds.), *Wired Women: Gender and New Realities in Cyberspace* (pp. 242–63). Seattle: Seal Press.

Mennecke, B., McNeill, D., Roche, E., Bray, D., Townsend, A., & Lester, J. (2008). *Second Life* and other virtual worlds: A roadmap for research. *Communications of the Association for Information Systems*, 22(20), 371–88.

Miller, D. (2003). Determine ownership in virtual worlds: Copyright and license agreements. *The Review of Litigation*, 22(2), 435–71.

Miller, L. (1995). Women and children first: Gender and the settling of the electronic frontier. In J. Brook & I. Boal (eds.), *Resisting the Virtual Life: The Culture and Politics of Information* (pp. 49–58). San Francisco, CA: City Lights Books.

Mitchell, W. (1999). Replacing place. In P. Lunenfeld (ed.), *The Digital Dialectic: New Essays on New Media* (pp. 112–28). Cambridge, MA: MIT Press.

Morningstar, C., & Farmer, R. (1990). The lesson's of Lucasfilm's *Habitat*. In M. Benedikt (ed.), *Cyberspace: First Steps*. Cambridge, MA: MIT Press.

Nakamura, L. (2002). *Cybertypes: Race, Ethnicity and Identity on The Internet*. New York: Routledge.

Nutt, C. (2007). Haro on making *Habbo* a success. *Gamasutra.com*. http://www.gamasutra.com/php-bin/news_index.php?story=15397.

Ondrejka, C. (2004). Escaping the gilded cage: User created content and building the metaverse. *New York Law School Review*, 49(1), 81–101.

Reid, L. (1995). Virtual worlds: Culture and imagination. In S. Jones (ed.), *Cybersociety: Computer-Mediated Communication and Community* (pp. 164–83). Thousand Oaks, CA: Sage.

Reynolds, R. (2008). The virtual policy network. http://www.virtualpolicy.net/index.html.

Rheingold, H. (1993). *The Virtual Community: Homesteading on the Electronic Frontier*. Reading, MA: Addison-Wesley.

Riley, D. (2007). Could *Barbie Girls* become the largest virtual world? *TechCrunch*. http://www.techcrunch.com/2007/07/15/could-barbie-girls-become-the-largest-virtual-world/.

Robbins, S. (2008). Institutional Education vs Social Media Learning: What's the future of learning? *Ubernoggin*. http://ubernoggin.com/archives/195.

Steinkuehler, C., & Williams, D. (2006). Where everybody knows your (screen) name: Online games as 'third places.'" *Journal of Computer-Mediated Communication*, 11(4). http://jcmc.indiana.edu/vol11/issue4/steinkuehler.html.

Stephenson, N. (1992). *Snow Crash*. New York: Bantam Books.

Stone, R. A. (1995). *The War of Desire and Technology at the Close of the Mechanical Age*. Cambridge, MA: MIT Press.

Suler, J. (1999). Do boys (and girls) just wanna have fun? Gender-switching in cyberspace. http://www-usr.rider.edu/~suler/psycyber/genderswap.html.

Taylor, J. (1997). The emerging geographies of virtual worlds. *Geographical Review*, 87(2), 172–93.

Taylor, T. L. (1999). Life in virtual worlds. *American Behavioral Scientist*, 43(3), 436–49.

Tetzlaff, D. (2000). Yo-ho-ho and a server of warez: Internet software piracy and the new global information economy. In A. Herman & T. Swiss (eds.), *The World Wide Web and Contemporary Cultural Theory* (pp. 99–126). New York: Routledge.

Virtual Worlds Management. (2008). Youth Worlds Analysis, *Virtual Worlds Management*, April. http://www.virtualworldsmanagement.com/2008/youthworlds.html.

Watson, A., Grant, R., Bello, H., & Hoch, D. (2008). Brave new worlds: How virtual environments can augment traditional care in the management of diabetes. *Journal of Diabetes Science and Technology*, 2(4), 697–702.

Webb, S. (2001). Avatar culture: Narrative, power and identity in virtual world environments. *Information, Communication & Society*, 4(4), 560–94.

Wellman, B. (2004). The three ages of Internet studies: Ten, five and zero years ago. *New Media & Society*, 6(1), 123–29.

Woodland, R. (2000). Queer spaces, modem boys and pagan statues. In K. Bell (ed.), *The Cybercultures Reader* (pp. 416–31). New York: Routledge.

Yee, N., Bailenson, J., Urbanek, M., Chang, F., & Merget, D. (2007). The unbearable likeness of being digital: The persistence of nonverbal social norms in online virtual environments. *Cyberpsychology & Behavior*, 10(1), 115–21.

16

Internet, Children, and Youth

Sonia Livingstone

Introduction – The "Digital Generation"

In late modernity, "self-actualisation is understood in terms of a balance between opportunity and risk" (Giddens, 1991, p. 78). For the first generation to fully experience the Internet in industrialized countries, negotiating this balance has fast become integral to growing up. Framing this is a story of "great expectations," circulated among both parents and children, and strongly fostered by governments and business. But what fuels these expectations? Are they being realized? What are the real benefits of using the Internet? Or the risks?

Children and young people are usually among the earliest and most enthusiastic users of information and communication technologies, and households with children lead the diffusion process. It is often argued that children are more flexible, creative users than adults, having fewer established routines or habits and being oriented toward innovation and change. As young people make the transition from their family of origin toward a wider peer culture, they find that the media offer a key resource for constructing their identity and for mediating social relationships. Does this live up to the popular rhetoric regarding youthful "cyberkids" (Facer & Furlong, 2001) or "the digital generation" (Buckingham, 2006; Tapscott, 1997)?

The demands of the computer or web interface render many parents "digital immigrants" in the information-age inhabited by their "digital native" children (Prensky, 2001). Only in rare instances in history have children gained greater expertise than parents in skills highly valued by society – thus young people's new-found online skills are justifiably trumpeted by both generations. Yet this chapter will argue, following research revealing that children as well as adults may struggle in mastering the Internet (Livingstone, 2008a), that children and young people are divided in their take-up of online opportunities. For some, the Internet is an increasingly rich, diverse, engaging, and stimulating resource of growing importance in their lives. For others, it remains a narrow and relatively unengaging if occasionally useful resource. Boys, older children, and middle-class children all benefit from more and better quality access to the Internet than girls, younger, and working-class children, and although access does not wholly determine use, it certainly sets the conditions within which children explore, gain confidence and skills, and so take up more or fewer online opportunities (Livingstone & Helsper, 2007).

A simple tally of online activities reveals how children and young people are using the Internet to explore, create, learn, share, network, and even subvert. Consider this list of online activities, here asked of 9–19-year-olds in the UK who use the Internet at least weekly (84% of the population in 2004; Livingstone & Bober, 2005):

- 90% do schoolwork
- 94% search for information
- 72% send/receive email
- 70% play games
- 55% do instant messaging
- 55% (aged 12+) visit civic/political site
- 46% download music
- 44% (12+) search careers/education information
- 44% completed a quiz
- 40% (12+) search goods/shop online

- 40% visit sites for hobbies
- 34% made a website
- 26% (12+) read the news
- 28% visit sports sites
- 25% (12+) seek personal advice
- 23% search information on computers/Internet
- 22% voted for something online
- 21% visit chat rooms
- 17% post pictures or stories
- 10% visit a porn site on purpose

For many Internet users, the move is well underway from being primarily an information receiver (typically of mass-produced content on a one-to-many model of communication, albeit often an actively interpretative receiver) to being also a content creator (of peer-produced content, typically on a one-to-one or some-to-some model of communication). A recent Pew Internet survey in the US found more than half of online teens are creating content in one way or another (Lenhart & Madden, 2005). The rise of social networking is rapidly advancing these and other forms of user-generated content creation and sharing, opening up possibilities for participation well beyond a few media-savvy aficionados (boyd & Ellison, 2007; Livingstone, 2008b).

Yet as children and young people move beyond the initial hiccups of acquisition and early exploration, there is evidence that many make the unfamiliar familiar by establishing a fairly conservative pattern of use primarily defined by pre-existing interests and preferences, notwithstanding the huge diversity of possible activities and contents. These familiar use practices tend to be mass-media related, particularly fandom for certain television programs, popular music groups, football teams, and so forth; thus strongly branded contents predominate among children's favorite sites (Ofcom, 2007), and these are often organized as sticky sites or walled gardens (Burbules, 1998; Grimes & Shade, 2005). In short, consumer culture more than new creativities frames many young people's engagement with the Internet. As the European project, *Mediappro* (2006, p. 16) observed, "the evidence here was that creative work was limited, with a minority of young people developing their own websites or blogs, and some evidence that these products could easily become inert."

How, then, should we understand the apparent gap between the great expectations and the often disappointing realities of children's Internet use? And what implications does this have for the unfolding balance between online opportunities and risks in the lives of children and young people?

Theoretical Framings

Research on children, young people and the Internet is structured around a strong tension between two competing conceptions of childhood. On one view, children are seen as vulnerable, undergoing a crucial but fragile process of cognitive and social development to which the Internet tends to pose a risk by introducing potential harms into the social conditions for development, necessitating in turn a protectionist regulatory environment. On the contrary view, children are seen as competent and creative agents in their own right whose "media-savvy" skills tend to be underestimated by the adults around them, the consequence being that society may fail to provide a sufficiently rich environment for them.

Piaget's developmental psychology has provided the dominant research paradigm for the former view (Piaget & Inhelder, 1969), with the focus on the individual child's cognitive development in "ages and stages" through an active and curious exploration of the environment, including the media environment (e.g. Dorr, 1986; Valkenburg, 2004). Its strength is a careful account of children's interests and abilities at different ages, including a theory of developmental transitions from one age to the next. Its weakness is a relative neglect of the ways in which the process of development towards adulthood is shaped by the activities, expectations, and resources of a host of socializing agencies and institutions – parents, teachers, technology and content providers, marketers, welfare bodies, politicians, governments. The importance of these in mediating social relations, including providing a social "scaffolding" for learning, is now being articulated by those following Vygotsky ([1934] 1986) (e.g. Erstad & Wertsch, 2008; Kerawalla & Crook, 2002).

The new sociology of childhood emerged as a reaction to Piagetian individualism and universalism (James, Jenks, & Prout, 1998). Qvortrup (1994) characterizes this approach as stressing three elements. First, it stresses the structural aspects of childhood, with its dynamics and determinants, rather than a naturalistic conception of the individual child and its development. Second, it emphasises relational elements, seeing neither "the child" in isolation from others, nor "the household" as sufficiently descriptive of its members; rather these relationships are worthy of study in and of themselves. Third, it prioritizes the present – children as people now, their relationships and cultures considered worthy of study in their own right, rather than looking forward by regarding children as merely persons-to-be and so as indicative of the adults they will become. Thus Corsaro (1997) observes that through their daily actions, often invisible to adult eyes, children construct their social worlds as real places where real meanings (rather than fantasy or imitation) are generated, and thus they contribute to social structures which have consequences for both children and adults. This involves, too, a politicization of childhood – childhood is seen as not only a demographic but also a moral classification, central to the project of making children count – and so addressing their needs and rights – when apportioning the resources of society (Qvortrup, 1994).

In seeking to avoid the extremes, and to integrate the insights of each approach, social scientists rely on the contingent and contextualized knowledge derived from detailed, preferably child-centered empirical work. In so doing, they either draw upon or even integrate two somewhat contrasting but potentially compatible approaches regarding the Internet – diffusion and domestication theory. As statisticians chart the rise in Internet access across and within countries, and as governments rely on the public to gain access at home, evidence for the gradual diffusion of the Internet from the "innovators" and "early adopters" through the mass market until eventually reaching the "laggards" is readily obtained (Rogers, 1995). But this neat account of the spread of a more-or-less stable technology through the market is quickly complicated and qualified once one explores the nature of use. For the Internet itself means different things to different users and at different points in the passage through design, production, marketing, consumption, and use (Livingstone, 2002; Silverstone, 2006).

Beyond the obvious practical and financial barriers that face ordinary users, ethnographic studies of technology use and domestic consumption practices draw attention to the symbolic struggles involved in going online (Bakardjieva, 2005; Van Rompaey, Roe, & Struys, 2002). Mothers have traditionally regulated their children's media use, and fathers have traditionally been relied on to fix household appliances, but the Internet may challenge both their competence and, in consequence, their social status in the family. Living rooms have long been places of leisure, but now they contain an object from the office. Living rooms have also been places for shared activities – eating, watching television, talking – but now they contain something that monopolizes one person's attention and excludes the others.

Research on children, youth, and the Internet requires, in short, a theory of both childhood and youth and, further, of the Internet. Already in the decade of so of research on the enticing intersection between young people and this young technology (Livingstone, 2003), there has emerged a neat synergy between classificatory approaches based on age (i.e. theories of child development) and on technology (diffusion theories of technology), just as there has emerged a parallel synergy between the social constructionist account of childhood and the ethnographic or domestication account of the appropriation of the Internet in everyday life. Often, therefore, research splits along these lines. In this chapter, I seek a more synthetic account of children, young people, and the Internet, focusing on three prominent areas of online opportunity – explorations of the self, traditional and alternative modes of learning, and opportunities for civic participation; to balance the optimism that these opportunities often occasion, I also consider the mounting evidence for online risks to children and young people.

Explorations of the Self

In late modernity, characterized by globalization, commercialization, and individualization, Buchner argues that:

> every child is increasingly expected to behave in an "individualised way" . . . children must somehow orient themselves to an *anticipated* life course. The more childhood in the family is eclipsed by influences and orientation patterns from outside the family . . . the more independent the opportunity (and drive) to making up one's own mind, making one's own choice . . . described here as the *biographization* of the life course. (Buchner, 1990, pp. 77–8)

In undertaking what Giddens (1991) called the "project of the self," children and young people are experiencing the Internet as a valued new place for social exploration and self-expression (Holloway & Valentine, 2003). Drotner (2000) proposes three key ways in which young people may be said to be "cultural pioneers" in their use of new media technologies, centering on innovation, interaction, and integration. Under "innovation," she notes how young people combine multiple media, multitask, blur production and reception, and so make creative use of the opportunities available. By "interaction," she points to how young people engage with each other within and through different media and media contents, opening up opportunities for intertextuality and connectivity. And by "integration," she points to the transformation of the distinction between primary (or face-to-face) and secondary (mass-mediated) socialization, resulting in diverse forms of mediated communication (see also Lievrouw & Livingstone, 2006).

For a prime example of the way in which an online, converged media environment affords distinctive forms of social identity, consider the popularity of witchcraft and "wiccan" subcultures across many media, linking primetime television shows (such as *Buffy the Vampire Slayer, Sabrina the Teenage Witch, Charmed, Bewitched*) with online communities – playing with identities, creating alternative worlds, writing fan fiction, sustaining niche networks and so forth. This testifies to the fascination of many, especially girls and young women, with subaltern notions of female power, spirituality and adventure, these providing a possible cultural repertoire with which to resist disempowering norms of femininity (precisely without, typically, embracing the term "feminism"). Clark (2002) argues that the wiccan subculture affords powerful mediated identifications that contrast with the relatively powerless position of teenagers in everyday life. Further, it allows for an exploration of morality and, indeed, an identification with "goodness" (for these are typically good, not evil, witches) that sidesteps acceptance of dominant adult morality (as often expressed, especially in the US, through organized religion).

In terms of content, then, "for the young, the media are part of a range of cultural signs available for processes of interpretation that are situated in time and space and dependent on constraints of production, distribution and resources for reception" (Drotner, 2000, p. 59). Or as 14-year-old Elena said, in my study of social networking sites, "I think layouts really show like who you are. So look at the rainbow in that. I think that would make you sound very like bubbly . . . I like to have different ones . . . it's different likes, different fashion, different feelings on that day" (Livingstone, 2008b, p. 399).

If media generally enable particular ways of constructing and participating in mainstream and alternative youth cultures and lifestyles (Ziehe, 1994), the specific technological affordances of the Internet play a role here too, for the Internet is a far from neutral, singular, or disinterested actor in reshaping everyday cultures (Hutchby, 2001). Boyd (2008) argues that social networking is particularly characterized by persistence (being recorded, it permits asynchronous communication), searchability (affording the easy construction of new, extended or niche networks), replicability (enabling multiple versions which do not distinguish the original from the copy) and, last, invisible audiences (resulting in a radical uncertainty about who is "listening"); one might add that there is also a radical uncertainty about who is "speaking," facilitated by online anonymity. All of these features of the online environment serve to disembed communication from its familiar anchoring in the face-to-face situation of physical co-location, an embedding that, traditionally, provided certain guarantees of authenticity, authority, and trust. As communication becomes re-embedded in new, more flexible, distributed, peer-oriented relations of sociability (Thompson, 1995), new conventions of authority and authenticity are emerging, as are new forms of play, manipulation, and deceit.

Creative, especially "self-authoring," practices may be especially significant when the participants are those "whose lives are often storied by others," as Vasudevan (2006: 207) observes when examining the online identity practices of African American adolescent boys. Again because their lives are often represented more powerfully by others than themselves, the exuberance and diversity of a girls' subculture online seems especially compelling. Mazzarella and Pecora (2007) argue that this affords a means of affirming the experiences of those who otherwise, being on the edge of adolescence, stand to lose their "voice" in the face of a mainstream public culture in which commercializing, pathologizing, or marginalizing messages predominate. So, extending the critical work of McRobbie and Garber (1976) on girls' magazines, and that of others on teenage bedrooms as a site of identity construction and display (Lincoln, 2004; Livingstone, 2007), Stern (2008) argues that web content created by, rather than for, girls enables the construction of a self-presentation by which girls can speak to each other "in a different voice" (Gilligan, 1993).

As Kearney (2007, p. 138) observes with some optimism, "contemporary female youth are not retreating to private spaces; they are *reconfiguring* such sites to create new publics that can better serve their needs, interests, and goals." Illustrating the point, Guzzetti (2006) discusses two girls aged 17–18, Saundra and Corgan, who had co-created an online magazine or "zine" that integrated activist themes of social justice and feminism with punk rock and entertainment content. Guzzetti argues that the development of digital literacies required to sustain the zine was embedded in social practices via the online community activities surrounding zines, rather than simply reflecting individual skill. Thus it enabled identity work that affirmed these young women as authentic members of the punk community, a world in which their expertise was essential, their performances valued, and within which they could escape stereotyped notions of gender. As she also showed, these benefits influenced Saundra's offline writing, stimulating a satirical and witty writing style with significant consequences for her social and cultural capital.

However, some critics are more concerned with the defining trend in post-traditional society of individualization than they are with opportunities for creativity. Contrary to the optimism of Kearney and others, one may read the privatization of public spaces and, for children, the rising importance of bedroom culture as well as the growing role of online culture, as evidence of the individualization of culture. For, being closely linked also with consumerism, these new freedoms afford new occasions for targeted advertising and marketing, and the development of "taste" and lifestyle is shaped significantly by powerful commercial interests in the fashion and music industries online as offline. Not only are advertisements are commonly placed at the top or centre of homepages, blogs, chat rooms and social networking sites, but also the user is encouraged to define their identity through consumer preferences (music, movies, fandom). Indeed, the user is themselves commodified insofar as a social networking profile in particular can be neatly managed, exchanged or organized in various ways by others precisely because it is fixed, formatted, and context-free (Marwick, 2005).

Learning – Traditional and Alternative

There is little doubt that the main ambition society holds out for children and the Internet centers on learning – both informally at home and though formal education in school. The perceived educational benefits of domestic Internet use have fuelled its rapid diffusion, and the Internet is becoming, it seems, as central to education as books, classrooms, and teachers. It is not yet, however, part of the educational infrastructure, not yet so thoroughly embedded in the social structures of everyday life as to be "invisible," taken for granted. Rather, while most schools in developed nations provide Internet access to their pupils, just how this is achieved, maintained, and valued is still fraught and problematic.

Infrastructure, as Star and Bowker (2002) explain, means that a service has become linked into the conventions of a community of practice; undoubtedly, this is underway – consider the changes in teacher training, curriculum redesign, and education budgets as well as classroom practice that have accompanied the introduction of education technology into schools – but the many difficulties and debates over how to fund, implement, and evaluate these changes testify to the efforts still required. Infrastructure also, Star and Bowker add, embodies particular standards, expectations, and values; here too debates rage on, with contestation accompanying such diverse matters as government targets for school information and communication technology (ICT) provision, parental expectations of a "good" school, pupils' understanding of learning values and practices, and teachers' expectations of educational outcomes.

Given the considerable financial investment in ICT hardware and software in schools, it may seem surprising that convincing evidence of an improvement in learning outcomes remains elusive. A recent report to Congress in the US found that test scores in classrooms using reading and mathematics software for a full year were little different from those using traditional teaching methods (Dynarski et al., 2007). This study found some indication that more use could improve results for reading (but not mathematics) among nine-year-olds and that, among five-year-olds, results were larger when class sizes were smaller. Since, for the most part, ICT investment uses resources that might otherwise be used to reduce class sizes, this latter finding is not encouraging – and indeed the same might be said of all the study results. A British government evaluation of the ICT in Schools Programme obtained similarly mixed and weak findings regarding improvements in national test scores (Harrison et al., 2003; see also Condie & Munro, 2007).

Other sources of evidence are surprisingly sparse. Thiessen and Looker (2007) asked whether learning to complete a range of computer and educational software tasks transfers positively to reading, finding that up to a certain point, more ICT use on educational tasks was associated with improved reading achievement scores, but beyond that, more ICT use was associated with lower scores – hence the often contradictory or inconclusive findings obtained by those seeking wider educational benefits of ICT use in the classroom or home. Not only is the amount of use crucial, so too is the quality of use, as Lei and Zhao (2007) found when examining the student learning outcomes in an American middle school (with pupils aged 12–13 years). Improvements in grade point averages were associated with subject-related technology uses but, unfortunately, these tended to be among the least popular activities. This contradicts the easy assumption that because children like using technology, this in and of itself gives them the confidence and motivation that enhances learning. It also contradicts the hope for a positive transfer from entertainment and communication uses to those that specifically facilitate school grades. Instead, it suggests that the technology uses that aid learning are the unpopular or difficult tasks (i.e. designed specifically to teach a certain topic), not the free and fun searching, game playing, or informal exploration.

Is education best assessed through increases in test scores, whether measured as grade point averages, reading ages, or exam results? Surely the potential of the Internet is greater than this – as, more importantly, is the potential of a child to learn. While government departments call for ICT to improve test scores, reduce disadvantage, and ensure delivery of the basic skills of reading, writing, numeracy, and science, critics reject the lack of imagination in this agenda, seeing it as wedded to a twentieth-, even a nineteenth-century conception of drill-and-skill education (Smith & Curtin, 1998). The alternative proposition, however, remains somewhat speculative, namely the claim that ICT enables the development – in or, better, outside the classroom – of precisely the soft skills vital for meeting the new demands of the global service and information economy of the twenty-first century (e.g. Gee, 2008; Jenkins, 2006). Hence the argument that playing certain computer games within the classroom may foster constructive learning practices and encourage learner motivation (Merchant, 2007). But, "soft skills have yet to be adequately defined and their importance, relative to formal qualifications, for different groups of people and at different stages in the life cycle is unknown" (Sparkes, 1999, p. 7).

Many remain optimistic. Nyboe and Drotner (2008) describe a school-based Danish animation project that deliberately broke with school routine and teacher–pupil hierarchies to enable pupils to co-design a digital animation over a two-week period. The process of decision-making, design, construction, and implementation all emerged from lively and often playful peer interaction – showing how learning itself is social rather than purely individual, being enabled by discussion, negotiation, imagination, conflict resolution. Significantly, as often argued but too rarely demonstrated, the project proved effective in terms of pupils' learning not only about software, media production, and team working but also in terms of gaining the media literacy required to analyze and critique the multiplicity of representational forms and knowledge claims that surround them in daily life. This, then, was a case in which peer culture was harnessed to deliver learning outcomes valued by teachers, children and, most likely, future employers, capitalizing on the observation that "mobile texting, online gaming, and blogging as well as digital editing of visuals and sound are all embedded within youthful communities of practice" (Nyboe & Drotner, 2008; see also Cassell, 2004).

At present, the great expectations associated with the search for alternatives have been neither supported nor disproved by evidence; nor, however, has the huge investment sunk into injecting ICT into the traditional model yet proved its worth. Whether society can harness the Internet to deliver the more radical and ambitious vision, whether it even really desires its alternative pedagogy, and whether education can resist the commercializing pressures to co-opt, constrain, and commodify the routes to knowledge opened up by this vision all remain to be seen (Buckingham, Scanlon, & Sefton-Green, 2001). For there is, undoubtedly, both money and power at stake here – "vying for position . . . are not only educators but also publishers, commercial hardware and software producers, parents, governments, and the telecommunications players of the corporate world" (Hawisher & Selfe, 1998, p. 3).

Opportunities to Participate

In recent decades, political scientists have been charting, with mounting concern, the steady decline in political participation by the public, across many countries, as measured by such indicators as voter turnout, party loyalty, and representation in decision-making bodies. Since this decline has coincided with the spread of mass media into daily life, media critics have scrutinized every dimension of the media's relations with political institutions and the public sphere. While some ask whether the media are responsible for the withdrawal from civil society, others are intrigued that the public seems to be reconstituting community online, discovering common interests with a potentially huge network of likeminded peers, developing new skills, building alternative deliberative spaces, raising the possibility of a virtual public sphere.

For many, the Internet is inherently "democratic" for, even though its features – interactivity, global scale, fast connectivity, unlimited capacity, etc – are not radically new, the Internet's possession of them in combination introduces a qualitative shift in the potential for democratic communication (Bentivegna, 2002). Intriguingly, there appears to be a promising match between the style of deliberation afforded by the Internet and that preferred by the very population segment – young people – who are in many ways the most disengaged from traditional forms of political activity. The very architecture of the Internet, with its flexible, hypertextual, networked structure, its dialogic mode of address, and its alternative, even anarchic feel, particularly appeals to young people, contrasting with the traditional, linear, hierarchical, logical, rule-governed conventions often used in official communications with youth.

For children and young people, then, the Internet appears to be "their" medium; they are the early adopters, the most media-savvy, the pioneers in the cyber-age, leading for once rather than being led, thus reversing the generation gap as they gain confidence and expertise. Online, we are witnessing a flourishing of the kinds of life-political or single-issue networks, campaigns, or groupings, whether on a local or a global scale, which may be expected particularly to appeal to young people (Bennett, 1998). These groupings are generally project-focused, idealistic in their hopes but pragmatic in the low level of obligation expected of members. They are characterized by openness and spontaneity, generating ad hoc, low-commitment, self-reflexive, and strategic communications within a flexibly defined, peer-based network (Coleman, 1999).

Today, the number and variety of initiatives to harness the Internet to encourage youthful participation has exploded, with the Internet widely hailed as the technology to bring new, more participatory, forms of civic engagement, political deliberation, and e-democracy to the polity. In a key report a few years ago, the

Center for Media Education in the US charted "an abundance of civic and political activity by and for youth," much of this using the Internet to "invite young
people to participate in a wide range of issues, including voting, voluntarism, racism
and tolerance, social activism and, most recently, patriotism, terrorism and military
conflict" (Montgomery, Gottlieb-Robles, & Larson, 2004, p.2). They argued for
the creation, and economic viability, of a "youth civic media" online (CME, 2000).

All of this energy and creativity designed to mobilize the Internet so as to enable
youthful participation is, at heart, a response to two fundamental and somewhat
contradictory shifts in society. The first, we have already seen, is the claim that
youth are apathetic, lacking the political commitment of previous generations,
alienated from the political system. Here the Internet is seen as a means of
countering a downward trend in participation, and the focus is "citizens in the
making" or "citizens-in-waiting" who must be prepared for their future adult
responsibilities (Lister et al., 2003). The second shift is historically radical, for it
positions children and young people for the first time as citizens now. The extension of the twentieth century movement for civil rights, women's rights, and human
rights also to encompass children's rights, and children's voices, is formalized in
the United Nation's Convention on the Rights of the Child (1989).

In other words, some initiatives are motivated by the challenge of stimulating
the alienated, while others assume young people to be already articulate and
motivated but lacking structured opportunities to participate. Some aim to
enable youth to realize their present rights while others focus instead on preparing them for their future responsibilities. These diverse motivates may, however,
result in some confusion in mode of address, target group, and, especially,
form of participation being encouraged. As the *Carnegie Young People Initiative*
(Cutler & Taylor, 2003, p. 11) noted, with concern, "the benefits and impacts
of children and young people's participation are not clearly identified" in many of
the projects they reviewed.

What does the evidence say about whether the Internet can be used to enable
political participation (or, reverse the apparent political apathy) among children
and young people, and under what conditions might this be brought about? The
results are, in some ways, encouraging. Nearly one in five of those aged 18–35
in the UK had contributed to an online discussion about a public issue of importance to them, while for those over 35 the figure falls to 5 percent (though people
aged 55 and above were more likely to have contacted a local politician about
the issue), reviving hope that the Internet could help rather than hinder youthful civic engagement (Couldry, Livingstone, & Markham, 2007). Young people
are more likely to participate online than take part in more traditional forms
of politics: while only 10 percent of 15–24-year-olds took part in any form of
political activity offline, three times that many did something political on the Internet
(Gibson, Lusoli, & Ward, 2002). In the US, 38 percent of 12–17-year-olds said
they go online to express their opinion (Lenhart, Rainie, & Lewis, 2001).

However, generally, evaluations of online initiatives are less than optimistic (Phipps,
2000). Not all voices are heard equally online (Bessant, 2004), there being many

impediments to open online exchange (Cammaerts & Van Audenhove, 2005). An American survey of 15–25-year-olds found the Internet an even less effective means of engaging disaffected young people than traditional routes, though very effective at mobilizing the already-interested (Levine & Lopez, 2004). Commonly, it is the already-engaged for whom the combination of new media and alternative politics seems especially potent (Dahlgren & Olsson, 2007), possibly because so many of the rest are socialized – by media and other means – not into a culture of activism but rather into one of inefficacy and distrust.

Contrary to the popular discourses that blame young people for their apathy and their lack of motivation or interest, it seems that young people learn early that they are not listened to. Hoping that the Internet can enable young people to "have their say" thus misses the point, for they are not themselves listened to. This is both a failure of effective communication between young people and those who aim to engage them, and a failure of civic or political structures – of the social structures that sustain relations between established power and the polity, or what Meyer and Staggenbord (1996) term the "opportunity structures" that facilitate, shape, and develop young people's participation. What matters, in short, "is not whether new media are capable of capturing, moderating and summarizing the voice of the public, but whether political institutions are able and willing to enter into a dialogical relationship with the public" (Coleman, 2007, p. 375).

Risky Encounters

With headlines full of pedophiles, cyber-bullies, and online suicide pacts, it is unsurprising that much academic research is wary of research on online risks, for these moral panics, amplified by the popular media, have their own pernicious consequences, including the call for censorship or other restrictions on freedom of expression and the deflection of public anxieties about economic and social change onto technology. Public anxiety regarding risk in relation to children and the Internet is exacerbated by the coincidence of three factors: first, the extraordinary rapidity of the Internet's diffusion and development, faster than any previous medium (Rice & Haythornthwaite, 2006) and so outpacing adults' ability to adjust; second, an endemic cultural fear of the new, encouraged by media panics framing the Internet both as responsible for scary threats to children's safety and as escaping traditional forms of regulation; and third, the novelty of a reverse generation gap whereby parental expertise (and, therefore, authority) in managing children's Internet use is exceeded by children's ability both to use the technology and to evade adult management.

Yet these public anxieties regarding the "child in danger" (and the "dangerous child," Oswell, 1998) remain, for the most part, familiar ones, having accompanied previous mass media from the nineteenth-century comic through the advent of film, television, and computer games, up until and including the Internet and mobile media of the twenty-first century. As Critcher puts it: "The pattern is standard. A new medium, product of a new technology or a new application of an old one, emerges and finds a mass market. Its content is seen as criminal or violent or horrific. It constitutes a danger to children who cannot distinguish between reality and fantasy." (Critcher 2008, p. 100)

In Western thinking about childhood, and for parents especially, risk anxiety has become "a constant and pervasive feature of everyday consciousness" (Jackson & Scott, 1999, p. 88). In relation to the Internet, one reason is that the opportunities and the risks are inextricably linked – on reflection, we cannot sustain the commonsense polarization of opportunities and risks, the idea that young people engage in some activities of which society approves and others of which society disapproves. Rather, these are often the same activities, not only because teenagers especially like to test adult authority, challenging adult-imposed rules and boundaries and evading parental scrutiny, but also because of the design of online contents and services.

To take up an opportunity one must, very often, take a risk. To make a new friend online, one risks meeting someone ill-intentioned. To engage even with the children's BBC website, one must provide personal information online. To meet your offline friends on a social networking site, you must tell the truth about your name and age. To search for advice about sexuality, one will encounter pornographic content also, since there is no consensual line between them. Thus we must examine the way that websites and services have been designed, socially shaped by producers, content providers, and users: the Internet does not create risk for children but it mediates the relation between risk and opportunity, and could be made to do so differently.

Research is now accumulating an array of evidence for online risk (Millwood Hargrave, & Livingstone, 2009), notwithstanding a series of conceptual and methodological difficulties with identifying and assessing risk, especially given the ethical issues involved in asking children about the risks that concern policymakers – illegal content, contact with pedophiles ("grooming"), exposure to extreme or sexual violence or other harmful or offensive content including racist material, commercial persuasion, biased or exploitative content, abuse of personal and private information, cyber-bullying, stalking, harassment, gambling, financial scams, self-harm (suicide, anorexia, etc), illegal activities (hacking, terrorism). Such a list invites classification, dividing content risks from contact risks, for example (Hasebrink, Livingstone, Haddon, & Ólafsson, 2009); here the former represent an extreme version of risks long addressed, and regulated, on mass media, while the latter present new challenges, for little or no regulation restricts who can be in touch with anyone else, particularly when age can be disguised online.

With the explosion of user-generated content, some hosted on commercial (i.e. professional) websites (e.g. social networking, gaming, or blogging sites) and some circulated peer-to-peer (e.g. via email or instant messaging), the distinction between content and contact is breaking down. The reluctant recognition that children and teenagers may be perpetrator as well as victim has led to the proposal of a third category, namely conduct risks (Hasebrink, Livingstone, Haddon, & Ólafsson, 2009). Offline, conduct between people, whether strangers or acquaintances, is socially regulated by behavioral norms and accepted sanctions. While not suggesting that social conventions are absent online, they are more flexible and more easily circumvented without sanction.

What is the scale of these online risks to children and young people? Across Europe, 18 percent of parents/carers state that they believe their child has encountered harmful or illegal content on the Internet (Eurobarometer, 2006). National surveys in Norway, Sweden, Ireland, Denmark, and Iceland found that a quarter to a third of 9–16-year-old Internet users had accidentally seen violent, offensive, sexual or pornographic content online (Larsson, 2003). A 2006 update in Ireland found that 35 percent had visited pornographic sites, 26 percent had visited hateful sites (mostly boys), and 23 percent had received unwanted sexual comments online (again more boys); further, one in five chatters was upset, threatened, or embarrassed online, and 7 percent had met an online contact offline. Of these, 24 percent turned out not to be a child but an adult, and 11 percent said the person tried to physically hurt them (Webwise, 2006). In the US, a survey of 1500 10–17-year-olds in 2006 found that, compared with an earlier survey in 2000, online exposure to sexual material had increased (34 percent versus 25 percent of young Internet users), as had online harassment (9 percent versus 6 percent), though unwanted sexual solicitations – often from acquaintances rather than strangers – had reduced (13 percent versus 19 percent); 4 percent had been asked for nude or sexually explicit photos of themselves, and the proportion who had been distressed by such experiences increased (9 percent versus 6 percent) (Wolak, Mitchell, & Finkelhor, 2006).

In countries where Internet diffusion is more recent, risk figures are rather higher, presumably because here especially, youth encounter online risk in advance of regulators and policymakers. In Bulgaria, one in three Internet users have met in person somebody they got to know online, one in three have experienced insistent and persistent attempts to communicate with them (often about sex) against their will, and four in ten are unaware of the risks of meeting online contacts offline (Mancheva, 2006). In Poland, a 2006 survey found that two in three Internet users make friends online and many give out personal information; almost one in two had gone to a meeting with someone encountered online, and half of them went alone; one in four of these described the behavior of the other person as "suspicious" (CANEE, 2006).

These and other experiences do indeed seem to go beyond what society expects for children and young people, though perhaps not beyond what society has long silently tolerated (Muir, 2005). Although arguments are mounting against unrealistic expectations of a zero-risk childhood, policymakers find it difficult to specify a level of acceptable risk when it comes to children, the result being that media panics effectively construe all risk as unacceptable. In reaction, critics counter with children's resilience to harm, their sophistication in using the Internet, and the historical "fact" that risk has always been part of childhood.

The challenge is to move beyond these polarized positions, for we can conclude neither that the Internet is too risky to allow children access nor that it affords no threat whatsoever. The theory of the risk society (Beck, 1992) offers three useful directions for thinking about how, now that so many are online, risk is being reconfigured for (and by) today's children and young people.

First, the theory of the risk society problematizes the *identification of risk*, rejecting the notion of risk as a natural hazard "out there" and seeking to understand how it is precisely a consequence of the institutions, innovations, and practices of modernity.

Second, the theory of the risk society invites us to inquire into the social, political, and economic (as well as the technological) reasons for the *intensification of risk* in late modernity. A third dimension of the risk society thesis is that of the *individualization of risk* in Western capitalist societies. For the discourse of risk is, today, closely accompanied by a discourse of empowerment, this being largely lifted from the life-political movements which spawned it (especially feminism) and re-embedded within official establishment discourses as a means of legitimating the individualization of risk – in other words, the increasing exposure of the individual to the consequences of their own risk-related decisions. As Harden (2000, p. 46) observes, "while anxieties about risk may be shaped by public discussion, it is as individuals that we cope with these uncertainties." For children, teenagers, and their parents, already absorbed in the fraught emotional conflicts of negotiating boundaries of public and private, dependence and independence, tradition and change, this is indeed a new burden (Livingstone & Bober, 2006).

Conclusions

Everybody is affected, in one way or another, by the ubiquity of new online technologies (Lievrouw & Livingstone, 2006), this resulting in the blurring of hitherto distinctive social practices of information and entertainment, work and leisure, public and private, even childhood and adulthood, national and global. Nonetheless, children, young people, and their families tend to be in the vanguard of new media adoption. They benefit from the early take-up of new opportunities afforded by the Internet, although significant inequalities in quality of access, use, and skill remain. However, the risk of harm to children's safety and social development is attracting growing academic, public, and policy attention. Here too, children and young people are often in the vanguard, exploring new activities, especially peer networking, in advance of adult scrutiny and regulatory intervention and, perhaps too often, encountering negative experiences that are unanticipated, for which they may be unprepared, and which may challenge their capacity to cope.

Although new media "are usually created with particular purposes or uses in mind, they are commonly adopted and used in unanticipated ways – reinvented, reconfigured, sabotaged, adapted, hacked, ignored" (Lievrouw & Livingstone, 2006:

5). A child-centered approach is enabling researchers to explore just how this works – for better or for worse, advancing children's interests or the contrary – across the scope of their lives. They use the Internet for communicating, learning, participating, playing, connecting, and so forth in far more ways than I have had space to review here, though evidence of just how they use it can reveal not only exciting possibilities but also some limitations to the sometimes convenient or complacent perception of children as "the Internet generation," supposedly natural "experts" in using the Internet (Buckingham, 2006; Livingstone, 2008a).

A balanced picture has emerged that bodes well for further initiatives to encourage, celebrate, and support children's effective use of the Internet while not legitimating any withdrawal of the public resources that such initiatives will surely require. I have argued that research does not, and should not, focus solely on the activities of children and young people, for instead a dual analysis is required that encompasses the social and the technological, at the level of both individual and institutional practices. When examining children's and young people's Internet expertise and literacies, for example, we must consider not only their capabilities and skills but also the technological affordances designed into the interfaces they are faced with, and the institutional interests that lie behind. To take a simple example, having seen teenagers reveal personal information publicly online, rather than declaring that teenagers lack a sense of privacy online, we should instead ask whether they understand just how privacy controls work on social networking sites and, especially, whether these could be better designed (Livingstone, 2008b). Similarly, instead of despairing that online as offline, few young people become engaged in civic forums, we should instead – or also – ask what it takes to get political actors to engage with, and respond to, young people online.

Young people's Internet literacy does not yet match the headline image of the intrepid pioneer not because young people lack imagination or initiative but because the institutions that manage their Internet access and use are constraining or unsupportive – anxious parents, uncertain teachers, busy politicians, profit-oriented content providers. In recent years, popular online activities have one by one become fraught with difficulties for young people – chat rooms and social networking sites are closed down because of the risk of pedophiles, music downloading has resulted in legal actions for copyright infringement, educational institutions are increasingly instituting plagiarism procedures, and so forth. Although in practice the Internet is not quite as welcoming a place for young people as popular rhetoric would have one believe, in this respect it is not so different from offline social spaces. The future balance of opportunities and risks for children and young people online remains to be seen.

References

Bakardjieva, M. (2005). *Internet Society: The Internet in Everyday Life*. London: Sage.
Beck, U. (1992). *Risk Society: Towards a New Modernity*. London: Sage.

Bennett, L. (1998). The uncivic culture: Communication, identity, and the rise of lifestyle politics. *PS: Political Science and Politics*, 3(4), 740–61.

Bentivegna, S. (2002). Politics and new media. In L. Lievrouw & S. Livingstone (eds.), *The Handbook of New Media* (pp. 50–61). London: Sage.

Bessant, J. (2004). Mixed messages: Youth participation and democratic practice. *Australian Journal of Political Science*, 39(2), 387–404.

boyd, d. (2008). Why youth ♥ social network sites: The role of networked publics in teenage social life. In D. Buckingham (ed.), *Youth, Identity, and Digital Media* (pp. 119–42), MacArthur Foundation Series on Digital Learning. Cambridge: MIT Press.

boyd, d., & Ellison, N. (2007). Social network sites: Definition, history, and scholarship. *Journal of Computer-Mediated Communication*, 13(1). http://jcmc.indiana.edu/vol13/issue1/boyd.ellison.html.

Buchner, P. (1990). Growing up in the eighties: Changes in the social biography of childhood in the FRG. In L. Chisholm, P. Buchner, H. H. Kruger, & P. Brown (eds.), *Childhood, Youth and Social Change: A Comparative Perspective* (pp. 71–84). London: Falmer Press.

Buckingham, D. (2006). Is there a digital generation? In D. Buckingham & R. Willett (eds.), *Digital Generations* (pp. 1–13). Mahwah, NJ: Lawrence Erlbaum.

Buckingham, D., Scanlon, M., & Sefton-Green, J. (2001). Selling the digital dream: Marketing educational technology to teachers and parents. In A. Loveless & V. Ellis (ed.), *Subject to Change: Literacy and Digital Technology* (pp. 20–40). London: Routledge.

Burbules, N. C. (1998). Rhetorics on the web: Hyperreading and critical literacy. In I. Snyder (ed.), *Page to Screen: Taking Literacy Into the Electronic Era* (pp. 102–22). New York: Routledge.

Cammaerts, B., & Van Audenhove, L. (2005). Online political debate, unbounded citizenship, and the problematic nature of a transnational public sphere. *Political Communication*, 22(2), 179–96.

Cassell, J. (2004). Towards a model of technology and literacy development: Story listening systems. *Journal of Applied Developmental Psychology*, 25(1), 75–105.

Child Abuse and Neglect in Eastern Europe (CANEE) (2006). *Research on Risky Behaviours of Polish Children on the Internet*. http://www.fdn.pl/nowosci/?lang_id=2.

Clark, L. S. (2002). US Adolescent religious identity, the media, and the "funky" side of religion. *Journal of Communication*, 52(4), 794–811.

CME (2000). Citizen youth: CME looks beyond election day. *eCME News*, 1(2).

Coleman, S. (1999). The new media and democratic politics. *New Media & Society*, 1(1), 67–73.

Coleman, S. (2007). E-democracy: The history and future of an idea. In D. Quah, R. Silverstone, R. Mansell, & C. Avgerou (eds.), *The Oxford Handbook of Information and Communication Technologies* (pp. 362–82). Oxford: Oxford University Press.

Condie, R., & Munro, B. (2007). *The Impact of ICT in Schools – A Landscape Review*. Coventry: Becta.

Corsaro, W. A. (1997). *The Sociology of Childhood*. Thousand Oaks, California: Pine Forge Press.

Couldry, N., Livingstone, S., & Markham, T. (2007). *Media Consumption and Public Engagement: Beyond the Presumption of Attention*. Basingstoke: Palgrave Macmillan.

Critcher, C. (2008). Making waves: Historic aspects of public debates about children and mass media. In K. Drotner & S. Livingstone (eds.), *International Handbook of Children, Media and Culture* (pp. 91–104). London: Sage.

Cutler, D., & Taylor, A. (2003). *Expanding and Sustaining Involvement: A Snapshot of Participation Infrastructure for Young People living in England*. Dunfermline, Fife: Carnegie Young People Initiative.

Dahlgren, P., & Olsson, T. (2007). From public sphere to civic culture: Young citizens' Internet use. In R. Butsch (ed.), *Media and Public Spheres* (pp. 198–209). New York: Palgrave Macmillan.

Dorr, A. (1986). *Television and Children: A Special Medium for a Special Audience*. Beverley Hills, CA: Sage.

Drotner, K. (2000). Difference and diversity: Trends in young Danes' media use. *Media, Culture & Society*, 22(2), 149–66.

Drotner, K. (2008). Boundaries and bridges: Digital storytelling in education studies and media studies. In K. Lundby (ed.), *Digital Storytelling, Mediatized Stories: Self-Representations in New Media*. New York: Peter Lang.

Dynarski, M., Agodini, R., & Heaviside, S., et al. (2007). *Effectiveness of Reading and Mathematics Software Products: Findings from the First Student Cohort*. Washington, DC: US Department of Education, Institute of Education Sciences.

Erstad, O., & Wertsch, J. (2008). Tales of mediation: Narrative and digital media as cultural tools. In K. Lundby (ed.), *Digital Storytelling, Mediatized Stories: Self-Representations in New Media*. New York: Peter Lang.

Eurobarometer (2006). *Safer Internet*. Luxembourg: European Commission: Directorate General Information Society and Media.

Facer, K., & Furlong, R. (2001). Beyond the myth of the "cyberkid": Young people at the margins of the information revolution. *Journal of Youth Studies*, 4(4), 451–69.

Gee, J. P. (2008). Learning and Games. In K. Salen (ed.), *The Ecology of Games: Connecting Youth, Games, and Learning* (vol. 3, pp. 21–40). Cambridge, MA: MIT Press.

Gibson, R., Lusoli, W., & Ward, S. (2002). *UK Political Participation Online: The Public Response. A Survey of Citizens' Political Activity via the Internet*. Salford: ESRI. www.ipop.org.uk.

Giddens, A. (1991). *Modernity and Self-Identity: Self and Society in the Late Modern Age*. Cambridge: Polity.

Gilligan, C. (1993). *In a Different Voice: Psychological Theory and Women's Development* (2nd edn.). Cambridge, MA: Harvard University Press.

Grimes, S. M., & Shade, L. R. (2005). Neopian economics of play: Children's cyberpets and online communities as immersive advertising in NeoPets.com. *International Journal of Media and Cultural Politics*, 1(2), 181–98.

Guzzetti, B. J. (2006). Cybergirls: Negotiating social identities on cybersites. *E-Learning*, 3(2), 158–69.

Harden, J. (2000). There's no place like home: The public/private distinction in children's theorizing of risk and safety. *Childhood*, 7(1), 43–59.

Harrison, C., Comber, C., & Fisher, T., et al. (2003). *ImpaCT2: The Impact of Information and Communication Technologies on Pupil Learning and Attainment*. Coventry: Becta.

Hasebrink, U., Livingstone, S., Haddon, L., & Ólafsson, K. (2009). Comparing children's online opportunities and risks across Europe: Cross-national comparisons for EU Kids Online. EU Kids Online Deliverable D3.2 for the EC Safer Internet Plus program, 2nd edn. http://eprints.lse.ac.uk/24368/.

Hawisher, G. E., & Selfe, C. L. (1998). Reflections on computers and composition studies at the century's end. In I. Snyder (ed.), *Page to Screen: Taking Literacy into the Electronic Era* (pp. 3–19). London and New York: Routledge.

Holloway, S. L., & Valentine, G. (2003). *Cyberkids: Children in the Information Age*. London: Routledge Falmer.

Hutchby, I. (2001). Technologies, texts and affordances. *Sociology*, 35(2), 441–56.

Jackson, S., & Scott, S. (1999). Risk anxiety and the social construction of childhood. In D. Lupton (ed.), *Risk and Sociocultural Theory: New Directions and Perspectives* (pp. 86–107). Cambridge: Cambridge University Press.

James, A., Jenks, C., & Prout, A. (1998). *Theorizing Childhood*. Cambridge: Cambridge University Press.

Jenkins, H. (2006). *Convergence Culture: Where Old and New Media Collide*. New York: New York University Press.

Kearney, M. C. (2007). Productive spaces: Girls' bedrooms as sites of cultural production. *Journal of Children and Media*, 1(2), 126–41.

Kerawalla, L., & Crook, C. (2002). Children's computer use at home and at school: Context and continuity. *British Educational Research Journal*, 28(6), pp. 751–71.

Larsson, K. (2003). Children's online life – and what parents believe: A survey in five countries. In C. Von Feilitzen & U. Carlsson (eds.), *Promote or Protect? Perspectives on Media Literacy and Media Regulations* (pp. 113–20). Goteborg, Sweden: Nordicom.

Lei, J., & Zhao, Y. (2007). Technology uses and student achievement: A longitudinal study. *Computers & Education*, 49, 284–96.

Lenhart, A., & Madden, M. (2005). *Teen Content Creators and Consumers*. Washington, DC: Pew Internet and American Life Project.

Lenhart, A., Rainie, L., & Lewis, O. (2001). *Teenage Life Online: The Rise of the Instant-Message Generation and the Internet's Impact on Friendships and Family Relationships*. Washington, DC: Pew Internet and American Life Project.

Levine, P., & Lopez, M. H. (2004). *Young People and Political Campaigning on the Internet – Fact Sheet*. Center for Information and Research on Civic Learning and Engagement (CIRCLE), University of Maryland. www.civicyouth.org.

Lievrouw, L., & Livingstone, S. (2006). Introduction. In L. Lievrouw & S. Livingstone (eds.), *Handbook of New Media: Social Shaping and Social Consequences* (updated student edn., pp. 1–14). London: Sage.

Lincoln, S. (2004). Teenage girls' bedroom culture: Codes versus zones. In A. Bennett & K. Harris (eds.), *After Subculture: Critical Studies of Subcultural Theory* (pp. 94–106). Hampshire: Palgrave MacMillan.

Lister, R., Smith, N., Middleton, S., & Cox, L. (2003). Young people talk about citizenship: Empirical perspectives on theoretical and political debates. *Citizenship Studies*, 7(2), 235–53.

Livingstone, S. (2002). *Young People and New Media: Childhood and the Changing Media Environment*. London: Sage.

Livingstone, S. (2003). Children's use of the Internet: Reflections on the emerging research agenda. *New Media & Society*, 5(2), 147–66.

Livingstone, S. (2007). From family television to bedroom culture: Young people's media at home. In E. Devereux (ed.), *Media Studies: Key Issues and Debates* (pp. 302–21). London: Sage.

Livingstone, S. (2008a). Internet literacy: Young people's negotiation of new online opportunities. In T. McPherson (ed.), *Digital Youth, Innovation, and the Unexpected* (vol. 4, pp. 101–22). Cambridge, MA: MIT Press.

Livingstone, S. (2008b). Taking risky opportunities in youthful content creation on the Internet. *New Media & Society*, 10 (special issue: Authority and participation with digital storytelling), 393–411.

Livingstone, S., & Bober, M. (2005). *UK Children Go Online: Final Report of Key Project Findings*. London: London School of Economics and Political Science.

Livingstone, S., & Bober, M. (2006). Regulating the Internet at home: Contrasting the perspectives of children and parents. In D. Buckingham & R. Willett (eds.), *Digital Generations* (pp. 93–113). Mahwah, NJ: Lawrence Erlbaum.

Livingstone, S., & Helsper, E. J. (2007). Gradations in digital inclusion: Children, young people, and the digital divide. *New Media & Society*, 9, 671–96.

Mancheva, G. (2006). "Child in the net" national campaign. National Center for Studies of Public Opinion, September 12. Summary at http://www.bnr.bg/RadioBulgaria/Emission_English/Theme_Lifestyle/Material/childinthenet.htm.

Marwick, A. (2005). *"I'm a Lot More Interesting than a Friendster Profile": Identity Presentation, Authenticity and Power in Social Networking Services*. Paper presented at the Association of Internet Researchers 6. http://www.aoir.org/?q=node/652&PHPSESSID=50eb48e5a551e1e8a27cd5d18909c240.

Mazzarella, S. R., & Pecora, N. (2007). Revisiting girls' studies: Girls creating sites for connection and action. *Journal of Children and Media*, 1(2), 105–25.

McRobbie, A., & Garber, J. (1976). Girls and subcultures. In S. Hall & P. Jefferson (eds.), *Resistance Through Ritual: Youth Cultures in Post War Britain* (pp. 209–22). Essex: Hutchinson University Library.

Mediappro (2006). *A European Research Project: The Appropriation of Media by Youth*. Brussels: Mediappro.

Merchant, G. (2007). Mind the gap(s): Discourses and discontinuity in digital literacies. *E-Learning*, 4(3), 241–55.

Meyer, D., & Staggenborg, S. (1996). Movements, countermovements, and the structure of political opportunity. *American Journal of Sociology*, 101(6), 1628–60.

Millwood Hargrave, A., & Livingstone, S. (2009). *Harm and Offence in Media Content: A Review of the Evidence*, 2nd edn. Bristol: Intellect.

Montgomery, K., Gottlieb-Robles, B., & Larson, G. O. (2004). *Youth as E-Citizens: Engaging the Digital Generation*. Washington, DC: Center for Social Media, American University. http://www.centerforsocialmedia.org/ecitizens/youthreport.pdf.

Muir, D. (2005). *Violence against Children in Cyberspace: A Contribution to the United Nations Study on Violence against Children*. Bangkok, Thailand: ECPAT International.

Nyboe, L., & Drotner, K. (2008). Identity, aesthetics and digital narration. In K. Lundby (ed.), *Mediatized Stories*. New York: Peter Lang.

Ofcom (2007). *The Future of Children's Television Programming: Research Report*. Ofcom.

Oswell, D. (1998). The place of childhood in Internet content regulation: A case study of policy in the UK. *International Journal of Cultural Studies*, 1(1), 131–51.

Phipps, L. (2000). New communications technologies: A conduit for social inclusion. *Information, Communication and Society*, 3(1), 39–68.

Piaget, J., & Inhelder, B. (1969). *The Psychology of the Child*. London: Routledge and Paul Kegan Ltd.

Prensky, M. (2001). Digital natives, digital immigrants. *On the Horizon*, 9(5), 1–6.

Qvortrup, J. (1994). *Childhood Matters: Social Theory, Practice and Politics*. Avebury: Aldershot.

Rice, R., & Haythornthwaite, C. (2006). Perspectives on Internet use: Access, involvement and interaction. In L. Lievrouw & S. Livingstone (eds.), *Handbook of New Media: Social Shaping and Social Consequences* (updated student edn., pp. 92–113). London: Sage.

Rogers, E. M. (1995). *Diffusion of Innovations* (vol. 4). New York: Free Press.

Silverstone, R. (2006). Domesticating domestication: Reflections on the life of a concept. In T. Berker, M. Hartmann, Y. Punie, & K. J. Ward (eds.), *The Domestication of Media and Technology* (pp. 229–48). Maidenhead: Open University Press.

Smith, R., & Curtin, P. (1998). Children, computers and life online: Education in a cyber-world. In I. Snyder (ed.), *Page to Screen: Taking Literacy into the Electronic Era* (pp. 211–33). London: Routledge.

Sparkes, J. (1999). *Schools, Education and Social Exclusion*: Centre for Analysis of Social Exclusion.

Star, L., & Bowker, G. (2002). How to infrastructure. In L. Lievrouw & S. Livingstone (eds.), *Handbook of New Media: Social Shaping and Consequences of ICTs*. London: Sage.

Stern, S. (2008). Producing sites, exploring identities: Youth online authorship. In D. Buckingham (ed.), *Youth, Identity, and Digital Media* (vol. 6, pp. 95–117). Cambridge, MA: MIT Press.

Tapscott, D. (1997). *Growing Up Digital: The Rise of the Net Generation*. New York: Mc-Graw Hill.

Thiessen, V., & Looker, E. D. (2007). Digital divides and capital conversion: The optimal use of information and communication technology for youth reading achievement. *Information, Communication & Society*, 10(2), 159–80.

Thompson, J. B. (1995). *The Media and Modernity: A Social Theory of the Media*. Cambridge: Polity.

United Nations. (1989). Convention on the Rights of the Child. Retrieved January 29, 2008, from http://www2.ohchr.org/english/law/crc.htm.

Valkenburg, P. M. (2004). *Children's Responses to the Screen: A Media Psychological Approach*. Mahwah, NJ: Lawrence Erlbaum.

Van Rompaey, V., Roe, K., & Struys, K. (2002). Children's influence on Internet access at home: Adoption and use in the family context. *Information, Communication and Society*, 5(2), 189–206.

Vasudevan, L. (2006). Making known differently: Engaging visual modalities as spaces to author new selves. *E-Learning*, 3(2), 207–16.

Vygotsky, L. ([1934] 1986). *Thought and Language*. Cambridge, MA: MIT Press.

Webwise (2006). *Survey of Children's Use of the Internet: Investigating Online Risk Behaviour*. Dublin, Ireland: Webwise.

Wolak, J., Mitchell, K. J., & Finkelhor, D. (2006). *Online Victimization of Youth: Five Years On*. Durham, NH: University of New Hampshire: National Center for Missing and Exploited Children.

Ziehe, T. (1994). From living standard to life style. *Young: Nordic Journal of Youth Research*, 2(2), 2–16.

17

Internet and Games

T. L. Taylor

As an Internet and games researcher, I have long had a foot in these two scholarly communities which have grown up nearly simultaneously. Writing a chapter on the subject of the two therefore provides an interesting opportunity to trace their interweaving. Whether it is the actual playing of games online or, just as important, the ways the Internet has been a powerful medium in forming and sustaining game culture writ large, neither the history of the Internet nor the history of computer games can be told without reference to the other. They are deeply interwoven and have co-constructed each other along the way. In the following I will map out a bit of this history and then unpack several key areas of research in the field, including work on the social and psychological aspects of online play, as well as some persistent critical issues that continue to warrant our attention.

Brief History of Online Gaming

While this chapter will give an overview of some key research areas within the domain of the Internet and games, a short overview of critical development points is warranted to help give some context. It is important to remember that if we start our history of online gaming with the near past of, for example, massively multi-player online games (MMOG), we miss some earlier influential markers – points which suggest that for decades now the space of play has found a home within networked domains. Even in 1969 we can see computational technology linked with networking being used for games, as in a version of *Spacewar!* which ran on PLATO, originally a computer-based educational system developed in the 1970s. These very early systems, precursors to the Internet as we know it now, hosted a number of games that got played by research scientists, faculty, and students.[1]

While many of these early networked games were accessible only to people working with restricted-access computers and directly tied to university and research networks, the bulletin board system (BBS) scene brought networked gaming to a larger population.[2] Homegrown BBSs dating back to the late 1970s hosted some of the first computer games. Using modems to connect users to each other, these systems form a fascinating early branch of online gaming history. By the mid 1980s a BBS protocol system called the Door allowed users to access a variety of games, directly linking actual play with being on the system. *Legend of the Red Dragon* (still being maintained), for example, was a popular early role-playing game (released in 1989) for BBS users which allowed them to collectively work on game goals. In addition BBSs were used to exchange game files or tips with other users, thus helping grow a more general game culture. With the development of larger commercial or state-sponsored systems (in the US CompuServe and in France Minitel stand out as notable examples) much of the networking functionality found in grassroots BBSs (including games) was brought to a larger public.

With the global development and expansion of the Internet across a growing number of university and research organizations there was also an emergence of new forms of computer gaming. In 1979 the first MUD (multi-user dungeon) was developed by Richard Bartle and Roy Trubshaw while they were at Essex University. Using text and basic telnet protocol, MUD systems allowed users to simultaneously enter online virtual worlds together. Early systems had a close kinship to *Dungeons and Dragons* (1974) game structures and were influenced by fantasy literature like *The Lord of the Rings* (1954), while later adaptations of the genre broadened out to provide worlds that were more building and chat focused (such as in the TinyMUD and MOO architectures). As a genre, MUDding plays a powerful historical role in the history of both our current 3D massively multiplayer online games and in non-game worlds for the ways it developed the notion of synchronous engagement and play in a virtual space.

Somewhat different from these (often fantasy) world environments was the development of the first-person shooter (FPS) genre and its networked play. *Doom* (1993) marks one of the earliest and most notable games of its type, allowing players on a network to simultaneously enter a space together to shoot monsters and opponents. While primarily played on LAN networks it is an important historical node for bringing together the genre of FPS with multi-user play. Built on an often strong team-based component these games have grown to be a popular genre, with titles like *Counter-Strike* (1999) sustaining not just a vibrant game community but also a professional gaming scene.

While MUDs originate in the pre-web period and FPS titles like *Doom* helped launch a new genre of networked gaming, simultaneous to their development was the porting to the Internet of more traditional titles. Versions of chess, accessed via telnet, or even *Scrabble* were for example quite popular in the earliest days of the Internet. And once graphical browsers for the web were created traditional board and card games also found a home on websites like Yahoo! Games or the Internet Gaming Zone (now MSN Games) where users could play things like bridge, hearts, *Monopoly*, and backgammon for free. So while computers and the Internet allowed for the creation and expansion of some new forms of gaming, they also helped sustain a much longer tradition of board and card games and titles that were familiar to many people who might not otherwise consider themselves "gamers."

This history is not a simple linear progression in which current forms have overtaken earlier ones. Even now one might still go online and play a game of chess using simple telnet and ASCII text, visit a MUD, or play the newest map of an FPS. The history of Internet gaming is one in which new genres and formats emerge but passionate player communities also remain around old favorites and indeed are sustained as networking and information tools become available. Websites and wikis have allowed communities of interest to form around objects that may have long passed out of popular fashion.

The final threads in contemporary Internet gaming take several forms: MMOGs, web browser-based games, and networked console (and even phone) gaming. MMOGs have received a fair amount of press in the last several years as their player-base has broadened out. Owing a strong debt to both early MUDs but also 3D gaming technology, MMOGs – which date back to titles like *Meridian 59* (1996) and *Ultima Online* (1997) – now provide millions of players around the world with an opportunity to game together with other players, using avatars, in fantastical environments. Quite often MMOG players also use voice tools to chat and coordinate their adventures, a development that is relatively new to online gaming.

While traditional MMOGs are based on large-scale worlds and often have heavy time investments and computational requirements, there is a growing category of multiplayer games that are more amenable to casual players due to their accessible mechanisms and user interface, as well as potentially shorter, flexible play sessions. Generally speaking they are also not based on massive virtual world spaces, backstories, and lore but instead are structured around tighter and smaller scenarios. Titles such as *PuzzlePirates* or *KartRider*, while often not boasting as many simultaneous players as some of the larger standalone MMOGs, are nonetheless a popular genre and growing in stature. Popular websites like PopCap or Pogo host hundreds of games, often produced by small to mid-sized development companies. There are also a number of initiatives as developers work on tying the web to online games and virtual worlds (*Metaplace* and *Warbook* are notable in this regard). And though often less reported on in popular media, web browser-based gaming supports a huge number of players as well, often reaching a more diverse demographic than normally associated with gaming (IGDA 2006). Web-based games, while commonly seen as more "casual" due to their shorter per-game duration than many other forms, nonetheless support dedicated playing.

Finally, the newest development in online gaming is coming through the growth of console-based play. While there were some attempts that tried as early as 1998 to connect players to each other (the Sega Dreamcast and its popular title *Phantasy Star Online* being notable) we now see real development of networking gaming through these devices. With the widespread growth of broadband access in the home and the enthusiasm for networked games via titles like

World of Warcraft, many console game developers have expanded their offerings to not only include online multiplayer components, but allow players to share their game data online, comparing statistics and achievements and in general building the gamer community. Xbox Live now boasts 10 million users and both the PlayStation 3 and the Wii have networking capabilities built in. With this trend in functionality console players get opportunities to play with others from around the world, and build communities around games (the Xbox Live gamer tags and achievements are both interesting examples in this regard).

While thus far I have focused on briefly discussing games that could be played online, the Internet has also been a powerful factor in not only sustaining play but distributing games themselves. From the early BBS days sharing games was an important function networking provided. While the past decade has witnessed the rise of the high-profile commercial game developer with big budget titles and boxed products, we are in many ways returning to the early roots of game culture where titles get distributed and shared via online mechanisms. The Internet allows for a renaissance for smaller developers who use their websites to distribute titles and support fledging game communities around them.

Commercial distribution venues like Valve's Steam provide both mainstream and independent developers a platform for sharing games. Microsoft's game development tool, XNA, and its distribution methods are another branch facilitating these kinds of productions. In addition, all the major consoles now boast digital distribution mechanisms for their games and content via their XboxLive, PS Network, and WiiWare systems. Whether it is providing new titles for distribution and download or adding additional content to existing games players have already purchased, many companies are starting to take advantage of closely linking the Internet with their products.

Finally the Internet has for a very long time now been a prime distribution mechanism for fan communities to share old games and develop emulation systems for long-extinct gaming devices. Whether it was distributing old games via the Usenet system or harnessing the power of newer BitTorrent technology, players have long been using whatever communication tools available to keep their (often niche) game cultures alive. While the rest of this chapter will focus more on actual play and game culture on the Internet, we should keep in mind the ways it is also a powerful tool for distribution, a key component of gaming.

Player (and Character) Identity

Of the many genres of games played online there is a sub-set that has attracted a fair amount of scholarly attention over the years for the special ways games of this sort intersect with complex psychological processes. Online multiplayer games – from early MUDs to more contemporary MMOGs – immerse players in virtual worlds that they simultaneously inhabit with others. Using avatars, originally text-based but now typically graphical representations of one's self, players create identities and engage with others in communities online. Because of the particular mechanism of creating a character tied to a digital representation one issue that has arisen in scholarship concerns the nature of online identity and the line between our online and offline selves.

The notion that one could go online and experiment with identity has been explored by a number of authors over the years who investigated multi-user games. Sherry Turkle's (1995) early influential work documented the way MUD players used those characters and systems as a way of often "working through" complex psychological issues.[3] In a MUD, they might explore a side of themselves that remained in the background or taboo offline. They might tackle emotionally weighty issues through their relationships and actions in the online world. The importance of this work, and that of other authors like Stone (1995) and Dibbell (1998) is that they sought to introduce into the conversation questions about how our understanding of ourselves is affected in online spaces and the potentials for experimentation. Given the popularity of games that allow for character creation in multiplayer environments the status of one's online identity remains regularly discussed by not only academics but players themselves.

Simultaneous to research on the more experimental side of identity in these spaces was work that sought to problematize the notion that one simply goes online and sheds offline traits, value sets, or frameworks. Work by scholars like Lori Kendall (2002), Beth Kolko (2000), and Lisa Nakamura (1995) have made important contributions by highlighting the ways things like race, gender, class, and powerful offline inequalities continued to exert themselves in important ways in these new spaces. These themes have also been picked up by some contemporary game studies scholars who continue to highlight the ways offline identity structures operate in online spaces, for example the way race, ethnicity, gender, embodiment, and sexuality continue to exert themselves within networked game worlds (Consalvo, 2003; Kennedy, 2005; Lahti, 2003; Leonard, 2006; Steinkuehler, 2005).

If we look at gender and online gaming, for example, we can see that while there has long been a stereotype that these technologies are not of interest to women and indeed an industry that has historically sidelined them as gamers, women have long been engaged players, often despite barriers to entry. While the game industry slowly seems to be taking notice, wanting to include women and girls more, often the framework for doing so relies on clichéd understandings of gender and leisure. There also remains at times the thorny issue of representation in games, and in particular the complicated relationship between aesthetics and play (Carr et al., 2006; Dovey & Kennedy, 2006; Krzywinksa, 2005). Finally, in some segments of game culture women often find they have to run a kind of gauntlet to participate, that the domain is not only governed by young men, but governed by ones invested in constructing and enforcing particular forms of masculinity. And while there is a growing body of literature on women and games, there has been very little exploring masculinity specifically and how it is constructed and enacted via computer gaming. As such there remain a number of areas within game studies that still call for serious attention to the ways gender intersects this growing form of contemporary play. The work done by feminist game scholars who try to tell a complex story which weaves together the issue of offline identity, player experience, game culture, and the specificities of gameplay has been an important conceptual intervention in understanding the nuanced relationship between player and game.

Nuance is central in approaching the study of online gaming in particular. A study of a game world can have important differences from that of a non-game space in that there are key ludic elements at work in shaping not only what occurs, how but it is meaningfully interpreted and understood by players (and at times pushed back on and altered). One of the most important iterations on this issue of player and character identity in online games has been the ways game studies scholars have tried to pay particular attention to how the specificities of the game space – with mechanics and logics of its own – complicate the terrain. Game scholars interested in the issue of player experience and game culture must give additional consideration to grounding their analysis within the game sphere specifically and think about how the requirements and structures of the game challenge a notion that people simply go online and freely experiment and construct play experience.

Identity creation and performance in, for example, a role-play space may have different nuances and outcomes than what happens in a player-versus-player scenario or in a non-game virtual world (Tronstad, 2007). Questions of identity experimentation have taken a slightly different turn then in the work of scholars who have looked at the role-play aspects of many of these spaces. Work by people like Torill Mortensen (2003) and Marinka Copier (2007) have tried to situate the kinds of character development we see in these spaces within a framework where gameplay intersects with identity construction, social action, and collective meaning. This merging of what we might think of as a ludological approach with more traditional Internet studies helps us refine analysis around the specificities of game worlds in particular.

The focus on in-game behavior and practices can also be found in Richard Bartle's (1996) influential work on player types and their typical orientations to online multiplayer games. Though refined in his later book (2004), his basic typology of killer, achiever, socializer, and explorer continues to be a frame investigated by many others. The work is notable for the way it provides both a relational framework – both between the categories but also via a consideration of how such identities and activities are informed by their location within a game structure. Scholars like Nick Yee (2002) have sought to expand this line of inquiry through researching the relationship between online and offline identities in play spaces. He has, in particular, examined the complex motivations for play in online games and how playtime is influenced and informed by offline issues. His ambitious Daedalus Project, for example, on MMOGs, has collected over a period of six years data from 40,000 people who have visited his site and answered a number of questions about their experience of online play, including things like identity development and gender swapping.

Studying Communities In and Around Games

The issues of socialization, communication, and distributed play go to the heart of Internet game culture. Online gaming allows people to either play with strangers from around the world or create shared situations with their already existing family and friends. It is important to consider the two prongs of how the social can be formulated here. The first is in looking at the actual play situations themselves, mediated through the Internet. The second area however is the way the Internet facilitates the ongoing production of game culture writ large.

Playing with others

From FPS clans to MMOG guilds to groups of people who play Yahoo! bridge together every week, online games have been hugely influential in allowing people to come together online and interact in and around play spaces. This aspect of online gaming is one of the oldest and it crosses genres. Sometimes the nature of playing together is cooperative – as in the *World of Warcraft* guild that attempts for numerous weeks to finally take down a powerful monster in the game or the *Battlefield 1942* team that refines tactics and teamwork. At other times play is primarily competitive or oppositional – seeking out the top spot on a high-score list, moving up the rankings ladder in one's favorite game, or competing in a player-versus-player match. And because network technology is a powerful way of bringing together distributed populations, we also have an instantiation of playing together that is about sharing and communication, such as when people visit each other's *Animal Crossing* towns via the Internet or swap items for their game worlds (as with *The Sims*).

Playing together online dovetails with many of the experiences tracked in Internet studies over the last several decades. Game groups are communities of practice who build systems of membership and norms. Their members are often passionately engaged not only with the game, but with their community and the relationships with each other (Jakobsson & Taylor, 2003). Many report that they stay with a title long after the game itself has interested them simply because of the people there. The social side of games, and a player's experience of one over the years as they progress, reveals a nuanced lifespan of a game with varying activities and networks that range from casual group interactions and solo play to large-scale coordinating raiding (Chen, 2009; Jakobsson, 2006; Simon, 2007; Thomas & Seely Brown, 2007). And as technologies are developed and extended into gaming spaces we see additional patterns of socialization and bonding emerge, for example with guilds that use voice communication (Williams, Caplan, & Xiong, 2007). Playing together online has proven to be one of the most powerful developments not only in game culture, but in the ways mainstream society is reinserting play through games into everyday life and increasingly legitimizing the notion that we may spend leisure time in these spaces.

Creating game culture

Beyond synchronous playing together however is the powerful way the Internet has been used to create and sustain game culture more generally. Player communities are brought together via websites to talk about games, and sometimes even thorny issues like cheating (Consalvo, 2007). Forums are widely used by groups of players in guilds, clans, and teams to organize their activities and create a community of players. Websites which host databases or wikis are regularly used for the production of collective knowledge about particular titles which are regularly used by players to facilitate their play. Video sites allow people to distribute walkthroughs and footage of skill demonstrations, and to produce machinima (Lowood, 2006). And most recently podcasts have allowed huge numbers of people to become amateur broadcasters, putting together shows covering their favorite games or topics of interest.

The network aspect has allowed for a kind of complex globalization of game culture, one which taps into issues of cultural importation and, often uneasily, socialization. In addition to the games that support players from different parts of the world on the same server (*Lineage 2* is a prime example of how the Japanese and American player-base is supported on shared worlds, although at times ambivalently), the Internet has been a powerful mechanism for people who are interested in titles that may otherwise be inaccessible to them due to sales restrictions or language and cultural barriers. Collective work to provide tools for breaking region coding, translation for titles, and websites that (often illegally) sell titles across national and regional borders have helped created a more global game culture (Sun, Lin, & Ho, 2003). Though regionalism still holds powerful sway (game companies themselves often actively segment markets for example and indeed communities can face globalization of their player-base in often fractious ways) game culture as mediated through the Internet is nonetheless fairly massive, distributed, and global.

Digital Play Industry and The Co-Construction of Games

Though their history is rooted in the homebrew, research, and fan communities, games have become a significant commercial industry and online gaming traverses a number of sectors that range from global production houses to policy and legal decisions by governments. Games are a growing and influential part of a larger media economy and as such they are also involved in broader conversations happening in that sphere around participation, reuse, audience influence, and cross-media engagement (Deuze, 2007; Jenkins, 2006). Questions about the status of games as media co-constructed objects (built from the passionate engagement of both formal designers and players) must engage with work that explores a structural analyses of gaming *vis-à-vis* its location in larger transnational industries that regularly intersect with governmental bodies (Ernkvist & Ström, 2008; Jin & Chee, 2008: Kline, Dyer-Witheford, & De Peuter, 2003). Considerations of the structure of the game industry, its processes and imaginations about its players, and in turn players' relationship to their games and altering them provide valuable ground to explore (Kerr, 2006; O'Donnell, 2008).

Player-designers

As can be seen in several of these critical issues raised above, one of the things that becomes apparent is the complex relationship between the imagined user for whom systems are designed and how systems actually get used in practice. Player communities often create new rules and norms around how they interact with game systems and indeed sometimes developers provide tools to help them then translate those practices and desires into technologies that feed back into the game (as with modding, the practice of player-modification of games). What this produces is a more complex picture of games – one in which gamers don't simply take products at face value and play them as intended off the shelf, they produce an emergent culture in and around them. While there are a few examples of developers integrating active players into their development process (Banks, 2002), the implications of this trend – be it in developing tools and methods for ongoing iterative development or participatory design, or in providing communities ways of managing themselves and influencing developers meaningfully – have yet to be explored fully in design practice.

Through their practices players transform the spaces they inhabit, often having productive impacts on how professional game designers make the spaces. Modding in computer games has, for example, proven to be a powerful method for players' productive engagement in reconfiguring games to cycle back into official releases of a title (Postigo, 2003, 2007; Sotamaa, 2007). But in addition to creating software, the practices of communities – in forming norms for their server, rules for how to play that may not be in the manual, practices for socializing new players into how things are done, and regulations for community behavior – also point to the productive power of users (Steinkuehler, 2006; Taylor, 2006, 2007). These emergent practices of playing together shape what games are and how current and future designers create titles.

Managing emergence

Game culture has long been contested territory. Whether it be governments wanting to regulate how much their citizenries play, companies seeking to carve out territories that are controlled through region encoding, or developers holding a tight rein on how actual play unfolds in their game worlds, the issue of governance and the regulation of gamers and their play is key (Grimmelman, 2006; Humphreys, 2005; Pargman, 2000; Smith, 2007; Taylor, 2006c). In-game protests by MMOG players are not infrequent, though regularly shut down by game managers and deemed illegitimate activity. Community managers for various games participate not only in fostering the community but also in regulating conversation and gameplay. As many games become small micro-societies companies are often confronted with having to tackle complex social issues and regulatory decisions. And in addition to the management work happening within games, ongoing activities of adept players to circumvent formal systems of control are widely prevalent. Rogue servers, cracked and bootleg copies of software (distributed over the Internet or via physical copies), and third-party applications that assist gameplay in ways deemed illegitimate by game companies all highlight the tension that can exist between what some players feel they should be allowed to do and what game developers claim governance over.

Very closely tied to the issues of regulation and governance is an ongoing debate about the legal status of game artifacts and the player activity around them (Hunter & Lastowka, 2004). With the growth of the modding community, machinima, and the amount of time and investment many players put into their game characters, the issue of whose game it is and, most importantly, what the legitimate boundaries are for use, re-use, and modification become ever more pressing. While on the one hand game developers are actively enlisting their player-base to refine and improve their games (with everything from beta-testing to modding user-interfaces) they are also always drawing a line in the sand in which they claim seemingly immovable intellectual property (IP) and ownership rights. This approach, one we see in the culture broadly, where IP rights have been well extended and vigorously defended, can at times seem out of step with the passionate enlistment of the labor of many players. Given the way ongoing game development and refinement can look more like a circuit between developers, designers, and players (versus a one-way distribution path), notions of co-creation present themselves in constant dialogue to an often regressive formulation of ownership and governance.

One emerging issue that intersects not only the governance and IP issue, but questions about the relationship between online and offline, in-game and out-game, is around real-money trade (RMT), that is, when players use their offline currency to purchase things for their in-game play. Hotly debated by both scholars and players, RMT provides a fascinating test case to explore larger conceptual and definitional issues (Dibbell, 2006). Sometimes RMT takes the form of authorized goods that players can buy from the game developer themselves, but just as regularly it comes in the form of illegal purchasing from game-currency sellers or power-leveling services of in-game goods, money, and services. While some game companies have been instituting formal mechanisms for players to pay "real world" cash for in-game artifacts or mechanisms, there remain a number of developers and designers who feel such practices undermine the meritocracy of the game or, in the case of unauthorized selling, compromise the inherent IP rights of the authors. As gaming takes on an increasingly distributed and networked character via the Internet such issues, which go to the heart of what it means to be engaged in play online and the relationship between domains, are sure to be ones we debate for years to come.

Conclusion

While we are now several decades into Internet research and well approaching a decade for game studies there remain some key areas that continue to pose challenges for those interested in the social and political aspects of online gaming. For the most part these issues hit massively multiplayer gaming most directly, though some other genres are also touched by them. One larger conceptual debate that intersects most of the areas described above – be it research done on player experience and characters, game culture, emergent play, and regulatory/governance issues – is the status of what is termed the "magic circle." Coined by Johan Huizinga (1955), the magic circle notion invokes the idea that game space is bracketed off and separated from our normal everyday life norms and practices – that it operates with special rules distinct from how we usually govern our behavior and that when we step into it, we agree to these rules and adopt this new ludic stance.

Within game studies there is ongoing debate around the notion of the magic circle along several axis: the benefits and costs of this conceptual framework, any normative assumptions that are used when it is invoked, and finally whether or not it has meaningful empirical basis. Some authors have expressed concern about when the boundaries of the "virtual" game space become porous to the "real" or when the rules of the game world are overtaken by those of offline life (Castronova, 2005, 2007). As we have seen in both game and Internet studies however, actual actors regularly cross and blur these lines, prompting such a position to be more normative than empirical in its framing. By contrast there is a growing body of work that is simultaneously problematizing this approach by introducing empirical work on the everyday experiences of play and the role of contingency in games (Malaby, 2006, 2007; Taylor, 2006a, 2006b). Indeed if we look to both work in traditional Internet studies and a range of research within game studies, the issue of the boundary line (offline/online, in-game/out-game) has historically been quite thorny and continues to be widely debated by researchers, developers, and players.

Another area in the developing landscape of the Internet and games worth our sharp focus revolves around globalization. Given that the rhetoric of the Internet is powerfully woven through with this notion more can certainly be done to investigate how it is operating in game culture. While there are many examples of game titles crossing national boundaries, very little has been done in documenting the complicated ways this occurs – both within the development process but also in relation to the labor of gamers who circulate products and information. There has also been very little research done exploring whether or not game culture is one in which globalization is increasing or actually contracting, for example via the use of regional encoding and enforcement schemes, breaking massively multiplayer game worlds into regionally based servers, and other forms of localization. Finally, while there have been some studies looking at cross-cultural comparisons of play in computer games (Chen, Duh et al., 2006), much more could be done to tease out the relation between "the global" and "the local" in terms of practices (in both play and design). While there are important specificities in game forms and play practices worldwide, games simultaneously often inhabit a global economy and game culture writ large, and much more could be done to understand how network technology is shaping this part of the domain.

Traveling hand-in-hand, the growth of the Internet and the development of networked play present us with fascinating new areas of leisure, work, and exploration – both as scholars and gamers. Internet and game studies have fruitful points of dialogue with each other, though the specific ludic qualities of online play at times require an additional layer of analysis that contextualizes the particular structure of engagement. Whether it be in an interpersonal microanalysis of role-playing characters in a MMOG or large-scale structural studies of networked distribution mechanisms in the game industry, the range of activities taking place in online games lends itself to valuable work that helps us discuss everything from the nature of identity or the work/play boundary, to systems of authority and control. As such, online games are not simply a niche culture, but increasingly a vibrant site for understanding broader critical social processes.

Notes

Big thanks to Mia Consalvo, Mikael Jakobsson, Kelly Joyce, Richard Bartle, and Raph Koster (and his blog readers) for assistance with this chapter.

1 For an excellent timeline history of online worlds, many of which were computer games, see Raph Koster's (2002) Online Worlds Timeline at http://www.raphkoster.com/gaming/mudtimeline.shtml.

2 Though not commonly thought of within the scope of the Internet, it is important to remember that early BBSs, with their links into FidoNet, provided some of the first paths into email and newsgroups for non-university/research-based computer users. The larger commercial and public systems mentioned also provided an important bridge technology for non-university-based users.

3 Indeed Turkle picks up this notion of the computer as not only a computational device but one we enlist in our psychological processes in her book *The Second Self* (1984).

References

Banks, J. (2002). Gamers as co-creators: Enlisting the virtual audience – A report from the net face. In M. Balnaves, T. O'Regan, & J. Sternberg (eds.), *Mobilising the Audience* (pp. 188–212). St Lucia, Queensland: University of Queensland Press.

Bartle, R. (1996). Hearts, clubs, diamonds, spades: Players who suit MUDs. *Journal of MUD Research*, 1(1). http://www.mud.co.uk/richard/hcds.htm.

Bartle, R. (2004). *Designing Virtual Worlds*. Indianapolis: New Riders.

Carr, D., Buckingham, D., Burn, A., & Schott, G. (2006). *Computer Games: Text, Narrative and Play*. Cambridge: Polity.

Castronova, E. (2005). *Synthetic Worlds: The Business and Culture of Online Games.* Chicago: University of Chicago Press.

Castronova, E. (2007). *Exodus to the Virtual World: How Online Fun is Changing Reality.* New York: Palgrave Macmillan.

Chen, M. (2009). Communication, coordination, and camaraderie in *World of Warcraft. Games and Culture.*

Chen, V. H., Duh, H. B., Kolko, B., Whang, L. S., & Fu, M. C. (2006). Games in Asia Project. Conference on Human Factors in Computing Systems, Montréal, Québec, Canada.

Consalvo, M. (2003). Hot dates and fairy-tale romances: Studying sexuality in video games. In M. J. P. Wolf & B. Perron (eds.), *The Video Game Theory Reader* (pp. 171–94). New York: Routledge.

Consalvo, M. (2007). *Cheating: Gaining Advantage in Videogames.* Cambridge, MA: MIT Press.

Copier, M. (2007). Beyond the magic circle: A network perspective on role-play in online games. Dissertation thesis, Utrecht School of the Arts, Utrecht, The Netherlands.

Deuze, M. (2007). *Media Work: Digital Media and Society.* Cambridge: Polity.

Dibbell, J. (1998). *My Tiny Life: Crime and Passion in a Virtual World.* New York: Henry Holt and Company.

Dibbell, J. (2006). *Play Money: Or, How I Quit My Day Job and Made Millions Trading Virtual Loot.* New York: Basic Books.

Dovey, J., & Kennedy, H. W. (2006). *Game Cultures: Computer Games as New Media.* Berkshire, UK: Open University Press.

Ernkvist, M., & Ström, P. (2008). Enmeshed in games with the government: Governmental policies and the development of the Chinese online game industry. *Games and Culture,* 3(1), 98–26.

Grimmelmann, J. (2006). Virtual power politics. In J. M. Balkin & B. S. Noveck (eds.), *The State of Play: Law, Games, and Virtual Worlds* (pp. 146–57). New York: New York University Press.

Huizinga, J. (1955). *Homo Ludens: A Study of the Play Element in Culture.* Boston: Beacon Press.

Humphreys, S. (2005). Productive users, intellectual property and governance: The challenges of computer games. *Media Arts Law Review,* 10(4). http://www.law.unimelb.edu.au/cmcl/malr/10-4-4%20Humphreys%20formatted%20for%20web.pdf.

Hunter, D., & Lastowka, G. (2004). The laws of the virtual worlds. *California Law Review,* 92(1). http://papers.ssrn.com/sol3/papers.cfm?abstract_id=402860.

IGDA (International Game Developers Association) (2006). *Casual Games Whitepaper.* http://www.igda.org/wiki/index.php/Casual_Games_SIG/Whitepaper.

Jakobsson, M. (2006). Questing for knowledge: Virtual worlds as dynamic processes. In R. Schroeder & A-S Axelsson (eds.), *Avatars at Work and Play: Collaboration and Interaction in Shared Virtual Environments.* Dordrecht: Springer.

Jakobsson, M., & Taylor, T. L. (2003). The Sopranos meets EverQuest: socialization processes in massively multi-user games. *FineArt Forum,* 17(8). http://www.itu.dk/~tltaylor/cv.html.

Jenkins, H. (2006). *Convergence Culture: Where Old and New Media Collide.* New York: New York University Press.

Jin, D. Y., & Chee, F. (2008). Age of new media empires: A critical interpretation of the Korean online game industry. *Games and Culture,* 3(1), 38–58.

Kendall, L. (2002). *Hanging Out in the Virtual Pub: Masculinities and Relationships Online.* Berkeley: University of California Press.

Kennedy, H. (2005). Psycho men slayers: Illegitimate, monstrous and out there: female Quake clans and inappropriate pleasures. In J. Hollows & R. Moseley (eds.), *Feminism in Popular Culture.* London: Berg.

Kerr, A. (2006). *The Business and Culture of Digital Games: Gamework/Gameplay.* London: Sage.

Kline, S., Dyer-Witheford, N., & De Peuter, G. (2003). *Digital Play: The Interaction of Technology, Culture, and Marketing.* Montreal: McGill-Queen's University Press.

Kolko, B. (2000). Erasing @race: Going white in the (inter)face. In B. Kolko, L. Nakamura, & G. B. Rodman (eds.), *Race in Cyberspace* (pp. 183–202). New York: Routledge.

Koster, R. (2002). *Online World Timeline.* http://www.raphkoster.com/gaming/mudtimeline.shtml.

Krzywinksa, T. (2005). Demon girl power: Regimes of form and force in videogames Primal and Buffy the Vampire Slayer. Women in Games Conference, Dundee, Scotland.

Lahti, M. (2003). As we become machines: Corporealized pleasures in video games. In M. J. P. Wolf & B. Perron (eds.), *The Video Game Theory Reader* (pp. 157–70). New York: Routledge.

Leonard, D. J. (2006). Not a hater, just keepin' it real: The importance of race- and gender-based game studies. *Games and Culture,* 1(1), 83–8.

Lowood, H. (2006). High-performance play: The making of machinima. *Journal of Media Practice,* 7(1), 25–42.

Malaby, T. M. (2006). Parlaying value: Capital in and beyond virtual worlds. *Games and Culture,* 1(2), 141–62.

Malaby, T. M. (2007). Beyond play: A new approach to games. *Games and Culture,* 2(2), 95–113.

Mortensen, T. E. (2003). Pleasures of the player flow and control in online games. Dissertation, Volda University College, Volda, Norway.

Nakamura, L. (1995). Race in/for cyberspace: Identity tourism and racial passing on the Internet. *Works and Days,* 13(1–2), 181–93.

O'Donnell, C. (2008). The work/play of the interactive new economy: Video game development in the United States and India. Dissertation, Science and Technology Studies, Rensselaer Polytechnic University, Troy, NY.

Pargman, D. (2000). *Code Begets Community: On Social and Technical Aspects of Managing a Virtual Community.* Linköping: Linköping University.

Postigo, H. (2003). From Pong to Planet Quake: Post-industrial transitions from leisure to work. *Information, Communication, and Society,* 6(4), 593–607.

Postigo, H. (2007). Of mods and modders: Chasing down the value of fan-based digital game modifications. *Games and Culture,* 2(4), 300–313.

Simon, B. (2007). Never playing alone: The social contextures of digital gaming. *Loading . . .* 1(1), 11–17.

Smith, J. H. (2007). Who governs the gamers? In J. P. Williams & J. H. Smith (eds.), *The Players' Realm: Studies on the Culture of Video Games and Gaming.* Jefferson, NC: McFarland & Company.

Sotamaa, O. (2007). On modder labour, commodification of play, and mod competitions. *First Monday,* 12(9). http://www.uic.edu/htbin/cgiwrap/bin/ojs/index.php/fm/article/view/2006/1881.

Steinkuehler, C. (2005). Cognition and learning in massively multiplayer online games: A critical approach. Dissertation, University of Wisconsin at Madison. Retrieved July 7, 2005, from http://website.education.wisc.edu/steinkuehler/papers/Steinkuehler_ch6b.pdf.

Steinkuehler, C. (2006). The mangle of play. *Games and Culture*, 1(3), 199–213.

Stone, A. R. (1995). *The War of Desire and Technology at the Close of the Mechanical Age.* Cambridge, MA: MIT Press.

Sun, C., Lin, H., & Ho, C. (2003). Game tips as a gift. Digital Games Research Association Conference, Utrecht University, The Netherlands.

Taylor, T. L. (2006a). *Play Between Worlds: Exploring Online Game Culture.* Cambridge, MA: MIT Press.

Taylor, T. L. (2006b). Does WoW change everything?: How a PvP server, multinational playerbase, and surveillance mod scene caused me pause. *Games and Culture*, 1(4), 1–20.

Taylor, T. L. (2006c). Beyond management: Considering participatory design and governance in player culture. *First Monday*, special issue no. 7. http://www.uic.edu/htbin/cgiwrap/bin/ojs/index.php/fm/article/view/1611/1526.

Thomas, D., & Seely Brown, J. (2007). The play of imagination: Extending the literary mind. *Games and Culture*, 2(2), 149–72.

Tronstad, R. (2007). Character identification in World of Warcraft: The relationship between capacity and appearance. In H. G. Corneliussen & J. W. Rettberg (eds.), *Digital Culture, Play, and Identity: A World of Warcraft Reader.* Cambridge, MA: MIT Press.

Turkle, S. (1984). *The Second Self: Computers and the Human Spirit.* New York: Simon & Schuster.

Turkle. S. (1995). *Life on the Screen: Identity in the Age of the Internet.* New York: Simon & Schuster.

Williams, D., Caplan, S., & Xiong, L. (2007). Can you hear me now? The social impact of voice in online communities. *Human Communication Research*, 33, 427–49.

Yee, N. (2002). *The Daedalus Project.* http://www.nickyee.com/index-daedalus.html.

18

Social Networks 2.0

Nancy K. Baym

"Web 2.0" is supposed to represent a new era of online communication in which users generate the content and fortunes may be made on a "dot.com" after all (Scholz, 2008). Of all the platforms taken as examples of Web 2.0, none seems to generate as much attention as social networking sites (SNSs), the domain on which this chapter will focus. MySpace has launched numerous national and regional efforts to legislate online interaction, people have been jailed for creating fake Facebook profiles, and pundits have worried that all of these sites have led the masses to forget the true meaning of "friend."

One might begin by questioning how much of Web 2.0 and online social networking is really new. As someone who has been studying online interactions since the early 1990s, I shake my head at the idea that the contemporary Internet is "user generated" while that which preceded it is not. The very phrase "user generated" only makes sense when there is an alternative, in this case something like "professionally generated for profit." Until 1994, this alternative did not exist. On an Internet with no World Wide Web, sponsored by the United States government, all of the content was generated by the people, for the people. We only call Web 2.0 "user generated" because a well-established class of professional content providers now dominates the Internet.

As this suggests, one thing that is new about Web 2.0 is that the domains in which people generate their content are now often for-profit enterprises. MySpace, YouTube, and Facebook are the best-known exemplars but are by no means unique. In the early 1990s when users created newsgroups and mailing lists in order to share content, they were the sole beneficiaries. Today when people create content, they continue to benefit, but so too do corporations such as Fox Interactive, Google, and the (as of this writing) privately held Facebook. I will return to this point toward the end of the chapter. For now, let us just note that successful SNS entrepreneurs are doing very well. Facebook sold 1.6 percent of their stock to Microsoft in 2007 for $240 million, suggesting a total valuation of $15 billion. In 2008 the popular European network Bebo was sold to America Online for

$850 million. When Last.fm was purchased in its entirety in 2007 for a comparatively paltry $280 million, it was more than enough to make instant multimillionaires of its three founders.

The ability of users to create content may not be new, but there are new phenomena afoot in SNSs. This chapter strives to identify what is novel in social networking online and to situate these sites in the larger context of the Internet's social history, as well as the history of human relationships preceding that first fateful log-on of 1969 (Hafner, 1998). After defining SNSs and briefly discussing their history, I turn to the three major themes that have characterized social research about the Internet since its beginnings: identity, relationships, and community (Baym, 2002; Silver, 2000a). The chapter closes with a brief discussion of the areas most ripe for future research.

Social Network Sites

The concept of a social network emerged in sociology in the 1950s, filling a middle ground between individuals and communities. Rather than describing an entirely new social formation, it represented a new way of looking at social structures. Allan (2006) grounds the study of social networks in early work by Barnes (1954) and Batt (1957). He points in particular to Wellman's work on "personal communities" throughout the last several decades. Wellman (e.g. 1988; Wellman et al., 2003) argues that a crucial social transformation of late modernism is a shift away from tightly bounded communities toward increasing "networked individualism" in which each person sits at the center of his or her own personal community. The concept replaces neither community nor individual, but brings a cultural shift enabled and accelerated by the Internet and related technologies to the fore.

Starting with any individual, one can identify a social network by expanding outwards to include that person's acquaintances and the interconnections among those acquaintances. The specific criteria by which social network scholars consider links worthy of inclusion in the network may vary from close ties to everyone a person knows in any capacity (Allan, 2006), a definitional quandary reflected in the decisions SNS users must make about which personal connections they will create through a site. To the extent that members of different people's social networks overlap and are internally organized, they may constitute groups, but social networks are egocentric and no two individuals will have identical social networks.

On the Internet, SNSs fill a middle ground between homepages and blogs in which the individual is primary, and online communities in which the group is primary. boyd and Ellison (2007) defined SNSs as "web-based services that allow individuals to (1) construct a public or semi-public profile within a bounded system, (2) articulate a list of other users with whom they share a connection, and (3) view and traverse their list of connections and those made by others within the system" (n.p.). It is not always clear what exactly should count as an SNS.

Some respondents to a survey I ran on Last.fm, a site which meets all of boyd's and Ellison's criteria said they didn't consider the site an SNS, and their answers to the question of which other SNSs they use indicated definitional boundaries that are fuzzy at best. YouTube and Twitter meet the criteria outlined by boyd and Ellison, yet most people use the former only as a video-viewing site and, with only 140 character updates as content, it's not clear that the latter is comparable to other SNSs.

Boyd and Ellison (2007) use the term "social *network* site" rather than "social *networking* site," in order to emphasize that these sites are more often used to replicate connections that exist offline than to build new ones. Their choice of noun over verb positions Web 2.0 as an extension of pre-existing social phenomena rather than as a transformation. Boyd and Ellison (2007) locate the origins of SNSs with the advent of SixDegrees.com in 1997, followed by AsianAvenue, BlackPlanet and MiGente, then LiveJournal and Cyworld (1999) and Lunarstorm (2000), all prior to the supposed advent of "Web 2.0." MySpace began in 2003, and Facebook in 2005.

Despite the similarities among sites, boyd and Ellison (2007) note that "the nature and nomenclature of these connections may vary from site to site" (n.p.), and that despite some technologically consistent features, SNSs are diverse (see also Hargittai, 2007). Most share profiles that include space for avatars (often, but by no means only, photographs of oneself), listings of personal information and interests, and listings of friends that, depending on the system's infrastructure may be mutual (as in Facebook and MySpace) or, less often, one-way (as on Twitter and LiveJournal). As Golder, Wilkinson, and Huberman (2007) say, "these links between people constitute the 'network' part of the social network, and enable sharing with friends" (p. 43).

Sites vary in their foci, technological affordances, regions in which they are most used, uses to which they are put, and social contexts that emerge through them. Consider, for instance, the contrasts between Last.fm and Facebook. Last.fm, based in England, is focused on music. Social networking is subsidiary to their primary goal of enabling music discovery. In contrast, Facebook, based in California, originated as a means to connect students within the same universities. Their mission is to support and create new personal relationships. Their music dimension remains marginal to their core focus. Facebook is enormously popular in the US and is rapidly gaining ground internationally. Last.fm is very popular in the UK and Europe, but (as of this writing) relatively unknown in the US (despite having been acquired by the American company CBS Corp).

The two sites differ in their affordances. Neither allows much flexibility in page design, as MySpace and LiveJournal do, but Facebook allows users more breadth in shaping their profile. Facebook users can add applications (including several from Last.fm) in order to shape their self-presentation, play games with their friends, and promote causes they find important. They can maintain photo albums, import blog posts, share items and videos from elsewhere on the net. Last.fm users can do very few of these things, but they can display the music they listen to in real time, create radio streams for others to hear, tag music and bands, author band wiki entries, and see personalized charts of their own and others' listening habits, which cannot be done on Facebook. Both sites allow users to create groups, and both recommend people with whom one might connect – Facebook by calculating the number of shared friends, Last.fm by calculating the number of shared listens. Not surprisingly, the two sites result in differing social contexts. While Facebook is seen as a space in which to socialize playfully with peers, Last.fm is all and only about music – one may socialize, but it's most likely going to be about music. Some of its users do not use its social features, friending no one, yet still have satisfying interaction with the site, a situation that would be unimaginable on Facebook.

Looking more broadly at the current array of SNSs available, one sees far more diversity than these two sites indicate. One point of variation is intended user population. Many are designed for very specific audiences, a tiny sampling of which might include BlackPlanet for African Americans, Schmooze for Jewish people, Jake for gay professional men, Ravelry for knitting enthusiasts, FanNation for sports fans, Vinorati for wine buffs, or Eons for aging baby boomers.

SNSs also vary considerably in their use across global regions. A map put together by French newspaper *Le Monde* shows national differences in SNS usage – MySpace and Facebook dominate North America, Orkut dominates Latin America with Hi5 coming in second, Bebo is most popular in Europe, Friendster in Indonesia, and LiveJournal in Russia. In addition to these international networks, smaller countries have their own regional sites such as LunarStorm in Sweden or Arto in Denmark. CyWorld is immensely successful in South Korea (*Le Monde*, 2008).

One lesson to take from the range of SNSs on offer and the variation in their features and geographical uptake is that "researchers should tread lightly when generalizing from studies about the use of one SNS to the use of another such service" (Hargittai, 2007, n.p.). Comparative work exploring the differences among sites and the social consequences of those variations will ultimately prove more valuable than efforts to focus on single sites or reduce the phenomena to a single field with uniform outcomes.

Identity

Authenticity

Since SNSs are built around individual profiles, questions of identity are germane to their analysis and have been the subject of most research. Internet researchers have a longstanding fascination with identity. Early online systems were text only, meaning that people who did not already know one another were often anonymous. This was seen as a danger, leading to increased "flaming" (Lea, O'Shea, & Spears, 1992) and worse, but also as an opportunity for identity play (O'Brien; 1999; Stone, 1995; Turkle, 1995). Despite the early focus on anonymity and deception, many early researchers (e.g. Baym, 1993; Curtis, 1997; Wellman, 1997) argued that identity play and deception were less common than identities closely tied to those claimed offline. In a study of personal homepages with particular relevance for studies of SNSs, Wynn and Katz (1998) showed that people usually contextualize themselves within offline communities by creating links to the sites of organizations with which they are associated.

As reflected in the choice of Milgrim's (1967) term "six degrees" for the first site, SNSs are grounded in the premise that both online and offline people would rather connect with those who share acquaintances. This can create trust and, at least in the abstract, render the dangers – and opportunities – of online anonymity passé (Donath & boyd, 2004). Yet this has not deterred public anxiety about the connections formed through SNSs. To the contrary, fears about deception and child predation have dominated the public discourse about SNSs in the United States and many other countries. The fear of technologically enabled dangerous liaisons is as old as communication technologies (Marvin, 1988; Standage, 1998). Though it is wise to beware of the limits of trust – both online and off – our understanding of SNSs is not improved by succumbing to the moral panic surrounding the authenticity of online identities (Marwick, 2008).

Audience and privacy

Another concern often tied to SNSs that is as old as communication technologies is privacy. Marvin (1988) recounts worries that callers could see into one's home via telephone lines in the early days of that technology. Standage (1998) tells of people fearing that messages sent across telegraph would be overheard by those beneath the wires. Identity is an inherently social concept. It makes no sense to claim an identity for no one; identities are performed for and perceived by others, and identities demand flexibility as different audiences require different aspects of one's self to be emphasized (Goffman, 1959). A crucial issue is thus audience. For whom is an identity created? By whom is it perceived? From whom might one want it hidden?

As Ellison, Steinfield, and Lampe (2007) argue, "popular press coverage has focused almost exclusively on the negative repercussions of Facebook use," mostly regarding "misalignments between users' perceptions about the audience for their profile and the actual audience" (n.p.). SNSs vary in the extent to which they allow users to control the accessibility of their profiles to search engines and other users. Orkut and Last.fm do not allow users to hide their profiles. On Orkut, not only are profiles visible to other users, but the chain of connection between any profile and a registered viewer is also displayed (Fragoso, 2006). In its default settings, Facebook makes all profiles visible to all members of a user's "network" (originally their university), though not to people outside the network or with no Facebook account. In a large university or city network, this can make a profile visible to tens of thousands of people if not more (my university network has nearly 40,000 members, city networks can have many times that). Default privacy settings are important since users rarely change them (Gross & Acquisti, 2005). In their study of Facebook, Gross and Acquisti (2005) found that users revealed a good deal of personal data and rarely limited access to that information.

In one of the few studies of rural American SNS users, Gilbert, Karahalios, and Sandvig (2008) found that rural women set profiles to private more often than did their urban counterparts, but that men didn't differ on this. These findings are consistent with Larson (2007), whose study of rural American Internet users found a great deal of mistrust about using the medium for interpersonal purposes. These studies raise unanswered questions about who modifies settings, how, and for what reasons.

Because SNSs often connect people who know one another, users may feel "a sense of false security" (boyd & Heer, 2006, n.p.) as they create personae for their "friends," not thinking of their online identity performance as the public or semi-public searchable act it is. When a profile is accessed by an unexpected viewer the results can be embarrassing or life-altering. Information posted in an SNS can be used outside of context with strong negative consequences, including lost jobs, revoked visas, imprisonment, and tarnished reputations (Snyder, Carpenter, & Slauson, 2006).

Even when SNS users have limited their profiles' visibility, they face the problem of collapsed contexts (boyd & Heer, 2006). As almost all SNSs are currently structured, friendship is a binary – one either is or is not a friend – despite the fact that in other social contexts, people have many degrees of friend and are selective about which information they reveal to whom. Facebook has "friends lists" that can be used to constrain which information people on each list can see, and Flickr allows people to limit the visibility of photographs to "friends" and/or "family." It is much more common, however, for all "friends" to have access to the same personal data, regardless of the degree to which one trusts any of them individually (Gross & Acquisti, 2005). Kim's and Yun's (2007) interviews with CyWorld users showed that one motivation for managing "minihompies" (profiles) was self-reflection. Thus, an important audience for one's online identity may be oneself, a person who presumably warrants far greater disclosure than even the closest peers.

Identity categories

Most SNSs provide predetermined sets of categories through which to build identities. The most important identity signals may be one's name and photograph. Their authenticity can be crucial to creating trust. MySpace, Last.fm, and many other sites do not care in the least what name one chooses. On Last.fm, it is unusual to see a real name and avatar pictures rarely depict the users. Cyworld, on the other hand, allows people to pick pseudonyms only after their identity has been verified and "the site's search functions are able to validate the name, date of birth, and gender of other users" (Kim & Yun, 2007, n.p.). Facebook requires real names, although their system for recognizing authenticity is flawed, resulting in multiple profiles bearing the names of celebrities, businesses, or websites. Baron (2008, p. 82) jokes, "if this rule is being followed, then Karl Marx, Anne Boleyn, and Kermit the Frog are alive and well." One survey of Facebook (Gross & Acquisti, 2005, n.p.) found that 89 percent of user names seemed to be real. Only 8 percent were clearly false and just 3 percent partial. Eighty percent had pictures that made them identifiable.

Unlike other online identity platforms, once users chose their names, SNSs provide them with categories to fill in on their profiles. Though the categories vary, most provide slots for demographic information including age, place of residence, and general interests – usually tastes in popular culture. Lampe and colleagues (2007) used automated data collection to collect profile information from all available profiles on their university's Facebook system and found that on average users filled in 59 percent of fields available to them. Gross and Acquisti (2005) found that 98.5 percent of Facebook users disclosed their full birthdates.

The ways in which predetermined categories both shape and constrain identity construction is most striking in the case of racial identity. In her analysis of BlackPlanet, Byrne (2007) reports that until 2005, members' only options for racial identification were black, Asian, Latino, Native American, and white. Following Nakamura (2002), she argues this "forces users into dominant notions of race" (n.p.), leaving little room for intercultural diversity or intra-racial identities. Other SNSs, such as MySpace, Last.fm, or Facebook do not provide any category for race, which, one might argue, reflects an effort to render race irrelevant or, following Silver (2000b), an assumption that the users, like most of the developers, are white.

Like race, nationality can be a charged identity category in SNSs. Last.fm displays all users' nationality if they've selected it from a drop-down list of options, leading to some distress from people such as Scots, who may not identify as residents of the United Kingdom (which is provided in the drop-down menu), but as residents of Scotland (which is not). The most striking example of this is Orkut (Fragoso, 2006). Orkut, owned by Google, launched as a US-based SNS in 2004. People could join only when invited by an existing member. Within a short time, Brazilians outnumbered every other country's members, a phenomenon which usually has been attributed to Brazilians' purported sociable and outgoing nature, an explanation which is surely inadequate (Fragoso, 2006). People began to construct their identities in terms of nationalism, leading to intense conflicts that were often grounded in language wars as Portuguese speakers colonized what had been English-language discussion groups.

Less charged, but more personally revealing are taste categories. Interest categorizations in online profiles originate in online dating sites (Fiore & Donath, 2005), where they are taken to imply interpersonal compatibility. The early SNS Friendster offered five categories (general interests, music, movies, television, and books) which are also used on MySpace, Facebook, and Orkut (Liu, 2007). Drawing on Simmel, Liu (2007) argues that this sort of taste identification is a way of performing individuality.

Both Liu (2007) and Donath (2007) emphasize the status-carrying potential of such lists. Donath (2007) describes identity cues in social networking sites as "signals of social position in an information based society" (n.p.). Liu (2007), uses Bourdieu to argue that "one's tastes are influenced both by socioeconomic and aesthetic factors. Socioeconomic factors – such as money, social class, and education – can shape tastes, because access to cultural goods may require possession of these various forms of capital" (n.p.).

Given that taste cues can generate status, their authenticity becomes problematic. People may list things they do not actually care for, or omit things they do care about, in order to create a public image in line with what they think others find attractive (Liu, Maes, & Davenport, 2006). In SNSs where people don't know one another through other means, audiences cannot distinguish false self-representations from honest ones, and hence can't punish inauthenticity (Donath, 2007). In SNSs where people do know one another, people have more reason to be honest, but then face the problems associated with collapsed audience contexts (Donath & boyd, 2004).

Another marker of status may be how many friends one has (boyd, 2006; Fono & Raynes-Goldie, 2006). In their work on Facebook, Lampe and colleagues (2007) found that number of friends was modestly positively correlated with self-descriptive content. In particular, people who included information on their profiles that indicated trustworthiness and thus made association with them less risky for others were more likely to have more friends.

Visible friends

Identity construction in SNSs is also distinguished from other forms of online communication in that one's connections are visible to others. Furthermore, others may contribute visible content to one's profile. Offline, where people often meet one another's friends, we all make strategic choices about which friends to expose to which other friends. In SNSs, all friends (and sometimes strangers) can see one's friends list. These lists provide context for interpreting a person and, as such, they can affect one's credibility and even perceived attractiveness (Walther et al., 2008). Donath and boyd (2004, p. 72) were among the first to note that displaying one's connection carries potential risk to one's reputation, writing that "[s]eeing someone within the context of their connections provides the viewer with information about them. Social status, political beliefs, musical taste, etc., may be inferred from the company one keeps." Thus, whatever one writes within a profile may be supported or undermined by the visible connections one has. SNSs themselves can vary in their trustworthiness by encouraging rampant friend collecting on the one extreme and making it difficult to add unknown friends on the other (Donath, 2007). LinkedIn, for instance, requires that one already knows the email address of a person or have a shared connection willing to make an introduction before that person can be added as a connection.

Drawing on research in social psychology showing that physical attractiveness may be affected by the attractiveness of one's peers, Walther and colleagues (2008) examined whether people with more attractive Facebook friends would be rated as more attractive by viewers. Using the same profile photo, but manipulating the attractiveness of friends' photos, they found that surrounding oneself with attractive friends increases perceptions of one's own attractiveness, while linking visibly to unattractive people may lessen one's own physical appeal.

Friends can also affect one's image by writing on one's "wall" or "shoutbox" (Walther et al., 2008), tagging photographs with one's names, and commenting on content one has uploaded. In some SNSs, people can do this even if they have not been accepted as a friend. "This makes participative social networking technologies different from Web pages, e-mail, or online chat" (Walther et al., p. 29), "because all those technologies allow the initiator complete control over what appears in association with his- or herself." Content posted by others may contribute disproportionately to one's image because it is may be seen as less biased by a desire to look good. In their experiment, Walther and colleagues found a double standard. For women's profiles, positive wall posts increased perceptions of physical attractiveness while negative posts decreased such perceptions. For men, negative wall posts indicating excessive drinking and sexual innuendo increased perceptions of attractiveness.

Multiple media

Perhaps the most neglected area of research regarding the use of identity is how people use non-verbal social cues such as video and photographs to create their identities. Lüders (2007), in her close study of a small number of Norwegian young people, showed that they simultaneously use multiple SNSs to create public personae that combine writing, video, and photography. Often their posts were mundane, and in most cases were tied to an identifiable offline persona. It is more difficult to study visual content than verbal content, but as visual means of self-construction become increasingly common, researchers must develop more robust ways to make sense of these phenomena.

Relationships

Personal profiles form the core content of SNSs, but it is the connections among those profiles and the relationships those connections represent that makes them networks. Personal relationship maintenance has always been one of the Internet's most popular uses, as the success of email has long demonstrated, but it has been one of the field's most neglected topics as the fascination with identity construction has too often obscured observation and analysis of relational processes. When attention has focused on interpersonal relationships in Internet research, it has often addressed the formation of new relationships between those who meet online rather than the more mundane maintenance of relationships between those who already knew one another (Baym, 2002).

To briefly summarize the work on new relationship formation, naturalistic pre-SNS relationship research often examined how online groups provided contexts for relationship creation (e.g. Baym, 2000; Kendall, 2002; Lea & Spears, 1995; Parks & Floyd, 1994), while experimental work (e.g. Walther, 1992, 1996) created task-oriented groups in order to study relational processes. There were often comparisons between "online" and "offline" relationships. Generally, such research has found that "online" relationships are less developed than "offline" ones (Mesch & Talmud, 2006; Parks & Roberts, 1998). However, in longitudinal studies, the differences between on and offline friendships were shown to diminish over time (Chan & Cheng, 2004; McKenna, Green, & Gleason, 2002).

Far less research has examined how the Internet helps people with existing ties to maintain their relationships. Stafford, Kline, and Dimmick (1999) and Dimmick, Kline, and Stafford (2000) found that people used email to support and maintain meaningful relationships, especially long-distance ones. My research (Baym, Zhang, & Lin, 2004; Baym et al., 2007) showed that college students very rarely used the Internet to communicate with people they did not communicate with in other ways.

Relational maintenance

Ellison and colleagues (2007) note that "in earlier online relationship work, the direction of social network overlap was usually movement from online to offline" (n.p.). Research on SNSs has emphasized movement in the opposite direction. While recognizing that SNSs "may facilitate making new friends" (Ellison et al., 2007, n.p.), they seem to be more often used for keeping in touch with people one has met elsewhere. Lenhart and Madden (2007) found that 91 percent of US teens who use SNSs report that they do so in order to connect with friends. Boyd (2006) also found that a primary use of MySpace for teens is socializing when they are not able to be together in an unmediated way. SNSs can also be useful for micro-coordination, as people organize their joint activities on the fly (Humphreys, 2007; Ling, 2004). Mayer and Puller (2008) pulled data from Facebook users at Texas A&M University to see how they met and found that of those who gave a reason, 26 percent met through a school organization, 16 percent through another friend, 14 percent had attended the same high school, and 12 percent had taken a course together. Only 0.4 percent met online. Relationship maintenance, rather than relational creation, has also been found to be a primary motive for using Cyworld (Choi, 2006) and MySpace (boyd, 2006). In contrast, Baym and Ledbetter (2009) found that although most Last.fm friendships were between people who had met elsewhere, almost half (47.1 percent) began through the site, although these did not generally become close.

On the whole, there is very little direct communication among friendship pairs in SNSs. In their analysis of 362 million fully-anonymized message headers on

Facebook, Golder and colleagues (2007) found that only 15.1 percent of friends ever exchanged messages. In their analysis of over 200,000 MySpace messages, Gilbert and colleagues (2008) found that 43.5 percent of friends never commented on one another's profiles, and only 4 percent exchanged 10 or more comments. Baron's (2008) research found that 60 percent of Facebook users wrote on others' walls either never or less than once a week. However, scant direct SNS communication does not imply little relational communication (Baym & Ledbetter, 2009; Haythornthwaite, 2005). Baym and Ledbetter (2009) found, for instance, that while 31.5 percent of friendship pairs on Last.fm only communicated via that SNS, on average friends used 2.13 additional media including instant messaging (42 percent), other websites (34.7 percent), face-to-face communication (33.55 percent), and email (31.3 percent). Furthermore, simply having access to one another's updates on an SNS may facilitate a sense of connection (e.g. Humphreys, 2007). Baron (2008, p. 85) cites a respondent who describes it as "a way of maintaining a friendship without having to make any effort whatsoever," thereby offering the interactants more control.

We know very little about the content or functions of message exchanges within SNSs. There is evidence, though, that in some cases they may allow exchanges more emotionally risky than could take place through other means. Larsen's (2007) work on Arto.dk, shows that participants, in particular adolescent girls, often leave emotionally effusive messages proclaiming their love and admiration for one another on each other's profiles, a form of communication out of keeping with Danish norms. Kim's and Yun's (2007) research likewise suggests that for Koreans, who may avoid emotional communication face to face, Cyworld can offer a venue for such communication, with one informant reporting that she had "been able to save many relationships thanks to my minihompy" (Kim & Yun, 2007, n.p.). Communication through these sites may also help some people convert weak-tie relationships into strong ones (Donath & boyd, 2004; Ellison et al., 2007).

Who friends whom

Although people seem to use SNSs primarily for the maintenance of existing relationships, people do use them to create new relationships which can range from highly specialized weak ties to intimate partnerships. Haythornthwaite (2005) coined the term "latent tie" to refer to potential relationships within a social circle that could be but have not been activated (i.e. friends of friends). By making friends lists visible and, in some cases, offering automated recommendations of latent ties, the architecture of SNSs facilitates the conversion of latent ties to weak ties (Ellison et al., 2007).

The theory of latent ties would predict that people are most likely to form relationships with those within their wider social circle. Indeed, most people on SNSs are connected through very few degrees of separation (Adamic, Büyükkökten, & Adar, 2003) and are more likely to join a "friend" network if their friends within it are also friends with one another (Backstrom et al., 2006). Kumar, Novak, and

Tomkins (2006) analyzed all the metadata from Flickr and Yahoo Groups and showed that consistent social structures emerge between the SNS site Flickr and the interest-based groups of Yahoo. Most users in both sites are part of what they call the "giant component," in which people are tightly connected through just a few degrees of separation. In fact, 59.7 percent of Flickr users are at only one degree of separation, and 50.4 percent are that tightly connected in Yahoo groups. Without the giant component, the average degree of separation between individuals is 4 or 5. At the perimeter of these giant components are "stars" – clusters built around individuals that remain isolated from other star-based sub-communities but which eventually merge into the giant component. Both sites also have many isolates or "singletons" who have no connections to others. From most users' points of view, then, SNSs seem to be very homogenous areas in which everyone knows one another (boyd & Heer, 2006).

In addition to sharing common acquaintances, friends on SNSs are often bound together by demographic and life-circumstance similarities, although the findings on homophily in SNSs are mixed. On Dodgeball, Humphreys (2007) found that users were demographically alike. Golder and colleagues (2007) found that 49 percent of messages exchanged in Facebook were between people attending the same university. Gilbert and colleagues (2008) found that rural MySpace users tended to have on-site friends that lived an average of 88.8 miles away, while urban users lived an average of 201.7 miles from their friends, suggesting that geographic homophily is stronger or more important for rural users. On Last.fm, however, a plurality of Last.fm friendships were between people who lived in different countries and just over 30 percent reported living in the same part of the country (Baym & Ledbetter, 2009).

The foregrounding of taste in SNS profiles, and Mayer and Puller's (2008) findings that racial divisions are largely taste-based, suggests that shared taste may be a strong incentive in SNS friending practices. The evidence on this is mixed. On Last.fm, we found that friends were more likely than not to share musical taste (Baym & Ledbetter, 2009), whether they met on site or elsewhere. However, Liu (2007) examined 127,477 MySpace profiles and found that "on average, MySpace users tended to differentiate themselves from their friends, rather than identifying with their friends' tastes" (n.p.), perhaps in order to build unique identities within their social circles.

Mayer and Puller (2008) showed that online, as offline, college social networks at both large and small American universities are racially segregated. Racial seg-mentation within Facebook was as high as it was offline. Rather than resulting from institutional forces that make it difficult for people to meet across racial lines, their simulations indicate that preferences drive this segregation.

Hargittai (2007) shows that these factors influence which SNSs people are likely to join in the first place. People self-select SNSs based in part on which services their friends use. She surveyed a diverse sampling of first-year college students and found that Hispanic students were more likely to use MySpace than Facebook, and white, Asian, and Asian American students were more likely to use

Facebook than MySpace. She warns that this may be "potentially limiting the extent to which they will interact with a diverse set of users on those services" (Hargittai, 2007, n.p.). These concerns may also be extended to rural SNS users who have a third as many friends and receive fewer comments on their MySpace walls than urban users (Gilbert et al., 2008).

One important consequence of maintaining and building relationships through SNSs is the increased social capital that may result. To the extent that such sites promote closer ties with those to whom one is already close, they offer increased "bonding capital," enabling a wide range of social support across a wide range of situations. To the extent that they support new and existing acquaintances, they may create "bridging capital," the access to resources that can only come from those unlike oneself (Ellison et al., 2007; Haythornthwaite, 2005; Williams, 2006). In the first significant study examining these questions in SNSs, Ellison and colleagues (2007) showed that intensive Facebook use is associated with both of these forms of capital. Furthermore, intense Facebook use seemed to enhance bridging social capital, giving people access to more resources of different types than they would likely have otherwise (Ellison et al., 2006). The warnings sounded by Hargittai and by Gilbert and colleagues about homophily in SNSs suggests that already-disadvantaged users may have less access to the bridging capital SNSs can provide.

Ambiguity

Donath (2007) posits that SNSs "may transform the concepts of friendship, personal acquaintance, and public celebrity," a possibility she wisely connects to "related cultural reconfigurations, from the reduced autonomy of American youth to the increased attention to the private lives of public figures" (n.p.). One striking difference between relationships maintained through SNSs and those maintained via other means, is that within SNSs, relationships are explicitly labeled by the systems' infrastructure. In most cases the label is "friend." Twitter uses the term "follower" as well as "friend" (one reads "friends" but is read by "followers"). Flickr allows people to be categorized as "friend," "contact" or "family." Cyworld uses the term *ilchon* which, as Kim and Yun (2007) explain, is loaded with significance since it "metaphorically extends the Korean cultural concept of blood ties to virtual interpersonal relations" (n.p.). LinkedIn, oriented toward professionals, uses the affectively neutral yet equally ambiguous terms "contact" and "connection."

Many scholars of friendship have noted the ambiguity of personal links (e.g. Parks, 2006; Rawlins, 1992). Online, as well as off, "the very term 'friendship' is both vague and symbolically charged and may denote many different types of relationship" (Kendall, 2002, p. 141). Partners within the same relationship may differ in how they categorize it. In SNSs, however, the minimal range of relationship labels and the technical necessity of labeling connections enhances this ambiguity. Definitional ambiguity can be useful. "In the face-to-face world," writes

Donath (2007), "people are circumspect about explicitly defining the parameters of their friendships. This is often a matter of saving face – of not embarrassing someone by pointing out the limits of one's affection for him or her" (n.p.). On the other hand, ambiguity can create problematic misunderstandings. Pairs may differ on what kind of relationship their "friendship" represents (Fono & Raynes-Goldies, 2006); people may be held to account for the behaviors of "friends" they barely know (boyd & Heer, 2006; Donath & boyd, 2004); people may not be sure or disagree about what obligations such links entail (Kim & Yun, 2007).

To some extent, SNSs have emergent friending norms, but ambiguity can still lead to conflict (boyd, 2006; Fono & Reynes-Goldie, 2006). One of boyd's teenage interviewees described MySpace's "Top 8" feature that allows people to list eight of their friends above all the others as "psychological warfare." People may also disagree about friending norms. Speaking of LiveJournal, Fono and Raynes-Goldies (2006) note that the term friend "has no fixed signified from which the entire population can derive shared meaning. It is this reflexivity and multiplicity of meaning that causes much of the social anxiety, conflict and misunderstanding" (n.p.). Similarly, "the ilchon metaphor created varying levels of relational tensions, depending on the degree of intimacy that the word ilchon connoted to users" (Kim & Yum, 2007, n.p.).

The little work that has been done looking directly at the nature of the ties on SNSs suggests that most are weak ties. Baron (2008) found that students reported an average of 72 "real" friends but 229 Facebook friends, a figure almost identical to the result found in Ellison and colleagues (2007) that two thirds of Facebook friends were not considered "actual" friends. Baym and Ledbetter (2009) found that while some reported close relationships on Last.fm, on average they rated their on-site relationships just below the midpoint on measures of relational development.

SNSs can also lead to new sorts of relationships such as those that emerge between fans and celebrities. The fan/band relationship was integral to the growth of MySpace (boyd & Ellison, 2007). Though this is often seen as a form of identity work on the fans' part and audience building on the part of the celebrities, Baym and Burnett (2008) showed that for many musicians the connections fostered through sites like MySpace develop into a new sort of emotionally rewarding relationship between fan and friend. This phenomenon may not apply just to celebrities, but also to micro-celebrities or even relative unknowns, as friend links may be formed simply because a person admires another user's "amusing web links, provocative conceptual musings, and attractive artistic output" (Fono & Raynes-Goldie, 2006, n.p.; see also Lange, 2007)

Community

Much, perhaps most, of the Internet research prior to SNSs focused on interest-based online groups and communities (rarely distinguishing between the two concepts). Hardly any work looks at community in the context of SNSs, leaving a wide-open terrain for future scholarship. As we have seen, most SNSs are based on individuals rather than interests; even those that are interest-focused are organized around individual profiles and dyadic connections. Although most SNSs offer ways to create user groups within the sites, these are usually poorly organized afterthoughts rather than key elements of the social structures. As boyd and Ellison (2007) say, this constitutes "a shift in the organization of online communities" (n.p.). My research (Baym, 2007) showed that music fans organize themselves loosely across sites that include multiple SNSs as well as blogs and news sites, with the result that coherent community can be difficult to create or sustain.

Online community research has shown, for instance, that online groups develop norms and behavioral standards (e.g. Baym, 1993; Lea et al., 1992; McLaughlin, Osborne, & Smith, 1995) and internal hierarchies (e.g. Galegher et al., 1998), and provide social support (e.g. Kollock, 1999; Preece & Ghozati, 1998). With the exception of social-capital analysis, there are no parallels within SNS research, although these phenomena are likely at play. There has, however been work showing that social norms emerge within SNSs, making them somewhat akin to communities in their own right. I have mentioned boyd (2006) and Fono's and Reynes-Goldie's (2006) claims that sites develop friending norms. Donath (2007) argues that SNSs develop norms for what constitutes truth in terms of "the mores of our community." Humphreys (2007) points to Dodgeball-wide behavioral norms, although in parallel to friending norms, she notes that "normative Dodgeball use is not only emerging but contested" and that sub-groups "may have different tolerance levels, expectations, and definitions of acceptable or 'correct' Dodgeball use" (Humphreys, 2007, n.p.).

Social norms are also rooted within the behavioral contexts in which users live. Donath (2007) argues that SNSs "place people within a context that can enforce social mores" by making them "aware that their friends and colleagues are looking at their self-presentation" (n.p.). SNSs can thus invoke and encourage group norms that extend beyond the sites. This might include issues of taste (Liu et al., 2006), and also of behavior. Focus group interviews undertaken by Walther and colleagues (2008) found that "statements reflecting both excessive and morally dubious behavior" (p. 38) were viewed unfavorably in Facebook profiles, although, as we have seen, their experiments suggested this might only be true for women. Golder and colleagues (2007) found strong temporal rhythms to messaging norms in Facebook some of which are "robust and consistent across campuses and across seasons" (n.p.), and others which are more similar within a university.

Missing Topics

SNSs are relatively new and academic research is notoriously slow. By the time you read this, there will doubtlessly be dozens if not hundreds more articles published on the topic. There is no shortage of work to be done. The length of the above three sections is itself an indication of some of the understudied areas. We have a good understanding of the self-presentation issues involved in SNS profiles, although there has been little work on how people are actually perceived in these sites. We have a good sense of the diversity of reasons people friend one another on SNSs, but know very little about these relationships or the roles of SNSs in creating, maintaining, and sometimes terminating them. We know next to nothing about how online communities use SNSs or how and if community emerges through these sites.

The research to date has focused on MySpace and Facebook, with occasional forays into other sites. We need comparative work that examines SNSs in varied national and topical contexts, work on users other than college students and adolescents, and analysis of how people organize their social experience across multiple sites and how they integrate these sites into the whole of their interpersonal encounters. We need studies that look rigorously at media such as photography and video. Sustained longitudinal studies will help us understand how these sites function over time rather than in the snapshot moments that are currently studied.

All of these areas are ripe for future analysis. But perhaps the area most crying out for sustained critical analysis is the one I touched on at the start of this essay: ethics. What are the practical and ethical implications of the move from socializing in not-for-profit spaces to proprietary profit-driven environments? Users may think that sites like Facebook belong to them, but they are wrong (Baron, 2008). As SNSs become practical necessities for many in sustaining their social lives, we become increasingly beholden to corporate entities whose primary responsibility is to their shareholders, not their users. Their incentive is not to help us foster meaningful and rewarding personal connections, but to deliver eyeballs to advertisers and influence purchasing decisions. The terms of use of many of these sites are deeply problematic – my students are shocked when I show them what they have agreed to without reading – and we have little choice but to trust that these sites will not abuse the content we have uploaded or expel us without recourse when we have invested so heavily. Questions are also raised about the lines between just reward for the content users provide and exploitation of users through free labor. At the same time, users are not without influence. When Facebook implemented their Beacon system tracking user purchases and other activities across the Internet and announcing them to their friends, a user backlash forced them to change their plans. The power struggles between owners/staffs and users are complex and thus far all but ignored in scholarship.

One might argue that if one doesn't like the terms of service or site redesigns enacted without user input, one should simply leave, but, as Petersen (2008) discusses, that is not feasible when an SNS is where one's data and connections are stored: "The users of Flickr that I interviewed all say they would not dream of moving to another site, unless they could take their network with them as well as all their pictures with comments, tags and notes" (n.p.).

Another ethical issue that has been little touched upon by scholars is the potential for data-tracking by those running the sites and search providers. Users have little, if any, choice to opt out of how their data are used once they have placed them on an SNS. As the above discussion of privacy suggests, they are also not well-informed about the uses to which the data they place online may be put. Zimmer (2008) has articulated the concerns around what he terms "Search 2.0," warning about "the growing integration of Web 2.0 platforms – and the personal information flows they contain" and the extent to which "search providers are increasingly able to track users' social and intellectual activities across these innovative services, adding the personal information flows within Web 2.0 to the stores of information can leverage for personalized services and advertising" (n.p.).

I do not mean to imply that SNSs should be viewed as a threat. They offer numerous benefits, including the abilities to carefully craft a public or semipublic self-image, broaden and maintain our social connections, enhance our relationships, increase access to social capital, and have fun. Those who provide these services are generally not charging us for their use. Yet they are without doubt restructuring the nature of social networks both online and off, and we must be cautious about studying them from within the lifeworlds they promote rather than stepping outside to understand them in their larger cultural and commercial contexts.

References

Adamic, L. A., Büyükkökten, O., & Adar, E. (2003). A social network caught in the web. *First Monday*, 8(6). Retrieved July 30, 2007, from http://www.firstmonday.org/issues/issue8_6/adamic/index.html.

Allan, G. (2006). Social networks and personal communities. In A. Vangelisti & D. Perman (eds.), *The Cambridge handbook of personal relationships* (pp. 657–71). Cambridge: Cambridge University Press.

Backstrom, L., Huttenlocher, D., Kleinberg, J., & Lan, X. (2006). Group formation in large social networks: Membership, growth, and evolution. *Proceedings of 12th International Conference on Knowledge Discovery in Data Mining* (pp. 44–54). New York: ACM Press.

Barnes, J. (1954). Class and committees in a Norwegian island parish. *Human Relations*, 7, 39–58.

Baron, N. (2008). *Always on: Language in an Online and Mobile World*. New York: Oxford.

Batt, E. (1957). *Family and Social Network*. London: Tavistock.

Baym, N. (1993). Interpreting soap operas and creating community: Inside a computer-mediated fan culture. *Journal of Folklore Research*, 30(2–3), 143–76.

Baym, N. (2000). *Tune in, Log on: Soaps, Fandom, and Online Community*. Thousand Oaks, CA: Sage.

Baym, N. (2002). Interpersonal life online. In S. Livingston & L. Lievrouw (eds.), *The Handbook of New Media*. London: Sage.

Baym, N. (2007). The new shape of online community: The example of Swedish independent music fandom. *First Monday*, 12(8). http://firstmonday.org/issues/issue12_8/baym/index.html.

Baym, N., & Burnett, R. (2008). Constructing an international collaborative music network: Swedish indie fans and the Internet. Paper presented at International Communication Association, May, Montreal.

Baym, N., & Ledbetter, A. (2009). Tunes that bind? Predicting friendship strength in a music-based social network. *Information, Communication, & Society*, 12(3).

Baym, N., Zhang, Y. B., & Lin, M. (2004). Social interactions across media: interpersonal communication on the Internet, telephone, and face-to-face. *New Media & Society* 6(3), 299–318.

Baym, N., Zhang, Y. B., Kunkel, A., Lin, M.-C., & Ledbetter, A. (2007). Relational quality and media use. *New Media & Society*, 9(5), 735–52.

boyd, d. (2006). Friends, Friendsters, and MySpace Top 8: Writing community into being on social network sites. *First Monday*, 11(12). http://www.firstmonday.org/issues/issue11_12/boyd/.

boyd, d., & Ellison, N. B. (2007). Social network sites: Definition, history, and scholarship. *Journal of Computer-Mediated Communication*, 13(1), article 11. http://jcmc.indiana.edu/vol13/issue1/boyd.ellison.html.

boyd, d., & Heer, J. (2006). Profiles as conversation: Networked identity performance on Friendster. *Proceedings of Thirty-Ninth Hawai'i International Conference on System Sciences*. Los Alamitos, CA: IEEE Press.

Byrne, D. N. (2007). Public discourse, community concerns, and civic engagement: Exploring black social networking traditions on BlackPlanet.com. *Journal of Computer-Mediated Communication*, 13(1), article 16. http://jcmc.indiana.edu/vol13/issue1/byrne.html.

Chan, D. K. S., & Cheng, G. H. L. (2004). A comparison of offline and online friendship qualities at different stages of relationship development. *Journal of Social and Personal Relationships*, 21(3), 305–20.

Choi, J. H. (2006). Living in Cyworld: Contextualising Cy-Ties in South Korea. In A. Bruns & J. Jacobs (eds.), *Use of Blogs* (pp. 173–86). New York: Peter Lang.

Curtis, P. (1997). Mudding: Social phenomena in text-based virtual realities. In S. Kiesler (ed.), *Culture of the Internet* (pp. 121–42). Mahwah, NJ: Lawrence Erlbaum.

Dimmick, J., Kline, S. L., & Stafford, L. (2000). The gratification niches of personal e-mail and the telephone: competition, displacement, and complementarity. *Communication Research*, 27(2), 227–48.

Donath, J. (2007). Signals in social supernets. *Journal of Computer-Mediated Communication*, 13(1), article 12. http://jcmc.indiana.edu/vol13/issue1/donath.html.

Donath, J., & boyd, d. (2004). Public displays of connection. *BT Technology Journal*, 22(4), 71–82.

Ellison, N., Steinfield, C., & Lampe, C. (2007). The benefits of Facebook "friends": Exploring the relationship between college students' use of online social networks and social capital. *Journal of Computer-Mediated Communication*, 12(3), article 1. http://jcmc.indiana.edu/vol12/issue4/ellison.html.

Fiore, A. T., & Donath, J. S. (2005). Homophily in online dating: When do you like someone like yourself? Paper presented at ACM Computer–Human Interaction, Portland, Ore.

Fono, D., & Raynes-Goldie, K. (2006). Hyperfriendship and beyond: Friends and social norms on LiveJournal. In M. Consalvo & C. Haythornthwaite (eds.), *Internet Research Annual* vol. 4, *Selected Papers from the AOIR Conference* (pp. 91–103). New York: Peter Lang.

Fragoso, S. (2006). WTF a crazy Brazilian invasion. In F. Sudweeks, H. Hrachovec, & C. Ess (eds.), *Proceedings of CATaC 2006* (pp. 255–74). Murdoch, Australia: Murdoch University.

Galegher, J., Sproull, L., & Kiesler, S. (1998). Legitimacy, authority, and community in electronic support groups. *Written Communication*, 15(4), 493–530.

Gilbert, E., Karahalios, K., & Sandvig, C. (2008). The network in the garden: An empirical analysis of social media in rural life. *CHI 2008* (pp. 1603–12), Proceeding of the twenty-sixth annual SIGCHI conference on Human factors in computing systems, April 5–10, Florence, Italy.

Goffman, E. (1959). *The Presentation of Self in Everyday Life*. Doubleday: Garden City, New York.

Golder, S. A., Wilkinson, D., & Huberman, B. A. (2007). Rhythms of social interaction: Messaging within a massive online network. In C. Steinfield, B. Pentland, M. Ackerman, & N. Contractor (eds.), *Proceedings of Third International Conference on Communities and Technologies* (pp. 41–66). London: Springer.

Gross, R., & Acquisti, A. (2005). Information revelation and privacy in online social networks. *Proceedings of WPES'05* (pp. 71–80). Alexandria, VA: ACM.

Hafner, K. (1998). *Where Wizards Stay up Late: The Origins of the Internet*. New York: Simon & Schuster.

Hargittai, E. (2007). Whose space? Differences among users and non-users of social network sites. *Journal of Computer-Mediated Communication*, 13(1), article 14. http://jcmc.indiana.edu/vol13/issue1/hargittai.html.

Haythornthwaite, C. (2005). Social networks and Internet connectivity effects. *Information, Communication, & Society*, 8(2), 125–47.

Humphreys, L. (2007). Mobile social networks and social practice: A case study of Dodgeball. *Journal of Computer-Mediated Communication*, 13(1), article 17. http://jcmc.indiana.edu/vol13/issue1/humphreys.html.

Kendall, L. (2002) *Hanging Out in the Virtual Pub: Masculinities and Relationships Online*. Berkeley: University of California Press.

Kim, K.-H., & Yun, H. (2007). Cying for me, Cying for us: Relational dialectics in a Korean social network site. *Journal of Computer-Mediated Communication*, 15(1), article 11. http://jcmc.indiana.edu/vol13/issue1/kim.yun.html.

Kollock, P. (1999). The economies of online cooperation: gifts and public goods in cyberspace. In M. Smith & P. Kollock (eds.), *Communities in Cyberspace* (pp. 220–42). New York: Routledge.

Kumar, R., Novak, J., & Tomkins, A. (2006). Structure and evolution of online social networks. *Proceedings of 12th International Conference on Knowledge Discovery in Data Mining* (pp. 611–17). New York: ACM Press.

Lampe, C., Ellison, N., & Steinfeld, C. (2007). A familiar Face(book): Profile elements as signals in an online social network. *Proceedings of Conference on Human Factors in Computing Systems* (pp. 435–44). New York: ACM Press.

Lange, P. G. (2007). Publicly private and privately public: Social networking on YouTube. *Journal of Computer-Mediated Communication*, 13(1), article 18. http://jcmc.indiana.edu/vol13/issue1/lange.html.

Larsen, M. C. (2007). Understanding social networking: On young people's construction and co-construction of identity online. Paper presented at Internet Research 8.0, Vancouver.

Larson, K. A. (2007). *The Social Construction of the Internet: A Rural Perspective.* Master's dissertation, Department of Communication Studies, University of Kansas, Lawrence, Kansas.

Le Monde (2008). World map of social network sites. http://www.lemonde.fr/web/infog/0,47-0@2-651865,54-999097@51-999297,0.html.

Lea, M., & Spears, R. (1995) Love at first byte? In J. Wood & S. Duck (eds.), *Understudied Relationships: Off the Beaten Track* (pp. 197–240). Thousand Oaks, CA: Sage.

Lea, M., O'Shea, T., Fung, P., & Spears, R. (1992) "Flaming" in computer-mediated communication: observations, explanations, implications. In M. Lea (ed.), *Contexts of Computer-Mediated Communication* (pp. 89–112). London: Harvester Wheatsheaf.

Lenhart, A., & Madden, M. (2007). *Teens, privacy, & online social networks.* Pew Internet and American Life Project Report. http://www.pewInternet.org/pdfs/PIP_Teens_Privacy_SNS_Report_Final.pdf.

Ling, R. (2004). *The Mobile Connection: The Cell Phone's Impact on Society.* San Francisco: Elsevier.

Liu, H. (2007). Social network profiles as taste performances. *Journal of Computer-Mediated Communication*, 13(1), article 13. http://jcmc.indiana.edu/vol13/issue1/liu.html.

Liu, H., Maes, P., & Davenport, G. (2006). Unraveling the taste fabric of social networks. *International Journal on Semantic Web and Information Systems*, 2(1), 42–71.

Lüders, M. (2007). *Being in Mediated Spaces.* Doctoral dissertation, Department of Media Studies, University of Oslo, Norway.

Marvin, C. (1988). *When Old Technologies Were New.* New York: Oxford.

Marwick, A. E. (2008). To catch a predator? The MySpace moral panic. *First Monday*, 13(6–2). http://www.uic.edu/htbin/cgiwrap/bin/ojs/index.php/fm/article/viewArticle/2152/1966.

Mayer, A., & Puller, S. L. (2008). The old boy (and girl) network: Social network formation on university campuses. *Journal of Public Economics*, 92(1–2), 329–47.

McKenna, K. Y. A., Green, A. S., & Gleason, M. E. J. (2002). Relationship formation on the Internet: What's the big attraction? *Journal of Social Issues*, 58(1), 9–31.

McLaughlin, M. L., Osborne, K. K., & Smith, C. B. (1995). Standards of conduct on Usenet. In S. Jones (ed.), *Cybersociety: Computer-Mediated Communication and Community* (pp. 90–111). Thousand Oaks, CA: Sage.

Mesch, G., & Talmud, I. (2006). The quality of online and offline relationships. *The Information Society*, 22, 137–48.

Milgram, S. (1967). The small world problem. *Psychology Today*, 2, 60–67.

Nakamura, L. (2002). *Cybertypes: Race, Ethnicity, and Identity on the Internet.* New York: Routledge.

O'Brien, J. (1999). Writing in the body: Gender (re)production in online interaction. In M. Smith & P. Kollock (eds.), *Communities in Cyberspace* (pp. 76–106). New York: Routledge.

Parks, M. R. (2006). *Personal Relationships and Personal Networks.* Mahwah, NJ: Lawrence Erlbaum.

Parks, M. R., & Floyd, K. (1996). Making friends in cyberspace. *Journal of communication*, 46(1), 80–97.

Parks, M. R., & Roberts, L. D. (1998). "Making MOOsic": The development of personal relationships on line and a comparison to their offline counterparts. *Journal of Social and Personal Relationships*, 15(4), 517–37.

Petersen, S. M. (2008). Loser generated content: From participation to exploitation. *First Monday*, 13(3). http://www.uic.edu/htbin/cgiwrap/bin/ojs/index.php/fm/article/viewArticle/2141/1948.

Preece, J., & Ghozati, K. (1998) In search of empathy online: A review of 100 online communities. In *Proceedings of the 1998 Association for Information Systems Americas Conference* (pp. 92–4).

Rawlins, W. K. (1992). *Friendship Matters: Communication, Dialectics and the Life Course*. NewYork: Aldine de Gruyter.

Scholz, T. (2008). Market ideology and the myths of Web 2.0. *First Monday*, 13(3). http://www.uic.edu/htbin/cgiwrap/bin/ojs/index.php/fm/article/viewArticle/2138/1945.

Silver, D. (2000a). Looking backwards, looking forward: Cyberculture studies 1990–2000. In D. Gauntlett (ed.), *Web.Studies: Rewiring Media Studies for the Digital Age* (pp. 19–30). New York: Arnold and Oxford University Press.

Silver, D. (2000b). Margins in the wires: Looking for race, gender and sexuality in the Blacksburg Electronic Village. In B. Kolko, L. Nakamura, & G. B. Rodman (eds.), *Race in Cyberspace* (pp. 133–50). New York: Routledge.

Snyder, J., Carpenter, D., & Slauson, G. J. (2006). MySpace.com: A social networking site and social contract theory. Proceedings of ISECON 2006. http://isedj.org/isecon/2006/3333/ISECON.2006.Snyder.pdf.

Stafford, L., Kline, S. L., & Dimmick, J. (1999). Home e-mail: Relational maintenance and gratification opportunities. *Journal Of Broadcasting & Electronic Media*, 43(4), 659–69.

Standage, T. (1998). *The Victorian Internet*. New York: Berkley.

Stone, A. R. (1995). *The War of Desire and Technology at the Close of the Mechanical Age*. Cambridge, MA: MIT Press.

Turkle, S. (1995). *Life on the Screen: Identity in the Age of the Internet*. New York: Simon & Schuster.

Walther, J. B. (1992). Interpersonal effects in computer-mediated interaction, *Communication Research*, 19(1), 52–90.

Walther, J. B. (1996). Computer-mediated communication: Impersonal, interpersonal and hyperpersonal interaction. *Communication Research*, 23(1), 3–43.

Walther, J. B., Van Der Heide, B., Kim, S. Y., Westerman, D., & Tong, S. T. (2008). The role of friends' appearance and behavior on evaluations of individuals on Facebook: Are we known by the company we keep? *Human Communication Research*, 34, 28–49.

Wellman, B. (1988). Networks as personal communities. In B. Wellman & S. D. Berkowitz (eds.), *Social Structures: A Network Analysis* (pp. 130–84). Cambridge: Cambridge University Press.

Wellman, B. (1997). An electronic group is virtually a social network. In S. Kiesler (ed.), *Culture of the Internet* (pp. 179–208). Mahwah, NJ: Lawrence Erlbaum.

Wellman, B., Quan-Haase, A. Q., Boase, J., Chen, W., Hampton, K., & de Diaz, I. I. (2003). The social affordances of the Internet for networked individualism. *Journal of Computer-Mediated Communication*, 8(3). http://jcmc.indiana.edu/vol8/issue3/wellman.html.

Williams, D. (2006). On and off the 'net: Scales for social capital in an online era. *Journal of Computer-Mediated Communication*, 11(2). http://jcmc.indiana.edu/vol11/issue2/williams.html.

Wynn, E., & Katz, J. E. (1998). Hyperbole over cyberspace: self-presentation and social boundaries in Internet home pages and discourse. *The Information Society*, 13(4), 297–328.

Zimmer, M. (2008). The externalities of Search 2.0: The emerging privacy threats when the drive for the perfect search engine meets Web 2.0. *First Monday*, 13(3). http://www.uic.edu/htbin/cgiwrap/bin/ojs/index.php/fm/article/viewArticle/2136/1944.

19

Newly Mediated Media: Understanding the Changing Internet Landscape of the Media Industries

P. David Marshall

The Internet is an elastic phenomenon that in its 30-year history has engulfed and absorbed greater and greater aspects of our cultural activity. It has come to represent an enormous and accessible library, an elaborate system for the trading of goods and services, and a behemoth of social networking and presentation of the self along with a host of other characterizations. Over its last 15 years, the Internet in its subsystem as the World Wide Web has progressively also become a media form – albeit a media form that is not as definable as its predecessors. This chapter looks more closely at how the Internet as media form has led to quite profound transformations of what could be characterized as traditional media in terms of economic models, forms of production, patterns of exhibition, and definitions of its audiences. At this moment, the media industries in a very real sense are being absorbed and ingested into a more complex system of exchange, agency, empowerment, and political economy that has begun to change fundamental media industries' business models. This absorption is not to say that existing media forms are disappearing; rather the traditional forms of television, film, newspapers, magazines and radio are presenting different and extended patterns of distribution, decidedly new formations and deadlines for the production of material, clearly shifted techniques for generating income, and new formations and even conceptualizations of audiences. The complexities of these newly *layered* media forms – something Henry Jenkins describes as a convergence *culture* that indicates our need to explore the cutting edge of a participatory media culture (Jenkins, 2006) – not only have repercussions for the media industries themselves but herald a wider cultural transformation of the role media play in contemporary culture.

The idea that the web is engulfing various media is certainly not new and has been explored through various strands of new media and Internet studies. Convergence, for instance, perhaps best expresses the phenomenon and futurist writers such as Gilder (1994), Pavlik (1996), and Negroponte (1995) first addressed these possibilities of how the computer interface would eventually usurp the other past screens of the household. Various authors have explored the way that media have integrated web-based forms in their content and the understanding of the web as a media form has also been advanced in key texts in the last decade (see Burnett & Marshall, 2003; Marshall, 2004). Lehman-Wilzig and Cohen-Avigdor attempted to understand the Internet's usurpation of older media in terms of an elaborate media lifecycle that indicated that the Internet was a multimedium that absorbed and transformed existing media (Lehman-Wilzig & Cohen-Avigdor, 2004). Fidler coined the term "mediamorphosis" to help describe how new media shifted the media environment into new but genetically related entities (Fidler, 1997).

Convergence between offline media and online media has been studied in often-distinct intellectual traditions depending on the media form or genre. For instance, online news which now naturally embodies print news and television news has been studied in two distinct ways. From the late 1990s, newspapers in particular were looked at in terms of how closely they "mirrored" their print versions which followed a longer debate about whether newspapers were in decline. (Allen, 2006) During the 2000s, much of the focus of online news research has been concerned with the newsblog (Singer, 2006, pp. 23–32), particularly after the terrorist attacks of September 11, 2001 (see Allen, 2002, pp. 119–40) and a wider engagement with what has been described as "citizen journalism."

Television has also been a source for some scrutiny of its transformation into a hybridized broadcast/Internet-based entity. Quite extensive writing has explored the way that both fan culture and reality television have grown partly because of new relationships to audiences and activity produced by the Internet (see for example Marshall, 2004; Jenkins, 2006; Andrejevic, 2009). Also, recent work on how public television broadcasters are dealing with their public mission in an area of multiple access points for content has been particularly fruitful in investigating the convergence of broadcast and online culture (Deuze, 2007).

In contrast to this work on news and television, film as a medium has been investigated quite differently when linked with the concept of convergence: a series of analyses has explored the implications of the digital in transforming film into the prevalent form of the DVD as well as a new digital aesthetic (Darley, 2000; Harries, 2000) and very little academic work has been done about the movement of content or exhibition – even in terms of piracy and illegal downloading – concerns onto the web. Perhaps one of the more influential approaches has been forwarded by Bolter and Grusin who identify how new media "remediates" past media and further explain that digital cinema with its special effects and spectacle was producing something that connected cinema to its origins – a cinema of attrac-tions (Bolter & Grusin, 2000, pp. 155–58).

It is also worth detailing the intellectual and academic institutional movement grouped around creative industries which has also articulated a sense of the inter-connection of creativity itself with the movement and transformation of information into knowledge and design, and thus has provided another area where media convergence has been investigated (see for example Hartley, 2005). In these analyses, creative industries have formed a seamless intersection of work and knowledge-creation that was very much wedded to the way that information moved through the Internet, with former boundaries between creative practices in their digital transformation now much more unified (Deuze, 2007). In Richard Florida's characterizations these new economies of information development and design were instrumental in the development of megacities that serviced the new interlocking creative class (Florida, 2003, 2008).

Despite all of this past work on how media have been newly mediated by the Internet, it is often difficult to get a clear map of the labyrinthine intersections and connections that link traditional media and online mediations. Like hyperlinks themselves, traditional media are housed in elaborate layered architectures and industrial models that often try to ensure a positive traffic flow between their original forms and their online forms. To explore the new layered look of the media and to generate a basic map of the media industries in terms of their online presence and the wider industrial intentions, I have divided the rest of the chapter into an analysis along five axes:

1   Promotion
2   Replication
3   Income
4   Alliances
5   Replacement

These axes play slightly different roles with each traditional media and what follows is a reading of their various forms of reactions to the new realities of the media industry. It is also important to emphasize in any analysis of the Internet and its interplay with media and culture that its impact is tempered by the technological infrastructure. In other words, the Internet's role in any nation or region is determined by the accessibility of connected computers and the speed of the connection. Thus, if broadband connection is relatively inaccessible in a given country and limited and inaccessible dial-up access to the Internet is still the dominant manner of connection, there will be a disconnect from the transnational flows of this new media industry. The implications of that disconnection will vary quite dramatically, with clear examples in a country like India where certain wealthier class fractions and certain regions are participating in this new layered media environment while much of the rest of the culture is playing in a different media mix. What is often called the digital divide (that is as much within nations as between nations) produces quite different media ecologies and even micro-media environments. Thus, the analyses that follow will have gradations of reality depending on the impact of the Internet and the web in different cultures.

Promotion

In 1998, I published an article that explored the way that the media represented themselves on the Internet (Marshall, 1998). It was clear then that there was

a great deal of activity on the Internet by the various media, but this didn't necessarily imply a full embrace of the Internet's interactive logos. What was evident
in 1998 was that promotion was front and centre in most traditional media's web
presence. In other words, the objective of the websites was to pull the user back
into the audience of the television network, the newspaper, or the radio station,
and the website was an elaborate and quite sophisticated form of advertising.
This promotional aesthetic and objective was perhaps most strongly evident with
television and film, and perhaps most weakly represented by print media. Web
presence for traditional media was motivated in the 1990s by the same rationale
that has kept corporations advertising: they are not sure whether the promotion
works, but they ultimately fear that things will be worse for their sales if they do
not promote. Indeed, the massive proliferation of businesses of all kinds having
a website was and continues to be one of promotion and presence in the vast
majority of cases. It remains the exception that a particular business incorporates
the web's possibilities fully into its structure and central business plan.

Ten years later the idea of promotion remains the very core in the websites
of most media corporations. What has changed is the level of sophistication
and resources that are put in place to maintain the promotion. On a basic level,
the web's form of promotion is often about corporate brand identity. Thus with
newspapers, it is important that no matter what else is contained on the website,
there remains the masthead which functions as a brand identity. The reality
of newspaper sites is that they no longer draw their content solely from their
newspapers and this form of brand promotion presents a useful mirage of coordination that hides the new alliances that are elemental parts of their online
coverage. These new alliances which allow an online version of a newspaper to
be much more dynamic will be explored in more detail in the alliance axis of this
chapter. Suffice it to say that newspapers circulate on the Internet as brands of
authoritative news discourse that course through a number of channels so that
they appear with regularity when any user searches for news.

The authoritative quality of news brands such as the *New York Times* or Canada's
Globe and Mail continues to carry weight in an online world that is populated by
so many competing blogs and vlogs (video blogs) that make claims to be channels
for the discussion of news events. Nonetheless, this diversity of sources actually
pushes newspapers to promote quite loudly on the Internet. Two further realities
of news coverage make this need to promote all the more central to newspapers.
First, at least on the web, there is little that distinguishes CNN, Fox News, the
BBC World Service, or even National Public Radio (NPR) from the activities of
a newspaper site. Along with the *New York Times* and the *Sydney Morning Herald*,
television news sites are populated with the same mélange of text, links to other
stories, videos, and slideshows. Indeed all are also populated with blogs from the
journalists and opportunities to write in to the site. What has changed is that news
sites, whether originating from newspapers or television, are competing to be seen
and heard on the Internet in roughly the same register. They are news gatherers
collectively speaking that serve as resource centre sites (Bruns, 2005) around the

production and dissemination of news. Secondly, the web has allowed institutions to speak for themselves much more publicly than in the past. Thus, the online newspaper's role of disseminating the information that comes from an institution is sometimes for some users an unnecessary form of mediation. For instance, someone very interested in the particular sport of tennis may go directly to the coverage provided by the Association of Tennis Professionals who have a sophisticated website, rather than trawl through newspaper efforts to cover that sport and report that coverage. Users then are seeking out more direct sources – what used to be press releases in the pre-Internet flow of news – that are sometimes the sources that newspapers have used to cover an individual event in a perfunctory way. Newspapers then in their online presence are not only competing with other news gatherers, they are also competing with institutions and organizations who are the sources of interest for users.

Newspapers online work through their forms of promotion and the collective memory of their value to make themselves distinctive from these other flows of information. In the recent past, newspapers in their hardcopy version have celebrated the individual columnist and the opinions of reporters (Marshall, 2009). The sustained online focus on promoting the individual journalist is a further extension of newspapers into the online world as journalists' opinion blogs become more prominent and visible in the massive blog world. There is a risk in the promotional expansion of the newspaper into news blogs: the newspaper's former claim to authority and objectivity is recast in this movement further into opinion journalism that ultimately resembles the blogosphere itself. Newspapers as entities risk being subsumed into these flows and their distinctive identities derived from their history are similarly susceptible to absorption.

Just as with newspapers, promotion remains the focal point of film and television sites; however film and television websites have achieved levels of sophistication that make it harder to discern where the promotional dimension of their forms of entertainment ends and the actual product begins. This blurring of the line between promotion and cultural form via online worlds has been developing for some time and it is worthwhile reprising some of the influential steps that have helped define the online life of film and television over the last ten years.

One of the seminal moments related to film at least was the unique promotion via the Internet of the independently made but eventually centrally distributed film *The Blair Witch Project* (1999). The basic premise of the horror fictional film was that a camera crew investigating a part of Connecticut haunted by the Blair Witch had disappeared and all that remained was the discovered video footage and cameras. The website intentionally blended the idea of whether the event was fact or fiction and in a viral way attracted an online following about what had actually happened to the young camera crew. The site contained interviews with supposed friends and family as well as other evidence and clues that would help solve the mystery of the camera crew's disappearance. What was unique about the site were two elements: it provided a great deal of material that surrounded the story that was not in the end in the film, and it predated the release of the film by months in order to create interest in the film. The interest in the film and its mystery helped it successfully launch at the Sundance Film Festival as the new distributors tried to continue the viral interest in the film in the types of promotion developed for it.

Other films experimented with long promotional lead times online. Spielberg's *AI* (2000) produced the now famous murder mystery game – known widely as "the Beast" derived from information on promotional posters a year before the release of the film. Ultimately, the game absorbed a core audience of a million searchers but became an entity unto itself and disconnected from the film. (Jenkins, 2006, pp. 123–5) Nonetheless, it established a potential pattern of expanding the promotion of a film outwards via the Internet prior to its release. *The Matrix* (1999–2002) series also created a continuous form of promotion via the Internet throughout the three-film release. Blockbuster films such as *Dark Knight* (2008) have managed to maintain a high visibility in advance of their release by a selective dissemination of material both through mainstream media, but more significantly through the Internet and advanced information about the film's content. The Internet thus has become the long promotional trailer for the film industry to build hype that becomes the material that fans are drawn to. Significantly, the film industry's love affair with existing cultural icons from other forms (particularly comic books) allows for film to build on existing fan loyalties (one can think here of the *X-Men* films) that serve as clusters attracted to any advanced online publicity for films.

Part of the rationale for both television and film production to present online a kind of promotional ethos is the survivalist relationship to the power of the Internet to transform their highly controlled systems of distribution and exhibition. Although there are many sites supporting the ripping of films and programs shortly after their release (and occasionally before their release), the official corporate websites for film and television have countered these developments with newly created exclusive promotional content that allows the potential audience to become further engaged in the fiction. This technique of deepening the product with additional short productions has been much more successfully attached to television series than films. For example, the intertextual promotional work around *Lost* (2005–) invites the viewer to look for clues online through replays of particular segments. In addition, sneak previews have been available on the official site in advance of the next installment to create a potential viral buzz around possible scenarios. *Lost*'s online producers have added fabricated though very real websites for key fictional corporations that are essential to the plot of the series: the mysterious Hanso corporation as well as the airline company Oceanic, whose plane's crash initiated the series narrative, both have quite functional web spaces that work to deepen the televisual text with extended realities online. Other major American series such as *Heroes* (2006–) and *Prison Break* (2006–) have produced similar elaborate websites. Other series have developed Myspace and Facebook sites for the fictional characters – for example the key characters in the Australian mockumentary series *Summer Heights High* (2007) all have Myspace sites – which once again are highly complex structures of online promotion of the television series.

One of the central effects of the Internet on film and television then is a new blending of promotion and production. With the elaborate effort to enrich the experience of the story for the more devoted fan of a particular program, it becomes quite unclear where the screenplay and actor's work ends and that of promotion and advertising begins. From Jenkins' perspective, this elaboration of content is "transmedia storytelling" (Jenkins, 2006, p. 21) and the online work is increasingly becoming a part of the experience of a television series that is planned for by the media production companies and network distributors. What is also developing is that television and film programs are being organized for redistribution through online forms specifically for promotion. YouTube thus represents for media production companies a source for the promotion of their product as much as it has been seen as a threat to the control of copyright and distribution. One of the effects of YouTube and other online video sources is that they privileged the dissemination of the "clip" or short segment which serves as a herald for the full film or television program.

Although the form of online promotion by traditional media has morphed since 1998, promotion remains an organizing feature of media websites. Promotion is now quite dramatically integrated into the structure of storytelling itself and definitively connected to fans' investment and loyalty to specific series and productions. For television and film, it remains a truism that these forms of elaboration are means and methods of maintaining the connection to the source of production in order to prevent rampant piracy. For print media, promotion becomes the method to produce an "authenticity" brand of trust among the clutter of online information sources.

Replication

The axis of replication analyzes the degree to which the online source is a copy of the traditional media form. The idea that the online home provides the possibility for complete access to what would normally have passed through other channels is one end of the spectrum; its opposite is the idea that the online home does not reproduce the content of the traditional media (and is often then a source of pure promotion – an indexical sign to the real source).

The degree of replication varies with each media form. Radio stations have now routinely made their websites another access point to their signals through online live streaming. The computer itself becomes a receiver. For the business of radio, the different delivery system is simply a way to expand the "signal." New office environments are filled with networked computers that allow workers to have their favorite radio stations streamed through their personal computers: the small radios and stereos have generally disappeared in many offices. A further element in the reason for radio's wholesale adoption of and replication via the web is its relative technological ease. Audio streams live at a much faster rate, which makes a radio signal more available than video streams. The Canadian CBC has 31 feeds of its programs to cater to stations across the country. Australia's ABC is not as generous in its reconstruction and streams seven signals of its flagship networks.

Radio's replication via the Internet is not as straightforward as just another form of signal carriage. Most radio stations' websites are catering for some major changes in distribution of audio programming. Publicly owned radio stations have generally made it part of their mission to replicate further their programs by making them available through "podcasts" or in MP3 format for downloading. Thus CBC Radio through its various networks or Australia's Radio National will ensure that most of their special programs are "saved" online for this expanded method of both distribution and audience timeshifting. The BBC maintains a seven-day archive of its programs. NPR in the United States has 622 different podcasts to choose at the time of this survey that are available in conjunction with the streams of their individual local stations. The visible embrace of podcasts for radio serves to change radio culture somewhat into a culture of valued programs and information sources. It is also recognized that podcasts allow users to both time- and place-shift into formats that are being accessed via their iPods, phones, and car MP3.

To characterize radio's form of replication is to acknowledge that websites of traditional media are at times hyperversions of their broadcast selves. For both commercial and publicly owned radio, websites also become the home for contests, blogs of on-air personalities, and methods for sending emails to specific programs and hosts. Their replication is a form of structured interactivity that has in many ways augmented the way radio had used the phone call as its feedback loop to its audience for the last half of the twentieth century. Layered onto that structure of connection to an audience is how radio stations' websites provide other kinds of information – news reports, weather, sports – that are presented in a text way that goes beyond the structured program flow of this same information on air.

Both television and radio broadcasting share some elements that make their websites hyperversions that go beyond replication. Consistently, radio and television provide extensive guides to their programs, the kind of material that would be sent out to newspaper media listings and TV guides without the excising of at least some of the promotional literature for each program. With radio, the website is relatively comfortable with the guide providing clear links to downloading program content. Television's means of replication is much more circumspect as it attempts to control its assets and intellectual property to ensure that there is some generation of income via the website and the original television broadcast. Thus, the major American television networks ensure that there is a secondary release of major series online one day after the release on air. The American network ABC for example has a countdown clock to the next on-air screening of the series *Lost* and in another portion of the website you can watch the past episodes and see a bulletin that the show will be available the day after its screening. Interestingly, old content is more freely available via websites. Thus, it is very possible on NBC to screen old episodes of the 1970s series *Battlestar Galactica,* but there is much more controlled distribution of material related to the current *Heroes* series. Nonetheless, the website replicates programming with an online difference that viewing episodes online is designed to ensure that the audience member "catches up" to the current installment in any series. There are different and distinctive forms of online distribution of American programs that have an international profile; the Seven network distributes *Lost* in Australia, but, unlike its American counterpart, it has no day-after online screenings. Replication on the Australian site is filled with short preview clips and an elaborate series of short clips from each episode that identify some key clues for understanding the convoluted *Lost* plot. There is no question that the international and relatively borderless structure of online culture has affected the structure of domestic and national television markets and their patterns of distribution. The gap in the release of series between the US and Australia has narrowed, with the *Lost* series one week behind its American premieres. The speed of this transfer also underlines the massive online economy of piracy of individual episodes. Likewise, episodes are regularly divided up and distributed via YouTube – at least before the corporate copyright lawyers attempt to shut down these forms of sharing.

In contrast to television, newspapers have had a much longer history of online replication. The relative ease with which text and image could be reproduced via the web meant that the challenge and the threat of online publishing of news have been ever-present since the mid-1990s for newspapers. Different models have been advanced over the years. What has developed is a general model that the online "paper" does indeed replicate the hardcopy version: major stories are aligned to a newspaper's homepage but they are signaled much more clearly through the use of an image and caption. Opening paragraphs are visible for these stories, but readers online have to click on a link to go further into the story. The key difference in the production of newspapers online is that the content is designed to change regularly and rapidly. Stories then are subject to updates in a manner that is impossible for the printed versions of newspapers, and major newspapers work to have the sense of continuing developing news. And, as discussed further in a subsequent section, it is also worth indicating that newspapers are not limited to their own content production: they work to have a number of marquee videos to supplement their content. Some newspapers such as the *Wall Street Journal* ensure that only subscribers can access the more official version. This relationship to the authentic version is another variation of online publication. Through different types of software reading devices online, papers like the *New York Times* can be downloaded in page-perfect versions. But what is more interesting and probably of greater long-term value for its online production is the development of a service called *My Times* which allows you to organize the content of the paper to suit your personal interests. This trend in newspaper production where information is reconstructed in personalized web frameworks matches the movement and development of online distribution of news and intersects with pre-existing services on the web such as MyYahoo! and the more recent Google News. Equally interesting is how the content of the newspaper becomes very elastic online. The

Wall Street Journal ensures that each article ends with the columnist's email address. It is also a recognized need by newspapers that their journalists are producing associated blogs for the extensions of their work. Indeed, as with radio, newspaper websites via blogs can be extended versions of published interviews. As well, the *Wall Street Journal* works to establish that it is a database of material for further in-depth searches. Its *My Online Journal* allows the subscriber to track specific companies (up to 10) and obtain wider reach across 28 industry sectors, along with specific stock information. What becomes evident in business-oriented newspapers is that they are competing to become the principal portal for players in the business world. A plenitude of podcasts and business videos are part of the parsing of information for retrieval for subscribers.

In general, the media industries are replicating themselves online, but realizing in that replication that they have to structure, compartmentalize, and produce multitudinous possibilities of flow and user patterns. The replication then becomes a way in which a form of individualization of use is at least made credibly real as the various industries try to ensure their visibility via the web.

Income

At the very hub of change and transformation of media industries is the way in which they sustain themselves and, in at least their capitalist incarnations, how they generate forms of profit. One of the features of mid- to late-twentieth century media corporations was their incredibly stable and profitable business models which allowed the newspaper baron Lord Beaverbrook to label ownership of a television station as a "licence to print money." The stability of these business and economic models has been explored in many works that looked at the political economy of media. To summarize it here, the media industries have worked with three basic models. The first and most prevalent is the advertising-supported model, the second is a subscription-based model, and the third is a government-supported model. It should be added that there are and have been hybrids that blended all three of these models. What you find in most media forms is some blending of at least two of the business models. What provided the income stability was the conceptualization of the audience and its size. The measurement techniques of the audience provided a generally agreed-upon acknowledgement of the power and influence of the various media and this recognition led the media collectively to be seen as part of the key defining elements of the modern public sphere.

As the audiences and subscribers have been gradually bled away from the traditional media, the models of income support, which have been dependent on both the stable conceptualization of the audience and the related acceptance of the media's power, have been challenged. It could be said in the 1970s for instance that television in a given country somehow embodied the public sphere in its programs and in its relationship to political and cultural agendas. Nearing the end of the first decade of the twenty-first century, it could be said that television does not occupy such a central role and the claim to synonymity between the public sphere and television is unsustainable. In many countries, a milestone has now been reached: the number of hours each week devoted to the Internet has now surpassed household TV viewing hours.

As these media entities have become diffused, they have moved laterally – that is, they have become multimedia entities. As detailed above, different media have produced strong web-based presences. In the 1990s, this model was characterized by media websites that were designed to bring viewers back to the anchoring original entity. Television stations would provide elaborate program guides; newspapers would indicate the pre-eminence of the hardcopy. The technique was to promote and to maintain the brand. Online homes were therefore not the site or source for the generation of much income. Indeed, like many dot.com startups in the 1990s, media entities recognized that the income models of the Internet were not real but more projections of the likely development of income in the future.

If we look more closely at the development of the online incarnations of media forms, the kinds of income generated resemble those of their broadcast origins. Advertising has become the lingua franca of the Internet. With television websites, these "commercials" tend to focus overly on advertising their own products. What is interesting is the multimedia mix of types of advertising, something that would be harder to realize in the broadcast world. Thus online television sites are filled with animated gifs, text- and image-based advertising, sound-bites, and very traditional commercials. Online television – when it does permit the streaming of programs – usually tops and tails the particular segment with the marquee sponsor. The marquee sponsor highlights television's efforts to replicate its broadcast income model. For example, the program *Lost* via the network ABC may have a relationship with Nissan where their advertisements in a very controlling way begin any particular streaming with a 30-second spot. This model returns television to something resembling single-program sponsorship that was instrumental in developing early American radio and 1950s television. However, with the webpage clutter that envelopes any television network website, the exclusivity of this kind of sponsorship is continually challenged and its value to the advertiser is thus limited.

One of the clear advantages of the Internet as a source of income generation is its capacity to produce this multimedia environment. Newspapers thus are no longer limited to text and display advertisements (although these still predominate its presentational model). Animation and short videos become part of the mix of how newspapers sell themselves and generate online income. This difference is reflected in both content generation and advertising to create the effect that newspapers online are designed to be an information portal. For instance, the *Boston Globe* is part of an online entity entitled Boston.com that highlights the *Globe*'s (and one of the local television station's) capacity to serve as the source for all things related to Boston.

The model of subscription has been harder to generate in the mediation of media online. Certainly through various techniques the brands of different media are seen to offer some sort of premium in quality. For instance, newspapers provide a premium service to those who subscribe both online and in their paper form. The *Wall Street Journal* also has recognized that it has constructed its news for a business readership and it has constructed tiered relationships to content. Trade presses like *Advertising Age*, whose core audience in the advertising industry is composed of a younger demographic and may already be very web-oriented, have made it a seamless subscription that connects printed versions to online versions. Indeed, the strength of *Advertising Age* is its ready building of related brands and sources from their online homes. Because of their video format, the online version of reviews of new commercials allows the easy perusal of the new video content, something quite unachievable through the printed version. And thus it could be said that in some instances, the online subscription may be critical to the income of particular media sources that are more closely related to the entertainment industry itself.

In general, income generation continues to be the bête-noire of the media industry and its online incarnations. With the movement of the share of advertising revenue increasingly into online structures, there is no question that the revenue streams of traditional media are expanding as well. The danger of this slower expansion is that different models of delivery of content could emerge that would take away the advantages now held by the recognized brands of media.

Alliances

The web has produced many media marriages as older entities try to intersect with some of the newer techniques of how audiences access their news, information, and entertainment. Similarly, web-based companies sometimes see the value in connecting with and collaborating with established media names in order to shore up their capacity to present reputable content. These arrangements and marriages of convenience operate at different levels of commitment and the best way to refer to them is as alliances.

Some alliances are incredibly powerful and have had remarkable longevity where brands become associated. For instance, MSN (Microsoft Network) and NBC established a news network, MSNBC, which has taken on a life of its own. Originally, the alliance served to provide a news web presence to MSN at a time when its parent Microsoft was engaging in the famed browser wars with Netscape. MSNBC also provided an instant structure for a website for NBC at a time when its parent company General Electric was launching into the production of an all-news cable channel. Ownership of MSNBC originally was a shared 50-50 for the cable channel but it has since become primarily owned by its parent NBC Universal. The online version MSNBC continues to be equally owned. Moreover, the online msnbc.com, in its challenge of the online versions of other newsgathering entities established content deals with the *New York Times* among other prominent sources. It is also worthy of note that a similar arrangement was struck between the most powerful commercial network in Australia, Channel 9, and MSN in 1997, where the new entity was entitled ninemsn and became one of the largest Australian web portals (because it is the default homepage of the Microsoft packaged computers). In 2006, in a very similar fashion, Yahoo! Australian Seven Network launched Yahoo7 which was a 50-50 venture between Yahoo! and the television broadcaster.

Other alliances are more subtle, yet perhaps more comprehensive in the movement of video from television to the Internet. In March 2007, a distribution deal by both NBC Universal and News Corporation was developed for the movement/distribution of high-quality video through key Internet-related sites such as AOL, MySpace, MSN, and Yahoo! (News Corporation, 2007). As the Internet becomes a more likely destination for the viewing of video content, the larger media entities are working out arrangements for breaking down their content for its reassembling in shorter formats via these websites. In conjunction with this movement of content is a recognition that advertising income must also be generated, and arrangements with major sponsors have accompanied the video distribution.

Alliances are more subtly constructed with the news services of major newspapers and the homepages constructed by Google or MSN. News stories from particular newspapers are "pushed" at users in a more or less regular pattern. The news stories are also country-specific – in other words, those users located in the US would receive feeds from American news services that would cater specifically to that national audience. In the directory and category structure of Yahoo!, wire services have often been privileged along with key newspapers. What appear to be relatively random choices of stories are clearly agreements between the Internet portal and the news provider. This relationship once again underlines an alliance between content provision and what is equivalent to a channel on the Internet.

Finally, alliances sometimes are user driven which can shift the relative power that any Internet entity might appear to have. The rapid expansion of RSS feeds from Internet sources to the homepages of users has allowed users to blend their favorite blog sites and interests with news and sports stories that are regularly surveyed and posted as headlines to the client/user. Thus the alliance is not so much to the entire media entity, but rather to a selection of content with a particular media content-provider. There may be a mélange of web-based journals and traditional online versions of newspaper stories that are further blended with regular feeds from new YouTube videos and weather services to comprise a complete homepage that is at least hosted by services such as Google or MSN.

Replacement

In the early days of the Internet, it was a regular and repetitive feature of newspapers and magazines to report on the potential moral panics, dangers, and risks of using the web. In contrast, traditional media despite these sensational reports presented themselves as safe, recognizable, and ultimately reliable. What has changed over the web's first 15 years is that there is less of an adversarial relationship between traditional media and the web and more of an acknowledgement of integration. The greatest corporate efforts to challenge the pre-eminence of print media occurred in the first five years with the launch of Internet magazines such as the Microsoft-initiated *Slate* (1996) and the independent *Salon* (1995). Ultimately these online-only magazines never threatened the traditional magazines directly and certainly didn't lead to massive shifts in media business models as their own experiments with online subscription either faltered (with *Salon*) or failed completely (in the case of *Slate*). Both *Slate*, which is now owned by the *Washington Post* group, and *Salon* continue to exist and depend primarily on advertising for their revenues; ultimately however, they are rivaled by the online presences of magazines and other television-based media sources.

The online magazine development and their quiet denouement provide an example of how difficult it has been for online sources of media content to thrive on the Internet and to serve as replacements of traditional media. It may appear at first glance that YouTube has successfully developed a model that is replacing the way in which video is viewed and distributed. After all, the service has millions of viewers, it has constructed the possibility of having your own "channel" for distribution of content, and it has successfully captured the international imagination of a generation of online users. For all its successes there is something incomplete in the way that YouTube operates. YouTube is much more about the distribution of existing content rather than "live" content and the liveness of television still provides a sense of its pre-eminence. YouTube often reconstructs the content of popular culture for further distribution. Through mash-ups and different music renditions, through distribution of shorter segments of television programs, and then through comments by different viewers, Youtube has constructed an elaborate series of communities connected to different aspects of video culture – but it is not live. Indeed, one of the key failures of the Web has been many of its live online events over the last decade. Although there have been some successes in "netcasts" in recent years particularly in relationship to concerts and benefit events, it would be fair to conclude that streaming of live programs has had limited appeal when events are designed for massive audiences.

Where there has been emerging success in online video is in much more niche markets. There is no question that the pornography industry has migrated dramatically to an online distribution of its content with continued and remarkable success. Sports coverage is also beginning to evolve into a model where the most devoted can gain access to greater online video content. For example, men's professional tennis has produced through the UK-based Tennis Properties Limited and Perform Media Services a series of live-streamed and downloadable matches related to its major international tournament series known as Masters. Devoted fans can choose to subscribe for an entire year, individual tournaments, or a particular day's coverage. YouTube and Facebook are used as sites to promote the fully subscribed online channel, but they are also places for fans to comment and discuss their own interpretations of tennis matches. What is developing through these extensions of live video is that the web is providing means and methods for the ready expansion of interpreting, editing, and transforming content that reconnects the video to the new and now central-to-the-experience-of-the-web exigencies of social networks.

As discussed above, television has now entered into thinking of its various network websites as locations for the distribution of video content. Perhaps what is most interesting in this development is that the public broadcasters are moving at a faster pace than many of the commercial networks. Under the mandate of serving the public and ensuring that their content reaches the widest possible public, the BBC and the Australian ABC have launched streamable program-content for their viewers. The BBC's iPlayer that was launched in 2006 is designed to facilitate "catch-up TV in the same tradition as the American networks now advance, but also a massive archive of content (James Bennett, 2008). The ABC's iView similarly is designed to recognize the different and non-television portals that Australians are using to access video content: certain programs in their entirety are available on the service.

These directions by existing broadcasters are not complete replacements of their broadcast worlds – they are extensions to a new platform very much like adding a new channel to a broadcaster's reach and distribution. Corporations that are replacing television with online delivery remain in niche and specialty markets. What may develop in future years are successful and new developments of media cultures in online worlds such as *Second Life*. At the moment, the existing media players have followed the hundreds of thousands of users and set up shop in *Second Life* in anticipation of its future value. Given that the social network model is primary to the experience of online worlds and may not match the organization of existing media entities, it is possible that genuine replacement media will emerge from these new sites of virtual experience. That kind of development is still in its infancy.

Conclusion

There is no question that there is a new layer of mediation that organizes and orchestrates our media use and our media industries. The Internet has served to extend existing media corporations quite dramatically; but in those extensions their form and their cores are transformed and mutating further. The nature of the Internet – one would have to say its core nature – is very much connected to new forms of interpersonal communication and personalized mediated explorations. The media industries have operated with great success throughout the twentieth century as "aggregators" – that is, they have been able to pull together massive audiences around particular cultural forms and practices. The organization of the advertising industry has underlined how well this model of aggregates has worked. The media industries' production of aggregates as audiences has been compensated handsomely by advertisers. The change now is that aggregation is not quite enough as the old media and new media intersect. The development of audiences in this newly mediated and Internet sense also implies the development of information about the audience/aggregate for more accurate targeting of advertised messages. The generation of information necessitates engagement and interaction by the users of the Internet at a level that goes so far beyond older media's system of fan mail and talkback radio. The movement of media content and its ultimate value is at least partially determined by how much chatter and interpersonal exchange occurs through its form: Do social network site-users link or connect to certain videos or certain kinds of music and do they pass that on through their own personal site to others? Do blogs and LiveJournal sites cluster around a given cultural form? Do users feel so connected to a given media form to post it on YouTube and then further connect it to their MySpace and Facebook sites (for further discussion, see boyd & Ellison, 2007; Beer, 2007)? Do search engines such as Google in their elaborate algorithms that rank web-pages chart new aggregations of interest that may be connected to the old-media-generated content but have mutated to the discussions, mash-ups, and vids produced by active users? These various activities isolate on the information that is generated about the former aggregates developed by the media industries – what Thrift has called "knowing capitalism" – and they underline how media themselves are now involved in these layers of production that are happening at this user level (Thrift, 2005).

While these developments of new layers of mediation through interpersonal use are real and advancing, it is important to conclude that the media industries also realize that the past models are still working – perhaps not as strongly, but still quite well. The clear adaptation that is occurring is recognizing how a cultural form or product moves through its uses via the Internet and whether the values generated by that kind of information become subcontracted to companies with Internet expertise or whether the existing media industries recognize these new layers as fundamental to their business models and absorb these emerging entities. The newly mediated media industries are now becoming increasingly involved with how the Internet's interpersonal mediation is producing an equally newly mediated audience.

References

ABC Television Network (2008). *Lost* webpages. Retrieved May 6–7 from http://abc.go.com/primetime/lost/index?pn=index.

Advertising Age (2008). Retrieved July 25 from www.adage.com.

Allen, S. (2002). Reweaving the Internet: online news of September 11. In S. Allen & B. Zelizer (eds.), *Journalism after September 11* (pp. 119–40). New York: Routledge.

Allen, S. (2006). *Online News: Journalism and the Internet.* Maidenhead: Open University Press.

Andrejevic, M. (2009). The twenty-first century telescreen. In G. Turner & J. Taye (eds.), *Television Studies After Television* (pp. 31–40). London: Routledge.

Association of Tennis Professionals (2008, July 20). Retrieved from www.atptennis.com.

Association of Tennis Professionals (2008, July 26). Masters Series TV. Retrieved from http://www.atpmastersseries.tv/page/loginOrBuy.

Australian Broadcasting Corporation (2008). Retrieved May 5–6 from www.abc.net.au.

Beer, D. (2007). Social network(ing) sites . . . revisiting the story so far: A response to Danah boyd and Nicole Ellison. *Journal of Computer-Mediated Communication*, 13(2), 516–29.

Bennett, J. (2008). Interfacing the nation: remediating public service broadcasting in the digital television age. *Convergence*, 14, 277–94.

Bennett, James (2008). Television studies goes digital. *Cinema Journal*, 47(3), 158–65.

Bolter, J. D., & Grusin, R. (2000). *Remediation: Understanding New Media*. Cambridge, MA: MIT Press.

Boston Globe online (2008). Retrieved July 29 from www.Boston.com.

boyd, D., & Ellison, N. (2007). Social networking sites: Definition, history, and scholarship. *Journal of Computer-Mediated Communication*, 13(1), 210–30.

British Broadcasting Company (2008). Retrieved May 4 from www.bbc.co.uk.

Bruns, A. (2005). *Gatewatching: Collaborative Online News Production*. New York: Peter Lang.

Burnett, R., & Marshall, P. D. (2003). *Web Theory*. London: Routledge.

CBC Radio (2008). Retrieved April 3 from http://www.cbc.ca/radio/.

CBC Television (2008). Retrieved April 3 from www.cbc.ca/television/.

Darley, J. (2000). *Visual Digital Culture*. London: Routledge.

Deuze, M. (2007). Convergence culture in the creative industries. *International Journal of Cultural Studies*, 10 (June), 243–63.

Facebook (2008). Association of Tennis Professionals Masters Series. Retrieved July 26 from http://www.facebook.com/pages/ATP-Masters-Series/17413858957.

Fidler, (1997). *Mediamorphosis: Understanding New Media*. Thousand Oaks, CA: Sage.

Florida, R. (2003). *The Rise of the Creative Class*. New York: Basic Books.

Florida, R. (2008). *Who's Your City?* New York: Basic Books.

Gilder, G. (1994). *Life after Television*, rev. edn. New York: Norton.

Globe and Mail online (2008). Retrieved March 23 from www.globeandmail.com.

Harries, D. (ed.) (2000). *The New Media Book*. London: BFI.

Hartley, J. (ed.) (2005). *Creative Industries*. Boston: Blackwell.

Jenkins, H. (2006). *Convergence Culture: Where Old and New Media Collide*. New York: New York University Press.

Lehman-Wilzig, S., & Cohen-Avigdor, N. (2004). The natural life cycle of new media evolution: Inter-media struggle for survival in the internet age. *New Media & Society*, 6(6), 707–30.

Marshall, P. D. (1998). Promotional desires: Popular media's presence on the Internet. *Media International Australia*, 86, 63–76.

Marshall, P. D. (2004). *New Media Cultures*. London and New York: Arnold/Oxford.

Marshall, P. D. (2009). New media as transformed media industry. In J. Holt & A. Perren (eds.), *Media Industries: History, Theory, and Method* (pp. 81–90). Oxford: Wiley-Blackwell.

National Public Radio (2008). Retrieved April 3 from http://www.npr.org.

Negroponte, N. (1995). *Being Digital*. Rydalmere, New South Wales: Hodder & Stoughton.

News Corporation (2007). NBC Universal and News Corp. announce deal with Internet leaders, AOL, MSN, MySpace, and Yahoo! to create a premium online video site with unprecedented reach. Retrieved March 22, 2007, and August 1, 2008, from http://www.newscorp.com/news/news_329.html.

New York Times online (2008). Retrieved March 20 from www.nyt.com/.

Pavlik, J. V. (1996). *New Media Technology: Cultural and Commercial Perspectives*. Boston: Allyn & Bacon.

Singer, J. P. (2006). Journalists and news bloggers: Complements, contradictions, and challenges. In A. Bruns & J. Jacobs (eds.), *Uses of Blogs* (pp. 23–32). New York: Peter Lang.

Sydney Morning Herald online (2008). Retrieved March 22 from www.smh.com.au.

Thrift, N. (2005). *Knowing Capitalism*. London: Sage.

Yahoo!7 (2008). *Lost* webpages. Retrieved May 6–7 from http://au.yahoo.com/lost.

YouTube (2008). Association of Tennis Professionals. Retrieved July 26 from http://www.youtube.com/atp.

20

Online Pornography: Ubiquitous and Effaced

Susanna Paasonen

There is little doubt as to the centrality of pornography in terms of Internet history, its technical development, uses, business models, or legislation. In one overview after another, pornography is said to comprise a major part of websites and downloads, to take up the most bandwidth, and to generate the most profit of all web content. At the same time, pornography remains one of the more under-studied areas of Internet research. The lack of scholarly attention helps to support the circulation of unverified estimates concerning the volume and centrality of pornography. Furthermore, it illustrates a gap between the online phenomena that have become central objects of scholarly analysis, and the ubiquitous everyday uses of the medium (Cronin & Davenport, 2001, p. 34).

Pornography, Technology, and Moral Panics

The Internet, and web distribution in particular, have had considerable effects on the cultural visibility and accessibility of pornography. As porn distribution has branched and shifted online, consumers have the possibility of anonymous access to virtually endless variety of pornographies from the confines and comforts of their own home: from free porn sites to premium pay-sites, live shows and archives of literary erotica, a plethora of sexually explicit material is readily available. Pornography was certainly present already in pre-web bulletin board systems (BBS) and Usenet newsgroups in the form of both amateur representations and com-mercial images, and Usenet remains a central forum for peer exchanges (Mehta & Plaza, 1997; Barron & Kimmel, 2000; Mehta, 2001; Dery, 2007a; see Slater, 1998, on picture exchange on Internet relay chat). It was nevertheless the easy usability and the graphical interfaces of the World Wide Web which, since the first launch of Mosaic in 1993, marked a departure in ways of distributing and consuming pornography. While pornographic content has been central to a myriad of previous and parallel media technologies (video in particular springs to mind), both the facility of accessing porn online and the broad range of available choices have worked to mark the Internet as *the* medium for porn.

Pornography has often been considered the first profitable form of online content production that suffered little from the dot.com crash of the early 2000s. It has been generally identified as an engine driving the development of media technology that is soon adapted to novel platforms and that generates fast profits (O'Toole, 1998; Lane, 2000; Filippo, 2000; Perdue, 2002). In this sense, it is hardly surprising that porn entrepreneurs were quick to make use of online distribution. These were initially independent operations whereas larger companies already operating on video and in print media branched out to the Internet after the mid-1990s (Perdue, 2002, p. 63). Pornography is quite justly known as a pioneering form of commercial content production and a driving force in the development of web technologies and business practices, from web hosting services to credit card processing, banner advertisement, web promotion, and streaming video technology (Filippo, 2000, p. 125; O'Toole, 1998, p. 285; Bennett, 2001, p. 381; Perdue, 2002). Porn also continues to take up considerable amount of bandwidth in web traffic due to the use of images and video. Some claim that porn comprises as much as 40 to 80 percent of all Internet traffic (Thornburgh & Lin, 2002, pp. 72–3; Perdue, 2002, pp. 33–5) although the development of peer-to-peer networks and file sharing has certainly made such estimates more difficult to verify. The overall profitability of porn production and distribution is undoubted, yet the variety of practices and business models, together with the difficulty of accessing reliable data concerning access and profit, make estimates difficult (Paasonen, Nikunen & Saarenmaa, 2007, p. 6).

According to the easily accessible statistics on the volume and use of online porn – such as those published by sites promoting filtering software (e.g. Net Nanny, CYBERsitter, Cyberpatrol, and Maxprotect), or sites promoting the protection of children and families like HealthyMind.com or FamilySafeMedia.com, arguably with some Christian-conservative undertones – porn comprises 14 percent of all websites and a quarter of all web searches. Studies published in peer review journals, however, offer much more moderate figures. According to a study by Spink, Partridge, and Jansen (2006), pornography comprises merely 3.8 percent of all web searches in comparison to 16.8 percent in 1997 (see also Jansen & Spink, 2006). The amount of pornographic sites or the total volume of the porn industry on a global scale is difficult to estimate due to conflicting information: as Coopersmith (2006, p. 2) points out, "gathering reliable data about web usage is inherently difficult because of its rapid growth, incomplete coverage of websites and poor research methodology." Estimates also seem to be published for certain ends in mind: sites promoting filtering software or lobbying for the regulation of adult content, for example, are likely to inflate their figures in order to feed both fears concerning the ubiquity of pornography and consumer interests towards their products. Filtering software, again, makes little distinction between hardcore pornography, sex education, and erotic poetry, conflating and equally filtering all. While estimates on the actual volume and role of porn in terms of Internet content, economy, and usage vary drastically it is the more inflated figures that tend to be most widely referenced. The proportional volume of sites deemed "adult" was considerable in terms of all web content for a large part of the 1990s but as other forms of content increased, the relative volume of pornography has consequently decreased (Coopersmith, 2006, pp. 3–4). It seems, however, common knowledge that the Internet is awash with pornography.

Both the volume and the easy availability of online pornography has given rise to various moral panics, especially ones concerning children: children's exposure (voluntary and involuntary) to porn, online distribution of child pornography, and pedophile networking have all been widely addressed in the media as well as in academic studies (e.g. Freeman-Longo, 2000; Jenkins, 2001; Heins, 2001; Thornburgh & Lin, 2002; Levy, 2002; Greenfield, 2004; Kleinhans, 2004). Pornography, addiction, and the exposure of children to materials deemed "adult" have been associated with the medium at least since the 1995 *Times* article, which rather liberally categorized over 80 percent of all photographs online as pornographic and framed online pornography as a source of cultural anxiety concerning control and autonomy (Chun, 2006, pp. 77–80; Patterson, 2004, pp. 104–05). The theme of children dominates discussions of online pornography to the degree that database searches for anglophone articles on the topic result in numerous hits on pedophiles and sex crimes. While these are certainly issues of concern, it is noteworthy that the recurring co-articulations of Internet, pornography, and children work to frame online pornography in highly partial terms of social harm and risk. This says little of the actual range of online pornographies or their uses.

It should also be noted that the discourse of moral panics and danger is more active and prevalent in the US than in different European countries. While the Bush administration waged a war on porn online and offline, this should not be generalized as a global trend. As Kuipers (2006) illustrates in her comparative analysis of Dutch and US debates on online pornography, the construction of moral panics in the US involves "highly emotional and polarized debates, sustained media attention, the founding of organizations of distressed citizens, skewed and exaggerated representation of the nature and amount of pornography and sex on the internet and numerous attempts at government regulation" (p. 390). US debates are structured by the principle of freedom of speech on the one hand, and the practices of filtering, prohibiting, and shielding on the other. In contrast, education and professional guidance are central to Dutch responses to online porn. The notion of freedom of speech is not very dominant in the Netherlands, which is less rooted in libertarian discourses concerning the Internet (pp. 386, 391; White, 2006, on censorship and regulation in the US). In my view, the same goes for several other European countries.

Search engines routinely exclude pornography from their freely published listings of the most popular search terms. Studies of Internet economy and history, again, tend to pay little attention to pornography (for exceptions, see Lane, 2000; Perdue, 2002). The tendency to avoid and marginalize pornography as a topic

owes to the ethical and political questions associated with it – from the exploitation of children and adult performers to the sexism of porn imageries, addictive
usage, and traffic in women (Hughes, 1999). During the "sex wars" of the 1980s,
feminist anti-pornography critiques defined pornography as exploitation of and
violence against women – as a form of sexist harassment and objectification (e.g.
McKinnon, 1987; Dworkin, 1989). Other anti-pornography advocates saw porn
as decaying the moral fiber and family life of the nation, and the two camps were,
in spite of their drastic political differences, occasionally aligned. Opposing voices
championing freedom of speech, again, argued for pornography as a form of
fantasy while also defending gay, lesbian, and queer forms of pornography (e.g.
Califia, 1994; Rubin, 1995). These debates, often caught in an unfortunate
"tired binary" (Juffer, 1998, p. 2) similar to that described by Kuipers in the
context of online porn, were waged largely in the US but they continue to shape
discussions on sexually explicit media as ones of either for or against on an international scale. This is also perhaps why scholars have been far less interested in
commercial mainstream porn catering to male consumers than in various subcultural,
artistic, independent, and amateur pornographies that are seen to shape and even
subvert the codes and conventions of pornography (e.g. Kibby & Costello, 2001;
Villarejo, 2004; Jacobs, 2004; Waskul, 2004; Halavais, 2005; Jacobs, Janssen, &
Pasquinelli, 2007). All in all, discussions on online pornography are still difficult
to detach from the binary logic structured around the anti-pornography and anti-
anti-pornography camps, moral panics, and debates concerning censorship and
freedom of speech (Ess, 1996). This also speaks of the dominance of North American
perspectives in studies of both pornography and the Internet.

Netporn and Alt Porn

Online porn has meant unprecedented visibility of sexual subcultures, diverse sexual
preferences, niches, and tastes. European scholars in particular have discussed this
proliferation under the term *netporn*, denoting "alternative body type tolerance
and amorphous queer sexuality, interesting art works and the writerly blogosphere,
visions of grotesque sex and warpunk activism" (Jacobs, Janssen, & Pasquinelli,
2007, p. 2). This definition marks netporn apart from porn on the net – the latter
referring to the circulation and reproduction of pornographies from print or video
online, and the former to experimental and artistic practices representing alternative aesthetics, politics, and economies, such as free sharing or activist uses of
the profits generated. Some identify netporn as exchanges and networked
experiences specific to the Internet that resist the commodity logic of the porn
industry (Shah, 2007). Others consider netporn an umbrella term for the diversity
of pornographies that have mushroomed online since the 1990s.

Of the practices categorized as netporn, alt porn (also referred to as "alternative"
"indie" and "alt.porn") has received most scholarly attention to date. Alt porn,
as represented by the well-known and commercially successful sites SuicideGirls

and BurningAngel, features female models with tattoos, piercings, punk and Goth coiffures. Alt porn sites incorporate the softcore pornographic into the subcultural, inviting users to read the models' blogs and profiles and to join a community based on shared cultural codes, music, lifestyle, or general attitude (Mies, 2006; Attwood, 2007; Magnet, 2007). In her analysis of SuicideGirls, Magnet (2007) argues that its articulations of female sexuality and agency are conditioned and dominated by maxims of profit. While alt and indie porn sites have been seen to challenge the porn industry in terms of their ethics, aesthetics, and economies (Mies, 2006), the two are not necessarily antithetical. Cramer and Home (2007, p. 165) go as far as to call indie porn "the research and development arm of the porn industry." In a more moderate phrasing, Attwood (2007) points out that the porn industry has turned towards alt porn when seeking out new audiences and uses for its online platforms.

The example of alt porn helps to illustrate both the dominance and the insufficiency of dualistic thinking when addressing online pornography. The alternative and the mainstream, the commercial and the non-commercial, the amateur and the professional – in addition to the already mentioned divisions between the anti-porn and anti-anti-porn stances – structure debates on porn at the very moment when such boundaries and opposites have become elastic indeed. So-called mainstream porn incorporates various fringes and extremities into its menu in order to attract new groups of users. *Hentai*, pornographic Japanese anime, which regularly displays fantastically exaggerated BDSM (bondage-domination-sadism-masochism) and non-consensual sex, is one example of this. As Dahlqvist and Vigilant (2004) illustrate, *hentai* was considered too extreme for video distribution in the 1990s, whereas it has since been incorporated as a niche into the diet of mainstream web porn sites. The bizarre catches the eye, attracts attention, and – perhaps – makes the visitor a paying user. Addressing this fragmentation of the mass market and the overall genre of pornography, Dery (2007b) argues that online pornographers aim to grab users "by their eyeballs" by showing them images amazing in their novelty, eccentricity, or extremity in order to mark themselves apart from that which is already familiar.

In her analysis of the rhetoric of freedom and choice related to online pornography, Chun (2006) shows that porn sites offering endless subcategories and special preferences simultaneously form micro-markets and increase the visibility of fetishes and kinks that were previously deemed subcultural or highly marginal (also Bennett, 2001, p. 384). Porn distributed in newsgroups and BBSs was difficult to index whereas portals, meta-sites, and search engines have enabled a broad variety of categories for users to choose from and "all these categories are one click away from each other" (Chun, 2006, p. 106). Such development is evident in the rise of the genre which Langman (2004) has titled "grotesque degradation," with its extreme and often aggressively sexist sub-genres – including sites advertising "painful anal," "cum guzzling sluts," or scatophilia. This logic of differentiation means that "the mainstream" is far from being something stable or unified but is instead constantly divided into endless categories, choices and preferences that online users need to navigate (Patterson, 2004, pp. 106–07). This also means that discussions of pornography as an assumedly unified and homogeneous entity are increasingly difficult and unconvincing.

Amateurs Abound

In addition to alt and indie porn, web distribution has increased the visibility of all kinds of marginal pornographies as the authors of artistic erotica, shoe fetish image galleries, vegan or fat porn are all making use of the web as a publishing platform (Tola, 2005). In comparison to magazine, video, or DVD publishing, the web is much more flexible and affordable for small producers (Lane, 2000, pp. 223–7; Thornburgh & Lin, 2002, pp. 82–3). Female porn entrepreneurs, often performing on the sites they run, have found novel forms of agency on the web, redefining the conditions of their work across the hierarchies of gender and race (Podlas, 2000; DeVoss, 2002; Miller-Young, 2007). For similar reasons, amateur pornographies have flourished online. Amateurs have been making porn in a range of media (still film cameras, Polaroid, or digital cameras) for decades whereas the "video revolution" of the 1980s – with easy-to-use video cameras and recorders – gave rise to amateur porn as a genre that was soon incorporated by the porn industry (O'Toole, 1998, p. 180; Patterson, 2004, pp. 110–11; Esch & Mayer, 2007, p. 10). Amateur pornographers can run their own sites and share their images and videos either privately or openly among anonymous users in forums ranging from newsgroups to professionally run websites with membership fees, streaming videos, and interaction possibilities (Lane, 2000, pp. 209–12; Patterson, 2004, pp. 110–19; Coopersmith, 2006, p. 2).

User-generated content has become increasingly central to business and site concepts of the so-called Web 2.0 (an industry-coined concept broadly describing the rise of wikis, blogs, podcasts, social networks, and communities in which users are content producers – or, according to the neologism, "produsers"). This is reflected in the high visibility of amateur pornographies and other sexually explicit representations produced – and partly also circulated – outside the porn industry. It also involves the blurring of the very notion of the pornographic: sexualized personal profiles on dating sites (according to popular practice men, for example, often choose to represent themselves through pictures of their genitalia) or explicit personal online exchanges (Attwood, 2006, pp. 79–81) can be seen as exemplifying the ways in which pornographic imagery or terminology provides templates for individual expressions of desire and arousal. As Mowlabocus (2007) points out, gay male pornography has become integral to gay self-representations online, particularly on dating sites. To the degree that these representations can be viewed as pornography – that is, as images viewed for arousal without any other interaction involved, all this involves a certain self-commodification (also McLelland, 2006, p. 81).

Amateur representations draw from the conventions of commercial pornography but they are more than mere approximations or imitations thereof. As the "documentary aura" of 1970s hardcore porn films "complete with wrinkles and wayward pubic hairs" (Patton, 1991, p. 375) has given way to increasingly stylized, polished, and airbrushed video productions, particularly in the US, claims for the realness of the sexual acts and the people performing them are made elsewhere. The rawness and realness of amateur porn – the idea that the performers are not actors and that they assumedly do what they do because they like doing it – is an attraction that the porn industry has tapped into by appropriating "amateur" as a sub-genre. The rise of "gonzo porn" since the late 1980s (i.e., videos shot by male director–performers claiming to show everyday sexual adventures as they occur) and diverse reality site and video concepts in the 1990s similarly speak of the attraction and centrality of "the real" in pornographic depiction (Esch & Mayer, 2007). The attraction of realness and immediacy is equally central to online live shows such as those performed on webcams (Bennett, 2001, pp. 387–8; Chun, 2006, pp. 102–04).

In his studies of Usenet alt.fetish groups, Sergio Messina has titled the amateur porn images distributed in them as *realcore* – that is, as a genre that stands apart from the traditional markers of hardcore and softcore in its authenticity and overall realness (in Dery, 2007a). According to Messina, realcore is about the real desires of the performers who also desire to be seen: hence the audience has an integral role in the circuits of desire and pleasure involved in amateur porn. Since such pornographies exist outside the "complex" of the porn industry – in the sense of large production companies, casting agencies, star performers, commodity logic, and distribution networks – they are also considered more ethical and less problematic as consumable images. The same applies to alt porn and other variations of "netporn."

Porn exchanges have been active in peer-to-peer (P2P) networks, although these have also been heavily regulated due to the possibilities of exchanging child pornography (Greenfield, 2004; Phillips, 2005; Coopersmith, 2006, pp. 14–15). Jacobs sees P2P practices in general as challenging both the normative codes of porn and the clear division of porn performers and their audiences (in Tola, 2005; also Juffer, 1998, p. 11). Such blurring of the boundaries marking porn producers and performers apart from consumers and viewers can be seen as a more general trend evident within amateur porn. For some, this represents the democratization of pornography: anyone can produce their own pornography and, if they so desire, make a business out of it (Coopersmith, 2006, pp. 10–11). There is, however, no guarantee that audiences will find the content or that profits are actually made as most users browse for free porn.

Experiences of porn consumption are embedded in particular frameworks that are economic, aesthetic, social, as well as technological. These vary drastically between different media, as well as different online pornographies and their platforms: amateur image swapping one-on-one differs from distributing the same images in newsgroups, or uploading them to an amateur porn image gallery or a personal profile in an adult dating service. As Klastrup (2007) points out in an extra-pornographic context, online platforms of distribution, storage, and publication involve codes and terms that shape and inspire both amateur productions and the ways of interpreting and interacting with them. These specificities need to be accounted for, if we are to understand some of the "social life" that these texts have.

Methodological Challenges

In discussions of online pornography, mainstream commercial pornography catering primarily to male heterosexual consumers and following the generic codes and conventions, as developed from print to screen, is positioned as the norm, yet it is rarely investigated or analyzed in itself. Given the scholarly attention directed towards alternative and independent pornographies, as well as extreme and abusive imageries, this aversion appears both striking and telling. The mainstream is, perhaps, assumed to be something too familiar and obvious to necessitate closer analysis. According to this logic, further investigations could only repeat that which we already know about pornography. At the same time, the shortage of actual studies addressing mainstream online porn means that this knowledge is based on assumptions and ad hoc discoveries.

Pornography tends to be generic even for a popular genre. With some risk of generalization, pornographic depiction draws on a limited and stylized range of terminology, characters, scenarios, and acts. Since these are easily recognizable, they are also easy to access in the sense of requiring little preparation on the part of the user. This leads to certain predictability as one video or image bears close resemblance to countless others. Furthermore, porn relies on clearly cut divisions and hierarchies. The roles of the seducer and the seduced or the dominant and the submissive are easily recognizable, and intertwined with identity categories such as age, gender, class, or ethnicity (Paasonen, 2006). Studies of pornography that limit themselves to stating this, or interpreting relations of control directly as ones concerning social power, however, largely miss the generic modality and specificity of pornography. While making claims for the realness of the bodies, acts, and pleasures shown, pornography is fundamentally unrealistic – or fantastic – in its hyperbolic display. Highly stylized and standardized, porn contrasts fantasy scenes with actual bodies, resulting in a highly carnal and visceral relation between the text and its consumer (Patton, 1991, pp. 378–9). The development of pornography as a genre has been addressed in the framework of film studies (centrally Williams, 1989). The new technologies of production and distribution call for closer investigations of how the genre has been shaped by networked communication. In any case, considerations of online pornography *as content* should pay special attention to its particular modalities and historically constructed specificities and characteristics, rather than providing readings that are either literal or make use of pornography as a cultural, social, or political metaphor. This is also a methodological question, and one necessitating more critical attention in studies of the Internet.

It is not exaggerated to claim that debates on pornography – popular, journalistic, and academic – are heavy with political investments, be these conservative-Christian, feminist, queer, or libertarian in character. Anti-pornography feminists oppose porn as a form of sexist oppression whereas other anti-porn advocates oppose it as something obscene, morally corrupt, and generally offensive. Some see pornography as emblematic of mass culture and the logic of sameness (and hence as predictable, repetitive, and generally poor content) and yet others as contributing to the general sexualization of culture, and as harmful to minors. Defenses of pornography, again, range from arguments for freedom of speech and trade to the importance of sexual fantasy and play, identity politics, and the visibility of diverse sexualities. The plethora of available online pornographies guarantees that virtually any stance on porn can be backed up with multiple examples supporting one's argument.

Anyone studying pornography is, quite justly, bound to face the question as to why she has chosen to study the examples she has, and to what degree her findings are to be generalized. This is due both to the range and diversity of different pornographies, and to histories of purposeful sampling: anti-pornography authors, for example, have been accused of using decontextualized BDSM imageries as evidence of porn as violence (Rubin, 1995, pp. 245–6). Similarly, reading online pornography as symptomatic of late modern capitalism and masculinity in crisis, Langman (2004) focuses on extreme and misogynistic examples to prove his point. Authors approaching online porn from a more positive angle, again, tend to focus on examples that challenge gender normativity, porn clichés and the commodity logic of the porn industry (Villarejo, 2005; Dery, 2007a; Shah, 2007).

One solution to the problems of focus and representativeness has been found from relatively large sampling enabling quantitative analysis. Following this principle, Mehta's (2001) study of pornography on Usenet in the mid-1990s involves a content analysis of 9,800 randomly selected images coded according to acts performed and the age of the performers, presented in statistical terms. Large samples, rather than analysis of singular sites, make it possible to argue something about general trends and conventions. This is also why I initially launched my own investigations into online porn through a sample of 366 email porn spam messages: rather than seeking out any particular kind of pornography, I chose to study the examples sent to my university account (Paasonen, 2006). While partial, I found such sampling justifiable in terms of both scope and method. The overall question concerning method and analysis is, however, considerably more complex.

Content analysis and other forms of "grounded theory" mean that the researcher theorizes on the basis of the research material, as analyzed though coding. This implies certain objectivity, "just looking" at what there is to be found, rather than approaching research material through a preconceived framework. Yet, given the political and affective investments involved in pornography and public debates concerning it, how is such neutrality to be achieved? Or, given the diversity of different forms of online pornography, can one come up with representative samples (Buzzell, 2005, p. 32)? Large sampling is no guarantee for representativeness as such. In a 1995 study descriptively titled "Marketing pornography on the information superhighway: A survey of 917,410 images, descriptions, short stories, and animations downloaded 8.5 million times by consumers in over 2,000 cities in forty countries, provinces, and territories," Rimm addressed an exhausting volume of online pornography harvested mainly from BBSs with the aid of "linguistic parsing software," which meant analyzing image descriptions, rather than the images themselves. As critics of the study have pointed out, it tended to "inflate the prevalence of certain acts and underestimated others" while also suggesting that Internet "technology brings to the surface the perversity lying within us all" (Mehta, 2001, p. 696; Chun, 2006, p. 84). Certain problems are also involved in analyzing and making claims about images and animations that one has actually never seen.

Content description is to a degree already an interpretation that is filtered through the values, premises, and personal investments of the researcher in question. What one scholar identifies as violent pornography, another does not, and this influences both the coding and the results. Some might label the ubiquitous sites featuring "teen" and "barely legal" young women as child porn whereas others would decline to do so. Identifying elements such as the age or ethnicity in porn images is often difficult (due to low image resolution, cropping, partial focus or possible mutual partners) and can necessitate creative readings (see also Mehta, 2001, pp. 699–700). Due to the role of interpretation and reading, there is a need to integrate methods of textual analysis – such as representational analysis, iconography, or close reading – into the palette of social sciences research methods (Paasonen, 2007). There is, however, relatively little discussion to date on research methods and their various implications in studies of pornography. Methodological discussions are bound to become increasingly pertinent as online pornography becomes less under-studied than it is today. As several researchers have already pointed out, this broadening of scholarly attention towards online pornography should also mean hearing from its consumers – their choices, preferences, and experiences (Lillie, 2002; Buzzell, 2005; Attwood, 2005; McKee, 2006). A focus on pornographic texts, independent of the exact method used, produces knowledge about their forms, conventions, and relative prevalence. While researchers can interpret their meanings and implications, such investigations cannot account for the meanings attached to them in experiences and acts of consumption.

Local and Global

In addition to methodological issues, more attention needs to be paid to the international variations, traffic, and economy of online porn: currently, case studies tend to be much too focused on US examples. It is hardly breaking news that pornography is business on a global scale: that products and capital circulate, that people move and that business is networked. Online distribution has helped to efface some of the meanings of location as people access porn from servers around the world and upload their own contributions virtually independent of their physical whereabouts. In addition to global circulation and access to porn, local productions address smaller niche audiences (in terms of language and cultural context as well as sexual preferences). Hence Italian or Finnish users have the choice of accessing porn that is locally produced and features well-known performers as well as semi-amateur "girls next door," or browsing pornographies produced elsewhere and distributed in a range of languages. The US continues to dominate porn production and distribution but it is countered by local practices and business strategies: in Europe, companies network in order to resist US dominance on the market.

From the perspective of the porn industry, online distribution has obvious benefits. It necessitates no manufacture of physical products (such as DVDs or magazines) and bandwidth expenses replace those involved in retail. Online distribution also enables bypassing local legislation as content deemed illegal in one country can be hosted on a server situated elsewhere. Locally, the question is then one of regulating access – something that has been done with child pornography but less with other kinds of pornographies in Western countries. In a global perspective, the regulation of online pornography (and of the Internet in general) varies considerably, as do understandings concerning the category of pornography (Kuipers, 2006; Paasonen, Nikunen, & Saarenmaa, 2007, pp. 15–16). At the same time, the proliferation of online pornographies, mainstream and fringe alike, questions the very notion of the pornographic. All this makes context specificity imperative when producing knowledge about online pornographies, their aesthetics, audiences, or economies. Rather than contributing to the dichotomous dynamics prevalent in popular media discourses, academic studies should be committed to accounting for the diversities and possible complexities involved.

In terms of porn use, the Internet has opened up a maze of options that necessitates some navigation skill. Porn addiction has become a central theme of public debate and concern, even if forms of addictive or compulsive use most often associated with the Internet – namely porn and gambling – are hardly specific or native to the medium in question (e.g. Cooper et al., 1999; Putnam & Maheu, 2000; Schneider, 2000; Griffiths, 2000). The discourse of addiction has perhaps worked to simplify the specific dynamics involved in searching and browsing for online porn. As Patterson (2004) points out, the experiences of accessing membership sites and searching for free porn vary considerably. Whereas the former mainly involves choosing from a relatively limited selection, the latter involves searching, frustration, waiting, and delay. While online porn promises immediate gratification, the actual pleasures of surfing for porn are different and based on the desire for something new. This perpetual movement is crucial to the experience and pleasure of web browsing (pp. 109–10; also Lillie, 2002, p. 38). The continuous motion from one document to another is not necessarily initiated by the user herself since pornographic sites have been long known to make use of pop-ups and to "mouse-trap" users by forwarding them to forever new pages as they try to close the browser window (Chun, 2006, pp. 124–5; Coopersmith, 2006, p. 9). Furthermore, hyperlinks often lead to directions unintended by the user: to use one example, meta-site links for free porn in virtually any category are likely to lead to any number of pay-sites (Bennett, 2001, p. 385).

It is not sufficient to consider the Internet a platform or "container" for pornography that has merely taken up the functions of magazines, DVDs, or VHS tapes in the distribution and consumption of porn. Rather, "sexual desires are being mediated through the pleasures of the technology itself, and the particular fantasies it has to offer" (Patterson, 2004, p. 119). In the case of online porn, these involve possibilities of interaction, anonymity, realness, and transparency – the interaction of bodies, interfaces, and network technologies that give rise to particular kinds of expectations and experiences (Lillie, 2002, pp. 37–41; also Uebel, 2000). Uses of Internet porn are by and large private, yet the medium also enables new kinds of interactions, intimacies, intensities, and exchanges that are social in nature (Lillie, 2002; Reading, 2005). These experiences and possibilities mark a departure from pornographies distributed in other media. At the same time, it is important not to overemphasize the differences between "traditional" porn and "cyberporn." Digital and network technologies have opened up new forms of circulation and exchange while also incorporating and appropriating familiar aesthetics, commodity forms, and practices of usage. Consequently, considerations of online pornography need to pay attention to intermedial ties and developments in order not to detach digital exchanges from their historical contexts.

Research methods, local contexts, and intermedial connections all represent challenges to studies of online porn. In addition, the movements of porn economy remain a challenge to scholarly analysis, online as well as offline, since information on the economies of porn enterprise is hard to come by. It also seems that the volume of free pornography currently available is compromising the success of commercial sites that have previously been seen as impervious to economic oscillations. Not only are DVD sales on the decrease, but also commercial porn sites are finding it difficult to compete with free user-generated pornographies. At the time of writing, YouPorn, the pornographic version of the video publishing service YouTube launched in 2006, was the highest-ranking adult site. Necessitating no subscription fees, with users sharing videos among themselves, YouPorn – like its multiple competitors with similar business concepts – makes its profits on advertisement revenues and premium membership fees. The massive popularity of such sites represents a shift in the economies and perhaps also in the aesthetics and ethics of online porn. Pornographic content production may not be the most popular example in discussions of produsage, Web 2.0, or participatory culture. Given the central role of pornography in the development of online business and web technologies, these recent developments may nevertheless be telling of fundamental transformations in commercial content production and distribution more generally.

References

Attwood, F. (2005). What do people do with porn? Qualitative research into the consumption, use and experience of pornography and other sexually explicit media. *Sexuality & Culture*, 9(2), 65–86.

Attwood, F. (2006). Sexed up: Theorizing the sexualization of culture. *Sexualities*, 9(1), 77–94.

Attwood, F. (2007). No money shot? Commerce, pornography and new sex taste cultures. *Sexualities*, 10(4), 441–56.

Barron, M., & Kimmel, M. (2000). Sexual violence in three pornographic media: Towards a sociological explanation. *The Journal of Sex Research*, 37(2), 161–8.

Bennett, D. (2001). Pornography-dot-com: Eroticising privacy on the Internet. *Review of Education/Pedagogy/Cultural Studies*, 23(4), 381–91.

Buzzell, T. (2005). Demographic characteristics of persons using pornography in three technological contexts. *Sexuality & Culture*, 9(1), 28–48.

Califia, P. (1994). *Public Culture: The Culture of Radical Sex*. Pittsburgh: Cleis Press.

Chun, W. H. K. (2006). *Control and Freedom: Power and Paranoia in the Age of Fiber Optics*. Cambridge, MA: MIT Press.

Cooper, A., Putnam, D. E., Planchon, L. A., & Boies, S. C. (1999). Online sexual compulsivity: Getting tangled in the net. *Sexual Addiction & Compulsivity*, 6(2), 79–104.

Coopersmith, J. (2006). Does your mother know what you *really* do? The changing nature and image of computer-based pornography. *History and Technology*, 22(1), 1–25.

Cramer, F., & Home, S. (2007). Pornographic coding. In K. Jacobs, M. Janssen, & M. Pasquinelli (eds.), *C'Lick Me: A Netporn Studies Reader* (pp. 159–71). Amsterdam: Institute of Network Cultures.

Cronin, B., & Davenport, E. (2001). E-rogenous zones: Positioning pornography in the digital economy. *The Information Society*, 17(1), 33–48.

Dahlqvist, J. P., & Vigilant, L. G. (2004). Way better than real: Manga sex to tentacle hentai. In D. D. Waskul (ed.), *Net.seXXX: Readings of Sex, Pornography, and the Internet* (pp. 91–103). New York: Peter Lang.

Dery, M. (2007a). Naked lunch: Talking realcore with Sergio Messina. In K. Jacobs, M. Janssen, & M. Pasquinelli (eds.), *C'Lick Me: A Netporn Studies Reader* (pp. 17–30). Amsterdam: Institute of Network Cultures.

Dery, M. (2007b). Paradise lust: Pornotopia meets the culture wars. In K. Jacobs, M. Janssen, & M. Pasquinelli (eds.), *C'Lick Me: A Netporn Studies Reader* (pp. 125–48). Amsterdam: Institute of Network Cultures.

DeVoss, D. (2002). Women's porn sites – Spaces of fissure and eruption, or, "I'm a little bit of everything." *Sexuality & Culture*, 6(3), 75–94.

Dworkin, A. (1989). *Pornography: Men Possessing Women*. E. P. Dutton, New York.

Esch, K., & Mayer, V. (2007). How unprofessional: The profitable partnership of amateur porn and celebrity culture. In S. Paasonen, K. Nikunen, & L. Saarenmaa (eds.), *Pornification: Sex and Sexuality in Media Culture* (pp. 99–111). Oxford: Berg.

Ess, C. (1996). Philosophical approaches to pornography, free speech, and CMC. Cyberspace as Plato's *Republic*: Or, why this special issue? *Computer-Mediated Communication Magazine*, 3(1). Retrieved February 28, 2008, from http://www.december.com/cmc/mag/1996/jan/ed.html.

Filippo, J. di (2000). Pornography on the web. In D. Gauntlett (ed.), *Web.Studies: Rewiring Media Studies for the Digital Age* (pp. 122–9). London: Arnold.

Freeman-Longo, R. E. (2000). Children, teens, and sex on the Internet. *Sexual Addiction & Compulsivity*, 7 (1/2), 75–90.

Greenfield, P. M. (2004). Inadvertent exposure to pornography on the Internet: Implications of peer-to-peer file-sharing networks for child development and families. *Applied Developmental Psychology*, 25(6), 741–50.

Griffiths, M. (2000). Does Internet and computer "addiction" exist? Some case study evidence. *CyberPsychology & Behavior*, 3(2), 211–18.

Halavais, A. (2005). Small pornographies. *ACM SIGGROUP Bulletin*, 25(2), 19–22.

Heins, M. (2001). *Not in Front of the Children: "Indecency," Censorship, and the Innocence of Youth*. New York: Hill and Wang.

Hughes, D. (1999). The Internet and global prostitution industry. In S. Hawthrone & R. Klein (eds.), *CyberFeminism: Connectivity, Critique and Creativity* (pp. 185–21). Melbourne: Spinifex.

Jacobs, K. (2004). The new media schooling of the amateur pornographer: Negotiating contracts and singing orgasm. Retrieved February 28, 2008, from http://www.libidot.org/katrien/tester/articles/negotiating-print.html.

Jacobs, K., Janssen, M., & Pasquinelli, M. (2007) Introduction. In K. Jacobs, M. Janssen, & M. Pasquinelli (eds.), *C'Lick Me: A Netporn Studies Reader* (pp. 1–3). Amsterdam: Institute of Network Cultures.

Jansen, B. J., & Spink, A. (2006). How are we searching the World Wide Web? A comparison of nine search engine transaction logs. *Information Processing and Management*, 42(1), 258–9.

Jenkins, P. (2001). *Beyond Tolerance: Child Pornography on the Internet*. New York: New York University Press.

Juffer, J. (1998). *At Home with Pornography: Women, Sex, and Everyday Life*. New York: New York University Press.

Kibby, M., & Costello, B. (2001) Between the image and the act: Interactive sex entertainment on the Internet. *Sexualities: Studies in Culture and Society*, 4(3), 353–69.

Klastrup, L. (2007). From texts to artefacts: Storytelling version 3.0. Paper presented at the NordMedia 2007 conference, Helsinki, 16–19 August.

Kleinhans, C. (2004). Virtual child porn: The law and the semiotic of the image. In P. Church Gibson (ed.), *More Dirty Looks: Gender, Pornography and Power*, 2nd edn. (pp. 71–84). London: BFI.

Kuipers, G. (2006). The social construction of digital danger: Debating, defusing and inflating the moral dangers of online humor and pornography in the Netherlands and the United States. *New Media & Society*, 8(3), 379–400.

Lane, F. S. III (2000). *Obscene Profits: The Entrepreneurs of Pornography in the Cyber Age*. New York: Routledge.

Langman, L. (2004). Grotesque degradation: Globalization, carnivalization, and cyberporn. In D. D. Waskul (ed.), *Net.seXXX: Readings of Sex, Pornography, and the Internet* (pp. 193–216). New York: Peter Lang.

Levy, N. (2002). Virtual child pornography: The eroticization of inequality. *Ethics and Information Technology*, 4(4), 319–23.

Lillie, J. (2002). Sexuality and cyberporn: Towards a new agenda for research. *Sexuality & Culture*, 6(2), 25–47.

MacKinnon, C. (1987). *Feminism Unmodified: Discourses on Life and Law*. Cambridge, MA: Harvard University Press.

Magnet, S. (2007). Feminist sexualities, race and the Internet: An investigation of Suicidegirls.com. *New Media & Society*, 9(4), 577–602.

McKee, A. (2006). The aesthetics of pornography: The insights of consumers. *Continuum: Journal of Media & Cultural Studies*, 20(4), 523–39.

McLelland, M. (2006). The best website for men who have sex with men: Cruisingforsex.com. In A. McKee (ed.), *Beautiful Things in Popular Culture* (pp. 79–86). Oxford: Blackwell.

Mehta, M. D. (2001). Pornography in Usenet: A study of 9,800 randomly selected images. *CyberPsychology & Behavior*, 4(6), 695–703.

Mehta, M. D., & Plaza, D. (1997). Content analysis of pornographic images available on the Internet. *The Information Society*, 13(2), 153–61.

Mies, G. (2006). Evolution of the alternative: History and controversies of the alt-erotica industry. *American Sexuality Magazine*. Retrieved February 28, 2008, from http://nsrc.sfsu.edu/MagArticle.cfm?Article=631&PageID=0.

Miller-Young, M. (2007). Sexy and smart: Black women and the politics of self-authorship in netporn. In K. Jacobs, M. Janssen, & M. Pasquinelli (eds.), *C'Lick Me: A Netporn Studies Reader* (pp. 205–16). Amsterdam: Institute of Network Cultures.

Mowlabocus, S. (2007). Gay men and the pornification of everyday life. In S. Paasonen, K. Nikunen, & L. Saarenmaa (eds.), *Pornification: Sex and Sexuality in Media Culture* (pp. 61–72). Oxford: Berg.

O'Toole, L. (1998). *Pornocopia: Porn, Sex, Technology and Desire*. London: Serpent's Tail.

Paasonen, S. (2006). Email from Nancy Nutsucker: Representation and gendered address in online pornography. *European Journal of Cultural Studies*, 9(4), 403–20.

Paasonen, S. (2007). Strange bedfellows: Pornography, affect and feminist reading. *Feminist Theory*, 8(1), 43–57.

Paasonen, S., Nikunen, K., & Saarenmaa, L. (2007). Pornification and the education of desire. In S. Paasonen, K. Nikunen, & L. Saarenmaa (eds.), *Pornification: Sex and Sexuality in Media Culture* (pp. 1–20). Oxford: Berg.

Patterson, Z. (2004). Going on-line: Consuming pornography in the digital era. In L. Williams (ed.), *Porn Studies* (pp. 104–23). Durham, NC: Duke University Press.

Patton, C. (1991). Visualizing safe sex: When pedagogy and pornography collide. In D. Fuss (ed.), *Inside/Out: Lesbian Theories, Gay Theories* (pp. 373–86). New York: Routledge.

Perdue, L. (2002). *Erotica Biz: How Sex Shaped the Internet*. New York: Writers Club Press.

Phillips, D. (2005). Can desire go on without a body? Pornographic exchange and the death of the sun. *Culture Machine/InterZone*. Retrieved February 28, 2008, from http://culturemachine.tees.ac.uk/InterZone/dphillips.html.

Podlas, K. (2000). Mistresses of their domain: How female entrepreneurs in cyberporn are initiating a gender power shift. *CyberPsychology & Behavior*, 3(5), 847–54.

Putnam, D. E., & Maheu, M. M. (2000). Online sexual addiction and compulsivity: Integrating web resources and behavioral telehealth in treatment. *Sexual Addiction & Compulsivity*, 7(2), 91–112.

Reading, A. (2005). Professing porn or obscene browsing? On proper distance in the university classroom. *Media, Culture & Society*, 27(1), 123–30.

Rimm, M. (1995). Marketing pornography on the information superhighway: a survey of 917,410 images, descriptions, short stories, and animations downloaded 8.5 million times by consumers in over 2,000 cities in forty countries, provinces, and territories. *Georgetown Law Journal*, 83(5), 1849–934.

Rubin, G. (1995). Misguided, dangerous and wrong: An analysis of anti-pornography politics. In G. Dines & J. M. Humez (eds.), *Gender, Race and Class in Media: A Text-Reader* (pp. 244–53). Thousand Oaks, CA: Sage.

Schneider, J. P. (2000). Effects of cybersex addiction on the family: Results of a survey. *Sexual Addiction & Compulsivity*, 7(1), 31–58.

Shah, N. (2007). PlayBlog: Pornography, performance and cyberspace. In K. Jacobs, M. Janssen, & M. Pasquinelli (eds.), *C'Lick Me: A Netporn Studies Reader* (pp. 31–44). Amsterdam: Institute of Network Cultures.

Slater, D. (1998). Trading sexpics on IRC: Embodiment and authenticity on the Internet. *Body & Society*, 4(4), 91–117.

Spink, A., Partridge, H., & Jansen, B. J. (2006). Sexual and pornographic web searching: Trend analysis. *First Monday*, 11(9). Retrieved February 28, 2008, from http://www.firstmonday.org/issues/issue11_9/spink/index.html.

Thornburgh, D., & Lin, H. S. (2002). *Youth, Pornography, and the Internet*. Computer Science and Telecommunications Board, National Science Council. Washington, DC: National Academy Press.

Tola, M. (2005). Re-routing the (a)sex drives of Big Dickie: Interview with Katrien Jacobs. Retrieved February 28, 2008, from http://www.networkcultures.org/netporn/index.php?onderdeelID=1&paginaID=13&itemID=70.

Uebel, M. (2000). Toward a symptomatology of cyberporn. *Theory & Event*, 3(4). Retrieved February 28, 2008, from http://muse.jhu.edu/journals/theory_and_event/v003/3.4uebel.html.

Villarejo, A. (2004). Defycategory.com, or the place of categories in intermedia. In P. Church Gibson (ed.), *More Dirty Looks: Gender, Pornography and Power*, 2nd edn. (pp. 85–91). London: BFI.

Waskul, D. D. (2004). *Net.seXXX: Readings of Sex, Pornography, and the Internet*. New York: Peter Lang.

White, A. E. (2006). *Virtually Obscene: The Case for an Uncensored Internet*. Jefferson: McFarland.

Williams, L. (1989). *Hard Core: Power, Pleasure, and the "Frenzy of the Visible."* Berkeley: University of California Press.

21

Music and the Internet

Steve Jones

Historical accounts will differ, but for most people the first and most obvious connection between music and the Internet was made by Napster in 1999. Inevitably for Napster, its fortunes rose and fell quickly, and it carries little sentimental weight. Revered and reviled, it stands as a symbol of a past Internet era, although it seems unlikely to be thought of nostalgically, unlike the Sony Walkman, transistor radio, or phonograph. Ostensibly both brand and software, Napster, like the MP3s that were shared through it, was not a physical object that could be displayed as one might display an album cover or vintage radio. But without the object, to what extent is nostalgia possible?

It may be too soon for nostalgia, since the history of digital music is still unfolding. Several very good historical accounts of online music have already been published (Alderman, 2001; Duckworth, 2005; Ayers, 2006; Burkart, 2006) and so will not be recounted in detail here. While this chapter will mention past developments regarding music and the Internet, the intent is to provide context illustrating the consequences of this turbulent intersection of art and technology particularly in Western popular music. When music met the Internet the repercussions were both deep and wide, for the music industry, musicians, and music fans, the three foci of this chapter.

Music and the Internet: The Music Industry

From the perspective of the music industry, the story of music and the Internet is a tale of loss. The newspaper headline might read, "Lost Sales, Revenue, Devastate Music Industry." Beginning with sales of physical recordings, CDs in particular, the recording industry is indeed suffering (IFPI, 2010; RIAA, 2010). There is, however, another side to the story. For instance, other revenue streams have become available to record companies. Sales of digital downloads, while not profiting major record labels to the same degree as in years past, are now a significant income element. Royalties from digital performances of copyrighted music are now flowing to rights holders. Sales of ringtones also generate additional income.

But to look at sales figures or performance royalties is only to see the tip of the iceberg that seems ready to sink the music industry. While the music industry has blamed Internet-using music fans who have illegally uploaded and downloaded music since Napster's advent, such activity is only partly responsible for any slump in the music business. The Internet changed sales and consumption patterns in additional ways, and it did so quite early in its ascendance during the 1990s as a new medium of communication (Holland, 1998).

One important change was the rise of online-only retail outlets. Without having to maintain brick-and-mortar facilities online retailers could be more flexible on pricing and promotions than traditional record stores. The 1990s and 2000s saw the shrinking and outright demise of several established retail chains, such as Tower Records, Sam Goody, and Virgin Megastore. In virtually all of those cases the major reason cited for closing stores or going out of business was the difficulty of competing with online retailers (though competition from "big box" retailers like Best Buy and Borders in the US must have been a contributing factor). The Internet also provided a large market for used recordings, one much larger than had been available to most music fans, particularly those outside urban areas. The greater availability of used records had consequences for the music retail chains, but it also had dire consequences for smaller, independently owned record stores, many of which relied on the used-record trade to stay in business.

The music industry was unprepared for uploading and downloading of digital music, whether illegal or legal. Rather than developing alternatives to illegal file-sharing tools like Napster and LimeWire, and sites like BearShare and RapidShare, the music industry focused most of its efforts on finding and shutting down file-sharing sites, and prosecuting those who illegally shared files. The Recording Industry Association of America (RIAA), a trade group representing major US record labels, was instrumental in suing people it believed were illegally sharing files (Electronic Frontier Foundation, 2008). In the meantime, mp3.com began operation in 1997, Apple introduced the iPod in 2001 and the iTunes music store in 2003, numerous streaming music sites sprang up, and in 2007 even Amazon launched an online music store. In short, the music industry failed to enter the digital retail space on its own terms, just as brick-and-mortar retail spaces were crumbling. One consequence of that failure was the ascendance of Apple's iTunes music store as the top US music seller in 2009, accounting for 26.7 percent of music sales in the US that year (Christman, 2010).

By the late 2000s streaming music services such as Last.fm, Pandora, and Lala began offering alternatives to downloading and to radio. Whereas before the Internet, music was marketed and promoted to an audience in a closed loop primarily between record companies and radio stations, by the 2000s there was clearly no longer any such loop. Listeners became aware of new music via multiple channels:

streaming music sites, friends, file sharing, websites, music blogs, Internet radio stations, and so on. Numerous means of discovering and attending to music were now competing with the traditional ways the industry reached audiences.

Another consequence of this proliferation was the lack of a secure system for payments for performances. Traditionally, performance royalties from broadcasting and other uses of music (in advertising, or in concert) were collected by performance rights organizations such as Broadcast Music, Inc. (BMI), the American Society of Composers and Publishers (ASCAP), and similar organizations with which composers and publishers of music could affiliate. (Analogous organizations performed such services in other countries.) Initially, none of those organizations had a mechanism for tracking streaming music or other online performances and collecting royalties, nor were those who played music online legally required to pay royalties. In 1995 the US Congress passed the Digital Performance in Sound Recordings Act. Three years later Congress passed the Digital Millennium Copyright Act. Those two laws created a legal requirement that those who transmit digital music via the Internet pay royalties. A non-profit organization, SoundExchange, was designated by the Librarian of Congress to collect and distribute those royalties to copyright owners. As of April 1, 2010, SoundExchange paid out over $360 million to rights holders (SoundExchange, 2010).

In sum, throughout the rise in popularity of the Internet, the music industry has generally been reactive rather than proactive in its approach to the new medium. There is little evidence that it will act differently in the near future. Meanwhile, the audience for music marches to its own beat.

Music and the Internet: The Audience

In contrast to the music industry, the music consumer has been largely proactive in taking advantage of new media for music. Almost as soon as software for downloading music became widely available, millions of US Internet users were downloading music. A 2000 report by the Pew Internet & American Life Project (Rainie, Fox, & Lenhart, 2000) estimated that 38 percent of all US Internet users had used the Internet to listen to or download music, and 14 percent had downloaded music for free that they did not already own in some other format (LP, CD, or cassette). Notably, the report was based on a survey of adult Internet users (18 years and older) and likely greatly underestimates the number of Internet users downloading music.

But perhaps most important about that data is that it was gathered a mere couple of years after the popularization of the MP3 format. While the format was patented in 1989, the first portable MP3 player was commercially available in the US beginning in 1997, and WinAMP, a free and widely used software for playing MP3 files on the Windows operating system, became available only in 1998. The very popular Rio series of portable MP3 players by Diamond Multimedia was also released in 1998, followed by the Creative Nomad players, introduced in 2000.

Also that year, Apple purchased the company that made SoundJam software, which allowed Macintosh computers to manage MP3 files on portable players, and renamed the software iTunes. The ascendance of the MP3 format as a means of storage, playback, and transfer of music files was swift and sure. Even though Apple's iPod was introduced only in late 2001, it was considered a latecomer to the field of portable MP3 players. Yet as of this writing (mid-2010) it continues to dominate the market.

Indeed, the word "iPod" has become synonymous with any MP3 player, just as "Kleenex" has become synonymous with "tissue." Words like MP3, iTunes, streaming, downloading, file sharing, and others, have become part of the lexicon surrounding popular music in the Internet age. While the focus of debates about digital music has largely centered on software, file-sharing sites, and portable devices, the habits and discourse of music fans have changed as much as or more than the technologies so frequently covered by the press. Discussions among music fans today are more likely to be about an artist's website, Twitter posts, or YouTube videos.

The portability of music is not very much in question. Like many who grew up in the 1960s and 1970s in the US, my lifelong impression of popular music has been that it is portable. In my childhood it came on records and on transistor radios, and soon thereafter it came on cassette tapes. My memory tells me that it was almost always something that could be copied, since by the early 1970s cassette tapes and recorders became available and relatively inexpensive.

But I never considered music to be free, nor did most other music fans. Even though one could swap cassette tapes or listen to the radio, the music one wanted to have on hand, at home, to own, came at a cost. The radio was fickle – it rarely played what you wanted – and the quality of dubbed and traded cassettes was so-so, at best. Thus we bought records, tapes, and, later, CDs. While music technology, the music business, and the state of computing and networking were far different in the 1960s, 1970s, and 1980s than now, most issues with which musicians, record companies, and fans struggled were ultimately not very different. It is primarily the scale of things and the relationships between listeners, fans, media, the music industry, and musicians that the Internet's development altered.

Exploring the sudden rise in popularity of the MP3 format and its centrality to contemporary upheavals in popular music would require a book unto itself. The brief outlines, though, are possible to sketch. First it is necessary to delve into the history of popular music in the US (and the Western world generally). The context for file sharing and music online is formed from the shared countercultural underpinnings of the popular music audience and the development of online communities and personal computing (Jones, 2002). Popular music contributed much common ground for shared community among US youth, both prior to World War II, and even more significantly after the war. To mainstream media, however, popular music was not a central concern, nor an important source of content. While a great deal of media attention focused on popular music from the late 1950s onward, it was generally regarded as a symptom of youth malaise (at best) or a sign of Communist infiltration (at worst). Broadcast media, particularly radio, increasingly began programming popular music from the 1950s but largely did so within commercial structures. Alternatives did not exist: the cost of entry for radio and TV was so high that it prohibited the formation of strong alternative media. By the late 1960s FM radio, and soon thereafter college radio stations, became an alternative to mainstream radio (and most, if not all, now have an online presence).

In the meantime, as access to computers on college campuses became more common by the 1960s, the earliest online communities emerged (most notably on the PLATO system and on the WELL, with the latter directly linked to the countercultural ethos via ties to the *Whole Earth Catalog*). Music discussions thrived on those systems, and also led to the creation of many newsgroups on Usenet, and, later, numerous World Wide Web sites.

Indeed, the real revolution in popular music in regard to the Internet is to be found in the availability of news, information, and discussion about music and musicians facilitated by Internet media. The formations of online communities oriented around particular types of music or particular musicians and bands offered people ways to discover new music and indulge tastes they would have had difficulty indulging via old media, alongside others with similar interests. Online communities, whether built by fans or commercial interests such as radio stations, record labels, or magazines, provided an alternative means of connecting both with music and music fans. They also became a means of connecting with musicians themselves, via social networking services like MySpace, Facebook, and Twitter (Baym, 2007; see also Baym, chapter 18, this volume).

This evolution is much lengthier and more complicated than what I have written here. The consequences for music fans are equally, if not more, complicated and lengthy. There are several that cannot be overlooked, but the one that deserves most attention is the notion of "sharing" itself.

Listening to music is an oddly schizophrenic thing. On the one hand, music is deeply personal. We all have our individual interpretations, memories, histories, and tastes that shape and inform our listening. Our preferences may change, but they are our preferences, influenced by others, but personal enough that showing an iPod playlist to someone is for many people too revealing an act (despite perhaps willingly sharing other kinds of personal information on Facebook). On the other hand, music is a communal experience, even when listening to it singly with headphones or earbuds, as it connects people in imagined communities and imagined communions, not only with its musicians but also with other listeners who have heard it, are hearing it, or will hear it. Even when it is not being experienced live, as an audience member, it is understood that there is an audience, an asynchronous one, a community of fans. The underlying message in the medium is that you are not alone. Perhaps nowhere is this combination of the personal and social better expressed than via the phenomenon of the mix tape, particularly well documented in *Cassettes From My Ex*, a collection of short essays by various authors about the mix tapes they once shared with someone else (Bitner, 2009).

With that as context, neither file sharing nor MySpace nor Twitter nor any other Internet-and-music-related phenomenon should seem strange or new. Research on adolescents from the 1980s and 1990s reveals that the stage was set for a combination of Internet and mobile phone technologies to predominate among young people well before those technologies were readily available. In a study of US teenagers' bedroom culture, Brown and colleagues wrote:

> Although many had television sets in their rooms at home, music systems and telephones were considered most essential to well-being. Emily's comment was fairly typical: "I can't be in here without music. I always have music on. When I'm sad, I listen to sad music, which doesn't exactly help in cheering me up. I listen to it much louder when I'm happy. And when I need to get pumped up, I listen to wild, loud music . . . like before a party." (Brown, Dykers, Steele, & White, 1994)

Emily's comments reveal not only the centrality of music in adolescent life, but two additional elements explaining the centrality of music to Internet use. First, Emily proves that she is not a passive music listener. Instead, she chooses particular music for particular actions and emotions. The ability to choose individual songs and to order them in particular ways is a key component of MP3 players and streaming websites. Emily's efforts at incorporating music into her world echo de Nora's findings that "music is used and works as an ordering material in social life" (de Nora, 2000, p. x). Second, the very mobility of new technologies for music listening such as the iPod and mobile phone mean that the elements "most essential to well-being" of adolescents are now portable, allowing them to maintain a sense of order and identity beyond the confines of the home, including other places while in transit.

Indeed, one of the key characteristics of music is that it is the only medium to which most people can attend while they engage in some other activity. It is the only *meanwhile* medium, one that can be alongside and with a person when they are driving, reading, commuting, studying, playing a game, talking, etc., and one that actively accompanies other activities and media (such as television and film) in ways that actively structure and order those activities. As de Nora (2000) put it:

> Music is active in defining situations because, like all devices or technologies, it is often linked, through convention, to social scenarios, often according to the social uses for which it was initially produced – waltz music for dancing, march music for marching, and so on [p. 11] . . . Building and deploying musical montages is part of a repertory of strategies for coping and for generating pleasure, creating occasion, and affirming self- and group-identity. (p. 16)

With a computer and Internet connection, or with an MP3 player or mobile phone, anyone can engage in defining situations for themselves. It is likely that at least part of the pleasure of setting an iPod to shuffle mode, or using Pandora's recommendations, is to hear the juxtapositions of music, mood, and social situations.

But the situation is more complicated still. While on the one hand such personalization of the experience of music is now commonplace, as online retailers, MP3 players and streaming websites will allow individuals to create custom playlists, such choices are almost never made without connection to a computer system that undertakes additional "personalization" by examining a listener's choices and recommending other music. So while it is more than ever possible to create customized, individual collections of music, many, if not most, such collections and playlists are now based on invisible interactions with machines. Recommendations from friends may still play a role. Even so, as the availability of communities of like-minded listeners has grown, and as the online definition of "friend" may mean something altogether different from its definition offline, it is hard to believe that the process of discovering music has not changed greatly. For that matter, the process of collecting music (Straw, 1997), of creating a "collection" in the sense one might have amassed records not long ago, has greatly changed, too (Shuker, 2004).

Whether this is good or bad is of less importance than that it highlights a new means by which music and affect are brought together by means other than human interaction. Grossberg wrote that what "distinguishes different modes of cultural affect (moods, mattering maps, emotions, desire, the multiplicity of pleasures, etc.) . . . (is) the different ways in which they are organized, which in turn define the different manifestations of their virtual effects" (1997, p. 28). Thus, another way to understand the connection between music and the Internet is through the affective investments that popular music enables and maintains. The means by which the Internet amplifies and focuses those investments through a combination of choice, cost, portability, and, perhaps most importantly, connection to and interaction with friends and fans, as well as machines, and musicians, are therefore of critical importance.

Music and the Internet: Musicians

Any discussion of music and the Internet is incomplete without considering the consequences of the Internet's popularity for musicians. The consequences are many, too many to be examined in a single book chapter. Yet, strangely, they have been explored very little by scholars and the media.

The most common trajectory of discussion goes along the lines of noting the potential loss of income to established artists from file sharing, and the potential gain in exposure and income to independent artists. The logic of this narrative rests on two assumptions: that those who download MP3 files would have otherwise purchased recordings, and that the Internet gives exposure to independent artists that they would not have had from traditional music media like radio and magazines. But in both cases it reduces music-making to an industrial process related primarily to commercial transactions.

Yet other areas of activity in which musicians engage are just as affected by Internet use. Much has been written about the creative process in popular music, particularly with regard to the role technology plays in music production (Frith, 1981, 1996; Jones, 1992; Negus, 1992; Théberge, 1997). But not much is known about the role technology plays in the creative process *vis-à-vis* exposure to music and musical knowledge. Record producer Joe Boyd (2006) noted in his auto-biography that during his time in England in the early 1960s not many musicians had phonographs:

> The most poverty-stricken folk singer in Cambridge or Greenwich Village had at least a record player and a refrigerator and many drove cars. In England, pilgrimages would be made with a newly purchased LP to the flat of someone with the means to play it. Keith Richards . . . and Mick Jagger had a single blues record between them when they first met. It was one I knew well, a Stateside four-track EP licensed from the Excello label. . . . They played it until it was so worn they could barely hear the music through the scratches. One way of looking at the Stones' sound is as a South-East London adaptation of the Excello style. If they had owned more records, their music might have been less distinctive. (pp. 65–6).

The notion of "influences" on a musician is routinely bandied about among musicians and fans as a means of situating a particular performer or song within an existing framework of histories, options, and genealogies, as well as a means of determining authenticity. There are many anecdotes about musicians learning from one another, hearing songs on the radio, being inspired by recordings, and playing along with records as a means of learning how to play an instrument. Such stories are usually accompanied by tales of how difficult it was to find a particular recording or style of music (or, in some cases, how easy it was to find, e.g. The Beatles had an advantage over musicians in other towns in England as Liverpool was a port city and ships and sailors routinely brought in records from overseas; Cohen, 1991). Furthermore, in an era of rampant digital sampling of music, the sheer variety and availability of countless recordings changes the options for those who create music employing samples. Doubtless the Internet will play a role as a new generation of musicians encounters new forms of music, and a vast array of it without much difficulty.

The matter of musical influences begs for study from the perspective of social networking and network analysis. Books such as *Rock Family Trees* (Frame, 1983) try to show how members of bands intertwined, but imagine if scholars like Christakis and Fowler (2009) or Barabási (2002) undertook a network analysis of the connections between musicians, or songs. Musicians have always relied on networks of people, from other musicians to fans to patrons to businesspeople, in order to get their music heard, and in some cases in order to survive. Little is known about the means the Internet provides musicians to network in such fashion via technology.

Obviously, musicians have always relied on audiences, and the Internet has changed the relationship between musician and audience, and musician and fan, in important ways. Prior to the Internet's popularity, it was rare for most any fan or audience member to have direct contact with a popular musician. Once an artist or band reached a certain level of popularity, a marketing and publicity effort kicked in, one making every effort to present them in a particular way to a particular

audience deemed to be their fan base. Cusic (1996) noted that record companies typically used radio and print media, and to a lesser extent television, to inform
consumers about new music, new bands, concerts, and tours.

While the basic trajectory of publicity and marketing efforts has remained the
same to this day, the addition of new media not only to reach journalists and
radio but also to reach fans directly has very much changed publicity and marketing strategies as well as the relationship between musician and audience. Social
networking sites like MySpace and Facebook are now a viable means by which
bands can present themselves to fans and grow a fan base. Sites such as Pandora,
Last.fm, MOG, Jango, and others, have similarly been a means by which bands
and fans can promote music. Many bands employ online "street teams" to promote
new releases or concerts. The need for, if not the very existence of, traditional
publicity and marketing is being challenged.

This is important to musicians for two reasons. First, whereas it had once been
the case that a band's image was created with or for them and then presented to
the audience at key moments in a band's career (e.g. when a new album is released
or a tour announced) such efforts are now part of a daily routine that might involve
posting to a blog, social networking site, or email list. Second, fans now often
have direct access to musicians. They might comment on a musician's blog post,
or email a question to a list, and get a response.

What makes phenomena such as these, enabled by new media, so critical, is not
that they change the industrial processes of publicity and marketing, but that they
change the relationships between musicians and fans, and thus change musicians
and fans themselves. Fandom and affect are tightly coupled to the ways fans imagine musicians and music, and to the ways musicians imagine an audience and music.
Prior to the Internet's diffusion, the most direct source of feedback between musician and audience was at a concert, which, although potentially quite powerful
(particularly in large numbers), is rather binary (e.g. cheering or booing), and not
usually mutual (beyond, e.g., "Thank you, Cleveland!" if I may exaggerate the
point). Another source of feedback was fan letters, but those were likely not often
read by musicians, and even less often garnered a response (beyond, perhaps, an
8 × 10 glossy photo).

This is stereotyping to an extent, and it is primarily describing musicians and
bands signed to major record labels. It also overlooks many musicians and bands
in the pre-Internet era who did pay attention to their audience and fans (particularly punk bands, for instance). Nevertheless, fans and musicians are able to connect and maintain a relationship via new media to an unprecedented degree, and
it is still to be seen how the formation of such relationships and maintenance of
communication will matter to fans and musicians in the long run. It is not as if
musicians are necessarily any more adept at using new media than they might be
at doing their own marketing and publicity. And, there is the fact that musicians'
schedules are not suddenly cleared so that they can find time to write blog posts,
answer emails, etc. That they will use new media to communicate with fans is
nevertheless expected.

Popular music itself has been changed by new media, too. The individual song is again emphasized, as it was prior to the days of album-oriented rock in the 1960s. Consumers may now choose to purchase individual tracks from Amazon, the iTunes music store, and other digital music sites, and can avoid purchasing entire albums for just the song or songs they wish to own. Audio quality is a concern among many musicians, recording engineers, and producers, since the MP3 file format is a compressed one, well below that of an audio CD, and many MP3 files have obvious sonic artifacts that can distort the sound of a recording. Even the nature of the artwork that has for the last 50-plus years enclosed all manner of physical recordings, from 45s to LPs, 8-track tapes to cassettes and CDs (Jones & Sorger, 1999/2000), is changing, as musicians strive to find meaningful ways to package music that needs no packaging.

Music-making itself is undergoing changes due to the easy means by which musicians can share audio files and collaborate. Where it had once been necessary to either bring musicians together in the same room for a recording, or have them appear in a recording studio and shuttle tapes from one session to another, it is now possible to send and receive high-quality digital audio files online from one studio to another, or even for a musician to work at home or on the road with such files. In some cases musicians are able to collaborate in real time via the Internet. Though issues with network and device latency usually prevent truly synchronous performance or recording, as bandwidth increases the latency issues will be overcome, and even if they may not be able to play together, musicians and producers can still listen, see, and discuss the evolution of a recording via videoconferencing. Even the practice of touring has changed, as bands can now easily maintain contact with record labels while on the road, stream audio and/or video from concerts, and ask audience members to make set list requests online.

But for all the changes the Internet is bringing to the extraordinary and mundane aspects of music-making and of being a musician, it is not yet at all clear that the Internet can or will provide a means by which musicians can create an alternative to the existing music industry. Negus (1992) noted that:

> Ultimately, the recording industry cannot "control" or "determine" what is going to be commercially successful. All entertainment corporations can do is struggle to monopolize access to recording facilities, promotional outlets, manufacturing arrangements and distribution systems, and be in a position to appropriate the profits. (p. 152)

While the Internet may be a technology of disintermediation and help weaken the monopolies enjoyed by the music industry, it will not be a simple matter to replace that which is disintermediated with alternatives that will have the potential to scale. Some recording artists, such as Radiohead, Prince, and Aimee Mann, for example, have already tried alternative approaches but have met with mixed success, at best. The music industry is adapting, too, and may yet find its footing and regain at least some of its commercial dominance.

Conclusion

The debates about music and the Internet are ultimately about commerce and art, and are thus extraordinarily complicated and, perhaps, irresolvable. However, it is imprudent to focus either on the commercial aspects or the artistic ones alone, or to examine them out of the historical context in which these debates have occurred for decades. While new media, particularly network technologies, have created havoc as well as opportunities for the music industry, fans, and musicians – music, as both art and commerce, has always been changing. While the rate of change is now dizzying, new media are providing means by which music will remain prevalent in everyday life even as debates about art and commerce continue.

References

Alderman, J. (2001). *Sonic Boom: Inside the Battle for the Soul of Music.* London: Fourth Estate Classic House.

Ayers, M. D. (2006). *Cybersounds: Essays on Virtual Music Culture.* New York: Peter Lang.

Barabási , A.-L. (2002). *Linked: The New Science of Networks.* Cambridge, MA: Perseus.

Baym, N. (2007). The new shape of online community: The example of Swedish independent music fandom. *First Monday,* 12(8). Retrieved May 24, 2010, from http://people.ku.edu/~nbaym/2007BaymFirstMonday.pdf.

Bitner, J. (2009). *Cassettes From My Ex.* New York: St Martin's Griffin.

Boyd, J. (2006). *White Bicycles: Making Music in the 1960s.* London: Serpent's Tail.

Brown, J. D., Dykers, C. R., Steele, J. R., & White, A. B. (1994). Teenage room culture: Where media and identities intersect. *Communication Research,* 21(6), 813–27.

Burkart, P. (2006). *Digital Music Wars: Ownership and Control of the Celestial Jukebox.* New York: Rowman & Littlefield.

Christakis, N. A., & Fowler, J. H. (2009). *Connected: The Surprising Power of Our Social Networks and How They Shape Our Lives.* New York: Little & Brown.

Christman, E. (2010). Album sales decline slows in Q1: Digital sales dip. Reuters. Retrieved May 22, 2010, from http://www.reuters.com/article/idUSTRE6390D720100410.

Cohen, S. (1991). *Rock Culture in Liverpool: Popular Music in the Making.* Oxford: Oxford University Press.

Cusic, D. (1996). *Music in the Market.* Bowling Green, OH: Bowling Green State University Press.

De Nora, T. (2000). *Music in Everyday Life.* Cambridge: Cambridge University Press.

Duckworth, W. (2005). *Virtual Music: How the Web Got Wired for Sound.* New York: Routledge.

Electronic Frontier Foundation. (2008). RIAA vs. the People: Five years later. Retrieved May 22, 2010, from http://www.eff.org/files/eff-riaa-whitepaper.pdf.

Frame, P. (1983). *Rock Family Trees.* London: Omnibus Press.

Frith, S. (1981). *Sound Effects: Youth, Leisure, and the Politics of Rock 'n' Roll.* New York: Pantheon.

Frith, S. (1996). *Performing Rites.* Cambridge, MA: Harvard University Press.

Grossberg, L. (1997). *Bringing it All Back Home: Essays on Cultural Studies.* Raleigh, NC: Duke University Press.

Holland, B. (1998, February 28). RIAA's '97 figs. reflect changes in the U.S. mkt. *Billboard*, pp. 1, 81.

IFPI (2010). IFPI digital music report 2010. Retrieved May 22, 2010, from http://www.ifpi.org/content/library/DMR2010.pdf.

Jones, S. (1992). *Rock Formation: Music, Technology and Mass Communication.* Newbury Park, CA: Sage.

Jones, S. (2002). Building, buying or being there: Imagining online community. In K. A. Renninger & W. Shumar (eds.), *Building Virtual Communities* (pp. 368–76). Cambridge: Cambridge University Press.

Jones, S., & Sorger, M. (1999/2000). Covering music: A brief history and analysis of album cover design. *Journal of Popular Music Studies*, 11(12), 68–102.

Negus, Keith. (1992). *Producing Pop: Culture and Conflict in the Popular Music Industry.* London: Edward Arnold.

Rainie, L., Fox, S., & Lenhart, A. (2000). 13 million Americans "freeload" music on the Internet; 1 billion free music files now sit on Napster users' computers. Pew Internet & American Life Project, Washington, DC. Retrieved May 22, 2010, from http://www.pewinternet.org/~/media//Files/Reports/2000/MusicReportFull.pdf.

RIAA (2010). 2008 Consumer profile. Retrieved June 1, 2010, from http://76.74.24.142/CA052A55-9910-2DAC-925F-27663DCFFFF3.pdf.

Shuker, R. (2004). Beyond the "high fidelity" stereotype: defining the (contemporary) record collector. *Popular Music*, 23, 311–30.

SoundExchange (2010). SoundExchange and SENA ink agreement for independent labels. Retrieved May 22, 2010, from http://soundexchange.com/2010/03/18/soundexchange-and-sena-ink-agreement-for-independent-labels/.

Straw, W. (1997). Sizing up record collections: Gender and connoisseurship in rock music culture. In S. Whitely (ed.), *Sexing the Groove: Popular Music and Gender* (pp. 3–16). London: Routledge.

Théberge, P. (1997). *Any Sound you Can Imagine: Making Music/Consuming Technology.* London: University Press of New England.

22

Why and How Online Sociability Became Part and Parcel of Teenage Life

Marika Lüders

Introduction

During the last few years, personal and social media forms have blossomed online, attracting ever more users. Newsgroups, mailing lists, and MUDS (multi-user dungeons) in the 1980s and early 1990s were populated by a narrow segment of technologically interested Internet users. But email, instant messaging, blogs, photo- and video-sharing, and social network sites (SNSs) have become mainstream phenomena. In this chapter, (inter)personal tools for communication are labeled "personal media" to account for media forms that facilitate mediated interpersonal communication and personalized expressions (as a contrast to mass media)[1] (see also Lüders, 2008). The success of online personal media seems to reflect a human willingness to embrace tools that support social interaction between offline meetings (just as we have previously embraced letters and telephones) (see Licoppe & Smoreda, 2005). Whereas diaries, letters, telephones, and snapshot photography are also examples of personal media, the focus here is on online personal media, as their networked qualities suggest important changes if compared to the historical significance of the analogue antecedents. These changes and the growing importance of online sociability, particularly among young users (as suggested by e.g. Henderson & Gilding, 2004; Lenhart et al., 2007; Lewis & Fabos, 2005; Ofcom, 2008; Storsul et al., 2008; Kim & Yun, 2007), will be addressed in this chapter. Two questions will be attended to. First, *how should we understand the personal and social significance of online sociability?* This question reflects the focus of a considerable amount of research and will also suggest reasons for the extraordinary growth in use of personal media. Second, *having an online presence arguably challenges privacy issues, yet how should we appropriately assess the correlative challenges and risks with regard to privacy?*

The Escalation of Online Sociability

Extensive research has been conducted on the Internet as a social space and suggests why online personal forms of communication have become so popular. In short, personal media are perceived as meaningful by users, because they resonate with fundamental human desires concerning self-expression, socializing, play, and being creative. Common research questions have accordingly focused on the consequences of online practices for identity-related issues, the social relationships of individual users, as well as the interdependence of online and offline spaces.

In this section, research and theory concerning personal media as sites for self-expressions, socializing, and creative play will be discussed. A range of scholarly perspectives will be introduced, including sociology, media and communication research, psychology, and human–computer interaction (HCI). I also include analysis and interview-quotes from a three-year study of personal media usage among young Norwegians to illustrate and emphasize interesting aspects (Lüders, 2007). The informants were promised anonymity, and their names have accordingly been changed.

Self-performance and socializing

As the following pages will show, personal media have undoubtedly become part and parcel of everyday teenage life. Being online is basically one of several ways of being in the world. Online diaries, photosharing services, and SNSs situate the individual in the centre of her or his network (boyd & Ellison, 2007), and users play the role as themselves, maintaining (and strengthening) existing social ties (boyd, 2006; boyd, 2007; boyd & Ellison, 2007; Choi, 2006; Ellison, Steinfield, & Lampe, 2007; Hinduja & Patchin, 2008; Kim & Yun, 2007; Liu, 2007). According to a PEW study, 91 percent of US teens who use SNSs do so to connect with friends (Lenhart & Madden, 2007). However, according to the same study, 49 percent of social network users said that they used the networks also to make new friends. Moreover, some SNSs may be more oriented towards maintaining existing relations than other types of personal media. For example, Lüders (2009) portrays how the young Norwegian bloggers interviewed extended their personal social networks and strengthened social ties thanks to their extensive online presence. New friends were eventually included into their closer social circles, particularly after face-to-face meetings (Lüders, 2009). Dwyer and colleagues (2007) similarly found that MySpace users were significantly more likely to meet new people than Facebook users. MySpace users further reported a more extensive usage of additional personal media to strengthen new online relationships.

Whether friendships have been initiated offline or online, sociability is a keyword for understanding the attraction of personal media. Sociability as a concept characteristic of the significance of social interaction for societies was introduced by Georg Simmel (Simmel & Wolff, 1964). To Simmel, sociability is a particular play-form of association, in which people take part in interaction free of any disturbing material accent. Sociability characterizes interaction for its own sake and has no objective purpose with regard to the content of the interaction taking place. The main purpose is simply being together and acknowledging the other in one's life. Just as playful interaction is important in people's offline lives, sharing a playful togetherness has emerged as an appealing aspects of online spaces (see e.g. Baym, 1995; boyd, 2007; Lüders, 2009). Judith Donath (2004) applies the concept of "sociable media" to account for both old and new forms of media that enhance communication and the formation of social ties among people.

The application of Simmel's concept of sociability to online forms of communication illustrates that research and theory-building concerning online interactions and presentations of selves have not been developed from scratch. Rather, existing knowledge of self-performances and the significance of socializing have greatly inspired attempts to analyze and discuss their online counterparts. One of the most cited and relevant perspectives has been Erving Goffman's ([1959] 1990) work on context-dependent, face-to-face performances. According to Goffman, we take on specific characters to please our current audience: we adapt to social situations and perform according to common expectations of the roles we embody (Goffman, [1959] 1990). These expectations differ according to interactional contexts; e.g. a social, career-minded, family person embodies different roles in front of her/his children, spouse, friends, and colleagues. In everyday social situations we are consequently deliberately conscious of matching our presentations of self to expectations of the roles we embody.

Goffman's ideas have been revised to fit both electronically mass mediated forms of interaction (Meyrowitz, 1986) and mediated forms of interpersonal interaction (e.g. boyd, 2007; Ellison, Heino, & Gibbs, 2006; Kendall, 2002; Markham, 1998; Papacharissi, 2002; Sveningsson Elm, 2007, 2009). In face-to-face performances, expressions given off (e.g. drifting eyes, blushing cheeks, or other presumably unintentional cues) are difficult to control. Studies on mediated forms of communication have found that the physical absence of others makes users feel more in control with their mediated self (e.g. Bargh, McKenna, & Fitzsimons, 2002; Henderson & Gilding, 2004; Lewis & Fabos, 2005; Lüders, 2009; Markham, 1998; McKenna, Green, & Gleason, 2002), or, in Goffmanian terms, users have more control of expressions given off (Goffman, [1959] 1990). Possibilities for impression management are hence perceived as better (although far from total) in mediated interactions. In other words, there are unique qualities with mediated forms of communication, and these qualities affect how individual users choose and manage to present themselves. Mediated communication is sometimes characterized by candidness as a consequence of users having more time to create expressions, and greater control over self-representations. However, a multitude of self-presentational strategies are common. Some users create profiles which accurately describe their personality; others present themselves with deliberately false but humorous content (see also Livingstone, 2008). As 15-year-old Kristine says: "My profile just contains a lot of crap. Like claiming that I'm a widow and that I work with sewage. I don't pretend to be serious." This is far from the identity-experimenting role-playing typically often emphasized in studies conducted on computer-mediated forms of communication in the 1990s (Jones, 1997; Rheingold, 1993; Turkle, 1997). That is, whereas Sherry Turkle (1997, p. 177) proposed that, "[w]hen we step through the screen into virtual communities, we reconstruct our identities on the other side of the looking glass," Kristine of course does not reconstruct her self as a widowed sewage-worker. Rather, her profile actions should be regarded as play and superficial fun.

In online social spaces, users are not merely present on the basis of their own expressions. Rather, postings by other people on one's own profile will affect the perceptions that visitors get of the target profile maker. In a study of the role of friends' appearance on Facebook, Joseph B. Walther and colleagues (2008) found that the presence of physically attractive friends on the Facebook wall had a significant effect on perceptions of the physical attractiveness of the profile's owner, and, intriguingly, "things that others say about a target may be more compelling than things an individual says about his- or herself. It has more warrant because it is not as controllable by the target, that is, it is more costly to fake" (Walther et al., 2008, p. 33). Given that users commonly experience online spaces to be intertwined with offline spaces, friends-conveyed person-characteristics such as those uncovered in the aforementioned study may potentially have considerable consequences for how users are perceived by friends and contacts overall. Interestingly, the presence of others in one's own online life is also less ephemeral and more visible than the presence of others in one's own offline life. For example, unless purposely deleted, comments and photos that friends post on each others' walls stay there for all to see, whereas an oral compliment is bound to the place and time of the utterance.

Studies of self-performance and socialization are commonly situated within a context emphasizing the structures and features of network societies, arguing that modern Western societies have experienced the emergence of limited-purpose, loose relationships, more fluid, yet meaningful social networks (Benkler, 2006, p. 357). Instead of depending on locally embedded, thick, and stable relations (such as indicated by Tönnies' (1955) concept of *Gemeinschaft*), individuals in network societies are "more dependent on their own combination of strong and weak ties" (Benkler, 2006, p. 362); people navigate complex networks according to needs (Benkler, 2006, p. 362; Rheingold, 2002) and purposes of socialization, collaboration, and sense of belonging (Wellman, 2002). Interesting questions arise, such as those proposed by Donath (2007): Will this transform society by facilitating trustworthy individualized social networks of a scale and complexity never seen before? This raises further questions, particularly with regard to social competence. Users already employ digital personal media to assist processes of socializing, and as mediated forms of communication interact with offline spaces of socialization, social competence appears to include the ability to juggle between forms of mediated and immediate interaction. Important social situations are found in mediated as well as immediate spaces, and within certain population groups where mediated participation is especially high, choosing not to, or not being allowed to, participate in mediated spaces could be as unfortunate as not being part of the clique.

Nevertheless, few studies have been conducted on the characteristics of the social competence required from users in online spaces. Social competence is described within psychological research and clinical studies as the ability and capacity to interact rewardingly with others, and the capacity to adapt to social contexts and demands (Cavell, 1990; Spence, 2003). The context in these discussions is limited to face-to-face situations, accentuating the importance of verbal as well as non-verbal responses that influence the impression we make upon others during social interactions: facial expressions, posture, gestures, physical distance, tone of voice, and clarity of speech (Spence, 2003, p. 84). When social life is situated within mediated spaces, communication must be adapted to the obvious fact that the body is not fully present. Yet, as in face-to-face interactions, the content and the form of communicated messages are vital, as well as knowing the rules of conduct and digital play. Such knowledge can probably only be fully acquired through actual experience. With reference to Michael Polanyi's (1958) work on personal knowledge, the tacit element of social competence suggests that we assimilate social knowledge by being part of specific societal groups: social competence is arguably a type of knowledge with limited capability for transfer. Rather social knowledge develops in actual interactions with others (online or offline) to become part of our background knowledge. This would suggest that participation in online social spaces is important for youth to develop a relevant and comprehensive social competence. It also suggests that in order to investigate the character of social competence in online spaces, researchers need to take an active part in those spaces. Examining online social competence is particularly important as online and offline social venues are intertwined, and as interactions in online spaces hence have real-life consequences.

Considering the particular importance of peer feedback and reciprocity for adolescents (boyd, 2007), and the excellent opportunities for supporting and visualizing peer processes online, the popularity of sites such as MySpace, Flickr, and LiveJournal is reasonable. In the next section, creative play is discussed as an important (though under-researched) aspect of personal media. Contemporary network-mediated subjects are made up of more than their textual footpaths. Utilizing creative desires to construct interesting multimodal presences generates a potentially appealing presence towards others (as well as towards oneself). Social competence in online spaces is consequently connected to mundane forms of creativity.

Creative play

In 2005, PEW reported that 57 percent of American online teens create content for the Internet in a variety of ways, such as creating blogs and webpages; sharing original content such as artwork, photos, stories, or videos; or remixing content found online into a new creation (Lenhart & Madden, 2005, p. i). Today, numbers are likely to be significantly higher, both because of the growth in use of social network sites, and because these sites typically integrate different creative practices into one service. Jean Burgess (2007) suggests the term vernacular creativity to account for the ordinary, everyday, informal (not institutionally learned), and common forms of creativity at play when people create and share expressions and stories (whether online or offline). The opportunity to share vernacular creative acts online appears to strengthen the motivation users have for creating content (Cohen, 2005). In order to fully understand use of personal media and the concomitant pleasures, pains, and gains of digital play, additional research attention to the creative aspects involved should be included.

Creativity has been defined and comprehended in various ways (for discussions, see e.g. Pope, 2005; Weiner, 2000). Whereas creativity used to be conceptualized as a divine ability, it is now commonly understood as part of what constitutes human beings. Moreover, creativity is not necessarily (or even ever) an isolated phenomenon:

> "being creative" is, at least potentially, the natural and normal state of anyone healthy in a sane and stimulating community and . . . realising that potential is as much a matter of collaboration and "co-creation" as of splendid or miserable isolation. (Pope, 2005, p. xvi)

Creativity as natural, normal, and collaborative is more apparent than ever. Technologies which a few years ago would appear at least as semi-professional have now become affordable and manageable for huge user-groups, making it easier to create and share expressions with others. The explosion in content created and shared by amateurs has been so extensive that it is perceived as fundamentally changing the media industry (Bowman & Willis, 2003; Deuze, 2006; Jenkins, 2006; Uricchio, 2004). And whereas critical voices are also present, arguing that the growth in amateur content represents the demise of the public sphere (Keen, 2007), Tim Berners-Lee's (1999) idea of intercreativity reflects the reality in a more appealing and perhaps accurate way:

> not just the ability to choose, but also the ability to create. . . . We should be able not only to interact with other people, but to create with other people. *Intercreativity* is the process of making things or solving problems together. (Berners-Lee, 1999, p. 183)

Berners-Lee's optimistic depiction of participation, co-operation, and co-creation forecasts the Web 2.0 discourse exploding around 2005. Originally popularized by Tim O'Reilly (2005), the term "Web 2.0" describes a turning point, with the web emerging as a platform, flexible programming models (XML, RSS, Ajax), and, most famously, web services embracing "collective intelligence," "wisdom of crowds," user-participation, and creation.

Returning to a discussion of personal media, opportunities for participants to create and share expressions should be included in order to comprehensively explain their growth. It is likely that SNSs have blossomed partly because they support and facilitate creative play. Besides, creative play constitutes a basis for socializing, and creative efforts by friends and contacts are valued highly by users of personal media (Lüders, 2007, p. 164). Social and creative play resonates with the notion of *homo ludens*, introduced by Johan Huizinga ([1938] 1963) and often cited in gaming literature (e.g. Rodriguez, 2006). To Huizinga play is "free," i.e. play has no other motive than the experience it affords. We play because it is fun, and not because we want to fulfill a practical task. A *homo ludens* approach to personal media is an interesting one, although thus far not cited within the literature on online sociability. A focus on play does not imply that we cannot learn from creative play, only that learning is not the explicit aim. Also recall how sociability is comprehended as a particular play-form of association with no objective purpose, emphasizing how play and sociability are (of course) deeply entangled.

The playful character of personal-media actions and the idea of vernacular creativity may also explain why youth do not necessarily regard their online actions as increasing their technical, writing, and creative skills. PEW found that even though teens are embedded in a technology-rich world, they do not regard textual online communication as proper writing (Lenhart et al., 2008). Moreover, young people pose tough criteria for evaluating content as creatively valuable (Lüders, 2007). Yet, whereas youth do not always think of their own writing as "writing" or their photographs as creatively interesting, these informal and out-of-school playful actions may have significance, as users would be expected to develop a sense of technical competence and multimodal literacy. Some of the adolescents I have followed indeed have creative ambitions as such, and in talking to these young content creators, the importance of feedback from online peers for developing multimodal competences is explicitly stated: Camilla (aged 17) emphasizes the importance of receiving comments and learning what visitors to her DeviantArt profile think of her drawings and photos, and 15-year-old Marte comments, "constructive criticism helps me improve my skills" (Lüders, 2007, p. 165).

Undoubtedly, those with creative ambitions find a multitude of self-development opportunities online, but it is not clear what significance, if any, playful social network actions have. This is an interesting area for future research given the societal priority given to discussions about digital competence and digital (access and production) divides. Complicating matters further, creating and sharing (often private) content online is, as already mentioned, potentially connected to privacy hazards, suggesting that users must develop a competence to live in publicly available spaces without unnecessarily compromising personal privacy.

Young, Dim, and Vulnerable?

The previous sections demonstrate why personal media have been embraced by young people worldwide. This development has been met by warnings about the dangers faced by users exposing their private life online (for an overview of common concerns, see Hinduja & Patchin, 2008). Nevertheless US teenagers seem to take public concern about privacy seriously: among the 55 percent of online teens with social network profiles, 66 percent say that their profile is not visible to all Internet users, and among those whose profiles can be accessed by anyone, 46 percent report posting fake information to protect themselves (or to be playful and silly) (Lenhart & Madden, 2007). The need to protect the private sphere is regarded as important across cultures, yet how to ensure privacy may vary (Newell, 1998; Woo, 2006). There may for example be cultural differences as to whether citizens trust the state to protect them (citizens have a *right* to privacy) or whether they believe that only the individual can protect her/his privacy. An interesting question consequently arises: Do these high statistics in the US reflect the latter belief?

Whether privacy is regarded as a right or an individual responsibility, apprehension arises because network technologies elevate interactions and personal expressions from private lives into sometimes publicly available spaces. This creates complex situations concerning the roles we take on in interactions with others. Recall Goffman's work on context-dependent performances. Whereas online spaces can be private, semi-public, or public, a distinguishable feature appears to be an intermingling of different roles within the same arena, complicating processes of evaluating the appropriateness of self-expressions. The characteristics of digital personal and interactional arenas hence further increase the complexity of modern societies and the intricacy experienced by subjects about their "inner self," the exterior reality, and the connections in-between.

Uploading personal content additionally raises (at least) two fundamental privacy issues. First of all, it is often difficult to assess and interpret the meaning of the terms of services regarding privacy. While problematic, online content and service providers have developed a commercial logic where they offer their material for free in return for users giving away personal information (Shapiro, 1999). This aspect of privacy-related issues with regard to online social spaces is becoming increasingly difficult to assess, as major actors such as Facebook and Google have implemented features for dynamic information exchanges with third-party social application developers. Secondly, users have little control over the content published by their friends and contacts, or over the republication of their own content in other contexts. Consequently, whether or not users trust the service provider, can they trust their online friends (and foes)?

Users face two unfavorable options: protecting their privacy by not being present online, despite potentially undesirable personal and social consequences; or, alternatively, choosing to have an online presence and so jeopardizing their personal privacy. As discussed above, mediated forms of socialization are characterized by other qualities than face-to-face communication, and, especially for young users, not being online means not taking part in an important social arena. These spaces are not always characterized by the most significant forms of communication, but they are nevertheless significant as arenas for phatic communication (denoting small talk and communication without a purpose beyond acknowledging the presence of others).

Risk-Assessment in Networked Publics

> **Kristian (aged 17):** After all, the Internet is no more public than the world outside, . . . I don't care if a stranger sitting on the next table in a Chinese restaurant eavesdrops on my personal conversation with a friend.

All due respect to Kristian – the Internet *is* more public to the extent that actions are available to an audience independent of time and space, i.e. expressions stretch beyond a here and now, as is the case for public blogs, social profiles, and photo-sharing services (see also boyd, 2007). All the same, Kristian does have a point that often seems to disappear when distinctions between private and public arenas are discussed: private actions take place within public spaces both online and offline. Concurrently, intimate and private expressions and actions can be protected within private spaces offline as well as online. It is, in other words, necessary to differentiate between private and public online spaces.

The differing private or public character of online spaces is here depicted as one of two axes for comprehending online privacy risks. (See Figure 22.1.) The second axis is constituted by whether users are present online as anonymous beings, disclosing no traits which can identify them; or whether they have a disclosed presence online, revealing personal information such as full name, photos, and

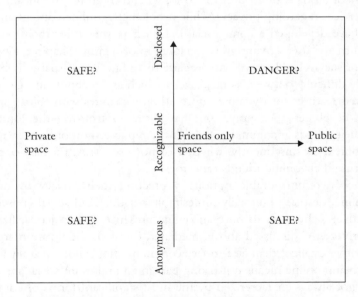

Figure 22.1 Potential Precarious Zones for Personal Information.

friends. Both axes have a middle region. Some blogs (such as LiveJournal) and SNSs allow users to restrict their content as accessible for "friends only," and users may choose to have a restricted or recognizable presence online, revealing first name and information which cannot easily be used to track them offline. A disclosed presence in public online spaces is typically regarded as precarious, whereas an anonymous presence in private online spaces is regarded as safe.

The lower right and upper right corners of the proposed model describe situations where the private sphere enters (or alternatively invades) public spheres. The development of media technologies has been connected to the increasing presence of the private sphere in the public long before the Internet (for discussions see e.g. Barthes, [1980] 1982; Bauman, 2000; Jerslev, 2004; Meyrowitz, 1986; Thompson, 2005). Network cultures strongly reinforce this tendency, and questions concerning privacy issues have consequently been regarded as very important (see for example Dwyer, Hiltz, & Passerini, 2007; Lenhart & Madden, 2007; Livingstone, 2008; Sveningsson Elm, 2007).

In public contexts people are normally anticipated to act in accordance with the expectations of several other groups (Goffman, [1959] 1990; Meyrowitz, 1986). Problems arise as young users regard online publics to be different. Online diaries, homepages, and SNSs can for example be perceived as private, even when they are publicly available:

KRISTOFFER (18):   For a long time I had a title on my weblog saying that if you know me, don't say that you have read this.
MARIKA: Why?
KRISTOFFER: Because then it would affect what I write. Then I would begin to think in relation to that person. I try to write my thoughts, but if I know that a person reads it I begin to think of that person as a recipient. And I just want my message to get across; this is my message to myself.

Similarly Walther and colleagues (2008) argue that Facebook users tend to think of their profiles as private, if not technologically then by convention. Recall Kristian's comment about eavesdropping on other people's conversations at restaurants. Although Kristian claims not to care, most people regard eavesdropping as rude (even if sometimes unavoidable). Just because you are able to look into somebody else's life, does not mean you should do it.

Yet, with the complex privacy preferences present in personal media applications, is there still a need to be worried? The answer is a definite yes, precisely *because* of the complex privacy preferences available. With Facebook currently being the example par excellence, privacy settings are way too complex, as described also by Livingstone (2008, p. 406), who found that the teenagers she interviewed experienced great difficulties in assessing the present privacy settings of their profiles. Managing the privacy settings was so complex that the teenagers interviewed did not know how to change settings according to their own liking. Similar observations concerning the asymmetry between desires to protect privacy and actual behaviors are made by Acquisti and Gross (2006), Stutzman (2006), and Barnes (2006). There is additionally a difference between being and feeling anonymous as users may include personal information, yet still feel that their online presence is relatively anonymous (Kennedy, 2006). Users may regard their privacy to be safe, basically because the magnitude of online expressions to a large extent serves as a safety barrier (boyd, 2007; Lange, 2007).

A complex relation between opportunity and risk is a characteristic feature of adolescence and thus not particularly distinctive to the Internet (Livingstone, 2008). Referring to psychologist Erik H. Erikson's classic work on teenage identity exploration processes, Livingstone argues that developing and gaining confidence in one's own self is part of being a teenager. This self-exploratory process includes figuring out whom to trust, what personal information to reveal, and how to express emotion. Risky use of online social spaces consequently fits neatly into a psychological framework of adolescence. Donath (2007) similarly argues that while excessive risk-taking online may seem irrational to outsiders, it may, when viewed as a signal, be seen as a way of expressing fitness or aptness to social contexts: "From lion-hunting Masai warriors to cigarette-smoking, drag-racing American teenagers, people (often young) perform risky acts to prove that they are so fit or skilled that they can afford to be daring" (unpaginated). Risk-taking in the form of online presences can also be explained with reference to the continuous risk assessments required of individuals in modern societies (Giddens, 1991). We take more or less calculated risks, believing that the outcome is worth the risk taken (comparable to bicycling, driving a car, investing in stock markets) (Lüders, 2007). Besides, even users who adopt a recognizable/disclosed presence in public online spaces, often regard themselves as having a specific control over their own online self-performance:

> **Linnea (18):** And you're more anonymous even if your name is there, or even if they know somebody who knows me and they might have read my diary. You can be a little bit different from who you are. And you start with a clean sheet. *Presenting yourself as you see yourself* [emphasis added], . . . You can choose what you want to tell.
>
> . . . it's all me, but it's small parts of me. Maybe it's the parts I'm more satisfied with that I write more about.

Linnea only publishes her first name online, but she is far from anonymous, and the content of what she shares with others in publicly available online spaces is honest and personal. As such, her online presence would by many be regarded as perilous.

One of the most interesting conflict dimensions between researchers and commentators of online sociability concern whether or not participants really should be encouraged to withhold information. As I have discussed elsewhere (Lüders, 2008), deceptive strategies may be somewhat at odds with conceptions of what normally constitutes virtuous conduct. Yet online, concealing one's identity (or even lying) is regarded as appropriate and, ironically, the morally right thing to do (see also J. E. Cohen, 2000; Woo, 2006). Bjørn K. Myskja (2008) discusses a related problem with regard to online trust, and applies Kant's moral philosophy and political theory to account for how Kant's pragmatic approach can be distinguished from his uncompromising ideal morality. Hence whereas according to Kant's moral philosophy we have a moral duty to refrain from lying, according to his pragmatic approach, there is such a thing as well-intended deception. We pretend to be better because as human beings we have so many objectionable characteristics. As such, deceiving others about our true nature makes us act as better humans. Myskja argues that online spaces provide ideal conditions for well-intended deceptions and further that online trust depends on the fact that we exercise self-censorship or deception. There exists a reciprocal acknowledgement that we are not completely honest, and this may promote reciprocal trust (Myskja, 2008). Concomitantly it can be argued that lying about one's identity online is not immoral. Common online practice suggests that participants are being themselves, although presenting a somewhat refined self-version. This is as expected from a Kantian pragmatist position, but perhaps users are nevertheless more inclined to comply with his moral philosophy?

Taking as a premise the belief that users of SNSs should refrain from posting revealing personal information, Hinduja and Patchin (2008) found that a number of users indeed post personal and identifying information, though not to the extent that many believe. Hinduja and Patchin strongly emphasize the risks associated with publishing information such as one's first or full name, portrait photos, or what school one attends. Although they are unaware of "any incident where the revelation of personal information by adolescents on MySpace pages has led to personal victimization" (p. 140), they do not delve much deeper into a discussion of whether publishing personal information necessarily represents risky behavior. Whereas it may initially appear as if the upper right corner of the proposed model – characterized by a disclosed public presence – is the most hazardous position to take, this might not be correct, because of the interplay in use of different personal media. That is, youth who are anonymous in MySpace might accept initiatives for further communication in instant messaging, phone conversations, and eventually face-to-face meetings. It is more important to focus on the context of young users: Youth who engage in a pattern of different kinds of online risky behavior, such as frequently chatting with unknown others, visiting sex sites, and talking about sex online with unknown others, experience greater risks for victimization, yet these kids are typically also experiencing problems in offline contexts (sexual abuse, parental conflict, and offline interpersonal victimization) (Ybarra et al., 2007).

Future research should attempt to examine self-performances and sociability from an unbiased point of view where a priori expectations do not steer gathering and analysis of data.

Concluding Discussion

It is no longer possible to research the social life of teenagers in the Western world without including online sociability as a crucial aspect. Assumptions about implications are common (e.g. claiming that online sociability replaces offline sociability), and research is therefore important in order to counter speculations with empirically based knowledge. As the use of personal media potentially reaches a stage of saturation (implying "everyone" within a social community has integrated sociable tools into their everyday lives), the implications of use become unpredictable. Will the dynamics of societal social networks change during the next few years? Are social networks becoming more ephemeral with weak and strong ties constantly changing? Or are implications too easily exaggerated? And how does trust develop between individuals in complex and individualized networks? This is also related to how individuals may be able to control their own self-performance, but not how their friends and foes represent them, suggesting relevant studies of the intermingling of interpersonal expressions.

This chapter further directs the attention towards social competence in online spaces. Whereas knowledge about social competence in offline contexts is extensive, more research is needed to disclose important social skills in online spaces. Given the interdependence between socialization online and offline, young people who for some reason do not have access to these spheres could potentially feel socially isolated. What are the social consequences of non-use for youth whose friends and acquaintances spend a considerable amount of time socializing online? Discussions about digital divides are consequently crucial as non-access may have serious social disadvantages. Similarly, approaching personal media actions as playful and creative is worth exploring further, for example from a textual and/or cultural studies perspective. Research on personal media should also examine how users acquire the technical competence, literacy, and skills to participate in mediated spaces without having to compromise individual privacy. The complex structures characterizing networked publics represent a fundamentally novel aspect of modern life, as network technologies elevate interactions and personal expressions from private life into sometimes publicly available spaces. This raises a wealth of intriguing and important questions, and as discussed it is not apparent what "risky online behavior" is. Future research should hence examine online behavior and privacy from sociological, legal, and psychological perspectives (e.g. cultural differences with regard to privacy), from an HCI-perspective (how to create safe and user-friendly personal media where users can actually comprehend terms of services and privacy preferences), and from a philosophical point of view (e.g. whether participation in personal media challenges truths and conducts we take for granted, and, if so, how this occurs). These questions are all the more important as personal information is treated as a commodity within an emerging personal-media industry.

The development of communication media has profound impact on the process of self-formation by uncoupling experience from encounters in the physical world, and we would have a very limited sense of the world without mediated forms of communication (Thompson, 1995). As such, mediated practices are not only about the significance of our own memory traces for our own sense of self, but also augment the complex abundance of personal life traces of others. These traces influence our perceptions of the world. This is true for mass mediated as well as interpersonal forms of communication and explains the common fascination with tools that help us participate in the creation of a collective world. Hence, although extensive research has already been conducted on the usage and significance of online personal media, the potential outcomes for society indicate that these services will continue to serve as an interesting area for research.

Note

1   "Personal media" is chosen instead of the more commonly used term "social media" in order to emphasize the contrast to mass media. Mass media are arguably highly social. Moreover personal media are concerned with intrinsic personal motivations as well as sociability. This is particularly evident with analogue personal media forms such as the diary, scrapbooking, and the photo-camera, but also the case when personal expressions traverse to online environments.

References

Acquisti, A., & Gross, R. (2006). Imagined communities: Awareness, information sharing, and privacy on the Facebook. Paper presented at the proceedings of the sixth Workshop on Privacy Enhancing Technologies, Cambridge: Robinson College.

Bargh, J. A., McKenna, K. Y. A., & Fitzsimons, G. M. (2002). Can you see the real me? Activation and expression of the "true self" on the Internet. *Journal of Social Issues*, 58(1), 33–48.

Barnes, S. B. (2006). A privacy paradox: Social networking in the United States. *First Monday*, 11(9). http://firstmonday.org/htbin/cgiwrap/bin/ojs/index.php/fm/article/view/1394/1312.

Barthes, R. ([1980] 1982). *Camera Lucida: Reflections on Photography*. New York: Hill and Wang.

Bauman, Z. (2000). *Liquid Modernity*. Cambridge: Polity.

Baym, N. (1995). The emergence of community in computer-mediated communication. In S. Jones (ed.), *CyberSociety: Computer-Mediated Communication and Community* (pp. ix, 241). Thousand Oaks, CA: Sage.

Benkler, Y. (2006). *The Wealth of Networks: How Social Production Transforms Markets and Freedom*. New Haven, CN: Yale University Press.

Berners-Lee, T. (1999). *Weaving the Web*. London: Orion Business Books.

Bowman, S., & Willis, C. (2003). We media. How audiences are shaping the future of news and information. The Media Center at the American Press Institute. http://www.mediacenter.org/pages/mc/research/we_media/.

boyd, d. (2006). Friends, friendsters, and Fop8: Writing community into being on social network sites. 11(12). Retrieved 17 January, 2007, from http://firstmonday.org/issues/issue11_12/boyd/index.html.

boyd, d. (2007). Why youth ♥ social network sites: The role of networked publics in teenage social life. In D. Buckingham (ed.), *Youth, Identity, and Digital Media* (pp. 119–42), MacArthur Foundation Series on Digital Learning. Cambridge, MA: MIT Press.

boyd, d., & Ellison, N. E. (2007). Social network sites: Definition, history and scholarship. *Journal of Computer-Mediated Communication*, 13(1). http://jcmc.indiana.edu/vol13/issue1/boyd.ellison.html.

Burgess, J. (2007). Vernacular creativity and new media. Doctoral dissertation. Queensland University of Technology, Brisbane.

Cavell, T. A. (1990). Social adjustment, social performance, and social skills: A Tri-component model of social competence. *Journal of Clinical Child Psychology*, 19(2), 111–22.

Choi, J. H. (2006). Living in cyworld: Contextualizing cy-ties in South Korea. In A. Bruns & J. Jacobs (eds.), *Use of Blogs (Digital Formations)*, (pp. 173–86). New York: Peter Lang.

Cohen, J. E. (2000). Examined lives: Informational privacy and the subject as object. *Stanford Law Review*, 52, 1373–438.

Cohen, K. R. (2005). What does the photoblog want? *Media, Culture & Society*, 27(6), 883–901.

Deuze, M. (2006). Participation, Remediation, Bricolage: Considering principal components of a digital culture. *The Information Society*, 22(2), 63–75.

Donath, J. (2004). Sociable media. In W. S. Bainbridge (Ed.), *Berkshire Encyclopedia of Human–Computer Interaction*, vol. 2. Great Barrington, MA: Berkshire Publishing Group.

Donath, J. (2007). Signals in social supernets. *Journal of Computer-Mediated Communication*, 13(1). http://jcmc.indiana.edu/vol13/issue1/donath.html.

Dwyer, C., Hiltz, S. R., & Passerini, K. (2007). Trust and privacy concern within social networking sites: A comparison of Facebook and MySpace. Proceedings of AMCIS 2007. Retrieved 28 May, 2008, from http://csis.pace.edu/~dwyer/research/DwyerAMCIS2007.pdf.

Ellison, N., Heino, R., & Gibbs, J. (2006). Managing impressions online: Self-presentation processes in the online dating environment. *Journal of Computer-Mediated Communication*, 11(2). http://jcmc.indiana.edu/vol11/issue2/ellison.html.

Ellison, N., Steinfield, C., & Lampe, C. (2007). The benefits of Facebook "friends": Social capital and college students' use of online social network sites. *Journal of Computer-Mediated Communication*, 12(4). http://jcmc.indiana.edu/vol12/issue4/ellison.html.

Giddens, A. (1991). *Modernity and Self-Identity: Self and Society in the Late Modern Age*. Cambridge: Polity.

Goffman, E. ([1959] 1990). *The Presentation of Self in Everyday Life*. London: Penguin.

Henderson, S., & Gilding, M. (2004). "I've never clicked this much with anyone in my life": Trust and hyperpersonal communication in online friendships. *New Media & Society*, 6(4), 487–506.

Hinduja, S., & Patchin, J. W. (2008). Personal information of adolescents on the Internet: A quantitative content analysis of MySpace. *Journal of Adolescence*, 31(1), 125–46.

Huizinga, J. ([1938] 1963). *Homo ludens: om kulturens oprindelse i leg*. København: Gyldendal.

Jenkins, H. (2006). *Convergence Culture: Where Old and New Media Collide.* New York: New York University Press.

Jerslev, A. (2004). *Vi ses på tv: medier og intimitet.* København: Gyldendal.

Jones, S. (1997). *Virtual Culture: Identity and Communication in Cybersociety.* London: Sage.

Keen, A. (2007). *The Cult of the Amateur: How Today's Internet is Killing Our Culture.* New York: Doubleday.

Kendall, L. (2002). *Hanging Out in the Virtual Pub: Masculinities and Relationships Online.* Berkeley: University of California Press.

Kennedy, H. (2006). Beyond anonymity, or, future directions for Internet identity research. *New Media & Society,* 8(6), 859–76.

Kim, K.-H., & Yun, H. (2007). Cying for me, Cying for us: Relational dialectics in a Korean social network site. *Journal of Computer-Mediated Communication,* 13(1). http://jcmc.indiana.edu/vol13/issue1/kim.yun.html.

Lange, P. (2007). Publicly private and privately public: Social networking and YouTube. *Journal of Computer-Mediated Communication,* 13(1). http://jcmc.indiana.edu/vol13/issue1/lange.html.

Lenhart, A., Arafeh, S., Smith, A., & Macgill, A. R. (2008). Writing, technology and teens. Pew Internet and American Life Project, Washington, DC. Retrieved 3 August, 2008, from http://www.pewinternet.org/PPF/r/247/report_display.asp.

Lenhart, A., & Madden, M. (2005). Teen content creators and consumers. Pew Internet and American Life Project, Washington, DC. Retrieved 12 September, 2006, from http://www.pewinternet.org/PPF/r/166/report_display.asp.

Lenhart, A., & Madden, M. (2007). Teens, privacy and online social networks. Pew Internet and American Life Project, Washington, DC. Retrieved 20 April, 2007, from http://www.pewinternet.org/PPF/r/211/report_display.asp.

Lenhart, A., Madden, M., Macgill, A. R., & Smith, A. (2007). Teens and social media. Pew Internet and American Life Project, Washington, DC. Retrieved 3 August 2008, from http://www.pewinternet.org/PPF/r/230/report_display.asp.

Lewis, C., & Fabos, B. (2005). Instant messaging, literacies, and social identities. *Reading Research Quarterly,* 40(4), 470–501.

Licoppe, C., & Smoreda, Z. (2005). Are social networks technologically embedded? How networks are changing today with changes in communication technology. *Social Networks,* 27(4), 317–35.

Liu, H. (2007). Social network profiles as taste performances. *Journal of Computer-Mediated Communication,* 13(1). http://jcmc.indiana.edu/vol13/issue1/liu.html.

Livingstone, S. (2008). Taking risky opportunities in youthful content creation: teenagers' use of social networking sites for intimacy, privacy and self-expression. *New Media & Society,* 10(3), 393–411.

Lüders, M. (2007). *Being in Mediated Spaces: An Enquiry into Personal Media Practices.* Oslo: Department of Media and Communication, Faculty of Humanities, University of Oslo.

Lüders, M. (2008). Conceptualizing personal media. *New Media & Society,* 10(5), 683–702.

Lüders, M. (2009). Becoming more like friends: a qualitative study of personal media and social life. *Nordicom Review,* 30(1), 201–16.

Markham, A. N. (1998). *Life Online: Researching Real Experience in Virtual Space.* Walnut Creek, CA: Altamira Press.

McKenna, K. Y. A., Green, A. S., & Gleason, M. E. J. (2002). Relationship formation on the Internet: What's the big attraction. *Journal of Social Issues*, 58(1), 9–31.

Meyrowitz, J. (1986). *No Sense of Place: The Impact of Electronic Media on Social Behavior.* New York: Oxford University Press.

Myskja, B. K. (2008). The categorical imperative and the ethics of trust. *Ethics and Information Technology*, 10(4), 213–20.

Newell, P. B. (1998). A cross-cultural comparison of privacy definitions and functions: A systems approach. *Journal of Environmental Psychology*, 18(4), 357–71.

Ofcom (2008). *Social Networking. A Quantitative and Qualitative Research Report into Attitudes, Behaviours and Use.* London: Ofcom.

Oksman, V., & Turtiainen, J. (2004). Mobile communication as a social state: Meanings of mobile communication in everyday life among teenagers in Finland. *New Media & Society*, 6(3), 319–39.

O'Reilly, T. (2005). What is Web 2.0? Design patterns and business models for the next generation of software. Retrieved 14 June, 2006, from http://www.oreillynet.com/pub/a/oreilly/tim/news/2005/09/30/what-is-web-20.html.

Papacharissi, Z. (2002). The presentation of self in virtual life: characteristics of personal home pages. *Journalism & Mass Communication Quarterly*, 79(3), 643–60.

Polanyi, M. (1958). *Personal Knowledge.* London: Routledge and Kegan Paul.

Pope, R. (2005). *Creativity: Theory, History, Practice.* London and New York: Routledge.

Rheingold, H. (1993). *The Virtual Community: Homesteading on the Electronic Frontier.* Reading, MA: Addison-Wesley.

Rheingold, H. (2002). *Smart Mobs: The Next Social Revolution.* Cambridge, MA: Perseus.

Rodriguez, H. (2006). The Playful and the Serious: An approximation to Huizinga's *Homo Ludens. Game Studies*, 6(1).

Shapiro, A. L. (1999). *The Control Revolution: How the Internet is Putting Individuals in Charge and Changing the World We Know.* New York: PublicAffairs.

Simmel, G., & Wolff, K. H. (1964). *The Sociology of Georg Simmel.* New York: Free Press.

Spence, S. H. (2003). Social Skills Training with Children and Young People: Theory, Evidence and Practice. *Child and Adolescent Mental Health*, 8(2), 84–96.

Storsul, T., Arnseth, H. C., & Bucher, T., et al. (2008). *Nye nettfenomener. Staten og delekulturen.* Oslo: University of Oslo.

Stutzman, F. (2006). An evaluation of identity-sharing behavior in social network communities. *Journal of the International Digital Media and Arts Association*, 3(1), 10–18.

Sveningsson Elm, M. (2007). Taking the girl's room online. Similarities and differences between traditional girls room and computer-mediated ones. Paper presented at the INTER: A European Cultural Studies Conference, Norrköping, Sweden.

Sveningsson Elm, M. (2009). Exploring and negotiating femininity: Young women's production of style in a Swedish internet community. *YOUNG*, 17(3), 241–64.

Thompson, J. B. (1995. *The Media and Modernity: A Social Theory of the Media.* Cambridge: Polity.

Thompson, J. B. (2005). The New Visibility. *Theory, Culture & Society*, 22(6), 31–51.

Tönnies, F. (1955). *Community and Association.* London: Routledge and Kegan Paul.

Turkle, S. (1997). *Life on the Screen: Identity in the Age of the Internet.* London: Phoenix.

Uricchio, W. (2004). Beyond the great divide. Collaborative networks and the challenge to dominant conceptions of creative industries. *International Journal of Cultural Studies*, 7(1), 79–90.

Ybarra, M. L., Mitchell, K. J., Finkelhor, D., & Wolak, J. (2007). Internet prevention messages: Targeting the right online behaviors. *Archives of Pediatrics & Adolescent Medicine*, 161(2), 138–45.

Walther, J. B. (2007). Selective self-presentation in computer-mediated communication: Hyperpersonal dimensions of technology, language, and cognition. *Computers in Human Behaviour*, 23(5), 2538–57.

Walther, J. B., Van Der Heide, B., Kim, S.-Y., Westerman, D., & Tong, S. T. (2008). The role of friends' appearance and behavior on evaluations of individuals on Facebook: Are we known by the company we keep? *Human Communication Research*, 34(1), 28–49.

Weiner, R. P. (2000). *Creativity and Beyond. Culture, Values, and Change*. Albany: State University of New York Press.

Wellman, B. (2002). Little boxes, glocalization, and networked individualism. In M. Tanabe, P. van den Besselaar, & T. Ishida (eds.), *Digital Cities II: Computational and Sociological Approaches* (pp. 10–25). Berlin: Springer.

Woo, J. (2006). The right not to be identified: Privacy and anonymity in the interactive media environment. *New Media & Society*, 8(6), 949–67.

Index

CONTENTS

ON THE ROAD WITH FODOR'S

WE'RE ALWAYS THRILLED to get letters from readers, especially when they sound like this:

It took us an hour to decide what book to buy and we now know we picked the best one. Your book was wonderful, easy to follow, very accurate, and good on pointing out eating places, informal as well as formal. When we saw other people using your book, we would look at each other and smile.

Our editors and writers are deeply committed to making every Fodor's guide "the best one"—not only accurate but always charming, brimming with sound recommendations and solid ideas, right on the mark in describing restaurants and hotels, and full of fascinating facts that make you view what you've traveled to see in a rich new light.

About Our Writers

The information in these pages is a collaboration of a number of extraordinary writers.

A professor of communication at Ateneo de Manila University, **Doreen G. Fernandez** is the author of several books; she wrote the Manila dining section.

Nigel Fisher is the editor of the montly travel publication *Voyager International*. He has traveled extensively thoughout Asia and the world and has had a hand in writing or updating nearly every chapter in this guide.

Born and raised in Manila and now a New York resident, Philippines chapter author **Luis H. Francia** is a teacher, poet, film critic/curator, and a freelance writer for such publications as the *Village Voice, Asiaweek,* and *Cinemaya,* a film quarterly based in New Delhi.

Pilar Guzman, a freelance writer and illustrator, thought she had retired from travel writing after several stints working on one of Fodor's Italy guides, but there was no way she could pass up the chance to write our new chapter on Vietnam. She's now devoting her spare time to accurately recreating a dish of *pho,* Vietnam's delicious noodle soup.

Our Singapore dining critic, **Wendy Hutton,** is a New Zealander by birth, but she's worked in Southeast Asia as a writer since 1967. She has written and edited many books on Asian food, including what some believe to be the definitive work on Singapore's culinary culture and cuisine, *Singapore Food.*

We'd also like to thank Singapore Airlines for its help with transportation and gracious transatlantic service; Royal Thai Airlines; and Ann's Tourist in Ho Chi Minh City.

On the Web

Check out Fodor's Web site (http://www.fodors.com/), where you'll find travel information on major destinations around the world and an ever-changing array of travel-savvy interactive features.

How to Use This Book

Organization

Up front is **Essential Information.** Its first section, **Important Contacts A to Z,** gives addresses and telephone numbers of organizations and companies that offer destination-related services and detailed information and publications. **Smart Travel Tips A to Z,** the Gold Guide's second section, gives specific information on how to accomplish what you need to in Southeast Asia as well as tips on savvy traveling. Both sections are in alphabetical order by topic.

Destination: Southeast Asia is meant to provide an overview of the best of the region, from our top picks to suggested vacation itineraries. The **individual country chapters** are arranged alphabetically. Each chapter covers exploring, dining, lodging, arts and nightlife, sports, and shopping in the country's best destinations; the chapter ends with an A to Z section, which tells you how to get there and get around, and how to plan and enjoy your trip. The final country chapter, **Other Destinations,** covers four less-visited Southeast Asian nations; information on each country is arranged as in the individual country chapters.

At the end of the book you'll find **Portraits,** including suggestions for pretrip reading, both fiction and nonfiction. A **Vocabulary** and **Index** follow.

Icons and Symbols

★   Our special recommendations
✕   Restaurant
🏠   Lodging establishment
✕🏠   Lodging establishment whose restaurant warrants a detour
⚠   Campgrounds
☕   Good for kids (rubber duckie)
☞   Sends you to another section of the guide for more information
✉   Address
☎   Telephone number
🕐   Opening and closing times
💰   Admission cost (Those fees we give apply only to adults; substantially reduced fees are often available for children, students, and senior citizens. In those countries where favorable rates of exchange make most admission fees negligible, we note only if admission is charged or free.)

Addresses

You may notice that not all listings in this guide include street addresses. In the older and less-industrialized cities and towns of Southeast Asia, systems of street naming and numbering often are not as rationalized as those in North America and Europe. Often a given attraction—a temple or monument or market—is a large-enough local landmark that a street number is superfluous (much like Grand Central Station or the Eiffel Tower), or the town is sufficiently small that the establishment is readily findable; when in doubt, ask a local or take a taxi. Similarly, we do not provide postal codes for all hotels, often because there is none; in other cases, postal codes exist, but are not widely used.

Hotel Facilities

We always list the facilities that are available—but we don't specify whether they cost extra. When pricing accommodations, always ask what's included.

Restaurant Reservations and Dress Codes

Reservations are always a good idea; we note only when they're essential or when they are not accepted. Book as far ahead as you can, and reconfirm when you get to town. Unless otherwise noted, the restaurants listed are open daily for lunch and dinner. We mention dress only when men are required to wear a jacket or a jacket and tie.

Credit Cards

The following abbreviations are used: **AE,** American Express; **DC,** Diners Club; **MC,** MasterCard; and **V,** Visa.

Please Write to Us

You can use this book in confidence that all prices and opening times are based on information supplied to us at press time; Fodor's cannot accept responsibility for any errors. Time inevitably brings changes, so always confirm information when it matters—especially if you're making a detour to visit a specific sight. In addition, when making reservations be sure to speak up if you have a disability or are traveling with children, if you prefer a private bath or a certain type of bed, or if you have specific dietary needs or any other concerns.

Were the restaurants we recommended as described? Did our hotel picks exceed your expectations? Did you find a museum we recommended a waste of time? If you have complaints, we'll look into them and revise our entries when the facts warrant it. If you've discovered a special place that we haven't included, we'll pass the information along to our correspondents and have them check it out. So send your feedback, positive *and* negative, to Southeast Asia Editor, 201 East 50th Street, New York, New York 10022—and have a wonderful trip!

Karen Cure

Karen Cure
Editorial Director

CHINA

Guangzhou
Macau HONG KONG

Mandalay   Hanoi
BURMA   LAOS   Luang   Haiphong
(MYANMAR)   Prabang   HAINAN
Vientiane
Pegu   Chiang   Hue
Rangoon   Mai   Danang
(Yangon)   THAILAND
Bangkok   Korat   VIETNAM
Andaman   Angkor Wat
Sea   CAMBODIA
Isthmus of   Phnom Penh   Ho Chi Minh City
Kra   Gulf of   (Saigon)
Thailand
Phuket   South China
Songkhla   Sea   Kota
Kinabalu
George Town   WEST   MALAYSIA   BRUNEI   SABAH
Medan   MALAYSIA   Kuala Lumpur   SARAWAK
Kuching   BORNEO
SINGAPORE
SUMATRA   KALIMANTAN
KEPULAUAN   Jambi   I N D O N E S I A
Palembang   Banjarmasin
GREATER   SUNDA   ISL
Jakarta
INDIAN   Bandung   Java Sea
OCEAN   Yogyakarta   JAVA   Surabaya
BALI   LE
LOMBOK

Strait of Malacca
Karimata Strait

0   500 miles
0   750 km

N

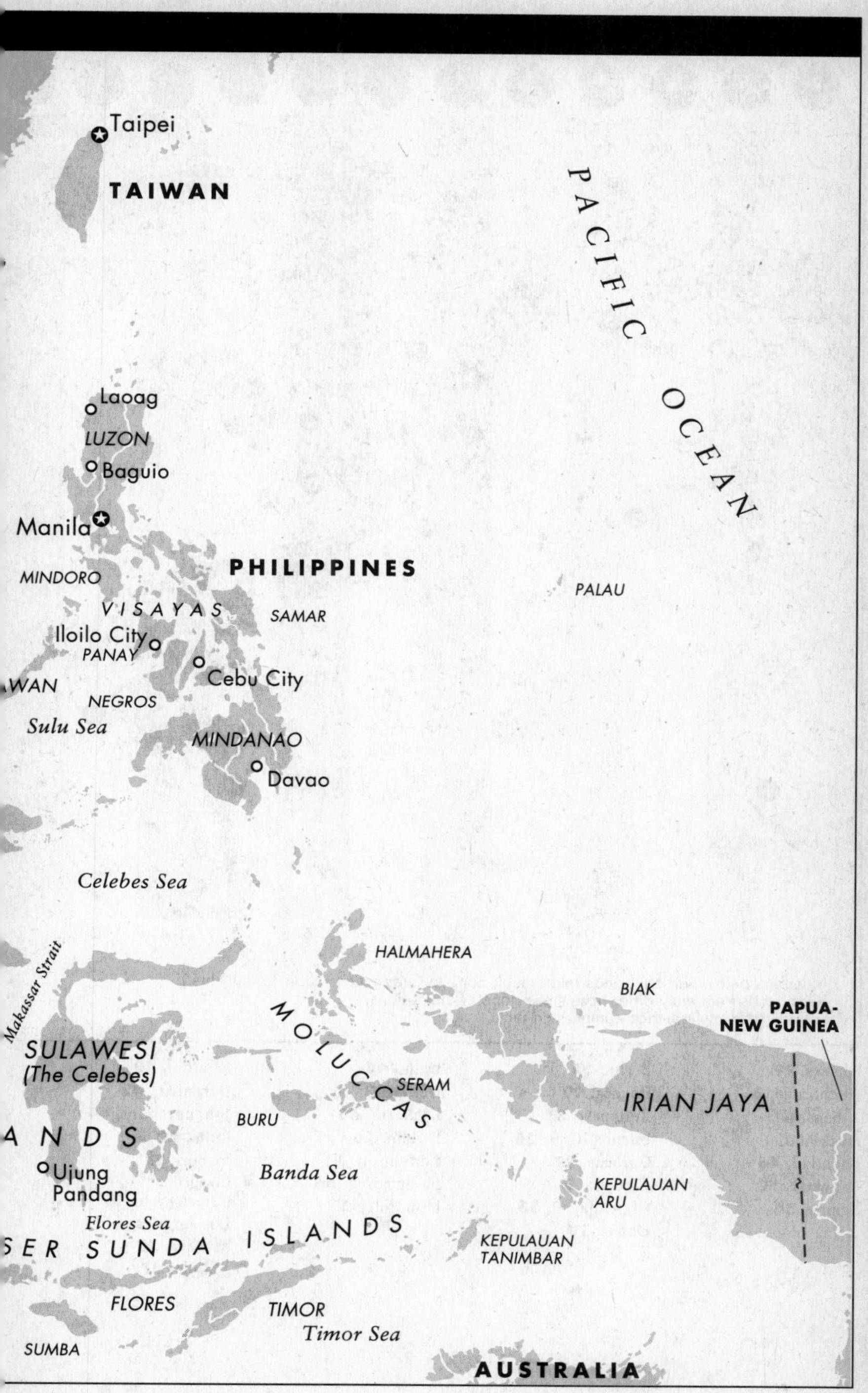

Taipei

TAIWAN

PACIFIC OCEAN

Laoag

LUZON

Baguio

Manila

MINDORO

PHILIPPINES

PALAU

V I S A Y A S

SAMAR

Iloilo City

PANAY

Cebu City

NEGROS

WAN

Sulu Sea

MINDANAO

Davao

Celebes Sea

HALMAHERA

BIAK

**PAPUA-
NEW GUINEA**

Makassar Strait

SULAWESI
(The Celebes)

M O L U C C A S

SERAM

IRIAN JAYA

BURU

A N D S

Ujung
Pandang

Banda Sea

*KEPULAUAN
ARU*

Flores Sea

S E R   S U N D A   I S L A N D S

*KEPULAUAN
TANIMBAR*

FLORES

TIMOR

Timor Sea

SUMBA

AUSTRALIA

World Time Zones

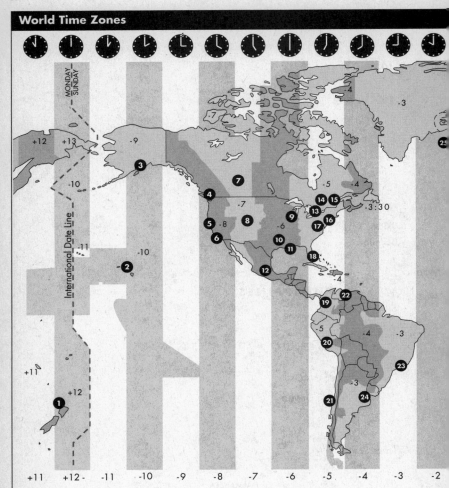

MONDAY
SUNDAY

International Date Line

+12 +13 -9 -4 -3

-10 -7 -5 -4 -3:30

-11 -10 -6

+11 -4

+11 +12 -5 -4 -3

+12 -3

Numbers below vertical bands relate each zone to Greenwich Mean Time (0 hrs.).
Local times frequently differ from these general indications,
as indicated by light-face numbers on map.

+11 +12 - -11 -10 -9 -8 -7 -6 -5 -4 -3 -2

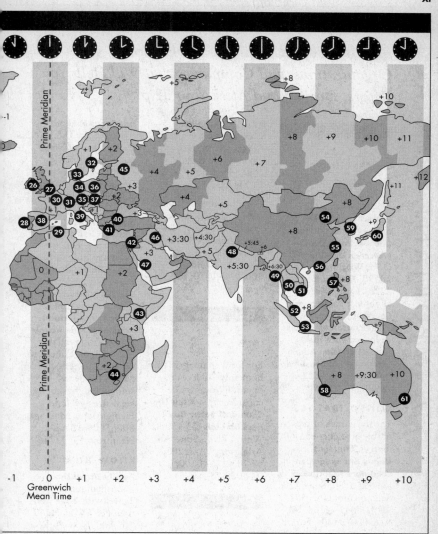

Mecca, **47**
Mexico City, **12**
Miami, **18**
Montréal, **15**
Moscow, **45**
Nairobi, **43**
New Orleans, **11**
New York City, **16**

Ottawa, **14**
Paris, **30**
Perth, **58**
Reykjavík, **25**
Rio de Janeiro, **23**
Rome, **39**
Saigon (Ho Chi Minh City), **51**

San Francisco, **5**
Santiago, **21**
Seoul, **59**
Shanghai, **55**
Singapore, **52**
Stockholm, **32**
Sydney, **61**
Tokyo, **60**

Toronto, **13**
Vancouver, **4**
Vienna, **35**
Warsaw, **36**
Washington, D.C., **17**
Yangon, **49**
Zürich, **31**

IMPORTANT CONTACTS A TO Z

An Alphabetical Listing of Publications, Organizations, and Companies that Will Help You Before, During, and After Your Trip

A

AIR TRAVEL

COMPLAINTS

To register complaints about charter and scheduled airlines, contact the U.S. Department of Transportation's **Aviation Consumer Protection Division** (✉ C-75, Washington, DC 20590, ☎ 202/366–2220). Complaints about lost baggage or ticketing problems and safety concerns may also be logged with the **Federal Aviation Administration (FAA) Consumer Hotline** (☎ 800/322–7873).

CONSOLIDATORS

For the names of reputable air-ticket consolidators, contact the **United States Air Consolidators Association** (✉ 925 L St., Suite 220, Sacramento, CA 95814, ☎ 916/441–4166, FAX 916/441–3520). For discount air-ticketing agencies, *see* Discounts & Deals, *below.*

PUBLICATIONS

For general information about charter carriers, ask for the Department of Transportation's free brochure **"Plane Talk: Public Charter Flights"** (✉ Aviation Consumer Protection Division, C-75, Washington, DC 20590, ☎ 202/366–2220). The Department of Transportation also publishes a 58-page booklet, **"Fly Rights,"**

available from the Consumer Information Center (✉ Supt. of Documents, Dept. 136C, Pueblo, CO 81009; $1.75).

For other tips and hints, consult the Consumers Union's monthly **"Consumer Reports Travel Letter"** (✉ Box 53629, Boulder, CO 80322, ☎ 800/234–1970; $39 1st year).

B

BETTER BUSINESS BUREAU

For local contacts in the hometown of a tour operator you may be considering, consult the **Council of Better Business Bureaus** (✉ 4200 Wilson Blvd., Suite 800, Arlington, VA 22203, ☎ 703/276–0100, FAX 703/525–8277).

C

CAR RENTAL

The major car-rental company represented in Southeast Asia is **Avis** (☎ 800/331–1084, 800/879–2847 in Canada).

CHILDREN & TRAVEL

FLYING

Look into **"Flying with Baby"** (✉ Third Street Press, Box 261250, Littleton, CO 80163, ☎ 303/595–5959; $4.95 includes shipping), cowritten by a flight attendant. **"Kids**

and Teens in Flight," free from the U.S. Department of Transportation's Aviation Consumer Protection Division (✉ C-75, Washington, DC 20590, ☎ 202/366–2220), offers tips on children flying alone. Every two years the February issue of *Family Travel Times* (☞ Know-How, *below*) details children's services on three dozen airlines. **"Flying Alone, Handy Advice for Kids Traveling Solo"** is available free from the American Automobile Association (AAA) (✉ Send stamped, self-addressed, legal-size envelope: Flying Alone, Mail Stop 800, 1000 AAA Dr., Heathrow, FL 32746).

KNOW-HOW

Family Travel Times, published quarterly by Travel with Your Children (✉ TWYCH, 40 5th Ave., New York, NY 10011, ☎ 212/477–5524; $40 per year), covers destinations, types of vacations, and modes of travel.

TOUR OPERATORS

If you're outdoorsy, look into family-oriented programs run by the **American Museum of Natural History** (✉ 79th St. and Central Park W, New York, NY 10024, ☎ 212/769–5700 or 800/462–8687).

CRUISING

The following lines operate seasonal cruises of Southeast Asia:

Crystal Cruises (✉ 2121 Ave. of the Stars, Los Angeles, CA 90067, ☎ 800/446–6620).

Cunard Line Limited (✉ 555 5th Ave., New York, NY 10017, ☎ 800/528–6273).

Orient Lines (✉ 1510 S.E. 17th St., Suite 400, Fort Lauderdale, FL 33316, ☎ 305/527–6660 or 800/333–7300).

Princess Cruises (✉ 10100 Santa Monica Blvd., Los Angeles, CA 90067, ☎ 310/553–1770).

Radisson Seven Seas Cruises (✉ 600 Corporate Dr., Suite 410, Fort Lauderdale, FL 33334, ☎ 800/333–3333).

Renaissance Cruises (✉ 1800 Eller Dr., Suite 300, Box 350307, Fort Lauderdale, FL 33335-0307, ☎ 800/525–2450).

Royal Caribbean Cruise Line (✉ 1050 Caribbean Way, Miami, FL 33132, ☎ 305/539–6000).

Seabourn Cruise Line (✉ 55 Francisco St., San Francisco, CA 94133, ☎ 415/391–7444 or 800/929–9595).

Silversea Cruises (✉ 110 E. Broward Blvd., Fort Lauderdale, FL 33301, ☎ 305/522–4477 or 800/722–9955).

Star Clippers (✉ 4101 Salzedo Ave., Coral Gables, FL 33146, ☎ 800/442–0551).

CUSTOMS

CANADIAN CITIZENS

Contact **Revenue Canada** (✉ 2265 St. Laurent Blvd. S, Ottawa, Ontario K1G 4K3, ☎ 613/993–0534) for a copy of the free brochure **"I Declare/ Je Déclare"** and for details on duty-free limits. For recorded information (within Canada only), call 800/461–9999.

U.K. CITIZENS

HM Customs and Excise (✉ Dorset House, Stamford St., London SE1 9NG, ☎ 0171/202–4227) can answer questions about U.K. customs regulations and publishes a free pamphlet, **"A Guide for Travellers,"** detailing standard procedures and import rules.

U.S. CITIZENS

The **U.S. Customs Service** (✉ Box 7407, Washington, DC 20044, ☎ 202/927–6724) can answer questions on duty-free limits and publishes a helpful brochure, **"Know Before You Go."** For information on registering foreign-made articles, call 202/927–0540 or write U.S. Customs Service, Resource Management, 1301 Constitution Ave. NW, Washington DC, 20229.

COMPLAINTS➤ Note the inspector's badge number and write to the commissioner's office (✉ 1301 Constitution Ave. NW, Washington, DC 20229).

D

DISABILITIES & ACCESSIBILITY

COMPLAINTS

To register complaints under the provisions of the Americans with Disabilities Act, contact the U.S. Department of Justice's **Disability Rights Section** (✉ Box 66738, Washington, DC 20035, ☎ 202/514–0301 or 800/514–0301, FAX 202/307–1198, TTY 202/514–0383 or 800/514–0383). For airline-related problems, contact the U.S. Department of Transportation's **Aviation Consumer Protection Division** (☞ Air Travel, *above*).

ORGANIZATIONS

TRAVELERS WITH HEARING IMPAIRMENTS➤ The **American Academy of Otolaryngology** (✉ 1 Prince St., Alexandria, VA 22314, ☎ 703/836–4444, FAX 703/683–5100, TTY 703/519–1585) publishes a brochure, **"Travel Tips for Hearing Impaired People."**

TRAVELERS WITH MOBILITY PROBLEMS➤ Contact **Mobility International USA** (✉ Box 10767, Eugene, OR 97440, ☎ and TTY 541/343–1284, FAX 541/343–6812), the U.S. branch of a Belgium-based organization (☞ *below*) with affiliates in 30 countries; **MossRehab Hospital Travel Information Service** (☎ 215/456–9600, TTY 215/456–9602), a telephone information resource for travelers with physical disabilities; the **Society for the Advance-**

ment of Travel for the Handicapped (⊠ 347 5th Ave., Suite 610, New York, NY 10016, ☎ 212/447–7284, FAX 212/725–8253; membership $45); and **Travelin' Talk** (⊠ Box 3534, Clarksville, TN 37043, ☎ 615/552–6670, FAX 615/552–1182) which provides local contacts worldwide for travelers with disabilities.

TRAVELERS WITH VISION IMPAIRMENTS➤ Contact the **American Council of the Blind** (⊠ 1155 15th St. NW, Suite 720, Washington, DC 20005, ☎ 202/467–5081, FAX 202/467–5085) for a list of travelers' resources, or the **American Foundation for the Blind** (⊠ 11 Penn Plaza, Suite 300, New York, NY 10001, ☎ 212/502–7600 or 800/232–5463, TTY 212/502–7662), which provides general advice and publishes **Access to Art** ($19.95), a directory of museums that accommodate travelers with vision impairments.

IN THE U.K.➤ Contact the **Royal Association for Disability and Rehabilitation** (⊠ RADAR, 12 City Forum, 250 City Rd., London EC1V 8AF, ☎ 0171/250–3222) or **Mobility International** (⊠ rue de Manchester 25, B-1080 Brussels, Belgium, ☎ 00–322–410–6297, FAX 00–322–410–6874), an international travel-information clearinghouse for people with disabilities.

PUBLICATIONS

Several publications for travelers with disabilities are available from the **Consumer Information Center** (⊠ Box 100,

Pueblo, CO 81009, ☎ 719/948–3334). Call or write for its free catalog of current titles. The Society for the Advancement of Travel for the Handicapped (☞ Organizations, *above*) publishes the quarterly magazine **Access to Travel** ($13 for 1-year subscription).

The 500-page **Travelin' Talk Directory** (⊠ Box 3534, Clarksville, TN 37043, ☎ 615/552–6670, FAX 615/552–1182; $35) lists people and organizations who help travelers with disabilities. For travel agents worldwide, consult the **Directory of Travel Agencies for the Disabled** (⊠ Twin Peaks Press, Box 129, Vancouver, WA 98666, ☎ 360/694–2462 or 800/637–2256, FAX 360/696–3210; $19.95 plus $3 shipping).

TRAVEL AGENCIES & TOUR OPERATORS

The Americans with Disabilities Act requires that all travel firms serve the needs of all travelers. That said, you should note that some agencies and operators specialize in making travel arrangements for individuals and groups with disabilities, among them **Access Adventures** (⊠ 206 Chestnut Ridge Rd., Rochester, NY 14624, ☎ 716/889–9096), run by a former physical-rehab counselor, and **CareVacations** (⊠ 5019 49th Ave., Suite 102, Leduc, Alberta T9E 6T5, ☎ 403/986–8332; in Canada, 800/648–1116), which has group tours and is especially helpful for cruises.

TRAVELERS WITH MOBILITY PROBLEMS➤ Contact **Accessible Journeys** (⊠ 35 W. Sellers Ave., Ridley Park, PA 19078, ☎ 610/521–0339 or 800/846–4537, FAX 610/521–6959), an escorted-tour operator exclusively for travelers with mobility impairments; **Hinsdale Travel Service** (⊠ 201 E. Ogden Ave., Suite 100, Hinsdale, IL 60521, ☎ 630/325–1335), a travel agency that benefits from the advice of wheelchair traveler Janice Perkins; and **Wheelchair Journeys** (⊠ 16979 Redmond Way, Redmond, WA 98052, ☎ 206/885–2210 or 800/313–4751), which can handle arrangements worldwide.

TRAVELERS WITH DEVELOPMENTAL DISABILITIES➤ Contact the nonprofit **New Directions** (⊠ 5276 Hollister Ave., Suite 207, Santa Barbara, CA 93111, ☎ 805/967–2841).

TRAVEL GEAR

The **Magellan's** catalog (☎ 800/962–4943, FAX 805/568–5406), includes a section devoted to products designed for travelers with disabilities.

DISCOUNTS & DEALS

AIRFARES

For the lowest airfares to Southeast Asia, call 800/FLY–4–LESS.

CLUBS

Contact **Entertainment Travel Editions** (⊠ Box 1068, Trumbull, CT 06611, ☎ 800/445–4137; $28–$53, depending on destination), **Great American Traveler**

(✉ Box 27965, Salt Lake City, UT 84127, ☎ 800/548–2812; $49.95 per year), **Moment's Notice Discount Travel Club** (✉ 7301 New Utrecht Ave., Brooklyn, NY 11204, ☎ 718/234–6295; $25 per year, single or family), **Privilege Card International** (✉ 3391 Peachtree Rd. NE, Suite 110, Atlanta, GA 30326, ☎ 404/262–0222 or 800/236–9732; $74.95 per year), **Travelers Advantage** (✉ CUC Travel Service, 49 Music Sq. W, Nashville, TN 37203, ☎ 800/548–1116 or 800/648–4037; $49 per year, single or family), or **Worldwide Discount Travel Club** (✉ 1674 Meridian Ave., Miami Beach, FL 33139, ☎ 305/534–2082; $50 per year for family, $40 single).

STUDENTS

Members of Hostelling International–American Youth Hostels (☞ Students, *below*) are eligible for discounts on car rentals, admissions to attractions, and other selected travel expenses.

PUBLICATIONS

Consult *The Frugal Globetrotter,* by Bruce Northam (✉ Fulcrum Publishing, 350 Indiana St., Suite 350, Golden, CO 80401, ☎ 800/992–2908; $16.95 plus $4 shipping). For publications that tell how to find the lowest prices on plane tickets, *see* Air Travel, *above.*

G
GAY & LESBIAN TRAVEL

ORGANIZATIONS

The **International Gay Travel Association** (✉

Box 4974, Key West, FL 33041, ☎ 800/448–8550, FAX 305/296–6633), a consortium of more than 1,000 travel companies, can supply names of gay-friendly travel agents, tour operators, and accommodations.

PUBLICATIONS

The 16-page monthly newsletter **"Out & About"** (✉ 8 W. 19th St., Suite 401, New York, NY 10011, ☎ 212/645–6922 or 800/929–2268, FAX 800/929–2215; $49 for 10 issues and quarterly calendar) covers gay-friendly resorts, hotels, cruise lines, and airlines.

TOUR OPERATORS

Toto Tours (✉ 1326 W. Albion Ave., Suite 3W, Chicago, IL 60626, ☎ 773/274–8686 or 800/565–1241, FAX 773/274–8695) offers group tours to worldwide destinations.

TRAVEL AGENCIES

The largest agencies serving gay travelers are **Advance Travel** (✉ 10700 Northwest Fwy., Suite 160, Houston, TX 77092, ☎ 713/682–2002 or 800/292–0500), **Club Travel** (✉ 8739 Santa Monica Blvd., W. Hollywood, CA 90069, ☎ 310/358–2200 or 800/429–8747), **Islanders/Kennedy Travel** (✉ 183 W. 10th St., New York, NY 10014, ☎ 212/242–3222 or 800/988–1181), **Now Voyager** (✉ 4406 18th St., San Francisco, CA 94114, ☎ 415/626–1169 or 800/255–6951), and **Yellowbrick Road** (✉ 1500 W. Balmoral Ave., Chicago, IL 60640, ☎ 773/561–1800 or 800/

642–2488). **Skylink Women's Travel** (✉ 2460 W. 3rd St., Suite 215, Santa Rosa, CA 95401, ☎ 707/570–0105 or 800/225–5759) serves lesbian travelers.

H
HEALTH

FINDING A DOCTOR

For its members, the **International Association for Medical Assistance to Travellers** (IAMAT, membership free; ✉ 417 Center St., Lewiston, NY 14092, ☎ 716/754–4883; ✉ 40 Regal Rd., Guelph, Ontario N1K 1B5, ☎ 519/836–0102; ✉ 1287 St. Clair Ave. W., Toronto, Ontario M6E 1B8, ☎ 416/652–0137; ✉ 57 Voirets, 1212 Grand-Lancy, Geneva, Switzerland, no phone) publishes a worldwide directory of English-speaking physicians meeting IAMAT standards.

MEDICAL ASSISTANCE COMPANIES

The following companies are concerned primarily with emergency medical assistance, although they may provide some insurance as part of their coverage. For a list of full-service travel insurance companies, *see* Insurance, *below.*

Contact **International SOS Assistance** (✉ Box 11568, Philadelphia, PA 19116, ☎ 215/244–1500 or 800/523–8930; ✉ Box 466, Pl. Bonaventure, Montréal, Québec H5A 1C1, ☎ 514/874–7674 or 800/363–0263; ✉ 7 Old Lodge Pl., St. Margarets, Twickenham

TW1 1RQ, England, ☎ 0181/744–0033), **Medex Assistance Corporation** (✉ Box 5375, Timonium, MD 21094, ☎ 410/453–6300 or 800/537–2029), **Near Travel Services** (✉ Box 1339, Calumet City, IL 60409, ☎ 708/868–6700 or 800/654–6700), **Traveler's Emergency Network** (✉ 1133 15th St. NW, Suite 400, Washington, DC 20005, ☎ 202/828–5894 or 800/275–4836, FAX 202/828–5896), **TravMed** (✉ Box 5375, Timonium, MD 21094, ☎ 410/453–6380 or 800/732–5309), or **Worldwide Assistance Services** (✉ 1133 15th St. NW, Suite 400, Washington, DC 20005, ☎ 202/331–1609 or 800/821–2828, FAX 202/828–5896).

PUBLICATIONS

The Safe Travel Book, by Peter Savage (✉ Jossey-Bass Publishers, Inc., 350 Sansome St., San Francisco, CA 94104 ☎ 800/956–7739, FAX 800/605–2665; $12.95 plus $5 shipping) is authoritative.

WARNINGS

The hot line of the **National Centers for Disease Control** (✉ CDC, National Center for Infectious Diseases, Division of Quarantine, Traveler's Health Section, 1600 Clifton Rd., M/S E-03, Atlanta, GA 30333, ☎ 404/332–4559, FAX 404/332–4565, http://www.cdc.gov) provides information on health risks abroad and vaccination requirements and recommendations. You can call for an automated menu of recorded information, use the fax-back service to request printed matter, or get information on line.

I

INSURANCE

IN CANADA

Contact **Mutual of Omaha** (✉ Travel Division, 500 University Ave., Toronto, Ontario M5G 1V8, ☎ 800/465–0267(in Canada) or 416/598-4083).

IN THE U.K.

The **Association of British Insurers** (✉ 51 Gresham St., London EC2V 7HQ, ☎ 0171/600–3333) gives advice by phone and publishes the free pamphlet **"Holiday Insurance and Motoring Abroad,"** which sets out typical policy provisions and costs.

IN THE U.S.

Travel insurance covering baggage, health, and trip cancellation or interruptions is available from **Access America** (✉ 6600 W. Broad St., Richmond, VA 23230, ☎ 804/285–3300 or 800/334–7525), **Carefree Travel Insurance** (✉ Box 9366, 100 Garden City Plaza, Garden City, NY 11530, ☎ 516/294–0220 or 800/323–3149), **Tele-Trip** (✉ Mutual of Omaha Plaza, Box 31716, Omaha, NE 68131, ☎ 800/228–9792), **Travel Guard International** (✉ 1145 Clark St., Stevens Point, WI 54481, ☎ 715/345–0505 or 800/826–1300), **Travel Insured International** (✉ Box 280568, East Hartford, CT 06128, ☎ 203/528–7663 or 800/243–3174), and **Wallach & Company** (✉ 107 W. Federal St., Box 480, Middleburg, VA 22117, ☎ 540/687–3166 or 800/237–6615).

L

LODGING

APARTMENT & VILLA RENTAL

Ccontact **Property Rentals International** (✉ 1008 Mansfield Crossing Rd., Richmond, VA 23236, ☎ 804/378–6054 or 800/220–3332, FAX 804/379–2073). Members of the travel club **Hideaways International** (✉ 767 Islington St., Portsmouth, NH 03801, ☎ 603/430–4433 or 800/843–4433, FAX 603/430–4444, info@ hideaways.com; $99 per year) receive two annual guides plus quarterly newsletters and arrange rentals among themselves.

M

MONEY

ATMS

For specific foreign **Cirrus** locations, call 800/424–7787; for foreign **Plus** locations, consult the Plus directory at your local bank.

CURRENCY EXCHANGE

If your bank doesn't exchange currency, contact **Thomas Cook Currency Services** (☎ 800/287–7362 for locations). **Ruesch International** (☎ 800/424–2923 for locations) can also provide you with foreign banknotes before you leave home and publishes a number of useful brochures, including a "Foreign Currency Guide" and "Foreign Exchange Tips."

WIRING FUNDS

Funds can be wired via **MoneyGram**SM (for locations and information in the U.S. and Canada, ☎ 800/926–9400) or **Western Union** (for agent locations or to send money using MasterCard or Visa, ☎ 800/325–6000; in Canada, ☎ 800/321–2923; in the U.K., ☎ 0800/833833; or visit the Western Union office at the nearest major post office).

P
PACKING

For strategies on packing light, get a copy of *The Packing Book*, by Judith Gilford (✉ Ten Speed Press, Box 7123, Berkeley, CA 94707, ☎ 510/559–1600 or 800/841–2665, FAX 510/524–4588; $7.95 plus $3.50 shipping).

PASSPORTS

See the individual country chapters for passport and visa requirements.

CANADIAN CITIZENS

For fees, documentation requirements, and other information, call the Ministry of Foreign Affairs and International Trade's **Passport Office** (☎ 819/994–3500 or 800/567–6868).

U.K. CITIZENS

For fees, documentation requirements, and to request an emergency passport, call the **London Passport Office** (☎ 0990/210410).

U.S. CITIZENS

For fees, documentation requirements, and other information, call the State Department's **Office of Passport Services** information line (☎ 202/647–0518).

PHOTO HELP

The **Kodak Information Center** (☎ 800/242–2424) answers consumer questions about film and photography. The *Kodak Guide to Shooting Great Travel Pictures* (available in bookstores; or contact Fodor's Travel Publications, ☎ 800/533–6478; $16.50 plus $4 shipping) explains how to take expert travel photographs.

S
SAFETY

"Trouble-Free Travel," from the AAA, is a booklet of tips for protecting yourself and your belongings when away from home. Send a stamped, self-addressed, legal-size envelope to Trouble-Free Travel (✉ Mail Stop 75, 1000 AAA Dr., Heathrow, FL 32746).

SENIOR CITIZENS

EDUCATIONAL TRAVEL

The nonprofit **Elderhostel** (✉ 75 Federal St., 3rd Floor, Boston, MA 02110, ☎ 617/426–7788), for people 55 and older, has offered inexpensive study programs since 1975. Courses cover everything from marisne science to Greek mythology and cowboy poetry. Costs for two- to three-week international trips—including room, board, and transportation from the

United States—range from $1,800 to $4,500.

ORGANIZATIONS

Contact the **American Association of Retired Persons** (✉ AARP, 601 E St. NW, Washington, DC 20049, ☎ 202/434–2277; annual dues $8 per person or couple). Its Purchase Privilege Program secures discounts for members on lodging, car rentals, and sightseeing.

STUDENTS

HOSTELING

In the United States, contact **Hostelling International–American Youth Hostels** (✉ 733 15th St. NW, Suite 840, Washington, DC 20005, ☎ 202/783–6161, FAX 202/783–6171); in Canada, **Hostelling International–Canada** (✉ 205 Catherine St., Suite 400, Ottawa, Ontario K2P 1C3, ☎ 613/237–7884); and in the United Kingdom, the **Youth Hostel Association of England and Wales** (✉ Trevelyan House, 8 St. Stephen's Hill, St. Albans, Hertfordshire AL1 2DY, ☎ 01727/855215 or 01727/845047). Membership (in the U.S., $25; in Canada, C$26.75; in the U.K., £9.30) gives you access to 5,000 hostels in 77 countries that charge $5–$40 per person per night.

ORGANIZATIONS

A major contact is the **Council on International Educational Exchange** (✉ Mail orders only: CIEE, 205 E. 42nd St., 16th Floor, New York, NY 10017, ☎ 212/822–2600, FAX 212/822–2699, info@ciee.org). The **Educational**

Travel Centre (✉ 438 N. Frances St., Madison, WI 53703, ☎ 608/256–5551 or 800/747–5551, FAX 608/256–2042) offers rail passes and low-cost airline tickets, mostly for flights that depart from Chicago.

In Canada, also contact **Travel Cuts** (✉ 187 College St., Toronto, Ontario M5T 1P7, ☎ 416/979–2406 or 800/667–2887).

T
TELEPHONES

For local access numbers abroad, contact **AT&T** USADirect (☎ 800/874–4000), **MCI** Call USA (☎ 800/444–4444), or **Sprint** Express (☎ 800/793–1153).

TOUR OPERATORS

Among the companies that sell tours and packages to Southeast Asia, the following are nationally known, have a proven reputation, and offer plenty of options.

GROUP TOURS

SUPER-DELUXE➤ **Abercrombie & Kent** (✉ 1520 Kensington Rd., Oak Brook, IL 60521-2141, ☎ 708/954–2944 or 800/323–7308, FAX 708/954–3324) and **Travcoa** (✉ Box 2630, 2350 S.E. Bristol St., Newport Beach, CA 92660, ☎ 714/476–2800 or 800/992–2003, FAX 714/476–2538).

DELUXE➤ **Globus** (✉ 5301 S. Federal Circle, Littleton, CO 80123, ☎ 303/797–2800 or 800/221–0090, FAX 303/795–0962), **Maupintour** (✉ Box 807, 1515 St. Andrews Drive, Lawrence, KS 66047,

☎ 913/843–1211 or 800/255–4266, FAX 913/843–8351), and **Tauck Tours** (✉ Box 5027, 276 Post Rd. West, Westport, CT 06881, ☎ 203/226–6911 or 800/468–2825, FAX 203/221–6828).

FIRST-CLASS➤ **General Tours** (✉ 53 Summer St., Keene, NH 03431, ☎ 603/357–5033 or 800/221–2216, FAX 603/357–4548), **Orient Flexi-Pax Tours** (✉ 630 Third Ave., New York, NY 10017, ☎ 212/692–9550 or 800/545–5540), **Pacific Bestour** (✉ 228 Rivervale Rd., River Vale, NJ 07675, ☎ 201/664–8778 or 800/688–3288), and **Pacific Delight Tours** (✉ 132 Madison Ave., New York, NY 10016, ☎ 212/684–7707 or 800/221–7179).

BUDGET➤ **Cosmos** (☞ Globus, *above*).

PACKAGES

Independent vacation packages are available from major airlines and tour operators. Among U.S. carriers, contact **Delta Dream Vacations** (☎ 800/872–7786) and **United Vacations** (☎ 800/328–6877). Many of the operators listed under group tours, above, also sell independent packages. Contact **DER Tours** (✉ 11933 Wilshire Blvd., Los Angeles, CA 90025, ☎ 310/479–4411 or 800/937–1235), **Orient Flexi-Pax Tours, Pacific Bestour,** and **Pacific Delight Tours.**

FROM THE U.K.

Tour operators with packages to Southeast Asia include **British Airways Holidays** (✉ Astral Towers, Betts

Way, London Rd., Crawley, West Sussex RH10 2XA, ☎ 01293/723–350), **Kuoni Travel** (✉ Kuoni House, Dorking, Surrey RH5 4AZ, ☎ 01306/740–500), **Bales Tours** (✉ Bales House, Junction Rd., Dorking, Surrey RH4 3HB, ☎ 01306/876–881 or 01306/885–991, and **Hayes and Jarvis** (✉ Hayes House, 152 King St., London W6 0QU, ☎ 0181/748–5050).

Travel agencies that offer cheap fares to Southeast Asia inlude **Trailfinders** (✉ 42–50 Earl's Court Rd., London W8 6FT, ☎ 0171/937–5400), **Travel Cuts** (✉ 295a Regent St., London W1R 7YA, ☎ 0171/637–3161, and **Flightfile** (✉ 49 Tottenham Court Rd., London W1P 9RE, ☎ 0171/700–2722).

THEME TRIPS

Customized tours of Southeast Asia are the specialty of **Pacific Experience** (✉ 366 Madison Ave., No. 1203, New York, NY 10017, ☎ 212/661–2604 or 800/279–3639, FAX 212/661–2587).

Travel Contacts (✉ Box 173, Camberley, GU15 1YE, England, ☎ 011/44/1/27667–7217, FAX 011/44/1/2766–3477), which represents over 160 tour operators, can satisfy just about any special interest in Southeast Asia.

ADVENTURE➤ Action-packed tours of Southeast Asia are sold by **Adventure Center** (✉ 1311 63rd St., No. 200, Emeryville, CA 94608, ☎ 510/654–1879 or

800/227–8747, FAX 510/
654–4200), **Mountain
Travel-Sobek** (✉ 6420
Fairmount Ave., El
Cerrito, CA 94530, ☎
510/527–8100 or 800/
227–2384, FAX 510/
525–7710), and **Wilderness Travel** (✉ 801
Allston Way, Berkeley,
CA 94710, ☎ 510/
548–0420 or 800/368–
2794, FAX 510/548–
0347).

ARCHAEOLOGY➤ **Archeological Tours** (✉ 271
Madison Ave., New
York, NY 10016, ☎
212/986–3054, FAX 212/
370–1561) delves into
the fascinating culture
of Indonesia.

BICYCLING➤ Bike tours
of Southeast Asia that
include Bali are available from **Backroads**
(✉ 1516 5th St., Berkeley, CA 94710-1740, ☎
510/527–1555 or 800/
462–2848, FAX 510/
527–1444).

LEARNING VACATIONS➤
For educational programs contact **Earthwatch** (✉ Box 403, 680
Mt. Auburn St., Watertown, MA 02272, ☎
617/926–8200 or 800/
776–0188, FAX 617/
926–8532), which
recruits volunteers to
serve in its EarthCorps
as short-term assistants
to scientists on research
expeditions, and **Smithsonian Study Tours and
Seminars** (✉ 1100
Jefferson Dr. SW, Room
3045, MRC 702, Washington, DC 20560, ☎
202/357–4700, FAX 202/
633–9250).

NATURAL HISTORY➤
Questers (✉ 381 Park
Ave. S, New York,
NY 10016, ☎ 212/
251–0444 or 800/468–
8668, FAX 212/251–
0890) explores the wild

side of Southeast Asia
in the company of
expert guides.

SCUBA DIVING➤ Dive
packages are available
from **Rothschild Dive
Safaris** (✉ 900 West
End Ave., No. 1B, New
York, NY 10025-3525,
☎ 212/662–4858 or
800/359–0747, FAX 212/
749–6172).

WALKING AND HIKING➤
Backroads (✉ 1516
5th St., Berkeley, CA
94710-1740, ☎ 510/
577–1555 or 800/462–
2848, FAX 510/527–
1444) guides travelers
across the wondrous
landscape of Bali.

YACHT CHARTERS➤ Try
Lynn Jachney Charters
(✉ Box 302 Marblehead, MA 01945, ☎
617/639–0787 or 800/
223–2050, FAX 617/
639–0216) and **Ocean
Voyages** (✉ 1709
Bridgeway, Sausalito,
CA 94965, ☎ 415/
332–4681, FAX 415/
332–7460).

ORGANIZATIONS

The **National Tour
Association** (✉ NTA,
546 E. Main St., Lexington, KY 40508, ☎
606/226–4444 or 800/
755–8687) and the
**United States Tour
Operators Association**
(✉ USTOA, 211 E.
51st St., Suite 12B, New
York, NY 10022, ☎
212/750–7371) can
provide lists of members and information
on booking tours.

PUBLICATIONS

Contact the USTOA
(☞ Organizations,
above) for its **"Smart
Traveler's Planning
Kit."** Pamphlets in the
kit include the "Worldwide Tour and Vacation Package Finder,"

"How to Select a Tour
or Vacation Package,"
and information on the
organization's consumer protection plan.
Also get a copy of the
Better Business Bureau's **"Tips on Travel
Packages"** (✉ Publication 24-195, 4200
Wilson Blvd., Arlington, VA 22203; $2).

TRAVEL GEAR

For travel apparel,
appliances, personal-
care items, and other
travel necessities, get
a free catalog from
Magellan's (☎ 800/
962–4943, FAX 805/
568–5406), **Orvis
Travel** (☎ 800/541–
3541, FAX 540/343–
7053), or **TravelSmith**
(☎ 800/950–1600,
FAX 415/455–0554).

ELECTRICAL
CONVERTERS

Send a self-addressed,
stamped envelope to
the **Franzus Company**
(✉ Customer Service,
Dept. B50, Murtha
Industrial Park, Box
142, Beacon Falls, CT
06403, ☎ 203/723–
6664) for a copy of the
free brochure "Foreign
Electricity Is No Deep,
Dark Secret."

TRAVEL AGENCIES

For names of reputable
agencies in your area,
contact the **American
Society of Travel Agents**
(✉ ASTA, 1101 King
St., Suite 200, Alexandria, VA 22314, ☎
703/739–2782), the
**Association of Canadian
Travel Agents** (✉ Suite
201, 1729 Bank St.,
Ottawa, Ontario K1V
7Z5, ☎ 613/521–
0474, FAX 613/521–
0805) or the **Association
of British Travel Agents**
(✉ 55-57 Newman St.,
London W1P 4AH, ☎

0171/637–2444, FAX 0171/637–0713).

U

U.S. GOVERNMENT TRAVEL BRIEFINGS

The U.S. Department of State's American Citizens Services office (✉ Room 4811, Washington, DC 20520; enclose SASE) issues **Consular Information Sheets** on all foreign countries. These cover issues such as crime, security, political climate, and health risks as well as listing embassy locations, entry requirements, currency

regulations, and providing other useful information. For the latest information, stop in at any U.S. passport office, consulate, or embassy; call the interactive hot line (☎ 202/647–5225, FAX 202/647–3000); tap into the department's computer bulletin board (☎ 202/647–9225); or access the full menu of updated sheets on the World Wide Web (http://travel.state.gov/travelžwarnings).

W

WEATHER

For current conditions and forecasts, plus the local time and helpful travel tips, call the **Weather Channel Connection** (☎ 900/932–8437; 95¢ per minute) from a Touch-Tone phone.

The *International Traveler's Weather Guide* (✉ Weather Press, Box 660606, Sacramento, CA 95866, ☎ 916/974–0201 or 800/972–0201; $10.95 includes shipping), written by two meteorologists, provides month-by-month information on temperature, humidity, and precipitation in more than 175 cities worldwide.

SMART TRAVEL TIPS A TO Z

Basic Information on Traveling in Southeast Asia and Savvy Tips to Make Your Trip a Breeze

A
AIR TRAVEL

Nonstop flights from the United States to points in Southeast Asia are rare. A direct flight, which requires at least one stop, or a connecting flight, which requires a change of airplanes, will often be your only choice. Some flights, especially nonstops, may be scheduled only on certain days of the week. Depending upon your destination, you may need to make more than one connection. This is especially true for less popular cities.

Flights to Southeast Asia may be transpacific or transatlantic. Westbound, the major gateway cities are Los Angeles, San Francisco, Seattle, and Portland (Oregon). Eastbound, the major gateways are New York, Detroit, Chicago, and Dallas. Stopover points may include Tokyo, Taipei, Hong Kong, or Seoul. Your best bet is to **use Tokyo for your stopover, as it has the greatest number of connecting flights.** Tokyo is usually your fastest choice even from East Coast departure points. If time is less important, with some carriers you can **add a stopover in Europe or the Middle East to your transatlantic flight** for a small charge.

CUTTING COSTS

Shop around, since you never know who may have the best deal. Make sure to call the airlines directly, get price quotes from a travel agent or tour operator who is experienced in booking travel to Southeast Asia, and contact a few consolidators. The Sunday travel section of most newspapers is a good place to look for deals.

MAJOR-AIRLINE FARES

Usually, you must **book in advance** and meet certain restrictions, such as minimum-stay requirements, to get cheaper fares. However—unlike on most North American and European flights—even the least-expensive airfares from the major airlines are often refundable. It's smart to **call a number of airlines and always ask for special fares** (☞ *below*), which may be available only to foreign nationals. Also **check different routings,** and if you are making several stops, try not to backtrack in order to make connections. The lowest fares may require only a confirmed departure date—you can often leave your return open or change your plans for a $50–$100 fee. Fares are generally comparable whether you are flying transpacific or transatlantic; your main savings will be in time.

From the U.K.➢ To save money on flights, **look into an APEX or**

Super-PEX ticket. APEX tickets must be booked in advance and have certain restrictions. Super-PEX tickets can be purchased at the airport.

SPECIAL FARES

If you plan to visit multiple countries in Southeast Asia, **check into "Circle Pacific" fares or around-the-world "Globetrotter Fares."** These are flat-rate fares that are subject to advance-purchase restrictions, usually of 7–14 days, and other rules. "Circle Pacific" fares allow four stopovers, although travel may not be allowed to such countries as Vietnam, Burma, Laos, and Cambodia. Additional stopovers can be purchased for $50–$100. Around-the-world fares also have routing restrictions and require one transatlantic and one transpacific crossing. You should **look for around-the-world fares that are mileage-based, rather than fares that require travel in one direction;** the former are easier to use and allow backtracking and multiple visits to a single city.

CONSOLIDATORS

Consolidators buy tickets for scheduled flights at reduced rates from the airlines then sell them at prices below the lowest available from the airlines directly—usually without advance restrictions.

Sometimes you can even get your money back if you need to return the ticket. Carefully read the fine print detailing penalties for changes and cancellations. If you doubt the reliability of a consolidator, **confirm your reservation with the airline.**

ALOFT

AIRLINE FOOD➤ If you hate airline food, **ask for special meals when booking.** These can be vegetarian, low-cholesterol, or kosher, for example; commonly prepared to order in smaller quantities than standard fare, they can be tastier.

JET LAG➤ To avoid this syndrome, which occurs when travel disrupts your body's natural cycles, try to maintain a normal routine. At night, **get some sleep.** By day, move about the cabin to **stretch your legs, eat light meals, and drink water—not alcohol.**

SMOKING➤ Smoking is not allowed on flights of six hours or less within the continental United States. Smoking is also prohibited on flights within Canada. For U.S. flights longer than six hours or international flights, **contact your carrier regarding their smoking policy.** Some carriers have prohibited smoking throughout their system; others allow smoking only on certain routes or even certain departures of that route.

WITHIN SOUTHEAST ASIA

Most of your international travel within the region is likely to be by air. Unless you are a very savvy traveler, it's best to **buy all your air tickets for travel within Southeast Asia before you leave home.** There are several options. First, **compare the cost of buying one ticket that includes all of your stopovers with the cost of buying individual tickets for each leg of your trip.** Also consider a "Visit Asia" fare for travel between three cities in different countries—usually at about half the normal coach fare. The flagship carriers of many Southeast Asian countries have "multicoupon" fares, which allow a certain number of flights within that country for a set fare. Addition coupons may also be purchased.

B
BUS TRAVEL

Most Asians don't own cars, so public transport is actually far more developed in Asia than in America, but it is, of course, crowded. The main problem is language; in many countries signs are not in Roman letters. City buses can be very confusing, so get written instructions from your hotel clerk to show the driver. In your free time, buses can give you very cheap sightseeing tours.

C
CAMERAS, CAMCORDERS, & COMPUTERS

IN TRANSIT

Always **keep your film, tape, or disks out of the sun;** never put these on the dashboard of a car. Carry an extra supply of batteries, and **be prepared to turn on your camera, camcorder, or laptop computer for security personnel** to prove that it's real.

X-RAYS

Always **ask for hand inspection at security.** Such requests are virtually always honored at U.S. airports, and are usually accommodated abroad. Photographic film becomes clouded after successive exposure to airport X-ray machines. Videotape and computer disks are not harmed by X-rays, but **keep your tapes and disks away from metal detectors.**

CUSTOMS

Before departing, **register your foreign-made camera or laptop with U.S. Customs.** If your equipment is U.S.-made, call the consulate of the country you'll be visiting to find out whether it should be registered with local customs upon arrival.

CAR RENTAL
CUTTING COSTS

To get the best deal, **book through a travel agent who is willing to shop around.** Ask your agent to **look for fly-drive packages,** which also save you money, and **ask if local taxes are included** in the rental or fly-drive price. These can be as high as 20% in some destinations. Don't forget to find out about required deposits, cancellation penalties, drop-off charges, and the cost of any required insurance coverage.

Also **ask your travel agent about a com-**

pany's customer-service record. How has it responded to late plane arrivals and vehicle mishaps? Are there often lines at the rental counter, and—if you're traveling during a holiday period—does a confirmed reservation guarantee you a car?

Always **find out what equipment is standard** at your destination before specifying what you want; automatic transmission and air-conditioning are usually optional—and very expensive.

INSURANCE

When driving a rented car, you are generally responsible for any damage to or loss of the rental vehicle, as well as any property damage or personal injury that you cause. Before you rent, **see what coverage you already have** under the terms of your personal auto insurance policy and credit cards.

If you do not have auto insurance or an umbrella insurance policy that covers damage to third parties, purchasing CDW or LDW is highly recommended.

LICENSE REQUIREMENTS

An International Driver's Permit is a good idea; it's available from the American or Canadian automobile associations, or, in the United Kingdom, from the AA or RAC.

SURCHARGES

Before you pick up a car in one city and leave it in another, **ask about drop-off charges or one-way service fees,** which can be substantial.

Note, too, that some rental agencies charge extra if you return the car before the time specified on your contract. To avoid a hefty refueling fee, **fill the tank just before you turn in the car**—but be aware that gas stations near the rental outlet may overcharge.

When traveling with children, **plan ahead** and **involve your youngsters** as you outline your trip. When packing, **include a supply of things to keep them busy** en route. On sightseeing days, try to **schedule activities of special interest to your children,** like a trip to a zoo or a playground. If you **plan your itinerary around seasonal festivals,** you'll never lack for things to do. In addition, **check local newspapers for special events** mounted by public libraries, museums, and parks.

BABY-SITTING

For recommended local sitters, **check with your hotel desk.**

DRIVING

If you are renting a car, don't forget to **arrange for a car seat when you reserve.** Sometimes they're free.

FLYING

As a general rule, infants under two not occupying a seat fly at greatly reduced fares and occasionally for free. If your children are two or older **ask about special children's fares.** Age limits for these fares vary among carriers. Rules also vary

regarding unaccompanied minors, so again, check with your airline.

BAGGAGE➤ In general, the adult baggage allowance applies to children paying half or more of the adult fare. If you are traveling with an infant, **ask about carry-on allowances** before departure. In general, for infants charged 10% of the adult fare you are allowed one carry-on bag and a collapsible stroller, which may have to be checked; you may be limited to less if the flight is full.

SAFETY SEATS➤ According to the FAA, it's a good idea to **use safety seats aloft** for children weighing less than 40 pounds. Airline policies vary. U.S. carriers allow FAA-approved models but usually require that you buy a ticket, even if your child would otherwise ride free, since the seats must be strapped into regular seats. However, some U.S. and foreign-flag airlines may require you to hold your baby during takeoff and landing—defeating the seat's purpose. Other foreign carriers may not allow infant seats at all, or may charge a child rather than an infant fare for their use.

FACILITIES➤ When making your reservation, **request children's meals or freestanding bassinets** if you need them; the latter are available only to those seated at the bulkhead, where there's enough legroom. If you don't need a bassinet, **think twice before requesting bulkhead seats**—the only storage space for in-flight necessities is in inconveniently distant overhead bins.

GAMES

Milton Bradley and Parker Brothers have travel versions of some of their most popular games, including Yahtzee, Trouble, Sorry, and Monopoly. Prices run $5 to $8. Look for them in the travel section of your local toy store.

LODGING

Most hotels allow children under a certain age to stay in their parents' room at no extra charge; others charge them as extra adults. Be sure to **ask about the cutoff age.**

CUSTOMS & DUTIES

To speed your clearance through customs, **keep receipts for all your purchases abroad** and **be ready to show the inspector what you've bought.** If you feel that you've been incorrectly or unfairly charged a duty, you can **appeal assessments in dispute.** First ask to see a supervisor. If you are still unsatisfied, **write to the port director** at your point of entry, sending your customs receipt and any other appropriate documentation. The address will be listed on your receipt.

IN CANADA

If you've been out of Canada for at least seven days, you may bring in C$500 worth of goods duty-free. If you've been away for fewer than seven days but for more than 48 hours, the duty-free

allowance drops to C$200; if your trip lasts between 24 and 48 hours, the allowance is C$50. You cannot pool allowances with family members. Goods claimed under the C$500 exemption may follow you by mail; those claimed under the lesser exemptions must accompany you.

Alcohol and tobacco products may be included in the seven-day and 48-hour exemptions but not in the 24-hour exemption. If you meet the age requirements of the province or territory through which you reenter Canada, you may bring in, duty-free, 1.14 liters (40 imperial ounces) of wine or liquor *or* 24 12-ounce cans or bottles of beer or ale. If you are 16 or older, you may bring in, duty-free, 200 cigarettes, 50 cigars or cigarillos, and 400 tobacco sticks or 400 grams of manufactured tobacco. Alcohol and tobacco must accompany you on your return.

An unlimited number of gifts with a value of up to C$60 each may be mailed to Canada duty-free. These do not affect your duty-free allowance on your return. Label the package "Unsolicited Gift—Value Under $60." Alcohol and tobacco are excluded.

IN THE U.K.

From countries outside the EU, including those covered in this book, you may import, duty-free, 200 cigarettes, 100 cigarillos, 50 cigars, or 250 grams of tobacco; 1 liter of spirits or 2 liters

of fortified or sparkling wine or liqueurs; 2 liters of still table wine; 60 milliliters of perfume; 250 milliliters of toilet water; plus £136 worth of other goods, including gifts and souvenirs.

IN THE U.S.

You may bring home $400 worth of foreign goods duty-free if you've been out of the country for at least 48 hours and haven't already used the $400 allowance, or any part of it, in the past 30 days.

Travelers 21 or older may bring back 1 liter of alcohol duty-free, provided the beverage laws of the state through which they reenter the United States allow it. In addition, regardless of their age, they are allowed 100 non-Cuban cigars and 200 cigarettes. Antiques, which the U.S. Customs Service defines as objects more than 100 years old, are duty-free. Original works of art done entirely by hand are also duty-free. These include, but are not limited to, paintings, drawings, and sculptures.

Duty-free, travelers may mail packages valued at up to $200 to themselves and up to $100 to others, with a limit of one parcel per addressee per day (and no alcohol or tobacco products or perfume valued at more than $5); on the outside, the package must be labeled as being either for personal use or an unsolicited gift, and a list of its contents and their retail value must be attached. Mailed items do not affect your duty-free allowance on your return.

D

DISABILITIES & ACCESSIBILITY

When discussing accessibility with an operator or reservationist, **ask hard questions.** Are there any stairs, inside *or* out? Are there grab bars next to the toilet *and* in the shower/tub? How wide is the doorway to the room? To the bathroom? For the most extensive facilities, meeting the latest legal specifications, **opt for newer accommodations,** which more often have been designed with access in mind. Older properties or ships must usually be retrofitted and may offer more limited facilities as a result. Be sure to **discuss your needs before booking.**

DISCOUNTS & DEALS

You shouldn't have to pay for a discount. In fact, you may already be eligible for all kinds of savings. Here are some time-honored strategies for getting the best deal.

LOOK IN YOUR WALLET

When you **use your credit card to make travel purchases,** you may get free travel-accident insurance, collision damage insurance, medical or legal assistance, depending on the card and bank that issued it. American Express, Visa, and MasterCard provide one or more of these services, so **get a copy of your card's travel benefits.** If you are a member of the AAA or an oil-company-sponsored road-assistance plan, always **ask hotel or car-rental reservationists for auto-club discounts.** Some clubs offer additional discounts on tours, cruises, or admission to attractions. And don't forget that auto-club membership entitles you to free maps and trip-planning services.

SENIORS CITIZENS & STUDENTS

As a senior-citizen traveler, you may be eligible for special rates, but you should mention your senior-citizen status up front. If you're a student or under 26 you can also get discounts, especially if you have an official ID card (☞ Senior-Citizen Discounts *and* Students on the Road, *below*).

DIAL FOR DOLLARS

To save money, **look into "1-800" discount reservations services,** which often have lower rates. These services use their buying power to get a better price on hotels, airline tickets, and sometimes even car rentals. When booking a room, always **call the hotel's local toll-free number** (if one is available) rather than the central reservations number—you'll often get a better price. Ask the reservationist about special packages or corporate rates, which are usually available even if you're not traveling on business.

JOIN A CLUB?

Discount clubs can be a legitimate source of savings, but you must use the participating hotels and visit the participating attractions in order to realize any benefits. Remember, too, that you have to pay a fee to join, so **determine if you'll save enough to warrant your membership fee.** Before booking with a club, **make sure the hotel or other supplier isn't offering a better deal.**

GET A GUARANTEE

When shopping for the best deal on hotels and car rentals, **look for guaranteed exchange rates,** which protect you against a falling dollar. With your rate locked in, you won't pay more even if the price goes up in the local currency.

DRIVING

Given the traffic situations within the city limits of major Southeast Asian destinations, it's probably best to **leave the driving to the cabbies and chauffeurs** who rule the roads here. For the adventurous who like to explore the countryside on their own, local and international car rental agencies are located in the major cities. Many Asian countries require (or would like you to have) an International Driver's License.

Generally, self-drive car rental is recommended only with caution. In certain locations such as Bali (Indonesia), the east coast of Malaysia, or Phuket (Thailand), renting cars is common practice, but in other locales traffic conditions and poor roads can make driving haz-

SMART TRAVEL TIPS / THE GOLD GUIDE

ardous. Hiring a car with a driver is usually reasonably inexpensive in Asia, and can be arranged through your hotel on arrival. Even less expensive and perhaps preferable are organized tours or day trips with car and guide, which will give you a chance to see the countryside and still enjoy the convenience of city facilities (including air-conditioning) on your return at night.

H
HEALTH

Although the countries in Southeast Asia do not require or suggest vaccinations before traveling, the United States Centers for Disease Control offer the following recommendations:

Tetanus-diphtheria and polio vaccinations should be up-to-date—if you haven't been immunized since childhood, **consider bolstering your tetanus vaccination.** You should also be immunized against (or immune to) measles, mumps, and rubella. If you plan to visit rural areas, where there's questionable sanitation, you'll need to **get an immune-serum globulin vaccination as protection against hepatitis A.** If you are staying for longer than three weeks and traveling into rural areas, antimalaria pills and a typhoid vaccination are recommended. If staying for a month or more, you should be vaccinated against rabies and Japanese encephalitis; for six months or more, against hepatitis B as well. For news on current outbreaks of infectious

diseases, ask your physician and check with your state or local department of health.

A major health risk in Southeast Asia is posed by the contamination of drinking water and fresh fruit and vegetables by fecal matter, which causes the intestinal ailment known as traveler's diarrhea. It usually lasts only a day or two. Paregoric, a good antidiarrheal agent that dulls or eliminates abdominal cramps, requires a doctor's prescription in some Southeast Asian countries. Two drugs recommended by the National Institutes of Health for mild cases of diarrhea can be purchased over the counter: Pepto-Bismol and loperamide (Imodium). If you come down with the malady, rest as much as possible and **drink lots of fluids** (such as tea without milk—chamomile is a good folk remedy for diarrhea). In severe cases, rehydrate yourself with a salt-sugar mixture added to purified water (½ tsp. salt and 4 tbsp. sugar per quart/liter of purified water). The best defense is a careful diet. **Stay away from unbottled or unboiled water, as well as ice, uncooked food, and unpasteurized milk and milk products.**

According to the Centers for Disease Control (CDC), there is a limited risk of malaria and dengue in certain areas of Southeast Asia. If you plan to visit remote regions or stay for more than six weeks, **check with the CDC's International Travelers Hotline**

(Center for Preventive Services, Division of Quarantine, Traveler's Health section, 1600 Clifton Rd., MSE03, Atlanta, GA 30333, ☎ 404/332–4559). Depending on your specific itinerary, your personal medical condition and history, and the presence of drug-resistant strains of malaria, the CDC recommends mefloquine (Larium), doxycycline, or chloroquine (Analen) as an antimalarial agent.

Malaria-bearing mosquitoes bite at dusk and at night, so travelers to susceptible regions should **take mosquito nets, wear clothing that covers the body, and carry repellent containing Deet** and a spray against flying insects for living and sleeping areas. No vaccine exists against dengue, so if it is in the area, travelers should use aerosol insecticides indoors as well as repellents against the mosquito.

DIVERS' ALERT
Scuba divers take note: **Do not fly within 24 hours of scuba diving.**

I
INSURANCE

Travel insurance can protect your monetary investment, replace your luggage and its contents, or provide for medical coverage should you fall ill during your trip. Most tour operators, travel agents, and insurance agents sell specialized health-and-accident, flight, trip-cancellation, and luggage insurance as well as comprehensive policies with some or all of these coverages. Comprehensive policies may also reimburse you for delays due to weather—an important consideration if you're traveling during the winter months. Some health-insurance policies do not cover preexisting conditions, but waivers may be available in specific cases. Coverage is sold by the companies listed in Important Contacts A to Z; these companies act as the policy's administrators. The actual insurance is usually underwritten by a well-known name, such as The Travelers or Continental Insurance.

Before you make any purchase, **review your existing health and homeowner's policies** to find out whether they cover expenses incurred while traveling.

BAGGAGE

Airline liability for baggage is limited to $1,250 per person on domestic flights. On international flights, it amounts to $9.07 per pound or $20 per kilogram for checked baggage (roughly $640 per 70-pound bag) and $400 per passenger for unchecked baggage. Insurance for losses exceeding the terms of your airline ticket can be bought directly from the airline at check-in for about $10 per $1,000 of coverage; note that it excludes a rather extensive list of items, shown on your airline ticket.

COMPREHENSIVE

Comprehensive insurance policies include all the coverages described above plus some that may not be available in more specific policies. If you have purchased an expensive vacation, especially one that involves travel abroad, comprehensive insurance is a must; **look for policies that include trip-delay insurance,** which will protect you in the event that weather problems cause you to miss your flight, tour, or cruise. A few insurers will also sell you a waiver for preexisting medical conditions. Some of the companies that offer both these features are Access America, Carefree Travel, Travel Insured International, and TravelGuard (☞ Insurance *in* Important Contacts A to Z).

FLIGHT

You should **think twice before buying flight insurance.** Often purchased as a last-minute impulse at the airport, it pays a lump sum when a plane crashes, either to a beneficiary if the insured dies or sometimes to a surviving passenger who loses his or her eyesight or a limb. Supplementing the airlines' coverage described in the limits-of-liability paragraphs on your ticket, it's expensive and basically unnecessary. Charging an airline ticket to a major credit card often automatically provides you with coverage that may also extend to travel by bus, train, and ship.

HEALTH

Medicare generally does not cover health care costs outside the United States; nor do many privately issued policies. If your own health insurance policy does not cover you outside the United States, **consider buying supplemental medical coverage.** It can reimburse you for $1,000–$150,000 worth of medical and/or dental expenses incurred as a result of an accident or illness during a trip. These policies also may include a personal-accident, or death-and-dismemberment, provision, which pays a lump sum ranging from $15,000 to $500,000 to your beneficiaries if you die or to you if you lose one or more limbs or your eyesight, and a medical-assistance provision, which may either reimburse you for the cost of referrals, evacuation, or repatriation and other services, or automatically enroll you as a member of a particular medical-assistance company (☞ Health Issues *in* Important Contacts A to Z).

U.K. TRAVELERS

You can buy an annual travel insurance policy valid for most vacations during the year in which it's purchased. If you are pregnant or have a preexisting medical condition make sure you're covered before buying such a policy.

TRIP

Without insurance, you will lose all or most of your money if you cancel your trip regardless of the reason. Especially if your airline ticket, cruise, or package tour is nonrefundable and cannot be changed, it's essential that you **buy trip-cancellation-and-interruption insurance.** When considering how much coverage you need, look for a policy that will cover the cost of your trip plus the nondiscounted price of a one-way airline ticket should you need to return home early. Read the fine print carefully, especially sections that define "family member" and "preexisting medical conditions." Also **consider default or bankruptcy insurance,** which protects you against a supplier's failure to deliver. Be aware, however, that if you buy such a policy from a travel agency, tour operator, airline, or cruise line, it may not cover default by the firm in question.

L

LODGING

Accommodations in Southeast Asia range from shoebox rooms with community or seatless toilets to five-star luxury. Every major city and important resort has at least one and probably several luxurious, international-style hotels (many are part of such international chains as Sheraton, Regent, Hyatt, Hilton, Holiday Inn, and Inter-Continental) that are famous for their service and amenities. If you can afford to splurge, this is the place to do it, for the prices of even the very top hotels are still far lower than comparable digs in Europe.

Most bottom-end accommodations are clustered in a particular area of the city, and you will probably want to see your room before committing to stay

there—and comparison-shop for the best deal. Also, **plan on spending more time getting from cheaper hotels to the major sights.** They are usually not on the beaten tourist path. In Bangkok, try the Banglampoo section of town, especially along Khao San Road. In Kuala Lumpur, try the Jalan Tuanku Abdul Rahman. In Manila, look in the Ermita and Quiapo sections. In Singapore, try Bencoolen Street and Beach Road.

You can find budget dormitory and hotel accommodations at the YMCAs in Bangkok, Kuala Lumpur, Manila, and Singapore, or at hostels in Thailand, the Philippines, Indonesia, and Malaysia. They vary greatly in quality but are generally inexpensive and clean.

You will also find some interesting Asian alternative lodging opportunities. In Sarawak, Malaysia, for example, you can stay in tribal longhouses and observe the native lifestyle, joining in meal preparation and evening entertainments. In northern Thailand, stays in village huts are part of many overnight treks to the hill tribes. For more, *see* the individual chapters.

A good rule is to **reserve your hotel rooms at least two months prior to arrival.** This is especially true in December and January, in autumn, at Chinese New Year, and over Easter, the busiest times. The international chains have U.S. reservations offices. If you do arrive

in an Asian capital without a hotel reservation, you will generally find a reservations desk at the airport that may be able to provide an immediate booking. This service is usually efficient and free, and often special discounts are available.

APARTMENT & VILLA RENTAL

If you want a home base that's roomy enough for a family and comes with cooking facilities, **consider taking a furnished rental.** This can also save you money, but not always—some rentals are luxury properties (economical only when your party is large). Home-exchange directories list rentals—often second homes owned by prospective house swappers—and some services search for a house or apartment for you (even a castle if that's your fancy) and handle the paperwork. Some send an illustrated catalog; others send photographs only of specific properties, sometimes at a charge; up-front registration fees may apply.

M

MEDICAL ASSISTANCE

No one plans to get sick while traveling, but it happens, so **consider signing up with a medical assistance company.** These outfits provide referrals, emergency evacuation or repatriation, 24-hour telephone hot lines for medical consultation, cash for emergencies, and other personal and legal assistance. They also dispatch medical personnel and arrange for the relay of medical records. Coverage varies by plan, so **read the fine print carefully.**

MONEY

ATMS

CASH ADVANCES> Before leaving home, **make sure that your credit cards have been programmed for ATM use in Southeast Asia.** Note that Discover is accepted mostly in the United States. Local bank cards often do not work overseas either; **ask your bank about a Visa debit card,** which works like a bank card but can be used at any ATM displaying a Visa logo.

TRANSACTION FEES> Although fees charged for ATM transactions may be higher abroad than at home, Cirrus and Plus exchange rates are excellent, because they are based on wholesale rates offered only by major banks.

EXCHANGING CURRENCY

For the most favorable rates, **change money at banks.** You won't do as well at exchange booths in airports or rail and bus stations, in hotels, in restaurants, or in stores, although you may find their hours more convenient. To avoid lines at airport exchange booths, **get a small amount of the local currency before you leave home.**

TRAVELER'S CHECKS

Whether or not to buy traveler's checks depends on where you are headed; **take cash to rural areas and small towns, traveler's checks to cities.** The most widely recognized checks are issued by American Express, Citicorp, Thomas Cook, and Visa. These are sold by major commercial banks for 1%–3% of the checks' face value— it pays to **shop around.** Both American Express and Thomas Cook issue checks that can be countersigned and used by either you or your traveling companion. So you won't be left with excess foreign currency, **buy a few checks in small denominations** to cash toward the end of your trip. Before leaving home, **contact your issuer for information on where to cash your checks** without a incurring a transaction fee. Record the numbers of all your checks, and keep this listing in a separate place, crossing off the numbers of checks you have cashed.

WIRING MONEY

For a fee of 3%–10%, depending on the amount of the transaction, you can have money sent to you from home through Money-Gram^{SM} or Western Union (☞ Money Matters *in* Important Contacts A to Z). The transferred funds and the service fee can be charged to a Master-Card or Visa account.

P

PACKING FOR
SOUTHEAST ASIA

Pack light, because porters can be hard to find and baggage restrictions are tight on international flights—be sure to check on your airline's policies before you pack. And either leave room in your suitcase or bring expandable totes for all your bargain purchases.

If you'll be traveling through several different types of climate, your wardrobe will have to reflect this. Light cotton or other natural-fiber clothing is appropriate for any Southeast Asian destination; drip-dry is an especially good idea, because the tropical sun and high humidity encourage frequent changes of clothing. Avoid exotic fabrics, because you may have difficulty getting them laundered.

Southeast Asia is generally informal: A sweater, shawl, or lightweight linen jacket will be sufficient for dining and evening wear, except for top international restaurants, where men will still be most comfortable in (and may in fact be required to wear) a jacket and tie. A sweater is also a good idea for cool evenings or overly air-conditioned restaurants.

The paths leading to temples can be rough; in any case, a pair of sturdy and comfortable walking shoes is always appropriate when traveling. Slip-ons are preferable to lace-ups, as shoes must be removed before you enter most shrines and temples.

It might be wise to bring your favorite toilet articles (in plastic containers, to avoid breakage and reduce the weight of luggage). Make sure that bottles containing liquids are

THE GOLD GUIDE / SMART TRAVEL TIPS

tightly capped to prevent leakage. Allow for the tropical sun by bringing along a hat and sunscreen. Mosquito repellent is a good idea, and toilet paper is not always supplied in public places. Bring an extra pair of eyeglasses or contact lenses in your carry-on luggage, and if you have a health problem, **pack enough medication** to last the trip or have your doctor write you a prescription using the drug's generic name, because brand names vary from country to country (you'll then need a duplicate prescription from a local doctor). It's important that you **don't put prescription drugs or valuables in luggage to be checked,** for it could go astray. To avoid problems with customs officials, carry medications in the original packaging. Also, don't forget the addresses of offices that handle refunds of lost traveler's checks.

ELECTRICITY

To use your U.S.-purchased electric-powered equipment, **bring a converter and an adapter.** The electrical current in the countries covered in this book is 220 volts, 50 cycles alternating current (AC), except the Philippines, which, like the United States, runs on 110-volt, 60-cycle AC current.

If your appliances are dual-voltage, you'll need only an adapter. Hotels sometimes have 110-volt outlets for low-wattage appliances near the sink, marked FOR SHAVERS ONLY;

don't use them for high-wattage appliances like blow-dryers. If your laptop computer is older, carry a converter; new laptops operate equally well on 110 and 220 volts, so you need only an adapter.

LUGGAGE

Airline baggage allowances depend on the airline, the route, and the class of your ticket; ask in advance. In general, on domestic flights and on international flights between the United States and foreign destinations, you are entitled to check two bags. A third piece may be brought on board, but it must fit easily under the seat in front of you or in the overhead compartment. In the United States, the FAA gives airlines broad latitude regarding carry-on allowances, and they tend to tailor them to different aircraft and operational conditions. Charges for excess, oversize, or overweight pieces vary.

If you are flying between two foreign destinations, note that baggage allowances may be determined not by piece but by weight—generally 88 pounds (40 kilograms) in first class, 66 pounds (30 kilograms) in business class, and 44 pounds (20 kilograms) in economy. If your flight between two cities abroad *connects* with your transatlantic or transpacific flight, the piece method still applies.

SAFEGUARDING YOUR LUGGAGE➤ Before leaving home, **itemize your bags' contents** and

their worth, and label them with your name, address, and phone number. (If you use your home address, cover it so that potential thieves can't see it readily.) Inside each bag, **pack a copy of your itinerary.** At check-in, **make sure that each bag is correctly tagged** with the destination airport's three-letter code. If your bags arrive damaged—or fail to arrive at all—file a written report with the airline before leaving the airport.

PASSPORTS & VISAS

If you don't already have one, **get a passport.** It is advisable that you **leave one photocopy of your passport's data page** with someone at home and keep another with you, separated from your passport, while traveling. If you lose your passport, promptly call the nearest embassy or consulate and the local police; having the data page information can speed replacement.

CANADIAN CITIZENS

You need only a valid passport to enter any of the countries covered in this book; see below for stay-length limitations and visa requirements. Passport application forms are available at 28 regional passport offices, as well as post offices and travel agencies. Whether for a first or a renewal passport, you must apply in person. Children under 16 may be included on a parent's passport but must have their own to travel alone. Passports are valid for five years and are usually mailed within two to three weeks of application.

U.K. CITIZENS

Citizens of the United Kingdom need only a valid passport to enter any of the countries covered in this book; see below for stay-length limitations and visa requirements. Applications for new and renewal passports are available from main post offices and at the passport offices in Belfast, Glasgow, Liverpool, London, Newport, and Peterborough. You may apply in person at all passport offices, or by mail to all except the London office. Children under 16 may travel on an accompanying parent's passport. All passports are valid for 10 years. Allow a month for processing.

U.S. CITIZENS

All U.S. citizens, even infants, need only a valid passport to enter any of the countries covered in this book; see below for stay-length limitations and visa requirements. Application forms for both first-time and renewal passports are available at any of the 13 U.S. Passport Agency offices and at some post offices and courthouses. Passports are usually mailed within four weeks; allow five weeks or more in spring and summer.

VISA REQUIREMENTS

☞ Contacts and Resources *in* the A to Z section for each country.

S

SENIOR-CITIZEN DISCOUNTS

To qualify for age-related discounts, **mention your senior-citizen status up front** when booking hotel reservations, not when checking out, and before you're seated in restaurants, not when paying the bill. Note that discounts may be limited to certain menus, days, or hours. When renting a car, **ask about promotional car-rental discounts**—they can net even lower costs than your senior-citizen discount.

SHIP TRAVEL

If you're interested in visiting a variety of Southeast Asian cities, **consider a cruise to the region.** Southeast Asia is one of the hottest destinations in cruising, and you can sail in many different styles. Choices range from a traditional ocean liner to a clipper-type tall ship to a luxury yacht. Ports of call include Bangkok, Singapore, and Ho Chi Minh City. To get the best deal, **book with a cruise-only travel agency.**

STUDENTS ON THE ROAD

To save money, **look into deals available through student-oriented travel agencies.** To qualify, you'll need to have a bona fide student ID card. Members of international student groups are also eligible (☞ Students *in* Important Contacts A to Z).

T

TELEPHONES

LONG-DISTANCE

The long-distance services of AT&T, MCI, and Sprint make calling home relatively convenient, but in many hotels you may find it impossible to dial the access number. The hotel operator may also refuse to make the connection. Instead, the hotel will charge you a premium rate—as much as 400% more than a calling card—for calls placed from your hotel room. To avoid such price gouging, travel with more than one company's long-distance calling card—a hotel may block Sprint but not MCI. If the hotel operator claims that you cannot use any phone card, ask to be connected to an international operator, who will help you to access your phone card. You can also dial the international operator yourself. If none of this works, try calling your phone company collect in the United States. If collect calls are also blocked, call from a pay phone in the hotel lobby. Before you go, **find out the local access codes** for your destinations.

TOUR OPERATORS

A package or tour to Southeast Asia can make your vacation less expensive and more hassle-free. Firms that sell tours and packages reserve airline seats, hotel rooms, and rental cars in bulk and pass some of the savings on to you. In addition, the best operators have local representatives

THE GOLD GUIDE / SMART TRAVEL TIPS

available to help you at your destination.

A GOOD DEAL?

The more your package or tour includes, the better you can predict the ultimate cost of your vacation. Make sure you know exactly what is covered, and **beware of hidden costs.** Are taxes, tips, and service charges included? Transfers and baggage handling? Entertainment and excursions? These can add up.

Most packages and tours are rated deluxe, first-class superior, first class, tourist, or budget. The key difference is usually accommodations. Remember, tourist class in the United States might be a comfortable chain hotel, but in Southeast Asia you might share a bath and do without hot water. If the package or tour you are considering is priced lower than in your wildest dreams, **be skeptical.** Also, **make sure your travel agent knows the accommodations** and other services. Ask about the hotel's location, room size, beds, and whether it has a pool, room service, or programs for children, if you care about these. Has your agent been there in person or sent others you can contact?

BUYER BEWARE

Each year a number of consumers are stranded or lose their money when operators—even very large ones with excellent reputations— go out of business. To avoid becoming one of them, take the time to **check out the operator—** find out how long the company has been in business and ask several agents about its reputation. Next, **don't book unless the firm has a consumer-protection program.** Members of the USTOA and the NTA are required to set aside funds for the sole purpose of covering your payments and travel arrangements in case of default. Non-member operators may instead carry insurance; look for the details in the operator's brochure—and for the name of an underwriter with a solid reputation. Note: When it comes to tour operators, **don't trust escrow accounts.** Although there are laws governing those of charter-flight operators, no governmental body prevents tour operators from raiding the till.

Next, **contact your local Better Business Bureau and the attorney general's offices** in both your own state and the operator's; have any complaints been filed? Finally, **pay with a major credit card.** Then you can cancel payment, provided that you can document your complaint. Always **consider trip-cancellation insurance** (☞ Insurance, *above*).

Big vs. Small➤ Operators that handle several hundred thousand travelers per year can use their purchasing power to give you a good price. Their high volume may also indicate financial stability. But some small companies provide more personalized service; because they tend to specialize, they may also be more knowledgeable about a given area.

USING AN AGENT

Travel agents are excellent resources. In fact, large operators accept bookings made only through travel agents. But it's good to **collect brochures from several agencies** because some agents' suggestions may be skewed by promotional relationships with tour and package firms that reward them for volume sales. If you have a special interest, **find an agent with expertise in that area;** ASTA can provide leads in the United States. (Don't rely solely on your agent, though; agents may be unaware of small-niche operators, and some special-interest travel companies only sell direct.)

SINGLE TRAVELERS

Prices are usually quoted per person, based on two sharing a room. If traveling solo, you may be required to pay the full double-occupancy rate. Some operators eliminate this surcharge if you agree to be matched up with a roommate of the same sex, even if one is not found by departure time.

TRAVEL GEAR

Travel catalogs specialize in useful items that can **save space when packing** and make life on the road more convenient. Compact alarm clocks, travel irons, travel wallets, and personal-care kits are among the most common items you'll find. They also carry dual-voltage appliances, currency converters and foreign-language phrase books. Some catalogs even carry miniature coffeemakers and water purifiers.

U
U.S.
GOVERNMENT

The U.S. government can be an excellent source of travel information. Some of this is free and some is available for a nominal charge. When planning your trip, **find out what government materials are available.** For just a couple of dollars, you can get a variety of publications from the Consumer Information Center in Pueblo, Colorado. Free consumer information also is available from individual government agencies, such as the Department of Transportation or the U.S. Customs Service. For specific titles, *see* the appropriate publications entry in Important Contacts A to Z, *above*.

THE GOLD GUIDE / SMART TRAVEL TIPS

1 Destination: Southeast Asia

ASIA REVEALED

ANY ATTEMPT TO generalize about Southeast Asia is doomed to failure. This vast, varied region encompasses every level of civilization, from booming, bustling Singapore—with its ultraluxury hotels, sophisticated restaurants, and world-class shopping—to the tribal villages of Sulawesi and of Borneo, where head-hunting was a way of life discarded only within recent memory.

A large part of Southeast Asia's fascination lies in the quiet beauty found in its rice-paddy landscapes—the glimpse into a simpler time that the West has left behind. But no matter where you go, do not expect to leave modern life entirely behind. As tourism among these societies grows, it subtly or grossly succeeds in changing them irrevocably.

WHAT'S WHERE

Indonesia

Indonesia is made up of five large and 13,600 small islands totaling more than 1,506,486 sq km (581,655 sq mi), with a population of 175 million. Its principal tourist destinations are Bali and Java. Java, the smallest of the main islands, has the capital city of Jakarta (population close to 11 million), which is bursting at its seams with an influx of people and investment swamping its Dutch-influenced past: Local markets are crammed with regional produce and crafts, museums display the heritage of former kingdoms, the cuisine is a curious mixture of Indonesian, Chinese, and Dutch, and the architecture includes both pompous projects by recent governments and those of nobler days, some of the world's great Buddhist and Hindu monuments, and the palaces of sultans in Yogyakarta and Solo.

Bali is only about 145 km (90 mi) long but has more than 3 million people and probably more than 10,000 temples. Since the destruction of Tibet, this is one of the very last completely traditional societies in which all facets of life—agriculture, economics, politics, technology, social customs, and the arts—are welded together by religion. The beaches of Bali's southern coast are highly developed to accommodate tourists, but it is in the interior that you can fully appreciate Bali's passionate and beautiful way of life. Lombok, the island to the east of Bali, is quickly becoming a resort attractive to those who find Bali too commercialized.

Sumatra, to the north, with its ethnic minorities, hill stations around Brastagi, a cool resort at Lake Toba, and isolated culture on Nias, has lately become a regular tourist stop, as have the Toraja Highlands on the island of Sulawesi. Allow a minimum of two weeks to see Indonesia, more if you plan to go beyond Jakarta and Bali.

Malaysia

Malaysia's more than 329,748 sq km (127,316 sq mi) are divided into two parts, peninsular and eastern Malaysia. Its population of 16 million is made up of about 56% Malays, 34% Chinese, and 10% Indians. Peninsular Malaysia, with 83% of the population, contains the chief cities, sights, and resorts. English is common in the major cities, and the country is prosperous, although Western visitors will still find prices very low. The scenery is spectacular, with jungles and rugged hills in the interior, plantations and superb beaches in some of the coastal areas.

The capital, Kuala Lumpur (population 1.6 million), is clean and comfortable—if rather dull—with striking Victorian-Moorish architecture. The city is a 50-minute flight from Penang (the other main tourist center) and is near the Genting and Cameron highlands. The island of Langkawi, between Penang and the Thai border, is becoming a popular resort with the opening of deluxe hotels.

The states of Sarawak and Sabah in northern Borneo constitute eastern Malaysia. For tourists, this is frontier country. It has limited facilities (other than a few new luxury resorts) but offers wild jungle and mountain scenery and fascinating close-up glimpses of tribal life. Malaysia's major highlights can be seen in seven to 10 days. (Be aware that a United States travel advisory for Malaysia warns that convicted drug traffickers will receive the death penalty.)

The Philippines

The Philippines has a population of 65 million and an area of nearly 300,000 sq km (115,831 sq mi), including seven major and 7,100 minor islands. The economic, political, and cultural center is Manila (population 8 million). Tourism is concentrated in Cebu and the Metro Manila area, where there are modern hotels, restaurants, and shops. Elsewhere on the main island of Luzon, hill resorts, beaches, subtropical scenery, and friendly people also draw visitors. The nation contains about 55 ethnic groups, each with its distinctive language, customs, and traditions. The five major cultures are the Ilocanos, Tagalogs, Visayans, Bicolanos, and Muslims. A couple of days will suffice to visit Manila, but if you want to see the upcountry areas and the exotic southern islands such as Cebu, plan on spending two weeks or more.

Singapore

Singapore is something of an anomaly: an independent city-state, an efficient economy, a tightly run welfare system, and a remarkable multiracial social environment. With a population of 2.6 million and about 582 sq km (225 sq mi), Singapore has lost the mystery and romance of the "exotic Orient." What you will find instead is a bright, clean, modern tropical city that has neither the glamour of Hong Kong nor, mercifully, its brutal contrasts of wealth and squalor. Although the population is predominantly Chinese, Singapore's national culture is truly multiracial. A major port and shopping center, Singapore boasts excellent tourist facilities. Sightseeing takes only two or three days, but shopping often keeps visitors busy much longer.

Thailand

Thailand, with a population of 54 million and an area of almost 513,998 sq km (198,455 sq mi), has become one of the world's top tourist destinations. Most of the traffic flows through the capital city of Bangkok (population 8 million), which has wonderful hotels, restaurants, nightclubs, shops, banks, and other big-city facilities. The level of development makes the city very convenient, but the headlong rush into the 21st century has taxed its infrastructure to its limit.

Outside the capital, chief excursions are to important temples and ruins, mostly in smaller towns in the Bangkok basin—a hot, flat, wet, rice-growing plain that epitomizes subtropical Asia. The eastern and northeastern parts of the country are arid and poor; the areas' riches lie in their fantastic ruins, their spicy food, and a traditional Thai lifestyle. In the north, Chiang Mai, the rapidly developing second city, is a pleasant provincial town on a cool mountain plateau, with several good hotels and a tranquil atmosphere. A number of beach resorts have established themselves on the world map. Pattaya was the first: almost 137 km (85 mi) south of Bangkok, it is Asia's largest—and possibly tackiest—resort. Phuket, an island in the Andaman Sea, is now the most favored resort. Toward the Malaysian border are miles of sand beaches, fishing villages, and jungle regions. At least two weeks are needed to get a feel for this fascinating land.

Vietnam

Altough it's rarely more than 150 km (90 mi) from the shores of the South China Sea to the western border, Vietnam snakes along the edge of the Indochinese peninsula for nearly 1,700 km (1,050 mi). The far northwest, bordered by China and Laos, is a remote mountainous region still inhabited by culturally unique hill tribes. Toward the coast lies Hanoi, the capital, surrounded by the fertile Red River Delta. South of Hanoi, Vietnam narrows; verdant fields hug hundreds of miles of largely unspoiled coastline, and low mountains and hills 50 km–200 km (30 mi–125 mi) inland form the western border with Laos and Cambodia. The former imperial city of Hue, Danang, and the sight-rich town of Hoi An are found midway down the coast of this central region; the beach town of Nha Trang and the mountain resort of Dalat are toward the southern end, surrounded by a wider swath of low mountains known as the Central Highlands. South of the mountains, Vietnam flattens into a broad floodplain that is home to Ho Chi Minh City (formerly Saigon) and the lush Mekong Delta.

Other Destinations

Brunei

Brunei, primarily a stopover between Sabah and Sarawak in East Malaysia, covers less than 5,760 sq km (2,226 sq mi). The tiny Malay sultanate is rich in oil revenues but still limited as to tourist facilities. Its population of 200,000 is found mostly in the sleepy tropical capital, Bandar Seri Begawan, and in kampongs on stilts at the waters' edge nearby. You can visit the country's attractions in a couple of days.

Burma (Myanmar)

Isolated for so long and still under a repressive government, Burma is just now opening up to tourism. Only a few destinations have facilities for the Western traveler who requires some comfort, but these are enough to hold anybody's interest for more than a fortnight. Rangoon (now called Yangon) is a capital city reawakening; it's also home to one of the most glorious pagodas in the Buddhist world, Shwedagon Pagoda. Mandalay is the old capital of Myanmar kings. Pagan (Bagan), another ancient capital, still has thousands of pagodas remaining from the 11th century. Inle Lake, often said to be the most beautiful in Southeast Asia, is a tranquil haven of floating islands.

Cambodia

Cambodia is recovering from years of civil war and still requires some fortitude from its visitors. Any inconveniences are worth it, however, to set eyes on one of the wonders of the world, Angkor, a magnificent temple complex built in the 10th–13th centuries, but not rediscovered until the late 18th century. To reach Angkor, you must go by way of Phnom Penh, the country's capital, a city that's trying to overcome memories of the horrific "killing fields" of the Khmer Rouge.

Laos

Laos sways to a slow rhythm of life, and the smiles of its people and charm of its small towns reward the visitor. Vientiane, the capital city, can be seen in less than a day before proceeding to Luang Prabang, with its enchanting palaces and temples.

PLEASURES & PASTIMES

Beaches

Southeast Asia has some of the world's most exotic beaches, ranging from remote volcanic stretches in the Philippines to resort-strewn sites on Bali. The following is a brief rundown of the best beaches in each country. (*See* individual chapters for more information.)

Indonesia

The island of Lombok (a 20-minute flight from Bali) has a warm, dry climate and lovely unspoiled beaches. Surfers head for the waves at Kuta Beach in Bali, where an annual festival is held with local and Australian participation.

Malaysia

The Batu Ferringhi strip on Penang Island has fine, golden-sand beaches, many of them shaded by willowy casuarina and coconut trees. Pangkor and Langkawi islands, off Malaysia's northwest coast, offer more remote stretches of sand, while Tioman Island (where the movie *Bali Hai* was filmed) provides idyllic scenery and water-sports facilities.

Philippines

This tropical archipelago of more than 7,000 islands has an abundance of beaches, from pebble-strewn coastlines and black volcanic stretches to shady white expanses. Some of the most picturesque spots are on the smaller islands, particularly on Boracay, Iloilo, Palawan, and Cebu. Puerto Galera on Mindoro Island has several good beaches and is four hours from Manila by bus and ferry.

Thailand

With its long coastlines and warm waters, Thailand offers many opportunities for beach lovers. Ko Samet, a popular Thai vacation spot, has many fine-sand beaches dotted with bungalows and cottages. Phuket, though much more commercial, boasts long, sandy beaches, cliff-sheltered coves, waterfalls, mountains, and waters that are excellent for scuba diving. Ko Samui in the Gulf is yet another excellent choice.

Vietnam

Vietnam's unspoiled beaches, clear waters, and coral reefs beckon travelers. The south-central coast, with Nha Trang as the resort hub, boasts some of Vietnam's most beautiful beaches, as does the much less crowded Dai Lanh, 83 km (51 mi) north of Nha Trang. Equally beautiful are the beaches of Danang. Vung Tau, the popular seaside resort, is not as beautiful but is certainly convenient from Ho Chi Minh City.

Dining

Hotels usually have several restaurants, from coffee shops serving both Western and Oriental cuisine to posh places staffed by famous European chefs. At the other end of the scale are outdoor stalls and markets where you can eat happily for a song.

Note: Though wine is available in Southeast Asia, it is relatively expensive. Furthermore, wine is not always the best accompaniment to local cuisines—whiskey or beer is often preferred. Mekong from Thailand is an excellent rice whiskey, and Thailand's Singha and Singapore's Tiger beers win international awards. If you are dining on European fare, consider Australian wines—they appear to survive the tropics better than do the French. If you want wine with Cantonese fare, check the wine list for Chinese wine (be sure that it is made from grapes and not rice)—Dynasty, for example, is a reasonable white Chablis-type wine.

Chinese

Many Southeast Asian countries have significant ethnic Chinese populations, and Chinese restaurants are everywhere. The best-known regional Chinese cuisine is **Cantonese,** with its fresh, delicate flavors. Characteristic dishes are stir-fried beef in oyster sauce, steamed fish with slivers of ginger, and deep-fried duckling with mashed taro.

Though the cooking of the **Teochew** (or Chao Zhou), mainly fisherfolk from Swatow in the eastern part of Guangdong Province, has been greatly influenced by the Cantonese, it is quite distinctive.

Teochew chefs cook with clarity and freshness, often steaming or braising, with an emphasis on fish and vegetables. Oyster sauce and sesame oil—staples of Cantonese cooking—do not feature much in Teochew cooking.

Characteristic Teochew dishes are *lo arp* and *lo goh* (braised duck and goose), served with a vinegary chili-and-garlic sauce; crispy liver or prawn rolls; stewed, preserved vegetables; black mushrooms with fish roe; and a unique porridge called *congee,* which is eaten with small dishes of salted vegetables, fried whitebait, black olives, and preserved-carrot omelets.

The **Szechuan** style of cooking is distinguished by the use of bean paste, chilies, and garlic, as well as a wide, complex use of nuts and poultry. The result is dishes with pungent flavors of all sorts, harmoniously blended and spicy hot. Simmering and smoking are common forms of preparation, and noodles and steamed bread are preferred accompaniments. Characteristic dishes are hot-and-sour soup, sautéed chicken or prawns with dried chilies, tea-smoked duck, and spicy string beans.

Pekingese cooking originated in the Imperial courts. It makes liberal use of strong-flavored roots and vegetables, such as peppers, garlic, ginger, leeks, and coriander. Dishes are usually served with noodles or dumplings and baked, steamed, or fried bread. The most famous Pekingese dish is Peking duck: The skin is lacquered with aromatic honey and baked until it looks like dark mahogany and is crackly crisp.

The greatest contribution made by the many arrivals from China's **Hainan** island, off the north coast of Vietnam, is "chicken rice": Whole chickens are poached with ginger and spring onions; then rice is boiled in the liquid to fluffy perfection and eaten with chopped-up pieces of chicken, which are dipped into a sour-and-hot chili sauce and dark soy sauce.

Fukien cuisine emphasizes soups and stews with rich, meaty stocks. Wine-sediment paste and dark soy sauce are used, and seafood is prominent. Dishes to order are braised pork belly served with buns, fried oysters, and turtle soup.

Hunanese cooking is dominated by sugar and spices and tends to be more rustic. One of the most famous dishes is beggar's chicken: A whole bird is wrapped in lotus leaves and baked in a sealed covering of clay; when it's done, a mallet is used to break away the hardened clay.

Hakka food is very provincial in character and uses ingredients not normally found in other Chinese cuisines. Red-wine lees are used to great effect in dishes of fried prawns or steamed chicken, producing delicious gravies.

Indian

Southern Indian cuisine is generally chili-hot, relies on strong spices like mustard seed, and uses coconut milk liberally. Meals are very cheap, and eating is informal: Just survey the cooked food displayed, point to whatever you fancy, then take a seat at a table. A piece of banana leaf will be placed before you, plain rice will be spooned out, and the rest of your food will be arranged around the rice and covered generously with curry sauce. The really adventurous should sample fish-head curry, with its hot, rich, sour gravy.

Generally found in the more posh restaurants, **Northern Indian** food blends the aromatic spices of Kashmiri food with a subtle Persian influence. Northern food is less hot and more subtly spiced than southern, and cow's milk is used as a base instead of coconut milk. Northern Indian cuisine also uses yogurt to tame the pungency of the spices and depends more on pureed tomatoes and nuts to thicken gravies. The signature Northern Indian dish is tandoori chicken (marinated in yogurt and spices and cooked in a clay urn) and fresh mint chutney, eaten with *naan, chapati,* and *paratha* (Indian breads).

Malay and Indonesian

Malay cuisine is hot and rich. Turmeric root, lemongrass, coriander, *blachan* (prawn paste), chilies, and shallots are the ingredients used most often; coconut milk is used to create fragrant, spicy gravies. A basic method of cooking is to gently fry the *rempah* (spices, herbs, roots, chilies, and shallots ground to a paste) in oil and then, when the rempah is fragrant, add meat and either a tamarind liquid, to make a tart spicy-hot sauce, or coconut milk, to make a rich spicy-hot curry sauce. Dishes to look for are *gulai ikan* (a smooth, sweetish fish curry), *telor sambal* (eggs in hot sauce), *empalan* (beef

boiled in coconut milk and then deep-fried), *tahu goreng* (fried bean curd in peanut sauce), and *ikan bilis* (fried, crispy anchovies). The best-known Malay dish is *satay*—slivers of marinated beef, chicken, or mutton threaded onto thin coconut sticks, barbecued, and served with a spicy peanut sauce.

Indonesian food is very close to Malay; both are based on rice, and both are Muslim and thus do not use pork. A meal called *nasi padang*—consisting of a number of mostly hot dishes, such as curried meat and vegetables with rice, that offer a range of tastes from sweet to salty to sour to spicy—originally comes from Indonesia.

Nonya

When Hokkien immigrants settled on the Malay Peninsula, they acquired the taste for Malay spices and soon adapted Malay foods. Nonya food is one manifestation of the marriage of the two cultures, which is also seen in language, music, literature, and clothing. Nonya cooking combines the finesse and blandness of Chinese cuisine with the spiciness of Malay cooking. Many Chinese ingredients are used—especially dried ingredients like Chinese mushrooms, fungus, anchovies, lily flowers, soybean sticks, and salted fish—along with the spices and aromatics used in Malay cooking.

The Nonya cook uses preserved soybeans, garlic, and shallots to form the rempah needed to make *chap chay* (a mixed-vegetable stew with soy sauce). Other typical dishes are *husit goreng* (an omelet fried with shark's fin and crabmeat) and *otak otak* (a sort of fish quenelle with fried spices and coconut milk). Nonya cooking also features sourish-hot dishes like *garam assam,* a fish or prawn soup made with pounded turmeric, shallots, *galangal* (a hard ginger), lemongrass, shrimp paste, and preserved tamarind, a very sour fruit.

Thai

Although influenced by the cooking of China, India, Java, Malaysia, and even Portugal, Thai cuisine is distinctly different in taste. Thai food's characteristic flavor comes from fresh mint, basil, coriander, and citrus leaves; extensive use of lemongrass, lime, vinegar, and tamarind keeps a sour-hot taste prevalent. On first tasting a dish, you may find it stingingly hot (tiny chilies provide the fire), but the taste of fresh herbs will soon surface. Not to say that all Thai food is hot—a meal is designed to have contrasting dishes, some of which are spicy, while others are mild. The Thais do not use salt in their cooking. Instead, *nam pla* (fish sauce) is served on the side, which you add to suit your taste.

Popular Thai dishes include *mee krob,* crispy fried noodles with shrimp; *tom yam kung,* hot and spicy shrimp soup, *tom kaa gai,* small pieces of chicken in a coconut based soup, (both are popular with foreigners); *gai hor bai toey,* fried chicken wrapped in pandanus leaves; and *pu cha,* steamed crab with fresh coriander root and a little coconut milk. Thai curries—such as chicken curry with cashews, salted egg, and mango—may contain coconut milk and are often served with dozens of garnishes and side dishes. Most meals are accompanied by rice and soup.

For drinks try Singha beer, brewed in Thailand, or *o-liang,* the national drink—a very strong, black iced coffee sweetened with palm-sugar syrup.

Shopping

Some people travel to Southeast Asia exclusively to shop. Finely tailored clothing and unique handcrafts, such as graceful ceramics, colorful textiles, and intricately engraved silver, can be found at rock-bottom prices here.

Although prices in department stores are generally fixed, be prepared to bargain with the smaller shopkeeper. It is the accepted practice in this region of few set prices. If you have time, comparison-shop for similar items in several stores to get a feel for prices. The final price will depend on your bargaining skill and the shopkeeper's mood, but generally will range from 10% to 40% off the original price.

If you can, carry your purchases with you instead of trusting shopkeepers and postal services to ship them safely home. If you're shopping for larger items, such as ceramic vases or furniture, the upscale shops are generally reliable. Some credit card companies, such as American Express, guarantee that items purchased with their card will arrive home safely.

With any purchase, make sure you get a receipt for the amount paid, both for potential returns and for Customs. Also, check on Customs and shipping fees to make sure your bargain doesn't turn into a costly white elephant.

The following is a quick rundown of some of the most popular buys in individual Southeast Asian countries.

Indonesia

Batik, shadow puppets, silver jewelry, wood masks and statues from Bali.

Malaysia

Batik, pewterware, gold jewelry, silver, woven fabrics.

Philippines

Traditional clothing such as the Barong Tagalog, bamboo furniture, cigars, rum, rattan baskets, and brassware.

Singapore

Contemporary fashions, electronic equipment, and silk.

Thailand

Silk, gems, jewelry, silverwork, ready-to-wear clothing, lacquerware, and pottery.

Vietnam

Custom-made clothing, lacquerware, wood carvings, contemporary painting, and pottery.

Sports

Western-style participant sports and unique Southeast Asian spectator sports are becoming more popular with travelers to the region. The following will give you an idea of which countries provide facilities for your chosen sport.

Bicycling is a popular diversion in Singapore. Fine **deep-sea fishing** is available around Pattaya (in the Thai Gulf) and Ranong and Phuket (in the Indian Ocean off Thailand's west coast). **Golf** aficionados will find quality courses in Thailand, Singapore, and the Philippines. If you plan to visit Thailand in March and April, look for **kite-fighting.** Many of Indonesia's wild rivers provide exciting **river rafting** opportunities. Southeast Asia's wealth of beaches and reef means that excellent spots for **scuba diving and snorkeling** abound; particularly recommended are Phuket and several marine national parks in Thailand, a number of islands of the Philippines (Batangas, Bohol, Cebu, and

Palawan), and Malaysia's Langkawi Island. **Tennis** facilities are available in Singapore and the Philippines, as well as at many resort hotels around the region. Thailand and the Philippines offer opportunities for **windsurfing.**

NEW & NOTEWORTHY

Indonesia

This vast archipelago of 3,000 miles has the more potential for tourism than any other country in the world, yet most of its tourist development is on the island of Bali—so much so that many people know where Bali is, but not Indonesia! And yet more **new hotels** are under construction. The Four Seasons, which already has the best resort on the island, is opening another hotel resort just outside Ubud. The Ritz-Carlton should open its hotel on Jimbaran Bay by 1997. Across the straits on the neighboring island off Lombok, a massive resort development is still planned for the southern shores around Kuta. It will spoil the natural drama of these shores, so go there while it remains pristine.

Other tourist destinations are developing much more gradually. Usually hotels outpace the number of tourists. This has kept the cost of hotel rooms down throughout the country. Yogjakarta has a new Radisson which is very pleasant and whose prices are a steal. Ujung Padang also has a new Radisson (Radisson plans to have close to 50 hotels in Asia by the end of the century) as does Jakarta. In Jakarta many new hotels have opened, the best of which has been the Regent. Most of these hotels are catering to the business traveler and, despite Indonesia's accelerating economy, there are always hotel rooms available. For you, this can mean discounted prices. Surabaya, like Jakarta, is growing its manufacturing and commercial interests more than its tourist base, but it has several new hotels including a Weston, a Shangri-la, and a Mandarin Oriental.

Malaysia

Kuala Lumpur is the center of Malaysia's booming economy. New skyscrapers are rising almost every month. Among them will be **new hotels** from such well-known management companies as Mandarin Oriental, Hyatt, and Ritz-Carlton. All are in the Golden Triangle and should open in 1997 and early 1988. New hotels are also scheduled to open on Langkawi, Malaysia's answer to Phuket. As a result, this island, declared a duty-free zone, is likely to lose its charm to rapid, quick-rich development schemes. There is even a charter airline from Germany bringing in thousands of visitors on packaged tours. In the meantime, the east coast is neglected. Strict adherence to Islam has curtailed licensing laws, and poor road links to the more populous west side of the peninsula have kept tourists (and hotel development) at bay.

On the island of Borneo, Saba is developing the region around Kota Kinabalu. By 1997, the new Shangri-la will be in full swing and other hotels are under construction. In Sarawak, big promises are made by the governor to develop Miri as a vacation base. Certainly these two states, Saba and Sarawak, are more active in promoting themselves than the federal government's tourist promotion board is in promoting Malaysia.

Highways are improving in Malaysia. The expressway (a toll road) is now complete running all the way up the west side of the peninsula from Johore Bahru in the south to the Thai border. The road across the top of the Malay Peninsula just south of the Thai border is finished, making the drive between Penang and Kota Bahru possible in six instead of ten hours. Though the twists and turns give drivers shoulder-ache, the scenery over the mountains is splendidly dramatic.

In the air, Malaysia Airlines has **expanded air routes** and offers the visitor a Discover Malaysia Pass, which is worth investigating if you want to see all of the nation. The one caveat is that it requires one international flight on Malaysia Airlines; however, that can be a short one such as an $80 flight from Medan, Indonesia.

Philippines

The **continuing volcanic activity** at Mt. Pinatubo, northwest of Manila, should not inconvenience most travelers, but it continues to wreak havoc in the lives of local residents. There are ongoing efforts to control the flow of lahar from the mountain, notably the construction of a permanent dike to channel the mud away from settled areas.

A number of new **transportation projects** should make it easier to get around Manila and Luzon. Manila's Light Elevated Transit line is being expanded; construction of additional track and stations is due to start in 1997. A new highway, dubbed "Skyway," will be built to nearby southern towns; a new expressway will be added going north, toward Central Luzon. There's also talk of adding an international airport at the former U.S. base at Olongapo, a three-hour drive north of Manila.

Singapore

Singapore is always adding **new and sparkling hotels** to its huge inventory of rooms—in excess of 30,000. Three of the new ones, the Ritz-Carlton, the Inter-Continental, and the Four Seasons, are in the luxury category, with the Ritz-Carlton being the most dramatic. The Shangri-la group has opened the more economical Traders Hotel, designed for the traveler who wants convenience, comfort, and efficiency, but not the high tariff. The **new convention center** at Suntec City (it, too, has a new 1,000-room hotel, the Marina Pontiac) is expected to increase the number and size of conventions held in Singapore.

The **Singapore Art Museum,** which opened in 1996 on Bras Basah Road, was a decade in the making. Its permanent collection encompasses some 3,000 works from Singapore, Indonesia, Malaysia, Brunei, the Philippines, Thailand, and Vietnam. Thematic exhibitions are drawn from this vast resource. The entire collection is accessible through the museum's Electronic Gallery, called E-mage, where visitors can call up digitized images of artworks on computer monitors. The goal of the museum is to study and present the region's modern art, although there are some pre-20th-century works as well.

Thailand

Of all the countries in Southeast Asia, Thailand runs ahead of the pack in the variety of **accommodations** it provides for the tourist. Bangkok has a surfeit of hotels, whose competition benefits the traveler. The Grande Sheraton Sukhumvit opened in mid-1996 and the Westin should be in full swing by 1997. The Sofitel, across the Chao Phraya River from the Oriental, should also be open by then. Other hotels, one of them the Regent, have spent millions on refurbishing their rooms and facilities. In the north, the Regent Chiang Mai opened in 1996 to immediate praise for its Lanna Thai architecture, comfort, and service. New hotels of international stature, like the Korat Princess, have opened in provincial capitals and elsewhere.

In Phuket, the new Sheraton and Banyan Tree resorts add to the luster of Bang Thao Bay, making five hotels whose facilities are open to guests at any of them. On Ko Samui, new hotels have sprung up on Chaweng Beach, where the action is, and also in quieter more secluded hideaways. Pattaya is pouring millions of dollars into its infrastructure, to bring it back to first-class status.

New airlines and air routes are opening up the country. Bangkok Airways has built an airport outside the meticulously restored ancient capital of Sukhothai, which has in the past been slightly off the beaten track. Now four flights a week arrive from Chiang Mai and Bangkok. A new service by Orient Airlines offers flights out of Chiang Mai direct to southern Thailand and the northeast without a stop in the capital. Bangkok is going ahead with plans for a second airport at Nang-Ngu Kao, 20 miles east of town, to relieve congestion at Don Muang. The intention is to keep Thailand's promise of being the transportation hub of Southeast Asia.

Bangkok is finally getting around to improving its traffic congestion. A **new skytrain** should be operational by the end of 1997 which will cross the city from north to south and east to west. At the same time, **expressways** are being built that will speed traffic across the city. This probably won't completely solve the traffic problem, since every day 600 cars are added to the streets.

In a couple of years, we expect that Thailand's **border crossings** with Cambodia, Laos, and Myanmar will open to foreigners. Even now, they may travel into Laos and to Vientiane, 20 kilometers (12 mi) away. Once Cambodia neutralizes the Khmer Rouge and cleans up long-buried land mines, Angkor Wat at Siem Reap will be accessible across the Thai border. For years Myanmar has allowed visitors to enter only by air or sea; now, in its desperate desire for foreign exchange, it has eased its visa restrictions and begun to permit entry by land from Mae Sai in northern Thailand to Kengtung.

New tourist destinations are also opening up. Vacationing Thais have moved down the coast from Pattaya to Ban Phe, near Rayong, and the hardier traveler goes even farther, to yet-to-be-developed islands like Ko Chang, near the Cambodian border. Thailand's last tourist frontier is the northeast, called I-San. It has always been the country's poorest region, at the mercy of the monsoons. To appease environmentalists, the Thai government created many national parks and built rustic cabins for hikers and nature lovers. I-San also has old Khmer temples to explore, even while they are still in the process of restoration. The newly constructed Friendship Bridge at Nong Khai, crossing the Mekong river to Laos, is further opening up this region.

Vietnam

Saigon's hotels and restaurants have always catered to foreigners, from the colonizing French to the occupying American troops, and today Vietnam is surprisingly travel-friendly. The government in Hanoi, though much less accustomed to foreigners, has reversed its famed xenophobic trend by loosening travel restrictions, beefing up travel facilities, and agreeing to a number of joint ventures with foreign companies and investors. The frenetic results are not always pleasant, as in the current boom of **new high-rise luxury hotels.** The Omnis, Sofitels, and Hyatts that go up overnight seem to homogenize the cityscapes. Still, the Vietnamese are so keen on tourism that most lodging establishments—from mom-and-pop minihotels to five-star palaces—offer a wide range of **travel services.** Tours, in particular, are widely available: everyone from the central government to the corner café owner runs excursions, so nearly every attraction in every corner of the country is accessible.

Although the country is undergoing a **major road-improvement program,** precarious road conditions and suicidal driving habits persist, making car travel nerve-racking. The government has put a lot of money into **reliable air service,** and state-run Vietnam Airlines has seen considerable improvements. Planes generally run efficiently and frequently to destinations throughout Vietnam and to certain destinations outside of Vietnam. American carriers are negotiating with the Vietnamese government for regular air service from the United States to Vietnam.

Other Destinations

Brunei
Interest in ecotourism continues to grow. Look into excursions to Brunei's largely unexplored interior jungle.

Burma (Myanmar)
In desperation to bring foreign exchange into the country and prop up its dictatorship, SLORC, the ruling party, has opened the nation's doors to tourism. Visas are quickly given and there is no longer the need to purchase local currency at the official exchange rate (nine kyats to the dollar instead of 120 on the not-so-black market). Foreign investment is also welcomed. The result has been a rapid increase in hotel construction, development of a rudimentary tourist infrastructure, and an opportunity to visit a country that has been off limits for so long. Only your conscience can tell you whether by visiting you are supporting one of the most inhumane governments in the world or helping the Burmese get an economic foothold and combat political repression.

Cambodia
Siem Reap, the base from which to visit the Khmer ruins of Angkor is still, as of press time, open to tourists, and the hotels there have been refurbished to meet the needs of the international traveler. Phnom Penh has quieted down since most of the United Nations personnel have moved out and reduced the inflationary pressure. An express bus now runs between Phnom Penh and Ho Chi Min City, Vietnam. Other parts of the country tend to be a little risky, especially around the Khmer Rouge's stronghold in the northwest.

Laos
Laos is opening up to foreign tourists in gentle steps. Bureaucratic procedures still

mean that visas take a week to process, but they are easily obtainable. New hotels are opening in Vientiane and the former capital, Luang Prabang. Outside of these two cities, accommodation is pretty rudimentary and scheduled travel uncertain, but the intrepid traveler can find his way around and is welcome.

FODOR'S CHOICE

No two people will agree on what makes a perfect vacation, but it's fun and helpful to know what others think. We hope you'll have a chance to experience some of Fodor's Choices yourself in Southeast Asia. For detailed information about each entry, refer to the appropriate chapter.

Museums

Indonesia

★**National Museum, Jakarta.** The country's most complete collection of Indonesian antiquities and ethnic artwork is on display here.

★**Puppet Museum, Jakarta.** Watch a shadow-puppet play or view an extensive collection of traditional Indonesian puppets, as well as examples from Thailand, China, Malaysia, India, Cambodia, and elsewhere.

Philippines

★**University of San Carlos Museum, Cebu City.** This extensive collection includes seashells, fauna, and anthropological relics, as well as traditional clothing and ornaments of various tribal minorities.

Singapore

★**Empress Place.** This cultural exhibition center has absolutely top-notch displays, many of which are of antiquities from mainland China.

★**Pioneers of Singapore/Surrender Chambers.** Wax figures and tableaux provide fascinating, three-dimensional recounting of Singapore's early days.

Thailand

★**National Museum, Bangkok.** The history of Thai art and culture is all here.

Palaces and Unique Structures

Indonesia

★**Traditional Clan Houses of the Toraja, Sulawesi.** The carved and painted *tongkonans* are built on piles and topped by massive roofs shaped like a ship or buffalo horns.

Philippines

★**Malacañang Palace, Manila.** Notable colonial Spanish architecture and interior decor here demand a look, especially the three chandeliers in the reception hall, beautiful hardwoods used for the grand staircase, portraits of former presidents, and exquisite music room.

★**Intramuros, Manila.** This ancient walled city, built by the Spaniards in the 16th century, is still formidable, with cannon emplacements atop the 30-foot-thick walls and a strategic location facing the bay.

Thailand

★**Suan Pakkard Palace, Bangkok.** The harmony of Thai architecture at home.

Shrines and Places of Worship

Indonesia

★**Borobudur Temple, Central Java.** It took perhaps 10,000 men 100 years to build this giant stupa, which illustrates the earthly and spiritual life of the Buddha with thousands of relief carvings and statues.

★**Prambanan Temple Complex, Central Java.** These remarkable 9th-century temples celebrate the Hindu pantheon.

Philippines

★**Quiapo Church, Manila.** This 16th-century church is home to the famed Black Nazarene, a dark statue of Jesus of Nazareth said to perform miracles.

★**San Agustin Church, Manila.** The second-oldest stone church in the country has 14 side chapels, a trompe l'oeil ceiling, and hand-carved 17th-century seats of molave, a beautiful tropical hardwood.

★**Paoay Church, Ilocos Norte.** The frontal crenellations and turrets, massive curlicued buttresses, exterior stairways, and niches give the impression of a Javanese temple.

Singapore

Fuk Tak Chi Temple. The different deities and overpowering aura of the other world here may make you a believer.

Sultan Mosque. This is the focus of the Malay community.

Thailand

Wat Benjamabophit (Marble Temple), Bangkok. Classical lines of perfection harmonize the spirit.

Wat Chaimongkol, Chiang Mai. A personal temple by the river.

Wat Phanan Choeng, Ayutthaya. Memories and fate are embedded in this monument.

Wat Phra Keo (Temple of the Emerald Buddha), Bangkok. Ornate and dramatic, it is a spiritual magnet.

Wat Traimitr (Temple of the Golden Buddha), Bangkok. An image that shines with the love of gold.

Vietnam

Jade Emperor's Pagoda, Ho Chi Minh City. A Vietnamese "It's a Small World," this pagoda is lined with carnival-like sculptures and reliefs of gods and mythical figures.

Marble Mountain, Quang Nam-Danang. Remarkable cave temples house dozens of statues of the Buddha, some said to have magical powers.

Other Destinations

Ankgor Temple Complex, Cambodia. More than 300 structures, including the monumental Angkor Wat, comprise one of the world's greatest architectural marvels.

Pagan Archeological Zone, Burma. More than 2,000 stupas, shrines, and monasteries still remain from the 6,000 built during the Pagan Dynasty.

Shwedagon Pagoda, Rangoon, Burma. This 320-foot-high, 2,500-year-old pagoda is covered with about 70 tons of gold and encrusted with thousands of diamonds.

Sultan Omar Ali Saifuddin Mosque, Bandar Seri Begawan, Brunei. This superb example of modern Islamic architecture—built in 1959 of imported white marble, gold mosaic, and stained glass—may be the most beautiful mosque in Southeast Asia.

The Natural World

Indonesia

Lake Toba, Sumatra. One of the largest lakes in Southeast Asia and one of the highest in the world, Lake Toba sits nearly 3,000 feet above sea level, surrounded by steep green mountains that plunge headlong into the 1,500-foot deep water.

Mt. Bromo, Java. You can stand on the rim of this active volcano just before dawn and watch it spew steam from a bubbling cauldron of water, ash, and sulphur.

Malaysia

Cameron Highlands. Cool forested trails are a welcome relief from the steamy concrete towns of the lowlands.

Mt. Kinabalu from anywhere in Sabah. Nature in its glory.

Philippines

Banaue Rice Terraces, northern Luzon. These spectacular, man-made rice paddies, terraced into the mountainsides more than 2,000 years ago, look like giant steps to the sky.

Mt. Mayon, southern Luzon. What may be the world's most symmetrical (and still active) volcano towers 8,189 feet over the Bicol countryside.

St. Paul Subterranean National Park, Palawan. The world's longest known underground river courses beneath this national rainforest park, through gigantic caverns that drip with unusual stalactite/stalagmite formations.

Singapore

Botanic Gardens. Escape from brick and mortar to appreciate tropical flora.

Zoological Gardens and Night Safari. The open plan of Singapore's zoo frees you from watching nature's creations from behind bars.

Thailand

Golden Triangle, northern Thailand. Misty mountains lure hikers with great trekking and unique hill-tribe villages.

Phang Nga Bay, off Phuket. These limestone rocks mysteriously rise out of the sea.

Vietnam

⭐**Halong Bay, off Halong City.** Jutting dramatically from the South China Sea, Halong Bay's limestone archipelago is a waterbound sculpture garden.

⭐**Hai Van Pass, north of Danang.** This stretch of Highway 1, perched on top of the Truong Son Mountain Range, has an unforgettable panorama of the startlingly limpid South China Sea.

⭐**Sapa, northern Vietnam.** Hill-tribe cultures thrive in the verdant highlands, undisturbed by the modern age.

Dining

Indonesia

⭐**Kupu Kupu Barong, Bali.** Amazing views of rice terraces and the Ayung River accompany tasty international and Indonesian dishes. $$$

⭐**The Spice Garden, Jakarta.** Spicy Szechuan dishes are served in refined surrounds. $$$

⭐**Sari Kuring, Jakarta.** Very good Indonesian seafood is typified by grilled prawns that melt in the mouth. $$

⭐**Ny Suharti, Yogyakarta.** Forget charm and atmosphere and all the other items on the menu: You are here for the best fried chicken in Java, perhaps in all of Indonesia. $

Malaysia

⭐**Lai Ching Yuen, Kuala Lumpur.** The city's best Cantonese fare is are served in room resembling two Chinese pavilions. $$$$

⭐**Restauran Makanan Laut Selayang, Kuala Lumpur.** Delicious seafood is the specialty here, but adventuous diners can also try steamed river frogs and soups of squirrel, pigeon, or turtle. $$

⭐**Eden, Penang.** This funky spot in downtown Georgetown makes fresh oxtail soup every day and does a magnificent Tunisian saddle of lamb. $$

Philippines

⭐**Bistro Remedios, Manila.** Pampanga regional cooking is served here in a setting of traditional furniture and paintings of Philippine landscapes. $$$

⭐**Lantaw Gardens, Cebu City.** Feast on a splendid, well-priced buffet in an open-air, garden setting while enjoying a folk-dance show and scenic views of the city. $$$

⭐**Alavar's, Zamboanga City.** This restaurant, a rambling house facing the sea, is justifiably famous for wonderful seafood. $$

⭐**Cafe by the Ruins, Baguio City.** An airy place with a patio setting, this café serves excellent home-cooked Philippine cuisine. $$

⭐**Sunset Terrace, Iloilo City.** Dine on excellent, well-priced seafood while enjoying riverside views. $$

Singapore

⭐**Li Bai.** Superior surroundings set the tone for "nouvelle Chinoise," the best of creative Cantonese cuisine. $$$–$$$$

⭐**Dragon City.** Many Singaporeans call this the best place to enjoy the emphatic cuisine of Szechuan. $$–$$$

⭐**Banana Leaf Apollo.** Come for robust South Indian curries, including the famous Singaporean Fish Head Curry. $

Thailand

⭐**Le Normandie, Bangkok.** For French food and an elegant evening out, this is the choice. $$$$

⭐**Amanpuri, Phuket.** Watching the Andaman Sea break on the rocks while dining on beautifully presented cuisine instills romance. $$$

⭐**Sala Rim Naam, Bangkok.** For dinner on royal Thai cuisine and a show of classical dancing, the Oriental's Sala Rim Naam is the best. $$$

⭐**Spice Market, Bangkok.** Newcomers to Thai food should come here to try one of the world's finest cuisines. $$$

⭐**Hong Tauw Inn, Chiang Mai.** Northern Thai fare, well prepared and authentic, is the promise kept by the English-speaking Thai owner. $$

⭐**Prachak, Bangkok.** The best roast duck in town is served for less than a dollar. $

⭐**White Orchid, Phuket.** Try this tiny outdoor café for fresh fish and a welcome smile. $

Vietnam

★**Camargue, Ho Chi Minh City.** Unique Eurasian cuisine is accented by an elegant open-air villa setting. $$$$

★**Lemongrass, Ho Chi Minh City.** Masterful Vietnamese standards and tasteful Franco-Viet decor make this an expat standby. $$$

★**Ngoc Suong, Nha Trang.** Try some of the world's freshest and finest seafood while dining in a delightful garden. $$

★**Ong Tao, Hue.** Imperial cuisine at its finest is served within the ruins of the ancient Imperial Enclosure. $$

★**Café des Amis, Hoi An.** Five heavenly courses of seafood or vegetarian ambrosia are served nightly; come again the next night, as the unwritten menu changes daily. $

★**Hue Restaurant, Hanoi.** Wonderful pork-wrapped sugarcane and other delicious standards are served at this casual sidewalk café. $

★**Ngoc Suong, Ho Chi Minh City.** Seafood perfection is served in a tree-houselike setting. $

Lodging

Indonesia

★**Four Seasons, Bali.** Given the captivating view of the sea, you may never want to leave your private villa and pool to explore Bali. $$$$

★**Kupu Kupu Barong, Ubud, Bali.** In serenity, hugging the side of a hill, it looks over rice terraces and the Ayung River. $$$$

★**Mandarin Oriental, Jakarta.** Expect refined, personal service in an atmosphere of understated elegance. $$$$

★**Oberoi, Legian, Bali.** Find tranquility and privacy in thatched cottages on the beach. $$$$

★**Kul Kul Beach Resort, Kuta, Bali.** This property has an intimate, Balinese feel, yet it's close to the action of Legian and Kuta. $$–$$$

★**Kusuma Sahid Prince Hotel, Solo.** A former prince's residence becomes your home away from home. $$

Malaysia

★**Datai, Langkawi.** Nature dictated the layout and structure of this luxury hideaway on the Andaman Sea. $$$$

★**Kuching Hilton, Kuching, Sarawak.** Quality service, fine dining, and the view from your room of the twilight playing on the Sarawak River will be etched in your memory. $$$$

★**The Regent, Kuala Lumpur.** Luxurious guest rooms and grand public spaces make this the capital's smartest hotel. $$$$

★**Pangkor Laut Resort, Pangkor Laut.** Stay in a stilted house perched above the sea or in a leafy bungalow on this private island. $$$–$$$$

Philippines

★**The Peninsula, Manila.** The Pen exudes an informal elegance, and the well-kept rooms are spacious enough to seem more like suites. $$$$

★**Davao Insular Hotel, Davao City.** The airy rooms at this hotel—on 20 lush acres with coconut groves, gardens, and a beachfront—come with verandas. $$$

★**Fort Ilokandia, Vigan, Northern Luzon.** Tiled walkways nestled among sand dunes connect several two-story buildings, whose style and room decor suggest the Old Quarter residences of Vigan. $$$

★**Philippine Plaza, Manila.** Luxurious and grand—a veritable resort sans beachfront—the Plaza has an enormous lobby and a huge circular swimming pool that's one of Asia's best. $$$

★**Casa Amapola, Baguio City.** This quiet pension—once a family residence—retains a pleasing family-style informality. $–$$

Singapore

★**Goodwood Park.** In a city bent on high-tech modernity, this is a bastion of tradition and gentility. $$$$

★**Ritz-Carlton.** Wallow in your bathtub and watch the ships lying at anchor in Singapore harbor. $$$$

★**Duxton Hotel.** In a city of skyscrapers, this boutique hotel in Chinatown is a wonderful exception. $$

★**Ladyhill Hotel.** Small and personable, this pleasant retreat feels like a home away from home. $

★**RELC International House.** For the best value in inexpensive lodgings, this is the spot. $

Thailand

★**Dusit Rahwadee, Krabi.** The only way to the duplex thatched bures on this magical headland is by long-tailed boat. $$$$

★**Oriental, Bangkok.** Nostalgia for the old days and views of the river bring us back here time and time again. $$$$

★**The Regent, Bangkok.** For refined classical elegance including the best service, the Regent wins our vote. $$$$

★**The Regent, Chiang Mai.** With Lanna Thai architecture built around rice fields and surrounded by the hills, the superb luxury is taken for granted. $$$$

★**Santiburi, Ko Samui.** Steps away from your teak-floored bungalow is white sand shaded by swaying palms. $$$$

★**Tara Mae Hong Son, Mae Hong Son.** Blending into the valley and feeling at one with nature. $$

★**Panviman Resort, Ko Pha Ngan.** Staggered up the cliff side, the bungalows look over the bay. $–$$

★**The Atlanta, Bangkok.** Music played at tea time and old movies shown after dinner are part of what makes this small hotel a throwback to better times. $

★**River View Lodge, Chiang Mai.** One of the few small, charming, and personable hotels in the north. $

Vietnam

★**Hotel Continental, Ho Chi Minh City.** The setting for Graham Greene's *The Quiet American,* the Continental is the most elegant accommodation in town. $$$$

★**Omni Saigon, Ho Chi Minh City.** This super-slick new pleasure dome offers every conceivable service. $$$$

★**Sofitel Hanoi/Metropole Hanoi.** Besides the beautifully renovated French-colonial architecture, there's impeccable food and service, to boot. $$$$

★**Dalat Sofitel/Dalat Palace.** Set on the cool slopes of rolling green hills, this perfectly restored Old World resort is an ideal retreat, especially for golfers. $$$–$$$$

★**Hotel Majestic.** New restorations have uncovered a slice of colonial Saigon in its heyday. $$$

Other Destinations

★**Strand Hotel, Rangoon, Burma.** Not only is this the best hotel in Rangoon, it is also one of the best in Asia—all the conveniences of the late 20th century, provided with impeccable Edwardian graciousness. $$$$

Beaches

Indonesia

★**Lombok Island.** Magnificent waves roll in on the deserted south-coast beaches.

Malaysia

★**Langkawi.** With so many coves and beaches, you'll walk untrodden sands.

★**Pangkor Laut.** A palm-grove beach on a private island with a charming hotel—what more could you want?

★**Damai Beach, Sarawak.** Golden sands stretch along the shore under the tropical sun.

Philippines

★**Boracay Island, Panay.** One of the country's most beautiful beaches is here, with sands as fine as sugar.

★**Mactan Island, Cebu.** Spend a few days lazing around at one of the resorts here.

★**Samal Island, Davao.** Some of the Davao City area's nicest beaches are on Samal Island.

★**Santa Cruz Island, Zamboanga.** This small island has a wonderful pink-coral beach and a lagoon in the middle.

Thailand

★**Pansea Beach, Phuket.** With a different beach for every day of your fortnight's Phuket island vacation, little Pansea Beach should be kept for the romantic interlude.

★**Nai Harn, Phuket.** As the sun sets dodging the tiny offshore islands, your tan will be golden.

★**Ao Phrang Bay, Krabi.** Limestone pinnacles that rise curiously out of the blue sea will rivet your attention while you laze on the sands.

★**Haad Tong Nai Pan Noi, Ko Pha Ngan.** No textbook has ever described such a perfect horseshoe bay.

★**Ko Chang.** Only your footsteps will be printed in the sands of these islands.

Vietnam

★**Nha Trang.** Catch this beautiful resort beach before it becomes another Pattaya.

★**Doc Let, north of Nha Trang.** Doc Let is accessible only by hiring a private car, but beach-going doesn't get much better than these white sands and clear waters.

★**Dai Lanh Beach, north of Nha Trang.** Sand dunes meet the sea at this semicircular beach, still virtually untouched by tourism.

Shopping

Indonesia

★**Antique wayang-kulit in Bali or Yogyakarta.** These puppets conjure up the shadows of Hindu epics.

★**Batiks and leather in Yogyakarta.** Fabulous designs on batik and crafted bags in leather are real temptations.

★**Stone and wood carving on Bali.** Guardians sculpted in stone and garuda masks in wood are essential to keep evil spirits at bay.

Malaysia

★**Karyaneka Handicrafts Center, Kuala Lumpur.** All the regional crafts are here.

★**Batik Malaysia Berhad, Kuala Lumpur and Penang.** The best quality and patterns of Malay fabric are found here.

★**Selangor pewter, throughout Malaysia.** Malaysia is famous for its tin, and has been producing pewter for centuries.

★**Jonker Street, Melaka.** You never know what Chinese or Nonya artifact may catch your eye in the antiques shops here.

Philippines

★**Yakan Village, Zamboanga.** The handwoven tribal cloth from this village is remarkable.

★**Baguio Public Market, Baguio City.** Handicrafts, antiques, and fresh produce are available in abundance.

★**Madrazo Fruit District, Davao City.** Most fruit vendors will let you sample the more exotic produce before you buy.

Singapore

★**Arab Street.** Stores and shops spill out onto the sidewalk with an array of Malay and Indonesian wares.

★**China Silk House.** This boutique has a deservedly high reputation for Chinese silks.

★**P. Govindasamy Pillai.** Come here for the best-quality Indian silks.

Thailand

★**Sapphires and rubies in Bangkok.** The center for gems is here.

★**Thai silk in Chiang Mai and Bangkok.** In all patterns, Thai silk is irresistible.

★**Night Bazaar in Chiang Mai.** So much for so little, be it fake or authentic, is for sale here.

Vietnam

★**Hoi An.** This perfectly preserved ancient port is almost entirely dedicated to seamstress boutiques and to souvenir shops that sell pottery and paintings by local artists.

★**Linh Phuong Maison de Couture, Ho Chi Minh City.** This shop specializes in custom clothing made from Japanese and Vietnamese silks and cottons.

★**Sapa Weekend Market.** Hill tribes from around the Sapa area convene at this colorful outdoor market to sell and exchange their chartreuse-embroidered, indigo-dyed clothing, as well as other handicrafts and food staples.

★**Tien Dat, Hanoi.** The best tailor in town for casual custom clothing, Tien Dat has the finest silks and cottons.

GREAT ITINERARIES

The itineraries that follow suggest ways in which destinations can be combined to create an itinerary that suits your interests, and give an idea of reasonable (minimum) amounts of time needed in various destinations.

The Capitals Tour

Southeast Asia is more diverse than Europe, yet there is a temptation on a first visit to cover the entire area on one European-style Grand Tour. Such a trip is physically and mentally taxing and cannot begin to do justice to the complexities of Asian cultures. However, as time is often limited, this whirlwind tour encompasses the capitals and a few of the highlights of Southeast Asia in three weeks.

Begin the tour in Bangkok. It's an exciting, exotic city yet has all the amenities that you could wish for in an international capital. Enjoy a leisurely round of sightseeing interspersed with shopping. Go up to Chiang Mai in northern Thailand before flying into Burma. From there, fly to Kuala Lumpur, before a stop in Singapore. Then it's on to Jakarta, Bali, and Manila.

Duration: Three weeks

Transportation
Be aware that stopping in all the major regions of Southeast Asia requires the use of different airlines. Coming from the United States, you may want to consider using Thai Airways International or Northwest Airlines, a U.S. airline that best covers all the capital cities in Southeast Asia, as your major carriers. Coming from Great Britain, British Airways covers many of Asia's capital cities.

Itinerary
BANGKOK: FOUR NIGHTS➤ Arrive in Bangkok and catch up on some zzz's before exploring Thailand's capital city with a look at some of its 300 temples. Go on a morning tour to Damnoen Saduak's floating market and a full-day tour to explore Ayutthaya, Thailand's ancient capital.

CHIANG MAI: TWO NIGHTS➤ Fly to Chiang Mai. (Alternatively, take the night train the evening before from Ayutthaya.) Visit the major temples in and around town, including Doi Suthep. Spend a morning at the elephant training camp at Mae Sa and an afternoon browsing the craft showrooms and workshops along San Kamphaeng Road.

MANDALAY AND PAGAN: THREE NIGHTS➤ Use Air Mandalay to fly to the unofficial capital of Upper Burma for one night, before continuing on to Pagan for two nights.

RANGOON (YANGON): ONE NIGHT➤ Fly down to Rangoon for the night, making sure that you have time to visit the Shwedagon Pagoda.

SINGAPORE: THREE NIGHTS➤ Fly to Singapore. You may want to give yourself the morning in Chiang Mai for a little extra shopping time. Once in Singapore, explore the various ethnic neighborhoods—Chinatown, Little India, the Arab district—take an evening stroll along the Padang, the heart of colonial Singapore, check out the myriad shops on Orchard Road, and dine sumptuously on Singapore's multi-ethnic cuisines. Make a day excursion to Malaysia to visit the historic city of Malaka. If you wish, you could fly from Yangon to Kuala Lumpur, capital of Malaysia, then travel by car passing through Malacca to Singapore.

BALI: FOUR NIGHTS➤ Fly to Bali. You'll want more than three days to explore the temples, the craft shops, and the town of Ubud, and more than one day on the beaches, so make plans to return next year.

MANILA: THREE NIGHTS➤ Fly to Manila. Explore the Philippine capital, especially Intramuros, the walled city. Take an afternoon to visit Corregidor Island, the famous World War II battle site, or the natural beauty of Lake Taal, or the gardens of the Hidden Valley.

The Indochina Tour

Take a circular tour of French Indochina using Bangkok as a starting and ending point.

Duration: Two weeks

Transportation
Northwest Airlines has the best flights from the United States to Thailand. British Airways flies in from London. Use Thai Airways International from Bangkok to Phnom Penh.

Itinerary
THAILAND: THREE NIGHTS➤ Start in Bangkok with a leisurely round of sightseeing interspersed with shopping and dining. Make a couple of side trips out of Bangkok to visit the former Thai capital, Ayutthaya, and another one to Damoen Saduak and the Bridge over the River Kwai. If you want to add some beach

time, go to Gulf of Thailand to Hua Hin or Pattaya.

CAMBODIA: THREE NIGHTS➤ Fly to Phnom Penh from Bangkok and overnight before going to Siem Reap for two nights to visit the fantastic Khmer ruins at Angkor.

VIETNAM: SIX NIGHTS➤ Fly on to Ho Chi Minh City to spend time exploring former Saigon and taking a day trip out to Caodai Holy See. Unless you have an extra three days, go by air rather than by road north to Hanoi for three nights to explore this fascinating mix of the old and the new.

LAOS: THREE NIGHTS➤ From Hanoi take a plane to Luang Prabang, the former capital of Laos and still its royal and artistic center. After two nights here, travel down the Mekong or fly to Vientiane, Laos' present capital.

THAILAND: TWO OR MORE NIGHTS➤ Cross over the Mekong on the new Friendship Bridge to Nong Khai. If you have the time amble down through the I-San to Bangkok or take the night train to the nation's capital. When you are ready and its time, board the plane for home.

The Orient with an Iberian Flavor

Take a trip to the Philippines. In Manila, you'll feel the presence of the Spanish colonial past, and outside the capital you'll experience the beauties of its nature. Next, make excursions first to the north, then to the south.

Duration: 7–10 days
Transportation
Philippines Airlines is the national carrier, Northwest is the leading U.S. carrier, and British Airways flies in from London.

Itinerary
MANILA: THREE NIGHTS➤ Fly to Manila. Tour Malacañang Palace, the Manila Cathedral, and, especially, Intramuros, the walled city built in the 16th century. Exploring out of the Tourist Belt, you'll want to visit the 16th-century Quiapo Church, famed for its black Nazarene statue of Jesus, and nearby Quiapo market, with its colorful and exotic produce. You will surely pass the Coconut Palace, a white elephant and pet project of Imelda Marcos. Farther afield are the Pagsanjan

Falls, the cascading drama of which was used in the film *Apocalypse Now*. You'll also want to visit the caldera Lake Taal with its baby volcano pushing up from the crater's languid waters. The charm of Villa Escudero, a coconut plantation with a unique museum, and the nearby tropical gardens of Hidden Valley, will also draw you.

BAGUIO: THREE NIGHTS➤ Leave Manila and make the six-hour overland trip by bus or car, or take the 45-minute Philippines Air Lines flight, to north Luzon and the highlands. Use the vacation and provincial capital city of Baguio as your base. If you desperately need a beach, there are the resorts of Bauang, with fine sandy beaches, and the hour's drive there is panoramic and thrilling. If you have an extra couple of days, make the eight-hour drive to the Banaue Rice Terraces, which look like giant steps to the sky. Nearby are the Ifugao villages with pyramid-shape huts perched on rocky crags. On the way back, pass through the tribal villages of the Bontoc, where the people still wear their traditional tasseled G-strings and little else.

CEBU CITY: TWO NIGHTS➤ Via Manila, fly to Cebu City, the capital of the Visayas and a base for visiting the southern provinces, which can include a trip to explore Zamboanga City and time to relax on the beach on Santa Cruz Island. If you can take a few extra days, head to Boracay Island, which has the Philippines' most beautiful beaches.

Hitting the Beaches

Increasingly Southeast Asia is becoming a sun and beach center. Each destination could be the entire vacation. However, you could cover several beaches in one three-week trip.

The Andaman Sea is known for its crystal-clear turquoise waters. From south Thailand to northern Malaysia, beaches beckon along the shore and hundreds of islands offshore offer Robinson Crusoe–style exploring.

Duration: Three weeks
Transportation
Thailand is served by Thai Airways International and Northwest Airlines from the United States, and Thai Airways International and British Airways from

Great Britain. With the exception of a visit to Langkawi, all travel is by plane. To reach Langkawi from the Phuket area take a bus, via Hattyai, into Malaysia. (There are flights from Phuket to Hattyai and Penang.) You may also travel the whole distance from Bangkok to Singapore by combinations of rail, bus, and ferry.

Itinerary

BANGKOK: TWO NIGHTS➤ Arrive in Thailand and spend at least one day exploring the capital city.

PHUKET: FIVE NIGHTS➤ Fly to Phuket. Enjoy the island's 12 beaches, but do take a cruise out to Phang Nga Bay and "James Bond" island.

PHI PHI: THREE NIGHTS➤ Take the morning boat to Phi Phi Island and the cruise around the islands where you can snorkel and scuba dive.

HATTYAI: ONE NIGHT➤ Cross by ferry to Krabi and take the bus to Hattyai and into Malaysia. Cross over to Langkawi. You may want to stay overnight in Hattyai. As an alternative to road and ferry, you can fly from Phuket to Langkaw, changing planes in Penang.

LANGKAWI: THREE NIGHTS➤ Spend a couple of days beachcombing, soaking up the sun, and cooling off in the warm waters of this tropical island retreat.

PENANG: FOUR NIGHTS➤ Take a ferry from Langkawi to Penang or cross to the mainland and travel south to cross over the bridge to the island of Penang, where you can mix sightseeing with relaxing on the beach. You can alaso fly from Langkawi to Penang.

SINGAPORE: ONE NIGHT➤ Fly to this island republic and take advantage of the shopping, delicious foods, and creature comforts before returning home.

2 Indonesia

In this land of contrasts and diversity, cultural attractions compete for your time with the pursuit of the pleasure principle. From the temples and beaches of Bali to the great architectural wonders around Yogjakarta, from fascinating animist rites on Sulawesi to the capital rush into the 21st century in Jakarta, Indonesia will enthrall you.

By Nigel Fisher
and Lois
Anderson

THE SHEER SIZE OF INDONESIA is mind-boggling. This nation is the world's fourth-most populous and covers 13,677 islands (more than half of them uninhabited) that stretch for more than 3,200 miles from the Pacific to the Indian Ocean. From north to south, the islands form a 1,100-mile-long bridge between Asia and Australia.

From Jakarta's tall steel-and-glass office buildings to Irian Jaya's thatched huts, Indonesia embraces an astonishing array of cultures. Today Indonesia's 165 million people—Asmats, Balinese, Bataks, Dayaks, and on down through the alphabet—speak as many as 300 languages, though a national language, Bahasa Indonesia, is officially recognized as a means of binding the population together.

It's this size and diversity that make Indonesia so fascinating. A visitor has the option of relaxing in one of Bali's luxury resorts or taking a river trip through the jungles of Borneo. If you do venture off the beaten path—really the best way to fall in love with Indonesia's many charms—remember that patience is a key to enjoying your trip. Since tourism is a new priority for Indonesia, the infrastructure is often rudimentry. Only in areas slated for tourist development can travelers expect to find services approaching international standards. Elsewhere, expect only modest accommodations and casually scheduled transport.

Don't mistake this lack of development for a lack of history, however. The nation has seen a succession of conquerors and revolutions, even receiving its name from one of its earliest colonizers: "Indonesia" comes from two Greek words—"indos," meaning Indian, and "nesos," meaning islands—a testament to the Indian traders who roamed the islands in the 1st century AD. By the 7th century, powerful Buddhist and Hindu kingdoms had emerged, and by the 1300s the Majapahit Hindu empire had united much of what is now Indonesia. The empire lasted for two centuries, although during that time Arab traders began setting up communities and spreading the teachings of Islam (the religion now followed by about 85% of the population).

Contact with the west came in 1509, when Portuguese traders arrived. A century later they were displaced by the Dutch, and by the 18th century, Dutch rule encompassed most of Indonesia, known to the West as the Dutch East Indies. Except for a brief interlude of British rule during the Napoleonic Wars of 1811–16, the Dutch remained in power until the outbreak of World War II. After the surrender of the occupying Japanese in 1945, a bloody fight for Indonesian independence ensued. In 1949 Indonesia won its sovereignty, and the name Dutch East Indies became one more piece of colonial history.

The man behind the independence movement was Sukarno, who became president of the new republic and implemented a leftist nationalist policy. He forcibly prevented ethnic groups from forming their own republics and extended Indonesia's borders by annexing part of New Guinea, now the province of Irian Jaya. Despite imprisoning his opposition, he lost control of the movement, the economy suffered under an annual inflation rate of 650%, and Indonesia dissolved into chaos.

On the night of September 30, 1965, communists (or so it was said) abducted and murdered six top generals and their aides and, it is alleged, were about to seize power. Major-General Suharto intervened, and blood flowed by the gallon. Anyone accused of being a communist was slaughtered. Rampaging mobs massacred thousands—some estimates place the number of dead at 500,000.

Indonesia

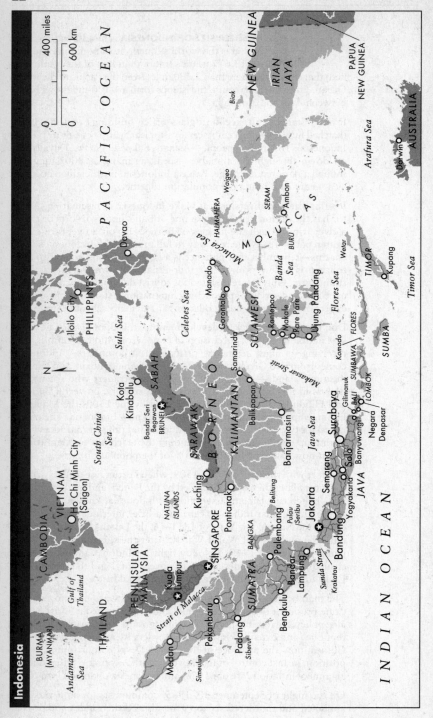

Suharto became president in 1967 and continues to rule, claiming that his country requires a "guided democracy." Now in his sixth "elected" term, he has succeeded in welding the diverse nation into one. However, his repressive policies toward the independence-minded people of Timor, the one island that remained more Portuguese than Dutch, have placed Indonesia in the spotlight because of human-rights violations. Awareness of Jakarta's heavy-handedness is spreading, and voices of dissent are gaining volume. Much will depend on how Suharto is able to transfer power when he steps down. His sons are being groomed to take over, but an undercurrent of dissatisfaction with his family's accumulation of wealth may derail the succession. Indonesia may enter the next century on another great wave of change.

Pleasures and Pastimes

Balinese Dance

Dance is everywhere in Bali: at celebrations, temple rituals, weddings, birthdays, processions to the sea, tooth-filing and purification ceremonies, and, occasionally, exorcisms. The dancers move low to the ground, with bent knees, arched backs, and controlled steps, arms at right angles with elbows pointing up and fingers spread wide. The female dancers flutter their long-nailed fingers. They'll move slowly across the stage, then turn quickly but precisely with a staccato movement. Head movements are staccato, too, without facial expression except for their darting and flashing eyes. They wear petaled or gold headdresses. The men have to do battle and get killed, and their movements are more varied.

Most dances are accompanied by the traditional *gamelan* orchestra of gongs, drums (mostly hand-beaten), a type of xylophone with bronze bars, two different stringed instruments, and a flute. Balinese dancing is far more exuberant than Javanese, and the Balinese gamelan is sharper, with more crescendo. Behind every dance is a legend with a moral theme.

BARONG

The Barong is a dance of Good versus Evil. The Good is Barong, a dragon with a huge, bushy, lionlike head and a long flower-bedecked beard. Bells ring as he snaps his head. The two dancers inside use complicated motions to make Barong humorous and good natured, but ferocious when he meets Evil, in the form of the witch Rangda. Rangda's horrifying mask is white, with bulging eyes and tusks extending from her mouth. Her long braided hair sweeps down to the floor amid evil red mirrored streamers. She rushes threateningly back and forth across the stage. There are also beautiful female dancers with petaled headdresses, tasseled girdles, and gold-and-green sarongs, and male warriors whose prince is crowned with gold and flowers. Rangda forces the warriors to turn their kris blades on themselves, but Barong's powers keep the blades from harming them. A bird dancer enters and is killed—the required sacrifice to the gods—and Rangda is banished.

LEGONG

The Legong is a glittering classical dance. The story involves a young princess kidnapped by an enemy of her father. Three young girls in tight gold brocade and frangipani headdresses perform several roles. Their movements are rapid and pulsating; they punctuate the music with quick, precise movements and flashing eyes. It is an exacting dance—girls start training for the roles at five and retire before they are 15.

KECAK

The dramatic Kecak, the Monkey Dance, depicts the monkey armies of Hanuman, who rescued Rama and his love, Sita, from the forests of Ceylon in the *Ramayana,* the great Hindu epic. No gamelan is used; all sound comes from the chorus, who, in unison, simulate both the gamelan and the chattering, moaning, bellowing, and shrieking of monkeys. This dance is always performed at night under torchlight. The dark figures, again in unison, make wild arm gestures and shake their fingers. (The Kecak is not a classical dance but a product of this century.)

OTHER DANCES

At least 200 dances, with a story for every occasion, have been handed down from generation to generation. The **Keris** is an ancient temple dance performed by two bare-chested men in a trance who continually stab themselves (the blades don't pierce their skin). The **Joged** is a social dance in which a female dancer selects a partner from the audience, who dons a sash and joins her. The **Sanghyang** is a sacred dance to ward off epidemics caused by demons. The **Janger** is a lively women's dance to songs accompanied by flute and drum. The **Baris** is a warrior dance accompanied by the full gamelan orchestra.

Dining

The choice of foods in Indonesia is wide ranging: Indonesian, Chinese, and Western cooking are available in every major town and resort. To meet the needs of an increasing number of Japanese tourists, you'll also find Japanese restaurants in Jakarta and Bali.

Warungs are Indonesian street-food stalls, sometimes with benches and tables in the open, under canvas, or sheltered by a sheet of galvanized tin. The food here—usually rice dishes and *soto ayam,* the native chicken soup—varies from drab to tasty, but is always cheap: you can eat well for Rp 1,000. Warungs are often clustered together at a *pasar malam,* or night bazaar.

Rumah makans are just like warungs, only with fixed walls and roofs. Another step up is the *restoran,* a very broad category. Most are Chinese-owned and serve both Indonesian and Chinese cuisine. The dining rooms of tourist hotels generally offer Chinese, Indonesian, and Western fare; the native specialties are usually toned down. If you enjoy spicy food, you'll be happier at more authentic eateries.

Rice *(nasi)* is the staple of the Indonesian diet. It's eaten with breakfast, lunch, and dinner, and as a snack. But it normally serves as a backdrop to an exciting range of flavors. Indonesian food can be very hot, particularly in Sumatra. Your first sample might be *sambal,* a spicy relish made with chilis that is placed on every restaurant table. Indonesians cook with garlic, shallots, turmeric, cumin, ginger, fermented shrimp paste, soy sauce, lime or lemon juice, lemongrass, coconut, other nuts, and hot peppers. Peanut sauce is a common ingredient, and two dishes frequently encountered are *gado gado,* a cold vegetable salad dressed with spiced peanut sauce, and *saté* (or *satay*), slices of skewered meat charcoal-broiled and dipped in a flavored peanut sauce.

Naturally, fresh fish and shellfish abound throughout Indonesia. Fish *(ikan)* is often baked in a banana leaf with spices, grilled with a spicy topping, or baked with coconut. Shrimp come cooked in coconut sauce, grilled with hot chilis, made into prawn-and-bean-sprout fritters, or, in Sulawesi, with butter or Chinese sweet-and-sour sauce.

For dessert, Indonesians eat fresh fruit: papaya, pineapple, rambutan, salak, and mangosteen. Because this is a mostly Muslim country, wine and alcohol are expensive additions to a meal; beer is your best bet.

The following terms appear frequently on Indonesian menus:

bakmi goreng—fried noodles with bits of beef, pork, or shrimp, tomatoes, carrots, bean sprouts, cabbage, soy sauce, and spices

dendeng ragi—thin squares of beef cooked with grated coconut and spices

gudeg—chicken with jackfruit

ikan—fish

kelian ayam—Sumatran chicken curry

nasi champur—steamed rice with bits of chicken, shrimp, or vegetables with sambal; often topped with a fried egg and accompanied by *krupok,* delicious puffy prawn crisps

nasi goreng—fried rice with shallots, chilies, soy sauce, and ketchup; may include pork (in Bali), shrimp, onions, cabbage, mushrooms, or carrots; often studded with tiny fiery green peppers in Sumatra

nasi rames—a miniature rijsttafel

rijsttafel—literally, "rice table"; steamed rice with side dishes such as sayur lodeh, gudeg, or kelian ayam

sambal—a spicy, chili-based relish

satay—grilled skewered *ayom* (chicken), *babi* (pork), *daging* (beef), *kambing* (lamb), or ikan, with a spicy peanut sauce

sayur lodeh—a spicy vegetable stew

soto ayam—chicken soup, varying from region to region but usually including shrimp, bean sprouts, spices, chilies, and fried onions or potatoes.

Price categories throughout the chapter are based on the following ranges:

CATEGORY	COST*
$$$$	over Rp 60,000 (US$30)
$$$	Rp 40,000–Rp 60,000 (US$20–US$30)
$$	Rp 20,000–Rp 40,000 (US$10–US$20)
$	Rp 10,000–Rp 20,000 (US$5–US$10)
¢	under Rp 10,000 (US$5)

per person for a three-course dinner, excluding tax, service, and drinks.

Lodging

You'll find superb resorts—such as the Four Seasons on Bali and Mandarin Oriental in Jakarta—that cost half what you would expect to pay in the Caribbean. More hotels open every year in Bali's popular areas; Ubud has yet to have mammoth hotels and so maintains some small-town feel, but the number of smaller hotels (20–50 rooms) multiplies every year.

The government classifies hotels with star ratings, five stars being the most luxurious. Its criteria are somewhat random, however. No hotel without a garage gets four stars, for example, and most tourists don't need a garage. Besides hotels, most Indonesian towns offer three types of rooming houses: *penginapan, losmen,* and *wisma.* Theoretically, the penginapan is cheapest, with thin partitions between rooms, and the wisma most expensive, with thicker walls. The term "losmen" is often used generically to mean any small rooming house. Facilities vary widely: Some Bali losmen are comfortable and social, others dingy and dirty; at the bottom range in the less touristed areas you get a clean room with shower and Asian toilet for less than $5 a night.

Price categories throughout the chapter are based on the following ranges:

CATEGORY	COST*
$$$$	over Rp 300,000 (US$150)
$$$	Rp 200,000–Rp 300,000 (US$100–US$150)
$$	Rp 150,000–Rp 200,000 (US$75–US$100)
$	Rp 80,000–Rp 150,000 (US$40–US$75)
¢	under Rp 80,000 (US$40)

for a standard double room in high season, excluding 10% service charge and 11% tax.

Scuba Diving and Snorkeling

Scuba diving is becoming popular, and licensed diving clubs have sprung up around the major resort areas. Bali (off Sanur and the north coast), Lombok's Gili Islands, Flores, and North Sulawesi have some of the world's best diving. The best times for diving in Indonesia are March–June and October–November.

Shopping

Arts and crafts in Indonesia are bargains by U.S. standards. If you have the time, custom-made items can be commissioned. Consider bringing pictures or samples of items that you would like built or reproduced—anything from clothing and jewelry to furniture and board games.

From Java the best buys are batik cloth and garments, traditional jewelry, musical instruments, leather wayang puppets, and leather accessories. In Bali, look for batiks, stone and wood carvings, bamboo furniture, ceramics, silver work, traditional masks, and wayang puppets. Sumatra is best for thick handwoven cotton cloth; carved-wood panels and statues, often in primitive, traditional designs; and silver and gold jewelry. From Sulawesi, there's filigree silverware, handwoven silks and cottons, hand-carved wood panels, and bamboo goods. Be aware that machine-produced goods are sometimes sold to tourists as handcrafted.

Exploring Indonesia

Because of its fertile lands, Java has supported some of Indonesia's mightiest kingdoms. For the same reason, the island has become overcrowded, accounting for 60% of the nation's population. At least 14 million people live in and around Jakarta, the capital. Jakarta already has a range of international hotels, and more are under construction. Efforts are being made to improve the museums, whose displays do not do justice to their rich holdings. Offshore, in the Java Sea, are the Pulau Seribu, the Thousand Islands, with resort hotels. Excursions are also available to Krakatau (Krakatoa), the island whose volcano erupted with such violence in 1883. Within a two-hour drive of Jakarta are hill towns offering an escape from the tropical heat, tea plantations, botanical gardens, and the volcanic crater of Tangkuban near Bandung, a pleasant university town in the mountains.

As a tourist destination, Jakarta doesn't hold a candle to the rest of the country, but it serves as a convenient gateway to other Indonesian destinations. Central Java, for example, has the architectural wonders of the 9th-century Buddhist Borobudur and Hindu Prambanan temples. Both are within a short drive of Yogyakarta and Solo (Surakarta), towns rich in culture and handicrafts.

Across a 2-mile-wide strait from East Java is the magical island of Bali, with a proud, smiling people whose religion is a unique form of Hinduism blended with Buddhism and animism. Here, distinctive architecture and holy mountains compete for attention with surf-swept beaches and sophisticated hotels.

From Bali, islands stretch eastward like stepping-stones. Immediately east is Lombok, offering virgin beaches and the hospitality of Balinese Hindus and Sasak Muslims. Northeast of Bali is Sulawesi, home to the Bugis, who for centuries have sailed their stout *prahus* (boats) on the Java Sea. Part of the island is inhabited by the Toraja, whose unique animist culture celebrates death as the culmination of life.

To the west of Java is Sumatra, with the popular resort at Lake Toba, where on Samosir Island the Batak people have ornately carved traditional houses built on poles, with high, saddle-shape roofs. To the south, around Bukit Thinggi, a quiet hill town north of Padang, the Minangkabau live in distinctive houses with buffalo-horn-shape roofs.

Great Itineraries

It could easily take an active traveler years to explore all of Indonesia, and even to see the limited number of destinations covered in this book would still require a whirlwind month or two of traveling. We cover here only those areas that have a range amenities for all travelers and have sights or attractions that are of particular interest. If you haven't been to Bali, then that island should be on your itinerary. It would be very easy to spend an entire vacation at one of Bali's resorts—**Kuta, Nusa Dua,** and **Sanur** are the best known—but assuming that you have the itch to see more, then Java's **Yogyakarta** and the famed temple of **Borobudur** should be your second destinations. After that, we recommend North Sumatra or Sulawesi or, if possible, both. **Jakarta** would be the last on our list: It may be the dynamic heart of the nation, but it's a difficult city to get to know, the traffic is horrendous, and it has few noteworthy architectural sights.

IF YOU HAVE 7 DAYS
Fly into Bali and spend the first two days exploring the temples and villages, using **Ubud** as your base; be sure to see at least one dance performance. Then take an hour's flight to **Yogyakarta** and spend two nights there, making sure to visit **Borobudur, Prambanan,** and the sultans' palaces in Yogyakarta and **Solo.** Then return to Bali for a couple of days at a beach resort before flying out.

IF YOU HAVE 10 DAYS
Enter Indonesia by way of **Medan** (there are flights from KL and Singapore, as well as service by boat), taking three days to visit **Brastagi** and **Lake Toba.** Depart from Sumatra and spend two nights in **Jakarta.** On the sixth day take the early morning flight into **Yogyakarta** and visit **Prambunan** in the afternoon. Next morning drive out to **Borobudur** and then take the late afternoon flight to Bali. Split your final days between the beach and sightseeing around the island.

IF YOU HAVE 14 DAYS
With two weeks in Indonesia, you could follow the 10-day itinerary and add a side trip from Bali to Sulewesi. Fly into **Ujung Padung** and proceed to **Rantapao** for a two- to three-day exploration of Torajaland.

When to Tour Indonesia

In the peak tourist months, June and July, popular areas (especially Torajaland) are crammed with visitors. Bali hotels also tend to be fully booked around Christmas and New Year's. The best months for traveling are April–May and September–October, when you are most likely to miss both the seasonal rains and the crowds. (*Also see* When to Go *in* Indonesia A to Z, *below.*)

Be aware that many of the national museums are closed on Mondays. Also, in observance of the Muslim holy day, museums usually close by 11 AM on Friday instead of the usual 2 PM or 3 PM closing.

JAKARTA

Indonesia's capital is a place of extremes. Modern multistory buildings look down on shacks with corrugated-iron roofs. Wide boulevards intersect with unpaved streets. Elegant hotels and high-tech business centers stand just a few blocks from overcrowded kampongs. BMWs accelerate down the avenues while pedicabs plod along the back streets.

Although the government is trying to prepare for the 21st century, Jakarta has trouble accommodating the thousands who flock to it each year from the countryside. Because of the number of migrant workers who come to the city each day, it is difficult to accurately estimate the city's population. The census reports 8.5 million, but the true number is closer to 14 million. The crowds push the city's infrastructure to the limit. Traffic grinds to a standstill, and a system of canals, built by the Dutch to prevent flooding in below-sea-level Jakarta, cannot accommodate the heavy monsoon rains, so the city is sometimes under water for days. The heat and humidity take getting used to. But air-conditioning in the major hotels, restaurants, and shopping centers provides an escape. Early morning and late afternoon are the best times for sightseeing.

As a tourist destination, Jakarta has a limited number of sights, but the government is intent on creating attractions for the overseas visitor, and private enterprise is building new luxury hotels, opening varied and good restaurants, and creating entertaining nightlife.

Exploring Jakarta

At Jakarta's center is the vast, parklike Merdeka Square, where Sukarno's 433-foot Monas Monument is topped with a gold-plated flame symbolizing national independence. Wide boulevards border the square, and the Presidential Palace (Suharto does not live here), the army headquarters, City Hall, Gambir Railway Station, the National Museum, and other government buildings are located here.

The square and the area immediately south along Jalan M.H. Thamrin (*jalan* means "street") comprise the Menteng district. This is the downtown of New Jakarta, home to most banks, large corporations, and international hotels. New Jakarta extends southwest, continuing through the district known as Kebayoran to Blok M, where many expatriates live.

North and west of Merdeka Square, around the port of Sunda Kelapa at the mouth of the Ciliwung River, is the Kota area, known as Old Batavia. This is Old Town, where the Portuguese first arrived in 1522. A century later, in 1619, the Dutch secured the city, renamed it Batavia, and established the administrative center for their expanding Indonesian empire.

Dutch rule came to an abrupt end when, in World War II, the Japanese occupied Batavia and changed its name back to Jayakarta. The Dutch returned after Japan's surrender, but by 1949 Indonesia had won independence and, abbreviating the city's old name, established Jakarta as the nation's capital.

We deal with the old and the new areas separately, followed by exploration of Jakarta's parks, offshore islands, and other attractions within easy reach.

Old Batavia

Jakarta is both old and new. The old section, known as Old Batavia or Kota, is down by the port, where the Dutch administration was centered. As Jakarta expanded after World War II, Old Batavia was neglected. Its stately colonial buildings fell into decay, the streets and sidewalks caved in, and the old shop-houses served as warehouse and repair shops. In recent years, an appreciation for Jakarta's heritage has awakened and the revitalization of Old Batavia is under way. Under the Taman Fatahillah Restoration project, begun in the early 1970s but slow to get off the ground, many of the old buildings have been restored and the area is experiencing an economic rejuvenation, as new small businesses occupy these spaces. The very comfortable Omni Batavia hotel opened in 1996, paving the way for a beautification of historic Jakarta; although some sections are a little scary to walk alone in at night, this too will likely change.

Numbers in the text correspond to numbers in the margin and on the Jakarta map.

A GOOD WALK

As it's best seen early in the morning, start your walk at the **fish market** ①. You'll save the entrance fee to **Sunda Kelapa Harbor** if you get there by walking through the back of the fish market. Here you'll see a riot of vessels that ply Indonesian waters, transporting goods from the outer islands to and from Jakarta. Head south on Jalan Pasar Ikan and stop in at the **Maritime Museum** ②, then veer left, over to Jalan Cengkeh, the street leading down to the heart of Old Batavia, **Fatahillah Square** ③. This was the city's central plaza in the days of the Dutch. On the west side of Fatahillah Square is the **Puppet Museum** ④, and on the east side is the **Jakarta Fine Art Gallery** ⑤, in the former Palace of Justice. The old Town Hall, on the south side of the square, is now the **Museum of Old Batavia** ⑥. Behind Town Hall, on Jalan Pangeran Jayakarta opposite the Kota Railway Station, is the **Portuguese Church** ⑦, the oldest church in Jakarta. Then head south of the square to explore **Glodok,** Old Batavia's Chinatown; wander around and marvel at the wealth of activity crammed into the narrow streets.

TIMING

In order to experience the frenetic activity of the fish market, start your tour early, around 7 AM. If you are taking the walk on Sunday, there is an abbreviated wayang kulit, or shadow play, performed at 10 AM at the Puppet Museum. Since the heat builds as the day progresses, try to finish your walk soon after midday. Remember that many sights are closed after 11 AM on Friday and after 1 PM on Saturday.

SIGHTS TO SEE

❸ **Fatahillah Square.** At the heart of the old city, once called Batavia and now known as Kota, is Fatahillah Square, cobbled with ballast stones from old Dutch trading ships. In the center of the square is a fountain, a reproduction of one originally built here in 1728. Near the fountain, criminals were beheaded, while their judges watched from the balconies of Town Hall (☞ Museum of Old Batavia, *below*). Just to the north is an old Portuguese cannon whose muzzle tapers into a clenched fist, a Javanese fertility symbol; childless women have been known to straddle the cannon for help in conceiving.

❶ **Fish Market** (Pasar Ikan). This market is as remarkable an introduction to the denizens of Indonesia's seas as a visit to an aquarium—and more chaotic and exciting. It's colorful, noisy, smelly, and slimy, and there are great photo opportunities. Be sure to come early, when it's in full swing. ✉ *Sunda Kelapa Harbor.*

Glodok. Much of Glodok, Old Batavia's Chinatown, has been demolished, but there are still sights and smells to bring back those days when Chinese immigrants were brought in as laborers and worked like slaves to become merchants. Wander around Glodok Plaza (a shopping center and office building—the area's landmark), and you can still find small streets crowded with Chinese restaurants and shops selling Chinese herbal medicines. Glodok is also an entertainment district at night, but unless you know your way around, it's better left to the locals.

❺ **Jakarta Fine Art Gallery** (Belai Seni Rupa Jakarta). This gallery is in the former Palace of Justice, built between 1866 and 1870, on the east

30

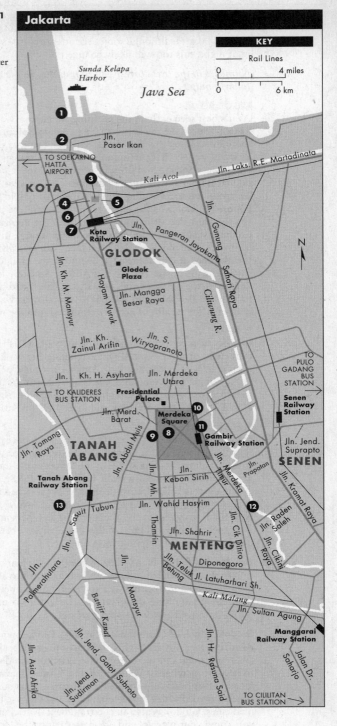

side of Fatahillah Square. The permanent collection includes paintings by Indonesia's greatest artists; contemporary works, such as wood sculptures; and the Chinese ceramic collection of Adam Malik, a former Indonesian vice-president. A museum in the southeast of the Menteng district, the **Adam Malik Museum** (✉ Jln. Diponegoro 29, ☎ 021/337400 or 021/337388), displays an even larger sampling from his collection. ✉ *Jln. Taman Fatahillah 2,* ☎ *021/676090.* 🎫 *Admission.* 🕐 *Daily 9–2.*

NEED A BREAK? **Café Batavia** (✉ Jln. Taman Fatahillah 14, ☎ 021/691–5531), on the north side of Fatahillah Square, is a friendly place in which to enjoy Indonesian hors d'oeuvres, an Indonesian or European entrée, or a bit of ice cream. Its collection of nostalgic bric-a-brac, including a sketch of Winston Churchill, makes for gay and cheerful decor. Choose a table by the window and watch the goings-on down below on the square.

❷ Maritime Museum (Museum Bahari). On Jalan Pasar Ikan, two former Dutch East Indies warehouses have been restored to house a museum of maritime history. One warehouse is devoted to models of Indonesian sailing vessels; the other contains ancient maps and documents that tell the history of the spice trade. Neither exhibit is very thorough. ✉ *Jln. Pasar Ikan 1,* ☎ *021/669–0518.* 🎫 *Admission.* 🕐 *Tues.–Thurs. 9–2, Fri. 9–11, Sat. 9–1, Sun. 9–3.*

❻ Museum of Old Batavia (Museum Sejarah Jakart). On the south side of Fatahillah Square is the old Town Hall, built by the Dutch in 1707. Preserved as a historic building, it now houses this museum often referred to simply as the Jakarta Museum. The history of Batavia is chronicled with antique maps, portraits, models of ancient inscribed Hindu stones, antique Dutch furniture, weapons, and coins. Unfortunately, the exhibits have few explanations in English, and the museum is rather gloomy. Beneath the halls are the dungeons where criminals once awaited trial. Prince Diponegoro, the Indonesian patriot who nearly managed to evict the Dutch from Java in 1830, was imprisoned here on his way to exile in Menado. All you see of the dungeons are the double-barred basement windows along Jalan Pintu Besar. ✉ *Jln. Taman Fatahillah 1,* ☎ *021/679101.* 🎫 *Admission.* 🕐 *Tues.–Thurs. 9–2:30, Fri. 9–noon, Sat. 9–1, Sun. 9–3.*

❼ Portuguese Church. Opposite Kota Railway Station, behind the Museum of Old Batavia, is the oldest church in Jakarta. The exterior is plain, but inside you'll see 17th-century carved pillars, copper chandeliers, solid ebony pews, and plaques commemorating prominent Dutch administrators. ✉ *Jln. Pangeran Jayakarta.*

★ ☞ ❹ Puppet Museum (Museum Wayang). On the west side of Fatahillah Square, in a former Protestant church, is an extensive collection of traditional Indonesian wayang kulit figures (the intricately cut leather shadow puppets used to perform stories from the Hindu epics the *Ramayana* and the *Mahabarata*). The museum also has wayang golek figures (wood puppets used in performing Arabic folk tales or stories of Prince Panji, a legendary Javanese prince associated with the conversion of Java to Islam), as well as puppets from Thailand, China, Malaysia, India, Cambodia, and elsewhere. Abbreviated wayang kulit shadow plays are performed on Sunday morning at 10. Also on display are puppets used for social education, including those used in the Yogyakarta family-planning program. ✉ *Jln. Pintu Besar Utara 27,* ☎ *021/679560.* 🎫 *Admission.* 🕐 *Tues.–Thurs. and Sun. 9–2, Fri. 9–11, Sat. 9–1.*

Sunda Kelapa Harbor. At the back of the fish market is the wharf, where Makassar and Bugis sailing ships (called *prahus*) are lined up at oblique angles to the piers. They look like beached whales, but they still sail the Indonesian waters as they have for centuries, trading between the islands. You can negotiate a small boat (punt) for about Rp 2,500–3,000 for a 30-minute tour of the harbor. Because the government plans to develop a tourist marina here and moor the trading ships elsewhere, this scene may soon change. ✉ *Admission.* ⊙ *Daily 8–6.*

New Jakarta

In many developing countries, especially those undergoing an economic boom, the capital becomes a symbol of the country's pride in shaking off the yoke of economic, and often colonial, servitude. In Jakarta, this attitude has led to the constuction of wide avenues, tall skyscrapers (many of which are bank offices), palatial government buildings, and extravagant monuments. Modern Jakarta has little aesthetic appeal, but it is an interesting example of how a newly independent nation attempts to thrust itself into the modern age.

A GOOD TOUR

New Jakarta is almost impossible to cover on foot. The distances between sights are long, the streets aren't pedestrian-friendly, and the equatorial heat will melt you. Taxis are very cheap. Use them to get from one sight to another.

Start your tour in vast Merdeka Square, at the towering **National Monument** ⑧, taking its interior elevator up to the top for a bird's-eye view of the city. Then go to the monument's basement to visit the **Museum of National History.** Next head to the west side of Merdeka Square and the **National Museum** ⑨ to see the best collection of Indonesian antiquities and ethnic artwork. From the museum, you may want to make a circle around the square in a taxi. On the northwest corner is the Presidential Palace; on the northeast corner the **Istiqlal Mosque** ⑩, Indonesia's largest mosque (guided tours are available); and a bit farther down the east side **Emmanuel Church** ⑪. Keep the taxi and continue south down Jalan Cikini Raya to the **Jakarta Cultural Center** ⑫, known by the acronym TIM, where you are bound to find a cultural performance of some kind in progress. (If you walk, it's about 15 minutes from the south side of the square.) Directly west from TIM and about 10 minutes by taxi is the **Textile Museum** ⑬, with a collection of more than 300 kinds of textiles made in Indonesia and a small workshop demonstrating the batik-making process.

TIMING

It should not take much more than a half a day to cover these sights. Do plan to take some time, at least a couple of hours, at the National Museum. If possible time your visit to coincide with one of the free tours given in English—Tuesday, Wednesday, and Thursday at 9:30 AM—and you'll appreciate the museum a thousand times more; on Sunday morning there is Javanese or Sudanese gamelan music from 9:30 to 10:30. Museums close at 11 on Friday, 1 PM on Saturday, and 2 PM on other days except Monday, when they are closed all day.

SIGHTS TO SEE

⓫ **Emmanuel Church.** This classical Dutch Protestant church, off Merdeka square in the shadow of the MONAS monument, was built in 1835. Today its modest simplicity seems wonderfully incongruous in contrast to the grandeur of the surrounding monuments. ⊠ *Jln. Merdeka Timor 10.*

⓾ **Istiqlal Mosque.** On the northwest corner of Merdeka Square is Indonesia's largest mosque. Individual visitors who have not come to pray are not encouraged, but if you wish to visit to appreciate the mosque's size and open layout, you can arrange to join a guided tour through your hotel or a travel agent. ✉ *Jln. Veteren.*

✋ ⑫ **Jakarta Cultural Center** (Taman Ismail Marzuki or TIM). There is something happening at the Jakarta Cultural Center from morning to midnight. Most evenings, either the open-air theater or the enclosed auditorium stages some kind of performance, from Balinese dance to imported jazz, from gamelan concerts to poetry readings. Your hotel will have a copy of the monthly program. Two art galleries display paintings, sculpture, and ceramics. Also within the complex are an art school, an art workshop, a cinema, a planetarium, and outdoor cafés. ✉ *Jln. Cikini Raya 73,* ☎ *021/342605.* ✍ *Admission.* ⊙ *Daily 8–8. Shows at the planetarium are Tues.–Sun. 7:30, and Sun. 10, 11, and 1.*

Museum of National History. In the basement of the National Monument (☞ *below*) is the Museum of National History, with a gallery of 48 dioramas illustrating Indonesia's history and struggle for independence. The Hall of Independence contains four national treasures: the flag raised during the independence ceremony in 1945; the original text of the declaration of independence; a gilded map of the Indonesian Republic; and the Indonesian coat of arms, which symbolizes the five principles of the Indonesian Republic (belief in one supreme god; a just and civilized humanity; unity of Indonesia; consensus arising from discussion and self-help; and social justice). ✉ *Jln. Silang Monas,* ☎ *021/681512.* ✍ *Admission.* ⊙ *Tues.–Thurs. and Sat. 9–2:30, Fri. 9–11:30 AM.*

❽ **National Monument** (Monumen Nasional or MONAS). Merdeka Square is dominated by the towering National Monument, a Russian-built tower commemorating Indonesia's independence that local wags have taken to calling "Sukarno's last erection." Some of this bitterness may stem from the fact that the World Bank supplied funds for 77 pounds of pure gold to coat the "flame of freedom" atop the column while many Indonesians starved. But the monument now stands for Indonesia's impressive economic development, and for the visitor it serves as a useful landmark. Take its interior elevator up to just below the flame for a panoramic view of the city. ✉ *Merdeka Square.* ✍ *Admission.* ⊙ *Sat.–Thurs. 9–4, Fri. 9–11.*

★ ❾ **National Museum** (Museum Nasional). On the west side of Merdeka Square stands the National Museum, recognizable by the bronze elephant in front—a gift from the King of Thailand in 1871. The museum has the most complete collection of Indonesian antiquities and ethnic artwork in the country. There are five sections: Hindu and Buddhist stone carvings from the 7th to 15th centuries; an exhibit of prehistoric skulls, weapons, and cooking utensils dating back 4,000 years; Indonesian ethnic crafts; a treasure room with gold trinkets, jeweled weapons, and Buddhist statues; and one of the largest collections of Chinese ceramics outside China. Free tours are given in English on Tuesday, Wednesday, and Thursday at 9:30 AM, and on Sunday morning you can hear gamelan music from 9:30 to 10:30. To the right, as you face the museum, is the **museum shop,** selling artifacts such as shadow puppets—made for tourist sale, but of good quality—and books on Indonesia. ✉ *Jln. Merdeka Barat 12,* ☎ *021/360976.* ✍ *Admission.* ⊙ *Tues.–Thurs. 9:30–2, Fri. 9:30–11, Sat. 9:30–1, Sun. 9:30–3.*

⑬ **Textile Museum** (Museum Tekstil). With its rich collection of Indonesian fabrics and small workshop demonstrating the batik-making process, the Textile Museum will give you an idea of what to expect by way of design and quality in the textiles you'll come across traveling about the country. ✉ *Jln. K. Sasuit Tubun 4,* ☎ *021/365367.* ✍ *Admission.* ⊙ *Tues.–Thurs. 9–2, Fri. 9–11, Sat. 9–1, Sun. 9–2.*

Jakarta's Green Spaces

Jakarta has made an attempt to attract visitors and to give local residents recreational opportunites. At the same time, the government wants to make Jakarta an example of the diversity that is Indonesia. Thus, many of the city's parks are celebrations of the different ethnic and cultural groups of the nation.

A GOOD ROUTE

You may not want to visit both of these recreational attractions—choose the one that best satisfies your interests. North of Kota and stretching east along the bay is **Dunia Fantasi at Ancol**; billed as Southeast Asia's largest recreation area, it provides entertainment around the clock. About 12 km (7 mi) southeast of Merdeka Square and 30 minutes by taxi is the **Beautiful Indonesia in Miniature Park.** Its 250 acres hold 27 full-size traditional houses, as well as various museums.

TIMING

You may want to spend the afternoon at Dunia Fantasi at Ancol after touring Old Batavia, since it is north of Kota. However, avoid it on the weekends, when it's thronged with Jakarta families. You'll want to allow a good half a day at Taman Mini Indonesia Indah, perhaps arriving in time for lunch.

SIGHTS TO SEE

☾ **Beautiful Indonesia in Miniature Park** (Taman Mini Indonesia Indah). The Batak house of North Sumatra, the Redong longhouse of the Kalimantan Dyaks, the cone-shape hut of Irian Jaya, and the Toraja house of South Sulawesi are just a few of the 27 full-size traditional houses—one from each Indonesian province—on display at the Beautiful Indonesia in Miniature Park. There are even miniature Borobudur and Prambanan temples. Other attractions at the 250-acre park include a 30-minute movie, *Beautiful Indonesia,* shown daily from 11 to 5; the Museum Indonesia, with traditional costumes and handicrafts; a stamp museum; the Soldier's Museum, honoring the Indonesian struggle for independence; the Transportation Museum; and Museum Asmat, highlighting the art of the master carvers of the Asmat people of Irian Jaya. The park also has an orchid garden, an aviary, a touring train, cable cars, horse-drawn carts, paddleboats, and places for refreshment. English-speaking guides are available, if you call in advance. The park is about 12 km (7 mi) southeast of Merdeka Square and 30 minutes by taxi. ⊠ *12 km (7 mi) south of central Jakarta, off Jagorawi Toll Rd.,* ☎ *021/849525.* ⊡ *Admission.* ☉ *Museums, daily 9–3; outdoor attractions, daily 9–4.*

☾ **Dunia Fantasi at Ancol.** A village unto itself, the 24-hour park has hotels, nightclubs, shops, and amusement centers, including an oceanarium with dolphin and sea lion shows, a golf course, a race-car track, swimming pools, and water slides. Africa is represented by a comedy of mechanized monkeys, America by a Wild West town, Europe by a mock Tudor house, and Asia by buildings from Thailand, Japan, India, and Korea. Rides, shooting galleries, and food stalls surround these attractions, all located on 1,360 acres of land reclaimed from the bay in 1962. ⊠ *Taman Impian Jaya Ancol,* ☎ *021/681512.* ⊡ *Admission.* ☉ *Daily 24 hrs.*

Dining

All the major hotels have Western and Indonesian restaurants, and many of the latter also offer Chinese food. Outside the hotels, dining options range from restaurants providing a formal atmosphere and fine cuisine to inexpensive street stalls.

British

$$ ✕ **George and Dragon.** For a change from rice dishes, try this restaurant for fish-and-chips or steak, kidney, and mushroom pie. The atmosphere is informal, and the bar, the first British pub in Jakarta, is very friendly. The decor is warm and cozy, with lots of wood. ✉ *Jln. Teluk Betung 32,* ☎ *021/325625. AE, V.*

Chinese

$$$$ ✕ **Spice Garden.** The Taiwanese chef at this elegant, high-ceiling restau-
★ rant prepares 160 spicy Szechuan specialties, including sliced braised chicken with hot-pepper oil, and abalone soup with fermented black beans. Try the excellent bird's nest soup and stir-fried lobster in hot black-bean sauce. The crimson-and-gold decor includes batik wall hangings by renowned designer Iwah Tirta. ✉ *Mandarin Oriental Hotel, Jln. M.H. Thamrin,* ☎ *021/321307. Reservations essential. AE, DC, MC, V.*

French

$$$ ✕ **Le Bistro.** Candlelit and intimate, with checked tablecloths and copper pots, the decor here puts you in the mood for the classic Provençal menu—simple food, prepared with herbs, from the south of France. Try the roast chicken with rosemary and thyme. At the back of the dining room is a circular piano bar where you can have an after-dinner liqueur. ✉ *Jln. K.H. Wahid Hasyim 75,* ☎ *021/364272. AE, DC, V.*

Indian

$$ ✕ **George's Curry House.** Next door to the George and Dragon (☞ *above*) and under the same management, this London-style eatery serves Indian, Sri Lankan, and Sumatran curries. Specialties include *tandoori murk,* chicken marinated in yogurt and spices, then charcoal-roasted. ✉ *Jln. Teluk Betung 32,* ☎ *021/325625. Reservations essential on weekends. AE, V.*

$ ✕ **Omar Khayyam.** In addition to an Indian buffet lunch, there is an extensive menu of specialties, including very good curries and tandoori dishes. The restaurant's decor pays homage to the eponymous Persian poet: Some of his poetry is inscribed on the walls. Try the chicken *tikka makhanwalla,* boneless tandoori chicken with tomato, butter, and cream sauce; or the marinated fish, wrapped in a banana leaf and deep-fried. ✉ *Jln. Antara 5–7,* ☎ *021/356719. Reservations not accepted. No credit cards.*

Indonesian

$$ ✕ **Handayani.** This is a true neighborhood restaurant, with friendly service and some English-speaking help. Decor is not its strong point—lines of tables and chairs fill a bare room—but Handayani is popular with locals for its Indonesian food. The extensive menu offers such dishes as chicken bowels steamed in banana leaves, beef intestine satay, goldfish fried or grilled, and lobster-size king prawns cooked in a mild chili sauce. The *nasi goreng Handayani* is a special version of the Indonesian staple. ✉ *Jln. Abdul Muis 35E,* ☎ *021/373614. DC, V.*

$$ ✕ **In the Streets of Jakarta.** Around the pool on Friday night, the Hilton hotel creates a completely visitor-friendly version of the food stalls found throughout the city, with satays, Indonesian fried chicken, and various rice dishes. Since the Hilton is in the expatriate district, you'll see many Europeans dropping in for Friday night dinner. ✉ *Jakarta Hilton International, Jln. Jend. Gatot Subroto,* ☎ *021/583051. Reservations essential Fri. night. AE, DC, MC, V.*

$$ ✕ **Manari.** The menu at this popular restaurant, where locals often take their foreign guests, is primarily Indonesian, with additional selections from China (Canton) and Thailand. The food is really secondary, however, to the varied dinnertime cultural performances—dances and

Jakarta Dining and Lodging

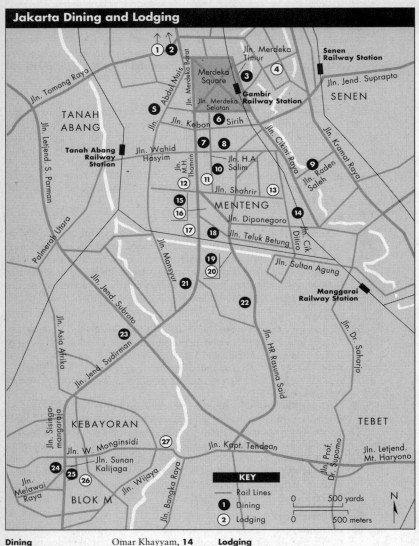

Dining

Asiatique, **19**
George and Dragon, **18**
George's Curry House, **18**
Green Pub, **7, 22**
Handayani, **5**
In the Streets of Jakarta, **23**
Le Bistro, **8**
Manari, **21**
Mira Sari, **24**
Natrabu, **6**
Oasis, **9**
Omar Khayyam, **14**
Paregu, **25**
Pondok Laguna, **2**
Sari Kuring, **3**
Spice Garden, **15**
Tora-Ya, **10**

Lodging

Grand Hyatt, **12**
Hotel Borobudur Inter-Continental, **4**
Hotel Wisata International, **17**
Interhouse, **26**
Jayakarta Tower, **1**
Kebayoran Inn, **27**
Mandarin Oriental, **16**
Marcopolo, **13**
President Hotel, **11**
Regent, **20**

songs from Indonesia's multi-ethnic heritage. ⊠ *Jln. Jend. Gatot Sub-roto 14,* ☎ *021/516102. Reservations essential. AE, MC, V.*

$$ ✕ **Mira Sari.** Comfortable rattan chairs with soft pillows, fresh flowers on the tables, and warm, friendly service make this a congenial spot. Regional Indonesian specialties are served in an air-conditioned dining room, in the garden, or on the terrace. The menu includes a very good version of Indonesian chicken soup, excellent spiced grilled fish, prawns grilled with spices and chilies, and roast or fried spiced chicken. ⊠ *Jln. Patiunus 15,* ☎ *021/771621. Reservations essential. No credit cards.*

$$ ✕ **Natrabu.** Decor at this popular Padang restaurant is minimal: bare tabletops and side booths, red Sumatran banners hanging from the ceiling, and a model of a Minangkabau house set in a corner. Waiters wearing Padang headscarves deliver bowls of food from the moment you sit down. You can order, or you can select from the dishes they bring you—you pay for the ones you try. ⊠ *Jln. H.A. Salim (often called Jln. Sabang) 29A,* ☎ *021/335668. Reservations not accepted. MC, V.*

$$ ✕ **Pondok Laguna.** This is one of Jakarta's most popular restaurants.
★ The large dining room, divided by water pools and falls, is always crowded with families and young couples. The noise level is fairly high and the service casual. Some of the staff speak English; all are anxious to help foreign guests. Fish is the main item served—either fried or grilled and accompanied by different sauces ranging from hot to mild. Whatever you choose, expect it to be fresh and cooked to perfection. ⊠ *Jln. Batu Tulis Raya 45,* ☎ *021/359994. Reservations not accepted (except for 8 or more). AE, DC, MC, V.*

$$ ✕ **Sari Kuring.** This restaurant near Merdeka Square serves very good
★ Indonesian seafood, especially the grilled prawns and the Thai fish "à la Sari Kuring," marinated in spices then quickly fried. The restaurant is large, but connected on many levels by stone steps, so there is some feeling of intimacy. If you are unable to secure a table here, try next door at **Sari Nusantara** (☎ 021/352972), where the fare is similar except for a slight Chinese influence in the cooking and fewer spices in the sauces. ⊠ *Jln. Silang Monas Timur 88,* ☎ *021/352972. AE, V.*

International

$$$ ✕ **Asiatique.** The concept of marrying Asian spices with Western culinary concepts is not new in California, but it is in Jakarta, where chef Derek Watanabe, a graduate from New York's Culinary Institute of America, is the innovator. He brings together elements from different Asian cuisines to produce tempting combinations. Most dishes can be ordered as an appetizer or main course, and a broad selection of appetizers is a good way to satisfy your curiosity. Especially good are the lemongrass-spiked tandoori salmon and the fried chili and lobster with peppers and lotus root. ⊠ *Regent Hotel, Jln. H.R. Rasuna Said,* ☎ *021/252–3456. AE, DC, MC, V. No lunch.*

$$$ ✕ **Oasis.** Fine international cuisine, as well as a traditional rijsttafel, assure that even after decades, the Oasis is still the most popular restaurant among Western visitors. A specialty is medallions of veal Oscar, in a cream sauce with mushrooms, crabmeat, and asparagus. The atmosphere lives up to the cuisine in this lovely old house decorated with tribal art and textiles. A combo alternates with Batak singers to provide music nightly. ⊠ *Jln. Raden Saleh 47,* ☎ *021/326397. Reservations essential. AE, DC, V. Closed Sun.*

Japanese

$$$ ✕ **Tora-Ya.** Some say this is Jakarta's best Japanese restaurant. The several attractive small dining rooms, each with a clean, spare decor, reflect the Japanese aesthetic. The service is low-key and very good. Both sushi and *kaiseki* (banquet) cuisine are offered. ⊠ *Jln. Gereja Theresia 1,* ☎ *021/310–0149. Jacket and tie. AE, DC, V.*

Mexican

$$ ✕ **Green Pub.** The two branches of the Green Pub are recommended not only for their Mexican food but for live country-and-western music (6:30–9) and jazz (9:30–1). The decor is somewhere between a Western saloon and a Mexican ranch, with tapestries adorning the walls. The burritos and enchiladas are quite authentic, and recently the menu was expanded to include such Tex-Mex dishes as barbecued spare ribs. ✉ *Jakarta Theater Bldg., Jln. M.H. Thamrin 9,* ☎ *021/359332;* ✉ *Jln. H.R. Rasuna Said, Setia Budi Bldg. 1,* ☎ *021/517983. Reservations not accepted. AE, V.*

Vietnamese

$$ ✕ **Paregu.** This is the place for the best Vietnamese food in town. The decor is simple, with Oriental embellishments, and service is top-notch. Try the Vietnamese version of spring rolls; the fried rice with scrambled eggs, chicken, shrimp, and a blend of herbs and spices; and the herbed seafood. ✉ *Jln. Sudan Cholagogue 64,* ☎ *021/774892. No credit cards.*

Lodging

Jakarta has some world-class accommodations with all the modern amenities. Most international hotels are south of Merdeka Square. Besides the Mandarin Oriental, the Grand Hyatt, the Regent, and Borobudur Inter-Continental (all listed below), the other leading hotels are the Jakarta Hilton, between the new center and Blok M, and the Hyatt Aryaduta, near Gambir Station. A recent spate of openings, including the Shangri-La high-rise, has brought a surfeit of five-star hotels—which means that actual rates should be far better than the published ones.

$$$$ 🏨 **Grand Hyatt.** Glitter and shining-marble modernity characterize this 1992 hotel. You enter the four-story atrium lobby and mount a palatial staircase (or take the escalator) to the reception area. One more short flight up brings you to the expansive Fountain Lounge, where you can watch the stalled traffic on Jalan M.H. Thamrin. On the fifth floor is the pool garden, an extensive area of greenery with a patio restaurant. Rooms are spacious, each with two bay windows; bathrooms have a separate shower stall and toilet. Furnishings are in the ubiquitous pastels, but pleasant nonetheless. Beneath the Hyatt is the Plaza Indonesia (☞ Shopping, *below*), with restaurants and nightclubs in addition to 250 shops. In a city that sprawls, this proximity to a "social center" is an advantage. ✉ *Jln. M.H. Thamrin, Jakarta 10230,* ☎ *021/390–1234 or 021/310–7400,* 🖷 *021/334321; U.S.* ☎ *800/233–1234. 413 rooms, 47 suites. 5 restaurants, pool, massage, 6 tennis courts, exercise room, jogging, squash, business services. AE, DC, MC, V.*

$$$$ 🏨 **Hotel Borobudur Inter-Continental.** Billed as "your country club in Jakarta," this large, modern hotel complex boasts 23 acres of landscaped gardens and excellent facilities. Floor-to-ceiling windows at the back of the Pendopo Lounge look out onto the tropical gardens, which makes it a delightful place for afternoon tea, cocktails, or snacks. Most of the compact guest rooms, except those on floors 9 and 16, have a modern Javanese design; the Garden Wing has suites with kitchens. Reserve a room overlooking the gardens and the swimming pool, not facing the parking lot. ✉ *Jln. Lapangan Banteng Selatan, Box 329, Jakarta 10710,* ☎ *021/380–5555,* 🖷 *021/380–9595; U.S.* ☎ *800/327–0200. 712 rooms, 140 suites. 4 restaurants, bar, room service, pool, miniature golf, 8 tennis courts, badminton, health club, jogging, racquetball, squash, dance club, playground, business services, meeting rooms. AE, DC, MC, V.*

$$$$ ★ ▦ **Mandarin Oriental.** This is the most sophisticated hotel in Jakarta. The elegant circular lobby has three tall, beautifully carved Batak roofs, each housing a Sumatran statue. An open mezzanine above the lobby provides comfortable seating for tea or cocktails and some fine shops, including a gallery for Ida Bagus Tilem, Bali's master wood-carver. Guest rooms are spacious and have top-quality furnishings: thick russet carpeting, floral bedspreads, off-white draperies on the picture windows, and dark-wood furniture. Complimentary afternoon tea and hors d'oeuvres are delivered to your room. Most rooms are "executive," with butler service; a nominal extra fee gives you use of the executive lounge for concierge assistance, and complimentary breakfast and cocktails. The location is central, and with the Plaza Indonesia shopping complex and the Grand Hyatt across the square, there are shops, restaurants, and bars within a two-minute walk. On-site restaurants include the Spice Garden (☞ Dining, *above*). ⊠ *Jln. M.H. Thamrin, Box 3392, Jakarta 10310,* ☎ *021/314–1307,* ℻ *021/314–8680; U.S.,* ☎ *800/526–6566. 455 rooms. 4 restaurants, bar, room service, pool, sauna, health club, business services, meeting rooms. AE, DC, MC, V.*

$$$$ ★ ▦ **Regent.** Designed by the same architects who created the Regent in Hong Kong, this property sits on six acres of land in the Golden Triangle, the city's booming business district, and makes the most of space and natural light. Ten different shades of granite and marble are set off by honey-color teak paneling and Indonesian art. Guest rooms are large—a minimum of 500 sqare feet—and the double layers of masonry between rooms keep them soundproof. Double-glazed sliding widows lead out onto a small balcony. Framed Indonesian tapestries adorn the walls. The marble bathrooms have a deep tub and a separate shower stall. Telephones have two lines, modem data ports, and a voicemail system. The Regent Club, on the 17th floor, has a commodious lounge with great city views and provides complimentary breakfast and evening cocktails. Service throughout the hotel is friendly and enthusiastic. ⊠ *Jln. H.R. Rasuna Said, Jakarta 12920,* ☎ *021/252–3456,* ℻ *021/252–4480; U.S.* ☎ *800/545–4000. 378 rooms. 3 restaurants, bar, pool, sauna, 2 tennis courts, health club, business services, meeting rooms. AE, DC, MC, V.*

$$$ ▦ **Hotel Wisata International.** Ranked as a three-star hotel by the government, the ungainly Wisata is off Jakarta's main thoroughfare. Corridors are long and narrow, guest rooms compact but clean. Each room has a king-size bed; a television and safe take up most of the remaining space. Rooms on the executive floor are only marginally larger. Still, the price, the convenient restaurant off the lobby, and the central, safe location make the Wisata a reasonable choice. ⊠ *Jln. M.H. Thamrin, Jakarta 10230,* ☎ *021/230–0406,* ℻ *021/324597. 165 rooms. Bar, coffee shop, meeting rooms. AE, DC, MC, V.*

$$$ ▦ **President Hotel.** Like many other hotels in the Japanese Nikko Hotel group, the President has a spare, utilitarian atmosphere but is equipped with all the modern amenities. Guest rooms are simple, with blue-and-navy striped fabrics and plain wood furniture. The bathrooms are small. The President offers good Japanese food at its Ginza Benkay restaurant, Japanese and Indonesian at the Kahyangan, and Chinese at the Golden Pavilion. ⊠ *Jln. M.H. Thamrin 59, Jakarta 10350,* ☎ *021/230–1120,* ℻ *021/314–3631. 354 rooms. 3 restaurants, bar, coffee shop, meeting rooms. AE, DC, MC, V.*

$$ ★ ▦ **Jayakarta Tower.** This tourist-class hotel is within walking distance of Old Batavia. The marble lobby is accented with hand-blown-glass chandeliers and carved-wood panels. Each spacious room has a double or two twin beds, with Javanese patterned spreads, plus a table and two chairs and a vanity/desk. Executive rooms have minibars. In the house are the Dragon, a Chinese restaurant, and a coffee shop, which

serves Western and Indonesian specialties; ask to see the Thai menu at both. Next door is the Stardust Discotheque. The hotel is now affiliated with KLM's Golden Tulip hotels, and reservations may be made through the airline. ⊠ *Jln. Hayam Wuruk 126, Box 803, Jakarta 11001,* ☎ *021/629–4408,* FAX *021/626–5000. 435 rooms. 2 restaurants, coffee shop, room service, pool, health club, dance club, meeting rooms. AE, DC, MC, V.*

$ ⊞ **Interhouse.** Centrally located in Kebayoran—the expatriate neighborhood and shopping district—this hotel offers comfortable, though not large, air-conditioned rooms with pleasant, homey furnishings and usually pastel decor. ⊠ *Jln. Melawai Raya 18–20, Box 128/KBYB, Jakarta 10305,* ☎ *021/720–6694,* FAX *021/720–6988. 130 rooms. Restaurant. AE, V.*

$ ⊞ **Kebayoran Inn.** Just south of the center of Jakarta, this is a quiet, residential-type lodging. The clean, air-conditioned rooms are simply decorated, with an Indonesian batik or ikat here and there. ⊠ *Jln. Senayan 87, Jakarta 12180,* ☎ *021/716208,* FAX *021/560–3672. 61 rooms. Restaurant. AE, V.*

$ ⊞ **Marcopolo.** This basic, economical hotel caters to businesspeople
★ and tourists alike. The staff is helpful, and while the carpeted rooms are plain, they are clean, adequate, and fully air-conditioned. The restaurant serves good Chinese and European food. ⊠ *Jln. T. Cik Ditiro 19, Jakarta 10350,* ☎ *021/325409,* FAX *021/310–7138. 181 rooms. Restaurant, pool, nightclub. AE, V.*

Nightlife and the Arts

The Arts

For information on Jakarta art events, good sources to check are the *Indonesian Observer* and the City Visitor Information Center (☎ 021/354094).

DANCE AND THEATER

Beautiful Indonesia in Miniature Park (☞ Jakarta's Green Spaces *in* Exploring Jakarta, *above*) offers various regional dances on Sunday and holidays from 10 to 2. ⊠ *Off Jagorawi Toll Rd.,* ☎ *021/849525.*
Bharata Theater stages performances of traditional *wayang orang* (dance-dramas), depicting stories from the *Ramayana* or the *Mahabharata,* every night but Monday and Thursday from 8:15 to midnight. Sometimes the folk play *Ketoprak,* based on Javanese history, is also performed. ⊠ *Jln. Kalilio, no phone.*
Jakarta Hilton Cultural Program offers programs of regional dance weekly. Every afternoon from 4 to 6, the famous and very old Cakra Delam Raya Gamelan orchestral set is played. ⊠ *Indonesia Bazaar, Hilton Hotel, Jln. Jend. Sudirman,* ☎ *021/583051.*
Taman Ismail Marzuki arts center hosts plays, music and dance performances, art shows, and films. Monthly schedules of events are distributed to hotels. ⊠ *Jln. Cikini Raya 73,* ☎ *021/342605.*

PUPPET SHOWS

The **National Museum** hosts biweekly performances of leather shadow-puppet plays, depicting stories from the *Ramayana* or the *Mahabharata,* or wood-puppet plays, usually depicting Islamic legends. ⊠ *Jln. Merdeka Barat 12,* ☎ *021/360976.*

The **Puppet Museum** offers performances; check with the museum for dates and times. ⊠ *Jln. Pintu Besar Utara 27,* ☎ *021/679560.*

Nightlife

Jakarta Week, which lists forthcoming entertainment, can be found at your hotel. Where necessary, your concierge can make reservations.

Blue Ocean Restaurant and Nite Club has seating for 2,000. Shows vary from magicians to acrobats and singers. ⊠ *Jln. Hayam Wuruk 5,* ☎ *021/ 366650.* 🎫 *Rp 25,000.*

Captain's Bar offers a comfortable, relaxed evening of music by a small international or local group. ⊠ *Mandarin Oriental Hotel, Jln. M.H. Thamrin,* ☎ *021/321307.* 🕙 *Nightly 8 PM–1 AM.*

Ebony Videotheque is a lively, posh two-floor disco with a large screen for viewing old movies and a Saturday-night floor show. Waitresses are dressed in Nubian attire. ⊠ *Kuningan Plaza, Jln. Rasuna Said C11– 14,* ☎ *021/513700.* 🕙 *Sun.–Thurs. 9 PM–2 AM, Fri.–Sat. 9 PM–3 AM.*

Fire Discotheque incorporates the newest gadgetry: 12-color laser lighting and a huge video screen. Up the spiral staircase, in the balcony lounges, the decor and noise are more subdued. ⊠ *Plaza Indonesia L3– 003, Jln. M.H. Thamrin,* ☎ *021/330639.*

Green Pub (☞ Dining, *above*) is an expat pub where you can listen to music performed by local singers and bands. ⊠ *Jakarta Theater Bldg., Jln. M.H. Thamrin 9,* ☎ *021/359332.*

Hard Rock Cafe offers the same pleasures here as at its other venues. American fare is served, and in the evening, live music starts at about 9 PM. The stage has a huge, stained-glass window backdrop depicting Elvis Presley. ⊠ *Sarinah Bldg., 2nd floor, Jln. M.H. Thamrin 11,* ☎ *021/390–3565.* 🕙 *Daily 11 AM–1 AM.*

Jaya Pub, across from the Sarinah department store, is a long-established piano bar. It's popular with expatriates and Indonesians alike, in part because the owners are two former Indonesian movie stars, Rimi Melati and Frans Tumbuan. ⊠ *Jln. M.H. Thamrin 12,* ☎ *021/327508.* 🕙 *Daily noon–2 AM.*

The Stardust, housed in a former theater, claims to be Asia's largest disco. ⊠ *Jayakarta Tower Hotel, Jln. Hayam Wuruk 126,* ☎ *021/629– 4408.* 🕙 *Nightly 9 PM–2 AM.*

Tanamur, a Jakarta institution, has good jazz and soft rock and is usually the most crowded disco in town. What goes on as couples huddle against the dimly lit walls is better not believed; for those without a date, a bevy of hostesses are ready to dance and drink with guests. ⊠ *Jln. Tanah Abang Timur 14,* ☎ *021/353947.* 🕙 *Nightly 9 PM–2 AM.*

Outdoor Activities and Sports

Diving

Dive Indonesia (⊠ Hotel Borobudur Inter-Continental, Jln. Lapangan Banteng Selatan, ☎ 021/370108) specializes in underwater photography and arranges trips to Flores and Sulawesi. **Jakarta Dive School and Pro Shop** (⊠ Hilton Hotel, Bazaar Shop 32, Jln. Jend. Sudiman, ☎ 021/ 583051, ext. 9008) offers open-water lessons and equipment rental.

Golf

Jakarta has two well-maintained 18-hole golf courses open to the public, both extremely crowded on weekends. The **Ancol Golf Course** (⊠ Dunia Fantasi at Ancol, ☎ 021/682122) has pleasant sea views. **Kebayoran Golf Club** (⊠ Jln. Asia-Afrika, Pintu 9, ☎ 021/582508) is popular with expats.

Health and Fitness Centers

The **Clark Hatch Physical Fitness Center** has two facilities (⊠ Hotel Borobudur Inter-Continental, Jln. Lapangan Banteng Selatan, ☎ 021/ 370108; ⊠ Jakarta Hilton Hotel, Jln. Jend. Gatot Subroto, ☎ 021/ 583051) with up-to-date equipment, plus massage, heat treatment, sauna, and whirlpool. Other gyms are: **Executive Fitness Center** (⊠ Ground floor, South Tower, Kuningan Plaza, Jln. H.R. Rasuna Said, ☎ 021/578– 1706), **Medical Scheme** (⊠ Setia Budi Bldg. L., Jln. H.R. Rasuna Said,

Kuningan, ☎ 021/515367), and **Pondok Indah Health and Fitness Center** (✉ Jln. Metro Pondok Indah, ☎ 021/764906).

Jogging

The **Hash House Harriers/Harriettes,** an Australian jogging club, has a chapter in Jakarta (✉ HHH Box 46/KBY, Jakarta, ☎ 021/799–4758). Men run Monday at 5 PM, women Wednesday at 5 PM, and there's socializing in between. Write or call for meeting places and running routes.

Squash

Nonguests can play squash at three top hotels when the courts are not fully booked: **Hotel Borobudur Inter-Continental** (✉ Jln. Lapangan Banteng Selatan, ☎ 021/370108), **Jakarta Hilton International** (✉ Jln. Jend. Gatot Subroto, ☎ 021/583051), and **Mandarin Oriental** (✉ Jln. M.H. Thamrin, ☎ 021/321307).

Swimming

Most of Jakarta's tourist hotels have pools. **Dunia Fantasi at Ancol** (☞ Exploring Jakarta, *above*) has a four-pool complex with a wave pool.

Shopping

Department Stores

Pasaraya (✉ Jln. Iskandarsyah 1½, in Blok M, ☎ 021/7390170), Jakarta's largest department store, tempts you to visit its multistory complex to see Indonesia's latest in women's fashions and handicrafts by paying your taxi fare if you are staying at a five-star hotel. Check with your hotel's concierge for a coupon.

Plaza Indonesia (✉ Jln. M.H. Thamrin, ☎ 021/310–7272), under the Grand Hyatt and across the square from the Mandarin Oriental, is a central and convenient shopping center. Among its 250 stores are upscale boutiques, art and antiques galleries, bookshops, travel agents, Sogo's food store, and restaurants.

Plaza Senoyan (✉ Jln. Asia-Africa 8, ☎ 021/572–5555), the city's newest shopping complex, has upmarket boutiques with designer-label fashions.

Markets

Jalan Surabaya Antiques Stalls (✉ Pasar Barang Antik Jalan Surabaya, in Menteng residential area), Jakarta's daily (9–6) "flea market," has mundane goods at either end, but in the middle you might find delftware, Chinese porcelain, old coins, old and not-so-old bronzes, and more. You *must* bargain.

Pasar Melawai (✉ Jln. Melawai, in Blok M) is a series of buildings and stalls with everything from clothing to toys, cosmetics, and fresh foods. English is spoken; hours are daily 9–6.

Specialty Stores

ANTIQUES

For serious antiques shopping, try the shops along these streets: Jalan Paletehan I (Kebayoran Baru), Jalan Maja Pahit and Jalan Gajah Mada (Gambir/Kota), Jalan Kebon Sirih Timur and Jalan H.A. Salim (Mentang), and Jalan Ciputat Raya (Old Bogor Rd.).

Cony Art Antiques (✉ Jln. Malawai Raya 180E, ☎ 021/716554), in the Kebayoran district, is worth a visit for antique Chinese porcelain.
Madjapahit Art and Curio (✉ Jln. Melawai III/4, ☎ 021/715878), behind Sarinah Jaya Department Store, is a reputable store.
NV Garuda Arts, Antiques (✉ Jln. Maja Pahit 12, Kota, ☎ 021/342712) is a reliable shop.

HANDICRAFTS

Sarinah (⊠ Jln. M.H. Thamrin 11, Menteng, ☎ 021/327425) is a department store whose third floor is devoted entirely to handicrafts, which you can also find in abundance at its larger sister store, Pasaraya (☞ *above*).

TEXTILES

Batik Berdikari (⊠ Jln. Masjid in Palmerah, southwest of Merdeka Sq., ☎ 021/5482814), a shop with a factory on the premises, presents various types of Indonesian batik and displays the ways batik is made, either hand-drawn or printed.

Batik Danar Hadi (⊠ Jln. Raden Saleh 1A, ☎ 021/342748) carries a large selection of batik.

Batik Mira (⊠ Jln. MAR. Raya 22, ☎ 021/761138) has expensive but excellent-quality batik. Its tailors will do custom work, and customers can ask to see the factory at the rear of the store.

Batik Semar (⊠ Jln. Tornang Raya 54, ☎ 021/567–3514) has top-quality batik with many unusual designs.

Bin House (⊠ Jln. Panarukan 33, ☎ 021/335941) carries Indonesian handwoven silks and cottons, including ikat, plus antique textiles and objets d'art.

Plaza Indonesia (☞ *above*) shopping complex has chic, fashionable batiks for sale, especially on the first floor.

PT Ramacraft (⊠ Jln. Panarukan 25, ☎ 021/333122) is the name of both the label and company run by Iwan Tirta, a famous designer of batik fabrics and clothing for men and women.

Jakarta A to Z

Arriving and Departing

BY BUS

All three bus terminals are off Merdeka Square; buy tickets at the terminals or at travel agencies. **Pulo Gadang** (⊠ Jln. Perintis Kemerdekaan, ☎ 021/489–3742) serves Semarang, Yogyakarta, Solo, Surabaya, Malang, and Denpensar. Use **Cililitan** (⊠ Jln. Raya Bogor, ☎ 021/809–3554) for Bogor, Sukabumi, Bandung, and Banjar. **Kalideres** (⊠ Jln. Daan Mogot) is the depot for Merak, Labuhan, and major cities in Sumatra.

BY PLANE

Jakarta's airport, **Soekarno Hatta,** is a modern showpiece, with glass-walled walkways and landscaped gardens. While most of the area is not air-conditioned, it's breezy and smartly clean. There is a small duty-free shopping area. Terminal One handles international flights, and Terminal Two serves all Garuda Indonesia Airways flights (both international and domestic) and all other domestic airlines. Between the two terminals, a **Visitor Information Center** (☎ 021/550–7088) is open 8 AM–10 PM, closed Sunday and when they feel like it. In both terminals there are **Indotel desks** (☎ 021/550–7179) where hotel reservations may be made, often at discounted rates.

From Soekarno Hatta Airport to Downtown: The airport is 35 km (20 mi) northwest of Jakarta. A toll expressway takes you three-quarters of the way to the city quickly, but the rest is slow going. To be safe, allow a good hour for the trip on weekdays.

Taxis *from* the airport add a surcharge of Rp 2,300 and the road toll (Rp 4,000) to the fare on the meter. The surcharge does not apply going *to* the airport. Blue Bird Taxi (☎ 021/325607) offers a 25% discount on the toll charge either way. The average fare to a downtown hotel is Rp 20,000. However, if it is raining and there are likely to be traffic jams, you will need to negotiate a fare—Rp.40,000 should do it.

On request, some hotels, such as the Mandarin Oriental, will arrange to have a chauffeur-driven car waiting for you. The cost is Rp 55,000.

Air-conditioned buses, with DAMRI in big letters on the side, operate every 20 minutes between the airport and six points in the city, including the Gambir Railway Station, Rawamangun Bus Terminal, Blok M, and Pasar Minggu Bus Terminal. The cost is Rp 3,000.

(☞ Indonesia A to Z, *below,* for information on international arrivals and departures and on domestic carriers and flights.)

BY TRAIN

Use the **Tanah Abang Railway Station** (✉ Jln. KH Wahid Hasyim, south-west of Merdeka Sq., ☎ 021/340048) for trains to Sumatra. Trains for destinations other than Sumatra—to Bogor and Bandung or to the east Java cities of Semarang, Yogyakarta, Solo, Surabaya, Madiun, and Malang—start from one of two other stations: the **Kota Railway Station** (✉ Jln. Stasiun Kota, south of Fatahillah Square, ☎ 021/678515 or 021/679194) or the **Gambir Railway Station** (✉ Jln. Merdeka Timur, on the east side of Merdeka Sq., ☎ 021/342777 or 021/348612). Be sure you have the correct station: The Bima train for Yogyakarta, for example, departs from Kota, but the Sinja Maya departs from Gambir.

Tickets may be purchased at the station at least an hour before departure for long distance trains, or from travel agencies, including: **Carnation** (✉ Jln. Menteng Raya 24, ☎ 021/384–4027 or 021/386-5728) and **P.T. Bhayangkara** (✉ Jln. Kebon Sirih 23, ☎ 021/327387).

Getting Around

BY BUS

Non-air-conditioned public buses charge a flat Rp 350; the (green) air-conditioned buses charge Rp 600. All are packed during rush hours, and pickpockets abound. The routes can be labyrinthine, but you can always give one a try and get off when the bus veers from your desired direction. For information, contact these companies: **Hiba Utama** (☎ 021/413626 or 021/410381), **P.P.D.** (☎ 021/881131 or 021/411357), or **Mayasari Bhakti** (☎ 021/809–0378 or 021/489–2785).

BY CAR

Though self-drive rental is available, it is not advised. Traffic congestion is horrendous and parking is very difficult. However, if you rent a car, be aware that traffic police supplement their income by stopping you, even for infractions that you never knew you made. The police will suggest Rp 70,000 to forget the matter; you are expected to negotiate, and Rp 30,000 should make you both happy.

Cars may be rented from: **Avis** (✉ Jln. Doponegoro 25, ☎ 021/331974), **Hertz** (✉ Jln. Tenku, C.K. Ditoro 11E, ☎ 021/332610), or **National** (✉ Hotel Kartika Plaza, Jln. M.H. Thamrin 10, ☎ 021/333423).

BY LIMOUSINE

Air-conditioned, chauffeur-driven cars can be hired for a minimum of two hours, at hourly rates of Rp 11,375 for a small Corona or Rp 21,000 for a Mercedes. Daily charters cost Rp 105,000 and Rp 210,000, respectively. Try Blue Bird Taxi (☞ *below*) or Hertz (☞ *above*).

BY TAXI

A cheap and efficient way of getting around, Jakarta's metered taxis charge Rp 900 (47¢) for the first km and Rp 450 (23¢) for each subsequent 100 m. Taxis may be flagged on the streets, and most hotels have taxi stands. Be sure that the meter is down when you set off, and avoid taxis with broken meters or none at all, or you will be seriously overcharged. For a radio-dispatched taxi, call **Blue Bird Taxi** (☎ 021/798–9000 or 798-9111).

Contacts and Resources

DOCTORS AND DENTISTS

A group-practice clinic, **Bina Medica** (✉ Jln. Maluku 8–10, ☎ 021/344893) provides 24-hour service, ambulance, and English-speaking doctors. **Doctors-on-Call** (☎ 021/683444, 021/681405, or 021/514444) has English-speaking doctors who make house calls. Payment in cash is required. English-speaking staff are available at the 24-hour clinic and pharmacy **SOS Medika Vayasan** (✉ Jln. Prapanca Raya 32–34, ☎ 021/771575 or 021/733094).

Dental services are provided at the **Metropolitan Medical Center** (✉ Wisata Office Tower, 1st floor, Jln. M.H. Thamrin, ☎ 021/320408). **SOS Medika Clinic Service** (✉ Jln. Prapanca Raya 32–34, Kebayoran Baru, ☎ 021/733094) provides dental care.

EMBASSIES AND CONSULATES

Australia (✉ Jln. H.R. Rasuna Said Kav. C15–16, ☎ 021/522–7111). **Canada** (✉ Jln. Jend. Sudirman Kav. 29, 5th floor, Wisma Metropolitan 1, ☎ 021/510709). **United Kingdom** (✉ Jln. M.H. Thamrin 75, ☎ 021/330904). **United States** (✉ Jln. Medan Merdeka Selatan 5, ☎ 021/3442211, FAX 021/386–2259)

EMERGENCIES

Ambulance, ☎ 119. **Police,** ☎ 110. **Traffic accidents,** ☎ 118. For emergency transport, **Blue Bird Taxi** (☎ 021/325607) may be more reliable than public services. Consult your hotel concierge, if possible, for advice in English.

ENGLISH-LANGUAGE BOOKSTORES

Major hotel shops carry magazines, newspapers, paperbacks, and travel guides in English. For a wide book selection, try **PT Indira** (✉ Jln. Melawi V/16, Blok M, ☎ 021/770584). **Family Book Shop** (✉ Kemang Club Villas, Jln. Kelurahan Bangka, ☎ 021/799–5525) has quite a few titles. The largest selection is at the **Times Bookshop** (✉ Jln. M.H. Thamrin 28–30, ☎ 021/570–6581), on the lower floor of Plaza Indonesia.

GUIDED TOURS

Gray Line (✉ Jln. Hayam Wunuk 3–P, ☎ 021/639–0008) covers most of Jakarta and surrounding attractions. Tourists who show up at **Jakarta City Touist Center** (✉ Lapangan Binteng, Bantung Square, no phone), which opens 8 AM, may join any of the tours operating that day, usually at a discounted rate.

Hotel tour desks will book the following tours or customize outings with a chauffeured car: **City Tour** (six hours) covers the National Monument, Pancasila Monument, Beautiful Indonesia in Miniature Park, and Museum Indonesia; **Indocultural Tour** (five hours) visits the Central Museum, Old Batavia, the Jakarta Museum, and a batik factory; **Beautiful Indonesia Tour** (three to four hours) takes you by air-conditioned bus through the Beautiful Indonesia in Miniature Park (☞ *above*), where the architecture and customs of different regions are displayed; **Jakarta by Night** (five hours) includes dinner, a dance performance, and a visit to a nightclub.

Tours beyond Jakarta include the following: a nine-hour trip to Pelabuhanratu, a former fishing village that is now a resort; an eight-hour tour to the safari park at Bogor and the Botanical Gardens, 48 km (30 mi) south of Jakarta at a cool 600 feet above sea level, and to

Puncak Mountain Resort; and a two-day tour into the highlands to visit Bandung and its volcano, with stops at Bogor and Puncak.

LATE-NIGHT PHARMACIES

SOS Medika Vayasan (⊠ Jln. Prapanca Raya 32–34, ☎ 021/771575 or 021/733094) is open 24 hours. **Melawai Apotheek** (⊠ Jln. Melawai Raya 191, ☎ 021/716109) has a well-stocked supply of American medicines.

TRAVEL AGENCIES

Travel agencies arrange transportation, conduct guided tours, and can often secure hotel reservations more cheaply than you could yourself. **Natourin** (⊠ 18 Buncit Raya, Jakarta 12790, ☎ 021/799–7886) has extensive facilities and contacts throughout Indonesia. Large government-owned travel agencies with branch offices at most Indonesian tourist destinations include the following: **Nitour** (⊠ Duta Merlin, Jln. Gajah Mada 3–5, ☎ 021/346346); **Satriavi** (⊠ Jln. Prapatan 32, ☎ 021/380–3944); and **Pacto Ltd. Tours and Travel** (⊠ Jln. Surabaya 8, ☎ 021/332634), the Indonedian representative of American Express.

VISITOR INFORMATION

The comprehensive *Falk City Map of Jakarta* is available at bookstores for Rp 9,200. The *Jakarta Program,* available at most hotel newsstands for Rp 4,000, is a monthly magazine listing attractions and events.

The **City Visitor Information Center** has brochures and maps locating city sights and hotels. You can also get information here on bus and train schedules to other Java destinations. ⊠ *Jakarta Theatre Bldg., Jln. M.H. Thamrin 9, ☎ 021/354094; ☉ Mon.–Thurs. 8–3, Fri. 8–11:30 AM, Sat. 8–2.*

The **Indonesian tourist office** is charged with dispensing information on destinations across the archipelago, but it's difficult to find and the assistance given is minimal. ⊠ *Jln. K.H. Abdurrohim 1, at Dimas Pariwisata, Kuningan Barat, Jakarta 12710, ☎ 021/525–1316, FAX 021/520–2256.*

SIDE TRIPS FROM JAKARTA

The Thousand Islands

16–32 km (10–20 mi) offshore; an hour or two by boat.

North of Jakarta in the Java Sea are the little Pulau Seribu, or Thousand Islands (*pulau* means island)—really a misnomer, because there are only 250 of them. Their white-sand beaches, lined with coconut palms, offer a retreat from the heat and bustle of the capital.

For a day trip, you can hop over to **Pulau Seribu** by motorboat from Marina Jaya Ancol (☎ 021/681512), or take a hovercraft (the port is at Jln. Donggala 26A, Tanjun Priok, ☎ 021/325608).

Lodging

Several islands have rustic getaways; accommodations are available on Pulau Putri (☎ 021/828–1093), Pulau Matahari (☎ 021/380–0521), Pulau Bidadari (☎ 021/680–048), and Pulau Laki (☎ 021/314–4885). Contact each island's Jakarta office (listed above) to make reservations and to arrange transport to the island. Room rates are usually quoted as all-inclusive packages that include food and transport.

$$$ ⚐ **Kotok Island Resort.** On 42 unspoiled acres of coconut groves and tropical foliage, this resort two hours from Jakarta by boat owns all the island except the eastern tip, which belongs to a private Japanese club. The resort has 22 bungalows with bamboo walls and basic bamboo furniture, plus a tiled shower bathroom. Eight units are air-conditioned, but thanks to the sea breezes, the rest are comfortable with just an overhead fan. This is a back-to-nature environment, and the accommodations are rustic, with primitive plumbing. The dining room—an open-air pavilion over the water—serves well-prepared Indonesian specialties, especially grilled fresh fish. Licensed instructors give scuba-diving courses and there's good snorkeling. The resort provides a launch service—the run takes 90 minutes– from Jakarta. ⊠ *Reservation office: Duta Merlin Shopping Arcade, 3rd floor, Jln. Gajah Mada 3–5, Jakarta,* ☏ *021/634–2948,* FAX *021/633–6120. 22 rooms. Restaurant, bar, dive shop. No credit cards, unless you book through a travel agent.*

Bogor

60 km (36 mi) south of Jakarta.

The sprawling, smoky city of Bogor hides several attractions. Drop in at Jalan Pancasan 17 to see a **gong foundry,** one of the few remaining on Java, where instruments of the gamelan orchestra are still made using traditional methods.

Behind the white-porticoed Presidential Palace are **Botanical Gardens** (Kebun Raya Bogor) founded in 1817 by the first English governor-general of Indonesia, maintained by the Dutch, and adopted by Sukarno. The 275-acre garden has 15,000 species of plants, hundreds of trees, an herbarium, cactus gardens, and ponds with enormous water lilies. The monument in the park is of Olivia Raffles, first wife of Sir Stanford Raffles, who died here at the Bogor Palace. Guides are available at Rp 6,000 an hour. ⊞ *Admission.* ⊙ *Daily 9–5.*

En Route The road from Bogor winds through tea plantations and rain forests, past waterfalls and lakes. This is the Puncak region, where on clear days you'll get views of the Gede, Pangrango, and Salak mountains. Just over the summit of Puncak Pass is **Puncak Pass Hotel,** a famous stop for travelers that serves up excellent afternoon teas and vistas. At the **Safari Park,** 75 km (46 mi) from Jakarta on the road to Puncak, you can fondle lion cubs, ride elephants, and watch other animals roam; the park is open daily 9–5.

Bandung

187 km (120 mi) southeast of Jakarta.

At the turn of the century the Dutch came here to escape the heat of Jakarta. Situated on a plateau at 2,500 feet and shadowed by majestic volcanoes, Bandung was transfomed into an oasis of Dutch culture as European architects put up Art Deco buildings and café society copied fashions from Paris and Amsterdam. Bandung became the cultural and intellectual heart of Indonesia, and there was even speculation that the capital might be transferred to this mountain-fresh hill town.

The city's status waned after World War II: With independence, the political focus shifted to the tightly centralized government in Jakarta. The Sudanese, the ethnic group that dominates this region, reasserted their own complex language, dances, and customs, and now Bandung is an appealing mix of European and Asian cultures. With overcrowding burdening Jakarta's infrastructure, Bandung is starting to attract high-tech businesses with its intellectual environment and its universities, which include the prestigious Institut Teknologi Bandung. Although the brochures exaggerate the attractions of the city, it does have a pleasant climate—warm days and cold nights—and it's small enough to cover on foot.

In the days when Bandung called itself the "Parijs van Java," **Jalan Braga** was the "Rue St. Honoré." There aren't many remnants of these glory days, but the classic Art Deco Savoy Homann Hotel (☞ Lodging, *below*) has been restored at great pains by its current owners. Near the Savoy hotel on Jalan Asia-Africa is the **Freedom Building** (Gedung Merdeka), where in 1955 Chou En-lai, Ho Chi Minh, Nehru, Nassar, and U Nu attended the famous Asia-Africa Conference of nonaligned nations.

Walking north back past the Savoy Homann, you'll reach the *alun-alun* (town square), the heart of Bandung; it's a little drab and derelict now, but with the current rejuvenation it may soon regain its rightful glory. Continue north along Jalan Braga for 2 km (1¼ mi), passing rather forlorn-looking colonial buildings. At the **Geological Museum** (⌗ Jln. Diponegoro), open daily 9–5, you'll find replicas of the fossils of Java Man (*Australopithecus*). North of the Geological Museum is the **Institut Teknologi Bandung,** designed by Maclaine Pont, a proponent of the Indo-European integrated style, exemplified here by the *Minangkabau* (Sumatran) upturned roofs; beyond the institute are the Dago Tea House and a nearby waterfall with a splendid panorama of the city.

Lodging

$$ ⌗ **Savoy Homann.** It's neither the priciest nor the most up-to-date in
★ town (for that, try the Grand Hotel Preager), but the Savoy Homann is loaded with character. Built in the 1880s, it acquired its Art Deco design in 1930. In the evening, guests gather at the bar in the central courtyard to listen to the band. The superior rooms are the size of small suites, usually with a sitting area, and look onto either the street (windows are double-glazed) or the courtyard. The English-speaking staff is very friendly. ⌗ *Jln. Asia-Afrika 112, Bandung 40261,* ☎ *022/250–0303,* FAX *022/250–0301. 153 rooms. Restaurant, bar, coffee shop. AE, DC, MC, V.*

$$ ⌗ **Sheraton Inn.** Though it's in a residential neighborhood 15 minutes by taxi from downtown, many travelers—especially businesspeople—prefer the modern facilities, the well-trained staff, and the quiet of this hotel. The best of the rooms overlook the circular courtyard and its pool. Dining is a relaxed affair, either on the circular terrace facing the pool or inside with air-conditioning. The Sheraton-style architecture and ambience are more American than Indonesian. ⌗ *Jln. Ir. H. Juanda 390, Box 6530, Bandung 40065,* ☎ *022/210303,* FAX *022/210301; U.S.,* ☎ *800/325–3535. 111 rooms. Restaurant, 2 tennis courts, business services. AE, DC, MC, V.*

Outdoor Activities and Sports

In many nearby villages, Sunday morning is the time for the weekly *adu domba* (ram fights). Facing off two at a time, the prize rams bang, crash, and lock horns until one contestant decides that enough is enough and scampers off. It's as much a social event as a serious sport (though the wagerers take it seriously) and shouldn't be missed if you're around on the weekend.

Bandung A to Z

ARRIVING AND DEPARTING

Though there are flights from Jakarta, the train trip—approximately three hours from Gambir Station, with nine departures daily—is more scenic: The train travels through flat rice lands before climbing through the mountains along curving track and over tressled bridges built by the Dutch in 1884. The road offers equally spectacular views, and many minibuses make the trip each day—though fretful passengers may spend more time watching the next curve than the scenery.

From Bandung, travelers can continue on to Yogyakarta by air or rail (eight hours). The night train has second-class compartments with reclining seats, air-conditioning, and blankets. The day train lacks these amenities, and sometimes it lacks second-class carriages. The optimal way to get from Bandung to Yogyakarta is to hire a car with a driver, which costs approximately U.S.$100 and may be arranged through your hotel.

Lembang

16 km (10 mi) north of Bandung.

The hills surrounding Bandung are known as Parahyangan (Abode of the Gods) and are sacred to the Sudanese. The first stop on a tour of this area is usually the hill town of Lembang, which offers a comfortable night's stay. **Tangkuban Perahu Nature Reserve,** 10 km (6 mi) beyond Lembang, features the only active volcano in Indonesia whose rim is accessible by car: From the entrance, the narrow road winds 4 km (2½ mi) up to the crater's edge. The souvenir stands and hawkers are a nuisance, but the crater, boiling and seething with sulfurous steam, is dramatic. Several kilometers away are the **Crater Hot Springs,** with public baths that visitors may use to soothe nervous tension and cure skin problems.

Lodging

¢ ⊞ **Lembang Grand Hotel.** Built in 1926 and used by the Dutch as a hill resort, the Grand still stands and offers simple accommodation. ⊠ *Jln. Raya Lembang 228,* ☎ *022/82393. 26 rooms. Pool, 2 tennis courts. MC, V.*

Krakatau Volcano

2 to 4 hours by boat from Carita Beach, which is 150 km (95 mi) west of Jakarta.

You'll need to make an overnight trip to see the famous Krakatau (Krakatoa) volcano, in the Sunda Strait between Sumatra and Java. This volcano, Anak Krakatau, is actually the child of Krakatau, the volcano that erupted in 1883, killing 36,000 people and creating marvelous sunsets around the world for the next two years. Anak Krakatau emerged from the sea between three other islands by early 1928 or 45 years after its father's eruption. The popular place to overnight is **Carita Beach,** a quiet resort that's pleasant in its own right.

Lodging

$$ ⊞ **Carita Krakatau Beach Hotel.** There are two advantages to this hotel: Air-conditioned buses leave daily from the hotel's reservation office in Jakarta (⊠ Hotel Wisata International, Jln. M.H. Thamrin, ground-floor arcade, ☎ 021/320252), and the hotel arranges trips (including the two-hour sea crossing) to the volcano. The rooms are modest, but most of the time guests are out on the beach or taking refreshment at the terrace restaurant. ⊠ *Carita Beach,* ☎ *0254/21043; Jakarta,* ☎ *021/314–0252. 45 rooms. Restaurant, waterskiing. MC, V.*

Krakatau Volcano A to Z

ARRIVING AND DEPARTING

You can travel from Jakarta to Carita Beach by public bus in about three hours, but the minivans of **P.J. Krakatau** (⊠ Unjung Kulon Tours, Hotel Wisata International, ☎ 021/314–0252) are a lot more comfortable.

Boats leave Carita Beach around 8 AM for the volcano; the trip takes 2½ hours on speedboats, four hours on slower boats. You'll have two hours on Anok Krakatoa. Count on spending Rp 100,000 for the speedboats. Don't venture out if the seas are up—the waters get rough, and some boats never return.

YOGYAKARTA

618 km (371 mi) east of Jakarta.

Every Indonesian has a soft spot for Yogyakarta, or Yogya (pronounced *joe-jakarta* or *joeg-ja*), a city of some 300,000 on a fertile plain in the shadow of three volcanoes. In many respects, it is the heart of Indonesia. Students from Yogya's Gajah Mada University account for some 20% of the city's population, and dance and choreography schools, wayang troupes, and poetry workshops make it an artist's mecca. Every evening, classical drama and dance performances are staged somewhere in the city. Leading Indonesian painters and sculptors display their work in numerous galleries, and crafts shopping is a major activity. The batik here and in Solo (☞ Central Java, *below*) is said to be superior even to Bali's.

Exploring Yogyakarta

Yogya sprawls. Unless you stay at the Garuda or one of the less expensive city hotels, chances are you will be a few miles from Jalan Malioboro, the main thoroughfare.

Numbers in the margin correspond to points of interest on the Yogyakarta map.

Sights to See

❺ Affandi Museum. Out toward the airport, about 8 km (5 mi) southeast of Yogya, is the home and studio of Indonesia's best-known painter, Affandi (1907–90). A permanent collection of his works, along with paintings by young artists, is exhibited in an oval, domed extension to the traditional paddy-field house. ⊠ *Jln. Laksda, Adisucipto 67, no phone.* ☎ *Free.* ⊙ *Daily 9–3.*

❹ Diponegoro Monument. This is the reconstructed residence of Prince Diponegoro, who rebelled against the Dutch and led a bloody guerrilla battle in the Java War (1825–30). The house is now a museum, displaying the prince's krises (daggers), lances, and other revered possessions. ⊠ *Tegalrejo (4 km [2½ mi] west of Yogyakarta),* ☎ *0274/563068.* ☎ *Donation.* ⊙ *Open by appointment only.*

Jalan Malioboro. This is where the action is, day and night. It is the main shopping street, not only for established shops but also for sidewalk vendors. These set up cardboard stands selling handicrafts until about nine in the evening, then convert to food stalls serving Yogya's specialties: *nasi gudeg* (rice with jackfruit in coconut milk) and *ayam goreng* (marinated fried chicken). Malioboro is a fascinating street to stroll, and if you arrive by 8 PM, you can catch both the shops and the food. But even with intensive bargaining, prices are high. You can find better deals at the new indoor market, **Pasar Beringharjo,** at the top of the street; it's worth visiting just to see the stacked merchandise—everything from jeans to poultry.

❶ Kraton. At the southern end of Malioboro stands the Kraton, or sultan's palace. The large, grassy square in front of it—a walled city within the city—is the **alun-alun,** where the townspeople formerly gathered to trade, gossip, and hear the latest palace news. The Yogya Kraton has special significance to Indonesians as the bastion against Dutch colonialism. During the War of Independence (1945–49), Yogya's Sultan Hamengku Buwono allowed the Indonesian freedom

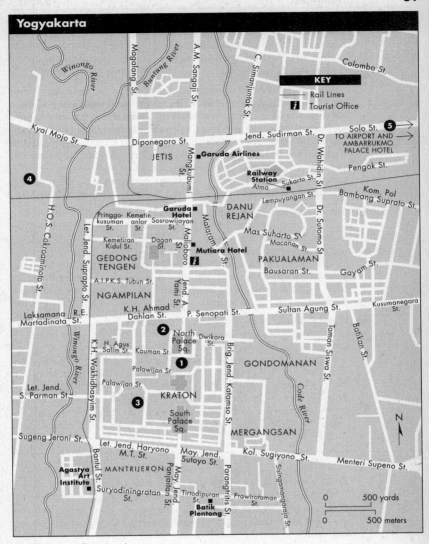

Yogyakarta

KEY
— Rail Lines
i Tourist Office

Affandi Museum **5**

Diponegoro
Monument, **4**

Kraton, **1**

Sono Budoyo
Museum, **2**

Water Palace, **3**

fighters—including guerrilla commander Suharto, now the nation's president—to use the Kraton as a military base. Built in 1756, it is a vast complex of pavilions and buildings, part of which—strictly off-limits to the public—is home to the present sultan. The complex is protected by 400 guards (in blue shirts) and 1,000 servants (in red shirts).

At the center of the green-trimmed white palace is the **Golden Pavilion,** (Bengsal Kengono) an open hall with carved teak columns and a black-and-gold interior, where weddings, cremations, and coronations are held. The complex includes a gallery exhibiting a collection of gamelan instruments. Try to time your visit to catch the Sunday classical dance rehearsal (10:30 and noon, except during Ramadan). In another pavilion is a collection of sedan chairs. The last one was used in 1877; now a Rolls-Royce transports the sultan on ceremonial occasions. *No phone.* ✉ *Admission.* ☉ *Sun.–Thurs. 8:30–1, Fri.–Sat. 8:30–11:30.*

➋ Sono Budoyo Museum. Of Yogya's several museums, the most interesting and well-maintained is the Sono Budoyo Museum, on the square in front of the Kraton. Inside this traditional Javanese-style building is a collection of crafts and batiks from Java and Bali. Its archaeological treasures include a small gold Buddha, and the display of wayang golek, the wood puppets used in Muslim theater, is charming. ☏ *0274/ 562775.* ✉ *Admission.* ☉ *Tues.–Thurs. 8–1, Fri. and Sun. 8–11, Sat. 8–noon.*

➌ Water Palace (Taman Sari). Behind the Kraton is a recreational water palace constructed by the same sultan who built the main palace. A large artificial lake, sunken bathing pools, underground passageways, and towers where gamelan orchestras serenaded the royal party were all part of this noble retreat. It was abandoned in the 18th century and fell into ruin; the restored sections give a sense of what the privileged enjoyed. Visit the ornate bathing pools used by the princesses, the underground mosque, and the tower from which the sultan watched his concubines lounge by the water. *No phone.* ✉ *Admission.* ☉ *Sun.–Thurs. 8–1, Fri. 8–11.*

Dining

For Western food, you will probably wish to dine at one of the major hotels. Most of the international-style hotels also offer a performance of segments from the *Ramayana,* charging an extra fee to see this show. For Indonesian fare, try the local restaurants. They are inexpensive and good.

$$$ ✕ **Floating Restaurant.** This restaurant looks Moroccan, with a pavilion overlooking gardens, and low tables—with ikat-covered floor cushions—as well as Western-style tables. At the center is a copious buffet of Indonesian specialties, which may include *gudeg* (chicken with jackfruit), the most famous dish of central Java, and *pepes ikan* (marinated fish baked with coconut). An Indonesian singer and instrumentalist provide background music. The place also has a barbecue buffet with Western dishes such as pasta carbonara, as well as Indonesian specialties, accompanied by native dance-drama. ✉ *Ambarrukmo Palace, Jln. Laksda Adisucipto,* ☏ *0274/566488. Reservations essential. AE, DC, MC, V.*

$$ ✕ **Pesta Perak.** Smartly decorated with wrought-iron furniture and a
★ sultan-costumed maître d', Pesta Perak has excellent Javanese cuisine. Its rijsttafel includes satays, gudeg, and fish wrapped in banana leaves. An à la carte menu is also offered, but customers rarely choose this. A gamelan trio plays traditional music. Use a *becak*, a three-wheel pedicab, to get there and have it wait for you; the fare from Jalan Malioboro,

including waiting time, is less than Rp 4,000. ⊠ *Jln. Tentura Rakyat Mataran 8,* ☎ *0274/586255. MC, V.*

$$ ✗ **Pringsewu Garden Restaurant.** For relaxed alfresco dining at tables tucked between shrubs and trees, this restaurant is a delight. It offers some of the best fare in the region, served by a friendly staff attired in colorful batiks. The cooking is from West Sumatra. Try the *ayam goreng mantega* (fried chicken with a butter sauce) or the *ikan mas baket* (grilled golden fish in ginger sauce). ⊠ *Jln. Magelang Km 6,* ☎ *0274/564993. AE, DC, MC, V.*

$$ ✗ **Sintawang.** Though the tables are Formica, the restaurant is clean and offers a wide range of outstanding seafood, either cooked Javanese-style or grilled for Western palates. Try the *udang bakar* (marinated and grilled prawns), *pais udang* (prawns spiced and grilled in a banana leaf), or *ikan asam manis* (fish in a sweet-and-sour sauce). ⊠ *Jln. Magelang 9,* ☎ *0274/512901. Reservations not accepted. AE, DC.*

$ ✗ **Legian Garden Restaurant.** Choose a table next to the open windows at the edge of its terrace and watch fellow tourists *jalan jalan* (amble around) on the street below. Since the food is pretty average (primarily Western, with a few Indonesian alternatives), you may just want to stop by for a beer. ⊠ *Jln. Perwakilan 9 (off Jln. Malioboro), 1st floor,* ☎ *0274/564644. Reservations not accepted. No credit cards.*

$ ✗ **Ny Suharti.** It's worth the Rp 3,500 cab ride here from Malioboro
★ for the best fried chicken in Java, perhaps in all of Indonesia. Forget charm and atmosphere and the other items on the menu: You are here for a bird—boiled, marinated in spices, then cooked up crisp. Order one for two people, with rice on the side, and enjoy it outside on the veranda. If you pay by credit card, a 3% surcharge will be added to your bill. ⊠ *Jln. Laksda Adisucipto, Km 7,* ☎ *0274/515522. Reservations not accepted. MC, V.*

Lodging

Although there are some full-service hotels in Yogyakarta that meet international standards, many hotels and guest houses do not have such facilities as private bath and air-conditioning. The ones listed below do. Should you decide to seek budget accommodation, a good selection of small hotels is to be found off Jalan Malioboro, across from the Garuda and two blocks from the railway station. So many hotels have opened of late (with more to come) that good discounts—as much as 50%—are available to travelers who ask.

$$$ ⊞ **Ambarrukmo Palace.** Yogyakarta's premier tourist hotel is built on the grounds of a former royal country retreat. Guest rooms are large, decorated with light Indonesian-pattern fabrics and mahogany furniture, and equipped with all the amenities, including color TV and minibars. The best rooms have balconies overlooking the gardens. Some are a little worn, so don't be reluctant to ask for another. This is an active hotel, popular with American tour groups. Every evening offers a different event, usually dances from the *Ramayana.* ⊠ *Jln. Laksda Adisucipto, Yogyakarta 55281,* ☎ *0274/566488,* FAX *0274/ 563283. 266 rooms. 3 restaurants, bar, room service, pool, travel services. AE, DC, MC, V.*

$$$ ⊞ **Garuda.** The draw for this imposing old hotel is a central location. The standard guest rooms are plainly furnished but do have all the latest conveniences, including color TV with VCR and minibar. The newer rooms are slightly better than the older ones (which have a faint odor), but they've all suffered from the steady stream of tour groups leaving black scrape marks on the walls and stains on the carpets. The restaurant offers Indonesian and Western food and dinner performances from the *Ramayana.* ⊠ *Jln. Malioboro 60, Yogyakarta 55271,*

☎ 0274/566353, FAX 0274/563074. *235 rooms. 2 restaurants, coffee shop, pool, tennis court, exercise room, business services, travel services. AE, DC, MC, V.*

$$ 🏨 **Hotel Santika.** This relatively characterless 1992 hotel—a 10-minute walk from the bustle of Jalan Malioboro—is built around a courtyard with pool. The carpeted guest rooms are furnished in deep rose fabrics and are uniform but clean and efficient; the choice ones face the courtyard, as those on the street can be noisy. (Rooms are just under $100 for a double, but you can often negotiate discounts.) The spacious lobby and lounge area is designed to receive tour groups; the coffee shop is a convenient place to wait for traveling companions. ✉ *Jln. Jend. Sundiman 19, Yogyakarta 55233,* ☎ 0274/563036, FAX 0274/ 562047. *148 rooms. Restaurant, coffee shop, pool, health club, meeting rooms, travel services. AE, DC, MC, V.*

$$ 🏨 **Radisson Yogya Plaza.** New in 1996, there is a pleasing freshness to this hotel, which calls itself a resort within a city. Guest rooms, most with king-size beds, are modern and functional; the best for light and quiet are those overlooking the courtyard, where you'll find the pool, with a café and terrace off to the side. In the evenings, a local band plays—sometimes a string quartet, sometimes a gamelan orchestra— and later a performance of the *Ramayana* is given. Off the large atrium lobby, which contains a comfortable sitting area, the dining room serves Western and Indonesian fare and excellent buffet breakfasts. The downside to this property is that it's more than a 30-minute walk to downtown Yogyakarta; a shuttle bus does run back and forth, but distance precludes a spontaneous walk. ✉ *Jln. Gejayan, Complex Columbo, Yogyakarta 55821,* ☎ 0274/584222, FAX 0274/584200. *120 rooms. 2 restaurants, bar, pool, massage, 2 tennis courts, health club, business services, meeting rooms. AE, DC, MC, V.*

$ 🏨 **Batik Palace Hotel.** For modest accommodations in the center of Yogyakarta, this hotel offers worn but clean rooms, each with twin beds, table, and chair. The lobby, decorated with batiks and crafts, is a comfortable place to relax. ✉ *Jln. Mangkubumi 46, Box 115, Yogyakarta 55153,* ☎ 0274/562229, FAX 0274/562149. *38 rooms. Restaurant, pool. V.*

$ 🏨 **Mutiara.** In the heart of Yogya on Jalan Malioboro, this downtown hotel consists of two buildings. The newer south wing has fresher rooms that, in spite of their pale-green-and-orange-flecked decor, are worth the extra $5. Cracked plaster and stained carpets notwithstanding, all the rooms are swept clean, fresh towels are supplied though the day, and the cheerful staff is always ready to give advice. The restaurant serves meals all day long, but stick to the breakfast. A small combo plays every evening on the ground floor. ✉ *Jln. Malioboro 18, Yogyakarta 55153,* ☎ 0274/563814, FAX 0274/561201. *109 rooms. Restaurant, coffee shop, pool. AE, DC, MC, V.*

$ 🏨 **Rose Guest House.** The rooms here are very modest, but they do have private baths and either air-conditioning or overhead fans. The tariff includes breakfast and airport transfer, so this hotel is an extremely good value. ✉ *Jln. Prawirotaman 22, Yogyakarta 55153,* ☎ 0274/ 727991. *29 rooms. Restaurant, pool. No credit cards.*

¢ 🏨 **Data Guest House.** Along Jalan Prawirotaman to the south of the Kraton are a score of inexpensive guest houses. Data is one of the best, with clean rooms and reasonable prices, and its position down a narrow street makes it one of the quietest. The very basic double room (around $15) has two narrow beds, a cold-water shower, no windows, and is fan-cooled. Twice as much will get you a "garden view" (the guest house's fancy term for their courtyard), air-conditioning, and hot and cold showers. Since there are only eight of these deluxe rooms, reserve ahead. The owners speak excellent English and are only too happy to assist in travel planning. Prices include a modest American buffet breakfast. (Be sure you find Data Guest House—many other hotels in the neighborhood have "Data" within their names.) ⊠ *26/1 Jln. Prawirotaman, Yogyakarta 55153,* ☎ *0274/372064. 32 rooms. Breakfast room. AE, DC, MC, V.*

The Arts

Yogyakarta is a cultural center and virtually everyday you can find performances of the traditional arts. Most often there will be a gamelan orchestra playing in your hotel, but a performance in the sultan's palace is not to be missed. Performances of segments from the *Ramayana* are performed at different venues throughout the city, but the most dramatic setting is at Prambanan (☞ Central Java, *below*). Wayang kulit shows, usually based on stories from the *Ramayana,* are also given.

Dance, Music, and Theater

The **Kraton,** the sultan's palace, hosts traditional gamelan music on Monday and Wednesday from 10:30 to noon. Every Sunday from 10:30 AM to 12:30 PM, the **Kraton Classic Dance School** performs dance rehearsals at the palace.

Actors perform stories from the *Ramayana* nightly at 7 PM at the **People's Park** (Taman Hiburan Rakyat; ⊠ Jln. Brig. Jen. Katamso). Shows last about two hours.

Puppet Shows

Leather-puppet shadow plays (wayang kulit) are performed Sunday through Friday from 3 to 5 PM at the **Agastya Art Institute** (⊠ Jln. Gedongkiwo MDIII/237, Yogyakarta).

Eight-hour wayang kulit performances of the full *Ramayana* or *Mahabharata* are usually held every second Saturday of the month at **Sasono Hinggil,** just south of Yogya's Kraton, on the opposite side of the alun-alun. These plays begin at 9 PM and last until dawn. Shorter versions lasting two to three hours are given at other times. Your hotel should have the schedule, or check at the information booth outside the theater.

At the **Yogyakarta Crafts Center** (⊠ Jln. Laksda Adisucipto, opposite the Ambarrukmo Palace Hotel), called Ambar Budaya, hour-long wayang kulit performances take place every Monday, Wednesday, and Saturday at 9:30 PM.

Shopping

Shopping for batiks is a delight, and you should find the time to watch the batik-making process at one of the many small factories. Yogyakarta is also a center for painters, and their works are displayed in scores of galleries. Leather goods are well made and inexpensive. Yogyakarta may be a shopper's dream, but be selective—there's a lot of tacky merchandise alongside the treasures—and bargain gracefully. After you have offered your next-to-last price, walk away; you will probably be called back. There are any number of scams to lure you into shops—for instance, the claim that a student art exposition is being held and the works are being sold without commercial profit. Don't believe it!

Jalan Malioboro is lined with shops; the handicraft stalls turn into food stalls around 9 PM. Most of the merchandise is junk, but it's worth picking through. This is a convenient area to buy T-shirts or shorts, but prices are high.

Good prices, prices that locals may pay, can be obtained at the modern indoor market, **Pasar Beringharjo,** at the top end of Jalan Malioboro, across from the Kraton. This fascinating market offers countless spices and foodstuffs, as well as pots and pans, clothes, and transistors.

Batik

The patterned Indonesian textiles called batik—made by drawing on fabric with wax, then dyeing the unwaxed areas—can be found in all the stalls in Yogyakarta. Many prints with batik design are machine-made, however, so beware. Before you buy, try to visit the batik factories, where you can watch the process and shop in the showrooms. One place to see the batik-making process is **Batik Plentong** (⊠ Jln. Tirtodipurun 28, ☏ 0274/562777), which has everything from yard goods to pot holders and batik clothing, hand-stamped and hand-drawn. Visit **Iman Batik Workshop** (⊠ Jln. Dagen 76B, just off Jln. Malioboro), where Iman Nuryanto, the owner, holds visiting exhibitions of local artists. Don't pay more than 50% of the asking price. The **Koperasi (Cooperative) Fine Arts School** (⊠ Jln. Kemetiran Kidul, no phone), south of the railway station, has batik designed by talented artisans, but be sure to bargain well.

Handicrafts

Handicrafts in Yogyakarta include batik "paintings," batik-patterned T-shirts and other apparel or household items, small hand-tooled leather goods, pottery (items decorated with brightly colored elephants, roosters, and animals from mythology are made in Kasongan, just south of Yogya), and wayang kulit (leather) and wayang golek (wood) puppets. All the shops and stalls on Jalan Malioboro and around the Kraton sell puppets and other handicrafts. The **Yogyakarta Handicrafts Center** (⊠ Jln. Adisucipto, no phone), not far from the Ambarrukmo Palace Hotel, sells handicrafts by artisans with disabilities.

Leather

Leather is a great buy in Yogyakarta. The shops and stalls on Jalan Malioboro offer a wide variety of goods. You'll find good quality and design at **Kusuma** (⊠ Jln. Kauman 50, parallel to Malioboro, ☏ 0274/565453); there's room for modest bargaining, but no credit cards are accepted.

Silver

Many silversmiths have workshops and salesrooms in **Kota Gede,** 6 km (3½ mi) southeast of Yogya. The largest in Kota Gede, **Tom's Silver** (⊠ Jln. Ngaksi Gondo, Kota Gede 3-1 A, ☏ 0274/525416), offers quality workmanship. Also try **MD Silver** (⊠ Jln. Keboan, Kota Gede, ☏ 0274/375063).

Yogyakarta A to Z

Arriving and Departing

BY BUS

Night buses from Jakarta take about 14 hours and cost about Rp 12,250. Buses also run from Denpasar on Bali (12 hours), Bandung (7 hours), and Surabaya (8 hours). (☞ Getting Around by Bus *in* Indonesia A to Z, *below*.) For information in Jakarta, contact: **Antar Lintas Sumatra** (⊠ Jln. Jati Baru 87A, ☏ 021/320970) or **PT. ANS** (for Java, Bali, and Sumatra), Jalan Senen Raya 50, Jakarta, ☏ 021/340494.

BY CAR

Although the scenery may be beautiful, the long drive from Jakarta is slow going, and service areas are few and far between. It is advisable to hire a driver when traveling through Indonesia.

Adisucipto Airport is 10 km (6 mi) east of Yogyakarta; airport tax is Rp 6,600. From Jakarta's Soekarno-Hatta Airport, **Garuda** (Yogyakarta, ☎ 0274/563–706; Jakarta, ☎ 021/334425) offers several daily flights; flying time is about 45 minutes. Seats fill up quickly, so reservations are essential. There are also flights into Yogya from Denpasar (Bali) and Surabaya (Java) on both Merpati and Sempati.

Between the Airport and Center City. A minibus runs until 6 PM from the Adisucipto Airport to the terminal on Jalan Senopati for Rp 250; from there you can catch a three-wheel becak to your hotel. Taxis to or from downtown charge Rp 5,500. The major hotels send their own minibuses to the airport.

BY TRAIN

Trains from the Gambir Railway Station in Jakarta leave several times daily for Yogya. The trip takes 7–12 hours and costs Rp 6,700–Rp 21,500, depending on whether the train is an express or a local and on the class of the ticket. The most comfortable trip is via the *Senja Utama Express*, which leaves Gambir at 7:20 PM and arrives in Yogya at 4:50 AM. The train has sleeping compartments. The fares are Rp 18,000 for B class, Rp 21,000 for A class, and Rp 44,000 for executive class. There are also day and night trains from Bandung (an eight-hour trip) and from Surabaya (seven hours).

Getting Around

BY BECAK

Yogya has 25,000 becak, or three-wheel pedicabs, and they are the main form of public transportation. Prices need serious negotiation. The proper fare is about Rp 500 per kilometer.

BY BICYCLE

Bicycles may be rented for Rp 4,000 a day from the **Hotel Indonesia** (⌂ Sosromenduran IV). The **Restaurant Malioboro** (⌂ Jln. Malioboro 67) also has bikes for rent, as do other shops.

BY MOTOR SCOOTER

A.A. Rental (⌂ Jln. Pasar Kembang 25, ☎ 0274/4489) has motor scooters for about Rp 16,000 a day. Scooters may also be rented from **Yogya Rental** (⌂ Jln. Pasar Kembang 86).

BY TAXI

Catch taxis in front of the larger hotels, such as Garuda or Mutiara; in general, they do not cruise the streets. Taxis are metered; the flag fall charge is Rp 800 and covers the first kilometer.

Contacts and Resources

EMERGENCIES

Ambulance, ☎ 118. **Fire,** ☎ 113. **Police,** ☎ 110.

GUIDED TOURS

Hotels and travel agencies can arrange the following tours, either in a private chauffeured car or as a group tour by bus:

Yogya City. A three-hour tour including the sultan's palace, Sono Budoyo Museum, Kota Gede silverworks, and batik and wayang workshops.
Borobudur. An eight-hour tour of Yogyakarta, the countryside, and the Borobudur, Mendut, and Pawon temples.
Prambanan. A three-hour tour of the temple complex.
Yogya Dieng Plateau. A 10-hour tour of the Dieng Plateau, with its spectacular scenery, sulfur springs, and geysers, plus a visit to Borobudur.
Art and Handicrafts. A five-hour tour of the local craft centers for leather puppets, wood carving, silverwork, batik, and pottery.

Yogya's main companies are as follows: **Nitour** (✉ Jln. K.H.A. Dahlan 71, ☎ 0274/375165). **Satriavi** (✉ Hotel Ambarrukmo Palace, ☎ 0274/566488, ext. 7135). American Express card holders can contact **Pacto Ltd. Tours and Travel** (✉ Hotel Ambarrukmo Palace, Jln. Adisucipto, ☎ 0274/566488, ext. 7130). The locally operated **Setia Tours** (✉ Garuda Hotel, Jln. Malioboro, ☎ 0274/566328, ext. 151) is also helpful.

Yogyakarta's **Tourist Information Office** has maps, schedules of events, bus and train information, and a helpful staff. There is also a tourist booth at the railway station. ✉ *Jln. Malioboro 16,* ☎ *0274/562811.* ⏱ *Mon.–Sat. 8–8.*

CENTRAL JAVA

Central Java nurtured some of Indonesia's great Indian kingdoms in the 8th and 9th centuries, including the Buddhist Sailendras, who built the Borobudur temple, and the Hindu Sanjayans, who made Prambanan their religious center. Today tourists generally use Yogyakarta as a base for visiting these temples, the best-known architectural and cultural sites of Indonesia. However, if you prefer less commercialism and tourist hustling, the ancient city of Solo, 64 km (40 mi) to the east, could be your best bet. Solo is quieter and less commercial, but also a cultural center, and from here, too, you can easily drive out to Sukuh Temple and to Sangiran, the site where Java Man was discovered.

Five hours by road to the northeast of Yogyakarta is Surabaya, which is more of a commercial and manufacturing city than a tourist destination. However, it is a base for setting out to explore the island of Madura and, to the east, to witness Mt. Bromo, an active volcano from whose rim you can peer down into nature's cauldron. From Mt. Bromo, you can continue east by bus for Bali.

Numbers in the margin correspond to points of interest on the Central Java map.

Borobudur Temple

★ ❶ *42 km (26 mi) northwest of Yogyakarta. Guided coach tours run from Yogya hotels, or hire a minibus and guide (usually more informed) from a Yogya travel agency. Or take the public bus toward Samarung, then change at Muntilan for the Ramayana bus to Borobudur.*

That the temple of Borobudur took perhaps 10,000 men 100 years to build becomes credible the moment you set eyes on its cosmic structure, in the shadow of the powerful volcanoes that the Javanese believe are the abode of God. Try to go early in the morning—plan to end your two-to three-hour visit before noon—while the temperature is still relatively cool.

Borobudur was abandoned soon after completion in AD 850, and the forest moved in. The man who founded modern Singapore, Thomas Stamford Raffles (then the English lieutenant-governor of Java), and his military engineer, H.C.C. Cornelius, rediscovered the temple in 1814. A thousand years of neglect had left much of it in ruins, and the temple has undergone two mammoth restorations, first from 1907 to 1911, and then again from the 1960s to the 1980s with the help of UNESCO and $25 million.

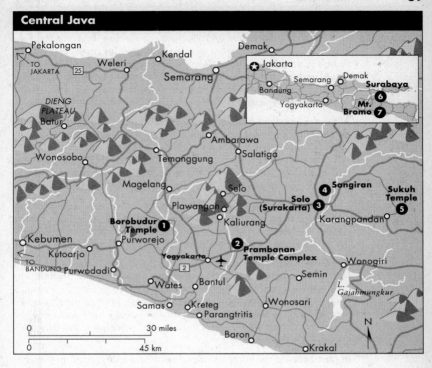

Central Java

The temple is a giant stupa: Five lower levels contain 1,500 relief carvings depicting the earthly life of Siddhartha in his passage to enlightenment. Start at the eastern staircase on the first level and walk clockwise around each gallery to follow the sequence of Lord Buddha's life.

Above the reliefs are 432 stone Buddhas. Even higher, above the square galleries, are three circular terraces with 72 latticed stupas that hide statues depicting the Buddha's departure from the material world and existence on a higher plane. The top stupa symbolizes the highest level of enlightenment. Looking out at the surrounding mountains from the upper level of Borobudur, you feel some of the inspiration that created this grand monument. If you go around each of the nine galleries, you will have walked 4.8 km (3 mi) closer to heaven. On weekends the complex is fairly crowded—another reason to come early. In 1990, a museum opened on the grounds of Borobudur, charging an additional admission that its contents do not justify. *No phone.* ✉ *Admission.* ⊙ *Daily 6:15–5.*

OFF THE BEATEN PATH

CANDI PAWON AND MENDUT – About 1.5 km (1 mi) east of Borobudur, on the way back to the main road, is a small temple, Candi Pawon, built around the same time as Borobudur. It is thought that worshipers purified themselves here on their way to Borobudur. Another kilometer or so farther east is the small temple Mendut, also from the 9th century. The exterior of this friendly temple is superbly carved with some 30 large relief panels depicting scenes from the Buddha's previous incarnations. Inside stands a magnificent 10-foot statue of Buddha, flanked by the bodhisattvas Avalokitesvara and Vajrapani.

Prambanan Temple Complex

★ ❷ *16 km (10 mi) northeast of Yogyakarta, a 30-min drive via the Solo
road. If you book through a tour agency, you can combine a visit to
Prambanan with a visit to Borobudur, or you can combine Prambanan with a trip to Solo, 46 km (29 mi) farther from Yogya. Minibuses
go out to Prambanan from the Jalan Solo terminus in Yogya. If you
hire a taxi, the round-trip will cost Rp 35,000.*

When the Sanjayan kingdom evicted the Buddhist Sailendras, the Sanjayans wanted to memorialize the return of a Hindu dynasty and, supposedly, undermine Borobudur. To this end they built Prambanan.
When the 9th-century complex was rediscovered in 1880, it had fallen
into ruin from centuries of neglect and enveloping vegetation. In 1937
reconstruction began, and the work continues to this day.

The temple was built with an outer stage for commoners, a middle stage
for high-ranking nobility, and a main temple area for royalty. Of the
original 244 temples, eight major and eight minor temples are still standing, in the highest central courtyard of the Prambanan plain.

The center temple, dedicated to Shiva the Destroyer, is the highest (155
feet) and the best-restored; Vishnu's is to the north, and Brahma's to
the south. Originally the temples were painted—Shiva's red, Brahma's
white, Vishnu's a dark gray—but only traces of the paint remain. To
the east of these temples are three smaller ones, which contained the
"vehicles" of each god: Shiva's bull, Vishnu's elephant, and Brahma's
goose. Only the bull survives.

In part because the complex was dedicated to Shiva, and in part because Shiva's temple is the best restored, this is where you will want
to spend most of your time. Over the entrance is the head of Kali, a
protection against evil from land. On the balustrade, the *naga* (serpent)
guards against evil from the sea. The base is decorated with medallions
with lions (an imported figure) and half-bird, half-human figures
flanked by trees of good hope. Above these, on the outer balustrade,
are carvings of classical Indian dancers and celestial beings.

The inner wall of the balustrade is carved with lively, sometimes
frivolous, reliefs telling the story of the *Ramayana.* From the east gate,
walk around the temple clockwise to follow the story in sequence. The
reliefs show free-flowing movement, much humor, and a love of nature. In contrast to Borobudur's reliefs, these carvings combine a celebration of the pleasures and pains of earthly life with scenes from Hindu
mythology. They are more fun to look at (monkeys stealing fruit and
bird-women floating in air), but the drama they portray—the establishment of order in the cosmos—is just as serious.

In the main chamber, at the top of the east stairway, a four-armed statue
of Shiva the creator and destroyer stands on a lotus base. In the south
chamber, Shiva appears as divine teacher, with a big beard and big stomach. The statue in the western chamber is Ganesha, Shiva's elephant-
headed son. And in the northern chamber, Shiva's consort, Durga, kills
the demon buffalo. An **archaeological museum** was opened in 1990,
but its contents do not add much to your appreciation of the imposing architecture of the temples. However, you may want to stop at the
information desk at the entrance to clarify any questions you have about
the complex. *No phone.* 🎫 *Admission.* ☉ *Daily 6–5.*

The Arts

Within walking distance of the temple is the **Prambanan theater complex,** where performances of the *Ramayana* are given in the evening,
either at the Ramayana Theatre (open-air) or the Trimurti Theatre (in-

door). The Ramayana ballet—an elaborate presentation with scores of dancers, a full-blown orchestra, and armies of monkeys strutting around the stage—is performed at various times through the year. From January through March, performances are usually once a week on Thursday. April through June and October through December, there are at least three performances (Tuesday, Wednesday, and Thursday). July through September features up to five performances a week—always on Tuesday, Wednesday, and Thursday, and usually on Saturday and Sunday. Hotel tour desks can arrange tickets and transportation, or you can share a taxi from the Tourist Information Center in Yogyakarta (✉ Jln. Malioboro 12) at 6:30. Public buses pass by the theater's entrance, but they can be unreliable, and the drivers tend to gouge foreigners. ✉ Jln. Raya Yogya-Solo, Km 16, Prambanan, ☎ 0274/63918. 🎫 Rp 15,000.

OFF THE BEATEN PATH	**CANDI SAMBISARI –** The numerous other Buddhist and Hindu temples between Yogyakarta and Prambanan are in various states of ruin but merit at least a day of exploring. A great way to see them is to rent a bike and pack a lunch. Signs on the Yogya–Solo road point the way to the temples. Most are off the road, down small paths, and charge a small admission. Candi Sambisari, a small temple located off the highway and 2 mi back toward Yogya, is set in a sunken garden and is usually deserted—ideal for a quiet rest.

Solo

❸ 60 km (38 mi) northeast of Yogyakarta.

Solo (also known as Surakarta or Sala) is less Westernized than Yogya, with fewer tourists and much less hustling. Solo has its own traditional batik designs and its own style of dance. And while its people are devoutly Muslim, their daily life is less religious.

On the west side of town is the **Mangkunegaran Palace,** a complex of carved, gilded teak pavilions. The outer center pavilion, or pendopo, serves as the audience hall and is typical of a Javanese royal building. The Italian marble floor laid in 1925, the guardian lions from Berlin, and the 50-foot roof supported by teak pillars make the pendopo very grand. Its ceiling is painted with a flame motif bordered by symbols from the Javanese zodiac, designed with the eight mystical colors (yellow to ward off sleep, green to subdue desire, purple to keep away bad thoughts, etc.). The effect is gaudy but dramatic.

The museum, in the ceremonial pavilion just behind the main pendopo, displays dance ornaments, masks, jewelry, chastity belts for men and women, and wayang kulit and wayang golek. At center stage is the enclosed bridal bed (originally a room reserved for offerings to the rice goddess). To the left of the museum are the official reception rooms: a formal dining room, with a Javanese-style stained-glass window (made in Holland) and an ivory tusk carved with depictions of the wedding of Arjuna, one of the heroes of the Mahabharata; a mirrored parlor area; and a "bathing" room for royal brides. No phone. 🎫 Admission. ⊙ Mon.–Thurs. and Sat. 9–noon, Fri. 9–11 AM.

Solo has a second palace, **Kraton Kasuhunan** (sometimes called Kraton Solo). This kraton suffered terrible damage from a fire in 1985 that gutted the elaborate ceremonial pavilion. Now the palace is being rebuilt. The museum—one of Central Java's best—was unharmed by the fire. It contains a priceless collection of silver and bronze Hindu figures and Chinese porcelain, but the real treat is three royal carriages given to the sultanate by the Dutch in the 18th century. The English-speaking guide will help you appreciate the collection. ☎ 0271/44046. ⌧ Admission. ☉ Sat.–Thurs. 9–noon.

Dining and Lodging

$$ **✕ Kasuma Sahid.** Without a doubt this is the place to dine in Solo. **★** Part of the Prince Hotel, this formal restaurant is light and airy, with white linen and polished silver. The menu, offering Indonesian specialties, features chicken with jackfruit and fish wrapped in banana leaves, with the restaurant's own special blend of spices. Western dishes with a nouvelle French influence and Indonesian accent are featured as well. ⌧ Jln. Sugiyopranoto 20, ☎ 0271/46356. Reservations not accepted. AE, DC, MC, V.

$$ **✕ Kusuma Sari.** This spotless restaurant is excellent for Indonesian fare, be it ayam goreng or a snack such as resoles ragout (chicken wrapped in a soft pancake)—and you can dine until 11 PM nightly. The tile floors, glass-topped wood tables, and plate-glass windows don't offer a lot of atmosphere, but choose a table by the window and watch the flow of pedestrians and becaks on the town's main street. ⌧ Jln. Slamet Riyadi 111, ☎ 0271/37603. Reservations not accepted. No credit cards.

$$$ **▦ Kusuma Sahid Prince Hotel.** Three two-story buildings and outly- **★** ing bungalows are set back from the street on 5 acres of landscaped gardens. The lobby veranda—the original pendopo agung (prince's court-yard)—is a wonderful place for tea or a cooling drink. The quiet guest rooms are well maintained, and all the accoutrements, from the linens to the orchids, are quite fresh. Some rooms have a view of the enormous pool, while those in the newer wing have up-to-date furnishings and always-welcome climate control. ⌧ Jln. Sugiyopranoto 22, ☎ 0271/46356, ℻ 0271/44788. 103 rooms. Restaurant, bar, room service, pool, shops, meeting rooms, travel services. AE, DC, MC, V.

$ **▦ Mangkunegaran Palace Hotel.** Adjacent to the palace and owned by Prince Mangkunegoro, this hotel has great potential, but it desperately needs the renovation that is being performed only intermittently. Inspect your room before signing in. If you don't mind cracked plaster and a musty smell, the Mangkunegaran is the least expensive palace you are ever likely to stay in. The most appealing space is the dining room, which has a batik-painted ceiling just like the palace's. ⌧ Istara Mangkunegaran, ☎ ℻ 0271/35683. 50 rooms. Restaurant, pool. AE, DC, MC, V.

$ **▦ Wisata Indah.** Though the plastered walls have hand smudges and the bathrooms are the bucket-dip (mandi) style, the hot water is hot, the sheets are freshly laundered, and the staff is friendly and helpful. Outside each room are tables and chairs for breakfast (included in the rate) and meals that may be ordered from the bellboys. Negotiate the room rate before you sign in. ⌧ Jln. Slamet Riyadi 173, ☎ 0271/46770. 27 rooms. MC, V.

The Arts

At Solo's **Mangkunegaran Palace,** a gamelan orchestra performs each Saturday from 9 to 10:30 AM. Dance rehearsals are held on Wednesday from 10 to noon and on Monday and Friday afternoon.

Shopping

Solo's main shopping street is **Jalan Secoyudan.** In addition to a score of goldsmiths, you'll find antiques stores selling curios from the Dutch colonial days, as well as krises and other Javanese artifacts.

Between Jalan Slamet Riyadi and Mangkunegaraan Palace and just off Diponegoro is **Pasar Triwindu,** Solo's daily flea market, where hundreds of stalls sell everything from junk to old coins to batik. Bargain like crazy! **Jalan Slamet Riyadi** has antiques shops.

BATIK

Solo has its own batik style, often using indigo, brown, and cream, as opposed to the brighter colors of Yogya's batiks. Prices are better in Solo, and you have some 300 batik factories to choose from. Aside from the shops along Jalan Secoyudan, visit **Pasar Klewer,** a huge batik market just outside the Kraton Solo with a fine selection of goods on the second floor. An established shop that sells batik and demonstrates the batik-making process is **Dinar Hadi Batik Shop** on Jalan Dr. Rajiman (no phone).

Sangiran

❹ *15 km (9 mi) north of Solo. Take a bus to Kaliso, then walk 30 min. to the site; or take a taxi (Rp 15,000 round-trip from Solo).*

Sangiran is where Eugene Dubois discovered Java Man (or *Homo erectus,* as the species is now known) in 1891. (It is not to be confused with Sanggarahan, a village just outside Yogya known for its pleasure houses.) The museum contains a replica of Java Man's cranium and models of these ancestors of *Homo sapiens* who lived some 250,000 years ago, plus fossils of other forms of life, such as now-extinct elephants. *No phone.* 🖼 *Admission.* 🕙 *Mon.–Sat. 9–4.*

Sukuh Temple

❺ *35 km (21 mi) east of Solo. A hired car (Rp 20,000) is the most convenient way to get here; the journey takes a good hour along winding, hilly roads. You can also come by bus, but it requires three changes: At Tertomoyo catch the bus to Tawangmangu, then get off at Karangpandan for a minibus to Sukuh.*

Sukuh Temple stands mysteriously and exotically alone and contains elements of Hinduism, Buddhism, and animism. Looking like an abbreviated pyramid, the delightful temple is full of cult symbols and objects with erotic suggestions. The structure dates from the 15th century, but no one knows who built it or what cults were celebrated. Because few tourists make it here, the place has a mystical atmosphere, enhanced by the lush surrounding rice terraces. 🖼 *Admission.* 🕙 *Daily 9–4.*

Surabaya

❻ *258 km (150 mi) northeast of Solo.*

Surabaya isn't on the traditional tourist route, but with a rapidly expanding business and industrial base—it now ranks as the nation's third-largest city—it is looking for visitors. Hope springs eternal in the human breast!

Surabaya does not offer exotic attractions. It was virtually leveled on November 10, 1945, when the Dutch and their allies tried to reclaim the city after the Japanese surrender. The Surabayans resisted, and the day came to symbolize the country's determination to throw off the colonial yoke; it is now celebrated throughout Indonesia as Revolutionary Heroes' Day.

Beyond serving as a port for ferries to the little-visited islands of Madura (famous for its bullfights and the adroitness of its women) and Sulawesi (☞ *below*) and as a transfer point for international flights to Singapore, Hong Kong, and Japan, Surabaya is a good base from which to visit Mt. Bromo. Although there are monuments to see in the old town, you may want to use the city simply for a night's rest before traveling on.

Lodging

Besides the hotels below, Surabaya also boasts new Shangri-La, Westin, and Hilton properties.

$$$ ⊡ **Hotel Majapahit.** Built in 1910 by the Sarkies brothers (of Singapore's Raffles fame) in the center of town, this is one of Indonesia's few heritage hotels. Its expansive courts and green lawns became derelict after World War II, but in 1994 the Mandarin Oriental Hotel Group, which manages such distinguished properties as the Oriental in Bangkok, took over; a $27 million restoration was completed in 1996. Many of the original design features have been retained—including stained-glass windows, terrazzo floors, and colonial-style balconies and verandas—and modern luxuries have been added. Rooms on the ground floor are large, but upstairs rooms are slighty quieter. The Presidential Suite, the largest of its kind in Indonesia, is over 8,600 square feet. Furnishings are Javanese, and some are antiques. Batiks from Yogjakarta add splashes of color. Aside from the pool bar, the Majapahit boasts three restaurants: Sarkies for Oriental seafood, Indigo for Eurasian, and Shima for Japanese. ⊠ *Jln. Tunjungan 65, Surabaya 60011,* ☎ *031/545–4333,* ℻ *031/545–4111. 150 rooms. 3 restaurants, bar, pool, tennis court, health club, business services, meeting rooms. AE, DC, MC, V.*

$$$ ⊡ **Hyatt Regency Surabaya.** This large, modern hotel has an 11-story wing and the 27-story Regency Tower with Regency Club rooms, meeting rooms, two business centers, and offices. An added convenience is an airline ticketing office. Rooms are typical Hyatt—comfortable, beige, fairly large, and furnished with wooden cabinets, king-size beds, and ferns in huge clay pots. The main lobby is a popular spot for locals who come to drink and listen to a trio playing sentimental favorites. Expats gather in the Tavern for drinks and light meals. ⊠ *Jln. Jend. Basuki Rakhmat 124-8, Surabaya 60275,* ☎ *031/511234,* ℻ *031/ 521508; U.S.,* ☎ *800/233–1234. 500 rooms. 2 restaurants, coffee shop, pool, exercise room, shops, business services, meeting rooms, travel services. AE, DC, MC, V.*

Mt. Bromo

★ ❼ *Tosari, a village on the mountain, is 90 km (55 mi) southeast of Surabaya, 340 km (210 mi) east of Solo.*

It's truly a thrill to approach the circular crater of this active volcano and then look down into what seems like the depths of hell—a bubbling cauldron of water, ash, and sulphur that spews clouds of hot steam. The elemental eeriness of this sight is compounded by having to get up very early in the morning, hike to the top through the chilly air, and worship the sun as it comes up.

Part of the pleasure of visiting Mt. Bromo is that you're allowed much closer to the rim than you would be at more "touristy" volcanoes (those in Hawaii, for example), but be surefooted: In 1994 one American peering down the 350 feet to the crater's bottom fell in and never came out. Additionally, before you make any Bromo-related travel plans, verify that the mountain is open: Sometimes the volcano is so active that the government prohibits tourists from visiting.

One common way to visit Mt. Bromo is on an organized tour that will place you at the rim of the caldera just before dawn. You can either leave Surabaya in the afternoon and catch a short night's rest in a small bungalow hotel, or leave in the wee hours of the morning and return by lunchtime. Either way, you'll have a walk in the chilly predawn hours, so take a sweater.

The largest tour agency is **Orient Express** (✉ Jln. Jend. Basuki Rakhamat 78, Surabaya 60262, ☎ 031/515253, FAX 031/511811), which will meet you at the airport or anywhere else in Surabaya. **Day tours** (☎ U.S.$40 per person) depart Surabaya at 1 AM. **Overnight tours** (☎ U.S.$85 per person) depart at 3 PM for the Bromo Cottages in Tosari, where the accommodation is simple, modern, and clean. You rise at 3:30 AM and travel by Jeep up Mt. Penanjakan (9,088 feet) for views of the spectacular sunrise. Afterward the Jeep takes you to the sea of sand—an area of fine volcanic ash bleached by the sun—and then to the stairway to the rim of the Bromo crater; finally it's back to the cottages for breakfast before returning to Surabaya.

You can also rent a chauffeured car and do the trip independently for about Rp 100,000, plus the fee for a jeep on the last leg of the journey. Try **P.T. Zebra Nusantart** (✉ Jln. Tegalsari 107, Surabaya, ☎ 031/ 511777); the firm also has a representative at the Surabaya Hyatt).

If you prefer public transport, take the bus from Surabaya's Bungurasih Bus Station to Probolinggo and change for a bemo up to Pasuruan; from there take a minibus up to Tosari. To get from Tosari to the crater's rim, another 7½ km (4½ mi), you can rent a four-wheel-drive vehicle (about U.S.$25) or walk (if you're fit—it's a two-hour uphill trudge). If you go by car, after the sun has risen ask the driver to take you to the sand sea and walk back from there to Tosari or to Cemoro Lawang. At Cemoro Lawang, a popular base from which to hike up to the northern rim of the caldera—it takes a couple of hours—there are cars going down to Ngadisari, where minibuses ply the route to Probolinggo. In Probolinggo you can board buses for Banyuwangi, Bali, or back to Surabaya.

Central Java A to Z

Arriving and Departing

SOLO
Minibuses leave for Solo throughout the day (7–5) from Yogyakarta's Terminal Terban (Rp 1,500) or may be caught along Jalan Sudirman or Jalan Solo. From Solo's Gilligan bus terminal, take a bemo (Rp 300) or a becak (Rp 750) the 3 km (1.8 mi) into town. A shared taxi from Yogya to Solo costs Rp 2,500 per person. The train from Yogya, invariably behind schedule, takes one hour; third-class fare is only Rp 500. Silk Air now flies into Solo from Singapore three times a week.

SURABAYA
There are flights to Surabaya's Juanda Airport (20 km from downtown) on Garuda, Merpati, and Sempati airlines from most Javanese cities as well as from Bali and Lombok. There is also train service from Jakarta, Yogyakarta, and Solo. Another train line links Surabaya to Banyuwangi, on the eastern tip of Java; from there ferries depart every 30 minutes for the 20-minute crossing to Bali. This is a slow train, though, and most non-air travelers to Bali prefer the night express buses.

Contacts and Resources

EMBASSIES AND CONSULATES
United States (✉ Jln. Raya Dr. Sutomo 33, Surabaya, ☎ 031/568–2287, FAX 031/567–4492).

EMERGENCIES
Ambulance, ☎ 118. **Fire,** ☎ 113. **Police,** ☎ 110.

VISITOR INFORMATION

Solo Tourist Information Office. ⊠ *Jln. Slamet Riyadi 275,* ☎ *0271/ 46501.* ⊘ *Mon.–Sat. 8–5.*

Surabaya Tourist Office. ⊠ *Jln. Darmakali 35,* ☎ *031/575448.*

BALI

The "magic" of Bali has its roots in the fact that the island is religiously distinct from the rest of Indonesia: unlike their Muslim neighbors, the Balinese are Hindus. Their faith also contains elements of Buddhism and of ancient animist beliefs indigenous to the archipelago. Hindu culture came to Bali as early as the 9th century; by the 14th century, the island was part of the Hindu Majapahit empire of East Java. When that empire fell to Muslim invaders, Majapahit aristocrats, scholars, artists, and dancers fled to Bali, consolidating Hindu culture and religion there.

To the Balinese, every living thing contains a spirit; when they pick a flower as an offering to the gods, they first say a prayer to the flower. All over the island, from the capital city of Denpasar to the tiniest village, plaited baskets filled with flowers and herbs lie on the sidewalks, on the prows of fishing boats, and in markets. These offerings are made from dawn till dusk, to placate evil spirits and honor helpful ones. Stone figures guard the entryways to temples, hotels, and homes. The black-and-white-checked cloths around the statues' waists symbolize the balance between good and evil. Maintaining that harmony is the life work of every Balinese.

Although the island is only 140 km (84 mi) long by 80 km (48 mi) wide, a week would not be enough to appreciate Bali's beaches, temples, volcanoes, and towns. With Indonesia's most developed tourist infrastructure, Bali has several beach areas on the southern coast, where 90% of its visitors stay. Each has its distinctive appeal and they are within easy reach of one another.

Numbers in the margin correspond to points of interest on the Bali map.

Kuta and Legian

❶ *14 km (8 mi) north of Ngurah Rai Airport.*

Kuta has one of the world's most splendid golden-sand beaches. The first resort to be developed on Bali, it is now extremely commercial—and somewhat tawdry. It appeals mainly to young Australians on package holidays that (even with airfare) cost less than a beach vacation at home. Kuta's main street, just two blocks from the beach, is crammed with boutiques, Western fast-food chains, bars, discos, and, after hours, hustling ladies of the night. But the sunsets are as spectacular as ever, and as you walk east along Kuta to Legian, the beach becomes less crowded.

Legian Beach is a little quieter and less congested; it's for those who like to be close to the action but not right in it—though both Kuta and Legian are for 24-hour partying, not peace. Just to the south of Kuta—really part of Kuta Bay—is another area of hotels, promoted under the name Tuban and designed to attract families and those looking for quieter vacations.

Dining and Lodging

Kuta offers a fairly wide range of restaurants. Western food abounds, though it's mostly of the fast-food variety. Hotels offer better Western cooking. Water is not potable; ice is made under government supervision with the claim that it is safe.

$$$ ✕ **Oberoi.** In an open pavilion with a bamboo ceiling, you dine around a pool with a fountain surrounded by trees and flowers. A Swiss chef and Balinese sous-chef turn out both an Indonesian buffet and an à la carte menu with a Continental flair. Try the crepe "le Oberoi," with its filling of crabmeat, cream, onions, and white wine, or the coconut-breaded shrimp, deep-fried and served with a ginger cream sauce. The Oberoi also prepares Indian specialties. ⊠ *Legian Beach, Jln. Kayu Aya,* ☎ *0361/751061. Reservations essential during busy season. AE, DC, MC, V.*

$$ ✕ **Glory Bar & Restaurant.** There are dozens of seafood restaurants in Kuta all offering the same fare. What puts the Glory a cut above is the freshness of its fish, mud crabs, and lobster. The atmosphere is convivial, and prices are fair. The wide-ranging Indonesian buffet on Wednesday night includes corn soup, fried chicken, sweet-and-sour pork, batter-fried fish, satay, and noodles. ⊠ *Jln. Legian Tengah 529, Legian,* ☎ *0361/751091. Reservations not accepted. AE, DC. MC, V.*

$$ ✕ **Indah Sari.** On Kuta's main drag, this seafood-and-barbecue restaurant serves well-prepared dishes, from prawns to grouper, that you can order either spicy or bland. The open-fronted restaurant can get boisterous, but the freshness of the food makes up for the lack of personal service and intimacy. ⊠ *Jln. Legian, Kuta,* ☎ *0361/751834. Reservations not accepted. AE, MC, V.*

$$ ✕ **Poppies.** A high wall surrounding the garden and well-spaced tables that permit you to hear your dining companions make this one of the few spots where you can escape the beer-chugging revelries of Kuta. The relaxed alfresco atmosphere is the drawing card; the food, mostly Western dishes, is average to good. ⊠ *Poppies La., off Jln. Legian, Kuta,* ☎ *0361/751059. Reservations not accepted. MC, V.*

$$ ✕ **Warung Kopi.** Five marble-topped tables facing the street and another 10 in the rear garden provide an oasis from the surrounding honkytonk scene. The menu is eclectic: Indonesian fish, vegetable, and rice dishes; Indian curries; Western beef and lamb. It's also fine for just a beer and an appetizer or coffee and dessert. ⊠ *Jln. Legian Tengah 427, Legian,* ☎ *0361/753602. Reservations not accepted. MC, V.*

$ ✕ **Bakung Mas Garden.** This peaceful and romantic restaurant belongs to the Segara Village Hotel. There are only six tables under the thatched roof, and a tiny bar in case you have to wait. The food has a Chinese influence: Try the stir-fried vegetables with pork or the *semur daging* (thinly sliced beef with a rich sauce of mushrooms and onions). ⊠ *Jln. Bakung Sari, Kuta,* ☎ *0361/788407. Reservations not accepted. No credit cards.*

$$$$ 🏨 **Oberoi.** Among the luxurious Oberoi's assets is its location, at the
★ far western end of Legian Beach away from the crowds. Its 33 acres offer tranquillity and privacy, with thatched cottages and private villas spaced among gardens of bougainvillea, hibiscus, and frangipani. The lobby and lounge building, with a coral exterior and polished stone floors inside, faces the sea. Rooms are beautifully furnished in dark wood, with ikat bedcovers and draperies. Each cottage has its own veranda; the villas have balconies and garden courtyards. The luxurious villas have private pools and traditional Balinese inner courtyards. Service is personal and friendly, and Balinese dance is performed on most evenings in an amphitheater. ⊠ *Box 451, Denpasar 80001,* ☎ *0361/ 751061,* 𝖥𝖠𝖷 *0361/752791; U.S.,* ☎ *800/5–OBEROI. 63 cottages, 12 villas. Restaurant, bar, outdoor café, room service, 4 tennis courts, windsurfing, laundry service, car rental. AE, DC, MC, V.*

Bali

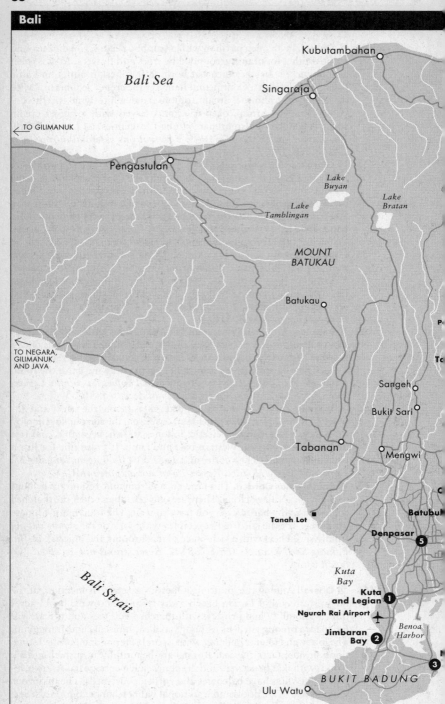

Bali Sea

Kubutambahan

Singaraja

← TO GILIMANUK

Pengastulan

Lake Buyan

Lake Bratan

Lake Tamblingan

MOUNT BATUKAU

Batukau

←
TO NEGARA,
GILIMANUK,
AND JAVA

Sangeh

Bukit Sari

Tabanan

Mengwi

Tanah Lot

Batubu

Denpasar ⑤

Kuta Bay

Bali Strait

Kuta and Legian ①

Ngurah Rai Airport ✈

Jimbaran Bay ②

Benoa Harbor

③

BUKIT BADUNG

Ulu Watu

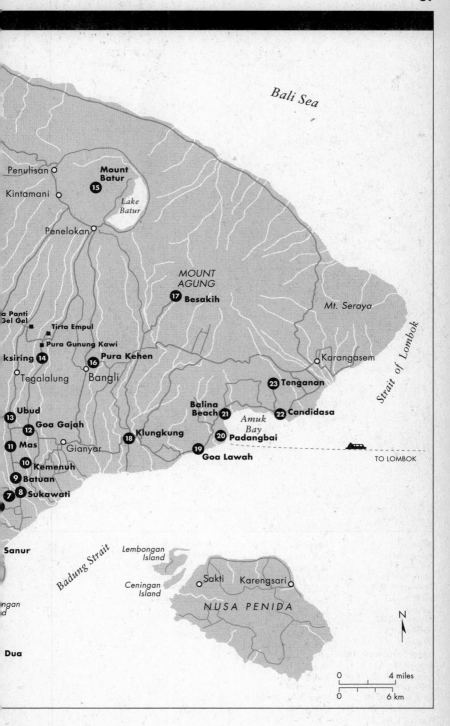

Bali Sea

Penulisan

Mount Batur 15

Kintamani

Lake Batur

Penelokan

MOUNT AGUNG

Besakih 17

Mt. Seraya

a Panti Gel Gel

Tirta Empul

Pura Gunung Kawi

ksiring 14 **Pura Kehen** 16

Tegalalung **Bangli**

Karangasem

Strait of Lombok

Tenganan 23

Ubud 13

Goa Gajah 12

Balina Beach 21

Amuk Bay

Candidasa 22

Mas 11

Gianyar

Klungkung 18

Padangbai 20

Goa Lawah 19

TO LOMBOK

Kemenuh 10

Batuan 9

Sukawati 8 7

Sanur

Badung Strait

Lembongan Island

Ceningan Island

Sakti Karengsari

NUSA PENIDA

ngan d

Dua

N

0   4 miles

0   6 km

Bali Beach Resorts Dining & Lodging

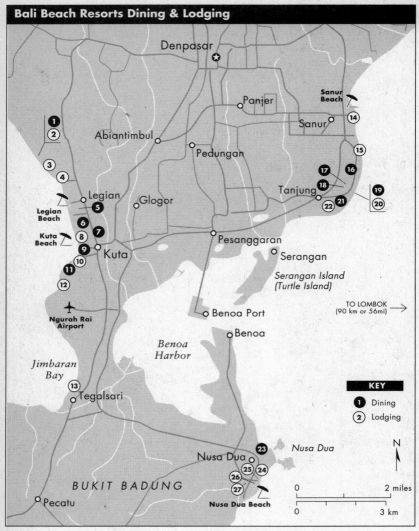

Dining

Bakung Mas Garden, **11**

Glory Bar & Restaurant, **6**

Indah Sari, **7**

Kertosa Restaurant, **23**

Le Gong, **18**

Oberoi, **1**

Penjor Restaurant, **16**

Poppies, **9**

Ronny's Pub & Restaurant, **21**

Spice Islander, **19**

Telaga Naga, **17**

Warung Kopi, **5**

Lodging

Bali Dynasty, **12**

Bali Hilton International, **26**

Bali Hyatt, **20**

Bali Imperial, **3**

Buala Club, **27**

Four Seasons Resort, **13**

Grand Hyatt Bali, **25**

Hotel Sanur Beach, **22**

Kul Kul Beach Resort, **10**

Kuta Palace Hotel, **4**

Oberoi, **2**

Sari Yasa Samudra Bungalows, **8**

Segara Village, **14**

Sheraton Lagoon Nusa Dua, **24**

Tandjung Sari, **15**

$$$ ☷ **Bali Imperial.** Set beyond the crowds along the Kuta/Legian strip but within a 10-minute walk of the action, this 1994 resort is a quiet oasis. The relaxed, expansive lobby is glass and marble. Guest rooms have high ceilings, light wood furniture, shining wood floors, either two twins or one king-size bed, balconies looking onto either the sea or the garden, and marble bathrooms with separate shower stalls. Butler service brings complimentary coffee or tea. The resort is under the same management as the Imperial Hotel in Tokyo—hence the emphasis on service; with a staff-to-guest ratio of three to one, attention is immediate. ⊠ *Box 384 (Jln. Dhyanapura), Legian Beach, Denpasar 80001, ☎ 0361/ 754545, ꜰꜰ 0361/751545; U.S., ☎ 212/692–9001; U.K., ☎ 0171/355– 1775. 121 rooms, 17 bungalows. 2 restaurants, room service, 2 pools, 2 tennis courts, travel services. AE, DC, MC, V.*

$$–$$$ ☷ **Kul Kul Beach Resort.** Kul Kul is architecturally the most interesting
★ and attractive hotel on Kuta beach. The sundeck is built over rocks on one side of the pool, and you clamber down boulders to have a dip or get a drink. Accommodations consist of modern bungalows that include sitting rooms and bedrooms furnished in Balinese style—rattan and bamboo—with deluxe bathrooms. The attentive service of the staff adds to the sense of harmony guests feel amid the resort's Balinese architecture. The restaurant has a comprehensive menu ranging from Italian pasta dishes to New Zealand lamb and beef to fresh fish to Indonesian rice dishes. In the evening, a wayang kulit performance is given in English, an Indonesian singer entertains in the bar, and a video is shown on a wide screen. ⊠ *Jln. Pantai Kuta, Legian Kelon, Kuta, Box 97, Denpasar 80361, ☎ 0361/752520, ꜰꜰ 0361/752519. 55 rooms. Restaurant, bar, pool, dance club. AE, MC, V.*

$$ ☷ **Bali Dynasty.** Tuban has more than enough restaurants, shops, and nightclubs, but it's still less congested than nearby Kuta. At the Dynasty, two wings branch out from the main building to house the guest rooms. These have a standard rectangular layout with a double or twin beds against one wall, a writing table along the other, and a couple of easy chairs; an extra $10 gets you a garden view. The pool is close to the beach. There is a Western-style restaurant and a particularly good Chinese restaurant, the Golden Lotus, whose Singaporean chef has a sure hand with spices. ⊠ *Box 2047, Jln. Kartika Plaza, Tuban 80361, ☎ 0361/752403, ꜰꜰ 0361/752402; U.S., ☎ 800/942–5050; U.K., ☎ 0181/747–8485. 225 rooms, 12 suites. 2 restaurants, 2 bars, pool, tennis court, dance club, travel services. AE, DC, MC, V.*

$$ ☷ **Kuta Palace Hotel.** Set on 11 acres on Legian beach, this hotel consists of two-story buildings surrounding a courtyard with gardens and pools. Rooms are simply but pleasantly decorated in Balinese-patterned fabrics and a cream-and-rust color scheme. All have air-conditioning, refrigerators, and views. ⊠ *Box 3244, Denpasar 80001, ☎ 0361/ 751433, ꜰꜰ 0361/752074. Restaurant, pool, room service, 4 tennis courts, laundry service. AE, DC, MC, V.*

$ ☷ **Sari Yasa Samudra Bungalows.** Across the road from Kuta beach, this collection of cottages offers bare-bones accommodations with ceiling fans and only limited hours of hot water in the private baths. It's virtually without aesthetic appeal but cleaner and newer than its sister property, Yasa Samudra, next door. ⊠ *Box 53, Denpasar 80001, ☎ 0361/751562, ꜰꜰ 0361/752948. 31 rooms. Restaurant, bar, pool. No credit cards.*

Nightlife and the Arts

Tourist life on Bali focuses on sightseeing and beach activities; by late evening, most areas quiet down, with one exception: Kuta Beach. Here the activity begins with drinks at cafés—one of the most consistently popular is Poppies (☞ Dining, *above*)—in the early evening, which may continue well into the night or shift to the discos. Most of these have a modest cover charge of Rp 2,000–Rp 3,000.

DANCE CLUBS AND MUSIC

Gado-Gado (⊠ Jln. Dhyana Puru, ☎ 0361/775225), open Wednesday–Sunday) is an open-air disco near the ocean. There's no cover at the **Hard Rock Cafe** (⊠ Jln. Legian 204, Kuta, ☎ 0361/755661) unless a live band is billed; generally, the action starts rolling at 9 PM and grinds down at 2 AM. **Kayu Api** (no phone), at the intersection of Jalan Legian and Jalan Melasti, has live music, often of international caliber. **Koala Blu** (⊠ Jln. Kuta) attracts mostly Australians. For informality, drop in at the **Kuta Jaya Jazz Corner** (⊠ Jln. Raya. Pantai Kuta, ☎ 0361/752308).

KARAOKE

There's a karaoke bar at the **Kul Kul Beach Resort** (☎ 0361/51952) on Jalan Pantai Juta at the boundary between Kuta and Legian townships. Here, on an open-sided stage, a small band plays the top 20 interspersed with large-screen video. A delightful veranda lounge offers a lower noise level. Another popular karaoke bar is at the Bali Dynasty's **Karaoke & Waves Discotheque** in Tuban (☎ 0361/752403).

Shopping

For Asmat art from Irian Jaya and other village artifacts, take a look at the wares in **Asmat** (⊠ Jln. Tunjung Mekar 55, Kuta, ☎). **The Grace Shop** (⊠ Jln. Legian Tengah 435, Kuta, ☎ 0361/752003) offers a range of Balinese antiques. For toys, try the **Joger Handcraft Center** in Kuta Beach (⊠ Jln. Raya Kuta, ☎ 0361/53959).

Jimbaran Bay

❷ *20 km (12 mi) south of Denpasar.*

A new resort area is springing up along Jimbaran Bay, on the western side of the Bukit Peninsula to the south of Kuta. Once a sleepy fishing village, it is now a playground for guests staying at the InterContinental and Bali's most luxurious resort, the Four Seasons. An offshore reef offers protection from the waves, providing gentle swimming waters.

Lodging

$$$$
★
🏨 **Four Seasons Resort.** This extravagant 35-acre resort is a village of luxury bungalows rising from the shore some 150 feet up the hill. The most elevated bungalows are the farthest from the public areas, including the beach and pool, but they have the best view of Jimbaran Bay. (Never fear: There's an electric taxi to beat the hike.) Once you enter your villa courtyard through a pair of carved and painted Balinese double doors, you're in your own personal oasis. Stepping stones, surrounded by luminous green pebbles, lead to a private pool. The gentle sound of splashing water spouts from a poolside fountain. The open-side living-and-dining pavilions look onto the pool and bay beyond, and each garden is totally private. The bedrooms have wonderful peaked bamboo-and-alang-alang–thatch roofs; eight larger bungalows have two bedrooms. Bathroom have huge, deep tubs and separate shower areas, plus another shower outdoors in a small courtyard garden. Down by the beach, the pool spills over a 20-foot waterfall into a free-form soaking area below. The Four Seasons is very much a self-contained resort; there are no villages within a couple of miles, and the nearest building is the Bali Inter-Continental, a mile or so down the beach. The quoted rate is expensive—about $425 a night—but seasonal discounts can usually reduce the rate. ⊠ *Jimbaran, Denpasar 80361,* ☎ *0361/701010,* FAX *0361/701020. 147 bungalows. 2 restaurants, pool, massage, spa, 2 tennis courts, snorkeling, windsurfing, boating. AE, DC, MC, V.*

Nusa Dua

❸ *30 km (18 mi) south of Denpasar.*

Nusa Dua, a former burial ground, consists of two tiny islands linked to the mainland with a reinforced sand spit. Unlike Kuta and Sanur, this is an entirely planned resort, with no indigenous community. Its large, self-contained hotels include a Grand Hyatt, a Sheraton, and a Hilton. Visitors who stay here must travel inland to see the real Bali, but Nusa Dua's beaches are wide and peaceful, and its hotels luxurious.

Dining and Lodging

$$$ ✕ **Kertosa Restaurant.** This formal Continental restaurant has the atmosphere of a European hotel, despite the Balinese stone sculptures on pedestals. The menu is international with a French flavor, and there's an extensive wine list—a costly luxury in Bali. ⊠ *Nusa Dua Beach Hotel,* ☎ *0361/977120. AE, DC, MC, V.*

$$$–$$$$ 🏨 **Bali Hilton International.** A spectacular floodlit waterfall sets the scene at this huge property. Five-story buildings on either side of the vast open-sided reception area create a U around a courtyard filled with lagoons. It takes 10 minutes to walk from the reception area to the buildings closest to the beach, though if you have a car you can drive. Most rooms look onto the lagoon courtyard rather than the sea. The Executive Court rooms are slightly larger and have separate showers. ⊠ *Box 46, Nusa Dua 80361, Bali,* ☎ *0361/771102,* 🖷 *0361/771199; U.S.,* ☎ *800/ HILTONS. 537 rooms. 4 restaurants, coffee shop, in-room safes, pool, 4 tennis courts, exercise room, squash, theater, meeting rooms. AE, DC, MC, V.*

$$$–$$$$ 🏨 **Grand Hyatt Bali.** You need a map to find your way around the four compounds of hotel rooms, let alone the beach. Each compound has its own small lagoon or swimming pool, so that all guest rooms have water views. Rooms are large, with king-size beds facing small sitting enclaves with banquette seats. The bathrooms, with separate shower stalls, have wooden shutters that may be opened to the bedrooms, creating a greater sense of space. Regency rooms (15%–20% costlier) offer separate lounge areas where complimentary breakfasts and evening cocktails are served. The hotel is designed to seem Balinese, from a temple to a night market of food stalls to a fish restaurant using Balinese fishing nets for decor. The complex's size makes it attractive to large groups and package tours. ⊠ *Box 53, Nusa Dua 80361, Bali,* ☎ *0361/ 777–1188,* 🖷 *0361/777–2038, U.S.,* ☎ *800/233–1234. 750 rooms. 5 restaurants, coffee shop, in-room safes, 6 pools, 6 tennis courts, exercise room, squash, theater, meeting rooms. AE, DC, MC, V.*

$$$–$$$$ 🏨 **Sheraton Lagoon Nusa Dua.** Much smaller than most hotels on Nusa Dua, the Sheraton Lagoon forms a U facing the sea. The central courtyard is a series of connected swimming lagoons and waterfalls; rooms face either these lagoons (the ones at ground level have swimming ladders from the balcony and a 20% higher tariff) or the gardens. The excellent service employs the butler concept, whereby one staff member is responsible for all a guest's wants. Most of the restaurants and activities are close to the beach. ⊠ *Box 2044, Nusa Dua 80361,* ☎ *0361/771327,* 🖷 *0361/771326, U.S.,* ☎ *800/325–3535. 276 rooms including 65 suites. 4 restaurants, in-room safes, pool, wading pool, 2 tennis courts, exercise room, theater, business services, tour services. AE, DC, MC, V.*

$$$ 🏨 **Buala Club.** At the southern end of Nusa Dua beach, this quiet hotel offers an all-inclusive vacation, with free activities and personalized service. Accommodations are in a two-story Balinese-style building surrounded by gardens. Rooms are simple but pleasant, with ikat-patterned fabrics; all have a private balcony or veranda. ✉ *Box 6, Nusa Dua 80363,* ☎ *0361/771310,* FAX *0361/771313. 50 rooms. 3 restaurants, bar, pool, horseback riding, beach, snorkeling, windsurfing, meeting rooms. AE, DC, MC, V.*

Nightlife and the Arts

In Nusa Dua, the hotels all offer evening entertainment, either Balinese dance or a live band playing current international favorites. For glittering action and dancing to live music, try **Soarrosa** at the Bali Resort Palace hotel in nearby Tanjung Benoa.

Outdoor Activities and Sports

The 18-hole, 6,839-yard course of the **Bali Golf & Country Club** (☎ 0361/771791), on the Bukit Peninsula near the hotels of Nusa Dua, offers $125 greens fees (including caddy) and $27 club rental.

Sanur

❹ *9 km (5 mi) east of Denpasar.*

Sanur Beach was Bali's second beach resort. Its hotels, restaurants, and shops are more spread out, so the pace here is less hectic than in Kuta. The beach is less dramatic, too: Instead of wild waves, there's a coral reef that keeps the water calm—especially appealing to windsurfers.

Dining and Lodging

$$$ ✕ **Spice Islander.** The elegant Balinese decor, with gilded table bases
★ and heavy rattan chairs, is a great setting in which to get acquainted with Balinese cuisine. A rijsttafel buffet with no fewer than 30 dishes—all labeled with their ingredients—is laid out on a lotus altar in the center of the room. Among the delicacies: *crancam ayam* (chicken soup with ginger), *kalio hati dengan kentang* (spicy chicken livers with potato), *opar sapi* (beef in coconut curry sauce), *satay lilit* (skewered pork and beef), and *gudeg yogya* (a dish made of jackfruit). ✉ *Bali Hyatt, Sanur,* ☎ *0361/588271. Reservations suggested during busy season. AE, DC, MC, V.*

$$$ ✕ **Telaga Naga.** With a name meaning "dragon's pond," this is the best Chinese restaurant in Bali. Two lily ponds create a floating pavilion atmosphere, and the Singaporean chef specializes in Cantonese and Szechuan cuisine. Try the minced chicken with chili and cucumber, followed by fried lobster with chili and black bean sauce. ✉ *Near the Bali Hyatt, Sanur,* ☎ *0361/88271. Reservations essential. AE, DC, MC, V.*

$$ ✕ **Le Gong.** The gong hangs in a central garden, and although the restaurant is on Sanur's main street, its woven bamboo walls and set-back tables give it a relaxing atmosphere. To make the most of the traditional Balinese menu, order a few dishes and share them. Some suggestions: soto ayam, prawns in butter sauce, fish grilled with spices, and nasi goreng. Fresh papaya or pineapple makes a refreshing dessert, but the coup de grâce is the Balinese equivalent of a banana split, swathed in a honey treacle. ✉ *Jln. Legong, Semawang-Sanur,* ☎ *0361/588066. No credit cards.*

$$ ✕ **Penjor Restaurant.** Set back from the main street, this bamboo-walled restaurant surrounds an open courtyard where tables are laid in fine weather. Each night a different Balinese dance-drama is presented, and the set menu rotates Balinese, Indonesian, Chinese, and Indian dinners. Owner Ida Bagus Ketut Oka speaks English fluently and loves to chat with his guests. ✉ *Batu Jumbar, Sanur,* ☎ *0361/88226. AE, DC, MC, V.*

$$ ✕ **Ronny's Pub & Restaurant.** For a choice of primarily Western dishes that include fresh fish, sirloin steaks, and nonspicy satay, this open-sided restaurant is better than most of the stops along the Sanur strip between the Hyatt and Sanur Beach hotels. Especially good are the grilled prawns served with butter rice and fresh vegetables. ⊠ *Jln. Sanur Beach, Sanur,* ☎ *0361/978370. Reservations not accepted. V.*

$$$$ ⚏ **Tandjung Sari.** This unique hotel is a peaceful "village" of Balinese-style bungalows set in tropical gardens that hide small stone temples and statues. The lobby is an open pavilion decorated with carvings. Bungalows have split bamboo walls and are furnished with handwoven fabrics, an antique or two, and a minibar. Most of the bathrooms have skylights. Prawns, curries, fritters, and a dozen other items—and, on Wednesday night, a superb rijsttafel—are served in a romantic setting just back from the beach. ⊠ *Box 25, Denpasar 80001,* ☎ *0361/ 288441,* FAX *0361/287930. 24 bungalows. Restaurant, bar, beach, pool, windsurfing, snorkeling. No credit cards.*

$$$ ⚏ **Bali Hyatt.** The queen of Sanur, this hotel sits on 36 acres of gardens along the beach. The open lobby has a soaring roof thatched with elephant grass and faces out to lush gardens that lead first to the pool and then the beach. The property lacks a certain style and flair, but the rooms are freshly furnished and those in the Regency wing are spacious. This Hyatt, in contrast to the Grand Hyatt at Nusa Dua, focusses on the individual traveler rather than groups. ⊠ *Box 392, Denpasar 80001,* ☎ *0361/288271,* FAX *0361/271693. 387 rooms. 5 restaurants, 4 bars, 2 pools, 3-hole golf course, 2 tennis courts, snorkeling, windsurfing, meeting rooms. AE, DC, MC, V.*

$$$ ⚏ **Hotel Sanur Beach.** Most of the action takes place around the pools, the beach, and the patio bars. The best rooms face the pool. All rooms have a private balcony, and most have huge double beds, though a few in the older wing have twins. There are also 26 self-contained bungalows for more privacy. Classical Balinese dance performances and buffet dinners are offered most nights. ⊠ *Box 3279, Denpasar 80001,* ☎ *0361/288011,* FAX *0361/287566. 298 rooms and 26 bungalows. 3 restaurants, coffee shop, 2 pools, 4 tennis courts, badminton, windsurfing, recreation room, meeting rooms. AE, DC, MC, V.*

$$ ⚏ **Segara Village.** At the north end of Sanur Beach, this small, family-owned hotel offers Balinese-style thatch-roof cottages. The open lobby houses both of the hotel's restaurants, so it can be busy. Rooms are air-conditioned and have a balcony or veranda and private bath. Decor is very simple, but the hospitality is genuine. ⊠ *Box 91, Denpasar 80001,* ☎ *0361/288407,* FAX *0361/287242. 40 rooms. 2 restaurants, 4 bars, room service, 2 pools, 2 tennis courts, bicycles, recreation room. AE, DC, MC, V.*

Nightlife and the Arts

Most hotels here have some form of entertainment with a live band. The largest disco is **Subek** (⊠ Jln. Danau Tamblingen 21, ☎ 0361/ 288888).

Outdoor Activities and Sports

BOATING

For yacht charters, contact **Jet Boat Tours** (⊠ Jln. Pantai Karang 5, Sanur, ☎ 0361/28839). Sanur's **Bali Hyatt** has two deep-sea fishing boats.

DIVING AND SURFING

You can get scuba equipment and a ride out to the reef at Sanur from **Bali Marine Sport** (⊠ Jln. Bypass Ngurah Rai, Sanur, ☎ 0361/87872) **Ocean Dive Center** (⊠ Jln. Bypass, Ngurah Rai, Sanur, ☎ 0361/88652) organizes dives out to reefs.

Nusa Lembongan, the island opposite Sanur Beach and next to Nusa Penida, offers surfing and diving. But for the best surfing, head to Ulu Watu, on the western side of the Bukit Peninsula at Bali's southern tip.

Both dive shops listed above rent boards and arrange transportation; you can also rent boards at the beaches, but they tend to be of lesser quality, and you are responsible for any damage done to them.

Denpasar

⑤ *10 km (6 mi) north of Kuta.*

Most of Bali's cultural attractions are inland, to the north and east of the capital, Denpasar. Tourists do not normally stay in this busy market town of about 40,000 people, but Denpasar is worth a half-day visit. You can book city tours through your hotel, or you can see Denpasar on your own, by taxi or bemo.

Pasar Banjung is the liveliest market in town. It is busiest in the early morning but continues until early afternoon. The large, two-story covered market, near the bridge off Jalan Gajahmada, is packed with spice vendors and farmers selling vegetables, meats, and flowers. The little girls who volunteer to guide you around the market get commissions from any vendor you patronize; of course, your price is raised accordingly.

If you come to Denpasar in the evening, head for the **night market** in the riverside parking lot of the multilevel shopping center at Kusumasari. The market is a gathering place for locals, who come to chat, shop, and feast on Balinese food.

At the center of the crossroads where Jalan Gajahmada intersects with Jalan Veteran is a large **statue of Brahma.** Its four faces look in the cardinal directions. To the left on Jalan Veteran is the **Hotel Bali** (⊠ Jln. Veteran 3, ☎ 0361/5681), in a building dating from the Dutch colonial period.

Continue through this intersection past Puputan Square—a park on the right-hand side, with its Sukarno-inspired heroic statue of the common man—to reach **Pura Agung Jagatnatha,** Bali's state temple. To find the entrance, go right at the end of the park onto Jalan Letkol, and it's on your left. The temple's center stupa is surrounded by a moat and rises eight levels; at the top is a statue of Shiva with flames coming out of his shoulders. The stupa is supported by the cosmic turtle (on whose back the real world symbolically sits) and protected by a huge carved face with a red-cloth tongue. *Nagas* (serpents) entwine the base; around the bottom are relief carvings.

Farther down Jalan Letkol is the **Bali Museum,** with Balinese art dating from prehistoric to present times. The buildings are excellent examples of Balinese temple and palace architecture. ⊠ *Jln. Letkol. Wisnu,* ☎ *0361/2680 or 0361/5362.* ▧ *Admission.* ⊙ *Tues.–Thurs. and Sun. 8–2, Fri. 8–11 AM, Sat. 8 AM–12:30 PM.*

Another Denpasar attraction is **Abiankapas,** a large art complex. In the summer, dance performances are held in its auditorium. During the rest of the year, it offers changing exhibits of modern paintings, batik designs, and wood carvings. ⊠ *Jln. Abiankapas, no phone.* ▧ *Admission.* ⊙ *Daily 10–4.*

Shopping
The **Mega Art Gallery** (⊠ Jln. Gajahmada) sells new and antique puppets, wood carvings, and paintings.

Tanah Lot

15 km (9 mi) west of Denpasar.

This famous temple stands on a small rocky islet accessible only by a small causeway (except at high tide, when it turns into an island). Though visitors come here in droves for the postcard-like setting, the Balinese revere this pagoda-style temple as deeply as they do the mountain shrines. It has the added mystery of snakes that secret themselves in the rock holes and are said to guard the spirits residing at Tanah Lot. Ideally, you should arrive at Tanah Lot an hour before sunset, which will give you enough time to inspect the snakes; entering the caves on the shore, you can usually find a sleepy reptile resting in the cool. Cross the causeway to the temple, then return to the shore to watch it become silhouetted against the burning sky as the sun goes down. Not even the hawkers and the lines of snapping cameras (and the Meridien hotel is opening within sight of the temple in 1997) can spoil the vision.

Batubulan

❻ *19 km (12 mi) northeast of Denpasar.*

The main route leading to Ubud from Denpasar passes through several villages, each known for a different craft. The first village is Batubulan, famous for the stone carvers whose workshops and displays line the road. You'll see workshops where boys chip at the soft sandstone, and sculptures are for sale out front. Their wares range from the classic guardian figures that stand before Balinese temples and houses to smaller statues. Most workshops make small carvings for tourists. I. Made Sura is one of the better shops; it also carries some wood carvings, old wood ornaments, and carved doors.

At 9:30 each morning, dance-dramas are performed at each of the village's three theaters, located along the main road. The same show is performed at all three. Admission is around Rp 20,000, but most audience members are on all-inclusive area tours arranged from their hotels.

Tohpati

Just north of Batubulan.

Balinese batiks tend to be more colorful than the traditional Javanese style, and the designs are more floral than geometric. A good source of hand-drawn batiks is **Popiler** (☎ 0361/36498) in the village of Tohpati, on the outskirts of Batubulan. If you pay cash instead of using a credit card, you may increase your bargaining power by around 20% for the yard goods, paintings, garments, and household items here. Behind the shop, you're invited to watch girls outlining the designs with wax.

Singapadu

1.6 km (1 mi) north of Batubulan.

German businessman and Balinese resident Ed Swoboda chose Singapadu as the site of the **Taman Burung** (Bali Bird Park). The avaries (designed with Balinese thatched roofs) of the 4-acre park house birds from around the world, including such rare and endangered species native to Indonesia as Irian Jayan birds of paradise and Balinese hynah. A 160-seat restaurant makes a good stop for breakfast in a lush tropical setting. ⊠ *Jln. Serma Lok Ngurah Gambir, Singapadu,* ☎ *0361/299352.* ⊡ *Admission.* ⊙ *Daily 8–6.*

Celuk

❼ *2 km (1.2 mi) north of Batubulan.*

Celuk is a village of silversmiths. In workshops behind the stores, you can watch boys working the silver and setting semiprecious stones. As a rule, the jewelry you find here is 90%–92% silver, the tableware

60%–70%. Filigree pieces with detailed imaginative designs are the best items to buy, but don't buy in the morning when all the tour buses stop here—come back in the afternoon when prices return to a more reasonable level. If you have time, you can custom-order pieces. Remember that with a smile and a murmur you might drive the cost of a $125 bracelet down to $80. Especially where price tags are in dollars, bargaining is the rule.

At least 30 shops line the main road and surrounding streets, although a severe shortage of sidewalks can make browsing about on foot potentially life-threatening. The goods vary little from store to store—rings, earrings, and hair clips are perennial favorites—but some establishments display more merchandise. One shop with a large selection is **Dewi Sitha** (no phone), on the left side of the road going north.

Sukawati

❽ *4 km (2.5 mi) north of Celuk.*

Sukawati is the cane-weaving village, but local artisans also make wind-chimes and shadow puppets. Stalls lining the road sell baskets, hats, and some furniture. If you determinedly ask, you'll also be able to find some antique wayang kulits here.

Batuan

❾ *2 km (1.3 mi) north of Sukawati.*

Batuan is a weaving village and Bali's painting center. For the best of Batuan, ask any local to direct you to the studios of Mokoh, I. Made Budi, or Wayan Darmawan. The hand-cut, painted shadow puppets for sale on Bali are usually new, but you can buy antique ones at the **Jati Art Gallery** (⊠ Along the main road, no phone), which also sells paintings and artifacts, old masks and temple ornaments, handwoven ikat, batiks, wood carvings, and new puppets.

Find time in this village to visit the 10th-century **temple of Brahma** (Pura Puseh Pura Desa). The brick-and-sandstone temple has three parts. You enter the outer courtyard through a classic Balinese split gate. The bell tower, in the second courtyard, is hung with the ubiquitous black-and-white-checked cloth. In the main courtyard, a stone screen protects the temple from bad spirits: Because a bad spirit can't turn a corner, it can't go around the screen. In one corner of the main courtyard is a shrine to Brahma, where a hermaphroditic figure is guarded by two nagas. This is the main shrine and, as in every Balinese temple complex, it faces the home of the gods, Mt. Agung. (Oddly for an island people, the Balinese have always turned inward, toward the land—the sea is full of demons.) Nearby, another shrine has three roofs representing the god's three manifestations. The face over the gate entrances, known as Boma, guards against evil from the earth, the nagas against evil from the sea.

Kemenuh

❿ *3 km (1.3 mi) north of Batuan.*

In the village of Kemenuh, the **home of Ida B. Marka,** a famous woodcarver, is open to the public, providing a rare opportunity to look inside a Balinese home. The sales showroom is in front, but there is no pressure to make a purchase. Behind are a courtyard and a cluster of buildings that serve as the family complex. The centerpiece is the building used for weddings and other rites of passage; this is where the oldest family member sleeps. Other structures include the family temple, a granary, and a cooperative workshop where other villagers help to carve and polish.

Mas

⓫ *5 km (3 mi) north of Kemenuh.*

There are some 4,000 wood-carvers on Bali, and most of them are in Mas. The village is also known for its mask making, samples of which can be found in shops down the back lanes. The masks, which make great wall hangings, range in price from $2 to $50, depending on their size and complexity.

The home of **Ida Bagus Tilem** (⊠ Ubud Rd., ☎ 0361/6414), Indonesia's most famous wood-carver, is in Mas; his work, which has been exhibited internationally, is sold in his small shop. **Taman Harum Cottages** (⊠ Box 216, Denpasar, ☎ 0361/35242) in Mas, with 17 compact adjoining duplexes, offers wood-carving classes to its guests and has its own shop, the **Tantra Gallery**, which display works of master carver Nyana. Another gallery worth searching out is the **Tinem Gallery** (☎ 0361/35136), with the works of Nyana's brother, Ida Bagus Nyana.

Goa Gajah

⓬ *After Mas and just before Ubud, take a right turn onto the road toward Pejeng and Gianyar. A parking lot on the right indicates the entrance to Goa Gajah.*

Discovered in 1923 by a farmer cultivating his field, the cave temple of Goa Gajah (Elephant Cave) is thought to have been built in the 11th century. In the courtyard, water spouts from the hands of six stone nymphs into two pools. It is believed that worshipers would purify themselves here before passing through the mouth of the giant Boma face carving on the entrance. The Balinese consider the face protective even though it contains the same symbolic features as the Kali face found at other Hindu temples. To enter the cave, worshipers must pass through her mouth.

The cave itself is pitch dark—hope that your guide has a flashlight. To the left is a niche with a statue of Ganesha, the elephant-headed god and son of Shiva. In the center, to the right of a crumbled statue, are three *linga* (upright carved stones symbolizing male fertility), each with three smaller *yoni* (female forms).

NEED A BREAK?	At the top of the hill, above the cave, is **Puri Suling** (no phone), a pleasant restaurant with a terrace that looks out over the rice fields and down to the cave area. In addition to dull Western food, the restaurant serves excellent Indonesian specialties.

Ubud

⓭ *25 km (15 mi) north of Denpasar, 5 km (3 mi) north of Mas.*

Ubud gained fame as an art colony and has since grown into the island's main cultural center, with art galleries, crafts shops, and traditional Balinese dance performances taking place in town or nearby every day. However, as it has grown as a tourist center, Ubud has become more commercial. Many artists still have their workshops in this region, but in recent years, hotels, guest houses, restaurants, ice-cream parlors, shops, and souvenir stalls have been multiplying.

Ubud and Vicinity

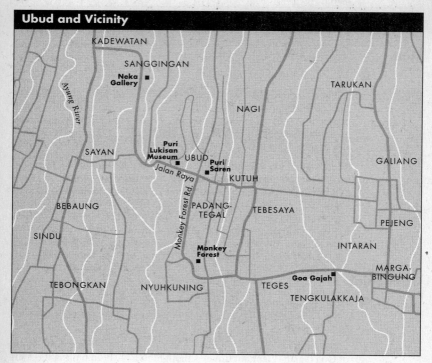

It may no longer be a quiet haven in which to immerse yourself in Balinese culture, but Ubud does still offer the best opportunity to brush against authentic Balinese life, at least when compared to the resort areas along the coast. It also makes an excellent base for exploring the interior of Bali. Step out of town and walk the many trails that lead through the surrounding countryside to small villages, and you will still find the "real Bali."

Ubud was placed on the world map when artists Walter Spies from Germany and Rudolf Bonnet from Holland introduced to the Balinese the three dimensional form and convinced them that using real people, not courtly officials, in a free flowing environment was legitimate art. From the point on, a naturalism was born in Balinese art. The place to see this evolution is at the **Puri Lukisan Museum,** which exhibits the range of art from the 1930s to the present. Set in a garden at the west end of the main street, with rice paddies and water buffalo in the background, the work is arranged chronologically, so you can follow the development from formal religious art to more natural, realistic depictions of dances, festivals, and rice harvesting. ⊠ *North side of main road, Jln. Raya, west of intersection with Monkey Forest Rd.,* ☎ *0361/ 975136.* 🎟 *Admission.* ⏱ *Daily 10–4.*

For a broad overview of Balinese (and Indonesian) styles, visit Ubud's finest collection of paintings at the **Neka Gallery,** at the east end of the main street. The works are organized by style in seven buildings, one of which has painting by foreign artists, including Spies and Bonnet. Be sure to visit Building Three, devoted to paintings by Affandi, and Building Two, which has works by I Gusti Nyoman Lempadi. ⊠ *Jln. Raya.* 🎟 *Admission.* ⏱ *Daily 9–4.*

In the center of town is **Puri Saren,** a prince's palace that is also a hotel. The complex is beautiful, but not very well maintained. The prince's living quarters are at the end of the courtyard; guest accommodations are in surrounding buildings. One contains an old tiger costume from the Barong dance, and a peacock walks the grounds. On Monday and Friday dances are performed in the courtyard; the dancers rehearse on Sunday.

Across from Puri Saren is Monkey Forest Road, which in recent years has filled up with souvenir and T-shirt shops and inexpensive restaurants. (Farther along are small hotels, losmen, and homestays where you can find simple accommodation for under U.S.$20 a night.) Keep walking and you'll reach the **Monkey Forest,** where a small donation will get you a close-up view of monkeys so accustomed to tourists that the little monsters will lift items from your pocket or tear jewelry off your neck and scamper off with their loot into the trees.

Dining and Lodging

$$$ ✕ **Kupu Kupu Barong.** Perched on a terrace in the hotel of the same
★ name, this restaurant—which has been newly refurbished, retiled, and rethatched—overlooks the spectacular green gorge of the Ayung River. Marble-top tables and rattan chairs add charm. The best views are from the upstairs dining room, though it takes longer for drinks to arrive from the bar. The menu includes Indonesian and international fare. Try the smoked duck with Balinese side dishes; the pan-fried lobster topped with shallots, mushrooms, and coriander; or the fish grilled on bamboo skewers and served with a light peanut sauce. ⊠ *Kedewatan,* ☎ *0361/923172. Reservations essential during high season. AE, V.*

$$ ✕ **Ananda Cottages.** Part of the Ananda Cottages hotel, this open-air restaurant is surrounded by rice paddies. Its menu lists Western and Indonesian specialties, including *satay pusut* (skewered meat in a spicy peanut sauce) and *betutu bebek* (Balinese duck). ⊠ *Jln. Raya,* ☎ *0361/ 958001. Reservations not accepted. No credit cards.*

$$ ✕ **Lotus Café.** Owned and managed by a Balinese and his Australian wife, this peaceful and charming restaurant in the center of Ubud has blue-and-white-tile-topped tables in a small garden with a Hindu temple at the back. The menu is creative and refreshing. Try the avocado with diced peanuts, or perhaps the roasted chicken. The homemade pasta is remarkably good, too. ⊠ *Jln. Raya, no phone. Reservations not accepted. No credit cards.*

$$ ✕ **Murni's Warung.** On the side of a small ravine, this simple terraced restaurant with bamboo furniture offers both Indonesian and Western cooking. The duck *tu tu* is a Balinese specialty of duck stuffed with spices and thoroughly baked so that the meat falls off the bones. The restaurant has two dining rooms: One is at street level and bustles with activity; the other, a steep flight down, is often empty and has the best views of the waterfall 50 feet away. ⊠ *Campuan,* ☎ *0361/995233. Reservations not accepted. No credit cards.*

$$$$ ▥ **Amandari.** Owned by Ammanresorts (which has two other resorts
★ on Bali, Amankila and Amanusa), this boutique hotel employs the same formula for success—luxury and elegance in a modern architectural style that reflects local custom. The Amandari overlooks the rice terraces of the lush Ayung gorge. Serene stone walls enclose individual thatch-roof villas, ensuring privacy. Inside are elegant, light-filled suites, beautifully appointed with dark wood, marble floors, and heavy cream upholstery; each has a spacious shower and dressing area and a sunken outdoor tub. In the duplex suites, a spiral stair leads to an upstairs bedroom. Prices ($400–$800) vary depending on size, view, and whether the suite has a private pool. The spacious public areas include the open-air lobby, a book and CD library, and a restaurant overlooking the dramatic infinity-edge pool. Drivers are available to take

you to and from downtown Ubud. ✉ *Box 33, Ubud 80571,* ☎ *0361/975333,* 🕾 *0361/975335; U.S.,* ☎ *800/447–7462 or 212/223– 2848; U.K.,* ☎ *0800/282684. 29 suites, 6 with private pool. Restaurant, bar, room service, pool, massage, tennis court, bicycles, hiking, rafting, travel services. AE, DC, MC, V.*

$$$$ 🏨 **Kupu Kupu Barong.** The loveliest, even if not the most luxurious, of ★ Bali's country lodgings, this beautiful and intimate hotel sits on the precipice of a deep valley, with glorious views of rice terraces and the Ayung River below. You approach the dining room via a path trellised with banana leaves, hibiscus, and clove trees. The rooms vary in size and cost ($350–$450); all require stout legs, since they're built into the hillside. The older bungalows are individually designed to blend with the hilly landscape, with woven rattan or stone-face walls and unique crafted furnishings. The duplexes have Indonesian wood paneling and luxuriously large bathrooms. The restaurant (☞ *above*) is delightful. The food and beverage manager is an avid collector of Balinese art with plenty of advice on Ubud's shops, which are reachable via a free shuttle service. Children under 12 are not welcome. ✉ *Desa Kedewatan, Ubud 80571,* ☎ *0361/795478,* 🕾 *0361/795079; U.S.,* ☎ *800/561– 3071; U.K.,* ☎ *0171/742–7780. 19 suites, 1 with private pool. Restaurant, 2 bars, room service, 2 pools, massage, bicycles, rafting, travel services. AE, DC, MC, V.*

$$ 🏨 **Puri Bunga Village Hotel.** With only 14 rooms and a very personable manager, this is a quiet oasis overlooking the Ajung River, with the same views as the Amandari and the Kupu Kupu at a quarter of the price. All but two rooms face the valley, so reserve accordingly. Rooms are quite spacious, though not spectacular in their furnishings. All come with a small bar area to make cocktails and morning coffee. Two junior suites have whirlpools, and the "honeymoon" suite is the most luxurious and private. A small pool in the garden adjoins the open-sided restaurant. You are better off having your own wheels here; otherwise it means a 10-minute taxi ride into Ubud's center. ✉ *Box 141, Kedewatan Village, Ubud 80000,* ☎ *0361/975488,* 🕾 *0361/ 975073. 14 rooms. Restaurant, pool. MC, V.*

$$ 🏨 **Tjampuhan.** On the main road just out of Ubud, atop a ravine overlooking a holy river, Tjampuhan was once an artists' colony and still includes the former house of German painter Walter Spies. The lobby is no more than an open terrace off the road, with paths leading to the bungalows. These have carved and gilded wood doors, woven bamboo walls, bamboo furniture, and handwoven fabrics and batik as decorations. During the rainy season, the rooms tend to be a little damp; because of the terracing, small children can take quite a tumble. You ring for breakfast with bamboo bells. ✉ *Box 15, Denpasar 80364,* ☎ *0361/ 728871,* 🕾 *0361/795155. 40 bungalows. Restaurant, bar, pool, 2 tennis courts, bicycles, car rental. MC, V.*

$ 🏨 **Agung Raka.** Four of the guest rooms at this lodging in a develop- ★ ing area off Monkey Forest Road are duplexes: downstairs are a covered patio and a small lounge area; up steep wooden stairs is the main bedroom with a canopied bed and a small balcony overlooking the rice fields. The bathroom and shower are outside, enclosed but open to the sky. The rate—about U.S.$50—includes breakfast. The remaining rooms, which cost about a quarter less, are in small two-story houses; the ground-floor ones have patios, the upstairs ones balconies. The duplexes are the better value. ✉ *Pengoseken, Ubud 80000,* ☎ *0361/ 975757,* 🕾 *0361/975546. 12 rooms. Restaurant, pool. MC, V.*

$ 🏨 **Ananda Cottages.** This friendly, relaxed hotel is set in the rice paddies in Campuhan, up the hill outside Ubud. The open-air lounge and lobby surround a central garden; the "cottages" are thatch-roof, brick bungalows with two units above and two below. Room decor is simple, with rattan furniture and ikat bedcovers. The upper rooms have better views and baths. ⊠ *Box 205, Denpasar 80364, no phone, telex 35428 Ubud IA. 30 rooms. Restaurant, bar, pool. No credit cards.*

$ ▦ **Ubud Village Hotel.** The two-story buildings surrounding an attractive garden and pool are in Ubud's busy central area, but set back from the road. Rooms are comfortable, clean, and well maintained if you can stand the occasional chip in the bathtub's enamel. The preferred ones are on the upper floors; they catch the breezes from the rice paddies and offer a little more privacy than the fan-cooled ground-floor rooms. There is a small restaurant, and Continental breakfast is included in the rates. ⊠ *Jln. Monkey Forest, Ubud 80571, ☎ 0361/795571, FAX 0361/795069. 32 rooms. Restaurant, pool. MC, V.*

¢ ▦ **Sehati.** A cross between a homestay and guest house (there are any number of both in Ubud), Sehati offers six double rooms, each with a private bathroom with a hot water shower, for about $20 a night. The choice room, No. 5, has a fine veranda facing a small forested ravine. A light breakfast is included in the room charge. ⊠ *I Wayan Jembawan 7 (behind the post office), Ubud 80571, ☎ 0361/975460. 6 rooms. No credit cards.*

Nightlife and the Arts

Ubud shuts down early—by the time most dance performances let out, around 9 or 9:30, many cafés and restaurants are beginning to close. One or two spots along Jalan Raya stay open later.

DANCE PERFORMANCES

Ubud is the dance center of Bali, and you should make an effort to see at least two or three performances during your visit—not a problem, considering at least three troupes perform nightly.The dances performed at hotels are often commercially adapted and shortened; the ones performed in other venues around Ubud will be more genuine. (☞ Pleasures and Pastimes, *above,* for a discussion of some of the most popular dances.) Try to attend at least one performance in the village of Peliatan, whose troupes enjoy some reknown; the atmospheric setting of Puri Saren, Ubud's palace, also makes a pleasant venue for dance. If possible, avoid seeing the Kecak dance in Bone village, as traffic noise distracts from the chant.

Consult your hotel or the *Bali Tourist Guide* and the *Bali Guide to Events* for current schedules, or go to **Ubud Tourist Information** (⊠ Jln. Raya, just west of Monkey Forest Rd., ☎ 0361/96285), which has a weekly dance-performance schedule and sells tickets (Rp 5,000–Rp 7,000) that include transportation to performances not held in Ubud proper.

Outdoor Activities and Sports

GOLF

The 18-hole, 6,432-yard **Bali Handera Country Club** (⊠ Bedugul, 45 minutes north of Ubud, ☎ 0361/788994) is possibly the only course anywhere that's set in a volcanic crater, with beautiful landscaped gardens on the sides of the fairways. Daily greens fees are $87 on weekends and $72 during the week. Caddies, whether male or female, are $7 a round, and there are accommodations, decorated with modern Balinese furniture and batiks, available for $70–$120 a double.

RAFTING

It takes 2½ hours to drift and bump through gorges and rapids down the Ayung River, ending in the gentle valley near Ubud. Several outfits organize rubber raft trips for around $55, including the reliable Australian outfit **Bali Adventure Rafting** (⊠ Jln. Tunjung Mekar, Legian, ☎ 0361/751292).

Shopping

Ubud's main street is lined with shops selling art, textiles, clothing, and other handicrafts. On most days you'll also find a street market. First visit the Neka Art Gallery (☞ *above*) to get an overview of Balinese fine art, then head for the **Rudana Gallery** (✉ Jln. Cokgederai, ☎ 0361/26564), which exhibits collectors' pieces of hand-painted batik and paintings at affordable prices. Once you have grasped the concepts behind Balinese art, get directions to the workshops of A.A. Gd. Sobart, Gusti Ketut Kobot, I.B. Made Poleng, Mujawan, Sudiarto, or I. Bagus Nadra.

Look for handcrafted furniture, one of the best buys on Bali, at **Mario Antiques** (✉ Peninjauan Sukawati, Gianyar, ☎ 0361/98541), just outside Ubud.

Aside from painting, Ubud has its own style of wood carving, slightly more ethereal than you'll find in Mas. A good place to see both old and newer work is the **Nyana Tilem Gallery** (Mas Road, no phone).

OFF THE BEATEN PATH
TEGALALUNG – The roads north out of Ubud pass through lovely countryside with patchwork rice fields in different stages of cultivation. Men ankle-deep in mud plant and weed, while ducks paddle and dip for their lunch. Out in the fields stand shrines to Dewi, the goddess of rice, and stilted, roofed structures where the farmers rest or eat. In the small village of Tegalalung, artisans carve intricate flower designs into wood. It's delicate work where a slip of the chisel can ruin the whole piece. You don't have to buy anything—though to do so would make the artisans happy—to watch and marvel at the craftmanship.

Tampaksiring

⑭ *19 km (12 mi) north of Udud.*

The town of Tampaksiring is an excellent base for visiting three sacred sites in Balinese religion. Out of Tampaksiring follow the sign to **Pura Gunung Kawi,** a monument to an 11th-century ruler and one of the oldest in Bali. From the access road, a stone stairway leads down to a lush green valley. Pass through a stone archway to the canyon floor and two rows of memorial temples, carved in niches in the face of two cliffs. According to legend, the giant Kebo Iwa carved these niches in one night with his fingernails.

Beyond the outskirts of Tampaksiring, the road forks. To the right is the famous temple at **Tirta Empul.** People from all over Bali come to bathe in the holy spring, said to have been created when the god Indra pierced a stone to produce magical waters that revived his poisoned army.

At the **Pura Panti Pasek Gel Gel** holy spring, a few miles north of Tirtal Empul, the hawkers are less demanding, and fewer tourists interrupt the sanctity of the temple than at Tirtu Empul. The temple is dedicated to Vishnu, whose many responsibilities include water and irrigation. The main shrine stands in the center of a pool filled with holy water and fat goldfish. Bathing pools are segregated by sex and age.

Mt. Batur

⑮ *62 km (37 mi) north of Ubud.*

North of Sebatu, the vanilla-and-clove-bordered road climbs quickly. Roadside stalls sell fruits and vegetables, replacing the souvenir and handicraft kiosks of the lower altitudes. And then there's the majestic bulk of 4,757-foot Mt. Batur. Dark lava flows are visible within the volcano's vast crater—nearly 18 mi in diameter and 600 feet deep—

where a new volcano has arisen and cool Lake Batur has formed. **Penelokan,** a village at the edge of the old crater, affords a great view of the lake and caldera.

NEED A BREAK? Except when the low clouds move in, as they often do later in the day, **Puri Selera** (☎ 0361/88226, no credit cards), about a kilometer out of Penelokan toward Batur, offers superb views of the crater. The local fare is reasonably good, but what you're paying for is the view.

Along the road on the rim of the crater is **Kintamani,** a quiet town with losmen used by hikers who climb Mt. Batur. Guided hikes up Batur can be arranged at a cost of about Rp 10,000 per person with a minimum of four in the group. To find a guide, ask at the Hotel Miranda, the losmen on the left as you enter the village.

In the village of Penulisan, an old stairway leads up a hill to the ancient temple of **Pura Sukawana.** Most of the decaying sculptures are from the 11th century, but look closely and you will find older, pagan phallic symbols. The view, which stretches across Bali to the Java Sea, is breathtaking, especially at sunrise.

Pura Kehen

 35 km (21 mi) south of Mt. Batur. The drive south from Penelokan to Bangli is a quick run downhill. On the outskirts of Bangli is an S-curve; here take a left, and at the foot of the hill is Pura Kehen.

Pura Kehen is a 12th-century temple dedicated to Shiva. A great flight of steps leads up to this terraced temple. In the first courtyard is a giant holy banyan tree with a bell tower used to summon the villagers for ceremonies and other events. The entrance to the inner courtyard is up two steep, parallel flights of steps. At the top center are the "closed gate" and the Boma face, blocking evil spirits. Within the inner courtyard, the main shrine sits on a cosmic turtle, symbolizing the spiritual world, entwined by nagas, symbolizing the material. Material binds the spiritual—another example of Balinese harmony. The Meru in the center has 11 roofs, the highest honor to the gods.

Besakih

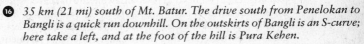 *40 km (25 mi) northeast of Bangli, 45 km (28 mi) north of Klunkung, 60 km (35 mi) north of Denpasar. Besakih may be reached from Bangli (if you're coming from Mt. Batur), Klungkung (the best route if you're coming from Ubud, Denpasar, or points south), and from Candidasa—take the road inland to Amlapura where the road splits, take the road to Rendang, then turn right to climb the 11 km (7 mi) to the temple.*

Pura Besakih, known as the mother temple of Bali, is the most sacred of them all. Situated on the slopes of Mt. Agung, the complex has 30 temples—one for every Balinese district—on seven terraces. It is thought to have been built before Hinduism reached Bali and subsequently modified. The structure consists of three main parts, the north painted black for Vishnu, the center white for Shiva, and the south red for Brahma. You enter through a split gate.

Much of the temple area was destroyed in 1963 when Mt. Agung erupted, killing 1,800 believers, but diligent restoration has repaired most of the damage. Visitors are not allowed into the inner courtyard, but there is enough to see to justify the steep 2-km-long (1¼ mi) walk from the parking lot past souvenir stands and vendors.

Klungkung

⓲ *46 km (29 mi) east of Denpasar, 28 km (18 mi) southeast of Ubud.*

To the southeast of the main road between Ubud and Denpasar is Klungkung, a former dynastic capital. In the center of town stands the **Kerta Gosa** (Hall of Justice), built in the late 18th century. The raised platform in the hall supports three thrones—one with a lion carving for the king, one with a dragon for the minister, and one with a bull for the priest. The accused brought before this tribunal could look up at the painted ceiling and contemplate the horrors in store for convicted criminals: torches between the legs, pots of boiling oil, decapitation by saw, and dozens of other punishments to fit specific crimes. To the right of the Hall of Justice is the **Bale Kambang** (Floating Pavilion), a palace surrounded by a moat. It, too, has a painted ceiling, this one of the Buddhist *Suta Sota.*

Goa Lawah

⓳ *10 km (6 mi) east of Klungkung.*

East of Klungkung, the road drops south to run along the coast and through the area of Kusamba, speckled with the thatched roofs of salt-panning huts. Just beyond is Goa Lawah, the bat cave. Unless you long to see thousands of bats hanging from the ceiling, you may not want to subject yourself to the aggressive hawkers, postcard sellers, and young girls who throw you a flower, then angrily demand payment when you leave. The cave is said to lead all the way to Mt. Agung.

Padangbai

⓴ *5 km (3 mi) east of Goa Lawah.*

Continuing east from Goa Lawah along the coast takes you to Padangbai, a pleasant small town and the port for a ferry to Lombok. There is less traffic here now that the Madura Express hydrofoil competes for the run to Lombok out of Benoa.

Balina Beach

㉑ *5 km (3 mi) east of Padangbai.*

The curving stretch of Balina Beach, at the other end of Amuk Bay, is a quiter version of Candidasa.

Lodging

$ ▣ **Balina Beach.** Popular among scuba and snorkel enthusiasts for its diving club, this hotel has one- and two-story thatched cottages scattered near the sandy beach 3 km (1.8 mi) west of Candidasa. The best rooms, upstairs in the two-story bungalows, have sitting rooms and porches. All have private baths and ceiling fans; their rattan decor is simple. ⊠ *Partai Buitan, Manngis Karang Asem 80870,* ☎ *0361/8777. 41 rooms. Restaurant, bar, dive shop. V.*

Outdoor Activities and Sports

The **Balina Diving Association** (⊠ Balina Beach, ☎ 0361/80871) arranges dives out to Nusa Penida.

Candidasa

㉒ *14 km (9 mi) east of Padangbai, 29 km (18 mi) east of Klungkung.*

Candidasa, once a budget traveler's escape from Kuta, now boasts a dozen small hotels and restaurants as well as inexpensive guest houses.

The waters here are gentle because of a reef 270 m (300 yd) offshore—good for snorkeling—but at high tide the sea swallows the beach.

Lodging

$$$$ ⌂ **Amankila.** Luxury thatched-roof pavilions are positioned on a hill-side looking out across the Bandung Straits to Lombok. Each private villa includes an outdoor terrace with large daybed, table, and chairs; a bedroom with a canopied king-size bed; and a spacious bathroom with a sunken tub and separate shower. All pavilions are the same size; the price (U.S.$360–U.S.$560) is higher for those with an ocean view or a private pool. The main pool is built into the hillside, forming a terrace of its own, while the beach is a stiff downhill climb away. ✉ *Manggis, near Candidasa,* ☎ *0366/21993,* ⅎ *0366/21995; U.S.,* ☎ *800/447–7462 or 212/223–2848; U.K.,* ☎ *0800/282684. 35 suites, 7 with private pool. 2 restaurants, bar, room service, pool, massage, hiking, snorkeling, windsurfing, library, travel services. AE, DC, MC, V.*

$ ⌂ **Puri Buitan Cottages.** Opened in late 1988, the Puri Buitan has added to its room capacity as Candidasa has become increasingly popular. A mile from the center of the village, the beach here is quiet, and a reef keeps the sea perfect for swimming. Rooms are simple and clean, with the larger first-floor units good for families. ✉ *Box 464, Denpasar 80001, no phone. 34 rooms. Restaurant, pool. V.*

Tenganan

㉓ *8 km (5 mi) north of Candidasa.*

On the western side of Candidasa, a road turns inland to Tenganan, an ancient walled village of the Balinese who preceded the Majapahit. The village consists of two parallel streets lined on either side with identical walled compounds. Inside the compounds, houses face each other across a grassy central strip, where the public buildings stand—no cars allowed. Tenganan people seldom marry outside the village and they adhere to their traditions—it is, for example, the only place in Indonesia where double ikat is still woven. The design is dyed on individual threads of both the warp and the filling before being woven (in single ikat, the dye goes only on the warp threads).

Bali A to Z

Arriving and Departing

BY BOAT

Ferries make the 35-minute crossing frequently between Ketapang in eastern Java and Gilimanuk in western Bali. Inquire at the pier. (☞ Lombok A to Z, *below,* for information on ferry serice between Bali and Lombok.)

BY BUS

Buses from Yogyakarta to Denpasar (16 hours) use the ferry; an air-conditioned bus costs Rp 16,500. Bus service is available also from Jakarta and Surabaya. Tickets may be purchased through any travel agent.

BY PLANE

Bali's airport, **Ngurah Rai,** is 13 km (8 mi) southwest of Denpasar, at the southern end of the island between Kuta and Sanur; departure tax is Rp 20,000 for international flights, Rp 7,000 for domestic ones. Garuda Indonesia is the main carrier, with flights from Los Angeles, Hong Kong, Kuala Lumpur, Jakarta, Yogyakarta, Ujung Pandang, and other domestic airports. Qantas flies to Bali from Australia, Singapore Airlines flies in from Singapore, and Thai Airways International from Bangkok.

Between the Airport and Hotels. Most hotels have a car or minivan waiting to meet arriving planes, and certainly will if you let them know in advance. Otherwise, order a taxi at the counter outside customs; the fixed fare varies from Rp 5,000 to Rp 10,000, depending on the location of your hotel (Rp 6,500 for Kuta; Rp 10,000 for Legian; Rp 15,000 for Sanur; Rp 34,000 for Ubud).

Getting Around

BY BEMO

Bemos (minibuses) ply the main routes from Denpasar to Sanur and Kuta and from Kuta to Ubud.

BY CAR

Renting cars or jeeps in Bali is convenient and popular. Daily rates vary from Rp 90,000 at Avis to Rp 36,000 at a small operator, including insurance (with a Rp 540,000 deductible) and unlimited mileage. If you rent from an upscale hotel, the cost of the car will be considerably higher than if you rent off the hotel property. Legally you have to have an international driver's license, though some agencies will not ask for it.

Try **Lina Biro Jasa** (⊠ Jln. Bakungsari, Kuta, ☎ 0361/51820), a local company. **Avis** has several branches (⊠ Jln. Danau Tamblingan, Sanur, ☎ 0361/289138; also at the Bali Hyatt, Sanur, ☎ 0361/8271; Nusa Dua Beach Hotel, ☎ 0361/71210; and Hotel Sanur Beach, ☎ 0361/288011).

Alhough prices vary, depending on the places you wish to visit (and the distance covered), a car with driver will run about $65 per 12 hours. Most hotels and agencies can provide drivers.

BY TAXI

Taxis are available in the main tourist areas. Kuta, Sanur, Nusa Dua, and Denpasar have metered taxis. Make sure that the meter is used. The charge is Rp 450 per kilometer. The 15-minute ride from Kuta to Nusa Dua, for example, is Rp 9,000; from Sanur to Nusa Dua, Rp 15,000. For longer journeys, rates are more negotiable—count on about Rp 15,000 per hour. To order a cab, call the **dispatcher** (☎ 0361/701000 or 0361/289090).

Contacts and Resources

EMBASSIES AND CONSULATES

Australia (⊠ Jln. Prof. Moch, Yanin 51, Denpasar, ☎ 0361/235092). **United States** (⊠ Jln. Segara Ayu 5, Sanur, ☎ 0361/288478; ⊠ Jln. Hayam Wuruk 188, Denpasar, ☎ 0361/233605).

EMERGENCIES

Ambulance, ☎ 118. **Fire,** ☎ 113. **Police,** ☎ 110.

GUIDED TOURS

Private Tours: The best way to explore Bali is with a private car and a knowledgeable guide. Without a guide, you may miss much of what is so intriguing about the island. Should you visit the craft villages north of Denpasar, remember that most guides get a commission on your purchases. If your guide stops at every shop along the road, speak up—there is too much to see in Bali to spend all your time this way. A car, driver, and guide can be hired from most travel agencies (☞ *below*) or from your hotel travel desk. For a personal guide, contact **I Made Ramia Santana** (⊠ Jln. Planet 9, Denpasar, ☎ 0361/725909).

Organized Tours. The following standardized tours take groups in buses or vans virtually every day and will usually collect you from your hotel. (☞ Travel Agencies, *below,* for recommended tour operators.)

Denpasar City Tour (three hours) includes the Art Center and the Bali Museum.

Kintamani Tour (eight hours) includes the Barong and kris dance performance; silversmith-and-goldsmith, wood-carving, and painting villages; the sacred spring at Tampaksiring; and Kintamani, with its view of Batur volcano and Lake Batur.

Sangeh and Mengwi Tour (four hours) visits the Bali Museum in Denpasar, Sangeh and the sacred monkey forest, and the Pura Taman Ayun temple at Mengwi. Ubud Handicraft Tour (five hours) visits the handicraft villages north of Denpasar; Ubud, the artists' center; the museum in Ubud; and Goa Gajah, the elephant cave.

Besakih Temple Tour (seven hours) offers fantastic views on the way to the temple on the slopes of Mt. Agung and includes the ancient hall of justice in Klungkung and the bat cave. A full-day (10-hour) tour includes Besakih and Kintamani, the handicraft villages, Ubud, and other temples.

Afternoon Tanah Lot Sunset Tour (five hours) includes the monkey forest, the temple at Mengwi, and sunset at Tanah Lot.

Turtle Island Tour (four hours) goes by fishing boat from Suwung, near Benoa harbor, to Serangan, an island just off the coast of Sanur, to watch the giant sea turtles.

PHARMACIES

Bali Farma Apotik (✉ Jln. Melatig, Denpasar, ☎ 0361/22878) provides reliable service and advice. **Indonesia Farma Apotik** (✉ Jln. Diponegoro, Denpasar, ☎ 0361/27812) is a recommended pharmacy.

TRAVEL AGENCIES

Nitour (✉ Jln. Veteran 5, Denpasar, ☎ 0361/736096) is a reliable tour operator.

Pacto Ltd. Tours and Travel (✉ Bali Beach Hotel, Jln. Tanjung Sari, Sanur, ☎ 0361/788449, ext. Pacto) provides tour and travel services and also represents **American Express**; card holders can buy travelers checks, get mail, report lost cards, and receive other AmEx services.

Satriavi Tours & Travel (✉ Jln. Cemara 27, Semawang, Sanur, ☎ 0361/287494; Nusa Dua Beach Hotel, ☎ 0361/971210, ext. 719; Hotel Sanur Beach, ☎ 0361/288011) is an established agency that offers the most comprehensive selection of tours and also arranges custom tours. One new tour is a day's trek through villages that are off the beaten track. Since Satriavi is a subsidiary of Garuda Indonesia Airlines, it is well equipped to handle onward flight reservations.

VISITOR INFORMATION

Denpasar: **Dipardi Bali** (✉ Jln. Raya Puputan Renon, ☎ 0361/238184).

Kuta: **Bali Tourist Information Center** (✉ Central Tourist Plaza, ground floor, Jln. Benasati 7, Legian, ☎ 0361/754090).

Ubud: **Ubud Tourist Information** (✉ Jln. Raya Ubud, ☎ 0361/96285).

LOMBOK

The island of Lombok lies just 45 km (27 mi) east of Bali but seems to exist several decades back in time. The beaches are superior to those of Bali and the level of commercialism is substantially lower. Also, Lombok has a climate considerably drier than Bali's, which is a distinct advantage during the rainy season, from December through May. You can take a 20-minute flight to the island, spend the day exploring, and return by nightfall—though the island really deserves more time.

Lombok, meaning chili pepper in Javanese, is home to two cultures, the Balinese Hindu and the Sasak Moslem. Most of the Balinese, who ruled the island until 1894, live on the western side of the island around Ampenan, Mataram (the provincial capital), and Cakranegara (known for its handwoven textiles). Here you will find Balinese temples of interest, though none are as fully developed as in Bali.

Come enjoy Lombok while you can, as the unspoiled atmosphere is changing fast: Senggigi Beach is now crowded with hotels, the beaches on the Gili coral atolls are lined with low-priced bungalows, and the Indonesian president's son has bought up the beautiful beaches to the south to make way for a Nusa Dua–type megaresort of international hotels.

Mataram

24 km (14 mi) north of Lembar (the port for Bali ferries).

Mataram, Lombok's provincial capital, is not a tourist destination. You may want to make a brief visit to **Pura Meru,** the largest Balinese temple on Lombok. Constructed in 1720, Puru Meru is arranged around three courtyards full of small meru shrines. The three most important—those to Shiva, Vishnu, and Brahma—are in the central courtyard.

Cakranegara

3 km (2 mi) east of Mataram.

Stop in Cakranegara to see the **Taman Mayura,** once a Balinese royal palace, now a large artificial pool filled with lotus. In the center of the pool is Bale Kembang, a floating pavilion that is similar to but smaller and less ornate than the one in Klungkung, Bali.

Cakranegara's handwoven textiles are well known; visit **Pertenunan Rinjani** (✉ Jln. Pejanggik 46, ☎ 0364/23169) on the town line of Mataram for handwoven ikat. The public market in Cakranegara is good for silver and gold and for straw baskets.

At **Sweta,** a market area and the main bus terminal on Lombok, located just outside Cakranegara, you can shop for spices and beautifully made cane baskets that entrepreneurs buy and take back to Bali to sell at inflated prices.

Narmada

10 km east of Cakranegara.

Lombok's most famous temple-palace complex is **Narmada Taman,** built in 1727. The architecture is an interesting mix of Hindu, Islamic, and Sasak, but the temple is notable for its man-made lagoons symbolizing the lakes of the holy mountain, Mt. Rinjani, in the north of Lombok. The faithful explain that the replica of the lake was to permit the aging king to fulfil his relious obligations. However, more likely it was to permit the gentleman to spy on the maidens washing in the pools.

Five kilometers (3 mi) north of Narmada is **Lingsar Temple,** built in 1714 by the first migrating Balinese and reconstructed in conjunction with Sasak Moslems as a symbol of their unity. Nearby is **Suranadi,** a cool hill town with a Hindu temple, especially venerated for its spring water and eels. Both promise good fortune to the pilgrim.

Senggigi Beach

12 km (7 mi) north of Mataram.

The route north out of Mataram by way of the old port of Ampenan passes by some ugly petroleum storage tanks contrasting with gaily colored fishing boats before the coutryside opens up and the beaches beckon. The curving beach with a rather narrow strip of sand was once the backpackers escape from the crowed beaches of Bali. Since then, while some inexpensive accommodations are still available, more expensive resort hotels have moved in to dominate the beach. It is still a pleasant place to relax, but a far cry from a quiet hideway.

Lodging

$$–$$$ **Intan Laguna.** A vast, lagoon-shape swimming pool is this hotel's focal point. The design of the bungalows is a modern interpretation of Balinese architecture; guest rooms are spacious with tile floors and unadorned walls. These may crowd the property and detract from the feeling of openness that it now has. The open-air dining room, cooled by the sea breezes, offers some of the best fare on the island. ⊠ *Intan Laguna, Box 50, Mataram 83123, Lombok* ☎ *0364/93090,* ℻ *0364/93185; on Bali,* ☎ *0361/52191,* ℻ *0361/52193. 146 rooms. 2 restaurants, bar, pool, 2 tennis courts, exercise room, shops. AE, DC, MC, V.*

$$–$$$ **Senggigi Beach Hotel.** The location of this hotel, on a small peninsula jutting into the Lombok Strait, will always make this a choice resort; sunsets are particularly splendid. Thatched roof cottages—with several rooms per building—are scattered over 25 acres of grass and coconut trees. White sandy beaches form the perimeter. The open-sided dining room, overlooking the pool, serves mostly buffet-style meals both for breakfast and dinner. Guest rooms are modest: Most have twin beds, with scant furniture other than a table, chairs, and a television. Bathrooms have showers only. ⊠ *Senggigi, Box 1001, Mataram 83125, Lombok,* ☎ *0364/93210,* ℻ *0364/93200; on Bali, contact Hotel Sanur Beach. 182 rooms. Restaurant, room service, pool, 2 tennis courts, badminton, snorkeling, windsurfing, boating, tour services. AE, DC, MC, V.*

$$–$$$ **Sheraton Senggigi Beach Resort.** Rooms at this 1992 resort are in three-story buildings around a compact enclave of landscaped gardens, with a free-form pool as the central focus. An island stage in the pool is used for dance performances. All rooms look onto the gardens and pool, and many offer a glimpse of the beach beyond. The main restaurant offers indoor and outdoor dining, and the reception and lounge areas are open. Rooms are slightly larger and newer than at the Senggigi Beach Hotel. ⊠ *Jln. Raya Senggigi, Box 1156, Mataram 83015, Lombok,* ☎ *0364/93333,* ℻ *0364/93140; U.S.,* ☎ *800/325–3535. 158 rooms. Restaurant, pool, 2 tennis courts, health club, windsurfing, sailing, snorkeling, travel services. AE, DC, MC, V.*

$ **Graha Beach.** Set on the beach, this is one of the best of several inexpensive hotels and losmen in Senggigi. The facilities are limited to a restaurant serving primarily local food, though a few Western and Chinese dishes are offered. Clean, air-conditioned rooms have twin beds, tile floors, and TV; each has a private shower and toilet. There is a small souvenir shop and money exchange. Tours of the island can be arranged—prices are negotiable. ⊠ *Senggigi Beach, Mataram, Lombok,* ☎ *0364/93401. 29 rooms. Restaurant, travel services, car rental. No credit cards.*

¢ **Pondok Wisata Rinjani.** This inexpensive property is usually filled with budget travelers, who stream in around 6 PM. The Rp 15,000 rooms are the first to go, then the slightly larger Rp 20,000 ones. Both have twin beds and private bathrooms with Western-style showers. The Rp 10,000 rooms have mandi toilets (a tank with a dipper). All rooms are clean, with fresh sheets. The restaurant and bar, open all day, serve as the lounge area. A band plays Western music in the evening. ⊠ *Senggigi Beach, Senggigi, Lombok,* ☎ *0364/93274. 45 rooms. Restaurant, bar. No credit cards.*

Gili Islands

30 km (18 mi) north of Mataram.

A 30-minute drive north of Senggigi brings you to the Bangsai ferry dock, near Pamenang, where a small boat will ferry you across to one of three coral atolls known as the Gili Islands, all of which have cottage bungalows very popular with backpackers. Most accommodations consist of very simple bamboo huts ($10–$20) with mandi toilets, but each island has a few upmarket places with electricity. Most losmen rent snorkeling equipment, and dive trips can be arranged. Bring cash, as credit cards are rarely accepted and travelers checks can be difficult to exchange.

Gili Air is closest to shore and requires only a quick 10-minute sea crossing in a motorized prahu. Here dazzling white sand meets crystal-clear water, and the coral reef is home to brightly colored tropical fish. For even more pristine waters, the next atoll, **Gili Meno,** has a greater abundance of sea life—red-lined triggerfish, starfish, five-line damsel, and the occasional shark—and, for scuba divers, there is unique blue coral 50–80 feet below the surface. Visibility isn't what it was 10 years ago, however, and during the rains (January–March) it can diminish to 50 feet. **Gili Trawangan** is the most distant island and has a small village of 700 fishermen. The beaches are excellent here, the diving is the best of the three islands, and there are plenty of losmen.

Rambitan

22 km (13 mi) south of Mataram.

The south of the island is scattered with small Sasak villages. On the road to Kuta, stop at the government "protected village" Rambitan, often referred to as Sade. The long sloping thatched roofs of traditional Sasak houses are clustered together, and a few of the villagers sell batik sarongs at ridiculously low prices. Try to get a glimpse into the houses. Each house has two main areas: The outer area is where the men sleep; the inner area is reserved for the women.

Kuta

30 km (18 mi) south of Mataram.

Kuta is a tiny village on the shores of the Indian Ocean. The curving sandy beach, known as Putri Nyale Beach, is virtually deserted, frequented only by a few hardy travelers staying at the losmen on the other side of the road.

Tanjung Aan

35 km (20 mi) south of Mataram.

Farther east along the coast is the horseshoe-shaped Tanjung Aan, the most beautiful beach on Lombok. With its fine, soft, white sand, the beach is postcard-perfect—and usually deserted, except for a few hopeful vendors selling watermelons and brave hearts windsurfing. All this may change—the beach is slated for development, with wealthy businessmen from Jakarta putting up the money for 25 luxury hotels.

Lombok A to Z

Arriving and Departing

BY BOAT

Two ferries a day make the four-hour crossing from Lembar, south of Ampenan in Lombok, to Padangbai, east of Denpasar; the fare is Rp 5,000. The major travel agencies will be able to tell you about schedules.

Since the ferry docks some distance from the tourist centers on both Bali and Lombok (it takes three bemos to travel from Lembar Harbor to Senggigi), a bus/ferry package—between Ubud, Kuta, or Sanur on Bali and Mataram or Senggigi on Lombok—is a better alternative. **Perama Travel** (☎ 0364/51561) organizes the packages, and most small travel agents can make the booking. Fares are reasonable—e.g., Rp 13,000 from Kuta to Senggigi.

BY HYDROFOIL

A 248-passenger hydrofoil, the **Mabua Express** (schedules on Bali, ☎ 0361/772370; on Lombok, ☎ 0364/37224), runs between Benoa, just north of Nusa Dua, and Lembar on Lombok, a 2½-hour one-way trip. It currently makes two round-trips a day—morning and afternoon—at a one-way price of $25 for the upper deck and $17.50 for the lower.

BY PLANE

Merpati and Sempati airlines run a shuttle service, with flights every hour beginning at 7 AM, from Denpasar to Lombok's Mataram airport. The last flight is at 3 PM. Purchase tickets (Rp 62,000 one-way) at the airport an hour before departure. Returning from Lombok to Denpasar, you can only reserve a seat if you have a connecting flight. Flights have a tendency to be late, and are frequently cancelled.

Getting Around

Public transport on Lombok consists of crowded bemos (minibuses) and the *cidomo,* a horse-drawn cart that seats four or five and costs approximately Rp 500 per kilometer.

Taxis are available from the airport and at hotels; a taxi from the airport to Senggigi should cost less than Rp 7,000 (though you'll be asked for at least Rp 10,000 initially).

Rental cars cost about Rp 45,000 a day or Rp 75,000 with driver.

Contacts and Resources

EMERGENCIES

Ambulance, ☎ 118. **Fire,** ☎ 113. **Police,** ☎ 110.

GUIDED TOURS

Satriavi Tours & Travel (✉ Senggigi Beach Hotel, ☎ 0364/23430, ext. 8602) organizes different tours of the island.

VISITOR INFORMATION

Regional Office of Tourism (✉ Jln. Singosari 2, Mataram, ☎ 0364/21730).

SULAWESI

To the north and east of Bali and Java is the island of Sulawesi, formerly called the Celebes. Four long peninsulas radiate from a central mountainous area, giving the island an orchid shape. Its geography is dramatic—from rice fields to rain forests and mountains to hidden bays, from which Bugis pirates once raided merchant ships. As if cast off in some strange upheaval, Sulawesi has become the last home of such unique animals as the babirusa (a pig-deer with upward-curving tusks) and the anoa (a pygmy buffalo). At present, Sulawesi is virtually unspoiled, and its tourist infrastructure is confined mostly to the main city, Ujung Pandang, and Tanatoraja (Torajaland).

The Toraja people are Sulawesi's prime attraction. The Toraja live in the northern mountains of south Sulawesi, practicing an ancient animist religion alongside Christianity. Tourism has affected the Toraja, but their customs, rituals, and social structure have survived the centuries. Perhaps the only obvious change in the last 500 years is that now buffalo and pigs are sacrificed instead of humans. With their traditional clan houses—the carved and painted *tongkonans*—built on piles and topped by a massive roof shaped like a ship or buffalo horns, and their public sacred rituals, the Toraja offer the visitor a fascinating glimpse of Indonesia's multifaceted population.

The Toraja comprise only a small minority of Sulawesi's inhabitants, however. The Makassarese and the Bugis are more numerous, and the journey from Ujung Pandang to Tanatoraja passes through Bugis country. Though many now have settled on land to cultivate rice, the seafaring Muslim Bugis still ply the Asian seas in their sailing ships, called *prahus,* trading among Indonesia's islands.

Numbers in the margin correspond to points of interest on the Sulawesi and Torajaland map.

Ujung Pandang

❶ *About 1 hr by plane from Denpasar; 328 km (205 mi) south of Rantepao.*

Most visitors fly into Ujung Pandang and use it as a starting point for travel in Sulawesi. The city, called Makassar by the Dutch, is a bustling commercial center. Although it's the fifth-largest Indonesian city, Ujung Pandang has little to hold the tourist's attention.

The principal site is **Fort Rotterdam,** now officially called Benteng ("fort") Ujung Pandang, though most people still use its old name. Located by the harbor in the center of the Old City, it began as a fortified trading post for the Sulawesi Goanese dynasty and a defense against pirates. The fort was first captured and rebuilt by the Portuguese in 1545, then captured by the Dutch in 1608 and reinforced again. Several municipal offices are housed in the fort complex, including the Conservatory of Dance and Music, and sometimes you will see dance classes for children held on the open stage in the center of the fort. On Saturday night at 8, dance performances are often held here. The staff at your hotel should know whether any are scheduled. ✆ *Free.* ☉ *Daily 8–5.*

The fort includes the **Galigo Museum** (the Ujung Pandang State Museum), divided into ethnology and history sections. The ethnographic museum is the more interesting, with a large collection of artifacts from different areas of Sulawesi. ✆ *Admission to each museum.* ☉ *Tues.– Thurs. 8 AM–1 PM, Fri. 8 AM–10 AM, weekends 8–4.*

Just 3¼ km (2 mi) north of Ujung Pandang is **Paotare,** a harbor where the Bugis prahus come to unload their cargo, mend their sails, and prepare for their next passage. Sunsets from here are marvelous, but the pier has missing planks and gaping holes, so watch where you step.

Across the harbor of Ujung Pandang is **Samalona Island,** which has been developed into a recreational center, mostly appealing to locals. It can be reached in 45 minutes. Sports include snorkeling and waterskiing. If you do visit, go during February to October, the hot and dry season.

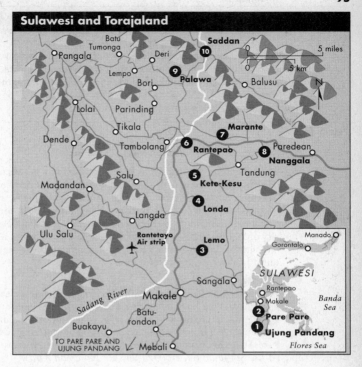

Sulawesi and Torajaland

Dining and Lodging

$$ ✕ **Restaurant Surya.** Super Crab, as this restaurant is called, serves some of the best seafood in Ujung Pandang. It is always crowded, and you will probably have to wait for a table. The proprietor, Jerry, speaks English, so you won't have any problem with the menu. The large, bright room has no decor or atmosphere, but the crab-and-asparagus soup is delicious, as are the gigantic prawns. ✉ *Jln. Nusakambangan 16,* ☎ *0411/317066. Reservations not accepted. No credit cards.*

$$$ 🏨 **Makassar Golden Hotel.** This hotel at the harbor has Toraja-style
★ roofs on its main building. Most rooms face the sea and have wall-to-wall carpeting, with beige decor and woven bedcovers in a Toraja design. Makassar also has cottages facing the sea. All rooms have private bath, minibar, and TV with video programs. ✉ *Jln. Pasar Ikan 50,* ☎ *0411/314408,* FAX *0411/320951. 69 rooms. 2 restaurants, pool, dance club. AE, DC, MC, V.*

$$$ 🏨 **Radisson Ujung Pandang.** What this 1996 hotel lacks in charm it makes up in smart efficency and a grand location on the waterfront. Rooms are boxlike but comfortable and well-equipped, with such amenities as hair driers and in-room safes. The coffee shop looks out onto the water and offers a combined taste of Western and the Orient—tiger prawns with a hint of lemon grass and barbecued duck with a light curry sauce, for example. There is also a Chinese restaurant serving Szechuan and Cantonese fare. ✉ *Jln Somba Opu, 235, Ujung Padang 90111,* ☎ *0411/3333111,* FAX *0411/333222. 90 rooms. 2 restaurants, health club, meeting rooms. AE, DC, MC, V.*

$$ 🏨 **Makassar City Hotel.** Toraja-style carved-wood panels are the theme here. The hotel is affordable and centrally located, but its facilities and furnishings have seen better days: rooms are spacious, with sitting areas, king-size beds, color TV, and minibar, but stains on the carpets and scuff marks on the walls attest to their age. The lounge has tired crushed-velvet sofas and lumpy leather chairs. ✉ *Jln. Khairil Anwar 28,* ☎ *0411/317055,* ℻ *0411/311818. 89 rooms. Restaurant, bar, pool, meeting room. AE, DC, MC, V.*

$ 🏨 **Hotel Ramayana.** Between the airport and Ujung Pandang, this place is clean but purely utilitarian. It's conveniently located across from the Liman Express office, which runs buses to Torajaland. ✉ *Jln. G. Bawakaraeng 121,* ☎ *0411/442479,* ℻ *0411/322165. 35 rooms. Restaurant, travel services. No credit cards.*

Pare Pare

2 *180 km (108 mi) north of Ujung Pandang.*

The four-hour drive north to Pare Pare, halfway between Ujung Pandang and Rantepao, is through flat countryside of rice fields, with the Makassar Strait on the left. The area is inhabited by Bugis, whose houses, on stilts and with crossed roofbeams, line the road. In some you'll see fish hanging from the rafters, curing in the sun. Pare Pare itself is a city of 90,000 and Sulawesi's second-largest town. From its port, boats cross the Makassar Sea to Kalimantan. There is little to see in Pare Pare, but it has two decent restaurants.

Dining

$ ✗ **Bukit Indah.** Perched on a hill, this smart, pristinely clean restaurant has a view of the bay and catches a nice breeze. The crab-and-corn soup is delicious, as are the fried frogs' legs. To reach Bukit Indah, take a right turn up the hill from the main street just before entering downtown Pare Pare. Six clean, simple rooms are available if you wish to stay the night. ✉ *Jln. Sudiman 65,* ☎ *0421/21886. No credit cards.*

$ ✗ **Sempurna.** On Pare Pare's main street is a clean, Formica-furnished, air-conditioned restaurant that serves tasty Indonesian and Chinese food. Try the sweet-and-sour shrimp. ✉ *202 Jln. Bau Massepe,* ☎ *0421/21573.*

En Route From Pare Pare the road twists and turns inland, leaving the sea to the west as it climbs into limestone hills forested with tropical pine and palms. Shimmering in the distance are the steely blue mountains that locked out intruding cultures for centuries. Not until 1980 was the road paved. Before then, the rutted, stony track took hours to cover. Dominated by Bamba Buang mountain, the scenery becomes increasingly dramatic. According to legend, the souls of the Torajan dead assemble here to journey to the "gate of God." As the road continues into the mountains of Tanatoraja, look to the right across the small valley and you'll recognize the "Lady Mountain," where two ridges split off, suggestive of a woman's legs. In the distance is Rura, said to be the very first Toraja village.

NEED A BREAK? Located 248 km (153 mi) from Ujung Pandang and 54 km (32 mi) before Makale is a roadside restaurant, **Puntak Lakawan,** with a terrace affording spectacular views—an exciting introduction to Tanatoraja. Travelers stop here for the views, the strong coffee, and the "tourist only" Western toilet facilities—not for the food.

Tanatoraja

328 km (205 mi) north of Ujung Pandang.

Tanatoraja's two main towns are Makale, the administrative center, and Rantepao, the commercial and tourist center and the settlement with the best selection of hotels. You'll need at least two or three days to visit Tanatoraja, plus two to get there and back. Plan on a longer stay if you want to get off the beaten track to the remote villages. The best time for a trip is at the beginning or end of the dry season, April through October. Vast numbers of Europeans descend in June and July, so try to avoid those months.

If you have time, the ideal way to experience Tanatoraja is by hiking through the hills along small paths from one village to the next. Visiting them by bus is possible, with short hikes, but it is slow going. You can also hire a minivan or four-wheel-drive jeep with a guide. Wear strong, ankle-supporting shoes, because you'll do some walking over rutted tracks or roads. Each tour guide has his favorite villages for visiting. He should be able to learn about any scheduled ceremonies. Encourage him to do so, for witnessing one is an event you won't forget.

The **funeral ceremony** is the most important event in the life of a Toraja. Though families traditionally gave as lavish a funeral as possible to demonstrate the prestige of the dead to the gods, a competition for status has now entered the ceremony. Wealth is measured in buffalo: the more buffalo sacrificed at the funeral, the more honor to the dead, the family, and the clan. Even Toraja who have converted to Christianity continue the funeral ritual to demonstrate their prestige, keep tradition, and make sure the dead have plenty of influence with the gods.

When a clan erects a new tongkonan, there's a large **housewarming ceremony** with the whole clan present, which may mean hundreds of people. Buffalo and pigs are sacrificed—again to display status.

Of the hundreds of villages nestling in the valleys throughout Tanatoraja, the following are some of the more accessible. To varying degrees, they give the visitor a chance to see aspects of animist culture and architecture. The farther you go from Rantepao and Makale, the fewer tourists the inhabitants will have seen, and the more welcoming they are. If you have time and spirit, head into the northwestern or eastern part. These areas are the least infiltrated. Most of the inhabitants will know a few words of Bahasa Indonesia, but no English. Most villages on the regular tourist route require a donation of Rp 1,500 or more. In theory, this helps the villagers maintain their buildings.

Between Makale and Rantepao

③ ④ ⑤ *13 km (8 mi) from Makale to Lemo, 15 km (9 mi) from Lemo to Londa, 9 km (5.5 mi) from Londa to Kete-Kesu, and 10 km (6 mi) from Kete-Kesu to Rantepao.*

Bypass Makale, the first large town, and head for Rantepao, the center of travel and the hub of the network of roads that peel off into the countryside to the Toraja villages. The more heavily traveled tourist villages, such as **Lemo, Londa,** and **Kete-Kesu** lie between Makale and Rantepao. Some are the sites of limestone burial caves with *tau taus,* wood effigies carved for noble Toraja and placed on a balcony at the cave entrance. The spirit of the ancestor honored thus will help the descendants enjoy a better life.

Rantepao

⑥ *24 km (15 mi) from Makale.*

Rantepao is a small, easygoing town. Its big event occurs every sixth day, when the "weekly" market at the town crossroads attracts just about everyone from the surrounding villages. Even on off days, the market shops sell wood carvings, cloth, and other Toraja-crafted goods. Rantepao also has small restaurants and inexpensive hotels. The more comfortable accommodations are a bit out of town, however, either back on the road to Makale or on the road east toward Marante.

DINING AND LODGING

$ ✕ Pondok Torsina. Set in the rice fields a few kilometers south of Rantepao, this small hotel and restaurant serves good Indonesian food on a veranda overlooking the paddies. Try the asparagus soup, shrimp in spicy butter sauce, and grilled fish. The Toraja owner is very helpful in filling in the information gaps left by your guide. ✉ *Tikunna Malenong,* ☎ *0423/21293. Reservations not accepted. No credit cards.*

$ ✕ Restaurant Rachmat. Near the traffic circle with a model of a Toraja house, this Chinese-operated restaurant offers tasty Indonesian and Chinese dishes. ✉ *Jln. Abdul Sari 8. Reservations not accepted. No credit cards.*

$$ ⊡ Hotel Misiliana. Make sure to book rooms in the new part of this
★ hotel, where a courtyard garden has a row of traditional houses with rice barns opposite. Guest rooms surround the courtyard in two- or four-unit bungalows designed to complement the houses. The rooms are spotless, furnished with twin beds in colorful native covers, and have modern tile bathrooms. Breakfast and dinner are included in the room price, and both meals offer a fixed menu—Europeanized Indonesian fare of no distinction. The cultural show in the evening is not worth the entrance fee. ✉ *Jln. Raya Makele, Box 01,* ☎ *0423/852293,* FAX *0423/21212. 80 rooms. Restaurant. DC, V.*

$$ ⊡ Toraja Cottages. Just 3 km (2 mi) east of Rantepao, and set among
★ tropical gardens, this hotel consists of rows of attached cottages terraced around the main building. The guest rooms, with twin beds, are small but clean. Westernized Indonesian food is served in an open veranda restaurant with rattan furniture, and, amusingly, a model of the Statue of Liberty on a corner table. A small bar off the lobby functions as a gathering place at this popular tourist hotel, which has a variety of activities and services available, including tours and gift shops. ✉ *Kamp. Bolu,* ☎ *0423/21268,* FAX *0423/21369. Reservations and information: Jln. Johar 17, Jakarta Pusat, Jakarta,* ☎ *021/321346; or Jln. Somba Opu 281, Ujung Pandang,* ☎ *0411/84146. 58 rooms. 2 restaurants, bar, pool. AE, DC, V.*

$ ⊡ Pia and Poppies Hotel. Mr. Paul worked for years as a chef at different Bali resorts before coming back to Rantepao to open his own inn. His wonderful property is sleepy and serene, with panoramic valley views from the terrace and skylit, rock-inlaid showers. Mr. Paul and his family also preside over one of the most sophistacted Torajan dining rooms around; save room for the pumpkin soup. ✉ *Jln. Pong Tika 27A, few blocks south of Rantepao on road to Makale, no phone. 10 rooms. Restaurant. No credit cards.*

Marante
❼ *9 km (5 mi) from Rantepao.*

At Marante you'll find burial caves in a limestone cliff. The remnants of poles used to support hanging coffins and some old carved coffins are here. There is also a funeral bier shaped like a traditional house— a ship to carry the deceased to the next life. At one end of the village is a modern home with a prow projecting from the roof and a wood buffalo head attached to its front post—a fabulous anachronism.

LODGING

$$$ ⊡ Marante Highland Resort. This new resort hotel is in Tana Toraja,
★ the village known for its tongkonan, just outside Marante. Rooms are either in the main building or in one of the traditionally-designed houses built with roofs that look like upside-down boats. These rooms are the best, with Indonesian fabrics and terraces that look over the

landscaped grounds. All rooms have a good long bath. The pool has an adjoining terrace café, the coffee shop serves Western food and a few Indonesian dishes, and the Asian Barbecue restaurant offers an array of dishes from Southeast Asia. Excursions to the surrounding villages and cliffside gravesites may be arranged through the hotel. ✉ *Jln. Jurusan Palapo, Box 52, Rantepao,* ☎ *0423/216169,* FAX *0423/ 21122. 111 rooms. 3 restaurants, pool, games room, shops, tours, meeting room. AE, DC, MC, V.*

Nanggala
8 *16 km (10 mi) from Rantepao.*

This quiet village is one of the best examples of traditional Toraja life. The tongkonan and other houses are built on poles with soaring prow-shaped roofs, lined up facing north (whence the ancestors came); *lumbung* (granaries or rice barns, smaller than the houses but similar in shape) stand opposite. The tongkonan is cared for by the clan leader. A noble clan may decorate all the walls with carved and painted designs symbolizing the buffalo, the sun, and important crops. A middle-ranking clan is permitted to decorate only the front gable. When you see a wood buffalo head or the horns of sacrificed buffalo affixed to the front pole of the house, you're looking at the house of a noble clan.

Palawa
9 *12 km (7 mi) from Rantepao.*

North of Rantepao, off the road to Saddan, is the very old village of Palawa, where hundreds of horns of sacrificed buffalo hang on the houses and where eight traditional homes contain shops selling Toraja carvings, textiles, old coins, and junk.

Saddan
10 *17 km (10.5 mi) from Rantepao.*

In the weaving center of Saddan, Toraja women weave and sell their colorful designs, which use mainly primary colors in geometric patterns. You can also purchase the beautiful vegetable-dyed ikat textiles from Galumpang, an area north and west of Tanatoraja known for its weaving.

Sulawesi A to Z

Arriving and Departing
BY BOAT
Pelni ships from Surabaya (☎ 031/21041) or Ambon (☎ 0311/3161–2049) pass through Ujung Pandang (☎ 0411/317962) every seven days and moor at Pelabuhan Hatta Harbor, a short becak ride from the center of town. Because Ujung Pandang is the gateway to eastern Indonesia, many other shipping companies take passengers from here aboard freighters to the Moluccas and other eastern islands and to Kalimantan, on Borneo. Pelni also has a subsidiary, **Perintis**, which serves many of the outer ports of Indonesia. For information, contact Pelni at one of the above numbers, or call the head office in Jakarta (☎ 021/416262).

BY PLANE
Garuda flies to Ujung Pandang's **Hasanuddin Airport** from Jakarta and Surabaya on Java, and from Denpasar on Bali. Garuda also has service from Ambon, Biak, and Jayapura. The smaller Merpati, Bouraq, and Mandala also serve Ujung Pandang.

Between the Airport and Downtown. Taxis from the Ujung Pandang airport cost about Rp 15,000. Purchase a coupon inside the terminal, next to the baggage claim. In Rantepao, a cab to town costs Rp 15,000.

Merpati Airlines flies between Ujung Pandang and the simple **Rantetayo airstrip** in Tanatoraja two times a day, Monday through Saturday. The runway can become unserviceable in the rainy season, causing frequent flight cancellations. The airport is 24 km (15 mi) from Rantepao.

Getting Around

Because the country between Ujung Pandang and Rantepao is fascinating, the ideal way to visit Tanatoraja is to make the outbound journey by road and return by air.

BY BECAK

For journeys of less than 3¼ km (2 mi), bicycle rickshaws are popular. Bargain hard—a trip in town should cost about Rp 1,000, even if the driver begins by asking Rp 5,000.

BY BEMO

In Ujung Pandang, bemo minivans run along Jalan Jend. Sudirman/Ratulangi; Jalan Hasnuddin/Cendrawash; and Jalan Bulusaraung/Mesjid Raya to Maros (sometimes detouring to the airport). Public minibuses to towns outside Ujung Pandang leave from Jalan Sarappo whenever they're full.

BY BUS

A large company, with the newest buses serving towns outside Ujung Pandang, is **Liman Express** (☎ 0411/5851).

The bus to Tanatoraja from Ujung Pandang takes nine hours, plus an hour lunch break. There are morning and evening departures in both directions. At Rp 15,000, it's an economical way to go. Since the countryside is not to be missed, make sure to make at least one trip during daylight.

BY CAR

Self-drive rental cars are not available—or permitted—on Sulawesi.

BY TAXI

You can hail cruising cabs in Ujung Pandang or find them waiting outside hotels. Taxis are unmetered; you negotiate the fare. Two large companies are: **Mas. C.V.** (☎ 0411/4599) and **Omega** (☎ 0411/22679).

BY TOUR BUS

Travel agencies either take clients one way from Ujung Pandang to Rantepao by minibus and fly them back, or go both ways by minibus. The advantage of such a tour is the guide. (☞ Guided Tours, *below*, for tour companies in Ujung Pandang.)

Contacts and Resources

EMERGENCIES

Ambulance, ☎ 118. **Police,** ☎ 110 or 7777.

GUIDED TOURS

Intravi (✉ Jln. Urip Sumoharjo 225, ☎ 0411/319747) is a reputable agency. Besides arranging tours, **Pacto Ltd. Tours and Travel** (✉ Jln. Jend. Sudirman 56, ☎ 0411/873208) represents American Express. **Ramayana Tours** (✉ Jln. Bulukunyi 9A, ☎ 0411/871791) is particularly good for tours into Torajaland because many of its guides come from there. It also offers excursions to the southeast peninsula, famous for boatbuilding and a reclusive Muslim village, and arranges customized tours, such as a jeep trip across the island and a canoe visit to the weavers of Galumpang in central Sulawesi.

VISITOR INFORMATION

In Ujung Pandang, the **South Sulawesi Tourist Office** (✉ Jln. Sultan Alauddin 105 B, ☎ 0411/83897) is open Monday–Thursday and

Saturday 7–2, Friday 7–11 AM. For most tourist information, the tourist office is not worth much; your hotel can supply as much, if not more, information.

SUMATRA

Traveling in Sumatra is for the adventurous and tolerant; those who want exact schedules, fixed prices, luxury, and planned itineraries will probably not enjoy the island. The Indonesians are freewheeling entrepreneurs, but all the basic tourist amenities are available, as are local people to help direct you to what you want. Sumatrans are friendly and welcoming, and many speak a few words of English. Taxis and a comprehensive bus system link the towns, and the domestic airlines connect the provincial capitals.

The sights below are located around the northern, more developed half of the island. A visit to Brastagi and Lake Toba requires two nights. Add another night if you visit the orangutans in Gunung Leuser National Park, and at least two more if you travel to Nias Island.

Numbers in the margin correspond to points of interest on the North Sumatra map.

Medan

1 *2-hr flight northwest of Jakarta, 1-hr flight south of Singapore.*

Medan, the capital of North Sumatra and the third-largest city in Indonesia, has a population of 2 million people jostling in a city designed for 500,000. The streets are bedlam—cars, taxis, bemos, motor scooters, bicycles, and pedestrians going in all directions on streets that have started to be repaired but have never quite been finished. The two major sights are the large, multidome **Mesjid Raye Mosque**, built in 1906 and one of Indonesia's largest, and the Sultan's Palace, the **Isetana Sultan Deli**. Special permission from the tourist office is required to visit the inside of the palace.

A major reason for coming to Medan is to visit the **Orangutan Rehabilitation Station** in Gunung Leuser Park. The best way to do this is to hire a taxi and guide for about U.S.$75 for the 2½-hour drive. (One-way taxi fare is about U.S.$30.) Leave Medan by about 11 AM to reach the park by 2 PM. You will then have a 30-minute walk in tropical heat up to the ranger's hut. A further 15-minute hike up the mountain takes you to the feeding platform where rangers, at 3:30 PM, spend 35 minutes feeding and inspecting the orangutans, preparing them for life in the wild. You need to be relatively fit to make the 45-minute hike, which involves rugged terrain and crossing a creek by raft, but the experience is well worth the effort.

If you arrive in Medan by plane, the only way into town is by taxi. A fixed rate of 4,800 Rps applies. An extremely helpful tourist office, between the new domestic and international terminals, has lists of accommodations in the region and will happily make reservations and arrange transportation for you.

Lodging

$$$$ ⊞ **Natour Dharma Deli Medan.** This high-rise chain hotel in the center of Medan comes close to rivaling the Tiara Medan as the city's best. But don't expect more than boxy rooms with two queen-size beds, two chairs, and a coffee table, plus a cabinet that serves as both work desk and resting place for the (satellite) television. The outdoor pool has bar service and shaded areas that offer an escape from the equatorial sun.

North Sumatra

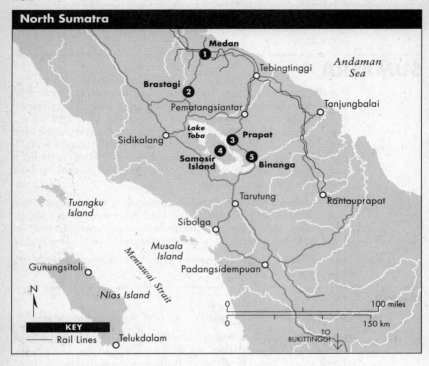

The coffee shop is an all-purpose restaurant offering Indonesian, Chinese, and Western food. ⊠ *67 Jalan Balai Kota, Medan 20111,* ☎ *061/327–011,* 𝔽𝔸𝕏 *061/327–153. 180 rooms. Coffee shop, pool, exercise room. AE, DC, MC, V.*

$$$$ 🏨 **Tiara Medan Hotel.** This clean, smart hotel, with a fresh-looking dining room offering standard Chinese, European, and Indonesian fare for lunch and the more formal Amberita Restaurant for dinner, is Medan's best. Guest rooms are well maintained, spacious, and air-conditioned. The hotel offers a conference center and recreational facilities. ⊠ *Jalan Cut Mutia, Medan 20152,* ☎ *061/516000,* 𝔽𝔸𝕏 *061/51076. 204 rooms. 2 restaurants, bar, room service, pool, 2 tennis courts, health club, squash, business services, meeting rooms, travel services. AE, DC, V.*

$ 🏨 **Waiyat Hotel.** This is a good budget hotel with well-swept rooms, most of which have a private bathroom. The staff is friendly, speaking a little English. ⊠ *Jln. Asia No 44, Medan 20214,* ☎ *061/27475. 70 rooms. Restaurant. No credit cards.*

Brastagi

❷ *68 km (41 mi) southwest of Medan.*

Brastagi, two hours from sweltering Medan, is a refreshing hill station 4,600 feet above sea level that maintains an Old World air from when it was used by Dutch planters to escape the heat. You can stay in Brastagi's charming colonial hotel.

Several groups of the Karo Bataks have their villages in the highlands, and one worth a visit is **Lingga,** 15 km (9 mi) from Brastagi. Here you can see 250- to 300-year-old multifamily tribal houses that are still used today. Karo Bataks, as well as the Toba Bataks, are descendants from proto-Malay tribes who originally inhabited the border areas of what is now Myanmar (Burma) and Thailand. They chose this mountainous region for its isolation, and their patrilineal society remains virtually intact.

Lodging

$$–$$$ 🏨 **Bukit Kubu Hotel.** This wonderful old colonial-style hotel is the area's
★ best. Ask for a double suite with a view of the mountains (the price is
only U.S.$5 more than the standard rooms). Lunch is served on a breezy
terrace; dinner, inside, in the surprisingly formal dining room. Starched
linen and billowing lace curtains are reminiscent of the 1930s, when
Dutch planters came here to relax. Today, the hotel is popular with
wealthy folk from Medan who come for weekends in the cool mountain air. ✉ *Jalan Sempurna 2, Brastagi 22151,* ☎ *0628/20832. Booking office: Jalan Jenderal Sudirman 36, Medan,* ☎ *061/519636. 40
rooms. Restaurant, laundry service. AE, V.*

Prapat

❸ *176 km (110 mi) south of Medan.*

From Brastagi it is an easy two-hour drive (by bus or taxi) to Prapat.
The last 30 minutes of the journey are the most dramatic. The road
winds through tropical vegetation to a pass, where Lake Toba suddenly
is visible spread out below.

Lodging

$$$$ 🏨 **Hotel Patra Jasa.** About 5 km (3 mi) from Prapat, on a bluff overlooking the lake, this hotel is the best retreat in the area. For peace and
quiet, nothing can beat it, but the location makes every trip into Prapat an excursion, and its facilities are somewhat limited. Guest rooms
are located in pavilions surrounding the main lodge, about 10 rooms
in each. Hot water is available most of the time. ✉ *Jalan Siuhan, Peninsula Prapat, Prapat 21174,* ☎ *0625/41196,* ℻ *0625/41536. 45 rooms.
Restaurant, pool, 2 tennis courts, 9-hole golf course. AE, V.*

$$$ 🏨 **Natour Hotel Parapat.** The best rooms here are in the bungalows facing Lake Toba. They are comfortably large, worn, but reasonably well
furnished and have the benefit of lounge and patio. All the bungalows
are scattered on a terraced slope covered with flower beds. This is the
best hotel in Prapat. ✉ *Jalan Marihat 1, Prapat 21174,* ☎ *0664/41012,*
℻ *0664/41019. 85 rooms. Dining room, bar, room service. AE, V.*

¢ 🏨 **Risis Hotel.** For a budget hotel that is clean and friendly, this small
whitewashed building on the street that leads into the market square
is the best. Some rooms come with a private bath, all have bare walls
and floors and minimal furniture. ✉ *Jalan Haranggaol 39, Prapat 21174,*
☎ *0664/41392. 20 rooms. No credit cards.*

Lake Toba and Samosir Island

★ ❹ *Samosir Island is 30 minutes by boat from Prapat.*

Lake Toba (Donau Toba), one of the largest lakes in Southeast Asia
and one of the highest in the world, sits 2,950 feet above sea level, surrounded by steep slopes that plunge headlong into the water to depths
of 1,475 feet. Prapat may be the major resort town *on* Lake Toba, but
most visitors prefer to stay *in* the lake—on Samosir, a hilly 300-square-mile island in the middle of the lake that's home to the Toba Bataks.

The main tourist destination on Samosir is **Tomok,** where you'll find
the tombs of King Sidabutar, who ruled in the 1800s; his son; his grandson; and several warriors of rank. Nearby are several Batak houses with
curving roofs and intricately carved beams and panels. To reach these
cultural attractions, walk a quarter-mile up from the ferry dock past

stalls selling souvenirs, artifacts, and batik cloth. Keep in mind the actual purchase price is 30%–40% of the initial asking price.

Tuk Tuk, on a peninsula that juts into the lake, is reached either by road from Tomok (a 30-minute walk) or by ferry; small hotels line the peninsula's shoreline. Next is **Ambarita,** a village where, in the past, miscreants had their heads lopped off. You can still see the courtyard where the king held council. Ancient, weathered stone chairs and tables form a ring in front of the chief's traditional house.

At the northern tip of the island is the village of **Simanindo,** site of a fine old traditional house, once the home of a Batak king. The village has been declared an open-air museum, and the one house not to miss is the Long House (Rumak Bolon), with its fine carvings and the sculpted depiction of the god Gajah Dompak. His job was to frighten off evil spirits, and by the look of him, he must have been good at it.

A public ferry runs from Prapat's market square to Tomok, but the most popular way to get to Samosir is by the boat that boards passengers from the shore near the Hotel Parapat for a round-trip fare of Rp 3,000. Other boats go to Tuk Tuk, Ambarita, and Simanindo, and fares for these trips are slightly higher. You may also charter a powerboat for a three-hour trip to Tomok, Tuk Tuk, Ambarita, and Simanindo, which will cost about Rp 40,000. For travel around Samosir, minibus taxis make irregular trips and there are motorbikes for rent for about Rp 15,000 an hour.

Lodging

If you cannot obtain a room at Tuk Tuk's Carolina Cottage, there is the the nearby **Samosir** (no phone), with a lovely open-sided restaurant/lounge and a bit of its own beach, or **Silintong** (☎ 0622/41345). Near Tomok, try the **Toba Beach Hotel** (☎ 0622/41275).

$–$$ ⊞ **Carolina Cottage.** Accommodations here are in Batak houses perched
★ on the edge of the lake. All have spectacular views, but only a few have hot running water. The service is friendly and helpful. The best rooms, in cottages on stilts above the lake, are No. 40 and No. 41. Continental breakfasts, snacks, and dinners are served. ⊠ *Tuk Tuk Siadong, Danau Toba,* ☎ *0625/41520. 23 rooms with bath. Restaurant, bar. No credit cards.*

Binanga

❺ *15 km (9 mi) from Prapat on the road to Bukittinggi.*

Binanga (sometimes known as Lumban Binanga) is the site of five traditional Batak houses. Park at the side of the road (you'll see a sign) and walk down the hill past some new houses and terraced paddy fields to the cluster of these Batak houses that are 150 to 200 years old. Few tourists come here, so Binanga has much less commercial bustle than the villages on Samosir.

Sumatra A to Z

Arriving and Departing

BY BOAT

The MS *Gadis Langkasura* ferry makes two trips a week between Penang, Malaysia, and Medan (Belawan Harbour). Sleeping berths are shared by four people, and economy passengers have reclining seats. Schedules continually change, so check with the Indonesian Tourist Promotion Office in Singapore before you commit yourself to this route. Cost: M\$65 for a berth; M\$55 for an economy seat. Check with the Indonesian Tourist Promotion Office for schedules.

Garuda Indonesian Airways and Singapore Airlines have daily hour-long flights from Singapore to Medan. The least expensive way of reaching Medan is by hydrofoil from Singapore to Batam and by plane to Medan. Domestic airlines are considerably cheaper than international airlines, and all major towns in Indonesia are connected by air routes.

Getting Around

Distance traveling in Sumatra can be done by plane, bus, and shared or private taxi. Air travel is to be preferred; overland travel is an often tedious business, made more unpredictable in the rainy season,when mud slides can close roads for hours. Buses range from air-conditioned express buses to crowded local ones. Driving your own rented car is not advised; the risk of an accident is too great.

Taxis do not use meters; it is necessary to negotiate the fare before you enter the taxi. For a shared taxi, try **Indah Taxi** (⊠ Brig-jen Katamso 60, Medan, ☎ 06/510036). Private taxis can be found at hotels, bus stations, and airports.

Contacts and Resources

VISITOR INFORMATION
The best place to pick up tourist information about Sumatra is at Singapore's **Indonesian Tourist Promotion Office** (⊠ 15–07 Ocean Bldg., 10 Collyer Quay, Singapore 0104, ☎ 534–2837). Some information can be obtained from **North Sumatra Regional Office of Tourism** (⊠ Jl. Alfalah 22, Kampung Baru, Medan 20146, ☎ 061/762220). A helpful office is the **Provincial Tourist Service** (⊠ Jl. Jend. A. Yani No. 107, Medan 20151, ☎ 061/511101) and their office at Medan airport.

RIAU ARCHIPELAGO

From the tallest buildings in Singapore, you can see the nearby islands of Indonesia. In 30 minutes, you can cross the straits on a hydrofoil ferry south to the islands of the Riau Archipelago. The two main islands are Batam and Bintan. Batam is undergoing a vast development project that includes a duty-free industrial zone and a tourist complex. However, while it may appeal to Singaporeans looking for cheap shopping or a weekend away from the constraints of their city, its interest for the long-haul traveler is limited. Lying to its east is the more interesting island of Bintan, which is also slated for development, but primarily for tourists.

Bintan

Bintan's main town is **Tanjung Pinang,** where the primary activity is shopping at Pasar Pelantar Dua. You can rent a motorboat at the pier to take you up the Snake River through the mangrove swamps to the oldest Chinese temple in Riau; as the boatman poles his way up the small tributary choked with mangroves, it's thrilling to come upon the isolated 300-year-old temple with its murals of hell.

Every morning two ferries depart at 10 AM, 10:30 AM, and 3 PM for the 90-minute trip (S$51 one-way) from Finger Pier at Singapore's World Trade Centre and return at 9:30 AM, 10 AM, and 2 PM. Contact **Dino Ferries** (☎ 270–2228) or **Auto Batam** (271–4866), though reservations aren't usually necessary, except on weekends.

Lodging

$$$$ 🏨 **Banyan Tree Bintan.** Nestled in a secluded bay, this is the most luxurious resort in the Riau islands. Perched on the hill slopes, all 27 villas face the sea and three of them are two-bedroom mansions with their

own large private plunge pool. The other villas, all large at 1,500 square feet, have private outdoor whirlpools on the sun deck. The accent is is on spa treatments and massages, but this does not detract from the romantic mood—have dinner served al fresco on your terrace before watching a video in the privacy of your villa. You can also dine on Asian and Western fare at the restaurant alongside the rock-edge swimming pool. ⊠ *Tanjung Said, Bintan,* ☎ *0771/81347,* FAX *0771/ 81348. 27 villas. Restaurant, pool, massage, 2 tennis courts, windsurfing, golf, meeeting rooms. AE, DC, MC, V.*

$ ▦ **Riau Holidays Inn.** If you're stuck in Tanjung Pinang, this is the best of a pretty seedy bunch of city hotels. The rooms are a little depressing and smelly, but the bar lounge, which is built on stilts and looks out over the port, is a good local hangout. ⊠ *53 Jalan Pelanta Dua,* ☎ *0771/22573. 50 rooms. Restaurant, bar.*

Outdoor Activities and Sports

To get to the beach, you'll need to take a taxi 40 km (24 mi) to Trikora Beach on the east coast, where you can use the facilities of the resort hotel, the **Trikora Country Club** (no phone), a true hideaway with an excellent beach that's good for swimming and snorkeling.

INDONESIA A TO Z

Arriving and Departing

By Boat

FROM MALAYSIA

A ferry departs every morning except Tuesday and Sunday from Penang, Malaysia, and arrives in Belawan (the port of Medan) on Sumatra five hours later. The cost is M$110 one way. Return trips depart around noon from Belawan every day except Monday and Saturday. There is another ferry, the KM *Maharani Express I,* from Port Klang (Kuala Lumpur) to Medan. The boat leaves two times a week, takes five hours, and costs M$130. Note that the same boat also goes to Dumai, but Westerners require a visa to enter Indonesia through Dumai.

FROM SINGAPORE

A popular route to avoid international airfares is to take a ferry from Singapore to the Riau Archipelago's Batam—there are departures every hour during the day—and pick up a domestic flight to anywhere in Indonesia, be it Medan or Jakarta and on to Bali. Another ferry route from Singapore is to Tanjung Pinang, just a 90-minute ferry ride, and where one can connect with Merpati flights to other Indonesian destinations.

By Plane

AIRPORTS

International flights to Jakarta's **Soekarno Hatta Airport** land at Terminal One, with the exception of Garuda Indonesia Airways flights, which are processed through Terminal Two. There is an airport tax of Rp 21,000 for international departures.

CARRIERS

Garuda Indonesian Airways (☎ 021/380–1901; in the U.S., ☎ 212/ 370–0707, 800/342–7832 outside of New York), the national carrier, offers a direct, two-stop flight from Los Angeles to Jakarta or Bali; however, most people, including Indonesians, prefer a foreign carrier. Many travelers use one airline into Singapore or Bangkok, then transfer to Garuda or Singapore Airlines for the remaining leg into Indonesia. This process was somewhat simplified in 1996, when Northwest Airines was granted rights to fly into Jakarta from their hub in Tokyo, thus permitting direct travel (with a change of plane) from the U.S.

The following airlines fly to Indonesia: **Continental** (☎ 021/334417); **Northwest Airlines** (☎ 021/520–3152); **Qantas** (☎ 021/230–0655); **Singapore Airlines** (☎ 021/570–4422); **Thai International** (☎ 021/314–0607); and **United Airlines** (☎ 021/570–7520).

FLYING TIMES
Transpacific flying time to Bali is 19 hours from Los Angeles, 23 hours from Chicago, and 25 hours from New York. Flying the eastbound route, the flight time from New York is 20 hours to Singapore, then another two hours to Jakarta.

Getting Around

By Bajaj
Popular in Jakarta, this three-wheeled, two-passenger motor vehicle is less comfortable and less expensive than a taxi but can be faster, since it can scoot through the traffic. They are hailed on the street, and you negotiate the fare.

By Becak
These three-wheeled pedicabs are useful for short distances. In Jakarta they are permitted only in the outlying neighborhoods, but elsewhere in Indonesia they are plentiful. Becak drivers are tough bargainers, but if one doesn't meet your price, another may.

By Bemo
A bemo is a converted pickup truck or minivan—a standard form of transport for short trips. Most bemos follow regular routes and will stop anywhere along the way to pick up or discharge passengers. You pay when you get out. Try to learn the fare (they vary according to distance) from another passenger; otherwise you'll be overcharged. An empty bemo will often try to pick up Western travelers, but beware: unless you clarify that it's on its regular route, you will be chartering it as a taxi.

By Boat
Ferries run between many of the islands. Hotel travel desks and travel agencies have schedules; you buy your tickets at the terminals. For longer trips, **Pelni** (✉ Jln. Angkasa 18, Jakarta, ☎ 021/416262), the state-owned shipping company, serves all the major ports with ships accommodating 500 to 1,000 passengers in four classes. First-class cabins are air-conditioned and have private bathrooms. Schedules and tickets are available from Pelni's head office or at travel agencies.

By Bus
The main means of land travel in Indonesia, buses offer varying degrees of comfort. Long-distance expresses are air-conditioned and have reclining seats; some even show video programs. Local buses can be crowded and steaming hot. It's an inexpensive means of transport—the 14-hour trip between Jakarta and Yogyakarta, for instance, costs Rp 17,500 on an air-conditioned express. Tickets and schedules are available from terminals, travel desks, or travel agencies. Tourist offices also provide schedules. For Java and Sumatra, contact **Antar Lintas Sumatra** (✉ Jln. Jati Baru 87A, Jakarta, ☎ 021/320970). For Java, Bali, and Sumatra, **PT. ANS** (✉ Jln. Senen Raya 50, Jakarta, ☎ 021/340494).

By Car
GASOLINE
Gas prices are higher than in the States, the equivalent of around $1.65 for a U.S. gallon. Stations are few and far between, so don't set out with less than a quarter tank.

RENTALS

Self-drive rental cars are available only in Jakarta, Yogyakarta, and Bali—and only for use in the vicinity. You'll need an international driver's license. Elsewhere, and for long-distance trips, your rental car includes a driver. A helpful hint: Indonesians love to talk. If your driver gets too chatty, feign sleep so he'll concentrate on the road. But do talk to him occasionally or suggest rest stops to keep him awake and alert.

The rental charge for a self-drive four-wheel-drive vehicle from a national firm such as Avis runs about $45 a day with a collision damage waiver (CDW). You can find better rates from local rental firms, but make absolutely sure that the car is fully insured.

ROAD CONDITIONS

Indonesia's main roads are in fairly good condition, but side and back roads can be poor. Tourist areas often get very congested, with small trucks, bemos, scooters, bicycles, and pedestrians adding to car traffic.

RULES OF THE ROAD

Driving is on the left, as in Great Britain. Road signs reading HATI HATI mean "warning."

By Horse Cart

Horse-drawn carts are disappearing fast, but they remain popular in Padang, Lombok, and other tourist areas. The cost depends on your bargaining skill.

By Plane

Reservations are strongly advised on popular routes—between Jakarta and Yogyakarta, for example. Expect delays, especially during the monsoon rains, which can make air travel impossible.

There is an airport tax of Rp 9,000 for domestic departures.

CARRIERS

Garuda Indonesian Airways (☞ Arriving and Departing, *above*) and **Merpati** (☎ 021/348760) cover all 27 provinces. Under the current restructuring of government-owned airlines, Garuda Indonesia Airways will hand over many of its domestic flights to Merpati Airlines. Garuda will retain the routes between major airports, but for shorter hauls Merpati—using either jets or propeller planes—will be the government carrier.

A new private airline, **Sempati** (☎ 021/809–4407), is challenging both Garuda and Merpati with better service and lower fares. Locally owned **Bouraq** (☎ 021/659–5194) flies into small towns with limited landing facilities, such as destinations in Kalimantan.

AIR PASSES

You can save up to 60% on domestic flights by buying your tickets in Indonesia instead of overseas. However, if you don't use these tickets, you will not receive a full refund. Garuda offers a **Visit Indonesia Pass** to a minimum of three destinations within Indonesia for U.S.$300 and an additional U.S.$100 for each additional destination.

By Taxi

Registered taxis and hired cars may be hailed on city streets—look for the yellow number plates. Except in Jakarta, Surabaya, parts of Bali, and at most airports, you negotiate the fare with the driver before setting out. Most hotels have taxi stands.

By Train

Only Java has a useful passenger railroad, running east–west across the island. It offers three travel classes, with air-conditioned sleepers available for trips between Jakarta and Yogyakarta and on to Solo and

Surabaya. Southern Sumatra has train service between Panjang and Palembang. Except for the Jakarta–Yogyakarta and the Jakarta–Bandung expresses, trains can be slow (and late), and they're not always air-conditioned. You can get schedules and tickets at hotel travel desks, travel agencies, or train stations; schedules are also available at tourist offices.

Contacts and Resources

Customs and Duties

Two liters of liquor and 200 cigarettes may be brought into Indonesia duty-free. Restrictions apply on the import of radios and television sets.

Visitors may not export more than 50,000 rupiah per person.

Dining

Even in Jakarta, you will see well-dressed Indonesians eating with their fingers. Most food comes cut into small pieces, and finger bowls are provided. Tourists normally receive forks.

Electricity

The electrical current in Indonesia is 220 volts, 50 cycles alternating. You should bring an adapter and converter, or, if your appliances are dual voltage, just an adapter. Wall outlets take a variety of plug styles.

Etiquette and Behavior

Indonesians are extremely polite. Begin encounters with locals by saying "Selemat," ("blessings," or "peace"). Shaking hands has become a common practice, but do not offer to shake hands with an Indonesian woman unless she proffers her hand first. And try not to use the word "No." Indonesians find it ugly and impolite and will go to great lengths to avoid giving direct refusals. When dining, avoid touching food with your left hand.

The more formal or sacred an occasion, the more formally dressed you should be. When visiting mosques, women should wear something on the head and should not enter during menstruation. Men should wear long trousers and have at least their upper arms covered. Do not walk in front of those who are praying. At Balinese temples, you must often wear a sash to enter; one can usually be rented on-site for a few rupiah. As shorts (and other above-the-knee clothing) are considered improper temple attire, avoid them or borrow a sarong when visiting any holy place.

Health and Safety

Drink only bottled water, and avoid ice in any beverage (although ice at luxury hotels, such as those on Bali, is often made from distilled water and may be safe). It's best to steer clear of raw, unpeeled fruits and vegetables.

Civil unrest is generally confined to the island of Timor, where there is an ongoing separatist movement; two Timorese activists were awarded the Nobel Peace Prize in 1996. Street crime is minimal, though Jakarta has its share of pickpockets.

Language

Although some 300 languages are spoken in Indonesia, Bahasa Indonesia has been the national language since independence. English is widely spoken in tourist areas.

Mail

POSTAL RATES

Two kinds of airmail are available: regular *(pos udara)* and express *(kilat)*. Kilat rates to the United States or the United Kingdom are Rp 1,200

and Rp 1,300 respectively for postcards and Rp 1,600 and Rp 1,700
for 1 gram (.035 oz) letters.

RECEIVING MAIL

In Jakarta, have letters sent to the main post office (☉ Mon.–Thurs.
8–4, Fri. 8–11 AM, Sat. 8 AM–12:30 PM) addressed to you c/o Central
Post Office, Jalan Pos Utara, Jakarta, and marked *poste restante.* Your
surname should be written in underlined capitals, with only the initial
of your given name, to avoid misfiling. Major post offices outside Jakarta
also accept poste restante.

Money and Expenses

CURRENCY

Indonesia's unit of currency is the rupiah. Bills come in denominations
of 100, 500, 1,000, 5,000, 10,000, 20,000, and 50,000 Rp, coins in
25, 50, 100, 500, and 1,000 Rp. The exchange rate at press time was
Rp 2,300 to the U.S. dollar, Rp 1,700 to the Canadian dollar, and Rp
3,700 to the pound sterling.

TAXES

Hotels and formal **restaurants** add a 7.5% government tax and a 10%
service charge to their bills. On Lombok, the tax is 11%. Departing
passengers on international flights pay an **airport departure tax** of around
Rp 21,000. For domestic travel, airport taxes are from Rp 6,500 at
the smaller airports to Rp 9,000 at Jakarta.

WHAT IT WILL COST

Prices in Indonesia depend on what you're buying: The basic cost of
living is low and domestic labor is cheap, but you pay a premium for
anything imported. Thus, renting a car is expensive, hiring a driver is
not; camera film is expensive, food is not. Regionally, costs rise in direct relation to tourism and business development. Prices in Bali and
Jakarta are relatively high, particularly at deluxe hotels and restaurants.
Sumatra and Sulawesi, by contrast, are bargains. In general, Indonesia's prices are comparable to or somewhat lower than Malaysia's and
definitely lower than Thailand's.

Major cities have shopping complexes and department stores where
prices are fixed, but at small shops and street stalls bargaining is not
only necessary but part of the pleasure. Negotiating a price is, in fact,
having a dialogue with the vendor, and a certain respect is established
between you and the vendor. Bargaining is an art. You'll develop your
own technique. In the meantime, try offering half the asking price, even
a third in the tourist areas. You will finish somewhere in between. Shops
with higher-quality merchandise are likely to take credit cards, but payment in cash puts you in a better bargaining position.

Sample Prices: Continental breakfast at hotel, $3; bottle of beer at hotel,
$2.50; bottled water, 75¢; Indonesian dinner at good restaurant, $15;
1-mile taxi ride, 75¢; double room, moderate $50–$75, very expensive over $115 ($250 in Jakarta and Bali).

National Holidays

The following are national holidays; some are tied to a religious calendar, hence the dates vary from year to year: New Year's Day (Jan.
1); Idul Fitri, the end of Ramadan (Jan./Feb.); Isra Miraj Nabi Mohammed, Mohammed's Ascension (Feb./Mar.); Good Friday
(March/April); Ascension Day, 40 days after Easter (April/May);
Waicak, Birth of Buddha, (May/June); Haji, commemorating Mecca
pilgrimages (July); Independence Day (Aug. 17); Birth of Mohammed
(Oct.); Christmas Day (Dec. 25).

Opening and Closing Times

Banks are open from either 8 or 8:30 AM to noon or 2 PM. Bank branches in hotels stay open later. **Government offices** are open Monday–Thursday 8–3 and Friday 8–11:30 AM. Some are also open on Saturday 8–2. **Business offices** have varied hours; some are open weekdays 8–4, others 9–5. Some offices work a half day on Saturday. Most **museums** are open Tuesday–Thursday and weekends 9–2 (although some larger museums stay open until 4 or 5), Friday 9–noon. Most **shops** are open Monday–Saturday 9–5.

Outdoor Activities and Sports

Swimming pools, health clubs, tennis, badminton, and sometimes squash and racquetball are available at the major hotels. There are golf courses near the larger cities and in resort areas. Special adventure tours can be arranged through tour operators. Traditional sports include bull races in Madura, Java; bullfights (bull against bull) at Kota Bharu, near Bukit Thinggi, Sumatra; and cockfighting (though it is illegal) in Java, Bali, and Sulawesi.

For scuba-diving information, call the Indonesian diving organization, **Possi** (✉ Jln. Prapatan 38, Jakarta, ☎ 021/348685).

Passports and Visas

Passports must be valid for at least six months from arrival date, and all travelers must have proof of onward or return passage. Visas are not required of U.S., Canadian, and U.K. citizens for stays of up to 60 days, as long as you enter the country through one of the major gateways. These include the airports at Ambon, Bali, Bandung, Batam, Biak, Jakarta, Manado, Medan, Padang, Pontianak, and Surabaya, as well as sea ports in Bali, Balikpapan, Batam, Jakarta, Kupang, Pontianak, Semarang, and Tanjung Pinang. Other ports of entry may require a visa.

Telephones

To call Indonesia from overseas, dial the country code, 62, and then the area code, omitting the first 0.

DIRECTORY ASSISTANCE AND OPERATOR INFORMATION

For operator and directory assistance, dial 108 for local calls, 106 for the provinces, and 102 for international.

LOCAL CALLS

Jakarta's telephone system has improved, and most business establishments have phones, but the rest of the country is less well supplied. In most cases you are best off using hotel phones despite the small surcharges; that way you don't need to amass quantities of coins, and an operator can help with translation and information. Your best chance of finding a phone is in hotel lobbies.

For local calls, three minutes costs Rp 100. Older public phones take Rp 100 coins, but the newer ones accept only phone cards—a recent introduction restricted to the larger cities and tourist areas. For long distance, dial the area code before the number.

INTERNATIONAL CALLS

Major Indonesian cities are now hooked into the International Direct Dialing (IDD) system via satellite. Dial 001 plus the respective country code. For towns without the IDD hookup, go through the operator (in tourist destinations many speak English). If you want to avoid using hotel phones, the most economical way to place an IDD call is from the nearest **Kantor Telephone & Telegraph** office.

You may make collect calls to Australia, Europe, and North America; for other countries, you need a telephone credit card. Reduced rates on international phone calls are in effect 9 PM–6 AM daily. When calling the States, you can also dial the following **access numbers** to reach a U.S. long-distance operator: MCI (☎ 001–801–11); Sprint (☎ 001–801–15).

Tipping

Some **restaurants** include the service charge; if not, tip 10%. Most **hotels** add a 10% service charge, but bell boys look for around Rp 1,000 per bag; you may also want to tip room-service personnel if you order something very small (on which 10% is negligible) or if you request a special service (to come get the plates in exactly 45 minutes, etc.). **Porters** at the airport should receive Rp 500 per bag. **Taxi drivers** are not tipped except in Jakarta and Surabaya, where Rp 500, or the small change, is the minimum. For a **driver of a hired car**, Rp 5,000 for half a day would be the minimum tip. **Private guides** expect a gratuity, perhaps Rp 5,000 per day.

Visitor Information

At press time, there was no Indonesian tourism office in Canada. Contact the **Embassy of Indonesia** (⊠ 287 MacLaren St., Ottawa, Ontario, Canada K2P 0L9, ☎ 613/236–7403, FAX 613/563–2858) or the consulates in Toronto and Vancouver.

In the United Kingdom, contact the **Indonesian Tourist Office** (⊠ 3 Hanover St., London W1R 9HH, ☎ 0171/493–0030, FAX 0171/493–1747).

In the United States, contact the **Indonesia Tourist Board** (⊠ 3457 Wilshire Blvd., Los Angeles, CA 90010, ☎ 213/387–2078, FAX 213/380–4876).

When to Go

Indonesia's low-lying regions are uniformly hot and humid year-round. Temperatures can reach 90°F (32°C) soon after midday, and they drop no lower than 70°F (21°C) at night. The weather at higher altitudes is up to 20°F (11°C) cooler.

The best months to visit Indonesia are April–May and September–October, when crowds are lighter and you're not so likely to get drenched: The west monsoon, from November through March, brings heavy rains. It can drizzle for several days in a row or pour half the day, with only occasional dry spells. Since most of Indonesia's attractions are under the open sky—temples and other architecture, beaches, and outdoor festivals—the monsoon can very literally dampen your enjoyment.

In the peak tourist months, June and July, popular areas (especially Torajaland) are crammed with visitors. Bali hotels also tend to be fully booked around Christmas and New Year's. Unless you will be staying solely on Bali, consider carefully before visiting during Ramadan.

CLIMATE

The following are average temperatures in Jakarta:

Jan.	84F	29C	May	88F	31C	Sept.	88F	31C
	74	23		74	23		74	23
Feb.	84F	29C	June	88F	31C	Oct.	88F	31C
	74	23		74	23		74	23
Mar.	85F	30C	July	88F	31C	Nov.	85F	30C
	74	23		74	23		74	23
Apr.	86F	30C	Aug.	88F	31C	Dec.	85F	30C
	74	23		74	23		74	23

FESTIVALS AND SEASONAL EVENTS

Festival dates depend on the type of calendar prevalent in the region where they take place. Most of Indonesia uses the Islamic calendar; the Balinese use a lunar calendar. The **Indonesia Calendar of Events,** with listings for the entire archipelago, is available at Garuda airline offices, or contact tourist information offices.

January–February: **Idul Fitri,** two days marking the end of Ramadan (a month of fasting during daylight), is the most important Muslim holiday. Festivals take place in all the villages and towns of Muslim Indonesia.

March: **Nyepi,** the Balinese New Year, falls on the vernal equinox, usually around March 21. New Year's Eve is spent exorcising evil spirits, which are first attracted with offerings of chicken blood, flowers, and aromatic leaves, then driven away with noise as masked youths bang gongs and tin pans. The island falls silent: No fires or lamps may be lit, and traffic is prohibited.

May: **Waicak Day,** a public holiday throughout Indonesia, celebrates the Buddha's birth, death, and enlightenment.

The **Ramayana Ballet Festival** is held at the Prambanan temple near Yogyakarta during the full-moon week each month, beginning in May and contiuing through October. A cast of 500 performs a four-episode dance-drama of the *Ramayana* epic.

July: **Galungan,** Bali's most important festival, celebrates the creation of the world, marks a visit by ancestral spirits, and honors the victory of good over evil. Celebrants make offerings in family shrines and decorate their villages. On the 10th and last day they bid farewell to the visiting spirits with gifts of *kuningan,* a saffron-yellow rice.

August: **Independence Day** is celebrated on the 17th throughout Indonesia with flag-raising ceremonies, sports events, and cultural performances.

October: The town of Pamekasan on Java holds **bull-racing finals** in mid October. A jockey stands on skids slung between two yoked bulls. The animals are decorated, and there's mass dancing before they run. The winner is the bull whose feet cross the finish line first.

Sekaten commemorates the birth of Mohammed. In Yogyakarta the sultan's antique gamelan—a unique Indonesian musical instrument—is played only on this day. The concert is performed in the gamelan pavilion of the kraton, the sultan's palace complex. Then the celebrants form a parade, carrying enormous amounts of food from the kraton to the mosque, where they distribute it to the people.

December–January: **Kesodo** ceremonies are held by the Hindu Tengerese at the crater of Mt. Bromo on Java.

3 Malaysia

Malaysia is, for one thing, an extraordinary olfactory experience. In the cities the acrid smell of chilies frying in street-vendor stalls mingles with the sweetness of incense wafting out of Indian shops, the pungency of curry powders from spice merchants, the delicate scents of frangipani and other tropical flowers that bloom everywhere, and the diesel fumes from taxis and buses. The jungle has a damp, fermenting aroma that will haunt your imagination long after you've returned to everyday life at home.

THE EARLIEST INHABITANTS of the Malay Peninsula were Neolithic Negrito peoples whose descendants— the Orang Asli—still live simply in jungle uplands. Several waves of progressively more Mongoloid groups brought Iron and Bronze Age cultures to the peninsula and spread out over the entire archipelago. Later, with the emergence of the Java-based Majapahit, the Malay Peninsula came under the influence of a Hindu-Javanese empire that exerted little political control but strong cultural influence. This can be seen in the *wayang kulit* (shadow puppet plays)—a form of storytelling—still performed in villages, and in many traditional ceremonies and customs.

Updated by
Nigel Fisher

In the 15th century, Islam entered Malaya from northern Sumatra and became the official religion of the powerful state of Melaka during the reign of Sultan Iskandar Shah. Islam solidified the system of sultanates, in which one person and his family provided both political and religious leadership. (Today Malaysia still has nine sultans; every five years one is elected to serve a term as constitutional monarch. The head of government in this parliamentary democracy is the prime minister.)

For the next 200 years the peninsula was a hornets' nest of warring sultanates, marauding pirate bands, and European adventurers who, searching for spices and gold, introduced guns and cannons. The Portuguese conquered Melaka, and were soon followed by the Dutch, who established a stronghold in Java and outposts in Sumatra and Melaka. British settlements in the Straits of Melaka, Singapore, and Penang flourished. In 1824 a treaty with the British separated Malaya from Dutch-held Sumatra, and the two regions, so similar in historical development, cultural traditions, and religious customs, began to split and follow the lead of the new European colonists.

In the middle of the 19th century, millions of Chinese fled from war and famine in their homelands and sought employment in Malaya's rapidly expanding tin industry. Soon after their arrival, another new industry developed: rubber. Rubber requires intensive labor, and workers were again brought in from outside—this time from India. Other groups came from India to trade, open shops, or lend money. The British in India had also trained many civil servants and professionals, and they, too, came to Malaya to practice.

The Indian community maintained strong ties with home. Even today it is not unusual for an Indian to request a bride or groom from his or her ancestral village—many marriages are still arranged—and Indians often return to their native land at retirement, something the Chinese can no longer do.

These patterns of life in Malaya were well established until World War II. Malays continued their traditions in *kampongs,* or communal villages, where time flowed slowly. The sultans prospered under British protection, combining the pleasures of East and West. The Chinese, growing ever more numerous and powerful, became the economic backbone of the peninsula, with the Indians performing various middleman roles. The British maintained a benevolent rule. Each community flourished separately, with little cultural interchange.

The war had little impact on life in Malaya until the Japanese attack on Pearl Harbor and subsequent invasion of Malaya threw the complacent population into turmoil. Japanese forces landed in the northern state of Trengganu and moved rapidly down through the jungle,

Malaysia

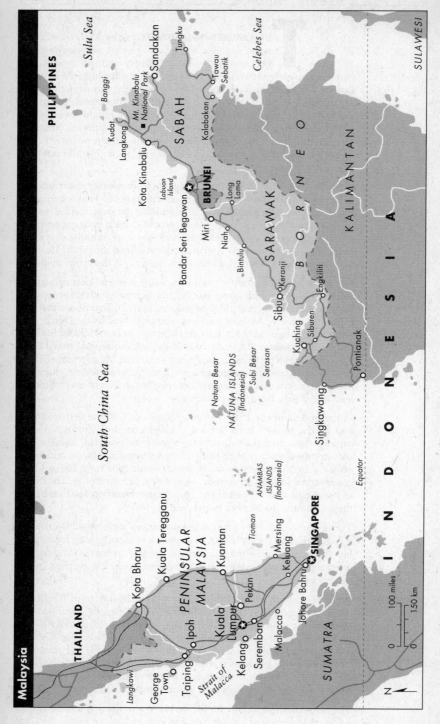

taking Singapore in March 1942. Life on the Malay Peninsula changed overnight.

The British, of course, had farthest to fall. Many women and children were evacuated to Australia, but the men remained. Former planters, bankers, executives, and soldiers were suddenly thrust from a life of ease into hardship or jail. Many prisoners perished during the construction of the infamous "Death Railway" in Siam. The survivors had to endure the indignities of captivity, which completely undermined their image as "superior" whites.

The Chinese received particularly harsh treatment from their Japanese conquerors. They faced constant harassment from Japanese forces, who jailed and executed thousands. Many Chinese fled to the jungle, where, aided by remnants of the British army, they formed guerrilla bands. As in Europe, those most adept at underground organization were Communist-trained. By the end of the war, Communist influence among the Chinese was much enhanced by the years spent in the jungle fighting the Japanese.

The war left the people floundering in economic uncertainties. Until independence under a federation of Malayan states was declared in 1957, politics consisted mostly of power struggles between the two major racial groups. The Malays, realizing that independence would remove British protection and leave the Chinese in control, became politically active. The Chinese, despite their economic clout and with their ranks decimated by the occupation, failed to organize politically. Thus, the years of separatism took their toll on national unification and development. Bitter disputes raged among the local leadership. In 1948 the Chinese guerrilla forces began a campaign of terrorism, harassing plantation workers, owners, and managers. Travel along the jungle roads was hazardous, and many Malays and British were killed in ambush. The insurgents were gradually pushed back into the jungle, and in 1960 emergency policies were lifted.

Such ethnic factionalism plagued the new federation until 1963, when the nation of Malaysia was created. It included two British protectorates in northern Borneo—Sabah and Sarawak—that were to serve as an ethnic balance against the power of the Chinese in Singapore. Indonesia, however, viewed Malaysia as a threat, and President Sukarno declared confrontation—a sort of miniwar that finally fizzled out in 1967.

Today Malaysia's racial and political power balance is still delicate. In spite of legislation to promote "Bumiputra," or numerically dominant ethnic Malay interests, the Chinese still control much of Malaysia's commerce and industry. Much has been done to defuse tensions among the ethnic groups, but pressures continue, as evidenced in the movements to strengthen Muslim law (for example, by arresting Muslims who break the Ramadan fast) and give greater emphasis to the Malay language. Over the last few years, the press has been increasingly muzzled and criticism of politicians suppressed; citizens are becoming more careful about what they say, and to whom.

Pleasures and Pastimes

Malaysia offers some of the world's best coral reefs, long stretches of white-sand beaches (both developed, with plenty of water-sports facilities, and deserted), the highest mountain in Southeast Asia, hill resorts that provide recreation and escape from the tropical sun, spectacular limestone outcroppings (at Ipoh), vast areas of primary jungle, and networks of rivers perfect for white-water rafting. More facilities are available for the international traveler, though the major destinations remain Melaka, Kuala Lumpur, Penang, and Langkawi on the west coast; Kuantan and Tioman Island on the east coast; the Cameron and Genting highlands in the center; Kota Kinabalu in Sabah; and Kuching in Sarawak.

Beaches

Despite Malaysia's extensive coastline, there are relatively few beach resorts, in part because of the country's slow tourist development and in part because not all the shore is suitable for resorts. Penang Island was the first to promote its beaches, even though they are not as soft or broad as some found elsewhere in the country. Pangkor and Langkawi islands, off the northwest coast, have good golden-sand beaches. Today Langkawi, with its multiple swimming coves, is promoted by the Malaysia government as the alternative to Thailand's Phuket.

On the east coast, Kuantan, Desaru, and Tioman Island offer resort life; north of Kuantan, miles of quiet and lovely sandy beaches and picturesque villages await those willing to swap luxuries for a more traditional Malay experience. Though this will be bound to change, for the moment the lack of public transport and ferry services has kept development limited to the area around Kuantan.

Over on Borneo, Sarawak's rivers tend to bring silt down to the ocean, making for muddy waters. One exception is Dumai, just outside Kuching, where a resort complex has developed. In Sabah, the beaches in Tanjung Aru are of golden sand, but the real joy is going to the pristine islands off Kota Kinabalu.

Dining

Street food is a main event throughout Malaysia; locals share tables when it's crowded. Look at what others are eating, and if it looks good, point and order. One favorite is the *popiah,* a soft spring roll filled with vegetables. The *meehon* and *kweh teow* (fried noodles) are especially tasty and cheap. Pay each provider for the individual dish he or she makes. Be cautious with the *nasi kandar,* a local favorite, for the chilies rule the spicy prawns and fish-head curry. Try Malaysia's favorite breakfast dish, *nasi lemak*—a bundle of rice with salt fish, curry chicken, peanuts, slices of cucumber, and boiled egg.

Because fruit is so plentiful and delicious, Malaysians consume lots of it, either fresh from the ubiquitous roadside fruit vendors or fresh-squeezed—try especially star fruit or watermelon juice. Mangoes, papayas, rambutans, mangosteens, and finger-size bananas are widely available. The "king" of fruits is the durian, but be prepared: The smell is not sweet, even though the taste is. Hotels have strict policies forbidding durians in guest rooms, so most buyers select a fruit, have the seller cut it open, then eat the yellow flesh on the spot (it's sort of like vanilla pudding).

Surprisingly, "real" Malay food is not as widely available in Malaysia's restaurants as Chinese or even American fast-food fare, including Kentucky Fried Chicken and A&W. Other cuisines are also well represented. Thai and Japanese restaurants are legion, and the cuisine of the Nonya, or Straits-born Chinese—a combination of Malay, Chinese, and Thai tastes—is gaining popularity. Three styles of Indian cooking—southern Indian, Mogul, and Indian Muslim (a blend of Southern Indian and Malay)—can be found in Kuala Lumpur. Eating Indian rice and curry with your hands on a banana leaf, as is done in the Southern Indian restaurants, is an experience to be savored.

The following terms are likely to appear on the menus you'll see in Malaysia:

asam—sour, a reference to the sourness of the *asam* fruit, used in some curries

dim sum—Chinese snacks, eaten at breakfast or lunch, made with meat, prawns, or fish, and usually steamed or deep-fried

garoupa—a local fish with tender flesh and a sweet flavor

green curry—a Thai curry with fewer chilies than Indian, made with small green *brinjals* (eggplants) and meat

ice kacang—shaved ice heaped over red beans, jelly, sweet corn, and green rice-flour strips, flavored with syrup or coconut sugar

kacang (pronounced "ka-chang")—signals the presence of beans or nuts

kaya—a jam made from steaming a mixture of eggs, sugar, and coconut cream

kerabu—a hot-and-sour Thai salad of chicken, jellyfish, mango, squid, beef, or almost anything else, dressed with onions, lemongrass, lime juice, and small chilies

Nonya—Chinese born in Malaysia who have assimilated and adapted Malay customs

rendang—meat simmered for hours in spices, chilies, and coconut milk until nearly dry

roti—bread

sambal—a thick, hot condiment of chilies, local roots and herbs, and shrimp paste

tandoori—meat or seafood roasted in a clay oven, Northern Indian style

tomyam—Thai soup cooked with seafood or meat in asam juice, sometimes very hot and sour

Price categories throughout the chapter are based on the following ranges:

CATEGORY	COST*
$$$$	over M$80 (US$30)
$$$	M$50–M$80 (US$20–US$30)
$$	M$20–M$50 (US$8–US$20)
$	under M$20 (US$8)

per person, based on 3 dishes shared between 2 people, excluding tax, service, and drinks.

Golf

Golf is part of the British legacy in Malaysia, and you'll find excellent courses throughout the country. Among the best are the Royal Selangor Golf Club in Kuala Lumpur and the Bukit Jambul Golf and Country Club in Penang.

Hiking

East Malaysia specializes in hiking, either full-scale backpacking through dense jungle or shorter hiking trips combined with road and river transport. The best climb in Southeast Asia is Sabah's Mt. Kinabalu, the second highest mountain in Asia. Paths through Kinabalu Park, at its base, offer rewarding but less arduous walking.

There are also superb hiking trails on peninsular Malaysia. Jungle trekking can be arranged in Taman Negara, a national park north of Kuala Lumpur. For leisurely hikes in cooler temperatures, try the hills of the Cameron Highlands.

Malaysia has reserved several broad expanses, both on peninsular Malaysia and on Borneo, as national parks. The government tourist office produces a useful brochure describing these parks and their trails along with what primitive accommodation is available.

Jungle Trips

Borneo is among the last wildernesses in Southeast Asia. Rain forest and jungle, threaded by numerous rivers and rapids, cover most of the land, and intrepid travelers explore it on foot, by jeep, or by longboat. Because the tourist industry is only now being developed, you won't trip over other tourists, and native lifestyles are for the most part uncorrupted and authentic. You can trek through the jungle interior, ride a longboat upriver, and stay overnight in a tribal longhouse.

Lodging

For a long time Malaysia had been in the shadow of Singapore to the south and Thailand to the north. Only recently has its economy spurted and the rush is on to develop the country as a tourist destination. In the major cities, especially in Kuala Lumpur, the growth of luxury hotels, primarily geared to the business traveler, is almost overwhelming. These are splendid marble and glass shining towers providing smiling service and every comfort. In the smaller provincial capitals, hotels are on a more modest scale and fall into the three- and four-star categories, which while lacking grandeur provide quality comfort. Further down the scale are the bare-bones hotels where the furnishings are worn and the plaster walls have cracks but the bed linen is fresh and the bathrooms are flushed clean. In the major resorts, the full range of accommodations are offered, from modern, self-contained resort complexes to the inexpensive cramped Chinese hotel with a bathroom down the hall.

Malaysia has very few exceptional hotels of character and charm. Only three come to mind: Pangkor Laut, on a private island, brings back the exotic feeling of a Malay village; Datai, on Langkawi, is architecturally innovative and marvelously designed to blend into the environment; Carcosa Seri Negara, in Kuala Lumpur, the former governor's mansion, has been restored resplendently. Unfortunately, the E&O Hotel in George Town, Penang, a hotel of the same vintage as Singapore's Raffles and the Rangoon Strand, is undergoing a restoration that could destroy its original charm. For exotica, though, Malaysia offers the chance to stay in the longhouses of the Dyaks, the indigenous peoples of Sarawak, and small thatched beach bungalows, albeit with primitive plumbing, on small islands of the peninsula's east coast.

Price categories throughout the chapter are based on the following ranges:

CATEGORY	COST*
$$$$	over M$300 (US$115)
$$$	M$225–M$300 (US$90–US$115)
$$	M$150–M$225 (US$60–US$90)
$	M$150–M$50 (US$20–US$60)
¢	under M50 (under US$20)

for a standard double room in high season, excluding 10% service charge and 5% tax.

River Trips

Because of the thick rain forests of Sarawak, most transportation in the interior is by river. River boats serve much like buses do in peninsular Malaysia. Taking these river boats to the towns and villages along the banks of Sarawak's rivers is an opportunity to experience the indigenous life of peoples who, only a decade or so ago, would place strangers in a pot and boil them. A visitor taking a trip up one of the rivers for a night or two in a longhouse will find the "forest primeval." Insects hum, invisible creatures croak and grunt, water gurgles and sighs. Equally mysterious are the groaning and screeching of trees that, burdened by age and debris, finally crash through the jungle growth. Sabah's scenic white-water rivers guarantee exciting outdoor adventures.

Scuba Diving

Sipadan Island, off Sabah's east coast in the Celebes Sea, is the best dive spot in Malaysia, and one of the best in the world. A coral reef and green sea turtles are among the attractions. Tioman Island is located on coral fringes and has diving facilities.

Shopping

Malaysia's hand-printed batiks, with layers of rich colors and elaborate traditional designs, have become high fashion worldwide. Shirts and simple skirts and dresses can be purchased off the rack in most sizes, or you can buy lengths of fabric and have garments made at home.

Pewter is another Malaysian specialty, since it's made from one of the country's prime raw materials, tin. The best-known manufacturer is Selangor Pewter, which markets its goods through its own showrooms as well as in department stores, gift shops, and handicraft centers throughout the country.

Malaysian handicrafts, especially those from Sarawak in East Malaysia, are well made and appealing: typical products are rattan baskets in pretty pastels, handwoven straw goods, and handmade silver jewelry from Kelantan. The Dayak people in Sarawak create weavings called *pua kumbu,* which use primitive patterns and have a faded look like that of an antique Persian carpet. Tribal sculptures have an allure similar to their African counterparts. Perhaps the most unusual handcrafted material is *kain songket,* an extraordinary tapestrylike fabric with real gold threads woven into patterns. (For an overview of Malaysian goods, check out the Central Market and the Karyaneka Handicraft Center in Kuala Lumpur.)

Exploring Malaysia

Malaysia is composed of two parts. East Malaysia comprises the states of Sabah and Sarawak on the island of Borneo, which also includes the Indonesian state of Kalimantan as well as the Republic of Brunei. West Malaysia, the southern portion of the Malay Peninsula (which also includes part of Thailand), is also called peninsular Malaysia or Malaya, as the country was known before the addition of the East Malaysian states in 1963.

Though East Malaysia has a larger area, it is mostly jungle, and 80% of the nation's population lives on the peninsula. This population— some 15.6 million—is about 56% indigenous Malays, 34% ethnic Chinese, 9% Indians, and 1% others, including the Kadazan, Dayak, and other tribes of East Malaysia. Although Malaysia is officially a Muslim country, some Malays remain animists, the Chinese are mostly Buddhists and Christians, and most Indians are Hindu. The East Malaysian states are primarily Christian, thanks to the 20th-century missionaries who helped develop the area.

This mix of cultures is one of Malaysia's main fascinations. It confronts visitors especially in the cities, where, interspersed with businessmen in Western garb and teenagers in T-shirts and jeans, you'll see Malay women in floral-print sarongs, Muslim women with traditional head coverings, Chinese in the pajama-type outfits called *samfoo,* and Indian men in dhotis. It manifests itself in a lively and varied street-food scene, with a proliferation of vendors selling everything from exotic fruits and juices to *hokkien* noodles to Malay *satay* to fish grilled with pungent Asian spices. And it proclaims itself joyously in the street festivals and religious ceremonies that these different cultures celebrate throughout the year.

On the west coast of the peninsula is Kuala Lumpur, Malaysia's capital and the gateway through which most visitors enter the country. It is a sprawling, clamorous, modern city that nevertheless retains many reminders of the past, though perhaps not a lot of charm. The island of Penang, on the other hand, is an exciting combination of beach resort area and university town, with charm to spare. It is a wonderful place to tool around on a bicycle through streets lined with lively shops and graceful colonial architecture. North of Penang is the duty-free island of Langkawi, whose idyllic setting has attracted the attention of resort hotel developers. For a sense of Malaysia's colonial history, a visit to Melaka, with ruins and restored buildings from successive European colonizers, is a must.

The peninsula's east coast is less developed, allowing a glimpse of a quieter Malaysia. The area around Kuantan offers excellent beaches and some first-rate resorts; Mersing, to the south, is the jumping-off point for Tioman Island, where the film *South Pacific* was shot. The scenery is as idyllic today as it was then, and a resort hotel offers a perfect base for a water-sports and jungle-hiking island vacation. Much of the rest of the peninsula is covered with rubber estates, oil palm plantations, and cool hill stations.

Sabah and Sarawak, on Borneo, deliver all the adventure that the word *Borneo* promises, including trips through dense jungle by backpack and longboat to visit the descendants of headhunters at their longhouses, where you can stop over for the night—a rare opportunity to learn about a culture so very different from what you've left at home.

Great Itineraries

A visit to Malaysia can be simply in search of sun, sea, and relaxation, in which case Pangkor Laut, Penang, Langkawi, Kuantan, and the east coast, or Tanjung Aru in Sabah could be the destination. Alternatively, such is the diversity of Malaysia, a trip could be specifically geared to special-interest travel such as river trips in Borneo or hiking through the national parks. Here, though, we suggest itineraries, within limited time frames, that cover as much of Malaysia's diversity as possible.

IF YOU HAVE 3 DAYS

With this limited time, you'll probably wish to spend it in **Kuala Lumpur,** though we strongly recommend that you try to get out into the country. **Melaka,** with its colonial past, is only a three-hour drive away, or you may want to consider limiting Kuala Lumpur to only one day and spend two up in the **Cameron Highlands** or at the beach on the island of **Pangkor Laut.**

IF YOU HAVE 7 DAYS

Start your visit with two full days in **Kuala Lumpur** before going north to the **Cameron Highlands** to stay at Ye Old Smokehouse for two nights. Then continue north up to **Penang** to spend one night in **George Town.** The following morning take either the ferry or a plane to **Langkawi** for two days of sun and a beach vacation.

IF YOU HAVE 10 DAYS

While 10 days will not permit you to cover all of Malaysia's highlights, it does offer some flexibility. Give yourself a full day in **Kuala Lumpur** and then pick up a car to drive to the **Cameron Highlands** for the night. Next day continue on to Penang to spend the night in **George Town.** From there, on the following day, drive over the mountains to peninsular Malaysia's east coast and drive south to **Kuantan.** You'll want to rest up and spend a couple of nights there. On the morning of the sixth day drive down to **Johore Bahru** to drop off the car and pick up a flight to **Kota Kinabalu** in Sabah. Give yourself at least a couple of days here. From Kota Kinabalu you may want to fly into **Bandar Seri Begawan** in Brunei for the night before continuing on to **Kuching** in Sarawak. Spend a minimum of two nights in Sarawak, making sure that you have a chance to go into the interior for a river trip and visit to a Dayak village. From Kuching, you can take a direct flight back to peninsular Malaysia or Singapore.

When to Tour Malaysia

On the Malay Peninsula's east coast the wet season runs from late October through February, and on Borneo it is slightly longer, with rains beginning in November and persisting through April. Since these rains can be heavy, flooding is common. Islam is the state religion of Malaysia, and Islamic law is quite strictly enforced. Friday is the holy day, and government offices close as well as museums and many of the government-supervised sights. Another law of Islam is that during the month of Ramadan, Muslims are not allowed (if caught, offenders are punished) to eat or drink from sunup to sundown. Restaurants are therefore often closed during the day, especially those serving Malay food. Incidentally, the stress of fasting during Ramadan makes believers a little grumpy. and not their normal hospitable selves. (*Also see* When to Go *in* Malaysia A to Z, *below.*)

KUALA LUMPUR

In Kuala Lumpur, gleaming skyscrapers sit next to century-old, two-story shop-houses. On six-lane superhighways, rush hour traffic often appears to be an elongated parking lot, but nearly a quarter of the population still lives in kampongs, traditional communal units, within the city, giving KL (as it is commonly called) as much a rural as an urban feel.

Kuala Lumpur was founded by miners who discovered tin in this spot where the Kelang and Gombak rivers formed a broad delta. Those pioneers were a rough, hardy lot, and the city retains some of that early boomtown character. Despite its bustling, cosmopolitan style, Kuala Lumpur is at heart an earthy place, where people sit around the *kedai kopi* (coffeehouse) and talk about food, religion, and business. It also is the center of the federal government, and since government is dominated by the easygoing Malays and business by the hyperactive Chinese, the tone of the city is schizophrenic at best.

While not one of the world's great destination cities, Kuala Lumpur does offer first-rate hotels, excellent and varied cuisines, a lively blend of cultures, a rich mix of architectural styles from Moorish to Tudor to international modern, a generally efficient infrastructure, and the lowest prices of any major Asian city.

Exploring Kuala Lumpur

394 km (246 mi) northwest of Singapore, 481 km (300 mi) south of Alor Setar (near the Thai border).

In the last 20 years, Kuala Lumpur has mushroomed both outwards and upwards in a most confusing manner. Most visitors spend the majority of their time in an area known as the Golden Triangle, the city's economic center and home to most of the major tourist attractions. Here you'll find symbols of Malaysia's dynamic economy, with the towering Petronas Twin Towers Complex as the most recent addition. Other notable landmarks include the Shangri-la Hotel and the Hilton. The old colonial center of the city is marked by the grand railway station, while nearby Chinatown was the scene of trading and commerce.

Numbers in the text correspond to numbers in the margin and on the Kuala Lumpur map.

A Good Walk

In this walking tour, we cover the area known as the Golden Triangle. The ideal place to begin exploring Kuala Lumpur is Malaysia's **National Museum** ①, a short walk from the KL Visitors Center. The museum provides an opportunity to place the nation in a historical perspective, giving a notion of the country's culture. Relax afterwards in the **Lake Gardens** ② before visiting the **National Art Gallery** ③, next door to the Visitors Center. Across the street are the **main railway station** ④ and the administrative offices of KTM, the national rail system. Walk up Jalan Sultan Hishamuddin to the **National Mosque** ⑤, which can accommodate 10,000 worshipers. The entrance is on Jalan Lembah Perdana. At Jalan Cenderasari, go under the road via the pedestrian walkway to the **Dayabumi Complex** ⑥, which has the city's the main post office and a stamp museum. Stroll through the glistening red-marble lobby of the Dayabumi tower to the shopping-arcade level. Across the plaza in the other direction is the **British Council** ⑦. On the town side of the plaza, cross the pedestrian bridge to the **Central Market** ⑧, a renovated Art Deco building that holds a lively bazaar with tempting food stalls. Exit the way you came in or via the other side door onto a street called Leboh Pasar Besar, which means "big market." Cross the river and go up a block to the high-tech twin-story **Petronas Twin Towers Complex** ⑨, Kuala Lumpur's current pride and joy.

Pass by **Jamek Bandaraya Mosque** ⑩, the city's oldest mosque, **St. Mary's Anglican Church** ⑪, **India Mosque** ⑫, and the vendors selling herbal medicine and cosmetics, then head north up Jalan Tuanku Abdul Rahman, past a few remaining turn-of-the-century, two-story shophouses with decorative flourishes along the roofline. You'll be in the center of the city when you reach the massive **Sultan Abdul Samad Building** ⑬, where you may want to stop in at Infokraf Malaysia, a branch of the national handicrafts center. Along this strip of Jalan Tuanku Abdul Rahman are a number of colorful sari shops, bookstores, stationery shops, Indian Muslim restaurants, and stores of an indeterminate nature. Notice the **Coliseum Theater** ⑭, a city landmark and one of the capital's first movie houses. Across the road from the theater, on Jalan Bunus, lots of little shops and vendors congregate in the shadow of the bustling Mun Loong department store. Around the theater's parking lot, near the traffic signal, are public toilets *(tandas)* and a number of American fast-food outlets. Or stop in at the **Coliseum Cafe** ⑮, a city landmark that has superb sizzling steaks and British pints.

Continue north on **Batu Road** ⑯, as the locals call Jalan Tuanku Abdul Rahman, a popular shopping street. Inspect the pewter creations at the **Selangor Pewter showroom** ⑰. At the meeting of Jalan Dang Wangi and Jalan Tuanku Abdul Rahman, the Odeon Theatre occupies one corner, and the huge shopping center of **Pertama Complex** ⑱ takes up another. Continue up Jalan Dang Wangi and turn left onto Jalan Ampang. Turn right at the next corner and you'll see the Concorde Hotel.

Turn right on Jalan Raja Chulan. In the next block you'll see a row of outdoor food stalls along Jalan Kia Peng, just behind the Hilton Hotel in the parking lot. Locals insist that this hawker area, **Anak Ku** ⑲, is among the best in the city. Continue on to the **Karyaneka Handicraft Center** ⑳, which has displays and demonstrations by local artisans. As

Kuala Lumpur

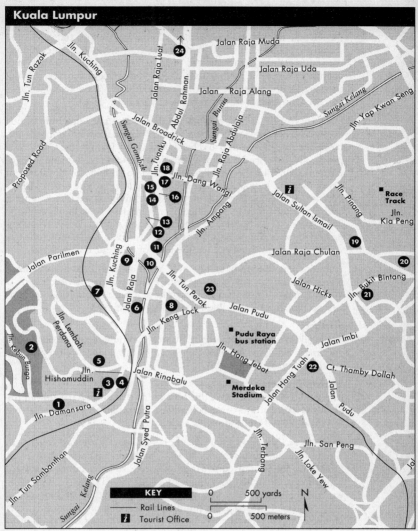

KEY

— Rail Lines

i Tourist Office

0   500 yards   N

0   500 meters

Anak Ku, **19**

Batu Caves, **24**

Batu Road, **16**

British Council, **7**

Central Market, **8**

Coliseum Cafe, **15**

Coliseum Theatre, **14**

Dayabumi Complex, **6**

India Mosque, **12**

Jalan Bukit
Bintang, **21**

Jamek Bandaraya
Mosque, **10**

Karyaneka
Handicraft Center, **20**

Lake Gardens, **2**

Main railway
station, **4**

Maybank
Building, **23**

National Art
Gallery, **3**

National Mosque, **5**

National Museum, **1**

Pertama Complex, **18**

Petronas Twin Towers
Complex, **9**

Pudu Prison, **22**

St. Mary's Anglican
Church, **11**

Selangor Pewter
showroom, **17**

Sultan Abdul Samad
building, **13**

you leave the center, turn left and head for the next block, which is **Jalan Bukit Bintang** ㉑, then turn right. A couple of blocks along on the left you'll find the Kuala Lumpur Shopping Center, and across the street, the Regent Hotel. Two shopping complexes at the next intersection, the Bukit Bintang Plaza in front and the Sungai Wang Plaza behind it, form one of the largest shopping areas in the city. Among the tenants are boutiques, bookshops, and the Metrojaya and Parkson department stores, possibly the city's finest.

Head east up Jalan Pudu one block. On the corner at Jalan Imbi stands the **Pudu Prison** ㉒ with its painted tropical-landscape wall—topped with barbed wire. Turn around and head back down Jalan Pudu. On the imposing hill just ahead is the new **Maybank Building** ㉓, housing the Numismatic Museum. Beyond Pudu Raya, Jalan Pudu becomes Jalan Tun Perak. Beyond Leboh Ampang you'll come again to the Kelang River. To your right is the Bank Bumiputra, built in the shape of a kampong house. On the other side of Jalan Tun Perak is Wisma Batik, with the Batik Malaysia Berhad (BMB) on the first and second floors. This shop has a wide selection of batik fabrics, shirts, dresses, and handicrafts upstairs. At the next intersection, the loop of our tour is completed.

A unique attraction about 11 km (7 mi) north of the city is the **Batu Caves** ㉔, vast caverns in a limestone outcrop some of which form a Hindu temple. To reach the caves, take a taxi for about M$25 round-trip or a local bus from Pudu Raya Bus Terminal.

Timing

The walk can be done in several hours, but you'll get more out of it if you linger along the way. Don't hesitate to talk to locals—they are, by and large, open and friendly.

Sights to See

⑲ Anak Ku. Locals insist that this hawker area is among the best in the city. It is easy to find—just behind the Hilton Hotel you'll see a row of outdoor food stalls along Jalan Kia Peng.

㉔ Batu Caves. About 11 km (7 mi) north of the city are vast caverns in a limestone outcrop discovered in 1878 by American naturalist William Hornaday in one of his forays for new species of moth larvae. The Batu Caves are approached by a flight of 272 steps, but the steep climb is worthwhile. A wide path with an iron railing leads through the recesses of the cavern. Colored lights illuminate the stalagmites and other formations. It is here that the spectacular but gory Thaipusam festival (held around February) takes place in its most elaborate form. In the main cave is a Hindu temple dedicated to Lord Subramaniam. Behind the Dark Cave lies a third cave called the Art Gallery, with elaborate sculptures of figures from Hindu mythology. The caves are staggering in their beauty and immensity: The Dark Cave is 366 m (1,200 ft) long and reaches a height of 122 m (400 ft). The caves are open daily 7 AM–9 PM. To reach the caves, take a taxi for about M$25 round-trip, or a local bus from Pudu Raya Bus Terminal.

⑯ Batu Road. On Batu Road—as locals call Jalan Tuanku Abdul Rahman—are a number of colorful sari shops, bookstores, stationery shops, Indian Muslim restaurants, and stores of an indeterminate nature. You can stop for a frosty mug of root beer at the A&W or a bowl of steaming noodle soup at one of the open-air coffee shops with marble-top tables and bentwood chairs. In the daytime, shopping families fill the streets while a troupe of blind musicians with bongo drums and electric piano entertains passersby. After midnight the street life changes dramatically, as *pondans* (transvestites) chat up men who cruise by in cars.

Across the road from the theater on Jalan Bunus, lots of little shops and vendors press on in the shadow of the bustling **Mun Loong department store.** Farther along Batu Road, at Number 223, is the **Peiping Lace Shop,** which features Chinese linens, lace, jewelry, and ceramics. **China Arts,** next door, is a branch of Peiping Lace that sells furniture; the rambling shop is filled with decorative coromandel screens, carved writing desks, teak and camphor chests, and antique vases.

❼ **British Council.** Across the Dayabumi Complex plaza and on a hill beyond the main road is the British Council. The public reading room has all sorts of English books and magazines and is a pleasant place to rest. ✉ *Jln. Bukit Aman,* ☎ *03/298–7555.* ⊙ *Tues.–Fri. 10–6:30, Sat. 10–4:45.*

❽ **Central Market.** This lively bazaar, housed in a renovated Art Deco building in the heart of Kuala Lumpur, used to be the city's produce market. It was converted into a series of stalls and shops in 1986. Now the 50-year-old market, painted apricot and baby blue, is the commercial, cultural, and recreational hub of downtown from 10 to 10 daily. Some 250 tenants do business within the two-story, block-long market. Demonstrations of such disappearing arts as batik block printing, Kelantan silversmithing, and the weaving of kain songket draw crowds to an area called the kampong. Cultural programs are presented daily, highlighting such Malaysian entertainments as wayang kulit, gamelan orchestras, Chinese opera, lion dances, and traditional Malay dances.

The Central Market gives visitors a chance to study the whole gamut of Malaysian goods. It has local cakes called *kuih,* herbal products used as medicines and for cooking, Malaysian kites, batik clothing, jewelry, antiques, copper relief pictures, rattan baskets, and wood and bamboo crafts. In addition, some 40 food vendors serve Malaysian dishes at reasonable prices. This is a great place to sample new dishes. Or, in the evening, drop by the small Riverbank Restaurant for light Continental fare and live jazz.

⓯ **Coliseum Cafe.** Built in 1921, the Coliseum Cafe (☞ Dining, *below*) is a city landmark, known for two things: It has the best steak in town, and it's the favorite watering hole for rowdy locals. The delightfully seedy atmosphere exudes history, so with a little imagination you can conjure up visions of British rubber planters in the 1930s ordering a *stengah,* or half-pint of ale. A sizzling steak with all the trimmings costs about M$13.50, a great value. The place is usually crowded and doesn't take reservations, but waiting in the pub can be an event in itself.

Coliseum owners Wong Chin-wan and Loi Teik-nam sit behind the bar working and chatting with customers: young Europeans traipsing around Asia on a student budget, and regulars—a mix of expatriates, Chinese, Indians, and Malays, including a number of journalists and a cartoonist nicknamed Lat. Lat is an institution: his cartoons—which appear in the *New Straits Times* and have been collected into nearly a dozen books—often reflect the national mood. ✉ *98–100 Jln. Tuanku Abdul Rahman,* ☎ *03/292–6270.*

⓮ **Coliseum Theater.** If you enjoy seeing local films when you travel, drop by the Coliseum Theater, which showcases the best of Malaysian and Indonesian cinema. Tickets are inexpensive, and all seats are reserved. Note that the cheap seats are downstairs in front and first class is in the balcony—the reverse of what you might expect. These movies usually have only Chinese subtitles, but you can usually figure out what's going on because they are quite action-oriented.

⑥ Dayabumi Complex (Kompleks Dayabumi). Constructed in 1984, the Dayabumi Complex off Jalan Cenderasari has three elements—the main post office building, the spectacular, gleaming white office tower with its lacy Islamic motif, and the plaza connecting the two.

In the post office, philatelists can buy colorful and exotic stamps. Around the corner from the main lobby is a tiny **Stamp Museum** (Galeri Setem), which is opened on request on weekdays between 8 and 6, Saturdays 8 to noon. Inside, you can study recent stamps spotlighting native musical instruments, animals, butterflies, and orchids.

At the center of the two-level plaza area is a huge fountain. From the upper level, you can get a good view of the commercial district. One landmark on the horizon is the Hindu temple **Sri Mahamariamman** in Jalan Bandar, which houses the tall silver chariot used in a procession to the Batu Caves for the Thaipusam festival. Originally built in 1873, the ornate temple has images of numerous deities in tile, gold, and precious stones; it was rebuilt in 1985 by craftsmen from India.

Stroll through the glistening red-marble lobby of the Dayabumi tower, the major tenant of which is Petronas, the national oil company. Occasionally, art exhibits in the lobby feature local work. On the shopping-arcade level is a host of shops, including the **Pasaraya Supermarket** and the trendy **Rupa Gallery** (Lot 158), which specializes in architectural artworks (☞ Shopping, *below*).

⑫ India Mosque (Masjid India). This modern Indian Muslim mosque is the centerpiece of Little India. One attraction here are the street vendors selling local *ubat* (medicine) or *jamu* (cosmetics) with all the theatricality of carnival barkers and snake-oil salesmen. They lure potential customers with elaborate stories and "magic" acts in which audience members participate.

㉑ Jalan Bukit Bintang. This street leading off the Jalan Sultan Ismail is one of the most active in Kuala Lumpur's Golden Triangle. A group of new buildings—the **Regent Hotel** and the **Kuala Lumpur Shopping Center** on one side and, on the other, the **Bukit Bintang Plaza** and **Sungai Wang Plaza,** home to some of the best shops in Malaysia—makes you aware what a tiger economy Malaysia has become. Yet, across from the taxi stand are racks of a strange green produce that resembles a porcupine more than a fruit: the Malaysian durian, which grows in the jungle and is highly prized by city dwellers. Hawkers contribute to the atmosphere with the pungent smell of chilies frying and peanuts steaming. At night, crowds often gather around a pitchman selling medicines.

Farther south, Jalan Bukit Bintang is a jumble of modest hotels, goldsmiths and other shops, and finance companies. Past the Federal Hotel, in front of the Cathay and Pavilion cinemas, vendors hawk the usual candies and some unusual drinks, such as coconut squeezed fresh before your eyes. Off Bukit Bintang is a night hawker food market with some of the best seafood and Chinese dishes in town—an area popular with ladies of pleasure looking for income.

⑩ Jamek Bandaraya Mosque (Masjid Jamek Bandaraya). At the point where the Kelang and Gombak rivers flow together is the city's oldest mosque. Its two minarets are only slightly taller than the coconut palms on the grounds. A vendor beside the main gate sells tape recordings of those hypnotic prayer chants.

⑳ Karyaneka Handicraft Center. The Karyaneka Handicraft Center is a campus of museums and shops that sell regional arts and crafts. Each of 13 little houses is labeled with the name of a Malaysian state. Inside, goods from that area are on display and demonstrations are presented by local artisans. The main building, shaped like a traditional Malay house, stocks goods from the entire country, including a wide selection of rattan baskets and straw purses and mats; batik-design silk shirts, dresses, scarves, and handkerchiefs; delicate silver jewelry; native sculptures from Sarawak; and lengths of kain songket. ⊠ *186 Jln. Raja Chulan,* ☎ *03/243–1686.* 🎟 *Free.* ⊘ *Sun.–Fri. 9–6, Sat. 9–6:30.*

Behind the Karyaneka Handicraft Center, across a little stream, are two small museums. The **Crafts Museum** has changing exhibits. The **International Crafts Museum** has a modest collection of work from around the world. The botanical gardens that border the stream offer a quiet spot to rest.

❷ Lake Gardens (Taman Tasik Perdana). Behind the National Museum are the scenic Lake Gardens, more than 200 acres where you can enjoy a leisurely stroll and join city dwellers relaxing, picnicking, and boating on the lake. Also in the park are the **National Monument,** a bronze sculpture dedicated to the nation's war dead, and an **orchid garden** with more than 800 species.

❹ Main Railway Station. The imposing Moorish structures that have become a postcard shot of Kuala Lumpur make up the city's main railway station and the administrative **offices of KTM** (Kereta-api Tanah Melayu), the national rail system. Built in the early 20th century and renovated since, they were designed by a British architect to reflect the Ottoman and Mogul glory of the 13th and 14th centuries. The KTM building blends Gothic and Greek designs and distinctive, wide exterior verandas.

㉓ Maybank Building. On the imposing hill at the corner of Jalan Pudu and Jalan Keng Lock stands the Maybank Building, designed to resemble the handle of a *kris* (an ornately decorated dagger), the national emblem. Up the escalators, you can enter and walk around the soaring five-story bank lobby during banking hours. The new **Numismatic Museum,** which exhibits Malaysian bills and coins from the past, can supply information on the nation's major commodities, and adjoins a gallery of contemporary art. ☎ *03/280–8833, ext. 2023.* 🎟 *Free.* ⊘ *Daily 10–6; closed public holidays.*

★ ❸ National Art Gallery. This four-story building was the old Majestic Hotel until its conversion into the National Art Gallery in 1984. The permanent collection serves as an introduction to the art of Malaysia and its people. It also reflects native artists' visions and concerns. They tend to work in contemporary modes—conceptual pieces, pop images, bold sculptures, humorous graphics, and realistic landscapes. The gallery is a bit funky, with its ceiling fans, linoleum-covered floors, and some dimly lit rooms, but it's still a treat. The museum shop sells witty posters, prints and cards, and artsy T-shirts at reasonable prices. ⊠ *1 Jln. Sultan Hishamuddin,* ☎ *03/230–0157.* 🎟 *M$1.* ⊘ *Daily 10–6, except for the Fri. prayer break.*

❺ National Mosque (Masjid Negara). The contemporary architecture of the National Mosque features a towering 240-foot minaret spire, a purple roof, and geometric-patterned grillwork. Though not the largest mosque in Asia, it can accommodate 10,000 worshipers. The entrance is on Jalan Lembah Perdana. Signs remind visitors to dress modestly and to remove their shoes when entering, and that certain areas are off-limits, especially during prayer times. The mosque complex also houses a library and a mausoleum. ⊠ *Jln. Sultan Hishamuddin* ⊘ *Sat.–Thurs. 9–6, Fri. 2:45–6.*

➊ National Museum (Muzim Negara). The distinctive architecture of the National Museum makes it easily identifiable; the building is modeled after an old-style Malay village house, enlarged to institutional size. On its facade are two large mosaic murals depicting important moments in history and elements of Malay culture.

A number of exhibits are located behind the museum. The **transportation shed** displays every form of transport used in the country, from a Melaka bullock cart, with its distinctive upturned roof, to pedaled trishaws, still in use in Penang. Don't miss the Malay-style house, called **Istana Satu** ("first palace"). Built on stilts, the simple little wood structure is open and airy—perfectly adapted for the tropics—and features decorative wood carvings. Burial totem poles from Sarawak line the path to the museum.

The cultural gallery, to the left as you enter the museum, emphasizes Malay folk traditions. One exhibit explains wayang kulit, the shadow plays performed with puppets cut out of leather and manipulated with sticks. You can see how a simple light casts the images on the screen, though the exhibit doesn't capture the theatrical magic the storyteller creates as he spins out rich folk legends. You'll also see a tableau of an elaborate Malay wedding ceremony and exhibits on etiquette, top spinning, Islamic grave markers, colorful cloth headdresses, and a form of the martial-arts called *silat*. Chinese culture in Malaysia is highlighted at the far end of the gallery. A model Nonya (Peranakan, or Straits-born Chinese) home shows classical Chinese furniture, such exquisite antiques as carved canopy beds, and a table-and-chair set with mother-of-pearl inlay.

The historical gallery has models of homes from different regions and a collection of ceramic pottery, gold and silver items, and other artifacts, plus traditional costumes, now seen only at festivals or on hotel doormen. Exhibits trace the stages of British colonization from the arrival of the old East India Company in the late 18th century to its withdrawal in the mid-20th. Photos and text outline the Japanese occupation during World War II and Malaysia's move toward federation status in 1948 and independence in 1957. A natural-history exhibit upstairs is devoted to indigenous wildlife, with stuffed flying lemurs, birds, insects, and poisonous snakes. ✉ *Jln. Damansara,* ☎ *03/238–0255.* 📷 *Free.* ⊙ *Daily 9–6; closed for Fri. prayers, 12:15–2:45 PM.*

⓲ Pertama Complex (Kompleks Pertama). At the meeting of Jalan Dang Wangi and Jalan Tuanku Abdul Rahman, the Odeon Theatre occupies one corner, and the huge Pertama Kompleks another. Pertama ("first") is typical of most town shopping centers: clothing, shoe, appliance, and record shops, plus several recreational spots, including a video-games room, a pool hall, and a nightclub. ✉ *Jln. Dang Wangi and Jln. Tuanku Abdul Rahman.*

➒ Petronas Twin Towers Complex. Malaysia's aspirations of attaining developed-nation status by the year 2020 are symbolized by this building, completed in 1996 and currently the world's tallest structure. It's pretty ghastly, but the Malays are proud of it. The twin 88-story towers are linked to each other by a 175-foot-long skybridge at the 41st and 42nd floors. The complex includes a shopping and entertainment center that, when totally occupied, will have two department stores, over 300 specialty shops, two food courts, and an indoor theme entertainment theater. Also planned are a surau (an Islamic prayer hall), a 645-room Mandarin Oriental Hotel, and a 50-acre park that will preserve some of the trees from the playing fields of the Selangor Turf Club, the private club that formerly occupied the site.

★ ㉒ **Pudu Prison.** The walls of Kuala Lumpur's main prison are covered with a beautifully painted tropical landscape—and topped with barbed wire. The mural, painted by inmates, is the longest in the world, according to the *Guinness Book of World Records*. You'll also note a warning that death is the mandatory sentence for drug trafficking in Malaysia, and the news reports will confirm that the law is enforced. ✉ *Jln. Imbi and Jln. Pudu.*

⑪ **St. Mary's Anglican Church.** Close to the Sultan Abdul Samad Building is this pristine church with its red-tile roof and manicured grounds. Services are held in Tamil and English.

⑰ **Selangor Pewter showroom.** Tin was a major Malaysian export of and so it was only natural that the country would develop a pewter industry. The most famous name is Selangor, and the Selangor Pewter showroom has a full range of the sorts of wares made in Malaysia for more than 100 years. Most designs are simple and of superior quality. A few items, such as a photo frame encrusted with Garfield the Cat, are pure kitsch. In its Heritage Collection, Selangor has replicas of *caping,* fig leaf–shape "modesty discs" that nude children once wore to cover their genitals; now teenagers wear them on chains as pendants. In the back of the shop you can see a demonstration of the pewter-making process. ✉ *231 Batu Road.*

⑬ **Sultan Abdul Samad Building.** This massive structure, erected in 1897 with Moorish arches, copper domes, and clock tower, is considered the center of the Old City. Preservationists fought to have it restored in the early 1980s. Originally occupied by the state secretariat (Dewan Bandaraya), it now houses the judicial department and high courts, along with a handicrafts museum called **Infokraf Malaysia,** a branch of the national handicrafts center. ✉ *Corner of Jln. Tun Perak. Museum,* ☎ *03/293–4929.* ▦ *Free.* ☉ *Sat.–Thurs. 9–6.*

Dining

Though Kuala Lumpur is not a coastal city, it delights in the ocean's produce. Seafood is the rage among locals, who wash it down with ice-cold beer, and outdoor restaurants serving both have sprung up in the city and on its fringes. Indian, Chinese, Japanese, Thai, and Nonya cuisine are also all available—so much so, in fact, that it can be difficult to find a "Malaysian" restaurant. The lack of purely Malay restaurants is offset by the hotels, which serve Malay buffets and à la carte dishes. Food festivals featuring regional specialties from the different Malaysian states are also common.

Eating out almost anywhere is informal. Jackets and ties are seldom worn except at the swankiest five-star hotels. Most places accept credit cards. The more expensive restaurants add a 10% service charge and 5% sales tax, in which case tipping is not necessary. Lunch is normally served from 11:30 AM to 2:30 PM, dinner from 6:30 to 11. Seafood restaurants are usually open from 5 PM to 3 AM.

Chinese

$$$$ ✕ **Lai Ching Yuen.** Master Chef Choi Wai Ki came from Hong Kong
★ to establish Kuala Lumpur's foremost Cantonese restaurant. The extensive menu features shark's fin, bird's nest, abalone, pigeon, chicken, and duck, as well as barbecue specialties; the drunken prawns are superb. The dining room is designed as two Chinese pavilions, with illuminated glass etchings, modern Chinese art, silver panels, a Burmese teak ceiling, and silver-and-jade table settings creating an elegant ambience. Traditional music on Malay instruments accompanies dinner.

Kuala Lumpur Dining and Lodging

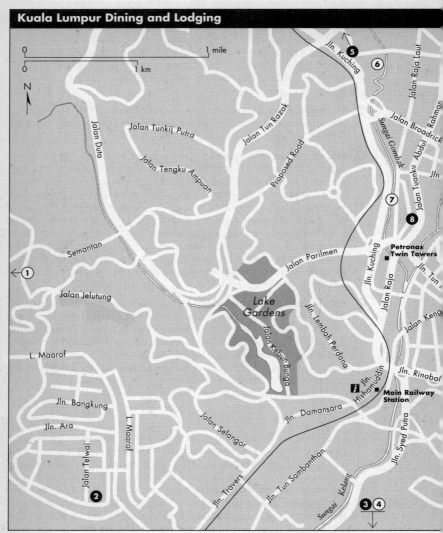

Dining
Ala'din, **2**
Bon Ton, **13**
Chikuyo-tei, **21**
Ciao, **19**
Coliseum Cafe, **8**
Happy Hour Seafood Restaurant, **25**
Kedai Makanan Yut Kee, **9**
Lafite Restaurant, **10**
Lai Ching Yuen, **22**

Lotus Restaurant, **3**
Melaka Grill, **16**
Nonya Heritage, **24**
Regent Grill, **22**
Restoran Makanan Laut Selayang, **5**
Satay Anika, **27**
Teochew Restaurant, **28**
Terrace Garden, **20**
Yazmin, **18**

Lodging
Carcosa Seri Negara, **1**
Cardogan Hotel, **31**
Concorde Hotel, **12**
Equatorial, **14**
Federal Hotel, **30**
Holiday Inn City Centre, **7**
Holiday Inn on the Park, **15**

Kuala Lumpur Hilton, **17**
Lodge Hotel, **32**
P. J. Hilton, **4**
Pan Pacific, **6**
Park Avenue, **29**
Park Royal of Kuala Lumpur, **26**
Regent, **23**
Shangri-La, **11**

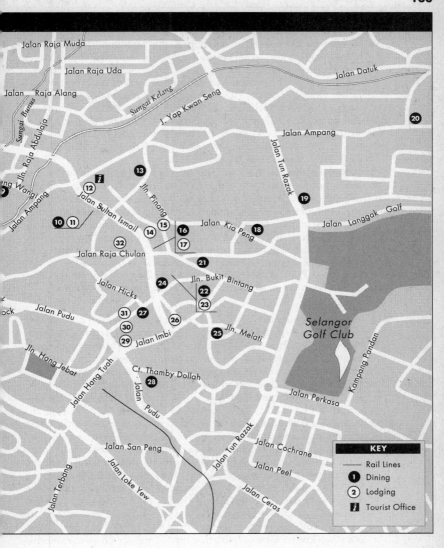

✉ *The Regent, 126 Jln. Bukit Bintang,* ☎ *03/241–8000. Reservations essential. Jacket and tie. AE, DC, MC, V.*

$$ ✕ **Teochew Restaurant.** Spanning two shop buildings, this restaurant is soothingly decorated in cream and brown, with well-spaced tables and screened-off private dining rooms. It's popular on weekends and holidays, when 100 varieties of dim sum are served for breakfast and lunch. Typical Teochew Chinese specialties include noodles made entirely of fish; sea cucumber stuffed with scallops, crab, mushrooms, and water chestnuts; and sizzling prawns. Try also the *oh wee,* a sweet yam dessert with ginkgo nuts, served with tiny cups of bitter Teochew tea. ✉ *270–272 Jln. Changkat Thamby Dollah, off Jln. Pudu,* ☎ *03/ 241–5851. Reservations essential. MC, V.*

$ ✕ **Kedai Makanan Yut Kee.** This 60-year-old family-run Hainanese
★   restaurant is one of the few that has not been torn down in the name of progress. Big and airy but rather noisy from the city traffic, the casual dining area is filled with marble-top tables and regular customers who insist on their favorite seats. Recommended are *roti babi,* a sandwich with pork filling dipped in egg and deep-fried, and asam prawns. The black coffee is the best around, and the Swiss roll filled with kaya makes a fine dessert. As befits the the coffee-shop feel, meals are served starting at 7 AM; it closes at 6. ✉ *35 Jln. Dang Wangi,* ☎ *03/298– 8108. Reservations not accepted. No credit cards. Closed Mon.*

European

$$$$ ✕ **Lafite Restaurant.** Named for France's finest vineyard, Lafite serves classic European cuisine in a romantically lit setting with pastel-hued wallpaper and upholstery. Oil paintings and fine crystal are on display, and an impressive wine cellar is the dining room's centerpiece. Specialties include rabbit loin with figs and port wine, trio of seafood in yellow-pepper sauce, and poached pear with almond cream. The Table Surprise Lafite is a lavish Continental dinner buffet. ✉ *Shangri-La Hotel, 11 Jln. Sultan Ismail,* ☎ *03/232–2388. Reservations essential. AE, DC, MC, V.*

$$$$ ✕ **Melaka Grill.** In a setting designed to re-create an ancient Chinese courtyard, this restaurant has a unique, colorful ambience accented by crisp linens, elegant crockery, and sparkling crystal. The style of cooking is European, though ingredients are primarily fresh local products, such as tiger prawns. An excellent value is the one-price luncheon where, for M$45, guests may select four courses from a number of options— a duck liver parfait with Kalahari truffles for an appetizer, perhaps, followed by a lobster bisque soup, and then sukiyaki in a seashell for the main course; dessert is selected from the trolley. For dinner, there is a seven-course *menu dégustation* for M$68, as well as an extensive à la carte menu. ✉ *Kuala Lumpur Hilton, Jln. Sultan Ismail,* ☎ *03/ 242–2122. Reservations essential. Jacket and tie. AE, DC, MC, V.*

$$$$ ✕ **Regent Grill.** Choosing between Shangri-La's Lafite, the Hilton's Melaka Grill, or the Regent Grill is a gourmet's dilemma. The Grill is new, aims to impress, and is a little more expensive than the other two. Wood paneling, leather upholstery, and stark earth-tone walls make the white German Schoenwald china and Schoff Zweisel crystal stand out. The menu varies, but frequent items are lamb chops served on a bed of herbs, medallions of venison, and a pumpkin and scallop soup or goose liver terrine to start. The wine list is comprehensive—there are some 300 selections, many of which are surprisingly affordable, though you may be tempted by the Château Margaux 1929 at M$7,800. ✉ *The Regent, 160 Jln. Bukit Bintang,* ☎ *03/241–8000. Reservations essential. Jacket and tie. AE, DC, MC, V.*

$$$ ✕ **Terrace Garden.** Soothing shades of green and gray, white walls, blackframed windows, and pale green trellis dividers blend well in this restaurant converted from a house. Dolly Lim runs the place sweetly and efficiently; Dolly Augustine sings evergreen numbers for entertainment. The chef recommends U.S. tenderloin stuffed with spinach leaves and smoked salmon; the lobster Thermidor is the best around. Finish with mocca Bavaria, a three-layer cream custard with Tía Maria sauce, or the blueberry pie. On Friday and Saturday there's a barbecue in the open-air extension. ⊠ *308 Jln. Ampang,* ☎ *03/457–2378. Reservations essential on weekends. AE, DC, MC, V.*

$$ ✕ **Coliseum Cafe.** The aroma of sizzling steak—the house specialty—fills the air in this old café established before World War II. A nostalgic, slightly seedy colonial ambience prevails, with the waiters' starched white jackets a bit frayed and the walls cracked and brown with age. Steaks are served with brussels sprouts, steak fries, and salad. Another favorite here is crab baked with cheese. The Sunday lunch, or *tiffin,* of light curry dishes, is not to be missed. ⊠ *98–100 Jln. Tuanku Abdul Rahman,* ☎ *03/292–6270. Reservations not accepted. No credit cards.*

Indian

$$ ✕ **Ala'din.** The deep pink table settings in this cozy Northern Indian spot contrast with creamy white walls; trellis screens separate the tables; sitar music soothes the senses. The curries (with yogurt and cream, rather than coconut) are served with various Indian breads, and the chicken, crab, and rabbit tandooris are popular. Another winner is mutton *karai*—meat simmered in a clay pot with coriander, black pepper, and capsicums. For dessert there's *rasmalai,* a rich custard with semolina and almonds. ⊠ *6 Jln. Telwai Empat, Bangsar Baru,* ☎ *03/255–2329. Reservations not accepted. AE, DC, MC, V.*

$$ ✕ **Lotus Restaurant.** The fun at this Southern Indian restaurant is eating from a banana leaf with your hands. Heaped on the leaf are rice, pickles, and such spicy goodies as chili-hot crabs and mutton curry. Try also the *dosai,* a thin, crisp Indian pancake with a hint of sourness. *Badam halva,* an almond-and-milk drink, takes away the curry sting, as does the restaurant's cool cream-and-sky-blue interior. Mind how you close up the banana leaf after eating: Folding it toward you means you enjoyed the meal, folding it away from you shows you were displeased. The house's long hours mean you can stop in from 7 in the morning to 11 at night. ⊠ *15 Jln. Gasing, Petaling Jaya,* ☎ *03/792–8795. Reservations not accepted. No credit cards.*

Italian

$$ ✕ **Ciao.** The owner, Leo Spadavecchia, will enthusiastically guide you to a table and talk you through the menu. Listen well, because the choicest items often aren't written down. Follow the *antipasto rustico* with one of the pasta dishes. For the main course, consider the hearty, traditional veal marsala or, for lighter fare, the fresh fish with tomatoes baked in foil. ⊠ *428 Jln. Tun Razak,* ☎ *03/986–2617. Reservations essential. AE, MC, V. Closed Mon. No lunch weekends.*

Japanese

$$$ ✕ **Chikuyo-tei.** Despite the rather dismal entrance into the basement of an office complex, Chikuyo-tei—the oldest Japanese restaurant in the city—has a warmly lit, woody interior with tatami rooms and sectioned-off dining areas. It serves excellent *unagi kabayaki* (grilled eel) and *nigirisushi,* a variety of sushi made with tuna, herring, salmon eggs, and squid. The *teppanyaki*—meat, seafood, and vegetables sliced, seasoned, and cooked on a hot plate in front of you—is popular. ⊠ *See Hoy Chan Plaza, Jln. Raja Chulan,* ☎ *03/230–0729. Reservations essential. AE, DC, MC, V. No lunch Sun.*

Malay

$$ ✕ **Yazmin.** Good Malay food in pleasant surroundings is hard to find, so this restaurant in a white colonial bungalow on shady, sprawling

grounds attracts visitors from around the world. Guests dine in an airy upstairs hall with front windows overlooking a bamboo grove. Evocative black-and-white photographs taken by a sultan grace the walls, and the owner/hostess is Raja Yazmin, a Malay princess. The best dishes are the *rendang tok* (beef simmered with spices and coconut), *roti canai* (unleavened bread), and *rendang pedas udang* (prawns cooked in coconut, chilies, and herbs). On most evenings, a buffet is offered, followed by a cultural show of traditional Malay dances. This pleasant combination has, however, caught the eye of tour operators, so some evenings a crowd swamps the buffet tables, watches the show, then leaves en masse. A bit disquieting. ⊠ *6 Jln. Kia Peng,* ☎ *03/241–5655. Reservations essential. AE, DC, MC, V. Closed 4 days at end of Ramadan.*

Nonya

$$ ✕ Bon Ton. Although this bistro-style restaurant with Southeast Asian artifacts on its walls also serves European dishes, the Nonya set meal, with chicken and lamb, is an excellent way to experience the native cuisine. The Indian blackened fish with tandoori yogurt and cucumber relish is also well worth trying. The ambience is quiet and relaxed, though the small chairs can become uncomfortable if you linger too long. ⊠ *7 Jln. Kia Peng,* ☎ *03/241–3611. AE, MC, V.*

$$ ✕ Nonya Heritage. White lace curtains and ethnic wood carvings grace this cozily lit restaurant, which serves hot-and-sour, spicy, and rich cuisine. The Nonya Golden Pearl, a deep-fried ball of minced prawns and fish with a salted egg yolk in the middle, is a good start. Then try the spicy fried rice in a pineapple, the *melaka sotong* (squid) with chilies, the asam fish-head curry, or the kerabu. ⊠ *44–4 Jln. Sultan Ismail,* ☎ *03/243–3520. Reservations not accepted. AE.*

Satay

$ ✕ Satay Anika. Meat marinated with spices, threaded on sticks like a kebab, grilled over charcoal, and served with a nutty, spicy sauce used to be a delicacy found only in street stalls. Now you can enjoy it in the cool comfort of a restaurant in Kuala Lumpur's busiest shopping complex. Plainly furnished and well lit, Satay Anika is owned by a family that has been cooking satay for four generations. A portion of beef, mutton, chicken, or beef liver satay is 10 sticks. Wash it down with Malaysian fruit juices, and try the ice kacang for dessert. (A number of other restaurants on this floor offer a wide range ethnic dishes from Malay to Chinese.) *Lower ground floor, Bukit Bintang Plaza, Jln. Bukit Bintang,* ☎ *03/248–3113. No credit cards.*

Seafood

$$ ✕ Happy Hour Seafood Restaurant. Strings of lights drape the front of this restaurant, and its tables spill out onto the walkway, which has a little more atmosphere than the brightly lit, functional room indoors. Steamed, baked, or fried crabs filled with rich red roe are the specialty. Other good choices are the prawns steamed with wine and ginger, and the deep-fried garoupa. ⊠ *53 Jln. Barat, off Jln. Imbi,* ☎ *03/248–5107. AE, DC, V. No lunch.*

$$ ✕ Restoran Makanan Laut Selayang. This excellent restaurant is very
★   plain: Food, not decor, is its raison d'être. You can eat outside, under a zinc roof, or in a simple air-conditioned room that seats 30 at three large, round tables. Adventurous diners can try steamed river frogs and soups of squirrel, pigeon, or turtle. Also good are the deep-fried soft-shell crabs and the prawns fried with butter, milk, and chilies. The house specialty is *fatt thieu cheong* ("monk jumps over a wall"), a soup of shark's fin, sea cucumber, dried scallops, mushrooms, and herbs, which must be ordered in advance. If you are not in the mood for seafood, one great dish here is black chicken—a small Malaysian bird with black

skin and white feathers—steamed in a coconut. ⊠ *Lot 11, 7½ mi, Selayang,* ☎ *03/627–7015. AE, V.*

Lodging

Almost all the tourist hotels are north of the train station, with the best concentrated near the intersection of Jalan Sultan Ismail and Jalan Bukit Bintang, the heart of the commercial district and one corner of the Golden Triangle. The range is broad. Those at the top level can compete with the world's best in terms of luxury and service; at the lower level, you can find nearly unbeatable prices—for example, at the Meridian International Youth Hostel on Jln. Hang Kasturi (☎ 03/232–5819), where US$7 will get you a clean room for the night. Other inexpensive accommodations can be found on Jalan Tuanku Abdul Rahman.

$$$$ 🏨 **Carcosa Seri Negara.** These two adjacent colonial mansions on an estate 7 km (4 mi) from downtown once housed the Governor of the Straits Settlement. There are seven suites in Carcosa, the main house, and six in Seri Negara, the guest house, with a golf-cart shuttle (or an eight-minute walk) between the two. Suites vary in size, grandeur, and price, but all are appointed with late-19th-century furniture. They can be stiff and slightly dreary, but those with a veranda have streams of light pouring in. They're not for families or scene makers, but they're ideal for anyone seeking genteel Victorian accommodation. The dining room is one of Kuala Lumpur's best. And if you don't stay or dine here, then come for the Seri Negara's afternoon tea. ⊠ *Taman Tasik Perdana, 50480 Kuala Lumpur,* ☎ *03/282–1888,* FAX *03/282–7888; U.S.,* ☎ *800/447–7462 or 212/223–2848. 13 suites. Restaurant, tea shop, pool, 2 tennis courts, massage, sauna, exercise room, business services. AE, DC, MC, V.*

$$$$ 🏨 **Kuala Lumpur Hilton.** Though dated, the city's first high-rise luxury hotel still maintains its world-class standards for service and quality. The mood of crisp elegance is set in the lobby, with fresh flowers and glowing chandeliers. The pastel-decorated rooms have bay windows, sitting areas, and desks. Rooms with the best views look down onto the hotel's pool and the Turf Club's racetrack. The Cantonese restaurant, Tsui Yuen, is one of the city's best. ⊠ *Jln. Sultan Ismail, 50250 Kuala Lumpur,* ☎ *03/248–2322 or 800/HILTONS,* FAX *03/244–2157. 581 rooms, including executive suites. 4 restaurants, coffee shop, pool, 2 tennis courts, health club, squash, business services, meeting rooms. AE, DC, MC, V.*

$$$$ 🏨 **Pan Pacific.** This 1986 hotel stands next to the Putra World Trade Center and across from The Mall shopping complex—a location more suited to conventioneers than to tourists. Its multilevel lobby includes glass-walled elevators and live music in the lounge. The rooms are richly appointed with comfortable furniture. The VIP floor has butler service. ⊠ *Box 11468, 50746,* ☎ *03/442–5555 or 800/937–1515,* FAX *03/443–1167 or 03/441–7236. 600 rooms and suites. 3 restaurants, coffee shop, pool, health club, business services. AE, DC, MC, V.*

$$$$ 🏨 **Park Royal of Kuala Lumpur.** Because of its location near the shopping district, this 21-story hotel is a popular meeting place, especially the serene garden lounge off the lobby. Despite the presence of many tour groups, the staff is exceptionally good-humored and helpful, and the room rate is lower than at other hotels in this category. The Grill is extremely popular for its European fare (baked duck breast, roast prime rib) and for its unique flap fans, which sway backward and forward. ⊠ *Jln. Sultan Ismail, 50250,* ☎ *03/242–5588 or 800/835–SPHC,* FAX *03/241–5524. 360 rooms. 3 restaurants, health club, business services. AE, DC, MC, V.*

$$$$ ☰ **P.J. Hilton.** Located in Petaling Jaya near the industrial zone, this luxury hotel caters to visiting executives who wish to be near many of Kuala Lumpur's multinational corporations and halfway between the Subang airport and downtown. Its rooms and public areas are less grand than the Hilton's, but the accommodations are quite spacious. The sedate lobby lounge is as comfy as a living room. ✉ *2 Jln. Barat, 46200 Petaling Jaya,* ™ *03/755–9122 or 800/HILTONS,* FAX *03/755–3909. 398 rooms. 3 restaurants, pool, health club, 2 tennis courts, squash, nightclub. AE, DC, MC, V.*

$$$$ ☰ **Regent.** This hotel, located across from the KL Plaza Shopping
★   Center, opened in 1990 and has maintained its crisp newness. Spacious guest rooms with natural woods and pastel fabrics, and opulent marble bathrooms with huge tubs and separate glass-enclosed showers, create a feeling of spaciousness, and there is plenty of light. The large atrium lobby is stepped, with each level separated by flower boxes. The fifth-floor pool looks over the city and a crowded public pool across the avenue. The Regent Grill and the Lai Ching Yuen vie for top culinary honors with the Hilton's and Shangri-La's European and Chinese restaurants. ✉ *126 Jln. Bukit Bintang, 55100,* ™ *03/241–8000 or 800/545–4000,* FAX *03/242–1441. 454 rooms. 3 restaurants, coffee shop, tea shop, pool, sauna, health club, squash, business services, meeting rooms. AE, DC, MC, V.*

$$$$ ☰ **Shangri-la.** Since opening in 1985, this central hotel has attracted a glamorous set that parades through its spacious and opulent lobby. Businesspeople keep coming back for its business services, meeting rooms, and convenience to the city's financial institutions. All guest rooms are large and furnished with dark wood furniture to give them a traditional feel. While the Shangri-la tries to keep up with its newer competitors, the glitz is wearing a little thin, the scuff marks showing more and more, and the facilities becoming a little tired. The higher floors are quieter, and guests paying a premium to stay on the Horizon floor receive more personalized service. In addition to the gourmet Japanese, French, and Chinese dining rooms, there is a poolside café for daytime relaxation and a pub for congenial socializing in the evening. ✉ *11 Jln. Sultan Ismail, 50250,* ™ *03/232–2388 or 800/44–UTELL,* FAX *03/230–1502. 722 rooms. 4 restaurants, pub, pool, 2 tennis courts, health club, squash, dance club, business services, meeting rooms. AE, DC, MC, V.*

$$$ ☰ **Equatorial.** This 16-story hotel near the Hilton doesn't have a warm or appealing layout, but it serves well the businessperson on a budget. The deluxe rooms are spacious and equipped with such amenities as a hair dryer and telephone in the bathroom. Rooms in the rear are quieter. The basement café serves a "hawker" buffet of authentic local dishes, and the reasonably priced lunches at its Japanese restaurant, the Kampachi, have become deservedly well known. ✉ *Jln. Sultan Ismail, 50250,* ™ *03/261–7777 or 800/44–UTELL,* FAX *03/261–9020. 300 rooms. 4 restaurants, pool, business services, meeting rooms. AE, DC, MC, V.*

$$$ ☰ **Federal Hotel.** This Japanese-owned hotel in the heart of the shopping district is distinguished by a revolving rooftop restaurant and an 18-lane bowling alley downstairs. The front of the hotel, with its street-level coffee shop, is decidedly urban, but the landscaped pool area is tropical in atmosphere. The guest rooms have large windows and the usual amenities. ✉ *35 Jln. Bukit Bintang, 55100,* ™ *03/248–9166 or 800/44–UTELL,* FAX *03/248–2877. 450 rooms. Restaurant, coffee shop, pool, dance club, meeting rooms. AE, DC, MC, V.*

$$$ ☰ **Holiday Inn City Centre.** Alongside the Gombak River, this 18-story hotel faces a major thoroughfare, so the atmosphere is urban. Its central location is a prime asset. The hotel's lobby is compact and busy. Guest rooms have refrigerators and minibars, along with the usual ameni-

ties, but the hotel is due for a thorough refurbishing. ✉ *12 Jln. Raja Laut, Box 11586, 50750,* ☎ *03/293–9233 or 800/HOLIDAY,* FAX *03/293–9634. 250 rooms. Restaurant, bar, coffee shop, pool, exercise room, squash, business services. AE, DC, MC, V.*

$$$ 🏨 **Holiday Inn on the Park.** Just off the main drag, this 14-story hotel is surrounded by trees and is the smarter of the city's two Holiday Inns. Many guest rooms are decorated in ghastly corporate green-and-white, but they do offer complimentary extras such as in-room movies and coffee- and tea-making facilities. The continuous passage of tour groups has taken its toll on the furnishings, however. ✉ *Box 10983, Jln. Pinang, 50732,* ☎ *03/248–1066 or 800/HOLIDAY,* FAX *03/248–1930. 200 rooms. 4 restaurants, pool, sauna, tennis court, exercise room. AE, DC, MC, V.*

$$$ 🏨 **Park Avenue.** Formerly the Prince, this high-rise hotel is near the major shopping district. Its rooms were renovated when the hotel changed hands in 1989. An 18th-floor restaurant serves Western fare. ✉ *Jln. Imbi, 55100,* ☎ *03/242–8333,* FAX *03/242–6623. 300 rooms. 2 restaurants, coffee shop, pool, dance club, business services. AE, MC, V.*

$$–$$$ 🏨 **Concorde Hotel.** Once the government-owned Merlin Hotel, this large, centrally located building has been completely—and impersonally—refurbished. But the rooms are bright and fresh and the price is right. Pay more for the concierge floor if you want more personalized service, including complimentary breakfast. The large lobby is often filled with tour groups. ✉ *2 Jln. Sultan Ismail, 50250,* ☎ *03/244–2200,* FAX *03/244–1628. 600 rooms and suites. 3 restaurants, coffee shop, pool, health club, 3 concierge floors. AE, DC, MC, V.*

$$ 🏨 **Cardogan Hotel.** It's mainly a business hotel with few frills, but the rooms, most with king-size beds, are clean, smart, and equipped with air-conditioning, television, and minibars. The staff is cheerful, and the coffee shop is good for a quick meal. Best of all is the Golden Triangle location, close to many restaurants and hawker stands. ✉ *64 Jln. Bukit Bintang, 55100,* ☎ *03/244–4856,* FAX *03/244–4865. 61 rooms and suites. Coffee shop, exercise room, business services. MC, V.*

$ 🏨 **Lodge Hotel.** Across from the Hilton in the Golden Triangle, this hotel offers basic air-conditioned accommodation. Everything is a little shabby—carpets have stains and bathrooms need some plaster repair—but the rooms are clean and service is friendly. The swimming pool is tiny, but the coffee shop stays open, albeit sleepily, 24 hours a day. ✉ *Jln. Sultan Ismail, 50250,* ☎ *03/242–0122,* FAX *03/241–6819. 50 rooms. Bar, coffee shop, pool. DC, V.*

Nightlife and the Arts

A free monthly guide called "This Month," published by the Kuala Lumpur Tourist Association, is available at hotels and MTPB offices. The "Metro Diary" column in the daily *Star* also lists cultural events, including films, seminars, and clubs.

Most government-sponsored cultural events are in the folk rather than the fine-arts vein. Traditional cultural programs are regularly presented on Friday evening from 8 to 9 on Level 2 of the Putra World Trade Center. Free performances are held nightly at 7:45 on the Central Market's outdoor stage. Contemporary offerings sometimes include fashion shows or jazz concerts. The schedule of events is published in a monthly brochure distributed to hotels.

Dance Clubs

While pubs close around 11 PM, the action at the discos only cranks up about then and continues until 2 AM. Some discos have live bands as well as a DJ. Some places have a cover and others may have a drinks minimum. Many discos combine a restaurant and a disco so guests can choose to eat, dance, or both.

Club Oz (⊠ Jln. Sultan Ismail, ☎ 03/232–2388) at the Shangri-La Hotel is a top dance club. At the **Hip-E Club** (⊠ Damansara Utama, ☎ 03/719-6569), the band plays a repertoire of Deep Purple, Led Zeppelin, and more for a hip crowd Wednesday–Sunday. Popular and easy to find is the **Shark Club** (⊠ Jln. Sultan Ismail, ☎ 03/241-7878), where you can enjoy live music or shake your thing in the disco; outside is a casual restaurant where you can refuel. The Hilton's **Tin Mine** (⊠ Jln. Sultan Ismail, ☎ 03/242–2222)—long a hot spot for Malaysian film, TV, and fashion celebrities—remains the city's premier disco. Slightly outside of town, **Uncle Chili's** (⊠ Jln. Barat in Petaling Jaya, ☎ 03/755–9122), at the P.J. Hilton, has live bands.

Hotel Lounges

At the lounges and clubs of the major hotels, the atmosphere is international, the tabs pricey. Most have entertainment nightly except Sunday. The **Aviary Lounge** at the Hilton (⊠ Jln. Sultan Ismail, ☎ 03/242–2222) becomes darkly romantic when its highly regarded jazz combo, the Jazzmates, plays Monday through Saturday. The **Lobby Lounge** of the Pan Pacific Hotel (⊠ Jln. Putra, ☎ 03/442–5555) has a piano bar with singer. The Federal Hotel features nostalgic tunes in its **Sky Room Supper Club** (⊠ 35 Jln. Bukit Bintang, ☎ 03/248–9166). The **Casablanca Club** at the Holiday Inn City Centre (⊠ Jln. Raja Laut, ☎ 03/293–9233) has pop singers. The **Blue Moon Lounge** of the Equatorial Hotel (⊠ Jln. Sultan Ismail, ☎ 03/261–7777) offers a live combo.

Pubs and Bars

Pubs are modeled after their British counterparts, while bars are American-style, with country-and-Western, blues, jazz, or pop bar bands. The main problem with either type of nightspot is location, which is frequently in the suburbs and difficult to find, even for taxi drivers.

The quirkiest nightspot in KL may be the **Anglers Pub** (⊠ 22 Jln. SS2/67, Petaling Jaya), which shows fishing videos in the early evening, with musical entertainment afterward. **Carlos Hacienda** (⊠ 364 Jln Tun Razak, ☎ 03/242-8470) offers Mexican food outside in cabanas; take your margarita into the disco and burn off calories or just wander into the pub and play darts. For homesick baseball fans, there is **Damn Yankees** (⊠ East Block, Wisma Selangor, Jln. Ampang, ☎ 03/264-9159), a sports bar where pictures of athletes adorn the walls, Mexican-Amercian food is served, and live bands play all evening long. The **DJ Pub** (⊠ 37 Jln. SS22/19, Damansara Jaya, ☎ 03/717–0966), part of the Executive Club, opens at 4:30 PM and often has bands. The **Hard Rock Cafe** (⊠ Wisma Concorde, 2 Jln. Sultan Ismail, ☎ 03/244-4062) has come to Kuala Lumpur; it's in the building adjacent to the Concorde Hotel and by 10 PM a line forms outside. For a relaxing pint, the **Pub** (⊠ 11 Jln. Sultan Ismail, ☎ 03/232-2388) at the Shangri-la has a cozy wood-paneled ambience in which to relax, have a snack, and play backgammon. At **Riverbank** (⊠ Central Market, ☎ 03/274-6651), a smallish spot tucked away in a corner of the market, you can sit on the terrace above the river while a DJ inside plays music. **Spuds** (⊠ Ground floor, Annex Bldg., Jln. Raja Chulan, ☎ 03/248–5097) is a wine bar with live music that stays open until 2 AM. The timber and rattan interior is comfortable for a drink or a bite of local or Western food.

Outdoor Activities and Sports

Beaches

The beach nearest Kuala Lumpur is at Port Dickson, about an hour and a half away. Intercity buses from Pudu Raya station take passengers to the terminal in Port Dickson; local buses there will drop you off anywhere you want along the coast road. Alternatively, you can charter a limousine for M$200. The beach stretches for 16 km (10 mi) from the town of Port Dickson to Cape Rachado, with its 16th-century Portuguese lighthouse. A good place to begin a beach walk is the fifth milestone from town. On the coast road, stalls offer fruits of the season.

Golf

Hotels can make arrangements for guests to use local courses, including the **Selangor Golf Club** (☎ 03/984–8433), which enjoys the best reputation.

Horse Racing

Malaysians, especially the Chinese, have a passion for horse racing, and a regional circuit includes race days in Kuala Lumpur, Penang, Ipoh, and Singapore. Races are held on Saturday and Sunday year-round.

Shopping

Malaysia offered few bargains until duty-free shopping reduced prices a few years ago. Now most quality radios, watches, cameras, and calculators are slightly cheaper in Kuala Lumpur than in Singapore; look for a duty-free sticker in shop windows. Fashion, too, has come to Kuala Lumpur, and at prices far better than in Singapore. You can also pick up inexpensive clothing, from jeans to shirts, for much less than in the United States and Europe. If you can't find a particular product or service, call **Infoline** (☎ 03/230–0300), a telemarketing company that will try to steer you in the right direction. It also gives advice on restaurants and nightspots.

(Many of the following shops and centers are discussed in greater detail in Exploring, *above*.)

Antiques

For Nonya antiques, try **Le Connoisseur** (☎ 03/241–9206) in Yow Chuan Plaza. The shop is normally open only in the afternoon, but call Mrs. Cheng to visit at other times. For Chinese arts and crafts, look in at **Peiping Lace Co.** (✉ 223 Jln. Tuanku Abdul Rahman, ☎ 03/298–3184) **China Arts** (✉ 235 Jln. Tuanku Abdul Rahman, ☎ 03/292–9250), next door to the Peiping Lace Co., has Chinese arts and crafts. For Nonya and colonial antiques, visit the **Treasure Chest** (✉ Jaya Supermarket, Petaling Jaya, ☎ 03/755–3942).

Art

The **Rupa Gallery** (✉ Dayabumi Shopping Center, ☎ 03/755–9142) specializes in architectural artwork, including delightful watercolor-print notecards of shop-houses and line-drawing prints of Kuala Lumpur landmarks by Victor Chin. Watercolors and portraits finished or in progress can be found at the **Central Market.**

Near the Turf Club's old racetrack on Jalan Ampang is a little arts and design center called **10 Kia Peng** (✉ Off Jln. P. Ramlee and Jln. Pinang, ☎ 03/248–5097). In the renovated stables of an old mansion there, 14 prominent sculptors, painters, wood-carvers, calligraphers, and printers hold workshops and sell their art at reasonable prices. A gallery has regular exhibitions, and hawker stalls provide snacks daily 10–6.

Handicrafts

For rattan baskets, straw handbags, wood carvings, Kelantan silver jewelry, and batik fashions, try **Karyaneka Handicrafts Center** (⊠ Jln. Raja Chulan, ☎ 03/241–3704). The stalls of the **Central Market** (⊠ Jln. Cheng Lock, ☎ 03/274–6542) offer handicrafts as well as a wide range of other souvenirs, including portraits, painted tiles, jewelry, and antiques. The best selection of batik is at **Batik Malaysia Berhad** (⊠ Jln. Tun Perak, ☎ 03/291–8606), which has a wide selection of batik fabrics, shirts, dresses, and handicrafts. Traditional and modern pewter designs are available at the **Selangor Pewter** showrooms (⊠ 231 Jln. Tuanku Abdul Rahman, ☎ 03/298–6244).

You can visit the **Selangor Pewter Factory,** a few miles north of the city in the suburb of Setapak. In its showroom, visitors can see how pewter is made from refined tin, antimony, and copper, and formed into products such as pitchers and candelabras. Duty-free souvenirs can be bought here, too. ⊠ 4 Jln. Usahawan 6, Setapak, ☎ 03/422–3000. ⊙ Mon.–Sat. 8:30–4:45, Sun. 9–4.

Jewelry

Try **Jade House** (☎ 03/241–9640), on the ground floor of KL Plaza. **Jewellery by Selberan,** with showrooms in KL Plaza (☎ 03/241–7106) and Yow Chuan Plaza (☎ 03/243–6386) does fine work with precious gems.

Shopping Centers

The Mall on Jalan Putra is the largest in Southeast Asia. Its anchor tenant is the Yaohan department store, but it has numerous specialty shops as well. The Weld on Jalan Raja Chulan is one of the decidedly upscale malls in Kuala Lumpur: It has a marble interior and an atrium, and its shops include Crabtree & Evelyn, Benetton, Bruno Magli, and Etienne Aigner.

The most popular shopping centers are the Bukit Bintang Plaza, Sungai Wang Plaza, and KL Plaza, all in the same vicinity on Jalan Bukit Bintang and Jalan Sultan Ismail. All have major department stores, such as Metrojaya and Parkson, plus bookstores, boutiques, and gadget shops. The atrium area almost always has an exhibition of some sort: comic books, fitness equipment—whatever. Also worth a visit are Yow Chuan Plaza, on Jalan Tun Razak, and the Pertama Kompleks at Jalan Tuanku Abdul Rahman and Jalan Dang Wangi.

Street Markets

At Kuala Lumpur's street markets, crowded hawker stalls display everyday goods, from leather handbags to pocketknives to pop music cassettes. Bargaining is the rule, and only cash is accepted. The largest night market is on **Petaling Street** in Chinatown. The smaller of the city's two nightly markets is **Chow Kit** on upper Jalan Tuanku Abdul Rahman. On Saturday night, between 6 and 11, **lower Jalan Tuanku Abdul Rahman** near the Coliseum Theatre is closed for a market, where you'll find everything from the latest bootleg tapes to homemade sweets. In the **Kampung Baru** area on Sunday, another open-air bazaar (called *pasar minggu*) offers Malay handicrafts and local food.

Kuala Lumpur A to Z

Arriving and Departing

BY BUS

Regional buses bring passengers to the main **Pudu Raya terminal** on Jalan Pudu, across from the new Maybank skyscraper, where you can get a taxi or local bus to your city destination. Kuala Lumpur–Singapore express buses cost M$17; Kuala Lumpur–Butterworth, M$15.50.

For Kota Bahru and other destinations on the east coast, buses and shared taxis use the Putra Bus Station opposite the Putra World Trade Center.

BY CAR

The roads into and out of Kuala Lumpur are clearly marked, but traffic jams are legendary. It's best to avoid the morning and late-afternoon rush hours if possible. Tropical downpours also tie up traffic.

BY PLANE

Sultan Abdul Aziz Shah Airport, formerly named and still known as the Subang Airport, 26 km (16 mi) southwest of downtown, is the gateway to Malaysia.

From Sultan Abdul Aziz Shah Airport to Downtown: Taxi service to city hotels runs on a queue-and-coupon system. You buy the coupon outside customs from the kiosk near the queue, paying by zone; prices run M$24–M$28 to the downtown area. Beware of unscrupulous drivers trying to lure you into private "taxis"—before you get in, look for a license posted on the dash of the passenger side and a meter.

Public bus 47 runs between the airport and the central bus station downtown, where you can catch another bus to your final destination. Fares are cheap (M$1.60), but the "every thirty minutes" service is erratic and unavailable after midnight, when international flights often arrive. Buses to the airport start running at 6 AM. Travel time is about 45 minutes, depending on traffic.

(☞ Malaysia A to Z, *below,* for information on international arrivals and departures and on domestic carriers and flights.)

BY TRAIN

All trains from Butterworth and Singapore deposit passengers at the **main railway station** (☎ 03/274–7435) on Jalan Sultan Hishamuddin, a short distance from the city center. There are always cabs at the taxi stand. The second-class air-conditioned train fare to Kuala Lumpur from either Singapore or Butterworth is approximately M$28, first class is about M$60.

Getting Around

Because Kuala Lumpur sprawls, it is a tough city to explore. It's not made for walking—distances between sights seem a long way in the heat and humidity, sidewalks have potholes, and crossing streets requires a reckless disregard for danger. On the other hand, you don't want to sit in a taxi, stalled in the traffic. The best plan is to arm yourself with a map, choose the sights that you wish to see, and dress in comfortable walking shoes and loose, light clothing (cotton breathes and keeps you cooler than synthetics); when the distances are far between, hop on a "bas mini" (minibus) and get off when it deviates from the direction in which you want to go. A new light-rail system, under construction at press time, may help matters.

BY BUS

Bus service covers most of the metropolitan area, and bus stops are usually marked. Before you get on, ask the driver whether his route serves your destination. Fares are based on distance, 20 sen for the first km and 5 sen for each additional 2 km. Just tell the conductor where you want to go, and have small change ready, because ticket sellers don't like to break large bills. **Minibuses,** about half the size of regular buses, have separate stops and charge 50 sen for rides of any distance. The two major **bus terminals** are Pudu Raya on Jalan Pudu and the Kelang terminal on Jalan Sultan Mohamed.

Taxis are plentiful, except when its raining. You can catch them at stands, hail them in the street, or request them by phone (pickup costs extra). Most taxi drivers speak passable English, but make sure they understand where you want to go and know how to get there before you get in.

Taxis are metered, and do make sure that the meter is turned on—taxi drivers are notorious for not using their meters and charging tourists more than twice the correct fare. Air-conditioned cabs charge 20% more, but are still reasonable: M$1.50 for the first 2 km, 10 sen each additional 200 meters. A 50% surcharge applies between midnight and 6 AM, and extra passengers (more than two) pay an additional 20 sen each per ride. Luggage, if placed in the trunk, is and additional M$1. You can also hire a cab by the hour for M$30 the first hour and M$20 per hour afterward.

Radio-dispatch taxi companies include the following: **Comfort Radio Taxi** (☎ 03/733–0495). **Kuala Lumpur Taxi Assn.** (☎ 03/221–4241). **Teletaxi** (☎ 03/221–1011).

Contacts and Resources

DOCTORS AND DENTISTS

The telephone directory lists several government clinics, which treat walk-in patients for a cash fee; these are open during normal business hours.

EMBASSIES AND CONSULATES

Australia (✉ 6 Jln. Yap Kwan Seng, ☎ 03/242–3122). **Canada** (✉ Plaza MBF, 5th floor, Jln. Ampang, ☎ 03/261–2000). **United Kingdom** (✉ Wisma Damansara, 5 Jln. Semantan, ☎ 03/254–1533). **United States** (✉ 376 Jln. Tun Razak, ☎ 03/248–9011).

EMERGENCIES

For **police, ambulance,** and **fire,** dial 999.

ENGLISH-LANGUAGE BOOKSTORES

Because English is widely used in Malaysia, reading material is easy to find, especially on Jalan Tuanku Abdul Rahman, in the 100-block area, and in the Sungei Wang Plaza on Jalan Sultan Ismail.

GUIDED TOURS

The **Malaysian Tourist Promotion Board** (MTPB) maintains a list of all licensed tour operators; you can also get brochures in most hotel lobbies and information from local travel agents. **Mayflower Acme Tours** (✉ 18 Jln. Segambut Pusat, ☎ 03/626–7011; ✉ Ming Court Hotel lobby, ☎ 03/261–1120) is one of the biggest operators. **Reliance** (✉ 3rd floor, Sungei Wang Plaza, Jln. Sultan Ismail, ☎ 03/248–0111) is a major tour operator.

TRAVEL AGENCIES

American Express (✉ MAS Bldg., 5th floor, Jln. Sultan Ismail, ☎ 03/261–0000). **Thomas Cook** (✉ Wisma Bouftead, Jln. Raja Chulan, ☎ 03/241–7022). *Also see* Guided Tours, *above.*

VISITOR INFORMATION

The **KL Visitors Center** supplies city maps, directions, and assistance in finding hotels. ✉ *3 Jln. Hishamuddin,* ☎ *03/230–1369.* ☉ *Weekdays 8–4:15, Sat. 8–12:45 PM.*

The **Malaysia Tourist Information Center** (MATIC) offers information on Kuala Lumpur and Malaysia; additionally, various travel agencies represented in the building can supply bus and train schedules, car rental information, as well as hotels and tours. There are also information counters at the airport and the main railway station. ✉ *109 Jln. Ampang,* ☎ *03/242-3929.* ☉ *Weekdays 8–4:15, Sat. 8 AM–12:45 PM.*

The **Malaysian Tourist Promotion Board** (MTPB) has information on all of Malaysia. ✉ *26th floor, Menara Dato Onn, Putra World Trade Center, Jln. Tun Ismail,* ☎ *03/293–5188.* ☉ *Mon.–Thurs. 8–12:45 and 2–4:15, Fri. 8–noon and 2:30–4:15, Sat. 8–12:45 PM.*

SIDE TRIPS FROM KUALA LUMPUR: CENTRAL MALAYSIA

South of Kuala Lumpur is the agreeable region of Negri Sembilan, home to the city of Melaka. This port town was colonized first by the Portuguese, then by the Dutch, and finally by the British—a colonial heritage that makes Melaka unique on the Malaysian map and attracts visitors for a day's sightseeing. North of Kuala Lumpur and inland are cool, lovely higlands areas; on the coast, there are the delightful resort islands of Pulau Pangkor and Pangkor Laut.

Numbers in the margin correspond to points of interest on the Central Malaysia map.

Melaka

❶ *155 km (97 mi) south of Kuala Lumpur, 245 km (153 mi) northwest of Singapore.*

Once the most important port in Southeast Asia, Melaka (Malacca) is now a relatively sleepy backwater. Created as the capital of a Malay sultanate, it was captured in 1511 by the Portuguese, who built fortifications and held it until 1641, when the Dutch invaded and took possession. The city thrived as a port-of-call to many a ship from China, India, Arabia, and South America, but it eventually lost out to Singapore. (The Sultan of Johore, the man who signed over the rights of the island of Singapura to Raffles in 1819, has his tomb here in the **Tranquerah Mosque,** a 150-year-old building of Sumatran design.)

The British took over Melaka in Victorian times and remained in control until Malay independence in 1957. After a long period of languishing in the doldrums, Melaka is now enjoying a rebirth. Construction has sprawled out along the coast and a vast land reclamation project is in the works at the mouth of the Melaka River estuary. However, visitors come to Melaka because it's Malaysia's most historic town, with impressive buildings and ruins dating from all its periods of colonial rule.

One of the oldest of Melaka's Portuguese ruins, dating from 1521, is **St. Paul's Church,** atop Residency Hill. The statue at the summit commemorates St. Francis Xavier, who was buried here before being moved to his permanent resting spot in Goa, India, where he began his missionary career. The **Church of St. Peter**—built in 1710 and now the church of the Portuguese Mission under the jurisdiction of the bishop of Macau—is interesting for its mix of Western and Asian architecture. It is about a half-mile east of the city center, on Jalan Bendahare. The only surviving part of the Portuguese fortress **A Famosa** is the Porta de Santiago entrance gate, which has become the symbol of the state of Melaka. Near the Porta de Santiago, the **Muzium Budaya,** a museum with collections on Muslim culture and royalty, is housed in a re-creation of a traditional wood palace.

The Dutch influence in Melaka is more prevalent. **Christ Church** was built in 1753 of salmon-pink bricks brought from Zeeland (Nether-

Central Malaysia

lands) and faced in red laterite. Across the street from Christ Church is the **Stadthuys,** the oldest remaining Dutch structure in the Orient. This complex of buildings was erected between 1641 and 1660 and used until recently for government offices. It has now been restored and converted into a museum with artifacts from both the Dutch and Portuguese eras. The Stadthuys is good and solid, in true Dutch style: note the thick masonry walls, the heavy hardwood doors, and the windows with wrought-iron hinges.

Melaka's history, of course, predates the arrival of the Western colonialists. Six centuries ago, a Chinese Ming emperor's envoy set up the first trade arrangements in this ancient Malay capital; a daughter of the emperor was sent to Melaka as wife to Sultan Mansor Shah. She and her 500 ladies-in-waiting set up housekeeping on **Bukit China** (Chinese Hill). The early Chinese traders and notables who lived and died in Melaka were buried on this hill, and their 17,000 graves remain, making Bukit China the largest Chinese cemetery outside China. Stop off at the **Sultan's Well,** at the foot of Bukit China. Tossing a coin into the well—a custom that dates to the founding of Melaka by Raja Iskandar Shah in the 14th century—is said to ensure your return to the city.

On the west bank of the Melaka River, the **Chinese quarter**—narrow streets lined with traditional shop-houses, ancient temples, and clan houses (note the interesting carved doors)—reflects the long Chinese presence. **Cheng Hoon Teng Temple** is one of the city's oldest Chinese temples. You'll recognize it by its ceremonial masts, which tower over roofs of the surrounding old houses, and by the porcelain and glass animals and flowers that decorate its eaves. Built in the Nanking style, the temple embraces three doctrines: Buddhist, Taoist, and Confucian. You can tell the monks apart by their robes; the Taoists expose their right shoulder. On your way out, you can buy sandalwood (the scent that permeates the temple) as well as papier-mâché houses and cars and symbolic money ("hell money"), used to burn as offerings during funeral ceremonies.

Close by on Temple Street are the papier-mâché doll makers, who fashion legendary figures from Chinese mythology. Wander on, turning right onto Jalan Hang Lekiu and right again onto Jalan Hang Jelat, and you'll find good pork satay at No. 83 and several coffee shops selling wonderful noodles. From Jalan Hang Jebat take a left onto Jalan Kubu, then another left onto Jalan Tun Tan Cheng Lock. This street was once called "Millionaires' Row" for its glorious mansions, built by the Dutch and then taken over by wealthy Babas in the 19th century.

Lodging

$$$ ▣ **Ramada Renaissance.** This 24-story Ramada operates smoothly for
★ both the business traveler and the tourist. The guest rooms are bright, decorated in pastel colors, and equipped with IDD phones, color TV and video, and refrigerator; those overlooking the gardens and shore are obviously more pleasant than those at the back. In addition to the Renaissance floor, with concierge services, there are two no-smoking floors. In the evening there is usually live entertainment in the Famosa Lounge, and throughout the year the hotel offers various festivities as well as special room packages that may be 60 per cent lower than the listed room rates. ✉ *Jln. Bendahara, 75100,* ☎ *06/284–8888,* FAX *06/ 284–9269. 295 rooms. 2 restaurants, room service, pool, exercise room, squash, dance club, business services, meeting rooms, travel services. AE, DC, MC, V.*

$$ ▣ **City Bayview.** Opened in 1987, this modern 14-story high-rise stands in contrast to the older buildings of Melaka. The look of the hotel is strictly functional, with no personality, but the rooms, with motel-like furniture and IDD phones, are clean and satisfactory. ✉ *Jln. Bendahara, 75100,* ☎ *06/239–7888,* FAX *06/236–7699. 181 rooms. 2 restaurants, coffee shop, pool, exercise room, dance club, laundry service, business services, meeting rooms. AE, DC, MC, V.*

Nightlife

Melaka's sights are brought to life nightly in a **sound-and-light show,** in which the city's history is told to the accompaniment of Malay music, sound effects, and illuminated monuments. The first show is at 8:30 PM; the second, narrated in English, is at 10:30 PM.

Melaka A to Z

ARRIVING AND DEPARTING

By Boat. The ferry from Melaka to Dumai on Sumatra (Indonesia) takes four hours, costs M$80, and departs (usually) every day at 10 AM. You'll need a visa to enter Indonesia.

By Bus. Express bus service from Kuala Lumpur to Melaka is offered by **Jebat Express** (in Kuala Lumpur, ☎ 03/282202; in Melaka, ☎ 06/ 222503) for M$6.50. **Melaka Barat Express** (☎ 06/249937) runs to Port Dickson. **Ekspress Nasional** (☎ 06/220687) goes to Butterworth. The **Melaka–Singapore Express** (☎ 06/224470) covers the obvious route. In Singapore, try **Majulah Travel and Express** (01–38 Golden Mile Tower, 6001 Beach Rd., ☎ 291–6533); the one-way fare for the 2½ hour journey from Singapore is M$18.

By Car. The toll-road expressway between Kuala Lumpur and Johore Baru passes Melaka 15 km to the east of downtown and has an exit for the city. Several local tour operators organize day trips to Melaka in an air-conditioned limousine for M$200. Day tours by coach are about M$70. These may be arranged through most hotels.

By Taxi. A taxi from Kuala Lumpur to Melaka costs approximately M$90 (a shared taxi M$22.50). A round-trip is less than twice the one-way, but a Kuala Lumpur taxi driver is unlikely to know his way around Melaka. To order a taxi from Melaka to Kuala Lumpur, phone the taxi depot (☎ 06/223630).

By Train. Melaka does not have a train station, but train travelers can get off in Tampin, 38 km (24 mi) north of the city. From Tampin, take a taxi to Melaka (about M$3). For information, call the KTM office (☎ 06/223091 in Melaka) or the train station in Tampin (☎ 06/411034).

CONTACTS AND RESOURCES

Guided Tours. The best-known tour guide in Melaka is **Robert Tan Sin Nyen** (✉ 256-D Jln. Parameswara, 75000, ☎ 06/244857). You can take a 45- or 90-minute **river tour** (☎ 06/236538) of the city from the dock on Jalan Quayside, behind the information center.

Visitor Information. The **Melaka Tourist Information Center** (☎ 06/236538) is in the heart of the city on Jalan Kota.

Negri Sembilan

❷ *South of Kuala Lumpur.*

Between Kuala Lumpur and Melaka is an area called Negri Sembilan ("Nine States"). It's not a major tourist destination, although residents of Kuala Lumpur come for a day's outing or a splash on the beach. Negri Sembilan is unique in Malaysia, for it's an internal union of ancient matriarchal states—tribal lines descend from women rather than from men.

Seremban, Negri Sembilan's capital, is a pleasant city 64 km (37 mi) south of Kuala Lumpur with attractive botanical gardens. An old Malay palace has been moved to the gardens and serves as a museum; there is also a reconstructed Malay house, an example of early Minangkabau (or Sumatran) architecture. The people of this area are related to the inhabitants of West Sumatra; homes in both places have the same buffalo-horn-shape peaked roofs.

At **Sri Menanti,** a few miles west of Seremban, is the sultan's headquarters, where you can visit both a new *istana* (palace) and an old one, the latter in Sumatran style, as well as an ancient royal burial ground. The drive to Sri Menanti takes you through hilly country, where bougainvillea and hibiscus abound.

Port Dickson, on the coast, is a seaside resort area, where casuarina trees line the shore. Near the Melaka border, south of Port Dickson, is **Pengkalan Kempas.** Here are three famous stones, inscribed in cuneiform, that remain an archaeological mystery, and the **tomb of Sheik Ahmad,** dated 1467.

Pulau Pangkor and Pangkor Laut

❸ *84 km (52 mi) south of Ipoh, 175 km (109 mi) north of Kuala Lumpur, 180 km (112 mi) south of Penang.*

Just off the coast of the state of Perak, 90 minutes west of Ipoh, is the island of **Pulau Pangkor.** While the island is known for its fishing, visitors also come for the beaches on its western shore. Aside from the major stretches of sand at Teluk Nipah, Teluk Belanga, and Pasir Bogok, there are quiet coves and untrodden bays at Tortoise Bay and Teluk Chempedak.

However, what really makes the journey from Kuala Lumpur worthwhile is a stay on **Pangkor Laut,** a small private island across a narrow channel from Pulau Pangkor. A variety of accommodations is available, from the 245-room Pan Pacific Resort (☎ 05/685–1399) to small chalets.

Lodging

$$$–$$$$
★

🏨 **Pangkor Laut Resort.** There are very few places in Malaysia where you will want to stay because of the hotel. One exception is the Pangkor Laut Resort, on a small private island across a mile-wide channel from Pulau Pangkor. As you approach Pangkor Laut, you see small houses standing on stilts some 50 feet offshore—it looks like a traditional Malay fishing kampong, except rather smarter and less congested. These water villas, connected by walkways 15 feet above the water, have private balconies hanging over the sea and peaked roofs that keep the air circulating. Two of the villas hold suites, which have at least four private decks, a huge bathroom with its bath suspended over the water, and a raised platform with four glass-paned trapdoors reflecting light from the sea 15 feet below. For those who prefer terra firma, other villas line the palm-studded sandy beach and nestle in the forested hills. These villas, too, have oversized baths—those at the beach villas are outside—cream-color cotton spreads, and polished wood floors. Limousine service is available from Penang and Kuala Lumpur. ⊠ *Pangkor Laut Island, 32200 Lumut, Perak,* ☎ *05/699–1100,* 🆑 *05/699–1200. 186 villas. 4 restaurants, 2 pools, snorkeling, windsurfing, massage, 3 tennis courts, health club, squash, spa, library. AE, DC, MC, V.*

Pulau Pangkor and Pangkor Laut A to Z

ARRIVING AND DEPARTING

The jumping-off point for Pulau Pangkor is the coast town of Lamut, reached by an hour's taxi ride from Ipoh, the state capital, which is served by Malayan Railways. A shuttle ferry runs to and from the island.

Cameron Highlands

★ ❹ *190 km (118 mi) north of Kuala Lumpur.*

There are few places left in this world so slavishly faithful to colonial values as the Cameron Highlands. Built as a hill station for the British plantation owners and senior civil servants, the genteel and civilized tone is epitomized by Ye Olde Smokehouse rest house, a semiprivate hotel. Here is a re-creation of the ambience of an English inn, where you can snort a pink gin by the fireplace and place yourself back in Blighty.

Indeed, the whole landscape of the Cameron Highlands makes you feel as if you're hallucinating—it's England in the middle of Malaysia and less than 200 miles from the equator. Once you pass through the town of Tanah Rata, not only does the terrain change, but the architecture as well. As tropical foliage gives way to Scottish crispness, Tudor and Edwardian bungalows appear. The sense of Britain is remarkably re-created, even down to the worker homes built as English row houses. Just as in colonial India, the "rules of deportment" are followed here even more than they would be in Great Britain—tie and jacket for dinner, order from the bar and wait until the maître d' invites you to your table, return to lounge for brandy and port (though ladies are not pared away), and so on. Very genteel and a jolly good show.

Instead of renting a car, you may prefer a chauffeured, air-conditioned car at MS$180 (US$69) for the six-hour drive from Penang to the Cameron Highlands and a similar amount for the five- to six-hour drive from the Cameron Highlands to Kuala Lumpur's airport. A word of caution: despite assurances that drivers will go all the way up the mountain to Ye Olde Smokehouse, they will try to leave you at the taxi station in Tanah Rata. Your best recourse is to refuse to pay the fare until the driver has arranged for a second taxi to go the rest of the way up the hill.

Lodging

$$$ ⊞ **Ye Old Smoke House.** Although there are other hotels in the Cameron
★   Highlands, to really breathe the true spirit of this hill station you need to splurge and stay at Ye Old Smoke House. Treat yourself and flagrantly indulge—take the most expensive suite (MS$374). Stuffed with delightful British clutter, suites have superb mountain views and plenty of odd corners to sit in. If you have to skimp, the less expensive suites are nearly as charming and are roughly half the price (MS$200). ⊠ *Golf Course Rd., 39100 Cameron Highlands,* ☎ *05/941214,* ℻ *05/ 941213. 20 suites. Restaurant, bar. AE, MC, V.*

Outdoor Activites and Sports

Time at the Cameron Highlands is spent breathing deeply the glorious mountain air and walking. The highly touted "jungle walks" are exciting, but may be rather too exciting for some. The trails are not well marked at all, and the maps are merely suggestive. Most people find their way in the end—at least on the easier trails—but energy is better spent on walking and admiring the scenery than wondering if the search party will find you. If you walk more than the Tenderfoot Trail, take a guide; for a small reimbursement, many of the younger staff members at Ye Olde Smokehouse are willing and informative. For the fairly forgiving No. 4 Trail, the fee is about MS$25 (US$10) for the two-hour trek.

PENANG

Malaysia's major holiday island, and one of considerable historical interest, is Penang. With safe anchorage and linked to Kuala Lumpur by rail since early colonial days, Penang developed as a cosmopolitan city. Today, with its bridge connecting it to the mainland and its sister city, Butterworth, Penang is a thriving commercial and industrial center. For the visitor, though, Penang's appeal is the throb and local culture and the beach resorts along the island's north coast.

Called the Pearl of the Orient for its natural beauty, as well as for its charming and graceful colonial architecture, Penang respects tradition but is neither stodgy nor sleepy. The island's beaches—in particular the glorious stretch at Batu Ferringhi—may have made it justly famous as a beach-vacation destination

Penang's population is primarily Hokkien Chinese, with a sizable Indian community living in downtown George Town and Malays residing in the countryside. Batu Ferringhi on the north coast has all the resort activity you could wish for, yet is never overcrowded. The airport is in the southeast of the island and George Town is in the northeast. The north coast has the most popular beaches and the resort hotels. (Don't plunge into the sea unless it's clear of jellyfish; the tide sometimes brings them in along the coast, and their sting can be serious.) For a low-key sun-and-beach vacation, make tracks for the island of Langkawi, less than an hour's flight from Penang.

George Town

602 km (360 mi) north of Kuala Lumpur.

George Town is a vibrant university town that is the intellectual center as well as the conscience of the country, a place where ideas are generated and venerated. It is also a great place to tour on foot, by bicycle, or by trishaw, stopping off frequently to sample the many fun shops and world-famous cuisine found around every corner.

Numbers in the margin correspond to points of interest on the George Town map.

❶ Just in front of the Tourist Information Office, near the Swettenham Pier, stands a **Victorian clock tower,** donated to the city by a Penang millionaire to commemorate Queen Victoria's diamond jubilee. The tower is 60 feet tall, one foot for every year of her reign up to 1897.

❷ Head from the Victorian clock tower up Jalan Tun Syed Barakbah past **Fort Cornwallis,** the harborside site where city founder Captain Sir Francis Light of the British East India Company first landed on the island in 1786. On the outside, the 1810 compound's moss-encrusted ramparts and cannons give the impression of a mighty fortress, but it never saw any real action. On the inside are an open-air amphitheater, shade trees, and public toilets, as well as some annoying local hustlers offering to serve as guides.

❸ The **Esplanade**—an open, grassy field next door—is a pleasant site for a stroll, especially in the evening, when the sea breezes roll in and the hawkers set up their mobile stands. It is is often used for recreational sports and festival events. A monument surrounded by palms honors soldiers who died in World War I.

❹ Penang's center used to be Beach Street, near the ferry terminal, the heart of the banking district. But since construction of the Penang Bridge in the mid-1980s reduced pedestrian traffic, the city center has gravitated toward Komtar, once the tallest building in Malaysia. The **Municipal Council Building,** a stately turn-of-the-century structure with arched windows, no longer houses the city government, which moved to Komtar several years ago. The building is now used for special exhibitions.

❺ The **Dewan Sri Pinang** next door to the Municipal Council Building is the city's major auditorium, seating some 1,300 for concerts, theater, and other events. Coming cultural activities are posted on a billboard in front. The **Penang Library** is on the first floor.

❻ The colonial structure across the street from Dewan Sri Pinang houses the **High Court.** Malaysia uses the British legal system, and the courts conduct much of their business in English. Cases are open to the public, and visitors are free to wander in and immerse themselves in a local legal drama. Inside the compound is a marble statue dedicated to James Richardson Logan, a lawyer and newspaper editor who devoted his life to public service, advocating freedom of speech, law, and order.

❼ Behind the High Court, on Lebuh Farquhar, is the **Penang Museum and Art Gallery.** The statue outside the 1821 building, which was used as the Penang Free School for more than a century, is of Sir Francis Light. On the first floor is a small museum packed with old photographs, maps, and relics of the city's past. An art gallery upstairs constantly changes exhibits, which range from contemporary works to traditional Malaysian art. ▨ *Free.* ☉ *Daily 9–5 (closed Fri. 12:15–2:45).*

❽ Next door to the Museum and Art Gallery is the **Cathedral of the Assumption,** one of the oldest Roman Catholic churches in Malaysia.

❾ Past the City Bayview Hotel is the **Eastern and Oriental Hotel,** commonly known as the E&O. Its reputation as one of Asia's early grand hotels, in the tradition of Raffles in Singapore and the Strand in Rangoon, faded in the post colonial era, though it was still full of genteel charm and a place to visit. In 1996 it was closed for a total and mas-

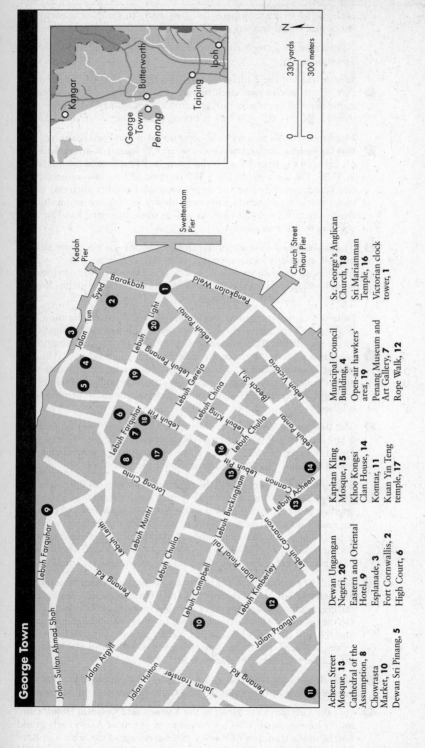

George Town

Acheen Street Mosque, **13**
Cathedral of the Assumption, **8**
Chowrasta Market, **10**
Dewan Sri Pinang, **5**

Dewan Ungangan Negeri, **20**
Eastern and Oriental Hotel, **9**
Esplanade, **3**
Fort Cornwallis, **2**
High Court, **6**

Kapitan Kling Mosque, **15**
Khoo Kongsi Clan House, **14**
Komtar, **11**
Kuan Yin Teng temple, **17**

Municipal Council Building, **4**
Open-air hawkers' area, **19**
Penang Museum and Art Gallery, **7**
Rope Walk, **12**

St. George's Anglican Church, **18**
Sri Mariamman Temple, **16**
Victorian clock tower, **1**

sive renovation, including the building of an adjacent tower for condominiums; it is due to reopen in 1998, hopefully with its old character brought back to life.

Heading inland from the Eastern & Oriental Hotel is **Penang Road,** the city's main shopping area. In the first block is a series of handicraft and antiques shops, all carrying a variety of Asian jewelry and gift items such as Thai and Indonesian wood carvings. In the next block, in front of the Continental, Malaysia, and Ambassador hotels, you'll find a number of trishaw drivers—mostly older men—who will solicit you aggressively. A suggested trishaw sightseeing route: Head up Lebuh Muntri past some of the city's best examples of traditional architecture, turn left onto Love Lane, up to Farquhar Street again, and then turn left onto Lebuh Leith past the 18th-century Cheong Fatt Tse Mansion, one of the oldest remaining Chinese homes in Asia.

At Lebuh Chulia, you'll see lots of European, Australian, and American backpackers, who seek out the cheap hotels and seedy bars in this area. The next street is Lebuh Campbell, another main drag for shopping. The shops here sell fabrics, shoes and clothing, costume jewelry, and inexpensive bags and luggage.

⑩ South of Lebuh Campbell off Penang Road is the **Chowrasta Market,** an indoor market selling all sorts of local produce. In front of the entrance, shops sell more produce, plus pickled and dried nutmeg, papaya and mango, and candies made from gingerroot, coconut, and durian. The durian cake, called *dodol,* is sold in little triangular pieces or foot-long rolls.

NEED A
BREAK?

Near the market, across the road from the Choong Lye Hock movie theater, is an old-fashioned coffee shop with marble-top tables. The **Teik Hoe Cafe** is nearly hidden by the souvenir vendor who works the sidewalk out front. Although the place looks scruffy, it's a great spot to people-watch over a cup of local coffee (pronounced "ko-pee" in Malay). The blend is strong, with a smooth mocha flavor. The parade of shoppers and passersby makes fine entertainment.

In the labyrinth of stalls in the alley next door to the **Penang Bazaar** (a dry-goods market), you'll find such basics as underwear, belts, and handbags. At the corner, a street hawker sells *chendol,* a local dessert that looks bad—wormlike strands of green jelly served in coconut milk over ice—but tastes good.

Across the plaza, in front of the Capitol Theatre, street vendors peddle luxury knockoffs. Fake Gucci watches sell for about M$24; ersatz Polo cologne and Chanel No. 5 perfume go for half that. Pirated pop and country cassette tapes sell for a little more than M$2.70 each. The concession stand for the theater is outside, so the confections Asians enjoy are available: Try the dried cuttlefish, called the chewing gum of the Orient. And the young portrait artist who often works here does good charcoal likenesses for just over M$27.

⑪ The Tower of the East, as **Komtar** was dubbed when it was still the tallest building in the ASEAN region, is totally out of scale with the diminutive neighboring buildings. The long flight of stairs you see leads up to a food court on the fifth floor. On the lower levels is a shopping complex named after the country's second prime minister, Tun Razak. At **Chin's Art Gallery,** next to an MAS office, you can have a stone chop (seal) engraved with your initials for M$54–M$135, depending on the size and quality of the stone. Among the tower's busiest tenants are hip young tailors with trendy haircuts and smart outfits who scurry about fitting customers with garments cut from the bolts of fabric they stack in every corner of their tiny shops. In the center of the mall are a number of fast-food outlets serving hamburgers, fried chicken, and pizza. One of the best Chinese restaurants in the city, Supertanker (☞ Dining, *below*), is on the upper level.

A two-lane street and pedestrian walkway runs through the ground floor of Komtar. Here you'll notice the **Centre Point** pool parlor—not your typical smoke-filled dive. The teenage boys who surround the tables are practicing for tournaments, when they dress in black bow ties and vests and compete before hushed, well-mannered crowds. On the 58th floor is the **Tower Tourist Center,** an observation deck with cultural performances at 8:30 and 9:15 every evening but Monday. Buy the M$5 ticket on the ground floor, and hold onto it—you can redeem it for beverages. A **duty-free shop** is one floor down; one floor up is the **Tower Palace Restaurant** (☎ 04/262–2222), which offers buffet lunches, dinner dances, and a karaoke bar. The Shangri-La Penang (☞ Lodging, *below*) is also here.

⑫ A number of antiques stores have congregated around **Rope Walk,** on Jalan Pintal Tali. Turn right onto Lebuh Kimberly, then, past a row of highly decorated shop-houses with elaborately carved doors, turn left onto Carnarvon Street, and then right on Acheen. At the next corner is the **Tang Lee Trading Co.,** which manufactures the cheap summer sandals called flip-flops.

⑬ At the junction of Lebuh Acheen and Cannon Lebuh Pitt is the **Acheen Street Mosque,** the oldest in Penang. To enter, you must get permission from officials. Turn left and you'll be on Cannon Street.

⑭ On the north side of Lebuh Acheen, look for a small sign posted above an entrance to an alley, which announces the **Khoo Kongsi Clan House,** a complex of structures that may be the most elaborately decorated in Malaysia. Recently restored, the **Leong San Tong** (Dragon Hall) temple is a showcase of Chinese architecture and art, constructed by 19th-century master craftsmen from China. Virtually no surface is unadorned. Notice the relief sculptures depicting Chinese legends and the heavily gilt dragons. The open theater across the square is used for opera performances. Visitors are welcome weekdays 9–5, Saturday 9–1. Permission to enter must be obtained from the office.

⑮ Pitt Street is often called the street of harmony, because all four major religions are represented along its few blocks. The **Kapitan Kling Mosque** is at the Lebuh Buckingham intersection. Built in the early 1800s, the mosque has been recently renovated and continues to serve the Indian Muslim community. You need permission to enter.

Along this section of Pitt Street is a row of small jewelry shops run by the Indians who deal in gold and semiprecious stones. Many are also licensed money changers. These street bankers can handle almost any type of foreign currency and work much longer hours than regular banks. Some are also numismatists who sell to collectors.

⑯ Past the gates of the **Teochew Association House,** on the corner of Pitt and Lebuh Chulia, is the **Sri Mariamman Temple** on Queen Street, in the heart of the Indian district. The entranceway is topped by a *gopuram,* a tower covered with statues of Hindu deities. Inside, the ceiling features the symbols for the planets and signs of the zodiac. The most prized possession of the faithful is a statue of Lord Subramaniam, which is covered with gold, silver, diamonds, and emeralds. The statue is paraded about during the Thaipusam festival. Visitors can enter the temple, with permission.

⑰ The **Kuan Yin Teng** temple, dedicated to the goddess of mercy, Kuan Yin, is the busiest in the city, perhaps because it's associated with fertility. Built in 1800, this temple serves the Cantonese and Hokkien communities. A block east of Kuan Yin Teng, on Farquhar Street, is the

⑱ stately **St. George's Anglican Church,** with its gracious flowering trees and gazebo. Built in 1818 by convicts, this symbol of the British role in Penang's early history is now attended mostly by Indians.

⑲ On the corner of Lebuh Light and King Street at an **open-air hawkers' area,** old Chinese men often bring their caged pet birds when they come for a cup of coffee and a breath of morning air. In this area, you may also note elderly men writing letters on old portable typewriters. These public scribes serve clients who need help dealing with the bureaucracy or illiterates who simply want to write a friend.

Travelling east on Lebuh Light before you reach the Victorian clock tower

⑳ you'll see the **Dewan Ungangan Negeri,** a majestic colonial building with massive columns. This is the state assembly, and the luxury cars parked out front belong to its illustrious members. You're now across from Fort Cornwallis again—near the ferry if you're hopping back to the mainland and a waterfront cab ride away from the beach hotels.

Dining

For elegant dining with attentive service, the major hotels are your best bet, but reserve one evening for dining alfresco along Guerney Drive. For about 2 km (1.2 mi), the sea laps one side of the road and restaurants and hawkers' stalls line the other. Seafood, understandably, is the specialty. Most of the cooking is Hokkien, though there are also good Malay hawker stalls. There are other hawker centers at Lebuh Campbell, the Esplanade, and Jalan Macalister; don't miss them. Local specialties include *char koay teow,* flat rice noodles fried smooth and soft with bean sprouts, prawns, and eggs; chicken curry *kapitan,* spicy chicken cooked with ginger, coconut milk, and lemon juice; Hokkien *mee* noodles, beans and sprouts in a spicy shrimp soup topped with fried onions; *inchee kabin,* deep-fried chicken pieces marinated with coconut milk, ginger, chili, and spices; *chandol,* a dessert of green bean noodles and kidney beans in fresh coconut milk and ice; and *bubur cha cha,* a Nonya dessert of sweet potatoes, yams, and beans in fresh coconuts.

CHINESE

$$ ✕ **Supertanker.** The noise and crowds at Supertanker are its testimonials: locals love the food and the prices. Favorites on its Teochew menu are the crisp roast suckling pig and the porridges. ✉ *Komtar,* ☎ *04/ 261–6393. AE, MC.*

$ ✕ **E. T. Steamboat.** At this restaurant named after the do-it-yourself Chinese stew, waiters bring vegetables, seafood, tofu, and a fondue pot full of rich broth to your table; you custom-cook your own dinner. For variety, try *lowbak* (pork rolls) or *tom yom,* a spicy Thai soup. *Two locations:* ✉ *Komtar and* ✉ *4 Jln. Rangoon,* ☎ *04/436–6025. AE, MC.*

EUROPEAN

$$$ ✕ **Brasserie.** Candles and fresh flowers on the tables soften the so-
★ phisticated French decor of wood-paneled walls, lace curtains, and black-and-white floor tiles. At lunch you select your main course (seafood or meat) from the menu and then help yourself from the buffet for appetizers, soups, salads, and dessert. For dinner, the menu takes the nouvelle approach to European gourmet cooking, with small, attractive portions of lamb, duck, steak, or tiger prawns. Try the frogs'-leg ravioli and the sherbet with cassis. ✉ *Shangri-La Hotel, Jln. Magazine,* ☎ *04/262–2622. Reservations essential. AE, DC, MC, V.*

$$ ✕ **Eden.** A downtown restaurant with a funky decor, Eden makes fresh
★ oxtail soup every day and does a magnificent Tunisian saddle of lamb.
The lunch menu caters to Westerners, with sandwiches, salads, and ice
cream sundaes. ✉ *15 Jln. Hutton,* ☎ *04/437–7263. AE, DC, MC, V.*

INDIAN MUSLIM

$ ✕ **Hameediyah.** This simple downtown restaurant excels with its *nasi
kandar* (rice with mutton), fish and chicken curry, or *murtabak*, an In-
dian-style pizza filled with spicy mutton and onions. ✉ *164 Lebuh
Campbell,* ☎ *04/261–1095. No credit cards. Closed Fri.*

MALAY

$ ✕ **Golden Phoenix.** Once you claim your table in this hawker-stall area,
remember its number so the different vendors will know where to de-
liver your food. The open-air accommodations are somewhat primi-
tive, but the food is authentic, and you get a fine sea breeze from across
the road. Try *laksa asam* (a sour soup made with local fish), or *chien*
(a fried oyster omelet), or the crisp roast duck. You can wash it down
with juices made from starfruit and watermelon. The stallls remain open
until 2 AM nightly. ✉ *Gurney Dr., no* ☎. *No credit cards.*

$ ✕ **Minah.** This simple open-air restaurant is in Minden, near the uni-
★ versity. You fill your plate by pointing to what you want as it goes by:
curry dishes, satay, beef rendang, or sambal. Try the *goreng pisang* (fried
bananas) for dessert. ✉ *Glugor Rd.,* ☎ *04/8881234. No credit cards.*

NONYA

$$ ✕ **Dragon King.** People come here for the food, not the atmosphere
or decor, which is modest. This is a good place to sample Nonya cui-
sine, a spicy local blend of Malay and Chinese food; try the spicy curried chicken and the kerabu salad. Come early—they close at 9. ✉ *9
Lebuh Bishop,* ☎ *04/261–8035. AE, MC, V.*

Lodging

$$$$ 🏨 **Equatorial Hotel.** Although not in George Town proper and far
from the beaches, this hotel is close to the airport, the industrial zone,
and the golf course. Note the unique 10-story atrium garden with bub-
ble elevators. One restaurant, The View, offers a range of Western dishes
with a smattering of Asian ones; the view, by the way, is of the ships
moving through the straits. ✉ *1 Jln. Bukit Jambul, 11900 Bayan
Lepas, Penang,* ☎ *04/643–8000 or 800/44–UTELL,* 𝔽𝔸𝕏 *04/644-
8000. 415 rooms and suites. 3 restaurants, coffee shop, 2 tennis courts,
golf privileges, health club, squash, meeting rooms. AE, DC, MC, V.*

$$$$ 🏨 **Shangri-La Penang.** The glitziest hotel in George Town is next to the
Komtar complex downtown. Its efficient rooms are comfortably decorated with large floral drapes and bedspreads and offer great views of
the city. The Shang Palace, a Cantonese restaurant, serves dim sum daily
and the Brasserie (☞ Dining, *above*) prepares nouvelle French cuisine.
Guests are a mix of tourists and business travelers seeking modernity
and efficiency. ✉ *Magazine Rd., 10300 Penang,* ☎ *04/262–2622,* 𝔽𝔸𝕏
04/262–6526; in U.S. ☎ *800/942–5050; in U.K.* ☎ *081/747–8485.
426 rooms, 16 suites. 3 restaurants, coffee shop, lobby lounge, pool,
health club, dance club, business services. AE, DC, MC, V.*

$$ 🏨 **Eastern & Oriental Hotel.** Known as the E&O, this delightful small
hotel was opened in 1885 by the Sarkie brothers (of Singapore's Raf-
fles). It closed in 1996 for two years of renovations, and the staff, some
of whom had been there 25 years, were let go. Heritage and charm
have always been the primary attractions here, and it remains to be
seen how renovations and new ownership will affect the hotel. In any
case, the E&O's location cannot change, and, hopefully, the waterfront
gardens and pool area will remain Victorian gems. ✉ *10 Farquhar St.,
10300 Penang,* ☎ *04/635322,* 𝔽𝔸𝕏 *04/634833.*

$ ⊡ **Bellevue.** Atop Penang Hill, this little hotel can only be reached by funicular railway. Its attractions are spectacular views, an aviary and pretty gardens, cool air, and privacy. ⊠ *Bukit Bendera, 11300 Penang,* ☎ *04/889–2256, no* FAX *. 12 rooms. Restaurant, bar. No credit cards.*

$ ⊡ **Malaysia.** All the rooms in this hotel, conveniently located downtown on upper Penang Road, have bath, TV, and fridge. ⊠ *7 Penang Rd., 10000 Penang,* ☎ *04/263–3311,* FAX *04/263–1621. 126 rooms. Restaurant, bar, exercise room, dance club. AE, MC, V.*

Nightlife and the Arts

Arts events held at the City Hall auditorium downtown are advertised with posters and in the newspapers. Festivals include street events, such as Chinese opera.

BARS

Downtown George Town still has seedy bars, with dim lights and ladies of indeterminate age and profession. Try the **Hong Kong Bar** (⊠ Lebuh Chulia, ☎ 04/261–9796). The **Liverpool Bar** (⊠ Lebuh Bishop, ☎ 04/261–2153) attracts an expatriate crowd for lunch. **Sumn's** (⊠ Lebuh Pantai, ☎ 04/261–0193), in the central business district, offers darts in the evening. At the **Cheers Beer Garden** (⊠ 22 Jln. Argyll, ☎ 04/263–7971), Ken and Pat run their pub with an eye to assisting the traveler.

DANCE CLUBS

Street One, in the Shangri-La (⊠ Jln. Magazine, ☎ 04/262–2622), features the latest lighting effects and sound equipment from London, with special events most nights. **Cinnamon Tree** (⊠ Orchid Hotel, ☎ 04/880–3333) is the popular spot for the young and hip.

LOUNGES

Penang's nightlife revolves around the major hotels, where discos cater to the trendy set and sedate lounges host those who enjoy listening to live music while chatting over a drink. Combos tend to stick to "Candy Man" and "Feelings." In the downtown Shangri-La Hotel's **Lobby Lounge** (⊠ Jln. Magazine, ☎ 04/262–2622), a string quartet—playing everything from classical pieces to waltzes to pop—alternates evenings with a Latin combo. For a drink with a panoramic city view, head for the revolving restaurant atop the **City Bayview Hotel** (⊠ Farquhar St., ☎ 04/263–3161).

Outdoor Activities and Sports

GOLF

Penang has two 18-hole golf courses open to the public—Batu Gantung and Bukit Jambul. For information, fees, and tee times, call the golf section of the Penang Turf Club (☎ 04/366–2333) or the Bukit Jambul Country Club (☎ 04/8842255).

HIKING

For jungle hiking, the best bet is the **Recreational Forest** (called Rima Rekreasi in Malay), 1½ km (1 mi) past the village of Telok Bahang. The tropical forest also has a museum, a children's playground, and picnic tables. A Malayan Nature Society brochure with six other treks around the hills of Penang is available at tourist information centers.

HORSEBACK RIDING

For information about trail or beach rides, contact the **Bay Riders** (☎ 04/445-6892, code 24277).

JOGGING

In Air Itam, joggers or walkers may also want to explore the track around the reservoir that provides Penang with drinking water. The path cuts through a tropical forest and across the dam. There is no bus service up to the area, so getting there is a workout in itself. It's best as an early morning outing.

Shopping

Penang Road is the main shopping area, with Lebuh Campbell and Jalan Burmah as offshoots. Look for antiques and junk in the Rope Walk district, now listed on maps as Jalan Pintal Tali. Don't hesitate to bargain, but remember that shopkeepers play the game full-time. You'll see signs for duty-free prices on certain goods. Most shops are open 10–10.

ANTIQUES

The **Saw Joo Ann** antiques shop, on the corner of Lebuh Hong Kong, has high-quality Malaysian artifacts. If it's not open during normal business hours, ask at the coffee shop next door and someone will come to let you browse.

CRAFTS

On Upper Penang Road, shops sell crafts from Malaysia, Thailand, Indonesia, China, and India. **Selangor Pewterware** (☎ 04/366–6742) has a showroom next to the E&O Hotel on Lebuh Farquhar. The best selection of batik prints is at the **BMB** shop (☎ 04/262–1607) in Komtar. **Penang Butterfly Farm** (✉ 803 Mk. 2, Jln. Taluk Bahang, ☎ 04/881–1253) sells artifacts from all of Southeast Asia.

MARKETS

The **Chowrasta Market** (☞ Exploring, *above*) on Penang Road is an indoor wet market with shops and stalls outside. On Sunday morning, a **flea market,** offering a mixture of junk and antiques, is held on Jalan Pintal Tali.

Batu Ferringhi

The Batu Ferringhi Beach, with fine, golden sand shaded by casuarina and coconut trees, has made Penang one of the best-known holiday islands in Southeast Asia. In the '60s, the beaches on Penang's north coast were the haunting ground of down-and-out, dope-smoking backpackers. Once developers placed their sights on huge profits to be made from sun and beach resorts, the police started to harrass the long-hairs to such a point that they were forced to take their backpacks to islands in the north, particularly Phuket in Thailand, where they discovered the sea was bluer and the bays had softer sand. Penang's north coast then became a strip of resort hotels starting from about 16 km out of George Town to Telok Bahang. Most of the coastline is broken up into small rocky coves. The one exception is the shore at Batu Ferringhi, and that is where the majority of resort hotels cluster.

Though not Miami Beach, Batu Ferringhi does have a similar ambience—a strip of fancy hotels that primarily provide blocks of rooms to package tours. (You'd never want to pay the published room rate prices here unless you don't mind your fellow guests' paying half that amount.) Batu Ferringhi may be a popular choice for a week's stay at a beach resort, but it has fewer charms for the daytripper. Public facilities, such as showers and changing rooms, are nonexistent. Don't go to a great effort to drive out.

Dining

ITALIAN

$$$ ✕ **Il Ritrovo.** This Italian bistro, cozily decorated with travel posters and candles in wine bottles, draws locals and tourists alike. Its excellent three-course meal is good value. Chef Luciano does a perfect *antipasti tutti mare* (seafood antipasto), followed by an impressive range of pasta, veal, lamb, and chicken dishes and classic Italian *dolci*. A Filipino band enhances the atmosphere by playing requests. ⊠ *Casuarina Beach Hotel, Batu Ferringhi,* ☎ *04/881–1711, ext. 766. Reservations essential. AE, DC, MC, V. Closed Mon.*

$$$ ✕ **La Farfalla.** Farfalla's swank decor includes a white grand piano and a different ice sculpture every night. It overlooks the pool and sea, but the place is so pretty you may not notice the view. Try the *carpaccio d'agnello con zucchine* (thin strips of lamb with zucchini) or the *saltimbocca alla Romana* (veal stuffed with cheese and ham). You may be more impressed by the chic setting and the presentation than the creativity of the chef. ⊠ *Penang Mutiara, Telok Bahang,* ☎ *04/881–2828. Reservations essential. AE, DC, MC, V.*

SEAFOOD

$$$ ✕ **Eden Seafood Village.** This open-air beachfront restaurant caters to tourists with a nightly cultural show. Its Chinese-style specialties include crab cooked in a spicy chili-tomato sauce, steamed prawns dipped in ginger sauce, lobster, and fried squid. ⊠ *Batu Ferringhi,* ☎ *04/881–1852. Reservations essential. AE, DC, MC, V.*

Lodging

$$$$ 🏨 **Penang Mutiara.** This luxury resort at the end of Batu Ferringhi Beach
★ opened in late 1988 and has set a new standard for glitz and glitter in Malaysia. All rooms have an ocean view and are decorated with rattan furniture, batik wall prints, and Malay-pattern rugs. Balconies drooping with bougainvillea, ceiling fans, and shutters give additional tropical flavor. The sparkling-white marble lobby features fountains and waterfalls and floor-to-ceiling windows. Restaurants include La Farfalla for Italian fare (☞ Dining, *above*) and a seafood restaurant aptly named Catch. ⊠ *Jln. Teluk Bahang, 11050 Penang,* ☎ *04/881–2828 or 800/44–UTELL,* FAX *04/881–2829. 443 rooms. 5 restaurants, 2 bars, 2 pools, 4 tennis courts, health club, sailing, windsurfing, dance club. AE, DC, MC, V.*

$$$ 🏨 **Shangri-La Golden Sands.** The beachfront Golden Sands has lush tropical landscaping around two pools and an open-air lounge and café, with a spectacular indoor-outdoor garden effect. Each room is decorated in soft pastels accented with cane and has a private balcony with a view of sea or hills. Such activities as jungle walks and sandcastle-building competitions are arranged, and special poolside events, such as Chinese buffet dinners or barbecues, are held most nights. The hotel's most popular restaurant, Peppino, serves a wide variety of antipasti, pizzas, and nine types of pasta. ⊠ *Batu Ferringhi Beach, 11100 Penang,* ☎ *04/881–1911,* FAX *04/881–1880, U.S. res.* ☎ *800/942–5050. 310 rooms. 2 restaurants, bar, coffee shop, 2 pools, wading pool, sailing, snorkeling, windsurfing. AE, DC, MC, V.*

$$$ 🏨 **Shangri-La Rasa Sayang.** This is the top of the luxury hotels that line overcrowded Batu Ferringhi Beach. Between the main building and beach is a large pool that is turned into a fountain floodlit by colored lights in the evening. The hotel has programmed activities day and night. Popular with Japanese tourists, it offers a restaurant with teppanyaki, sushi bar, and tempura, as well as a European and a Chinese restaurant. ⊠ *Batu Ferringhi Beach, 11100 Penang,* ☎ *04/881–1811 or 800/942–5050,* FAX *04/881–1984; U.S. res.* ☎ *800/942–5050; U.K. res.* ☎ *081/747–8485. 520 rooms. 3 restaurants, bar, coffee shop, 2 pools, putting green, 4 tennis courts, health club, squash, volleyball, sailing, snorkeling, windsurfing, dance club, meeting rooms. AE, DC, MC, V.*

$$ 🏨 **Casuarina Beach Hotel.** Large, cozy rooms, a low-key pace, and attentive service make this established resort a favorite. Named for the willowy trees that mingle with palms along the beach, this hotel has a pleasant pool area and offers champagne brunches and country-and-Western music nights. ⊠ *Batu Ferringhi Beach, 11100 Penang,* ☎ *04/*

881–1711, FAX *04/881–2155. 179 rooms. 3 restaurants, lounge bar, pool, sailing, snorkeling, windsurfing. AE, DC, MC, V.*

$$ 🏨 **Holiday Inn Penang.** This seven-story hotel surrounds a large pool right on the beach. Popular with Australians, it offers such activities as bike rides and jungle walks, snooker and ping-pong tournaments, and tennis and windsurfing lessons. Day rates available. ⊠ *Batu Ferringhi Beach, 11100 Penang,* ☎ *04/881–1601 or 800/HOLIDAY,* FAX *04/881– 1389. 54 rooms. 3 restaurants, 3 bars. AE, DC, MC, V.*

$ 🏨 **Lone Pine.** The best bargain on the beach, this hotel is a bit scruffy, with no pool and few amenities, but its beachfront area is shaded and pleasant. The air-conditioned rooms are spacious if Spartan; all have bath, TV, and fridge. Rates include breakfast and morning tea. ⊠ *97 Batu Ferringhi Beach, 11100 Penang,* ☎ *04/881–1511, no* FAX. *54 rooms. Restaurant, bar. AE, DC, MC, V.*

Nightlife and the Arts

CULTURAL EVENTS

Eden Seafood Village (☎ 04/881–1852) in Batu Ferringhi holds a cultural show for diners most evenings. The show features Malay dancers, Indians laden with bells, and noisy Chinese lion dancers.

Beyond Batu Ferringhi is the **Pinang Cultural Center** (⊠ Jln. Teluk Bahang, ☎ 04/881–1175), which re-creates a kampong with a *balai* (community center), an Orang Ulu longhouse, a padang for outdoor activities, and an exhibition hall. There are three 45-minute cultural performances daily (10:15, noon, and 3:15) with dances and traditional music. 🎫 *Admission.* ⏱ *Daily 9:30–5.*

LOUNGES AND CLUBS

The Penang Mutiara's serene **Palmetto Lounge** (⊠ Telok Bahang, ☎ 04/881–2828) has a resident pianist. For activity on the dance floor the **Cinta** in the Rasa Sayang Hotel (⊠ Batu Ferringhi, ☎ 04/811–1811, ext. 1151) draws an international crowd nightly.

Outdoor Activities and Sports

Several small bicycle-rental firms operate across the road from the major hotels in Batu Ferringhi, but be aware that the traffic often drifts quite close on the narrow roads.

Penang A to Z

Arriving and Departing

BY BOAT

There are now two ferries that ply between Penang and Medan in Sumatra. Except for Sunday, they depart daily from Penang at 10 AM and arrive at Medan's port of Belawan five hours later (no visa required for American and British citizens). The return trip departs from Belawan at 9 AM. The one-way fare is M$96. The terminal office is next to the Tourist Information Office on Leboh Pantai, near Fort Cornwallis.

BY BUS

The **main bus station** (☎ 04/634–4928) for intercity service is on the Butterworth side near the ferry terminal. Coach service to Singapore can be booked through **Hosni Express** (☎ 04/261–7746). The fare from Kuala Lumpur is around M$17.

BY CAR

You can either drive across the Penang Bridge from Butterworth (M$7 toll) or bring your car across on the car ferry (M$4–M$6, depending on the size of your vehicle; passengers pay 40 sen). The ferry operates 24 hours, but service after midnight is infrequent.

BY PLANE

Penang International Airport (☎ 04/883–1373), located in Bayan Lepas, about 18 km (11 mi) from George Town, is served by MAS, Singapore Airlines, Garuda, Cathay Pacific, and Thai Airways International. All departing passengers pay an airport tax: M$40 for international flights, M$10 to Singapore, and M$5 for domestic destinations. Penang is about a 40-minute flight from Kuala Lumpur.

Between the Airport and Hotels. Airport taxis use a coupon system with fixed fares. A one-way ride into the city costs M$17; to Batu Ferringhi it's M$25. A public bus (Yellow No. 66) just outside the airport entrance will take you to the terminal in the city center for a ringgit. Buses run hourly at night, more frequently during the day.

BY TRAIN

The train station serving Penang is at the ferry terminal on the Butterworth side. You can buy a ticket at the **Butterworth station** (☎ 04/331–2796) or at a booking station at the **ferry terminal** (✉ Weld Quay, ☎ 04/261–0290). It's not a long walk from Butterworth station to the ferry, but you'll have to carry your own luggage. On the Penang side, porters and taxi drivers will help.

Getting Around

BY BUS

Five bus companies operate in the Penang area. Each is identified by a different bus color and serves a different route. All buses operate out of a central terminus on Jalan Prangin, a block from Komtar. Passengers buy tickets from conductors on the bus and pay according to the distance traveled. For information on routes and schedules, call ☎ 04/262-9357.

BY CAR

Avis (☎ 04/337–3964 or 04/881–1522), **Hertz** (☎ 04/263–5914), and other major companies have counters at the airport and in George Town. **Sintat** (☎ 04/883–0958) has an airport counter only.

BY TAXI

Taxi stands are located near many hotels. Two taxi companies are **Syarikat George Town Taxi** (☎ 04/261–3853) and **Island Taxi** (☎ 04/262–5127). The minimum charge is M$3, more for air-conditioned cars. Though taxis have meters, they are never used. Establish the price before you get in.

BY TRISHAW

Not only tourists but some city residents, mainly elderly Chinese women, rely on trishaws—large tricycles with a carriage for passengers and freight—for transport around town. The pace is pleasant, and it's a relatively inexpensive way to sightsee. Negotiate the route and fare before you get in. A short trip is likely to cost only 5 ringgit. If you want to hire a trishaw for longer, the usual hourly rate for one person riding on a nice day would be about M$15. The driver will, of course, ask for more, but negotiate.

Contacts and Resources

DOCTORS

Contact the **Hospital Besar** (☎ 04/637–3333), on Jalan Residency at Hospital Road, on the edge of downtown. The **Specialists Center** (✉ 19 Jln. Logan, ☎ 04/636–8501) can also help.

EMERGENCIES

For **police** or **ambulance** service, dial 999. For **fire,** dial 994. The **Penang Adventist Hospital** (☎ 04/637–3344) also sends ambulances.

ENGLISH-LANGUAGE BOOKSTORES
The **Times Bookstore** is on the first floor of the Penang Plaza shopping complex (⊠ 126 Jln. Burmah, ☎ 04/262–3443). Other bookstores include: **City Book Center** (⊠ 11 Lebuh Bishop, ☎ 04/265–1593) and **Academic** (⊠ 23 Lebuh Bishop, ☎ 04/261–5780).

GUIDED TOURS
Local companies offer a number of general tours. The most popular is a 73-km (45-mi), 3½-hour drive around the island. From Batu Ferringhi it goes through Malay kampongs, rubber estates, and nutmeg orchards, stops at the Snake Temple, cruises past the Universiti Sains Malaysia campus and through George Town, then returns via the beach road. The principal tour companies also offer such excursions as Penang Hill and Temples, City and Heritage, and Penang by Night, in addition to trips to the world's largest butterfly farm (at Telok Bahang), and the Botanical Gardens.

Tour North East (⊠ Golden Sands Hotel, Batu Ferringhi, ☎ 04/881–1662; ⊠ Penang Plaza, 4th floor, ☎ 04/261–9563) will arrange private car or limousine tours at additional cost and offer side trips to Langkawi Island, Cameron Highlands, and Pangkor Island; most tours run just under three hours and cost M$90 per car. **Mayflower Acme Tours** (⊠ Shangri-La Inn on Jln. Magazine, ☎ 04/262–3724, or ⊠ Tan Chong Building, 23 Pengkalan Weld, ☎ 04/262–8196) is Penang's other major tour company and offers services similar to Tour North East.

Tour agents can arrange harbor cruises with **Waterfront Sdn. Bhd.,** which runs a sunset dinner cruise, a waterfront and Penang Bridge trip, and a Monkey Beach excursion.

TRAVEL AGENCIES
American Express (⊠ Pan Chang Bldg., 274 Victoria St., ☎ 04/462–88196). **Thomas Cook** (⊠ 1 Pengkalan Weld, ☎ 04/261–0511). **Malaysia Airline System** (MAS) is on the ground floor at Komtar. **Ace Tours and Travel** (⊠ Kompleks Tun, Abdul Razak, Penang Rd., 10000 Penang, ☎ 04/261–1205), which often sells airline tickets for less than MAS, is next door to the MAS office; ask for Mr. Joe Y.C. Ng.

VISITOR INFORMATION
The **Penang Tourist Association** distributes information from centers on level 3 of the Komtar building (☎ 04/261–4461) and downtown near Fort Cornwallis, at the intersection of Lebuh Pantai and Lebuh Light (☎ 04/261–6663). Both booths are open weekdays 8–noon and 2–4, and Saturday 8–12:30. The **MTPB** has a counter at the airport (☎ 04/643–0501; ⟳ Weekdays 8:30–4:45, Sat. 8:30–1) and an office in Komtar (☎ 04/262–0066).

LANGKAWI

One hour by ferry from Kuala Perlis.

The hottest resort destination in Malaysia is currently Langkawi, an archipelago of 101 islands at low tide (99 at high tide), north of Penang and just south of the Thailand border. Ten years ago it was a Robinson Crusoe hideaway; today it's Malaysia's primary beach resort.

In contrast to Penang's resort-cluttered north coast, Langkawi is still a relatively unspoiled spot where relaxation is the only game in town. Commercialism is arriving: envious of islands like Bali and Phuket, Malaysia is in a rush to develop Pulau Langkawi, the major island, as a big foreign-exchange earner. To encourage development and tourism, it has been made a duty-free zone; this means the cost of beer and whiskey is much less than on the mainland, but, as of yet, there is limited shopping beyond that.

It doesn't take much more than three hours to explore and to learn the local legends (Langkawi is being promoted as "the Isles of Legends"); after that, all that's left is to explore the beaches of Pulau Langkawi and the other 100 islands. There are boats for hire, and the major resorts rent snorkeling equipment; there are also organized trips to the other islands for picnics and diving. Take a boat, find your island, snorkel, dive, and laze away the day on your own beach!

Pulau Langkawi

Pulau Langkawi, the largest island, houses the airport, the ferry terminal, and the major hotel resorts, more of which are opening every year. In 1995 alone, a dozen new hotels (including the Mahsuri Westin, the Berjaya Langkawi Beach Resort, and Hotel Grand Continental) were added, and in 1996 a new Sheraton and Radisson also opened their doors. German charter companies are now bringing in Europeans by the planeload. Langkawi is losing its serenity, but for a few years yet it will remain a sun-and-sea haven with a lovely slow pace.

Lodging

The choice is varied, from luxurious resorts priced at US$300 a night to local hotels with fan-cooled rooms that cost about US$10. The following properties are the two best.

$$$$ ⊞ **Datai.** Tucked away on the northwestern tip of the island (a 40-minute
★ drive from most of the other attractions), fronting the turquoise Andaman Sea and backed by a tropical rain forest, this 1994 hotel ranks as one of the world's finest hideaways. The large open-air main building, which serves as a reception area and lounge, perches at the top of a small valley that carves its way steeply down to the beach, a 10-minute walk away. Open-air corridors link the lobby to the guest quarters, with the majority of the rooms looking down into the valley. The large rooms are decorated in silk and red balau, a warm Malaysian hardwood that shines from the floors to the walls; each boasts a bedroom with a king-size bed, a living room with bar and two daybeds for lounging, and a grand bathroom with two vanities, shower, bath, and luggage space. Villas and suites are almost twice as big and include a private deck with a sun lounge and elevated veranda. Food here is of a high standard—not innovative, but well orchestrated. ⊠ *Jln. Teluk Datai, 07000 Pulau Langkawi,* ☎ *604/950–2500,* ℻ *604/959–2600; in Kuala Lumpur* ☎ *603/245–3515,* ℻ *603/245–3540; in U.S.* ☎ *800/447–7462; in U.K.* ☎ *0800/181–535. 54 rooms, 40 villas, and 14 suites. 2 restaurants, bar, 2 pools, 18-hole golf course, 2 tennis courts, health club, windsurfing, boating, mountain bikes, meeting rooms. AE, DC, MC, V.*

$$$ ⊞ **Pelangi Beach Resort.** The service, amenities, architecture, and ambience are tops for a large Malaysian resort. The intent throughout the 51 one-and two-story buildings on 25 acres of beachfront is to create the atmosphere of a kampong. But the primary feeling is of a vacation resort with pool, swim-up bar, and so forth. The beach is not spectacular, but at low tide you can wade across to a nearby island for privacy. In the center of the large lobby is a relaxing lounge bar for tea and cocktails. Guest rooms are rather small, and the extensive use of (compressed) wood and heavy carpeting makes them seem smaller; fortunately, they come with balconies, as well as both air-conditioning and fans. About a third face the sea, another third a man-made lake, and the remainder the back lot; room rates reflect these locations. ⊠ *Pantai Cenang, 07000 Pulau Langkawi, Kedah,* ☎ *04/955–1001,* ℻ *04/955–1122; in Kuala Lumpur* ☎ *03/261–0393; in Singapore* ☎ *235–7788. 302*

rooms, 55 suites. 2 restaurants, room service, pool, sauna, 3 tennis courts, exercise room, squash, tour services. AE, DC, MC, V.

Langkawi A to Z

Arriving and Departing

FROM MAINLAND MALAYSIA

By Boat. It's a one-hour ferry ride from Kuala Perlis, on the mainland, to Langkawi. The ferry departs hourly during the day. You can also catch a morning ferry from Penang, a journey that takes approximately five hours.

By Plane. Langkawi has its own airport with several daily MAS flights from Penang and Kuala Lumpur. These flights are often fully booked, so make reservations far in advance and reconfirm those reservations.

FROM THAILAND

By Boat. The established route from Thailand to Langkawi is to arrive overland by bus at Kangar or by train at Arau and take a shared taxi from there to the ferry at Kuala Perlis.

There is also a ferry service to and from Satun on the southwestern Thai coast. (At press time, there was not sufficient traffic to justify daily service; check its schedule first before you commit to this route.) It takes about 90 minutes, departing from Langkawi at approxminately 9 AM and 3 PM and from Satun at approximately noon and 4:30 PM. If you travel to Satul by the morning ferry, a minibus from Hat Yai will get you to Krabi, Phuket, or Ko Samui by the end of the day.

By Plane. From Phuket, MAS and Thai International share a service to Langkawi, with three flights a week currently.

Getting Around

While buses do circle the island, their schedules are erratic. Taxis are the easiest, and are available at the airport and all the major hotels. The cost is approximately M$15 per hour and M$40 for a three-hour tour. Motorcycles are available for rent at M$25 per day.

THE EAST COAST

Whereas the west coast of peninsular Malaysia may be regarded as the industrial half of the country (albeit much still undeveloped), the east coast is puttering along with an economy based on fishing and agriculture. That is its delight.

Along the coastal roads, all the way from the south at Desaru up to the Thai border, towns are few; chances are that you'll spot a monkey or two crossing the road. Even though the beaches are tempting, there are few resort areas along the coast. The Malays are not typically beach goers and not so many Westerners visit the east coast, in part because without a car, travel is by sporadic bus services. The islands offshore, the most well-known of which is Pulau Tioman, have yet to be developed into large scale resorts, again in part because access to them is time-consuming, often a two to three hour ferry ride departing at unscheduled times. With the exception of the resort area just to the north of Kuantan, traveling the east coast is for the most part an adventure for the intrepid traveler.

Numbers in the margin correspond to points of interest on the East Coast map.

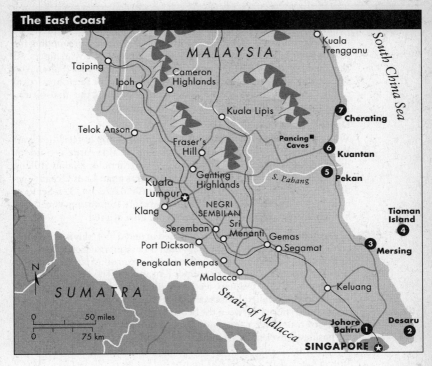

The East Coast

Johore Bahru

1 *368 km (221 mi) southeast of Kuala Lumpur, 30 km (18 mi) north of central Singapore.*

At the southern tip of peninsular Malaysia—and at the end of the causeway from Singapore—lies Johore Bahru, an old royal and administrative capital. Coming from Singapore, the apparent lack of town planning stands in sharp contrast to the city-state's orderliness. There is no center and there are no right angles; streets follow no grid or other logical plan but run into one another higgledy-piggledy. The pace, too, is noticeably different: Here, watches seem to have no minute hands.

But Johore Bahru's days as a laid-back escape from the planned sterility of its neighbor are waning, if not already over. Because labor costs are lower than in Singapore, the last few years have seen rapid commercial and industrial development. The pace is picking up, taxis are smarter, and first-class hotels are being built; congestion and pollution are also on the rise. Johore Bahru is still an excellent transportation hub, both for exploring the east coast and heading to and from Kuala Lumpur and Melaka, but more than a couple of hours there may prove tiresome.

The town's major sight is the **Istana Besar** (✉ Jln. Tun Dato Ismail), the old palace of the sultans of Johore. This neoclassical, rather institutional-looking building, erected in 1866, has been converted into a museum; it holds the hunting trophies of the late sultan as well as ceremonial regalia and ancient weapons. The new sultan's palace, the **Istana Bukit Serene** (✉ Jln. Straits View), was built in 1933 and is noted for its gardens, which are popular with joggers.

The **Sultan Abu Bakar Mosque** (✉ Jln. Gerstak Merah, off Jln. Tun Dato Ismail), built in 1900 in European Victorian style, is one of Malaysia's most beautiful, with sparkling white towers and domes surrounding the main prayer hall. It can accommodate more than 2,000 worshipers. At the cemetery on Jalan Muhamadiah, the **Royal Mausoleum** (Sultan Abu Bakar Mausoleum) has been the final resting place for the Johore royal family since it left Singapore. Visitors may not enter the mausoleum, but a number of impressive Muslim tombs surround it.

Dining and Lodging

While smart dining may be found at the Johore's top hotels, the Hyatt Regency and the Puteri Pan Pacific, the top local favorite is outdoor dining at one of the restaurants clustered together along Jalan Stulang Laut. Two of the popular restaurants are **Makunan Laut Ocean Garden** (☎ 07/222–7482) and **Khye Cheang** (☎ 07/222-4732). Seafood is the speciality—be sure to ask the prices before committing yourself—but Malay curries and Chinese dishes are also offered.

$$$$ 🏨 **Hyatt Regency Johore Bahru.** Opened in mid-1994, this is the grandest of Johore Bahru's modern hotels. Built on a slight rise facing the Straits of Johore, the mammoth building forms an arc around landscaped gardens through which a two tiered pool meanders. The guest rooms are large (more than 350 square feet) with all the latest technological gadgetry in bedside controls. Increase the feeling of space by keeping open the wooden shutter between the bedroom and the bathroom, which has plenty of room and a separate shower stall. The hotel is designed for the business traveler, with four restaurants (Western, Japanese, Szechuan, and Italian) for entertaining and meeting rooms for business. ✉ *Jalan Sungai Chat, Box 222, 80720 Jahore Bahru,* ☎ *07/223–1234,* FAX *07/223–2718. 406 rooms. 4 restaurants, bar, pool, 2 tennis courts, health club, business services, meeting rooms. AE, DC, MC, V.*

$$$ 🏨 **Puteri Pan Pacific.** This 500-room hotel opened in 1991 adjacent to the Kotaraya Complex—the city's newest and most prestigious office and shopping mall. The design makes use of round, timber-clad columns and colorful batiks in an open court lobby. Guest rooms, decorated in popular pastel colors, are fully equipped with modern amenities. ✉ *Jalan Salim, Box 293, 80000 Johore Bahru,* ☎ *07/223–3333,* FAX *07/233–6622. 500 rooms. 5 restaurants, in-room safes, room service, pool, business services. AE, DC, MC, V.*

Shopping

There are several handicraft centers, including **Sri Ayu Batik Industries** (✉ 136 Jalan Perwira Satu), where demonstrations of batik making and songket weaving are given.

Desaru

❷ *94 km (58 mi) east of Johore Bahru, 436 km (282 mi) southeast of Kuala Lumpur.*

An hour out of Johore on the road to Kota Thinggi (about 45 km or 30 mi), there is a junction; the right fork goes to Desaru. Since Singapore has no decent beaches, Desaru was developed to fill the bill. For a time, fast ferries brought droves of Singaporeans over on weekends; plans were made for a Disney World–style playground, with two more golf courses, more water-sports facilities, an additional 4,000 holiday homes, and more hotels along the 17-km (10.5-mile) stretch of jungle-fringed beach. That expansion has not, so far, materialized. Instead, Desaru has become a rather desultory playground.

Lodging

$$$–$$$$ ⊞ **Desaru View Hotel.** At this full-service luxury resort hotel set in seaside gardens, all rooms have balconies and views of the South China Sea, plus air-conditioning, color TV and video, and minibar. A wide variety of facilities—including the longest swimming pool in Malaysia—is available, and pickup in Singapore can be arranged. ⊠ *Tanjung Penawar, 81900 Kota Tinggi,* ☎ *07/822–1221,* FAX *07/822–1237. 134 rooms. 4 restaurants, bar, pool, 4 tennis courts, 18-hole golf course, miniature golf, horseback riding, bicycles, dance club, recreation room, meeting rooms. AE, MC, V.*

$$–$$$ ⊞ **Desaru Golf Hotel.** This medium-class hotel is family-oriented and set in a two-story building with double-peaked roof. Not all guest rooms have sea views. ⊠ *Tanjung Penawar, 81900 Kota Tinggi,* ☎ *07/822–1101,* FAX *07/822–1480. 100 rooms. Restaurant, coffee lounge, 2 tennis courts, 18-hole golf course, dive shop, playground, convention center. AE, MC, V.*

Golf

The **Desaru Resort Golf Club** (⊠ Box 57, 81907 Kota Tinggi, ☎ 07/821–187, FAX 07/821–855) has an undulating 18-hole course designed by Robert Trent Jones, Jr. and made more difficult by strong sea breezes.

Mersing

❸ *353 km (212 mi) southeast of Kuala Lumpur, 161 km (100 mi) north of Johore Bahru.*

The low-key market town of Mersing is a good three hour-drive from Johore Bahru on a road that cuts through rubber and palm plantations. An occasional monkey scampering across the road keeps you alert. Mersing still has its roots as a fishing village, but it also has become the gateway to Tioman Island and the other smaller islands lying offshore.

Strangely, Mersing has one of the most helpful local tourist offices, the **Mersing Tourist Information Center** (⊠ 1 Jln. Abu Bakar, ☎ 07/799–5212, FAX 07/799–3975). It's a good idea to drop in here—it's about 400 yards before you reach the ferry wharf—to get maps, your bearings, and reliable information on the hotels. If you are going to Tioman, you can book the ferry ride and the isalnd lodging of your choice at one of the many tourist offices around Mersing's harbor and in the adjacent Plaza R&R; try **Zaid Mohammed Lazim** (⊠:17 Jln. Abu Bakar, Plaza R&R, ☎ 07/799-4280, FAX 07/799-4434).

Lodging

$ ⊞ **Timotel.** The only reason for staying overnight in Mersing is if you have missed the ferry to the offshore islands. While there are several inexpensive Chinese hotels on Mersing's main street, this spot on the edge of town in a small shopping center and on the road to Kuantan is the newest (1995) and cleanest hotel in the area. All rooms have air-conditioning and either a king-size bed or twins. Furnishings are basic—carpet on the floor, TV on a side cabinet, coffee table, and chairs. Bathrooms have a tub and hand-held shower. A small dining area serves meals all day long. ⊠ *839 Jln. Endau, 86800 Mersing,* ☎ *07/799-5888,* FAX *07/799-5333. 44 rooms. Coffee shop. AE, MC, V.*

Tioman Island

❹ *Two hours by ferry from Mersing.*

Tioman Island, the largest and farthest offshore of the islands near Mersing, was Bali Hai in the movie *South Pacific.* This lush tropical island hasn't changed much since then, except for the tourists, and it is large enough to absorb them. Sunbathe in the sandy coves, swim in the clear waters, try the nine-hole golf course, or take walks through the jungle-clad hills (the highest is Gunjung Kajang at 3,400 feet). Plenty of water sports are available; brightly colored fish and coral make for enjoyable snorkeling. Boats and bicycles—your transportation around the island–are available for rent.

Tioman, while peaceful and quiet by most standards, does get a little busy with tourists. Those seeking quieter havens head for the other nearby islands. Three of them, which each have one resort offering simple bungalow accommodation, are **Pulau Cibu** (☎ 07/799–3167), **Pulau Rawa** (☎ 07/799–1204), and **Pulau Besar** (☎ 07/799–4995). The latter has slightly larger, more spacious bungalows than the others.

Boats are scheduled to leave Mersing harbor for the two-hour trip to Tioman and the other islands every day around noon, though because they are dependent on the tides, the actual departure time varies. The cost to any of the islands is M$25. Because the boats must wait for the morning tides to make the return from Tioman, a day excursion is not possible; you must stay overnight.

Lodging

The ferry makes five stops up the island's west coast at various accommodations, only one of which is a major resort (☞ *below*); it's located in the center of the island. If the room prices there strike you as too steep, you can drop by to use the facilities but stay at one of the inexpensive chalets around Kampung Telek and Kampung Air Batang.

$$$$ 🏨 **Berjaya Imperial Beach Resort.** A full renovation in 1993 transformed this property into a full-service hotel and resort complex. Rooms are decorated in soft colors and equipped with telephones, televisions, and minibars, and a conference center can accommodate business seminars and conferences. An attractive nine-hole golf course and a large swimming pool keep most guests occupied, and the activities desk can also arrange pony rides, diving and snorkeling, and boat trips around the island. ⊠ *Pulau Tioman, 86807 Mersing, Johor,* ☎ *09/414–5445,* 𝔽𝔸𝕏 *09/414–5718. 375 rooms. 2 restaurants, bar, coffee shop, pool, 9-hole golf course, 2 tennis courts, dive shop, jet skiing, meeting rooms. AE, MC, V.*

Pekan

❺ *107 km (63 mi) north of Mersing.*

Though there are numerous traditional kampongs and colorful fishing villages along the east coast between Mersing and Kuantan, the only main town is Pekan, the home of the sultan. You can see his modern palace, with its manicured lawns and, of course, its polo field, but only from outside the gates. Don't bypass this town, as the signposts invite you to; drive through the center instead. Built on the western shore of a river, it is delightfully old-fashioned, with two-story shop-houses lining the main street. At the **Silk Weaving Center** at Pulau Keladi, traditional Pahang silk is woven into intricate designs.

Kuantan

❻ *259 km (156 mi) east of Kuala Lumpur, 70 km (42 mi) north of Pekan, 325 km (155 mi) north of Johore Bahru.*

The major beach and holiday resort on Malaysia's east coast is Kuantan. The first hotel area begins just north of the city at the crescent-shaped sandy bay of Telok Champedak. To get there, take Jalan Telok

Sisek just past the Hotel Suraya. This small community consists of several hotels (including the Hyatt Kuantan), four or five restaurants and bars, discos, and a small but attractive curving beach. Sunbathers come for the company of other vacationers rather than solitude. If you prefer privacy, continue a few miles north. Here, smaller hotels dot a long stretch of virtually untrodden sands.

Dining and Lodging

$$$ ✕ **Kampong Café.** In a soft candlelit setting, with rattan chairs, taupe linens, and sparkling crystal and silver, the setting is already romantic, but it gets better. The restaurant is built on stilts; the view is of the South China Sea. The food is a mix of Malay and European and the best are the seafood dishes. ✉ *Hyatt Kuantan, Telok Chempedak,* ☎ *09/525–211. Reservations essential. AE, DC, MC, V.*

$$$ ⊞ **Hyatt Regency Kuantan.** The architects were Malaysian, but the de-
★ sign of this low-rise hotel gives one a feeling of Hawaii. Full advantage of the sea breezes is taken with the open side facing the South China Sea. Lush, cultivated gardens surround the hotel and two swimming pools are steps back from the golden sand beach. Rooms are in three courts running parallel to the beach. The farthest rooms from the lobby are in the Regency Court extension. The distinct advantage in staying here is the lounge, which serves an ample continental breakfast and an array of evening cocktails with hors d'oevres. The carpeted guest rooms have either king-size or twin beds and bathrooms with a separate shower stall. Since you have come here for the sea, it's worth the premium to reserve rooms facing the sea—sleep with the balcony doors open to the souds of the surf—rather than the vegetation and hills at the back of the courtyards. A six-story business wing to the rear of the main hotel has conference rooms and 52 business suites. A Filipino band plays for the late night crowd. ✉ *Telok Chempedak, 25730 Kuantan, Pahang Darul Makmur,* ☎ *09/513–1234,* 𝔽𝔸𝕏 *09/567–7577. 327 rooms. Restaurant, outdoor café, room service, 2 pools, sauna, golf privileges, 3 tennis courts, exercise room, squash, dance club. AE, MC, V.*

$–$$ ⊞ **Coral Beach Resort.** Formerly a Ramada-managed property, this is a modern resort hotel with a wide-open lobby area and a light-filled coffee lounge serving Malay and European fare. A Japanese and a Chinese restaurant are available for more elaborate dining. The resort's chief pleasure is its piece of the endless sands on the shore of the South China Sea. Rooms are similar to what you may expect of a former Ramada: Beds are either king-size or twins, furniture is utilitarian, and the bathrooms are adequate. The hotel promotes itself to tourists and for business seminars, so the mix of earnest, shirted delegates and fun-loving sunbathers seems a bit strained during the day, but by night the bars scattered around the property relieve the tension. The Coral Beach is 12 km north of Kuantan. ✉ *152 Sungai Karang, 26100 Beserah, Kuantan,* ☎ *09/544–7544,* 𝔽𝔸𝕏 *09/544–7543. 162 rooms. 2 restaurants, pool, 2 tennis courts, squash, health club, meeting rooms. AE, DC, MC, V.*

¢ ⊞ **Tanjung Gelang Motel.** This small, Chinese-owned motel has simple chalets packed rather tightly together, facing the beach. The motel's advantage is its price, around M$40 a night. There are no frills, just the basics and a small restaurant that serves mostly Chinese and European food, but the Coral Bay Resort and all its facilities are right next door. To reach this motel from Kuantan, you do need a car. ✉ *Km 15, Jln. Kemaman, 26100 Kuantan, Pahang Darul Makmur,* ☎ *09/544–7254,* 𝔽𝔸𝕏 *09/544–7388. 40 rooms. Restaurant. AE, MC, V.*

| OFF THE | **PANCING CAVES –** Some 25 km (15 mi) into the jungled hills west of |
| BEATEN PATH | Kuantan are the Pancing Caves (or, more correctly, Gua Charah). Trav- |

eling from Kuantan, you first pass rubber and oil-palm plantations before arriving at the bottom of a small hill. Now comes the hard part: To reach the caves, you must climb 220 steps. Buddhists still live here, and there are many altars. Don't miss the cave with the reclining Buddha some 9 meters (30 feet) long, carved by a Thai Buddhist monk who devoted his life to the task.

Cherating

⑦ *30 km (19 mi) north of Kuantan.*

Half an hour's drive north of Kuantan is the peaceful village of Cherating, a rustic haven of beachcombing along miles of white, clean beaches fanned by gentle breezes through the coconut trees. Club Med was one of the first to stake its claim on a fine stretch of beach here, responding to the spirit of the place with its Malay-style bungalows built on stilts. Since then, numerous three- and four-star hotels have sprung up along the main highway, but they always seem to have more than enough empty rooms to offer good discounts.

Opportunities for **turtle-watching**—one of the east coast's most popular attractions—begin at Cherating and continue north. The best viewing place is said to be Chendor Beach, an hour north of Kuantan or 20 minutes up from Cherating. Most nights between May and September (peak month is August), enormous leatherback turtles slowly make their way ashore to lay as many as 200 eggs each. Signs at the hotels will tell when and where to go, and the crowds do gather to watch as the 1,000-pound turtles laboriously dig their "nests" before settling down to their real work.

Lodging

$$$$ 🏨 **Club Med Cherating.** This Malaysian-style Club Med village is set on its own bay, surrounded by 200 acres of parkland. Accommodation is in twin-bedded bungalows with air-conditioning and showers. As with all Club Meds, the package is inclusive, with full sporting facilities, arts-and-crafts workshops, and buffet-style dining in the price. The resort was refurbished in 1994 and is quieter and more low-key than the Club Meds found in the Caribbean. ⊠ *Mile 29, Jln. Kuantan-Kemaman, Cherating, 26080 Kuantan,* ☎ *09/439–133 or 800/258–2633,* 🅵🅰🆇 *09/439–524. 300 rooms. 2 restaurants, pool, 6 tennis courts, aerobics, archery, exercise room, squash, windsurfing, children's program (ages 4–9 and 10–11). AE, MC, V.*

$$$$ 🏨 **Impiana Resort.** For more independence than at Club Med, here is a low-rise sprawl of modern luxury on 32 acres at the edge of Cherating's beach. The vast lobby, flooded by natural light and cooled by sea breezes, is the focal point. Beyond is the two-tiered swimming pool, and beyond that the sea. Guests choose between Malay, Chinese, or Western food from the three restaurants, or take something of everything from the evening buffet. Standard rooms are in the main building; there are also two- and three-bedroom chalets. Most rooms and chalets face the sea, and all have four-poster wooden beds, a ceiling fan, and air-conditioning. For recreation, there is a fully equipped water-sports center, which includes jet skiing. ⊠ *Km 32, Jln. Kuantan–Kemaman, Cherating, 26080 Pahang,* ☎ *09/439–000,* 🅵🅰🆇 *09/439–090. 250 rooms, including chalets. 3 restaurants, bar, meeting rooms. AE, DC, MC, V.*

$$ 🏨 **Cherating Holiday Villa Beach Resort.** Formerly affiliated with the Holiday Inn in Kuala Lumpur, this hotel has undergone a metamorphosis. From the central building that houses the reception and dining area, buildings fan out toward the beach, enclosing a swimming pool and gardens. The structures vary, with each taking some architectural aspect, usually a roof style, from a different region of Malaysia. Rooms are equally diverse, from modern, Western-style accommodations to chalets designed in the Malay style with bare wood floors and a minimum of furniture. Most are wood paneled, with sliding-glass doors facing the pool—more privacy, therefore, is found in the rooms on the second floor. The restaurant at night offers a mix of Italian-inspired fare and Malay cooking; a beach barbecue is held twice a week. As at the other hotels on the east coast of Malaysia, you'll need a car to get off the property. ⊠ *Lot 1303, Mukim Sungei Karang, Cherating, 26080 Kuantan,* ☎ *09/581–9500,* FAX *09/581–9178; in Kuala Lumpur* ☎ *03/262–2922,* FAX *03/262–2937. 94 rooms. 2 restaurants, coffee lounge, 2 pools, 3 tennis courts, 2 badminton courts, exercise room, squash. AE, MC, V.*

¢ 🏨 **Cherating Beach Mini-Hotel.** If your reason for staying in Cherating is beachcombing, then this small budget hotel is perfect. The rooms are very small and sparsely furnished, but the beach is at the front door. The staff is wonderfully low-key and friendly, and the restaurant does its best to cook up European food (though it's better at Malay dishes). ⊠ *Batu 28 Kampung, Jln. Kemaman, Cherating, 26080 Kuantan, Pahang Darul Makmur,* ☎ *09/592–527, no* FAX*. 35 rooms, most with shower and toilet. Restaurant. No credit cards.*

East Coast A to Z

Arriving and Departing

BY BUS

Johore Bahru, as the southern end of the line for peninsular Malaysia, has comprehensive bus connections. Bus service is fast and efficient and inexpensive. Sample fares: from Kuala Lumpur, M$15; from Melaka, M$10.30. Departures are frequent from Bangunan Mara Terminal. Both air-conditioned and non-air-conditioned buses are available. Bus 170 makes the run across the causeway between Johore Bahru and Singapore.

Contacts and Resources

Malaysian Tourist Promotion Board (⊠ Tun Abdul Razak Complex, 4th floor, Jln. Wong Ah Fook, Johore Bahru, ☎ 07/222–3591).

SARAWAK

Sarawak's modern history began in 1846, after Sir James Brooke settled a dispute between the local raja and the Sultan of Brunei. Establishing peace and bringing relief from marauding pirate bands, Raja Brooke instituted a benevolent family regency that lasted more than a century, until the arrival of the Japanese. Their intrusion was deeply resented by the tribal people, who eagerly resumed their practice of head-hunting, which had been banned by the Brooke rajas. But Sarawak has otherwise remained for the most part peaceful, unspoiled, and serene.

Sarawak remained as a colony under the British until it was annexed to the independent state of Malaysia in 1963. Thus the native peoples have little in common with West Malaysians, who absorbed much European and Chinese culture. The ancient languages, arts and crafts, and social customs remain relatively intact. Some tribes still live in traditional longhouses, communal bamboo structures that house from 10 to 40 families under one roof.

Sarawak is bigger and poorer than neighboring Sabah, with some 1.5 million people inhabiting its 125,000 sq km (48,250 sq mi). About 360,000 live around the capital city of Kuching, a pleasant and fairly modern town that still retains many of its Victorian buildings and Chinese shop-houses. About 80% of Sarawak's population is Chinese or Malay; as in Sabah, Christians outnumber Muslims.

Sarawak's principal tourist attractions are the Dayak and Iban long-houses upriver from Kuching. Guided trips give travelers a sense of river life as well as of the richness and power of the jungle. You can visit longhouses for a day or stay over for a night or more, sharing communal meals and admiring native dances. Another fascinating destination is the Niah Caves, which have yielded a wide range of archaeological finds, including human remains believed to date from 40,000 years ago.

Numbers in the margin correspond to points of interest on the Sarawak and Sabah map.

Kuching

❶ *920 km (575 mi) southeast of Kuala Lumpur, 832 km (520 mi) south-west of Kota Kinabalu.*

Kuching suffered little damage during the Second World War, and a walk around town will give the visitor some feeling for its history. You'll note the gentle, unhurried pace as you stroll along the newly landscaped waterfront, where there are benches, food stalls, and a small stadium in which dancers perform.

The town's oldest building is the 1840s **Tua Pek Kong** Chinese temple, downtown on Jalan Tuanku Abdul Rahman at Padungan Road. You can watch worshipers lighting incense and making paper offerings to the god of prosperity. Among the colonial buildings worth seeing is the **Court House,** the former seat of the British white rajahs, with its portico and Romanesque columns (the clock tower was added in 1883). This remains the venue for any event of pomp and circumstance. Behind the Court House on Jalan Tun Haji Openg stands the **Pavilion Building,** where, behind an elaborate Victorian facade, the Education Department now does its business.

Across the river is **Fort Margherita,** built in 1879 by rajah Charles Brooke. Today it's a police museum displaying cannons and other colonial weapons. Near Fort Margherita, **Astana** was the Brooke palace, built in 1870—three bungalows, complete with military ramparts and tower. Today Astana is the official residence of Sarawak's head of state, and is not open to the public.

The highlight of the city is the **Sarawak Museum,** one of the best in Southeast Asia—comprehensive and beautifully curated. In addition to exhibits of local insects and butterflies, sea creatures, birds, and other wildlife, there are displays on Dayak body tattoos, burial rites, face masks, and carvings. In the new building across the road are a delightful exhibit on cats *(kuching* means "cat" in Malay), a model of the Niah Caves showing how nests are gathered, a movie theater, an art gallery, and a crafts shop. ⊠ *Jln. Tun Haji Openg,* ☎ *082/244232.* 🎟 *Free.* ☉ *Mon.–Thurs. 9:15–5:30, Sat. and Sun. 9:15–6.*

For beach action, head for **Damai,** 35 minutes by taxi from Kuching. The Holiday Inn (☞ Lodging, *below*) can supply all the amenities you need for relaxing on the powdery white sands.

The **Cultural Village and Heritage Center** (⊠ Santubong, ☎ 082/422411) at Damai runs programs of such folk arts as dancing, kite flying, use of the blowpipe, and handicraft production. The reconstructed village displays the heritage of the seven major tribes indigenous to Sarawak. Elaborate dance shows are held twice-weekly (check the current sched-

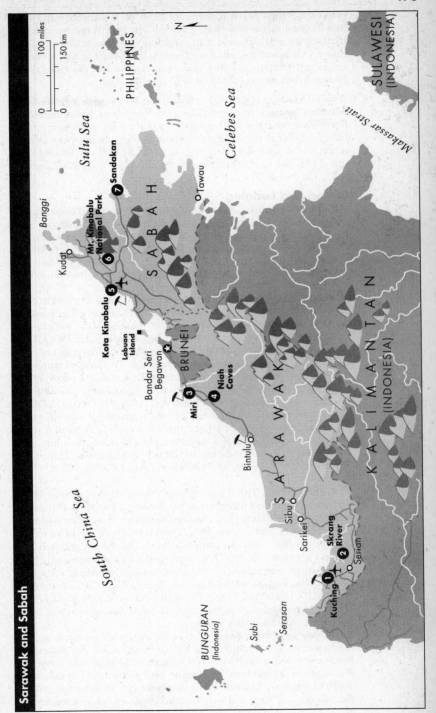

Sarawak and Sabah

ule at the Damai Beach Resort), and craft demonstrations and some folk-dancing performances are given daily at 2 PM. A restaurant serves local dishes and delicious rum punches, and plans call for a long-house-style accommodation for tourists. The Sarawak Economic Development Corporation directs the project, but call the **Holiday Inn Damai Beach Resort** (☎ 082/411777) for details.

About 22 km (14 mi) from Kuching is the **Semonggok Wildlife Rehabilitation Center,** where orangutans, other monkeys, honey bears, and hornbills formerly in captivity are prepared for return to their natural habitat. You can get a visitor's permit through the Forestry Department (✉ Mosque Rd., Kuching, ☎ 082/248739). ☎ 082/423111, ext. 1133, for tour arrangements. 🖾 Admission. ☉ Weekdays 8–4:25, Sat. 8–12:45.

Dining and Lodging

$$ ✕ **Beijing Riverbank.** The food—light refreshments and drinks downstairs, a more elaborate Cantonese and Western menu upstairs—is acceptable, but what draws people to this modest pagoda is its situation overlooking the river. ✉ Kuching Waterfront, ☎ 088/234126. MC, V.

$$ ✕ **Lok Thian.** This large restaurant, located near the Dewan Mesayakat, is renowned for its Cantonese barbecue. ✉ 319 Jln. Padungan, ☎ 088/3130. AE, DC, V.

$$ ✕ **Meisan Szechuan.** This gaudily decorated Chinese restaurant overlooks the Sarawak River. Waiters deliver 23 varieties of dim sum—all you can eat. ✉ Holiday Inn Kuching, Jln. Tuanku Abdul Rahman, ☎ 082/423111. Reservations essential on Sun. morning. AE, DC, MC, V.

$$ ✕ **Tsui Hua Lau.** Cantonese and Szechuan dishes highlight an extensive menu at this brightly lit, two-story restaurant. The unusual entrées include braised turtle, sea cucumber, and bird's nest soup (a bowl for 10 costs M$100). The barbecued duck and Szechuan-style shredded beef meet high standards. ✉ 22 Ban Hock Rd., ☎ 082/414560. AE, DC, V.

$$ ✕ **Waterfront Cafe.** On the river, this serene ground-floor coffee shop has a good view of the wharf and the water traffic. Its menu features Malay, Chinese, and Indian favorites plus Western specialties. The noodle dishes are delicious; the service is fine. ✉ Kuching Hilton, Jln. Tuanku Abdul Rahman, ☎ 082/248200. AE, DC, MC, V.

$$$$ 🏨 **Kuching Hilton.** This 15-story luxury hotel on the Sarawak River, ★ just across from Fort Margherita, has become a landmark for quality service and fine dining. The bleached furniture in its spacious rooms includes a desk with a view. One "Penthouse Floor" and two executive floors offer special amenities: separate check-in, a personal butler, and a private lounge. The views—and all the restaurants have them—are far better than the ones at the newer Riverside Majestic next door. ✉ Jln. Tuanku Abdul Rahman, Box 2396, 93748 Kuching, ☎ 082/248200 or 800/HILTONS, ℻ 082/428984. 322 rooms and 3 floors of suites. 4 restaurants, bar, pool, exercise room, business services, meeting rooms. AE, DC, MC, V.

$$$ 🏨 **Holiday Inn Damai Beach.** Except for the rather primitive accommodations at Santubong Fishing Village or at Santin, this is the only beach resort in Sarawak. Set on 90 acres in a tropical rain forest, it's about 24 km (15 mi) from Kuching on a lovely stretch of beach on the South China Sea. (A shuttle bus connects the two Holiday Inn properties.) Rooms are large and well furnished, with an outdoor feeling created by glass patio doors. The hotel offers water sports, jogging, and jungle treks among its plentiful opportunities for recreation. The word damai means "harmony and peace," but to find it one must walk away from all the activity—though an additional 80 deluxe rooms and 20 suites in the longhouse style have opened on the breezy hill slopes ad-

jacent to the main part of the hotel, and they're quieter and more attractive. ✉ *Box 2870, 93756 Kuching,* ☎ *082/411777 or 800/HOLIDAY (0171/722–7755 in the U.K.),* 𝖥𝖠𝖷 *082/428911. 302 rooms, including suites, studios, and chalets. 3 restaurants, snack bar, pool, sauna, 18-hole golf course, miniature golf, 2 tennis courts, exercise room, squash, sailing, snorkeling, windsurfing, bicycles, dance club, recreation room, business services, meeting rooms. AE, DC, MC, V.*

$$–$$$ 🏨 **Holiday Inn Kuching.** The first international hotel on the river seems to bustle all the time, perhaps because it's next to a major shopping arcade, but also because it receives most of the tour groups that come to Kuching. Arrangements can be made to split one's stay between this Kuching property and the Holiday Inn on Damai Beach. The rooms are compact, with typical Holiday Inn furniture along with the standard amenities. The view of the road is rather depressing, so request a room that looks out over the Sarawak River. A new executive floor has rooms with newer furniture and a shared lounge with a splendid view of the river. ✉ *Jln. Tuanku Abdul Rahman, Box 2362, 93100 Kuching,* ☎ *082/423111 or 800/HOLIDAY (0171/722–7755 in the U.K.),* 𝖥𝖠𝖷 *082/426169. 305 rooms. 2 restaurants, bar, pool, sauna, tennis court, exercise room, dance club , playground, business services. AE, DC, MC, V.*

$$ 🏨 **Aurora.** This well-located Asian hotel is clean and a good value. Its large rooms are cheaply furnished but have air-conditioning, TV, phone, and private bath. ✉ *McDougall Rd., Box 260, Kuching,* ☎ *082/240281,* 𝖥𝖠𝖷 *082/425400. 86 rooms. 2 restaurants, coffee shop. No credit cards.*

$–$$ 🏨 **Hotel Longhouse.** The city-center location does mean some street noise, but the cleanliness and the helpful staff make this place a good budget choice. ✉ *Jln. Abell, Padungan, 93100 Kuching,* ☎ *082/410333,* 𝖥𝖠𝖷 *082/323690. 26 rooms. Coffee shop. MC, V.*

Nightlife and the Arts

The **Holiday Inn Kuching** (☞ Lodging, *above*) has a small cultural show every Monday, Thursday, and Saturday evening at 7:30. A troupe of gong players and pretty female dancers perform a variety of dances from the state's different ethnic groups. (*Also see* Cultural Village and Heritage Center, *above*.)

Outdoor Activities and Sports

BEACHES

Idyllic Damai Beach is about 20 km (12 mi) northwest of Kuching, at the foot of Santubong Mountain. The Holiday Inn Damai Beach (☞ Lodging, *above*) allows non-guests to use its facilities for windsurfing, catamaran sailing, kayaking, and waterskiing.

GOLF

The **Sarawak Golf and Country Club** (☎ 082/23622) at Petra Jaya is open to guests of major hotels. The **Holiday Inn Damai Beach** (☞ Lodging, *above*) has a new 18-hole course.

Shopping

The handicrafts in Sarawak are among the most fascinating in the world. Especially distinctive are the handwoven blankets, or *pua kumbu*, whose intricate tribal designs have ceremonial significance. Baskets, hats, and mats are made from a combination of rattan, palm leaves, and reeds; their designs vary according to the ethnic group. The wood carvings often bear the motif of the hornbill, the national emblem. Pottery designs show a Chinese influence, as do brassware and silver objects.

The **crafts shop** next to the Sarawak Tourist Information Center has a large selection of all kinds of handicrafts, and other shops around the city stock similar goods. ⊠ *Tourist-office complex, Main Bazaar, Kuching, no phone.* ☉ *Daily 10–12 and 3–7.*

A **Sunday market** in the parking lot of Bank Bumiputra on Jalan Satok sells everything from fruit to heirlooms. For antiques, try along Wayang Street, Temple Street, and the Main Bazaar. Bargaining is expected.

Skrang River

❷ *Approximately 100 km (60 mi) east of Kuching.*

Few tourists come this far without making a trip to a tribal longhouse. Some are as close as a 1½-hour drive from Kuching; others involve longer rides and boat trips. You can visit for a day or stay for as long as a week. Either way, your hosts welcome you with a mixture of hospitality and polite indifference.

The Skrang River is a popular destination for longhouse excursions. A car or bus takes you through pepper plantations, run mostly by Chinese families, to the town of Serian, where you board a canoe for a beautiful ride through the jungle on the clear, green river. A longhouse awaits you at the end of the journey.

Despite what some tour operators may seem to suggest, unless you go deep into the forests (a difficult, arduous trek), you'll not be staying in an actual village longhouse, but at very modest bungalow hotels. These accommodations are quite spartan, but guest quarters do usually include mosquito netting, flush toilets, and running water. The attraction is seeing, close at hand, a lifestyle that has changed little in centuries. Tour operators give advice on dress and comportment.

Lodging

$$$$ 🏠 **Batang Ai Longhouse.** One exception to the typically spartan accommodations available on longhouse tours opened in late 1994. This resort, designed on the lines of a traditional Iban timber longhouse, stands on a small island in Batang Ai Lake, surrounded by mountains and rainforest. Guest rooms are comfortably furnished with native woods and have air-conditioning and ceiling fans. Another longhouse contains a large dining room with a terrace overlooking the lake. Evening meals are buffet-style. Batang Ai National Park is close by, and trekking tours and longboat excursions to Iban communities are the main options for daily activities. The resort is a four-hour drive, then a five-minute boat ride, from Kuching; Hilton International will make travel arrangements through a local tour operator. ⊠ *Reservations: Kuching Hilton, Jln. Tuanku Abdul Rahman, Box 2396, 93748 Kuching,* ☎ *082/248200 or 800/HILTONS,* 🖷 *082/428984. 100 rooms. Restaurant, meeting rooms. AE, DC, MC, V.*

Miri

❸ *544 km (340 mi) northeast of Kuching.*

Since 1910, when Shell first discovered oil offshore, Miri has been changing from a sleepy fishing village to a thriving boom town. With several flights daily on MAS out of Kuching and Kota Kinabalu, the city is flourishing as the administrative capital for northeastern Sarawak and as an economic center. With this rapid growth have come some reasonably comfortable hotels, karaoke clubs, and bars for the uncouth. A new Miri Resort Development is promised for the seafront by 1998, with a complex of plush hotels, restaurants, and a marina. In the meantime, the most exotic attraction is the Tamu Muhibbah native market, which sells all sorts of weird produce—from edible stems harvested in the jungles to Kuching laksu noodles swimming in coconut milk and good, old-fashioned monkey stew.

The main reason for coming to Miri is to connect with the bus, from the terminal behind the Park Hotel, either to Batu Niah, the town near the Niah Caves, or to Kuala Belait, the town across the border in Brunei. Miri is also the jumping-off point for river trips up the Baram River and for the longhouses of the Kayan and Kenyah tribes.

Lodging

$$$ ⊞ **Rihga Royal Hotel.** At the edge of the beach and a five-minute walk from the town center, this modern hotel sits on 20 acres of landscaped grounds. Three buildings form a courtyard that fans out to the grounds, the swimming pool, and guest chalets. Rooms in the main buildings and in the chalets are smart, efficient, and functional—in other words, quite boring, but the air-conditioning is individually controlled, and there are coffee- and tea-making facilities in each room. A cascading waterfall is the centerpiece of the atrium lobby, off which is a pub for a convivial chat and a game of darts (the general manager is British). ⊠ *Uyang Lawai, 98998 Miri,* ☎ *085/421121,* ℻ *085/421099. 170 rooms. 3 restaurants, pub, pool, health club, dance club, business services, meeting rooms. AE, DC, MC, V.*

Niah Caves

❹ *·109 km (68 mi) south west of Miri.*

The Niah Caves of Niah National Park are an archaeologist's mecca. The caves were occupied for thousands of years and contain stone, bone, and iron tools; primitive paintings and drawings; and Chinese ceramics. They are still used as a commercial resource by the local people, who gather guano from the cave floors for fertilizer and collect birds' nests from the ceilings for bird's-nest soup—a Chinese delicacy.

Niah National Park is a 40-minute flight from Kuching to Miri and then a bus or M$40 taxi ride from Miri. Adventurous travelers willing to negotiate the long path of 10-inch-wide boards that leads to the caves can explore with a guide. This trip is not for the lazy, but is greatly rewarding. A **hostel** (⊠ National Parks Office, ☎ 085/33361 or 085/36637) in Niah National Park provides simple accommodations.

Sarawak A to Z

Arriving and Departing

BY BOAT
The cruise ship *Muhibah* makes regular runs to the eastern states from Port Kelang and Kuantan in West Malaysia; contact **Feri Malaysia** (⊠ Menara Utama UMBC, Jln. Sultan Sulaiman, 5000 Kuala Lumpur, ☎ 03/238–8899).

BY PLANE
Malaysia Airlines is the primary carrier to Sarawak, although Royal Brunei also flies in to **Kuching International Airport** (☎ 082/454242); this spacious airport is about 11 km (7 mi) south of town, and the unmetered taxis charge M$12 for the trip.

Getting Around

BY BUS
In Kuching, the main terminal is on Mosque Road, where a posted map displays the routes. Among the companies serving the area are Kuching Matang Transport (☎ 082/422814) and Sarawak Transport (☎ 082/242579).

BY CAR

Four-wheel-drive vehicles are recommended for driving in the interior. Drivers can be hired, too. In Kuching, local rental companies have counters at the airport; Avis and Hertz are not represented. Prices are high—at least M$175 a day. Try **Makena Rent-a-Car** (☎ 082/411970).

BY FERRY

In Sarawak, ferries and riverboats are the popular form of transport. At least four ferries a day depart from Kuching for Sibu, where you can transfer onto a riverboat for destinations inland.

BY TAXI

In Kuching, drivers gather in front of the Holiday Inn. Outside these cities, taxis are not plentiful. Hiring a car with driver for three hours to see the main sights costs about M$50. Shared taxis and minibuses congregate near the bus terminals, and boat taxis and chartered launches have kiosks along the waterfront.

Contacts and Resources

EMERGENCIES

Dial 999.

GUIDED TOURS

It takes about three hours to cover Kuching's historic sites, including a drive past the central market and a Malay village, with a stop at the Sarawak Museum. You can take guided nature walks to the orangutan sanctuary, a crocodile farm, or the Bako National Park and Matang area. Tour organizers also arrange backpacking and spelunking excursions into mountain regions, national parks, and ancient caves.

Several travel agencies in Kuching offer a variety of tours throughout the state. You'll find the itineraries and prices comparable at: **Interworld Travel Service** (⊠ 85 Jln. Rambutan, Box 1838, Kuching, ☎ 082/252344), **Sarawak Travel** (⊠ 70 Padungan Rd., ☎ 082/243708), and **Borneo Island Tours** (⊠ Jln. Borneo, ☎ 082/423944). **Borneo Adventure** (⊠ 1st floor, Padungan Arcade, Jln. Song Thian Cheok, ☎ 082/245175) specializes in backpacking tours but has longhouse and hotel-based excursions as well.

VISITOR INFORMATION

MTPB (⊠ AIA Building, 2nd floor, Jln. Song Thian Cheok, Kuching, ☎ 082/246575).

Sarawak Tourist Association (⊠ Main Bazaar, 93000 Kuching, ☎ 082/240620; ⊠ *airport counter,* ☎ *082/456266).*

In Singapore: **Sarawak Tourism Center** (⊠ 268 Orchard Rd., 08–07 Yen San Bldg., 0923, ☎ 736–1602); the staff is not very helpful).

SABAH

Sabah, known as the Land Below the Wind because it lies below the typhoon belt, shares the northern third of the island of Borneo with Sarawak, Malaysia's other eastern state, and with the sultanate of Brunei, which is sandwiched between them. Its primary resource is its vast timber operations, on which fortunes have been built. Though forestry has plundered the coastal areas, much of Sabah is still primary jungle, with majestic tropical forests and abundant wildlife—and a relatively small population. With an area of some 77,700 sq km (30,000 sq mi), the state has about 1 million people, of which the Kadazans are the largest ethnic group. The Bajaus, who live along the west coast, are seafarers; many also farm and raise ponies. Chinese make up about a quarter of the population.

Borneo's forbidding interior made it far less attractive to early traders and explorers than neighboring countries, and so Sabah remained uncolonized by the British until the mid-19th century. In 1963 it was annexed to the independent state of Malaysia. Most Sabahans are Christians, so there is some religious tension between the Islamic state and its citizens. Native languages, arts and crafts, and social customs of Sabah are still retained and, in fact, away from the urban centers, Malay is treated like a second language, the official language to be sure, but not the everyday language used among friends.

Sabah's capital, Kota Kinabalu, is a relatively new town, rebuilt after the Japanese destroyed it during World War II. It contains little to interest the tourist but serves as a jumping-off point and transportation hub for exploring the state. Most travelers to Sabah visit Mt. Kinabalu, the legendary mountain in the primitive interior. This is the highest peak in Southeast Asia, at 13,500 feet. From a national park at its base, climbers can make the ascent in two days. For beachcombers, the seas around Sabah offer a kaleidoscope of marine life: You can snorkel, scuba dive, or putter about the reefs in glass-bottom boats.

Kota Kinabalu

❺ *1,584 km (990 mi) east of Kuala Lumpur.*

The capital, called Jesselton when Sabah was the British crown colony of North Borneo, was razed during World War II, thus its local name Api-Api (meaning "fires"). It was renamed in 1963, when Sabah and Sarawak joined independent Malaysia. Little of historic interest remains—the oldest part of the city is vintage 1950s. The multistory shophouses sell hardware and other practical goods; the upper floors are dwellings. The central market on the waterfront sells produce and handicrafts. Next to the central market is a smaller collection of stalls selling produce from the Philippines.

Kota Kinabalu's main draw is the **Sabah Museum,** on a hilltop off Jalan Penampang about 3 km (2 mi) from the city center. The building resembles a traditional longhouse, and its exhibits are a good introduction to local history, archaeology, botany, and ethnography. One features innumerable varieties of the large ceramic *tajau,* a household jar common throughout Asia. Another displays the many ingenious uses of bamboo, in toys, animal traps, musical instruments, and farm tools. A third gallery is devoted to head-hunting. ⊠ *Bukit Istana Lama,* ☎ *088/53199.* ⊡ *Free.* ☉ *Sat.–Thurs. 9–6.*

Three seas converge at the northern tip of Borneo, and their shores are all easily accessible from Kota Kinabalu. Just offshore are five small and delightful islands that make up the **Tunku Adbul Rahman National Park.** You can make a day trip to picnic and snorkel among the reefs at **Pulau Gaya** and walk the 20 km of trails through the mangrove swamps and tropical forests. The island of **Pulau Sapi** is the most popular for spending the day on the beach and snorkeling its clear waters. **Pulau Mamutik** is a quiet little island with a resthouse that has domitory-style bunk beds. **Pulau Manukan** has a campground, and **Pulau Sulug,** the farthest offshore, is the least visited. Contact the **Sabah Parks Office** (☎ 088/51591) in Kota Kinabalu for information on any of these islands.

Dining and Lodging

$$$ ✕ **Garden Terrace Restaurant.** The Tanjung Aru's open-fronted restaurant, decorated with antique overhead fans and rattan furniture, serves traditional Italian food in a setting made romantic by candlelight and the chirping of tropical creatures in the surrounding gardens. (The resort's casual Garden Room offers delectable seafood and grills.) ⊠ *Tan-*

jung Aru Beach Resort, Jln. Aru, ☏ 088/58711. *Reservations not accepted. AE, DC, MC, V.*

$$$ ✕ **Gardenia Steak and Lobster Bar.** This elegant restaurant has a Western-style menu listing lobster as well as New Zealand lamb with mint sauce. Business travelers and government officials eat here. ⊠ *55 Jln. Gaya,* ☏ *088/54296. Reservations essential during holidays. AE, DC, MC, V.*

$$ ✕ **Nam Hing.** The locals who patronize this Chinese restaurant order the dim sum, but there are also tasty seafood dishes—chili crab, squid, and prawns. The noise and gusto of the clientele provide a lively distraction from the bland decor. ⊠ *32 Jln. Haji Saman,* ☏ *088/51433. No credit cards.*

$ ✕ **Tioman.** Across from the Capitol Theatre, this restaurant features 30 types of noodle dishes, some in soups, some dry, and others fried. Also on the menu are 20 varieties of *congee* (rice porridge) and three delicious creamy dessert puddings—peanut, almond, and sesame. ⊠ *56 Bandaran Berjaya,* ☏ *088/219734. AE, DC, V.*

$$$$ ▥ **Hyatt Kinabalu.** The Hyatt, which appeals especially to business travelers, is anxious to keep its leading position downtown, so there has been considerable refurbishment, and a new extension has been added. Between the hotel and the waterfront is a pool in an Astroturf garden. Rooms are spacious and comfortable; many have views of the port and nearby islands. The top two floors have Regency Club (concierge) rooms. In the evening, a *pasar malam* has hawker food stalls. The 24-hour coffee shop is a magnet for late-night revelers. ⊠ *Jln. Datuk Salleh Sulong, 88994 Kota Kinabalu,* ☏ *088/221234 or 800/223–1234,* ᶠᴬˣ *088/225972. 289 rooms, 26 suites. 3 restaurants, pool, 2 bars, business services. AE, DC, MC, V.*

$$$$ ▥ **Tanjung Aru Beach Hotel.** This premier luxury resort, run by Shangri-
★ La International, is near the airport and 10 minutes from downtown (a bus shuttles guests downtown five times a day). No longer a quiet getaway, it has become a major resort hotel (double its size in 1994) that bustles with activity when it is fully occupied. For all the publicity the place receives, the rooms are rather ordinary, though the wicker furniture gives an airy feel, and each has a private balcony overlooking the hotel's 57 landscaped acres and the sea and islands beyond. The leisure center teaches and arranges windsurfing, scuba diving, waterskiing, sailing, white-water rafting, and glass-bottom boat rides. ⊠ *Locked Bag 174, 88999 Kota Kinabalu,* ☏ *088/225800 or 800/942–5050,* ᶠᴬˣ *088/244871. 500 rooms and suites. 3 restaurants, lounge bar, 2 pools, 9-hole golf course, 4 tennis courts, exercise room, dance club, business services. AE, DC, MC, V.*

$$ ▥ **Hotel Perkasa.** It stands on a hilltop facing Mt. Kinabalu, to which excursions can be arranged. Rooms offer a mountain view as well as heaters—a rarity in the tropics—to warm the brisk mountain air, but that's the extent of the luxury. The hotel is a 2½-hour drive from the airport. ⊠ *W.D.T. 11, 89300 Ranau,* ☏ *088/889511,* ᶠᴬˣ *088/889101. 74 rooms. Restaurant, lounge bar, golf privileges, tennis court, exercise room, business services, travel services. AE, DC, MC, V.*

$ ▥ **Way May Hotel.** In the center of Kota Kinabalu is a Chinese hotel that keeps its small twin-bedded rooms clean and offers friendly service to its guests. For meals, there are plenty of local restaurants a street or two away. ⊠ *36 Jln. Haji Saman, 88000 Kota Kinabalu,* ☏ *088/266118,* ᶠᴬˣ *088/266122. 24 rooms. MC, V.*

Nightlife and the Arts

CULTURAL SHOWS

A year-round opportunity to see Kadazan culture and taste its food is now available at a **folk village** at Karambunai, about 16 km (10 mi) out of Kota Kinabalu via the Tuaran Road. The village opened in 1990, and more native houses are under construction to permit artisans to make and sell their traditional crafts. Cultural shows at the model kampong are presented by the **Kadazan Cultural Association** (☎ 088/ 713696).

The Tanjung Aru Beach Hotel's **Garden Terrace restaurant** (☎ 088/ 58711) has cultural shows every Saturday at 8:30 PM. At the Sunday **market** in Kota Belud, visitors can watch Bajau dancing, pony riding, and cockfights.

DANCE CLUBS

The **Mikado** (✉ Hyatt Hotel lower level, ☎ 088/219888) is a recommended modern nightclub. You may want to try the **Tiffany Disco and Music Theatre** (✉ 9 Jln. Karamunsing, ☎ 088/210645) to see how the locals have a good time.

Outdoor Activities and Sports

BEACHES

The best beaches are on the islands of the **Tuanku Abdul Rahman National Park,** a 15-minute speedboat ride from the pier in downtown Kota Kinabalu. Here serenity and privacy prevail. Pretty coral formations and exotic marine life attract snorkelers and divers. Tour operators will arrange a picnic lunch for an outing. Contact the **Sabah Parks Office** (☎ 088/51591) in Kota Kinabalu for information.

DIVING

Divers will find some of the world's richest reefs off Sipadan Island. **Borneo Divers** (✉ Tuaran Rd., Kota Kinabalu, ☎ 088/53074) arranges diving excursions.

GOLF

Kota Kinabalu has two private golf courses that can be used by visitors who make arrangements in advance through their hotels. The 18-hole course at **Bukit Padang** is run by the Sabah Golf and Country Club. The nine-hole course at **Tanjung Aru** is under the auspices of the Kinabalu Golf Club.

WATER SPORTS

You can snorkel, scuba dive, windsurf, and sail off the beach at **Tanjung Aru,** only a few minutes from Kota Kinabalu, and on small islands accessible through the major hotels.

Shopping

Sabah handicrafts are less elaborate than Sarawak's, but they do have character. In Kota Kinabalu, **Borneo Handicrafts** (✉ Ground floor, Lot 51, Jln. Gaya, ☎ 088/714081; airport outlet, ☎ 088/230707) specializes in local products. A collection of various tribal arts is for sale at **Sabah Handicraft Center** (✉ Ground floor, Lot 49, Bandaran Berjaya, ☎ 088/ 221230).

For a wide assortment of goods in Kota Kinabalu, cruise through **Kompleks Karamunsing,** off Jalan Kolam. You can pick your way through the **Matahari Superstore** (☎ 088/214430) in the Segama district near the Hyatt if you need basic essentials. For jewelry, try **Yun On Goldsmiths** (☎ 088/219369) in the Wisma Merdeka building.

The **night market** in Kota Kinabalu usually sets up about 7 PM in front of the central market. One portable souvenir is mountain-grown Sabah tea.

OFF THE
BEATEN PATH **LABUAN ISLAND –** This tiny island at the mouth of the Brunei River and 8 mi off the coast of Sabah was ceded to the British in 1846 and remained a British protectorate for the next 115 years—except for the three years during which it was occupied by the Japanese. It gained its independence along with Malaysia in 1963, and in 1984 separed from the state of Sabah to become a duty-free port administered by Kuala Lumpur. Except for businessmen with petroleum interests, most visitors come to this Federal Territory on the far northwestern border on their way to Brunei. Morning ferries leave for the six-hour run to Labuan from the waterfront at Kota Kinabalu, or you can take a taxi to Menumbok, via Beaufort, and take the 40-minute ferry across to Labuan. Take a look at the **An'Nur Jamek Mosque**, which at a cost of US$11 million, is an impressive, futuristic piece of architecture and highly unorthodox. Other than that, you may want to hang out at one of the beaches facing the South China Sea or dine at one of the seafood restaurant in **Kampung Ayer,** a water village complex designed to attract visitors to the island.

Mt. Kinabalu National Park

❻ *113 km (68 mi) south of Kota Kinabalu.*

A favorite destination is Mt. Kinabalu National Park, about two hours from Kota Kinabalu. Nature lovers can walk miles of well-marked trails through jungle dense with wild orchids, carnivorous pitcher plants, bamboo, mosses and vines, and unusual geologic formations. The wildlife is shy, but you are likely to see exotic birds and possibly a few orangutans.

★ For some, the main event is scaling **Mt. Kinabalu,** at 13,500 feet the highest mountain in Southeast Asia—and thus a place of spiritual significance for the Kadazan people. Climbers can reach the peak in two days without too much exertion, and the view from the summit on a clear morning is worth every step. Climbers catch their second wind at the overnight rest house at Penar Laban (11,000 feet) before leaving at 2 AM to reach the summit by dawn. Rooms cost about M$28, and bunk beds in the nearby mountain shelters go for M$5; both should be reserved ahead through the Mt. Kinabalu Park Office (☞ *below*). Mountain guides are equipped with mobile telephones, and the park has a helipad.

To reach Mt. Kinabalu, take the minibus departing Kota Kinabalu for Ranau at 8 AM and noon (fare: M$10); it passes the park's entrance. You can stay at the **Kinabalu Lodge** in the park (deluxe room M$300, twin-bedded room M$50, dormitory accommodation M$10). Make reservations, before you arrive, at the **Mt. Kinabalu Park Office** (✉ Ground floor, Lot 3, Block A, Complex Sinsuran, Kota Kinabalu, ☎ 088/211585). Day and overnight tours can be arranged through **Popular Express Travel** (✉ 33 Jln. Tugu, Kampung Air, 88805 Kota Kinabalu, ☎ 088/214692, ℻ 088/225140).

Sandakan

❼ *386 km (241 mi) south of Kota Kinabalu.*

The small coastal trading town of Sandakan, reached by road or air, was completely destroyed by the Japanese in World War II. The town came back to life in the 1970s as center for the logging industry, but that natural resource has been exhausted. Now it is trying to survive as the provincial capital for the southwestern region of Sabah.

For the tourist, the reason to come to Sandakan is the **Sepilok Orang Utan Rehabilitation Center,** a jungle habitat for the near-human primates from Sandakan. Here, illegally captured animals are prepared for a return to the wild. There's no guarantee that you'll see the apes in this vast forest, but there's enough to make the trip worthwhile if you don't—including waterfalls, cool streams for swimming, and other rainforest wildlife. From Sandakan, buses go the 21 km (13 mi) several times a day (for schedules, ☎ 088/215106); you then have to walk 2 km (1.2 mi) from the entrance to the center. ☎ *089/214179 or 089/660811.* ▨ *Free.* ☉ *Daily 9–4.*

Three islands, Selinganm, Bakungan, and Gulian, just to the north of Sandakan, make up a **turtle sanctuary.** Every October and November green and hawksbill turtles come to their shores to nest and lay eggs in the warm sands. These hatcheries are open to the public, though you will need to make arrangements with a tour operator in Sandakan who will organize a boat and, if you wish, an overnight stay at the rest house.

Sabah A to Z

Arriving and Departing
BY BOAT
The cruise ship *Muhibah* makes regular runs to the eastern states from Port Kelang and Kuantan in West Malaysia; contact **Feri Malaysia** (✉ Menara Utama UMBC, Jln. Sultan Sulaiman, 5000 Kuala Lumpur, ☎ 03/238–8899).

BY PLANE
Malaysia Airlines is the primary carrier to Sabah; in addition, Royal Brunei, Philippine Airlines, Singapore Airlines, and Cathay Pacific fly into **Kota Kinabalu International Airport** (☎ 088/54811). A taxi ride from the airport to the city center costs M$13; purchase the taxi voucher from the counter marked TARSI.

Getting Around
BY BUS
Public bus companies serve the cities and the countryside, but poor road conditions make intercity travel rough. Kota Kinabalu's main terminal is in front of the port. **Leun Thung Transport Co.** (☎ 088/762655) goes from the city center to Tanjung Aru. **Tuaran United Co.** (☎ 088/31580) stops at all the villages along the road to Tuaran.

BY CAR
Four-wheel-drive vehicles are recommended for driving in the interior. Drivers can be hired, too. For rentals in Kota Kinabalu, try: **Avis** (☎ 088/56706), **Kinabalu** (☎ 088/23602), or **E&C** (☎ 088/57679).

BY TAXI
Cabs are more expensive here than in peninsular Malaysia, and they are unmetered. Ask at your hotel about the usual fares to various destinations; agree on the price with your driver before setting out. Hiring a car with driver for three hours to see the main sights costs about M$50.

In Kota Kinabalu you can always find a cab near the Hyatt downtown. Outside the city, taxis are not plentiful. Ask the staff at your hotel to call one for you, or inquire in the street about the location of the nearest taxi stand. Summoning cabs by telephone isn't very reliable, but you can try the **taxi company** (☎ 088/51863 or 088/25669) in Kota Kinabalu.

Sabah State Railways (☎ 088/54611) runs a scenic rail line from Kota Kinabalu south to Tenom. The 49-km (31-mi) stretch between Beaufort and Tenom passes through the spectacular Crocker Range and Padas Gorge, takes 1½–2 hours, and costs M$12.20 first class, M$4.25 economy.

Contacts and Resources

EMERGENCIES
Dial 999.

GUIDED TOURS
A Kota Kinabalu city tour covers the highlights in just two hours (note that the mosque and Sabah Museum are closed Friday). A countryside tour stops at Mengkabong, a stilted village of Bajau fisherfolk 30 km (19 mi) out of Kota Kinabalu, driving past rice fields and rural kampongs and the township of Tamparalim, reached by a rope suspension bridge. Other excursions include the Sunday market at Kota Belud, a day trip to Tenom, and the Sepilok Orang Utan Rehabilitation Center.

Tour operators in Kota Kinabalu include: **Api Tours** (✉ Bandaran Berjaya, ☎ 088/221230), **Bakti** (✉ Hyatt Hotel, Jln. Datuk Salleh Sulong, ☎ 088/534426), and **Popular Express Travel** (✉ 33 Jln. Tugu, 88305 Kota Kinabalu, ☎ 088/214692). **Marina** (✉ Tanjung Aru Beach Hotel, ☎ 088/214215) specializes in island trips and water sports. Api and Marina have white-water rafting as well as hiking safaris into the interior, including visits to native villages.

The diving season lasts from mid-February to mid-December; in August and September, the green sea turtles come ashore to lay their eggs. **Borneo Divers** (✉ Bag 194, Kota Kinabalu, ☎ 088/421371) arranges dive excursions to Sipadan and the reefs of Tunku Rahman National Park; the company also offers packages with Malaysia Airlines.

VISITOR INFORMATION
MTPB (✉ Block L, Lot 4, Bangunan STPC, Bandaran Sinsuran, Box 136, 93100 Kota Kinabalu, ☎ 088/211698).

Sabah Tourist Association (✉ Level 1, Kota Kinabalu International Airport, ☎ 088/211484, ext. 335).

MALAYSIA A TO Z

Arriving and Departing

By Plane

AIRPORTS
Sultan Abdul Aziz Shah Airport, commonly called Subang Airport, 26 km (16 mi) southwest of downtown Kuala Lumpur, is currently the main point of entry to Malaysia. The first sections of the brand-new **Kuala Lumpur International Airport** are scheduled to open in January 1998; this large, modern facility, 51 km (32 mi) from downtown, will have updated check-in, baggage-handling, and security procedures; two hotels; and direct rail and bus links into the capital.

CARRIERS
Malaysia Airlines (MAS; ☎ 03/261–0555; U.S. ☎ 800/552–9264), the national carrier, offers a direct flight, with one stop in Tokyo, from Los Angeles to Kuala Lumpur. **Northwest** (☎ 03/238–4355), with its

reliable schedule, is often more convenient for departures originating from the United States. Northwest also offers more flexibility, for example, flying into Kuala Lumpur and out of Singapore.

Among the many other airlines that serve Subang are **British Airways** (☎ 03/242–6177), **Singapore Airlines** (☎ 03/292–3122), and **Thai Airways International** (☎ 03/293–7100). During the day both MAS and Singapore Airlines fly hourly between Kuala Lumpur and Singapore; you can cut the fare in half by buying a standby air-shuttle ticket at the airport.

FLYING TIME
Flight time is 17 hours from Los Angeles, 21 hours from Chicago, and 23 hours from New York.

Getting Around

By Bus
Bus service is extensive and cheap, but only coaches traveling between major cities are air-conditioned. Local buses are usually crowded, noisy, and slow, but it's a great way to people-watch and sightsee at the same time.

By Car
EMERGENCY ASSISTANCE
Car-rental agents in most cities will assist with problems. The **Automobile Association of Malaysia** (✉ Hotel Equatorial, Kuala Lumpur, ☎ 03/261–3713 or 03/261–2727) can also offer advice in case of a roadside emergency.

GASOLINE
Stations charge about M$5.20 per gallon and offer full service. Except for a few 24-hour stations in cities, most places are closed at night.

PARKING
In the cities, on-street parking is plentiful, and meters are closely monitored. Public lots are also available. In some areas of Kuala Lumpur, you are expected to pay young hoodlums to "protect" your car while you are away; if you don't, they may vandalize your car. Locals believe it's worth a few coins for such insurance.

RENTAL AGENCIES
Car rental, for which you are advised to have an international driving license in addition to a valid permit from home, is available in major towns. The largest car-rental operation in Malaysia, **Avis** has offices all over the mainland; the main office is in Kuala Lumpur (✉ 40 Jln. Sultan Ismail, ☎ 03/242–3500). **Budget** (☎ 03/263–7748) has offices in Kuala Lumpur and counters at Subang and Penang airports. **Hertz** (☎ 03/248–6433) has offices in Kuala Lumpur, Penang, and Johore Bahru. **Mayflower** (☎ 03/261–1136) is part of Acme Tours, with a counter at the Ming Court Hotel in Kuala Lumpur. One-way rentals are popular and the surcharge is very modest. **Thrifty,** which often offers the best one-way rates, has offices in Kuala Lumpur (☎ 03/230–2591), Kuantan (☎ 09/528–400), Penang (☎ 04/830–958), and Singapore (☎ 02/272–2211).

RENTAL RATES
Rates run about M$125 a day with unlimited mileage. Inquire about special three-day rates and special weekend rates. These can offer significant rate reductions. One-way rentals are possible for additional drop-off fees.

ROAD CONDITIONS

The only superhighway in the country runs along the western side of the peninsula north–south from the Thai border past Penang, Ipoh, Kuala Lumpur, and Melaka to the causeway to Singapore at Johore Bahru. It is lightly traveled because of the tolls. Other roads, especially near industrial centers, have heavy traffic day and night. Slow-moving trucks, motorcycles, and bicycles make it somewhat treacherous. Back roads are narrow but paved, and the pace is relaxed—you'll weave around dogs sleeping in the road. Mountain roads are often single-lane, and you must allow oncoming cars to pass.

RULES OF THE ROAD

Seat belts are compulsory for drivers and front-seat passengers, and stiff fines are imposed on those caught without them. Driving is on the left side of the road. The police use radar traps frequently and fines are heavy—about M$300 for driving 20 kph over the limit. It is not a good idea to attempt bribery. Some common traffic signs: AWAS(caution), JALAN SEHALA (one way), KURANGKAN LAJU (slow down), and IKUT KIRI (keep left). Directions are *utara* (north), *selatan* (south), *timur* (east), and *barat* (west).

By Ferry

Feri Malaysia (☎ 03/238–8899) operates the cruise ship *Muhibah* between Kuantan (on the east coast of peninsular Malaysia), Singapore, Kuching (Sarawak), and Kota Kinabalu (Sabah). The ship offers air-conditioned cabins and suites, restaurants, a cinema, a disco, a gym, and a swimming pool. In port cities there's regular **ferry service** to the islands. To get to Pangkor, catch the ferry in Lumut; for Langkawi, in Kuala Perlis or Penang. Launches serve Tioman Island from Mersing and Pulau Gaya from Kota Kinabalu.

By Plane

Malaysia Airlines (☎ 03/261–0555) flies to 35 towns and cities in Malaysia. Domestic flights are relatively inexpensive and often fully booked, especially during school holidays and festivals. You must confirm reservations a day or so beforehand.

AIR PASSES

Malaysia Airlines offers a **Discover Malaysia Pass** that enables international visitors to travel on domestic routes for about half the normal fare. You may make flight reservations and purchase tickets overseas or in Malaysia. There is a catch, though. You will be required to show your that your entry into Malaysia will be or is on Malaysian Airlines. Since you probably don't want to fly with them across the Pacific, you can purchase the cheapest international Malaysian Airlines ticket, the flight from Medan (Indonesia) to Kuala Lumpur for $80.

By Taxi

Taxi operators near bus terminals call out destinations for long-distance, shared-cost rides; drivers leave when they get four passengers. Single travelers who want to charter a taxi pay four times the flat rate and leave whenever they want. The quality of service depends on the condition of the vehicle and bravado of the driver. In general, the cost is comparable to that of a second-class train ticket or non-air-conditioned bus fare.

City taxis are plentiful and relatively cheap. Rates in peninsular Malaysia are metered. However, taxi drivers in Kuala Lumpur will attempt not to use the meter and, instead, charge you a fixed, tourist-inflated price. Taxis in Sabah and Sarawak are not metered—set the fare with the driver in advance. Air-conditioned or late-night rides cost 20% more than what's on the meter.

By Train

Malayan Railways, known as KTM, offers cheap and relatively comfortable service on the peninsula. Beginning at Singapore, one branch leads northwest to Butterworth, the Penang station, via Kuala Lumpur; at Butterworth, a connection can be made with the International Express to Bangkok (which runs thrice weekly) or a local train to Hat Yai, Thailand. Another branch leads to Kota Bharu, at the northeast tip of peninsular Malaysia; at Pasir Mas, a trunk line connects KTM with the Thai railway, 23 km (14 mi) to the north. Both express and local service, and both air-conditioned and non-air-conditioned cars, are available. Passengers with tickets for distances over 200 km (124 mi) can stop off at any point on the route for one day per 200 km traveled: *The stationmaster must endorse the ticket immediately upon arrival at the stopoff station.* On long trips movies are shown, but the passing scenery is always more interesting. In some sections the route goes through jungle and you may see wild monkeys. Sleepers are available on overnight service for a supplemental charge. Dining-car food is simple, cheap, and tasty. For information on the rail line in Sabah, *see* Getting Around By Train *in* Sabah A to Z, *above.*

A luxury (and super-expensive) train service, the Eastern & Oriental Express, which is modeled after the Orient Express, makes the 41-hour trip between Singapore and Bangkok with stops in Malaysia at Kuala Lumpur and Butterworth (for Penang). For information in the United States, call ☎ 800/524–2420.

RAIL PASSES

A foreign tourist can buy the KTM Railpass, permitting unlimited travel for 10 days (US$55) or 30 days (US$120), at main railway stations in Malaysia and in Singapore. Passes are reduced for children between 4 and 12 years old and for youths under the age of 30 and who hold the ISIC, YIEE Card, or Youth Hostel Card.

Contacts and Resources

Customs and Duties

Such items as cameras, watches, pens, lighters, cosmetics, perfume, portable radio cassette players, cigarettes (up to 200), and liquor (1 liter) may be brought into Malaysia duty-free. Visitors bringing in dutiable goods, such as video equipment, may have to pay a deposit (up to 50% of the item's value) for temporary importation, which is refundable when they leave. If you have to pay a tax or deposit, be sure to get an official receipt. The importation of illegal drugs into Malaysia carries the death penalty.

Restrictions exist on the export of antiquities. If in doubt about any purchase, check with the director of the Museum Negara in Kuala Lumpur.

Electricity

The electrical current in Malaysia is 220 volts, 50 cycles alternating current (AC). You should bring an adapter and converter, or, if your appliances are dual voltage, just an adapter. Wall outlets take a variety of plug styles, including plugs with two round oversize prongs and plugs with three prongs.

Etiquette and Behavior

Being neatly dressed is respected by the Malays. Furthermore, as a Muslim country, bare skin is frowned upon. Neither women nor men should wear revealing clothes; shorts and sleeveless shirts and dresses will be conspicuous. Entering a mosque, women should wear something, a scarf for example, over their heads.

In Kuala Lumpur, there is an emphasis upon fashion and dressing up for dinner at the more expensive hotels and restaurants. Men do not have to wear a tie (though businessmen may want to during the day and perhaps at dinner). Smart casual is the best guide to dressing.

Health and Safety

As a general rule, food handlers are inspected by health-enforcement officers, but the best advice is to patronize popular places: consumers everywhere tend to boycott stalls with a reputation for poor hygiene.

As elsewhere in Southeast Asia, you should find out whether there are stinging jellyfish in the water before you wade in.

Language

The official language is Bahasa Malaysia, but English is widely spoken in government and business and is the interracial lingua franca. The Chinese speak several dialects, including Cantonese, Teochew, Hakka, and Hokkien. The Indians are primarily Tamil speakers. In the countryside, most people use a kampong version of Malay, even in Sabah and Sarawak, where native languages (Kadazan and Iban) predominate.

Lodging

Bathrooms in the city generally offer Western-style commodes, whereas Asian-style squat facilities are common in rural areas. Better hotels have in-house movies available on color television. The government censors the media, so there is only limited satellite programming, and only a half-dozen hotels are permitted to broadcast CNN.

Inexpensive Chinese hotels abound in Malaysia, though they are often a bit down-at-heel. Rest houses—government bungalows normally rented to officials—are available to tourists at low rates when government officers aren't using them, but they are difficult to book in advance, and you can count on their being full during school holidays. To check their location and availability, write or visit any Malaysian Tourist Promotion Board (MTPB) office (☞ Visitor Information, *below*).

Youth Hostels Association (⊠ Box 2310, 9 Jln. Vethavanam, off 3½-mi Jln. Ipoh, Kuala Lumpur, ☎ 03/660872) operates hostels throughout Malaysia. **Utell International** (☎ 800/44–UTELL in the U.S.) represents more than 30 hotels in Malaysia. For a complete list of accommodations, ask the MTPB for a copy of its hotel list.

Outdoor Activities and Sports

The MTPB produces a number of publications with sports and outdoors information; in particular, ask for the *Golf Handbook* and for the hill resorts booklet, which also discusses area hiking trails.

Mail

POSTAL RATES

Stamps and postal information are generally available at hotel front desks. Postcards cost 50 sen to Europe, 55 sen to the Americas; airmail letters M$1.10 (½ oz). Aerograms are the best value of all, at 50 sen.

RECEIVING MAIL

American Express (⊠ Bangunan MAS, 5th floor, Jln. Sultan Ismail, Kuala Lumpur) will hold mail for 30 days at no charge, as long as you can produce identification and either an American Express card or American Express traveler's checks.

Money and Expenses

Prices in most shops and larger stores are fixed, but you can discreetly ask for a discount. In street markets, flea markets, and antiques stores, bargaining is expected.

CURRENCY
Malaysian ringgit, also called Malaysian dollars, are issued in denominations of M$1, M$5, M$10, M$20, M$50, M$100, M$500, and M$1,000. The ringgit is divided into 100 sen, and there are coins worth 1, 5, 10, 20, and 50 sen and M$1. The exchange rate at press time was M$2.50 to the U.S. dollar, M$1.86 to the Canadian dollar, and M$4 to the pound sterling.

TAXES
A 5% tax is added to hotel and restaurant bills, along with a 10% service charge, in a system that the locals call "plus plus." (You'll see the "++" symbols where this applies.) Airport departure tax varies depending on destination. For domestic flights it's M$5; for flights to Singapore and Brunei, M$10; for other international flights, M$40.

WHAT IT WILL COST
The Malaysian ringgit has gained in value against the United States dollar in recent years, but since prices have remained relatively stable, Westerners get more for their money than they do, for example, in Singapore. As might be expected, prices in the cities are higher than elsewhere, Kuala Lumpur being the most expensive.

Sample Costs: Cup of tea in hotel coffee shop, $2; cup of tea in open-air *kedai*, 70¢; Chinese dim sum breakfast, $5; hotel breakfast buffet, $8; bottle of beer at a bar, $3; bowl of noodles at a stall, $1.50; 1-mile taxi ride, $1; typical bus fare, 25¢; double room, $30 budget, $75 moderate, $150 luxury ($200 in Kuala Lumpur).

National Holidays
The major national public holidays are Chinese New Year; Labor Day, May 1; Hari Raya Puasa, usually mid-May; King's Birthday, June 1; Hari Raya Haji, usually late July; Maal Hijrah, August 14; National Day, August 31; Prophet Muhammad's Birthday, October 23; Deepavali, November 8; and Christmas, December 25. Museums and government offices may be closed on state holidays as well.

Opening and Closing Times
Restaurants normally serve lunch from 11:30 AM to 2:30 PM, dinner from 6:30 to 11. Shops are generally open 9:30 AM–7 PM; department stores and supermarkets, 10–10. Many places are closed Sunday, except in the states of Johor, Kedah, Perlis, Kelantan, and Terengganu, where Friday is the day of rest. Banks are open weekdays 10–3 and Saturday 9:30 to 11:30 AM. Government office hours are Monday–Thursday 8–12:45 and 2–4:15, Friday 8–12:45 and 2:45–4:15, and Saturday 8–12:45.

Passports and Visas
Visas are not required of U.S., Canadian, or U.K citizens staying less than 90 days.

Telephones
To call Malaysia from overseas, dial the country code, 60, and then the area code, omitting the first 0.

DIRECTORY ASSISTANCE AND OPERATOR INFORMATION
For assisted local calls, dial 102; for assisted long-distance within Malaysia, dial 101; for assisted international calls, dial 108. Dial 103 for directory information.

LOCAL CALLS
Public pay phones take 10-sen coins (time unlimited on local calls). Remember to press the release button, which allows your coins to drop

down, when the person you call picks up the receiver. Telephone cards are becoming increasing popular for use at public pay phones.

INTERNATIONAL CALLS

You can direct-dial overseas from many hotel-room phones. If you want to avoid the hotel charges, local phone books give pages of information in English on international calling, rates, and locations of telephone offices.

Public phones using telephone cards are found at strategic locations throughout the country. There are two types of cards: Kadfon, good only for Telekom phone booths, and Unicard, for Uniphone booths. Instructions are displayed in the phone booths. The cards come in denominations of from M$3 to M$50 and can be purchased at airports, Shell and Petronas petrol (gas) stations, and most Seven-Eleven and Hop-In stores.

When calling the States, you can dial the following **access numbers** to reach a U.S. long-distance operator: AT&T (☎ 800–0011); MCI (☎ 800–0012); Sprint (☎ 800–0016). To use AT&T's UKDirect to Britain, dial ☎ 800–0044.

Tipping

Tipping is usually unnecessary, since a 10% service charge is automatically added to most restaurant and hotel bills. You'll know that's the case when you see the ++ symbol on menus and rate cards. Tip porters one ringgit per bag. It would be insulting to tip less than 50 sen. Malaysians usually tip taxi drivers with their coin change. Otherwise, when you want to acknowledge fine service, 10% is generous—not expected.

Visitor Information

For information and brochures, contact the **Malaysia Tourist Promotion Board** (✉ 595 Madison Ave., Suite 1800, New York, NY 10022, ☎ 212/754–1113, 𝕱𝕬𝕏 212/754–1116; ✉ 57 Traflagar Square, London WC2 5DU, ☎ 0171/930–7932). The tourist board also maintains a site on the Web (http://www.InterKnowledge.com/Malaysia).

When to Go

Malaysia's equatorial climate is fairly uniform throughout the year: Temperatures range from the low 90s during the day to low 70s at night. The mountains may be 10° cooler than the lowlands. Relative humidity is usually about 90%. Rain is common all year, but showers don't last long and shouldn't slow you down much. A rainy season brought on by monsoons lasts from November through February on the east coast of peninsular Malaysia, from October through April in Sarawak, and from October through February in Sabah. The heavy rains can cause delays.

During school holidays, locals tend to fill hotels, so book in advance if you plan to visit in early April, early August, or from mid-November to early January.

CLIMATE

The following are average temperatures in Kuala Lumpur:

Jan.	89F	32C	May	91F	33C	Sept.	89F	32C
	72	22		74	23		74	23
Feb.	91F	33C	June	91F	33C	Oct.	89F	32C
	72	22		74	23		74	23
Mar.	91F	33C	July	89F	32C	Nov.	89F	32C
	74	23		72	22		74	23
Apr.	91F	33C	Aug.	89F	32C	Dec.	89F	32C
	74	23		74	23		72	22

Malaysia's multiracial society celebrates numerous festivals, since each ethnic community retains its own customs and traditions. The dates of some holidays are fixed, but most change according to the various religious calendars.

January–February: During **Chinese New Year,** Chinese families visit Buddhist temples, exchange gifts, and hold open house for relatives and friends.

The Hindu festival **Thaipusam** turns out big crowds for a street parade in Penang and a religious spectacle at the Batu Caves near Kuala Lumpur. Indian devotees of the god Subramaniam pierce their bodies, cheeks, and tongues with steel hooks and rods.

Hari Raya Puasa, marks the end of Ramadan, the fasting month. It is a time of feasting and rejoicing and often includes a visit to the cemetery, followed by mosque services. Tourists are welcome at the prime minister's residence in Kuala Lumpur during open-house hours. (Because the Islamic calender follows the lunar cycle, each Gregorian year Ramadan begins roughly 10 days earlier; in the late 1990s, Hari Raya Puasa will fall in January and early February.)

May: The **Kadazan Harvest Festival** is celebrated mid-month in Sabah with feasting, buffalo races, games, and colorful dances in native costumes.

May–June: **Gawai Dayak,** a weeklong harvest festival, is celebrated in Sarawak with dances, games, and feasting in the longhouses.

June: The **Dragon Boat Festival** features boat races off Gurney Drive in Penang early in the month. On June 3 every state marks the **King's Birthday** (Yang Di-Pertuan Agong) with parades. In Kuala Lumpur's Merdeka Stadium, a trooping of the colors is held.

August: Merdeka Day, on the 31st, is Malaysia's Independence Day. Arches are erected across city thoroughfares, buildings are illuminated, parades are arranged, and in Kuala Lumpur there is a variety show in Lake Gardens.

August–September: On **All Soul's Day,** or the Feast of the Hungry Ghosts, Chinese honor their ancestors by burning paper objects (for the ancestors' use in the afterlife) on the street. Chinese opera is performed in various locations in Penang and other cities.

October–November: During **Deepavali,** the Hindu festival of lights that celebrates the triumph of good over evil, houses and shops are brightly decorated.

December: During the **Chingay Procession** in late December, Malaysian Chinese parade through the streets of Penang and Johore Bahru doing stunts with enormous clan flags on bamboo poles, accompanied by cymbals, drums, and gongs. It's a noisy, colorful, folksy pageant. **Christmas** is widely celebrated, with decorations, food promotions, music, and appearances of Father Krismas.

4 Philippines

A feast of islands awaits the traveler in the Philippines. Luzon has historic Metro Manila, with its vibrant nightlife, the breathtaking mountain ranges to the north, and Spanish-era architecture and churches. The Visayas are known for some of the country's best beaches and music-loving inhabitants, while Mindanao has a sizable Muslim population, towering Mt. Apo, and rare flora and fauna. All three regions enjoy translucent seas, tropical beaches, and highlands to trek.

By Luis H.
Francia

THIS ARCHIPELAGO OF 7,107 ISLANDS, extending between Taiwan to the north and Borneo to the south, sometimes seems like a misplaced Latin American country. Indeed, Filipinos are often referred to as the "Latins of the East." While the dominant racial stock is Malay—akin to the indigenous populations of Indonesia, Borneo, and Malaysia—most people's names are Hispanic and their faith Roman Catholic (the Philippines is the only predominantly Catholic nation in Asia). To add to this cultural mix, the government is headed by a democratically elected president and English is widely spoken here, making the Philippines the fourth-largest English-speaking nation in the world, after the United States, the United Kingdom, and India. These features reflect four centuries of Spanish and American colonization. As celebrated Philippine writer Carmen Guerrero Nakpil put it, the Philippines spent more than 300 years in a convent and 50 in Hollywood.

Historically, this cultural potpourri began around the 10th century, when the native Malays intermarried with Arab, Indian, and Chinese merchants who came to trade. Then, in 1521, Ferdinand Magellan—a Portuguese navigator in the service of the Spanish throne, heading the first expedition to circumnavigate the world—landed on the island of Homonhon, off the coast of Samar, and claimed the country for Spain. The intrepid Magellan moved on to Cebu (then known as Zubu and, as now, an important trading port) and was killed shortly thereafter by Lapu-Lapu, a native chieftain. Spanish rule was uneasy, periodically interrupted by regional revolts that culminated in 1896 in a nationwide revolution, the first of its kind in Asia. Nationalist aspirations were aborted, however, when the United States, after defeating Spain in the Spanish-American War, took over in 1898—but not without the ensuing bitter, five-year Philippine-American War, a conflict characterized by guerrilla tactics on the part of the underarmed Philippine soldiers.

American rule, interrupted by Japanese occupation during World War II, finally came to an end on July 4, 1946, when Manuel Roxas took over as the first postcolonial president. Except during the dictatorial rule of Ferdinand Marcos from 1972 until 1986 (when he was ousted by the bloodless four-day "People Power" revolution), the government has since been a democratically elected one. The new constitution adopted in 1987 under President Corazon Aquino limits presidential tenure to one term of six years. Elections in 1992 to determine her successor resulted in former general Fidel V. Ramos's winning the presidency. National presidential elections will be held again in 1998.

After more than two decades of unrest, a nationwide Communist insurgency—with its roots in agrarian and social injustice—has been on the decline, with ongoing peace talks between rebel leaders and the government. The same is true of a Muslim secessionist movement in southern Mindanao, though a small radical splinter group has engaged the Philippine military sporadically. The military itself, after several coup attempts in the late '80s, has adjusted to civilian leadership.

Because of its colonial history and its people's innate warmth, the Philippines today is a country open to strangers and tolerant of cultural idiosyncrasies. Filipinos are a gregarious, fun-loving people whose hospitality is legendary. ("No" is a word frowned upon; a Filipino will find countless ways to decline a request without sounding negative, smoothing over a potentially disruptive moment. Westerners should be aware that insistent straightforwardness is not necessarily prized and can be counterproductive.) Filipinos love to joke and tease and have

The Philippines

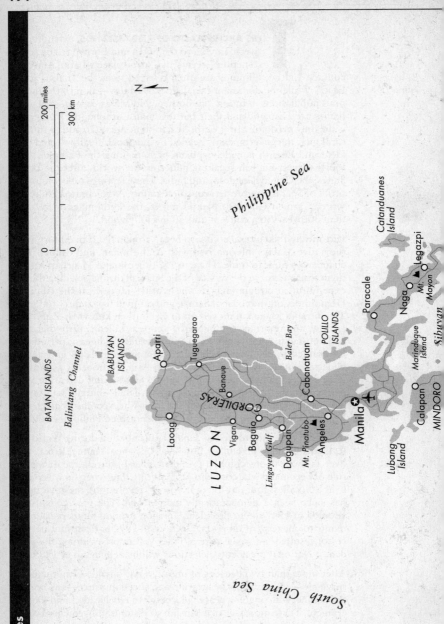

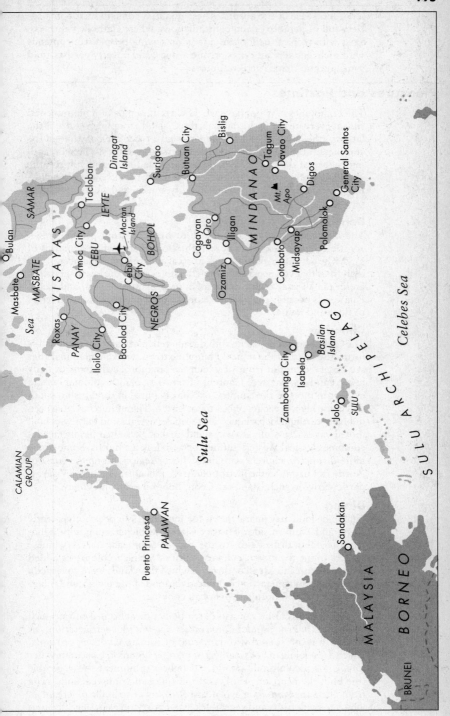

a natural sense of the absurd. These qualities come in handy in a society full of paradoxes and contradictions, where Catholic values coexist with tropical hedonism; a freedom-loving people still contends with such feudal practices as private armies; and poverty persists amid sunshine and rich natural resources.

Pleasures and Pastimes

The Philippines may not have world-class museums or a monumental ruin at every turn, but the nation's three island groupings—Luzon (the largest), the Visayas, and Mindanao—have twice the coastline of the continental United States and offer diverse attractions. The outstanding beauty of the land, the many picturesque towns and villages, the abundance of uncrowded islands and beaches, the excellent dining (especially on seafood), and the hospitality, music, and gaiety of its people more than satisfy most visitors.

Beaches

The Philippines has an abundance of beaches, from pebble-strewn coastlines and black volcanic stretches to brilliant white expanses of sand. The advantage of being on a tropical archipelago (remember, 7,100 islands!) is that you're never far from the sea. Some of the loveliest beaches are in the Visayas region, such as Boracay, Panay, Bohol, and Cebu. Palawan is possibly the least developed island and the wildest in terms of flora and fauna.

Churches

The Catholic church—along with the adjacent plaza and the town hall—forms the heart of the typical Philippine town, where communal rites are observed and in front of which the languorous rhythms of daily living can be witnessed. Churches from the Spanish colonial era are evident in most of the country, except of course in the Muslim south and in the higher reaches of Northern Luzon. These churches have been dubbed "earthquake baroque" for the massive walls and buttresses built (not always successfully) to withstand earthquakes; their ornate facades combine classical Western influences with folk art motifs. Some of the more distinctive churches are in the Ilocos region (along the coast of Northern Luzon), in the metropolitan Manila area, and in the Visayas, particularly on such islands as Cebu, Bohol, Leyte, and Panay.

Dining

Philippine food may puzzle the visitor, including as it does both patently Asian and Western sides. History is responsible: starting with a matrix of Malay dishes akin to the rest of Southeast Asia's, Chinese traders input their own culinary culture, Spanish colonizers added those of Spain and Mexico (through which the islands were governed), Indian and Arab interaction influenced the food of Mindanao, and American colonization brought American cooking.

The indigenous cuisine consists of seafood or meat broiled and steamed in vinegar (*paksiw* or *adobo,* for preserving without refrigeration), or stewed in broth soured with tamarind or tomato (*sinigang* or *tinola,* which are cooling in hot weather) or in other liquids like coconut water (*pinais*) or coconut milk (*laing*). Coconut is prominent—as vegetable (the bud, the heart of palm), as drink (juice of young coconut, *tuba* from the sap, *lambanog* when distilled), as coco milk or cream in which to cook fruits and vegetables (*ginataan*), and as flesh grated into desserts and sweets.

Rice is the staple, a shaper of other tastes. Ground into flour, it is transformed into myriad varieties of cake for snacks and festive occasions. One such is *bibingka,* baked in a clay oven with charcoal above and below and topped with freshly grated coconut, salted duck's egg, and slices of white cheese; another is leaf-wrapped *suman,* sticky rice cooked with coconut milk and eaten with ripe mangoes.

The Chinese connection is apparent in such foods as vegetable- or pork-filled *lumpia* (spring rolls), and especially in *pansit,* noodles (rice, mung bean, wheat, fresh or dried, fat or thin) sautéed with vegetables, pork, sausages, or seafood—the ingredients used differ from region to region.

Spanish dishes are the stuff of fiestas: *lechon,* spit-roasted suckling pig; chicken *relleno* stuffed with pork, sausage, and spices; *paella* rich with crabs, prawns, sausage, ham, and clams; *pochero,* a beef stew given local character with a vegetable relish; *callos* (tripe) with chickpeas and pimentos; *caldereta,* goat or beef stew with olive oil, bell peppers, and olives.

The American regime, which began in 1898, brought in convenience (sandwiches and salads), quick cooking (fried chicken, hamburgers), and a new food culture. The East-West range is therefore wide, but made more Philippine through time by local ingredients, dipping sauces (*patis* and *bagoong, calamansi* and chilies, vinegar, and garlic), cooking styles, and general fine-tuning.

In a nation whose 7,100-plus islands are home to some 90 ethno-linguistic groups, there are, of course, regional variations. The food of the Bicol people is chili-hot; so is that of some Muslims, like the Maranaws, whose food has a kinship with Indonesian cooking. Keep an eye out for the Bicol *pinangat* (shrimp or pork wrapped in taro leaves, cooked with coco cream and ginger, and chili-embellished) or the Maranaw catfish (cooked with turmeric, coco milk, and chilis).

The Ilocano north favors vegetable stews flavored with the salty shrimp or fish sauce called *bagoong,* often with the bitter-sweetness of *ampalaya* (bitter melon). Try *pinakbet,* which has become the pan-Philippine vegetable dish. Leyte and Samar have many dishes cooked in coconut milk (like chicken with ginger, or prawns). Tagalog dishes lean toward a controlled sourness, as in beef, pork, or chicken *sinigang.* Pampango food is one of the richest regional cuisines, including a plethora of sweets and such exotica as stuffed frogs (*betute*).

Almost all of these regional cooking styles—and most international cuisines—can be sampled in Metro Manila restaurants, as well as in food malls, markets with *turo-turo* ("point-point" arrays to choose from), and street stalls. But venturing into the provinces is the way to get a real taste of the Philippines.

Price categories throughout the chapter are based on the following ranges:

CATEGORY	COST*
$$$$	over P525 (US$20)
$$$	P250–P525 (US$10–US$20)
$$	P150–P250 (US$6–US$10)
$	under P160 (US$6)

per person for a three-course dinner, excluding tax, service, and drinks.

Lodging

Major urban areas, such as Manila, Cebu, Baguio, and Davao, have lodgings for every type of traveler, from the hedonist with deep pockets to the backpacker who must count pennies. Large towns usually feature a couple of reasonably priced, comfortable hotels and lower-scale inns and pensions. In the more rustic areas, accommodations tend, not surprisingly, towards the basic, though popular beach areas will have resorts which range from pricey air-conditioned cabanas to inexpensive cottages. The other cities offer mostly family-run hotels, sometimes short on amenities but generally well maintained and clean, with the staff invariably courteous and helpful.

For the more expensive hotels and beach resorts, it would be a good idea to make reservations during the peak season, coinciding with the cold season in the West, from November to February.

Price categories throughout the chapter are based on the following ranges:

CATEGORY	COST*
$$$$	over P5,600 (US$220)
$$$	P2,600–P5,600 (US$100–US$220)
$$	P1,500–P2,600 (US$60–US$100)
$	under P1,500 (US$60)

for a standard double room in high season, excluding 10% service charge and 13.7% tax.

Mountain Climbing

Mt. Pulog in the Cordilleras, Mt. Mayon in southern Luzon, Mt. Kanlaon on Negros Island, Mt. Hibok-Hibok on Camiguin Island, and Mt. Apo in Mindanao are all have known trails and experienced local guides who can be hired for mountain climbing and trekking.

Shopping

The Philippines can yield great bargains if you know what to look for and where. There are handicraft stores all over the country, usually near the public market in small- to medium-size cities and towns and in shopping centers in such large urban areas as Manila, Cebu, and Baguio. Because Manila is the commercial capital of the country, regional goods are available there, though prices are not usually advantageous. Focus on handicrafts special to the region you're visiting. For example, look for handwoven rattan baskets and backpacks from northern Luzon; handwoven cloth from northern Luzon, Iloilo City, and southern Mindanao; shellcraft from Cebu City and Zamboanga City; handwoven pandan mats with geometric designs from Zamboanga City and Davao City; brassware from southern Mindanao; bamboo furniture from central Luzon; gold and silver jewelry from Baguio City and Bulacan province; and cigars from Baguio City and the Ilocos region.

Bargaining is an accepted and potentially profitable way of shopping in public markets, flea markets, and small, owner-run stores. Department stores and big shopping areas have fixed prices.

Snorkeling, Scuba Diving, and Surfing

The tropical waters are ideal for a variety of water sports, from snorkeling to waterskiing. A number of resorts in different regions offer equipment and facilities.

The country has some of the best dive sites in the world, with more than 40 known spots, most concentrated around Palawan, the Visayas, and Batangas Province. Many more wait to be discovered. Most resorts rent out snorkeling equipment; the tonier ones have scuba gear as well.

Surfers have discovered the Philippines, though there are still only a handful of surf centers. Most are on the island of Catanduanes off southern Luzon, on the Pacific coast.

Exploring the Philippines

Great Itineraries

To begin to truly appreciate what the country has to offer, you will need at least two weeks, given the variety of attractions and their diverse locations. If you have less time, however, here are some suggested itineraries.

IF YOU HAVE 3 DAYS

Your best bet is to explore **Metro Manila,** with an all-day trip to Pagsanjan Falls, a two-hour drive from the city. In the city, two days should be sufficient to visit such sights as Intramuros, Malacañang, the Coconut Palace, Rizal Park, and such colorful neighborhoods as Binondo, Quiapo, and the tourist districts of Ermita and Malate.

IF YOU HAVE 7 DAYS

Follow the three-day itinerary above, then either join a tour or proceed on your own to the Cordilleras in Northern Luzon. Plan on an overnight stay in **Banaue** to visit the magnificent rice terraces, built more than two millenia ago. From Banaue, proceed to **Baguio** and spend a few days; nearby is **Sagada,** a picturesque town with unique limestone formations and burial caves.

IF YOU HAVE 10 DAYS

Spend two days in **Metro Manila,** then head north to the rice terraces in **Banaue** and to **Baguio.** On the fifth day, fly back to Manila and take a connecting flight to **Cebu.** Two days in the "Queen City of the South" should suffice to see the city's sights and to spend a day lazing about on a beach on nearby Mactan Island. The last two days could be spent either in **Zamboanga City,** on the western coast of Mindanao, or **Davao City,** on the eastern coast. Both cities have their own sights, Muslim communities, indigenous tribes, and beach resorts. Zamboanga is an older city, the southernmost bastion of Spanish rule in the archipelago, while Davao City is a boom town, the site of huge agribusiness and trading concerns.

When to Tour the Philippines

The country has two distinct seasons: dry and wet. Weather-wise the ideal time to visit is from mid-October to February (the peak tourist season being from late November to February), right after the monsoon rains and before the start of the scorchingly hot period of March to May. Besides having perfect beach weather, the hot months do coincide with the Lenten season, when reenactments of Christ's Passion take place in towns and cities and flaggelants, whipping themselves into a bloodied frenzy, stagger through the streets, particularly in Central Luzon. There are fiestas every month, but May is traditional fiesta time, when every town in the country seems to have some kind of celebration. If you happen to be in the Philippines in the rainy season, from June to mid-October, be sure to pack a raincoat and waterproof shoes; the monsoon season generally does not affect Mindanao. (*Also see* When to Go *in* Philippines A to Z, *below.*)

METRO MANILA

The urban sprawl that is metropolitan Manila (made up of the cities of Manila, Makati, Pasay, Quezon, Caloocan, plus 13 towns) is a fascinating, even surreal, combination of modernity and tradition. In Manila's streets you'll see horse-drawn *calesas* (carriages) alongside sleek Mercedes-Benzes, Japanese sedans, passenger buses, and the ubiquitous passenger jeepneys—once upon a time, converted World War II Jeeps but now manufactured locally.

Built by the Spanish conquistadors in 1571 as Intramuros, a fortified settlement on the ashes of a Malay town, Manila spread outward over the centuries, so that the oldest districts are those closest to Intramuros. Yet very few buildings attest to the city's antiquity, since it suffered extensive destruction during World War II, the most except for Warsaw, Hiroshima, and Nagasaki. Among the older districts are the bay-front Ermita and Malate, which make up the Tourist Belt, so-called because of their central location and density of hotels, clubs, restaurants, boutiques, and coffee shops. At the upper end of the scale is Makati, the country's financial center, with its wide, well-kept boulevards, high-rise apartment and office buildings, ultramodern shopping centers, and well-guarded walled enclaves of the fabulously rich.

Like most other Third World cities, however, Metro Manila also has its share of congestion, pollution, haphazard planning, and poverty. The large slum of Tondo is dominated by a huge pile of garbage known as "Smoky Mountain" for the endless burning of trash fires. Here the poor live in cardboard shanties and scavenge for a living.

But for all the city's stark contradictions, the 10 million inhabitants of the "noble and ever loyal city"—as Manila was described by its Spanish overlords—have a joie de vivre that transcends their day-to-day battles for survival. The fortuitous blend of Latin and Southeast Asian temperaments makes for an easygoing atmosphere, where fun is as important as business. Manilans bear their burdens with humor and a casual grace. If, like New Yorkers, they love to complain about their considerable hardships, it doesn't prevent them from crowding the city's myriad restaurants, bars, and clubs. The nightlife here may well be Southeast Asia's liveliest, certainly comparable to Bangkok's. Manila has discotheques, coffeehouses, nightclubs, massage parlors, topless bars, music lounges, and beer gardens. Certainly its bands—rock, Latin, or jazz—have the reputation for being the finest in Southeast Asia. Enjoy the city's mixture of the terrible and marvelous, for it is a microcosm of Philippine society.

Exploring Metro Manila

Metropolitan Manila is roughly a crescent in shape, with Manila Bay and the scenic Roxas Boulevard, which runs along it, forming the western boundary. Forming the eastern border is the Epifanio de los Santos Highway (EDSA). The Pasig River bisects the city into north and south, with the oldest districts, including the ancient walled city of Intramuros, near where the river empties into Manila Bay.

Intramuros

Manila's ancient walled city, built by the Spaniards in the 16th century, is a compact 7.5 square km (3 square mi). Within this small area, churches, schools, convents, offices, and residences were constructed— the latter reserved for the Spanish and Spanish mestizos only. In its heyday Intramuros must have presented a magnificent sight to visiting galleons, what with its seven drawbridges and encircling moat. The moat, filled in by the Americans to prevent the spread of disease, is now used as a golf course, but the 30-foot-thick walls are still formidable, with cannon emplacements and a strategic location facing the bay.

Numbers in the text correspond to numbers in the margin and on the Intramuros map.

A GOOD WALK

Fort Santiago ①, off Aduana Street, is where the Spanish placed their first settlement and where you should begin your explorations. Diagonally across from the fort is **Manila Cathedral** ②. Walking along General Luna Street, bordering the cathedral, you will come to **San Agustin Church** ③. Across the street is the Barrio San Luis Complex, which includes **Casa Manila** ④. General Luna ends at one of Intramuros's fortified gates, Puerta Real, which has a display of antique church silver.

Bearing left onto Muralla Road, note the famed (if largely reconstructed) walls—gray, stately, and radiating a feeling of invincibility. You will pass lookout towers and other fortifications. Muralla winds around in a semicircle, bringing you to Puerta Isabel. This gate houses a fascinating display of baroque floats bearing statues of saints.

TIMING

It's best to explore the Walled City in the early morning, when the heat isn't so fierce. Exploring Intramuros on foot should take about half a day—longer if you take your time—or you can rent a *caretela* (a horse-drawn cart that can carry several persons) on the grounds for about P300.

SIGHTS TO SEE

❹ **Casa Manila.** The main attraction of the **Barrio San Luis Complex** is not the shops but this splendid re-creation of a 19th-century Spanish patrician's three-story domicile, complete with carriage entrance, inner courtyard, and grand stairway. ✉ *Gen. Luna St., across from San Agustin Church,* ☎ *2/496–793 or 2/483–275.* ⌨ *Admission.* ☉ *Daily 9–6.*

❶ **Fort Santiago.** This stone fort overlooking the mouth of the Pasig River is on the site where the original Malay Muslim settlement stood. Previously used by the Spanish, Americans, and Japanese, it is now a pleasant park with an open-air theater where plays in Pilipino (the national tongue) are staged among the ruins. The fort has a grim history: Philippine revolutionaries (including the national hero José Rizal) were imprisoned here by the Spanish; they often drowned in the dungeons, which were below the high-tide level. ⌨ *Admission.* ☉ *Daily 8 AM–9 PM.*

❷ **Manila Cathedral.** Dedicated to the Immaculate Conception of the Virgin Mary, this Romanesque edifice (a reconstruction of the original 1600 structure) has three arched doorways that form an imposing facade. The middle door is made of bronze, with eight panels portraying the cathedral's history. Inside, the clerestory's stained-glass windows depict the history of Christianity in the Philippines. Underneath the main altar is a crypt where the remains of the former archbishops are entombed. Fronting the church is **Plaza Roma**, where bullfights were once staged. Its centerpiece is a monument to three Philippine priests executed in 1872 for their nationalism. ✉ *General Luna and Postigo Sts.* ☉ *Mon.–Sat. 6–5, Sun. 6–6.*

★ ❸ **San Agustin Church.** The second-oldest stone church in the country has 14 side-chapels and a trompe l'oeil ceiling. Up in the choir loft, note the hand-carved 17th-century seats of molave, a beautiful tropical hardwood. Adjacent to the church is a small **museum** run by the Augustinian order, featuring antique vestments and religious paintings and icons. ✉ *Gen. Luna and Real Sts.* ⌨ *Admission to museum.* ☉ *Church, daily 7–7:30 AM and 5–6 PM; museum, daily 9–12 and 1–5.*

North of the Pasig River

This is a poorer and more crowded part of the city, but it also has an older, more historic feel. The streets are narrower, with a mix of small businesses and residential buildings. Manilans say a foreigner should come here to get a true feel for down-home Philippine neighborhoods.

Numbers in the margin correspond to numbers on the Manila map.

SIGHTS TO SEE

Binondo. Forbidden by the Spanish from living in Intramuros, Chinese merchants and their families settled north of the Pasig River, and a sizable community—now known as Binondo—grew up here in the 18th century. Bounded by the river, Claro M. Recto Avenue, Del Pan Street, and Avenida Rizal, Manila's Chinatown is a jumble of narrow streets packed with jewelry shops, sporting-goods and clothing stores, apothe-

202

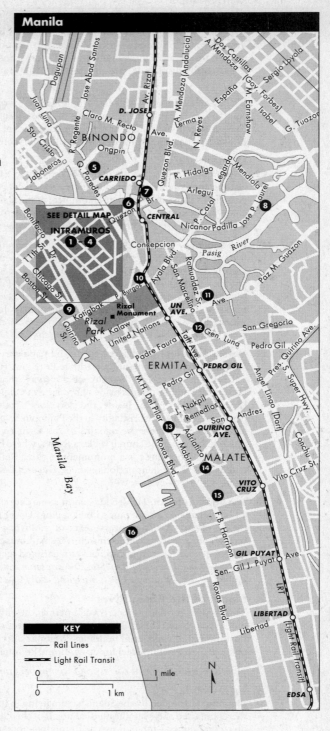

Casa Manila, **4**

Fort
Santiago, **1**

Manila
Cathedral, **2**

San Agustin
Church, **3**

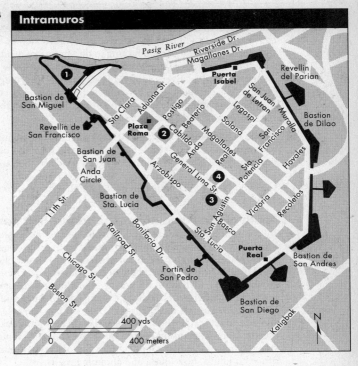

caries, kung-fu schools, movie houses showing Hong Kong flicks, magazine stalls, seedy hotels, brothels, and restaurants that usually offer Amoy and Fukienese cuisine. Stroll about, especially on Ongpin, the main street, or stop a calesa and have the driver take you around.

⑤ Binondo Church. This 16th-century church still has its original stone walls and is worth visiting. Note the replica of St. Peter's dome at the main altar and the Madonna encased in glass. The first Philippine saint, Lorenzo Ruiz, started here as an altar boy. ⊠ *Paredes St. at Plaza Calderon de la Barca.* ☉ *Daily 6 AM–7 PM.*

★ ⑧ Malacañang Palace. Once the seat of the colonial Spanish and American governor-generals, this palace is the official residence of Philippine presidents and is sometimes referred to as the Philippine White House. During her term, Corazon Aquino preferred to live in the guest house, a symbolic gesture meant to disassociate her from the dictatorial Ferdinand Marcos. Now open to the public, Malacañang's colonial Spanish architecture and interior decor are worth a look, especially the three chandeliers in the reception hall, the beautiful hardwoods used for the grand staircase, the portraits of former presidents, and the exquisite music room. The Marcoses' personal effects, which included Ferdinand's dialysis machine and Imelda's infamous hoard of shoes and bulletproof bra, have been replaced by selected memorabilia of past presidents. ⊠ *J.P. Laurel St.,* ☎ *2/427–131.* ▣ *Admission.* ☉ *Tues.–Thurs., guided tours only, 9–3:30; Fri.–Sat., general viewing, 9–3.*

★ ⑦ Quiapo Church. East of Binondo, not far from the foot of Quezon Bridge and facing **Plaza Miranda**—the local equivalent of Hyde Park, where orators of varying skills and persuasions harangue passersby—is this 16th century church, later enlarged. Its crowded environs are as close to an authentic Philippine neighborhood as you can get in Manila. On the side streets are vendors from whom you can buy amulets or herbal cures for a wide variety of ailments. The church is home to the famed **Black Nazarene,** a dark statue of Jesus of Nazareth made by a Mexican craftsman and brought via galleon from Mexico in the 18th century. Its devotees claim that praying to the statue can produce miracles. It isn't unusual to see supplicants crawling on their knees from the entrance to the altar. Every January 9, as part of the Quiapo Fiesta, the Nazarene is paraded, with bare-chested male devotees competing for the honor of pulling the float through the district's narrow streets. ⊠ *Plaza Miranda and Quezon Blvd.* ◷ *Daily 6 AM–7 PM.*

⑥ **Quinta Public Market.** Bargain-priced handicrafts, from handwoven mats to rattan baskets and straw brooms, are the specialty of this market near Quiapo Church. You can also get a snack or light meal of native dishes. Be mindful of your wallet or bag, and be especially wary of persons wanting to buy your dollars. ⊠ *Below Quezon Bridge.* ◷ *Daily 5 AM–8 PM.*

South of the Pasig River: The Tourist Belt and Around

By using Roxas Boulevard and Taft Avenue as the western and eastern limits, respectively, and Intramuros and Pablo Ocampo Senior Street as the north and south parameters, a visitor should get a pretty good idea of Ermita and Malate, or the Tourist Belt. On the boulevard are nightclubs, the Cultural Center of the Philippines complex, hotels, restaurants, apartment buildings, the huge Rizal Park, and Intramuros. On Taft Avenue are the Light Rail Transit, universities, shops, retail stores, and several hospitals. In between are bars and cocktail lounges, the infamous go-go joints (especially on M.H. Del Pilar and A. Mabini streets), massage parlors, coffeehouses, more restaurants and hotels, office buildings, boutiques, and shopping malls.

SIGHTS TO SEE

⑮ **Central Bank Money Museum.** A fascinating collection of currency specimens from all over the world is on display here. The Philippine segment is understandably the most complete. ⊠ *Roxas Blvd. at Pablo Ocampo Senior St.,* ☎ *2/507–051.* ⊡ *Admission.* ◷ *Tues.–Sun. 9–6.*

★ ⑯ **Coconut Palace.** South of Malate on Roxas Boulevard is this $10 million project of former first lady Imelda Marcos, so named because more than 70% of the construction materials were derived from the coconut tree. The grandiose structure, located within the Cultural Center Complex, faces Manila Bay and was constructed for Pope John Paul's visit in 1981 (he refused to stay here). Each of the seven (the Marcoses' lucky number) palatial suites is named and styled after a different region of the country. The Ilocos Room, for instance, has chairs with mother-of-pearl inlay and a coffee table laminated with tobacco leaves, while the Zamboanga Room features brassware and handwoven mats. Many of the bathroom fixtures are 24-karat gold. Several of Imelda's jet-set friends stayed here at one time or another, among them Van Cliburn and Brooke Shields. ⊠ *Cultural Center Complex,* ☎ *2/832–1125.* ⊡ *Admission.* ◷ *Tues.–Sun. 9–11:30 and 1–4:30.*

⑬ **Malate Church.** Photographers love to shoot the picturesque, well-kept facade of this gray stone church, an intriguing mixture of Romanesque and Baroque styles. Its interior, however, is unremarkable. Between the church and Roxas Boulevard is **Rajah Sulayman Park,** the centerpiece of which is a statue of Rajah Sulayman, a pre-Spanish (16th-century) ruler of Manila. ⊠ *Corner of Remedios and M.H. Del Pilar Sts.* ◷ *Mon.–Sat. 5:30–noon and 3–7, Sun. 5:30 AM–8 PM.*

NEED A
BREAK? Around Malate Church are innumerable places for lunch or a snack. You can walk eastward—i.e., away from the bay— on Remedios Street, and choose from several cafés around Remedios Circle. Besides the cafés listed in Nightlife and the Arts, *below,* try the 24-hour **Aristocrat** (⊠ Roxas Blvd. at San Andres St., ☎ 2/507671), a favorite with everyone from gangsters to businesspeople; prices are reasonable and the food is decent.

❾ Manila Hotel. On the edge of Rizal Park and a short stroll from the Rizal Monument is the doyen of Philippine hotels, built in 1912. This is where General Douglas MacArthur lived during much of his time in the Philippines; Ernest Hemingway also stayed here once. The lobby is spacious without making you feel lost, and gracious in that Old World style. Note the ceiling and woodwork, made entirely of precious Philippine hardwoods, the floors of Philippine marble, and the mother-of-pearl and brass chandeliers. ⊠ *Rizal Park at Bonifacio Dr.* ☎ *2/527–0011.*

NEED A
BREAK? Manila Hotel has an airy, pleasant poolside coffee shop, **Café Ylang-Ylang** (☎ 2/527–0011). The menu is quite good, offering local and Continental cuisine and sumptuous desserts. In the afternoons the café has a mouthwatering dessert buffet that the sweet of tooth will find irresistible.

🐾 ⑭ Manila Zoo. This small zoo in the Tourist Belt has the usual assortment of wild animals, including such local species as the tamaraw (a peculiar water buffalo), the rare mouse deer (the smallest deer in the world), and the Palawan pheasant. ⊠ *Quirino Ave. at Adriatico St.;* ☎ *2/586–216.* 🔳 *Admission.* 🕑 *Daily 7–6.*

❿ National Museum. Once the site of Congress, this building now houses varied displays, ranging from archaeological treasures to paintings, including an impressive array of the 19th-century artist Juan Luna's works. ⊠ *Rizal Park at Padre Burgos St.,* ☎ *2/494–450.* 🔳 *Admission.* 🕑 *Mon.–Sat. 9–noon and 1–5.*

⑫ Paco Park. On the south side of the Pasig River, this petite but beautiful circular park of moss-covered stone—with a picturesque chapel in the middle that's a favorite site for weddings—was a cemetery until it was declared a national park in 1966. Its two concentric walls served as burial niches for the Spanish elite. No burials have been performed here since 1912. Free concerts are offered on Friday at 6 PM. ⊠ *San Marcelino and General Luna Sts.,* ☎ *2/502–011 or 2/590–956.* 🔳 *Admission.* 🕑 *Daily 8–5.*

Rizal Park. Stretching from Taft Avenue toward the bay is a 128-acre oasis where Manilans can jog, do Tai Chi, stroll through the **Chinese Garden** (🔳 Admission), a pleasant arboretum, or just lie on the grass. The park is named after José Rizal, a national hero who was, among other things, a doctor, linguist, botanist, novelist, poet, educator, and fencer. Executed in 1896 by the Spanish because of his reformist views, he was originally buried at Paco Park but now lies under the **Rizal Monument,** designed by Swiss artist Richard Kissling and erected in 1912. Nearby, towering above the statue, is a stately 50-foot obelisk marking the spot where three local 19th-century priests were garroted by the Spanish for their nationalist views. The 24-hour guards, like honor guards everywhere, try to be as impassive as possible. Rizal's poem *Mi Ultimo Adios,* composed just before his death, is inscribed on a bronze slab set into a nearby octagonal wall; in addition to the original Spanish, it appears in English and several other languages.

The young and young-at-heart may enjoy a **Matorco ride,** a scenic drive along Manila Bay in open-air, double-decker buses that depart from and return to the Rizal Monument; buses run 6 AM–10 PM.

⑪ **Tabacalera Factory.** The full, rather grandiloquent name of this company is La Flor de Isabela, Companía General de Tabacos de Filipinas (Flower of Isabela, General Company of Philippine Tobacco). Founded during the Spanish colonial era, it has a well-deserved reputation for fine cigars. The factory offers free tours (call in advance) on which visitors can observe the time-honored process of cigar-making; cigars and humidors can be purchased and even personalized. ⊠ *900 Romualdez St., at United Nations Ave.,* ☎ *2/508–026, ext. 273 or 274.* ☉ *Mon.–Sat. 9–5.*

OFF THE BEATEN PATH   **A RIDE ON THE LRT –** The Light Rail Transit (LRT) is an excellent means of getting beyond the usual tourist sights. For only a few pesos, you can ride from one end of the 15-stop line and back (a 1¼-hour trip), taking in the heart of Manila. Baclaran, the southernmost terminal, is not far from Baclaran Church, which is packed with devotees for special services to the Virgin Mary every Wednesday. Moving north, you pass through congested neighborhoods and can often peer into offices, apartments, and backyards. It's worth getting off at the R. Papa station, taking a pedicab, and visiting the remarkable Chinese Cemetery (there's a small entrance fee). The mausoleums are virtual mansions with architectural styles that range from Chinese classical to baroque, a reminder that wealth makes a difference even in death. At the last stop, Monumento, walk a short distance to the monument marking the spot where Philippine revolutionaries began their struggle against Spain.

Dining

Most restaurants can accommodate diners who drop in, but reservations are a good idea on holidays and weekends. Most places close only on Christmas, New Year's Day, All Souls' Day, Maundy Thursday, and Good Friday. Hours are normally noon to 2:30 for lunch and 7 to 11 for dinner; some restaurants are also open for breakfast (7–10) and *merienda* (4–6).

Few require formal dress; jackets or the long-sleeved *barong tagalog* for men suffice for even the most upscale establishments, and most others draw the line only at athletic shorts, tank tops, and slippers. Restaurants build a 10% VAT into their charges. Ask if a service charge is included; it often is not, in which case a 10%–15% tip would be expected.

$$$$ ✕ **Champagne Room.** The dining room of the grand old Manila Hotel (☞ *Lodging, below*) is decorated with wrought-iron tracery and glass palm trees and opens out into a garden. Strolling musicians play light classical music and Philippine *kundiman*. An attentive staff serves classic French cuisine—coquilles St. Jacques, salmon, lobster, Chateaubriand, rack of lamb, soufflés, crepes—and the wine list is reasonable in range. ⊠ *Manila Hotel, Rizal Park, Manila,* ☎ *2/527–0011. AE, DC, MC, V. No lunch Sat. No dinner Sun.*

$$$$ ✕ **Le Soufflé Restaurant and Wine Bar.** The three chefs who own and
★   operate this restaurant, where large picture windows overlook a public garden, have designed a light, fresh cuisine, generally Mediterranean but with salutes to Asia and eclecticism. If they have the ingredients, they will accommodate requests not on the menu. Specialties range from pan-fried goose liver in raspberry sauce to shiitake mushroom salad, baked salmon in phyllo pastry, and desserts like chocolate soufflé with berry sauce and vanilla ice cream. ⊠ *2F Josephine Bldg.,*

Greenbelt Dr. at Makati Ave., Makati, Metro Manila, ☎ *2/812–3287 or 2/894–1269, 2/894–3253. AE, DC, MC, V.*

$$$ ✕ **Bistro Remedios.** Pampanga regional cooking is served here in a set-
★ ting of traditional furniture and paintings of Philippine landscapes. Taste the local culture in the form of betute (stuffed frog), *gising-gising* (chopped chili with minced pork in coconut cream), *adobong palos* (freshwater eel in coconut milk, *kamias*, and chili), crisp-fried beef ribs, cooling *guinumis* (gelatin, tapioca, coco milk, and shaved ice), or a break-fast of garlic rice, eggs, sausages, and a cup of thick hot chocolate. The Bistro keeps long hours: 7–2:30 and 6–midnight weekdays, 7 AM–2 AM Saturday, and 10–2 and 6–11 Sunday. ☒ *1903 Adriatico St., at Remedios St., Malate, Manila,* ☎ *2/521–8097. AE, DC, MC, V.*

$$$ ✕ **Blue Bacon & Green Eggs.** A whimsical name identifies this garden café, where the wrought-iron chairs have backs featuring mangoes, pep-pers, and squashes. The food is mainly in a Mediterranean mode: sal-ads, pastas (with scallops and mushrooms, perhaps, or smoked salmon and caviar), meats and grills, soufflées savory and sweet, seafood, cof-fees, and such family favorites of Spanish extraction as *Potaje de Miguel* (a mixed boil of ham, pork, chicken, garlic, and onion) and *tulingan* (frigate mackerel) in olive oil. Desserts include an *ube*-cream pie (a cream pie made with purple yam) that's worth trying. ☒ *27 Lan-tana St., at Boston St., Quezon City,* ☎ *2/721–7666 or 2/721–2717. AE, DC, MC, V.*

$$$ ✕ **City Garden Seafood Restaurant.** The secret behind the sucess of this Cantonese restaurant—an attractive space with high ceilings, marble walls, and impeccable housekeeping—are its Hong Kong chefs and man-ager Robert See and his staff, who suggest dishes and menus accord-ing to occasion, taste, and budget. Try a simple seafood soup with spinach puree, bean curd braised with X-O (dried scallops) sauce, live Zam-boanga tiger lobster sautéed with ginger and onions, or hard-to-get *ma-meng* (wrasse), simply steamed. ☒ *Bank Dr., St. Francis Square, Ortigas Center, Pasig City,* ☎ *2/635–3006. AE, DC, MC, V.*

$$$ ✕ **Flavours and Spices.** The first of the city's many Thai restaurants, this is also a store for spices and condiments. Try the popular fa-vorites: *tom yam* soup, chicken in *pandan* leaf, red/green/yellow cur-ries, catfish salad with green mango, *phad thai* noodles, little *takho* cakes, and crushed-ice desserts like *tub tim grob* or *ruam-mit*. A less common standout here is hotpot of soup in which you cook meats, seafood, and vegetables to then dip in a sesame-seed hot sauce. ☒ *Gar-den Sq., Greenbelt Commercial Center, Makati, Metro Manila,* ☎ *2/ 815–3029 or 2/819–1375;* ☒ *Ruby Rd. at Julia Vargas, Ortigas Cen-ter, Pasig City,* ☎ *2/632–7153. AE, DC, MC, V.*

$$$ ✕ **Kamayan Restaurant.** The name means "to eat with the hands," pic-nic- or provincial-style, and at these four restaurants, your food is served on leaf-lined wooden plates—forks are optional. Entrées span regional cuisines: *lechon de leche* (whole roast suckling pig), sautéed crab with a sauce of its own coral, *kinulob na kitang* (butterfish wrapped in ba-nana leaf with onions and tomatoes), prawns in crab fat. You get all this in a setting of paneled walls, *capiz*-shell windows, and staff in styl-ized Philippine costumes. ☒ *47 Pasay Rd., Makati, Metro Manila,* ☎ *2/815–1463 or 2/883604;* ☒ *207 EDSA, Greenhills, Mandaluyong,* ☎ *2/795–504 or 2/709224;* ☒ *532 Padre Faura, at M. Adriatico, Er-mita, Manila,* ☎ *2/521–9490 or 2/582537;* ☒ *15 West Ave., Quezon City,* ☎ *2/989–470. AE, DC, MC, V.*

$$$ ✕ **La Primavera.** This imaginative Italian restaurant, steadily good through the years, offers standards and variations. Prosciutto comes with mango; *linguini verdi* is enhanced by fish, shrimps, olives, capers and anchovies; pizzas come in a choice of crusts—regular, potato, and sunflower; the risotto is made with mushrooms and *lughanighetta*

Dining

Lodging

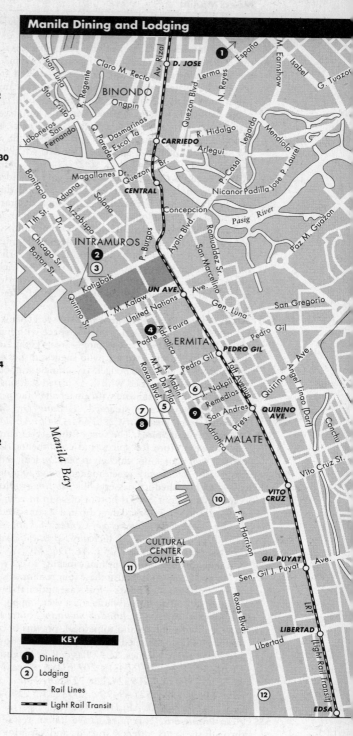

Manila Dining and Lodging

KEY

- **1** Dining
- **2** Lodging
- — Rail Lines
- ▬ Light Rail Transit

sausage; the seafood salad harmonizes salmon, *lapu-lapu* (spotted grouper), prawns, and smoked *tanguingue* (Spanish mackerel) thanks to a dill-mango dressing. A salad bar, cake trolley, and children's cart supplement the menu. ⊠ *Garden Square Bldg., Legaspi St. at Greenbelt Dr., Makati, Manila,* ☎ *2/818–1945;* ⊠ *GF, El Pueblo Real Building III, ADB and Julia Vargas Aves., Ortigas Commercial Center, Pasig City,* ☎ *2/632–7116 or 2/632–7117. AE, DC, MC, V.*

$$$ ✕ **La Tasca.** Manila has a well-deserved fame for the best Spanish cui-
★   sine in Asia, and La Tasca is one of the reasons why. The basic menu has such favorites as *sopa de ajo* (garlic soup), *paella* Valenciana or marinera (all seafood), *fabada asturiana* (bean stew with bacon), *bacalao a la vizcaina* (codfish), and desserts like *canonigo* (meringue, mangoes, and syrup). There are also changing specials and excellent staples, including steaks, prawns in a sauce of crab coral, and Swiss fondue. ⊠ *Legazpi St., Greenbelt Park, Makati, Metro Manila,* ☎ *2/893–8586 or 2/819–8435. AE, DC, MC, V. Closed Sun. No lunch Sat.*

$$$ ✕ **Sugi.** Japanese and Philippine chefs offer a wide-ranging menu: sushi, tempura, *teppanyaki* steak, grilled fish like *gindara* (silver cod), sukiyaki, *shabu-shabu* (thin-sliced, blanched beef served with dipping sauce), and *soba* (buckwheat) and *udon* (wheat) noodles. Check for special dishes like *kana koura age* (creamed crab with mushrooms), chicken with vegetables in a *wasabi*-flavored sauce, or Emperor's Soup (served in a tiny pot with a spout, slivers of squid, prawn, mushrooms, and radish sprouts within). The decor is Japanese, the service exemplary. ⊠ *Greenbelt Mall, Ayala Centre, Makati, Metro Manila,* ☎ *2/816–3886 or 812–8519;* ⊠ *Greenhills Commercial Center, Ortigas and Connecticut Aves., San Juan, Metro Manila,* ☎ *721–7111 or 723–9496. AE, DC, MC, V.*

$$$ ✕ **Via Mare Seafood Specialty Restaurant.** This is an institution—a gra-
★   cious setting for seafood in many guises. Fat live oysters are flown in daily from the Visayas, and prime seafood—salmon and trout, Alaskan cod and blue marlin, sole and *lapu-lapu*, scallops and lobsters—is transformed into such international and Philippine delights as timbale of salmon and sole, seafood grillades, and *calamares en su tinta* (squid in its own ink). ⊠ *Greenbelt Sq., Paseo de Roxas, Makati, Metro Manila,* ☎ *2/893–2306 or 2/893–2746;* ⊠ *Penthouse, Tektite East Tower, Ortigas Center, Pasig City,* ☎ *2/631–7980. AE, DC, MC, V. No lunch Sun.*

$$ ✕ **Cafe Ysabel.** In an old house (ca. 1927) set among trees is a kitchen that creates delicious Euro-American-Philippine cuisine. Most of the menu consists of owner/chef Gene Gonzalez's creations, including crepes and soufflés and 56 hot and cold coffees, decaf and not. More substantial meals range from sandwiches (*shawarma* to Reuben), pastas, and entrées French, Spanish and Italian, to dishes that evoke the turn-of-the-century cuisine of some now-vanished Pampanga town (Prawns Sulipan with mousselines of sole, or ox tongue with a mushroom velouté). ⊠ *455 P. Guevarra St., San Juan, Metro Manila,* ☎ *2/722–0349. AE, DC, MC, V.*

$ ✕ **Aristocrat Restaurant.** Since opening in 1936, the Aristocrat has been run by four sucessive generations of the Reyes family, and although there are now five other branches, the one beside the bay is the signature outlet. Popular dishes include chicken or pork barbecue with Java rice, satay sauce, and papaya pickles; *pansit luglog* (fat rice noodles with a shrimp and duck-egg sauce); chicken honey; and a Philippine breakfast of rice, dried beef or marinated milkfish, and coffee or chocolate. Drop by any time—it's open 24 hours. ⊠ *432 San Andres, at Roxas Blvd., Malate, Metro Manila,* ☎ *2/524–7671. No credit cards.*

$ ✕ **SM Megamall Food Court.** In the air-conditioned basement of the largest shopping mall in Metro Manila, some 40 food stores ring the tables, presenting a spectrum of current popular taste. The offerings include Philippine food: *bibingka* at **Ferino's,** *lechon* at **Lydia's,** *pansit* and regional dishes at **Aristocrat** and **Kamay Kainan;** Chinese vegetarian food at **Bodhi,** Cantonese food at **Golden Cantonese,** dim sum at **Maxim's;** Japanese food at **Moshi-Moshi;** Korean at **Kimchi;** French at **Le Coeur de France;** and American-style pizzas, hamburgers, fried chicken, pies, cookies, and salads. The food court opens at 10 and closes at 9. ⊠ *SM Megamall Bldg. A, EDSA and Julia Vargas St., Pasig, Metro Manila,* ☎ *2/633–5012. Reservations not accepted. No credit cards.*

Lodging

As the largest urban area in the country, metropolitan Manila has lodgings that run the gamut from small, intimate establishments to five-star hotels whose lobbies accentuate the grand and the grandiose. Almost all hotels are in two areas: the so-called Tourist Belt (Malate and Ermita districts) in downtown Manila, or in Makati, Manila's Wall Street and fashionable residential enclave. The former has more lodging options, while Makati has mainly upscale hotels. Unless otherwise noted, rooms in all listed hotels have private baths.

Ermita/Malate

The advantages of staying in the Tourist Belt are Manila Bay, with its fabled sunsets, and the area's assortment of restaurants, bars, clubs, coffeehouses, and shops. A number of museums are located here, such as the National Museum and the Central Bank Money Museum. The Cultural Center of the Philippines is right on Roxas Boulevard, the scenic main road flanking the bay.

$$$$ 🏨 **Century Park Sheraton.** The sunny, six-story lobby brings the outdoors inside with an aviary and artfully arranged tropical foliage. A string quartet serenades lobby loungers every evening from 4 to 8. The rooms, done in muted but cheery tones, are spacious. Ask for a full bay view; some rooms overlook the adjacent parking lot and shopping complex. ⊠ *Pablo Ocampo Senior St. (formerly Vito Cruz) at Adriatico St.,* ☎ *2/522–1011,* FAX *2/521–3413. 500 rooms. 8 restaurants, bar, coffee shop, deli, pool, exercise room, nightclub, business services. AE, DC, MC, V.*

$$$$ 🏨 **Manila Hotel.** The doyen of Manila's hotels, this is where General
★ MacArthur had his unofficial headquarters before World War II. Other luminaries have stayed here, including Ernest Hemingway and Douglas Fairbanks. The magnificent lobby exudes an Old World feeling, with floors of Philippine marble, narra and mahogany hardwood ceilings, and mother-of-pearl and brass chandeliers. The MacArthur Club, reached by private elevator, serves complimentary breakfast. Room decor re-creates the colonial era with nostalgic artwork and intricate wood-panelling recalling traditional motifs. Best rooms face the bay, with its sunsets, and the pool. ⊠ *Rizal Park, adjacent to Quirino Grandstand,* ☎ *2/527–0011,* FAX *2/527–0022. 570 rooms. 7 restaurants, bar, pool, 2 tennis courts, exercise room, business services. AE, DC, MC, V.*

$$$ 🏨 **Hyatt Regency.** Right on the boulevard, this medium-sized establishment has a spare but elegant lobby, graced by *capiz* (mother-of-pearl) chandeliers, that never seems crowded. The rooms—all with views of the bay—have wood and straw headboards and cane chairs. ⊠ *2702 Roxas Blvd.,* ☎ *2/833–1234,* FAX *2/833–5913. 265 rooms. 3 restaurants, bar, pool, exercise room, nightclub, business services, meeting rooms. AE, DC, MC, V.*

$$$ 🏨 **Manila Diamond Hotel.** The style of the lobby (or, as the staff describes it, the "tea lounge") combines art deco and postmodern design. The hotel fronts Manila Bay, and all the rooms have a view of the ocean. Room decor combines dark-wood panelling with art-deco touches; these eclectic motifs, combining ethnic and modernist designs, verge on the pleasantly gaudy. ⊠ *Roxas Blvd. at J. Quintos St.,* ☎ *2/526–2211,* FAX *2/526–2255. 495 rooms. 8 restaurants, bar, pool, hot tub, health club, business services, meeting rooms. AE, DC, MC, V.*

$$$ 🏨 **Philippine Plaza.** Luxurious and grand—a veritable resort sans
★ beachfront—the Plaza has an enormous lobby with two levels, the lower one graced by a carp pool and a waterfall. The huge circular swimming pool, with slides for the kids and a snack bar smack in the middle, is one of Asia's best. All rooms have terraces with views of Manila Bay. The furniture is rattan and the decor has a beige-and-white color scheme. ⊠ *Cultural Center Complex, Roxas Blvd.,* ☎ *2/832–0701,* FAX *2/832–3485. 673 rooms. 8 restaurants, bar, pool, miniature golf, 4 tennis courts, exercise room, nightclub, business services, meeting rooms. AE, DC, MC, V.*

$$ 🏨 **Admiral Hotel.** Fronting the bay, this businesslike place is unpretentious but efficient, with a quiet café in its small, informal lobby. Rooms are air-conditioned, neat, and modern but a bit small. Best are those with a view of the bay. The staff is friendly and attentive. ⊠ *2138 Roxas Blvd.,* ☎ *2/572–081 to –093,* FAX *2/522–2018. 110 rooms. Restaurant, coffee shop, pool, dance club. AE, DC, MC, V.*

$ 🏨 **Adriatico Arms.** This small, cozy hotel, with armchairs in the lobby and a combination coffee shop/deli, is in the heart of the Tourist Belt. The rooms are tastefully, if simply, furnished in basic black and white. ⊠ *560 J. Nakpil St., at Adriatico,* ☎ *2/521–0736,* FAX *2/588–014. 28 rooms. Coffee shop. AE, DC, MC, V.*

Makati

Only developed in the 1960s, this district, the business capital of the country and neighbor to the airport, is relatively uncongested compared to the Tourist Belt. The streets and sidewalks are wide, making it easier than elsewhere to walk around, and the hotels are concentrated around the gigantic Makati Commercial Center, which has everything from movie houses to money changers.

$$$$ 🏨 **Mandarin Oriental.** The ambience here is discreet and elegant, with
★ a small but stately lobby done in black marble with a cut-crystal chandelier. The rooms are scrupulously maintained and similarly elegant, with muted but rich colors. Service is unfailingly professional and courteous, another reason (along with the management's sensitivity to noise and security) that it's a favorite with busy travelers. ⊠ *Makati Ave. and Paseo de Roxas St.,* ☎ *2/750–8888,* FAX *2/817–2472. 470 rooms. 4 restaurants, bar, pool, exercise room, nightclub, business services, meeting rooms. AE, DC, MC, V.*

$$$$ 🏨 **New World Hotel.** A modernist 25-story edifice built in 1995, this property has what is termed an internationalist style, from its lobby to its rooms: ultramodern decor and furnishings meant to make traveling businesspeople feel that they're really not too far from home. All the rooms have centralized bedside controls for everything—television, lights, air-conditioning, etc. Staff are quiet, fast, and efficient. ⊠ *Esperanza St., at Makati Ave.,* ☎ *2/811–6888,* FAX *2/811–6777. 611 rooms. 3 restaurants, bar, coffee shop, lobby lounge, pool, barbershop, beauty salon, health club, business services. AE, DC, MC, V.*

$$$$ 🏨 **Peninsula.** The Pen, as Manilans call it, exudes an informal elegance,
★ expressed in the wide lobby—divided by a grand aisle with floral decor— and the understated furnishings and decor of the well-kept rooms, which are spacious enough to seem more like suites. The lobby is known as a "power spot," where politicians and other power brokers in Manila society like to gather for breakfast or a late-night drink. ⊠ *Makati and Ayala Aves.,* ☎ *2/815–3402,* FAX *2/815–4825. 535 rooms. 4 restaurants, bar, deli, pool, nightclub, business services. AE, DC, MC, V.*

$$$$ ☎ **Shangri-La Manila.** After the huge, luxurious, soaring, light-filled lobby, the rooms here are something of a disappointment: although spacious and sparking clean, the quarters have a bland, modern decor. A number of rooms have been added, increasing the hotel's capacity, and it has the metropolitan area's hottest restaurant/disco, Zu. ⊠ *Ayala Ave. at Makati Ave.,* ☎ *2/813–8888,* FAX *2/813–5499. 730 rooms. 4 restaurants, bar, deli, pool, exercise room, dance club, business services. AE, DC, V, MC.*

$$$ ☎ **Dusit Thani.** This hotel, formerly the Nikko Manila Garden, was poised to reopen in 1997. One aspect of the property that's sure not to have changed is its convenient location—smack in Makati Commercial Center, with snack bars, restaurants, bookstores, cinemas, boutiques, and department stores. ⊠ *Makati Commercial Center,* ☎ *2/857–911,* FAX *2/817–862. 523 rooms. 5 restaurants, bar, pool, exercise room, nightclub, business services, meeting rooms. AE, DC, MC, V.*

Nightlife and the Arts

The Arts

Good guides to the city's cultural life are the *Expat Weekly* and *What's on in Manila,* distributed free by major hotels, restaurants, and tourist information centers. Check the entertainment pages of the dailies, particularly the Sunday editions.

At the entrance to the offices of the **Cultural Center of the Philippines** (⊠ Roxas Blvd. facing Pablo Ocampo Senior St., ☎ 2/832–1125), you can pick up a monthly calendar of the center's offerings. The government-run center emphasizes music, theater, dance, and the visual arts and has a resident dance company and theater group. The center also hosts internationally known artists and musicians, sometimes in cooperation with the various cultural arms of the foreign embassies. The center's two art galleries display figurative and abstract art.

ART GALLERIES

Ateneo de Manila Gallery (⊠ Ateneo De Manila University, Katipunan Rd., Loyola Heights, Quezon City, ☎ 2/998–721) has one of the country's strongest collections of Philippine modern art. **Crucible Gallery** (⊠ Artwalk, 4th floor, Bldg. A, Megamall, ☎ 2/635–6061) exhibits contemporary Philippine artists. **Galleria Duemila** (⊠ Artwalk, 4th floor, Bldg. A, Megamall, ☎ 2/633–6687) focuses on young, contemporary European artists. **Heritage Art Center** (⊠ 33 4th Ave., at Main Ave., Cubao, Quezon City, ☎ 2/700–867) exhibits both traditional and nontraditional art. **Hiraya Art Gallery** (530 United Nations Ave., Ermita, ☎ 2/594–223) favors up-and-coming artists. **Kulay Diwa** (⊠ 25 Lopez Avenue, Lopez Village, Paranaque, ☎ 827–7735) shows a wide-ranging collection of contemporary Philippine art, on from modernist to indigenous themes. **Luz Gallery** (⊠ Makati Ave. at Ayala Ave., ☎ 2/815–6906) is a famous venue for well-established modern artists. The government-run **National Commission for Culture and the Arts Gallery** (⊠ 633 General Luna St., Intramuros, ☎ 527–2197) offers a wide range of painting, sculpture, and prints by Philippine artists.

CONCERTS

Free concerts are given at Rizal Park on Sunday beginning at 5 PM, usually featuring a program of popular Western and Philippine music. Well-known singers and musicians are featured. Paco Park and Puerta Real in Intramuros offer similar programs, at 6 PM on Friday and Saturday respectively.

DANCE

The **Cultural Center of the Philippines** (✉ Roxas Blvd.) has a resident dance company, Ballet Philippines (☏ 2/831–7082), and provides offices for Bayanihan Dance Company (☏ 2/832–3688), a world-famous folk-dance group. The ballet company is the Philippines' best, with guest dancers from around the world.

FILM

Metro Manila has many cinema houses, but most of the English-language films are the substandard B type. **Free films** are presented at Rizal Park's open-air theater at 5 PM on Saturday afternoon and after the concert on Sunday evening; the **Alliance Française de Manille** (✉ 220 Gil Puyat Ave., ☏ 2/813–2681), **Goethe House** (✉ 687 Aurora Blvd., Quezon City, ☏ 2/722–4671), the **University of the Philippines Film Center** (✉ Diliman campus, Quezon City, ☏ 2/963–640), and the **Thomas Jefferson Library** (✉ 395 Buendia Ave. Ext., ☏ 2/818–5484) regularly offer free film screenings, ranging from silent classics to contemporary movies.

During the two-week **Metro Manila Film Festival** in June and December, only Philippine films are shown in the cinemas. The **Mowelfund Film Institute** (✉ 66 Rosario Drive, Cubao, Quezon City, ☏ 2/721–7702) holds a yearly film festival, *Pelikula at Lipunan* (Film and Society), a selection of the best of commercial and independent Philippine cinema.

Nightlife

Metropolitan Manila is a pleasure-seeker's paradise, with a catholic array of nighttime activities, from the soothing to the sinful. You can listen to jazz or rock, have a drink at a bar while ogling scantily clad performers of either sex, dance madly at a disco, or have a snack and cappuccino in one of the lively coffeehouses.

BARS

There are really two types of bars in Manila: those with skimpily attired dancers and those without. The former play disco music, while the latter have more varied fare. There used to be a large concentration of "girlie" bars in the Tourist Belt, but the current mayor has had them shut down. Most have moved to Pasay City, along Roxas Boulevard. More have sprouted in Quezon City, around the Tomas Morato–Quezon Avenue intersection, ranging from basic pub–cum–strip-joints to upscale places offering high-priced drinks and high-priced hostesses who will drink with gentlemen patrons and listen sympathetically as they unburden their troubles.

Nongirlie bars are spread out in Makati and the Tourist Belt. In the Tourist Belt try **Tap Room** (✉ Manila Hotel, ☏ 2/470–011) for small jazz and pop ensembles. **Siete Pecados** (✉ Philippine Plaza Hotel, ☏ 2/832–0701) puts on brass acts and Latin groups. At **Oar House** (✉ A. Mabini St., at Remedios, ☏ 2/595–864) journalists gather to listen to classical ballads on tape. **Remembrances** (✉ 1795 A. Mabini, ☏ 2/521–7605) appeals to those who yearn for taped oldies-but-goodies. **Guernica's** (✉ 1856 Bocobo St., Malate, ☏ 2/521–4415) features Spanish music, ballads, and folk songs. In Makati, try Nina's Papagayo (✉ 1 Anza St., ☏ 2/887–925), well-known for its Spanish and Mexican music. **Sirena** (✉ Manila Peninsula, Ayala Ave., ☏ 2/819–3456) has lively bands that play top-40 hits.

CAFÉS

The largest concentration of cafés is in the Malate district, in and around Remedios Circle. **Blue Cafe** (✉ Nakpil St. at Bocobo St., ☏ 2/581–725) serves no food but has a cash bar, a gay crowd, and excellent sounds. **Cafe Adriatico** (✉ 1790 Adriatico St., ☎ 2/584–059) features classical music, Philippine food, and a low-key atmosphere. Tiny **Cafe Mondial** (✉ Adriatico St. at Pedro Gil St., ☎ 2/598–946) serves fresh-fruit shakes, delicious crepes, and finger sandwiches. In Quezon City there's the **Cine Cafe** (✉ 76-C Roces Ave., ☎ 2/969–421), a gay gathering spot with offbeat, often experimental, films on video monitors. **Penguin Cafe** (✉ 604 Remedios St., at Bocobo St., ☎ 2/631–2088), which doubles as an art gallery, has a great outdoor patio, an artistic crowd, and good homemade pasta.

CASINOS

Manila has three government-sanctioned casinos, each in a major hotel: **Grand Boulevard Hotel** (✉ 1990 Roxas Blvd., ☎ 2/507–818), formerly the Silahis, occupying the whole mezzanine, with a room reserved for high-rollers; **Holiday Inn-Manila Pavilion Hotel** (✉ Maria Orosa St. at United Nations Ave., ☎ 2/522–2911); and **Heritage Hotel** (✉ Roxas Blvd. at EDSA, Pasay City, ☎ 2/891–7856).

DISCOS

Manila discos tend to be cavernous. The beat is generic and follows Western fashions. In Quezon City, a popular gay disco is **Club 69** (✉ 690 Amoranto St., at Biak-na-Bato St., ☎ 2/712–3662), with shows featuring dancers and impersonators. **Euphoria** (✉ Hotel Inter-Continental, Makati Commercial Center, Ayala Ave., ☎ 2/815–9711) is a trendy yuppie hangout. **Studebaker's** (Quad III, Ayala Center, in front of Shangri-La Manila Hotel, Makati, ☎ 2/892–0959) has three floors: one for a café, the second for a karaoke lounge, and the third for an often crowded disco. **Zu** (✉ Shangri-La Manila Hotel, Makati Ave. at Ayala Ave., Makati, ☎ 2/813–8888) is the current hot spot, where everyone from yuppies to entertainment celebrities to fast-rising politicos come to see and be seen.

FOLK AND ROCK HOUSES

Chatterbox (✉ 41 West Avenue, Quezon City, ☎ 2/997–539) caters to the college-age grunge set. **Club Dredd** (✉ 570 EDSA, at Tuason St., ☎ 2/912–8464) favors hard-core rock. **Hobbit House** (✉ 1801 A. Mabini St., ☎ 2/521–7604) is memorable for its wait staff of little people and regular roster of folk singers; Freddie Aguilar, who's famous throughout Southeast Asia, performs twice a week. **Mayric's** (✉ 1320 Espana St., in front of the University of Santo Tomas, ☎ 2/732–3021) has bands that alternate between punk and grunge. In Quezon City, the **'70's Bistro** (✉ 46 Anonas St., ☎ 2/922–0492) has a mix of students and professionals listening to folk-rock bands.

NIGHTCLUBS AND CABARETS

Manila nightclubs offer floor shows that vary from performances of well-known bands and cultural presentations to highly choreographed "model" shows, in which a lot of skin is bared. **Lost Horizon** (✉ Philippine Plaza, Cultural Center Complex, ☎ 2/832–0701) usually has a lively pop band. **Zamboanga** (✉ 1619 Adriatico St., ☎ 2/572–835) serves Philippine cuisine and presents regional folk dances. **Top of the Century** (✉ Century Park Sheraton, Pablo Ocampo Senior St. at Harrison St., ☎ 2/522–1011) has well-known jazz and pop singers. **La Bodega** (✉ Manila Peninsula, Makati Ave. at Ayala Ave., ☎ 2/819–3456) has an intimate feel, with Spanish/Latin music and small pop ensembles.

Outdoor Activities and Sports

Basketball

Basketball is the Philippines' premier sport, an enduring legacy of the American colonial era. Tournaments are held by the professional **Philip-**

pine **Basketball Association** (☎ 2/833–4103), as well as by the **University Athletic Association of the Philippines** (UAAP) and the **Philippine Amateur Basketball League** (PABL). The major courts are at the Ultra Center in the nearby town of Pasig, Rizal Coliseum in Malate, and the Cuneta Astrodome in Pasay City.

Cockfighting

This national pastime is obviously not for animal lovers: During the fascinating prefight ceremonies, oddsmakers patrol the noisy and often cigarette-smoke-filled cockpit taking bets—sums can range from the petty to the astronomical—and handlers prepare their feathered charges with time-honored methods. Then the two cocks, equipped with razor-sharp spurs, fight to the death. A fight can last less than a minute if uneven, longer if the combatants are well matched. Sometimes the winner may be barely alive at the end and will wind up, like the loser, on the owner's dinner table.

In the metropolitan area, cockfights are usually held on Sunday. The big arenas are **La Loma Cockpit** (✉ 68 Calavite St., ☎ 2/731–2023) and the **Pasay Arena** (✉ Dolores St., Pasay City, ☎ 2/843–1746).

Golf

Capitol Hills Golf Club (✉ Old Balara, Diliman, Quezon City, ☎ 2/931–3050) is an 18-hole course in Quezon City. **Intramuros Golf Club** (☎ 2/478–470) has 18 holes right beside the historic walls of Intramuros. **Puerto Azul Beach and Country Club** (Ternate, Cavite, ☎ 2/574–731), a 90-minute drive from Manila, is a championship 18-hole course in a tropical resort by the sea.

Horse Racing

The **Santa Ana Race Track** (✉ J. Rizal St., Santa Ana, ☎ 2/879–951) and the **San Lazaro Hippodrome** (✉ Manila Jockey Club, Felix Huertas St., ☎ 2/711–125) feature races on Tuesday and Wednesday evenings and Saturday and Sunday afternoons.

Tennis

The city's numerous tennis courts include **Club Intramuros** (✉ Intramuros, ☎ 2/477–754), **Philippine Plaza Hotel** (✉ Cultural Center Complex, ☎ 2/832–0701), **Rizal Memorial Stadium** (✉ Pablo Ocampo Senior St., Malate, ☎ 2/583–513), and **Velayo Sports Center** (✉ Domestic Airport Rd., ☎ 2/832–2316).

Shopping

As the nerve center of the country, Manila has all the shopping options, from sidewalk vendors and small retail stores to market districts and shopping centers. Nothing beats shopping in the market districts for color, bustle, and bargains—in a word, for atmosphere. Here haggling is raised to a fine art. Located in the older areas of the city, each encompasses several blocks and is a neighborhood unto itself. Crowds can be intense, and, as in any urban area, they include pickpockets. Don't be paranoid, just alert. Shopping malls are found in relatively newer areas, such as Makati's commercial center, and in Quezon City. The malls are better organized and easier to get to, making up in convenience what they lack in charm; prices are fixed, however, so bargaining is pointless.

Market Districts

Baclaran. The many stalls on Roxas Boulevard near Baclaran Church specialize in ready-to-wear clothing. Prices are supposedly lowest on Wednesday, when the weekly devotions to Our Lady of Perpetual Help are held at the church. The disadvantages of Wednesday shopping are the crowds and worse-than-usual traffic jams.

Divisoria. North of Binondo, this is the largest old-fashioned market district, with everything from fresh produce, fruit, and cooking utensils to hardware, leather goods, and handicrafts. Savvy Manilans come to browse among the assorted stalls, emporia, and department stores until they see what they want at the right price.

A. Mabini Street. While not a market district per se, this street in the Tourist Belt is lined with small antiques and handicraft shops. Some of the more reputable stores are **Bauzon Antiques** (✉ 1219 A. Mabini, ☎ 2/522–3126), **Tesoro's** (✉ 1325 A. Mabini, ☎ 2/503–931), **T'boli Arts and Crafts** (✉ 1362 A. Mabini, ☎ 2/586–802), **Terry's Antiques** (✉ 1401 A. Mabini, ☎ 2/588–020), **Via Antica** (✉ 1411 A. Mabini, ☎ 2/522–0869), **Likha Antiques** (✉ 1475 A. Mabini, ☎ 2/588–125), and **Goslani's** (✉ 1571 A. Mabini, ☎ 2/507–338).

San Andres Market. This 24-hour Tourist Belt market is noted for its tropical and imported fruits. Bright and neatly arranged, the piles of mangoes, watermelons, custard apples, and jackfruit are above average. It's pricey, but you can bargain.

Shopping Malls and Centers

EDSA Malls. On EDSA between Shaw Boulevard and Ortigas Avenue, loom three gigantic air-conditioned shopping malls—**Robinson's, Shangri-La,** and **SM.** All three have shops selling clothing, electronics, record and books, as well as fast-food areas, fine restaurants, art galleries, cinemas, and several department stores (Robinson's, Shoemart, and Rustan's). There's even a skating rink. All three are linked, making for one monstrous bazaar, where sophisticated urbanites, foreigners, and visitors from the provinces all mingle in air-conditioned comfort. Shops and fast-food restaurants close at 9 PM, while fine-dining establishments close at 10. The malls themselves shut at midnight, or whenever the last film screening lets out.

Harrison Plaza. This huge Tourist Belt center adjacent to the Century Park Sheraton, on Adriatico and Pablo Ocampo Senior Streets, has department stores, supermarkets, jewelers, drugstores, boutiques, record and electronics shops, video rentals, restaurants and snack bars, and four movie houses. Opening hours vary, but all shops close at 7:30 PM, except the fast-food restaurants, which are open until 8:30.

Makati Commercial Center. Bounded by Makati Avenue on the west, Ayala Avenue on the north, Epifanio de los Santos Highway on the east, and Pasay Road on the south, this is the biggest such center in the country, including several shopping malls and such gigantic department stores as Shoemart and Landmark, two hotels, sports shops, money changers, etc. There are small plazas where the weary can rest and watch humanity stream by. Opening hours vary; shops and fast-food restaurants close at 9 PM, fine dining establishments close at 10, and the malls themselves close at midnight or whenever the last movie lets out.

Metro Manila A to Z

Arriving and Departing

BY BUS

There are about 20 major bus companies in the Philippines and almost as many terminals in Manila. Those closest to downtown Manila and Makati can be found at Plaza Lawton (now called Liwasang Bonifacio, but bus signboards still use "Lawton") and along a portion of EDSA in Pasay City, not far from Taft Avenue. Another important terminal is farther north on EDSA, on the corner of New York Street, in the district of Cubao, Quezon City. The only way to get tickets is to go to a terminal; you can purchase tickets in advance.

Bus companies include: **BLTB** (✉ EDSA at Aurora St., Pasay City, and at Plaza Lawton, ☎ 2/833–5501). **Dangwa** (✉ 1600 Dimasalang, Sampaloc, ☎ 2/731–2859). **Pantranco** (✉ 325 Quezon Blvd. Ext., near Roosevelt Ave., Quezon City, ☎ 2/833–5061) **Philtranco** (✉ EDSA and Apelo Cruz St., Pasay City, ☎ 2/833–5061 to –5064). **Victory Liner** (✉ EDSA at Aurora St., Pasay City, ☎ 2/833–0293, 2/833–5019, or 2/833–5020).

BY CAR

The best routes for leaving or entering the city are the Epifanio de los Santos Avenue (known as EDSA), the South Superhighway, the C-5 Highway (finished in 1995), and the EDSA-North Diversion link. EDSA is the main artery connecting Pasay, Makati, Mandaluyong, Quezon, and Caloocan. The North Diversion begins in Caloocan, at a junction of EDSA, and leads to points north. The South Superhighway originates in Manila, passes through Makati with EDSA as a junction, and leads to points south. C-5 is a circumferential road that connects Pasig (a district adjacent to the EDSA malls) to the South Superhighway and destinations further south, allowing motorists to bypass the often congested stretch of EDSA where it passes through Makati and Mandaluyong.

Parking is not a problem, even in congested Manila. In the Tourist Belt and in Makati, there's a P10 fee for parking, collected in advance, with no time limit. Be on the lookout for designated tow-away zones in Makati.

BY PLANE

Ninoy Aquino International Airport (☎ 2/832–3011 or 2/832–1901) is the international air hub of the Philippines.

From Ninoy Aquino International Airport to Downtown: The major Manila hotels have airport shuttles, so look around for one before using another means of transport. Normally a metered taxi to Makati should cost no more than P75, or P100 to the Tourist Belt area, but airport taxi drivers charge a higher, agreed-upon price of P300. Avis (☎ 2/833–7897) has a taxi-coupon service, with rates averaging P300. Or you can go to the departure area on the third level and flag a taxi that has just brought departing passengers. Limousine service is available for $40–$50; check at the arrivals hall. For rental cars, Hertz, Avis, and National have booths in the arrival area. To the right of the airport building at the end of the driveway are stops for public buses, such as the Love Buses (☎ 2/951–203), that pass by the Tourist Belt via Makati. Public buses leave every 15 minutes. Though inexpensive, they're not recommended if you have a lot of luggage, and they make many stops.

Metropolitan Manila is served by the **Manila Domestic Airport** (☎ 2/832–0991 or 2/832–0932) for domestic flights.

From Manila Domestic Airport to Downtown: In light traffic, it's a 30-minute ride from the airport to Makati's hotels; getting to the Tourist Belt takes close to an hour. Manila Domestic Airport is essentially a one-building affair, and cabs line up on the driveway. Normally a metered cab ride to Makati should cost no more than P75, and to the Tourist Belt in Manila, P100, but airport taxi drivers charge a higher, fixed price: P200–P500, depending on your destination. But a scant 15 meters from the terminal is the busy Domestic Airport Road, where you can hail a passing cab and pay lower, metered rates.

(☞ Philippines A to Z, *below,* for information on international arrivals and departures and on domestic carriers and flights.)

BY TRAIN
Manila's main rail terminal, **Tutuban Station** (☎ 2/210–011), is in the Tondo district. Two other stations are in the Paco and Makati districts. Commuter trains operate on a north–south axis during rush hours, from Paco, in Manila, to Alabang, a southern suburb. Minimum commuter fare is P1.50.

Getting Around
Manila isn't a city for walking, though you can do so within certain areas, particularly in the Tourist Belt, on Roxas Boulevard, and in some parts of Makati. Sidewalks are generally narrow, uneven, and sometimes nonexistent. Instead, choose from a vast array of transportation, public and private, from horse-drawn carriages to elevated trains.

BY BUS AND JEEPNEY
The routes of public buses and jeepneys (a cross between a van and a Jeep) crisscross Metropolitan Manila and are the cheapest form of travel for areas not served by the LRT, the light-rail system. Buses make sense for longer trips, while jeepneys are best for short ones. For example, a bus is recommended to reach Quezon City from Ermita, but within Ermita, or from one district to the next, take a jeepney. The latter can accommodate 12 to 15 passengers and is perhaps the city's most colorful form of public transport, gaudily decorated and with the driver's favorite English slogan emblazoned in front. Average fares range from P3 to P10.

An excellent means of transport is the **Love Bus** (☎ 2/951–203), a fleet of air-conditioned coaches that make fewer stops than the regular, non-air-conditioned ones. Fares average P15.

BY CAR
Between the frustration and the smoke emissions, traffic jams in Manila can reduce drivers to tears. If you don't have to drive within the city, don't. Public transportation is plentiful and cheap. If you do drive, improvisation—such as sudden lane changing—is the rule rather than the exception. Many of the nonarterial roads are narrow and become clogged during morning (7:30–10) and afternoon (3:30–7:30) rush hours. On the other hand, a car gives you flexibility, parking isn't a problem, and you don't have to deal with cabs, the meters of which may run faster than a speeding bullet.

Some car-rental agencies: **Ace** (☎ 2/812–3386). **Avis** (☎ 2/742–2871). **Car Express** (☎ 2/876–717). **Dollar** (☎ 2/844–3120). **Hertz** (☎ 2/832–5325 or 2/868–0520). **National** (☎ 2/818–8667 or 2/833–0648).

BY CARETELA OR CALESA
Good for short hops within a neighborhood are the horse-drawn carriages called *caretelas* (the larger size) and *calesas*. They are available mostly in the older neighborhoods, such as Binondo (Chinatown) and are quite inexpensive (about P15 a ride).

BY LIGHT RAIL
The **Light Rail Transit** (LRT, ☎ 2/832–0423) is an elevated, modern railway, with 16 stops on a north–south axis; additional stations are under construction. It's the fastest, cleanest, and safest mode of transport in the city. The southern terminal is at Baclaran in Pasay City, the northern at Monumento in Caloocan City. Most stops are in Manila. Hours of operation are from 4 AM to 9 PM. Fare between any two stations is P5. Each station displays a guide to the routes.

BY LIMOUSINE

The major hotels have limousine service and use mostly Mercedes-Benzes. For a private limo service, try **Filipino Transport** (☎ 2/581–493), which charges P1,600 for eight hours and P180 per additional hour. Outside Manila, rates vary. For instance, Manila to Baguio overnight costs P6,000, and P2,000 per additional day. At least 24-hour notice is required.

BY PEDICAB OR TRICYCLE

Bicycles and motocycles with attached sidecars—known as pedicabs and tricycles, respectively—are found everywhere and provide amazingly inexpensive (P2–P5) short hops.

BY TAXI

Taxis are not as inexpensive as other means of public transport, but they're still pretty cheap: A metered 2-mile cab ride should cost about P75 (assuming you don't get caught in a traffic jam, a commonplace occurrence), plus tip. However, while rates are theoretically standard, a number of cab companies tolerate their drivers' tampering with the meters. If you feel the fare registered is exorbitant, say so politely. Often the driver will allow you to pay less than what's shown. Try to take a taxi from the better hotels, where cabs are always waiting and hotel doormen note down the taxi number, which is useful in case of problems. **Avis Taxi** (☎ 2/531–2495 or 2/532–0605) is a reputable cab company. **R & E** (☎ 2/341–464) is known for reliability and honesty.

Contacts and Resources

DOCTORS AND DENTISTS

Call the **Philippine Medical Association** (☎ 2/974–974 or 2/992–132) for medical referrals. The **Philippine Dental Association** (☎ 2/818–6144) can suggest a dentist. Finer hotels usually have a doctor and/or dentist either on premises or on call.

EMBASSIES AND CONSULATES

Australia (✉ Dona Salustiana S. Ty Tower, ground floor, 104 Paseo de Roxas, Makati, ☎ 2/817–7911). **Canada** (✉ Allied Bank Center, 9th floor, 6754 Ayala Ave., Makati, ☎ 2/810–8861). **U.K.** (✉ LV Locsin Bldg., 15th–17th floors, 6752 Ayala Ave., Makati, ☎ 2/816–7116 or 2/816–4849). **U.S.** (✉ 1201 Roxas Blvd., Manila, ☎ 2/521–7116, FAX 2/522–1608).

EMERGENCIES

The **Metropolitan Police Command** now has one line for all emergencies: ☎ 166.

There are **emergency rooms** at **Makati Medical Center** (✉ 2 Amorsolo St., at De La Rosa, near Ayala Ave., ☎ 2/815–9911 to –9944) and at **Manila Doctors' Hospital** (✉ 667 United Nations Ave., Ermita, near UN station on LRT, ☎ 2/503–011).

ENGLISH-LANGUAGE BOOKSTORES

National Book Store is a popular chain. In the Tourist Belt, try the **Harrison Plaza branch** (✉ M. Adriatico and Pablo Ocampo Senior Sts., ☎ 2/572–179); in Makati, try the **Quad Arcade branch** (☎ 2/892–5767) at the Makati Commercial Center. **Solidaridad** (✉ 531 Padre Faura, Ermita, ☎ 2/586–581), owned by well-known novelist F. Sionil Jose, is frequented by Manila's literati. The store offers political, literary, and popular titles.

GUIDED TOURS

The average city tour takes five hours and can be arranged by any of the following travel agencies: **American Express** (✉ Ground floor, PhilamLife Bldg., in front of Manila Pavillion Hotel, United Nations

Ave., ☎ 2/521–9492). **Baron Travel Corp.** (✉ Pacific Bank Bldg., H.V. De La Costa St. and Ayala Ave., Makati, ☎ 2/892–3462). **Manila Sightseeing Tours** (✉ 500 United Nations Ave., ☎ 2/521–2060). **Rajah Tours** (✉ 3/f Physicians' Tower, 533 United Nations Ave., ☎ 2/522–0541). **Thomas Cook** (✉ G/F Skyland Plaza, Gil Puyat Ave., Makati, ☎ 2/816–3701 or 2/812–2446).

The Department of Tourism (☞ Visitor Information, *below*) can provide a list of English-, Spanish-, Japanese-, French-, Italian-, German-, Indonesian-, and even Hebrew-speaking guides. Guides charge P350 for the standard city tour, and day tours to nearby Tagaytay and Pagsanjan are P650 and P850 (with lunch), respectively.

Sun Cruises (☎ 2/522–3613) offers daily cruises to Corregidor—the famous World War II battle site and island fortress at the mouth of Manila Bay. Cruise boats leave weekdays at 9 AM, weekends at 8 AM and 11 AM, from a dock right by the Cultural Center of the Philippines.

LATE-NIGHT PHARMACIES

Mercury Drug Store, a citywide chain, has 24-hour branches in Cubao, Quezon City (☎ 2/781–746); Quiapo, Plaza Miranda (☎ 2/733–2112); and Guadalupe Commercial Center, Makati, (☎ 2/843–4327).

VISITOR INFORMATION

The **Department of Tourism** has an information center on the ground floor of its main offices at the **Tourism Building** (✉ Agrifina Circle, Rizal Park, T.M. Kalaw Ave., Manila, ☎ 2/599–031, ext. 146, or 2/501–728). Other centers are located at: the mezzanine and arrival mall at **Ninoy Aquino International Airport** (☎ 2/832–2191), **Manila Domestic Airport** (☎ 2/832–3566), Nayong Pilipino Reception Unit at the **Nayong Pilipino Complex** (☎ 2/832–3767 or 2/832–3768) on Airport Road.

The **Tourist Security Division** (☎ 2/501–728 or 2/501–660, 24 hours) can assist in cases of theft, missing luggage, or other untoward incidents.

For information on the old walled city, contact **Intramuros Administration** (☎ 2/527–2811 or 2/527–3155).

SIDE TRIPS FROM METRO MANILA

Las Piñas

12 km (8 mi) from Manila. Go south from Rizal Park on Roxas Blvd., turn left on Airport Rd., turn right on Quirino Ave., and continue for 6 more mi to Las Piñas.

The world's only **bamboo organ** is housed in Las Piñas's 18th-century **San José Church.** The organ, built in 1795, has 121 metal pipes, 832 bamboo pipes, 22 registers, and a five-octave manual. Not far from San José church is the **Sarao Motor Works,** largest manufacturer of the ubiquitous and gaudy jeepney, its original prototype a converted U.S. Army Jeep.

Tagaytay Ridge

60 km (37 mi) south of downtown Manila. Take South Expressway to Carmona exit, from which clearly marked signs lead to Tagaytay.

Rice fields line the South Expressway, the tree- and flower-lined road that heads south from downtown Manila to Tagaytay Ridge, 2,500 feet above sea level. Here you can view what may be the world's smallest volcano, **Taal Volcano,** actually a volcano within a volcano: The ridge on which sightseers stand is actually the rim of a large, extinct volcano, and the lake below encloses Taal, another volcano, one that is dormant. With cool temperatures and scenic vistas, Tagaytay provides welcome relief from Manila's heat and congestion.

Villa Escudero

★ *97 km (61 mi) from Manila. Take South Expressway until it ends and then turn right toward Lucena City; bear left at Santo Tomás intersection onto the road to San Pablo City, which passes through Alaminos. Slow down as you approach the archway signaling the end of Laguna Province and the start of Quezon Province: the entrance to Villa Escudero is immediately after the archway, on your left.*

If the sight of smiling children in traditional dress serenading you with native instruments doesn't warm your heart, nothing will. These friendly youngsters greet visitors to Villa Escudero, a working 1,600-acre rice-and-coconut plantation with its own river and man-made falls, only a 90-minute drive from Manila. After being serenaded you can explore the **Escudero Museum,** with an eclectic and colorful collection that includes war memorabilia (such as cannons and tanks, which children always seem to enjoy), antique religious artifacts and altars, paintings, stuffed animals, and celadon pottery. ⊠ *Alaminos, Laguna.* ▨ *Admission.* ⊙ *Daily.* ☏ *2/590–554 or 2/521–8698.*

Lodging

¢ ▨ **Hidden Valley.** At this popular resort, the emphasis is on having as
★ natural an environment as possible, centered around natural springs and lush tropical miniforests. Overnight cottages are available. ⊠ *Entrance is to the right, before the archway,* ☏ *2/815–4522 or 2/819–7439. 18 rooms. Bar, pool, meeting rooms. AE, DC, MC, V.*

Pagsanjan

★ *130 km (80 mi) south of Manila. Take South Expressway to its end, then turn left toward Calamba (there are signs). Turn right at the first major intersection and follow signs to Pagsanjan.*

About an hour and a half southeast of Manila, the town of Pagsanjan was used by Hollywood director Francis Ford Coppola for his epic film *Apocalypse Now* (older residents complain the town hasn't been the same since). Pagsanjan is known for its river rapids and the numerous waterfalls that empty into the Magdapio River; the last set of falls, the **Magdapio Falls,** cascade from a height of about 100 feet. You can take to the river in small boats guided through the rapids by skillful oarsmen. A raft trip under the Magdapio Falls into a cave caps off the ride. This exhilarating trip offers a glimpse of rural life: villagers bathing and laundering in the river as well as an occasional water buffalo (*carabao* in Pilipino) cooling off. Be sure to dress appropriately, and wrap your camera and watch in plastic. Life preservers aren't provided, so you might want to think twice about bringing children along. The round-trip takes 2½–3 hours. The fee is P500 for two, or P250 per head. Although not obliged to, passengers are expected to tip the boatmen; P80 each is a reasonable sum.

Legazpi City

545 km (338 mi) from Manila or an hour by plane.

Legazpi City—near the tip of southern Luzon, an hour's flight from Manila—has what may be the world's most symmetrical (and still active) volcano, towering 8,189 feet over the Bicol countryside. Aside from
★ the lure of the two- to three-day climb, **Mt. Mayon** has a volcanol-

ogy/seismography station at about 2,500 ft, with a rest house offering panoramic views of the volcano and the surrounding terrain. The station has geological displays relating to volcanoes, earthquakes, and tidal waves. You can also see a seismograph in operation.

Just 5 km (3 mi) from Legazpi City are the **Cagsawa Bell Tower and Ruins,** all that remains of a church buried in an 1814 eruption; the more than 1,000 people who had sought refuge inside also perished. For more information on Lezgapi City, contact the **Department of Tourism office** (Peñaranda Park, Albay District, ☎ 5221/4492 or 5221/4026).

Hundred Islands National Park

254 km (158 mi) from Manila.

North of Manila, on the west coast of Luzon, is a collection of small islands (the largest being Governor's and Quezon) that have good to spectacular beaches and some good snorkeling. There are no commercial establishments, so if you choose to visit, bring food and refreshments. Some of the islands have no shade and some have snakes—the local boatmen who transport you among the islands will know which ones are which. Boats can be reserved in the small coastal town of Lucap, a 4½-hour drive from Manila, at the Public Assistance Center (which, like the entire town, has no phone).

NORTHERN LUZON

The Philippines is justly acknowledged for its beautiful waters and beaches, though the fact that the country is essentially mountainous is sometimes overlooked. In northern Luzon are the rugged Cordillera and the Sierra Madre ranges, with breathtaking views at elevations of from 3,000 to 9,500 feet, and the narrow but beautiful coastal plains of the Ilocos region. This area is home to ancient highland peoples—referred to collectively as Igorots and less Westernized than their lowland counterparts—whose origins can be traced to migratory groups older than the Malays. Over the centuries highland and lowland cultures have mingled through commerce, religion, education, and conflict. Nowhere is this more evident than in the charming city of Baguio: A good number of its inhabitants are lowlanders (businesspeople, retirees, artists), so you're as likely to hear Pilipino as well as Ilocano, the regional tongue. The city also has several universities, attracting students from all over Luzon.

Sitting at 5,000 feet above sea level among pine-covered slopes, Baguio is a lovely respite from the lowland heat and serves as a base from which to explore the rice terraces of Banaue or the towns and churches of the Ilocos region—especially the area around Vigan and Laoag. A combination of rugged terrain and coastal plains, Ilocos is known for its neat towns, its hardworking natives, and its gorgeous Spanish-era churches. (Note that it can be chilly at night, especially from November through February, and that rains are torrential during the wet season (mid-June through October) and can cause rock slides and make roads impassable.)

Numbers in the margin correspond to points of interest on the Northern Luzon map.

Baguio

❶ *246 km (153 mi) north of Manila, 196 km (121 mi) south of Vigan.*

At 5,000 feet above sea level, the air in Baguio is crisp, invigorating, and laden with the fragrance of pine trees. Billed as the "summer cap-

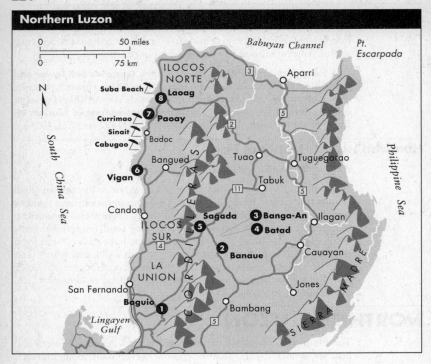

0   50 miles
0   75 km

N

Babuyan Channel   Pt. Escarpada

ILOCOS NORTE

Suba Beach

8 Laoag

3   Aparri

Currimao **7** Paoay

Sinait
Cabugao   Badoc

Bangued

Tuao

5

Tuguegarao

Vigan **6**

Tabuk

11

5

Candon

ILOCOS SUR   **5** Sagada   **3** Banga-An   Ilagan

4 Batad

2 Banaue   Cauayan

LA UNION   Jones

San Fernando

Baguio **1**

Bambang

5

Lingayen Gulf

South China Sea

Philippine Sea

CORDILLERAS

SIERRA MADRE

ital of the Philippines," this resort city was developed as a hill station during the American colonial era and is now the commercial, educational, and recreational hub of the Cordilleras. Avoid the city during the Christmas holidays and Easter week, when both the population of 150,000 and prices practically double. A day tour could begin at the Department of Tourism (☞ Contacts and Resources *in* Northern Luzon A to Z, *below*), where you can pick up maps and suggestions.

Start your tour at **Mines View Park,** a 15- to 20-minute ride by public jeepney from Session Road, the city's main downtown artery. Mines View is a promontory from which you can gaze at the surrounding mountains and abandoned silver mines. (Below the promontory, local children wait for you to toss coins, which they catch with baskets on poles.) Souvenir stalls sell wood carvings, brassware, walking sticks, jewelry, native blankets, and bamboo flutes.

Take a jeepney back to Baguio's downtown, and the vehicle will pass by **Mansion House.** Built in 1908 as the summer residence of the American governor-generals, it now serves as the getaway of Philippine presidents. Visitors enter through gates that replicate those of Buckingham Palace in London. ⊠ *Leonard Wood Rd.,* ☎ *74/442–2703.* ▢ *Admission.* ☉ *Daily 8–5.*

Across the road is the **Pool of Pines,** a 300-foot-long carp pool that's bordered by pine trees. From the vine-covered stone trellis at the far end, steps lead down to **Wright Park,** home to a rental stable (☞ Outdoor Activities and Sports, *below*).

At **Baguio Botanical Park** (⊠ Leonard Wood Rd.), a pleasant arboretum a short drive (again, towards downtown Baguio) from Mansion House, you will find sculptures of *anitos* (native gods) and examples of dwellings used by the different highland ethnic groups. For a small fee, natives dressed in traditional tribal finery will pose for photos.

Return to Session Road and look for what may be the Philippines' only cathedral painted a light, cheery pink. With its hints of Norman architecture, **Baguio Cathedral** won't inspire raves, but it is a good perch from which to get a panoramic view of Baguio and of Mt. St. Tomás, its highest peak. ✉ *Post Office Loop,* ☎ *74/442–4256.* ☉ *Mon.–Sat. 6–8 AM and 5–6 PM, Sun. 5–10 AM and 4–6 PM.*

| NEED A BREAK? | ✕ **Mario's** has a first-rate Caesar salad, good steaks, seafood, and daily chef's specials. Its success has spawned two branches in Metro Manila. ✉ *176 Session Rd.,* ☎ *74/442–4241. AE, DC, MC, V.* |

On one side of Baguio Cathedral is a long flight of steps leading to **Session Road,** downtown Baguio's half-mile-long main street, with bazaars, restaurants, movie houses, offices, and cafés. This (and Burnham Park, *below*) is where Baguio residents promenade.

★ Set between a hill and Magsaysay Avenue (at the bottom of Session Road), the **Baguio Public Market** is an indispensable part of the Baguio experience. A series of alleys with stalls on either side, it has sections devoted to fish and meat; fresh vegetables and strawberries, for which Baguio is famous; dry goods, from Igorot blankets and traditional loincloths to army surplus; regional handicrafts, with an emphasis on rattan backpacks, silver jewelry, and tribal ornaments; tailor shops; and antiques. The money changers here give a better rate than you'll find at hotels or banks.

South of Session Road lies the pleasant oasis of **Burnham Park.** Named for American landscape architect Daniel Burnham, who helped plan the city, the park's spacious grounds are perfect for an idyllic stroll or a picnic on the grass. It's popular with families and crowded on weekends. For kids, there's boating on the artificial lake and skating. Bicycles can be rented.

End your tour of the city at the **Baguio–Mt. Province Museum,** at Club John Hay (a former U.S. military base), which houses an excellent collection of artifacts, tribal clothing, weaponry, and dioramas. You'll need to take another jeepney, or a taxi (eminently affordable); just tell the driver you're going to John Hay. He'll know exactly where it is. ✉ *Loakan Rd. and South Dr.,* ☎ *74/442–7902.* ▨ *Admission.* ☉ *Daily 8–5.*

Dining and Lodging

Baguio City has a wide range of accommodations, from medium-size hotels to pension-style lodgings. Restaurants are informal and inexpensive, serving a wide range of Western-style, Chinese, and Philippine dishes.

$$ ✕ **Barrio Fiesta/Pinoy Hotpot.** You can dine on Philippine dishes, including food served in a hot pot, while admiring or critiquing the 10 giant Igorot wooden statues and other carvings that decorate the interior. ✉ *North Dr. and Session Rd.,* ☎ *74/442–6049. AE, DC, MC, V.*

$$ ✕ **Bonuan.** In a quiet neighborhood below the cathedral, this establishment specializes in seafood and Philippine cuisine. ✉ *10-B Happy Glen Loop,* ☎ *74/442–5175. AE, V.*

$$ ✕ **Cafe by the Ruins.** An airy place with a patio setting, this café serves
★ excellent home-cooked Philippine cuisine, including delicious tiny fried fish, fish-roe steak, and vegetarian spring rolls. The café makes its own pastas and bread. ✉ *23 Chuntug St.,* ☎ *74/442–4010. No credit cards.*

$$ ✕ **O Mai Kan.** Featuring an all-you-can-eat menu, this establishment offers a style of cooking they call "Mongolian": You fill a large bowl with

various meats and vegetables and select the spices you like, and the staff cooks it for you. ⊠ 12 Otek St. ☎ 74/442–5885. AE, DC, V.

$ ✕ **Biscotti en Chocolat.** The paintings hung on the wall here reveal the calling of the owners, two artists. A variety of coffees, pastries, and Mexican-type dishes like tacos and tamales are served. ⊠ *Unit 5, Nevada Sq., near Club John Hay, no phone. No credit cards.*

$ ✕ **Ionic Cafe.** Midway along Session Road, this hip place, favored by students and local bohemians, has good coffee, a full bar, salads, pastas, and sandwiches. Its second-floor windows afford excellent people-watching. ⊠ *Session Rd.,* ☎ *74/442–3867. No credit cards.*

$ ✕ **Solana's Manna.** This bakery offers mountain coffee, products made from *camote* (yam) flour, and breakfast and lunch dishes. ⊠ *Club John Hay,* ☎ *74/442–7902. No credit cards. No dinner.*

$ ✕ **Star Cafe.** This bright, busy Chinese restaurant has an extensive menu of tasty dishes, most of which are reasonably priced. ⊠ *Session Rd.,* ☎ *74/442–3148. AE, DC, MC, V.*

$$ ▦ **Benguet Prime Hotel.** Right in the heart of busy downtown, this architecturally challenged hotel has no lobby to speak of, but it is clean and convenient. Rooms are spacious, though the decor is plain. ⊠ *Session Rd. at Calderon Rd.,* ☎ *74/442–7066. 51 rooms. Restaurant, room service. AE, DC, V.*

$$ ▦ **Burnham Hotel.** The accommodations at this small hotel near Session Road, the heart of downtown Baguio, are clean and wood-paneled. Avoid rooms on the ground floor, as they can be noisy. ⊠ *21 Calderon Rd.,* ☎ *74/442–2331 or 74/442–5117,* ℻ *74/442–8415. 18 rooms. Restaurant, room service. AE, DC, V.*

$$ ▦ **Mountain Lodge.** A cozy establishment with a lobby fireplace and local artifacts as decor, the lodge is in a quiet area. The dining section includes a terrace. The rooms are clean and simply furnished. ⊠ *27 Leonard Wood Rd.,* ☎ *74/442–4544. 21 rooms. Restaurant, bar. DC, MC, V.*

$$ ▦ **Munsayac Inn.** Small but well maintained, this family-run hotel has a pleasant ambience. Long patronized by missionaries, the inn will appeal to those who like their lodgings on the quiet side. The rooms are neat, with locally woven blankets, TV, and a refrigerator. ⊠ *125 Leonard Wood Rd.,* ☎ *74/442–2451. 20 rooms. Restaurant, lobby lounge. AE, DC, MC, V.*

$–$$ ▦ **Casa Amapola.** In a quiet neighborhood, this pension—once a fam-
★ ily residence—retains a family-style informality. What was once the living room is now a lounge where guests meet informally, and there's a terrace where you can breakfast while watching the fog lift from the surrounding hills. In addition to the regular rooms, three three-story chalets with verandas and kitchens are available for those who like more privacy. ⊠ *46 First Rd., Quezon Hill,* ☎ *74/442–3406. 13 rooms, 3 chalets. Dining room. AE, V.*

$ ▦ **Cecile's Inn.** This lovely old wooden house next door to the Cafe by the Ruins has spacious, high–ceilinged (albeit plain) rooms, with a bed, small table, and dresser. ⊠ *23 Chuntug St.,* ☎ *74/442–4010. Lobby lounge. No credit cards.*

Nightlife and the Arts

THE ARTS

Baguio has a lively arts scene, with the arts collective, the **Baguio Arts Guild** (☎ 74/442–8489), and other civic groups organizing the biannual **Baguio Arts Festival** in late November. Poetry readings, art exhibits, dance, music, and performance art constitute a cornucopia of festival activity. **Christine's Art Gallery** (⊠ 23 Chuntug St., ☎ 74/442–

5041), adjacent to Cafe by the Ruins, is a showcase for contemporary local artists.

NIGHTLIFE

Pub Luz (⊠ 12 Chuntug St., across from City Hall, no phone) hosts folk and rock bands on weekends. **Rumors** (⊠ 55 Session Rd., no phone) is a low-key bar and lounge with tasty appetizers; you can also hear live music here from time to time. **Songs** (⊠ 181 Session Rd., at Carlu St., ☎ 74/442–4963) is a small, often smoky club featuring jazz or folk music; patrons are of all ages. **Spirits** (⊠ 22 Otek St., at Burnham Park, ☎ 74/442–3097) is a pleasant, lively disco in a rambling colonial-era gingerbread wooden house, which is itself worth a close look.

Outdoor Activities and Sports

GOLF

Try your irons at the 18-hole **Club John Hay** (⊠ South Dr. at Loakan Rd., ☎ 74/442–7902); fees are P550 weekdays, P750 weekends.

HORSEBACK RIDING

There are ponies and larger horses for both children and adults alike at **Wright Park**; the fee is less than P100 an hour. You can ride on some trails outside the park, but only with a guide. Guides don't usually give lessons, but if you'd like some instruction, the local DOT office advises you pay the guide an hourly fee of P120.

Shopping

Check out the handicraft section of the Baguio Public Market (☞ *above*) and the antiques shops right above it. **Easter Weaving School** (⊠ Easter School Rd., 10-min. drive from Session Rd., ☎ 74/442–4972) offers highland blankets and clothing woven on the premises. At **Munsayac's Handicraft** (⊠ 21 Leonard Wood Rd., ☎ 74/442–2451), good wood carvings, brass, and silverware can be found. For items made of *ikat* (an indigenous woven cloth), try **Narda's** (⊠ 151 Session Rd., ☎ 74/442–2992). Off Session Road there's the **St. Louis Silver Shop** (⊠ St. Louis High School, Assumption Rd., ☎ 74/442–2139), with conventional but high-quality artisanship. **Tucucan** (⊠ Upper Level, Maharlika Bldg., Baguio Public Market, ☎ 74/442–4169) has unusual artifacts, from baskets to beads.

Banaue

❷ *196 km (122 mi) from Baguio. Banaue is a 9-hour drive from Baguio or Manila; route from Baguio is shorter, but is all on mountain roads with dizzying switchbacks and long unpaved stretches.*

★ Looking like giant steps to the sky, the **Banaue Rice Terraces** are spectacular, man-made rice paddies terraced into the mountainsides of Mayaoyao and Carballo by the Ifugao, a highland tribe, more than 2,000 years ago. If placed end to end, these terraces would extend for 22,500 km (14,000 mi) or halfway around the world. Some of the terraces can be seen from Banaue itself, but the best views are in the countryside. **Viewpoint,** a 1½-hour hike (ask for directions) or a 20-minute drive from Banaue proper, is a promontory offering a panoramic view of the rice terraces. Wizened Ifugao women in native dress will pose for a little money.

Dining and Lodging

$$ ╳ **Banaue Hotel Restaurant.** This informal but excellent restaurant serves
★ American-style breakfasts, Continental food, and such Philippine regional dishes as *pinakbet* (vegetable stew with pork in a salty sauce). The dining room is large and airy, with bright red decor, native wall hangings, and a view of the hotel gardens. Service is superb. ⊠ *Banaue Hotel, Banaue,* ☎ *73/386–4007. AE, DC, MC, V.*

$ ✗ **Cool Winds.** Simple and inexpensive fare is the speciality of this spot near the town market, a favorite of locals and backpackers. ✉ *Town Market, Banaue, no phone. No credit cards.*

$$ 🏨 **Banaue Hotel.** Each room at this semiluxury hotel has a terrace and a good view of the town and valley; decor is reminiscent of a country lodge. ✉ *Banaue, ☎FAX 73/386–4087; in Manila, ☎ 2/812–1984. 90 rooms. Restaurant, lobby lounge, pool. AE, DC, MC, V.*

$ 🏨 **Sanafe Lodge.** Near the city market, Sanafe is a combination dormitory and hotel, with a small lobby overlooking rice terraces. Private rooms are small but clean; the less expensive dorm rooms—which sleep eight—are spartan but also clean. The resident manager is a gold mine of information concerning the area. ✉ *Banaue, ☎ 73/386–4085; in Manila, ☎ 2/721–1075. 14 rooms (8 with bath), 2 dorms. Restaurant. No credit cards.*

Nightlife and the Arts

The Banaue Hotel puts on a free cultural show of Ifugao dances for its guests nightly at 8, or after dinner. After the performance, the dancers try to get the guests to join in for an impromptu session.

Outdoor Activities and Sports

TREKKING

The main outdoor activity in the Banaue area is trekking, and guides can be hired at pre-arranged fees; on the average, expect to pay about P300. A number of well-marked trails go to and through the rice terraces, for hikes that range from a couple of hours to a whole day, and even overnight. **Banaue Hotel** (☞ Dining and Lodging, *above*) has a list of treks and guides and even has walking sticks available, free of charge.

Shopping

Near the town market, which has handicrafts stalls, is the small **Trade Center,** good for such souvenirs as baskets, handwoven backpacks, and wood carvings.

Banga-An and Batad

❸ ❹ *From Banaue, Banga-An is an hour's drive on rough roads or three hours on foot; Batad is a 1½-hour drive, four–five hours on foot. You can't drive into the villages themselves; to get there, you must park your vehicle on the main and only road and walk—down to Banga-An, or up a steep mountain trail to Batad.*

Even more spectacular than Banaue are the Ifugao villages of Banga-An and Batad, both set among the terraces. Along the way you'll see pine-covered slopes, green valleys dwarfed by clouded peaks, far-off, pyramid-shape Ifugao huts improbably perched on crags, and mountain streams irrigating the terraces. There life goes on pretty much as it has for centuries: Rice is still planted in age-old rituals and plowed regularly with the help of the ubiquitous water buffalo. Dogs, pigs, and ducks wander about and under the native huts, which are elevated on wood posts. Handicrafts—rattan backpacks, baskets, and ornaments—are sold for low prices.

Sagada

❺ *150 km (93 mi) northeast of Baguio, a dusty, seven-hour bus ride on narrow winding roads (compensated for by mountain vistas). Dangwa buses (☎ 74/442–4150) depart in early morning from terminal in front of Baguio public market.*

Deep in the central Cordilleras among the rice terraces is a small, tightly knit Igorot community. A favorite with adventurous backpackers, Sagada has several burial caves with hanging coffins, an underground river, waterfalls, limestone formations, and hiking trails. Although these places of interest can be visited in one day, it is well worth spending at least two days here to savor this unspoiled town's charm, striking scenery, and laidback atmosphere. This is a wonderful place to visit, but be respectful of local customs. Do not, for instance, take photographs of the townspeople without asking their permission. Never point: it's considered intolerably rude. And of course, don't disturb the hanging coffins.

You can begin a walk through town from **Masferre's Studio,** 15 minutes south from the town center. A Spaniard who settled in Sagada and married a local, Eduardo Masferre chronicled the lives of the Cordilleran peoples for several decades, starting in the 1930s. A collection of his photos, which have been exhibited in several countries, is on display here, and prints and postcards are on sale. ⊠ *Bontoc–Banga–an Road.* ▣ *Free.* ☉ *Irregular hours.*

Sagada Weaving, closer to town than Masferre's studio, is a well-known purveyor of such quality hand-loomed products as sturdy backpacks, shoulder bags, and blankets. You can watch the Igorot women skillfully plying their trade, incorporating traditional designs into their weaving. ⊠ *Main road.* ☉ *Daily 9–4.*

Across from Sagada Weaving, a trail winds down to a small valley where it's easy to spot the mouth of **Matangkib Cave** and the burial coffins stored in niches within. Respect for these remains is a must. Enter the cave (you'll need flashlights) and you can hear the roar of an **underground river.**

Not far from Sagada Weaving—proceeding south and on the same side of the road—is a trail cutting across a narrow river. The trail leads to the small **Bokong Waterfall,** set amidst rice terraces, with a deep pool that's perfect for cooling off in after a day of hiking.

Dining and Lodging
In this small village, most of the dining places are close to the town center, near the Town Hall and market. Prices are truly a bargain, but credit cards are useless here. The lodgings are equally a bargain, as none charges more than $4 a night.

$ ✕ **Country Cafe.** Come to enjoy the big fireplace and strong native coffee. Short-order meals, ice cream, and homemade cakes are available. ⊠ *North of town hall, on the road to Besao, no phone. No credit cards.*

$ ✕ **Log Cabin Cafe.** This quiet and friendly spot serves very good dishes that reflect some European influence. ⊠ *North of town hall, on the road to Besao, no phone. No credit cards.*

$ ✕ **Shamrock Cafe.** Overlooking the market, this café is one of the oldest in town and offers breakfast, lunch, dinner, snacks, and drinks. ⊠ *South of town hall, on the road to Demang, no phone. No credit cards.*

$ ▦ **Mapiya-aw Pension.** This pleasant guesthouse is surrounded by striking limestone formations and pine groves. The staff is friendly and helpful and will serve meals on request. ⊠ *East of town hall, on the road to Bontoc, no phone. 12 rooms. Laundry service. No credit cards.*

$ ▦ **Masferre Cafe & Inn.** The rooms here are large, and the restaurant has a view of rice terraces. It has a gift shop that sells Masferre postcards and T-shirts. ⊠ *South of town hall, on the road to Demang, no phone. 10 rooms. Laundry service. No credit cards.*

$ 🏠 **St. Joseph's Rest House.** The largest accomodation in the area is slightly elevated, with a good view of the town and the Episcopalian church across the way. Rooms are spartan but clean. ✉ *East of town hall, opposite the church. 15 rooms. Laundry service. No credit cards.*

Outdoor Activities and Sports

Besides the Matangkib Cave (☞ *above*), there are other caves in the Sagada area. If you want to go spelunking, visit the offices of the **Sagada Environmental Guides Association** at the town hall and get information and a guide; unfortunately, the association has no phone and keeps irregular hours. Rates depend on the size of the party but are eminently affordable. Hiking is the area's other main outdoor activity; you can head into the fields and pine groves by yourself, but if you would like to know the countryside better, the guides association can arrange to take you out.

Vigan

❻ *196 km (122 mi) north of Baguio, 78 km (48 mi) south of Laoag.*

The capital of the Ilocos Sur province, a scenic four-hour drive from Baguio, is Vigan, a small coastal city that dates from the early years of Spanish colonization. It has some of the best-preserved Spanish-influenced architecture in the country, suggesting how Manila's Intramuros would have looked had it not been destroyed during World War II.

Set in a colonial-era residence that used to be occupied by a revolutionary priest, the **Ayala Museum** has a collection of dioramas, artifacts, and paintings relating to the area's history. View period furniture and rooms, local artifacts, and 14 paintings depicting a local revolt. ✉ *Burgos St.,* ☎ *77/855–316.* 🎫 *Admission.* ⊙ *Tues.–Sun. 9–noon and 1–5.*

It's about a 10-minute walk from the Ayala Museum to the town's main landmark, the 16th-century **Vigan Cathedral** (also known as the Cathedral of St. Paul), a massive, whitewashed brick-and-wood structure with a tile roof. Chinese lions guard the portals and the gleaming silver altar within. It's a short stroll northwest of the cathedral to the **Old Quarter.** The buildings have whitewashed brick walls, tile roofs, sliding *capiz* (mother-of-pearl) windows, and lofty interiors. General Luna, Crisologo, De los Reyes, and Bonifacio streets have row upon row of these edifices—perfect backdrops for Westerns or gothic films, for which, in fact, they have been used. You can explore the old town on your own in a couple of hours, or contact **Ric Favis** (☎ 77/722–2286), an excellent guide who owns a home in the area; his rates average $10 per hour.

Dining and Lodging

On the Ilocos coast, seafood dishes and vegetables are the specialty. Try fried squid, fresh shrimp marinated in vinegar and peppers, and grilled catch of the day. In Vigan's plaza, you can taste the local delicacy, an *empanada* (turnover) stuffed with vegetables. Also worth trying are *ipon,* delicious small fish caught seasonally, and *pinakbet,* a vegetable dish with bits of pork and tiny shrimp, flavored with *bagoong,* a salty shrimp paste (also used as a condiment).

$ ✕ **Cool Spot.** Pick from the tasty regional dishes on display behind a glass counter in this wide, airy, thatch-and-bamboo hut. ✉ *Beside Vigan Hotel, Burgos St.,* ☎ *77/722–2588. No credit cards.*

$$ 🏠 **Cordillera Inn.** The rooms at this inn, a colonial-era building with broad stairways and good views of the Old Quarter, are on the bare side but clean. Climb up to the roof for an excellent panorama. ✉ *Gen-*

eral Luna St., at Crisologo St., ☎ 77/722–2526. 23 rooms. Restaurant, laundry service. No credit cards.

$ ⌂ **Villa Angela.** This lovely turn-of-the-century home with period furniture and a garden has been converted into a pension. The living room has family memorabilia on display. In keeping with the spirit of the place, the rooms have high ceilings, old-fashioned poster beds, mosquito nets, and mother-of-pearl windows. Meals can be ordered. ✉ *Quirino Blvd., at Liberation St., ☎ 77/722–2755 or 77/722–2766. 6 rooms. Laundry service. No credit cards.*

Shopping

Besides than the town markets, there's the *burnay,* or **potters' district,** of Vigan, about a 15-minute walk from the cathedral, where jars and urns can be bought for low prices from the potters themselves. The Old Quarter has antiques shops, such as **Ciudad Fernandina** (✉ 888 Plaza Burgos, ☎ 77/722–2888). In the town of Santiago, south of Vigan, there's **Cora's Ethnic Handwoven,** where the prized local weave is available.

En Route   North of Vigan are a number of good beaches—most of which have no resorts—near the towns of Cabugao, Sinait, Currimao, and Pangil. Sinait's beach, Pug-os, is a picture-pretty white-sand beach used by local fishermen to store their boats and nets.

Paoay

❼ *20 km (12 mi) south of Laoag.*

Between Vigan and Laoag are towns whose churches are fine examples of what a local writer once termed Filipino Baroque—unique, even rococo, combinations of Western and Asian styles. Among the most impressive are Santa Maria, with its stately broad steps; Magsingal, ★ with a small but intriguing museum nearby; and the majestic **Paoay Church** in Paoay, a sleepy town about 15 minutes from Laoag. The crenellations and turrets, massive curlicued buttresses, exterior stairways, and niches are reminiscent of a Javanese temple. Beside this splendid fusion of styles is a belfry made of limestone, used as an outpost during the Revolution of 1896 against Spain and by guerrillas during the Japanese occupation in World War II.

Laoag

❽ *278 km (172 mi) north of Baguio, 78 km (48 mi) or an hour's drive, from Vigan.*

Laoag, another coastal Spanish colonial town, doesn't have the wealth of architecture and sights of Vigan, though **Laoag Cathedral** and its **Sinking Bell Tower** are worth visiting. The 17th-century cathedral is heavily buttressed (a protection against earthquakes), with two exterior stone stairways, urn ornamentation, and foliate capitals. North of the church is a bell tower that has sunk about 1 m (1.09 yds), so that its portal is barely visible.

Dining and Lodging

$$$ ✕ **Pamulinawen.** Wood-paneled and spacious, Pamulinawen serves very ★ good Philippine cuisine, including pinakbet and beef *tapa* (cured, dried strips of meat served with a vinegar-and-garlic sauce), and some Continental dishes. ✉ *Fort Ilokandia Hotel, Baranggay 37, Calayag, ☎ 77/772–1166. AE, DC, MC, V.*

$$$ ⌂ **Fort Ilokandia.** This sprawling hotel is made up of several two-story ★ buildings whose style and room decor suggest the Old Quarter residences of Vigan. Tiled walkways connect the buildings, which are nestled

among sand dunes. The hotel has a good black-sand beach. ⊠ *Barang-gay 37, Calayab*, ☎ *77/772–1166,* FAX *77/772–1411. 264 rooms. Restaurant, bar, pool, dance club. AE, DC, MC, V.*

OFF THE BEATEN PATH   **THE BATANES –** The country's northernmost islands, the Batanes are closer to Taiwan than to Luzon. The rugged cliffs, rolling grassy fields akin to the Scottish moors, scenic coastline, and idyllic towns with unique stone-walled homes make for great treks. It's best to visit between November and May, as these isles are in the middle of the typhoon belt. PAL flies from Manila to Basco, the capital, thrice weekly, with a stopover in Laoag. Be sure to book your flight well in advance, as it is a popular destination with locals.

Northern Luzon A to Z

Arriving and Departing

BY BUS

A number of bus companies run daily trips from Manila to Northern Luzon on an hourly basis, with the most numerous being to Baguio, Vigan, and Laoag; for information, contact the Manila offices of Pantranco, Victory Lines, or Dangwa (☞ Arriving and Departing *in* Metro Manila A to Z, *above*). There are no nonstop bus routes to Sagada from Manila; you have to change buses in Baguio, at the terminal in front of the public market, or catch a jeepney from Banaue.

BY CAR

From Manila it's a mostly smooth six-hour drive to Baguio via the North Diversion highway, which begins at EDSA, links up to the MacArthur Highway, and leads to the zigzagging Kennon Road. If Kennon is closed for repairs, you can take Naguilian Road or the Marcos Highway (which has a Mt. Rushmore–like bust of the late dictator), farther north along the coast. Add an extra hour for these routes to Baguio. Because of rough road conditions, it isn't advisable to drive to Banaue—rather, take a public bus or join a tour group originating in Manila.

BY PLANE

Philippine Air Lines (PAL; ☎ 74/832–3166) has daily 45-minute flights from Manila Domestic Airport to Loakan Airport in Baguio; a cab ride from the airport into town should cost approximately P100. PAL has Monday and Friday flights to Laoag Airport; there are public jeepneys available at Laoag Airport that ply the Vigan–Laoag route.

Getting Around

BY BUS

Buses are used to get from one town to the next, and they are numerous and cheap. Terminals are located near the public markets. Baguio has two terminals, one in front of the public market on Magsaysay Avenue—where buses for Sagada can be boarded—and the other on Governor Pack Road, at the top of Session Road, where buses depart for Manila and Vigan.

BY CAR

On the coastal plains and around the cities of Baguio, Vigan, and Laoag, the roads range from good to excellent. Northeast of Baguio, however, deeper into the Cordilleras, they can be very bad, and public transportation is a better bet.

BY JEEPNEY

Plentiful and good for short routes, jeepneys begin and end their routes at or near the public market. They can also be hired for out-of-town trips. The average cost of a ride, for about a kilometer, is a mere P2.

BY TAXI

The region's only cabs are in Baguio. They are small Japanese models, and cheap: Rides within the central part of town average $2.

Contacts and Resources

EMERGENCIES

For emergencies in Baguio, contact the following: **Police,** ☎ 74/166. **Fire,** ☎ 74/160 or 74/442–3222. **General Hospital** (✉ Governor Pack Rd., ☎ 74/169). **St. Louis University Hospital** (✉ Assumption Rd., ☎ 74/442–5701).

LATE-NIGHT PHARMACIES

Baguio's **Mercury Drug Store** (✉ Session Rd. near Magsaysay Rd., Baguio, ☎ 74/442–4310) is open until 9 PM.

VISITOR INFORMATION

Department of Tourism (✉ Governor Pack Rd., Baguio, ☎ 74/442–7014, FAX 74/442–8848).

THE VISAYAS, MINDANAO, AND PALAWAN

While northerners are known for their industry and frugality, southerners are easygoing, gregarious, and musical (the best guitars come from this area). The land and seas are especially fertile, yet some of the worst pockets of poverty are also found here, arising out of centuries-old feudalism, an overdependence on cash crops, and the often tragic effects of militarization in areas where the New People's Army is active. It bears repeating that travelers need not worry about being caught up in the conflict: armed clashes almost always occur in remote rural areas. And left-wing insurgency is on the decline.

Geographically, the Visayas are the center of the Philippines. Bound on the north by Luzon and on the south by Mindanao, this group of islands has some of the best beaches and resorts in the country, unusual natural attractions, and non-Hispanicized minority cultures. Both Mindanao, the second-largest island in the country, and Palawan (the westernmost isle) are intriguing mixes of Christian, Muslim, and indigenous cultures. Large areas of both islands have been settled by mostly Christian migrants from Luzon and the Visayas. In the case of Mindanao, this has led to an ongoing Muslim secessionist movement, though peace talks are being conducted between the government and leaders of the movement. To really enjoy the region, take the time to appreciate the affectionate, fun-loving ways of its people, explore the beaches and beautiful scenery, and take in the charm of small towns and cities, many with old Spanish homes.

Numbers in the margin correspond to points of interest on the Visayas and Mindanao map.

Cebu City

❶ *1 hour by plane from Manila.*

This small but strategically important port has the advantages of a big city—restaurants, shops, lodgings, schools, and businesses—but few of the drawbacks. The "Queen City of the South" and capital of Cebu Island, it is not far from Homonhon, where Ferdinand Magellan claimed the country for Spain in 1521. The first Spanish settlement in the Philippines, Cebu is the oldest city in the country–founded by the Spanish conquistador Miguel Lopez de Legazpi in 1571. Little is left of the original town, however combined with other attractions, Cebu

The Visayas and Mindanao

Romblon
Odiongan
Tablas
Island
Sibuyan
Island
Masbate
MASBATE
Uson
Catarman
Laoang
Palapag
3
Balud
Calbayog City
SAMAR
4 **Boracay Island**
THE VISAYAS
Visayan
Sea
Sicogon Island
Catbalogan
Kalibo
Roxas City
Bantayan
Island
Biliran
Island
LEYTE
Burauen
Culasi
PANAY
Passi
Cadiz City
Escalante
Ormoc City
2
Baybay
Leyte
Gulf
Silay City
Iloilo City
2
Talisay
San Carlos City
CEBU
Matcan Island
Hilongos
Dinagat
Island
Miagao
3
Bacolod City
Strait
1 **Cebu City**
Strait
Maasin
Panaon
Island
Guimaras
Island
Guimaras
Naga
Carcar
BOHOL
Surigao City
Panay
Gulf
Kabankalan
Tanon Strait
Bohol
Bais City
Tagbilaran City
Chocolate Hills
Cauayan
NEGROS
Badian Island
Tanjay
Panglao
Island
Mindanao
Sea
Sipalay
Hinob-an
Bayawan
Santa Catalina
Dumaguete City
Siquijor
Island
Camiguin
Island
Cabadbaran
1
10
Palawan
Dapitan City
Dipolog City
Cagayan de Oro City
Gingoog City
Butuan City
Sulu
Sea
Oroquieta City
7
Iligan City
1
MINDANAO
Marawi City
Lake
Lanao
Valencia
Zamboanga Peninsula
N
Pagadian City
Quezon
Tagum
Parang
Cotabato City
Sultan Kudarat
3
Mt. Apo
National
Park **7**
Davao City **5**
Taluksangay
9
Moro
Gulf
Dinaig
Pikit
Magpet
Kidapawan
6
Samal
Island
8 **Zamboanga**
City
Santa Cruz Island
Lamitan
5
Davao
Gulf
Isabela
Basilan
Island
Celebes Sea
Polomolok
General
Santos City
Malita
Glan
N

0 _____ 100 miles

0 _____ 150 km

City makes for a fascinating and rewarding day-long tour. Most of the historical sights are within walking distance of one another in the downtown area near the ports.

Fort San Pedro is the oldest and smallest fort in the country, built in 1565. The three bastions with turrets for cannon give the fort its triangular shape. The parapets afford a good view of the sea—a necessity in the days when the settlement was a target for pirate raids. ⊠ *Port area,* ☎ *32/96518.* ☜ *Admission.* ◷ *Daily 8–noon and 1–5.*

From Fort San Pedro it's a 10-minute walk to Plaza Santa Cruz, where **Magellan's Cross,** the original cross brought over by the famed Portuguese navigator, is housed. You won't actually *see* the original: Residents believe the cross is miraculous and used to take slivers from it, so it has been encased within the hollow wooden cross that is displayed, suspended from the ceiling of an open-sided domed pavilion on Magallanes Street.

Opposite Magellan's Cross is the 18th-century **Basilica Minore** (closed daily noon–2 PM), built in typical Spanish Baroque style. The basilica houses the nation's oldest Catholic image—that of **Santo Niño,** the Holy Infant—brought over by Magellan and presented to Queen Juana of Zebu. Enshrined in glass and ornamented with gold and precious stones, the icon stands atop a side altar, venerated by a constant stream of devotees. Outside the church stand candle-bearing middle-aged women who, for a donation, will pray and dance to the Santo Niño on your behalf.

A short stroll from Basilica Minore is the oldest street in the country, named after Cristóbal Colón, otherwise known as Christopher Columbus. Formerly the heart of the Parian District (or Chinatown), **Colón Street** is now downtown Cebu's main drag. Here modernity crowds in on you in the form of movie houses, restaurants, department stores, and other commercial establishments.

NEED A
BREAK?

Colón Street is lined with eateries—try **Ding How Dim Sum** (⊠ 76 Colón St., ☎ 32/94946) where light Chinese meals are served in a busy, neon-lit environment.

From the eastern end of Colón Street, it's a short walk to **Casa Gorordo,** the former residence of Cebu's first bishop, Juan Gorordo. Now restored, the century-old wood house has a tile roof, mother-of-pearl windows, a wide veranda, and a fine collection of household furnishings from the last century. The ground floor is used as an art gallery for contemporary works by Philippine artists. ⊠ *Lopez Jaena St.,* ☎ *32/94576.* ☜ *Admission.* ◷ *Daily 9–noon and 2–6.*

★ The **University of San Carlos Museum,** a 20-minute walk from Casa Gorordo, has an extensive collection of seashells, fauna, and anthropological relics: local prehistoric stone and iron tools, burial jars, and pottery. Another section focuses on traditional clothing and ornaments of various tribal minorities. ⊠ *Rosario and Junquera Sts.,* ☎ *32/724–19.* ☜ *Admission.* ◷ *Weekdays 9–noon and 3–6, weekends and holidays by appointment.*

Incongruously set in an expensive suburb known as Beverly Hills is a **Taoist Temple,** dedicated to the teachings of the 6th-century BC Chinese philosopher Lao-tzu. You can get here by taxi (referred to as a P.U., for "public utility") for about P80. A flight of 99 steps leads up to it from the road. Come for the panoramic views of the city, the colorful and ornate Chinese architecture, and to have your fortune read. ⊠ *Beverly Hills,* ☎ *32/93652.* ☜ *Free.* ◷ *Daily until dark.*

Dining and Lodging

Sinugba is a Cebuano method of grilling fish and shellfish over coals. Western- and Asian-style dishes are also available. As the second-largest city in the Philippines, Cebu City has a full range of accommodations, from the inexpensive to the costly. A number of nearby islands, namely Badian and Mactan, have attractive beach resorts.

$$$ ✕ **Lantaw Gardens.** You can feast on a splendid, well-priced buffet—★ including seafood—in an open-air garden setting while enjoying a folk-dance show and scenic views of the city. Seating at long tables is available for groups. ⊠ *Cebu Plaza, Nivel Hills, Lahug,* ☎ *32/231–1231. AE, DC, MC, V.*

$ ✕ **Golden Cowrie.** This informal and lively screen-enclosed outdoor establishment serves inexpensive grilled seafood, as well as typical Philippine cuisine. ⊠ *Salina at La Guardia St.,* ☎ *32/92633. No credit cards.*

$ ✕ **Snow Sheen.** Get tasty but inexpensive Chinese food at this busy, unpretentious spot. ⊠ *Juan Luna and Capitolyo Sts.,* ☎ *32/255–1176. No credit cards.*

$ ✕ **Vienna Kaffeehaus.** The Austrian proprietor has re-created the am-★ bience of a Viennese coffeehouse, complete with food, newspapers, and magazines from Vienna. ⊠ *Manros Plaza, Maxilom Ave.,* ☎ *32/253–1430. No credit cards.*

$$$$ ▦ **Badian Beach Club.** On Badian Island, a small island off the southwest coast of Cebu—about a three-hour drive from the city—this resort has a lovely beachfront, scenic views of the bay, sailboats, and a variety of water sports, including scuba diving. The staff schedules a cultural show during the buffet dinners. ⊠ *Badian Island,* ☎ *32/253–3385. 20 cottages. Restaurant, beach. AE, DC, MC, V.*

$$$$ ▦ **Cebu Plaza.** A luxurious hotel, the Cebu Plaza has panoramic views,★ sprawling grounds, and a clientele consisting mainly of Japanese and Chinese tourists. The best rooms are those with a view of the city. ⊠ *Nivel Hills, Lahug, Cebu City,* ☎ *32/311–231,* FAX *32/2312–071. 417 rooms. 2 restaurants, bar, 2 karaoke bars, pool, 2 tennis courts, shops, dance club, meeting rooms. AE, DC, MC, V.*

$$$$ ▦ **Maribago Bluewater Beach Resort.** About 30 minutes from the city, this upscale resort has all the comforts and water sports you'd want. Locally made rattan furniture is used in the brightly decorated rooms. ⊠ *Mactan Island,* ☎ *32/253–7617. 76 rms. 3 restaurants, coffee shop, pool, barbershop, driving range, tennis court, exercise room. AE, DC, MC, V.*

$$$$ ▦ **Shangri-La's Mactan Island Resort.** Situated on a large landscaped site near the airport, this is a palatial luxury resort has a private beach cove. The well-maintained and comfortable rooms have a tropical-decor theme,and come with satellite TV and centralized controls. ⊠ *Mactan Island,* ☎ *32/310–288,* FAX *32/311–688; U.S., 800/942–5050. 407 rooms. 4 restaurants, coffee shop, lobby bar, 2 pools, massage, golf course, tennis court, exercise room, boating, fishing. AE, DC, MC, V.*

$$ ▦ **Montebello Villa.** Located in a quiet neighborhood, this hotel has nice gardens, cheerfully decorated rooms, and a cultivated colonial-era ambience. ⊠ *Banilad,* ☎ *32/313–681,* FAX *32/231–4455. 142 rooms. 2 restaurants, coffee shop, pool, 2 tennis courts, casino, meeting rooms, travel services. AE, DC, MC, V.*

$$ ▦ **Park Place Hotel.** In the heart of downtown, this neat and cozy establishment is patronized mostly by Westerners. ⊠ *Fuente Osmena,* ☎ *32/253–1131,* FAX *32/634–7509. 114 rooms. Restaurant, bar, café, shops, meeting rooms. AE, DC, MC, V.*

Outdoor Activities and Sports

BEACHES

In and around Cebu are a number of beaches and beach resorts (☞ Lodging, *above*). Day visitors can use the beaches for a fee.

TENNIS

Both the Cebu Plaza and Montebello Villa have tennis courts that nonguests can use for a fee.

Nightlife and the Arts

BARS

Love City (✉ Osmeña Blvd., ☎ 32/94077) is a raucous downtown bar with a mostly male clientele who come for beer and the go-go dancers. Europeans favor the friendly, informal **St. Moritz Bar** (✉ Gorordo Ave., Lahug, ☎ 32/231–0914), part of a hotel of the same name.

CASINO

At the **Cebu Casino** (✉ Nivel Hills, Lahug, ☎ 32/74361), not far from Cebu Plaza, the action at the tables runs from 5 PM to 5 AM.

DANCE CLUBS

Balls Disco (✉ Gen. Maxilom Ave., ☎ 32/79305) has live bands from 7 to 10 PM. From 10 on, the dance floor gets crowded with a mixed, mostly young crowd. The city's fashionable set dances at the strobe-lit **Bai Disco** (✉ Cebu Plaza Hotel, Nivel Hills, Lahug, ☎ 32/231–1131). **St. Gotthard** (✉ Fulton St., Lahug, ☎ 32/231–1401) is a lively disco with waitresses on roller skates.

Shopping

One of the best handicraft stores in the city is the **Cebu Display Center** (✉ 11–13 Magallanes, at Lapu-Lapu St., ☎ 32/52223 or 32/52224), which has an excellent collection of regional crafts, particularly shell-craft. Prices aren't inflated for tourists. You may want to visit **Carbon Public Market,** a 20-minute walk from Magellan's Cross and a good place for handicrafts.

OFF THE
BEATEN PATH

CHOCOLATE HILLS, BOHOL ISLAND – These are about 50 striking limestone hills, with an average height of 36 m (120 ft), that look like overturned teacups sans handles. About a two-hour bus ride from the market in Tagbilaran City—a half-hour flight from Cebu City, or one-and-a-half hours via Aboitiz's Supercat Ferry—the hills turn chocolate-brown during the dry months (February through May). In July they become green again, their grasses nourished by rain.

Iloilo City

② *½-hour flight from Cebu City to Iloilo Airport, a 10-minute ride from the city center.*

A small and gracious aggregate of six districts, Iloilo (pronounced "ee-lo-ee-lo"), capital of Iloilo Province on the island of Panay, has a genteel air and loads of southern charm. As always, it's a good idea to visit the Department of Tourism (☞ Visitor Information *in* Visayas, Mindanao, and Palawan A to Z) to pick up maps, brochures, and tips.

Near the city center and across from the provincial Capitol is the **Museo Iloilo,** which has an excellent collection of pre-Hispanic artifacts dug up mainly on Panay Island. These include fossils, Stone Age flake tools, and gold death masks. Other exhibits, some supplemented by video presentations, focus on liturgical art and the treasures of a British frigate shipwrecked nearby in the 19th century. ✉ *Bonifacio*

Dr. at General Luna St., ☎ 33/72986. ✉ Admission. ⊙ Daily 8–noon and 1–5.

The city and surrounding area have several churches worth visiting, all of them accessible by public transporation. As in most Philippine towns and small cities, churches are where you can best feel the civic and social pulse of Iloilo. In the Molo district of downtown Iloilo is a twin-spired Gothic structure erected in the late 19th century. **Molo Church** sits in a pleasant park and has an intricate facade, with a kind of domed pergola, complete with Greek columns. Note the row of female saints lining the nave.

Jaro Cathedral, 3 km (1.5 mi) from downtown, is larger than Molo Church but also shows Gothic influences. In front is a balcony with a statue of the Virgin that locals consider miraculous. Across the street is the church's reconstructed belfry. Nearby is a statue of **Graciano Lopez Jaena,** a journalist who wrote against the Spanish regime and died in Barcelona in 1896, at the outset of the revolution against Spain. Take some time to walk around the district and look at the grand, colonial-style residences, with their intricate grillwork and mother-of-pearl windows.

The 200-year-old **Miagao Fortress Church,** 40 km (25 mi) south of the city, has two bell towers—of different design, as they were erected by two different friars—that also served as watchtowers against invasions by Muslim pirates. If you promise to be careful, the bell ringer will let you climb one of them. The sandstone facade depicts, amid floral designs, St. Christopher planting a coconut tree.

Dining and Lodging

Iloilo is well known for its *pancit molo* (pork dumplings in noodle soup), *la paz batchoy* (a tripe stew), and pastries.

$$ ✕ **Sunset Terrace.** For the money, you get excellent seafood (try the
★ blue marlin and *tanguigue,* or local mackerel, local specialties, plus scenic views of the river and (if you time it right) a sunset to boot. ✉ *Hotel del Rio, M.H. Del Pilar St.,* ☎ *33/335–1171. AE, DC, MC, V.*

$–$$ ✕ **Grandma's Fried Chicken and Steakhouse.** If you're pining for the down-home taste of a platter of fried chicken or steak, this is the place to dine. ✉ *Delgado St., Amigo Plaza,* ☎ *33/70479. No credit cards.*

$–$$ ✕ **Igmaan.** The emphasis here is on informality and native cuisine, including quite a bit of seafood. On the breezy terrace of the Hotel Del Rio, you can view the broad Iloilo River and note the bamboo fish pens on the water. ✉ *Hotel del Rio, M.H. Del Pilar St.,* ☎ *33/335-1171. AE, DC, MC, V.*

$ ✕ **Ihawan.** A down-home atmosphere prevails, and the chicken barbecue and other grilled meats are top-notch. ✉ *Iznart St. at Yulo St.,* ☎ *33/76834. No credit cards.*

$$ ⌂ **Hotel Del Rio.** Although modest, this well-run property is quiet and
★ appealing. The clean, spacious rooms take advantage of breezes off the Iloilo River, which flows right beside the hotel. ✉ *M.H. Del Pilar St., Molo District,* ☎ *33/335–1171* FAX *33/70736. 57 rooms. 3 restaurants, bar, pool, dance club. AE, DC, MC, V.*

$$ ⌂ **Sarabia Manor.** This hotel has a cosmopolitan feel and a friendly, well-informed staff. Ceilings are rather low, but the rooms are otherwise spacious and quite well kept. ✉ *General Luna St. and Ybiernas St.,* ☎ *33/335–1021,* FAX *33/79127. 100 rooms. 3 restaurants, bar, pool, dance club. AE, DC, MC, V.*

Nightlife and the Arts

Galeria de Madia-as (✉ Washington St., Jaro, Department of Tourism, ☎ 33/78701 or 33/74511) is an art gallery presenting contemporary pieces. The **Iloilo Society of Arts Gallery** (✉ 2nd floor, B & C Square, Iznart St., ☎ 33/71026) displays works by contemporary artists.

Shopping

At **Asilo de Molo Molo** (✉ Avancena St., Molo, ☎ 33/74717), an orphanage for girls, the skills of fine embroidery, especially for church vestments, are taught by nuns. Embroidered gowns, dresses, and exquisite *barong tagalogs* are sold at firm prices. **Sinamay Dealer** (✉ Osmeña St., Arevalo, ☎ 33/4221) is a weaving store where fine cloth is spun from pineapple fiber. Shirts and dresses are made from the cloth, then hand-embroidered.

Guimaras Island

❸ *45-minute boat ride from Iloilo City.*

This lush island, just off the coast of the city, is justly famous for its luscious mangoes and has a number of fishing villages, rice- and cornfields, and a Trappist Monastery that doesn't encourage visitors. It's home to one of the more rustic, if moderately expensive, resorts in the area.

Lodging

$$$ 🏨 **Isla Naburot.** Stay here in native-style cottages while enjoying excellent meals, water sports, and diving facilities. There is no electricity and most of the food is home-grown or freshly caught. The owner's daughter is the chef here, and she will urge you to eat till you're near to bursting. ☎ 33/76616. *18 cottages. Fishing, snorkeling. No credit cards.*

Boracay Island

★ ❹ *2 hours by plane and boat from Manila.*

Famous among Europeans, this small, bow-tie-shape island off the coast of Panay has one of the Philippines' most beautiful beaches, with sands as fine and smooth as refined sugar. This is the only attraction, and lazing on the beach or engaging in the water sports available at the various resorts are the main activities.

Lodging

Boracay has accommodations ranging from the expensive to the basic—a few too many, in fact—and is crowded from November to June.

$$$ 🏨 **Friday's Beach Resort.** This well-maintained resort has cottages done in bamboo and thatch decor; each has a terrace. ☎ 2/521–2283, FAX 2/521–1072. *22 rooms. Restaurant, bar, snorkeling, fishing. AE, DC, MC, V.*

$$$ 🏨 **Mila's Boracay Beach Resort.** Bamboo and rattan interiors aside, the Spanish-style villas at this beachfront compound evoke the Mediterranean. ☎ 2/526–9976, FAX 2/526–9977. *36 rooms. Restaurant, bar, snorkeling, fishing. AE, MC, V.*

$$ 🏨 **Pink Patio.** Air-conditioned rooms at this motel-like resort, five minutes from the beach, face a pleasant garden. ☎ 2/812–9551, FAX 2/810–8282. *57 rooms. Restaurant, snack bar. AE, DC, MC, V.*

Nightlife

The central section of the beach has several distinctly different establishments: **Bazura Bar** is a disco, sometimes with all-night partying. **Beach-**

comber is a mellow spot, often with a folk singer entertaining. **Moondog's Shooter Bar** offers an array of imaginative tropical drinks.

Davao City

⑤ *1½ hours by plane from Manila.*

One of the largest cities in the world in terms of area (approximately 1,937 sq km, or 748 sq mi), Davao City is busy and booming. It's also probably the most ethnically diverse urban area in the country, with Muslim, Christian, Chinese, and indigenous tribal communities. It's bounded on the west by **Mt. Apo** (at 9,689 feet, the country's tallest peak), on the east by Davao Gulf, and is surrounded by banana plantations and fruit and flower farms.

★ Davao is justly famous for its tropical fruits, especially the *durian*, said to "smell like hell and taste like heaven." The **Madrazo Fruit District**, near the downtown area, is an excellent place to get to know these unusual fruits; most vendors will let you have a sample before you buy.

Lon Wa Buddhist Temple, the most intricate and largest in Mindanao, houses three altars, made of Italian marble, gold, and bronze respectively. Deceased faithful have their photos enshrined here. A resident Buddhist monk will tell your fortune if you ask. ⊠ *Road to the airport, no phone.* ⊡ *Donation requested.*

The **Dabaw Museum,** not far from the airport and the Davao Insular Hotel, has fascinating displays of tribal artifacts and costumes. ⊠ *Insular Village, Lanag St.,* ☎ *82/73296.* ⊡ *Admission.* ⊙ *Mon.–Sat. 8–5.*

Philippine Eagle Nature Center, a not-for-profit organization in Calinan, about 36 km (22 mi) from the city center, attempts to preserve the Philippine Eagle, an endangered species, through breeding in captivity. This majestic bird has a wing span of approximately six feet, and its diet includes monkeys. The fierce-looking warriors-of-the-air are truly an awesome sight. The center also has captive crocodiles. ⊠ *Malagos, Calinan,* ☎ *82/298–2663.*

Dining and Lodging

Because Davao Gulf is a rich fishing area, seafood is plentiful here and inexpensive. Lodgings are mostly limited to medium-size hotels, with reasonable rates.

$$ ✕ **Luz Kinilaw.** Fishermen bring in their yellowfin tuna catch near this shore-area reataurant, where the specialties are coal-grilled tuna tail and jaw and sashimi. ⊠ *Salmonan, Quezon Blvd.,* ☎ *82/64612. DC, V.*

$ ✕ **Molave.** This friendly eatery is well known for its unique, truly greaseless fried chicken. ⊠ *Matina District,* ☎ *82/53184. No credit cards.*

$ ✕ **Tai Huat Clay Pot.** The inexpensive and delicious Chinese food served here is popular with Davao's Chinese community. ⊠ *141 Magsaysay Ave.,* ☎ *82/64576. No credit cards.*

$$$ ▥ **Insular Century Hotel Davao.** Close to the airport and about 3 km
★ (2 mi) from town, this hotel sits on 20 lush acres with coconut groves, gardens, and a beachfront. Nearby is a small settlement of an indigenous tribe, the Mandaya. Twice a day *tuba* (coconut wine) gatherers climb the tall trees to collect the sap. The airy rooms, done in native-style decor, come with verandas. ⊠ *Lanang, Davao City,* ☎ *82/234–3050,* ℻ *82/629–59. 153 rooms. 3 restaurants, bar, coffee shop, pool, 2 tennis courts, squash, shops, meeting rooms. AE, DC, MC, V.*

$$ 🖼 **Apo View.** A regular clientele of locals and businessmen patronizes this downtown hotel, which has a pleasantly busy lobby and rooms that are comfortably furnished. ✉ *J. Camus and Bonifacio Sts.,* ☎ *82/221–6430,* FAX *82/221–0748. 105 rooms. Restaurant, bar, coffee shop, pool. AE, DC, MC, V.*

$$ 🖼 **Casa Leticia.** This small but friendly establishment has a cozy, casual lobby that is popular with locals. Rooms are clean and well maintained. ✉ *J. Camus and Palma Gil Sts.,* ☎ *82/224–0501. 41 rooms. Restaurant, coffee shop, bar. AE, DC, MC, V.*

Nightlife and the Arts

Toto's Bar Cafe (✉ J. Camus St., ☎ 82/224–0501), on the top floor of the Casa Leticia hotel, hops almost every night and especially on weekends; the owner himself often plays DJ. Photos of rock stars, album covers, and other rock memorabilia cover the walls, one of which backs a long wood-grain bar. Tables accommodate couples and big groups.

Shopping

The downtown **Aldevinco Shopping Center** is a complex of neat rows of small stores selling Mindanao tribal crafts, woven mats, Muslim brassware, antiques, batik cloth, and wood carvings. A 15-minute walk away is the **Madrazo fruit district,** which features exotic tropical fruits like lanzones, chico, atis, rambutan, and durian.

Samal Island

6 *15 minutes by motorized launch from Davao Insular Hotel.*

Some of the Davao City area's nicest beaches are on nearby Samal Island. The island has several resorts where you can spend the day or stay overnight.

Lodging

$$$$ 🖼 **Pearl Farm Beach Resort.** Formerly an aquaculture enterprise, this pricey resort has beautifully designed bungalows on a hillside overlooking Davao Gulf. ☎ *82/234–0601; Manila, 2/832–0893. 44 rooms. Restaurant, bar, pool. AE, DC, MC, V.*

$$$–$$$$ 🖼 **Paradise Park and Beach Resort.** This pleasant beach resort, complete with small zoo, is good for a day trip or overnight stay. ☎ *82/ 234–1229. 22 rooms. Restaurant, beach. AE, DC, MC, V.*

Mt. Apo National Park

7 *40 km (25 mi) west of Davao City.*

Davao City is a good base from which to explore the surrounding countryside, including Mt. Apo, at 9,689 feet the tallest peak in the country. The mountain, considered sacred by the indigenous people that live in and around it, is part of the Mt. Apo National Park. Trails pass through rainforests, sulfur springs, and, toward the summit, sparse vegetation. The average time for getting to the summit and back is five days; you can climb at any time of year, but it is best to do so between the months of March and May, when dry weather predominates. Check with the **Davao Tourist Office** (☎ 82/221–6798) for guides and other essential information.

OFF THE **CAMIGUIN –** A three-hour trip from Cagayan de Oro City on the north-
BEATEN PATH west coast of Mindanao, this lovely unspoiled isle is still heavily forested and has seven volcanoes. Hibok-Hibok, the largest of them, can be climbed with a hired guide. The best place to secure guides is Ardent Hot Springs, not far from Mambajao, which is also a good place to begin—and end—the climb. Accommodations are basic but cheap and

clean, and the local people are friendly. There are hot springs, trekking opportunities, beaches, and waterfalls.

Zamboanga City

❽ *45-minute flight from Cebu or Davao City.*

Zamboanga City is famous for its bright flowers (its early name, Jambangan, meant "land of flowers"), which grow profusely in every garden. The roadsides are lined with bougainvillea and bright-red-flowered *gumamela* bushes. It is also a city with a sizable Muslim population, made up mainly of the Yakan, Badjao, Samal, and Tausug tribes; the Christian and Muslim populations live for the most part peaceably but in separate enclaves.

Begin exploring the city at **Plaza Pershing,** the town square named after "Blackjack" Pershing, the first American governor of the region, which was formerly known as Moroland, and said to have spurred the development of the .45 pistol. Two blocks southeast of Plaza Pershing, on Valderrosa Street, is **City Hall;** built by the Americans in 1907, it's a curious combination of Arab and baroque styles.

East on Valderrosa Street from City Hall is **Fort Pilar,** an old Spanish fortress. Not far away is the Lantaka Hotel, where the **Department of Tourism** (☎ 62/991–0217) has its field office. Beyond Fort Pilar is **Rio Hondo,** a small riverine Muslim village with its own mosque. Many of the houses are on stilts. Men wear white skullcaps, and women wear the distinctive *malong,* brightly decorated wraparound dress.

Two interesting sights are north of downtown, toward Taluksangay (☞ *below*). The attraction of **Climaco Freedom Park** (named after a beloved mayor slain many years ago) is the Ecumenical Holy Hill: Stations of the Cross on a roadside cliff leading to a giant white cross at the top, where you get good views of the city. The unique offering in **Pasonanca Park** is the **Pasonanca Treehouse,** available for one or two nights of (bathroomless) lodging—a fun Tarzan-and-Jane experience for couples young at heart—if prior notification is given the city (contact the Department of Tourism, ☎ 62/991–0217).

Dining and Lodging

Zamboangeños like steamed crabs, barbecued meats, and raw fish marinated in vinegar and hot green peppers.

$$ ✕ **Alavar's.** Run by a husband-and-wife team (he cooks, she manages),
★ this restaurant is justly famous for wonderful seafood. Prawns, clams, and blue marlin are served in this rambling house facing the sea, but the specialty is *curacha,* crabs in a creamy, sweet-spicy sauce that is the chef's secret. Down your food with refreshing *buko* (young coconut) juice. ✉ *R.T. Lim Blvd.,* ☎ *62/991–2483. DC, MC, V.*

¢ ✕ **Palmeras.** Dine pleasantly in a shaded terrace set in a garden. Service is a bit slow, but the barbecued meats are worth the wait. ✉ *Santa Maria Rd.,* ☎ *62/991–3284. AE, V.*

$$ ▥ **Lantaka.** In the heart of the city and right by the waterfront, this establishment has well-appointed rooms and gracious service. The terrace abuts the sea, where Badjaos, a gypsylike tribe, sell mats and seashells from their outrigger boats. Watch the sunset and the sea from the lovely, open-air Talisay Bar. Unfortunately, the hotel cuisine is mediocre. ✉ *Valderrosa St.,* ☎ *62/991–2033,* FAX *62/991–1626. 112 rooms. Restaurant, coffee shop, bar, pool, meeting room, travel services. AE, DC, MC, V.*

$ 🏨 **Zamboanga Hermosa Inn.** This hotel has a small, informal lobby with a coffee shop. While not so central, it's in a quiet area of the city. The rooms here are small but comfortably furnished and clean. ⊠ *Mayor Jaldon St.,* ☎ *62/991–2042. 33 rooms. Restaurant, laundry service. DC.*

Shopping

CRAFTS

The **City Market** (⊠ Alano St., dawn to dark) is one of the most colorful in the country. The handicraft section, especially Row C, has the woven mats for which Zamboanga is noted, along with brassware, antiques, shellcraft, and batik from Indonesia.

★ For tribal weavings prized by Philippine designers, visit the **Yakan Weaving Village,** 5 km (3 mi) from the city on the west coast. The weave is so fine it takes at least a week to finish a meter of cloth.

SHELLS

Zamboanga is famous for its shells. **Rocan** (⊠ San José Rd., ☎ 62/2492) is a shell purveyor. **San Luis Shell Industries** (⊠ San José Rd., ☎ 62/2419) also has a wide selection of shells. The pickings are good at **Zamboanga Home Products** (⊠ San José St. at Jaldon, ☎ 62/2874).

OFF THE BEATEN PATH	**SANTA CRUZ ISLAND –** This small island has a wonderful pink-coral beach and a lagoon in the middle; the beach is open daily 7–4. At the beach's eastern end is a **Muslim burial ground,** ornamented with stars, crescents, and tiny boats—to provide passage to the next life. In this life, your passage to the island is best acomplished by renting a motorized *banca,* a native canoe fitted with outriggers, from the Lantaka Hotel (☞ *above*) in Zamboanga. The trip takes 20 minutes; rates are officially set at $8 round-trip. Be sure to bring water and refreshments, as there are no food or beverage stands.

Taluksangay

9 *16 km (10 mi) north of Zamboanga.*

This big Muslim village is up the coast from Zamboanga. At the back of the town's distinctive red-and-white mosque is a prominent Muslim family's burial plot with headstones shaped like boats and with the ever-present crescent. The community is made up of seaweed gatherers; everywhere piles of seaweed dry in the sun. Stroll along the many catwalks and watch as women weave and sell straw mats. Remember to bargain; prices quoted at first will be high.

Palawan

10 *90-minute flight from Cebu City or Manila to Puerto Princesa.*

Shaped like a long dagger, Palawan is the archipelago's westernmost island and one of its most isolated and least developed. There are beautiful beaches throughout, with excellent snorkeling and diving spots, and Palawan has flora and fauna not found elsewhere in the country, such as giant turtles, peacocks, mouse deer, scaly anteaters, purple herons, hornbills, and seven-color doves.

Lack of development does mean that Palawan requires a bit more forebearance on the part of the traveler. Outside the largest city, Puerto Princesa, roads are unpaved and tend to be almost impassable after a heavy rain. (The points of interest listed here are those accessible by public transporation.) And as the island has malaria-bearing mosquitoes, you should take preventive medication at least two weeks before arriving and bring insect repellent.

The usual port of entry is the capital, **Puerto Princesa.** It is the hub from which the rest of the island can be explored. Within the city itself, though pleasant and clean (it has regularly won honors as the cleanest city in the country), there isn't a great deal to see. The **Palawan Museum** (⊠ Old City Hall Bldg., J. Valencia St., no phone; ✆ Admission) does have good ethnographic and crafts displays. There is a tourism counter at the airport and a branch office at **City Hall** (☎ 48/433–2154).

★ North of the capital is **St. Paul Subterranean National Park,** a national rainforest park with the world's longest known underground river, **St. Paul's River,** most of which runs through St. Paul's Peak, the mountain that comprises almost all of the park. There is a small beach hamlet, **Sabang,** about a three-hour ride by jeepney from Puerto Princesa. At Sabang, you can hire a motorized *banca* to take you to the river and the gigantic caverns, with their unusual stalactite and stalagmite formations, through which it courses. At the river's mouth is a park ranger station where visitors need to obtain permits for a tour of the cave and the river. There is no charge, but be sure to tip the boatmen.

You can also hike from Sabang to the river, about two km (1¼ mi) away. A well-marked trail starts from the beach, goes up through virgin rainforest, and emerges at the main ranger station where visitors' passes can be obtained as well. From the station the hike continues by the beach and onto the **Monkey Trail,** a bamboo stairway that winds among limestone rocks and through forest inhabited by monitor lizards, parrots, and monkeys. ⊠ *St. Paul Subterranean River National Park office, 150 Manalo St., Puerto Princesa,* ☎ *48/433–2409.*

South of Puerto Princesa, about a five-hour bus ride, off the coastal town of Quezon, are the **Tabon Caves,** discovered in 1962. These caves—numbering about 200 but with only a small number explored—were among the earliest inhabited sites in the country. The skullcap of a woman has been carbon dated to 22,000 BC. No artifacts are to be seen in the caves; most are in the National Museum in Manila. But just being here and imagining life millennia ago as you look across to the ocean is well worth the experience.

At the branch of the **National Museum** in Quezon, *banca* trips to the Tabon caves can be arranged for reasonable prices. The museum has regional artifacts and marine specimens on display. ✆ *Admission.* ☻ *Mon.–Sat. 9–noon and 1–5.*

Dining and Lodging
PUERTO PRINCESSA

$$$ ✕ **Cafe Puerto.** This upscale restaurant serves Continental cuisine, including seafood and chops, in one of the city's more formal settings. ⊠ *Rizal Ave.,* ☎ *48/433–2266. AE, DC, M, V.*

$$ ✕ **Ka Lui's.** Puerto's free spirits hang out here to dine on fresh seafood
★ and delicious fruit shakes served on an airy bamboo veranda. The owner/chef has a small lending library on the premises, with a wide variety of English-language titles. ⊠ *Rizal Ave.,* ☎ *48/433–2580. No credit cards.*

$$$ ▦ **Asia World.** Although this concrete structure is incongruous in a city where preserving the environment is an issue, it well meets the demands of travelers who prefer urban comforts. Rooms are spacious, air-conditioned, and well maintained. ⊠ *National Highway,* ☎ *48/433– 2111; in Manila,* ☎ *2/833–9858. 127 rooms. 2 restaurants, bar, coffee shop, pool, travel services. AE, DC, MC, V.*

$$ 🏨 **Badjao Inn.** A pleasant low-key atmosphere and a veranda recommend this inn, although many of the rooms are cheerless. ⊠ *350 Rizal Ave.,* ☎ *48/433–2761. 26 rooms. Restaurant, laundry service. AE.*

$$ 🏨 **Casa Linda.** Constructed of bamboo, wood, and thatch, this inn has a veranda, as well as a courtyard garden and parrots. The staff is cheerful and helpful. ⊠ *Trinidad Rd.,* ☎ *4821/433–2606. 13 rooms. Restaurant, laundry service. AE.*

ELSEWHERE AROUND PALAWAN

Perhaps the most secluded luxury resorts in the Philippines are situated in northern Palawan, difficult to get to by land.

$$$$ 🏨 **Amanpulo.** A private island in the Cuyo Archipelago, roughly half way between northern Palawan and the Visayas' Panay Island, has been turned into a luxurious getaway. Spacious villas line white-sand beaches. ⊠ *Pamalican Island, in Manila,* ☎ *2/532–4040,* FAX *2/532–4040; in U.S.,* ☎ *800/447–7462 or 212/223–2848. 40 villas. Restarant, bar, room service, pool, massage, 2 tennis courts, boating, fishing, diving, snorkeling, library, meeting rooms. AE, DC, MC, V.*

$$$$ 🏨 **El Nido.** This resort, spread over two islands, is in a marine park and has its own ecological and environmental protection programs, such as a fish nursery and the prohibition of commercial fishing within its boundaries. Packages include meals, charter air transportation, lodging, and the use of water-sports facilities. ⊠ *Miniloc and Pangulasian islands, near the town of El Nido, northern Palawan; in Manila, call Ten Knots,* ☎ *2/810–7291 or 2/818–2623. 61 rooms. Restaurant, kayaking. AE, DC, MC, V.*

$$$ 🏨 **Marina del Nido.** One of the most unusual resorts in northern Palawan was built in 1994. Sailboats and yachts can moor here and their crews take in necessary supplies or just enjoy the resort's cuisine. For the landlubber, there are bungalows built in the native style with no airconditioning. The staff, drawn from the local community, can arrange diving and snorkeling tours, as well as camping trips in the rainforest. ⊠ *Malapacao Island; in Manila,* ☎ *2/831–1487. 4 cottages. Restaurant, boating, fishing, snorkeling. AE, DC, MC, V.*

Nightlife and the Arts

Nightlife in Puerto Princesa is limited to the lodgings, where people gather in lounges for a drink and conversation. Asia World has a discotheque, **Prism** (☎ 48/433–2111). **Bistro Valencia** (⊠ E. Valencia St., no phone) has local folksingers. Patrons are encouraged to try their vocal cords with the featured singers at **Erick's Sing-Along Bar** (⊠ Rizal Ave. Extension, no phone). **Kamayan Folkhouse and Restaurant** (⊠ Rizal Ave., ☎ 48/433–2019) serves native dishes as folk bands strut their stuff.

Shopping

Along Rizal Avenue, handicrafts, antiques, and baskets can be purchased at Mencoco, Culture Shack, or Karla's. The public market is a good source as well. Try Macawili Handicraft for baskets and brassware.

Visayas, Mindanao, and Palawan A to Z

Arriving and Departing

BY PLANE

Philippine Air Lines (☎ 32/254–4036) has daily flights from Manila to major cities in the region, with six to Cebu City's Mactan International Airport (on Mactan Island and 45 minutes from the city proper), five to Iloilo City, three to Davao City, two to Zamboanga, and one to Puerto Princesa. In the summer, PAL also has flights from Tokyo to Cebu. **Singapore Airlines/Silkair** (☎ 32/253–1343) has direct flights from Singapore to Cebu. The small **Lahug Airport**—30 minutes from Cebu City—is used by charter lines.

BY BOAT

Cebu is a busy port and a primary stop for interisland ships. All the major lines have trips between Cebu and ports all over the archipelago. The Cebu–Manila voyage takes 21 hours, Cebu–Davao, 12 hours. Some Cebu offices: **Aboitiz Shipping** (✉ Pier 4, Reclamation Area, ☎ 32/956–61 or 32/253–3143; in Manila, ☎ 2/276–332). **Escaño Lines** (✉ Reclamation Area, ☎ 32/772–53 or 32/621–22). **Negros Navigation** (✉ Port Area, ☎ 32/253–3831; in Manila, ☎ 2/816–3481 or 2/856–986).

WG & A (in Manila, ☎ 2/894–3211 or 2/893–2211) operates what it calls its SuperFerry service between the cities of Cebu, Iloilo, Davao, and Puerto Princesa; their cruise ships have suites, on-board entertainment, and dining.

BY BUS

If you can't get enough of bus travel, bridges and ferry service make it possible to travel overland from Manila to Davao City in Mindanao; the **Philtranco** (☎ 2/833–5061) bus lines make the trip in approximately 44 hours.

Getting Around

BY BUS

As elsewhere in the Philippines, bus is the main form of transportation between towns. Buses usually begin and end their routes in the vicinity of the public market, whether in Cebu or Puerto Princesa. Get to the market early in the morning to secure a good seat. Air-conditioned buses, not as common on islands other than Luzon, are of course more expensive.

BY CAR

Roads in the urban areas, especially in Iloilo City, are in good shape. The exception is Palawan, where roads are largely unpaved and often impassable during the rainy season. While having a car gives you freedom and privacy, rates for taxis and jeepneys are inexpensive, and local drivers know the area better than you do.

Car-rental agencies in **Cebu**: Avis (☎ 32/88527), Cattleya (☎ 32/73074), and Metro (☎ 32/92176 or 32/96245). In **Iloilo** it's Avis (☎ 33/271–171). In **Davao,** rent from Guani (☎ 82/221–5000). In **Puerto Princesa,** try Labuyo (☎ 48/433–2606 or –2580).

BY JEEPNEY

Jeepneys generally begin and end their trips at the public market. Fares are very low: A 2-km (1¼-mi) ride within Cebu City, for example, costs only P2.

BY PLANE

Cebu City's **Mactan International Airport** is the regional hub, providing a crucial link between Manila and Mindanao, other parts of the Visayas, and Palawan. Most regional destinations—such as charming Iloilo City, rich in old mansions and baroque churches—are only a 30-minute flight away. Zamboanga City, in southwest Mindanao, is only 45 minutes away by plane, while an hour away are eastern Mindanao's bustling Davao City—possibly the nation's most ethnically diverse city—and Puerto Princesa on Palawan Island. **Philippine Airlines** (☎ 32/254–4036) has daily flights from Mactan to Iloilo, Zamboanga, Davao, and Palawan.

BY TAXI

Taxis in Cebu are metered, while in Iloilo, Zamboanga, and Davao prices are agreed upon beforehand. The average taxi ride in Cebu costs P80. Trips to the airport and to out-of-town destinations start at P250. In Davao, a ride to the airport averages P80.

BY TRICYCLE

The tricycle, the ubiquitous motorized pedicab, is good for within-a-neighborhood trips. In Puerto Princesa, however, they are the main form of public transport. It is also possible to hire one for trips inside the city or to outside destinations. Prices are negotiable but are routinely a bargain.

Contacts and Resources

Area codes in the region are as follows: Cebu, 32; Iloilo, 33; Zamboanga, 62; Davao, 82; Palawan, 48.

CONSULATES

U.S. (⊠ Fourth floor, PCI Building, Gorordo Avenue, Cebu, ☎ 32/231–1261).

EMERGENCIES

Cebu, ☎ 32/95676 or 32/74642. **Iloilo,** ☎ 33/75511. **Davao,** ☎ 82/119.

GUIDED TOURS

Tours can be arranged in Manila (☞ Travel Agencies *in* Metro Manila A to Z, *above*). You can also consult local Department of Tourism offices (☞ Visitor Information, *below*) for suggestions and a list of guides. The larger hotels usually have tour operators' desks.

VISITOR INFORMATION

Cebu City Department of Tourism (⊠ GMC Plaza Bldg., 3rd floor, Legaspi Extension Road, ☎ 32/254–2811, or 32/254–6077; FAX 32/254–2711).
Davao City Department of Tourism (⊠ 7 Magsaysay Ave., at Magsaysay Park, ☎ 82/221–6798 or 82/221–6955).
Iloilo City Department of Tourism (⊠ Sarabia Hotel, General Luna St., ☎ 33/335–0245).
Puerto Princesa Department of Tourism (⊠ Provincial Capitol, ☎ 48/433–2983).
Zamboanga City Department of Tourism (⊠ Lantaka Hotel, Valderrosa St., ☎ 62/991–0217 or 62/991-9218, FAX 62/991–1626).

PHILIPPINES A TO Z

Arriving and Departing

By Plane

AIRPORTS

Manila's **Ninoy Aquino International Airport** (☎ 2/832–3011 or 2/832–1901) is the major air hub for the Philippines. Some international flights use Cebu City's **Mactan International Airport,** most commonly those originating from Japan, Singapore, and Australia. PAL offers flights to and from Hong Kong and Tokyo to Cebu. The **Laoag International Airport** is now an alternate port of entry into the country for travellers coming from Taipei.

The international airport departure tax is P500.

CARRIERS

Philippine Airlines, the national carrier, offers daily direct flights, with one stop in Honolulu, from San Francisco or Los Angeles to Manila. The carrier has nonstop flights four times a week from San Francisco, and thrice weekly from Honolulu. **Northwest,** now in its 50th year of service to the Philippines, has two flights direct to Manila, one via Tokyo, the other via Osaka; one leaves from Chicago, the other from Los Angeles, with flights connecting from all major U.S. cities. Other carriers to Manila include: **China Airlines, Continental, EVA Air, Japan Airlines, Korean Air,** and **Singapore Airlines.**

FLYING TIMES
Manila is 16 hours from San Francisco, 15 from Los Angeles, 20 hours from Chicago, and 22 hours from New York.

Getting Around

By Boat or Ferry

Much of the local populace travels by boat, the cheapest way to get from island to island. One-way rates from Manila to Cebu City (a 24-hour trip) range from P2,400 for luxury on **Aboitiz** superferries (☎ 2/202–726 or 2/894–3211) to P800 for first-class down to P400 for economy. Were you to fly, the same one-way trip on Philippine Airlines would cost about P1,700 but take only 70 minutes.

Speed, reliability, and safety vary from line to line: **Negros Navigation** (☎ 2/816–3481 or 262–539), **William** (☎ 2/219–821), **Sweet Lines** (☎ 2/912–2332), and **Aboitiz** (☞ *above*) lines generally have well-kept ships and good records. **Sulpicio** (☎ 2/201–771) and **Gothong** (☎ 2/214–121) lines have lesser reputations. Possibly the worst maritime disaster in modern history occurred when the Sulpicio Line's *Doña Paz,* with about 4,000 passengers on board (way above the limit), sank in 1987. Most drowned.

By Bus

The Philippines has an excellent bus system, with 20 major bus lines covering the entire archipelago. Service between major destinations is frequent, often on an hourly basis. This is a cheap way to travel, and it's generally safe. It's possible to go island-hopping by combining buses and island ferries. These routes are usually limited to islands close together, though today one can travel from Manila in Luzon to Davao City in Mindanao, on the Philtranco line, in 44 hours.

In metropolitan Manila, the country's largest urban area, there are several bus terminals (☞ Arriving and Departing *in* Metro Manila A to Z, *above*). Outside Manila, most bus terminals are next to public markets. Bus companies serving major routes have coaches with or without air-conditioning. The former offer films on videotape, but the quality is hideous. Some of the larger bus lines are: **Philtranco** (☎ 2/833–5061 to –5064). **BLTB** (☎ 2/833–5501). **Dagupan Bus Co.** (☎ 2/976–123 or 2/995–639). **Pantranco** (☎ 2/997–091). **Victory Liner** (☎ 2/833–0293, 2/833–5019, or 2/833–5020).

By Car

EMERGENCY ASSISTANCE
There are no road-service organizations, but if your car breaks down, passing motorists and townsfolk will gladly lend a hand.

GASOLINE
A liter costs close to P12.

RENTAL AGENCIES
The larger car-rental agencies are: **Avis** (☎ 2/741–0394 or 2/878–497). **Car Express** (☎ 2/876–717). **Dollar** (☎ 2/883–134 or 2/883–138). **Hertz** (☎ 2/832–5325, 2/868–685, or 2/831–9827). **National** (☎ 2/818–8667 or 2/833–0648). For chauffeured cars, try **Filipino Transport**

(☎ 2/581–493), which charges P1,600 for eight hours and P180 per additional hour.

RENTAL RATES

Outside Manila, rates vary. For instance, Manila to Baguio overnight costs P5,000, and P2,000 per additional day. At least 24-hour notice is required.

ROAD CONDITIONS

Road conditions vary from excellent, with smooth cement or asphalt highways (generally around metropolitan areas like Manila, Cebu City, and Baguio), to bad, where "road" is a euphemism for a dirt track that is dusty and badly rutted in summer and muddy during the rainy season.

While highway signs display speed limits—60 mph maximum and 35 mph minimum—they are not enforced, so you can go as fast as you dare on the open road. Use prudence in populated areas and where children or farm animals are nearby.

RULES OF THE ROAD

Driving is on the right, and you must have a valid foreign or international driver's license to rent a car. Drive defensively—this is not a car culture, so driving rules tend to be honored in the breach.

By Plane

AIRPORTS

Manila Domestic Airport (☞ Arriving and Departing *in* Metro Manila A to Z, *above*), used almost exclusively by Philippine Airlines, is the largest domestic hub. Cebu City's **Mactan International Airport,** the nation's second-busiest airport, is used mainly for domestic flights. Domestic airports charge a tax, which vary, with the average being P50.

CARRIERS

Philippine Air Lines (PAL), the nation's flag carrier, covers pretty much the entire archipelago, serving 43 cities and towns, and is aggressively modernizing its fleet in the face of competition from several smaller carriers; for flight information, call the **24-hour PAL reservation line** (☎ 2/816–6691). It's always wise to confirm your flight at least two days in advance. The carrier offers discounts to students with valid student IDs, and carry-on privileges for such sportsmen as golfers and scuba divers. PAL changes its flight schedule every quarter, though the changes don't usually affect major routes.

Smaller, privately owned companies have regular flights to some cities and resorts. These include: **Aerolift** (☎ 2/817–2369 or 2/818–4223). **Air Philippines** (☎ 2/832–1961). **Asian Spirit** (☎ 2/817–1176). **Cebu Pacific Air** (☎ 2/893–9607). **Grand Air** (☎ 2/833–8090). **Pacific Air** (☎ 2/832–2731, 2/832–2732, or 2/833–2390).

By Train

Only Luzon has a railway system, the **Philippine National Railways** (PNR, ☎ 2/210–011 or 2/561–1125), a single-rail system that has seen better days. Lines run to San Fernando in Pampanga Province, north of Manila, and as far south as Iriga, Camarines Sur in the Bicol region. (There are plans to extend rail service farther north, to La Union, and farther south, to Legazpi City.) Fares are slightly lower than those for bus travel, but trips take longer.

Contacts and Resources

Customs and Duties

Personal effects (a reasonable amount of clothing and a small quantity of perfume), 400 cigarettes or two tins of smoking tobacco, and 2 liters of liquor may be brought into the Philippines duty-free.

There are restrictions on the export of antiques, religious and historical artifacts, seashells, coral, orchids, monkeys, and birds (including endangered species such as the Philippine eagle).

Electricity

The electrical current in the Philippines, like in the United States, runs on 110-volt, 60-cycle AC current. Wall outlets take a variety of plug styles, including Continental-type plugs, with two round prongs, and plugs with two flat prongs.

Etiquette and Behavior

Two simple rules will smooth your way in the Philippines: Don't point and don't raise your voice.

Language

The Philippines is an English-speaking country, a legacy of its years as a U.S. colony. Communicating is rarely a problem, either in the cities or in the countryside. A second lingua franca is Pilipino, which is based on the regional language of Tagalog. Spanish is still spoken by many members of the country's elite; in Zamboanga City a form of creolized Spanish known as *Chavacano* is spoken.

Mail

POSTAL RATES
To most Western countries, stamps are P8 for a letter and P5 for a postcard or an aerogram.

RECEIVING MAIL
Letters sent care of Poste Restante to the General Post Office in Manila (✉ Plaza Lawton, Manila, ☎ 2/471–411) will be held for you. Otherwise, have your mail addressed to you c/o American Express, ground floor, PhilamLife Building, United Nations Avenue, Ermita, Manila.

Money and Expenses

CURRENCY
The unit of currency is the peso, made up of 100 centavos. Bills come in denominations of 2, 10, 20, 50, 100, 500, and 1,000 pesos. Coins range from 5 centavos to P2.

EXCHANGING MONEY
The exchange rate at press time was P20 to the Canadian dollar, P27 to the U.S. dollar, and P42 to the pound sterling. In Manila, better rates than the banks offer can be obtained from licensed money-changers in the Tourist District, especially on M.H. Del Pilar and A. Mabini streets.

TAXES
The international airport departure tax is P500, while domestic airports charge on the average P50. Hotels add a 10% service charge (as do most restaurants) and a government tax of 13.7%. In addition to a 4% sales tax, a value added tax (VAT) of 10% is charged by all businesses.

WHAT IT WILL COST
The Philippines remains a bargain, with low inflation. Predictably, metropolitan Manila is the most expensive destination. Other urban areas, such as Cebu City in the Visayas and Baguio in northern Luzon, are less expensive, and the surrounding provincial areas are cheapest of all.

Sample Costs: Cup of instant coffee, 25¢; fresh-brewed native coffee, 50¢–$1; bottle of beer, 50¢–$1¢; Coca-Cola, 60¢; hamburger, $1.50–$2.50; 1-mile cab ride, $2; double room, $10–$15, budget; $16–$60, moderate; $61–$120, expensive; above $120, luxury.

National Holidays

New Year's Day (Jan. 1); Holy Week (Maundy Thursday through Easter Sunday); Labor Day (May 1); Day of Valor (May 6); Independence Day (June 12); All Saints' Day (Nov. 1); Andres Bonifacio Day (Nov. 30); Christmas (Dec. 25); José Rizal Day (Dec. 30).

Opening and Closing Times

Banks are open 9–3; supermarkets, 9:30–7:30; public markets, dawn to dusk; museums, 9–noon and 1–5. Except for Holy Week, most shops remain open during holidays, though banks close. Museums close on holidays and Sunday.

Outdoor Activities and Sports

MOUNTAIN CLIMBING AND TREKKING

For information on hiking and mountaineering, call the Department of Tourism (☎ 2/501–703) or PAL Mountaineering Club (☎ 2/586–712).

SNORKELING, SCUBA DIVING, AND SURFING

Philippine Air Lines has its Flying Sportsman Privilege, allowing, for instance, divers an extra 30 kilograms free of charge on domestic flights. The carrier will issue a permit card good for one year. For more information, contact PAL (☎ 2/816–6691) or the Philippine Commission on Sports Scuba Diving (☎ 2/585–857 or 2/503–627).

Telephones

To call the Philippines from overseas, dial the country code, 63, and then the area code.

DIRECTORY ASSISTANCE AND OPERATOR INFORMATION

For directory assistance, dial 114. All operators speak English.

LOCAL CALLS

Local calls are untimed, except for those made on a pay phone, which cost P2 for the first three minutes. For domestic long-distance calls, you need to go through an operator by dialing 109, unless your phone has direct dialing, now being introduced in stages.

INTERNATIONAL CALLS

The big hotels have direct overseas dialing. Otherwise, dial 108. Whether or not the party is at the other end, a connection fee of about $1 is charged. Overseas rates person-to-person to the United States and the United Kingdom are $9.60 for the first three minutes and $2.32 for each additional minute; station-to-station, it's $7.20 for the first three minutes, $2.32 again for each additional minute. A cheaper alternative is AT&T's **USADirect** service, which charges $3.25 for the first minute and $1.40 for each additional minute, plus a service charge of $2.50 for station-to-station or $6 for person-to-person calls. For information, ☎ 412/553–7458, ext. 914, or 800/874–4000, ext. 314. If you're outside the United States, call collect—AT&T will pick up the tab.

Passports and Visas

Visas are not required of Canadian, U.K., or U.S. citizens for stays of up to 21 days, provided that travelers have a ticket for a return or onward journey.

Tipping

Tipping is now an accepted practice, and 10% is considered standard for waiters, bellboys, and other hotel and restaurant personnel; many restaurants and hotels tack on a 10% service charge. When there is a service charge, tipping becomes optional, but it is customary to leave loose change. At Ninoy Aquino International Airport, arrivals pay P30 per cart, and porters expect P10 for each piece of luggage (in addition to P10 per piece paid to the porter office). Hotel doormen and bell-boys should get about the same. For taxi drivers, P5 is fine for the average 1½-mile ride.

Visitor Information

Contact the **Philippine Center** (✉ 556 5th Ave., New York, NY 10036, ☎ 212/575–7915, FAX 212/302–6759; ✉ 3660 Wilshire Blvd., Suite 825, Los Angeles, CA 90010, ☎ 213/487–4527, FAX 213/386–4063; ✉ 447 Sutter St., Suite 507, San Francisco, CA 94108, ☎ 415/956–4060, FAX 415/956–2093). At press time, there was no Philippine tourism office in Canada.

When to Go

The Philippines has two seasons: dry and wet. The dry season generally runs from late October through May, with temperatures ranging from cool and breezy—even chilly—in the northern highlands to scorching hot in the lowland cities. Within this seven-month span, the coolest stretch is from November through February and, since it coincides with winter months in the West, is also the peak tourist season. During this period popular spots are crowded, major hotels have high occupancy rates, and airfares are higher. Still, there are plenty of beaches and unspoiled places where crowds are either sparse or nonexistent.

If you enjoy crackling summer heat, then March through May are the best months to visit. The Catholic penitential rites of Lent are observed in late March or early April, climaxing in nationwide rituals during Holy Week, when business and government offices shut down. May is harvest—and fiesta—time.

For travelers who find themselves in the Philippines during the rainy season—June through September—it's helpful to know that most of Mindanao lies outside the typhoon belt, which cuts across Luzon and most of the Visayas. Mindanao does get rain, but not much more than during the rest of the year. Manila, on the other hand, is subject to frequent floods, while the highlands of northern Luzon become waterlogged, and mud and rock slides frequently make the roads impassable. Be sure to pack a good raincoat and waterproof boots.

The following are maximum and minimum temperatures for Manila.

CLIMATE

Jan.	86F	30C	May	93F	34C	Sept.	88F	31C
	70	21		75	24		75	24
Feb.	88F	31C	June	92F	33C	Oct.	88F	31C
	70	21		75	24		74	23
Mar.	91F	33C	July	88F	31C	Nov.	88F	31C
	72	22		75	24		72	22
Apr.	93F	34C	Aug.	88F	31C	Dec.	86F	30C
	74	23		75	24		70	21

FESTIVALS AND SEASONAL EVENTS

The most spectacular festivals are in honor of Jesus Christ, as the Holy Infant (Santo Niño) or Son of God, and the Virgin Mary.

January: Three orgiastic, dancing-in-the-streets carnivals take place this month: the **Ati-Atihan** (the third weekend of the month, in Kalibo, Aklan), the **Sinulog** (the third weekend in January, in Cebu City), and the **Dinagyang** (the last weekend in January, in Iloilo City). In all three, the Holy Infant is the object of veneration. Kalibo's Ati-Atihan, the oldest and most popular, is also the noisiest, as competing town bands thump enthusiastically night and day. All three cities get crammed to the gills, and plane, ship, and room reservations must be made two or three months in advance.

In contrast, on January 9, the **Black Nazarene** procession of the Quiapo district in Manila is a more somber but equally intense show of devotion, as the faithful compete to pull the carriage holding a statue of Christ that is believed to be miraculous.

January–February: With the **Hari Raya Puasa,** Muslims celebrate the completion of Ramadan, a holy month of fasting and abstention that commemmorates the revelation of the Koran to the Prophet Mohammed by the Angel Gabriel. (Because the Islamic calender follows the lunar cycle, each Gregorian year Ramadan begins roughly 10 days earlier; during the late 1990s, Hari Raya Puasa will fall in January and early February.)

Late March–early April: Christ's final sufferings are remembered during the last week of Lent, Holy Week. In the provincial towns of Bulacan and Pampanga, in central Luzon, masked and bleeding flagellants atoning for their sins are a common sight in the streets. Small groups of old women and children gather at makeshift altars and chant verses describing Christ's passion. The **Turumba** in Pakil, Laguna (held the second Tuesday and Wednesday after Holy Week), honors Our Lady of Sorrows. Devotees dance through the streets trying to make her smile.

May: All over the country, the **Santacruz de Mayo** commemorates St. Helen's discovery of the Holy Cross in 324. The celebrations include colorful processions, complete with floats of each town's patron saint, beautifully gowned young women acting as May queens, and local swains dressed in their Sunday best. One of the more unusual feasts is in Lucban, Quezon Province, where multicolored rice wafers, called *kiping,* are shaped into window ornaments, usually in the form of fruits and vegetables.

September: The **Peñafrancia** (third weekend in September) is the biggest festival in the Bicol region, drawing as many as 10,000 spectators to Naga City in southern Luzon. A procession of floats on the river honors the Virgin of Peñafrancia.

December: 'Tis the season for carolers, midnight masses, and such feasts as the **Maytinis** festival of the town of Kawit, Cavite—a 90-minute drive from Manila. Christmas Eve is celebrated with 13 colorful gigantic floats. Be there by 6 PM to get a good view.

5 Singapore

Don't let first impressions lead you to write Singapore off as just another modern international capital. Although it may no longer be the exotic, romantic city so vividly documented by Conrad and Kipling, Singapore is yet a unique metropolis, where the flavor, spirituality, and gentle manners of the East peacefully coexist with the comforts, conveniences, and efficiency of the West.

By Nigel Fisher

Updated by
Christine Hill

TO ARRIVE IN SINGAPORE is to step into a world where the muezzin call to prayer competes with the bustle of capitalism; where old men play mah-jongg in the streets and white-clad bowlers send the ball flying down well-tended cricket pitches; where Chinese fortune-tellers and high-priced management consultants advise the same entrepreneur. This great diversity of lifestyles, cultures, and religions thrives within the framework of a well-ordered society. Singapore is a spotlessly clean—some say sterile—modern metropolis, surrounded by green, groomed parks and populated by 2.7 million extremely polite, well-mannered people.

While the Malays, Chinese, and Indians account for 97% of Singapore's population, other ethnic groups—from Eurasians to Filipinos, from Armenians to Thais—contribute significantly to the nation's cultural mix. Understandably, the British and the heritage of their colonial stay is profoundly felt even though Singapore became an independent nation in 1965.

In a part of the world where histories tend to be ancient and rich, Singapore is unique in having almost no history at all. Modern Singapore tends to date its history from the early morning of January 29, 1819, when a representative of the British East India Company, Thomas Stamford Raffles, stepped ashore at Singa Pura (Sanskrit for "lion city"), as the island was then called, hoping to establish a British trading settlement on the southern part of the Malay Peninsula. The two sons of the previous sultan, who had died six years earlier, were in dispute over who would inherit the throne. Raffles backed the claim of the elder brother, Tunku Hussein Mohamed Shah, and proclaimed him sultan. Offering to support the new sultanate with British military strength, Raffles persuaded him to grant the British a lease allowing them to establish a trading post on the island in return for an annual rent; within a week the negotiations were concluded. (A later treaty ceded the island outright to the British.) Within three years, the small fishing village, surrounded by swamps and jungle and populated by only tigers and 200 or so Malays, had become a boomtown of 10,000 immigrants, administered by 74 British employees of the East India Company.

As Singapore grew, the British erected splendid public buildings, churches, and hotels, often using Indian convicts for labor. The Muslim, Hindu, Taoist, and Buddhist communities—swelling rapidly from the influx of fortune-seeking settlers from Malaya, India, and South China—built mosques, temples, and shrines. Magnificent houses for wealthy merchants sprang up, and the harbor became lined with *godowns* (warehouses) to hold all the goods passing through the port.

By the turn of the century, Singapore had become the entrepôt of the East, a mixture of adventurers and "respectable middle classes." World War I hardly touched the island, although its defenses were strengthened to support the needs of the British navy, for which Singapore was an important base. When World War II broke out, the British were complacent, expecting that any attack would come from the sea and that they were well prepared to meet such an attack. But the Japanese landed to the north, in Malaya. The two British battleships that had been posted to Singapore were sunk, and the Japanese land forces raced down the peninsula on bicycles.

In February 1942 the Japanese captured Singapore. Huge numbers of Allied civilians and military were sent to Changi Prison; others were marched off to prison camps in Malaya or to work on the notorious "Death Railway" in Thailand. The 3½ years of occupation was a time of privation and fear; an estimated 100,000 people died. The Japanese surrendered on August 21, 1945, and the Allied military forces returned to Singapore. However, the security of the British Empire was never again to be felt, and independence for British Southeast Asia was only a matter of time.

In 1957 the British agreed to the establishment of an elected 51-member legislative assembly in Singapore. General elections in 1959 gave an overwhelming majority—43 of 51 seats—to the People's Action Party (PAP), and a young Chinese lawyer named Lee Kuan Yew became Singapore's first prime minister. In 1963 Singapore became part of the Federation of Malaysia, along with the newly independent state of Malaysia.

Mainly due to Malays' anxiety over a possible takeover by the ethnic Chinese, the federation broke up two years later and Singapore became an independent sovereign state. The electorate remained faithful to Lee Kuan Yew and the PAP. In 1990, Lee resigned after 31 years as prime minister, though as a senior minister he maintains his strong grip. His firm leadership of the party, his social and economic legislation, and his suppression of criticism led to his reputation as a (usually) benevolent dictator; yet Singaporeans recognize that his firm control had much to do with the republic's economic success and high standard of living. Lee is rumored to be grooming his son for the reigns of the PAP—though the fact that the party is receiving fewer votes than in the past suggests a disaffection with the (virtually) one-party system. In the meantime, Lee's hand-picked successor, Goh Chok Tong, has established a power base of his own during his years as prime minister.

Pleasures and Pastimes

Dining

Eating is an all-consuming passion among Singaporeans, and the visitor soon discovers why. There is a stunning array of delicious cuisine from all around the world, particularly from the three major cultures that make up the island nation: Chinese, Malay, and Indian. Food is a route to cultural empathy for the visitor, especially if it's consumed at a hawker's stall in one of Singapore's food centers, preferably of the old-style open-air variety. And though the cost of living in Singapore has escalated over the last decade, competition among the restaurants has kept dining inexpensive. The cleanliness of Singapore also makes dining a pleasure. You can eat with the same confidence at a roadside stand as in a gourmet five-star hotel dining room.

The following are dishes and food names you will come across often at the hawker centers.

char kway teow—flat rice noodles mixed with soy sauce, chili paste, fish cakes, and bean sprouts and fried in lard.
Hokkien prawn mee—fresh wheat noodles in a prawn-and-pork broth served with freshly boiled prawns.
laksa—a one-dish meal of round rice noodles in coconut gravy spiced with lemongrass, chilies, turmeric, shrimp paste, and shallots. It is served with a garnish of steamed prawns, rice cakes, and bean sprouts.
mee rebus—a Malay version of Chinese wheat noodles with a spicy gravy. The dish is garnished with sliced eggs, pieces of fried bean curd, and bean sprouts.
rojak—a Malay word for "salad." Chinese rojak consists of cucumber, lettuce, pineapple, *bangkwang* (jicama), and deep-fried bean curd, tossed with a dressing made from salty shrimp paste, ground toasted peanuts, sugar, and rice vinegar. Indian rojak consists of deep-fried lentil

and prawn patties, boiled potatoes, and deep-fried bean curd, all served with a spicy dip sweetened with mashed sweet potatoes.

roti prata—an Indian pancake made by tossing a piece of wheat-flour dough into the air until it is paper-thin and then folding it to form many layers. The dough is fried until crisp on a cast-iron griddle, then served with curry powder or sugar. An ideal breakfast dish.

satay—small strips of meat marinated in fresh spices and threaded onto short skewers. A Malay dish, satay is barbecued over charcoal and eaten with a spiced peanut sauce, sliced cucumbers, raw onions, and pressed rice cakes.

thosai—an Indian rice-flour pancake that is a popular breakfast dish, eaten with either curry powder or brown sugar.

CATEGORY	COST*
$$$$	over S$60 (US$42)
$$$	S$35–S$60 (US$25–US$42)
$$	S$15–S$35 (US$11–US$25)
$	under S$15 (US$11)

per person for a three-course meal, excluding tax, service charge, and drinks

Gardens and Parks

You can escape from the concrete and glass that is modern downtown Singapore to wonderfully kept gardens, such as the Botanic Gardens, or visit orchid farms. The more energetic can hike the trails of Bukit Timah Nature Reserve—the tigers have long gone, but the sounds and smells of the jungle are still there. If you want to see a tiger or two, as well as animals from as far away as the North Pole, Singapore has one the world's most pleasant zoos, designed on the open-moat concept. And because many animals are nocturnal, there is another zoo, the Night Safari, where tigers and rhinoceros wake up at dusk to feed.

Lodging

Although Singapore is not the same indulgent retreat it once was, it is hard to match the standard of comfort, efficiency of staff, and level of ancillary services that the Singapore hotel offers. The luxury hotels cater to every whim—and so they should at $300 a night—but good service, freshly decorated rooms, cleanliness, and modern facilities can be found for around $200. For less money, there are simple, clean hotels (often more personal than the larger ones), with rooms for about $90. If you are on a tight budget, the youth hostels are spotless, cosmopolitan, and cheap.

CATEGORY	COST*
$$$$	over S$375 (US$265)
$$$	S$275–S$375 (US$194–US$265))
$$	S$175–S$275 (US$124–US$194)
$	S$100–S$175 (US$71–US$124)
¢	under S$100 (US$71)

All prices are for a standard double room, excluding 4% tax and 10% service charge.

Shopping

Once upon a time Singapore, a duty-free republic, was a haven for shoppers. And though shopping is still the major pastime for Singaporeans, nowadays they are rich and sassy. The strong Singaporean dollar and expensive real estate have caused prices to shoot up, and except for a lucky find in an antique store, bargains no longer exist. Still, nowhere else will you find so many shops carrying the latest fashions and electronic equipment, so browsing rather than shopping becomes the pleasurable pastime. Look here, decide what you want, then purchase it when you reach another Asian capital—perhaps Kuala Lumpur or Bangkok.

Theme Parks

No other country of Singapore's size has put so much effort into creating attractions for both its citizens and tourists. Singapore may have spent millions destroying its heritage buildings, but private enterprise has also spent a fortune recreating the old at theme parks, usually designed to educate and entertain. Haw Par Villa emphasizes Chinese mythology, and the Tang Dynasty Village displays life in ancient China.

EXPLORING SINGAPORE

The main island of Singapore is shaped like a flattened diamond, 42 kilometers (26 miles) east to west and 23 kilometers (14 miles) north to south. At the foot are Singapore city, the docks, and, offshore, Sentosa and 59 smaller islands—most of them uninhabited. To the east is Changi International Airport, connected to the city by a parkway lined for miles with amusement centers of one sort or another. To the west are the industrial city of Jurong and several decidedly unindustrial attractions, including gardens and a bird park. At the center of the diamond is Singapore island's "clean and green" heart, with a splendid zoo, an orchid garden, and reservoirs surrounded by luxuriant tropical forest. Of the island's total land area, less than half is built up, with the balance made up of farmland, plantations, swamp areas, and forest. Well-paved roads connect all parts of the island, and Singapore city is served with excellent public transportation.

Colonial Singapore

Numbers in the text correspond to numbers in the margin and on the Colonial Singapore map.

A GOOD WALK

A convenient place to start exploring Colonial Singapore is at Clifford Pier, where most Europeans alighted from their ships. Walk up **Collyer Quay** ① toward the Singapore River, passing the old **General Post Office** ②, a proud Victorian building of gray stone. Walk down the short, tree-lined street alongside the GPO to cross the gracious old iron-link **Cavenagh Bridge** ③.

Once over the bridge, take a left onto North Boat Quay and walk past the **statue of Sir Thomas Stamford Raffles** ④, who is believed to have landed on this spot in 1819. Turn right onto St. Andrew's Road, where you'll see **Parliament House** ⑤, the oldest government building in Singapore, on your left, and on your right, **Victoria Memorial Hall** ⑥, built in 1905 as a tribute to Queen Victoria. Across the road from the theater is the old **Singapore Cricket Club** ⑦. Just past the Cricket Club on your right as you continue up St. Andrews Road is the **Padang** ⑧ or playing field. To your left are the **Supreme Court** ⑨ and **City Hall** ⑩, two splendidly pretentious, imperial-looking buildings. Continuing east on St. Andrew's Road, cross Coleman Street toward the green lawns that surround the Anglican **St. Andrew's Cathedral** ⑪.

To the northeast of the cathedral, within easy walking distance, is the huge **Raffles City** ⑫ complex. Take the MRT underpass north across Stamford Road, and walk through Raffles City to Bras Basah Road. Across the street is the venerable **Raffles Hotel** ⑬. After touring the hotel, turn right on Bras Basah Road to reach the **Singapore Art Museum** ⑭. After viewing the exhibits, cross Bras Basah Road, and walk up Armenian Street. Turn right onto Stamford Road, and the **National Museum and Art Gallery** ⑮, a silver-domed colonial building, will be on

Colonial Singapore

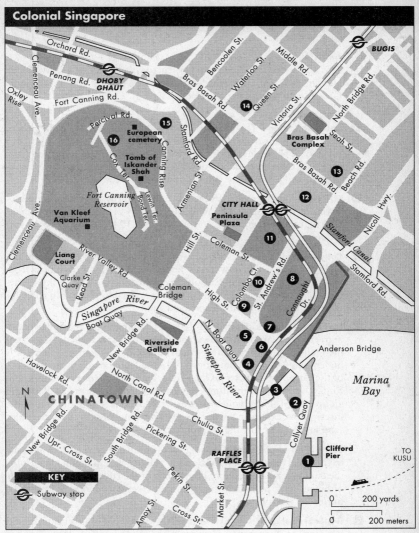

your left. You may wish to conclude the tour with a stroll through **Fort Canning Park** ⑯, pausing at the European Cemetery and the Tomb of Iskander Shah.

TIMING

This walking tour, with time factored in to wander through Raffles Hotel and view the exhibits at the Singapore Art Museum and the National Gallery, will take five to six hours.

SIGHTS TO SEE

❸ **Cavenagh Bridge.** This gracious old iron-link bridge is named after Major General Orfeur Cavenagh, governor of the Straits Settlements from 1859 to 1867. The bridge, built in 1868 from iron girders imported from Scotland, once carried the principal road across the river; now the **Anderson Bridge** bears the main burden of traffic.

❿ **City Hall.** Completed in 1929, this building now houses a number of government ministries, including the Ministry of Foreign Affairs. It was here that the British surrender took place in 1942, followed by the surrender of the Japanese in 1945.

❶ **Collyer Quay.** Land reclamation in 1933 pushed the seafront back and Collyer Quay, which now fronts Telok Ayer Street, is three blocks from its original site. Nearby **Clifford Pier** still reveals some of the excitement of the days when European traders arrived by steamship and Chinese immigrants by wind-dependent junks.

🦢 ⑯ **Fort Canning Park.** Until recently Fort Canning was hallowed ground, a green sanctuary from the surrounding city's mass of concrete commercialism. Alas, like almost everything else in Singapore, the park is undergoing extensive renovations. What still remains are the tombstones of the **European cemetery.** Once divided into areas for Protestants and for Catholics, the tombstones have been moved to form a wall around an open field. The plaques are weathered, and it is difficult to read the inscriptions, but their brevity suggests the loneliness of the expatriates who had sought fortune far from home.

Seven centuries ago **Fort Canning Rise** (now part of the park) was home to the royal palaces of the Majapahit rulers, who no doubt chose it for the cool breezes and commanding view of the river. The last five kings of Singa Pura, including the legendary Iskandar Shah, are said to be buried on the hill.

❷ **General Post Office.** The GPO recently moved out of this beautiful old building. The government has promised not to knock it down, but has not made a decision on how to use it.

⑮ **National Museum and Art Gallery.** Housed in a grand colonial building topped by a giant silver dome, the museum originally opened as the Raffles Museum in 1887. Included in its collection are 20 dioramas depicting the republic's past; the **Revere Bell,** donated to the original St. Andrew's Church in 1843 by the daughter of American patriot Paul Revere; the 380-piece **Haw Par Jade Collection,** one of the largest of its kind; ethnographic collections from Southeast Asia; and many historical documents. ⊠ *Stamford Rd.,* ☎ *330–9562.* 🎟 *S\$3.* ☺ *Tues.–Sun. 9–5:30.*

❽ **Padang.** The Padang (Malay for "field" or "plain") used to be a center for Singapore's political and social events but is now used primarily as a playing field.

❺ **Parliament House.** Designed in 1827 by Irish architect George Coleman, Parliament House is considered the oldest government building in Singapore. Out front is a bronze statue of an elephant, presented by King Chulalongkorn of Siam during his state visit in 1871.

⑫ **Raffles City.** The Raffles City complex of offices and shops contains Asia's tallest hotel, the **Westin Stamford.** You'll get a beautiful view of downtown Singapore and the harbor from the **Compass Rose** restaurant at the top of the hotel.

⑬ **Raffles Hotel.** Once a "tiffin house," or tearoom, the Raffles Hotel started life as the home of a British sea captain. In 1886 the Armenian Sarkies brothers took over the building and greatly expanded it, making it into one of the grandest hotels in Asia. The Raffles has had many ups and downs, especially during World War II, when it was first a center for British refugees, then quarters for Japanese officers, then a center for released Allied prisoners of war. After the war the hotel deteriorated. However, in late 1991, after two years of renovating and rebuilding some of the original structures and adding new buildings, the Raffles reopened as Singapore's most expensive hotel.

Tourists are channeled through new colonial-style buildings to visit the museum of Raffles memorabilia, open daily 10–9; attend a multimedia show (performances are at 10, 11, 12:30, and 1), and take refreshment in a reproduction of the **Long Bar,** where the famous Singapore sling was created in 1903. Casual visitors are discouraged from entering the original part of the hotel, but you may want to brazen it out just to see how unlikely it would be to find a Conrad at the tiny and stiff new **Writers Bar.**

⑪ **St. Andrew's Cathedral.** This Anglican church, surrounded by a green lawn, is the second built on this site. The first church was built in 1834; after being struck twice by lightning, it was demolished in 1852. The new cathedral, completed in 1862, with bells cast by the firm that made Big Ben's, is in 12th-century English Gothic style. The cathedral's lofty interior is white and simple, with stained-glass windows coloring the sunlight as it enters. Around the walls are marble and brass memorial plaques, including one in memory of 41 Australian army nurses killed in the 1942 Japanese invasion of Singapore.

⑭ **Singapore Art Museum.** Officially opened in 1996 in a restored 19th-century schoolhouse, the museum showcases contemporary art from all over Southeast Asia. ✉ *71 Bras Basah,* ☎ *332–3550 or 332–3222.* ⌸ *$3.* ☉ *Tues.–Sun. 9–5:30.*

NEED A BREAK? At the back of the Singapore Art Museum, you'll find one of Singapore's most pleasant casual lunch spots, **Olio Dome** (☎ 298–5054). While serving a Western menu of soups, salads, and sandwiches on toasted foccacia bread, the Dome specializes in coffee. A latte goes for S$4.90. You can eat outside on the curving neoclassical porch or inside in a 1920s-style bistro.

⑦ **Singapore Cricket Club.** Founded during the 1850s, the club became the main center for the social and sporting life of the British community. It now has a multiracial membership of over 4,000. The club is not open to passing sightseers, but you can sneak a quick look at the deep, shaded verandas around back, from which members still watch cricket, rugby, and tennis matches.

④ **Statue of Sir Thomas Stamford Raffles.** This statue near the Empress Palace on North Boat Quay is on the spot where Raffles first landed in Singapore early on the morning of January 29, 1819.

9 Supreme Court. In the neoclassical style so beloved by Victorian colonials, the Supreme Court boasts Corinthian pillars and the look of arrogant certainty. However, it is not as old as it seems, having been completed in 1939, just in time for the Japanese to use the building as their headquarters.

6 Victoria Memorial Hall. The Memorial Hall was built in 1905 as a tribute to Queen Victoria. Along with the adjacent **Victoria Theatre,** built in 1862 as the town hall, it is the city's main cultural center, offering regular exhibitions, concerts, and theatrical performances of all types (☞ Nightlife and the Arts, *below*).

Chinatown

In a country where 76% of the people are Chinese, it may seem strange to name a small urban area Chinatown. But Chinatown was born some 170 years ago, when the Chinese were a minority (if only for half a century) in the newly formed British settlement. In the belief that it would minimize racial tension, Raffles allotted sections of the settlement to different ethnic groups. The Chinese immigrants were given the area to the south of the Singapore River. Today, the river is still the northern boundary of old Chinatown, while Maxwell Road marks its southern perimeter and New Bridge Road its western one. This relatively small rectangle was crammed with immigrants from mainland China—many of them penniless and half starved. Within three years of the formation of the Straits Settlement, 3,000 Chinese had moved in; this number increased tenfold over the next decade.

In the shop-houses—two-story buildings with shops or small factories on the ground floor and living quarters upstairs—as many as 30 lodgers would live together in a single room. Life was a fight for space and survival. Crime was rampant. What order existed was maintained not by the colonial powers but by Chinese guilds, clan associations, and secret societies, which fought—sometimes savagely—for control of various lucrative aspects of community life.

Until recently, all of Chinatown was slated for the bulldozer, to be replaced by uniform concrete structures. Much of the original community was disassembled and entire blocks were cleared of shop-houses. However, the government finally recognized not only the people's desire to maintain Chinese customs and strong family ties, but also the important role these play in modern society. Chinatown received a stay of execution, and an ambitious plan to restore a large area of shop-houses is partially completed. Fortunately, enough of the old remains to permit the imaginative visitor to experience a traditional Chinese community.

Numbers in the text correspond to numbers in the margin and on the Chinatown map.

A GOOD WALK

Begin at the Elgin Bridge, built to link Chinatown with the colonial administration center, and walk down South Bridge Road. Turn right on Upper Circular Road; at No. 13 is **Yeo Swee Huat** ①, which sells paper replicas of houses, cars, and other worldly goods intended to be burned at Chinese funerals. Continue to New Bridge Road, turn left, and walk past the People's Park Centre, now home to the Singapore Handicrafts Centre. Cross Upper Cross Street and take a left onto Mosque Street. The old shop-houses here—now being redeveloped into offices—were originally built as stables. Turn right onto South Bridge Road. The **Jamae Mosque** ② will be on your right. On the next block is the **Sri Mariamman Temple** ③, the oldest Hindu temple in Singapore.

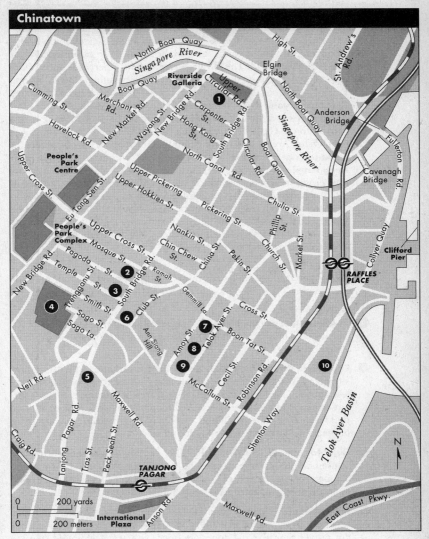

Chinatown

Al Abrar Mosque, **9**

Chinatown Centre, **4**

Guild for amahs, **6**

Jamae Mosque, **2**

Jinriksha Station, **5**

Nagore Durghe
Shrine, **7**

Sri Mariamman
Temple, **3**

Telok Ayer
Market, **10**

Thian Hock Keng
Temple, **8**

Yeo Swee Huat, **1**

If you take the next right, onto **Temple Street,** you will be in the core of Chinatown, an area known as Kreta Ayer. Trengganu Street leads to the new **Chinatown Centre** ④. Take **Sago Street** back to South Bridge Road and turn right; you'll come to the intersection of **Tanjong Pagar Road** and Neil Road. The old **Jinriksha Station** ⑤ here was once a rickshaw depot, but now it's a food court. After strolling down Tanjong Pagar Road to see the restored shop-houses, head back to South Bridge Road. Ann Siang Road, on the right side of South Bridge Road, is full of old shops and site of the **Guild for amahs** ⑥. From Ann Siang Road, turn left on to Club Street, and then right at Gemmill Lane. When you get to Telok Ayer Street, turn right to find the **Nagore Durghe Shrine** ⑦, an odd mix of minarets and Greek columns. Continue to the **Thian Hock Keng Temple** ⑧, the most interesting temple in Chinatown. A little farther down the street, and you'll see the **Al Abrar Mosque** ⑨, built in 1827. Return to the Nagore Durghe Shrine and take a right on Boon Tat Street. After crossing Robinson Road you'll the **Telok Ayer Market** ⑩, the largest Victorian cast-iron structure left in Southeast Asia. Here you can refresh yourself at the food court, then take the subway back to Raffles Place on Collyer Quay.

TIMING

Allow two to three hours for this walk, and factor in a half an hour each for the Thian Hock Keng and Sri Mariamman temples.

SIGHTS TO SEE

❾ **Al Abrar Mosque** (Kuchu Palli). This small structure dates from 1850. The original mosque, built in 1827, was one of the first for Singapore's Indian Muslims.

❹ **Chinatown Centre.** This market is mobbed inside and out with jostling shoppers. At the open-air vegetable and fruit stands, women—toothless and wrinkled with age—sell their wares. Inside, on the first floor, hawker stalls sell a variety of cooked foods, but it is the basement floor that fascinates: Here you'll find a wet market, where an amazing array of meats, fowl, and fish is bought and sold.

❻ **Guild for amahs.** Club Street is full of old buildings that continue to house clan associations, including the professional guild for amahs. Though their numbers are few today, these female servants were once an integral part of European households in Singapore.

❷ **Jamae Mosque** (Masjid Chulia). This simple, almost austere mosque was built in the 1830s by Chulia Muslims from India. So long as it is not prayer time and the doors are open, you are welcome to step inside for a look (you must be dressed conservatively and take your shoes off before entering).

❺ **Jinriksha Station.** This station was once the bustling central depot for Singapore's rickshaws, which numbered more than 9,000 in 1919. Now there is nary a one. The station has been converted into a food market on one side and an office block on the other. This is a good place to sit down with a cool drink.

❼ **Nagore Durghe Shrine.** This unusual structure was built by southern Indian Muslims between 1828 and 1830. Inside it is decorated with Christmas tree lights.

Sago Street. Here family factories make paper houses and cars to be burned for good fortune at funerals. A cake shop at **No. 36** is extremely popular for fresh baked goods, especially during the Mooncake Festival. Two doors up, at **No. 32**, is a store selling dry snakes and lizards, for increasing fertility, and powdered antelope horn, for curing headaches and cooling the body.

③ Sri Mariamman Temple. The oldest Hindu temple in Singapore, the building has a pagodalike entrance topped by one of the most ornate *gopurams* (pyramidal gateway towers) you are ever likely to see. Hundreds of brightly colored statues of deities and mythical animals line the tiers of this towering porch; glazed cement cows sit atop the surrounding walls.

Tanjong Pagar Road. The center of an area of redevelopment in Chinatown, the road has a number of shop-houses restored to their 19th-century appearance—or rather a sanitized, dollhouselike version of it. It now contains teahouses, calligraphers, mah-jongg makers, and other shops.

⑩ Telok Ayer Market. Already a thriving fishmarket in 1822, the market was redesigned by George Coleman in 1894. It reopened in 1992 as a planned food court, with hawker stalls offering the gamut of Asian fare. By day it's busy with office workers. After 7 PM Boon Tat Street closes to traffic and the mood turns festive: The hawkers wheel out their carts, and musicians give street performances until midnight.

⑧ Thian Hock Keng Temple (Temple of Heavenly Happiness). This temple was completed in 1841 to replace a simple shrine built 20 years earlier, in gratitude for safe passage to Singapore across the China Sea. It is one of Singapore's oldest and largest Chinese temples. Thian Hock Keng is richly decorated with gilded carvings, sculptures, tiled roofs topped with dragons, and fine carved stone pillars. The pillars and sculptures were brought over from China, the cast-iron railings outside were made in Glasgow, and the blue porcelain tiles on an outer building came from Holland. Outside, on either side of the entrance, are two stone lions. The one on the left is female and holds a cup, symbolizing fertility; the other, a male, holds a ball, a symbol of wealth. Inside, a statue of Ma-Chu P'oh, the goddess of the sea, dominates the room. While the main temple is Taoist, the temple at the back is Buddhist and dedicated to Kuan Yin, the goddess of mercy.

① Yeo Swee Huat. Here, paper models of the paraphernalia of life—horses, cars, boats, planes, even fake money—are made, to be purchased by relatives of the deceased (you can buy them, too) and ritually burned so that their essence passes through to the spirit world in flames and smoke.

The Arab District

Long before the Europeans arrived, Arab traders plied the coastlines of the Malay Peninsula and Indonesia, bringing with them the teachings of Islam. By the time Raffles came to Singapore in 1819, to be a Malay was also to be a Muslim. Traditionally, Malays' lives have centered on their religion and their villages, known as kampongs. These consisted of a number of wood houses, with steep roofs of corrugated iron or thatch, gathered around a communal center, where chickens and children would feed and play under the watchful eye of mothers and the village elders while the younger men tended the fields or took to the sea in fishing boats. The houses were usually built on stilts above marshes and reached by narrow planks serving as bridges. If the kampong was on dry land, flowers and fruit trees would surround the houses.

The area known as the Arab District, while not a true kampong, remains a Malay enclave, held firmly together by strict observance of the tenets of Islam. At the heart of the community is the Sultan Mosque, originally built with a grant from the East India Company to the Sultan of Jahore. Around it are streets whose very names—Bussorah, Baghdad, Kandahar—evoke the fragrances of the Muslim world.

The Arab District is a small area, bounded by Beach and North Bridge roads to the south and north and spreading a couple of blocks to either side of Arab Street. It is a place to meander, taking time to browse through shops or enjoy Muslim food at a simple café.

Numbers in the text correspond to numbers in the margin and on the Arab District map.

A GOOD WALK
This walk begins at the foot of Arab Street, just across Beach Road from the Plaza Hotel. (From Collyer Quay, take Bus 20 or Bus 50; from Raffles Boulevard or the Stamford and Orchard roads intersection, take Bus 107.)

The first shops on Arab Street are bursting with baskets of every description. Farther along, shops selling fabrics—batiks, embroidered table linens, rich silks and velvets—dominate. Turn right onto Baghdad Street and watch for the dramatic view of the **Sultan Mosque** ① where **Bussorah Street** opens to your left. Leave the mosque, turn right at the end of Muscat Street, right on Kandahar Street, and then left on Baghdad Street. Baghdad Street becomes Pahang Street at Sultan Gate, where traditional Chinese stonemasons create statues curbside. At the junction of Pahang Street and Jalan Sultan, turn right and, at Beach Road, left, to visit the endearing **Hajjah Fatimah Mosque** ②, built in 1845. Return to Jalan Sultan and take a right. Past Minto Road is the **Sultan Plaza** ③, which houses fabric stores.

Three blocks beyond where **Bugis Street** ④ becomes Albert Street—past the Fu Lu Shou shopping complex (mostly for clothes) and the food-oriented Albert Complex—is Waterloo Street. Near the corner is the **Kuan Yin Temple** ⑤, one of the most popular Chinese temples in Singapore.

TIMING
This walking tour should not take more than two hours, including some time to look around the temples and mosques, but take your time. This is one of the friendliest places in Singapore.

SIGHTS TO SEE
❹ **Bugis Street.** Until recently Bugis Street was the epitome of Singapore's seedy but colorful nightlife; tourists (and Singaporeans, too) used to delight in its red lights and bars. The government was not delighted, though, and the area was razed to make way for a new MRT station. So strong was the outcry that Bugis Street has been re-created, approximately 137 meters (150 yards) from its original site, between Victoria and Queen streets, Rochor Road, and Cheng Yan Place. The shop-houses have been resurrected; hawker food stands compete with open-fronted restaurants (Kentucky Fried Chicken has a dominant corner). The streets in the center of the block are closed to traffic. Though it's convenient for lunch or an early-evening meal, Bugis hasn't boomed as anticipated. Nightlife here is disappointing.

Bussorah Street. Interesting shops include a Malay bridal shop and purveyors of batiks and Arab-designed cushion covers, and an importer of leather goods from Jogjakarta. At No. 45 is the Malay-crafts store of Haija Asfiah, who will gladly explain in detail the origin and traditional uses of his goods.

❷ **Hajjah Fatimah Mosque.** In 1845 Hajjah Fatimah, a wealthy Muslim woman married to a Bugis trader, commissioned a British architect to build this mosque. The minaret is reputedly modeled on the spire of the original St. Andrew's Church in colonial Singapore, but it leans at a 6° angle. No one knows whether this was intentional.

❺ **Kuan Yin Temple.** The temple's dusty, incense-filled interior, its altars heaped with hundreds of small statues of gods from the Chinese pan-

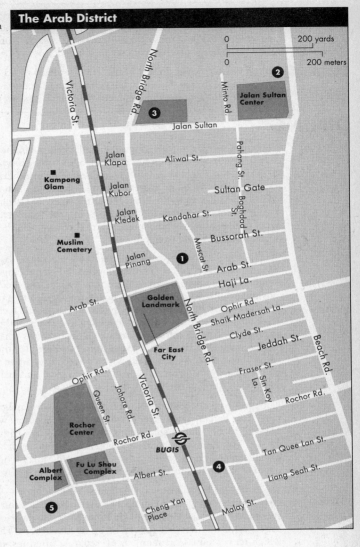

The Arab District

theon, transports the visitor into the world of Chinese mythology. People in search of help and advice about anything from an auspicious date for a marriage to possible solutions for domestic or work crises come here, shake *cham si* (bamboo fortune sticks), and wait for an answer. The gods are most receptive on days of a new or full moon. A small vegetarian restaurant next to the temple serves Chinese pastries, including mooncakes out of season.

North Bridge Road. North Bridge Road is full of fascinating stores selling costumes and headdresses for Muslim weddings, clothes for traditional Malay dances, prayer beads, scarves, perfumes, and much more. Interspersed among the shops are small, simple restaurants serving Muslim food.

❶ **Sultan Mosque** (Masjid Sultan). The first mosque on this site was built early in the 1820s with a S$3,000 grant from the East India Company. The current structure, built in 1928 by the same architects who designed the Victoria Memorial Hall, is a dramatic building with golden domes and glistening minarets. The walls of the vast prayer hall are adorned with green and gold mosaic tiles on which passages from the Qur'an are written in decorative Arab script.

❸ Sultan Plaza. Inside, dozens of traders offer batiks and other fabrics in traditional Indonesian and Malay designs, and one store on the third floor (No. 26) sells handicrafts from the Philippines.

DINING

Updated by
Wendy Hutton

Singapore offers the greatest feast in the East, if not in the world. Here you'll find excellent restaurants specializing in home-grown fare (known as *Nonya,* or *Peranakan* cuisine) and foods from Malaysia, Indonesia, Thailand, Vietnam, Korea, Japan, all parts of China, and North and South India, as well as from Western Europe and the United States. Gourmet cooking can be found as easily in small, unpretentious, open-front coffee shops as in the most elegant restaurants in the world, with service that's second to none.

At the other end of the scale are the hawker centers, agglomerations of individual vendor-chefs selling cooked foods in the open air. These vendors originally traveled from door to door selling their wares from portable stalls. Some years ago, Singapore decided to gather them in food centers to be monitored for hygiene. Visitors and locals alike find these centers a culinary adventure—find a seat at any of the tables, note the number of your table so you can tell the hawkers where to deliver your orders, then sit down, order a drink, and wait for the procession of food to arrive. Most dishes, which are paid for upon arrival, cost S$4 or slightly more; for S$12, you can get a meal that includes a drink and a slice of fresh fruit for dessert.

The most touristy center is Newton Circus. Other hawker centers include Lau Pa Sat, Telok Ayer Food Centre, on Shenton Way in the financial district; and Bugis Square, at Eminent Plaza (this one's open 7 AM–3 AM). An excellent covered center at Marina South has hundreds of stalls offering a vast selection of Chinese and Malay foods. You need a taxi to get there, but the ride is only about S$8 from Orchard Road.

Dim sum—called *dian xin* ("small eats") in Singapore—is a particularly Cantonese style of eating. Featured are a selection of bite-size steamed, baked, or deep-fried dumplings, buns, pastries, and pancakes, with a variety of savory or sweet flavorings. The selection, which may comprise as many as 50 separate offerings, may also include such dishes as soups, steamed pork ribs, and stuffed green peppers. Traditionally, dim sum are served three on a plate in bamboo steamer baskets on trolleys that are pushed around the restaurant. Simply wait for the trolleys to come around, then point to whichever item you would like. Dim sum is usually served for lunch from noon to 2:30 PM, though some teahouses in Chinatown serve it from 5AM to 9AM. An excellent place for dim sum is the Noble House (✉ 04–02 DBS Bldg., 6 Shenton-Way, ☎ 227–0933), a huge room heavy with Chinese decor. For a dim sum breakfast, try the New Nam Thong Tea House (☞ *below*).

High tea has become very popular in Singapore, and in many hotels, such as the Goodwood Park Hotel and the Holiday Inn Park View, is accompanied by light Viennese-style music. Though British-inspired, the Singapore high tea is usually served buffet style and includes dim sum, fried noodles, and other local favorites in addition to the regulation finger sandwiches, scones, and cakes. Teas are usually served between 3 and 6 PM and cost about S$20 per person, including tax.

DRESS

Except at the fancier hotel dining rooms, Singaporeans do not dress up to eat out. Generally, though, shorts, thongs, singlets (sleeveless cotton T-shirts), and track suits are not appropriate. Those sensitive to cold might bring a sweater, since many restaurants are air-conditioned to subarctic temperatures.

HOURS

Most restaurants are open from noon to 2:30 or 3 for lunch and from 7 to 10:30 PM (last order) for dinner. Seafood restaurants are usually open only for dinner and supper, until around midnight or 1 AM. Some hotel coffee shops (and the Indian coffee shops along Changi Road) are open 24 hours a day; others close between 2 and 6 AM. At hawker centers, some stalls are open for breakfast and lunch while others are open for lunch and dinner. Late-night food centers like Eminent Plaza in Jalan Besar are in full swing until 3 AM. Unless otherwise stated, restaurants listed below are open daily for lunch and dinner.

Chinese: Cantonese

$$$–$$$$ ★ ✕ **Li Bai.** Its dining room evokes richness without overindulgence: deep maroon wall panels edged with black and backlighted; elaborate floral displays that change with the seasons; jade table settings; ivory chopsticks. The service is very fine, as is the cooking, which is modern and innovative, yet deeply rooted in the Cantonese tradition. The chef's unusual creations include deep-fried diamonds of egg noodles in a rich stock with crabmeat and mustard greens; fried lobster in black bean paste; and double-boiled shark's fin with Chinese wine and *jinhua* ham. ✉ *Sheraton Towers Hotel, 39 Scotts Rd.,* ☎ *737–6888. AE, DC, MC, V.*

$$–$$$ ✕ **Lei Garden.** This aesthetically pleasing restaurant has built up a devoted following. The food represents the nouvelle Cantonese style with its pristine tastes and delicate textures. The menu also offers a long list of double-boiled tonic soups (highly prized by the Chinese), barbecued meats, seafoods, and a variety of shark's fin dishes. Dim sum is available; recommendations include Peking duck, grilled rib-eye beef, and fresh scallops with bean curd in black bean sauce. ✉ *Boulevard Hotel, 200 Orchard Blvd., Basement 2,* ☎ *235–8122. AE, DC, MC, V.*

$$–$$$ ✕ **Xin Cuisine.** The most innovative Chinese food in Singapore is served here. The cooking is excellent, the service expert, the setting cloistered and restful with elegant overtones: Dishes change regularly; watch for the monthly specials. We recommend the wok-fried salmon with shiitake and pickled ginger. The steamed fish is a good bet, and the desserts are all good for you—they either improve your complexion or cool you down. Double-boiled bird's nest, Chinese herbal pudding, and double-boiled *hasma* (snow frog jelly) with gingko nuts are just some of the endings to sample. ✉ *Concorde Hotel, 317 Outram Rd.,* ☎ *733–0188. AE, DC, MC, V.*

$ ✕ **Loy Sum Juan Restaurant.** This is not the place to go for glamour (it's tucked away on the second floor of a low-rent block of apartments on the fringe of Chinatown), but the food is both cheap and totally delicious. This is a good bet for traditional Cantonese cooking: Song Yu fish head steamed Hong-Kong style, abalone salad, and deep-fried chicken with prawn paste are among the specialties. The restaurant, which is just a stone's throw away from the Outram Park MRT station, is open for lunch and dinner. ✉ *02–88 Block 31, Outram Park,* ☎ *273–7231. Reservations not accepted. No credit cards.*

$ ✕ **New Nam Thong Tea House.** This Chinatown teahouse is absolutely inelegant and totally authentic. Breakfast here between 5 and 9:30 AM

270

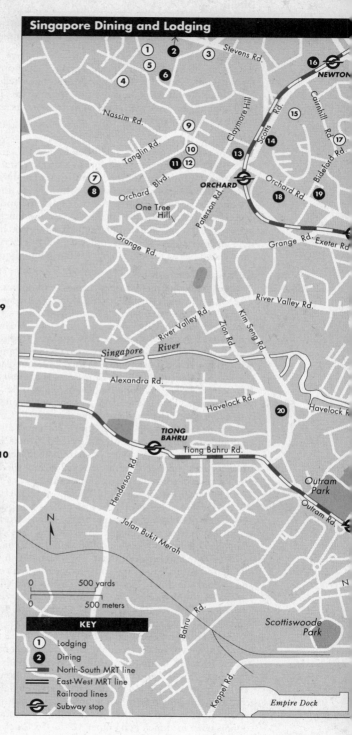

Singapore Dining and Lodging

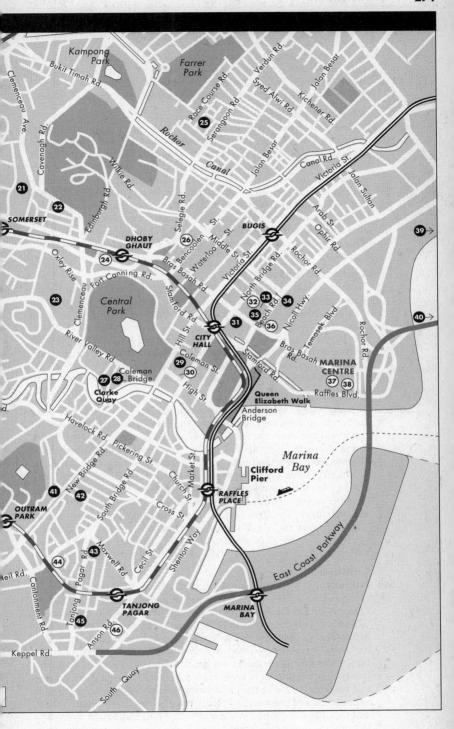

for a view of real Singapore life. Older folk, mainly men, congregate daily to gossip with friends and read the Chinese papers. Situated above an open-front shophouse, the teahouse is not air-conditioned and can be muggy, but it serves hearty, giant-size dim sum—*char siew pow* (steamed barbecued pork buns), *siew mai* (prawn-and-minced-pork dumplings), and other assorted dishes. Wash it all down with piping-hot Chinese tea. ⊠ *8–10A Smith St.,* ☎ *223–4229. Reservations not accepted. No credit cards.*

Chinese: Herbal

$$–$$$ ✕ **Imperial Herbal Restaurant.** In this unique restaurant, the kitchen is presided over by an herbalist rather than a chef, and there is a traditional pharmacy near the entrance where the herbs are stored (they can also be purchased for home cooking). The menu includes a wide range of dishes—a must is the delicate quick-fried egg white with scallops and herbs, served in a crunchy nest of potato threads. Eel fried with garlic and fresh coriander and eggplants with pine nuts are equally delicious, while the crispy fried ants on prawn toast are not only a conversation piece but totally inoffensive. Beer and wine are available as well as restorative tonics and teas. ⊠ *Metropole Hotel, 41 Seah St., 3rd floor,* ☎ *337–0491. AE, MC, V.*

Chinese: Hokkien

$$ ✕ **Beng Hiang.** Like Hakka food, Hokkien cooking is peasant-style: hearty, rough, and delicious. *Kwa huay* (liver rolls) and *ngo hiang* (pork-and-prawn rolls) are very popular and are eaten dipped in sweet plum sauce. *Hay cho* (deep-fried prawn dumplings) are another Hokkien staple. Beng Hiang also serves *khong bak* (braised pig's feet) and what is reputedly the best roast suckling pig in Singapore. The restaurant is in a restored shophouse just outside the main financial district. ⊠ *112–116 Amoy St.,* ☎ *221–6695. Reservations not accepted. No credit cards.*

Chinese: Szechuan

$$–$$$ ✕ **Dragon City.** Many Singaporeans consider Dragon City the best place
★ for Szechuan food. Set in a courtyard and entered through a flamboyant red moongate door, the restaurant is a large room that looks Chinese but is not particularly appealing. The food is where all the artistry is. Choose from such Szechuan staples as *kung po* chicken and prawns, in which the meat is deep-fried with whole dried chili peppers and coated with a sweet-and-sour sauce; or try the delicious minced-pork soup in a whole melon, steamed red fish with soybean crumbs, or smoked Szechuan duck. The service is fast. If you don't quite know how to order your meal, ask for Mr. Wang Ban Say, the restaurant's manager and one of the owners. ⊠ *Novotel Orchid Inn, Plymouth Wing, 214 Dunearn Rd.,* ☎ *250–3322. AE, DC, MC, V.*

Continental

$$$ ✕ **Bastiani's.** Mediterranean food with a New World accent stars in
★ this gorgeous restaurant in a restored riverside warehouse on Clarke Quay. A comfortable downstairs bar and outdoor patio are adjacent to Bastiani's cellars, while upstairs, the spacious dining room has a delightful terrace (where renegade smokers can indulge while eating). With its Oriental rugs on polished wooden floors, eclectic blend of furniture, and open kitchen hung with garlic, salamis, and the like, Bastiani's has a casual elegance hard to find in Singapore. The menu changes every two months, but always emphasizes fresh vegetables, herbs, grains such as couscous and polenta, and plenty of grilled or baked poultry, meat, and fish. Pizza is cooked in a wood-fired oven. More than 4,000 bottles of wine in the cellar should satisfy the most fastidious wine buff. ⊠ *Bastiani's, Clarke Quay,* ☎ *433–0156. AE, DC, MC, V.*

French

$$–$$$ ✕ **La Brasserie.** Often named as the favorite French restaurant in Singapore, this is an informal place, with garçons clad in ankle-length aprons serving hearty traditional fare like French onion soup, *émincé de veau à la crème* (sliced veal with mushrooms in cream sauce), and crème brûlée. Here you'll dine on the spirit of Paris as well as the food: red-checked tablecloths, wrought-iron lamps, exuberant French art, lace curtains, gleaming copper pans, and two attractive bar counters bring this brasserie to life. ✉ *The Marco Polo Singapore, Tanglin Rd.*, ☎ 474–7141. *AE, DC, MC, V.*

Indian

$$$ ✕ **Tandoor.** The food has a distinctly Kashmiri flavor at this luxurious restaurant, where Indian paintings, rust and terra-cotta colors, and Indian musicians at night create the ambience of the Moghul court. The tandoor oven, seen through glass panels across a lotus pond, dominates the room. Also cooked in the oven is the northern Indian leavened bread called *naan*; the garlic naan is justifiably famous. The tender spice-marinated roast leg of lamb is a favorite of the regulars. Spiced masala tea is a perfect ending to the meal. Service is exceptionally attentive. ✉ *Holiday Inn Park View, 11 Cavenagh Rd.*, ☎ 733–8333. *AE, DC, MC, V.*

$$–$$$ ✕ **Annalakshmi.** This Indian vegetarian restaurant, run by a Hindu religious and cultural organization, is considerably more elegant and consequently somewhat more expensive than most serving vegetarian cuisine. The paper-thin *dosai* pancakes are delicious in the special Sampoorna dinner (S$35), limited to 30 servings and presented on silver. The selection often includes cabbage curry, potato roast, *channa dhal* (chick pea stew), *kurma* (a mild vegetable curry spiced with cumin, coriander, cinnamon, and cardamom and cooked with yogurt or cream), *poori* (puffy, deep fried bread), *samosa* (deep-fried, vegetable-stuffed patties), and *jangri* (a cold dessert). ✉ *02–10 Excelsior Hotel & Shopping Centre, 5 Coleman St.*, ☎ 339–9993. *AE, DC, MC, V. Closed Thurs.*

$ ✕ **Banana Leaf Apollo.** Along Race Course Road are a host of South Indian restaurants that serve meals on fresh rectangles of banana leaf. The specialty here is fish-head curry (S$18–S$25, depending on size), and the taste is gutsy and chili-hot. The food itself is fabulous, though be warned that you may wind up with tears streaming! Each person is given a large piece of banana leaf; steaming-hot rice is spooned into the center; then two *papadam* (deep-fried lentil crackers) and two vegetables, with delicious spiced sauces, are arranged neatly around the rice. Optional extras such as the fish-head curry or spicy mutton may be added. ✉ *56/58 Race Course Rd.*, ☎ 293–8682. *Reservations not accepted. No credit cards.*

Italian

$$ ✕ **Pete's Place.** This is one of the city's most popular restaurants. The look is cozy Italian-country, with rustic brick walls and checkered tablecloths. The food is Italian-American, with staples like pizza and pastas. A salad bar with crisp, fresh vegetables, a wide array of dressings, and a large selection of breads is particularly popular, especially at lunchtime when you can opt for a light luncheon of soup and salad. A plus is Pete's proximity to two of the best shopping centers—Scotts and Far East. ✉ *Hyatt Regency Singapore, 10/12 Scotts Rd.*, ☎ 738–1234. *AE, DC, MC, V.*

$$ ✕ **Prego Restaurant.** On the ground floor of the Westin Plaza hotel, Prego is very popular for its reasonable prices and informality. The S$2 million transformation of the site of the former Palm Grill is a gamble that's paid off for the Westin. Italian staples include *focaccia all* *origano* (flat oregano bread with whole roasted garlic), ravioli, *pollo al rosmarino* (roast chicken with rosemary), and skewered prawns. ✉ *Westin Plaza, 2 Stamford Rd.,* ☎ *338–8585. AE, DC, MC, V.*

Japanese

$$$ ✕ **Nadaman.** There's nothing quite so exciting as watching a teppan-
★ yaki chef perform his culinary calisthenics at this 23rd-floor restaurant, with the Singapore skyline as a backdrop. The Nadaman offers sushi, sashimi (the fresh lobster sashimi is excellent), teppanyaki, tempura, and kaiseki. Try one of the *bento* lunches—fixed-price meals (around S$30) beautifully decorated in the Japanese manner and served in lacquer trays and boxes. The decor is distinctly Japanese, and the service is discreetly attentive. ✉ *Shangri-La Singapore, 22 Orange Grove Rd., 24th floor,* ☎ *737–3644. AE, DC, MC, V.*

$$$ ✕ **Sushi Nogawa.** Chef Nogawa himself presides, and his clientele is
★ so discerning that he is able to fly in tons of fresh Japanese produce throughout the year. The best dishes are seasonal (hence it's difficult to say what to expect). The adventurous can leave it all to the restaurant manager and hope to be surprised. There's *dobinmushi* (teapot soup) as well as tempura, more unusual stews, and even a fish-head dish. The small original restaurant, where afficionados sit cheek by jowl, is in the Crown Prince Hotel; the new, larger branch, at Takashimaya Shopping Centre on the opposite side of Orchard Road, offers less expensive food. Over at Takashimaya, you can choose from a number of set menus, including the most elegant of Japanese meals, the *kaiseki* banquet. ✉ *Crown Prince Hotel, 270 Orchard Rd.,* ☎ *732–1111;* ✉ *Takashimaya Shopping Centre, 391 Orchard Rd., Level 4,* ☎ *735–5575. AE, DC, MC, V.*

Malay and Indonesian

$$$ ✕ **Raffles Tiffin Room.** For a taste of nostalgia and of a typical British "curry tiffin," a visit to the Tiffin Room at Raffles is a must. Despite its popularity with tour groups, the light, airy restaurant with its marble floors is still gracious. A self-service buffet available for both lunch and dinner, the tiffin is a tempting spread of largely Indian dishes. Head straight for the mulligatawny, a spicy curry soup. There's a large array of spicy (but not necessarily chili-hot) vegetable, meat, poultry, and seafood dishes, and far more pickles, chutneys, and other condiments than a genuine Indian meal would provide. If you've still got room, the dessert table offers one or two local desserts as well as Indian and international favorites. ✉ *Raffles Hotel, 1 Beach Rd.,* ☎ *337–1886. AE, DC, MC, V.*

$$ ✕ **Aziza's.** Hazizah Ali has brought elegant Malay cooking out of the home and into her intimate street-front restaurant on the charming Emerald Hill Road, just up from Peranakan Place. It's the spicy cooking of the Malay Peninsula you get here—lots of lemongrass, galangal, shallots, pepper, coriander, cloves, and cinnamon. Try the *rendang* (beef simmered for hours in a mixture of spices and coconut milk), *gado gado* (a light salad with a spiced peanut sauce), or *bergedel* (Dutch-influenced potato cutlets). The oxtail soup is especially delicious. Ask for *nasi ambang* and you'll get festive rice with a sampling of dishes from the menu. The Orchard Road location and the friendly setting make this an easy place to experiment with Malay food. ✉ *36 Emerald Hill Rd.,* ☎ *235–1130. AE, DC, MC, V.*

$$ ✕ **Sukmaindra.** You'd expect this restaurant, in one of the many hotels owned by the Sultan of Brunei, reputedly the world's richest man, to be opulent. And you won't be disappointed; there are acres of marble with Moorish arches and marble columns supporting a sculptured geometric ceiling. Dishes to sample include oxtail soup stewed in a light blend of spices, satays, and *kepala ikan* (fish-head curry). For dessert, *chendol* (a noodle-like jelly) served with palm sugar and coconut milk is a delight. No alcoholic beverages are served. ⊠ *Royal Holiday Inn Crowne Plaza, Level 3, 25 Scotts Rd.,* ☎ *737–7966. AE, DC, MC, V.*

Nonya

$$ ✕ **Nonya and Baba.** This restaurant serving the authentic food of the Babas is situated near the Tank Road Hindu Temple. It's intimate but not particularly well decorated. Habitués like it for the food and the basic comforts it provides. Try the *ayam buah keluak, bakwan kepiting* (soup of crabmeat and pork dumplings), *babi pongtay, satay ayam* (fried chicken satay), or *sambal* "lady's fingers" (okra with a spicy sauce). ⊠ *262 River Valley Rd.,* ☎ *734–1382/6. Reservations not accepted. V.*

Seafood

$$–$$$ ✕ **Palm Beach Seafood.** Forty years ago, this restaurant was on a beach, with tables set under coconut trees—hence the name. It is now in a shopping and leisure complex next to the National Stadium and covers three floors, the downstairs restaurant seating around 550. What the place lacks in ambience, it more than makes up for in food, and the prices must be the best in town for seafood. The most popular dishes include chili crabs served with French bread to mop up the sauce (although you may prefer the black pepper crab); prawns fried in black soy sauce or in butter and milk with curry leaves; and deep-fried crisp squid. Don't miss the *yu char kway,* deep-fried crullers stuffed with a mousse of squid and served with a tangy black sauce. ⊠ *Leisure Park, 5 Stadium Walk, Kallang Park,* ☎ *344–3088. Reservations not accepted. AE, MC, V.*

$$–$$$ ✕ **UDMC Seafood Centre.** You *must* visit this place at the East Coast Parkway, near the entrance to the lagoon, to get a true picture of the way Singaporeans eat out, as well as real value (prices here are cheaper than in most other seafood restaurants). Walk around the eight open-fronted restaurants before you decide where to eat. Chili crabs, steamed prawns, steamed fish, pepper crabs, fried noodles, and deep-fried squid are the specialties. ⊠ *East Coast Pkwy. Restaurants include Chin Wah Heng,* ☎ *444–7967;* ⊠ *Gold Coast Seafood,* ☎ *242–7720;* ⊠ *Golden Lagoon Seafood,* ☎ *448–1894;* ⊠ *Jumbo Seafood,* ☎ *442–3435;* ⊠ *Kheng Luck Seafood,* ☎ *444–5911;* ⊠ *Lucky View Seafood Restaurant,* ☎ *241–1022;* ⊠ *Ocean Park Seafood Restaurant,* ☎ *242–7720; and* ⊠ *Red House Seafood Restaurant,* ☎ *442–3112. Reservations not accepted. AE, DC, MC, V. No lunch.*

Thai

$$–$$$ ✕ **Thanying.** Possibly the best Thai restaurant in Singapore, the Thanying is decorated in exquisite aristocratic Thai taste, and the food—redolent of kaffir lime leaves, basil, mint leaves, ginger, and coriander leaves—is cooked in the best palace tradition. The restaurant has been such a success that there is now a second Thanying along the attractive Clarke Quay. As with Chinese food, you normally order one dish per person plus one extra and share the entire meal. Try the *gai kor bai toey* (marinated chicken wrapped in pandanus leaves and char-grilled to perfection), an exquisite Thai salad like *yam sam oh* (shredded pomelo tossed with chicken and prawns in a spicy lime sauce), *pla khao sam rod* (garoupa, or grouper, deep-fried until it's so crispy you can practically eat the bones), and one of the Thai curries. And of course, don't miss out on the sour and hot *tom yam* soup. ⊠ *Amara Hotel, Level 2, 165 Tanjong Pagar Rd.,* ☎ *222–4688;* ⊠ *Clarke Quay, Block D,* ☎ *336–1821. AE, DC, MC, V.*

$$ ✕ **Yhingthai Palace.** The no-nonsense decor of this small, simple restaurant—just around the corner from the famous Raffles Hotel—makes it clear that food is the prime concern. Although the service can

be a little slow, the well-prepared and moderately priced Thai food is worth waiting for. The *yam ma muang* (sour mango salad) is an excellent and refreshing dish, while *hor mok talay,* seafood mousse served in charming terra-cotta molds, is light and full of flavor. If you enjoy spicy dishes with plenty of herbs, try to *phad kra kai* (stir-fried minced chicken). The *kuay teow phad Thai* (fresh rice noodles fried with seafood) are delicious, and one of the lemony *tom yam* soups is almost obligatory. ⊠ *13 Purvis St.,* ☎ *337–1161. AE, MC, V.*

LODGING

Over the years Singapore has been transformed from a popular destination for individual tourists to a conventioneers' mecca teeming with tour groups and delegates. Singapore's lodging has visibly changed to accommodate this profitable market: Extensive refurbishment and growth with less personal, more automated service has been the trend. Although at times hotel rooms can be scarce, with the overall decline in the number of tourists visiting Singapore, attractive discounts are usually available—and no thrifty visitor ever pays the published price.

Even with the discounts, Singapore's hotels are no longer inexpensive compared to New York's. The average price ranks just under Hong Kong's and considerably above those of Jakarta, Bangkok, Manila, and Kuala Lumpur. At deluxe hotels, a superior double room runs more than S$400 a night. A room with a private bath in a modest hotel should cost no more than S$200. At budget hotels with shared bathroom facilities, the rates are under S$85. And if all you're looking for is a bunk, walk along Bencoolen Street, where there are dormitory-style guest houses that charge no more than S$25 a night.

Your choice of hotel location may be influenced by your reason for visiting Singapore, but it should not be overemphasized. Singapore is a relatively compact city, and taxis and public transportation, especially the new subway, make travel between areas a matter of minutes. Furthermore, no hotel is more than a 30-minute cab ride from Changi Airport. If you are between planes and this is too far, the new Transit Hotel within the airport departure area charges on the basis of six-hour periods.

All hotels listed, unless otherwise noted, have rooms with private baths. All deluxe hotels have International Direct Dial (IDD) telephones with bathroom extensions, color televisions with Teletext for world news and information, room service, and minibars. The top luxury hotels have recently added database ports for modems and are currently connecting their business centers to the Internet. Most hotels have a travel desk.

$$$$ 🖬 **Goodwood Park.** This venerable Singapore institution began in
★ 1900 as a club for German expatriates and has since hosted the likes of the Duke of Windsor, Edward Heath, Noël Coward, and the great Anna Pavlova, who performed here. Today the hotel may be overshadowed by the glitz of the high-rises, but for personal service and refinement, it stands alone. Guests are greeted by name, high tea is accompanied by a string quartet, and guest rooms achieve the comfort of a country house. Parklane suites, each with a separate bedroom and living-dining room, can be rented for less than a double room in the main hotel; the drawback is the five-minute walk to the hotel's facilities. Restaurants include the **Gordon Grill,** the **Min Jiang,** and the **Chang Jiang** (☞ *Dining, above*). ⊠ *22 Scotts Rd., 0922,* ☎ *737–7411,* 𝖥𝖠𝖷 *732–8558; U.S. reservations 800/323–7500. 171 rooms, 64 suites. 3 restaurants, coffee shop, tea shop, 3 pools, beauty salon, baby-sitting, business services, meeting rooms. AE, DC, MC, V.*

$$$$ ★ 🏨 **The Oriental.** Inside this pyramid-shaped Marina Square hotel, architect John Portman has created a 21-story atrium with interior balconies that are stepped inward as they ascend; glass elevators glide from floor to floor. The reception area and lobby are on the fourth floor, free from the bustle of transients. Rooms are understated, with soft hues of peach and green, hand-woven carpets, and paintings of old Singapore. Of special note are the Italian-marble-tiled bathrooms, with telephones, radio and television speakers. One-bedroom suites have lovely sitting rooms and a separate guest washroom. The **Cherry Garden** (☞ Dining, *above*) prepares some of the best Hunanese food in Singapore. ✉ 01–200, 6 Raffles Blvd., 0103, ☎ 338–0066, FAX 339–9537. *640 rooms. 5 restaurants, pool, massage, sauna, golf privileges, 2 tennis courts, exercise room, jogging, squash, business services, meeting rooms, travel services. AE, DC, MC, V.*

$$$$ 🏨 **Raffles Hotel.** Opened by the Sarkies brothers in 1887 and visited by Conrad, Kipling, and Maugham, Raffles was the belle of the East during its heyday in the '20s and '30s but fell on hard times after World War II. True to form in this planned republic, millions of dollars have been spent to replace Singapore's noble old charm with a sanitized version of colonial ambience. The new Raffles is a glistening showpiece, though mostly from the outside; inside, it's sterile. The polished-marble lobby seems cold while guest suites have teak floors, 14-foot ceilings, overhead fans, and '20s-style furnishings that tend to be stiff. ✉ 1 Beach Rd., 0718, ☎ 337–1886, FAX 339–7650. *104 suites. 2 restaurants, pool, exercise room, business services. AE, DC, MC, V.*

$$$$ ★ 🏨 **Ritz-Carlton.** The most dramatic of the new spate of luxury hotels is the Marina Square Ritz-Carlton. It opened in 1996 to a fanfare so impressive that taxi drivers dubbed it the "wanna-be six-star hotel." All rooms are unusually large, with unobstructed views—from the tall beds and even the tubs—of the skyline or Marina Bay. Modern, minimal appointments are softened by Tibetan-style woven rugs and wooden floors. Floors 30 to 32 are Club Floors where, for a S$50 premium, guests enjoy complimentary breakfast, evening cocktails, and personalized concierge services. ✉ 7 Raffles Ave., 0397, ☎ 337–8888, FAX 338–0001. *610 rooms. 3 restaurants, pool, tennis court, health club, business services, meeting rooms. AE, DC, MC, V.*

$$$$ ★ 🏨 **Shangri-La.** Amid 15 acres of gardens in a residential area at the top of Orchard Road, the Shangri-La is a pleasant 10-minute walk from the shopping areas. The main lobby is handsome and pleasant, with easy chairs and tables for morning coffee and afternoon tea. The most attractive rooms are in the newer Valley Wing, which has its own entrance, check-in counter, concierge, boardrooms, and spacious guest rooms. Rooms in the Garden Wing are replete with warm fabrics and maple, cherry wood, and rattan furniture. The Tower Wing is the oldest, with the smallest rooms, but was refurbished in 1994. The Japanese **Nadaman** (☞ Dining, *above*) really draws a crowd. ✉ 22 Orange Grove Rd., 1025, ☎ 737–3644, FAX 733–7220. *821 rooms (136 in the Valley Wing). 4 restaurants, poolside bar and café, 4 tennis courts, putting green, exercise room, squash, dance club, nightclub, business services, meeting rooms. AE, DC, MC, V.*

$$$ ★ 🏨 **The Duxton.** This was Singapore's first boutique hotel—eight smartly converted shop-houses in the Tanjong Pagar district of Chinatown. It remains a breath of fresh air: intimate and tasteful with a hint of old Singapore's character before it sold out to steel girders and glass. The standard rooms, at the back of the building, are small, with colonial reproduction furniture. You may want to spend the extra S$50 for one of the small duplex suites. Since windows aren't double glazed, you can hear some street noise. Breakfast is included, and afternoon tea is served in the lounge. The excellent French restaurant, **L'Aigle d'Or** (☞ Dining, *above*), is off the lobby. ✉ *83 Duxton Rd., 0208,* ☎ *227–7678,* ℻ *227–1232; U.S. reservations 800/272–8188, U.K. reservations 0181/876–3419. 48 rooms. Restaurant, business services. AE, DC, MC, V.*

$$$ 🏨 **Hilton International.** It may be short on glitter and dazzle, but the rooms have all the standard amenities of a modern deluxe property. It's near Orchard and Scotts roads and shopping arcades with some of Singapore's most exclusive boutiques. Though the rooms on the street side have views, those on the back have been blocked by the adjacent Four Seasons; however, in back you can sleep with the sliding windows open, unlike in most Singapore hotels, which rely solely upon air-conditioning for ventilation. The former Givenchy suites are now executive club floors with 72 contemporary rooms and suites. Vodka aficionados can choose from 50 varieties at the **Kaspia** bar; locals come here for afternoon tea and the best cheesecake in Singapore. ✉ *581 Orchard Rd., 0923,* ☎ *737–2233,* ℻ *732–2917. 435 rooms. 4 restaurants, 2 bars, pool, health club, business services, meeting rooms. AE, DC, MC, V.*

$$$ 🏨 **Omni Marco Polo.** The word on the street is that this hotel may be transformed into separate apartments for long-term stays. In the meantime, the rooms in the Continental Wing have Chippendale reproductions, marble-tiled bathrooms, writing desks, and remote controls for television and lights. The Omni Continental Club concierge floor has a handsome split-level lounge for complimentary breakfast and cocktails, and a separate business center. There are three restaurants: the smart, formal **Le Duc,** with haute Continental cuisine; the cheerful **La Brasserie,** with bistro-style cooking (☞ Dining, *above*); and the coffee shop. ✉ *Tanglin Rd., Singapore 1024,* ☎ *474–7141; in U.S., 800/843–6664;* ℻ *471–0521. 573 rooms, 30 suites. 2 restaurants, bar, coffee shop, lobby lounge, in-room safes, pool, exercise room, dance club, business services, meeting rooms. AE, DC, MC, V.*

$$$ 🏨 **Orchard Hotel.** Close to the bustle of Orchard Road, several embassies, and the Botanical Gardens, this hotel, one of the largest in Singapore, is a popular spot. A recent renovation has inflated the prices but quelled the frequent mob scenes in the otherwise nondescript lobby. The light pastel rooms here are comfortable and functional. The Claymore Wing, a 300-room 17-story tower extension, is more expensive, with slightly larger rooms and built-in safes. The top four Claymore floors form the Premier Club, which has separate check-in, complimentary breakfast, and evening cocktails. ✉ *442 Orchard Rd., 0923,* ☎ *734–7766,* ℻ *733–5482. 679 rooms. 3 restaurants, outdoor café, pool, dance club, business services, travel services. AE, DC, MC, V.*

$$ 🏨 **Boulevard Hotel.** A floor-to-ceiling sculpture dominates the airy atrium lobby of this hotel, which caters to the traveling executive. Guest rooms have large work desks, IDD telephones, and pantries with coffee and tea makers. Rooms come in three sizes: standard; deluxe, with a corner pantry; and executive, with a work desk area. This hotel has not pushed up its rates like some of its competitors. It's at the top end of Orchard Road, away from the main thoroughfare. ✉ *200 Orchard Blvd., 1024,* ☎ *737–2911,* ℻ *737–8449. 528 rooms. 3 restaurants, coffee shop, 2 pools, beauty salon, exercise room, dance club, business services, travel services. AE, DC, MC, V.*

$ 🏨 **Cairnhill Hotel.** Not a particularly attractive building in itself, this
★ hotel on a hill commands good views of downtown Singapore. Its restaurant serves Pekingese and Szechuan food, as well as regional fare. It's a 10-minute walk from Orchard Road. *19 Cairnhill Circle, 0922,* ☎ *734–6622,* ℻ *235–5598. 220 rooms. Restaurant, coffee shop, pool, exercise room, business services, meeting room. AE, V.*

$ 🏨 **Ladyhill Hotel.** Unlike most other Singapore hotels, Ladyhill em-
★ phasizes home comforts and relaxation. In the main building are the guest rooms. "Superior" rooms in the surrounding cottages are spa-

cious enough for an extra bed, perfect for families with children. There is usually a poolside barbecue at night. The Ladyhill is in a residential area a good 10-minute walk uphill from Orchard Road (a hotel bus shuttles the weary back and forth). ⊠ *1 Ladyhill Rd., 1025,* ☎ *737–2111,* FAX *737–4606. 171 rooms. Restaurant, bar, coffee shop, pool, nightclub, meeting rooms. AE, V.*

$ ⊞ **RELC International House.** This is less a hotel than an international
★ conference center often used by Singapore's university for seminars. However, the upper floors of the building are bargain guest rooms: large and basically comfortable, with plenty of welcomed light, but be prepared for slapdash plaster repair work in the otherwise clean and functional bathrooms. The building is in a residential neighborhood, up a hill beyond the Shangri-La Hotel, a 10-minute walk to the Orchard and Scotts roads intersection. Because of its good value, it is often booked, so reservations are strongly advised. ⊠ *30 Orange Grove Rd., 1025,* ☎ *737–9044,* FAX *733–9976. 128 rooms. Coffee shop, coin laundry. No credit cards.*

$ ⊞ **Singapore Peninsula Hotel.** Near the Padang and between the fashionable Orchard Road and commercial district areas, this hotel offers the basic creature comforts. The lobby area is small and nondescript. The fairly spacious guest rooms are clean—the best are on the 17th floor—though you may have to tolerate water stains in the bathtub. All rooms have televisions with Teletext. There is no restaurant, but a coffee shop serves the basics. ⊠ *3 Coleman St., Singapore 0617,* ☎ *337–2200,* FAX *339–3580. 311 rooms, 4 suites. Bar, coffee shop, room service, minibars, in-room safes, pool, massage, sauna, exercise room, nightclub. AE, MC, V.*

¢ ⊞ **Hotel Bencoolen.** On the commercial street that leads from Orchard Road to Little India, this hotel's highlights are in-room IDD phones, its central location, and helpful staff. Usually, one can negotiate a discount on the room rate, making the Bencoolen a fine value. A rooftop restaurant serves Chinese and Continental fare. ⊠ *47 Bencoolen St., 0718,* ☎ *336–0822,* FAX *336–4384. 86 rooms. Restaurant. MC, V.*

¢ ⊞ **Metropole Hotel.** This is a very modest and basic hotel near Raffles City. The rooms are simply furnished and have televisions. The staff is quite helpful, which isn't always the case in budget hotels. ⊠ *41 Seah St., 0718,* ☎ *336–3611,* FAX *339–3610. 54 rooms. Restaurant, coffee shop, room service. AE, DC, MC, V.*

¢ ⊞ **YMCA International House.** This well-run YMCA at the bottom end of Orchard Road offers hotel-like accommodations for men and women, with double (S$70) and single (S$55) rooms, plus dormitories for budget travelers (S$20). S$5 will buy you temporary YMCA membership. All rooms have private baths, color TVs, and IDD phones. In addition to an impressive gym, there are a rooftop pool and squash and badminton courts. And there's a McDonald's at the entrance. ⊠ *1 Orchard Rd., 0923,* ☎ *336–6000,* FAX *337–3140. 60 rooms. Pool, exercise room, squash. AE, DC, MC, V.*

NIGHTLIFE AND THE ARTS

The Arts

The Singapore Tourist Promotion Board (STPB; ☎ 736–6622) has listings of events scheduled for the current month. You can also find the schedules of major performances in the local English-language newspaper, the *Straits Times,* or in the free monthly *Arts Diary* brochure available at most hotel reception desks.

CHINESE OPERA

Chinese operas—called *wayangs*—reenact Chinese legend through powerful movement, lavish costumes, outrageous masks, and heavy makeup. Performances are held on temporary stages set up near temples, in market areas, or outside apartment complexes. They are staged year round, but most frequently in August and September, during the Festival of the Hungry Ghosts. Gongs and drums beat, devils leap, maidens weep, and heroes reap the praise of an enraptured audience.

CONCERTS

Nanyang Academy of Fine Arts Chinese Orchestra (☎ 338–9176) gives regular concerts featuring traditional Chinese instruments producing classics and folk tunes. Performances are given at the Victoria Theatre and Memorial Hall four times a year. Three times a year, the 70-member **Chinese Orchestra of the Singapore Broadcasting Corporation** (☎ 338–1230 or 256–0401, ext. 2732) performs Chinese classical music at the Victoria.

CULTURAL SHOWS

"ASEAN Night" at the Mandarin Hotel offers traditional songs and dances from the various countries of ASEAN (the Association of South East Asian Nations). The shows are held poolside, and dinner is available during performances ⊠ *333 Orchard Rd.,* ☎ *737–4411.* ☒ *Dinner and show S$46.50, show S$26.25.* ۞ *Tues.–Sun., dinner at 7, show at 7:45.*

The **"Cultural Wedding Show"** is a 45-minute re-creation of a Peranakan wedding ceremony. The presentation is part of a three-hour immersion in the culture of Straits-born Chinese that includes a tour of Peranakan Place's Show House Museum and dinner at Bibi's restaurant, serving Nonya food. ⊠ *Peranakan Pl., 180 Orchard Rd.,* ☎ *732–6966.* ☒ *S$36.* ۞ *Weeknights at 6:30.*

"Instant Asia" is a 45-minute revue of Chinese, Indian, and Malay dance. At the end of the show, members of the audience are invited to participate. Although cliché and commercial, it's fun if the first time around. ⊠ *920 East Coast Pkwy.,* ☎ *345–1111.* ☒ *S$5, free to diners.* ۞ *Weeknights at 7:30.*

"Malam Singapura" is the Hyatt Regency's colorful 45-minute show of song and dance (mostly Malay) performed poolside with or without dinner. ⊠ *10–12 Scotts Rd.,* ☎ *733–1188.* ☒ *Dinner and show S$38, show S$18.* ۞ *Nightly, dinner at 7, show at 8.*

Nightlife

Music clubs, offering everything from serious listening to jazz to the thumping and flashing of discos, are becoming more popular as Singaporeans take up the Western custom of dating. The increasingly popular *karaoke* bars, where guests grip real microphones and sing along to the music track of a video, offer chronic shower singers the chance to go public.

Nightclubs with floor shows are also popular, and the bigger the place is, the better—some accommodate as many as 500 revelers. There is usually a cover charge or a first-drink charge (cover plus one free drink) of about S$15 weeknights and S$25 weekends.

COUNTRY-AND-WESTERN

Golden Peacock Lounge. This has long been a favorite of those who enjoy country music. ⊠ *Shangri-La Hotel, 22 Orange Grove Rd.,* ☎ *737–3644.* ☒ *Drinks from S$15.* ۞ *Nightly 8–2.*

DANCE AND THEATER NIGHTCLUBS

Golden Million. Here you can either dine or just listen to Hong Kong bands play a mixture of Mandarin, Cantonese, and Western music. The decor is expansive and rich, with lots of gold and red, oozing extravagance. ⊠ *Peninsula Hotel, 3 Coleman St., 5th floor,* ☎ *336–6993.* ◐ *Nightly 8–2.*

Lido Palace Niteclub. Chinese cabaret, a band, DJ-spun disco, karaoke, and, for those who wish to dine, Cantonese cuisine, are the highlights at the "palace of many pleasures." ⊠ *Concorde Hotel, 317 Outram Rd., 5th floor,* ☎ *732–8855.* ⊞ *1st drink S$30.* ◐ *Nightly 9–3, shows at 9:30 and 12:30.*

Neptune. At this sumptuous two-story establishment, designed as an Oriental pavilion, Cantonese food is served, and there is a gallery for nondiners. Local, Taiwanese, and Filipino singers entertain in English and Chinese; occasionally a European dance troupe is added to the lineup. ⊠ *Overseas Union House, Collyer Quay,* ☎ *224–3922 or 737–4411 (information and reservations).* ⊞ *S$8, dinner S$15.* ◐ *Nightly 8–2.*

DISCOS AND DANCE CLUBS

Caesars. The decor and the waitresses clad in lissome togas give this disco an air of decadent splendor. DJ-spun music plus imported live bands make it a hot venue. ⊠ *02–36 Orchard Towers, front block, 400 Orchard Rd.,* ☎ *235–2840.* ◐ *Sun.–Thurs. 8 PM–2 AM, Fri.–Sat. 8 PM–3 AM.*

Celebrities. At this establishment in the swank Orchard Towers, dance music spun by a DJ is interspersed with live pop music; the all-girl band Heaven Knows is a key attraction. There is ample room to drink at the 150-foot-long bar. ⊠ *B1–41 Orchard Towers, rear block, 400 Orchard Rd.,* ☎ *734–5221.* ◐ *Sun.–Thurs. 8 PM–2 AM, Fri.–Sat. 8 PM–3 AM.*

Fire. One of Singapore's steady favorites, Fire has live music danced to by a lively crowd. Upstairs would-be artists sing their lungs out in 12 computerized karaoke rooms. ⊠ *Orchard Plaza 04-19, 150 Orchard Rd.,* ☎ *235–0155.* ◐ *Nightly 9–2.*

Rumours. One of the largest discos in Singapore, this is a favorite among the younger set. The two-level glass dance floor is designed to make you feel as though you are dancing in space; the play of mirrors adds to the distortion. ⊠ *03–08 Forum Galleria, 483 Orchard Rd.,* ☎ *732–8181.* ◐ *Sun.–Thurs. 8–2, Fri.–Sat. 8–3.*

The Warehouse. Two former riverside warehouses now store up to 500 disco fanatics and the largest video screen in Singapore. This is a popular nightspot, especially for the younger crowd. ⊠ *332 Havelock Rd., next to the River View Hotel,* ☎ *732–9922.* ◐ *Sun.–Thurs. 8 PM–2 AM, Fri.–Sat. 8 PM–3 AM.*

Xanadu. With the flip of a switch, the American Western scene—complete with square dancing—is transformed into a tropical island night suitable for smooching. ⊠ *Shangri-La Hotel, 22 Orange Grove Rd.,* ☎ *737–3644.* ◐ *Nightly 9–3.*

JAZZ

Captain's Bar. For a sophisticated evening of jazz and rhythm and blues, this elegant but comfortable bar and lounge is just the place. ⊠ *Oriental Hotel, Marina Square,* ☎ *338–0066.* ◐ *Nightly 9–1.*

Duxton's Chicago Bar & Grill. In the renovated Tanjong Pagar district, this bar serves up barbecued spare ribs to the tune of jazz and blues American style. ⊠ *6 Duxton Hill,* ☎ *222–4096.* ◐ *Nightly 5–1.*

Harry's Quayside. This comfortable spot offers a mix of jazz, blues, and classic rock. Occasionally the band gets carried away and produces a jam session. Upstairs food is served with fine waterfront views. ✉ *28 Boat Quay,* ☎ *538–3029.* ◷ *Daily 11 AM–midnight.*

KARAOKE BARS

Park Avenue. Different sections permit different kinds of crooning, from French love songs in a library setting to John Denver in a Western landscape. ✉ *#04–08, 80 Marina Parade,* ☎ *440–9998.* ◷ *Nightly 8–2.*

PUBS AND BEER GARDENS

Brannigans. Decorated with knickknacks from around the world to celebrate the adventures of Captain David Brannigan, British wanderer, this popular watering hole is a convenient meeting spot. ✉ *Hyatt Regency, 10–12 Scotts Rd.,* ☎ *733–1188.* ◷ *Daily 11 AM–1 AM.*

Dickens Tavern. At this pub and lounge, regulars listen to bands while being served by friendly waitresses (not hostesses). It's a good place to visit if you do not want to have a raucous and expensive evening. ✉ *04–01 Parkway Parade, 80 Marina Parade Rd.,* ☎ *440–0215.* ◷ *Nightly 8–2.*

Flag & Whistle. Down in the renovated part of Chinatown, this English-style pub chatters with expat conversations punctuated with pints and fortified with British snacks. ✉ *10 Duxton Hill,* ☎ *223–1126.* ◷ *Daily 11 AM–midnight.*

Hard Rock Cafe. Hamburgers and light fare are served at this pub/café, and a live band plays in the evenings. ✉ *02–01, 50 Cuscaden Rd.,* ☎ *235–5232.* ◷ *Nightly 6–1.*

Wild West Tavern. One of Clarke Quay's plethora of restaurants and bars, this is less pricey than most and quite appealing for a beer and a chat. ✉ *12 Clark Quay,* ☎ *334–4180.* ◷ *Nightly 4–midnight.*

OUTDOOR ACTIVITIES AND SPORTS

Singapore is one of the best cities in Asia for outdoor activities, despite the heat, for it's one of few that's not polluted. The government has taken care to set aside a significant portion of the island for recreation, so you can choose anything from waterskiing to a jungle hike to beach volleyball. Be careful to drink lots of water, and try to schedule the most strenuous activities in early morning or late afternoon.

Beaches and Water Parks

East Coast Park. Here you'll find an excellent beach and a water-sports lagoon where you can rent sailboards, canoes, and sailboats. The **Aquatic Centre** has four pools—including a wave pool—as well as a giant water slide called the Big Splash. "Holiday chalets" set among the palm trees beside the beach can be rented by the day. Restaurants and changing facilities are available.

Sentosa Island. Sentosa offers a reasonable beach and a swimming lagoon, with changing and refreshment facilities, as well as rowboats, sailboards, and canoes for rent. Do not expect seclusion on the weekend—the island gets very crowded.

Desaru, Malaysia. The best beach area near Singapore is on peninsular Malaysia, 100 kilometers (60 miles) east of Johore Bahru. Excellent beaches and resort-type activities on the water, as well as an 18-hole golf course are available. You can charter a taxi from Johore Bahru for about M$60 (US$23), but it's easier to take the 450-passenger, 80-vehicle catamaran *Tropic Chief,* which makes a 45-minute run between the Marine Terminal at Changi and Tanjung Belungkar; from there a coach makes the 32-kilometer (20-mile) run to Desaru. Contact **Ferrylink** (⊠ Changi Ferry Rd., ☎ 733–6744; S$18 one-way; reservations essential). For overnight accommodations, Desaru has two hotels and several chalets (the Desaru View Hotel will collect you from Singapore).

Participant Sports

BICYCLING

You can rent a bike from one of the many **bicycle kiosks** that dot designated bike paths. Rates are about S$3–S$8 an hour, with a deposit of S$20–S$50.

FLYING

The **Republic of Singapore Flying Club** (⊠ East Camp Bldg., 140B Seletar Airbase, ☎ 481–0502 or 481–0200) offers visiting membership to qualified pilots and has aircraft available for hire (approximately S$270 per hour plus S$65 per hour for a temporary one-month membership). You cannot fly solo unless you have a Singapore license.

GOLF

Some of the top Singapore hotels, including the Oriental, have special arrangements for guests at local golf clubs, or you can make your own. The STPB has a brochure on clubs.

Changi Golf Club (⊠ 345 Netheravon Rd., ☎ 545–5133) is a hilly nine-hole course on 50 acres that's open to nonmembers on weekdays. **Jurong Country Club** (⊠ 9 Science Centre Rd., ☎ 560–5655) has an 18-hole, par 71 course on 120 acres. **Keppel Club** (⊠ Bukit Chermin, ☎ 273–5522) is the nearest 18-hole course to the city. **Seletar Country Club** (⊠ Seletar Airbase, ☎ 481–4746) is considered the best nine-hole course on the island. **Sembawang Country Club** (⊠ 17 Km Sembawang Rd., ☎ 257–0642) is an 18-hole, par 70 course. It is known as the commando course for its hilly terrain. **Sentosa Golf Club** (⊠ Sentosa Island, ☎ 275–0022) permits visitors to play on the 18-hole, par 71 **Tanjong course** on the southeastern tip of the island. The 18-hole **Serapong course** is also open to nonmembers on weekdays; but both courses are restricted to members on weekends and public holidays.

TENNIS

The top hotels have their own tennis courts, and several public clubs welcome visitors: **Alexandra Park** and **Kallang Squash and Tennis Centre** (☞ Squash and Racquetball, *above*) have courts. Also try the **Singapore Tennis Centre** (⊠ 1020 East Coast Pkwy., ☎ 442–5966) and **Tanglin Tennis Courts** (⊠ Minden Rd., ☎ 473–7236).

Spectator Sports

In addition to the sports listed below, international matches of golf, tennis, cycling, formula motor racing, swimming, badminton, and squash are held on and off. Most events are detailed in the newspapers; information is also available from the **National Sports Council** (☎ 345–7111).

CRICKET

From March through September, games take place on the Padang grounds in front of the old **Cricket Club** (☎ 338–9271) every Saturday at 1:30 PM and every Sunday at 11 AM. Entrance to the club during matches is restricted to members, but you can watch from the sides of the playing field.

POLO

The **Singapore Polo Club** (⊠ Thomson Rd., ☎ 256–4530) is quite active, with both local and international matches. Spectators are welcome to watch Tuesday, Thursday, Saturday, and Sunday matches, played in the late afternoon.

RUGBY

Rugby is played on the **Padang** grounds in front of the Singapore Cricket Club. Kickoff is usually at 5:30 PM on Saturdays from September through March.

SOCCER

Soccer is the major sport of Singapore; important matches take place from September through March in the **National Stadium** at Kallang.

SHOPPING

Singapore is a shopping fantasyland. What makes it so is not the prices but the incredible range of goods brought in from all over the world to be sold in an equally incredible number of shops. The prices, unfortunately, are no longer competitive with places like Kuala Lumpur, Bangkok, or even Hong Kong. Best buys are items indigenous to the region—leather, batiks, Oriental antiques, and silks. Watch for the Singapore Tourist Promotion Board logo—a gold Merlion (a lion's head with a fish tail) on a red background. This signifies that the retailer is recommended by the STPB and the Consumer's Association of Singapore.

Shopping Essentials

IMITATIONS

Singapore has recently tightened its copyright laws: It is illegal either to sell or to buy counterfeit products. (It's also illegal to bring them back to the States.) There are still street stalls and bargain stores offering Rolexes, LaCoste shirts, and Gucci purses at ridiculously low prices, but you can be certain they're fakes.

TOUTS

Touting—soliciting business by approaching people on the street with offers of free shopping tours and special discounts—is illegal (maximum fines were raised from S$200 to S$5,000 in 1989, and prison sentences of up to six months are possible). Nevertheless, it continues inside one or two shopping centers. Some taxi drivers tout as well. Avoid all touts and the shops they recommend. The prices will end up being higher—reflecting the tout's commission—and the quality of the goods possibly inferior.

BARGAINING

Bargaining is widely practiced in Singapore: the type of store determines the discount. Department stores and chain stores have fixed prices. It's a good idea to visit a department store first to establish the base price of an item, then shop around. Shops in upscale shopping complexes or malls tend to give a 10% discount on clothes. At a jewelry store, the discount can be as high as 50%, and carpet dealers also give hefty reductions. Stalls and shops around tourist attractions have the highest initial prices and, consequently, can be bargained down to give the greatest discounts.

HOW TO PAY

All department stores and most shops accept credit cards and traveler's checks. Many tourist shops will also accept foreign currency, but it is better to change traveler's checks and foreign currency at a bank before shopping. Except at the department stores, paying with a credit card will mean that your "discounted price" will reflect the commission the retailer will have to pay the credit card company.

RECEIPTS

Be sure to ask for receipts, both for your own protection and for Customs. Though shopkeepers are often amenable to stating false values on receipts, Customs officials are wary and knowledgeable.

GUARANTEES

Make sure you get international guarantees and warranty cards with your purchases. Check the serial number of each item against its card, and don't forget to mail the card in. Sometimes guarantees are limited to the country of purchase.

COMPLAINTS

Complaints about either a serious disagreement with a shopkeeper or the purchase of a defective product should be lodged with the STPB (✉ Tourism Court, 1 Orchard Spring Lane, Singapore 247729, ☎ 736–6622). The Consumers Association of Singapore (✉ 164 Bukit Merah Central, 04–3625, Singapore 150164, ☎ 270–4611) can also advise you regarding a vendor-related complaint.

Shopping Districts

Throughout the city are complexes full of shopping areas and centers. Many stores will have branches carrying much the same merchandise in several of these areas.

ORCHARD ROAD

The heart of Singapore's preeminent shopping district, Orchard Road is bordered on both sides with tree-shaded tiled sidewalks lined with modern shopping complexes and deluxe hotels that house exclusive boutiques. It is known for fashion and interior design shops, but you can find anything from Mickey Mouse watches to Chinese paper kites and antique Korean chests.

CHINATOWN

Once Singapore's liveliest and most colorful shopping area, Chinatown lost a great deal of its vitality when the street stalls were moved indoors (into the **Kreta Ayer Complex,** off Neil Road; the **Chinatown Complex,** off Trengganu Street; and the **People's Park Centre,** on Eu Tong Sen Street), but it is still fun to explore. South Bridge Road is the street of goldsmiths, specializing in 22K and even 24K gold ornaments in the characteristic orange color of Chinese gold. You *must* bargain here. On the same street are art galleries, such as the **Seagull Gallery** (✉ 62B, ☎ 532–3491) and the **Wenian Art Gallery** (✉ 95, ☎ 538–3750), and seal carvers in the **Hong Lim Shopping Centre** will carve your name into your own personal chop.

LITTLE INDIA

Serangoon Road is affectionately known as Little India. For shopping purposes, it begins at the **Zhu Jiao Centre,** on the corner of Serangoon and Buffalo roads. Some of the junk dealers and inexpensive-clothing stalls from a bazaar known as Thieves Market were relocated here when the market was cleared out. All the handicrafts of India can be found here: intricately carved wood tables, shining brass trays and water ewers, hand-loomed table linens, fabric inlaid with tiny mirrors, brightly colored pictures of Hindu deities, and even garlands of jasmine for the gods. At dozens of shops here you can get the six meters of voile, cotton, Kashmiri silk, or richly embroidered Benares silk required to make a sari. For the variety, quality, and beauty of the silk, the prices are very low.

ARAB STREET

The area really begins at Beach Road, opposite the Plaza Hotel. A group of basket and rattan shops first catches your eye. There are quite a few jewelers and shops selling loose gems and necklaces of garnet and amethyst beads. The main business is batiks and lace.

Shopping Centers

Centrepoint (⊠ 176 Orchard Rd.) has the **Robinsons** department store as its anchor tenant. **Delfi Orchard** (⊠ 402 Orchard Rd.) is full of wedding boutiques and jewelry shops, but **Waterford Wedgwood** and **Selangor Pewter** are also here, along with a well-stocked golf shop. **Far East Plaza** (⊠ 14 Scotts Rd.) has shops geared to the young and trendy. **Forum Galleria** (⊠ 583 Orchard Rd.) has a huge **Toys 'R' Us** (☎ 235–4322), as well as an assortment of boutiques. At **Lucky Plaza** (⊠ 304 Orchard Rd.), many jewelers are involved in a perpetual price-cutting war, to the delight of shoppers. This is the place at which to bargain furiously. **Ngen An City,** is taken up mostly by the Japanese store **Takashimaya** (☎ 738–1111), but there are a number of small boutiques as well.

Palais Renaissance, across the road from the Hilton Hotel (⊠ 390 Orchard Rd.), is Singapore's newest haute-fashion center; it's chic, opulent, and overpriced but a delight to wander through. **The Paragon** (⊠ 290 Orchard Rd.), one of the glossiest of the shopping centers, has more than 15 men's fashion boutiques. **The Promenade** (⊠ 300 Orchard Rd.) is Singapore's most elegant shopping center, in both design (a spiral walkway with a gentle slope instead of escalators) and tenants. Though **Raffles City,** bordered by Stamford, North Bridge, and Bras Basah roads, has a confusing interior, the Japanese department store **Sogo** rewards the harried shopper with an array of unique finds. Also here are a **Times** bookshop and fashion boutiques. Across the road is the **Raffles Hotel Shopping Complex,** with 60 boutiques selling high fashion and art. **Raffles Place,** overlying the Raffles Place MRT stop, caters mainly to the daily business crowd. **Ming Blue** (⊠ P1-22 Raffles Place, MRT station, ☎ 533–7153), a super place for knickknacks from all over the Orient. **Scotts Shopping Centre** (⊠ 6–8 Scotts Rd.)is one of the best places in Singapore for affordable fashion.

Department Stores

Singapore has one homegrown chain. **Metro** offers a wide range of affordable fashions and household products. The designs are up-to-the-minute, and the prices are good by local standards and unbelievably good by international standards. Look for Metros in Far East Plaza, Marina Square, and the Paragon.

Tang's (☎ 737–5500), also known as Tang's Superstore or C. K. Tang's, looks upmarket, but has some of the best buys in town. Accessories are excellent, especially the costume jewelry, and its household products are unsurpassed.

Both branches of the **Overseas Emporium** (⊠ People's Park Complex, ☎ 535–0555; People's Park Centre, ☎ 535–0967) offer Chinese silk fabric, silk blouses, brocade jackets, crafts, children's clothes, and china.

Singaporeans enjoy Japanese department stores such as **Isetan**—in Wisma Atria (⊠ 435 Orchard Rd., ☎ 733–7777), Shaw House (⊠ 350 Orchard Rd., ☎ 733–1111), and Parkway Parade (⊠ Marine Parade Rd., ☎ 345–5555). **Daimaru** (☎ 339–1111), in Liang Court, has some very unusual goods. **Yaohan,** whose biggest store is in Plaza Singapura (☎ 337–4061; others are at Parkway Parade and at Thomson Plaza on Thomson Rd.), is by far the most popular chain. **Sogo** (☎ 339–1100) has opened in Raffles City. The giant **Tokyu** (☎ 337–0077) is in Funan Center.

In case you're running low.

We're here to help with more than 118,000 Express Cash locations around the world. In order to enroll, just call American Express before you start your vacation.

do more ®

Express Cash

And just in case.

We're here with American Express® Travelers Cheques
and Cheques *for Two*® They're the safest way to carry
money on your vacation and the surest way to get a
refund, practically anywhere, anytime.
Another way we help you...

do more ®

**Travelers
Cheques**

The English **Robinsons** (☎ 733–0888), in Centrepoint, is Singapore's oldest department store. **John Little** (☎ 737–2222), at the Specialists Centre, has a full range of offerings but is now targeting the young and trendy. The **Marks & Spencers** in the basement of Lane Crawford at the corner of Scotts and Orchard is the biggest of several outlets in town.

Markets

FOOD MARKETS

Usually, a food market is divided into two sections: the dry market and the wet market. It is in the latter that squirming fish, crawling turtles, strutting chickens, and rabbits are sold for the pot while the floors are continually sluiced to maintain hygiene. The wet market at the **Chinatown Centre** is the most fascinating; the dry market at **Cuppage Centre** (✉ on Cuppage Rd., off Orchard Rd.), where the flower stalls are particularly appealing, is a better choice for the squeamish.

STREET MARKETS

In the **Sungei Road** area, site of the once-notorious Thieves Market, a few street vendors creep back each weekend. The stalls sell inexpensive shirts, T-shirts, children's clothes, and underwear, as well as odds and ends such as watches, costume jewelry, and sunglasses. The **Kreta Ayer** complex in Chinatown may be modern, but it has all the atmosphere of a bazaar. All the street vendors from Chinatown were relocated here. The shops sell cassette tapes, clothing from China, toys, and a lot of gaudy merchandise.

Some of Chinatown's elderly junk peddlers refuse to leave the streets. In the afternoon, they line up along **Temple Street** and lay out a strange variety of goods—old bottles, stamps, bits of porcelain or brass, old postcards, and the like—on cloths.

Specialty Shops

ANTIQUES

At the Tanglin Shopping Centre's **Antiques of the Orient** (☎ 734–9351), you'll find maps, ceramics, and furniture; try **Moongate** (☎ 737–6771), for porcelain. Off Orchard Road on Cuppage Road is a row of restored shop-houses. Here, **Babazar** (✉ 31A–35A Cuppage Terr., ☎ 235–7866) has jewelry, furniture, clothes, art, knickknacks, and antiques, and **Aizia Discoveries** (✉ 29B Cuppage Rd., ☎ 734–8665) has yet more antiques. **Keng of Tong Mern Sern** (✉ 226 River Valley Rd., ☎ 734–0761), near the Chettiar Temple, is a rabbit warren of antiques. For museum-quality Asian antiques, visit the **Paul Art Gallery** in Holland Park (✉ 62–72 Greenleaf Rd., ☎ 468–4697).

ART

For a range of art, try **Art Forum** (☎ 737–3448) and **Raya Gallery** (☎ 732–0298), both in the Promenade. There are also many galleries on South Bridge Road in Chinatown.

BATIK

A traditional craft item of Singapore, Malaysia, and Indonesia, batik is now also important in contemporary fashion and interior

design. **Blue Ginger Design Centre** (☎ 334–1171) and **Design Batik** (☎ 776–4337), both at Raffles Hotel, sell clothes and fabrics in modern designs. Blue Ginger is especially innovative. Traditional batik sarong lengths can be bought in the shops on Arab Street and in the **Textile Centre** on Jalan Sultan. **Tang's** stores sell inexpensive batik products, including a good range of men's shirts.

CAMERAS

Photographic equipment may not be the bargain it once was, but the range of cameras and accessories available can be matched only in Hong Kong.

If you do not care for negotiating prices, **Cost Plus Electronics** (⊠ B1–21 Scotts Shopping Centre, ☎ 235–1557), something of a supermarket of cameras and electronics, has low listed prices; no further discounts are given. For more-personalized service try **Cathay Photo** (☎ 339–6188) in Marina Square.

CARPETS

Attractively priced Afghan, Pakistani, Persian, Turkish, and Chinese carpets—both antique and new—are carried by reputable dealers.

Good shops include **Qureshi's** (⊠ 05–12, ☎ 235–1523) in Centrepoint, **Hassan's** (⊠ 01–15, ☎ 737–5626) in the Tanglin Shopping Centre, and **Amir & Sons** (⊠ 03–01, ☎ 734–9112) in Lucky Plaza. It is quite acceptable to bargain in these shops.

CURIOS

Curio shops sell a fascinating variety of goods including reverse-glass paintings, porcelain vases, cloisonné, wood carvings, jewelry (agate, jade, lapis lazuli, malachite), ivory carvings, embroidery, and idols. Shops such as the Orchard Towers' **Chen Yee Shen** (⊠ 01–12, ☎ 737–1174) and **Ivory Palace** (⊠ ☎ 737–1169) are great places for those who seek the unusual.

FUN FASHION

In department stores and small boutiques all over the island—but especially on Orchard Road—locally made ladies' fashions and Japanese imports sell for a song. Two of the better-known boutiques are **Mondi** (⊠ 300 The Promenade, ☎ 738–1318; 03–36 Centrepoint, ☎ 734–9672) and **Trend,** with two locations (⊠ Centrepoint, ☎ 235–9446; Plaza Singapura, ☎ 337–1038).

HIGH FASHION

Singapore has its own designers: **Tan Yoong** has his shop in Lucky Plaza (☎ 734–3783), and **Benny Ong** (who is based in London) sells through Tang's and China Silk House (☞ Silk, *below*). For European couture, check the arcades of the Hilton International and the Mandarin, as well as the more fashionable shopping centers. **Lanvin** (☎ 235–4039) is at the Hyatt Regency; **Gucci** is in the Hilton (☎ 732–3298) and the Paragon (☎ 734–2528); **Dior** (☎ 734–0374) is in Wisma Atria; **Nina Ricci** (☎ 732–9555) is in Isetan Scotts and Takashimaya.

Men's fashions are represented by **Dunhill** (☎ 459–2038) in the Hilton; **Mario Valentino** (☎ 338–4457) in Marina Square; **Hermès** (☎ 734–1353) in Liat Towers; and **Ralph Lauren** (☎ 738–0298) in Takashimaya. The Wisma Atria department store also carries Ralph Lauren, Givenchy, and Valentino.

JEWELRY

Singapore is a reliable place to buy jewelry, and there are so many jewelers that prices are competitive. Never accept the first price offered, no matter how posh the store. All jewelers give enormous discounts, usually 40% or more, but some, especially in hotels only when pressed.

In Chinatown, particularly along South Bridge Road and in People's Park, there are dozens of Chinese jewelers selling 22K gold. Many of these are old family firms. Prices are calculated by abacus based on the weight of the ornament and the prevailing price of gold. The bargaining procedure can take quite some time. On Orchard Road, the jewelry shops are often branches of Hong Kong firms or are local firms modeled along the same lines. They sell 18K set jewelry, often in Italian designs, as well as loose investment stones. **Larry's** (☎ 734–8763), with branches in Orchard Towers and Takashimaya, is popular. One of the many other small jewelers in Takashimaya is the **Hour Glass** (☎ 734–2420), which carries a large selection of designer watches.

LUGGAGE AND ACCESSORIES

Luggage is a bargain in Singapore. Every complex contains several stores carrying all the designer names in luggage and leather accessories. **Dunhill** (☎ 339–1111) is in the Daimaru in Liang Court; **Etienne Aigner** is in Shaw Centre (☎ 737–6141); **Louis Vuitton** (☎ 737–5820) is in the Hilton and in Takashimaya; **Hermès** is at Liat Towers (✉ 541 Orchard Rd., ☎ 734–1353) and at Daimaru in Liang Court (☎ 339–1111); and **Charles Jourdan** (☎ 737–4988) is in the Promenade. The **Escada** boutique (☎ 336–8283) at the Promenade and the Millennia Walk has a range of accessories and custom-made luggage.

PEWTER AND DINNERWARE

Malaysia is the world's largest tin producer, and pewter is an important craft item in the region. **Selangor Pewter,** the largest pewter concern in Singapore, has a great product range displayed at the main showrooms in the Paragon, Delphi, Clarke Quay, Raffles Hotel, Marina Square, and Raffles City. The main office is at 7500A Beach Road (☎ 334–1183).

REPTILE-SKIN PRODUCTS

Check the import restrictions on these goods. Singapore issues no export certificate for these or for ivory. The price of alligator, crocodile, and snake skins is lower here than anywhere else except Hong Kong. In the old shops around the Stamford Road–Armenian Street area, hard bargaining will yield dividends. The range is widest at big stores such as the showroom at the **Crocodilarium** (✉ 730 East Coast Pkwy., ☎ 447–3722). You can have bags and belts made to your specifications. The existing designs, especially for shoes, are often old-fashioned.

SILK

Indian silk, in sari lengths, is found in the dozens of sari shops in the Serangoon Road area. For 6 meters (6.5 yards) of silk, which could be the thin Kashmiri silk or the heavier, embroidered Benares silk, you pay only a fraction of what you would pay elsewhere. The major store for Indian textiles is **P. Govindasamy Pillai** (✉ 153 Dunlop St., ☎ 297–5311).

Chinese silk is easy to find in Singapore. All the emporiums have special departments for fabrics and tailored clothes. **China Silk House** (✉ Tanglin Shopping Centre, ☎ 235–5020, and Centrepoint, ☎ 733–0555) has a wide range of fabrics in different weights and types, plus silk clothing, including a line designed for the shop by Benny Ong. Thai silk, in different weights for different purposes, comes in stunning colors. Specialty shops sell it by the meter or made up into gowns, blouses, and dresses. **Jim Thompson** (☎ 737–1133), is one source. A much more extensive collection can be found at the **Miss Ming** shops in the Orchard Towers (☎ 235–2865).

TAILORING

Tailors who offer 24-hour service rarely deliver, and their quality is suspect. Allow four to five days for a good job. **Justmen** (☎ 737–4800) in the Tanglin Shopping Centre is one of a number of excellent men's tailors. For ladies, shops such as the Tanglin branch of **China Silk House** (☎ 235–5020) offer good tailoring.

SIDE TRIPS AROUND SINGAPORE

Using Singapore's excellent public transportation system, you can tour the island. Alternatively, you can use taxis or join one of the many organized tours that cover the attractions that interest you.

Numbers in the margin correspond to points of interest on the Side Trips Around Singapore map.

West Coast

Near the satellite city of Jurong, Singapore's main industrial area, are a number of attractions. The concept of a garden environment has been continued here to demonstrate that an industrial area does not have to be ugly.

Sights to See

❹ Chinese Garden. This 34.6-acre garden reconstructs an Imperial garden, complete with temples, courtyards, bridges, and pagodas. It is beautifully landscaped, with lotus-filled lakes, placid streams overhung by groves of willows, and twin pagodas. ⊠ *Off Yuan Ching Rd., Jurong,* ☎ *265–5889.* ▨ *Combined ticket with Japanese Garden, S$4.* ☉ *Mon.–Sat. 9–7, Sun. 8:30–7.*

❶ Haw Par Villa (Tiger Balm Gardens). The Haw Par Villa reopened in late 1990 as a cross between an amusement park and a multimedia presentation of Chinese mythology. The best time to start your half-day visit is at 9:30 AM, before the crowds and long lines. ⊠ *262 Pasir Panjang Rd.,* ☎ *774–0300.* ▨ *S$16.50 (includes all attractions).* ☉ *Daily 9–6. A taxi from Orchard Rd. will run S$10, or take Bus 10 or 30 from the Padang to Pasir Panjang Rd. (S$1.10).*

❺ Japanese Garden. Adjacent to the Chinese Garden, this delightful formal garden is one of the largest Japanese-style gardens outside Japan. Its classic simplicity, serenity, and harmonious arrangement of plants, stones, bridges, and trees induce tranquility. ⊠ *Off Yuan Ching Rd., Jurong,* ☎ *265–5889.* ▨ *Combined ticket with Chinese Garden, S$4; camera charge, S$.50.* ☉ *Mon.–Sat. 9–7, Sun. 8:30–7; last admission at 6.*

❷ Jurong Bird Park. Built on 50 landscaped acres, the park has the world's largest walk-in aviary, complete with a 30-meter (100-foot) man-made waterfall that cascades into a meandering stream. More than 3,600 birds from 365 species are here, including the colorful, the rare, and the noisy. If you get to the park early, try the breakfast buffet from 9 to 11 at the **Song Bird Terrace,** where birds in bamboo cages tunefully trill as you help yourself to sausages, eggs, and toast. From there you can walk over to the **Free Flight Show** (held at 10:30), featuring eagles and hawks. In the afternoon, at 3:30, you might catch the **Parrot Circus,** complete with bike-riding bird-gymnasts. ⊠ *Jurong Hill, Jalan Ahmad Ibrahim,* ☎ *265–0022.* ▨ *S$6; Panorail fare, S$2.* ☉ *Daily 9–6.*

❸ Jurong Crocodile Paradise. At this 5-acre park you'll find 2,500 crocs in various environments—in landscaped streams, at a feeding platform, in a breeding lake. You can feed the crocodiles, watch muscle-bound showmen (and a showlady) wrestle them, or buy crocodile-skin products at the shop. You can also watch the beasts through glass, in an underwater viewing gallery. ⊠ *241 Jalan Ahmad Ibrahim,* ☎ *261–8866.* ▨ *S$6.* ☉ *Daily 9–6; crocodile-wrestling shows at 11:45, 2, and 4.*

❻ Singapore Science Centre. The center is dedicated to the space age and its technology. Subjects such as aviation, nuclear sciences, robotics, astronomy, and space technology are entertainingly explored through audiovisual aids and computers that you operate. Visitors can walk into a "human body" for a closer look at the vital organs; there is also a flight simulator of a Boeing 747, plus computer quiz games and other computer/laser displays. The Omni Theatre presents two programs: "Oasis in Space," which travels to the beginning of the universe, and "To Fly," which simulates the feel of travel in space. All age groups are sure to get a thrill from the brave new world of science presented here. ⊠ *Science Centre Rd., off Jurong Town Hall Rd.,* ☎ *560–3316.* ▦ *S$3; Omni Theatre, S$9.* ⊙ *Tues.–Sun. 10–6.*

🐾 **❼ Tang Dynasty Village.** This theme park re-creates the 7th-century Chinese village of Chang'an (present-day Xian) with pagodas, gilded imperial courts, and an underground palace of the royal dead guarded by 1,000 terra-cotta warriors. Artisans make and sell traditional wares, and acrobats, rickshaws, and oxcarts all add to the authenticity. A tramway takes you around. The easiest way here by public transportation is the MRT to Boon Lay Station. ☎ *261–1116.* ▦ *S$15.45, with tramway.* ⊙ *Daily 9 AM–10 PM.*

The Heart of the Garden Isle

Singapore is called the Garden Isle with good reason. Obsessed as it is with ferroconcrete, the government has also established nature reserves, gardens, and a zoo. This excursion from downtown Singapore takes you into the center of the island to enjoy some of its greenery. If you have only a little time to spare, do try to fit in the zoo, at least—it is exceptional. The quickest way to reach the zoo is a 20-minute taxi ride—the fare is about S$12. Check at your hotel for bus service.

Sights to See

❿ Botanic Gardens. This is an ideal place to escape the bustle of downtown Singapore. The beautifully maintained gardens are spread over some 74 acres, with a large lake, masses of shrubs and flowers, and magnificent examples of many tree species, including 30-meter-high (98-foot-high) fan palms. An extensive orchid bed contains specimens representing 250 varieties, some of them very rare. The combined fragrances of frangipani, hibiscus, and aromatic herbs that pervade the gardens are a delight. ⊠ *Corner of Napier and Cluny Rds.,* ☎ *1800/479–7100.* ▦ *Free.* ⊙ *Weekdays 5 AM–11 PM, weekends 5 AM–midnight.*

Inside the Botanic Gardens, the three-hectare (7.4-acre) **Singapore Orchid Garden** provides a splendid display of more than 3,000 orchids. ⊠ *Botanic Gardens.* ▦ *S$2.* ⊙ *Daily 8:30–6; last ticket sold at 6, last person out at 7.*

🐾 **❾ Night Safari.** Right next to the zoo, the safari claims to be the world's first nighttime wildlife park. Here 80 acres of secondary jungle provide a home to 100 species of wildlife that are more active at night than during the day. Night Safari uses the same moat concept as the zoo to create an open natural habitat; the area is floodlit with enough light to see the animals' colors, but not enough to limit their nocturnal activity. Visitors are transported on a 45-minute tram ride along 3 kilometers (2 miles) of loop roads, stopping frequently to admire the beasts and their antics. ⊠ *80 Mandai Lake Rd.,* ☎ *269–3411.* ▦ *S$15.* ⊙ *Daily 7:30–midnight.*

🐾 **❽ Singapore Zoological Gardens.** Cliché though it may be, here the humans visit animals as guests in their habitat. The zoo is designed according to the open-moat concept, wherein a wet or dry moat separates the animals from the people. Try to arrive at the zoo in time for the buffet breakfast. The food itself is not special, but the company is. At 9:30 AM, Ah Meng, a 24-year-old orangutan, comes by for her repast.

Side Trips Around Singapore

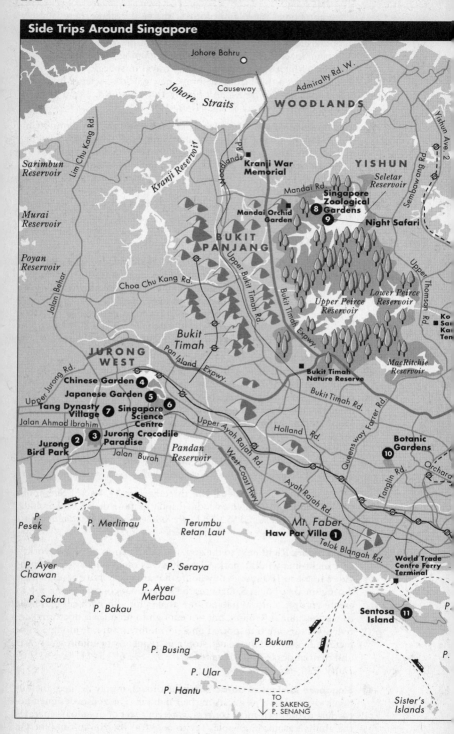

Johore Bahru

Causeway

Johore Straits

Admiralty Rd. W.

WOODLANDS

Sarimbun
Reservoir

Lim Chu Kang Rd.

Kranji Reservoir

Woodlands Rd.

Kranji War
Memorial

YISHUN

Yishun Ave. 2

Seletar
Reservoir

Sembawang Rd.

Murai
Reservoir

Mandai Rd.

Mandai Orchid
Garden

Singapore
Zoological
Gardens ⑧
⑨ **Night Safari**

Poyan
Reservoir

Jalan Behar

Choa Chu Kang Rd.

**BUKIT
PANJANG**

Upper Bukit Timah Rd.

Bukit Timah Expwy.

Upper Peirce
Reservoir

Lower Peirce
Reservoir

Upper Thomson Rd.

Ko
Sar
Ka
Ten

Bukit
Timah

Pan Island Expwy.

MacRitchie
Reservoir

**JURONG
WEST**

Upper Jurong Rd.

Chinese Garden ④

Japanese Garden ⑤

Tang Dynasty
Village ⑦   ⑥

Singapore
Science
Centre

Bukit Timah
Nature Reserve

Bukit Timah Rd.

Farrer Rd.

**Botanic
Gardens**
⑩

Jalan Ahmad Ibrahim

⑨ ③ **Jurong Crocodile
Paradise**

Upper Ayah Rajah Rd.

Holland Rd.

Queensway

Tanglin Rd.

Orchar

② **Jurong
Bird Park**

Jalan Buroh

Pandan
Reservoir

West Coast Hwy.

Ayah Rajah Rd.

P
Pesek

P. Merlimau

Terumbu
Retan Laut

Mt. Faber

Haw Par Villa ①

Telok Blangah Rd.

**World Trade
Centre Ferry
Terminal**

P. Ayer
Chawan

P. Seraya

P. Sakra

P. Bakau

P. Ayer
Merbau

**Sentosa
Island** ⑪

P.

P. Busing

P. Bukum

P. Ular

P. Hantu

TO
P. SAKENG,
P. SENANG

Sister's
Islands

0 | 4 miles
0 | 6 km

WEST MALAYSIA

P. Seletar

Johore Straits

S. Seletar

TO DESARU, MALAYSIA

Punggol Rd.

P. Serangoon

P. Ubin

TO P. TEKONG

Yio Chu Kang Rd.

PUNGGOL

S. Serangoon

P. Ketam

SERANGOON

Serangoon Harbour

CHANGI

Loyang Ave.

Meng hur See le

Central Expwy.

Upper Serangoon Rd.

Tampines Rd.

U. Changi Rd.

Changi Airport

■ **Crocodile Farm**

Changi Prison

Airport Blvd.

Siong Lim Temple

Paya Lebar Rd.

Pan Island Expressway

BEDOK

New Upper Changi Rd.

Changi Coast Rd.

Serangoon Rd.

Sims Ave.

Geylang Rd.

East Coast Rd.

Kallang Rd.

KATONG

Mountbatten Rd.

East Coast Parkway

■ **East Coast Park**

Nicoll Hwy.

■ **National Stadium**

■ **Crocodilarium**

N

Strait of Singapore

Brani

Buran Darat

Tekukor

P. Renggit

Kusu Island

Lazarus Island

St. John's Island

Subway & Rail Lines

- - - - North-South MRT line
———— East-West MRT line
——— Railroad lines
⊖ Subway stop

There are performances by fur seals, elephants, free-flying storks, and other zoo inhabitants at various times throughout the day. Elephant rides are available for S$2 adults, S$1 children. For S$1.50, visitors can travel from one section of the zoo to another by tram. ⊠ *80 Mandai Lake Rd.,* ☎ *269–3411.* ▨ *S$9; breakfast or tea S$15 before 9 AM or after 4 PM.* ☉ *Daily 8:30–6; breakfast with an orangutan Tues.–Sat. 9–10 AM; high tea at 3.*

Sentosa

⑪ Connected to Singapore by bridge, this highly developed island is Singapore's best-known amusement park. Though Sentosa is certainly not a must-see in Singapore, there are two good reasons to go: the visual drama of getting there and the fascinating wax museum.

ADMISSION

There are two main types of all-day (8:30 AM–10 PM) admission passes to the island, plus cheaper evening-only (5–10 PM) versions of the same. You may also choose the Sentosa Discovery Package (S$21.50), which includes transfer to and from the city's major hotels and admission to major attractions. Reservations may be made through your hotel desk or by telephoning 235–3111. For further information about Sentosa and its facilities, call 270–7888.

ARRIVING AND DEPARTING

To reach Sentosa, take the cable car (the more dramatic method, with small gondolas holding four passengers each), the ferry, or a shuttle bus. We recommend the cable car, which picks up passengers from two terminals on the Singapore side: the Cable Car Towers, next to the World Trade Centre, and the Mt. Faber Cable Car Station. As the trip from Cable Car Towers starts at the edge of the sea and is a bit shorter, it does not afford the spectacular, panoramic views you get swinging down from Mt. Faber. At 113 meters (377 feet), Mt. Faber is not particularly high, but it offers splendid views of Singapore city to the east and of industrial Jurong to the west. There's no bus to the Mt. Faber Cable Car Station, and it's a long walk up the hill, so a taxi is the best way to get there. The Cable Car Towers station is accessible by bus: From Orchard Road, take Bus 10 or 143; from Collyer Quay, Bus 10, 20, 30, 97, 125, or 146. ⊠ *Off Kampong Bahru Rd.,* ☎ *270–8855.* ▨ *S$6.50 round-trip, S$5 one way.* ☉ *Mon.–Sat. 10–7, Sun. and public holidays 9–9.*

GETTING AROUND

Once on Sentosa you can use the **monorail,** the first of its kind in Southeast Asia (operates daily 9 AM–10 PM). Unlimited rides are included in the price of the admission ticket. A free bus (daily 9–7) also provides transportation to most of the attractions.

Sights to See

Fort Siloso. Gun buffs will enjoy the range of artillery pieces here. Photographs document the history of the war in the Pacific, and dioramas depict the life of POWs during the harsh Japanese occupation. ▨ *S$1.* ☉ *Daily 9–7.*

Maritime Museum. A small but interesting collection of ship models, pictures, and other items document Singapore's involvement with the sea in business and in war. A collection of full-size native watercraft traces the development of local boatbuilding. ▨ *S$1.* ☉ *Daily 10–7.*

Merlion. This monument to bad taste is Singapore's tourism mascot—a 10-story, 37-meter off-white sea lion that emits laser beams from its eyes and smoke from its nostrils. It even glows in the dark. The ride up to the 10th story is by elevator, then you climb up two stories to the top and a view of Singapore and the Indonesian islands of Bataam and Bintan. ▣ *S$3.* ⊘ *Daily 9–10.*

Rasa Sentosa. This 450-room hotel, popular with families, has one of the better island beaches and a big pool.

★ ○ **Pioneers of Singapore/Surrender Chambers.** This wax museum stands out from all the rest of Sentosa's attractions. A series of galleries traces the development of Singapore and portrays the characters whose actions profoundly influenced the island's history. The second part of the museum is the **Surrender Chambers,** with wax tableaux depicting the surrender of the Allies to the Japanese in 1942 and the surrender of the Japanese in 1945. ▣ *S$3.* ⊘ *Daily 9–9.*

○ **Underwater World Sentosa.** Completed in 1991, Underwater World reverses the traditional aquarium experience by placing the visitor right in the water. Two gigantic tanks house thousands of Asian Pacific fish and other marine life; visitors walk through a 91-meter (100-yard) acrylic tunnel that curves along the bottom. ▣ *S$10.* ⊘ *Daily 9–9.*

SINGAPORE A TO Z

Arriving and Departing

By Plane

AIRPORTS

The major gateway to Singapore is **Changi International Airport** (☎ 011–65/541–9828). The Airbus (S$5) runs to and from all major hotels 6 AM–midnight.

CARRIERS

Singapore Airlines (☎ 800/742–3333), the national carrier, offers direct, one-stop flights from Los Angeles to Singapore. **United** (☎ 800/241–6522), winning a reputation for its Connoisseur (business) class, has direct one-stop flights from Los Angeles, San Francisco, and Seattle, and connecting flights (one stop, with a change in Tokyo) from New York and Chicago.

Among the many other airlines that serve Singapore are **British Airways** (☎ 0181/897–4000 or 0345/222–111 outside London), **China Airlines** (☎ 800/227–5118), **Cathay Pacific Airways** (☎ 800/233–2742 in the U.S.; 800/663–1338 in Canada), **Japan Airlines** (☎ 800/525–3663), **Korean Air** (☎ 800/438–5000), **Qantas** (☎ 0345/747–767 or 0800/747–767), and **Thai Airways** (☎ 0171/499–9113).

FLYING TIMES

Singapore is 18 hours from Los Angeles or San Francisco, 20 hours from Chicago, and 22 hours from New York. If you fly out of New York, via Helsinki aboard Finnair, flight time is 18 hours.

Getting Around

By Bus

Buses are much cheaper than taxis and—with a little practice—easy to use. During rush hours, they can be quicker than cabs, since there are special bus lanes along the main roads, and service is frequent—usually every five to 10 minutes on most routes. The excellent *Bus Guide,* available for S$1.20 at any bookstore, pinpoints major stops.

The minimum fare is S$.50, the maximum S$1.10 for non-air-conditioned buses, S$.60–S$1.70 for air-conditioned ones. Bus numbers are clearly marked, and most stops have a list of destinations with the numbers of the buses that service them. Most buses run from 5:30 or 6 AM until around 11:30 PM, while some run all night.

The new Singapore Trolley bus service starts at the Botanic Gardens and continues to Orchard Road, Tanjong Pagar, and the World Trade Centre. It's not very convenient, and it's expensive (S$9 adults, S$7 children), but it does make 22 stops and your ticket is good all day for unlimited journeys. You can buy the ticket (you'll need exact change) when you board. A one-ticket point-to-point fare is S$3.

For all information on bus travel within Singapore, contact the **Singapore Bus Service Passenger Relations Center** (☎ 287–2727).

By Car

GASOLINE
Unleaded gas starts at S$1.08 per liter in Singapore. A government ruling requires any car passing the Causeway out of Singapore to drive with at least half a tank of gas or be fined; the republic's huge losses in revenue as a result of Singaporeans' driving to Malaysia to gas up cheaply led to the understandably unpopular ruling.

RENTAL AGENCIES
The major car-rental companies represented in Singapore are Avis, Budget, Hertz, and National InterRent. Should you want to look up firms in the Singapore Yellow Pages, check under "Motorcar Renting and Leasing." The following are some local branches of international agencies: **Avis** (✉ Changi Airport, ☎ 542–8833; ✉ Boulevard Hotel, ☎ 737–1668), **Hertz** (✉ Changi Airport, ☎ 542–5300; ✉ Tanglin Shopping Centre, Tanglin Rd., ☎ 734–4646; ✉ 280 Kampong Arang Rd., 447–3388), **National** (✉ 73 Bukit Timah Rd., ☎ 338–8444), **Sintat** (✉ Changi Airport, ☎ 542–7288).

RENTAL RATES
Rates in Singapore begin at US$91 a day and US$548 a week for an economy car with unlimited mileage. This does not include tax on car rentals, which is 3%.

RULES OF THE ROAD
Singapore's speed limits are 80 kph (50 mph) on expressways unless otherwise posted, and 50 kph (31 mph) on other roads. Keep in mind that drivers must yield right of way at rotaries and drive on the left-hand side of the road. Unleaded gas starts at S$1.08 per liter in Singapore, significantly less in Malaysia. A government ruling requires any car passing the Causeway out of Singapore to drive with at least half a tank of gas or be fined; the republic's huge losses in revenue as a result of Singaporeans' driving to Malaysia to gas up cheaply led to the understandably unpopular ruling.

By Subway
The MRT, consists of two lines that run north–south and east–west and cross at the City Hall and Raffles Place interchanges. The system includes a total of 42 stations along 67 kilometers (42 miles). All cars and underground stations are air-conditioned, and the trains operate between 5:45 AM and midnight daily.

Tickets may be purchased in the stations from vending machines (which give change) or at a booth. Large maps showing the station locations and the fares between them hang above each vending machine. There's a S$2 fine for underpaying, so make sure you buy the right ticket for your destination. The magnetic tickets are inserted in turnstiles to let you on and off the platform. Fares start at S$.60 for about two stations; the maximum fare is S$1.60. The fare between Orchard Road Station and Raffles Place Station (in the business district) is S$.60.

For information on subway routes and schedules, call the **Singapore Tourist Promotion Board** (STPB; ☎ 736–6622) or inquire at your hotel.

By Taxi

There are more than 10,000 taxis in Singapore, strictly regulated and metered. The starting fare is S$2.40 for the first 1.5 kilometers (0.9 miles) and S$.10 for each subsequent 240 meters (900 feet). After 10 kilometers (6 miles) the rate increases to S$.10 for every 225 meters (820 feet). Every 30 seconds of waiting time carries a S$.10 charge. Drivers do not expect tips.

Be aware of several surcharges that may apply. A S$2.20 surcharge is charged for taxis booked by phone, and there is an additional S$1 surcharge for every booking half an hour or more in advance. Trips made between midnight and 6 AM have a 50% surcharge; rides from, *not to,* the airport carry a S$3 surcharge; and there are "entrance and exit fees" on taxis and private cars going into and out of the central business district, or CBD.

Unless a taxi displays a yellow permit, a S$1 surcharge is added to fares from the CBD between 4 and 7 PM on weekdays and noon and 3 PM on Saturdays. To the CBD, there's a S$3 surcharge for the purchase of an Area License, which is needed to enter the Restricted Zone between 7:30 AM and 6:30 PM Monday–Friday and between 7:30 AM and 2 PM Saturday and on the eve of five major public holidays. Passengers do not pay the fee if the taxi already has the sticker. A $1 surcharge is added for all trips in London cabs and a Station Wagon taxi; an extra 10% of the fare is charged for payment by credit card.

Find taxis at stands or hail them from any curb not marked with a double yellow line. Radio cab services are available 24 hours (☎ 552–1111); a S$2.20 surcharge is imposed, and the meter should not be switched on until after you have entered the taxi. A driver showing a red disk in the window is returning to his garage and may pick up passengers going only in his direction. Often, it's almost impossible to get through to reserve a cab, so it's better to just hail one or take the bus.

Under normal traffic conditions, the trip by taxi takes 20 to 30 minutes, depending on the location of your hotel. The fare ranges from S$13 to S$20, plus a S$3 airport surcharge (not applicable for trips *to* the airport, but be wary of taxi drivers who try imposing this charge anyway). Other surcharges apply when baggage is stored in the trunk or when more than two adults travel in the same cab.

By Train

The same company that operates the Venice Simplon–Orient Express now runs the Eastern & Oriental Express deluxe train once a week between Singapore and Bangkok, with a stop in Butterworth (Malaysia) permitting an excursion to Penang. The 1,943-kilometer (1,200-mile) journey takes 41 hours and includes two nights and one full day on board. The cabin decor is modeled on the Josef von Sternberg–Marlene Dietrich movie *Shanghai Express*. Fares, which vary according to cabin type and include meals, start at US$860 per person one-way. For information in the United States, call 800/524–2420.

Contacts and Resources

Customs and Duties

ON ARRIVAL

Duty-free allowances include 1 liter each of spirits, wine, and beer; all personal effects; and less than S$50 in foods such as chocolates, biscuits, and cakes. The import of drugs, obscene articles and publications, seditious and treasonable materials, toy coins and currency notes, cigarette lighters of pistol/revolver shapes, or reproductions of copyrighted publications, videotapes, records, or cassettes is prohibited. Chewing gum in amounts deemed large enough for resale is also prohibited, as are duty-free cigarettes.

ON DEPARTURE

Export permits are required for arms, ammunition, explosives, animals, gold, platinum, precious stones and jewelry, poisons, and medicinal drugs. The export of narcotic drugs is punishable by death under Singapore law.

Electricity

The electrical current in Singapore is 220 volts, 50 cycles alternating current (AC). You should bring an adapter and converter, or, if your appliances are dual voltage, just an adapter. Wall outlets take a variety of plug styles, including plugs with two round oversize prongs and plugs with three prongs.

Embassies and Consulates

Most countries maintain a diplomatic mission in Singapore. Call ahead to confirm hours. If you hope to obtain visas for neighboring countries, be aware that the visa-application process at Singapore consular offices may take several days.

Australia (⊠ 25 Napier Rd., ☎ 737–9311). **Canada** (⊠ 80 Anson Rd., ☎ 325–3200). **United Kingdom** (⊠ Tanglin Rd., ☎ 473–9333). **United States of America** (⊠ 30 Hill St., ☎ 338–0251).

Emergencies

Ambulance and fire, ☎ 995. **Police,** ☎ 999.

Guided Tours

A wide range of sightseeing tours covers the highlights of Singapore. They are a good introduction to the island and are especially convenient for business travelers or others on a tight schedule. Tours can take two hours or the whole day, and prices range from S$20 to S$109. Most are operated in comfortable, air-conditioned coaches with guides and include pickup and return. Tour agencies can also arrange private-car tours with guides; these are considerably more expensive. There is no need to book tours in advance of your visit; they can be easily arranged through the tour desks in hotels.

Health and Safety

FOOD AND DRINK

Tap water is safe, and every eating establishment—from the most elegant hotel dining room to the smallest sidewalk stall—is regularly inspected by the very strict health authorities.

Language

Singapore is a multiracial society with four official languages: Malay, Mandarin, Tamil, and English. The national language is Malay; the lingua franca is English. English is also the language of administration, is a required course for every schoolchild, and is used in the entrance examinations for universities. Hence, virtually all Singaporeans speak English with varying degrees of fluency. Mandarin is increasingly replacing the other Chinese dialects. However, many older Chinese do not speak Mandarin and communicate in SinEnglish, a Singaporean version of English that has its own grammar.

Mail

RECEIVING MAIL

American Express cardholders or traveler's-check users can have mail sent c/o American Express International, 3 Killeney Road, Winsland House 01-04/05, Singapore 239519. Envelopes should be marked "Client Mail." For more postal information, contact the General Post Office (GPO) in Fullerton Square, off Collyer Quay (☎ 533–6234).

Money and Expenses

CURRENCY

The local currency is the Singapore dollar (S$), which is divided into 100 cents. Notes in circulation are S$1, S$2, S$5, S$10, S$20, S$50, S$100, S$500, S$1,000, and S$10,000. Coins: S$.01, S$.05, S$.20, S$.50, and S$1.

At press time, the exchange rate was S$1.02 to the Canadian dollar, S$1.40 to the U.S. dollar, and S$2.16 to the pound sterling.

TAXES

There is a 3% sales tax in Singapore, called the GST. You can get refunds for purchases over S$500 at the airport as you leave the country. This government tax is added to restaurant and hotel bills; sometimes a 10% service charge is added as well. Visitors are also subject to a S$15 airport departure tax, which is payable at the airport. To save time and avoid standing in line, buy a tax voucher at your hotel or any airline office.

WHAT IT WILL COST

Singapore ranks up there with other world capitals as far as expenses go. Prices have risen consistently over the last 10 years, while the currency has also appreciated against the US dollar and other major currencies. While a gastronomical delight is still a little less than you would pay in Paris, hotel rooms are in the New York range. You can keep costs down by eating at the inexpensive hawker food centers, especially those in the major shopping malls, and by using public transportation.

National Holidays

Singapore has 11 public holidays: New Year's Day (January 1), Hari Raya Puasa, Chinese New Year, Good Friday, Hari Raya Haji, Labor Day (May 1), Vesak Day, National Day (August 9), Deepvali, and Christmas Day (December 25). Many dates vary year by year.

Opening and Closing Times

Businesses are generally open weekdays 9 or 9:30 to 5 or 5:30; some, not many, are also open on Saturday mornings.

In general, banking hours are weekdays 10–3, and Saturday 9:30–11:30 AM. However, branches of the Development Bank of Singapore stay open until 3 PM on Saturdays, and the bank at Changi Airport is open whenever there are flights. Many museums close on Monday; otherwise, they are generally open 9–5. Registered pharmacists work 9–6, though some pharmacies in the major shopping centers stay open until 10 PM. Of the 87 post offices on the island, most of them are open weekdays 8:30–5 and Saturday 8:30–1. The airport post office and the Takashimaya post office are open daily 8–8. Shop opening times vary. Department stores and many shops in big shopping centers are generally open seven days a week from about 10 AM to 9 PM (later some evenings); smaller shops tend to close on Sunday.

Passports and Visas

Visas are not required for stays of up to 14 days for Canadian, U.K., and U.S. citizens.

Telephones

To call Singapore from overseas, first dial the country code, 65, then the number.

LOCAL CALLS

From a pay phone, the cost is S$.10; insert a coin and dial the seven-digit number. Hotels charge anywhere from S$.10 to S$.50 a call. There are free public phones at Changi Airport, just past Immigration.

LONG-DISTANCE AND INTERNATIONAL CALLS

Use the Telecoms phone card if you'll be making several long-distance calls during your stay in Singapore. The cards can be purchased in denominations of S$2, S$5, S$10, S$20, and S$50 and permit you to make both local and overseas calls. The price of each call is deducted from the card total, and your balance is roughly indicated by the punched hole in the card. Phone cards are available from post offices, Telecoms Customer Services outlets, and many drugstores. Telephones that accept the phone card are most frequently found in shopping centers, post offices, subway stations, and the airport. For information, call 288–6633.

Tipping

Tipping is not customary in Singapore, and the government actively discourages it. It is prohibited at the airport and not encouraged in hotels that levy a 10% service charge or in restaurants. After experiencing some Singapore service, you may soon wish that they did allow tipping. Hotel bellboys are usually tipped S$1 per bag for handling luggage. Taxi drivers are not tipped by Singaporeans, who become upset when they see tourists tip.

Visitor Information

Contact the **Singapore Tourist Promotion Board** in the United States: ⊠ 590 Fifth Ave., 12th floor, New York, NY 10036, ☎ 212/302–4861, FAX 212/302–4801; ⊠ Two Prudential Plaza, 180 North Stetson Ave., Suite 1450, Chicago, IL 60601, ☎ 312/938–1888, FAX 312/938–0086; ⊠ 8484 Wilshire Blvd., Suite 510, Beverly Hills, CA 90211, ☎ 213/852–1901, FAX 213/852–0129; in Canada, ⊠ The Standard Life Centre, 121 King St. West, Suite 1000, Toronto, Ontario, M5H 3T9, ☎ 416/363–8898, FAX 416/363–5752.

When to Go

Singapore has neither peak nor off-peak tourist seasons. Hotel prices remain the same throughout the year, though during quiet spells many properties will discount room rates upon request (either in person or by mail). The busiest tourist months are December and July.

With the equator only 129 km (80 mi) to the south, Singapore is usually either hot or very hot. The average daily temperature is 80°F (26.6°C); it usually reaches 87°F (30.7°C) in the afternoon and drops to a cool 75°F (23.8°C) just before dawn. The months from November through January, during the northeast monsoon, are generally the coolest. The average daily relative humidity is 84.5%, though it drops to 65%–70% on dry afternoons.

Rain falls year-round, but the wettest months are November through January. February is usually the sunniest month; December, the most inclement. Though Singapore has been known to have as much as 512.2 mm (20 in) of rainfall in one 24-hour period, brief, frequent rainstorms are the norm, and the washed streets soon dry in the sun that follows.

CLIMATE

Jan.	86F	30C	May	89F	32C	Sept.	88F	31C
	74	23		75	24		75	24
Feb.	88F	31C	June	88F	31C	Oct.	88F	31C
	74	23		75	24		74	23
Mar.	88F	31C	July	88F	31C	Nov.	88F	31C
	75	24		75	24		74	23
Apr.	88F	31C	Aug.	88F	31C	Dec.	88F	31C
	75	24		75	24		74	23

FESTIVALS AND SEASONAL EVENTS

With so many different cultural and religious groups, Singapore is a city of festivals, from the truly exotic to the strictly-for-tourists. The dates and seasons of many of them vary from year to year according to the lunar calendar.

December–January: Ramadan is the month of daytime fasting among the city's Muslim population. Stalls on Bussorah Street and around the Sultan Mosque sell a variety of dishes, including Malay rice cakes wrapped in banana leaves, and fragrant puddings flavored with pandanus and coated in coconut syrup.

January–February: Thaipusam celebrates the victory of the Hindu god Subramaniam over the demon Idumban. After nightlong ritual purification and chanting, penitents enter a trance and pierce their flesh with knives, steel rods, and fishhooks, which they wear during the festival's spectacular procession. The 8-kilometer (5-mile) procession begins at the Perumal Temple on Serangoon Road, passes the Sri Mariamman Temple on South Bridge Road, and ends at the Chettiar Temple, where women pour pots of milk over the image of Lord Subramaniam.

The lunar New Year celebration known as the **Chinese New Year** lasts for 15 days, and most shops and businesses close for about a week. (In 1998 the New Year begins on January 27.) The end of the Chinese New Year is marked by the **Chingay Procession.** Chinese, Malays, and Indians all get into the act for this event. Accompanied by clashing gongs and beating drums, lion dancers lead a procession of Chinese stilt-walkers, swordsmen, warriors, acrobats, and characters from Chinese myth and legend. A giant dragon weaves through the dancers in its eternal pursuit of a flaming pearl. Check local newspapers for the parade route, which varies from year to year.

March or April: On the **Birthday of the Saint of the Poor,** the image of Guang Ze Zun Wang is carried from the White Cloud Temple on Ganges Avenue around the neighborhood and back to the temple through streets thronged with devotees. Spirit mediums—their cheeks, arms, and tongues pierced with metal skewers—join the procession.

April: Songkran (April 18) is a traditional Thai water festival that marks the beginning of the year's solar cycle. In Singapore's Thai Buddhist temples, images of Buddha are bathed with perfumed holy water, caged birds are set free, and blessings of water are splashed on worshipers and visitors. The liveliest (and wettest) celebrations are at the Ananda Metyrama Thai temple on Silat Road and the Sapthapuchaniyaram Temple on Holland Road.

May: Vesak Day commemorates the Buddha's birth, Enlightenment, and death. It is the most sacred annual festival in the Buddhist calendar. Throughout the day, starting before dawn, saffron-robed monks chant holy sutras in all the major Buddhist temples and captive birds are set free. Many temples offer vegetarian feasts, conduct special exhibitions, and offer lectures on the Buddha's teachings. Visitors are permitted at any temple; particularly recommended are the Kong Meng San Phor Kark See temple complex on Bright Hill Drive and the Temple of 1,000 Lights on Race Course Road. Candlelight processions are held at some of the temples in the evening.

June: The Arts Festival is a new biannual international event that features both Asian and Western attractions—concerts, plays, Chinese opera—with local and visiting performers. Performances take place throughout the city; the STPB will have the schedule.

August: National Day, the anniversary of the nation's independence, is a day of processions, fireworks, and dancing. The finest view is from the Padang, where the main participants put on their best show. Tickets for special seating areas are available through the STPB.

September: The Mooncake Festival, a traditional Chinese celebration, is named for special cakes—found for the most part only during this festival—that are the subject of legend. The festival is held on the night of the year when the full moon is thought to be at its brightest. There are lantern-making competitions and special entertainments, including lion and dragon dances. (Locations are published in local newspapers.) Mooncakes—sweet pastries filled with red-bean paste, lotus seeds, nuts, and egg yolks—are eaten in abundance.

September–October: During the nine-day Navarathri Festival, Hindus pay homage to three goddesses. The first three days are devoted to Parvati, consort of Shiva the Destroyer. The next three are for Lakshmi, goddess of wealth and consort of Vishnu the Protector. The final three are for Sarawathi, goddess of education and consort of Brahma the Creator. On all nights, at the Chettiar Temple on Tank Road, there are performances of classical Indian music, drama, and dancing from 7 to 10 PM. On the last evening the image of a silver horse is taken from its home in the Chettiar Temple and paraded around the streets. Thousands take part in the procession, best seen at the Sri Mariamman Temple.

October–November: During the Pilgrimage to Kusu Island, more than 100,000 Taoist believers travel to the temple of Da Bo Gong, the god of prosperity. If you want to join in, take one of the many ferries that leave from Clifford Pier.

November: Merlion Week is Singapore's version of Carnival, with food fairs, fashion shows, masquerade balls, and fireworks displays. The events start with the crowning of Miss Tourism Singapore and end with the international Singapore Powerboat Grand Prix. Brochures about the activities are available in every hotel.

November–December: Being a multicultural society, Singapore has taken Christmas to heart—and a very commercial heart it is. All the shops are deep in artificial snow, and a Chinese Santa Claus appears every so often to encourage everyone to buy and give presents, which they do with enthusiasm. A lighting ceremony takes place on Orchard Road during the last 10 days of November.

6 Thailand

A dynamic economy and an energetic people whose traditions are rooted in centuries of culture make Thailand the fulcrum of Southeast Asia. No other country in the region has so well combined a rush toward industrialization with a genuine reverence for heritage. You may discover that there are two Thailands: Pristine mountain jungles and virgin beaches sheltered by palm groves contrast with sleazy beach resorts and red-light districts, while peaceful temple complexes and gracious, first-class hotels are islands of calm within the traffic-filled sensory kaleidoscope of the capital.

By Nigel Fisher

THE KINGDOM OF THAILAND is unique among Southeast Asian nations in having developed its culture independently of Western colonialism. Thailand's origins may reach as far back as 5,600 years to the world's oldest Bronze Age civilization. Much later, from the 6th to the 13th centuries, known as the Dvaravati period, people from the southern Chinese province of Yunnan moved into the fertile basin of the Chao Phraya River. The Sukhothai period began when two Siamese chieftains banded together, captured the Khmer outpost of Sukhothai, and established the first Thai kingdom in 1238. Early in the Sukhothai period, Thailand's first great king, Ramkhamhoeng, came to power. Not only was he an outstanding warrior, but he made two lasting and significant contributions to Thai culture. He revised and adapted the Khmer alphabet to the requirements of the Thai language, and he invited Ceylonese monks to purify the Khmer-corrupted Theravada (sometimes called Hinayana) Buddhism and establish the religion in a form that is, for the most part, still practiced today.

By 1350, Sukhothai's strength had waned sufficiently for the rising and dynamic young state of Ayutthaya to usurp the reins of power. For four centuries and 33 kings, Ayutthaya was the heart and brain of Thailand. In the 1650s, the city's population exceeded that of London and—according to many foreign travelers—with its golden spires, waterways, and roads, it was the most glorious capital not just in Asia, but in all the world.

In 1766 the Burmese attacked the city. After a 15-month siege, they finally captured Ayutthaya and plundered it. Golden Buddhas were melted down, treasuries ransacked, and buildings burned. Thais who were unable to escape were killed or sent into slavery; by the time the Burmese left, Ayutthaya's population had dropped from 1 million to 10,000.

Under General Taksin, the Thais regrouped, established a capital on the Chao Phraya River at Thonburi (opposite present-day Bangkok), and set about successfully expelling the Burmese from Thailand. In 1782, Chao P'ya Chakri, a supporter of General Taksin, who had briefly been crowned king, became the first king of the current Chakri dynasty. (The present monarch, King Bhumibol Adulyadej, is the ninth in the line.) One of the first acts of P'ya Chakri, or Rama I (all kings of the Chakri dynasty are given the title Rama), was to move the Thai capital to Bangkok.

During the past 200 years, Thailand has had two prime concerns: staving off foreign encroachment on its sovereignty and restructuring its society to meet the demands of modern industrialism. It has managed to succeed quite well with both.

Western powers were first welcomed when they arrived in 1512, but the French (from whom the Thai word *farang*, meaning foreigner, is derived) tried to overthrow the legitimate government and install a puppet regime. The result was that the Thais not only threw out the French, but also closed their doors to all outsiders until the middle of the 19th century. When the West again threatened Thailand's sovereignty, King Mongkut (Rama IV, 1851–1868) kept the colonial forces at bay through a series of adroit treaties. His efforts were continued by King Chulalongkorn (Rama V, 1868–1910). Thai independence was eventually secured by the cession to the British of a little of what is now Malaysia and to the French of a little of Cambodia.

Thailand's other concern was adapting to modern social pressures. Under King Chulalongkorn, slavery was abolished, hospitals and schools were established, and some upper-class Thais received a European education so they could replace Western advisers. Under King Prajadhipok (Rama VII, 1925–1935), the world's economic depression brought its share of discontent to Thailand. The pressure for sweeping reform ended in 1932 with the military demanding the establishment of a constitutional monarchy on lines similar to that of Great Britain. Since then, quasimilitary governments and a strong bureaucracy have administered the country. Changes in government have been by coup as often as by election. Despite such occasional upheavals, the nation's policies have been remarkably consistent in fostering the expansion of the industrial economy. But in their increasing affluence, Thais are developing a desire for pluralistic representation and accepting less the dictates of unelected officials.

Throughout all this, the monarchy, which has enormous respect at all levels of society, has been a powerful stabilizing influence (it is an indictable offense to show disrespect for the monarch). The much-loved king is seen as the father of the nation, and the queen has won the heart of every Thai. This trust and respect for the royal family had a calming effect during the democracy demonstrations that brought down the military-backed government in 1992. They bind Thai society and permit the nation, unlike any other in Asia, to progress peacefully into the 21st century.

Pleasures and Pastimes

Architecture

No country is an island free from external influence, and over its thousand-year history Thailand, though staving off modern colonial rule, has been the beneficiary of many architectural and artistic styles. It is graced with the leavings of the early Lanna culture, of the Khmer empire, and with the classic Thai architecture of its Buddhist temples.

Beaches

Thailand's two shorelines, along the Gulf of Thailand and the Andaman Sea, lie slowly steaming below the Tropic of Cancer, a sun-worshiper's dream come true. The beaches come in every flavor: there are lively scenes with bars, discos, and jet skis; quiet coves with luxury hotels; islands with thatched bungalows; resorts for families; and stretches of sands with no footprints at all.

Dining

Food to the Thais is a consuming passion: they constantly eat and snack except when they're actually asleep. Throughout the day, a succession of corner food carts replaces one another, each vendor stirring up a different tasty morsel, depending on the time of day. The range of Thai cuisine is vast; no restaurant worth its salt has fewer than a hundred dishes on its menu. There are regional differences and specialties and, of course, seasonal delights. Thais know that eating out can be cheaper than eating in, and inexpensive restaurants often serve food as good as, sometimes better than the fare at fancy places. The best roast duck in Bangkok, for instance, comes from a tiny hole-in-the-wall and costs $1.10, rice included. And though some Thai food is as hot as the fires of hell, an equal number of dishes are mild—and the hot ones can be tempered. Thai food can easily become your passion too, if not second to none at least second to one.

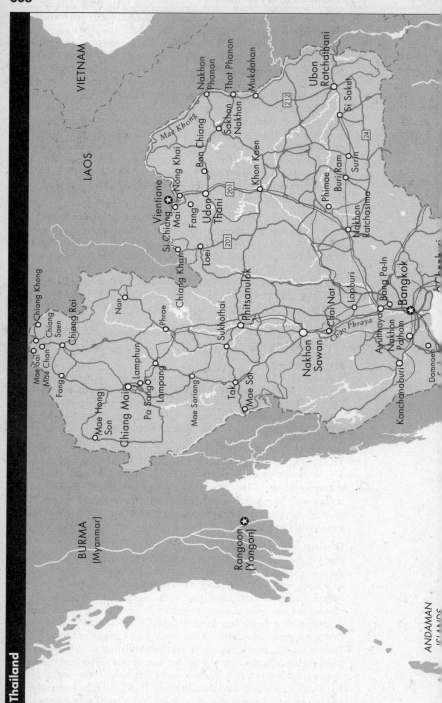

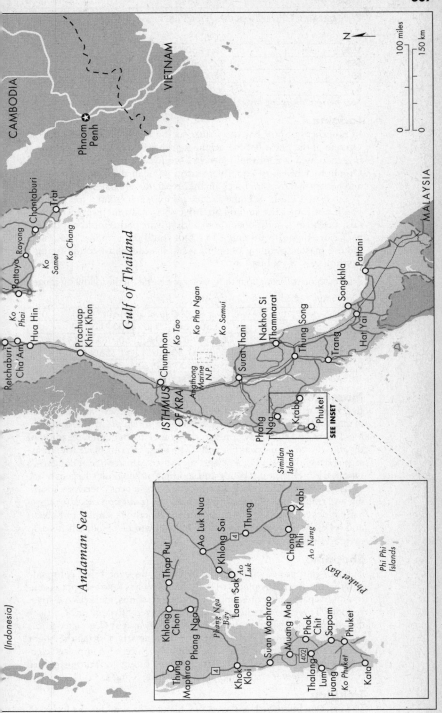

CAMBODIA

VIETNAM

Phnom Penh

Chantaburi

Trat

Pattaya · Rayong

Ko Chang

Ko Samet

Ko Phai

Hua Hin

Cha'Am

Petchaburi

Prachuap Khiri Khan

Gulf of Thailand

ISTHMUS OF KRA

Chumphon

Ko Tao

Ko Pha Ngan

Ko Samui

Angthong Marine N.P.

Surat Thani

Nakhon Si Thammarat

Thung Song

Trang

Songkhla

Hat Yai

Pattani

MALAYSIA

Phang Nga

Krabi

Phuket

SEE INSET

Similan Islands

Andaman Sea

(Indonesia)

100 miles

150 km

Inset:

Thap Put

Ao Luk Nua

Khlong Sai

Thung

Krabi

Chong Phli

Ao Nang

Phuket Bay

Phi Phi Islands

Khlong Chon

Phang Nga

Phang Nga Bay

Laem Sak

Ao Luk

Thung Maphrao

Khok Kloi

Suan Maphrao

Muang Mai

Phak Chit

Sapam

Phuket

Thalang

Lum Fuang

Ko Phuket

Kata

Price categories throughout the chapter are based on the following ranges:

CATEGORY	COST*
$$$$	over B500 (US$20)
$$$	B250–B500 (US$10–US$20)
$$	B100–B250 (US$4–US$10)
$	under B100 (US$4)

*per person, including tax

Lodging

In no other country has the visitor such a range of accommodation. On one of the finest beaches in the world, a few dollars can get you a bed cocooned in a mosquito net, in a wood hut under a thatched roof. On another beach of equal perfection you can dwell in such luxury and beauty that five-star hotels on the French Riviera pale in comparison. Though you could become jaded, taking such luxury for granted, you'll not forget the smiling attentive service. In the provincial capitals, a clean air-conditioned room with private bath should be your expectation. If you spend only $15–$20, you'll get a smaller room with flaking plaster, gurgling plumbing, and instead of air-conditioning a rhythmically wobbling fan.

Price categories throughout the chapter are based on the following ranges:

CATEGORY	COST*
$$$$	over B4,000 (over US$160)
$$$	B2,500–B4,000 (US$100–US$160)
$$	B1,500–B2,500 (US$60–US$100)
$	B500–B1,500 (US$20–US$60)
¢	under B500 (US$20)

*per double room, including service and tax

Massage

Every visit to Thailand should include a massage or two—and they come in many different varieties. Aside from those which promise lots of bubbles, soap, and full body contact, they range from gentle kneading of the muscles to joint-breaking pulls. The most famous place for a massage is Bangkok's Wat Po; you'll get the most expensive one at Bangkok's Oriental Hotel, the most gentle and soothing at Bangkok's Regent hotel. Those offered at the beach resorts tend to be a cross between soothing and traditional. The traditional massage (*nuat boroan*) aims to release blocked channels of energy and uses methods similar to Shiatsu and reflexology. Joint pains and headaches can be eased, but it's also invigorating.

Shopping

You can get hooked on shopping in Thailand—everything is for sale and there are so many places to look. Bangkok has fancy shopping centers and department stores, antiques and crafts shops, markets and street vendors. There are watches with recently affixed "Rolex" or "Cartier" trademarks and T-shirts with a crocodile slightly askew. Negotiated prices are irresistibly low. In many large cities and resorts, visiting the Night Market is part of an evening's entertainment. Except for imported electronics and luxury goods, Thailand's prices, though not duty-free, are considerably lower than Singapore's or Hong Kong's.

Trekking

The forested hills north and west of Chiang Mai would make for good trekking just for their misty, rugged beauty. But here you can take treks of a day or longer to visit isolated villages that are home to the hill tribes, ethnic groups who migrated from Burma and China, and who have kept their traditions over the last two centuries.

Exploring Thailand

It is in Bangkok that we begin, like most visitors to Thailand. The capital city, equidistant from the country's four corners, is in position to become the hub of Southeast Asia. A number of points of interest that lie within a day's striking distance of Bangkok. To the west, through forested hills close to the Burmese border, flows the River Kwai, known for its infamous bridge. North up the Chao Phraya River stand the ruins of Ayutthaya, the ancient, glorious capital, and the Khmer-influenced buildings at Lopburi. To the southwest are the floating market at Damnoen Saduak and Nakhon Pathom, where Buddhism first found a home in Thailand. And down both sides of the Gulf of Thailand lie convenient beach resorts.

The vast middle of Thailand stretches from the Burmese border to those of Laos and Cambodia. In the Central Plains stand the restored and partially rebuilt palaces and temples of Thailand's first capital, Sukhothai, and its satellite town, Sri Satchanalai. An hour east of Sukhothai is the busy transportation hub of Phitsanulok, and east of there lies the vast agricultural Northeast. Along its southern border are scattered grand sanctuaries and palaces left behind by the 13th-century Khmer empire.

The unofficial capital of Northern Thailand is Chiang Mai, whose cultural traditions matured apart from those of the central region. Its temple architecture stems from the Lanna kingdom, which preceded the Thai nation, its food is zestier, its language is slower, and its rivers faster-flowing. Northern Thailand is hilly, forested, and has stretches of no-man's-land on the Burmese border where the opium poppy grows. Throughout these forests live seven ethnic groups known collectively as the Hill Tribes. Today they maintain a village life independent of mainstream Thailand.

Beach resorts line the skinny peninsula stretching south from Bangkok to the Malaysia border. For now, three areas: Phuket, on the Andaman Sea; Krabi on the western shore facing it; and Ko Samui, an island in the Gulf of Thailand, have exploited nature's potential, but on these long coastlines the possibilities are endless.

Great Itineraries

IF YOU HAVE 7 DAYS

Spend your first two days in **Bangkok.** Start your first day with the most famous of all Bangkok sights, the Grand Palace, then go on to the gorgeously ornate Wat Phra Keo and Bangkok's oldest and largest temple, Wat Po. Explore Chinatown and visit Wat Traimitr, the Temple of the Golden Buddha. At the Chao Phraya, catch a river bus to the Oriental Hotel and have a cup of tea. In the evening, walk bustling Silom Road to check out the vendor stalls and catch a dinner show of Thai dancing. Next day, go to Wat Benjamabophit, which contains Bangkok's much-photographed Marble Temple. Spend the afternoon in the National Museum to gain an overview of Thai history and art. In the evening explore Bangkok's nightlife.

On the third day go to **Ayutthaya,** the glorious former capital. If you intend to head south to a beach resort next, travel to Ayutthaya by bus and return to Bangkok the same day by boat down the Chao Phraya River. For your remaining four days, enjoy sun, sea, and sand at a resort on **Phuket** or **Ko Samui,** both of which are short flights from Bangkok.

If you would rather spend your final days seeing more of Thailand's history and landscape, use your fourth day to continue north by train or bus to **Chiang Mai.** On the fifth day explore the wats of the inner city and in the afternoon check out the craft stores along Sankamphaeng Road. In the evening have a Thai massage, followed by a *khantoke* (northern Thai) dinner and cultural show. On the sixth day rise early and go to Wat Phrathat Doi Suthep, a temple on a mountain overlooking Chiang Mai. In the afternoon see Wat Chedi Yot and the **National Museum.** For the evening's entertainment go to the Night Bazaar. On your final day take an excursion south to the ancient wats at **Lamphun,** and buy cottons at **Pa Sang.**

IF YOU HAVE 10 DAYS

Spend your first two days in **Bangkok** and your third in **Ayutthaya.** Beach lovers can then head south to spend the remainder of their trip at southern beach resorts. If you go overland, break the 12- to 14-hour trip to **Ko Samui** or the Andaman Sea Resorts—**Phuket, Krabi,** and **Ko Phi Phi**—with a night or two at the adjoining Gulf Coast resort towns of **Hua Hin** and **Cha' Am;** or fly straight to Phuket and make the six-hour land/boat crossing to Ko Samui.

If you head north from Ayutthaya on your fourth day, spend the fifth and sixth days covering the major sights of **Chiang Mai**—not forgetting to shop and have a massage. On the seventh day fly to **Mae Hong Son** and make a three-day, two-night trek among the hill tribes. Or travel by raft to **Chiang Rai,** and spend the remaining days relaxing in nearby **Sop Ruak** and exploring the **Golden Triangle.**

IF YOU HAVE 14 DAYS

With a full two weeks you have plenty of options. After spending your first three days in and around **Bangkok,** you could devote your time to some of Thailand's less-developed paradises, like the Gulf Coast's **Ko Chang;** or **Ko Pha Ngan,** north of Ko Samui; or **Ao Nang,** near Krabi. You could also combine the best of both worlds: Travel north from Bangkok to Ayutthaya and Chiang Mai during the first week then fly south to **Phuket** or another of the southern resorts for the latter half of your trip.

To see more of Thailand's heartland, however, visit the central plains and I-San. After visiting Ayutthaya and returning to Bangkok by boat take the night train or an early morning flight to **Nakhon Ratchasima,** or Korat, which you'll use as your base for the fourth and fifth days. Take a day trip to **Prasat Hin Phimae** to visit the late-11th-century Khmer sanctuary. In the evening be sure to go to Korat's Night Bazaar. On the fifth day take a car or bus to **Prasat Him Khao Phanom Rung,** a supreme example of 12th-century Khmer architecture. On the sixth day either take a direct bus or fly via Bangkok to **Phitsanulok** and spend the night there. On the seventh and eighth days visit **Old Sukhothai** then continue north to explore Chiang Mai and its surroundings for the rest of the trip.

When to Tour Thailand

November through March is the best time to be in Bangkok. The city is at its coolest—85°—and driest. The Andaman Sea (Phuket, Krabi, and environs) has two seasons. During the monsoon season, May through October, hotel prices are considerably lower, but rough seas can make some beaches unsafe for swimming. The peak season is the dry period, from November through April. Typhoons hit Ko Samui from late October through December, and its peak season runs from January through early July, when prices drop by as much as 40%.

The central and northern part of Thailand has three seasons. The best time to visit is winter. From November to March the weather is cool in the hills at night; take a sweater and windbreaker if you are trekking. The region is hottest and driest from March to May—rather unbearably hot on the plains—and the rainy season, from June to October, makes unpaved roads difficult, especially during September.

BANGKOK

A foreigner's reaction to Bangkok is often as confused as the city's geography. Bangkok has no downtown, and the streets, like the traffic, seem to veer off in every direction. The oldest quarter clusters along the eastern bank of the Chao Phraya River, which snakes between Bangkok and Thonburi, where the capital was first established after the fall of Ayutthaya in 1767. There's even confusion about the city's name. Though to Thais it is Krung Thep, the City of Angels, foreigners call it Bangkok. When King Rama I moved his capital in 1782 from Thonburi across the Chao Phraya, he chose a site that foreign vessels knew from their navigational charts as the village of Bangkok.

In the last 20 years, this city has changed enormously. Before the Vietnam War, and before Bangkok became *the* R&R destination for American servicemen, it had a population of 1.5 million. Then, as U.S. dollars attracted the rural poor and development began, it grew to 8 million, 40 times the size of any other city in Thailand. Nowadays, space in which to live and breathe is inadequate. Air pollution is among the worst in the world (policemen directing traffic are now required to wear masks). Constant traffic jams the streets and *sois* (side streets and alleys), and no cure is in sight.

Yet, while hurtling headlong into the modern world, Bangkok strangely gives you a sense of history and timelessness, perhaps because King Rama I set out to build a city as beautiful as old Ayutthaya before the Burmese sacked it. Bangkok's contrasts require an adjustment on your part, but amid the chaos you soon come to appreciate the gentle nature of the Thais and their genuine respect for other people.

Exploring Bangkok

Learning your way around is a challenge. It may help to think of Bangkok as an isosceles triangle with the base abutting the *S* curve of the Chao Phraya and the apex, pointing east, ending down Sukhumvit Road, somewhere around Soi (lane) 40.

Sukhumvit, at the apex of this conceptual triangle, was once a residential neighborhood. In the last decade, it has developed into a district of hotels, shops, nightclubs, and restaurants. Now the area known as Bangkapi has become a satellite town, attracting industry and residential complexes.

Westward, toward the Chao Phraya, you come to spacious foreign embassy compounds, offices of large corporations, and modern international hotels. Slightly farther west, you reach the older sections of Bangkok. On the southern flank is Silom Road, a shopping and financial district. Parallel to Silom Road is Suriwongse Road, with more hotels, and between the two is the entertainment district of Patpong. Continue farther and you reach the riverbank.

Going west along Rama I Road in the center of the triangle, you pass the Siam Square shopping area and the National Stadium. Continue south toward the Hualamphong Railway Station, and between it and the river lies Chinatown, a maze of streets containing restaurants, goldsmiths, small warehouses, and repair shops.

In the northern part of the triangle, moving westward, you pass through various markets before reaching Thai government buildings, the Victory Monument, Chitlada Palace, the Dusit Zoo, the National Assembly, the National Library, and, finally, the river. Slightly south of this route, you can go west from the Democracy Monument to the National Museums and Theatre near the river, and then south to the Grand Palace, and Wat Phra Keo (the Temple of the Emerald Buddha).

Knowing your exact destination, its direction, and approximate distance are important in negotiating tuk-tuk fares and planning your itinerary. (But note that many sights have no precise written address.) Crossing and recrossing the city is time-consuming; many hours can be spent in frustrating traffic jams. Above all, remember that Bangkok is enormous and distances are great; it can take a half hour or more to walk between two seemingly adjacent sites.

Old Bangkok Along the Chao Phraya

Bangkok's major sightseeing attractions—the state palace and many of the famous, highly revered temples—are within a short distance of the Chao Phraya River in the part of Bangkok that was founded in 1782. Chinatown is also here. On the tour described below you'll experience one of Bangkok's greatest pleasures—after getting good and hot from looking at a wat or two, you'll be refreshed by crossing the cool Chao Phraya on a ferryboat before tackling another temple.

Numbers in the text correspond to numbers in the margin and on the Bangkok map.

A GOOD TOUR

Start at the **Grand Palace** ①, Bangkok's major landmark, and go on to the adjoining **Wat Phra Keo** ②. Walk south from the Grand Palace on Sanamchai Road to **Wat Po** ③. From Wat Po, walk west to the river and then north (toward the Grand Palace) about 250 yards to the Tha Thien jetty, to take the ferry across to **Wat Arun** ④. Return by the same ferry to the eastern shore and take a tuk-tuk to **Chinatown.** Get out at Pahuraht Road and as you take in the sights, walk east, then zigzag left to Yaowarat Road, and continue east until it leads into Charoen Krung. There, on the opposite corner stands **Wat Traimitr** ⑤.

TIMING

This is a full day's sightseeing. In miles this route probably amounts to no more than 5, but because of the heat you might want to hop into a taxi or a tuk-tuk for the stretch between Wat Phra Keo and Wat Po. Ideally, you would begin early in the morning, take a break for lunch to escape the heat of midday, and end the excursion in the late afternoon. Most sites are open everyday from 8–5, but the Grand Palace and Wat Phra Keo have stricter hours: daily 8:30–11:30 and 1–3:30. You might spend as much as 90 minutes at each. Wat Po, which opens at 7 AM will only take a half-hour, unless you have an hour-long massage. Allow time to climb the prang (tower) at Wat Arun. Chinatown is a maze of streets and markets, so two hours wandering through here can pass by quickly, though nonshoppers may find 30 minutes sufficient. During Chinese New Year, much of Chinatown closes down. Wat Traimitr can be a 15-minute stop, or you might like to sit there a while and restore your spirit.

SIGHTS TO SEE

Chinatown. Chinatown used to be Bangkok's prosperous downtown, but, as the city grew, the neighborhood lost some of its bustle. Red lanterns and Chinese signs do still abound, and modest restaurants line the streets. Pahuraht Road is full of textile shops, with nearly as many Indian dealers here as Chinese, and Yaowarat Road, the main thoroughfare, is crowded with gold and jewelry shops. The Thieves Market, at the northwest end of Yaowarat Road is fun to browse through.

❶ Grand Palace. In 1782, when King Rama I moved the capital from Thonburi, across the Chao Phraya, he built this palace and walled city, which subsequent Chakri monarchs enlarged. The compound is open to visitors, but not all the buildings, which are used only for state occasions and royal ceremonies—the king actually lives at Chitlada Palace in north Bangkok. Of the compound's buildings, the Dusit Maha Prasart, on the right, is a classic example of palace architecture; Amarin Vinichai Hall, on the left, the original audience hall, is now used for the presentation of ambassadors' credentials. Note the glittering gold throne. ▦ *Admission.* ☉ *Daily 8:30–11:30 and 1–3:30.*

❹ Wat Arun. Wat Arun means "Temple of the Dawn," but it's even more marvelous toward dusk, when the setting sun casts its amber tones. The temple's architecture is symmetrical, with a square courtyard containing five Khmer-style *prangs* (stupas)—the central prang (282 feet high) surrounded by its four attendant prangs in the corners. All the prangs are covered in mosaics of broken Chinese porcelain. ⊠ *West side of Chao Praya.* ▦ *Admission.* ☉ *Daily 8–5:30.*

★ **❷ Wat Phra Keo** (Temple of the Emerald Buddha). No building within the Royal Palace compound excites such awe as the adjoining royal chapel, the most sacred temple in the kingdom. No other wat in Thailand is so ornate and so embellished with murals, statues, and glittering gold.

As you enter the compound, take note of the 20-foot-tall helmeted and tile-encrusted statues in traditional Thai battle attire standing guard and surveying the precincts. They set the scene—mystical, majestic, and awesome. Turn right as you enter, and notice along the inner walls the lively murals (recently restored) depicting the whole *Ramayana* epic (*Ramakien* in Thai).

The main chapel, with its gilded, glittering, three-tier roof, dazzles your eyes. Royal griffins stand guard outside, and the perfect symmetry of the shining gold stupas in the court establish a feeling of serenity. Inside sits the Emerald Buddha. This most venerated image of the Lord Buddha is carved from one piece of jade 31 inches high. No one knows its origin, but history places it in Chiang Rai in 1464. From there it traveled first to Chiang Mai, then to Lamphun, and finally back to Chiang Rai, where the Laotians stole it and took it home. Eventually, the Thais sent an army into Laos to get it back, and it reached its final resting place when King Rama I built the chapel.

At the back of the royal chapel you'll find a scale model of Angkor Wat. As this complex, in Cambodia, is difficult to reach nowadays, this is a chance to sense the vastness of the old Khmer capital. ▦ *Admission.* ☉ *Daily 8:30–11:30 and 1–3:30.*

❸ Wat Po, or Wat Phra Jetuphon (Temple of the Reclining Buddha). The largest temple in Bangkok, Wat Po, is famous, in part, for housing the largest—151 feet—reclining Buddha in the country. Especially noteworthy are his 10-foot feet, inlaid in mother-of-pearl with the 108 auspicious signs of the Lord Buddha.

Walk beyond the chapel containing the Reclining Buddha and enter Bangkok's oldest open university. A hundred years before Bangkok was established as the capital, a monastery was founded to teach classical Thai medicine. The school still gives instruction in the natural methods of healing. Around the walls are marble plaques inscribed with formulas for herbal cures, and stone sculptures squat in various postures demonstrating techniques for relieving pain. The monks still practice ancient cures, and the **massage school of Wat Pho** has become famous.

Bangkok

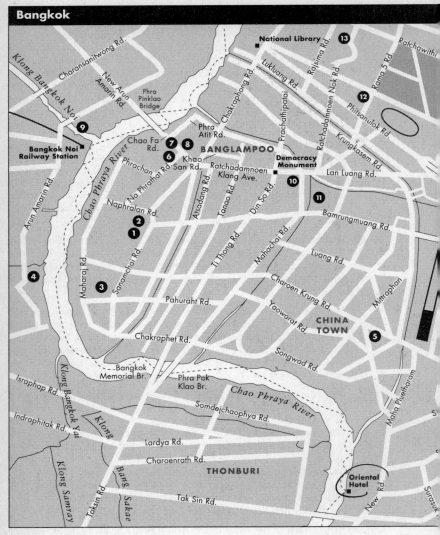

Grand Palace, **1**

National Art Gallery, **8**

National Museum, **6**

National Theatre, **7**

Pasteur Institute, **14**

Royal Ceremonial Barges, **9**

Vimarnmek Palace, **13**

Wat Arun (Temple of the Dawn), **4**

Wat Benjamabophit (Marble Temple), **12**

Wat Phra Keo (Temple of the Emerald Buddha), **2**

Wat Po (Temple of the Reclining Buddha), **3**

Wat Rachanada (Temple of the Metal Castle), **10**

Wat Saket (Temple of the Golden Mount), **11**

Wat Traimitr (Temple of the Golden Buddha), **5**

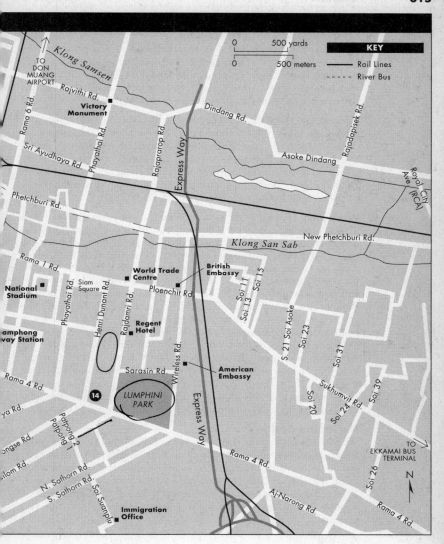

KEY

—— Rail Lines

- - - - River Bus

0   500 yards
0   500 meters

TO DON MUANG AIRPORT

Klong Samsen

Rajvithi Rd.

Victory Monument

Rama 6 Rd.

Phayathai Rd.

Rajaprarop Rd.

Dindang Rd.

Rajadapisek Rd.

Royal City Ave. (RCA)

Sri Ayudhaya Rd.

Express Way

Asoke Dindang

Phetchburi Rd.

Klong San Sab

New Phetchburi Rd.

Rama 1 Rd.

National Stadium

Siam Square

World Trade Centre

Phayathai Rd.

Henri Dunant Rd.

Rajdamri Rd.

Ploenchit Rd.

British Embassy

Soi 11

Soi 13

Soi 15

S. 21 Soi Asoke

Soi 23

Soi 31

Soi 39

amphong vay Station

Regent Hotel

Wireless Rd.

American Embassy

Soi 20

Soi 24

Sukhumvit Rd.

Rama 4 Rd.

Sarasin Rd.

14

LUMPHINI PARK

ya Rd.

ongse Rd.

Patpong 2

Patpong 1

Express Way

Rama 4 Rd.

TO EKKAMAI BUS TERMINAL

Soi 26

Rama 4 Rd.

ilom Rd.

N. Sathorn Rd.

S. Sathorn Rd.

Soi Suamplu

Immigration Office

Aj-Narong Rd.

N

The massage lasts one hour, growing more and more pleasurable as you adjust to it. Masseurs are available daily 7–5 for B150.

Don't be perturbed by the tall statues that good-naturedly poke fun at farangs (Westerners). These gangling 12-foot figures depict the most evil demons, which scare away all other evil spirits. With their top hats, they look farcically Western and, in fact, were modeled after the Europeans who plundered China during the Opium Wars.

These statues guard the entrance to the northeastern quarter of the compound and a very pleasant three-tier temple containing 394 seated Buddhas. On the walls, bas-relief plaques salvaged from Ayutthaya depict stories from the *Ramayana*. Around this temple area are four tall *chedis* (Thai-style pagodas where holy relics are kept), decorated with brightly colored porcelain, each representing one of the first four kings of the present dynasty. ▣ *Admission.* ⊙ *Daily 7–5.*

★ ⑤ **Wat Traimitr** (Temple of the Golden Buddha). The main temple of Wat Traimitr has little architectural merit, but off to the side, next to the money-changing wagon, is a small chapel containing the world's largest solid-gold Buddha, cast about nine centuries ago. Weighing 5½ tons and standing 10 feet high, the statue gleams with such richness and purity that even the most jaded are inspired by its strength and power (and value). The statue, sculpted in Sukhothai style, is believed to have been brought first to Ayutthaya. When the Burmese were about to sack the city, it was covered in plaster, and two centuries later, still in plaster, it was regarded as just another statue. When it was being moved to a new temple in Bangkok in the 1950s it slipped from the crane, and leaving the statue in the mud, the workmen called it a day. First thing in the morning, a temple monk, who had dreamed that the statue was divinely inspired, went to see the Buddha image. Through a crack in the plaster he saw the glint of yellow, and opening the plaster farther, he discovered that the statue was pure gold. ▣ *Admission.* ⊙ *Daily 9–5.*

Museums and Wats

Slightly inland from the river and north of the Grand Palace, stands a cluster of cultural and government buildings. The neighborhood, in itself not particularly attractive, is made less appealing by the jammed traffic on weekdays, but you must not miss the National Museum, with Thailand's most valued historic treasures and a great collection of Southeast Asian art. There are also two unusual temples a little farther east.

A GOOD TOUR

The **National Museum** ⑥ should be seen early in your visit. It really helps in understanding Thai history, art and architecture. Next door, in the **National Theatre** ⑦, classical Thai dance and drama performances are held (☞ Nightlife and the Arts, *below*). Next visit the **National Art Gallery** ⑧, opposite the theater, which has exhibits of modern and traditional Thai art. Next, take a ferry across the Chao Phraya (one of Bangkok's great pleasures) to visit the **Royal Ceremonial Barges** ⑨, and come back the same way. You can walk or take a tuk-tuk east, past the National Museum and the Democracy Monument, to **Wat Rachanada** ⑩, and then walk east, across Maha Chai Road, to **Wat Saket** ⑪, a notable landmark of the old city.

TIMING

This route is fairly compact. The museums are close together, and though it's not more than a 15-minute walk, you'll probably take a tuk-tuk or taxi to Wat Rachanada. Wat Saket is just a block away. Allow a good two or three hours at the National Museum and just under an hour at the National Art Gallery. Both are closed on Monday, Tuesday, and public holidays; go to the National Museum on Wednesday or Thursday at 9:30 AM for the free 90-minute lecture tour in English. Then, after lunch, visit Wat Rachanada and Wat Saket. It will take at least an hour by taxi from the Sukhumvit area to reach the National Theatre, and 40 minutes from the Silom Road area via the river bus.

SIGHTS TO SEE

⑧ National Art Gallery. Opposite the National Theatre, the National Art Gallery exhibits both modern and traditional Thai art. ⌧ *Chao Fa Rd.,* ☎ *02/281–2224.* 🎫 *Admission.* ⊘ *Tues.–Thurs. and weekends 9–noon and 1–4.*

★ **⑥ National Museum.** By far the best place to acquaint yourself with Thai history and art is at the extensive National Museum, which has one of the world's best collections of Southeast Asian art in general, and Buddhist and Thai art in particular. Most of the great masterpieces of the Sukhothai and Ayutthaya periods and works from the northern provinces have found their way here, leaving up-country museums rather bare of fine Thai art. Here you'll have a good opportunity to trace Thailand's long history, beginning with the ceramic utensils and bronzeware of the Ban Chiang civilization, thought to have existed 5,000 to 6,000 years ago. You might go first to the artifact gallery at the left of the ticket counter, for a historical overview. Afterward, explore the galleries that portray the Dvaravati and Khmer periods of more than 1,000 years ago. These will prepare you for the different styles of Thai art, from the Sukhothai period (1238–mid-14th century) on. ☎ *02/224–1333* 🎫 *Admission.* ⊘ *Wed.–Fri. and weekends 9–noon and 1–4. Cafeteria. Free 90-min orientation tours in English, 9:30 AM Wed., Thurs., by specialists in different aspects of Thai art and culture. Meet at entrance to main building.*

⑦ National Theatre. Next door to the National Museum is the National Theatre, where classical Thai dance and drama can be seen. ⌧ *Na Phra That Rd.,* ☎ *02/224–1342 for information on scheduled programs. Regular exhibitions of classical Thai dance, the last Fri. and Sat. of each month. (☞ Nightlife and the Arts, below).*

⑨ Royal Ceremonial Barges. These splendid ceremonial barges are berthed in a shed on the Thonburi side of the Chao Praya River. The beautifully crafted boats, carved in the early part of this century, take the form of famous mythical creatures of the *Ramayana.* The most impressive is the red-and-gold royal flag barge, *Suphannahongse* (Golden Swan), used by the king on special occasions. Carved from a single piece of teak, it measures about 150 feet and weighs more than 15 tons. Fifty oarsmen propel it along the Chao Phraya River, not counting two coxswains, the flag wavers, and the rhythm-keeper. 🎫 *Admission.* ⊘ *Daily 8:30–4:30.*

⑩ Wat Rachanada (The Temple of the Metal Castle). Across from Wat Sakret, Wat Rachanada intentionally resembles the mythical castle of the gods. According to legend, a wealthy and pious man built a fabulous castle, Loha Prasat, according to the design laid down for the disciples of the Lord Buddha. Wat Rachanada, built in metal, is meant to duplicate that castle and is the only one of its kind remaining. In its precincts are stalls selling amulets that protect the wearer from misfortune—usually of the physical kind, though love amulets and charms are also sold. 🎫 *Admission.* ⊘ *Daily 8–6.*

⑪ Wat Saket (Temple of the Golden Mount). East of the Democracy Monument you'll find Wat Sakret, a notable landmark of the old city. To reach the gold-covered chedi, you must make an exhausting climb up 318 steps winding around the mound. Every November, the compound is the site of Bangkok's largest temple fair, with food stalls, stage shows, and merrymaking. ☒ *Admission.* ⊘ *Daily 8–5.*

Scattered Bangkok

One of the delights of Bangkok is that it sprawls, seemingly without rhyme or reason, in delightful chaos. Temples, factories, palaces, office buildings, and private houses may all be found on one block. The negative is that getting from one major sight to another takes time, usually spent in stalled traffic.

SIGHTS TO SEE

⑭ **Pasteur Institute** (Red Cross Snake Farm). In 1923, the Thai Red Cross established this farm, where venom is milked and stored as the antidote for people bit by poisonous snakes. There are slide shows before the milking sessions, at 10:30 AM and 2 PM on weekdays and 10:30 on weekends. You can watch the handlers work with deadly cobras, kraits, and pit vipers, and even get typhoid, cholera, and smallpox vaccinations here. ☒ *1871 Rama IV Rd., at Henri Dunant, near top of Suriwong Rd,* ☎ *02/252-0161.* ☒ *Admission.* ⊘ *Daily 8:30–4:30.*

⑬ **Vimarnmek Palace.** This is the largest teak structure in the world, built by King Rama V, grandfather of the present king, as a four-story suburban palace. Now, with the capital's growth, it's in the center of administrative Bangkok, next to the National Assembly building. The palace fits its name, "Castle in the Clouds," its extraordinary lightness enhanced by a reflecting pond. King Rama's fascination with Western architecture shows in its Victorian style, but the building retains an unmistakably Thai delicacy. Most of the furnishings were either bought in the West or given by European monarchs. Some are exquisite—porcelain, handcrafted furniture, and crystal—and some have novelty value, like the first typewriter brought to Thailand. ☎ *02/281-1569.* ☒ *Admission.* ⊘ *Daily 9:30–4.*

★ ⑫ **Wat Benjamabophit** (Marble Temple). Bangkok's most photographed wat, built in 1899, is where Thailand's present king came to spend his days as a monk before his coronation. Statues of Buddha line the courtyard, and the magnificent interior has crossbeams of lacquer and gold, but Wat Benjamabophit is more than a splendid temple. The monastery is a seat of learning that appeals to Buddhist monks with intellectual yearnings. ☒ *Admission.* ⊘ *Daily 7–5.*

Dining

Thais are passionate about food—finding the out-of-the-way shop that prepares some specialty better than anyplace else, then dragging groups of friends to share the discovery, is a national pastime. Until your non-native digestion adjusts to the food, steer clear of the stands in markets and at roadsides. Most of these are safe, but as a general rule, you should stick to cooked food. The clean, well-maintained food shops on major roads and in shopping centers rarely cause problems and will give you a chance to taste authentic versions of popular Thai dishes at very low prices.

Non-Thai Asian

$$$$ ✗ **Genji.** The fact that this Japanese restaurant is in a large international hotel shouldn't deter even culinary purists—there is an excellent sushi bar and several small, private rooms. Try especially the succulent grilled eel. Set menus for lunch and dinner are well conceived, and Japanese breakfasts are also served. ☒ *Hilton International, 2 Wireless Rd.,* ☎ *02/253-0123. Reservations essential. AE, DC, MC, V.*

It helps to be pushy in airports.

Introducing the revolutionary new TransPorter™ from American Tourister®. It's the first suitcase you can push around without a fight. TransPorter's™ exclusive four-wheel design lets you push it in front of you with almost no effort – the wheels take the weight. Or pull it on two wheels if you choose. You can even stack on other bags and use it like a luggage cart.

TransPorter™ is designed like a dresser, with built-in shelves to organize your belongings. Or collapse the shelves and pack it like a traditional suitcase. Inside, there's a suiter feature to help keep suits and dresses from wrinkling. When push comes to shove, you can't beat a TransPorter™. For more information on how you can be this pushy, call 1-800-542-1300.

Shelves collapse on command.

Stable 4-wheel design.

American Tourister

Making travel less primitive®

Your passport around the world.

- Worldwide access
- Operators who speak your language
- Monthly itemized billing

MCI Calling Card

415 555 1234 2244
J.D. SMITH

Use your MCI Card® and these access numbers for an easy way to call when traveling worldwide.

Bahrain†	800-002
Brunei	800-011
China (CC)†	108-12
(Available from most major cities)	
For a Mandarin-speaking operator	108-17
Cyprus ♦†	080-90000
Egypt (CC) ♦†	355-5770
Federated States of Micronesia	624
Fiji	004-890-1002
Guam (CC)†	950-1022
Hong Kong (CC)†	800-1121
India (CC)†	000-127
(Available from most major cities)	
Indonesia (CC) ♦†	001-801-11
Iran ⁜	(Special Phones Only)
Israel (CC)†	177-150-2727
Japan (CC) ♦†	
To call U.S. using KDD ■	0039-121
To call U.S. using IDC ■	0066-55-121
Jordan	18-800-001
Korea (CC)†	
To call using KT ■	009-14
To call using DACOM ■	0039-12

Phone Booths ⁜	Press Red Button 03, then ✱
Military Bases	550-2255
Kuwait†	800-MCI (800-624)
Lebanon (CC) ⁜	600-624
Macao†	0800-131
Malaysia (CC) ♦†	800-0012
Philippines (CC) ♦†	
To call using PLDT ■	105-14
To call using PHILCOM ■	1026-12
For a Tagalog-speaking operator	105-15
Qatar ★	0800-012-77
Saipan (CC) ⁜†	950-1022
Saudi Arabia (CC)†	1-800-11
Singapore†	8000-112-112
Sri Lanka	(within Colombo) 440100
	(outside of Colombo) 01-440100
Syria	0800
Taiwan (CC) ♦†	0080-13-4567
Thailand ★†	001-999-1-2001
United Arab Emirates ♦	800-111
Vietnam ●	1201-1022

To sign up for the MCI Card, dial the access number of the country you are in and ask to speak with a customer service representative.

http://www.mci.com

$$$$ ✕ **Royal Kitchen.** Perhaps the most elegant of Bangkok's many Chi-
★ nese restaurants, the Royal Kitchen consists of a number of small, at-
mospherically decorated dining rooms. The menu is a reference resource
for southern Chinese delicacies, including such offerings as *Mieng
nok,* with finely minced, seasoned pigeon served on individual fragrant
leaves. At lunchtime, dim sum is served, and it, too, is probably
Bangkok's best, as beautiful to look at as it is subtle in taste. ⊠ *N.
Sathorn Rd., opposite YWCA and Thai Oil,* ☎ *02/234–3063. Reservations essential. Jacket and tie. AE, DC, MC, V.*

$$$ ✕ **Hok Thean Lauo.** A shuttle boat runs guests across the Chao Praya
from the River City Shopping Centre to one of Bangkok's top Can-
tonese restaurants. Sit at a table by the window, watching the streams
of rice barges labor up and down the river. Hok Thean Lauo is known
for its dim sum lunches, especially on Sunday. ⊠ *762 Ladya Rd.,
Klongsam,* ☎ *02/437–1121. Reservations essential Sundays. AE, DC,
MC, V.*

$$$ ✕ **Sweet Basil.** Thais dress up for a special meal and make the long
★ trek down Sukhumvit to Soi 62 (Ekimae) for splendidly presented
Vietnamese fare, in a fresh setting of crisp white tablecloths, glistening silver and glassware, ferns and flowers. Try the *bo la lat* (brochettes
of beef wrapped in a pungent leaf) and the *ban cuon tom* (dumplings
stuffed with shrimp and mushrooms) or the more usual but delicious
salads and crunchy *cha gio* (spring rolls with a sweet, tangy sauce). ⊠
23 Soi 62, ☎ *02/176–5490. Reservations essential. AE, DC, MC, V.*

$$–$$$ ✕ **Himali Cha Cha.** Cha Cha, the chef who was once Nehru's cook,
died in 1996, but his recipes are now prepared with matching ability
by his wife, who serves up the northern Indian cuisine in a pleasantly
informal setting. The tandoori chicken is locally famous, and the daily
specials, precisely explained, are usually to be recommended. Always
good are the breads and the fruit-flavored *lassis* (yogurt drinks)—especially the mango ones. ⊠ *1229/11 New Rd.,* ☎ *02/235–1569. AE,
DC, MC, V.*

$$–$$$ ✕ **Le Dalat.** This very classy Vietnamese restaurant, once a private house,
★ consists of several intimate and cozily decorated dining rooms. Try *naem
neuang,* which requires you to take a garlicky grilled meatball and place
it on a round of *mieng* (edible thin rice paper wrapper), then pile on
bits of garlic, ginger, hot chili, star apple, and mango, spoon on a vis-
cous sweet-salty sauce, and wrap the whole thing up in a lettuce leaf
before eating. A branch in Patpong I has a similar menu, but the decor
is by no means as attractive. ⊠ *51 Sukhumvit Soi 23, opposite Indian
Embassy,* ☎ *02/258–4192. Reservations essential. AE, DC, MC, V.*

$$–$$$ ✕ **Mandalay.** Here, at one of the two Burmese restaurants in Thailand,
★ the food looks similar to Thai, but tends not to be so spicy hot. Many
of Mandalay's highly seasoned, saladlike dishes are real surprises. You
should try one marvel called *lo phet* (made from marinated young tea
leaves, peanuts, sesame, garlic, toasted coconut, and several aromatic
herbs); remember the caffeine content of the tea leaves—too much will
keep you awake. There are also excellent, very thick beef and shrimp
curries and an unusual pork curry called *hangle.* On the walls are
Burmese antiques from the owner's famous shop, Elephant House. ⊠
*77/5 Soi Ruamrudee (Soi 11) Sukhumvit (behind the Ambassador
Hotel),* ☎ *02/250–1220. AE, DC, MC, V.*

$ ✕ **Coca Noodles.** On evenings and weekends, this giant, raucous restau-
rant is full of Chinese families eating a daunting variety of noodle dishes
with noisy gusto. Both wheat- and rice-based pastas are available, in
combination with a cornucopia of meats, fish, shellfish, and crunchy
Chinese vegetables. Try some of the green, wheat-based noodles called
mee yoke, topped with a chicken thigh, red pork, or crabmeat. Also,
on a gas ring built into the table, you can prepare yourself an intrigu-

Bangkok Dining and Lodging

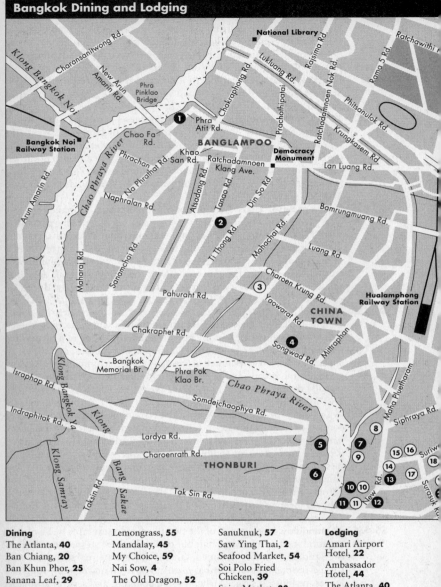

Dining

The Atlanta, **40**
Ban Chiang, **20**
Ban Khun Phor, **25**
Banana Leaf, **29**
Cabbages & Condoms, **46**
Coca Noodles, **26**
Genji, **36**
Himali Cha Cha, **13**
Hok Thean Lauo, **5**
Le Dalat, **49**
Le Normandie, **10**

Lemongrass, **55**
Mandalay, **45**
My Choice, **59**
Nai Sow, **4**
The Old Dragon, **52**
Pan Pan, **38, 53**
Prachak, **12**
The Regent Grill, **33**
River City Bar B-Q, **7**
Royal Kitchen, **31**
Sala Rim Naam, **6**
Salathip, **11**

Sanuknuk, **57**
Saw Ying Thai, **2**
Seafood Market, **54**
Soi Polo Fried Chicken, **39**
Spice Market, **33**
Sweet Basil, **58**
Thai Room, **28**
Thong Lee, **51**
Ton Po, **1**
Tumnak Thai, **50**

Lodging

Amari Airport Hotel, **22**
Ambassador Hotel, **44**
The Atlanta, **40**
Bel-Air Princess, **43**
Century Hotel, **35**
Dusit Thani, **30**
The Executive House, **16**
First House, **23**

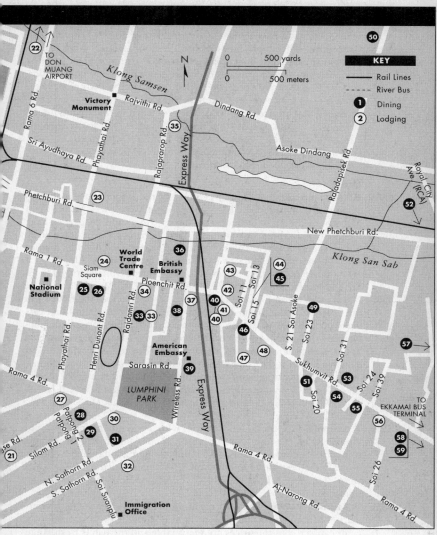

Grand China
Princess, **3**
Grand Hyatt
Erawan, **34**
Imperial Hotel, **37**
Landmark Hotel, **41**
La Residence, **18**
Manohra Hotel, **15**
Montien, **27**
Narai Hotel, **21**
New Trocadero, **14**

Oriental Hotel, **10**
Park Hotel, **42**
The Regent, **33**
River City Guest
House, **8**
Royal Orchid
Sheraton, **9**
Shangri-La Hotel, **11**
Sheraton Grande
Sukhumvit, **48**

Siam Inter-
Continental, **24**
Silom Plaza Hotel, **17**
Stable Lodge, **47**
Sukhothai, **32**
Tara Hotel, **56**
Tower Inn, **19**

ing Chinese variant of sukiyaki. ⊠ *In Siam Square Shopping Center facing 461 Henri Dunant Rd.,* ☎ *02/251–6337 or 02/251–3538. Another branch at* ⊠ *Suriwongse Rd.,* ☎ *02/236–0107. No credit cards.*

$ ★ ✕ **Prachak.** This simple, no-nonsense, tile-floor and bare-walls restaurant has superb roast duck (*ped*) and red pork (*moo daeng*). Families from wealthy neighborhoods send their maids here to bring back dinner, and by 6 PM there's often no duck or pork left. Nobody comes here for decor—it may even strike you as being a little grungy—but we've never had any stomach problems. The problem is in *finding* this "hole-in-the-wall": Look across from Bangrak Market (beside the Shangri-la hotel), diagonally across the road from a 7–11 store. ⊠ *1415 Charoen Krung (New Road), Silom Bansak,* ☎ *02/234–3755. Reservations not accepted. No credit cards.*

Thai

$$$$ ✕ **Lemongrass.** Elegance and a certain adventurousness have made this restaurant a favorite with Thais and resident Westerners. Embellished with Southeast Asian antiques, the dining rooms and the garden have plenty of atmosphere. Two southern Thai specialties are the notoriously hot fish curry, *kaeng tai plaa,* and the *kai yaang paak phanan,* a wonderfully seasoned dish that's like barbecued chicken. Be sure to try a glass of *nam takrai,* the cold, sweet drink brewed from lemongrass. ⊠ *5/1 Sukhumvit Soi 24,* ☎ *02/258–8637. AE, DC, MC, V.*

$$$$ ✕ **Sala Rim Naam.** At this elegant *sala* (room), across the river from the Oriental Hotel, some dishes are so beautifully presented that eating them feels like vandalism. Try some of the hot-and-sour salads, particularly the shrimp version called *yam koong.* Make reservations for 7:30 PM, and plan on staying afterward for the excellently staged Thai dancing. Lunch at the Sala Rim's excellent buffet is always less crowded, and during the hot season, special and rarely found light Thai recipes called *Khon Chere* are offered. ⊠ *Use free boat from Oriental Hotel,* ☎ *02/437–6211. Reservations essential weekends and Oct.–late-Feb. AE, DC, MC, V.*

$$$$ ✕ **Salathip.** Built as a Thai pavilion, with a veranda facing the Chao Phraya River, the restaurant provides an ambience that guarantees a romantic evening—reserve a table outside. On Sunday night, there's possibly the best buffet in Bangkok. ⊠ *Shangri-La Hotel, 89 Soi Wat Suan Phu, New Rd.,* ☎ *02/236–7777. Reservations essential for veranda. No lunch. AE, DC, MC, V.*

$$$$ ✕ **Seafood Market.** This vast restaurant still feels like the fish supermarket it used to be. Fluorescent lighting gives it the ambience of a giant canteen, but the prices are reasonable and the fish is fresh. Take a cart and choose from an array of vegetables and seafood—crabs, prawns, lobster, clams, oysters, flat fish, snapperlike fish, crayfish, and more. A waiter takes your selections away and cooks them any way you like.⊠ *388 Sukhumvit Rd., 02/258–0218. Reservations not accepted. AE, DC, MC, V.*

$$$ ✕ **Tumnak Thai.** This was once the biggest restaurant in the world (a claim is now made by the Golden Dragon, also in Bangkok). It seats 3,000, and a few waiters still zip around on roller skates. The bizarre *plaa buek,* a type of firm-fleshed, white, slightly sweet catfish (also cited in the *Guinness Book* as the world's biggest freshwater fish), is used in several dishes, including a tasty *tom yam* salad. Also worth trying is the sweet-fleshed *plaa yeesok* fish. Fame has pushed the prices up and made the service brusque, so come for fun, not a romantic dinner. ⊠ *131 Rajadapisek Rd.,* ☎ *02/274–6420. Reservations not accepted. AE, DC, MC, V.*

$$–$$$ ✕ **Ban Chiang.** The decor here is turn-of-the-century Bangkok, the painted walls adorned with prints, photographs, and a pendulum

clock. The extensive menu can be quite spicy: for example, the roast-duck curry and the shrimp-and-vegetable herb soup. The fried fish cakes and the grilled prawns are milder as is the chicken marinated in co-conut milk, then baked in pandanus leaves. ⊠ *14 Srivieng Rd.,* ☎ *02/236–7045. MC, V.*

$$–$$$ ✕ **Ban Khun Phor.** If you're in the area of Siam Square, try this popu-lar bistro diagonally across from the Novotel. The wooden tables mix with European Victoriana and Thai artifacts. The menu is varied, with such standard favorites as *tom khaa gai* (lemongrass coconut soup with chicken), roast duck with red curry, and even spicy stir-fried boar's meat. The best dish is the spicy crab soup. ⊠ *458/7–9, Soi 8, Siam Sq.,* ☎ *02/250–1733. Reservations not accepted. MC, V.*

$$–$$$ ✕ **Cabbages & Condoms.** Don't be disconcerted by this restaurant's name or by the array of contraceptive devices for sale: C&C is a fund-raiser for Thailand's birth-control program, the Population & Com-munity Development Association. The Thai food here is excellently prepared, with such dishes as chicken wrapped in a pandanus leaf, crisp fried fish with chili sauce, and shrimp in a mild curry sauce. There's a simply decorated dining room and a pleasant garden—one of the few places in Bangkok to sit outside without noise and air pollution. ⊠ *10 Sukhumvit Soi 12,* ☎ *no phone. AE, DC, MC, V.*

$$–$$$ ✕ **My Choice.** Middle-class Thais with a taste for their grandmothers' traditional recipes flock to this restaurant. The *ped aob,* a thick soup made from beef stock, is particularly popular, but foreigners may pre-fer the *tom khaa tala,* a hot-and-sour dish with shrimp, served with rice. The interior is plain, with Formica tables; it's better outside, where a few trees and vine-covered trellises shield you from a parking lot. ⊠ *Soi 36 Sukhumvit,* ☎ *02/258–6174. Reservations not accepted. AE, DC, MC, V.*

$$–$$$ ✕ **Old Dragon.** According to most counts, more than 150 bars and restau-rants straggle along Royal City Avenue (RCA). All look the same ex-cept for the Old Dragon, or Old Leng, a resurrected 100-year-old storehouse full of oddities out of the past—from wooden cinema seats to etchings of Chinese characters on old mirrors. Vorapoj Praponphan, the owner, says that except for the music machines, the cash register, and most of the guests, nothing in the place is younger than 50 years. Food is a mix of Chinese and Thai (snacks are also available). ⊠ *29/78–81 Royal City Ave.,* ☎ *02/203–0972. Open 6 PM–2 AM. MC, V.*

$$–$$$ ✕ **River City Bar B-Q.** As you're seated on the roof of the River City Shopping Centre, the waiter brings a burner and hot plate, and a mound of different meats and vegetables. You use your chopsticks to grill the food. Order some appetizers to nibble on while dinner is cooking—the northern Thai sausage is excellent. Request a table at the edge of the roof for a romantic view of the Chao Phrao River. ⊠ *5th Floor, River City Shopping Centre,* ☎ *02/237–0077, ext. 240. MC, V.*

$$–$$$ ✕ **Sanuknuk.** Named for one of the oldest surviving works of Thai lit-★ erature, Sanuknuk was originally conceived as a drinking place for the city's intellectual community. Its unique menu includes forgotten dishes that were resurrected by the owner and his wife through interviews with old women in up-country areas, and the eclectic decor features won-derful original work by the owner and many other prominent artists. Go with a Thai friend if you can, as the menu—a series of cards in a tape cassette box—is written in Thai. The many types of *nam phrik* (hot sauce) dishes and the soups like *tom khaa gai* (chicken with co-conut milk, lemongrass, and lime juice) are especially good. ⊠ *411/6 Sukhumvit Soi 55 (Soi Thong Law) at mouth of Sub-soi 23,* ☎ *02/390–0166 or 392–2865. Reservations essential on weekends. DC, MC, V. Closed at lunch and 3rd and 4th Sun. of the month.*

$$–$$$ ✕ **Spice Market.** Here is Thai home cooking as it was when domestic
★ help was cheap. The decor re-creates a once-familiar sight—the interior of a well-stocked spice shop, lined with sacks of garlic, dried
chilies, and heavy earthenware fish-sauce jars. The curries are superb,
and there is a comprehensive selection of old-fashioned Thai sweets.
From mid-January to the end of March, try the *nam doc mai* (Thai
mango) with sticky rice and coconut milk; knowledgeable foreigners
arrange trips to Bangkok at this time of year just for this dessert. ✉
Regent of Bangkok Hotel, 155 Rajadamri Rd., ☎ *02/251–6127.*
Reservations essential. AE, DC, MC, V.

$$–$$$ ✕ **Ton Po.** This is open-air riverside dining without tourist trappings;
★ the wide, covered veranda is right beside the Chao Phraya. Try the *tom
khlong plaa salid bai makhaam awn,* a delectable, very hot and sour
soup made from a local dried fish, chili, lime juice, lemongrass, young
tamarind leaves, mushrooms, and a full frontal assault of other herbal
seasonings. Equally good are the *kai haw bai toei* (chicken wrapped
in fragrant pandanus leaves and grilled) and *haw moke plaa* (a type
of curried fish custard, thickened with coconut cream and steamed in
banana leaves). ✉ *Phra Atit Rd. No phone. Reservations not accepted.*
AE, DC, MC, V.

$ ✕ **The Atlanta.** It is not often that we recommend a coffee shop in a
budget hotel, but the Thai cooking here is surprisingly good and very
inexpensive—all thanks to the innkeeper, Charles Henn, a fanatic
about food. The menu, which explains the ingredients of each dish,
makes interesting reading. Don't pass up the *yom yam khun* soup here—
it's especially smooth. New vegetarian dishes are being added every
week to the menu, which, if Henn has his way, will soon be recognized
as the best in Bangkok. Classical jazz is played at dinner time, followed
by a video movie of some repute. ✉ *Sukhumvit 78 Soi 2, Bangkok
10110,* ☎ *02/252–1650 or 02/252–6069.*

$ ✕ **Banana Leaf.** This is not only the best restaurant of this shopping
complex, but it's worth making tracks for if you are in the vicinity of
upper Silom Road. The people lining up to get in aren't coming for
the decor—it's just bare, painted walls, but the harried staff gives
quick, friendly service, and there's delicious Thai food at low prices.
Try the baked crab with glass noodles, hen's fingers salad, spicy papaya salad, grilled black band fish, or grilled pork with a coconut milk
dip. ✉ *Basement level, Silom Complex, Silom Rd.,* ☎ *02/231–3124.*
No credit cards.

$ ✕ **Nai Sow.** We searched for the best *tom yum khung* (hot/sour soup
with prawns) and found it here, a Chinese-Thai restaurant next door
to Wat Plaplachai in Chinatown. The owner, who never divulges his
recipes to his chefs, makes the essential mixture—which includes the
fatty juices from the prawns—in secret. Other equally tasty dishes range
from curried Thai beef to a mix of sweet and sour mushrooms. For an
unusual—and delicious—dessert, finish with the fried taro. Forget
decor: round tables and chairs are about the only furnishings. ✉ *3/1 Maitri-
chit Rd.,* ☎ *02/222–1539. Reservations not accepted. MC, V.*

$ ✕ **Saw Ying Thai.** Although this place has been open for almost 60 years
and has an extremely devoted clientele, it's rare to find a tourist here.
The menus on the wall are in Thai only, and none of the staff speaks
English, so try to bring a Thai friend. Be sure to order the *kai toon,* a
chicken soup with bamboo sprouts; also memorable are *plaa du thawd
krawb phad phed,* crisp-fried catfish stir-fried with curry spices and
herbs, and *khai jio neua puu,* an omelet full of crabmeat. This restaurant would rate a star were it more accessible in language or location.
✉ *Corner of Bamrungmuang and Tanao Rds. No phone. Reservations
not accepted. No credit cards.*

$ ✕ **Soi Polo Fried Chicken.** Although its beat-up plastic tables, traffic
★ noise, and lack of air-conditioning make this small place look like a
sure thing for stomach trouble, it is a popular lunch spot. The reason:
world-class fried chicken, flavored with black pepper and plenty of
golden-brown, crisp-fried garlic. The chicken should be sampled with
sticky rice and perhaps a plate of the restaurant's excellent *som tam*
(hot-and-sour raw papaya salad), a hydrogen bomb of a hot coleslaw
from the northeast. Come a bit before noon, or landing a table will be
a problem. ✉ *Walk into Soi Polo from Wireless Rd. (the restaurant is
the last of the shops on your left as you enter the soi). No phone. Reservations not accepted. No credit cards. No dinner.*

$ ✕ **Thong Lee.** This small but attractive shop-house restaurant has an
air-conditioned upstairs dining area. Although prices are very low,
Thong Lee has a devoted upper-middle-class clientele. The menu is not
adventurous, but every dish has a distinct personality. Almost everyone orders the *muu phad kapi* (pork fried with shrimp paste); the *yam
hed sod* (hot-and-sour mushroom salad) is memorable but very spicy.
✉ *Sukhumvit Soi 20. No phone. Reservations not accepted. No credit
cards.*

Western

$$$$ ✕ **Le Normandie.** This legendary restaurant perched atop the Orien-
★ tal Hotel commands a panoramic view across the Chao Phraya River.
Michelin three-star chef Georges Blanc is the restaurant's permanent
consultant, and the most highly esteemed chefs in France are periodically persuaded to take over in the kitchen. These artists usually import ingredients from home, and at such times the restaurant's patrons
enjoy what is literally the finest French food in the world. Even when
no superstar chef is on the scene, the cuisine is unforgettable. ✉ *48
Oriental Ave.,* ☎ *02/234-8690. Reservations essential. Jacket and tie.
AE, DC, MC, V. No lunch Sun.*

$$$$ ✕ **Regent Grill.** This strikingly designed, high-fashion French restaurant, formerly Le Cristal, has been enlarged to encompass a terrace overlooking the landscaped grounds of the Regent of Bangkok Hotel, and
it is now putting more emphasis on grilled dishes. Excellent endive salads and lobster dishes, one with a subtle goose liver sauce, are regularly featured. ✉ *155 Rajadamri Rd.,* ☎ *02/251-6127. Reservations
essential. Jacket and tie. AE, DC, MC, V. Dinner weekends only.*

$$ ✕ **Pan Pan.** The two branches of this Italian food-and-ice-cream chain
are enormously popular. The long list of generous and delicious pasta
dishes includes linguine with a sauce of salmon, cream, and vodka that
is a taste of high-calorie heaven, and "Chicken Godfather," with a cream-
and-mushroom sauce. Save room for the ice cream, which is of the thick,
dense Italian type. The branch on Sukhumvit Road offers an antipasto
buffet and a large selection of extremely rich desserts. ✉ *6-6/1
Sukhumvit Rd., near Soi 33,* ☎ *02/258-9304 or 258-5071;* ✉ *45 Soi
Lang Suan, off Ploenchit Rd.,* ☎ *02/252-7104. AE, DC, MC, V.*

$ ✕ **Thai Room.** Not a molecule of decor has changed since this restau-
rant opened in 1966, when it was packed with GIs on R&R from Viet-
nam. It is not unusual to see a veteran of that war quietly reminiscing.
Around him, however, will be local residents and tourists in from the
tawdry riot of Patpong, enjoying a spot that stays open until midnight.
The Mexican food is a peculiar hybrid of Mexican and Thai cuisines,
but the result is not unpleasing. Some of the Italian items, like the egg-
plant parmigiana, are very good by any standard, and the Thai food
can be excellent. ✉ *30/37 Patpong 2 Rd. (between Silom and Suriwongse
Rds.),* ☎ *02/233-7920. Reservations not accepted. AE, DC, MC, V.*

Lodging

The past surge in tourism taxed Bangkok's hotels to the limit, but the situation has considerably improved in the last two years with the opening of new ones. Nevertheless, from November through March, you may find your first choice fully booked unless you have reserved in advance.

Bangkok hotel prices are still lower than in Singapore and Hong Kong and are not expensive by European standards. Rates at wonderful deluxe hotels are about $250 for a double. There are many hotels in the $80–$100 range, and these, too, have every modern creature comfort. For $50, you can find respectable lodgings in a hotel with an efficient staff. Rooms in small hotels with limited facilities are available for around $10, and, if you are willing to share a bathroom, guest houses are numerous.

The four main hotel districts are next to the Chao Phraya and along Silom and Suriwongse roads; around Siam Square; in the foreign-embassy neighborhood; and along Sukhumvit Road. Other areas, such as Khao San Road for inexpensive guest houses favored by backpackers, and across the river, where modern high-rise hotels are sprouting up, are not included in the following list. The latter are inconveniently located, and finding a room in Khao San, especially in the peak season, requires going from one guest house to another in search of a vacancy—which is best done around breakfast time, as departing guests check out.

$$$$ 🏨 **Dusit Thani.** This low-key 23-story hotel with distinctive, pyramid-★ style architecture is the flagship property of an expanding Thai hotel group. Rooms are stylishly furnished in pastels, and the higher floors have a panoramic view. The very special Thai Heritage suites are furnished in classical Thai tradition with handcrafted furniture, but the standard rooms are in need of refurbishing. An extensive shopping arcade, a Chinese restaurant, and an elegant Thai restaurant are at street level. The pool area, a central courtyard filled with trees, is a peaceful oasis amid Bangkok's frenzy. ✉ *Rama IV Rd., 10500,* ☎ *02/233–1130, 800/223–5652,* ℻ *02/236–0450; in NY* ☎ *212/593–2988. 525 rooms, including 15 suites. 7 restaurants, bar, coffee shop, in-room VCRs, pool, health club, shops, nightclub, business services, meeting rooms. AE, DC, MC, V.*

$$$$ 🏨 **Grand Hyatt Erawan.** The Grand Hyatt is built on the site of the old Erawan Hotel, next to the much-revered Erawan shrine. The typically Hyatt lobby is a stylish four-story atrium with a domed, stained-glass roof. Guest rooms are large. The wood floors are strewn with area rugs, and each room has original art. The three Regency floors offer concierges and other services. Restaurants abound. The Italian fare at Spasso is especially creative. The pool terrace is covered with ferns and plants, and a physical therapist manages the elaborate health club. ✉ *494 Rajdamri Road, 10330,* ☎ *02/254–1234,* ℻ *02/253–5856; U.S. reservations,* ☎ *800/233–1234. 389 rooms and suites. 3 restaurants, bar, pool, 2 tennis courts, health club, squash, business services, meeting rooms. AE, DC, MC, V.*

$$$$ 🏨 **Landmark Hotel.** Though it calls itself high-tech, the Landmark's generous use of teak in its reception areas creates an ambience suggestive of a grand European hotel. Guest rooms, unobtrusively elegant, are geared to the international business traveler, with good desks and TV/video screens that can tune in to information banks linked to the business center. Service is swift and attentive. The hotel's elegant Hibiscus restaurant has a view of the city to accompany European fare. ✉ *138 Sukhumvit Rd., 10110,* ☎ *02/254–0404,* ℻ *02/253–4259.*

395 rooms and 55 suites. 4 restaurants, coffee shop, snack bar, pool, sauna, health club, 2 squash courts, shops, business services, meeting rooms. AE, DC, MC, V.

$$$$ ★ **Oriental Hotel.** The Oriental has set the standard toward which all other Bangkok hotels strive. The location on the Chao Phraya is unrivaled. The original building, now the Garden Wing, has been refurbished, and the rooms there—and the main building's luxury suites—are the hotel's best. You can attend a Thai cooking school, seminars explaining Thai culture, or a smart spa across the river. Among its well-known restaurants are China House, Sala Rim Naam, and Le Normandie. In addition, the hotel has a riverside barbecue every night. The hotel, in conjunction with the Royal Orchid Sheraton, has a helicopter service ($200) to and from the airport and a bus-riverboat shuttle ($28) that's faster than a taxi in the daytime. ⌧ 48 Oriental Ave., 10500, ☎ 02/236–0400, ℻ 02/236–1937; reservations in the U.K. ☎ 71/537–2988, in the U.S. 800/223–6800. 398 rooms. 3 restaurants, 2 tennis courts, health club, jogging, 2 squash courts, nightclub, business services. AE, DC, MC, V.

$$$$ ★ **The Regent.** Long one of Bangkok's leading hotels, the Regent is in the embassy district, now the geographical center of the city. Palatial steps lead to a formal lobby decorated with Thai classical art. Off a delightful courtyard are shops and restaurants, including the popular Spice Market. In 1996 a $15 million refurbishment enlarged many guest rooms and gave each a separate shower. They are decorated in timeless good taste, with Thai silk upholstery. Our favorite rooms overlook the racetrack, though some prefer the four "cabana rooms," whose private patios look onto a small garden with a lotus pond. Be sure to have the Regent's fragrant-oil massage. ⌧ 155 Rajdamri Rd., 10330, ☎ 02/251–6127, ℻ 02/253–9195. 363 rooms. 3 restaurants, pool, massage, health club, shops, business services. AE, DC, MC, V.

$$$$ **Royal Orchid Sheraton.** This 28-story palace rivals its neighbors, the Oriental and the Shangri-La, in riverfront luxury. All rooms face the river and are well appointed—the namesake flowers are everywhere. The restaurants are almost too numerous to mention, but the Thai one is memorable. You could equally well choose Japanese, Indian, or Italian cuisine. A glassed-in bridge leads to the River City Shopping Center next door, or try the beautiful free-form pool or the lushly landscaped pool next door at the Portuguese embassy. ⌧ 2 Captain Bush La., 10500, ☎ 02/234–5599 or 02/237–0022, ℻ 02/236–8320. 771 rooms. 9 restaurants and bars, wading pool, 2 tennis courts, health club, boat landing, shops, business services, meeting rooms, helipad. AE, DC, MC, V.

$$$$ ★ **Shangri-La Hotel.** The Shangri-La was one best hotels in Bangkok, but it's looking a little tired these days. The smiles seem permanently fixed, and the fairly large guest rooms, decorated in pastels, are showing signs of age. The staff is nevertheless professional and efficient, and the spacious marble lobby is a relief from the congestion of Bangkok. The lobby lounge offers a marvelous panorama of the Chao Phraya River. In the opulent Krungthep Wing, a separate tower across the gardens primarily designed for business people, all guest rooms have balconies looking over the river. The hotel now has helicopter service to the airport as well as the bus-riverboat shuttle ($28). ⌧ 89 Soi Wat Suan Phu, New Rd., 10500, ☎ 02/236–7777, ℻ 02/236–8579. 808 rooms and 60 suites. 16 restaurants and bars, shops, 2 pools, 2 tennis courts, health club, squash, business services. AE, DC, MC, V.

$$$$ **Sheraton Grande Sukhumvit.** Bangkok's newest, smartest, most spankingly gleaming hotel is the Sheraton Grande Sukhumvit, which opened in late 1996 and soars 33 floors above the business/shopping/embassy area. You'll never go hungry here: Riva's serves Californian cooking; the Orchid Café provides an international buffet; and the health club and swimming pool are laid out in an Oriental garden, which is also the setting for the Thai restaurant. The light-flooded guest rooms, on the upper floors, are a far cry from typical boxlike hotel rooms; each has a spacious bathroom angled off the bedroom, and the entrance hall and walk-in wardrobe have interesting diagonals. ⊠ *250 Sukhumvit Rd., 10110,* ☎ *02/653–0334,* ﬁ︎ *02/653–0400. 445 rooms 4 restaurants, pool, health club, business services. AE, DC, MC, V.*

$$$$ ⛻ **Sukhothai.** On 6 landscaped acres off Sakthorn Road (a high-traffic area with no tourist attractions), this 1991 hotel attempts to recapture the glory of Thailand's first kingdom in its architecture and ambience, but does not quite succeed. It does, however, offer quiet; the clutter and chaos of Bangkok seem a world away from its numerous courtyards. Public areas have stern pillars, sharp right angles, and prim little tables laid for tea. Standard rooms are spacious but not exceptionally well furnished, and the price is $250. The one-bedroom suites ($375) have splendid oversize, teak-floor bathrooms. Most of the guest rooms face one of the pond-filled courtyards. ⊠ *13/3 South Sathorn Rd., 10120,* ☎ *02/287–0222,* ﬁ︎ *02/287–4980. 212 rooms, including 76 suites. 2 restaurants, pool, health club, sauna, massage, tennis court, squash. AE, DC, MC, V.*

$$$ ⛻ **Amari Airport Hotel.** Connected to the terminal by an airbridge, this property is the only one within walking distance of the airport. The hotel is modern and utilitarian, with a helpful staff. Professional travelers will appreciate the 24-hour business center, and there's a free shuttle bus to town. Rooms are functional and efficient. The daytime (8 AM–6 PM) rate for travelers waiting for connections is B600 for stays up to three hours, and video screens in the public rooms display the schedules of flight arrivals and departures. ⊠ *333 Chert Wudhakas Rd., Don Muang, 10210,* ☎ *02/566–1020,* ﬁ︎ *02/566–1941. 440 rooms. 3 restaurants, coffee shop, room service, pool, exercise room, nightclub, laundry service, business services, meeting rooms. AE, DC, MC, V.*

$$$ ⛻ **Ambassador Hotel.** This hotel, with three wings of guest rooms, a complex of restaurants, and a shopping center, is virtually a minicity, which perhaps explains the impersonal service and limited helpfulness of the staff. Guest rooms are compact, decorated with standard pastel hotel furnishings. There is plenty to keep you busy at night: the Dickens Pub garden bar, the Flamingo Disco, and The Club for rock music. ⊠ *171 Sukhumvit Rd., Soi 11–13, 10110,* ☎ *02/254–0444,* ﬁ︎ *02/253–4123. 1,050 rooms, including 24 suites. 12 restaurants, coffee shop, snack bar, pool, massage, 2 tennis courts, health club, business services, meeting rooms. AE, DC, MC, V.*

$$$ ⛻ **Imperial Hotel.** After its major renovation in 1989, the Imperial be-
★ came the smartest hotel in this price category, but it is now under new management and changes are to be expected. The lobby's grand, high ceiling is magnificent, and the staff is friendly and eager to please. The bedrooms' pale cream walls are accented by bright, often red, bedspreads and draperies. It's on 6 acres in the embassy district, separated from the road by expansive lawns; inner gardens surround the pool and arcades. ⊠ *Wireless Rd., 10330,* ☎ *02/254–0023,* ﬁ︎ *02/253–3190. 400 rooms. 4 restaurants, pool, sauna, tennis court, putting green, health club, squash, pool, shops. AE, DC, MC, V.*

$$$ ⛻ **Montien.** This hotel across the street from Patpong, convenient to the corporations along Silom Road, has been remarkably well maintained over its two decades. The guest rooms are reasonably spacious, though not decoratively inspired. They do, however, have private safes. Prices are slightly higher than you would expect, but the hotel will give discounts. It's also the only hotel with in-house fortune-tellers who will read your palm or your stars for B250. ⊠ *54 Suriwongse Rd., 10500,* ☎ FAX *02/234–8060. 500 rooms. 2 restaurants, coffee shop, pool, nightclub, business services, meeting rooms. AE, DC, MC, V.*

$$$ 🏨 **Narai Hotel.** Conveniently located on Silom Road near the business, shopping, and entertainment areas, this friendly, modern hotel offers comfortable, utilitarian rooms, many decorated with warm, rose-color furnishings. At the low end of this price category, the hotel is a good value, given its cheerful rooms and high level of service. The most distinguishing feature is Bangkok's only revolving restaurant, La Rotonde Grill, on the 15th floor. ⊠ *222 Silom Rd., 10500,* ☎ *02/257–0100,* FAX *02/236–7161. 500 rooms, including 10 suites. 3 restaurants, coffee shop, pool, health club, nightclub, business services. AE, DC, MC, V.*

$$$ 🏨 **Siam Inter-Continental.** In the center of Bangkok on 26 landscaped acres, the Siam Inter-Continental has a soaring pagoda roof. Its modern Thai architecture, lofty lobby, and feeling of space make this hotel stand out. Each of the air-conditioned rooms is stylishly decorated with teak furniture, a trim, upholstered wing chair, and love seat. Especially attractive are the teak-paneled bathrooms with radios, telephones, and hair dryers. ⊠ *967 Rama I Rd., 10330,* ☎ *02/253–0355,* FAX *02/253–2275. 411 rooms and suites. 4 restaurants, 2 bars, pool, driving range, putting green, health club, jogging track, meeting rooms. AE, DC, MC, V.*

$$ 🏨 **Bel-Air Princess.** Two hundred yards down Soi 5 from bustling Sukhumvit is this quiet, well-managed hotel. It gets its fair share of tour groups, but for the most part the lobby and lounge area are cool and peaceful, and the downstairs restaurant is a good place to relax over a light meal. The spacious, carpeted guest rooms, with two queen-size beds or a king, are large enough for a round table and chairs. Personal safes, in-house movies, hair dryers, and tea/coffeemakers are pluses, and the bowl of fruit on each landing is a nice touch. Choose a room at the back of the hotel overlooking Soi 7 and beyond for the most light and a sprawling view. ⊠ *16 Sukhumvit Rd., Soi 5, 10110,* ☎ *02/253–4300,* FAX *02/255–8850. 160 rooms. 2 restaurants, pool, bar, health club. AE, DC, MC, V.*

$$ 🏨 **Century Hotel.** This location in the northern part of downtown is convenient to the airport. The rooms, though neat and clean, are small and dark. The coffee shop/bar is open 24 hours, a plus for travelers with early morning flights. ⊠ *9 Rajaprarop Rd., 10400,* ☎ *02/246–7800. 240 rooms. Bar, coffee shop, pool. AE, DC, MC, V.*

$$ 🏨 **Grand China Princess.** One good reason for staying in Chinatown is that it's the center of old Bangkok, with lots of exotic turn-of-the-century Asian ambience. Another reason is this hotel, which opened in October 1993. It occupies the top two-thirds of a 25-story tower with panoramic views. The furnishings are unexciting but functional, and all the rooms have safes and satellite television. Bathrooms are on the small side. Service is wonderfully friendly, and the reception floor (10th) has a welcoming bar, lounge, and coffee shop. ⊠ *215 Corner of Yaowaraj and Ratchawongse Rd., Samphantawongse, 10100,* ☎ *02/224–9977,* FAX *02/224–7999. 155 rooms. Restaurant, coffee shop, health club, business services. AE, DC, MC, V.*

$$ 🏨 **La Residence.** You would expect to find this small town-house hotel on the Left Bank of Paris, not in Bangkok. Though it's a little overpriced, La Residence suits the frequent visitor to Bangkok who wants a low-key hotel. The staff members, however, can be abrupt at times. The guest rooms are small, but the furnishings—pale wood cabinets, pastel draperies—give them a fresh, airy feel. The restaurant also serves as a sitting area for guests. ⊠ *173/8–9 Suriwongse Rd., 10150,* ☎ *02/233–3301. 23 rooms. Restaurant, laundry service. AE, DC.*

$$ ⊞ **Manohra Hotel.** An expansive marble lobby characterizes the pristine efficiency of this hotel between the river and Patpong. The Manohra is attractive and well run, with a helpful, friendly staff. Rooms have pastel walls, rich patterned bed covers, and dark-green carpets. There is a roof garden for sunbathing. A word of caution: If the Manohra is fully booked, the staff may suggest its sister hotel, the Ramada (no relation to the American-managed Ramada), which is overpriced and has small, poorly designed rooms.✉ *412 Suriwongse Rd., 10500,* ☎ *02/234–5070,* FAX *02/237–7662. 230 rooms. 2 restaurants, coffee shop, indoor pool, nightclub, meeting rooms. AE, DC, MC, V.*

$$ ⊞ **Park Hotel.** The lobby area, lounge, and bar are far from being designer decorated, but there is adequate room for checking in and comfortable seating. And there is a small pool in the garden. Ample light makes the guest rooms cheerful, and bathrooms are small and clean. The deluxe doubles have space for a desk. ✉ *Sukhumvit Soi 7, Sukhumvit Rd., 10110,* ☎ *02/255–4300,* FAX *02/255–4309. 139 rooms. Restaurant, coffee shop, bar, pool, travel services. MC, V.*

$$ ⊞ **Silom Plaza Hotel.** This hotel in the shopping area on Silom Road has an open lobby area with a lounge. The compact rooms have modern decor in soft colors; the more expensive ones have river views. The hotel caters to business travelers who want to be close to Silom Road. Service is quick. The facilities are limited, but all the entertainment you could wish for is nearby. ✉ *320 Silom Rd., 10500,* ☎ *02/236–0333,* FAX *02/236–7562. 209 rooms. Restaurant, coffee shop, indoor pool, sauna, health club, meeting rooms. AE, DC, MC, V.*

$$ ⊞ **Tara Hotel.** Built in 1989, the Tara is in the developing restaurant-
★ and-nightlife section of Sukhumvit Road. Guests register in a check-in lounge, where tea or coffee are served while the formalities are completed. The lobby is spacious, lined with teakwood carving. Guest rooms, which are on the small side, are decorated with pastels; many overlook the eighth-floor terrace garden with swimming pool. ✉ *Sukumvit Soi 26, 10110,* ☎ *02/259–0053,* FAX *02/259–2900. 200 rooms and 20 suites. Restaurant, coffee shop, pool, meeting room. AE, DC, MC, V.*

$$ ⊞ **Tower Inn.** For a reasonably priced, centrally located room, consider the Tower Inn, a tall skinny building near the Thai Airways office. The top floor has a health club and swimming pool, from which you can glimpse the Chao Phraya River. The rooms are spacious, with plenty of light. The furnishings are ordinary and utilitarian—two queen-size beds and a TV cabinet that serves as a desk. The bathroom is smallish—not one to linger in. You can usually negotiate a 30% discount, which brings the room rate down to B1,335 ($53). ✉ *533 Silom Rd., 10500,* ☎ *02/237–8300,* FAX *02/237–8286. 150 rooms. Restaurant, pool, health club, travel services. AE, DC, MC, V.*

$ ⊞ **Executive House.** The rooms are spacious for the price, the air-conditioning works, and, even if the decor is drab and a bit run-down, the rooms on the upper floors have plenty of light. The lack of tourist services makes this hotel more suited for visitors already familiar with Bangkok, although the reception staff will sometimes help with travel questions. The hotel is next to the Manohra Hotel, down a short driveway. ✉ *410/3–4 Suriwongse Rd., 10500,* ☎ *02/235–1206,* FAX *02/236–1482. 120 rooms. Coffee shop. MC, V.*

$ ⊞ **First House.** Tucked behind the Pratunam market on a soi off Phetchburi, the First House offers excellent value for a full-service hotel in this price range. The small lobby/sitting area serves as a meeting place where guests can read the complimentary newspapers. The compact rooms are carpeted and amply furnished but dark. Bathrooms are clean, though patches of rough plaster and drab fixtures don't encourage leisurely grooming. But the reasonable rates, the security, and the helpfulness of the staff make this hotel worth noting. ✉ *14/20–29 Petchburi Soi 19, Pratunam, 10400,* ☎ *02/254–0303. 84 rooms. Coffee shop, travel services. AE, DC, MC, V.*

$ 🏨 **New Trocadero.** This hotel, between Patpong and the Chao Phraya River, has been a Westerner's standby for six decades. Its smallish rooms, recently refurbished, have queen-size-plus beds and clean bathrooms. Service is friendly, and there's a helpful travel/tour desk in the lobby. The New Trocadero is associated with two adjacent, very similar hotels, the Peninsula and the Fuji. ✉ *343 Suriwongse Rd., 10500,* ☎ *02/234–8920,* FAX *02/236–5526. 130 rooms. Coffee shop, pool, travel services. AE, DC, MC, V.*

$ 🏨 **Stable Lodge.** Down a small, partly residential street off Sukhumvit Road, this small hotel seems more like a guest house. Since the new owners acquired the property (formerly Mermaid's), prices have climbed to around B1,000, but it is quiet and rooms are clean and neat, with queen-size beds. The more expensive rooms have private balconies. A pool in the garden is an added attraction. The coffee shop serves Thai and Western food all day. ✉ *39 Sukhumvit Soi 8, 10110,* ☎ *02/253–3410,* FAX *02/253–5125. 40 rooms, most with private baths. Restaurant, pool. AE, MC, V.*

¢ 🏨 **The Atlanta.** For decades the Atlanta has been an oasis for the ed-
★ ucated traveler—and one of the best values in town. Now Charles Henn, a part-time professor, caters to visiting academics and scholars, mature frugal travelers who come for more than Bangkok's cheap whiskey and ribald nightlife. The dining room and lobby lounge are straight out the 1950s, with leatherette banquettes and a circular sofa; it's often used for fashion shoots. The accommodations are simple and without TV, but clean and very spacious for the rock-bottom rates. (Half the rooms were repainted in 1996.) Some rooms have air-conditioning, some have fans and ventilators, and some have balconies; most have personal safes. Ask for a room on the quiet side. The hotel's big plus is the dining room (☞ Dining, *above*), where classical music is heard before 5 PM and jazz thereafter. ✉ *Sukhumvit 78 Soi 2, 10110,* ☎ *02/252–1650 or 02/252–6069,* FAX *02/656–8123 or 02/255–2151. 59 rooms. Restaurant, pool, travel services. No credit cards.*

¢ 🏨 **River City Guest House.** It's a shame this small hotel, a block from the water's edge, has no view of the river. But then if it had, the price of a room would probably quadruple. As it is, B600 gives you a modest air-conditioned room with a double bed and a table and chair. The small bathrooms have showers with hot and cold water, with exposed plumbing for decoration! The trick is to find the hotel. Walk up river from the Sheraton, past the River City Shopping Plaza and as the soi bends to the right, the hotel is on the right. This location gives you easy access to the marvelous sois of Chinatown and the river ferries, and puts you within walking distance of Suriwongse and Silom roads. ✉ *11/4 Soi Rong Nam Khang 1, New Rd. 24, 10100,* ☎ *02/235–1429,* FAX *02/237–3127. MC, V.*

Nightlife and the Arts

The English-language newspapers, the *Bangkok Post* and *The Nation,* have good information on current festivals, exhibitions, and nightlife. TAT's weekly *Where* also lists events.

Nightlife
A recent law requires that bars and nightclubs close at 2 AM, but Bangkok never sleeps, and many restaurants and street stalls stay open for late night carousing. Unfortunately, tourism has propagated the most lurid forms of nightlife geared to the male tourist. Live sex shows, though

officially banned, are still found in Patpong and other areas. Expect to be ripped off if you indulge.

CABARET

Most of the nightlife will be found on three infamous side streets that link Suriwongse and Silom roads. **Patpong I and II** are packed with go-go bars. The obscene club acts are generally found one flight up. Patpong III caters to homosexuals. A quieter version of Patpong is **Soi Cowboy,** off Sukhumvit Road at Soi 22, where bars have more of a publike atmosphere. The largest troupe of performing transvestites is reputed to be on stage at the **Calypso Garden** (✉ 688 Sukhumvit Rd., between Soi 24 and 26, ☎ 02/258–8987) with nightly shows at 8:15 and 10. For less ribald entertainment with live bands and internationally known nightclub artists, try the **Tiara** penthouse restaurant at the Dusit Thani Hotel.

BARS

Just beyond Soi Cowboy, in the curving side streets (Soi 23 to Soi 31) off Sukhumvit, are several small, pleasant bars, often with a small live band playing jazz or country music. At **Rang Phah** (✉ 16 Sukhumvit 23 Soi, ☎ 02/258–4321), you can sit in the garden and drink, eat a little, and gaze at the stars. **September** (✉ 120/1 Sukhumvit 23, ☎ 02/258–5785) is designed in a Victorian Thai style with a heavy teak bar. The friendly and cozy **Drunken Duck Pub** (✉ 59/4 Soi 31, Sukhumvit Road, ☎ 02/258–4500) has a three-piece band playing popular jazz. A country-and-western band plays at **Trail Dust** (✉ 43/2 Sukhumvit 31, ☎ 02/258–4590), a large tavern with a patio garden.

Friendly pubs and cafés, popular with yuppie Thais and expats, can be found along Sarasin Road (north of Lumphini Park). **Brown Sugar** (✉ 231/20 Soi Sarasin, ☎ 02/250–0103) has a clutter of small rooms humming with animated conversation. Those who want Western food and live music will always gravitate to the **Hard Rock Cafe** (✉ Siam Sq., ☎ 02/251–0792). An oasis in Patpong is the British-style **Bobbies Arms** (✉ Car Park Blvd., Second Level, Patpong 2 Rd., ☎ 02/233–6828), where you can get a decent pint of beer (chilled) and pub grub.

Only in Bangkok would you ever find a phenomenon like **Royal City Avenue.** By about 11 PM this strip is thronged with thousands of young Thais walking up and down. Enticing them are some 160 bars, which have rows of tables extending deep onto the avenue and often a dance floor inside. No one bar appears different from the others, except the Old Dragon (☞ Dining, *above*).

DISCOS

Most of the large hotels have their own disco/nightclubs. One of the best known is **Juliana's of London** at the Hilton. **Diana's** at the Oriental is said to be Bangkok's most extravagant club. If you're looking for the hot disco and pub center, head for **Silom Plaza** (✉ 320/14 Silom Rd., nearly opposite Patpong ☎ 02/234–2657), where discos and bars thumping out loud stereo music line the courtyard, and you can drink and eat at outdoor tables.

DINNER CRUISES

These two-hour evening cruises on the Chao Phraya River are strictly for tourists. Boats like the **Wan Foh** (☎ 02/433–5453)—built to look like a traditional Thai house—start at the Mae-Nam Building near the Shangri-La Hotel. A Western/Thai dinner is served. The difference between one ship and another is marginal. Your hotel staff will make reservations. Cost: B550 per person.

CULTURAL SHOWS

Silom Village (⊠ 286 Silom Rd., ☏ 02/234–4448, open 10 AM–10 PM) may perhaps be rather touristy, but it appeals also to Thais. The block-size complex has shops, restaurants, and performances of classical Thai dance. The best cultural show is at **Ruan Thep** (☏ 02/234–4581). Dinner starts at 7 and showtime is at 8:20. Dinner and a show costs B350; show only, B200.

The Arts

CLASSICAL THAI DANCE

Thai classical dance is the epitome of grace. Themes for the dance drama are taken from the *Ramayana* (*Ramakien* in Thailand). A series of con-trolled gestures uses eye contact, ankle and neck movements, and hands and fingers to convey the stories' drama. It is accompanied by a woodwind called the *piphat,* which sounds like an oboe, and per-cussion instruments. The two forms of Thai dance drama are the *khon* and the *lakhon.* In khon, the dancers (originally all men) wear fero-cious masks, and in the lakhon, both male and female roles are played by women.

In 1994, dance drama received a shot in the arm, with support from private industry and the donation by King Rama VII of the **Chalermkrung Royal Theatre** (66 New Rd., ☏ 02/222–0434). A troupe of 170 dancers now performs the Khon Masked Dance, with stunning light effects and high-tech sophistication. English translations are printed in the pro-grams and on screens above the stage. Performances are held Tuesday and Thursday at 8 PM; your hotel can make seat reservations.

Various restaurants offer a classical dance show with dinner. **Baan Thai** (⊠ Soi 22, Sukhumvit Rd., ☏ 02/258–5403) is a popular one for those staying at hotels in the eastern part of Bangkok. The **Sala Rim Naam** (⊠ Oriental Hotel, 489 Charoen Nakom Rd., ☏ 02/437–6211) puts on a good show and their buffet is excellent. At the **National Theatre** (⊠ Na Phra That Rd., ☏ 02/221–5861 or 02/224–1342), performances are given most days at 10 AM and 3 PM.

Outdoor Activities and Sports

Participant Sports

GOLF

There are good golf courses in and around Bangkok, and although week-end play requires advance booking, tee times are usually available during the week. Greens fees are approximately B500 weekdays and B1,000 on weekends. **Krungthep Sports Golf Course** (⊠ 522 Gp 10 Hua-mark, ☏ 02/374–0491), is attractively laid out with fairways flanked by bougainvillea and pine trees, and elevated greens surrounded by sand traps. The **Navatanee Golf Course** (⊠ 22 Mul Sukhaphiban 2 Rd., Bangkapi, ☏ 02/374–6127), designed by Robert Trent Jones, is thought to be the most challenging. The **Rose Garden Golf Course** (⊠ 4/8 Soi 3 Sukhumvit, ☏ 02/253–0295) is a pleasant, undemanding course.

MASSAGES

Thailand is known for its different schools of massage; the one you re-ceive in Had Yai is likely to differ from that of Chiang Mai or Bangkok. Even in Bangkok, they differ. The massage (B150) given at the famous **Wat Po school** is the best bargain and an experience not to be missed. A very gentle massage in very genteel surroundings may be had at the new **Health and Beauty Center** (☏ 02/236–0400) in the Oriental Hotel. Here in wood-paneled sophistication you can get facials, hydrotherapy, mud and seaweed wraps, and herbal treatments. A most relaxing mas-sage, with oils, is available at the **Regent Hotel** (☏ 02/251–6127).

Spectator Sports

HORSE RACING

Horse racing is a popular pastime in Bangkok. The **Royal Bangkok Sports Club** (02/251–0181) and the **Royal Turf Club** (02/280–0020), hold races on alternating Sundays.

THAI BOXING

The national sport of Thailand draws an enthusiastic crowd in Bangkok, where the bouts are the real thing. Understanding the rules is close to impossible; it's fast and furious, and the playing of traditional music heightens the drama. Though you will be out of your element, try to catch a match or two at one of the two main stadiums. **Lumphini** (⊠ Rama IV Rd., ☎ 02/251–4303) hosts bouts Tuesday and Friday–Sunday. **Ratchadamnoen** (⊠ Ratchadamnoen Nok Rd., near TAT office, ☎ 02/281–4205) has matches Monday, Wednesday, and Thursday. Bouts begin at 6 PM, or Sunday at 1 PM; tickets (B100–B500) may be bought at the gates.

Shopping

Browsing through the markets is fascinating, even if you're not in a buying mood. Everything (some say everyone) is for sale—from fake Rolex watches for US$8 to Paris originals costing thousands. And aside from the wonderfully cheap mass-produced knockoffs of international brands, you'll find good-quality merchandise and crafts made in Thailand: jewelry, silks, silverware, leather, and Oriental antiques are just some examples.

Shopping Districts

The main shopping areas are along Silom Road and at the Rama IV end of Suriwongse for jewelry, crafts, and silk; along Sukhumvit Road for leather goods; along Yaowarat in Chinatown for gold; and along Silom Road, Oriental Lane, and Charoen Krung Road for antiques. The Oriental Plaza and the River City Shopping Centre next to the Sheraton Orchid Hotel have shops with collector-quality goods; the shops around Siam Square and at the new World Trade Centre attract middle-income Thais and foreigners. Peninsula Plaza, across from the Regent Hotel, has very upmarket shops, and the newest and glitziest complex is Thaniya Plaza, between Silom and Suriwongse roads, near Patpong. If you're knowledgeable about fabric and cut, you can find bargains at the textile merchants and tailors who compete along Pahurat Road in Chinatown and Pratunam off Phetchburi Road.

Street Markets

Bangkok's largest market, where you can buy virtually anything, is the **Weekend Market.** If you want cheap chinaware or a tough pair of boots, come here. Sometimes you'll find great fashion buys. Even if you don't buy, a visit will open your eyes to exotic foods, flowers, and Thai life. ⊠ *Chatuchak Park, Paholyothin Rd. opposite Northern Bus Terminal,* ☽ *Weekends 9–9.*

Bargain lovers should sift through the merchandise at **Pratunam Market** (⊠ Corner of Phetchburi and Rajaprarop roads, near the Indra Regent Hotel). Hundreds of stalls and shops jam the sidewalk daily; the stacks of merchandise consist mainly of inexpensive clothing—jeans for $5 and shirts for $4.

A lively market for goods that are cheap, but inflated for the tourist, is in **Patpong I.** You'll see locals buying here too, between five and eight o'clock every evening, before the area's sex clubs get going. Between Yaowarat and Charoen Krung (New Road) in Chinatown lies the so-called **Thieves Market** (Nakorn Kasem), an area of small streets with old wood houses, where you can buy all sorts of items, from hardware to porcelains. **Soi Sampeng,** parallel to Yaowarat Road, has toys, household goods, and clothes. **Pahurat Cloth Market** (off Yaowarat Road)is known for its bargain textiles, batiks, and buttons. **Ta Phra Chan,** near Wat Phra Keo, where the Weekend Market was held before it moved, still has booths selling antiques and assorted goods. More antiques (both old and new) are found on **Ta Chang Road,** where there's also jewelry made by Thailand's northern hill tribes.

Specialty Stores

ART AND ANTIQUES

Suriwongse Road, Charoen Krung Road, and the Oriental Plaza (across from the Oriental Hotel) have many art and antiques shops. Good quality artifacts are found in the shops at the **River City Shopping Centre,** next to the Royal Orchid Sheraton Hotel. **Peng Seng** (⌧ 942 Rama IV, ☎ 02/234–1285, at the intersection of Suriwongse Rd.) is one of the most respected dealers in antiquities in Bangkok. The price may be high, but the article is likely to be genuine.

CLOTHING AND FABRICS

Thai silk gained its world reputation only after World War II, when technical innovations were introduced. Two other fabrics are worth noting: *mudmee* (tie-dyed) silk, produced in the northeast, and Thai cotton, which is soft, durable, and easier on the wallet than silk.

The Jim Thompson Thai Silk Company (⌧ 9 Suriwongse Rd., ☎ 02/234–4900) has become *the* place for silk by the yard and for ready-made clothes. There is no bargaining and the prices are high, but the staff is knowledgeable and helpful. A branch store has opened in the Oriental Hotel's shopping arcade. **Choisy** (⌧ 9/25 Suriwongse, 02/233–7794) is run by a French woman who offers Parisian-style ready-to-wear dresses in Thai silk. **Design Thai** (⌧ 304 Silom Rd., ☎ 02/235–1553) has a large selection of silk items in all price ranges (you can usually manage a 20% discount here.)

For factory-made clothing, visit the **Indra Garment Export Centre** (⌧ Rajaprarop Road, behind the Indra Regent Hotel), where hundreds of shops sell discounted items, from shirts to dresses.

The custom-made suit in 48 hours is a Bangkok specialty, but the suit often looks like a rush job. If you want an excellent cut, give the tailor more time. The best in Bangkok is **Marco Tailor** (⌧ 430/33 Siam Sq., Soi 7, ☎ 02/252–0689), where, for approximately B10,000, your suit will equal those made on Savile Row.

JEWELRY

The **Narayana-Phand** government store (⌧ 295/2 Rajaprarop, Payatai, ☎ 02/245–3293) has a selection of handcrafted jewelry; but prices are not negotiable. **Polin** (⌧ 860 Rama IV Rd., ☎ 02/234–8176), close to the Montien Hotel, has jewelry of interesting design. The **A. A. Company** (⌧ Siam Centre, ☎ 02/251–7283), across from the Hotel Siam Inter-Continental, will custom-make jewelry if you have three days to wait or are returning to Bangkok.

A long-established jewelry firm is **Johny's Gems** (⌧ 199 Faeng Nakorn Rd., ☎ 02/224–4065). If you telephone, they'll send a car to pick you up.

LEATHER

Leather is a good buy in Bangkok, with possibly the lowest prices in the world, especially for custom work. Crocodile leather is popular, but be sure to obtain a certificate that the skins came from a domestically raised reptile; otherwise U.S. Customs may confiscate the goods.

For shoes, try **River Booters** (⊠ River City Shopping Centre, ☎ 02/235–2966).

If you don't want to wait to buy silverware or items in niello or bronze in Chiang Mai, **Anan Bronze** (⊠ 157/11 Phetchburi Rd., ☎ 02/215–7739) should have something to take your fancy. **S. Samran** (⊠ 302/8 Phetchburi Rd., ☎ 02/215–8849) has a good selection at fair prices.

Bangkok A to Z

Arriving and Departing

BY BUS

Bangkok has three main bus terminals. **Northern/Northeast Bus Terminal** (⊠ Phaholyothin Rd., ☎ 02/272–0296 or 02/279–6222), often referred to as Morsit, serves Chiang Mai and the north. **Southern Bus Terminal** (⊠ Pinklao-Nakomchaisri Rd., Talingchan, ☎ 02/435–1199), on the Thonburi side of the river, is for Hua Hin, Ko Samui, Phuket, and points south. **Eastern Bus Terminal** (⊠ Sukhumvit Rd., Soi 40, Ekkamai, ☎ 02/391–2504 or 02/392–2391), usually referred to as Ekkamai, is for Pattaya and points southeast, to Rayong and Trat province.

BY PLANE

Bangkok's new **Don Muang Airport international terminal,** adjacent to what is now the domestic terminal, has a TAT desk (☎ 02/523–8972) with brochures and maps. Both terminals have luggage-checking facilities (☎ 02/535–1250). There is a tax of B250 for international departures and B30 for domestic departures.

Thai Airways International (⊠ 485 Silom Road ☎ 02/234–3100) is the national airline, and most of its flights come in and out of Don Muang. **Northwest Airlines** (⊠ 153 Rajdamri Rd., Peninsula Shopping Plaza, 4th Floor, ☎ 02/254–0789) is the major U.S. carrier.

A word of caution. The airport has more than its share of hustlers out to make a quick baht, who often wear uniforms and tags that make them seem official.

Between the Airport and Town

By Bus: New in 1996, an airport bus service that costs B70 runs approximately every 30 minutes between Don Muang and three sectors of downtown Bangkok. A detailed listing of each route is available from the airport TAT office and at the bus stop outside the arrivals hall.

By Helicopter: The quickest way downtown is the helicopter that lands at the Shangri-La Hotel. Anyone who will pay the $200 fare is welcome aboard.

By Minibus: Thai Airways has a minibus service between the airport and major hotels. They depart when they are full. Cost: B100.

By Riverboat Shuttle: A bus-and-boat service leaves every 30 minutes, 6 AM–9 PM. It's really for the benefit of guests at the Oriental, Royal Orchid Sheraton, and Shangri-La hotels, but others can use it if there's space. Fare is $28 (B700); overall time is under an hour.

By Taxi: Don Muang is 25 km (15 mi) from the city center. Be prepared for a 90-minute journey by taxi, though there are times when it can take less than 40 minutes. Obtain a reservation and prepay the fare at the counter (at either terminal), and a driver will lead you to the taxi. Count on paying at least B300–B350 from the international terminal and B250 from the domestic. Taxis to the airport from downtown

Bangkok are approximately B130. Use a metered taxi and agree to pay for the toll road, an extra B50.

By Train: The Bangkok Airport Express trains make the 35-minute run every 90 minutes from 8 AM to 7 PM. Check the schedule at the tourist booth in the arrival hall. Fare: B100. You can also take the regular trains from 5:30 AM to 9 PM. The fare is B5 for a local train, B13 for an express.

BY TRAIN

Hualamphong Railway Station (✉ Rama IV Rd., ☎ 02/223–0341), the city's main station, serves most long-distance trains. **Bangkok Noi** (✉ Arun Amarin Rd., ☎ 02/411–3102) on the Thonburi side of the Chao Phraya River, is used by local trains to Hua Hin and Kanchanaburi.

Getting Around

In late 1997 two routes of the new Skyway train should be operating: one going up Silom, along Rajdamri and on to northern downtown; the other going along Sukhumvit and Rama I Road to the Democracy Monument. This will be Bangkok's first attempt at rapid inner city transport and may speed up some travel, but meanwhile the horrendous traffic is made even worse by the ongoing construction.

BY BOAT

Water taxis and ferries ("river buses") ply the Chao Phraya River. The taxis are long-tailed boats that you can hire for about B300 an hour. Ferry fare is based on zones, but B5 will cover most trips. You'll also have to pay a B1 jetty fee. The jetty adjacent to the Oriental Hotel is a useful stop. In about 10 minutes and half a dozen stops, you can get to the Grand Palace, or to the other side of Krungthon Bridge in about 15 minutes. It is often the quickest way to travel north–south.

BY BUS

Though buses can be very crowded, they are convenient and inexpensive. For a fare of only B3.50 (any distance) on the ordinary non-air-conditioned buses and B6 to B16 on the less frequent air-conditioned ones, you can go virtually anywhere in the city. A new addition is Micro Buses, which are smaller, air-conditioned, do not permit standing passengers, and charge B30 for any distance. Buses operate from 5 AM to around 11 PM. The routes are confusing, but you can pick up a route map at most book stalls for B35.

BY SAMLOR

These unmetered three-wheeled polluters, also called tuk-tuks, are slightly cheaper than taxis and are best used for short trips in congested traffic. But the drivers are tough negotiators, and unless you are good at bargaining you may well end up paying more than for a metered taxi.

BY TAXI

Since 1993, meters have been installed in most Bangkok taxis. The tariff for the first 2 km (1.2 mi) is set at B35 and then increases a baht for about every 50 meters. If the speed drops to under 6 kph, there is a surcharge of one baht per minute. A typical journey of about 5 km (3 mi) runs about B60. (At press time taxi drivers were demonstrating for B50 for the first 2 km).

Contacts and Resources

EMBASSIES

Australia (✉ 37 Sathorn Tai Rd., ☎ 02/287–2680). **United Kingdom** (✉ 1031 Wireless Rd., ☎ 02/253–0191). **United States** (✉ 95 Wireless Rd., ☎ 02/252–5040).

The **Immigration Division** (✉ Soi Suan Sathorn Tai Rd., ☎ 02/286–9176) is the place to go for a Thai visa extension.

EMERGENCIES

General emergencies, ☎ 1699. **Ambulance,** ☎ 02/246–0199. **Fire,** ☎ 199. **Police,** ☎ 191.

You're advised to contact the **Tourist Police** (✉ Unico House, Ploenchit Soi Lang Suan, ☎ 02/221–6209) rather than the local police. There are tourist police mobile units at critical tourist areas, such as at Patpong in the evening.

ENGLISH-LANGUAGE BOOKSTORES

The English-language dailies, the *Bangkok Post* and *The Nation*, are available at newsstands.

Asia Books (✉ 221 Sukhumvit Rd., Soi 15, ☎ 02/252–7277; ✉ Peninsula Plaza, adjacent to Regent Hotel, ☎ 02/253–9786) has a wide selection of books and magazines. **Duang Kamol Bookshop** (main branch, ✉ 244–6 Siam Sq., ☎ 02/251–6335), known as DK Books, has stores in most neighborhoods.

GUIDED TOURS

Numerous tours cover Bangkok and its environs. With slight variation, they cover the following itineraries. **Floating Market Tour:** This half-day tour is a boat ride on the Chao Phraya and into the *klongs* (small canals), to the former site of a lively floating market. **Grand Palace and Emerald Buddha Tour:** Because you can easily reach the palace by yourself and hire a guide on the spot, you may want to visit these sights independently. **City and Temples Tour:** In half a day, you can visit some of Bangkok's most famous temples: Wat Po with the reclining Buddha; Wat Benjamabopit, famous for its marble structure; and Wat Traimitr, with the five-ton golden Buddha. This tour does not include the Grand Palace. **Thai Dinner and Classical Dance:** This evening tour includes a buffet-style Thai dinner with a show of classical dancing. You can manage it just as well on your own.

HOSPITALS

Chulalongkorn Hospital (✉ Rama I Rd., ☎ 02/252–8181), **Police Hospital** (✉ Rajdamri Rd., ☎ 02/252–8111).

TRAVEL AGENCIES

Bangkok used to be the world's leading center for discounted airline tickets. The prices are not as competitive as they used to be, but agencies still offer some good prices, usually on lesser-known airlines. Be sure to read the restrictions on the ticket carefully before you part with any money. It's safer to buy open tickets than those naming a specific flight and time. Large, established agencies include: **Diethelm** (✉ 544 Phoenchit Rd., ☎ 02/252–4041) and **World Travel Service** (✉ 1053 New Charoen Krung Rd., ☎ 02/233–5900).

VISITOR INFORMATION

The **Tourist Authority of Thailand** (TAT; ✉ 372 Bamrung Muang Rd., Pom Prap, 10100, ☎ 02/226–0060) tends to have more in the way of colorful brochures than hard information, but it can supply useful material on national parks and various routes to out-of-the-way destinations. The office is extremely inconvenient; it's not far from the Golden Mount, next to the Metropolitan Water Tower—where the traffic comes close to gridlock. There is also a TAT branch at the international terminal at Don Muang Airport (☎ 02/523–8973) open 8 AM–midnight.

SIDE TRIPS WEST OF BANGKOK

Around Nakhon Pathom the country has been settled for millennia—
the city was founded before the time of Christ. Kanchanaburi Province,
farther west, is so full of lush tropical beauty that you may want to go
hiking and thoroughly explore its gorges and waterfalls, or even take
an overnight rafting trip.

Nakhon Pathom

56 km (34 mi) west of Bangkok.

Nakhon Pathom is reputed to be Thailand's oldest city, dating from
150 BC. Its main attraction is **Phra Pathom Chedi,** the tallest Buddhist
monument in the world—at 417 feet, it stands a few feet higher than
the Shwe Dagon Chedi of Burma. The first *chedi* (Thai pagoda where
holy relics are kept) on this site was erected in the 6th century; the large
chedi you see today, built in 1860, encases the ruins of the original.

In the outer courtyard are four *viharn* (halls) facing in different directions and containing images of Lord Buddha in various postures. The
eastern viharn depicts Buddha beneath a bo tree; the western viharn
shows him in a reclining position (symbolizing his imminent death),
surrounded by his disciples; in the southern viharn, Buddha is being
protected by a Naga; and in the northern one he is standing. The terraces around the temple complex are full of fascinating statuary, including a Dvaravati-style Buddha seated in a chair, and the museum
contains some interesting Dvaravati (6th–11th century) sculpture. ✆
Museum: Wed.–Sun. 9–noon and 1–4.

Sanan Chan Palace, just west of Phra Pathom Chedi, was built during
the reign of King Rama IV. The palace is closed to the public, but the
surrounding park is a lovely place to relax in cooling shade.

Kanchanaburi

140 km (87 mi) west of Bangkok.

The movie *The Bridge Over the River Kwai,* adapted from Pierre
Boulle's novel, gave the area of Kanchanaburi a certain fame. Even if
this were not so, Kanchanaburi province would attract tourists. Lush
tropical vegetation and rivers with waterfalls and gorges make it one
of the most beautiful national parks in Thailand. The small, sleepy town
has little architectural merit, but its location, where the Kwai Noi and
Kwai Yai rivers meet to form the Mae Khlong River, is splendid. A reconstruction of the now famous bridge (it was successfully bombed by
the Allies toward the end of the war) stands just north; take Saeng Chuto
Road, the main street.

Between 1942 and 1945, more than 16,000 Allied prisoners of war
and 49,000 impressed Asian laborers died while being forced by the
Japanese, under abysmal conditions, to build a railway—the **Death Railway**—through the jungle from Thailand into Burma. One person died
for every railway tie on the track. At **Kanchanaburi War Cemetery,** with
row upon row of neatly laid-out graves, the 6,982 American, Australian,
British, and Dutch prisoners of war are remembered at a commemorative service every April 25.

Upriver is the **JEATH War Museum** (JEATH is an acronym for Japan,
England, America, Australia, Thailand, and Holland). Founded by a
monk from the adjoining temple, the museum consists of a reconstructed
bamboo hut—the type used to house the POWs—and a collection of
utensils, railway spikes, clothing, aerial photographs, newspaper clip-

pings, and illustrations designed to show the conditions the POWs lived under during the construction of the Death Railway. ☜ *Admission.* ⊙ *Daily 8–5.*

A quiet and sadly serene Allied burial ground, the **Chong-Kai War Cemetery,** lies across the river. To get there, take the ferry from the pier below the park off Patana Road. A 1-km (½-mi) walk inland from Chong-Kai is **Wat Thum Khao Pun,** one of the best cave temples in the area. A small temple stands outside and a guide entices you into the cave, where calm images of Buddha sit between the stalagmites and stalactites.

OFF THE BEATEN PATH

ERAWAN WATERFALL – If you want to visit some of the spectacular countryside of Kanchanaburi province, the Erawan Waterfall, perhaps the most photographed in Thailand, is worth the trip. It is in the beautifully forested Khao Salop National Park, 65 km (40 mi) northwest of Kanchanaburi, and is at its best in early autumn. You can take a tour bus from Kanchanaburi or the public bus (No. 8170), which leaves every hour for the 90-minute journey. It's a 1½-km (1-mi) walk or taxi ride to the foot of the falls. Allow two hours to climb up all seven levels of the falls, and wear tennis shoes or similar footwear. The rock at the top is shaped like an elephant; hence the name Erawan, which means elephant in Thai.

Dining and Lodging

$ ✕ **Pae Karn Floating Restaurant.** For authentic Thai food, try this little restaurant on a floating dock at the river's edge, just at the confluence of the Kwai Noi and Kwai Yai rivers. The food is better than the tourist restaurants around the bridge, but the decor amounts to no more than plain walls and a few tables. ✉ *Song Kwai Rd.,* ☎ *034/513–251. No credit cards.*

$ ✕ **River Kwai Floating Restaurant** The most attractive—and crowded— open-air restaurant is this one to the right of the bridge. Fish dishes, either cooked with Thai spices or lightly grilled, dominate the menu. The specialty is *yeesok,* a fish found in the Kwai Yai and Kwai Noi rivers. ✉ *River Kwai Bridge,* ☎ *034/512–595. No credit cards.*

$$$ ⊡ **Felix River Kwai Resort.** This luxury hotel, completed in 1992, has a tranquil setting along the river in sight of the bridge, within walking distance of most of Kanchanaburi's attractions. Polished wood floors and wicker headboards give a cool country airiness to the rooms. A large free-form pool amid the tropical plants sets the scene. ✉ *9/1 Moo 3, Tambon Thamakham, Kanchanaburi 71000,* ☎ *034/515–061,* FAX *034/515–095; Bangkok reservations* ☎ *02/255–3410. 150 rooms. Restaurant, pool, massage, health club. AE, DC, MC, V.*

$$ ⊡ **Kwai Yai Garden Resort.** This small resort 15 minutes by ferry from the Tha Kradan Pier, offers thatched bungalows, a few raft houses, a small restaurant, and a friendly staff. ✉ *125 Moo 2, Tambon Thamakham, Kanchanaburi 71000,* ☎ *034/513–611; Bangkok reservations: 02/513–5399. 12 rooms and 4 rafts. Restaurant, bar, travel services. MC, V.*

$$ ⊡ **River Kwai Hotel.** Across the bridge on the banks of the Kwai Yai, this hotel is a small complex of thatched bungalows, including some on rafts. The dining room and lounge, on one raft, offer a picturesque view of the bridge. ✉ *284/4–6 Saengchuto Rd., Kanchanaburi 71000,* ☎ *034/511–184,* FAX *034/511269. 77 rooms and 9 raft houses. Restaurant, travel services. MC, V.*

$$ ⊡ **River Kwai Village.** In the heart of the jungle in the River Kwai Valley, this resort village consists of log cabins and a few rooms on rafts. All non-raft rooms have air-conditioning and are simply furnished, with

teak and colored stones embedded in the walls. Eat at the casual restaurant on one of the anchored floating rafts. The resort will supply transportation from Bangkok. ✉ *72 Moo 4, Tambon Thasao, Amphoe Sai Yok, Kanchanaburi 71150,* ☎ *034/591055,* ⅲ *034/591054. 60 rooms and 7 raft houses. 2 restaurants, pool, meeting rooms, travel services. AE, DC, V.*

Outdoor Activities and Sports

RAFTING

Rafting trips on either the Kwai Yai or Mae Khlong rivers, which take at least a full day, let you experience the tropical jungle in a leisurely way. The rafts, which resemble houseboats, are often divided into sections for eating, sunbathing, and diving. For one-day rafting trips, the cost is approximately B300. Longer trips are also offered. Make advance reservations through the TAT office or a travel agent. If you book through a responsible travel agent, you may have to pay a bit more, but you'll also be more likely to get a raft in good condition and a skipper familiar with the currents.

Side Trips West of Bangkok A to Z

Arriving and Departing

By Bus: Air-conditioned and non-air-conditioned buses leave the Southern Bus Station (✉ Charan Sanitwong, ☎ 02/434–5557) frequently. The journey to Kanchanaburi takes about 2½ hours.

By Taxi: You can arrange to be picked up by a private car or taxi. Speak to your concierge, who will usually have a good resource. If you keep the car to visit both Nakhon Pathom and Kanchanaburi, the cost will be about B1,500.

By Train: Trains from the Bangkok Hualamphong and Bangkok Noi stations stop in Nakhon Pathom. The train for Kanchanaburi leaves Noi Station at 8 AM and 1:55 PM. The State Railway of Thailand also runs a special excursion train (B75 adults, B40 children) every Saturday, Sunday, and holidays; it leaves Hualamphong Station at 6:15 AM and returns at 7:30 PM, stopping at Nakhon Pathom, the River Kwai Bridge, and Nam-Tok, from which point minibuses take you to Khao Phang Waterfall. Buy your ticket in advance (☎ 02/223–3762).

Contacts and Resources

VISITOR INFORMATION

Kanchanaburi **Tourist Authority of Thailand** (TAT) (✉ Saeng Chuto Rd., Kanchanaburi, ☎ 034/511–200).

SIDE TRIPS TO THE GULF COAST

As the Bangkok metropolitan area becomes more and more congested, the Eastern Seaboard is growing rapidly, with most of the economic development around Chonburi and Rayong. The coast has been the attraction, chiefly the resort of Pattaya, with its water sports, fair grounds, and nightlife, but Pattaya has so exemplified the seedier aspects of tourism and so rapidly outpaced its infrastructure that many travelers continue into Chantaburi and Trat provinces as far as the Cambodian border. Not all the coastline is particularly attractive, and cultural sites are few and far between, but there are fishing villages along the way, a few decent beaches, delightful islands offshore, and provincial capitals inland for supplies.

In the 1920s the royal family built a palace at Hua Hin on the west shore of the Gulf of Thailand. The royal entourage would travel from Bangkok on special trains, and high society followed. Those were Hua

Hin's glory days. After World War II, Pattaya's star ascended, and Hua Hin became a quiet town once more, but Pattaya's seedy reputation has lately caused Thais and foreign visitors to reconsider Hua Hin and its near neighbor Cha' Am as desirable beach resorts close to the capital. In the last several years, the area has enjoyed a building boom.

Hua Hin and Cha' Am

189 km (118 mi) south of Bangkok.

This is a low-key destination, where nightlife is restricted mostly to the hotels. During the day, Hua Hin is a busy market town, but most tourists are at the beach. They come into town in the early evening to wander through the bazaars before dinner. There is no beachfront road to attract boisterous crowds, so stretches of beach remain deserted. They have gently sloping drop-offs, and the waters are usually calm. The only drawback is the occasional invasion of jellyfish—check for them before you plunge in.

On the east side of the highway at the northern boundary of Hua Hin stands the **royal summer palace,** where the king and queen spend the month of April and celebrate the anniversary of their royal wedding.

The highway to the southern provinces passes through the center of Hua Hin. In fact, it's the town's main street, with shops and cafés lining the sidewalk; a congested street of market stalls and buses runs parallel to it. The **Chatchai street market** is fun to walk through. Toward the southern end of town, across the tracks from the quaint wooden railway station lies the respected **Royal Railway Golf Course.** Nonmembers can play the par-72 course for B300–B500; you can rent clubs, and there's a coffee lounge for refreshments. Lining both sides of Damnernkasem Road, leading to the **public beach,** are shops for tourists and moderately priced hotels.

On your way to the beach, keep your eyes open for **Nab Chai Hat Lane,** just before the Sofitel, where Damnernkasem Road becomes closed to traffic. Several small restaurants here are excellent places to keep in mind for dinner. Most have their offerings displayed on slabs of ice. You choose the fish, negotiate a fair price, and then take a table and order any other dishes and drinks you want.

Dining and Lodging

$$$ ✕ Market Seafood Restaurant. The nautical decor sets the tone of the Royal Garden Resort's restaurant, which serves excellently prepared gulf seafood—clams, lobsters, mussels, sea-tiger prawns, and crabs. ⊠ *107/1 Phetkasem Rd.,* ☎ *032/511–881. AE, DC, MC, V.*

$$ ✕ Sang Thai. For interesting seafood dishes—from grilled prawns with bean noodles to fried grouper with chili and tamarind juice—this open-air restaurant down by Fisherman's Wharf has been consistently popular with Thais. Close your eyes to the ramshackle surroundings and floating debris in the water. Don't miss the *kang* (mantis prawns). ⊠ *Naresdamri Rd.,* ☎ *032/512–144. DC, MC, V.*

$$$$ 🏨 Royal Garden Resort. Adjacent to the Sofitel, this hotel has accommodations and service equal to those of its neighbor, but because it doesn't have the colonial ambience, the rates are a few hundred baht less. The hotel tends to draw a younger set, attracted by the nightclub and the proximity to the beach. Guest rooms are decorated with modern, unimaginative furniture. ⊠ *107/1 Phetkasem Rd., Hua Hin 77110,* ☎ *032/511–881;* FAX *032/512–422. Bangkok reservations,* ☎ *02/255–8822. 215 rooms. 2 restaurants, bar, coffee shop, pool, 4 tennis courts, snorkeling, boating, nightclub, playground. AE, DC, MC, V.*

$$$$ ☒ **Sofitel Hua Hin Resort.** Even if you don't stay here, the Old World
★ charm of this tastefully renovated hotel is worth a visit. Wide verandas fan out in an arc, following the lines of the wooden building, and
open onto gardens leading down to the beach. The gardens are splendidly maintained, with scores of different plants plus topiary figures
that look like shadows in the night. The lounges around the reception
area are open to the sea breezes, and the airiness revives memories of
Somerset Maugham. The best guest rooms are those on the second floor
with sea views. The units in an annex across the street are less attractive. ☒ *1 Damnernkasem Rd., Hua Hin 77110,* ☎ *032/512–021,* FAX
032/511–014; Bangkok reservations, ☎ *02/233–0974. 154 rooms. 2
restaurants, bar, coffee shop, pool, 4 tennis courts, snorkeling, boating, nightclub, meeting rooms. AE, DC, MC, V.*

$$$–$$$$ ☒ **Dusit Resort & Polo Club.** Although this resort opened in early 1991,
★ the polo grounds and riding stables have yet to be added. Even so, the
game establishes the tone—smart, exclusive, and luxurious. The spa-
cious lobby serves as a lounge for afternoon tea and evening cocktails,
drunk to the soft tunes of the house musicians. Beyond the ornamen-
tal lily pond out front is the swimming pool with bubbling fountains,
and beyond that is the beach. All the guest rooms have private bal-
conies and a pool or sea view. ☒ *1349 Petchkasem Rd., Cha' Am, Petch-
buri 76120,* ☎ *032/520–009,* FAX *032/520–296; Bangkok reservations,*
☎ *02/238–4790. 308 rooms and suites. 4 restaurants, 2 bars, in-
room safes, pool, wading pool, 2 tennis courts, exercise room, squash,
snorkeling, boating, parasailing, waterskiing, meeting rooms, shuttle
service to Hua Hin, car service to Bangkok. AE, DC, MC, V.*

$$$–$$$$ ☒ **Regent Cha' Am.** This modern beach resort has everything from water
sports to gourmet dining to shopping arcades. Some guest rooms are
in bungalows, a number of which face the beach, while others are housed
in one of two 12-story buildings set back from the beach. Gardens sep-
arate the bungalows, the main building, two large outdoor pools, and
two smaller outdoor pools. The hotel has its own car service from
Bangkok. ☒ *849/21 Cha' Am Beach, Petchburi,* ☎ *032/471–480,* FAX
032/471–492; Bangkok reservations, ☎ *02/251–0305,* FAX *02/253–
5143. 400 rooms. 3 restaurants, coffee shop, 4 pools, snorkeling,
boating, nightclub. AE, DC, MC, V.*

$$$ ☒ **Pran Buri Beach Resort.** This isolated holiday complex south of Hua
Hin offers a collection of small bungalow units along the shore. The
first row, facing the beach, is obviously the best. Though simply furnished, guest rooms have their own terraces and minibars, telephones,
and TV with in-house VCR. The main lodge contains the bar/lounge
and dining room, where Thai, Chinese, and Western food is served.
The atmosphere is laid-back, casual, and fun. ☒ *9 Parknampran
Beach, Prachuapkhirikhan 77220,* ☎ *032/621–701. Bangkok reservations:* ☎ *02/233–3871;* FAX *02/235–0049. 60 rooms. Restaurant, bar,
pool, 2 tennis courts, health club, sailing, snorkeling, meeting rooms.
AE, DC, MC, V.*

$–$$ ☒ **Hua Hin Raluek.** Centrally located on the main tourist street, this
hotel has bungalow cottages in its courtyard. Rooms have huge beds
and not much else, but the price is right. The terrace restaurant facing
the street stays open late and is a popular spot from which to watch
the parade of vacationers walking past. ☒ *16 Damnernkasem Rd., Hua
Hin 77110,* ☎ FAX *032/511–755. 61 rooms with bath. Restaurant/cof-
fee shop. MC, V.*

$–$$ ☒ **Thanan-Chai Hotel.** This hotel on the north side of Hua Hin sup-
plies the basic amenities of clean guest rooms, friendly service, and a
coffee lounge that serves breakfast and light fare all day. Its quiet location, friendly staff, and modest price are its assets, but you do have

to walk to the beach. ⊠ *11 Damrongraj Rd., Hua Hin 77110,* ☎ *032/511–940. 41 rooms. Coffee shop. MC, V.*

Pattaya

147 km (88 mi) southeast of Bangkok.

Pattaya is Thailand's total beach resort, offering everything from deep-sea fishing to golf, from windsurfing to elephant kraals. Overdevelopment, an unbridled sex trade, crowds, and water pollution have eroded its appeal, but now, after a few years in the doldrums, Pattaya is getting busier. The highway from Bangkok is congested; on weekends the two-hour trip often takes four. Raw sewage still flows into the once-crystal-clear bay, but the government and private enterprise have started a cleanup process. Perhaps by the year 2,000, the water may be safe once more for marine and human life.

Pattaya can be divided into three sections: The northernmost, Naklua Beach, attracts locals and has few tourist facilities. On a small promontory south of the Dusit Resort Hotel is the picturesque curving bay of Pattaya, along which runs Beach Road, lined with palm trees on the beach side and modern resort hotels on the other. At the southern end of the bay is the developed part of town—bars, nightclubs, restaurants, and open-front cafés dominate both Sunset Avenue (the extension of Beach Rd.) and the side streets.

☺ One worthwhile diversion in Pattaya is elephants. At the **Elephant Kraal,** 14 pachyderms display their skill at moving logs in a two-hour show, twice daily. There are also demonstrations by war elephants, an enactment of ceremonial rites, and the capture of a wild elephant. ⊠ *On main hwy., 5 km (3 mi) from Pattaya,* ☎ *038/428–640. Tickets and transport* ⊠ *1/11 Central Pattaya Rd.,* ☎ *038/422–958.* ▣ *Admission.* ☉ *Shows at 2:30 and 4:30.*

☺ **Nong Nuch Village** offers a folk show, an exhibition of monkeys picking coconuts, elephants bathing, and a small zoo and aviary. Despite its touristy nature, the village provides a pleasant break from sunbathing, particularly if you're traveling with children. Hotels can arrange transportation. ⊠ *15 km (9 mi) south of Pattaya, 163 km marker on Hwy. 1, Bang Saray,* ☎ *038/238–158.* ▣ *Admission.* ☉ *9–5:30 daily; folk show daily 10 AM and 3 PM.*

☺ Among the plenitude of commercial attractions, the **Bottle Museum** is special. Pieter Beg de Leif, a Dutchman, has devoted 14 hours a day for the last 15 years to creating more than 300 miniatures in bottles—tiny replicas of famous buildings and ships. ⊠ *79/15 Moo 9, Sukhumvit Rd.,* ☎ *038/422–957.* ▣ *Admission.* ☉ *Daily 10–9.*

Dining and Lodging

$$$ ✕ **Peppermill Restaurant.** Tucked away next to P.K. Villa, this distinctly French restaurant takes a classical approach to dining, with an emphasis on flambéed dishes. More creative dishes such as fresh crab in a white-wine sauce and poached fillet of sole with a lobster tail are also served. ⊠ *16 Beach Rd.,* ☎ *038/428–248. AE, DC, MC, V.* ☉ *Closed lunch.*

$$$ ✕ **San Domenico.** The Roman owner of this restaurant halfway between Pattaya and Jontien prides himself on pasta dishes, and you might want to try his filling pizzas, excited by Thai spices, or the buffet (B300). Be sure to have the Italian ice cream. ⊠ *Jontien Rd., S. Pattaya,* ☎ *038/426–871. MC, V.*

$$ ✕ **Angelo's.** For Italian food, this is a good choice. It's owned by a Milanese, who presides over the dining room, and his Thai wife, the

chef. Her fortes are lasagna and a wonderful fish casserole. ⊠ *N. Pattaya Rd.,* ☎ *038/429–093. MC, V.*

$$ ✕ **Nang Nual.** Next to the transvestite nightspot, Simon Cabaret, this restaurant is one of Pattaya's better places for seafood, cooked Thaistyle or simply grilled. A huge array of fish is laid out as you enter the restaurant. Point out what you want and say how you want it cooked. For carnivores, the huge steaks are an expensive treat. ⊠ *214–10 S. Pattaya Beach Rd.,* ☎ *038/428–478. AE, MC, V.*

$$ ✕ **Tak Nak Nam.** This floating restaurant in a Thai pavilion at the edge of a small lake has an extensive menu of Chinese and Thai dishes. Live classical Thai and folk music is played while you dine on such specialties as steamed crab in coconut milk or blackened chicken with Chinese herbs. ⊠ *252 Pattaya Central Rd., next to Pattaya Resort Hotel,* ☎ *038/429–059. MC, V.*

$ ✕ **Sportsman Inn.** If you want a respite from Thai food and some downhome English cooking, this is the best spot in Pattaya. The steak-and-kidney pie, bangers and chips, fish-and-chips, and such are well prepared. ⊠ *Soi Yod Sak (Soi 8),* ☎ *038/361–548.*

$$$$ ☶ **Royal Cliff Beach Hotel.** Pattaya's most lavish hotel, 1½ km (1 mi) south of town on a bluff jutting into the Gulf, is a self-contained resort with three wings. The 84 one-bedroom suites in the Royal Wing (double the price of standard rooms in the main building) have butler service, breakfast in the room at no charge, and reserved deck chairs. The Royal Cliff Terrace wing has two-bedroom and honeymoon suites with four-poster beds. The swimming pool sits on top of a cliff overlooking the sea. ⊠ *Jontien Beach, Pattaya, Chonburi,* ☎ *038/250–421,* 𝖥𝖠𝖷 *038/250–511; Bangkok reservations,* ☎ *02/282–0999. 700 rooms and 100 suites. 4 restaurants, 3 pools, sauna, miniature golf, 2 tennis courts, jogging, squash, 2 private beaches, windsurfing, boating, shops. AE, DC, MC, V.*

$$$ ☶ **Dusit Resort.** On a promontory at the northern end of Pattaya
★ Beach, this large hotel offers superb sea views. The beautifully laidout grounds include two pools that run around the promontory. Though the rooms are in need of some cheerful refurbishing, they have large bathrooms, balconies, oversize beds, and sitting areas. The Landmark Rooms are larger and have extensive wood trim. This retreat from the Pattaya tourists is only a B5 songthaew ride from all the action. ⊠ *240/2 Pattaya Beach Rd., Pattaya, Chonburi 20260,* ☎ *038/425–611,* 𝖥𝖠𝖷 *038/428–239; Bangkok reservations,* ☎ *02/236–0450. 500 rooms and 28 suites. 4 restaurants, 2 pools, massage, sauna, 3 tennis courts, billiards, health club, Ping-Pong, squash, windsurfing, boating, shops. AE, DC, MC, V.*

$$$ ☶ **Montien.** Though not plush, this hotel has a central location and design that take advantage of the sea breezes. With the hotel's generous off-season discounts, a room with a sea view can be one of the best values in town. The air-conditioned section of the Garden Restaurant has a dance floor and stage for entertainment. ⊠ *Pattaya Beach Rd., Pattaya, Chonburi 20260,* ☎ *038/428–155,* 𝖥𝖠𝖷 *038/423–155; Bangkok reservations,* ☎ *02/233–7060. 320 rooms. 2 restaurants, bar, coffee shop, snack bar, pool, 2 tennis courts, meeting rooms. AE, DC, MC, V.*

$ ☶ **Diamond Beach Hotel.** In the heart of Pattaya's nightlife section, this hotel is a bastion of sanity. Rooms are clean, and security guards make female guests feel safe. ⊠ *373/8 Pattaya Beach Rd., Pattaya, Chonburi 20260,* ☎ *038/428–071,* 𝖥𝖠𝖷 *038/424–888. 126 rooms. Restaurant, massage, travel services. No credit cards.*

$ ☶ **Nag's Head.** Owned by an Englishman, this small hotel offers clean, inexpensive, air-conditioned rooms with private baths. Its location on a busy road is not the best, but the friendly atmosphere makes this the top budget choice. ⊠ *179 Pattaya 2 Rd., Pattaya, Chonburi 20260,* ☏ *038/418–264. 15 rooms. Restaurant, bar. No credit cards.*

$ ▦ **Palm Lodge.** This no-frills hotel has the benefit of being central, quiet, and inexpensive. Guest rooms are sparsely furnished, without carpeting, bathrooms are basic, and the outdoor pool is small. The staff is reliable, however. ⊠ *Beach Rd., Pattaya, Chonburi 20260,* ☏ *038/428–780,* FAX *038/421–779. 80 rooms. Coffee shop, pool, laundry service. MC, V.*

Nightlife and the Arts

Entertainment in Pattaya revolves around the hundreds of bars, bar/cafés, discos, and nightclubs. Discos usually have a cover charge of B100, and drinks cost about B50. Of late, Pattaya has had a rash of AIDS cases and drug-related killings. Caution is advised. One popular night spot is the **Pattaya Palladium** (☏ 038/424–922), which bills itself as the largest disco in Southeast Asia. The **Marina Disco** in the Regent Marina Hotel (⊠ S. Pattaya Rd., 038/429–568) has a laser light show, live entertainment, and three DJs.

Outdoor Activities and Sports

GOLF

The Royal Thai Navy Course (⊠ Phiu Ta Luang Golf Course, Sattahip, Chonburi, ☏ 02/466–1180, ext. Sattahip 2217), 30 km (18 mi) from Pattaya, is Thailand's longest course (6,800 yds) and, with rolling hills and dense vegetation,is considered one of the country's most difficult. The **Siam Country Club** (⊠ Pattaya, Chonburi, ☏ 038/418–002), close to Pattaya, offers a challenging course with wide fairways, but awkward water traps and wooded hills. **Panya Resort Country Club** (⊠ Pattaya. ☏ 038/239–400) boasts three par-72 courses, where clubs can be rented and greens fees are B500 (B750 on weekends).

WATER SPORTS

All kinds of water sports are available, including windsurfing (B200 per hr), waterskiing (B1,000 per hr), and sailing on a 16-foot Hobie catamaran (B500 per hour). Private entrepreneurs offer these activities all along the beach, but the best area is around the **Sailing Club** on Beach Road. The water near shore is too polluted for diving and snorkeling.

Ko Chang and Mu Ko Chang National Park

1 hr by ferry from Laem Ngop, which is 15 km (9 mi) southwest of Trat; Trat is 400 km (250 mi) southeast of Bangkok.

Ko Chang is the largest and most developed of the 52 islands that comprise Mu Ko Chang National Park, many of them not much more than hummocks protruding from the sea. These islands are being discovered by Westerners and local tourists, and they have not yet been spoilt by the honky tonk commercialism found in Pattaya. That also means that their infrastructure is basic and accommodations rustic. Booking agents at travel agencies in Laem Ngob port, where you catch the ferry, can make reservations for you on the Ko Chang islands.

Ko Chang's best beaches are on the western shore. First comes **Haad Sai Khao** (White Sand Beach), with B100-a-night cots in huts crammed together along the narrow beach. Next in line is **Haad Khlong Phrao,** which has a long curving beach of pale golden sand. Accommodations here are more spaced out and tend to be larger and more expensive. Further down and at the end of the only road on the island is **Haad Kai Bae.** Here the beach, with both sand and pebbles, has a very gentle dropoff—safe for nonswimmers. Accommodations range from a few air-conditioned bungalows to small huts.

Ko Mak, one of the largest of the other islands, has a small village and a couple of basic resorts with bungalows. One of the most beautiful islands is tiny **Koh Wai,** (3 hrs by ferry from Laem Ngob), resplendent with idyllic beaches, tropical flora, and fantastic coral reefs. **Ko Kradat** is another small island with little development except for one bungalow resort. **Ko Kut,** the second largest of the Ko Chang group, is mountainous with lush tropical foliage.

Lodging

$$$ ⊞ **Ko Chang Resort.** This was one of the first comfortable resorts to be built on Ko Chang. It is a self-contained complex on the edge of the bay, with clean, rustic bungalows around a reception lounge and dining room. The rate for the air-conditioned units is fairly steep, and the small ones are very cramped. The advantage of the resort is that you can make the booking in Bangkok and it has its own boat service to the island. ⊠ *Ko Chang, Trat 23120,* ☎ *01/211–3834; Bangkok reservations,* ☎ *02/276–1233,* ℻ *02/276–6929. 45 rooms. Restaurant. MC, V.*

$–$$$ ⊞ **Sea View Resort.** Your option is either a small fan-cooled thatched bungalow just back from the sands of Kai Bae Beach or a larger air-conditioned unit with a private bath 100 yards inland on a slight rise. The resort is at the far end of the beach and therefor quieter than the others. Its pluses are an attractive terrace restaurant and a very gentle sloping sandy beach. ⊠ *Ko Chang, Trat 23120,* ☎ *01/321–0055; Bangkok reservations,* ☎ *02/276–1233,* ℻ *02/276–6929. 32 rooms. Restaurant. MC, V.*

¢–$$ ⊞ **Kae Bae Hut Bungalows.** Accommodations run the gamut from tiny
★ B50 bungalows back from the beach to much larger ones with air-conditioning and private baths facing the beach. Because it's near the center of Kae Bae Beach, guests can wander over to nearby restaurants for meals and entertainment. But, in fact, the food here is the best on the beach and the staff is the friendliest. ⊠ *Ko Chang, Trat 23120,* ☎ *01/329-0452. 25 rooms. Restaurant, dive shop. No credit cards.*

Side Trips to the Gulf Coast A to Z

Arriving and Departing

HUA HIN/CHA'AM

By Bus: Buses air-conditioned and non-air-conditioned, leave Bangkok's Southern Bus Terminal every half hour during the day for the three-hour trip.

By Car: A few hotels, such as the Regent and Dusit Thani, run minibuses between their Bangkok and Cha' Am/Hua Hin properties for a flat fee of B200. Nonguests may use these. Otherwise, you can hire a car and driver for approximately B1,750 or B2,500 to or from the Bangkok airport.

By Plane: Bangkok Airways (☎ 02/253–4014) serves Hua Hin from Bangkok with a daily 25-minute evening flight. Take a taxi from the airport, or ask your hotel to meet you.

By Train: The train from the Bangkok Noi station in Thonburi takes four long hours to reach Hua Hin's delightful wooden train station (⊠ Damnernkasem Rd., ☎ 032/511–073).

KO CHANG

Take a bus from Bangkok's Eastern Bus Terminal for the 5–6-hour trip to Trat, where you pick up a songthaew for the 20-minute run to Laem Ngob and the ferries for the various islands of the Ko Chang group.

By Bus: Buses depart every half hour from Bangkok's Eastern and Northern terminals. The fare is B66 per person. A bus runs between Don Muang Airport and Pattaya every two hours between 7 AM and 5 PM.

By Limousine/Bus: Direct buses make the three-hour drive between Pattaya's hotels and Bangkok's Don Muang Airport, every two or three hours from 6 AM to 9 PM.

By Minibus: Most hotels in Bangkok and Pattaya have a travel-agent desk that works directly with a minibus company. An Avis minibus that departs from Bangkok's Dusit Thani Hotel for its property in Pattaya is open to nonguests as well.

By Plane: Bangkok Airways (☎ 02/229–3456) runs twice-daily flights from Ko Samui, which land at U-Tapao Airport, 50 km (30 mi) east of Pattaya.

By Taxi: Taxis make the journey from either Don Muang Airport or downtown Bangkok for a quoted B2,500, quickly renegotiated to B1,800 or less. Coming back, the fare is about B1,000.

Getting Around

Sedans and Jeeps can be rented for B700–B900 a day, with unlimited mileage. **Avis** (✉ Dusit Resort Hotel, Pattaya, ☎ 038/429–901) offers insurance, though not all rental companies do. Motorbike rental costs about B250 a day.

Contacts and Resources

Local police in Hua Hin (☎ 032/511–027); Cha' Am (☎ 032/471–321). The **hospital** is in Hua Hin (✉ Phetkasem Rd., ☎ 032/511–743).

In Pattaya, for **police, fire department,** or an **ambulance,** dial 191. **Tourist Police** (✉ Pattaya 2 Rd., ☎ 038/429–371) or in emergencies ☎ 1699.

Hua Hin Tourist Information Center (✉ 114 Phetkasem Rd., near the railway station, ☎ 032/512–120. ◷ Daily 8:30–4:30). Pattaya **TAT** (✉ 382/1 Beach Rd., South Pattaya, ☎ 038/428–750. ◷ Daily 9–5).

SIDE TRIPS NORTH FROM BANGKOK

People visit these sites on excursions from Bangkok or on the way to Thailand's northern provinces. Try to get an early start for Ayutthaya in order to see as much as possible before 1 PM, when the heat becomes unbearable. Then take a long lunch and, if you have time, continue into the late afternoon and catch the sunset before you leave. Most people, though, find that a morning is sufficient. For a three-hour tour of the sights, tuk-tuks can be hired for approximately B450; a four-wheel bicycle cab for about B700. English-speaking guides can be hired around the station.

Ayutthaya

72 km (45 mi) north of Bangkok.

Ayutthaya became the kingdom's seat of power in 1350, and toward the end of the 16th century, Europeans described the city, with its 1,700 temples and 4,000 golden images of Buddha, as more striking than any capital in Europe. Certainly the Ayutthaya period was also Thailand's most glorious. In 1767, the Burmese conquered Ayutthaya and destroyed the temples with such vengeance that little remained standing. The city never recovered from the Burmese invasion, and today it is a small provincial town with partially restored ruins. The site is particularly striking at sunset, when the silhouetted ruins glow orange-brown and are imbued with a melancholy charm.

Ayutthaya lies within a large loop of the Chao Phraya River, where it meets the Pa Sak and Lopburi rivers. To completely encircle their capital by water, the Thais dug a canal along the northern perimeter, linking the Chao Phraya to the Lopburi. Although the new provincial town of Ayutthaya, including the railway station, is on the east bank of the Pa Sak, most of Ayutthaya's ancient temples and ruins are on the island. An exception is Wat Yai Chai Mongkol (a B20 tuk-tuk ride southeast of the railway station).

Wat Yai Chai Mongkol was built in 1357 by King U-Thong for meditation. The complex was totally restored in 1982; with the contemporary images of Buddha lining the courtyard and the neatly groomed grounds, it looks a little touristy. ⊠ *Admission.* ⊘ *Daily 8–5.*

The road continues to **Wat Phanan Choeng,** a small temple on the banks of the Lopburi. In 1324, one of the U-Thong kings, who had arranged to marry a daughter of the Chinese emperor, came to this spot on the river; instead of entering the city with his fiancée, he arranged an escort for her. But she, thinking that she had been deserted, threw herself into the river and drowned. The king tried to atone for his thoughtlessness by building the temple. ⊠ *Admission.* ⊘ *Daily 8–6.*

Returning to the main road, go left and cross over the bridge to the island. Continue on Rojana Road for about 1½ km (1 mi) to the **Chao Phraya National Museum.** Though Ayutthaya's best pieces are in Bangkok's National Museum, a guided visit here can highlight the evolution of Ayutthaya art over four centuries. ⊠ *Admission.* ⊘ *Wed.–Sun. 9–noon and 1–4.*

Just beyond the Chao Phraya National Museum, turn right onto Si Samphet Road. Pass the city hall on the left and continue for 1 km (½ mi) to **Wat Phra Si Samphet,** easily recognizable by the huge parking lot. Wat Phra Si Samphet was the largest wat in Ayutthaya and the temple of the royal family. Built in the 14th century, in 1767 it lost its 16-meter (50-foot) Buddha, Phra Sri Samphet, to the Burmese, who melted it down for its gold—374 pounds worth. The chedis, restored in 1956, survived and are the best examples of Ayutthaya architecture. Enshrining the ashes of Ayutthaya kings, they stand as eternal memories of a golden age. ⊘ *Daily 8–5.*

Naresuan Road crosses Si Samphet Road and continues past a small lake to nearby **Wat Phra Mahathat,** on the corner of Chee Kun Road. Built in 1384 by King Ramesuan, the monastery was destroyed by the Burmese. If you climb up what is left of the monastery's 42-meter (140-ft) *prang* (Khmer-style pagoda with an elliptical spire), you'll be able to envision just how grand the structure must have been. You can also admire the neighboring **Wat Raj Burana,** built by the seventh Ayutthaya king in memory of his brother.

For an educational overview of the 400 years of the Ayutthaya period, stop in at the new **Ayutthaya Historical Study Centre,** located near the Teacher's College and the U-Thong Inn. Models of the city as a royal capital, as a port city, as an administrative and international diplomatic center, and as a rural village depicting lifestyles in the countryside are displayed. ⊠ *Rotchana Rd.,* ☎ *035/245–124.* ⊠ *Admission.* ⊘ *Tues.–Sun. 9–4:30.*

Dining and Lodging

$$ ✕ **Pae Krung Kao.** If you want to dine outdoors on Thai food and watch the waters of the Pa Sak, this is the better of the two floating restaurants near the bridge. You can also come here for a leisurely beer. ⊠ *4 U-Thong Rd.,* ☎ *035/241–555. No credit cards.*

$$ ✕ **Tevaraj.** For good Thai food that does not spare the spices, head for this unpretentious restaurant behind Ayutthaya's railway station. The restaurant is short on decor, but the fish dishes and the *tom khaa* (soup made with coconut milk) are excellent. ⊠ *74 Wat Pa Kho Rd. No phone. No credit cards.*

$$ ▦ **Krungsri River Hotel.** For a long time the U-Thong Inn was the only reasonably smart hotel in Ayutthaya. The Krungsri is a welcome addition and it is conveniently close to the train station. The spacious marble-floored lobby is refreshingly cool after the outside heat, and the rooms, albeit not special in any way, are clean, fresh, and furnished with modern amenities. For atmosphere, choose a room overlooking the river. Because Ayutthaya has few overnight visitors, try to negotiate a discount from the published room rate. ⊠ *27/2 Rojana Rd., 13000,* ☎ *035/242996,* ℻ *035/242996. 200 rooms. Restaurant. MC, V.*

Bang Pa-In

20 km (12 mi) south of Ayutthaya.

A popular attraction outside Ayutthaya is the Bang Pa-In Summer Palace, within well-tended gardens in an architectural complex of striking variety.

Phra Thinang Warophat Phiman, nicknamed the Peking Palace, stands to the north of the Royal Ladies Landing Place in front of a stately pond. The replica of a palace of the Chinese imperial court, it was built from materials custom-made in China—a gift from Chinese Thais eager to win the favor of the king. It contains a collection of exquisite jade and Ming-period porcelain.

Take the cable car across the river to the unique wat south of the palace grounds. King Chulalongkorn built this Buddhist temple, **Wat Nivet Thamaprawat,** in Western Gothic style. Complete with a belfry and stained-glass windows, it looks as much like a Christian church as a wat. 🏛 *Admission to Bang Pa-In Palace Complex.* ☉ *8–3, closed Mon. and Fri.*

The **Bang Sai Folk Arts and Craft Centre** was set up by the queen in 1976 to train and employ families with handicraft skills. Workers at the center demonstrate the techniques and make and sell products that are sold throughout Thailand at the Chitrlada handicraft shops. The crafts on sale include fern-vine basketry, wood carvings, dyed silks, and handmade dolls. ⊠ *24 km (14½ mi) south of Bang Pa-In on the Chao Phraya River,* ☎ *035/366–6092.* 🏛 *Admission.* ☉ *Closed Wed.*

Lopburi

75 km (47 mi) north of Ayutthaya, 150 km (94 mi) north of Bangkok.

Lopburi is one of Thailand's oldest cities: the first evidence of its habitation dates from the 4th century. In 1664, King Narai made it his second capital—to escape the heat and humidity of Ayutthaya. He employed French architects to build his palace; consequently, Lopburi is a strange mixture of Khmer, Thai, and Western architecture.

Wat Phra Si Mahathat, built by the Khmers, is at the back of the railway station. It underwent so many restorations during the Sukhothai and Ayutthaya periods that it's difficult to discern the three original Khmer prangs—only the central one has survived intact. Several Sukhothai- and Ayutthaya-style chedis are also within the compound. ▦ *Admission.* ⊘ *8:30–4:30.*

Walk diagonally through Wat Phra Si Mahathat to **Narai Ratchaniwet Palace.** The preserved buildings, which took from 1665 to 1677 to complete, have been converted into museums. Surrounding the buildings are castellated walls and triumphant archways grand enough to admit an entourage mounted on elephants. The most elaborate structure is the **Dusit Mahaprasat Hall,** built by King Narai to receive foreign ambassadors. The roof is gone, but you'll be able to spot the mixture of architectural styles: The square doors are Thai and the dome-shaped arches are Western.

The next group of buildings in the palace compound—the **Chan Phaisan Pavilion** (1666), the **Phiman Monghut Pavilion** (mid-19th century), and the row of houses once used by ladies of the court—are now all museums. The ladies' residences now house the **Farmer's Museum,** which exhibits regional tools and artifacts seldom displayed in Thailand. ▦ *Admission.* ⊘ *Wed.–Sun. 9–noon and 1–4.*

North across the road from the palace (away from the station), you'll pass through the restored **Wat Sao Thong Thong.** Notice the windows of the viharn, which King Narai changed in imitation of Western architecture.

Beyond Wat Sao Thong Thong and across another small street is **Vichayen House,** built for Louis XIV's personal representative, De Chaumont. The house was later occupied by King Narai's infamous Greek minister, Constantine Phaulkon, whose political schemes eventually caused the ouster of all Westerners from Thailand. ▦ *Admission.* ⊘ *Wed.–Sun. 9–noon and 1–4.*

Walk east on the road between Wat Sao Thong Thong and Vichayen House to **Phra Prang Sam Yot,** a Khmer Hindu shrine and Lopburi's primary landmark. The three prangs symbolize the sacred triad of Brahma, Vishnu, and Siva. King Narai converted the shrine into a Buddhist temple, and a stucco image of the Lord Buddha sits serenely before the central prang once dedicated to Brahma.

About 250 yards down the street facing Phra Prang Sam Yot and across the railway tracks is the **San Phra Kan shrine.** The respected residents of the temple, Samae monkeys, often perform spontaneously for visitors. These interesting animals engage in the human custom of burying their dead.

Lodging

$$ 🏨 **Lopburi Inn.** This is the only hotel in Lopburi with air-conditioning and modern facilities. Even so, don't expect your room to have much more than a clean bed and a private bath. The dining room serves Thai and Chinese food, and the hotel has achieved a certain fame by having an annual dinner party for the town's resident monkeys. ✉ *28/9 Narai Maharat Rd.* ☎ *036/412–300,* FAX *036/411–917. 142 rooms. Restaurant, coffee shop. DC, V.*

Side Trips North of Bangkok A to Z

Arriving and Departing

AYUTTHAYA

By Boat: Though you can reach Ayutthaya by rail or road, the nicest way to get there (at least one-way) is by boat along the Chao Phraya River (☞ Guided Tours, *below*).

By Bus: Buses leave Bangkok's Northern Terminal on Phaholyothin Road (☎ 02/271–0101) every 30 minutes between 6 AM and 7 PM.

By Train: Between 4:30 AM and late evening, trains depart frequently from Bangkok's Hualamphong station, arriving in Ayutthaya 80 minutes later.

BANG PA-IN

By Boat: Boats make the 40-minute trip down the Chao Phraya from Ayutthaya; the fare is B150.

By Bus: Minibuses leave Chao Prom Market in Ayutthaya frequently, starting from 6:30 AM, for the 50-minute trip (B10).

By Train: Trains from Bangkok regularly make the 70-km (42-mi) run to Bang Pa-In railway station, from which a minibus runs to the palace.

LOPBURI

By Bus: Buses leave the Northern Terminal (✉ Phaholyothin Rd., ☎ 02/271–0101) for Lopburi every 30 minutes between 6 AM and 7 PM.

By Train: Three morning and two afternoon trains depart from Hualamphong station on the three-hour journey to Lopburi. The journey from Ayutthaya takes just over an hour. Trains back to Bangkok run in the early and late afternoon.

Getting Around

For a three-hour tour of Ayutthaya's sites, tuk-tuks can be hired within the city for about B400; a four-wheel samlor can be rented for about B650.

Contacts and Resources

EMERGENCIES

Ayutthaya Tourist Police (☎ 035/242–352).

GUIDED TOURS

Tours to Ayutthaya and Bang Pa-In take a full day. You may travel the 75 km (46 mi) both ways by coach or in one direction by cruise boat and the other by coach. The best combination is to take the morning coach to Ayutthaya for sightseeing before the day warms up, and return downriver. The most popular trip is aboard the **Oriental Queen**, managed by the Oriental Hotel (☎ 02/236–0400, ext. 3133). The **Ayutthaya Princess** (☎ 02/255–9200), a new boat whose exterior resembles a royal barge, offers the same itinerary for the same fare. It departs from both the Shangri-La and Royal Orchid Sheraton piers. To book either of these cruises, contact the respective hotels or any travel agent.

The **Chao Phraya Express Boat Co.** (✉ 2/58 Aroon-Amarin Rd., Maharat Pier, Bangkok, ☎ 02/222–5330) runs a popular Sunday excursion to the Bang Pa-In Summer Palace. The boat departs from Bangkok's Maharat Pier at 8:30 AM and reaches Bang Pa-In in time for lunch. On the downriver trip, it stops at the Bang Sai Folk Arts and Craft Centre before returning to Bangkok by 5:30 PM.

THE CENTRAL PLAINS AND I-SAN

While Bangkok is the economic heart of Thailand, and the south its playground, the soul of the country may be said to live in the vast central area that stretches from the Burmese border to Cambodia.

The early history of Thailand lies in the western part of this region, on the plains due north of Bangkok. Here the Thai nation was founded at Sukhothai in 1238, when the Khmer empire was defeated. After 112 years the seat of government was transferred briefly to Phitsanulok, and then south to Ayutthaya. In recent times, Phitsanulok has grown into a major provincial capital, while Sukhothai has become a small farming community. Fortunately, the wats and sanctuaries of Old Sukhothai were largely spared destruction, and their careful restoration shows us the classical art of early Thailand.

The eastern part, the sprawling plateau known as I-San, is rarely visited by tourists. Comprising one third of Thailand's land area, 17 provinces, and four of the kingdom's most populous cities, the Northeast is also the least-developed area and the poorest. Life, for the most part, depends upon the fickleness of the monsoon rains; work is hard and scarce. For many, migration to Bangkok has been the only option. Most tuk-tuk drivers in Bangkok are from I-San, and the bars of Patpong are filled with the daughters of I-San, sending their earnings back to their parents.

I-San's attractions are first, the Khmer ruins, which have been only partially restored; national parks; the Mekong river; and the traditional rural way of life. And while there are hotels in every town, and an efficient bus service reaches the smallest of hamlets, the accommodations are not deluxe and lack sophisticated amenities.

Numbers in the margin correspond to points of interest on the Central Plains and I-San and the Old Sukhothai maps.

Phitsanulok

1 *377 km (234 mi) north of Bangkok.*

For a brief span, Phitsanulok was the capital of Siam after the decline of Sukhothai and before the consolidation of the royal court at Ayutthaya in the 14th century. The new Phitsanulok, which had to relocate 5 km (3 mi) from the old site, is a modern provincial administrative seat with few architectural blessings. Wat Yai, however, merits a visit. Phitsanulok is also the closest city to Sukhothai with modern amenities and communications, which makes it a good base for exploring the region.

A major street runs from the railway station to the Kwae Noi River. The newer commercial and office area is along this street and a little farther south, around the TAT office. North of this main street are the market and Wat Phra Si Ratana (commonly known as **Wat Yai**), where the treasured statue of Lord Buddha sits in majesty. Built in 1357, Wat Yai has developed into a large monastery with typical Buddhist statuary and ornamentation. Particularly noteworthy are the viharn's wooden doors, inlaid with mother-of-pearl at the behest of King Boromkot in 1756. Behind the viharn is a 30-meter (100-foot) prang that you can climb, though you cannot see the Buddha relics.

All this is secondary, however, to what many claim is the world's most beautiful image of the Buddha, **Phra Buddha Chinnarat** cast during the late-Sukhothai period, the statue, in the position of subduing evil, was covered in gold plate by King Eka Thossarot in 1631. According to folklore the king applied the gold with his own hands. The statue's grace and air of humility have an overpowering serenity. The black backdrop, decorated with gilded angels and flowers, further increases its strength. It's no wonder that so many copies of this serene Buddha image have been made, the best known of which resides in Bangkok's Marble Temple. *Free.* ☉ *Daily 8–6.*

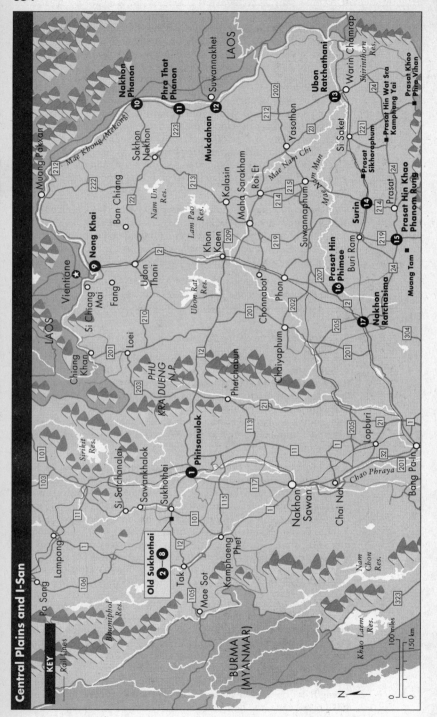

Central Plains and I-San

KEY

Rail Lines

LAOS

Pa Sang

Lampang

Si Satchanalai

Sawankhalok

Sukhothai

Old Sukhothai ② — ⑧

Tak

Mae Sot

Kamphaeng Phet

Phitsanulok ①

Nakhon Sawan

Chai Nat

Chao Phraya

Bang Pa-In

Lopburi

Phetchabun

Chaiyaphum

PHU DUENG N.P.

KRA

Loei

Chiang Khan

Si Chiang Mai

Fang

Vientiane

Nong Khai ⑨

Udon Thani

Ban Chiang

Nam Un Res.

Sakhon Nakhon

Nakhon Phanom ⑩

Phra That Phanom ⑪

Suwannakhet

LAOS

Mae Khong (Mekong)

Muang Pakxan

LAOS

Kalasin

Maha Sarakham

Khon Kaen

Lam Pao Res.

Ubon Rat Res.

Chonnabot

Phon

Roi Et

Mae Nam Chi

Yasothon

Mukdahan ⑫

Ubon Ratchathani ⑬

Warin Chamrap

Sirinthorn Res.

Prasat Khao Phra Vihan

Prasat Hin Wat Sra Kamphaeng Yai

Si Saket

Prasat Sikhoraphum

Surin ⑭

Prasat

Prasat Hin Khao Phanom Rung ⑮

Muang Tam

Buri Ram

Suwannaphum

Mae Nam Mun

Prasat Hin Phimae ⑯

Nakhon Ratchasima ⑰

Bhumiphol Res.

Sirikit Res.

Nam Chon Res.

Khao Laem Res.

BURMA (MYANMAR)

N

100 miles

150 km

Lodging

$$ ⊞ **Amarin Nakhon.** If a central location is a priority, this is Phitsanulok's best offering. The hotel is a bit dark and worn, but the staff is helpful and the rooms are clean. Each has two queen-size beds, leaving little space for other furniture. The coffee shop stays busy 24 hours a day, serving late-night customers from the hotel's basement disco. ⊠ *3/1 Chao Phraya Rd.,* ☎ *055/258–588,* FAX *055/258–945. 130 rooms. Restaurant, coffee shop, dance club. AE, DC, MC, V.*

$$ ⊞ **Rajapruk Hotel.** Of the two best hotels in town, this one is quieter
★ and more refined, and has newer furnishings. The owner's wife is American, and many staff members speak a few English words. Guest rooms are decorated with wood and warm colors that accentuate the hotel's feeling of intimacy. The hotel's main drawback is its location, away from the town center on the east side of the railroad tracks. ⊠ *99/9 Pha-Ong Dum Rd.,* ☎ *055/258–477,* FAX *055/251–395; Bangkok reservations,* ☎ *02/251–4612. 110 rooms. Restaurant, coffee shop, pool, beauty salon, nightclub, car-rental. AE, DC, MC, V.*

Sukhothai

56 km (35 mi) northwest of Phitsanulok, 427 km (265 mi) north of Bangkok.

An hour from Phitsanulok by road, Sukhothai has a unique place in Thailand's history. Until the 13th century, most of Thailand consisted of many small vassal states under the suzerainty of the Khmer Empire in Angkor Wat. But the Khmers had overextended their resources, allowing the princes of two Thai states to combine forces. In 1238 one of the two princes, Phor Khun Bang Klang Thao, marched on Sukhothai, defeated the Khmer garrison commander in an elephant duel, and captured the city. Installed as the new king of the region, he took the name Sri Indraditya and founded a dynasty that ruled Sukhothai for nearly 150 years.

The Sukhothai period was relatively brief—a series of only eight kings—but it witnessed lasting accomplishments. The Thais gained their independence, which has been maintained to the present day. King Ram Khamhaeng formulated the Thai alphabet by adapting the Khmer script to suit the Thai tonal language. And Theravada Buddhism was established and became the dominant national religion. In addition, toward the end of the Sukhothai dynasty, a distinctive Thai art flourished that was so wonderful the period is known as Thailand's Golden Age of Art.

By the mid-14th century, Sukhothai's power and influence had waned, permitting its dynamic vassal state, Ayutthaya, to become the capital of the Thai kingdom. Sukhothai was gradually abandoned to the jungle, and a new town of Sukhothai grew up 10 km (6 mi) away. In 1978, a 10-year restoration project costing more than $10 million saw the creation of the Sukhothai Historic Park—an area of 70 sq km (27 sq mi) with 193 historic monuments, though many of these are little more than clusters of stones. Only about 20 monuments can be classified as noteworthy, of which six have particular importance.

➋ Most of the significant pieces of Sukhothai art are in Bangkok's National Museum, but the **Ramkhamhaeng National Museum** has a sufficient sampling to demonstrate the gentle beauty of this period. The display of historic artifacts helps visitors form an image of Thailand's first capital city, and a relief map gives an idea of its geographic layout. ▨ *Admission.* ☉ *Wed.–Sun. 9–noon and 1–4.*

Old Sukhothai

3 In the 19th century, a famous stone inscription of King Ram Khamhaeng was found among the ruins of the **Royal Palace.** Sometimes referred to as Thailand's Declaration of Independence, the inscription's best-known quote reads: "This Muang Sukhothai is good. In the water there are fish, in the field there is rice. The ruler does not levy tax on the people who travel along the road together, leading their oxen on the way to trade and riding their horses on the way to sell. Whoever wants to trade in elephants, so trades. Whoever wants to trade in horses, so trades."

4 The magical and spiritual center of Sukhothai is **Wat Mahathat.** Sitting amid a tranquil lotus pond, Wat Mahathat is the largest and quite possibly the most beautiful monastery in Sukhothai. Enclosed in the compound are some 200 tightly packed chedis, each containing the funeral ashes of a nobleman. Towering above these minor chedis is a large central chedi, notable for its bulbous, lotus-bud prang. Friezes of 111 Buddhist disciples, hands raised in adoration, walk around the chedi's base. Though Wat Mahathat was probably built by Sukhothai's first king, Sri Indraditya, it owes its present form to a 1345 remodeling by King Lö Thai, who erected the lotus-bulb chedi to house two important relics—the Hair Relic and the Neck Bone Relic—brought back from Ceylon by the monk Sisatta.

5 Possibly the oldest structure of Sukhothai is **Wat Sri Sawai.** The architectural style is Khmer, with three prangs—similar to those found in Lopburi—surrounded by a laterite wall. The many stucco images of Hindu and Buddhist scenes suggest that Sri Sawai was probably first a Hindu temple, later converted to a Buddhist monastery.

6 Another one of Sukhothai's noteworthy attractions is the striking and peaceful **Wat Sra Sri,** which sits on two connected islands encircled by a lotus-filled lake; the rolling, verdant mountains beyond add to the monastery's serenity. The lake, called Traphong Trakuan Pond, supplied the monks with water and served as a boundary for the sacred area. In classical Sukhothai style, a Singhalese chedi dominates six smaller chedis. A large, stucco seated Buddha looks down a row of columns, past the chedis, and over the lake to the horizon.

Even more wondrous is a **walking Buddha** by the Singhalese-style chedi. The walking Buddha is a Sukhothai innovation and the epitome of Sukhothai's art: Lord Buddha appears to be floating on air, neither rooted on this earth nor placed on a pedestal above the reach of the common people.

❼ Just beyond the northern city walls is **Wat Phra Phai Luang,** second in importance to Wat Mahathat. This former Khmer Hindu shrine was also converted into a Buddhist temple. Surrounded by a moat, the sanctuary is encircled by three laterite prangs, similar to those at Wat Sri Sawai—the only one that's intact is decorated with stucco figures. In front of the prangs are the remains of the viharn and a crumbling chedi with a seated Buddha on its pedestal. Facing these structures is the *mondop* (square structure with a stepped pyramid roof, built to house religious relics), once decorated with standing Buddha images in four different poses. Most of these are now too damaged to be recognizable; only the reclining Buddha still has a definite form.

❽ The **Wat Si Chum,** southwest of Wat Phra Phai Luang, is worth visiting for its sheer size. Like other sanctuaries, it was originally surrounded by a moat serving as a perimeter to the mondop. The main sanctuary is dominated by Buddha in the Mara posture. The huge stucco image is one of the largest in Thailand, measuring 37 feet from knee to knee. Enter the mondop through the passage inside the left inner wall. Keep your eyes on the ceiling: More than 50 engraved slabs illustrate scenes from the *Jataka* (stories about the previous lives of Lord Buddha).

Lodging

$$ 🏨 **Northern Palace.** The best of Sukhothai's indifferent lodgings is this small, modern hotel on the Phitsanulok road, close to the town center. Rooms have twin beds and are furnished in light colors and kept clean. The bar and dining room serves as an evening gathering spot—often with live music—for locals and foreigners. ⊠ *43 Singhawat Rd., Amphoe Muang, 64000,* ☎ *055/612–081,* 𝔽𝔸𝕏 *055/612–038. 81 rooms. Restaurant, pool, nightclub. MC, V.*

$$ 🏨 **Pailyn Sukhothai Hotel.** This modern building has the most creature comforts of any hotel in the area and most of the better tour groups stay here. The big negative is that it's off by itself between Old and New Sukhothai, with no place of interest in the vicinity. ⊠ *Jarodvithithong, 64210,* ☎ *055/613–310,* 𝔽𝔸𝕏 *055/613–317; Bangkok reservations* ☎ *02/215–7110. 238 rooms. 3 restaurants, pool, sauna, health club, shuttle bus. MC, V.*

$$ 🏨 **Thai Village House.** This compound of thatched bungalows is usually fully booked with tour groups. Consequently, the staff is impersonal and unhelpful. The hotel's advantage is its location—a five-minute bicycle ride from the Historical Park. Guest rooms have two queen-size beds and little else except for private bathrooms. ⊠ *2/4 Jarodvithitong Rd., Muang Kao, 64000,* ☎ *055/611–049,* 𝔽𝔸𝕏 *055/612–583. 45 rooms with bath. Restaurant, shops. MC, V.*

$ 🏨 **Anasukho.** In a small Thai house down a narrow *soi* (lane) on the south side of the river, this guest house is run by a friendly Thai couple. The wood floors and beams and the small garden add to the feeling that this could be your home away from home. No food is served, but tea and coffee are always available. ⊠ *234/6 Jarodwitheethong Rd.*

and Soi Panison, Sukhothai 64000, ☎ 055/611–315. 3 rooms, with shared bath. No credit cards.

$ 🏨 **River View Hotel.** Steps away from the private bus terminal in the center of the new town, this very basic and rather institutional hotel is currently the best and most convenient budget choice. The air-conditioned rooms are mopped clean, and each has a private shower. ✉ *92 Nikorn Kasem Rd., 64000, ☎ 055/611–656, ℻ 055/613–373. 32 rooms. Dining room. No credit cards.*

Nong Khai

❾ *615 km (381 mi) northeast of Bangkok, 356 km (221 mi) north of Korat.*

The delight of Nong Khai is its frontier-town atmosphere: In 1994, the Friendship Bridge across the Mae Khong opened, joining Nong Khai to the capital of Laos, Vientiane, in a sweeping arc. Previously the only connection was a scurry of ferries from Tha Sadet, the boat pier, which has a small immigration and customs shed. Now the traffic crosses the river, switching on the Laotian side so drivers can change from driving on the right-hand side—as in Thailand—to the left-hand side, as in Laos. Non-Thais need Laotian visas to cross the river, which, at press time, cannot be obtained in Nong Khai (and take about three to seven days to secure in Bangkok).

Fanning out from Tha Sadet, the boat pier, on Rim Khong Road, are market stalls with goods brought in from Laos. On Nong Khai's main street, Meechai Road, the old wooden houses—for example, the governor's residence—show French colonial influences from Indochina. **Wat Pho Chai,** the best-known temple, houses a gold image of Buddha, Luang Pho Phra Sai, that was lost for many centuries in the muddy bottom of the Mae Khong. Its rediscovery, part of the local lore, is told in pictures on the temple's walls. **Village Weaver Handicrafts,** next to the temple, employs 350 families in the production of indigo-dyed mudmee cotton. You may want to take a B50 tuk-tuk ride 5 km (3 mi) west of town to visit **Wat Khaek,** something of an oddity created by Luang Pu, a monk, who believes that all religions should work together. The temple's gardens are a collection of bizarre statues representing gods, goddesses, demons, and devils from many of the world's faiths.

Lodging

$$ 🏨 **Mekong Royal.** The glaring white building standing back from the Mekong a mile out of town is operated by Holiday Inn management. While furnishings and architecture may not enthrall you, the rooms are spacious, amenities are new, and most of the rooms have great views over the Mekong into Laos. Best of all is the large pool. ✉ *222 Panungchonprathan Rd., 43000, ☎ 042/420–024, ℻ 042/421–280. 197 rooms. 2 restaurants, pool, health club. AE, DC, MC, V.*

$ 🏨 **Phanthawi.** This is Nong Khai's best hotel, but don't expect more than clean rooms with either air-conditioning or fans. The restaurant, on the open-fronted ground floor, serves also as a sitting area. The staff speaks limited English, but enough to direct guests to the appropriate bus stations. ✉ *Haisoke Rd., 43000, ☎ 042/411568. 67 rooms. Restaurant. MC, V.*

Nakhon Phanom

❿ *740 km (459 mi) northeast of Bangkok, 303 km (188 mi) south of Nong Khai, 252 km (156 mi) east of Udon Thani.*

Approximately three hours east of Udon Thani by bus is Nakhon Phanom, on the banks of the Mae Khong, a sleepy market town with the best hotel in the area, where you should spend the night.

Lodging

$–$$ ☷ **Si Thep Hotel.** About 400 yards from the Mae Khong river, this hotel is by far Nakhom Phanom's best. The property is back from a side street off the main road, so all the rooms are quiet. Rooms are standard and the well-used furnishings are slightly depressing, but all is clean, including the bathrooms. The restaurant has a terrace, should you want the evening air instead of air-conditioning. ⊠ *708/11 Si Thep Rd.,* ☎ *042/512395,* FAX *042/511–346. 87 rooms. Restaurant. MC, V.*

$ ☷ **Windsor Hotel.** This basic hotel has little going for it except its price, the friendly staff, and its location across from the bus stop for Phra That Phanom. Rooms contain little more than a bed. The sheets are well worn and patched, but clean, and though the walls are covered with handprints and smudges, the floors get mopped each day. The bathroom is Asian-style. ⊠ *692/19 Bamrungmuang Rd.,* ☎ *042/511946. 60 rooms. No credit cards.*

Phra That Phanom

⑪ *50 km (31 mi) south of Nakhon Phanom.*

Phra That Phanom is northeast Thailand's most revered shrine. No one knows just when Phra That Phanom was built, though archaeologists trace its foundations to the fifth century. The temple has crumbled and been rebuilt several times—it now stands 52 meters (171 ft) high, with a decorative tip of gold weighing 10 kg (22 lb). Though it's impressive, you may be equally moved by the small museum to the left of the grounds that houses its ancient bells and artifacts. Once a year droves of devotees arrive to attend the Phra That Phanom Fair during the full moon of the third lunar month, and the village becomes a mini-metropolis, with stalls of market traders and makeshift shelters for the pilgrims.

Mukdahan

⑫ *40 km (24 mi) south of Phra That Phanom.*

Mukdahan on the Mae Khong, Thailand's newest provincial capital, is opposite the Laotian town of Suwannakhet. It bustles with vendors in stalls and shops all along the riverfront, selling goods brought in from Laos—a fascinating array of detailed embroidery, lace, lacquered paintings, trays, and bowls, cheap cotton goods, and a host of souvenir items. The time out from shopping can be spent promenading along the riverfront, stopping occasionally to sample Thai and Laotian delicacies from one of the numerous food stalls.

Lodging

$$ ☷ **Mukdahan Grand Hotel.** The only Western-style hotel in town is this modern concrete building. The staff is welcoming and helpful, though little English is spoken. Rooms are plain, but adequately furnished with twin or king size beds, table and chairs. The restaurant serves a buffet breakfast, Thai and Western dishes for lunch and dinner. ⊠ *70 Songnang Sanid Rd., 49000,* ☎ *042/612–020,* FAX *042/612–021. 200 rooms. Restaurant. AE, MC, V.*

Ubon Ratchathani

⑬ *181 km (112 mi) south of Mukdahan, 227 km (141 mi) east of Surin.*

Ubon Ratchathani is southern I-San's largest city. Its best-known tourist attraction is the Buddhist-inspired Candle Procession in late July, when huge wax sculptures are paraded through town. At other times, especially after the rainy season, locals make for **Haad Wat Tai Island** in the middle of the Mun River, a site for food stalls. It's connected to the shore by a rope bridge (1 baht) that sends shivers of apprehension through those who cross. Try the local favorites: *pla chon*, a fish whose name is often translated as "snakehead mullet," or if your stomach is feeling conservative, the ubiquitous *kai yang* (roast chicken).

Lodging

$$ ⊡ **Patumrat Hotel.** Though the nearby Regent Palace is the newest four-star hotel in town, the Patumrat's service and personality guarantee its position as Ubon's leading hotel. Its drawback, as is the Regent's, is the location, a 20-minute walk from the center of town. ⊠ *173 Chayangkun Rd., 34000,* ☎ *045/241–501,* ℻ *045/243–792. 137 rooms. Restaurant, coffee shop. AE, DC, MC, V.*

$ ⊡ **Sri Kamol Hotel.** This clean, modern hotel in the center of town, a five-minute walk from the TAT office, has carpeted rooms with twin beds or king-size beds. The staff is welcoming, and a few of them speak good English. You can often negotiate a discount of 25% on the price of a room. ⊠ *26 Ubonsak Rd., 34000,* ☎ *045/255–804,* ℻ *045/243–793. 82 rooms. Restaurant. No credit cards.*

Surin

⓮ *227 km (141 mi) west of Ubon Ratchathani, 190 km (120 mi) east of Korat.*

Surin is famous for its annual elephant roundup in the third week of November. The roundup is essentially an elephant circus, albeit an impressive one, where elephants perform tricks in a large arena and their mahouts reenact scenes of capturing wild elephants. At other times, if you want to see elephants, you must travel to **Ban Ta Klang,** a village 60 km (37 mi) north of Surin, off Highway 214. This is the home of the Suay people, who migrated from southern Cambodia several centuries ago and whose expertise with elephants is renowned.

Lodging

$$ ⊡ **Tharin Hotel.** This is Surin's leading hotel. The lobby and public reception areas are kept shining, and light flooding in through tall glass windows reflects off the polished marble. Rooms have wall-to-wall carpeting, TV, and telephones. ⊠ *60 Sirirat Rd., 32000,* ☎ *045/514281,* ℻ *045/511580. 160 rooms and 35 suites. Restaurant, coffee shop, sauna, nightclub, meeting rooms. AE, MC, V.*

$ ⊡ **Petchkasem Hotel.** While the newer Tharin Hotel has smarter creature comforts, the Petchkasem has more character and is in the center of town. The carpeted guest rooms have air-conditioning, refrigerators, and color TV. ⊠ *104 Jitbamroong Rd., 32000,* ☎ *045/511–274,* ℻ *044/511–041. 162 rooms. Restaurant, lobby lounge, pool, nightclub, meeting rooms. AE, MC, V.*

¢ ⊡ **Pirom Guest House.** The owners, the Piroms, are enthusiastic about the I-San and love to explain the region to guests. Mr. Pirom often arranges tours to off-the-beaten-track villages. They have only five small, fan-cooled rooms, none with private bath, but most of the time is spent sitting in the garden. ⊠ *242 Krungsrinai Rd., 2 blocks west of market, 32000,* ☎ *044/515–140. 6 rooms. Breakfast room. No credit cards.*

Prasat Hin Khao Phanom Rung

⓯ *60 km (37 mi))south of Buri Ram, 65 km (39 mi) west of Surin, 90 km (54 mi) east of Korat.*

The restored hilltop sanctuary of Prasat Hin Khao Phanom Rung, is 7-km (4½-mi) by bus or taxi from the village of Nang Rung. It is a supreme example of Khmer art, built in the 12th century under King

Suriyaworamann II, one of the great Khmer rulers, and restored in the 1980s at a cost of $2 million. It's one of the few Khmer sanctuaries without later Thai Buddhist additions. The approach to the prasat sets your heart thumping—you cross an imposing *naga* bridge (one with snake balustrades), and climb majestic staircases to the top, where you are greeted by the magnificent Reclining Vishnu lintel. Step under the lintel and through the portal, and you are within the double-walled sanctuary. Intricate carvings in a style similar to those found in Lopburi cover the interior walls, and in the center of the prasat stands the great throne room dedicated to Brahma Lord Siva.

Prasat Hin Phimae

16 *58 km (36 mi) north of Korat; buses leave for Phimae every 15 min between 6 AM and 6 PM for the 1¼-hr trip.*

Prasat Hin Phimae, the other great Khmer structure of the Northeast (along with Phanom Rung) was probably built sometime in the late 11th or early 12th century, and though the ruins have been restored, they have not been groomed and manicured. Entering the prasat through the two layers—the external sandstone wall and the gallery—is to step back eight centuries, and by the time you reach the inner sanctuary, you're swept up in the creation and destruction of the Brahman gods engraved on the lintels. Gate towers (*gopuras*) at the four cardinal points guard the entrances, with the main one facing south, the route to Angkor.

The central white sandstone prang is 60 feet tall, flanked by two smaller buildings, one in laterite, the other in red sandstone; they make an exquisite combination of pink and white against the darker laterite, especially in the light of early morning and late afternoon. The principal prasat is surrounded by four porches, whose external lintels reflect scenes from the Ramayana and depict the Hindu gods. Inside, the lintels portray the religious art of Mahayana Buddhism. An open-air museum nearby displays a collection of lintels from Phimae and other northeast Khmer sites, which gives you a chance to learn to recognize the different styles of Thai-Khmer art.

You may want to drive about 2 km (1.2 mi) from the ruins to see **Sai Ngam,** the world's largest banyan tree, whose mass of intertwined trunks supports branches that cast a shadow of nearly 15,000 square feet. Some say that it is 3,000 years old. On weekends, the small nearby park has stalls selling *patnee* (noodles) and *kai yang* (roast chicken) for picnics.

Nakhon Ratchasima (Korat)

17 *54 km (60 mi) southwest of Phimae, 259 km (160 mi) northeast of Bangkok. Bangkok is four hours away by train, via Ayutthaya and Bangkok's Don Muang Airport, and there are direct buses to Bangkok, Pattaya (284 km, 176 mi), Rayong (345 km, 214 mi), Chiang Rai (870 km, 539 mi), Chiang Mai (763 km, 473 mi), and Phitsanulok (457 km, 283 mi).*

Most tourists use Nakhon Ratchasima (Korat) as a base for visiting Phimae and Buri Ram. It is I-San's major city, with a population of over 200,000, considered the gateway to the Northeast. Other than to do some basic shopping, you will probably not want to spend any daytime hours here, but between 6 and 9 PM, head to the **Night Bazaar** in the center of town. A block-long street is taken over by food stands and shopping stalls and is crowded with locals in a festive atmosphere.

A side trip to **Pak Thongchai Silk and Cultural Center,** 32 km (20 mi) south of Korat offers a chance to see the complete silk-making process, from the raising of silk worms to the spinning of thread and weaving of fabric. You can also buy silks at some 70 factories in the area. Try the **Srithai Silk** showroom (⊠ 333 Subsiri Road, ☎ 044/441588) in Pakthongchai.

Lodging

$$–$$$ 🏨 **Royal Princess.** This is the newest (1994) hotel in town, and it perhaps has just the edge over the Sima Thani. The staff is efficiently professional and helpful. The rooms are large, furnished in pastels, and most have queen-size beds. ⊠ *1/37 Surenarai Rd., 2 mi from downtown, Amphur Muang, 30000,* ☎ *044/256–629,* ℻ *044/256–601. 186 rooms. Restaurant, coffee shop, pool, 2 tennis courts, health club, business services, meeting rooms. AE, DC, MC, V.*

$$–$$$ 🏨 **Sima Thani Hotel.** This sparkling hotel is well-accustomed to tourists and businessmen. Each room has two queen-size beds, a table and chairs, and a good working desk. Bathrooms come with hair dryers, telephones, and toiletries. The extensive outdoor evening buffet has musicians and classic I-San dancers. ⊠ *Mittraphap Rd., Tambon Nai Muang, Amphur Muang, 30000,* ☎ *044/243–812,* ℻ *044/251–109. 135 rooms. Restaurant, coffee shop, piano bar, pool, massage, health club, meeting rooms. AE, DC, MC, V.*

$ 🏨 **Chansurang.** In the heart of town, minutes away from the Night Bazaar, this was once Korat's main hotel. Renovations have smartened up the rooms and added modern amenities. The restaurant serves Thai dishes, including I-San specialties, and Western food. ⊠ *2701/2 Mahadthai Rd., Amphur Muang, 30000,* ☎ *044/257–060,* ℻ *044/252– 897. 157 rooms. Restaurant, pool. MC, V.*

The Central Plains and I-San A to Z

Arriving and Departing

BY BUS

Many of the towns in the Northeast are served by direct air-conditioned and nonair-conditioned buses from Bangkok's Northern Bus Terminal on Phahonyothin Road. The fares are slightly lower than those for the train. There are also daily direct buses that connect Chiang Mai and the major provincial capitals in the Northeast.

Buses run frequently to Phitsanulok from Chiang Mai, Bangkok, and Sukhothai. Bus service also connects Phitsanulok to eastern Thailand. From Phitsanulok there is daily service to Loei and then on to Khon Kaen and Nong Khai. Long-distance buses arrive and depart from the intercity bus terminal, 2 km (1¼ mi) northeast of town.

Buses depart from Phitsanulok's intercity bus terminal, located on the northeast edge of town. The Sukhothai bus, however, makes a stop just before the Naresuan Bridge. These buses end their journey in New Sukhothai; you can take the minibus at the terminal to Old Sukhothai. Buses go directly to Sukhothai from Chiang Mai's Arcade Bus Station (☎ 053/242–664); the trip takes five hours and costs B100. The bus trip from Bangkok's **Northern Bus Terminal** (☎ 02/279–4484) takes seven hours and costs B140.

BY PLANE

All air traffic radiates from Bangkok, with daily flights on **Thai Airways International** between the capital and Khon Kaen, Udon Thani, Nakhon Phanom, Ubon Ratchathani, and Korat. Three direct flights each day connect Phitsanulok with Bangkok (B920) and Chiang Mai (B650).

In 1996 **Bangkok Airways** started operating direct flights to Sukhothai from Bangkok and Chiang Mai three times week. The airport, located between Sukhothai and Si Satchanalai is a 35-minute ride from Sukhothai. Alternatively, you can use Thai International into Phitsanulok and take an hour-long bus or taxi ride to Sukhathai.

BY TRAIN

Northeastern Railways has frequent service from Bangkok to Nakhon Ratchasima, where the line splits. One route runs east, stopping at Buri Ram, Surin, and Si Saket before terminating at Ubon Ratchathani; the other line goes north, stopping at Khon Kaen and Udon Thani, before arriving at Nong Khai. Both routes have daytime express and local trains and an overnight express train with sleeping cars. The Ubon Ratchathani sleeper leaves Bangkok at 9 PM to arrive at 7:05 AM, and departs from Ubon Ratchathani at 7 PM to arrive in Bangkok at 5:20 AM. The Nong Khai sleeper departs from Bangkok at 10:30 PM to arrive at 7:30 AM, and on the return trip leaves Nong Khai at 7 PM to be back in Bangkok at 6 AM.

Phitsanulok is about halfway between Bangkok and Chiang Mai. On the rapid express, it takes approximately six hours from either city. Some trains between Bangkok and Phitsanulok stop at Lopburi and Ayutthaya, enabling you to visit these two historic cities en route. A special express train between Bangkok and Phitsanulok takes just over five hours. Tickets for this service, which cost 50% more than those for regular second-class travel, may be purchased at a separate booth inside the Bangkok and Phitsanulok stations; reservations are essential.

Getting Around

I-SAN

Between cities, there are buses throughout the day, from about 6 AM to 7 PM. In towns, the bicycle samlors and songthaews are plentiful. Rental cars, with or without a driver, are available in the provincial capitals.

PHITSANULOK

Most sights in Phitsanulok are within walking distance, but bicycle samlors are easily available. Bargain hard for a proper fare—most rides should cost between B10 and B20.

SUKHOTHAI

Bicycle samlors are ideal for getting around New Sukhothai, but take either a taxi (B120) or a local bus (B5) to travel the 10 km (6 mi) from New Sukhothai to Old Sukhothai (Muang Kao) and the Historic Park. Buses depart from the local terminal, located 1 km (½ mi) on the other side of Prarong Bridge.

The best means of transportation around the Historical Park is a rented bicycle (B20 for the day). If you don't have much time, you can hire a taxi from New Sukhothai for B250 for a half day. The drivers know all the key sights. Within the park, a tourist tram takes visitors to the major attractions for B20.

Contacts and Resources

EMERGENCIES

Phitsanulok doesn't have a Tourist Police office, but the local police (☎ 055/240–199) are helpful in an emergency. For medical attention, try the **Phitsanuwej Hospital** (✉ Khun Piren Rd., ☎ 055/252–762). There is no Tourist Police office in Sukhothai, but the local police (☎ 055/611–199) are accustomed to helping foreigners. For medical emergencies, contact the **Sukhothai Hospital** (☎ 055/611–782).

VISITOR INFORMATION
Tourism Authority of Thailand/Tourist Police (✉ 2102–2104 Mittraphap Rd., Amphor Muang, Nakhon Rathchasima 30000, ☏ 044/243427; ✉ 209/7–8 Boromtrailokanat Rd., Amphoe Muang, Phitsanulok 65000, ☏ 055/252–742; ✉ 264/1 Khuan Thani Rd., Ubon Ratchathani 34000, ☏ 038/377008).

NORTHERN THAILAND

Northern Thailand is a mix of peoples and traditional cultures meeting the modern age. Chiang Mai, Thailand's northern capital, is for travelers the gateway to the region. Many take lodging here for a month or longer, making excursions and returning to rest. Guest houses and sophisticated hotels accommodate them, and well-worn tracks lead into the tribal villages. The opium trade still flourishes, flowing illegally into southern Thailand en route to the rest of the world. For the tourist, however, the attractions are forested hills laced with rivers, the cultures of the hill tribes, and the cool weather. (Those travelers who also seek the poppy while trekking often find themselves languishing in a Chiang Mai prison.)

The hill tribes around Chiang Mai have been visited so frequently that they have lost some of their character. Those in search of villages untainted by commercialism need to go farther afield, to areas around Tak, near the Burmese border, and Nan to the east. Even Mae Hong Son, west of Chiang Mai, known for its sleepy, peaceful pace and the regular gathering of the area's hill tribes, is developing its tourist trade. Two paved highways from Chiang Mai and now daily flights have opened up the region.

The Golden Triangle (Sop Ruak in Thai), the area where Thailand, Laos, and Burma (Myanmar) meet, has long captivated the Western imagination. The opium poppy grows here, albeit on a much diminished scale, and the hill tribes that cultivate it are semi-autonomous, ruled more by warlords than by any national government. Today, the tribes of Laos and Burma retain their autonomy, but Thailand's corner of the Golden Triangle has become a tourist attraction, with the tribes caught up in the tide of commercialism. Chiang Rai is the closest city. In 1990 it had only one luxury hotel; now there are at least three resort complexes, and two more have been built up where the rivers converge, overlooking Laos and Burma.

Numbers in the margin correspond to points of interest on the Northern Thailand and the Chiang Mai maps.

Chiang Mai

696 km (430 mi) north of Bangkok.

Chiang Mai's rich culture stretches back 700 years, to the time when several small tribes, under King Mengrai, banded together to form a new "nation" called Anachak Lanna Thai. They first made Chiang Rai (north of Chiang Mai) their capital, but in 1296 they moved it to the fertile plains between Doi Suthep mountain and the Mae Ping River and called it Napphaburi Sri Nakornphing Chiang Mai.

Lanna Thai eventually lost its independence to Ayutthaya and later, Burma. Not until 1774—when General Tuksin (who ruled as king before Rama I) drove the Burmese out—did the region revert to Thailand. After that, it developed independently of southern Thailand. Even the language is different, marked by a relaxed tempo. In the last 50 years communications have opened up between Bangkok and Chiang Mai; the small, provincial town has exploded beyond its moat and gates, and some of its innocence has gone.

① **Wat Suan Dok,** on Suthep Road, one of the largest of Chiang Mai's temples, is said to have been built on the site where bones of Lord Buddha were found. Some of these relics are reportedly housed in the chedi; the others went to Wat Prathat on Doi Suthep. At the back of the *viharn* (large hall where priests perform religious duties) is the *bot* (main chapel) housing Phra Chao Kao, a superb bronze Buddha cast in 1504. Chiang Mai aristocrats are buried in stupas in the graveyard.

On the superhighway, between its intersection with Huay Kaew Road and Highway 107, stands Wat Photharam Maha Viharn, more commonly known as **Wat Chedi Yot** (Seven-Spired Pagoda). Built in 1455,
② it is a copy of the Mahabodhi temple in Bodh Gaya, India, where the Lord Buddha achieved enlightenment; the seven spires represent the seven weeks that he subsequently spent there. The sides of the chedi have marvelous bas-relief sculptures of celestial figures.

③ From Wat Chedi Yot you can walk to the **National Museum,** a northern Thai-style building containing many statues of Lord Buddha and a huge Buddha footprint of wood with mother-of-pearl inlay. The upper floor's archaeological collection includes a bed with mosquito netting used by an early prince of Chiang Mai. ✉ *Admission.* ☉ *Weekdays 8:30–noon and 1–4:30.*

Chiang Mai's city walls contain several important temples—all in walking distance of one another. At the junction of Ratchadamnoen and Singharat roads, in the middle of town, stands Chiang Mai's prin-
④ cipal monastery, **Wat Phra Singh,** containing the Phra Singh Buddha image. The serene and benevolent facial expression of this statue has a radiance enhanced by the light filtering into the chapel. Be sure to note the temple's facades of splendidly carved wood, the elegant teak beams and posts, and the masonry. In a large teaching compound, student monks often have the time and desire to talk.

On Phra Pokklan Road just before it crosses Rajmankha Road stands
⑤ **Wat Chedi Luang.** In 1411, a vision commanded King Saen Muang Ma to build a chedi "as high as a dove could fly." He died before it was finished, as did the next king, and, during the next king's reign, an earthquake knocked down 100 feet of the 282-foot chedi. It is now a superb ruin. Don't miss the naga balustrades at the steps to the viharn—considered the finest of their kind.

⑥ **Wat Chiang Man,** Chiang Mai's oldest (1296) monastery, typical of northern Thai architecture, has massive teak pillars inside the bot. Two important images of the Buddha sit in the small building to the right of the main viharn. Officially, they are on view only on Sunday, but sometimes the door is unlocked.

Each of Chiang Mai's multitude of temples has merit, but the temple that counts is the one that inspires you. One that may, for example, is
⑦ **Wat Chaimongkol,** along the Mae Ping River, near the Chiang Mai Plaza Hotel. It's small, with only 18 monks in residence, and foreigners rarely visit. Though the little chedi is supposed to contain holy relics, its beauty lies in the quietness and serenity of the grounds.

Dining

$$ ✕ **Arun Rai.** This is the best-known restaurant in Chiang Mai for northern-Thai cuisine. Try the *phak nam phrik* (vegetables in pepper sauce), *tabong* (boiled bamboo shoots fried in batter), *sai oua* (pork sausage with herbs), or the famous frog's legs fried with ginger. The menu is available in English. The Arun Rai often has the delicacy *jing*

Northern Thailand

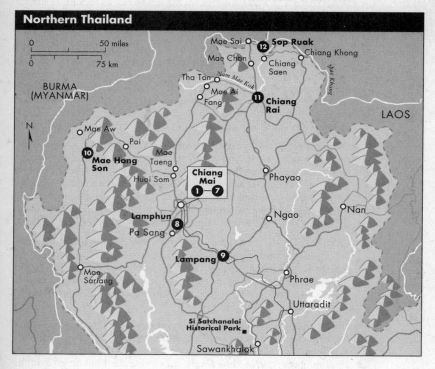

kung (a cricketlike insect) that you may want to try. ⊠ *45 Kotchasarn Rd.,* ☎ *053/276–947. Reservations not accepted. No credit cards.*

$$ ✕ **Baen Suan.** This delightful restaurant off the San Kamphaeng Road (the shopping/factory street) is a B40 tuk-tuk ride from downtown. The northern-style teak house sits in a peaceful garden, and the excellently prepared food is from the region. Try the hot Chiang Mai sausage (the recipe originally came from Burma), broccoli in oyster sauce, green curry with chicken, and a shrimp-and-vegetable soup. ⊠ *51/3 San Kamphaeng Rd.,* ☎ *053/242–116. Reservations essential. No credit cards.*

$$ ✕ **Hong Tauw Inn.** This relaxing, intimate restaurant has the atmosphere of a Thai bistro; linger, trying dishes from northern Thailand and from the central plains. There is an English menu, and the owner speaks it fluently. Excellent Thai soups, *sai oua* (northern sausages), crispy *pla mee krob* (fried fish with chili), and *nam phrik ong* (minced pork with chili paste and tomatoes) are among the popular dishes. ⊠ *Across from Rincome Hotel, 95/17–18 Nantawan Arcade, Nimanhaemin Rd.,* ☎ *053/215–027. MC, V.*

$$ ✕ **Kaiwan.** Not many Westerners come here, but the food is held in
★ high esteem by Thais. The best place to sit is upstairs at one of the picnic tables under the stars. For a not-so-spicy beef curry, try Kaeng Mat Sa Man, and for a zesty fried fish, go for the Pla Tot Na Phrik. ⊠ *181 Nimmanhaemin Rd., Soi 9, near the Rincome Hotel,* ☎ *053/221–147. MC, V.*

$$ ✕ **Nang Nuan.** Though this large restaurant has tables indoors, it's pleasant to sit on the terrace facing the Mae Nam Ping. As it's 3 km (2 mi) south of Chiang Mai, you'll take a tuk-tuk or taxi, but the *kai tom khaa* (chicken soup with coconut milk) and the *yam nua* (beef salad) are worth the trip. Grilled charcoal steaks and fresh seafood (displayed in tanks) are also on the menu. ⊠ *27/2 Ko Klang Rd., Nonghoy,* ☎ *053/281–955. AE, DC, MC, V.*

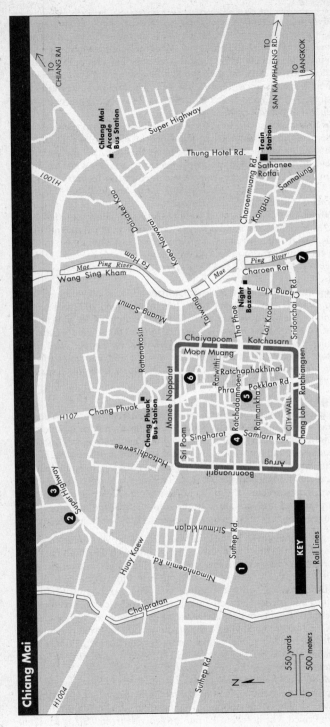

Chiang Mai

TO CHIANG RAI

H1001

Chiang Mai Arcade Bus Station

Super Highway

Thung Hotel Rd.

SAN KAMPHAENG RD.

TO BANGKOK

Train Station

Charoenmuang Rd.

Sathanee Rotfai

Sannalung

Kongsai

Dossket Kao

Kaeo Nawarat

Fa Ham

Mae Ping River

Wang Sing Kham

Muang Samut

Rattanakosin

Manee Nopparat

Chang Phuak

H107

Chang Phuak Bus Station

Hatsdhisewee

Sri Poom

Singharat

Ratchadamnoen

Samlarn Rd.

Ping River

Charoen Rat

Night Bazaar

Tha Phae

Loi Kroa

Sridonchai Rd.

Chang Klan

Chaiyapoom

Moon Muang

Kotchasarn

Ratwithi

Ratchaphakhinai

Phra

Pokklan Rd.

Rajmankha

CITY WALL

Chang Loh

Ratchangsen

Arrug

Boonruangrit

Mae

Taipang

Suthep Rd.

Sirimun klajon

Suhep Rd.

H107

Super Highway

Huay Kaew

Nimanhaemin Rd.

Cholpratan

H1004

KEY

Rail Lines

N

0 — 550 yards
0 — 500 meters

National Museum, **3**
Wat
Chaimongkol, **7**
Wat Chedi Luang, **5**
Wat Chedi Yot, **2**
Wat Chiang Man, **6**
Wat Phra Singh, **4**
Wat Suan Dok, **1**

$$ ✕ **Riverside.** In a 100-year-old teak house on the bank of the Mae Nam Ping, this restaurant serves Thai and Western food. The casual atmosphere attracts young Thais and Westerners, and with lots of beer flowing, the food gets only partial attention. The choice tables are on the deck jutting out over the river, with views of Wat Phrathat on Doi Suthep in the distance. There's live light jazz and popular music after 7 PM. ✉ *9–11 Charoen Rat Rd.,* ☎ *053/243–239. Reservations not accepted. No credit cards.*

$$ ✕ **Ta-Krite.** This small, intimate restaurant opens onto the street, and the service and ambience are casual. Cheerful blue tablecloths, wooden beams, and a veranda facing a garden set the tone. Try the watercress sweet-and-sour soup and the crispy, sweet rice noodles with shrimp and egg in a taro basket. For curry, choose the duck for its seasoned sauce. ✉ *17–18 Samkarn Rd. (just off main road),* ☎ *053/278–333. Reservations not accepted. No credit cards.*

$$ ✕ **Whole Earth.** On the road leading to the Chiang Plaza Hotel, this long-established restaurant serves delicious vegetarian and health foods. On the second floor of an attractive, old Thai house in a garden, the dining room takes full advantage of any breezes. ✉ *88 Sridonchai Rd.,* ☎ *053/282–463. Reservations not accepted. No credit cards.*

$ ✕ **Supotana Kaun.** For this superb northern Thai food you must travel
★ 7 km (4.3 mi) north on the Chiang Dao road (Hwy. 107) and also put up with traffic noise, zero decor, and crates of empty bottles lying around. What you are about to eat is worth all this. The house specialty is a light, airy omelet, the like of which you've never tasted; *paed thai* is so crisp and delicate it melts in your mouth. ✉ *Chiang Dao Rd., at traffic light where road from Chiang Mai Sports Complex joins from left,* ☎ *053/210980. No credit cards.*

Lodging

Lodgings cluster in four districts. The commercial area, between the railway station and the old city walls, holds little interest for most tourists. The area between the river and the old city has the largest concentration of hotels and is close to most of the evening street activity. Within the city walls small hotels and guest houses offer simple, inexpensive accommodations, centrally located. The west side of town, near Doi Suthep, has attracted the posh hotels; it's quieter but also farthest from points of interest. Some hotels add a surcharge in January and February, which brings prices here close to those at Bangkok hotels.

$$$$ ☷ **Regent Chiang Mai.** In the lush Mae Rim Valley 20 minutes north of
★ Chiang Mai, the most attractive hotel in northern Thailand nestles in 20 acres of landscaped gardens amid lakes, lily ponds, and terraced rice paddies. An arc of 16 two-story buildings in traditional Lanna style contains the suites, each with its outdoor *sala* (Thai gazebo) just perfect for breakfast and cocktails. Rooms are furnished with rich Thai cottons and Siamese art; floors are polished teak. Huge bathrooms overlook a garden. Once you're here, you're tempted not to leave; even catching the shuttle bus to Chiang Mai center seems too much effort. ✉ *Mae Rim-Samoeng Old Rd., 50180,* ☎ *053/298–181,* ℻ *053/298–189. 67 suites. 2 restaurants, bar, pool, 2 tennis courts, health club. AE, DC, MC, V.*

$$$ ☷ **Chiang Mai Orchid Hotel.** This is a grand hotel in the old style, with teak pillars in the lobby. Rooms are tastefully furnished and trimmed with wood. The Honeymoon Suite, we are told, is often used by the Crown Prince. The hotel is a 10-minute taxi ride from Chiang Mai center. ✉ *100–102 Huay Kaeo Rd., 50000,* ☎ *053/222–099,* ℻ *053/221–625; Bangkok reservations,* ☎ *053/245–3973. 267 rooms, including 7 suites. 3 restaurants, 2 bars, pool, beauty salon, sauna, health club, business services, meeting room. AE, DC, MC, V.*

$$$ ⊞ **Mae Ping Hotel.** This high-rise hotel has the advantage of a central location, but the service staff could use more training. Its rooms are decorated in ever-popular pastels. An executive club floor offers escape from the tour groups in the remainder of the hotel. The two restaurants serve Thai and Western food and Italian specialties. ⊠ *153 Sridonchai Rd., Changklana Muang, 50000,* ☎ *053/270–160,* FAX *053/270–181; Bangkok reservations,* ☎ *02/232–7712. 400 rooms. 2 restaurants, pool with bar, meeting rooms. AE, DC.*

$$$ ⊞ **Royal Princess.** This hotel is ideal if you'd like to step out the front door into the bustle of Chiang Mai's tourist center. The famous Night Bazaar is a block away, and street vendors are even closer. The rooms' lack of natural light makes them seem a little dreary. But the staff is well-trained and helpful, the lobby is pleasant, and the Jasmine restaurant serves the best Cantonese fare in Chiang Mai. ⊠ *112 Chang Rd., 50000,* ☎ *053/281–033,* FAX *053/281–044; Bangkok reservations,* ☎ *02/233–1130. 200 rooms. 2 restaurants, pool, airport shuttle, meeting room. AE, DC, MC, V.*

$$ ⊞ **Chiang Inn.** Behind the Night Market, the centrally located Chiang Inn offers well-kept guest rooms. As the hotel is set back from the street, the rooms are quiet. They are reasonably spacious and are done in local handwoven cottons. The hotel is usually swamped with tour groups, and its facilities are geared to that kind of traffic. ⊠ *100 Chang Khlan Rd., 50000,* ☎ *053/270–070,* FAX *053/274–299; Bangkok reservations,* ☎ *02/251–6883. 170 rooms, including 4 suites. 2 restaurants, pool, dance club, meeting room, travel services. AE, DC, MC, V.*

$$ ⊞ **River View Lodge.** Facing the Mae Nam Ping across a grassy lawn,
★ this lodge is an easy 10-minute walk from the Night Bazaar. Some seasoned travelers say it's the best place to stay in the city. The rooms are tastefully done with wood furniture crafted in the region and terra-cotta floor tiles; the more expensive ones have private balconies overlooking the river. The small restaurant is better for breakfast than for dinner, and the veranda patio is good for relaxing with a beer or afternoon tea. The owner speaks fine English and will assist in planning your explorations. ⊠ *25 Charoen Prathet Rd., Soi 2, 50000,* ☎ *053/271–109,* FAX *053/279–019. 36 rooms. Restaurant, pool. AE, DC, MC, V.*

$$ ⊞ **Zenith/Suriwongse.** This hotel around the corner from the Royal Princess, near the Night Bazaar, has undergone a refurbishment that brings it up to first-class standards. Its association with the French hotel chain attracts European tour groups. The rooms, redone in pastels, are bright and cheery, and the hotel compares favorably with the Royal Princess. ⊠ *110 Chang Khlan Rd., 50000,* ☎ *053/270–051,* FAX *053/270–063; Bangkok reservations,* ☎ *02/251–9883; U.S. reservations,* ☎ *800/221–4542. 170 rooms, including 4 suites. Restaurant, coffee shop, travel services, airport shuttle. AE, DC, MC, V.*

$–$$ ⊞ **River Ping Palace.** The complex of Siamese buildings at this little guest house shows you what Chiang Mai was like 50 years ago. Food is served at any time in the pleasant open-air restaurant that's also a sitting area. The wooden structures have smallish rooms decorated with old Thai furnishings and artifacts. The best room, No. 3, costs B1,600; in the smaller ones (B1,200) there's very little space around the double bed. Another drawback is that it's a B30 tuk-tuk ride south of the Night Bazaar. ⊠ *385/2 Charoen Prathat Rd., Chang Klan, 50100,* ☎ *053/274–932,* FAX *053–204–281. 5 rooms, most with bath. Restaurant. MC, V.*

$ ⊞ **Grand Apartments.** This new building in the old city offers air-conditioned rooms by the day or by the month, which makes it useful for an extended stay at very reasonable rates (B4,000 per month). The rooms are efficient and clean, and guests have access to telex, fax machines, and a laundry room. ⊠ *24/1 Prapklao Rd., Chang Puak Gate, 50000,* ☎ *053/217–291,* FAX *053/213–945. 36 rooms. Café. MC, V.*

¢   ☷ **Galare Guest House.** On the Mae Ping riverfront, this guest house
★   has many advantages: its good location, within five minutes' walk of
the Night Bazaar; friendly service from its staff; small but clean rooms
with air-conditioning or fans; and a restaurant. It offers more charm
and personal service than many of the other city hotels, and is the best
value in town. ⊠ *7 Charcoplathat Rd., 50000,* ☎ *053/273–885,* ℻
053/279–088. 25 rooms. Restaurant. No credit cards.

¢   ☷ **Lai Thai.** On the edge of the old city walls, a 10-minute walk from
the Night Bazaar, this friendly guest house offers rooms around a garden courtyard and a casual open-air restaurant that serves Thai, European, and Chinese food. The rooms are either air-conditioned or cooled
by overhead fans. Bare, polished floors and simple furniture give them
a fresh, clean look. Those at the back are quietest. There's a laundry
room.⊠ *111/4–5 Kotchasarn Rd., 50000,* ☎ *053/271–725,* ℻ *053/272–
724. 120 rooms. Restaurant, motorbikes, travel services. MC.*

Nightlife and the Arts

KHANTOKE DINNERS

No first visit to Chiang Mai should omit a khantoke dinner, whose menu
is usually sticky rice, which you mold into balls with your fingers; delicious *kap moo* (spiced pork skin); a super spicy dip called *nam prink
naw,* with onions, cucumber, and chili; and *kang ka,* a chicken-and-
vegetable curry—all accompanied by Singha beer. Frequently the khantoke dinner includes performances of Thai and/or hill-tribe dancing.
An evening's diversion usually starts at 7, costs about B650 for two,
and requires reservations.

One much publicized "dinner theater" puts on a repertory of dancing
and a khantoke dinner at the back of the **Diamond Hotel** (☎ 053/272–
080). Tour groups come here because there are good explanations of
the symbolism in the dancing. The **Old Chiang Mai Cultural Centre** (⊠
185/3 Wualai Rd., ☎ 053/275–097), designed like a hill-tribe village,
has nightly classical Thai and authentic hill-tribe dancing, after a khantoke dinner. The best place in the center of Chiang Mai to eat a khantoke dinner and see hill-tribe and classical Thai dances is the **Khum Kaew
Palace** (⊠ 252 Pra Pok Klao Rd., ☎ 053/214–315). The symbolism
of each dance is explained in Thai and English. The building is a distinctive traditional northern Thai house, where you sit cross-legged on
the floor or at long tables.

MASSAGE

Chiang Mai is a good place to try a traditional Thai massage. The cost
is B150 for a simple hour massage and B400 for a two-hour herbal
rubdown. **Petngarm Hat Wast** at the Diamond Hotel (⊠ 33/10 Charoen
Prathet Rd., Chiang Mai, ☎ 053/270–080) offers a range of traditional
massages. Good massages with or without herbs are also given at
Suan Samoon Prai (⊠ 105 Wansingkham Rd., ☎ 053/252–716).

PUBS AND BARS

The **Riverside** (☞ Dining, *above*) is one of the most popular pub
restaurants. For a casual evening, with a jazz trio, drop in at the European-style **Bantone** (⊠ 99/4 Moo 2, Huay Kaew Rd., ☎ 053/224–
444). At the **Cozy Corner** (⊠ 27 Moon Muang Rd., ☎ 053/277–964)
the pub atmosphere, chatty hostesses, and beer garden with a waterfall are all popular with the patrons, who come for hamburgers and
beer. Collect a T-shirt from the **Hard Rock Cafe** (⊠ 66/3 Loi Kroh Rd.,
near Thape Gate, ☎ 053/206–103). Described by *Newsweek* as "one
of the world's best bars," **The Pub** (⊠ 189 Huay Kaew Rd., ☎ 053/211–
550) can get a little crowded. Still, for draft beer, good grilled steak,
and a congenial atmosphere, this place is hard to beat. **The Domino Bar**
(⊠ 47 Moon Muang Rd. ☎ 053/278–503), an English-style pub with

snacks, is a meeting place where you may leave messages for fellow travelers.

Shopping

Always negotiate prices. Even if merchandise is priced, there is room for negotiation. Most shops honor major credit cards, and a further discount for cash is often possible. You will surely spend some time along the **Golden Mile,** a 16-km (10-mi) stretch of the road that runs east to San Kamphaeng. On both sides, large emporiums sell silver, ceramics, cottons and silks, wood carvings, hill-tribes' crafts and artifacts, lacquerware, bronzeware, and hand-painted umbrellas. Any taxi driver will happily spend a couple of hours taking you around for the giveaway rate of about B50 to B100, counting on your intent to buy: he receives a commission on your purchases.

One of Thailand's most exciting markets, the **Night Bazaar,** is a congestion of stalls selling anything from intricately woven Burmese rugs to designer-label shirts made in Thailand. The clothing can be very inexpensive, and, at times, good quality. Some objets d'art are instant antiques. This is shopper's heaven for crafts made in the rural villages throughout Burma, Laos, and northern Thailand—but inspect the goods thoroughly. The back of the stalls opens up into a sort of courtyard, with restaurants and some good hill-tribe products.

ANTIQUES

Borisoothi Antiques (✉ 15/2 Chiang Mai–San Kamphaeng Rd., ☏ 053/338–460) has a reputation for expertise in Thai and Burmese antiques, though it is always recommended that you have some expertise yourself before you settle on a purchase. Borisoothi also manufactures Ming Dynasty–style furniture.

CERAMICS

Siam Celadon (✉ 38 Moo 10, San Kamphaeng Rd., Km 10, ☏ 053/331–526) has the largest collection of Thai celadon. The deep, crackled, gray-green glaze is achieved with a wood-ash formula developed a thousand years ago. Celadon tends to be expensive, but prices are better here than in Bangkok.

ENGLISH-LANGUAGE BOOKS

D.K. Books (✉ 234 Tapae Rd., opposite Wat Buparam, ☏ 052/235–151) has a good selections of books in English, including guidebooks. **Suriwongse Centre** (✉ 54/1–5 Sri Douchai Rd., ☏ 053/252–052) carries a range of English-language books, with a large selection of Thai/English dictionaries.

HANDICRAFTS

Hilltribe and Handicraft Centre, Co, Ltd. (✉ 172 Moo 2, Bannong Khong, Chiang Mai-San Kamphaeng District, ☏ 053/331–977). Handicrafts and fabrics from the six hill tribes (Meo, Yao, Lisu, Igo, Muser, and Karen) are on display. Goods range from dolls dressed in multicolored traditional costumes to elaborate half-moon necklaces and clothes made from natural hemp. **Pen's House** (✉ 267/11 Chang Klarn Rd., Ampher Muang, ☏ 053/252–917). In hill-tribe-style houses various craftsmen "perform" their craft. Musical instruments are sold, including antique Karen elephant bells, for B30,000. Shoulder bags in traditional hill-tribe designs make especially good gifts.

JEWELRY

Chiang Mai is fast becoming Thailand's major center for trinkets, precious stones, and hill-tribe ornaments. **PN Precious Stones** (✉ Nai Thawan Arcade, opposite the Rincome Hotel, 95/6–7 Nimmanhemin Rd., ☏ 053/212–368) has quality gems. For hill-tribe jewelry and ornaments, visit the **Hill Tribe Products Promotion Centre** (main, ✉ 21/17 Suthep Rd., near Wat Suan Dok, ☎ 053/277–743; branch, ✉ 100/51–52 Huay Kaew Rd., opposite Chiang Mai University, ☎ 053/212–978).

LACQUERWARE

Chiang Mai Laitong (✉ 80/1 Moo 3, San Kamphaeng Rd., ☎ 053/338–237). This shop offers a vast array of lacquerware, ranging from small boxes to tables, and is a good place to see what is available. The clerks explain the seven-step process, and you can watch the artists at work.

SILK AND COTTON

San Kamphaeng (toward the end of the Golden Mile) has the best Thai silk at good prices. **Shinawatra** (on the Golden Mile) has the most stylish silk clothing and fabrics. **Jolie Femme** (✉ 8/3 San Kamphaeng Rd., past the superhighway intersection, ☎ 053/247–222) has Thai silk garments designed in the UK and will make clothes in 24 hours. **Neramit Custom Tailoring** (✉ 9½ Ratchawong Rd., ☎ 053/236–234) has a solid reputation built on 30 years of business.

SILVERWORK

The silversmiths along the Golden Mile are known for delicate work in silver close to 100% pure (look for the certifying marks). You'll see bowls with intricate hammered designs depicting the life of the Buddha or scenes from *Ramayana*. You can buy the chunky, attractive hill-tribe jewelry at the villages (that of the Meos has the most variety) or at **Thai Tribal Crafts** (✉ 208 Bamrung Rd., ☎ 053/241–043, closed Sun.), a nonprofit store run by church groups to promote self-help among the hill tribes.

UMBRELLAS

A fascinating traditional craft still continues at **Bo Sang** (north off the Golden Mile). Here villagers make paper umbrellas; the process begins by soaking mulberry wood and ends with the hand-painting of colorful designs on the finished product. **Umbrella Making Centre** (✉ 111/2 Bo Sang, Chiang Mai, ☎ 053/338–947), a manufacturer and retailer, has wonderful displays of hand-painted umbrellas and fans. **SA Paper and Umbrella Handicraft Centre** (✉ 999/16 Ban Nongkhong, San Kamphaeng Rd., ☎ 053/331–973) has a large selection of handmade paper, umbrellas, and fans.

Lamphun

8 *26 km (16 mi) south of Chiang Mai.*

Lamphun claims to be the oldest existing city in Thailand (but so does Nakhon Pathom). Originally called Nakorn Hariphunchai, it was founded in AD 680 by the Chamdhevi dynasty, which ruled until 1932. Unlike Chiang Mai, with its rapid growth, Lamphun remains a sleepy town, consisting of a main street with stores, several food stalls, and not much else. The town is known for its lamyai fruit, a sweet cherry-sized fruit with a thin shell. Buy yourself a jar of lamyai honey; you'll be in for a treat.

Lamphun's architectural prizes are two temple monasteries. Two kilometers (1¼ mi) west of the town's center is **Wat Chama Devi**—often called Wat Kukut (topless chedi) because the gold at its top has been removed. You'll probably want a samlor to take you down the narrow residential street to the wat. Since it is not an area where samlors generally cruise, it's a good idea to ask the driver to wait for you.

Despite a modern viharn at the side of the complex, the beauty of this monastery is in its weathered look. Suwan Chang Kot, to the right of the entrance, is the most famous of the monastery's two chedis. Built by King Mahantayot to hold the remains of his mother, the legendary Queen Chama Devi, first ruler of Lamphun, the five-tier sandstone chedi is square; on each of its four sides, and on each tier, are three Buddha images. The higher the level, the smaller the images. All are in the Dvaravati style—8th and 9th centuries—though many have obviously been restored. The other chedi was probably built in the 10th century, though most of what we see today is the work of King Phaya Sapphasit in the 12th century.

Lamphun's second major attraction, **Wat Phra That Hariphunchai,** is dazzling. Enter the monastery from the river, through a parking lot lined with stalls selling mementos. Go through the gates, guarded by ornamental lions, and you'll encounter a three-tier, sloping-roof viharn, a replica (built in 1925) of the original, which burned in 1915. Inside, note the large Chiang Saen–style bronze image of Buddha, Phra Chao Thongtip, and the carved *thammas* (Buddhist universal principals) to the left of the altar.

Leave the viharn by walking to the right past what is reputedly the largest bronze gong in the world, cast in 1860. The 165-foot Suwana chedi, covered in copper plates and topped by a golden spire, dates from 847. A century later, King Athitayarat, the 32nd ruler of Hariphunchai, raised its height and added more copper plating to honor the relics of Lord Buddha inside. On top of the chedi, he added a nine-tier umbrella, gilded with 14 pounds of pure gold. The museum, just outside the compound, has a fine selection of Dvaravati stucco work and Lamma antiques. ✉ *Admission.* ☉ *Museum open Wed.–Sun. 8:30–4.*

Lampang

⑨ *65 km (40 mi) southeast of Lamphun, 91 km (59 mi) southeast of Chiang Mai.*

The charming image of horse-drawn carriages in the town's quaint streets is still promoted by tourism officials, but the 20th century has come to Lampang. Concrete houses and stores have replaced the wooden buildings, cars and buses have taken over the streets, and only a few horses remain. Still, its wats, shops, and the few old-style wooden houses are sufficiently pleasant that you may wish to spend the night. Hotels in Lampang are the best that you will find between Chiang Mai and Phitsanulok.

Despite its rush into the 20th century, Lampang has some notable Burmese architecture remaining. Opposite the Thai International Airways office is **Wat Phra Fang,** easily recognizable by the green corrugated-iron roof on the viharn and the tall white chedi, decorated with gold leaf, at the top. Surrounding the chedi are seven small chapels, one for each day of the week. Inside each chapel is a niche with images of the Lord Buddha.

A well-preserved example of Lampang's Burmese architecture is **Wat Sri Chum.** Pay particular attention to the viharn: The eaves have beautiful carvings, and its doors and windows have elaborate decorations. Inside, gold-and-black lacquered pillars support a carved-wood ceiling, and to the right is a bronze Buddha cast in the Burmese style. Red-and-gold panels on the walls depict country temple scenes.

North of town, on the right bank of the River Wang, is **Wat Phra Kaeo Don Tao,** whose dominating visual element is the tall chedi, built on a rectangular base and topped with a rounded spire. Of more interest, however, are the Burmese-style shrine and the adjacent Thai-style sala. The 18th-century shrine has a multitier roof rising to a point. Inside, the walls are masterfully carved and inlaid with colored stones; the ornately engraved ceiling is inlaid with enamel. The Thai sala, with the traditional three-tier roof and carved-wood pediments, houses a Sukhothai-style reclining Buddha.

Wat Phra That Lampang Luang, south of Lampang, is one of the most venerated temples in the north. You'll spot the chedi towering above the trees, but the viharn to the left is the most memorable. The carved wood facade and two-tier roof complement its harmonious proportions; note the painstaking workmanship of the intricate decorations around the porticoes. The temple compound was once part of a fortified city, which has long since disappeared. It was founded in the 8th century by the legendary Princess Chama Dewi of Lopburi and destroyed about 200 years ago by the Burmese. The temple museum has excellent wood carvings, but its treasure is a small emerald Buddha, which some claim was carved from the same stone as its counterpart in Bangkok. ⊠ *Admission.* ☉ *Tues.–Sun. 9–4, closed Mon.*

Dining and Lodging

$$$ ✕ **Krua Thai.** For a stylish Thai meal, take a samlor to this popular restaurant in a northern-Thai–style house. Locals gather here in the many small, heavily timbered dining rooms to eat the mostly spicy Northern Thai food, but there are some Chinese dishes to offset the heat of chilis. ⊠ *Paholyothin Rd.,* ☏ *054/226–766), MC, V.*

$$ ✕ **Baan Rim Nam.** The name means "home by the river," and that is exactly what this traditional wood house was before it became a wonderful, atmospheric restaurant. The menu offers good Thai food (not too spicy for foreigners) and international dishes. ⊠ *328 Thip Rd.,* ☏ *322–501. MC, V.*

$ ✕ **U-Ping.** The fun local place to eat is this open-sided restaurant on the main street across from the access road to the Thip Chang hotel. Sports fans gather here to dine on the varied and well-prepared Thai food while watching local and international matches on the half-dozen TVs suspended from the ceiling. ⊠ *Thakraw Noi Rd.,* ☏ *054/226–824. No credit cards.*

$$ 🛏 **Wienthong Hotel.** Currently the best hotel in Lampang, the Wienthong has the most comfortable rooms and public areas. Rooms are kept clean and fresh, despite the continual flow of tour groups. The restaurant is the best in town for Western food. ⊠ *138/109 Paholyothin Rd.,* ☏ *054/225–801,* FAX *054–225–803. 178 rooms. Restaurant. AE, MC, V.*

¢ 🛏 **No 4 Guest House.** This old Thai-style teak house has a garden. The friendly owner teaches English at the local school. ⊠ *54 Pamai Rd., Vieng Nuea, Lampang, no phone. 25 rooms with shared bath. Breakfast room. No credit cards.*

Shopping

Lampang is known for its blue-and-white pottery. Buy it at shops in the city center, or visit any of the 60 factories in town. Generally, a samlor driver will take you to these factories for a few baht, because he receives a commission. **Ku Ceramic** (⊠ 167 Mu 6, Phahonyothin Rd., ☏ 054/218–313) has a good selection.

Mae Hong Son

⑩ *270 km (169 mi) northwest of Chiang Mai via Pai, 368 km (230 mi) via Mae Sariang, 924 km (574 mi) north of Bangkok.*

Just inside the Burmese border, this sleepy market town where villagers trade vegetables and wares is like the Chiang Mai of 30 years ago, but it is developing fast. Already it has two comfortable hotels, several small resorts, and at least a dozen guest houses.

The tourist lure is **visiting hill-tribe villages,** especially those of the Karen Long Necks (also called Padong), whose women wear copper bands around their necks, making them exceptionally long. Long Neck Karens have a legend that their ancestors were descended from the god of wind and a female dragon, and it is thought that the women extend their necks to imitate the dragon. Perhaps it is more true that the copper bands are a sign of wealth. The girls start to wear bands at six, adding another every three years until they are 21. They are never removed, even after death, except for cleaning, or in case of adultery, when the woman's relatives, out of shame, will forcibly remove them.

In Thailand there are three Karen Long Neck villages, all outside Mae Hong Son, with a total of 36 families, all of whom are accustomed to posing for photographs. There is a B300 fee for entering the village; half of the tax goes to the village, the other half to the local warlord, who uses the money to fund his army. The easiest village to reach is the one with six families, upriver from Mae Hong Son beyond the village of Nam Pieng Din. By arrangements made through your hotel or a local guide, you travel by boat, with a guide, for the 90-minute trip. (Cost: approximately B1,300.)

Within a three-hour drive of Mae Hong Son, the Shans, Lanna Thais, Karens, and Hmongs (Meo) also have villages, which are usually visited on guided treks of three or more days. You can leave the choice of village up to the guide—each has his favorites—but you should ask him whether he speaks the village language and discuss fully with him what is planned and how strenuous the trek is. Since guides come and go, and villages tend to change in their attitude toward foreigners, what is written today is out of date tomorrow (☞ Trekking, *below*).

Dining and Lodging

$–$$ ✕ **Bai Fern.** For food and music together this is the most popular restaurant in town, both with Thais and foreigners. The room is large, with paneled walls and teak columns. Subdued lights and whirling fans add to the festive mood. A band plays Thai Western songs that harmonize with the clatter of plates. Most of the menu is Thai, and spicy dishes are adapted to Western tastes on request. ✉ *87 Khun Lum Praphas Rd.,* ☎ *053/611–374. MC, V.*

$ ✕ **Kai-Mook,** just off the main street, is the best restaurant for al fresco
★ dining and excellent northern Thai cooking. Of the 10 or so restaurants along this street, Kai-Mook has the freshest and tastiest food. ✉ *71 Khun Lum Praphas Rd.,* ☎ *053/612–092. No credit cards.*

$$–$$$ ▦ **Holiday Inn.** This international-style hotel, about 1½ km (1 mi) out of town off the main road to Khun Yuam, bustles with tour groups coming and going; activity focuses around the pool in the daytime and in the disco at night. Rooms are standard, boring, slightly depressingly furnished in blue, well-worn but clean. The best of them have private balconies that look out over the gardens and the pool. Service is a little sloppy, but many of the staff speak English. ✉ *114/5–7 Khun Lum Praphas Rd., Mae Hong Son 58000,* ☎ *053/611–390,* ℻ *053/611–524. 144 rooms. Restaurant, pool, nightclub, travel services. AE, DC, MC, V.*

$$ ▦ **Tara Mae Hong Son.** This hotel is slightly less expensive than the
★ Holiday Inn and considerably more attractive. Its classic northern Thai architecture, with the huge lobby reception area and broad open porches, gives it an airy feeling. The restaurant faces the lush terraced valley, as does the beautifully landscaped pool. The decor emphasizes

wood with highly polished floors and bamboo chairs and tables. The service is enthusiastic and helpful. The hotel is 3 km (2 mi) out of town slightly beyond the Holiday Inn. ⊠ *149 Moo 8 Tambon Peng Moo, Amphur Muang, Mae Hong Son 58000,* ☎ *053/611–473,* 𝔽𝔸𝕏 *053/611– 252. In Bangkok,* ☎ *02/254–0023. 104 rooms. Restaurant, pool, travel services. AE, DC, MC, V.*

$–$$ 🏨 **Rim Nam Klang Doi.** On the Pai River, 5 km (3 mi) out of town, this is one of the better rural resorts and offers good value. Many of the rooms look out onto the river; others have views of the tropical landscaped grounds. The preferred rooms are fan-cooled with a private hot-water shower—you really don't need the more expensive air-conditioned rooms. A minivan shuttles you to town or back for B100. ⊠ *Ban Huay Dua,* ☎ *053/612–142,* 𝔽𝔸𝕏 *053/612–086) 34 rooms. Restaurant. MC, V.*

$ 🏨 **Piya Guest House.** This is the most comfortable guest house in the area, with the best location, facing serene Jong Kham lake in the center of Mae Hong Son. The owner has let the fan-cooled rooms around the courtyard deteriorate slightly and paid more attention to the air-conditioned rooms. Outside tables at the restaurant face the lake; those inside share space with a pool table. ⊠ *1 Soi 6, Khun Lum Praphat Rd., Mae Hong Son 58000,* ☎ *053/611–260,* 𝔽𝔸𝕏 *053/612–308. 11 rooms, most with bath. Restaurant. No credit cards.*

¢ 🏨 **Jean's Guest House.** This is truly a basic, bungalow guest house where a tiny room with a fan goes for B100. The advantage of staying here is that Jean speaks fluent English and can often serve as a good resource for finding local guides. ⊠ *6 Prachautith Rd., Mae Hong Son 58000* ☎ *053/611–662. 9 rooms. No credit cards.*

Outdoor Activities and Sports

TREKKING

In the 1960s a few intrepid travelers in northern Thailand started wandering the hills and staying at the villages; by 1980, tour companies were organizing groups with a guide and sending them off for three- to seven-day treks. Days are spent walking forest trails between villages, where nights are spent as paying guests. Accommodation is in huts, and at best a wooden platform with no mattress is provided. Food is likely to be a bowl of sticky rice and stewed vegetables. It can become very cold at night, so take warm clothes as well as sturdy hiking shoes. Also take insect repellent, against mosquitoes, and perhaps some disinfectant soap, in case the huts are grubby. Otherwise, travel light.

The level of difficulty varies: you might traverse tough, hilly terrain for several hours or travel by Jeep then take an easy 30-minute walk to a village. Perhaps a ride on an elephant or a half-day on a raft is thrown in to give the sense of adventure.

Typically, the easier the trek the more commercial the village; the search is for one that has not been saturated with Westerners, but they are becoming fewer and fewer. Because areas quickly become overtrekked and guides come and go, the only way to select a tour is to talk to other travelers and try to get the latest information. What was good six months ago may not be good today.

Unless you speak some Thai, know the local geography and understand something of the native customs. Don't go alone: You risk being robbed or worse by bandits. It's best to use the services of a certified guide. Since the guide determines the quality of the tour, it's important to pick one who's familiar with the local dialects and languages spoken and who knows which villages are the least tourist-ridden. He should also speak good English. It is also imperative that you discuss the villages and route; that way you'll at least seem to know the ropes. You usually can tell whether the guide is knowledgeable and respects the villagers, but question him thoroughly about his experience before you sign up.

Chiang Rai

⑪ *180 km (112 mi) northeast of Chiang Mai, 780 km (485 mi) north of Bangkok.*

Architecturally, little can be said for this city of two-story concrete buildings. Most of the famous old structures are gone. Today, Chiang Rai is a market town that works during the day and is fast asleep by 10 PM, though a recently established night bazaar, just off Phahalyothin Road, provides crafts stalls and open-air dining.

The Akha, Yao, Meo, Lisu, Lahu, and Karen tribes all live within Chiang Rai province. Each has a different dialect, different customs, handicrafts, costumes, and a different way of venerating animist spirits. Only in the past two decades have the tribes been confronted with the 20th century. Now, the villagers are learning to produce their handicrafts commercially for eager buyers in exchange for blue jeans and other commodities. You can visit some villages on day trips or make two- to five-day guided treks to the more remote ones (☞ Trekking, *above*).

Dining and Lodging

$ ✕ **Honarira.** If you decide not to dine at the night bazaar, then this restaurant is Chiang Rai's best for a casual outdoor meal under an umbrella of small trees. The menu (also in English) is a mix of northern and mainstream Thai, so you might start with some spicy sausages and follow with *pla tod chon* (deep fried serpent-head fish) and red curry beef. ☒ *402/1-2 Banphaprakan Rd.,* ☎ *053/715–722. No credit cards.*

$$$ 🏨 **Dusit Island Resort.** Sitting on an island in the Kok river, the Dusit
★ Island has the best location in Chiang Rai. The hotel has all the amenities of a resort, including the largest outdoor pool in the north. Furnished in a modern rendition of traditional Thai, the spacious rooms have air-conditioning, television, and large marble baths; all have a stunning view of the river. If you arrive in Chiang Rai by river, the boatman can drop you off at the hotel's pier. ☒ *1129 Kraisorasit Rd., Amphur Muang, Chiang Rai 57000,* ☎ *053/715–777,* 🖷 *053/715–801. Bangkok reservations,* ☎ *02/238–4790. 271 rooms. 3 restaurants, bar, pool, 2 tennis courts, health club, shops, nightclub, meeting room, airport shuttle, car rental. AE, DC, MC, V.*

$$$ 🏨 **Little Duck Hotel.** The first luxury resort in Chiang Rai, this hotel screams modernity. Guests are often conventioneers, who mill around the huge lobby. The rooms are bright and cheery, with light-wood fixtures and large beds. Service is brisk and smart, and the travel desk is ready to organize excursions into the neighboring hills. ☒ *450 Super Highway Rd., Amphoe, Muang, Chiang Rai 57000,* ☎ *053/715–620,* 🖷 *053/712–639; Bangkok reservations,* ☎ *02/255–5960. 350 rooms. 2 restaurants, 24-hr coffee shop, pool, tennis court, meeting rooms, travel services. AE, DC, MC, V.*

$$–$$$ 🏨 **Wiang Inn.** In the heart of town, this comfortable, well-established hotel has a small outdoor pool, a pleasant sitting area, and a restaurant with Chinese, Thai, and Western food. Spacious bedrooms, now slightly worn, make this the top hotel in Chiang Rai itself. ☒ *893 Phaholyothin Rd., Chiang Rai 57000,* ☎ *053/711–543,* 🖷 *053/711–877. 260 rooms. Restaurant, pool, health club, nightclub, travel services. AE, DC, V.*

$ ⊡ **Golden Triangle Inn.** Don't confuse this guest house with the resort at Bop Sop Ruak. It is a backpackers' base for trips into the hills. Rooms have private bathrooms and are either air-conditioned or fan-cooled. The restaurant/lounge offers Thai and Western fare. The owners arrange trips to Chiang Klong, where they have another guest house. ⊠ *590 Phaholyothin Rd., Chiang Rai 57000,* ☎ *053/711–339,* FAX *053/713–363. 20 rooms. No credit cards.*

Sop Ruak and the Golden Triangle

⑫ *67 km (42 mi) northeast of Chiang Rai, 247 km (153 mi) northeast of Chiang Mai.*

An hour outside Chiang Rai, on the banks of the Mae Khong River, is Chiang Saen. Turning left (north) at the T junction in Chiang Saen will take you to Sop Ruak, the village in the heart of the Golden Triangle where the opium warlord Khun Sa once ruled. A decade ago, Thai troops forced him back to Burmese territory, but visitors still flock here to see this notorious region, and the village street is lined with souvenir stalls to lure them from their buses. Some of the best views over the confluence of the Mae Sai, Mae Ruak and Mae Khong rivers, and into the lush hills of Burma and Laos, are from the new Golden Triangle Resort Hotel. Even if you are not staying at the hotel, pay a visit to check out the view. Another good viewing point is the pavilion along the path leading from behind the police station.

Lodging

$$$ ⊡ **Baan Boran Hotel.** The newest entry in the Golden Triangle is this
★   distinctive resort hotel, on a hill off the Mae Sai road 3 km (2 mi) out of Chiang Saen. All the guest rooms share the hotel's panoramic views over the confluence of the Ruak and Mae Khong rivers and beyond into Laos. They have rust-red fabrics and carpets, corner table/desks, couches, coffee tables, and picture windows opening onto balconies. ⊠ *Chiang Saen, Chiang Rai 57150,* ☎ *053/716–678,* FAX *053/716– 702; Bangkok reservations:* ☎ *02/251–4707. 106 rooms. 3 restaurants, bar, in-room safes, pool, meeting rooms, travel services, airport shuttle, car rental. AE, DC, MC, V.*

$$–$$$ ⊡ **Delta Golden Triangle Resort Hotel.** The views of the forested hills across the rivers are splendid from this resort. The architecture is northern Thai, with plenty of wood throughout. The superior ("executive") rooms have private balconies overlooking the Golden Triangle; third-floor rooms have the best view. The hotel has an elegant dining room, but it's more fun sitting out on the deck, sipping Mae Khong whiskey and imagining the intrigues in the villages across the border. Classical Thai dances are performed in the evening. ⊠ *222 Baan Sobruak, Chiang Saen, Chiang Rai,* ☎ *053/784–001,* FAX *053/784–006. Bangkok reservations,* ☎ *02/512–0392,* FAX *02/512–0393. 74 rooms. 2 restaurants, pool, 2 tennis courts, travel services. AE, DC, MC, V.*

Northern Thailand A to Z

Arriving and Departing

The State Railway links Chiang Mai to Bangkok and points south, but goes no farther north. As the trip from Bangkok takes about 13 hours and there's little to see but paddy fields, overnight sleepers are the best trains to take, and they are very comfortable. On most routes buses are faster and cheaper than trains, but if time is short, take a plane.

CHIANG MAI AND NEARBY

By Bus: Many state-run and private buses run day and night between Bangkok and Chiang Mai; the trip takes about 11 hours and costs approximately B300. On VIP air-conditioned buses with only 24 seats, it costs about B470. State-run buses leave from Bangkok's Northern Terminal (⊠ Phahonyothin Rd., ☎ 02/279–4484). Some of the private buses use Bangkok's Banglampoo section of town as the drop-off and pick-up point. Private tour coach operators such as Top North (☎ 02/252–2967 in Bangkok) and Chan Tour (☎ 02/252–0349 in Bangkok) have more luxurious buses and charge B30–B60 more for the Bangkok trip.

The easiest way to reach Lamphun from Chiang Mai is to take the minibus songthaew (fare B10), which leaves about every 20 minutes from the TAT office on Lamphun Road.

By Plane: Thai Airways International (☎ 02/234–3100 in Bangkok) has 10 or more flights daily between Bangkok and Chiang Mai, and direct daily flights between Phuket and Chiang Mai. The Bangkok flight takes about an hour and costs approximately B1,700. In 1996 Bangkok Airways (☎ 02/253–4014) started to fly three times a week between Chiang Mai and Bangkok with a stopover in Sukhothai. A new airline, the Orient Express (☎ 053/201566 in Chiang Mai, 02/267–3210 in Bangkok), connects Chiang Mai directly with Udon Thani, Ubon Ratchathani, Khon Kaen, Surat Thani, and Hat Yai. Convenient as these flights are, they are expensive. For example, a one-way ticket between Chiang Mai and Khon Kaen costs B1,490. Silk Air has direct flights between Chiang Mai and Singapore, and Air Mandalay flies three times a week between Mandalay and Chiang Mai (book through a travel agent). During the peak season, flights are heavily booked. The airport is about 10 minutes from downtown, a B80 taxi ride.

By Train: Trains depart from Bangkok's Hualamphong Railway Station and arrive at Chiang Mai (⊠ Charoenmuang Rd., ☎ 053/245–563). Overnight sleepers leave at 6 PM and 7:40 PM and arrive in Chiang Mai at 7:05 AM and 7:55 AM). The return train leaves at 5:15 PM from Chiang Mai and arrives in Bangkok at 6:25 AM. (Departure times are subject to minor changes.) The overnight trains are invariably well maintained, with clean sheets on the rows of two-tier bunks. The second-class carriages, either fan-cooled or air-conditioned, are comfortable (fare approximately B505). First class (two bunks per compartment) is twice the price. There is also the Nakhonphing Special Express that leaves Bangkok at 7:40 PM and arrives at Chiang Mai at 8:25 AM (return trip departs at 9:05 PM and arrives in Bangkok at 9:40 AM). This train does not have first-class compartments. There are hotel booking agents at Chiang Mai railway station. The tuk-tuk fare to the center of town ranges from B20 to B30. Most Bangkok–Chiang Mai trains stop at Phitsanulok at Lamphun, where a bicycle samlor can take you the 3 km (2 mi) into town for B30.

CHIANG RAI AND THE GOLDEN TRIANGLE

By Bus: Buses run throughout the day from Chiang Mai to Chiang Rai, departing from the Chiang Mai Arcade Bus Station. The express takes 2½ hours and costs about B80; the local takes 3½ hours and is even cheaper.

By Bus and Boat: The most exciting way to reach Chiang Rai is on a combination bus and boat trip. You leave Chiang Mai at 6:30 AM for a four-hour trip on a local bus to Tha Thon, north of Fang (or you can hire a car and driver for about B1,200 and leave your Chiang Mai hotel at 8 AM). In Tha Thon, after lunch at the restaurant opposite the landing stage, you leave on a long-tailed boats at 12:30 PM (buy your ticket at the kiosk). These public boats hold 10 passengers, and the fare is B160 per person. You may hire your own boat for B1,600, which you will have to do if you arrive after 12:30 PM. The trip down the Mae Kok River to Chiang Rai takes five hours, going through rapids and passing a few hill-tribe villages. The more adventurous can travel by unmotorized raft (best during October and November, when the water flows quickly), staying overnight in small villages on the three-day journey.

By Plane: Thai Airways International offers two nonstop flights daily into Chiang Rai from Bangkok (B1,820) and two flights from Chiang Mai (B230). Taxis meet incoming flights, but most tourist hotels have their own shuttle vans waiting for guests.

LAMPANG

By Bus: Both air-conditioned and non-air-conditioned buses connect Lampang to Thailand's north and northwest and to Bangkok. The bus station is 3 km (2 mi) away—take a samlor into town—but the ticket offices are in Lampang.

By Plane: Thai Airways International has one daily flight between Bangkok and Lampang.

By Train: From Chiang Mai, the train takes approximately 2½ hours to reach Lampang. From Bangkok, it takes 11 hours, and from Phitsanulok, five hours.

MAE HONG SON

By Bus: An express bus leaves Chiang Mai Arcade Bus Station in the morning for the 8-hour trip (fare B175). On the return trip you might want to get off the bus at Mae Taeng and connect with the bus from Chiang Mai that goes to Fang and Tha Thon (the village where boats leave for the river trip to Chiang Rai; ☞ Arriving and Departing, Chiang Rai and the Golden Triangle, *above*).

By Car: You can rent a car and drive from Chiang Mai, but unless you hire a driver to return the car, you're forced to make the long drive twice. The road has arm-wrenching bends but is also very scenic; the shortest and most attractive route is the northern route through Pai. The southern route, Highway 108 through Mae Sariang is longer, but it's easier driving and takes about two hours less time.

By Plane: Thai Airways International (☎ 02/513–0121 or 02/234–3100 in Bangkok) has two flights a day between Chiang Mai and Mae Hong Son. They tend to be fully booked, so make reservations in advance. The cost is amazingly low—B345 one way. Bangkok Airways has a direct daily flight between Bangkok and Mae Hong Son for B2180. The airport is within walking distance of town, though a tuk-tuk costs only B10.

Getting Around

CHIANG MAI AND NEARBY

Chiang Mai itself is compact and can be explored easily on foot or by bicycle, with the occasional use of public or other transport for temples, shops, and attractions out of the city center. In the small town of Lamphun all the sights are within a B20 bicycle samlor ride.

By Bus: Chiang Mai's Arcade Bus Station (☎ 053/274–638 or 242–664) serves Bangkok, Sukhothai, Phitsanulok, Udon Thani, and Chiang Rai (and towns within the province of Chiang Rai). The Chiang Phuak terminal serves Lamphun, Fang, Tha Ton, and destinations within Chiang Mai province.

By Car: A car, with a driver and guide, is the most convenient way to visit three of the five key temples located outside Chiang Mai as well as the Elephant Camp and hill-tribe villages. For a morning's visit to the 6-km-long (3.8-mi-long) long craft factory/shopping area, the price for a car should not be more than B100, as the driver will be anticipating commissions from the stores you visit. You can also make private arrangements with a taxi for a day's transportation, for approximately B1,000–B1,400, depending on mileage. Be sure to negotiate the price before you step in the car or, better yet, establish the price the evening before and have the driver collect you from your hotel in the morning. Do not pay until you have completed the trip. Two major agencies in Chiang Mai are **Hertz** (⊠ 90 Sridornchai Rd., ☎ 053/279–474) and **Avis** (⊠ 14/14 Huay Kaew Rd., ☎ 053/221–316).

By Motorcycle: Motorcycles are popular. Rental agencies are numerous, and most small hotels have their own agency. Shop around to get the best price and a bike in good condition. Remember that any damage to the bike that can be attributed to you will be, including its theft.

By Samlor: Most trips in a tuk-tuk within Chiang Mai should cost less than B30.

By Songthaew: These red minibuses follow a kind of fixed route, but will go elsewhere at a passenger's request. Name your destination before you get in. The cost is B5.

CHIANG RAI
Taxis and bicycle samlors are always available in Chiang Rai and in the surrounding small towns. Buses depart frequently for nearby towns (every 15 minutes to Chiang Saen or to Mae Sai, for example), or you can commission a taxi for the day.

LAMPANG
Horse-drawn carriages are available for tourists at a rank outside the government house, although some are usually waiting at the train station. The price for a 15-minute tour of central Lampang is B30. The hourly rate is approximately B100. The easiest and least expensive way to get around, however, is by samlor.

MAE HONG SON
Everything is within walking distance, though you may need a tuk-tuk or taxi to take you into town from your hotel. It is usual to take trips to the outlying villages and sights with a guide and chauffeured car. Should you hire a jeep, be sure that its four-wheel drive is in working order. Less expensive, if you want to explore on your own, are motorbikes, which can be rented from one of the shops along the town's main street.

Contacts and Resources
CONSULATES
Canadian Consulate (⊠ 151 Chiang Mai–Lamphun Superhighway, ☎ 053/850147). **U.K. Consulate** (⊠ 3rd Fl., IBM Building, 139/2 Huay Kaew Rd., ☎ 053/894–189). **U.S. Consulate** (⊠ 387 Wichayanom Rd., ☎ 053/252–629).

EMERGENCIES
In Chiang Mai and nearby, contact the following: **Police** and **ambulance** (☎ 191). **Tourist Police** (⊠ 105/1 Chiang Mai-Lamphun Rd., ☎ 053/248–974 or 1699). Also **tourist police boxes** (⊠ In front of the Night Bazaar and in the airport. **Lanna Hospital** (⊠ 103 Superhighway, ☎ 053/211–037).

In Chiang Rai, contact the following: **Chiang Rai police** (☎ 053/711–444). **Chiang Rai Hospital** (☎ 053/711–300). **Over Brook Hospital** (☎ 053/711–366).

In Mae Hong Son, contact the **Thai Tourist Police** (⊠ Rajadrama Phithak Rd., ☎ 053/611–812).

Every other store in Chiang Mai seems to be a tour agency, so you'd be wise to pick up a list of TAT-recognized agencies before choosing one. Also, each hotel has its own travel desk and association with a tour operator. Since it is the guide who makes the tour great, arrange to meet yours before you actually sign up. This is particularly important if you are planning a trek to the hill-tribe villages.

Prices vary quite a bit, so shop around, and carefully examine the offerings. Dozens of tour operators, some extremely unreliable, set up shop on a Chiang Mai sidewalk and disappear after they have your money, so *use* your TAT-approved list. **Top North** (⊠ 15 Soi 2, Moon Muang Rd., ☎ 053/278–532) and **Summit Tour and Trekking** (⊠ Thai Charoen Hotel, Tapas Rd., ☎ 053/233–351) offer good tours at about B350 a day (more for elephant rides and river rafting), and **World Travel Service** (⊠ Rincome Hotel, Huay Kaeo Rd., ☎ 053/221–1044) is reliable.

The four major hotels in Chiang Rai and the Golden Triangle Resort in Chiang Saen organize minibus tours of the area. Their travel desks will also arrange treks to the hill-tribe villages with a guide. Should you prefer to deal directly with a tour/travel agency, try **Golden Triangle Tours** (⊠ 590 Phahotyothin Rd., Chiang Rai 57000, ☎ 053/711–339).

ST&T Travel Center (⊠ 193/12 Sridonchai Rd., Amphur Muang, Chiang Mai, ☎ 053/251–922), on the same street as the Chiang Plaza Hotel, is good for plane, train, or bus tickets. Contact **Thai International Airways** (⊠ Phra Poklao Rd., Chiang Mai, ☎ 053/241–044), to arrange domestic and international bookings.

Chiang Mai Tourist Authority of Thailand (TAT) (⊠ 105/1 Chiang Mai-Lamphun Rd., on the far side of the river, ☎ 053/248–604).

Chiang Rai Tourist Information Center (⊠ Singhakhlai Rd., ☎ 053/711–433).

THE SOUTHERN BEACH RESORTS

The resorts of southern Thailand's long peninsula are pure hedonism. Everything is there for the wanting, from five-star luxury hotels to dirt cheap bungalows, from water sports to golf, from sleazy bars to elegant dining rooms, from beaches washed by azure waters to verdant hills, from exotic fruit to bountiful seafood to pizza and hamburgers. The Andaman Sea and the Gulf of Siam have become international playgrounds.

Phuket

Backpackers discovered Phuket in the early 1970s. The word got out about its long, white, sandy beaches and cliff-sheltered coves, its waterfalls, mountains, clear waters, scuba diving, fishing, seafood, and fiery sunsets—with rainbow colors shimmering off the turquoise Andaman Sea. Entrepreneurs built massive developments, at first clustering around Patong, and then spreading out. Most formerly idyllic deserted bays and secluded havens now have at least one hotel impinging on their beauty, and hotels are still being built despite a shortage of trained staff and an overburdened infrastructure.

Shaped like a teardrop pendant with many chips, Phuket is linked to the mainland by a causeway. Its indented coastline and hilly interior make the island seem larger than its 48-km (30-mi) length and 21-km (13-mi) breadth. Before the tourists came, Phuket was already making fortunes out of tin mining (it is still Thailand's largest tin producer) and rubber plantations. Although the west coast, with its glittering sand beaches, is committed to tourism, other parts of the island still function as normal communities, largely untainted by the influx of foreign holiday-makers. Typically, tourists go directly to their hotels on arrival, spend most of their vacation on the beach, and make only one or two sorties to visit other parts of the island. Hence, the sights and places (mostly beaches) are listed in a counterclockwise itinerary, beginning with Phuket Town, the provincial capital and only real town on the island.

Numbers in the margin correspond to points of interest on the Phuket map.

Phuket Town
❶ *862 km (539 mi) south of Bangkok.*

About one-third of the island's population lives in Phuket Town, the provincial capital, but very few tourists stay here. The town is busy, and drab modern concrete buildings have replaced the old Malay colonial-type architecture. A few hours of browsing through the tourist shops are not wasted, however. Most of the shops and cafés are along Phang-Nga Road and Rasda Road. By bus, you arrive in Phuket on the eastern end of Phang-Nga Road.

LODGING
$$$ 🏨 **Metropole.** If you should come to Phuket Town on business, you should stay at the best and newest hotel—the Metropole. A sparkling crisp marble lobby greets you; a spacious lounge bar on your left gives air-conditioned comfort during the day. Guest rooms are bright with picture windows and furnishings in pastel colors. ✉ *1 Soi Surin, Montri Rd., Phuket Town, 83000,* ☎ *076/214–022,* 📠 *076/215–990. 248 rooms. 2 restaurants, lobby bar, karaoke bar, pool, health club, business services, meeting rooms. AE, DC, MC, V.*

Bang Thao Beach
❷ *22 km (14 mi) northwest of Phuket Town.*

South of the headland sheltering Nai Thon Beach, the shore curves in to form Bang Thao Beach, formerly the site of a tin mine. Chemical seepage had left the place an ecological disaster, and it remained an eyesore until about 10 years ago, when a Thai developer bought the land and started a clean-up. He built one hotel, then another, and another, until the whole bay became a resort area with five major hotels offering in total 2,000 rooms and 27 restaurants.

LODGING
$$$$ 🏨 **Banyan Tree Phuket.** Of the five resort hotels at Laguna Beach on Bang Thao Bay, this is the most exclusive. Built along classical European lines, but with teak floors and Thai fabrics, you have a sense of entering a hedonistic Greek compound. Indeed, many guests come for the spa treatments, which include herbal massages, special diets, and exercise. When not being pampered at the spa, you can stay in your private villa—a secluded enclave whose bathroom, with an extra outdoor shower, is as big as the spacious bedroom. Thirty-four of these villas have their own small pools (B5,000 extra). Should you tire of the hotel's two restaurants, you can join the hoi polloi at any of the 28 restaurants at the other Laguna Beach hotels and bill your meals to your room. ✉ *33 Moo 4 Srisoonthorn Rd., Cherngtalay, Thalang, Phuket 83110,* ☎ *076/324–374,* 📠 *076/324–356. 98 villas. 2 restaurants, pool, 5 tennis courts, 18-hole golf course, massage, spa, health club, squash. AE, MC, V.*

Phuket

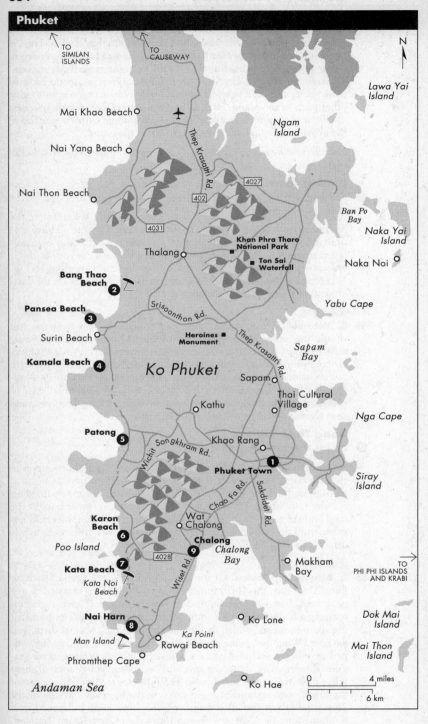

TO SIMILAN ISLANDS

TO CAUSEWAY

N

Lawa Yai Island

Mai Khao Beach

Ngam Island

Nai Yang Beach

Thep Krasattri Rd.

4027

Ban Po Bay

Nai Thon Beach

402

4031

Naka Yai Island

Khan Phra Tharo National Park

Ton Sai Waterfall

Thalang

Naka Noi

Bang Thao Beach 2

Srisoonthon Rd.

Yabu Cape

Pansea Beach 3

Heroines Monument

Thep Krasattri Rd.

Surin Beach

Ko Phuket

Sapam Bay

Kamala Beach 4

Sapam

Thai Cultural Village

Nga Cape

Kathu

Patong 5

Wichit Songkhram Rd.

Khao Rang

Phuket Town 1

Siray Island

Chao Fa Rd.

Sakdidet Rd.

Karon Beach 6

Wat Chalong

Chalong 9

Poo Island

4028

Chalong Bay

TO PHI PHI ISLANDS AND KRABI

Kata Beach 7

Wiset Rd.

Makham Bay

Kata Noi Beach

Dok Mai Island

Nai Harn 8

Ko Lone

Man Island

Ka Point

Rawai Beach

Mai Thon Island

Phromthep Cape

Andaman Sea

Ko Hae

0   4 miles

0   6 km

$$$ 🏨 **Dusit Laguna.** Facing a mile-long beach and flanked by two lagoons, this resort hotel is now part of the Laguna Beach complex. Its seclusion is gone, but the cross-dining plan extends your choices of where to eat and be entertained. The hotel rooms, with picture windows opening onto private balconies, have pastel decor and commodious bathrooms. There's barbecue dining on the terrace and, after dinner, dancing to the latest sounds. Evening entertainment changes nightly and may consist of a song-and-dance troupe of transvestites or classical Thai dance. ✉ *390 Srisoontorn Rd., Cherngtalay District, Thalang, Phuket 83110,* ☎ *076/324–320,* FAX *076/324–174; Bangkok reservations* ☎ *02/236–0450. 240 rooms, including 7 suites. 4 restaurants, pool, putting green, 2 tennis courts, windsurfing, boating, meeting rooms, travel services. AE, DC, MC, V.*

$$$ 🏨 **Sheraton Grande Laguna.** The beach is just across a grassy lawn, and a long, narrow pool meanders through the hotel complex before opening up into two larger, swimmable pools. The wonderfully spacious rooms are furnished minimally and decorated with indigenous art. All have small private balconies. For a large hotel the service is swift and polite. For more privacy and personal attention, rent one of the 85 one- or two-bedroom "villa suites" in a separate enclave with its own pool, and receive a complimentary breakfast as well as evening cocktails. Guests can dine at a range of restaurants, the best of which is the Marketplace, a group of food stands that present a sampling of Asian foods. ✉ *Bang Thao Bay, 10 Moo 4 Srisoonthorn Rd., Cherngtalay, Thalang, Phuket 83110,* ☎ *076/324–101,* FAX *076/324108. 343 rooms. 5 restaurants, 2 pools, 18-hole golf course, 4 tennis courts, windsurfing, boating, nightclub. AE, DC, MC, V.*

Pansea Beach
❸ *21 km (12 mi) northwest of Phuket Town.*

South of Bang Thao, in a small bay sheltered by a headland, stretches Pansea Beach, virtually a private enclave for two splendid hotels. The most famous of the two is the island's elegant—and certainly most expensive—resort, Amanpuri. Tucked in a small cove and designed to blend into the cliffside, it affords a complete sense of privacy. On the same beach with the same ideal location and cliffside backdrop, but at half the price, is the Chedi Hotel.

DINING AND LODGING

$$$$ ✕ **Amanpuri.** Make a special effort to visit, even if only for a drink, this beutiful resort dining room here is beautiful. The split-level building, with a thatched Thai roof and modern bamboo furniture, has spectacular sea views. The Continental cuisine has a definite Italian accent. Try the fresh fish on a bed of vegetables, topped with a sauce sparked by fresh ginger and lemongrass. ✉ *Pansea Beach,* ☎ *076/311–394. Reservations essential. AE, DC, V.*

$$$$ 🏨 **Amanpuri.** For relaxation amid tasteful and elegant surroundings, there is no finer place in Thailand—nor is any place quite as expensive. The most basic accommodation costs $350. The main building is completely open, with polished floors, modern bamboo furniture, and pitched, thatch roofs. Guests stay in individual pavilions, staggered up the hillside from the beach. The architectural style is distinctly Thai, with broad eaves and swooping roofs. Furnishings are handcrafted with local woods, and each suite has its private sundeck. A split-level bar perches on the hill, affording a romantic view of the sunset across the Andaman Sea. The swimming pool is up from the beach, and the beach itself is secluded. ✉ *Pansea Beach, Phuket 83110,* ☎ *076/324–333,* FAX *076/324–100; Bangkok reservations* ☎ *02/287–0226; in*

U.S. 800/447–7462. 40 pavilions and 13 villas. 2 restaurants, bar, pool, 2 tennis courts, windsurfing, boating, shops, travel services. AE, V.

$$ ▣ **Chedi.** Management of this cliffside hotel has been taken over by
★ the division of Amanresorts (who manage the Amanpuri) that handles properties in a lower price category. Nevertheless, they achieve a special ambiance and superior service. Some improvements are planned that may push prices up, but for the moment the Chedi is quite reasonable. Its beach is virtually private and is, in fact, a better beach than the Annapuri's. As you enter the lobby, you are greeted by a sweeping view of the Andaman Sea and a hexagonal-shape pool with gardens below. All the chalets along the hillside face the sea, but it is hidden from most by swaying palms. Each chalet has its own sundeck; inside it's compact but uncluttered and accentuated by wood floors and woven palm walls. The bathrooms have only showers and no baths. ⊠ *118 Moo 3, Chengthalay, Pansea Beach, Phuket 83110, ☎ 076/324017, ℻ 076/324252. 105 rooms. Restaurant, outdoor café, pool, 2 tennis courts, windsurfing, boating, business services, meeting rooms. AE, DC, MC, V.*

Kamala Beach
❹ *18 km (11 mi) west of Phuket Town.*

South of a small headland below Surin Beach you come to Kamala Beach, a small curving strip of sand with coconut palms and a few bungalows, a resort hotel, and a delightful tiny open-air restaurant.

DINING

$ ✕ **White Orchid.** At the far end of Kamala Bay Terrace Resort, where
★ the road peters out to a rutted track, is Eek's little lean-to restaurant with four tables under a thatched cover and two more sitting under palm trees at the water's edge. While the shack and kitchen may look primitive, all is clean. Eek is warm and welcoming, and she speaks English and French. The menu is limited to what she bought that day in the market. If tiger prawns are available, be sure to have those, and start with the spring rolls. ⊠ *Kamala Bay. No phone. No credit cards.*

Patong
❺ *13 km (8 mi) west of Phuket Town.*

Patong is Phuket's mini-Pattaya, complete with German restaurants, massage parlors, hustlers selling trinkets, and places like Tatum's, a combined coffeehouse, disco, and go-go dance floor. The 90 lodgings, ranging from deluxe hotels to small cottages, with more than 6,000 double rooms, attest to Patong's popularity. From about 7 PM on, the main street is lined with stalls selling everything from T-shirts to watches. Down the side streets, restaurants offer seafood and Western-style food, and beyond these, one bar crowds out another.

DINING AND LODGING

$$ ✕ **Baan Rim Pa.** For classical Thai cooking adapted to Western tastes, come to this restaurant on the cliff at the north end of Patong Beach. The large open terrace is one of the most attractive settings on Phuket, and the food is prettily presented in traditional style. If you like hot and spicy Thai fare, you may be disappointed. ⊠ *100/7 Kalim Beach Rd., Patong, ☎ 076/340–789. AE, MC, V.*

$$ ✕ **Chao Lay at Coral Beach Hotel.** Perched on a bluff overlooking the Andaman Sea and the beach, the Chao Lay open-front restaurant is an ideal spot to enjoy fantastic views and Thai cooking. Dishes include *tom kha gai* (slightly spicy chicken soup made with coconut milk), *mae krob* (Thai noodles), spring rolls, and grilled seafood. ⊠ *104 Moo 4, Patong Beach, ☎ 076/321–106. Reservations essential. AE, DC, MC, V.*

$$ ✕ **Mallee's Seafood Village.** An array of international dishes is offered at this restaurant in the center of Patong. Two Thai dishes worth trying are the charcoal-grilled fish in banana leaves and the steamed fish in a tamarind sauce. If you want Chinese food, try the shark steak in a green-pepper sauce; for European fare, consider the veal sausage with potato salad. On the other hand, you may simply want to sit at one of the sidewalk tables and indulge in pancakes with honey. ⊠ *94/4 Taweewong Rd., Patong,* ☎ *076/321–205. AE, DC, MC, V.*

$$$ ☷ **Diamond Cliff Hotel.** North of town, away from the crowds, this is one of the smartest and architecturally pleasing resorts in Patong. The beach across the road has mammoth rocks that create the feeling of several private beaches. The swimming pool is built on a ledge above the main part of the hotel, providing an unobstructed view of the coast and the Andaman Sea. Rooms are spacious, full of light, and decorated in pale colors to accentuate the open feel of the hotel. Dining is taken seriously, with the fresh seafood cooked in European or Thai style. ⊠ *61/9 Kalim Beach, Patong, Kathu District, Phuket 83121,* ☎ *076/340–501,* 𝔽𝔸𝕏 *076/340–507; Bangkok reservations* ☎ *02/246–4515. 140 rooms. Restaurant, lobby lounge, pool with bar, boating, travel services. AE, MC, V.*

$$ ☷ **Paradise Resort.** Of many similar moderately priced hotels in Patong, this one on the strip facing the beach has more appeal than those in the thick of the restaurants, shops, and bars. The Paradise has reasonably large rooms and clean bathrooms, a pool, and a coffee shop/dining room for light Thai and Western fare. ⊠ *93 Taweewong Rd. (next to the Holiday Inn), Patong 83121,* ☎ *076/340–172,* 𝔽𝔸𝕏 *076/295– 467. 16 rooms. Restaurant, pool, travel services. MC, V.*

$$ ☷ **Phuket Cabana.** This hotel's attraction is its location, in the middle of Patong, facing the beach. Laid-back and casual describe guests as well as staff, but the basic resort amenities are here, with a good tour desk and a reputable dive shop to arrange outings. Modest rooms are in chalet-type bungalows furnished with rattan tables and chairs. The Charthouse restaurant serves grilled Western food and a modest selection of Thai dishes. ⊠ *80 Taweewong Rd., Patong Beach, Phuket 83121,* ☎ *076/340–138,* 𝔽𝔸𝕏 *076/340–178; Bangkok reservations* ☎ *02/278–2239. 80 rooms. Restaurant, pool, dive shop, travel services, airport shuttle. AE, MC, V.*

Karon Beach

❻ *20 km (12 mi) southwest of Phuket Town.*

Karon Beach, south of Patong, is divided into two areas. Karon Noi, a small bay surrounded by verdant hills, is truly beautiful but virtually taken over by Le Meridien Hotel. Because of its good swimming and surfing, the other part, Karon Yai, is becoming increasingly popular, and several hotels and a minitown have sprung up.

DINING AND LODGING

$$ ✕ **On the Rock.** This 100-seat restaurant, perched on the rocks overlooking Karon Beach, has a wonderfully romantic setting. Three reef sharks lazily glide in an aquarium tank, glancing at the diners. Seafood is the specialty: Try the mackerel with fresh tomato and onion, the *her thalee kanom khrok* (a mixture of seafood with coconut milk, spiced with chili pepper), and the *pla goh tod na phrik* (snapper in a pepper and chili sauce) with rice. Those not partial to Thai fare can choose pasta dishes. ⊠ *Marina Cottages, south end of Karon Beach,* ☎ *076/381–625. AE, MC, V.*

$–$$ ⊞ **Marina Cottages.** The 50 small cottages here, straddling the divide
★ between Karon and Kata beaches, all have an ocean views, although
those closer to the beach are more spacious than those up the hill. All
have air-conditioning, tiled floors, balconies, and private bathrooms.
The pool, nestled among rock outcroppings, is surrounded by tropical foliage. ⊠ *Box 143, Phuket 83000,* ☎ *076/330–625,* FAX *076/330–
516. 104 rooms. 2 restaurants, pool, scuba diving. AE, MC, V.*

Kata Beach

❼ *22 km (13 mi) southwest of Phuket Town.*

Kata Beach is the next beach south of Karon Beach. The sunsets are
as marvelous as ever, but the peace and quiet are fading fast. Club Med
has moved in, but there are still stretches of sand with privacy, and the
center of town has only a modest number of bars. Nearby, on **Kata
Noi Beach** (*noi* means small) in the shelter of a forest-clad hill, a few
inexpensive bungalows share the quiet beach with the Kata Thani
Hotel, popular with tour groups.

LODGING

$$$ ⊞ **Boathouse Inn & Restaurant.** With all 33 rooms looking on to Kata
Beach, an excellent Thai restaurant facing the Andaman Sea, and a re-
laxing beach bar, this small hotel is a very comfortable retreat. The Thai-
style architecture adds a traditional touch to the otherwise modern
amenities. Guest rooms are furnished in reds and browns and have in-
dividually controlled air-conditioning, private safes, and bathrooms with
baths and massage showers. Sit on the veranda listening to gentle
music from a small band and sample the *kung thot keeow:* fried shrimp
paste with green curry, garnished with basil leaves and strips of red
chili, and served on thin, crisp pastry shells. ⊠ *2/2 Patak Rd., Kata
Beach, Phuket 83100,* ☎ *076/330–015,* FAX *076/330–561; Bangkok
reservations,* ☎ *02/253–9168; U.K. reservations, 071/537–2988; U.S.
reservations, 800/526–6566. 33 rooms. Restaurant, bar, beauty salon,
travel services. AE, DC, MC, V.*

$ ⊞ **Friendship Bungalows.** A four-minute walk from the beach, two rows
of single-story buildings contain modest, sparsely furnished, but spot-
lessly clean rooms, each with its own bathroom (there is usually hot
water). The owners are extremely hospitable. The small restaurant/bar
on a terrace offers good Thai food; Western food is also available. ⊠
6/5 Patak Rd., Kata Beach, Phuket 83130, ☎ *076/330–499. 30 rooms.
Restaurant. No credit cards.*

$ ⊞ **Mountain View.** Room prices on Phuket have been on the rise of
late, so we were pleased to find this reasonable three-story hotel at the
south end of Kata Noi beach. Though the facilities are minimal, it is
right across the street from the beach. Rooms are spare, and after their
new coat of paint, look fresh and clean. ⊠ *4/7 Kata Noi, Phuket
83130,* ☎ *076/330565,* FAX *076/330567. 33 rooms. Restaurant, bar.
MC, V.*

Nai Harn

❽ *18 km (11 mi) southwest of Phuket Town.*

The road south of Kata cuts inland across the hilly headland to drop
into yet another gloriously beautiful bay, Nai Harn. Protected by Man
Island, this deep bay has been a popular anchorage for international
yachtsmen. The beach is good for sunning and swimming in the dry
season, but beware of the steep drop-off.

DINING AND LODGING

$$$ ✕ **Chart Room at Phuket Yacht Club.** Though the exterior of the hotel
may be an eyesore, the main restaurant, the Chart Room, is lovely. With
one side completely open, it has a panoramic view of the bay and is-

lands. The menu now has a choice of European and Thai dishes, with an emphasis on seafood, though steaks are available. Try the baked fresh fish stuffed with prawns. ⊠ *Nai Harn Beach,* ☎ *076/381–156. Reservations essential. AE, DC, V.*

$$$$ ⊡ **Phuket Yacht Club.** Set in a picturesque westward-facing bay, this stepped, modern luxury hotel looks like an ambitious condominium complex. The architecture aside, its amenities and secluded location make the Phuket Yacht Club extremely pleasant. Though the furnishings are a tad worn, the guest rooms are large and have separate sitting areas and private balconies overlooking the beach and the islands. If your room is on the upper floors, your huge private balcony is completely private from other eyes. ⊠ *Nai Harn Beach, Phuket 83130,* ☎ *076/381–156,* 𝖥𝖠𝖷 *076/381–164; Bangkok reservations* ☎ *02/251–4707; in U.K. 071/537–2988; in U.S. 800/526–6566. 108 rooms, including 8 suites. 2 restaurants, pool with bar, 2 tennis courts, health club, boating, windsurfing, travel services. AE, DC, MC, V.*

Chalong
❾ *11 km (7 mi) south of Phuket Town.*

South of Phuket Town lies the huge, horseshoe-shape Chalong Bay, whose entrance is guarded by Ko Lone and whose waters are the temporary resting place for yachts making passage from Europe to Asia. Commercial fishing boats also anchor here, and you can catch a boat to Ko Hae and Ko Lone from the jetty. The town of **Chalong** has several good inexpensive outdoor seafood restaurants—try Kan Eang for delicious crabs and prawns.

A bit inland from Chalong Bay you'll find **Wat Chalong.** Phuket has 20 Buddhist temples—all built since the 19th century—but Wat Chalong is the largest and most famous. It enshrines the gilt statues, wrapped in saffron robes, of two revered monks who helped quell an 1876 rebellion by Chinese immigrants.

Cruise boats leave Chalong for popular **Ko Hae** (Coral Island), 30 minutes from shore, which has clear water for snorkeling and superb beaches for sunbathing. There is a café on the island and a resort with 40 bungalows. A few miles north of Ko Hae is **Ko Lone,** another island reached by boat Chalong, with a 30-room resort on its northern shore. Hiring a boat for half a day costs B800.

DINING

$$ ✕ **Jimmy's Lighthouse Bar and Grill.** The crowd who gathers here are mostly tourists, but the food, both Thai and Western, is good for lunch and dinner. ⊠ *45/33 Chao Fa Rd., Chalong,* ☎ *076/381–709. No credit cards.*

$$ ✕ **Kan Eang.** There are now two Kan Eang restaurants in Chalong. Thais make a point of going to Kan Eang 1; the food is more authentic and spicier than at nearby Number 2. At Number 1, choose a table next to the sea wall under the coconut palms, and order seafood. Include the succulent and sweet crabs in your order. ⊠ *Chalong,* ☎ *076/381–323. AE, MC, V.*

Ko Phi Phi

2-hr boat ride from Makham Bay, 11 km (6 mi) east of Chalong Bay, 9 km (5 mi) south of Phuket Town.

The proximity of the Phi Phi Islands to busy Phuket and the easy two-hour journey by ferry from Makham Bay have meant that tourists coming to escape Phuket's commercialism bring that very commercialism with them. While the islands are no longer completely unspoiled, you can still appreciate the silver-sand coves and limestone cliffs that drop precipitously into the sea. Several comfortable air-conditioned hotels have been built, and a number of very modest bungalow accommodations are available for budget travelers.

Of the two main islands, only **Phi Phi Don** is inhabited. It's shaped like a butterfly, with two hilly land portions linked by a wide sandbar, 2 km (1¼ mi) long. Most accommodations and the main mall with its shops and restaurants are on this sandbar, where boats come into a village called **Ton Sai.** No vehicles are allowed on the island; you can disembark at the hotels, on the north cape if you wish. In the evening, visitors stroll up and down the walkway along the sandbar, where small restaurants display the catch of the day on ice outside. There are no bars or discos on the island; though discovered, Ko Phi Phi is still very laid-back.

The most popular way to explore is by either a cruise boat or a long-tailed boat that seats up to six people. One of the most visually exciting trips is to the smaller island, **Phi Phi Lae.** The first stop is **Viking Cave,** a vast cavern of limestone pillars covered with what look like prehistoric drawings, but are actually only a few centuries old, depicting Portuguese or Dutch cutters. The boat continues on, gliding by cliffs rising vertically out of the sea, for an afternoon in **Maya Bay.** Here the calm, clear waters, sparkling with color from the live coral, are ideal for swimming and snorkeling. You can take a worthwhile 45-minute trip by long-tailed boat to **Bamboo Island,** which is roughly circular, with a superb beach around it. The underwater colors of the fish and the coral are brilliant. The island is uninhabited, but you can spend a night under the stars if you like.

Lodging

$$$ 🏨 **P. P. International Resort.** This isolated retreat on the north end of the island has standard double rooms and larger deluxe rooms in bungalows with sea views at twice the price. All rooms are air-conditioned and have small refrigerators and color TV. The terraced restaurant, serving Thai and European cuisines, has splendid views of the sea, and the fish is absolutely fresh. ✉ *Cape Laemthong, Phi Phi. Reservations:* ☎ *02/250–0768 in Bangkok,* ☎ *076/214–297 in Phuket,* ☎ *077/421– 228 in Ko Samui. 120 rooms. Restaurant, snorkeling, windsurfing, boating, travel services. AE, V.*

$$ 🏨 **Pee Pee Cabana and Ton Sai Village.** Facing the sea amid coconut palms, these two adjacent hotels offer the best accommodations in the center of Phi Phi. Ton Sai Village, abutting cliffs, is the quieter of the two, about a 10-minute walk from the ferry docks, and its rooms are slightly larger than those at Pee Pee Cabana. Both have either air-conditioned or fan-cooled rooms, and their outdoor restaurants serve food similar to that found in the village, but costing twice as much. ✉ *West end of Ton Sai Beach. Reservations:* ✉ *Pee Pee Marina Travel Co., 201/3–4 Uttarakit Rd., Amphoe Muang, Krabi 81000,* ☎ *075/611– 496,* ☎ 075/612–196. *100 rooms. Restaurant. No credit cards.*

$$ 🏨 **Pee Pee Island Village.** This hotel on the north cape offers modest accommodations in small thatched bungalows. It provides the same water sports and tours as its neighbor, P.P. International, but the service is more casual and the atmosphere more laid-back. Views from the hotel are less impressive, however, although guests do have panoramas of the sea and palm-clad hills. ✉ *Cape Laemthing, Phi Phi; Bangkok reservations* ☎ *02/277–0038, in Phuket* ☎ *076/215–014. 65 rooms. Restaurant, snorkeling, boating, travel services. AE, V.*

$ ⊞ **Krabi Pee Pee Resort.** In the center of the isthmus, this collection of small bungalows in a coconut grove offers clean, simple, fan-cooled rooms with private Asian-style squat toilets and showers. Guests don't seem to frequent the restaurant, but they do hang around the bar, which faces the bay. Compared with the other overpriced accommodations on the island, this "resort" is the best value. ⊠ *Lohdalum Bay, Phi Phi. Reservations in Krabi,* ☎ *075/611–484. 60 rooms. Restaurant, bar, dive shop. No credit cards.*

$ ⊞ **Pee Pee Resort.** This hotel consists of two rows of tiny, thatched, palm-woven huts facing the beach, each with its own Asian-style toilet. A mosquito net is supplied. A small café, attractively located on a small headland, offers basic Thai food. ⊠ *250 yards east of ferry dock, Ton Sai. No phone. 40 rooms. No credit cards.*

Krabi

867 km (538 mi) south of Bangkok, 180 km (117 mi) southeast from Phuket, 43 km (27 mi) by boat east of Ko Phi Phi.

Krabi, the provincial capital of the region, lies across Phuket Bay on the mainland. Once a favorite harbor for smugglers bringing alcohol and tobacco from Malaysia, it has become a fishing port and gateway to the province's islands and famous beaches. It is a pleasant, low-key town, but most visitors stop here only to do some shopping, cash traveler's checks, arrange onward travel, and catch up on the news at one of the restaurants on Uttarakit Road.

Dining and Lodging

$$ ✕ **Isouw.** This restaurant right on the main street of Krabi Town stands on stilts over the water. It is a wonderful place in which to sit, enjoy lunch, and watch the river traffic. It specializes in grilled fish with sweet-and-sour sauce, and the *mee krob* (fried Thai noodles) here has an abundance of fresh, sweet shrimp. ⊠ *256/1 Uttarakit Rd., Krabi,* ☎ *075/611–956. Reservations not accepted. No credit cards.*

$ ⊞ **Grand Tower Guest House.** This new guest house is extremely popular with backpackers. The rooms are clean and the facilities modern. The café serves basic Western fare, and the tour desk is knowledgeable. Also, many of the long-distance private bus companies stop here. ⊠ *73/1 Uttarakit Rd. Amphur Muang, Krabi,* ☎ *075/611–741. 27 fan-cooled rooms with baths. Restaurant, travel services. MC, V.*

Ao Nang

20 km (12 mi) from Krabi Town.

Ao Nang, less than 20 minutes by road from Krabi, is in the process of being discovered by land speculators. Aside from a few hotels, accommodations consist of rustic bungalows. The beaches have fine sand and calm waters, backed by verdant jungles and sheltered by islands. Days are spent on the beach or exploring the islands by boat, particularly Turtle Island and Chicken Island for snorkeling. You can rent boats from the local fishermen or from the Krabi Resort.

Lodging

$$$$ ⊞ **Dusit Rahwadee.** A true retreat, marvelously laid out on 26 landscaped acres, this resort is accessible only by boat (20 minutes from Krabi Town, 70 minutes from Phuket, and 10 minutes from Ao Nang Bay on the hotel launch). The modern Thai-style pavilions are circular, with spacious living rooms downstairs and spiral staircases to the magnificent bedrooms and sumptuous bathrooms with huge round tubs. The use of highly polished wood floors throughout adds to the cool luxury. Because nearly all the pavilions are between the two beaches that flank the headland, you are never more than a five-minute walk from a beach—you can hear but not see the waves roll in. Krua Pranang, the memorable Thai restaurant in a breezy pavilion one floor up, serves food as exciting as it is delicious.⌧ *67 Mu 5 Susan Hoy Rd., Tambol Sai Thai, Krabi 81000,* ☏ *075/620–740,* FAX *075/620–630; Bangkok reservations* ☏ *02/236–0450; in U.S. 800/223–6800. 98 pavilions. 2 restaurants, bar, in-room VCRs, in-room safes, pool, snack bar. AE, DC, MC, V.*

$$$ ☷ **Krabi Resort.** A small collection of thatched cottages on Ao Nang beach has now mushroomed into a large resort, where modern rooms in the new concrete addition are often preferred. There is also a pool in the garden, though the beach has greater attraction. Dinners are often feasts, with steaks or steamed fish in soy sauce; you can work off the calories later in the disco lounge. ⌧ *Ao Nang. Reservations: 55–57 Pattana Rd., Amphoe Muang, Krabi 81000,* ☏ *075/611–389,* FAX *075/612–160; Bangkok reservations* ☏ *02/251–8094. 80 rooms. Restaurant, pool, boating, nightclub. DC, MC, V.*

$ ☷ **Ao Nang Villa.** Along the same beach as the Krabi Resort are these more modest bungalows. Rooms vary from tiny and fan-cooled (B300) to reasonably spacious with twin beds and air-conditioning (B850). ⌧ *113 Ao Nang Beach, Krabi 81000,* ☏ *075/612–728,* FAX *075/611–837. 42 rooms. Restaurant. MC, V.*

$ ☷ **Emerald Bungalows.** On the quiet, sandy beach of Haad Noppharat, just north of Ao Nang, this hotel offers a choice of tiny bungalows with no bath or larger bungalows with private baths. Those facing the beach are the best and most expensive (B500). The restaurant specializes in seafood and is the place for socializing and reading. ⌧ *Haad Noppharat Beach, Moo 4, Tambol, Ao Nang. Reservations: 2/1 Kongca Rd., Krabi 81000,* ☏ *075/611–106. 36 rooms. Restaurant. No credit cards.*

Phang Nga Bay

100 km (62 mi) north of Phuket, 93 km (56 mi) northwest of Krabi.

Phang Nga Bay, made famous by the James Bond movie *The Man with the Golden Gun,* lies at the top of Phuket Bay. There are little islands to explore, offshore caves, and outcroppings of limestone rising 900 feet straight up from the sea—a unique sight. You really need a full day to see everything and to appreciate the sunsets, which are particularly beautiful on **Ko Mak.**

The best, really the only, way to visit this bay is by boat. A number of agencies on Phuket run half-day trips, or you can hire a boat locally. Most tourists don't arrive from Phuket until 11 AM. If you can get into the bay before then, it will be more or less yours to explore, with a boatman as your guide. To make an early start, you may want to stay overnight.

The key sights to visit are **Ko Panyi,** with its Muslim fishing village built on stilts; **Ko Phing Kan,** now known as James Bond Island; **Ko Tapu,** which looks like a nail driven into the sea; **Tham Kaeo grotto,** an Asian version of Capri's Blue Grotto; and **Tham Lot,** where a large cave has been carved into an archway large enough to allow cruise boats to pass through.

Lodging

$$ ☷ **Phang Nga Bay Resort.** This modern hotel's raison d'être is as a base for exploring the bay, and you can hire a boat here to do so. It's on an estuary 1½ km (1 mi) from the coast, and it does not have panoramic

views, but the rooms are comfortable and modern, the bathrooms are clean and large, and the dining room serves reasonable Chinese, Thai, and European food. ✉ *20 Thaddan Panyee, Phang Nga 82000,* ☎ *076/411–067;* 🄵🄰🄷 *076/411–057; Bangkok reservations* ☎ *02/259–1994. 88 rooms. Restaurant, coffee shop, 2 tennis courts, pool. AE, MC, V.*

Ko Samui

500 km (310 mi) south of Bangkok, 30 km (18½ mi) by boat east of Surat Thani.

In the southern Gulf of Thailand lies Ko Samui, the world's coconut capital, discovered by backpackers several years ago, now regarded as an alternative to Phuket. Already too commercial for some people, it still has far fewer hotels, restaurants, and café/bars than Phuket and is a haven of tranquillity compared with seedy Pattaya.

Ko Samui is half the size of Phuket, and could be easily toured in a day. But tourists come for the sun and beach, not for sightseeing, and they usually stay put. We cover the island clockwise. The best beaches, with glistening white sand and clear waters, are on the east coast; the others have either muddy sand or rocky coves. The sea surrounding the smaller islands nearby is still crystal clear, and the tiny islets of the **Angthong Marine National Park** (☞ *below*) are superb for snorkeling and scuba diving. The TAT has a list of guest houses on the islands, and most travel agencies can make reservations at some of them and at the hotels.

Numbers in the margin correspond to points of interest on the Ko Samui map.

New Port

❶ The car ferry from Don Sak on the mainland arrives at **New Port,** 6½ km (4 mi) south of Na Thon, the main town. Unless a hotel van is waiting for you, take a songthaew first to Na Thon, and then another to reach your final destination.

Na Thon

❷ Compared with the other sleepy island villages, **Na Thon** is a bustling town. The passenger ferry from Surat Thani docks here; shops, travel agencies, and restaurants line the waterfront, and local businesses and banks are on the parallel street one block back. Though Na Thon has a hotel, tourists seldom stay in town.

Maenam

❸ On the north coast east of Na Thon, the first major tourist area is **Maenam.** Its long, curving, sandy beach shaded by trees is lapped by gentle waters that are great for swimming. Inexpensive guest houses and the new luxury Santiburi resort hotel share the 5-km (3-mi) stretch of sand.

LODGING

$$$$ 🏨 **Santiburi.** This resort set on 23 acres is an exclusive hideaway. The
★ standard suites are private bungalows with highly polished wood floors, even in the huge bathrooms, which have two black washbasins, black oval bathtubs, and separate black-tile shower stalls. The contemporary Thai furnishings give a warm, open feel that's enhanced by a glass panel between the living room and bedroom. Each bungalow has its own TV, VCR, and CD player, with CDs and videotapes. Ask for a bungalow close to the palm-shaded beach. The main building, a modern Thai pavilion overlooking the oval swimming pool, has European and Thai restaurants, and guests amble up to the beach bar for informal meals. From this secluded oasis you can walk to the main road

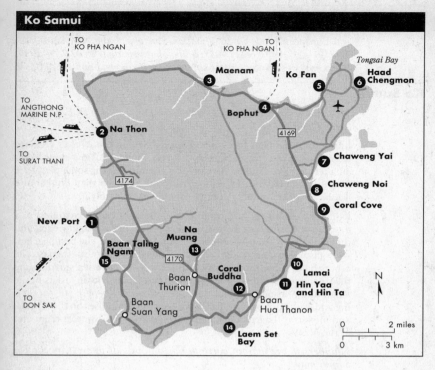

and take a songthaew to any place on the island. ✉ *12/12 Moo 1, Tambol Maenam, Ko Samui 84330,* ☎ *077/425–031,* FAX *077/425–040; Bangkok reservations* ☎ *02/238–4790; in U.S. 800/223–5652. 75 suites. 2 restaurants, pool, snack bar, 2 tennis courts, health club, squash, boating. AE, DC, MC, V.*

Bophut

4 A small headland separates Maenam from the next bay, **Bophut.** The sand is not as fine at Bophut and becomes muddy during the rainy season, but the fishing village is a popular gathering spot for backpackers. Many village homes have become crash pads; some might even be called guest houses, but this is changing: developers have moved in and fancier resorts are replacing the thatched bungalows.

Ko Fan

5 On the north shore near the northeast tip, you come to **Ko Fan,** a little island with a huge sitting Buddha image covered in moss. Try to visit at sunset, when the light off the water shows Big Buddha at its best. Back across the causeway on the beach facing the seated Buddha, there are a number of guest houses and bungalows frequented by backpackers who find Bophut too noisy and expensive.

Chengmon

6 Continue east along the north coast to **Haad Chengmon** (*haad* means beach), which is dominated by the headland Laem Rumrong. This is the end of the road for the few songthaews that take this route, and few tourists come here. Several guest houses are scattered along the shoreline, as well as an upscale resort, but you can still find peace and tranquillity.

LODGING

$$$$ 🏨 **Imperial Tongsai Bay Hotel.** The sister property to the Imperial Samui, the Tongsai Bay is an elegant resort retreat. It has whitewashed, red-tile hillside cottages, with balconies looking out to sea (when the view is not blocked by foliage), and 24 rooms in the three-story main building. The dining room has beautiful views; reserve a table on the terrace. Ko Samui is known for huge succulent oysters and king prawns, and Tongsai gets the best. A shuttle will take you to Na Thon and Chaweng. ⊠ *Tongsai Bay, Ko Samui,* ☎ *077/421–451,* 🆅🆇 *077/421–462; Bangkok reservations* ☎ *02/254–0023,* 🆅🆇 *02/253–3190. 80 rooms. Restaurant, bar, pool, 2 tennis courts, windsurfing, boating. AE, DC, MC, V.*

$$$ 🏨 **Boat House Hotel.** The Imperial Group's third property on Ko Samui, across the bay from Tongsai, is 34 rice barges, converted into duplex suites. Each has an enclosed upper deck with a lounge and wet bar and, below, a large bathroom with a grand oval tub, a dressing room/sitting area, and the bedroom. The hulls are original; the uncluttered interiors and upper decks are new, with highly polished teak and mahogany beams and paneling. The double beds are just a foot off the floor, while high above are suspended fishing nets. Very nice! Rooms built in two wings between the barges and the road are less expensive (B3,200 versus B5,400 for a barge suite) but have no sea view. Coral reefs are exposed at low tide, but the swimming is safe and in sheltered waters. ⊠ *Chengmon Beach, Ko Samui, Surat Thani 84140,* ☎ *077/421–451,* 🆅🆇 *077/421–462; Bangkok reservations* ☎ *02/254– 0023. 34 boat suites, 176 rooms. 2 restaurants, pool, 4 tennis courts, sailing, windsurfing, travel services. AE, DC, MC, V.*

Chaweng Yai and Chaweng Noi

Of the 11 beach areas of Ko Samui, Chaweng has the finest glistening white sand. But it is also the most congested, crammed with guest houses and tourists.

❼ **Chaweng Yai** (*yai* means large), the northernmost section, is separated from Chaweng Noi (*noi* means little) by a small point, Laem Koh Faan. Chaweng Yai is divided by a reef into two sections, of which the northern one is a quiet area popular with backpackers, and the southern, or main, part is crowded with hotels, tanned, scantily clad youths, and bulbous-breasted German hausfrauen. (Thais find it offensive that Western women sunbathe topless, and while they usually say nothing, they give a scornful smile.) Here you will find anything you want, from water-scooter rentals to money-changers and nightclubs.

❽ South of this busy beach is **Chaweng Noi,** which is only partially developed. It is quieter than Chaweng Yai, and the salt air has yet to be tainted by the odor of suntan oil. At the end of this beach there's an international resort, the Imperial Samui Hotel.

LODGING

$$$ 🏨 **Imperial Samui.** Chaweng's best international resort hotel, this property is attractively laid out at the top of a landscaped garden terrace with steps leading down to the beach. Guest rooms, which fan out from the main building, are standard, with modern furnishings and little appeal except for the view of the beach. Attention is focused on the swimming pool, next to the sea; a small island adorns the pool, complete with three coconut trees. The hotel is at the south end of Chaweng Noi, where the beach isn't crowded and the sea is clean. ⊠ *Chaweng Noi Beach, Ko Samui 84140,* ☎ *077/421–390; Bangkok reservations* ☎ *02/254–0023,* 🆅🆇 *02/253–3190. 77 rooms. Restaurant, bar, pool, sailing, windsurfing. AE, DC, MC, V.*

$$ 🏨 **Amari Palm Reef Hotel.** Half the rooms, in two wings that look onto the pool and garden, are simply functional, with small bathrooms and showers only. The more attractive accommodations are across the road from the beach. They're Thai-style cottages, in small compounds of teak bungalows, like a traditional Thai village. Mattresses are on low platforms above the polished mahogany floor. Large cottages have sleeping lofts, air-conditioning, and small terraces. This hotel is on the part of Chaweng Beach that's too shallow for swimming; you must walk 500 yards south for that. The hotel also has a swimming pool with a swim-up bar. ⊠ *14/3 Moo 2, Tambon Boput, Chaweng Beach, Ko Samui, Surat Thani 84140,* ☎ *077/422–015,* ℻ *077/422–394; Bangkok reservations* ☎ *02/251–4727. 104 rooms. 2 restaurants, bar, 2 pools, 2 tennis courts, squash. MC, V.*

\$\$　🏨 **Samui Pansea Hotel.** The Pansea, set back from the beach, may not be quite as smart as its neighbor, the Imperial Samui, but it costs less. Guest rooms come with fans or, for a few more dollars, air-conditioning. Equipment for water sports is available, and the restaurant offers views over the gulf. ⊠ *Chaweng Noi Beach, Ko Samui 84140,* ☎ *077/421–384;* ℻ *077/421–385. 50 rooms. Restaurant, coffee shop, bar, windsurfing. AE, MC, V.*

\$　🏨 **Fair House.** Right on the beach at Chaweng Noi, this hotel offers small, simple bungalows with air-conditioning or overhead fans, and rudimentary private bathrooms. Each bungalow has its own veranda, but only a few have a clear view of the beach. The open-fronted dining room has broad sea views, and the Thai cuisine—with a few Western dishes—is remarkably good. ⊠ *Chaweng Noi Beach, Ko Samui 84140,* ☎ ℻ *077/421–373. 26 rooms. Restaurant, bar. MC, V.*

\$　🏨 **O. P. Bungalow.** Of the inexpensive bungalow cottage hotels that line Chaweng Beach, this is the most efficiently run, and it has clean, simple rooms with hot-water geysers in the bathrooms. The narrow property has four rows of cottages stretching back from the beach to the road (rates are higher close to the beach). The rooms have tile floors and most have twin beds (with a few doubles). Room 502, with a double (and close to the beach), is a good one to ask for. An open-sided coffee shop down at the beach has reasonably priced Thai and Chinese food. ⊠ *Chaweng Beach, Ko Samui, Surat Thani 84320,* ☎ *077/422–424,* ℻ *077/422–425. 38 rooms. Restaurant. No credit cards.*

Coral Cove

❾ Beyond the Imperial Samui Hotel is **Coral Cove,** popular among scuba divers. But you don't have to be a diver to enjoy the underwater scenery: Just walk waist high into the water and look through a mask to see the amazing colors of the coral. For a Thai seafood lunch, walk up the rocks to Coral Cove Bungalows, where you also can rent snorkeling equipment.

Lamai

A rocky headland separates Chaweng from Ko Samui's second most
❿ popular beach, **Lamai.** It lacks the glistening white sand of Chaweng, but its clear water and rocky pools made this attractive area the first to be developed on Ko Samui (investors only later shifted their get-rich plans to Chaweng). Lamai has more of a steeply shelving shoreline than Chaweng, so few families come here, but it does make the swimming better. Lamai has a different feel from Chaweng; it's not so honky-tonk or congested, though there are plenty of restaurants and bars and enough shops to stir your acquisitive instincts.

Every visitor to Ko Samui makes a pilgrimage to Lamai for yet another reason: At the point marking the end of Lamai beach stand two rocks,
⓫ named **Hin Yaa and Hin Ta** (Grandmother and Grandfather Rock). Erosion has shaped the rocks to resemble weathered and wrinkled private parts—nature at its most whimsical.

LODGING

\$　🏨 **Golden Sand Beach Resort.** The open lobby and reception area of this hotel are off Lamai's main street. Guest rooms, in two-story buildings, angle out from the reception room and overlook a palm-fringed garden. While the rooms are small, most have air-conditioning (a few less expensive ones are fan-cooled) and each has its own balcony and private bathroom with a shower. The most expensive rooms have a sea view. ⊠ *124/2 Lamai Beach, Ko Samui, Surat Thani 84310,* ☎ *077/424–031,* ℻ *077/424–430. 82 rooms. Coffee shop, bar. MC, V.*

En Route At Baan Hua Thanon, a small Chinese fishing village, the road that
⑫ forks inland (the direct route to Na Thon) leads to the **Coral Buddha,** a natural formation carved by years of erosion. Beyond the Coral Buddha, toward Na Thon, lies the village of Baan Thurian, famous for its durian trees, where a track to the right climbs up into jungle-clad hills
⑬ to the island's best waterfall, **Na Muang.** The 30-meter (105-ft) falls are spectacular—especially just after the rainy season—as they tumble from a limestone cliff to a small pool. You can bathe in the pool, getting cooled by the spray and warmed by the sun. For a thrill, swim through the curtain of falling water; you can sit on a ledge at the back to catch your breath.

Laem Set Bay

⑭ This small rocky cape on the southeastern tip of the island is away from the crowds. It's a good 3 km (2 mi) off the main circle road, and without your own transport hard to reach, but it's worth the effort to get there to have a meal at the Laem Set Inn (☞ *below*).

LODGING

$–$$$$ 🏨 **Laem Set Inn.** The British owner, David Parry, and his Thai wife started the inn as a private club and have since enlarged it to make a very special hotel with widely varying rates. The buildings are reconstructions of traditional Thai houses or genuine old houses saved from destruction. The top-of-the-line Kho-Tan suite is an old rosewood house found on nearby Kho-Tan, dismantled, and reassembled here on a hillside overlooking the sea. It even has its own pool. Another suite was made from the old Ko Samui post office. More modest are the small thatched cottages (B1,250) with woven bamboo walls, which have only a small bathroom with a shower. Dining is given serious attention, and the kitchen has won accolades from the international press. The inn also offers cooking classes. Topless sun-bathing is not permitted. ⊠ *110 Mu 2, Hua Thanon, Ko Samui, Surat Thani 84310,* ☎ *077/424– 393, 077/233–300,* ℻ *077/424–394. 16 rooms. Restaurant, pool, snorkeling, boating, bicycles. MC, V.*

Baan Taling Ngam

⑮ Although the south and west coasts are less developed, their beaches, in general, are not so golden, the water not so clear, and the breezes not so fresh. But there is one very good reason for coming to the west coast, and that is a luxury hotel directly west of the village of Baan Taling Ngam, on a pretty stretch of shore with magnificent views of the sunset.

LODGING

$$$$ 🏨 **Baan Taling Ngam.** The name means "home on a beautiful cliff," which eminently suits this small and appealing hotel set dramatically on a cliffside facing west across the sea. Sunsets are phenomenal. The equally stunning swimming pool is set a couple of hundred feet above the sea, its water flowing over one side to disappear (seemingly) over the cliff. The guest rooms are also built into the cliffside, and each has a private terrace. The contemporary furnishings are given warmth by a generous use of wood paneling. Baan Taling Ngam is secluded, but

some may find it inconveniently far from most of the island's attractions—you'll need transport whenever you leave the property. ✉ *295 Mu 3, Taling Ngam, Ko Samui 84140,* ☎ *077/423–019,* FAX *077/423– 220; U.K. reservations* ☎ *071/537–2988; U.S. reservations 800/526– 6566. 40 rooms, 7 suites, 42 villas. 2 restaurants, pool, 2 tennis courts, health club, travel services. AE, DC, MC, V.*

OFF THE BEATEN PATH	**ANGTHONG MARINE NATIONAL PARK** – You should take one full day for a trip out to the 40 islets that make up the Angthong Marine National Park, which covers some 250 sq km (90 sq mi). The water, the multicolored coral, and the underwater life are superb, and the rocky islets form weird and wonderful shapes. Boats leave Na Thon daily at 8:30 AM for snorkeling and scuba diving; the cost is B250; the trip takes about one hour.

Ko Pha Ngan

12 km (7½ mi) by boat north of Ko Samui.

Since Ko Samui is no longer off the beaten track, travelers looking for the simple beach life now head for Ko Pha Ngan, which is at the turning point of its development. A decade ago, the few international wanderers stayed in fishermen's houses or slung hammocks on the beach. Now guest bungalows, cheap and simple, have sprung up on most of the best beaches, and investors are buying up beach properties. For now, though, the lack of transportation to and on the island limits Ko Pha Ngan's development, and one of the world's most idyllic places has yet to be spoiled.

Since the island's unpaved roads twist and turn, it's easier to beach-hop by boat. In fact, if you want to find the beach that most appeals to you, take a boat trip around the island on the ferries—it takes about nine hours. The southeast tip of the island is divided by a long promontory into **Haad Rin West and Haad Rin East,** the island's most popular and crowded areas. Boats from **Thong Sala,** the major town, take 40 minutes to reach Haad Rin East; their departure is timed to meet arriving passengers from the interisland boat.

If Haad Rin is too crowded, catch the onward boat up the east coast to **Haad Tong Nai Pan,** a perfect horseshoe bay divided by a small promontory. On the beach of the southern and larger half are several guest houses and a couple of small restaurants. The northern bay, **Tong Nai Pan Noi,** is the smaller and quieter of the two. Perhaps it has a few more years before being developed, but for now it's a beachcomber's paradise. Telephone cables have yet to link it with the world, and though there is a road, no self-respecting kidney will take the incessant bouncing of the 4-wheel-drive vehicle negotiating its curves and ruts. Glistening white sand curves around the turquoise waters of this half-moon bay, and coconut trees behind the beach hide the small houses of the villagers. At the ends of the bay are two small resorts.

Dining and Lodging

$ ✕ **Pannoi's.** The owner of this local restaurant goes fishing in the evening for tomorrow's menu. The guests, barefoot and shirtless, sit at rough-hewn wood tables set in the sand. A meal may consist of tender and succulent *ma pla* (horsefish, much like snapper) and a plateful of barbecued prawns with garlic and pepper. ✉ *Haad Tong Nai Pan Noi. No phone. No credit cards.*

$–$$ 🏠 **Panviman Resort.** This resort has thatched cottages and stone-and-stucco bungalows, some cooled by fan and others by air-conditioning. Each bungalow has a balcony, a large bedroom, and a spacious bathroom with a cold-water shower. During the day, electricity is turned off and the rooms become stifling, but who wants to be inside? There are also twin-bed, fan-cooled hotel rooms (half with ocean views) that cost B900. The circular wood restaurant, cooled by the breezes blowing over the promontory, serves Western food, but the Thai dishes are better. Guests gather here to watch the nightly video. ⊠ *Haad Tong Nai Pan, Ko Pha Ngan,* ☎ FAX *077/377–048; Bangkok reservations* ☎ *02/587–8491,* FAX *02/587–8493. 10 bungalows, 15 hotel rooms, 15 cottages. Restaurant. MC, V.*

$ 🏠 **Tong Tapan Resort.** These small thatched cottages on stilts perched on the side of the hill are home to international backpackers. ⊠ *North end of Haad Tong Nai Pan Noi. No phone. No credit cards.*

Southern Beach Resorts A to Z

Arriving and Departing

KO PHA NGAN

From Surat Thani, **Songserm** express boats (☞ Travel Agencies *in* Contacts and Resources, *below*) depart for Thong Sala on Ko Pha Ngan at 7 AM, 9 AM, and 2 PM (sometimes more often), stopping en route at Na Thon on Ko Samui. From Chumphon on the mainland, a ferry travels twice a week to Ko Pha Ngan. From Ko Samui, you can also take a small ferry boat from Bophut to Haad Rin at about 10 AM, and in good weather (but not when the seas are high), a long-tailed boat ferry leaves Maenam for Haad Tong Nai Pan at about 9 AM.

KO PHI PHI

Boats leave Makham Bay on Phuket twice a day for the two-hour journey; those run by **Songserm Travel Center** are the best. Two to four ferries a day make the two-hour trip between Krabi and Phi Phi Don.

KO SAMUI

By Boat: From Surat Thani (☞ *below*), two ferries cross to Ko Samui. The Songserm passenger boat leaves for Na Thon from its terminal 8 km (5 mi) out of town (a Songserm bus collects passengers from the row of travel agencies on the Surat Thani waterfront). Half the ferry ride is down the river's estuary and the other half across open water, taking, in all, about two hours, and the ferry goes on to Ko Pha Ngan. The other ferry, which takes cars and cargo, leaves from Donsak at the mouth of the river, 45 minutes by bus from Surat Thani, and lands at New Port. This ferry takes about 90 minutes. Combined bus-ferry tickets are available from one of the many tour/bus companies in Surat Thani. The last ferry to Ko Samui leaves around 4 PM, and the last ferry from Ko Samui departs at 3 PM. Times vary, so be sure to check the schedule.

By Plane: Ko Samui's small airport, on the island's northeast tip, is served by Bangkok Airways, which runs five flights daily between Bangkok and Ko Samui (B2,080) and between Phuket and Ko Samui (B1,300). Reservations are crucial during peak periods. Thai Airways International flies to Surat Thani on the mainland, from which you must transfer to Ko Samui. Orient Express flies between Ko Samui and Hat Yai. Taxis meet arrivals; their price is fixed—with little room for negotiation—for trips to various parts of the island. The most common price is B200. Some hotels have a limo/van service at the airport, but these cost the same as a taxi. Songthaews sporadically go between the airport and Na Thon, for B30.

Airline offices on Ko Samui include: **Bangkok Airways** (☎ 077/425–012; in Bangkok ☎ 02/229–3456). **Thai Airways International** (☎ 077/273–355). **Orient Express** (☎ 077/210–071).

By Train, Bus, and Ferry: The State Railway of Thailand offers a combined ticket that includes rail fare, a couchette in air-conditioned second class, bus connection to the ferry, and the ferry ride for B610. Passengers arrive at Ko Samui at about 10 AM the following day.

KRABI AND AO NANG

By Boat: Two to four ferries a day make the two-hour run between Krabi and Phi Phi. Bookings can be made on Phi Phi Don; the fare is B150.

By Bus: Air-conditioned buses depart from Bangkok's Southern Bus Terminal at 7 PM and 8 PM for the 290-km (180-mi) journey (fare B290) to Krabi.

By Shuttle or Songthaew: If you book accommodations in Ao Nang, transportation from Krabi will probably be arranged for you, or you can take a songthaew from Krabi for B20.

PHANG NGA BAY

First get yourself to the one-horse town of Phang Nga, served by a frequent buses from Krabi and Phuket, then take a songthaew 10 km (6¼ mi) to the bay. At the bay, hire a long-tailed boat to tour the islands.

PHUKET

By Bus: Non-air-conditioned buses leave throughout the day from Bangkok's Southern Bus Terminal. One air-conditioned bus leaves in the evening. Tour companies also run coaches that are slightly more comfortable, and often the price of a one-way fare includes a meal. The bus trip from Bangkok to Phuket takes 13 to 14 hours.

By Plane: Thai Airways International has daily 70-minute flights from Bangkok and 30-minute flights from Hat Yai. The airline also has direct flights from Chiang Mai, from Penang (Malaysia), and from Singapore. Bangkok Airways now offers two flights daily between Chiang Mai and Phuket and one daily flight between Phuket and Ko Samui.

Phuket's airport is at the northern end of the island. Most of the hotels are on the west coast, and many send minivans to meet arriving planes. These are not free, just convenient. For Phuket Town (32 km/20 mi southeast of the airport) or Patong Beach, take a Thai Airways minibus—buy the ticket (B70 and B100, respectively) at the transportation counter in the terminal. Sporadically, songthaews run between the airport and Phuket Town for B20.

By Train and Bus: The closest train station is at Surat Thani (☞ *below*), where trains connect to Bangkok and Singapore. A bus service links Phuket with Surat Thani. Traveling time between Phuket and Bangkok is five hours on the bus plus 11 hours on the overnight train. The State Railway of Thailand, in conjunction with Songserm Travel, issues a combined train and bus ticket. Panthip Tour also runs a daily bus between Phuket and Surat Thani.

SURAT THANI

By Bus: This town, at the crossroads of railway and bus lines, is the jumping-off place for all the southern beach resorts. The buses from Bangkok's Southern Bus Terminal cost less than the train (about B225 for air-conditioned buses), but they are also less comfortable. Private tour companies use more comfortable, faster buses. Express buses also go to Surat Thani from Phuket (5 hrs), from Krabi (4 hrs), and from Hat Yai (7 hrs).

By Train: Many express trains from Bangkok's Hualamphong railway station stop at Surat Thani on their way south. The journey takes just under 12 hours, and the best trains are the overnighters that leave Bangkok at 6:30 PM and 7:20 PM, arriving in Surat Thani soon after 6 AM. First-class sleeping cabins are available only on the 7:20 PM train. Two express trains make the daily run up from Trang and Hat Yai in southern Thailand.

Getting Around

KO SAMUI

By Bus: Na Thon on the west coast is the terminus for songthaews, which take either the north route around the island via Chengmon to Chaweng on the east coast, or the southern route along the coast to reach Lamai. Between Chaweng and Lamai you change songthaews at a transfer point for either the northern or southern route. The fare from Na Thon to Chaweng, the most distant point, is B30. Songthaews for the northern trip start from the waterfront north of the pier; those on the southern route start from south of the pier.

After about 6 PM songthaews become private taxis, and fares need to be established before setting out. During the day, songthaews may be rented as private taxis. The trip from Na Thon to Chaweng, for example, costs B250.

By Rental Car and Scooter: If you want to explore Ko Samui, it's best to rent your own transportation. Jeeps are expensive (around B1,200 plus B175 for CDW), but they're the safest, although most people choose motor scooters (about B175 per day), which can be rented at most of the resorts. Gravel, potholes, and erratic driving make riding dangerous, and each year some travelers return home with broken limbs, though crash helmets are now mandatory. Some never return at all.

Avis (✉ Santiburi Hotel, ☎ 077/425–031; Imperial Tongsai Bay Hotel, ☎ 077/421–451; and at the airport) **Hertz** is represented at the airport and at most of the luxury resorts. Scooters can be hired in Na Thon and most resort villages for about B150 up.

PHUKET

By Bus: Songthaews, the minibuses that seat 10 people, have no regular schedule, but all use Phuket Town as their terminal. Songthaews leave from Rangong Road near the day market and Fountain Circle, to ply back and forth to most beaches, and a few make the trip to the airport. If you want to get from one beach to another, you will probably have to go back into Phuket Town and change songthaews. Fares range from B10 to B40.

By Rental Car and Scooters: Your own transport, of course, is most convenient for exploring. Driving poses few hazards except for motor scooters. Potholes and loose gravel can cause a spill, and some minor roads are not paved. Crash helmets are required by law. Many hotels have rental desks, but their prices are 25%–40% higher than those in Phuket Town.

At Pure Car Rent (✉ 75 Rassada Rd., Phuket Town, ☎ 076/211–002), prices for a Jeep start at B770 per day, plus CDW of B120 per day. Motor scooters begin at B150 a day. The larger, 150-cc scooters are safer. Avis (☎ 076/327–358) and Hertz (☎ 076/321–190) have offices at the airport, as well as at some hotels.

By Taxi: Fares are, to a large extent, fixed between different destinations. If you plan to use taxis frequently, get a list of fares from the TAT office because drivers are not above charging more. A trip from Phuket Town to Patong Beach is B130 and to Bang Tao is B170.

Contacts and Resources

EMERGENCIES

On Ko Samui, contact the following: **General emergencies** (☎ 1699). **Tourist Police** (☎ 077/421–281 in Na Thon).

On Phuket, contact the following: **General emergencies** (☎ 1699). **Ambulance** (☎ 076/212–297). **Police** (☎ 076/212–046). **Tourist Police** (☎ 076/212–468).

On Surat Thani, contact the following: **Tourist Police** ☎ 077/281–300. **Surat Thani Hospital** ⊠ Surat-Phun Phin Road, ☎ 077/272–231.

GUIDED TOURS

A full-day **boat tour** goes from Phuket to Phang Nga Bay and other islands. World Travel Service (☞ Travel Agencies, *below*), runs a comprehensive tour to Phang Nga Bay. Another full-day tour visits the Phi Phi Islands for swimming and caving. The day-long Ko Hav (Coral Island) tour takes you snorkeling and swimming.

TRAVEL AGENCIES

Ko Samui: **Songserm Travel Center** ⊠ 64/1-2 Na Thon, ☎ 077/421–316). Also in Ko Pha Ngan (☎ 077/281–639).

Krabi: **Chan Phen Tour** (⊠ 145 Uttarakit Rd., ☎ 075/612–404, FAX 075/612–629). **Lao Ruam Kij** (⊠ 11 Khongka Rd., ☎ 075/611–930). There are also many other travel shops on Uttarakit Road.

Phuket: **New World Travel Service** (⊠ Hotel Phuket Merlin, Phuket Town, ☎ 076/212–866, ext. WTS, and Phuket Yacht Club ☎ 076/214–020, ext. WTS); **Songserm Travel Center** (⊠ 51 Satoon Rd., Phuket Town 83000, ☎ 076/222–570, FAX 076/214–391). **Panthip Tour** (☎ 076/210–425).

Surat Thani: **Songserm Travel Center** (☎ 077/272–928).

VISITOR INFORMATION

Krabi TAT (⊠ Uttarakit Rd., ☎ 075/612–740).

Phuket TAT (⊠ 73–75 Phuket Rd., near bus terminal, Phuket Town, ☎ 076/212–213). The TAT desk at Phuket airport offers limited help.

Surat Thani TAT (⊠ 5 Talat Mai Rd., Surat Thani 84000, ☎ 077/281–828) also handles Ko Phi Phi, Ko Pha Ngan, and Ko Tao, which have no proper representative. **Surat Thani Tourist Police** (☎ 077/281–300).

THAILAND A TO Z

Arriving and Departing

By Plane

AIRPORTS

The major gateway to Thailand is Bangkok's **Don Muang International Airport** (☎ 011–66–2/535–2081).

CARRIERS

In total, 35 airlines serve Bangkok, and more are seeking landing rights. The U.S. carrier with the most frequent flights is **Northwest Airlines** (☎ 800/447–4747). It has direct service through Tokyo (with a minimal stopover) from New York, Detroit, Seattle, Dallas, San Francisco, and Los Angeles. Incidentally, this airline's seats recline more than most, making sleeping much easier. Northwest also has a round-Asia fare, in conjunction with local airlines, which lets you hop from one capital to another.

To fly from the **west coast,** contact Cathay Pacific (☎ 800/223–2742), Garuda Indonesia (☎ 800/342–7832), Maylasia Airlines (☎ 800/421–8641), Thai Airways International (☎ 800/426–5204), and United Airlines (☎ 800/241–6522).

For departures from the **east coast,** contact All Nippon Airways (☎ 800/235–9262), Asiana Airlines (☎ 800/227–4262), China Airlines (☎ 800/227–5118), EVA Air (☎ 800/695–1188), Finnair (☎ 800/950–5000), Gulf Air (800/☎ 553–2824), Japan Airlines (☎ 800/525–3663), Korean Air (☎ 800/438–5000), Northwest Airlines, and Singapore Airlines (☎ 800/742–3333).

Daily departures to Thailand **from London** are scheduled aboard British Airways (☎ 0181/897–4000 or 0345/222–111 outside London), Qantas (☎ 0345/747–767 or 0800/747–767), and Thai Airways (0171/499–9113).

FLYING TIMES

From the West Coast, Bangkok is 18 hours from Seattle, 17 hours from San Francisco, 20 hours from Chicago, and 22 hours from New York. Add more time for stopovers and connections, especially if you are using more than one carrier.

Getting Around

By Bicycle Rickshaw

For short trips, bicycle rickshaws are a popular, inexpensive form of transport. They become expensive for long trips. Fares are negotiated. It is imperative to be very clear with these drivers about what price is agreed upon. They have a tendency to create a misunderstanding leading to a nasty scene at the end of the trip.

By Bus

Long-distance buses are cheaper and faster than trains, and there are buses into every corner of the country. A typical fare for the nine-hour trip between Chiang Mai and Bangkok is B400. The level of comfort depends on the bus company. Air-conditioned buses are superior, but the air-conditioning is always turned on full blast, and so you may want to take along an extra sweater. The most comfortable long-distance buses are operated by private travel/tour companies. For the most part, these private buses serve only resort destinations. Travel agents have the bus schedules and can make reservations and issue tickets.

By Car

Cars are available for rent in Bangkok and in major tourist destinations. If Thai driving intimidates you, you may wish to hire a driver. The additional cost is small, and the peace of mind great. If a foreigner is involved in an automobile accident, he or she—not the Thai—is likely to be judged at fault.

In Chiang Mai, Ko Samui, Pattaya, and Phuket, hiring a Jeep or motorcycle is a popular and convenient way to get around. Be aware that motorcycles skid easily on gravel roads or on gravel patches on the pavement. In Ko Samui, a sign posts the year's count of foreigners who never made it home from their vacation! Crash helmets are now required by law.

RENTAL AGENCIES

The major car-rental companies represented in Thailand are **Avis** (☎ 800/331–1084; in Canada, 800/879–2847), **Hertz** (☎ 800/654–3001; in Canada, 800/263–0600; in the U.K., 0345/555888), and **National InterRent** (sometimes known as Europcar InterRent outside North America; ☎ 800/227–3876; in the U.K., 0345/222–525).

RENTAL RATES

Rates in Thailand begin at $39 a day and $336 a week for an economy car with unlimited mileage. This include neither tax, which is 7% on car rentals, nor the Collision Damage Waiver, which is about $10 a day. With a significant surcharge over the basic one day's rental cost of B1,500 for a 1.6-liter car, Avis permits one-way rentals with drop-offs in most major cities. It is better to make your car rental reservations in Thailand as you can usually secure a discount.

ROAD CONDITIONS

The major roads in Thailand tend to be very congested, and street signs are often in Thai only. But the limited number of roads and, with the exception of Bangkok, the straightforward layout of cities combine to make navigation relatively easy. Driving at night in rural areas, especially north and west of Chiang Mai and in the south beyond Surat Thani is not advised, as highway robberies have been reported.

RULES OF THE ROAD

If your current driving license is not written in English, an international driving license is required. Driving is on the left; speed limits are 60 kph (37 mph) in cities and 90 kph (56 mph) outside.

By Plane

The major domestic carrier is **Thai Airways International** (✉ 485 Silom Rd., Bangkok, ☎ 02/234–3100). Its planes connect Bangkok with all major cities and tourist areas in Thailand with one exception. The closest Thai Airways flies to Ko Samui is Surat Thani, a two-hour bus-and-ferry ride from the island. For direct flights to Ko Samui, call **Bangkok Airways** (☎ 02/253–4014), which has three scheduled daily flights between Bangkok and Ko Samui, using 40-seat planes. Bangkok Airways also flies between Ko Samui and Phuket as well as a flight three times a week to Chiang Mai via Sukhothai.

On popular tourist routes during peak holiday times, flights are often fully booked. Make sure you have reservations, and make them well in advance of your travel date. Flights should be reconfirmed when you arrive in Thailand. Get to the airport well before departure time. Recently, the airlines have started to give away the reserved seats of late passengers to standby-ticket holders. Thai Airways has a good record for keeping to schedule. During the rainy season, however, you may experience delays due to the weather.

AIR PASSES

Thai Airways offers a travel package called the **Discover Thailand Pass.** For $259 you can take four flights to any of the airline's Thailand destinations. You must purchase the pass outside Thailand. Virtually all planes go through Bangkok, though Thai Airways has recently initiated daily nonstop service between Chiang Mai and Phuket. This pass has its limitations. For example, if you fly from Chiang Mai to Surat Thani, you must change planes in Bangkok, eaning that you will use two of your four flights.

By Samlor

Usually called tuk-tuks for their spluttering sound, samlors are three-wheel cabs that are slightly less expensive than taxis and, because of their maneuverability, the most rapid form of travel through congested traffic. All tuk-tuk operators drive as if your ride will be their last, but, in fact, they are remarkably safe. Tuk-tuks are not very comfortable, though, and subject you to the polluted air, so they're best used for short journeys.

By Taxi

Most Bangkok taxis now have meters installed, and these are the ones tourists should take. In other cities, fares are still negotiated. Taxis waiting at hotels are more expensive than those flagged down while cruising. Never enter the taxi until the price has been established. Most taxi drivers do not speak English, but all understand the finger count. One finger means B10, two is for B20 and so on. Ask at your hotel what the appropriate fare should be. Never pay more than what the hotel quotes, as they will have given you the high price. If in doubt, accept 65%–75% of the cabbie's quote.

With any form of private travel, never change your initial agreement on destination and price unless you clearly establish a new "contract." Moreover, if you agree to the driver's offer to wait for you at your destination and be available for your onward or return journey, you will be charged for waiting time, and, unless you have fixed the price, the return fare can be double the outbound fare.

By Train

The State Railway of Thailand has three lines, all of which terminate in Bangkok. The Northern Line connects Bangkok with Chiang Mai, passing through Ayutthaya and Phitsanulok; the Northeastern Line travels up to Nong Khai, near the Laotian border, with a branch that goes east to Ubon Ratchathani; and the Southern Line goes all the way south through Surat Thani—the stop for Ko Samui—to the Malaysian border and on to Kuala Lumpur and Singapore, a journey that takes 37 hours. (There is no train to Phuket, though you can go as far as Surat Thani and change to a scheduled bus service.)

Most trains offer second- or third-class tickets, but the overnight trains to the north (Chiang Mai) and to the south offer first-class sleeping cabins. Couchettes, with sheets and curtains for privacy, are available in second class. Second-class tickets are about half the price of first-class, and since the couchettes are surprisingly comfortable, most Western travelers choose these. Do not leave valuables unguarded on these overnight trains.

Fares are reasonable. An air-conditioned, second-class couchette, for example, for the 14-hour journey from Bangkok to Chiang Mai is B530; first class is B980. Tickets may be bought at the railway stations. Travel agencies can also sell tickets for the overnight trains. Reservations are strongly advised for all long-distance trains. Train schedules in English are available from travel agents and from major railway stations. For information on schedules and passes, call the **Bangkok Railway Station,** Advance Booking Office (☎ 02/223–3762 or 02/223–0341).

RAIL PASSES

The State Railway of Thailand offers two types of rail passes. Both are valid for 20 days of unlimited travel on all trains in either second or third class. The **Blue Pass** costs B1,500 (children B750) and does not include supplementary charges such as air-conditioning and berths; for B3,000 (children B1,500), the **Red Pass** does. Currently, a special discounted rate, available for nonresidents of Thailand, gives a reduction of B1,000 for the Red Pass and B400 for the Blue Pass.

You need to book seats ahead even if you are using a rail pass; seat reservations are required on some trains, and are a good idea on trains that may be crowded—particularly in summer on popular routes. You will also need a reservation if you purchase overnight sleeping accommodations.

Contacts and Resources

Customs and Duties

If you are bringing any foreign-made equipment from home, such as cameras, it is wise to carry the original receipt with you or register it with U.S. Customs before you leave (Form 4457). Otherwise, you may end up paying duty on your return.

One quart of wine or liquor, 200 cigarettes or 250 grams of smoking tobacco, and all personal effects may be brought into Thailand duty-free. Visitors may bring in any amount of foreign currency; amounts taken out may not exceed those declared upon entry. Narcotic drugs, pornographic materials, and firearms are strictly prohibited.

Electricity

To use your U.S.-purchased electric-powered equipment, bring a converter and an adapter. The electrical current in Thailand is 220 volts, 50 cycles alternating current (AC); wall outlets take either two flat prongs, like outlets in the United States, or Continental-type plugs, with two round prongs.

Etiquette and Behavior

Thais believe in accommodation rather than confrontation. Demands, displays of anger, and any behavior that upsets harmony are frowned upon.

Health and Safety

FOOD AND DRINK

In Thailand, the major health risk is posed by the contamination of drinking water, fresh fruit and vegetables by fecal matter, which causes the intestinal ailment known variously as Montezuma's Revenge and traveler's diarrhea. Stay away from ice, uncooked food, and unpasteurized milk and milk products, and drink only water that has been bottled or boiled for at least 20 minutes.

SHOTS AND MEDICATIONS

If you plan to visit rural areas, where there's questionable sanitation, you'll need a vaccination as protection against hepatitis A. Both Ko Samet and northern Thailand are known to have malarial mosquitoes, so take extra precautions if you visit these areas. The U.S. Centers for Disease Control recommend chloroquine (analen) as an antimalarial agent. In areas with malaria and dengue, also carried by mosquitoes, take mosquito nets, wear clothing that covers the body, apply repellent containing DEET, and use a spray against flying insects in living and sleeping areas. No vaccine exists against dengue, so if it's in the area, travelers should use aerosol insecticides indoors as well as repellents against the mosquito.

Language

Thai is the country's national language. As it uses the Khmer script and is spoken tonally, it is confusing to most foreigners. What may sound to a foreigner as "krai kai kai kai" will mean to a Thai, said with the appropriate pitch, "who sells chicken eggs?" In polite conversation, a male speaker will use the word "krap" to end a sentence or to acknowledge what someone has said. Female speakers use "ka." It is easy to speak a few words, such as "sawahdee krap" or "sawahdee ka" (good day) and "khop khun krap" or "khop khun ka" (thank you). With the exception of taxi drivers, Thais working with travelers in the resort and tourist areas of Thailand generally speak sufficient English to permit basic communication.

Mail

POSTAL RATES

Airmail postcard rates to the United States are B9; B8 to the United Kingdom. The minimum rate for airmail letters is B14.50 to the United States and B12.50 to the United Kingdom. Allow about two weeks for your mail to arrive at its overseas destination. If you want to speed that process, major post offices offer overseas express mail services (EMS), where the minimum rate (200 g or 8 oz) is B230.

RECEIVING MAIL

You may have mail sent to you "poste restante." Usually, there is a B1 charge for each piece collected. Thais write their last name first, so be sure to have your last name written in capital letters and underlined.

Money and Expenses

CURRENCY

The basic unit of currency is the baht. There are 100 satang to one baht. There are five different bills, each a different color: B10, brown; B20, green; B50, blue; B100, red; B500, purple; and B1,000, silver. Coins in use are 25 satang, 50 satang, B1, B5, and B10. One-baht coins and B5 coins both come in different sizes and can be easily confused—get the feel of them quickly. The B10 coin has a gold-colored center surrounded by silver.

EXCHANGING MONEY

The baht is considered a stable currency whose rate of exchange is pegged to the U.S. dollar. All hotels will convert traveler's checks and major currencies into baht, though exchange rates are better at banks and authorized money changers. The rate tends to be better in Bangkok than up-country and is better in Thailand than in the United States.

At press time, the exchange rate was B17.75 to the Canadian dollar, B25 to the U.S. dollar, and B37 to the pound sterling.

LOST CREDIT CARDS

To report lost or stolen credit cards, contact the following: **American Express** (☎ 02/273–3660). **Diners Club** (☎ 02/238–3660). **MasterCard or Visa** (☎ 02/246–0300).

TAXES

A 7% Value Added Tax is built into the price of all goods and services, including restaurant meals, and is essentially non-refundable.

WHAT IT WILL COST

The cost of visiting Thailand is very much up to you. It is possible to live and travel quite inexpensively if you do as Thais do—eat in local restaurants, use buses, and stay at non-air-conditioned hotels. Once you start enjoying a little luxury, prices jump drastically. For example, crossing Bangkok by bus is a 14¢ ride, but by taxi the fare may run to $10.

Sample Prices. Continental breakfast at a hotel, $8; large bottle of beer at a hotel, $6, but in a local restaurant it will be under $3; dinner at a good restaurant, $15; 1-mile taxi ride, $1.50; double room, $20–$60 inexpensive (**$**), $60–$100 moderate (**$$**), $100–$160 expensive (**$$$**).

National Holidays

New Year's Day, January 1; Chinese New Year (two days), February 7 and 8 in 1997 and January 27 and 28 in 1998; Magha Puja (on the full moon of the third lunar month), February 8 in 1997 and about January 29 in 1998; Chakri Day, April 6; Songkran, mid-April; Coronation Day, May 5; Visakha Puja, May, on the full moon of the sixth lunar month; Queen's Birthday, August 12; King's Birthday, December 5. Government offices, banks, commercial concerns, and department stores are usually closed on these days, but smaller shops stay open.

Opening and Closing Times

Thai and foreign **banks** are open weekdays 8:30–3:30, except for public holidays. Most **commercial concerns** in Bangkok operate on a five-day week and are open 8–5. **Government offices** are generally open 8:30–4:30 with a noon–1 lunch break. Many **stores** are open daily 8–8.

Passports and Visas

Canadian, U.K, and U.S. citizens need only a valid passport to enter Thailand for stays of up to 30 days.

Telephones

To call Thailand from overseas, dial the country code, 66, and then the area code, omitting the first 0.

DIRECTORY ASSISTANCE AND OPERATOR INFO

If you wish to receive assistance for an overseas call, dial 100/233–2771. For local telephone inquiries, dial 100/183, but you will need to speak Thai. In Bangkok, you can dial 13 for an English-speaking operator.

LOCAL AND LONG-DISTANCE CALLS

Public telephones are available in most towns and villages and take B1 coins or both B1 and B5 pieces. Long-distance calls can only be made on phones that accept both B1 and B5 coins. For a long-distance call in Thailand, dial the area code and then the number.

INTERNATIONAL CALLS

To make overseas calls, you should use either your hotel switchboard—Chiang Mai and Bangkok have direct dialing—or the overseas telephone facilities at the central post office and telecommunications building. You'll find one in all towns.

When calling the States, you can dial the following **access numbers** to reach a U.S. long-distance operator: AT&T (☎ 0019–991–1111; MCI (☎ 001–999–1–2001); Sprint (☎ 001–999–13–877). However, many hotels block these access numbers. Instead, you will be charged a premium rate—as much as 400% more than a calling card—for calls placed from your room. If the hotel operator claims that you cannot use any phone card, ask to be connected to an international operator, who will help you to access your phone card. If none of this works, try calling your phone company collect. If collect calls are also blocked, call from a pay phone in the hotel lobby. Some locations in Bangkok have AT&T USADirect phones, which connect you directly with an AT&T operator. You can also use those public phones which accept both B1 and B5 coins to reach a U.S. operator; your coin will be returned after the call.

Tipping

In Thailand, tips are generally given for good service, except when a price has been negotiated in advance. A taxi driver is not tipped unless hired as a private driver for an excursion. With metered taxis in Bangkok, however, the custom is to round the fare up to the nearest 5 baht. Hotel porters expect at least a B20 tip, and hotel staff who have given good personal service are usually tipped. A 10% tip is appreciated at a restaurant when no service charge has been added to the bill.

Visitor Information

Contact the offices of the **Tourism Authority of Thailand** (TAT, ✉ 5 World Trade Center, Suite 3443, New York, NY 10048, ☎ 212/432–0433, FAX 212/912–0920; 303 E. Wacker Dr., Suite 400, Chicago, IL 60601, ☎ 312/819–3990, FAX 312/565–0359; 3440 Wilshire Blvd., Suite 1100, Los Angeles, CA 90010, ☎ 213/382–2353, FAX 213/389-7544). Inquiries from Canada should be directed to the Chicago office. In the U.K., contact the **Thailand Tourist Board** (✉ 49 Albemarle St., London W1X 3FE, ☎ 0171/499–7679).

When to Go

Thailand has two climatic regions: tropical savannah in the northern regions and tropical rain forest in the south. Three seasons run from hot (March through May) to rainy (June through September) and cool (October through February). Humidity is high all year, especially during the hot season. The cool season is pleasantly warm in the south, but in the north, especially in the hills around Chiang Mai, it can become quite chilly. The cool season is the peak season. Prices are often twice as high then as in the low seasons, yet hotels are often fully booked.

CLIMATE

Following are average temperatures for Bangkok. The north will generally be a degree or two cooler.

Jan.	89F	32C	May	93F	34C	Sept.	89F	32C
	68	20		77	25		75	24
Feb.	91F	33C	June	91F	33C	Oct.	88F	31C
	72	22		75	24		75	24
Mar.	93F	34C	July	89F	32C	Nov.	88F	31C
	75	24		75	24		72	22
Apr.	95F	35C	Aug.	89F	32C	Dec.	88F	31C
	77	25		75	24		68	20

FESTIVALS AND SEASONAL EVENTS

The festivals listed below are national and occur throughout the country unless otherwise noted. Many events follow the lunar calendar, so dates vary from year to year.

January: New Year celebrations are usually at their best around temples. In Bangkok, special ceremonies at Pramanae Ground include Thai dances.

February: Magha Puja commemorates the day when 1,250 disciples spontaneously heard Lord Buddha preach the cardinal doctrine on the full moon of the third lunar month.

April: Songkran marks the Thai New Year and is an occasion for setting caged birds and fish free, visiting family, dancing, and water-throwing, in which everyone splashes everyone else in good-natured merriment. The festival is at its best in Chiang Mai, with parades, dancing in the streets, and a beauty contest.

May: On the full moon of the sixth lunar month, the nation celebrates the holiest of Buddhist days, Visakha Puja—commemorating Lord Buddha's birth, enlightenment, and death. Monks lead the laity in candlelit processions around their temples.

August: On the 12th, Queen Sirikit's birthday is celebrated with religious ceremonies at Chitlada Palace, and the city is adorned with lights galore.

November: Held on the full moon of the 12th lunar month, Loi Krathong is the loveliest of Thai festivals. After sunset, people throughout Thailand make their way to a body of water and launch small lotus-shaped banana-leaf floats bearing lighted candles. The aim is to honor the water spirits and wash away one's sins of the past year. Of all the fairs and festivals in Bangkok, the **Golden Mount Festival** is the most spectacular, with sideshows, food stalls, bazaars, and large crowds of celebrants.

December: On the 5th, the **King's birthday**, a trooping of the colors is performed in Bangkok by Thailand's elite Royal Guards.

7 Vietnam

The midday downpour is a given. The lush green of the landscape is only one sign that you're in monsoon country. Another is relentless flooding. But these are conditions the Vietnamese have learned to abide, even to revere. For thousands of years, they have followed the dictates of the predictable climate, obediently plowing, planting, and harvesting when the weather tells them to. Foreign oppressors may come and go, but the rhythmic cycle of monsoon and dry seasons endures.

By Pilar
Guzman

FOREIGN SUBJUGATION OF VIETNAM dates back some 2,000 years. The country's people, descended from nomadic tribes, have been massacred, plundered, and proselytized—most notably by the Chinese, the French, the Japanese, and the Americans. Yet they are amazingly resilient; from each of their foreign rulers they have taken what appealed to them, melding the most dissonant elements of foreign cultures into a culture uniquely their own.

The Chinese were the first to invade, and by the time they were finally driven out by Ngo Quyen in 938 AD they had ruled the country for 1,000 years. During that time the Vietnamese had learned from them the use of the metal plow, had absorbed Confucianism, and had adopted a rice-based agriculture that persists to this day. French rule began in the mid-19th century and ended at Dien Bien Phu in 1954. From that occupation the Vietnamese were left with the beginnings of an ambitious infrastructure of dikes, roads, and railways, a wealth of impressive urban architecture, and—a new alphabet, *quoc ngu*; the French Jesuit Alexandre de Rhodes had devised a way of writing their language in Latin-based letters. The legacy of the Americans from their nearly two decades of misguided involvement in the country's affairs is not so easy to define.

The country's leaders, to be sure, have by no means embraced gung-ho, American capitalism. Yet the attractions of venture capital from abroad have been difficult to resist. Blessed with endless miles of craggy coastline, with pristine seas and surreal limestone archipelagos, with fertile green deltas and richly forested highlands filled with wildlife, Vietnam is unquestionably an attractive tourist destination, and since 1994 various joint-venture construction projects have broken ground. Before long there will be any number of impressive five-star resorts and hotels to include in guides such as this.

Vietnam has abundant natural resources, and foreign capital is eager to exploit these as well. Yet perhaps its greatest resource is its people: hardworking, self-sacrificing, resourceful, educated—82% of the population can read and write—and endowed with an inexplicable natural grace. If you visit Vietnam, you cannot help but marvel at their endurance. Waifish, silk-clad women bear yokes hung with baskets of rice weighing 10 times their own weight, without a visible bead of sweat. Or they help to build roads, protected by only a conical hat and a perfectly white handkerchief tied over nose and mouth. You will also admire their panache: Do not be surprised to encounter a pair of bareheaded men careening on a motorbike through city traffic at the height of a midday downpour, the driver tooting his horn with a soggy cigarette in his mouth, his companion, arms outstretched, balancing a large pane of glass on his knees. That mixture of practicality and bravado is in some ways the essence of Vietnam.

Pleasures and Pastimes

Dining

Although there are upscale Vietnamese, French, and Chinese establishments in Ho Chi Minh City, relatively few exist in the rest of the country. Hanoi, at least, is bound to acquire them in the coming years. However, family-run restaurants and cafés with fresh seafood offerings, delicious meats, and tasty *an chay* (vegetarian dishes) are everywhere.

Vietnam's best eating isn't found in restaurants in any case, but at stalls on every street corner and in every marketplace. These soup, rice, and noodle kitchens are usually run by several generations of a single fam-

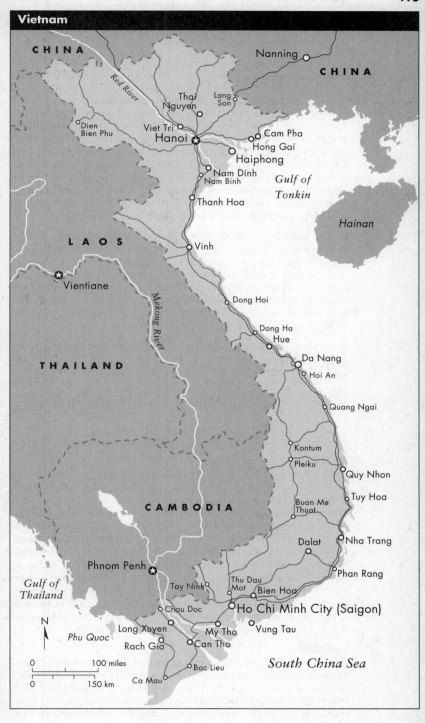

Vietnam

CHINA

CHINA

Red River

Nanning

Thai Nguyen

Lang Son

Dien Bien Phu

Viet Tri

Hanoi

Cam Pha

Hong Gai

Haiphong

Nam Dinh
Nam Binh

Gulf of Tonkin

Thanh Hoa

Hainan

LAOS

Vinh

Vientiane

Dong Hoi

Mekong River

Dong Ha
Hue

THAILAND

Da Nang

Hoi An

Quang Ngai

Kontum

Pleiku

Quy Nhon

Tuy Hoa

Buon Me Thuot

CAMBODIA

Nha Trang

Dalat

Phnom Penh

Phan Rang

Gulf of Thailand

Tay Ninh

Thu Dau Mot

Bien Hoa

Chau Doc

Ho Chi Minh City (Saigon)

N

Phu Quoc

Long Xuyen

My Tho

Vung Tau

Rach Gia

Can Tho

South China Sea

0   100 miles

0   150 km

Bac Lieu

Ca Mau

ily, and sitting down on the low plastic chairs at one of these self-contained sidewalk operations for a bowl of *pho* (noodles) feels like joining in a family gathering.

Pho with *bo* (beef), *ga* (chicken), *lon* (pork), *tom* (shrimp), or some combination thereof is served at all times of day, especially for breakfast. But the bowl of noodles is not merely an uninspiring staple, it is a work of art requiring the perfect balance of texture and taste. An ideal composition includes: heaps of crispy roughage, including basil, cilantro, parsley, and various herbs and shallots; the ubiquitous lime wedge, providing the requisite tangy-sour element; red chile, either coarsely chopped or puréed; and the indispensable condiment *nuoc nam,* a salty fermented-fish sauce that magically weds all of the flavors together. Don't be put off by the smell of this potent light brown liquid— skeptical foreigners have been known to become converts after a couple of experiences. But do take care not to overdo: it is usually served in a quick-pouring container, and a little bit goes a long way.

Besides noodles, *com* (rice) is another staple, and it is served with anything and everything. You should take advantage of the abundant and cheap seafood, especially in coastal towns. Beef and pork are also generally of high quality, but chicken tends to be somewhat tough. Dog meat isn't as inexpensive or plentiful as you might think, and the chance of encountering it shouldn't deter you from exploring Vietnam's back-alley food scene; if you want to avoid consuming dog inadvertantly, watch for dishes said to contain *thit cho.*

Price categories throughout the chapter are based on the following ranges:

CATEGORY	COST*
$$$$	over 275,000d (US$25)
$$$	165,000d–275,000d (US$15–US$25)
$$	77,000d–165,000d (US$7–US$15)
$	22,000d–77,000d (US$2–US$7)
¢	under 22,000d (US$2)

per person for a three-course dinner, excluding beverages.

Golf

As Vietnam has welcomed international businesspeople, golf courses have opened or re-opened, as the case may be, after a long, antibourgeois, dormant period. Completed resorts include the Dalat Pine Lake Golf Course, part of the newly renovated Dalat Palace Resort; the course, which has panoramic views of lush rolling hills and a pleasantly cool climate, dates from the 1920s, making it the oldest course in Southeast Asia. A shuttle service runs every Sunday morning from the Metropole in Hanoi to the King's Valley Golf Resort Country Club, which has an 18-hole course designed by Robert McFarland. Song Be Golf Resort, north of downtown Ho Chi Minh City, is another sprawling, luxurious, 18-hole course. The Vung Tau Entertainment Village's 27-hole course is 128 km (79 mi) south of Ho Chi Minh in the beach town of the same name. A number of other courses are under construction.

Lodging

Accommodations are surprisingly abundant and range from five-star pleasure domes to backpacker-friendly guesthouses. Vietnam's policy of economic renovation, which has opened the doors to more than US$20 billion in foreign investment, includes the construction of countless joint-venture luxury hotels. Hotel staffers are generally enthusiastic, but Western-style service is still a rarity.

"Minihotels" are increasing in number and get high marks even from those who can afford big-hotel luxury. Unique to Vietnam, these family-run operations range from the utilitarian to the plush, and usually provide friendly service, spotless rooms, and a homey environment. Although such facilities as restaurants, discos, and swimming pools are rare, guest rooms generally have air-conditioning and sometimes include satellite TV, phones, refrigerators, and proper bathtubs.

The rates quoted below are for accommodation during the summer months; reservations are recommended during July and August. Prices sometimes fluctuate mildly during the Tet, the new-year holiday, which falls in January or February (depending on the lunar cycle). At more upscale accommodations, rates often include breakfast. Price categories throughout the chapter are based on the following ranges:

CATEGORY	COST*
$$$$	over 2,200,000d (US$200)
$$$	1,100,000d–2,200,000d (US$100–US$200)
$$	550,000d–1,100,000d (US$50–US$100)
$	275,000d–550,000d (US$25–US$50)
¢	under 275,000d (US$25)

*for a standard double room in high season

Water Sports
With its endless stretches of pristine coastline, Vietnam has spectacular coral reefs and incredible sealife. Snorkeling, scuba diving, boating, and swimming are available in almost all seaside towns.   422

Exploring Vietnam

With billions of dollars in foreign investment jump-starting the economy, Vietnam has made its unspoiled highlands, dense forest, endlessly verdant deltas, and 3,450 km (2,140 mi) of breathtaking coastline accessible to tourism. As the capital of the Socialist Republic of Vietnam and original seat of Viet Minh power, Hanoi is the most sober and ideologically driven of Vietnam's cities. Trips around Hanoi include boat excursions through the limestone archipelagoes of Halong Bay and trekking tours through the Hoang Liem Mountains, where, in towns like Sapa, ethnic minority cultures persist despite sweeping changes in the rest of the country. South along the coast, Hue (the former imperial capital) and Hoi An are perhaps the country's most culturally rich areas. The area around unsavory Danang is known for its perfect beaches, like China Beach, and a spattering of Cham ruins. The south-central coast (the area around Nha Trang) is also known for its beaches and ruins, but trips through the Central Highlands to the resort town of Dalat and further inland to Kontum feature hiking through splendid mountain and lake districts. Only having been "freed" by North Vietnam in 1975, chaotic Ho Chi Minh (formerly Saigon), betrays its thoroughly Western heritage as the former capital of French Cochinchina and of South Vietnam. Among the most popular day-trip destinations are boat excursions to villages along the Mekong Delta, the country's breadbasket.

Great Itineraries
Even under the most stringent time constraints, touring just the two major cities would not only prove an unsatisfying experience, but a misleading representation of the country as a whole, as Vietnam's ethos is inextricable from its endless coast and exquisite rural landscape. Ho Chi Minh City, like the more conservative Hanoi, is not nearly as sight-intensive as beautiful Hue and the tiny riverfront town of Hoi An, nor nearly as representative of Vietnamese rice culture as the lush Mekong Delta. Therefore the itineraries given here try to combine city

and country, while accommodating visitors with limited time. Not included are destinations in the Central Highlands and along the south-central coast, areas of interest to beach goers and nature lovers but neither as historically significant nor as easy to get to as the cities and towns included below.

IF YOU HAVE 3 DAYS

Spend one day in **Ho Chi Minh City,** using it as a base for day trips to the **Cu Chi Tunnels** and **Mytho** in the Mekong Delta. Another option is to spend a day and a half in **Hue** and a day and a half in **Hoi An,** a three-hour car trip from Hue.

IF YOU HAVE 7 DAYS

Spend one day in **Ho Chi Minh City,** visiting Central Saigon (Dong Khoi Street, formerly Rue Catinat) from Notre Dame Cathedral to the Saigon River, the Ben Thanh market, the Jade Emperor's Pagoda, and the War Crimes Museum. A one-day boat trip along the **Mekong Delta** from Mytho offers a glimpse of the unique river life and its bustle of commercial activity. Fly to **Hue** for two days; tour the ancient citadel, and arrange a Perfume River boat trip to the Nguyen dynasty tombs and pagodas. A trip to the perfectly preserved 18th-century city of **Hoi An** is well worthwhile. Fly or take an overnight train to **Hanoi.** Spend two days touring the Old Quarter and the Hoan Kiem Lake District, Ho Chi Minh's Mausoleum, and the Temple of Literature. Make sure you catch a water-puppet show.

IF YOU HAVE 10 DAYS

Even if you have more time, three days in and around **Ho Chi Minh City** should suffice; the city does not have a large number of imposing sights, and a one-day boat trip in the **Mekong Delta** will give you an adequate glimpse of the region. Allow two days in imperial **Hue,** one day in **Hoi An,** two days in **Hanoi,** and a couple of days either in **Halong Bay,** one of Vietnam's most spectacular natural wonders, or northern **Sapa,** where you can take in the beautiful mountain scenery and see members of the various hill tribes trading at their colorful weekend market.

When to Tour Vietnam

There is no one best time to tour Vietnam. It exhibits a number of microclimates, so it can be hot and dry in one area while it's monsoon season in another. March and April have the best weather in the largest number of regions, while October and November run a close second. (☞ When to Go *in* Vietnam A to Z, *below.*)

HANOI

658 km (408 mi) from Hue, 763 km (473 mi) from Danang, 1,710 km (1,060 mi) from Ho Chi Minh City.

The self-appointed stronghold of "true" Vietnamese, anti-imperialist culture has learned to covet satellite TV and blue jeans. The country's leaders let in a flood of overseas investment from China, Malaysia, Singapore, Taiwan, and even the United States and Australia, and now the capital of the Socialist Republic of Vietnam relishes its new-found economic liberalization despite itself. What makes the city appealing for visitors is that while Western fashions, music, and food have managed to elbow their way into the once impenetrable north, Hanoi retains its ancient and French colonial architecture, broad tree-lined boulevards, and beautiful lakes.

The city dates back to the 7th century, when Chinese Sui dynasty settlers occupied the area and set up a capital called Tong Binh. Then, in 1010, King Ly Thai To is said to have seen a golden dragon ascending from Hoan Kiem Lake. The dragon is a traditional Chinese symbol for royal power, and the king took the omen literally: he relocated his capital to the shores of the lake, the site of present-day Hanoi, and named his new city Thang Long, or "City of the Ascending Dragon."

That was not the last of Hanoi's golden omens, however. In 1428, King Le Loi is said to have driven Vietnam's Chinese overlords from the country with the help of a magic sword. Celebrating his success after the war with a boating excursion on Hoan Kiem Lake, Le Loi was confronted by a gigantic golden tortoise that retrieved the sword for its heavenly owner. Hanoi continued to be the capital until Le Loi's dynasty was supplanted by the Nguyen dynasty in 1788, at which time it was demoted in favor of Hue.

The French used Hanoi as the "Eastern Capital," or Dong Kinh (hence "Tonkin"), of French Indochina. Once they were defeated by Ho Chi Minh's Viet Minh at Dien Bien Phu in 1954, the city was again declared the capital of Vietnam. Given the country's experience with foreign rulers, it is not surprising that the post-1975 socialist order sought to seal off the city and expelled non-native residents, even Chinese, many of whose families had lived in Vietnam for literally thousands of years.

Hanoi's reputation as hostile, anti-Western, and anti-outsider is in part justified; its bureaucracts are indeed defensive and difficult to deal with. Its ordinary citizens are nevertheless perfectly accommodating. Although northern Vietnamese are perhaps more introverted and formal than southerners, visitors should not mistake a provincial reserve—born of geographic, linguistic, and political isolation—for aloofness or xenophobia. Northern vendors are on the whole extremely polite, and unlike pushier Saigonese salesmen, refreshingly unaware of the schmoozier ways of capitalism.

Exploring Hanoi

Unlike Ho Chi Minh City, Hanoi is a very pleasant place for a leisurely stroll. The Hoan Kiem District, named after the lake at its center, is the hub of all local and tourist activity. Just north of the lake is the Old Quarter, a charming cluster of ancient streets. Unless you wish to make a pilgrimage to Ho Chi Minh's mausoleum in Ba Dinh or ride a bike to the picturesque West Lake, there is little occasion to leave the district. The modern city center to the south houses grand French colonial-style buildings that have been turned into embassies and hotels.

The Old Quarter

Between Hoan Kiem Lake, Long Bien Bridge, a former city rampart, and a citadel wall is the oldest part of the city. The area was unified by the Chinese, at which time ramparts were built. When Vietnam gained its independence from China in the 11th century, King Ly Thai To built his palace here, and the area came to be known as a crafts center. Artisans were attracted from all over the northern part of the country and formed cooperative living and working situations based on like skills and village affiliation. In the 13th century, the various crafts organized themselves into official guilds. The area is referred to as "36 Old Streets"—a misnomer, since there are nearly 70 of them. To this day, the streets are still named after the crafts practiced by the original guilds, and they maintain their individual character. Note the narrow "tube houses," combining workshops and living quarters. They were built extremely deep and narrow because each business was taxed according to the width of its storefront. In addition to the specialty shops that are still here, each street has its religious structures reflecting the beliefs of the village from which the original guilds had come.

Numbers in the text and in the margin correspond to points of interest on the Hanoi Old Quarter map.

A GOOD WALK

Begin your walking tour of the Old Quarter in the northern section of the Hoan Kiem District, at the **Dong Xuan Market** ①. Head south on Hang Duong Street, which turns into Hang Ngang Street, and then into **Hang Dao Street** ②. Hang Dao divides the Old Quarter and serves as a convenient corridor from which to adventure down any of the appealing side streets. Once you come to **Hang Bac Street** ③, a major thoroughfare, take a left.

Turning right down Hang Be Street brings you to the historic boat-building district. The bamboo *cai mang* rafts you see here were designed especially for the shallow rivers, lakes, and swamps of Hanoi. Hang Be takes you to Cau Go Street, where you turn right. This neighborhood was known for its flower market in colonial times, a vestige of which can be found at the intersection with Hang Dao, where you'll see the northern tip of **Hoan Kiem Lake** ④.

Rest a while here, enjoying the view of the lake, then continue up Cua Go until it veers to the left and becomes **Hang Gai Street** ⑤. Turning north on Hang Trong Street will bring you to **Hang Quat Street** ⑥. A quick jog to the left on Hang Non Street will bring you to Hang Thei Street, which turns into Thuoc Bac Street and eventually leads to **Hang Ma Street** ⑦. Hang Ma takes you back to Hang Chieu and the Dong Xuan Market.

TIMING

Since the area is filled with shops, this is the kind of walk that could take two hours or 10, depending on how much of a browser you are.

SIGHTS TO SEE

❶ Dong Xuan Market. Conveniently accessible by riverboat, this market, the oldest and largest in the city, once saw trading with the whole of Southeast Asia. The huge structure, to which the French had added a number of features, including a new facade, was destroyed by fire in 1994—ironically enough, on Bastille Day. Five people were killed and 3,000 workers left without jobs. The fire displaced 3,000 workers and took five lives. Now being rebuilt, the market is turning into something closer to a supermall.

❸ Hang Bac Street. This street was originally dominated by silversmiths and money changers, and still has a wide variety of jewelry shops. The Dong Cac jewelers' guild was established here in 1428, and later erected a temple (now gone) to three 6th-century brothers whose jewelry skills, learned from the Chinese, made them the patron saints of Vietnamese jewelry.

❷ Hang Dao Street. Since the 15th century, when it was one of the original silk-trading centers, Hang Dao Street has been known for its textiles. It first specialized in lovely pink silk, always in particular demand because the color symbolizes the Vietnamese lunar new year. By the 18th century, the street was still a major silk center but with a whole spectrum of colors. When the French colonized Vietnam, Hang Dao became the center for all traffic in silk, with massive biweekly trade fairs. Indians who settled here at the turn of the century introduced textiles from the west, and today the street features ready-made clothing.

❺ Hang Gai Street. The "Street of Hemp" now offers a variety of goods, including ready-made silk and silver products. This street is among the most popular with Western tourists.

➐ **Hang Ma Street.** Here you can find delicate *ma*, paper confections made to be burned in tribute to dead ancestors, alongside more modern niceties such as imported party decorations.

➏ **Hang Quat Street.** The "Street of Fans" now features a stunning array of religious paraphernalia, including beautiful funeral and festival flags.

➍ **Hoan Kiem Lake** (Ho Hoan Kiem). In the early morning, locals come to the lakeshore to play a little badminton and practice tai chi. You can visit the charming **Tortoise Pagoda** on the islet in the middle of the lake. Its name recalls the golden tortoise that reclaimed a magic sword here from King Le Loi.

NEED A BREAK?

Au Lac Café (☎ 04/828–7043), a coffee stand with outdoor seating, is on the southwest corner of Hoan Kiem Lake—actually on it, not just overlooking it. Snacks are available, but come to see and be seen: This very hip establishment is a favorite hangout for Westerners.

Around the Ho Chi Minh Mausoleum

From Hoan Kiem Lake, ask a cyclo or taxi driver to take you to the Ho Chi Minh Mausoleum, in the Ba Dinh District. Once there, you'll find several interesting sites are within easy walking distance.

Numbers in the text and in the margin correspond to points of interest on the Hanoi map.

A GOOD WALK

Start at the **Ho Chi Minh Mausoleum** ①, in the heart of the Ba Dinh District. Once you have passed by the unflinching guards and through the mausoleum, you'll be directed past the Presidential Palace and through Ho Chi Minh's Spartan residence, to the **One Pillar Pagoda** ②, and finally to the **Ho Chi Minh Museum** ③.

Return to the main entrance, at the intersection of Hung Vuong and Le Hong Phong Streets. Head east on Le Hong Phong until you reach Dien Bien Phu Street. Turn right on Dien Bien Phu; there, across from Chi Lang Park, site of Hanoi's Lenin Monument, you will see the Army Museum, home to bits and pieces of old planes and weaponry. Retrace your steps to the intersection of Le Hong Phong, Dien Bien Phu, and Hoang Dieu. Turn left on Hoang Dieu and continue until you reach Nguyen Thai Hoc Street, where you turn right. The Fine Arts Museum, at No. 66, has an uninspiring collection of lacquerware, sculpture, and painting. Turn left on Nguyen Thai Hoc Street when you leave the museum, then right on Van Mieu Street and right again on Quoc Tu Giam Street, where you will see the entrance to the **Temple of Literature** ④ on the right.

TIMING

Depending on the lines around Ho Chi Minh's Mausoleum, this walk could take anywhere from three to five hours.

SIGHTS TO SEE

➎ **Ho Chi Minh Mausoleum.** It is hard to overstate Ho Chi Minh's heroic stature among the Vietnamese. Originally called Nguyen Sinh Cung, Ho Chi Minh (literally "Bringer of Light") is the final and most memorable in a series of more than 50 pseudonyms that Vietnam's intrepid leader acquired during the course of his remarkable life. Born in 1890 in the Central Vietnamese province of Nghe An, Ho received traditional French schooling and became a teacher. From his father, who abandoned the family early on, Ho had, however, inherited a wanderlust that became fueled by a lifelong obsession with Vietnamese independence.

420

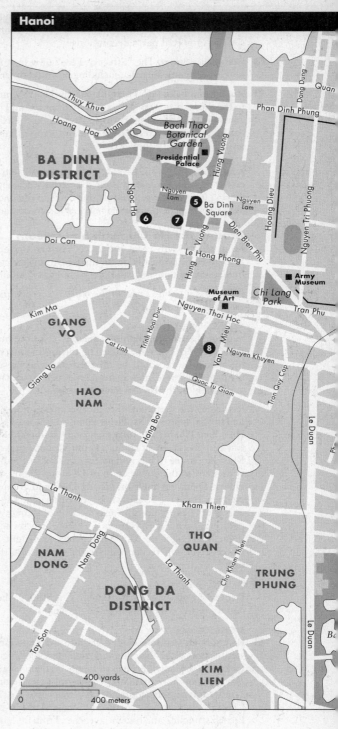

Hanoi

Thuy Khue

Hoang Hoa Tham

BA DINH
DISTRICT

Bach Thao
Botanical
Garden

Presidential
Palace

Phan Dinh Phung

Hung Vuong

Bung Bung

Quan

Hoang Dieu

Nguyen Tri Phuong

Ngoc Ha

Nguyen
Lam

5 Ba Dinh
Square

Nguyen
Lam

6 **7**

Le Vuong

Dien Bien Phu

Doi Can

Le Hong Phong

Hung

Army
Museum

Chi Lang
Park

Kim Ma

GIANG
VO

Cat Linh

Trinh Hoai Duc

Museum
of Art

Nguyen Thai Hoc

Tran Phu

Giang Vo

HAO
NAM

8

Van Mieu

Nguyen Khuyen

Tran Quy Cap

Quoc Tu Giam

Hang Bot

La Thanh

Kham Thien

Le Duan

NAM
DONG

Nam Dong

THO
QUAN

La Thanh

Cho Kham Thien

TRUNG
PHUNG

Tay Son

DONG DA
DISTRICT

KIM
LIEN

Le Duan

0   400 yards

0   400 meters

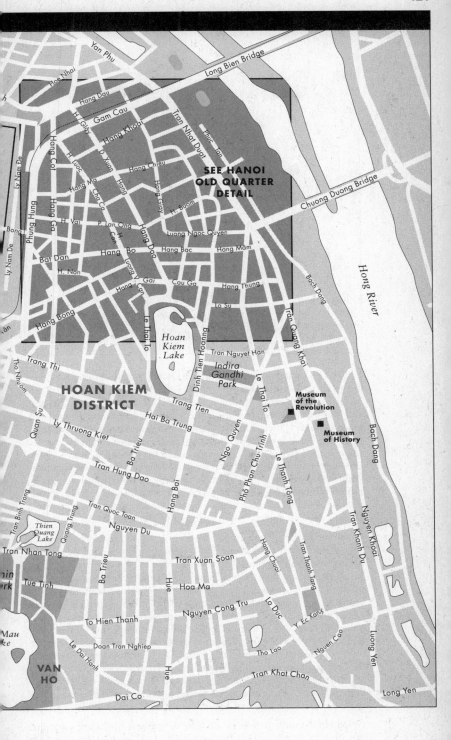

Long Bien Bridge

SEE HANOI
OLD QUARTER
DETAIL

Chuong Duong Bridge

Hong River

Hoan
Kiem
Lake

Indira
Gandhi
Park

**HOAN KIEM
DISTRICT**

Museum
of the
Revolution

Museum
of History

Thien
Quang
Lake

**VAN
HO**

Hoe Nhai

Yan Phu

Hang Dau

H. Giay

Gam Cau

Hang Khoai

Tran Nhat Duat

Phuc Tan

Hang Coi

Hang Ma

D. Xuan

Hang Chieu

Hang Giay

H. Buom

Phung Hung

H. Vai

P. Lan Ong

Cha Ca

Hang Dao

Luong Ngoc Quyen

Hang Ga

Hang Bo

Hang Bac

Hang Mam

Bat Dan

H. Non

Hang Gai

Cau Ga

Hang Thung

Hang Con

Hang Bong

Lo Su

Le Thai To

Dinh Tien Hoang

Tran Nguyet Han

Bach Dang

Tran Quang Khai

Trang Thi

Tho Nhuom

Quan Su

Ly Thruong Kiet

Hai Ba Trung

Trang Tien

Ba Trieu

Ngo Quyen

Le Thai To

Bach Dang

Tran Hung Dao

Hang Bai

Phô Phan Chu Trinh

Le Thanh Tong

Tran Quoc Toan

Nguyen Du

Quang Trung

Tran Binh Trong

Tran Nhan Tong

Ba Trieu

Hue

Tran Xuan Soan

Hang Chuoi

Tran Thanh Tong

Nguyen Khoai

Tran Khanh Du

Tue Tinh

Hoa Ma

Nguyen Cong Tru

La Duc

Y. Ec Xang

Nguyen Cao

Luong Yen

Mau
ke

To Hien Thanh

Le Dai Hanh

Doan Tran Nghiep

Hue

Tho Lao

Tran Khat Chan

Long Yen

Dai Co

Ly Nam De

Bong

Ly Nam De

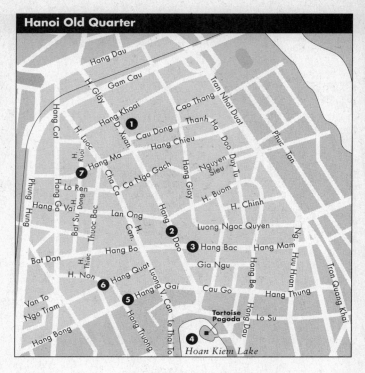

Hanoi Old Quarter

In 1911 he signed on to the crew of a French freighter; two years later, a stint aboard another French ship took him to the United States, where he settled for a year in Brooklyn and found work as a laborer. The next six years were spent in Paris, where besides mastering several languages—among them French, German, English, Cantonese, and Japanese—he moved in exclusive intellectual circles and first committed himself to political activism. After participating in the Versailles Peace Conference (where his modest proposal for basic democratic freedoms and constitutional structures for Vietnam was not adopted) and helping to found the French Communist Party, he left for Moscow in 1924. It soon became clear that to successfully foment a worker's revolution he would have to dedicate himself to organizing the Vietnamese.

By the end of the '20s, a number of poorly organized revolts had inspired aggressive French retaliations that were only compounded by a looming international economic depression. In June 1929, while based in Hong Kong, Ho consolidated the rebellious factions under the Indochinese Communist Party. However, it was not until 1941—after escaping arrest in Hong Kong, fudging documentation of his death, shuttling between China and the Soviet Union, and disguising himself as a Chinese journalist—that he was able to sneak back into Vietnam. Shortly thereafter he founded the Viet Minh Front to oust both the French and the occupying Japanese. The August Revolution of 1945, planned to coincide with the Japanese surrender, won North Vietnam for the Viet Minh. The Viet Minh's brilliant 1954 offensive against the French at Dien Bien Phu solidified North Vietnamese independence, and Ho ruled as president of the Democratic Republic of Vietnam until his death in 1969.

Given Ho's dominant role in modern Vietnamese history, it's not surprising how significant his mausoleum and the surrounding area are in Vietnam's ideological consciousness. Right outside the mausoleum is **Ba Dinh Square,** where Ho officially established the Democratic Republic of Vietnam by reading its Declaration of Independence in September 1945. Thousands of Vietnamese visit these revered sights each year to pay homage to "Uncle Ho." His embalmed body, touched up now and again in Russia, is displayed inside the mausoleum.

When you visit, be aware of the strict propriety required. Although you will see hoards of Vietnamese pilgrims moving in a solemn single-file procession, foreigners must sign in at a office at the front entrance just inside the gate, then leave their possessions at another checkpoint closer to the actual mausoleum, where uninformative non-mandatory brochures are for sale. Your purchase of them amounts to your entrance donation. No cameras, hats, or bags of any kind may be brought in the building, and you are expected to behave respectfully. This means not wearing shorts or tanktops or putting your hands in your pockets while inside. ✉ *Enter at corner of Hung Vuong and Le Hong Phong Sts.* 🏷 *Donation.* ☉ *Summer, daily 7:30–10:30* AM; *winter, Tues.–Thurs. and weekends 8–11* AM.

❻ Ho Chi Minh Museum. Don't expect to learn much about the life and importance of Ho Chi Minh at this museum unless you have a very articulate translator with you. Those who can read Vietnamese will appreciate a collection of manifestos, military orders, correspondence, and photographs from the Communist Party's early days to the present. Historical exhibits cover the October Revolution, the fight against fascism, Ho's revolutionary world movement, and Vietnam's struggle against imperialism. Labyrinthine murals and installations lead from the section called "Past" into the "Future," where you'll find everything from conceptual representations of peace to automobiles symbolizing America's military failure. Cameras and bags are forbidden inside the museum. There is an interesting gift shop. ✉ *3 Ngoc Ha St., Ba Dinh,* ☎ *04/826–3752 or 04/815–5425.* 🏷 *Admission.* ☉ *Tues.–Sun. 8–11:30* AM *and 1:30–4* PM.

❼ One Pillar Pagoda. The French destroyed this temple on their way out in 1954. It was reconstructed by the new government and still commemorates the legend of Emperor Ly Thai Tong. It is said that the childless emperor dreamt that the goddess of Mercy, seated on a lotus flower, handed him a baby boy. Sure enough, he soon met and married a peasant woman who bore him a male heir, and in 1049 he constructed this monument in appreciation. The distinctive single pillar is meant to represent the stalk of the lotus flower, a sacred Vietnamese symbol of purity. ✉ *Ong Ich Kiem St.* 🏷 *Free.*

❽ Temple of Literature (Van Mieu). An unusually well-preserved example of Vietnamese architecture, this monument to Confucius was built in 1070 by Emperor Ly Thahn Tong. Soon after its construction, the temple became Vietnam's first university, specializing in training students to pass the rigorous examinations for government and civil-service posts. The achievements of several centuries of the university's doctoral recipients are noted on 82 stelae, which rest on stone tortoises. It wasn't until 1802 that Emperor Gia Long moved his capital and the national university to Hue. The French, appropriately, later used the building as their school of civil administration, dubbing it the "Temple of the Crows" on account of the birds that tended to gather here. If you come before 3:20, there is a water-puppet show that is worth seeing. ✉ *Quoc Tu Giam St., Dong Ha,* ☎ *04/845–2917 or 04/823–5601.* 🏷 *Admission.* ☉ *Tues.–Sun. 8:30–11:30* AM *and 1:30* PM *to 4:30* PM.

Dining

Hanoi is certainly not known for its fine dining, but this is bound to change very soon. For a real culinary immersion, visit Ngo Cam Chi Street (off Hang Bong Street) in the Old Quarter for some local specialties. Try *banh cuon* (a rice pancake with savory stuffing), *pho mi xao* (Chinese wheat noodles), and *bun oc* (snails and rice noodles). The more upscale restaurants tend to be stodgy French or Chinese banquet-style establishments that are frighteningly reminiscent of the good old colonial days. The "fast food" advertised in café windows is a mistranslation for cheap rice or noodle dishes.

$$$$ ✕ **Le Beulieu.** At the best Western restaurant in Hanoi by far, a gracefully choreographed, pale pink–clad wait staff will replenish your table with the finest assortment of fresh breads in Asia. The impeccable service and ambience are paired with sublime, though not terribly innovative, French food. ✉ *Hotel Sofitel, 15 Pho Ngo Quyen St., Hoan Kiem District,* ☎ *04/826–6919. AE, DC, MC, V.*

$$$ ✕ **Banh Thai.** Frequented by international businessmen, this slightly upscale Thai restaurant offers excellent food and a decent ambience. ✉ *3B Cha Ca St., Hoan Kiem District,* ☎ *04/828–1120. No credit cards.*

$$$ ✕ **Club Opera.** The chef, whisked away from the late lamented Le Petit Bistrot in Saigon, prepares fine French cuisine in a starchily floral French villa setting. The upstairs section of the restaurant serves overpriced Vietnamese and Chinese cuisines. ✉ *59 Ly Thai To St., Hoan Kiem District,* ☎ *04/826–8802 (downstairs), 04/824–6950 (upstairs). AE, MC, V.*

$$$ ✕ **Galleon Steak House.** With black Angus beef imported from Australia, this steak house seems a little out of place in Vietnam. Still, the fresh meat can satisfy most any carnivorous hankerings. ✉ *50 Tran Quoc Toan St., Hoan Kiem District. AE, DC, MC, V.*

$$$ ✕ **Gustave's.** Considered one of the best restaurants in Hanoi, Gustave's offers dependable fine French dining that doesn't exactly push the creative culinary envelope. Since dishes are prepared with nothing but the finest and freshest ingredients, less is definitely more—the simple salmon tartare appetizer is superb. On the other hand, sauce-drenched lamb medallions, with the predictable carrot, potato, and parsley garnish, for example, smack of circa 1974 French cuisine. Equally passable, elegant, and time-warped are the grandiose French villa surroundings and decor. ✉ *17 Trang Tien St., Hoan Kiem District,* ☎ *04/825–0625. AE, DC, MC, V.*

$$$ ✕ **Indochine.** Indochine is the only upscale Vietnamese dining establishment in town worth trying. While consistently good traditional Vietnamese fare continues to bring customers back, expat critics complain that service is slacking. ✉ *16 Nam Ngu St., Hoan Kiem District,* ☎ *04/8246097. AE, MC, V.*

$$$ ✕ **Nha Hang Dong Nam A.** This no-ambience, white-tablecloth establishment offers banquet-style Chinese and Vietnamese fare. Though catering mostly to large groups, smaller parties still get Herculean portions of the finest meats and freshest fish. Westerners might be put off by the starchy, semiformal atmosphere. ✉ *126 Hang Trong St., Hoan Kiem District,* ☎ *04/826–8542. MC, V.*

$$$ ✕ **Richard's Court.** Part of the Hotel Villa Bleue, this restaurant offers faux-medieval intimacy and black Angus beef. Soups are seasonal and interesting, while entrées are a little bland. Ingredients, like the Australian and U.S. imported meats, are all very fresh. ✉ *82 Ly Thuong Kiet St., Hoan Kiem District,* ☎ *04/824–0607. AE, V.*

$$ ✕ **Al Fresco's.** This colorful south-of-the-border-cum-pizza restaurant/bar gets high marks from expats and travelers alike. Run by a friendly Aussie, the eclectic East-meets-West dining is coupled with a casual open-air ambience that makes it very easy to mingle. Things pretty much shut down by 10 PM. ⊠ *231 Ha Ba Trung St., Hoan Kiem District,* ☎ *04/826–7782. No credit cards.*

$$ ✗ Da Tano. This no-frills trattoria boasts the only real Italian chef in Hanoi. Pan-regional pasta is cooked to perfection. ⊠ *10 Hang Chao St., Hoan Kiem District,* ☎ *04/823–4850. No credit cards.*

$$ ✗ Gio Moi. Hanoi's answer to Mr. Chow's, this white-tablecloth establishment serves tasty authentic Chinese fare. ⊠ *63 Le Duan St., Lenin Park,* ☎ *04/822–9839. No credit cards.*

$$ ✗ Nam Phuong. Slightly upscale Vietnamese cuisine is served in a hip-but-elegant French villa setting. Although the tasty and beautifully presented dishes (like the beef in coconut milk that is served in a coconut) are satisfactory, portions are disappointingly scanty. ⊡ *19 Phan Chu Trinh St., Hoan Kiem District,* ☎ *04/824–0926. AE, MC, V.*

$$ ✗ Piano Restaurant & Bar. The live piano-and-violin duo serves as a pleasant backdrop to a good though unexceptional traditional Vietnamese meal. Stick to the very fresh boiled crab. The high-ceiling colonial French architecture, soft lighting, and antique yellow walls recreate turn-of-the-century charm. ⊡ *50 Hang Vai St., Hoan Kiem District,* ☎ *04/828–4423. No credit cards.*

$$ ✗ Saigon Sakura. Frequented by expats, this take-off-your-shoes Japanese restaurant serves an excellent calamari with vinegar marinade. What appears on the menu as risotto with shrimp is actually a very tasty cream rice that comes sizzling in a clay pot. ⊡ *17 Trang Thi St., Hoan Kiem District,* ☎ *04/825–7565.*

$ ✗ Five Royal Fish. In addition to a good Vietnamese menu (the curry is not great), homesick Westerners seem to enjoy their pizzas, sandwiches, and hamburgers. The shaded outdoor terrace here overlooks Hoan Kiem Lake, and if you go in the morning for a cup of coffee, you can watch locals practicing group tai chi on the shore. ⊠ *16 Le Thai To St., Hoan Kiem District,* ☎ *04/824–4368. No credit cards.*

$ ✗ Hue Restaurant. If you want the best food in Hanoi, come here for
★ imperial (Hue) cuisine and other traditional Vietnamese fare in a rustic outdoor/indoor setting. "Pork Pie" is a poor translation for culinary nirvana—a some-assembly-required platter of sugar-cane–wrapped ground pork that you roll with greens and vegetables in rice paper and dip into a delicious peanut sauce. For those who wince at this carnivorous frenzy, vegetarian delights are plentiful. (A warning: It's advised that you not drink too much, as the bathroom here is essentially a sloping floor.) ⊠ *6 Ly Thuong Kiet St., Hoan Kiem District,* ☎ *04/826–4062.*

¢ ✗ Ha Thanh Restaurant. Packed with locals at lunchtime, this Vietnamese equivalent of a greasy-spoon diner serves tasty heaping portions of Vietnamese and Chinese dishes. ⊠ *15A Hang Hanh St., Hoan Kiem District,* ☎ *04/828–5829. No credit cards.*

¢ ✗ Smiling Café. Brimming with young travelers, the Smiling not only serves some of the cheapest Vietnamese "fast food" but also doubles as a tourist agency that books boat and bus day trips out of Hanoi. As a hub of tourist activity, it is a great place to meet other travelers and exchange information while quaffing a refreshing fruit shake. ⊠ *10 Dinh Liet St., Hoan Kiem District,* ☎ *04/828–2109. No credit cards.*

Lodging

Hanoi is just beginning major construction of new luxury hotels, of which currently there is a limited crop. Although there are a couple of big Western-style hotels in the Ba Dinh District, that neighborhood is a good distance from the much more charming and walkable Hoan Kiem area. Instead, stay at one of the many clean minihotels, which have reasonable prices and often offer such modern amenities as cable

TV, IDD telephone, and great air-conditioning. Smaller properties are generally a better option than the huge hotels, many of which were built in the '60s and haven't been properly maintained or renovated. Be prepared for a strange trend in hotel decor that calls for mixing nice antique Chinese woodcarving with what appears to be green metal furniture from some defunct state institution.

$$$$ 🏨 **Daewoo Hotel.** Although one of the most sumptuous accommodations in town, the brand-new Daewoo is located away from the pedestrian hub of Hoan Kiem Lake, making it necessary to take cabs everywhere. With Hanoi's recent infusion of foreign investment and projected expansion, however, many businesses and restaurants are springing up in this area, the Ba Dinh District. ⊠ *Corner of Ngoc Thanh and Lieu Giai Sts., Ba Dinh District,* ☎ *04/831–5000,* FAX *04/831–5010. 411 rooms. 4 restaurants, 2 bars, air-conditioning, in-room safes, minibars, refrigerators, room service, pool, hot tub, sauna, aerobics, exercise room, dance club, laundry service and dry cleaning, concierge, business services, meeting rooms, travel services, car rental, parking. AE, DC, MC, V.*

$$$$ 🏨 **Hanoi Hotel.** This luxurious if charmless Western-style hotel seems to cater to businesspeople who have no interest in knowing that they are in Vietnam. It's quite a distance from the city center, but close to the Ho Chi Minh Mausoleum. Prices here are likely to come down as other joint-venture luxury hotels go up. ⊠ *D8 Giang Vo St., Ba Dinh District,* ☎ *04/825–4603,* FAX *04/825–9209. 76 rooms. 2 restaurants, 2 bars, air-conditioning, in-room safes, minibars, room service, massage, dance club, laundry service and dry cleaning, concierge, business services, meeting rooms, travel services, car rental. AE, DC, MC, V.*

$$$$ 🏨 **Metropole Hanoi/Hotel Sofitel.** By far the most beautiful hotel in
★   Hanoi, the exquisitely renovated Metropole dates from the turn of the century and combines old-world grandeur with modern convenience. An international management team ensures that the place runs like clockwork. Impeccably decorated rooms are luxurious if not incredibly spacious. ⊠ *15 Pho Ngo Quyen Ha Noi St., Hoan Kiem District,* ☎ *04/826–6919,* FAX *04/826–920,* FAX *04/826–6920. 244 rooms. Restaurant, 2 bars, air-conditioning, in-room safes, minibars, refrigerators, room service, pool, laundry service and dry cleaning, concierge, business services, meeting rooms, travel services, airport shuttle, car rental. AE, DC, MC, V.*

$$$ 🏨 **Hawaii Hotel.** Ignore the completely inappropriate name: This plush new minihotel offers spacious and tasteful rooms as well as a helpful staff. It is not too far from Thien Quang Lake and Lenin Park. ⊠ *77 Nguyen Du St., Hoan Kiem District,* ☎ *04/822–7517,* FAX *04/822–8698. 25 rooms. Restaurant, bar, air-conditioning, minibars, refrigerators, laundry service, business services, travel services, car rental. AE, DC, MC, V.*

$$$ 🏨 **Planet Hotel.** The proud host of the Italian soccer team in 1996, the Planet offers plush rooms and a great location in the Old Quarter overlooking West Lake. Wood touches offset the ultraslick modern edge and profusion of granite. ⊠ *120 Quan Thanh St., Hoan Kiem District,* ☎ *04/843–5888,* FAX *04/843–5088. 53 rooms. Restaurant, 2 bars, air-conditioning, in-room safes, minibars, refrigerators, room service, hot tub, sauna, health club, laundry service and dry cleaning, concierge, business services, travel services, car rental. AE, DC, MC, V.*

$$$ 🏨 **Saigon Hotel.** Despite its concrete '60s architecture, this property maintains high standards. The rooftop garden is a very pleasant place to have an evening drink. ⊠ *80 Ly Thuong Kiet St., Hoan Kiem District,* ☎ *04/826–8499,* FAX *04/826–6631. 44 rooms. Restaurant, 2 bars, air-conditioning, in-room safes, minibars, refrigerators, room service,* *massage, sauna, laundry service and dry cleaning, business services, meeting rooms, travel services, car rental. AE, DC, MC, V.*

$$$ 🏨 **Thang Loi Hotel.** Built during the '60s with help from the Cuban government, this was the first Western-style hotel in Hanoi. Poorly maintained '60s architecture literally floats on pontoons in the remote but peaceful West Lake. ✉ *Yen Phu St., West Lake District,* ☎ *04/826–8211,* 🖷 *04/825–2800. 178 rooms. 2 restaurants, 2 bars, air-conditioning, fans, minibars, refrigerators, room service, pool, barbershop, beauty salon, massage, sauna, tennis court, shop, laundry and dry cleaning, business services, meeting rooms, travel services, airport shuttle, car rental. AE, DC, MC, V.*

$$–$$$ 🏨 **Chains First Eden Hotel.** This 1996 establishment has all the makings of a first-class luxury hotel. Ideally located in the Old Quarter, the Eden is an excellent point of departure for walking tours through Hanoi. Rooms have all the amenities, and the staff is eager to please. ✉ *2 Phung Hung St., Hoan Kiem District.* ☎ *04/828–3897,* 🖷 *04/828–4066. 42 rooms. Restaurant, bar, air-conditioning, in-room safes, minibars, refrigerators, room service, health club, laundry service and dry cleaning, business services, travel services, car rental. AE, DC, MC, V.*

$$–$$$ 🏨 **Dan Chu Hotel.** The partial renovations here have not quite done justice to the lovely French architecture, which dates from the early part of the 20th century. Rooms are spacious and clean, with high ceilings, although their charms are compromised by ersatz Louis XVI decor. ✉ *29 Trang Tien St., Hoan Kiem District,* ☎ *04/825–4937,* 🖷 *04/826–6786. 56 rooms. Restaurant, bar, air-conditioning, minibars, refrigerators, room service, laundry service and dry cleaning, concierge, business services, travel services, car rental. AE, DC, MC, V.*

$$–$$$ 🏨 **Eden Hotel.** The Eden offers mini-hotel luxury and service at its finest
★ at a decent location near Thuyen Quang Lake. Bright rooms with carved-wood furniture have all of the conveniences. ✉ *94 Yet Kieu St., Hoan Kiem District,* ☎ *04/822–7465,* 🖷 *04/822–8235. 22 rooms. Restaurant, air-conditioning, minibars, refrigerators, laundry service and dry cleaning, concierge, travel services, car rental. AE, DC, MC, V.*

$$–$$$ 🏨 **Galaxy Hotel.** Although built in 1918, this granite-faced hotel has been fully renovated to accommodate business travelers and seems wholly modern. The comfortable rooms have typical hotel decor and are quieter than the hotel's proximity to the bustling Old Quarter would lead you to suspect. Attentive staff members speak English very well. ✉ *1 Phan Dinh Phung St., Hoan Kiem District,* ☎ *04/828–2888,* 🖷 *04/828–2466. 48 rooms. Restaurant, bar, air-conditioning, in-room safes, minibars, refrigerators, room service, laundry service and dry cleaning, concierge, business services, meeting rooms, travel services, car rental. AE, DC, MC, V.*

$$–$$$ 🏨 **Hoa Binh Hotel.** Situated in a grand old building, the three-star Hoa Binh is poised to accommodate an upscale crowd but seems to be lacking an experienced staff. The spacious rooms are clean and high-ceilinged, but betray sloppy renovations. ✉ *27 Ly Thuong Kiet, Hoan Kiem District,* ☎ *04/825–3315,* 🖷 *04/826–9818. 102 rooms. Restaurant, bar, air-conditioning, minibars, refrigerators, barbershop, laundry service and dry cleaning, business services, car rental. AE, DC, MC, V.*

$$–$$$ 🏨 **Prince Hotel** (Hoang Tu). This posh minihotel offers comfortable,
★ elegant rooms (some with a view of Hai Ba Trung Pagoda), excellent bathrooms, and a very enthusiastic English-speaking staff. Conveniently near the train station, the Prince is also not too far from the city center. ✉ *96A Hai Ba Trung St., Hoa Kiem District,* ☎ *04/824–8314,* 🖷 *04/824–8323. 25 bedrooms. Restaurant, bar, air-conditioning, minibars, refrigerators, laundry and dry cleaning, business services, car rental. AE, DC, MC, V.*

$$–$$$　🏨 **Thang Long Hotel.** The freshly painted rooms here have high ceilings and new bathroom facilities; many have balconies that overlook a lovely courtyard. Unfortunately, the otherwise elegant 1920s French structure suffers from puckering industrial red carpeting. ✉ *5 Nguyen Bieu St., Hoan Kiem District,* ☎ *04/823–1437,* FAX *04/823–1436. 18 rooms. Restaurant, bar, air-conditioning, minibars, refrigerators, laundry service, travel services, airport shuttle, car rental. AE, DC, MC, V.*

$$　🏨 **Dong Loi Hotel.** The fine '30s detailing at this hotel near the train station—beautiful moldings, fixtures, original doors, and high ceilings— is at odds with the newer wood paneling in the rooms, rattan furniture, and clear vinyl carpet runners. Rooms are clean, albeit a little dark, and have everything you need. ✉ *94 Ly Thuong Kiet St., Hoan Kiem District,* ☎ *04/825–5721,* FAX *04/826–7999. 30 rooms. 2 Restaurants, bar, air-conditioning, in-room safes, minibars, refrigerators, room service, massage, laundry service and dry cleaning, travel services, car rental. AE, MC, V.*

$$　🏨 **Ho Tay Villas.** If you are interested in complete silence, these villas, located 5 km (3 miles) outside of Hanoi at West Lake, offer peaceful accommodations that feel like a cross between an elegant estate and a socialist summer camp. Rooms are clean, with all of the amenities, but perhaps a little musty from age and proximity to the lake. ✉ *Dang Thai Mai St., Quan Tay Ho,* ☎ *04/845–2393,* FAX *04/823–2126. 10 villas. Restaurant, bar, air-conditioning, fans, minibars, refrigerators, laundry service, meeting rooms, travel services. No credit cards.*

$$　🏨 **Huyen Trang Hotel.** Not too far from Hoan Kiem Lake, this elegant new minihotel offers tasteful rooms and efficient and friendly service. ✉ *36 Hang Trong St., Hoan Kiem District,* ☎ *04/826–8480,* FAX *04/ 824–7449. 19 rooms. Restaurant, bar, air-conditioning, minibars, refrigerators, TV, billiards, laundry and dry cleaning, business services, car rental. AE, DC, MC, V.*

$$　🏨 **Phan Thai Hotel.** Modern minihotel conveniences, inoffensive decor, balconies, and a friendly staff make this a very decent accommodation. Conveniently located in the Old Quarter, it's near the Hoan Kiem Lake. ✉ *44 Hang Giay St., Hoan Kiem District,* ☎ *04/824–3667,* FAX *04/826– 6677. 16 rooms. Restaurant, air-conditioning, minibars, refrigerators, laundry service, travel services, car rental. AE, DC, MC, V.*

$$　🏨 **Viet My Hotel No. 9.** Within walking distance of the train station, the Viet My is in a lovely French colonial building from the '20s. Rooms have an old-world charm, with high ceilings and original gothic-arched double doors in each, although some are strangely configured and a little dark. ✉ *34/36 Nguyen Khuyen, Hoan Kiem District,* ☎ *04/823–2910,* FAX *04/824–1950. 24 rooms. Restaurant, bar, air-conditioning, fans, minibars, refrigerators, laundry service, travel services, car rental. AE, DC, MC, V.*

$$　🏨 **Villa Bleue Hotel.** Despite the fluorescent lights and neon back-lit welcome sign, this lovely renovated villa offers old-world charm, nice antiques, and some modern conveniences. Oddly enough, cheaper rooms seem to be nicer than the more expensive ones. The adjacent Richard's Court (☞ Dining, *above*) is a cavernous, pub-style restaurant. ✉ *82 Ly Thuong Kiet St.,Hoan Kiem District,* ☎ *04/824–7712,* FAX *04/824– 5676. 14 rooms. Restaurant, bar, air-conditioning, fans, minibars, refrigerators, laundry service, travel services, car rental. AE, MC, V.*

$–$$　🏨 **Freedom Hotel.** Amenities at this typical minihotel seem to come at the expense of completion of renovations in the stairwell. Still, rooms are clean and some have nice views. Nice antiques are mixed in with drab metal furniture. ✉ *57 Hang Trong St., Hoan Kiem District,* ☎ *04/826–7119,* FAX *04/824–3918. Restaurant, air-conditioning, fans, minibars, refrigerators, travel services, car rental. AE, MC, V.*

$ ▦ **Bodega V.** The 1996 Bodega offers tiny, immaculate rooms that are sparsely furnished but have excellent bathrooms and lots of light. The staff is very eager to please. ⊠ *32 Ly Thai To St., Hoan Kiem District,* ☎ *04/824–9867,* FAX *04/825–3145. 7 rooms. Restaurant, air-conditioning, fans, minibars, refrigerators, laundry service, travel services. No credit cards.*

¢–$ ▦ **Nam Phuong Hotel.** Just off Hang Trong Street, north of Hoan Kiem Lake, this hotel has old but charming rooms with balconies overlooking bustling Old Quarter streets. The staff is very accommodating. ⊠ *16 Bao Khanh St., Hoan Kiem District,* ☎ *04/825–8030,* FAX *04/825–8964. Air-conditioning, fans, minibars, refrigerators, laundry service, travel services. No credit cards.*

¢–$ ▦ **Vinh Quang Hotel.** Aside from the cheap East–West fusion decor, the Vinh Quang offers neat, efficient rooms and a great central location. The rooftop bar overlooks other Old Quarter rooftops. ⊠ *24 Hang Quat St., Hoan Kiem District,* ☎ *04/824–3423,* FAX *04/825–1519. Restaurant, bar, air-conditioning, fans, minibars, refrigerators, laundry service, travel services. AE, MC, V.*

¢–$ ▦ **Win Hotel.** At the top end of the budget accommodations, the Win is immaculate and homey all at once. Located on a quiet street just off Le Thai To, the hotel is just a stone's throw from Hoan Kiem Lake. ⊠ *34 Hang Hanh St., Hoan Kiem District,* ☎ *04/828–7371,* FAX *04/ 824–7448, 8 rooms. Air-conditioning, fans, minibars, refrigerators, laundry service, travel services, car rental. No credit cards.*

¢ ▦ **Camellia.** This small European-style building is in a quiet alleyway in the heart of the Old Quarter and offers rooms that overlook what could be a Parisian rooftop vignette. Naturally, charm at these prices comes at the expense of some of modern conveniences. Rooms are a little run-down but are reasonably clean. ⊠ *16A Trung Yen St. (off Dinh Liet St.),* ☎ *04/826–1512. 14 rooms. Air-conditioning, minibars, refrigerators, laundry service, travel services. No credit cards.*

Nightlife and the Arts

Bars, Pubs, and Nightspots

Apocalypse Now (⊠ 4 Hang Vai St., Hoan Kiem District, no phone) is a big expat hangout that's worth seeing for the cultural experience but not a quiet place to have a drink.

Le Club (⊠ 15 Ngo Quyen St., Hoan Kiem District, ☎ 04/826–6919), in the Hotel Sofitel, has a very pleasant ambience and good finger food.

Mailacafe (⊠ 1 Ngo Trang Tien St., Hoan Kiem District, ☎ 04/824–7579) is a quiet Vietnamese hangout.

Polite Pub (⊠ 5 Bao Khanh St., Hoan Kiem District, ☎ 04/825–0959) is one of the nicer, more popular bars in town; you can actually eat the ice, as well the bar food.

Tin Tin Pub (⊠ 14 Hang Non St., Hoan Kiem District, ☎ 04/826–0326) is a backpackers hangout with good food, ice-cold beer, and a casual ambience.

Stone Elephant (⊠ 2 Cua Dong St., Hoan Kiem District, ☎ 04/828–4545) is a hip expat hangout.

VIP Club (⊠ 60–62 Nguyen Du St., Hai Ba Trung District, ☎ 04/825–2690), part of former Boss Hotel, has an upscale karaoke scene with everything you would expect.

Volvo Discoteque (⊠ D8 Giang Vo St., Ba Dinh District, ☎ 04/825–4603) is the Hanoi Hotel's upscale disco.

Theater

At the **Municipal Theater** (✉ Intersection of Le Thanh Tong, Phan Chu Trinh, and Trang Tien Sts.), mediocre state-run evening show have replaced opera, for which the 1911 structure was originally built.

Water Puppets

Water-puppet performances are held Tuesday–Sunday 8–9 at the **Municipal Water Puppet Theater,** on the north shore of Hoan Kiem Lake. You can also catch an afternoon performance at the Temple of Literature (☞ Exploring, *above*).

Outdoor Activities and Sports

Other than renting a bike from a lakeside café, tourist agency, or hotel, there are not a large number of outdoor activities available in Hanoi.

Golf

King's Valley Golf Resort Country Club, about 45 km (28 mi) west of Hanoi in the Ha Tay Province, has an 18-hole course designed by Robert McFarland, as well as a new upscale hotel and villa complex; the greens fee is US$50. Other recreational services include tennis, horse-back riding, boating, and trekking excursions in Ba Vi National Park and Tan Vien Mountain. For information, ask at the Metropole Hanoi (☞ Lodging, *above*), which runs a weekly shuttle to the course.

Jogging

Perhaps the most pleasant place for a run is around Hoan Kiem Lake, where locals can be seen jogging and doing tai chi in the morning.

Swimming

With the purchase of drinks from the outdoor bar, nonguests are free to use the beautiful swimming pool at the **Metropole/Sofitel** (☞ Lodging, *above*).

Shopping

Department Stores

The **State General Department Store** (Back Hoa Tong Hop) on Hang Bai Street, just southeast of the lake between Hang Khai and Hai Ba Trung Streets, is a rip-off, but go to get a sense of the variety of arts and crafts available in Hanoi. It is a good way to get acquainted with prices, keeping in mind that things cost at least 15% more here than at smaller stores.

Shopping Districts

The area north of Hoan Kiem Lake is bustling with tiny shops carrying everything from shoes to clothes to antique timepieces. Hanoi is Vietnam's fine-arts capital, and running along the southern part of Hoan Kiem Lake, where Hang Khai turns into Trang Tien, are a number of antiques shops and arts-and-crafts galleries. Paintings and watercolors, as well as crafts like wood carvings, lacquerware, and puppets, can be found on Trang Tien and Hang Khai Streets. Any number of shops along Hang Gai and Duc Loi Streets, not far from Hoan Kiem Lake, can quickly and inexpensively produce custom-fitted clothes. Hang Gai is also good for souvenirs and antiques. Beautiful hand-embroidered linens can be found on Hang Bai, which becomes Hang Bong.

Street Markets

The largest of the street markets is **Dong Xuan Market** (☞ Exploring, *above*). The **19th of December Market,** on Ly Thuong Kiet between Hoa Lo and Quang Trung Streets, is not too far from the Hanoi Hilton. For a colorful experience, visit the tiny market on **Hang Bac Street,** north of Hoan Kiem Lake just off of Hang Dao in the Old Quarter, where makeshift tents are barely tall enough to accommodate Westerners. The occasional dog's head is a little alarming.

Specialty Stores

ART

Paintings, lacquerware, and sculpture by such contemporary Hanoi masters as Quach Dong Phuong, Bui Xuan Phau, Do Xuan Doan, and Truong Dinh Hao are on display and for sale at **ATC Art Gallery** (⊠ 48 Lang Ha St., Dong Da District, ☎ 04/835–3179, FAX 04/835–2081; ⊠ 22 Le Van Huu St., Hoan Kiem District, ☎ 04/825–0821, FAX 04/835–2081); the gallery is also represented in Ho Chi Minh City, Vung Tau, and Danang. Another fine art-and-crafts gallery is **Hanart** (⊠ 43 Trang Tien St., Hoan Kiem District, ☎ 04/825–3045). **Son Ha Art Gallery** (⊠ 35 Hang Than St., Hoan Kiem District, ☎ 04/826–9198) has a nice selection.

CLOTHES

At **Tien Dat** (⊠ 75 Hang Gai, Hoan Kiem District, ☎ 04/824–6244) the speedy, English-speaking Mr. Dat and his team custom-make clothes and hats for men, women, and children. The shop is not air-conditioned like some of the more expensive silk and clothing shops, but the work is of equal quality. A made-to-order woman's silk dress runs around US$15–US$20; reversible silk hats are around US$2. Mr. Dat also takes mail orders if you send him your dimensions and a detailed description of what you want. **Phuong Anh** (⊠ 56 Hang Hom, Hoan Kiem District, ☎ 04/826–1556) also does nice work.

EMBROIDERY SHOPS

Established in 1968, **Tan My** (⊠ 109 Hang Gai St., Hoan Kiem District, no phone) is the most famous embroidery shop in Hanoi. Employees from Thuong Tin province, which is known for its rich embroidery tradition, adorn tablecloths, silk clothing, and wall hangings with intricate designs. Ready-made work depicts everything from traditional Vietnamese floral patterns and dragon designs to scenes from Western fairy tales, or you can custom-order. **Tuyet Lan** (⊠ 65 Hang Gai St., Hoan Kiem District, ☎ 04/825–7967, FAX 04/826005816) also does beautiful embroidery, especially children's bed sheets, and accepts credit cards.

Hanoi A to Z

Arriving and Departing

BY CAR

To hire a car and driver, contact any hotel, Vietnam Tourism, or any other travel agency. The going rate is about US$35 per day for standard car or US$40 a day for a minivan.

BY PLANE

Noi Bai Airport is approximately 35 km (22 mi) north of the city. **Vietnam Airlines** (⊠ 1 Quang Trung St., ☎ 04/826–9294) offers non-stop international flights between Hanoi and Bancock, Seoul, Hong Kong, Taipei, Guangzhou, Dubai, Paris, Vientiane, and Phnom Penh. Domestic destinations served nonstop from Hanoi include Danang, Dien Bien, Ho Chi Minh City, Hue, Nha Trang, and Vinh. Flight schedules are often different for each day of the week. **Pacific Airlines** (⊠ 100 Le Duan St., Dong Da District, ☎ 04/851–5350) is the only other domestic carrier; ticket prices are comperable.

Between the Airport and the City Center: Buses to the airport depart from the Vietnam Airlines office (☎ 04/826–9294), around the corner from Trang Thi Street. Book a seat in advance. You can also hire a taxi with other travelers and split the fare (about 60,000d per person); travelers looking to share taxis congregate in front of the Vietnam Airlines office.

BY TRAIN

The ticket office at Hanoi's **main train station** (⊠ Opposite 115 Le Duan St., at the western end of Tran Hung Dao St., ☎ 04/825–3549) is open 7:30–11:30 and 1:30–3:30. There is a special counter where foreigners buy tickets. Another smaller train station, around the corner from the main one, services northern routes; the foreign booking agents at the main station will direct you.

Trains leave four times daily to Saigon (soft berth, US$97–US$125; 40 hours), but only one is express. Purchase a day in advance if you want to ensure a seat.

Getting Around

BY BICYCLE

Bikes can be rented at hotels and cafés along Hoan Kiem Lake for around 10,000d per day.

BY CYCLO

Cyclos (pedicabs) here are wider than anywhere else in Vietnam, so two people can ride comfortably; the fare is usually 5,000d–10,000d, depending on the distance.

BY MOTORBIKE

Motorbikes are a little safer here than in Saigon, though traffic is certainly not orderly. Hotels and cafés have rentals starting at about 90,000d a day.

BY TAXI

Taxis tend to congregate at the northwest corner of Hoan Kiem Lake, or you can order one by phone from **Hanoi Taxi** (☎ 04/853–5252), **Red Taxi** (☎ 04/835–3686), or **Taxi PT** (☎ 04/853–5171).

Contacts and Resources

CURRENCY EXCHANGE

ANZ (Australian New Zealand Bank; ⊠ 14 Le Thai To St., on western shore of Hoan Kiem Lake, ☎ 04/825–8190) exchanges money. **Vietcom Bank** (⊠ 78 Nguyen Du St., ☎ 826–8035) offers cash advances to Visa and MasterCard holders.

DOCTORS

Bach Mai International Hospital (Benh Vien Bach Mai; ⊠ Giai Phong St., ☎ 04/852–2004) has an international department with English-speaking doctors. **Viet Duc Hospital** (Benh Vien Viet Duc; ⊠ 48 Tranh Thai St., Hoan Kiem District, ☎ 04/825–3531) is open 24 hours for emergency surgery; staff speak English, French, and German. Procedures at the **Swedish Clinic** (⊠ Van Phuc St., opposite Swedish Embassy, ☎ 04/825–2464) may be covered by travel insurance.

EMBASSIES

Canada (⊠ 31 Hung Vuong St., ☎ 04/823–5500, FAX 04/823–5333). **United Kingdom** (⊠ 16 Ly Thuong Kiet St., ☎ 04/825–2510, FAX 04/826–5762). **United States** (⊠ 7 Lang Ha St., ☎ 04/843–1500, FAX 04/835–0447).

EMERGENCIES

Ambulance, ☎ 15. **Fire,** ☎ 14. **Police,** ☎ 13.

ENGLISH-LANGUAGE BOOKSTORE

Thong Nhat Bookstore has a selection of books in English. ⊠ Ngo Quyen and Trang Tien Sts., near Sofitel Metropole. ☉ Daily 8–noon and 1–8:30 (until 4:30, Mon. and Thurs.).

GUIDED TOURS

Depending on how many people are your group and on what organization you go through, day trips around Hanoi will range from US$15 to US$60. Tours can be arranged through any number of cafés, private agencies, or the state-run Hanoi and Vietnam Tourism; the cheapest tours are available from Green Bamboo Café (☞ Travel Agencies *and* Visitor Information, *below*), which has a sign-up list and a very affordable fixed price.

LATE-NIGHT PHARMACIES

☞ Viet Duc Hospital *in* Doctors, *above.*

POST OFFICE

The **post office** (Buu Dien Trung Vong) occupies a whole block across from Hoan Kiem Lake. Phone, fax, and telex services are available. ✉ *75 Dinh Tien Hoang St., Hoan Kiem District,* ☎ *04/825–7036,* ☉ *6:30 AM–8 PM.*

TRAVEL AGENCIES AND VISITOR INFORMATION

The following agencies offer visitor information, transportation booking and rental, and guided tours.

Ann's Tourist (✉ 26 Yet Kieu St., Hoan Kiem District, ☎ 04/825–2497).
Green Bamboo Café (✉ 42 Nha Chung St., Hoan Kiem District, ☎ 04/826–4949).
Hanoi Tourism (✉ 1 Ba Trieu St., Hoan Kiem District, ☎ 04/824-2330 or 826–5244, FAX 04/825–6418).
Tourist Smiling Café (✉ 100 Cau Go St., Hoan Kiem District, ☎ 04/824–4454).
Vietnam Tourism (✉ 30A Ly Thuong Kiet St., Hoan Kiem District, ☎ 04/825–6916, FAX 04/825–7583).

SIDE TRIPS FROM HANOI

The spectacular topography of the north includes the Hoang Lien Mountains or Tonkinese Alps, the Red River Delta, and Halong Bay's limestone islets, jutting up out of the South China Sea. Within their pristine natural environments, ethnic minority populations continue to live as they have for centuries—despite the government's attempts at cultural integration. Besides Sapa, Halong Bay, and Cat Ba Island National Park (☞ *below*), there are a number of destinations where you can explore this diverse environment.

Just 60 km (37 mi) southwest of Hanoi is a cluster of Buddhist shrines carved into the limestone of the Huong Tich Mountains. Day trips (a combined bus and boat excursion) to the **Perfume Pagoda,** as it is called, are available from any number of cafés (☞ Green Bamboo Café *in* Hanoi A to Z, *above*) or tourist organizations in Hanoi. Neighboring **Hoa Binh,** 74 km (46 mi) southwest of Hanoi, has a large concentration of ethnic hill tribes.

Bustling with a population of 1.3 million, **Haiphong** has been a hub of the North's industrial activity and one of its most significant seaports since the French settled it in 1874. Because of its strategic location on the northeastern coast, it became a dumping ground for bombers during the Franco-Viet Minh War in 1946 as well as during the Vietnam War. For buffalo fights, gambling, and some very nice stretches of beach, consider a side trip to **Do Son Beach,** 21 km (13 mi) southeast of Haiphong.

Ethnic minority villages abound in mountainous Lang Son Province as well as throughout the north central region. Cao Bang Province, 272 km (169 mi) north of Hanoi, is home to the Dao, Meo, and Tho minorities. The Dai live in stilted structures surrounded by the breathtaking rain forest, mountains, caves, waterfalls, lakes, and rivers of **Ba Be Lake National Park.** The Green Bamboo Café in Hanoi now offers a three-day, two-night excursion that includes a river boat trip.

National Highway 6 connects Hanoi with Dien Ben Phu via the **Northern Highlands.** Trekking tours (arranged from agencies/cafés in Hanoi) through Mai Chau, Moc Chau, and Son La offer a more intimate experience of ethnic minority villages if you take advantage of the trips that allow you to stay with families in their huts. At the northeastern tip of Vietnam, on the Laotian border, **Dien Ben Phu** was where the French capitulated to Viet Minh troops on May 6, 1954, after a stunning offensive led by Viet Minh General Vo Nguyen Giap. Dien Ben Phu was recently recognized as the capital of Lai Chau, since the former provincial capital Lai Chau has suffered catastrophic flooding from the Da River in recent years.

Halong Bay and Cat Ba Island National Park

160 km (99 mi) from Hanoi, 55 km (34 mi) from Haiphong.

Halong Bay's 3,000 islands of dolomite and limestone cover a 579-square-mile area, extending across the Gulf of Tonkin all the way to the Chinese border. According to Chinese legend, this breathtaking land-and seascape was formed by a giant dragon that came barreling out of the moutains toward the sea.

One of Halong Bay's most remarkable formations is Cat Ba Island. In 1938 a French archaeologist found traces of an ancient fishing culture on the island, which dates from the end of the Neolithic Era (2,000 BC). Today the population of over 12,000 continues to subsist on fishing and rice and fruit cultivation. Designated a national park in 1986, the Cat Ba is also home to tropical evergreen forests, beaches, lakes, grottoes, 15 kinds of mammals (including wild boars and hedgehogs), 21 species of birds, and 640 plant species. The sea life in the surrounding 35 square miles is also protected. Despite this protected status, Vietnamese tourists—who seem to be able to scale the slippery rocks in stiletto heels regardless of the weather—litter the trails with empty beer cans and junk-food wrappers.

Halong Bay and Cat Ba Island A to Z

ARRIVING AND DEPARTING

The only way to experience Halong Bay is by boat, and while you can see Cat Ba Island separately, it's usually most convenient to visit the island as part of a pre-arranged boat trip. Boat tours that include Cat Ba Island will organize a guided trekking tour of the national park. Avoid visiting during the cold, wet months of February through April or in the summer months, which bring tropical storms.

From Hanoi, you can rent a car for a couple of days for about US$100 and find a place to spend the night in Halong Bay, or you can join an all-inclusive group tour for US$24–US$38 (depending on how many days). The Green Bamboo Café (☞ Tourist Agencies *in* Hanoi A to Z, *above*) offers a couple of different group trips: a two-day tour of Halong Bay only and a three-day trip that includes Cat Ba Island. The terrifically unglamorous three-day trips include a two-night slumber party (to which countless insects and other creatures are invited) under the stars (or raindrops, as the case may be), amid exotic rock formations. Pricier excursions are available through private or state-run tourist agencies like Hanoi Tourism or Vietnam Tourism, but they offer little extra for the inflated cost.

Sapa

35 km (22 mi) from Lao Cai, 350 km (217 mi) from Hanoi.

Sapa is part of the northwestern province of Lao Cai, a name which literally means "town of sand." A pilgrimage to Sapa offers a glimpse of some of the country's most breathtaking mountain scenery as well as its virtually untouched ethnic minority cultures. The hill tribes cultivate rice and ginger and hunt wild game by traditional methods; they continue to worship the soul of rice, their ancestors, and the spirits of earth, wind, fire, rivers, and mountains as they always have. To see them in their traditional style of dress—layers of indigo-dyed, brilliantly embroidered cotton and elaborate headdresses—is to feel yourself caught in a time warp.

The local population is made up of the Hmong, the Dao, the Tay, the Giay, the Muong, the Thai, The Hoa (ethnic Chinese), and the Xa Pho, and is divided into 18 local communes with populations of between 970 and 4,500 inhabitants. These hill tribes, commonly known as "Montagnards" (the name given to them by the French), convene once a week to exchange everything from staples and handicrafts to live snakes. Any trip to Sapa should be planned to coincide with this colorful weekend market.

The French dubbed the area around Sapa the "Tonkinese Alps," and in 1932 colonial authorities displaced the minority residents and began building themselves villas in the town, turning it into a kind of health resort, a retreat from the oppressive heat of Hanoi. Between the end of French colonial rule and reunification, there were weak attempts to grant the ethnic minorities political representation. Since 1975 the government has pursued an "integration" program in which the state provides limited education and health care for free.

But neither representation nor the protection of Sapa's endangered cultural diversity seems to have any real place on the state agenda. Sadly, it appears that tourism may corrupt the integrity of the local populace and upset the area's fragile ecology. The minority groups themselves practice a "slash and burn" agriculture, and this (plus the depredations of two centuries of outside interests) has already reduced the virgin forest to a mere 4.5-square-mile area. Further destruction would be tragic, considering the area's remarkable natural gifts.

Sapa is part of the **Nui Hoang Lien Nature Reserve,** a mountainous, 7,400-acre landscape that includes Vietnam's highest peak, Fan Si Pan (1,950 feet). Covered by temperate and subtemperate forests, the reserve provides a habitat to 56 species of mammals, including tigers, leopards, monkeys, and bears, 17 of which (the Asiatic black bear, for example) are considered endangered. An impressive 150 species of birds, including the red-vented barbet and the collared finchbill, can be found only in the mountains of northwest Vietnam. Among the area's geological resources are minerals from sediments deposited in the Mesozoic and Paleozoic periods. From the Muong Hoa River to the peak of Fan Si Pan, the eastern boundary of the reserve is formed by a ridge of marble and calcium carbonate. Also found in this region is kaolinite, or "china clay," used in the making of porcelain.

Guided walking tours are recommended, and are easily arranged through hotels and guest houses. December and February see temperatures as low 26°F (–3.2°C). The rainy season is between May and September. Temperatures during the rest of the year fall between 60°F(15°C) and 85°F (30°C). Humidity averages about 87%.

Lodging

¢ 🖬 **Auberge.** With a restaurant terrace that overlooks the spectacularly
verdant and mountainous scenery, the Auberge offers basic, cozy, clean
rooms, some with fireplace. The food is also excellent. ⊠ *Auberge Dang-
Trung, Sapa Lao Ca,* ☎ *020/871243. 5 rooms without bath. Restaurant, laundry service, travel services, car rental. No credit cards.*

¢ 🖬 **Green Bamboo.** Run by the Green Bamboo Café in Hanoi, this moun-
tainside accommodation is perhaps the closest thing in town to a hotel.
Small, sunny, brand-new rooms have their own bathrooms. To get there,
follow the main road to its end, make a left, and continue on until you
see a white cliffside structure with green shutters. ⊠ *Reservations: Green
Bamboo Café, 42 Na Chung St., Hoan Kiem District, Hanoi,* ☎ *04/
826–4949. 15 rooms. No credit cards.*

Sapa A to Z

ARRIVING AND DEPARTING

For bus tours and private cars, it's a 10-hour trip on Highway 1 from
Hanoi to Lao Cai, then two hours from Lao Cai to Sapa on Highway
4. If you don't want to lose the whole day driving, the overnight train
(7:30 PM departure, 294 km, 12 hours) from Hanoi to Lao Cai, the
last stop before the Chinese border, is perhaps the best option (☞ Arriving and Departing *in* Hanoi A to Z, *above*). Reserve a hard sleeper
well in advance (soft berths are not available on this route); berths run
155,500d–173,000d.

From Lo Cai, the only way to reach Sapa is by road. Bus tickets
(25,000d) are available at a table to the right as you step off the train;
the two segregated buses (Vietnamese and non-Vietnamese) out front
leave when full. The bus from Lao Cai deposits passengers in front of
La Rose Hotel.

From Sapa, buses return to the Lao Cai train station twice daily, at 6:30
AM and 2 PM. Train schedules, reservations, and tickets are handled at
the post office (⊠ No address), just up the road from La Rose toward
the market, open daily 8–11:30 AM and 1–4 PM. This post office is
not to be confused with the larger building marked "Post Office," which
you will have seen on your left on the way into town.

GETTING AROUND

Sapa has essentially only a single street, intersected by a number of footpaths. Cars or motorbikes are of no use once you're there.

CONTACTS AND RESOURCES

The Green Bamboo (☞ Travel Agencies *and* Visitor Information *in* Hanoi
A to Z, *above*) is the only café/travel agency that organizes four-day
group trekking excursions to Sapa or a combined Sapa and neighboring Bac Ha Highlands tour; these trips cost US$50–US$65. Independent trekking excursions, on which you spend the night with an
indigenous family or tribe, can be arranged through private agencies
in Hanoi.

The Auberge (☞ Dining and Lodging, *above*) changes traveler's checks;
most other guest houses change hard currency only.

HUE

*658 km (408 mi) from Hanoi, 108 km (67 mi) from Danang, 1,097
km (680 mi) from Ho Chi Minh City.*

Bisected by the Perfume River and set 13 km (8 miles) inland in the
foothills of the Truong Song Mountains, Hue was the seat of 13
Nguyen dynasty emperors between 1802 and 1945. Although devas-

tated by the French in the 19th century and again by the Americans in the 20th, the monument-speckled former capital has a war-ravaged beauty. Despite gaping holes in its silhouette, one can still imagine its former splendor. A hub of political, intellectual, and religious activity, sight-rich Hue is appealing not only from an historical perspective but also for its excellent cuisine.

The city is now a very relaxing place to visit, but its history is anything but serene. In the 2nd century BC, when it was called Tay Quyen, the area was the seat of command for the Chinese Han army. In the second century AD, under the rule of local chieftains, it was renamed K'ui Sou. By the 15th century, after over four centuries of raids by northern Vietnamese raids, the area was absorbed by the Champa kingdom under the name Phy Xuan. After defeating the Nguyen lords, the Tay Son rebels planted themselves in Hue from 1786 to 1802, until the ousted Nguyen Anh returned, backed by the French. Nguyen Anh, who anointed himself Emperor Gia Long, christened Hue the new capital of a united Vietnam.

It was under Gian Long's rule that the city's architectural identity was established and that the prospect of French colonial rule was cemented. Under the direction of the French architect Olivier De Puymanel, Gia Long designed and implemented the city's surrounding fortress, a Chinese-style citadel consisting of three enclosed cities—the Capital City (Kinh Thanh), the Imperial City (Hoang Thanh), and the Forbidden Purple City (Tu Cam Thanh). A new Western-style city was established east of the citadel to accomodate the French Protectorate forces.

Voices of dissent protesting French presence in Tonkin were swiftly extinguished. In addition to pillaging every object of the royal court, the French burned the Imperial Library to the ground. Similarly, during the Tet Offensive of 1968, potential voices of opposition—merchants, monks, priests, and pundits—were systematically exterminated by occupying VC forces over a merciless three-week period. U.S. and South Vietnamese retaliation caused not only the destruction of most of the Imperial Enclosure and Forbidden Purple City but also took over 10,000 lives, most of whom were civilians.

Exploring Hue

A Good Walk

Since you will most likely be staying on the east bank, begin the walking tour at the Phu Xuan Bridge and Le Loi Street. Heading west, cross the bridge over the Perfume River. Once you have reached the west bank, turn left and then make your first right. You will now approach the **Citadel,** nearly 1,000 acres circumscribed by 66-foot-wide ramparts and a moat. Crossing the moat, you pass through the Ngan Gate. Just before the intersection you will see four of the Nine Holy Cannons on the right-hand side of the street. When you get to 23 Thang 8 Street, make a left and then an immediate right into the entrance of the **Imperial City.** In alignment with the entrance to the Imperial City is the 122-foot **Flag Tower,** which will appear on your left.

The Imperial City, once a complex of palaces and pavilions, preserves disappointingly few remnants of its past glory. Entering through the Noontime Gate (Cua Ngo Mon), take an immediate left toward the **Nine Dynastic Urns,** symbols of the formidable power of the Nguyen. Head toward the entrance and turn left, crossing the Golden Water Bridge (Trung Dao Bridge or Kim Thuy Kieu), which was for the emperor's use only. Straight ahead is one of the few structures in the imperial enclosure still intact, the richly and intricately decorated Palace of Supreme Harmony (Thai Hoa Dien).

Exiting through the back of the gift shop and heading toward the **Forbidden Purple City,** you pass on either side the Halls of the Mandarins, where mandarins dressed in the appropriate court attire before paying homage to the emperor. The area is now mostly rubble with some spotty vegetation. The Tet Offensive's destruction managed to spare the Royal Theater or Festival Hall (Duyet Thi Duong), on the right-hand side, and, behind it, the intimate and partially restored Imperial Library (Thai Binh Lau). Heading east from the Royal Theater, exit the imperial enclosure by way of the ornate Eastern Gate (Hung Khan Mon).

Make a right on Doan Thi Diem Street and then the first left on Le Truc Street. The **Imperial Museum** (formerly the Khai Dinh Museum), in a beautifully preserved structure that was formerly part of the palace, houses a fine collection of palace objects. Across the street is Hue's archeological center, once a kind of prep school for male members of royal court. It is just in front of the unimpressive Military Museum.

Make a left out of the museum and then another left onto Dinh Tien Hoan Street. Continue on through what feels like a quiet suburban residential neighborhood for about 1 km (½ mi). At the intersection with Tinh Tam, you'll see Tinh Tam Lake, which is often covered with lotus blossoms. Walk across a bridge to one of the islands for a little relaxation. Across Dinh Tien Hoang Street is another lake called Tang Tau, the former site of the Royal Library and still home to the Ngoc Huong Pagoda, a peaceful place to take a break from the heat.

Timing

The tour should take about three hours at a very leisurely pace. As always, early morning and late afternoon are the best times to walk around.

Sights to See

Citadel (Kinh Thanh). It seems ironic that Hue has a history of being easily overrun, for the Citadel appears to be impregnable. Built in the heart of the city by Emperor Gia Long in 1804, and reinforced with brick walls 6 feet deep under French rule, the Citadel is protected by a wide moat and 10 fortified gates. The outer ramparts enclose another sort of citadel, the Imperial City, which in turn contains the Forbidden Purple City (☞ *below*).

Flag Tower (Cot Co or Ky Dai). Atop the 56-foot central bastion of the Citadel stands Vietnam's tallest flagpole. The base of the 122-foot flagpole (formerly called the King's Knight) was originally built out of earth to serve as the Imperial Palace's central observation post; it has since been knocked down and re-erected several times. After the capture of Hue during the 1968 Tet Offensive, bold North Vietnemese flew the National Liberation Front flag from the tower for the city's three and a half weeks of Viet Cong occupation.

Forbidden Purple City (Tu Cam Thahn). This is where the Emperor conducted his private affairs. The complex was divided into masculine and feminine sides, representing different affairs that the Vietnamese considered superior and inferior, respectively. You now find only bare architectural ruins, as the area was heavily bombed by the U.S. after the Viet Cong seized Hue during the Tet Offensive. Even so, it is well worth strolling around in. UNESCO has been at work restoring what it can.

Imperial City (Hoang Thanh). The main Noontime Gate was once reserved solely for the use of the Emperor. Next to it is the Flag Tower (☞ *above*), and inside it is Thai Hoa Palace, now furnished with a gift shop. A dollar will get you an imperial tune from the authentically costumed minstrels. In its heyday, this is where the Emperor held special ceremonies, throngs of mandarins paying homage to him on his elevated throne.

Imperial Museum. Built in 1923, the museum's walls are inscribed with Vietnamese *nom* characters. Many of the most precious holdings of the museum were destroyed in the war, but it still features a good collection of art objects, traditional musical instruments, and old weapons.

Nine Dynastic Urns (Cuu Dinh O The-Mieu). Although they feature traditional designs that date back 4,000 years, these urns were actually cast in 1835 and weigh around 5,000 pounds each. Gia Long, the founder of the Nguyen dynasty, is featured on the central one, the most intricate of the nine.

Dining

There are few proper dining establishments in Hue, but the food from the stalls here is some of the best in Vietnam. Imperial cuisine, distinguished by the elegant radial symmetry of its presentation, is said to be the most sophisticated in all of Vietnam. Specialties include *banh khoai,* a shrimp- and sprout-stuffed crepe, and *bun bo Hue,* rice noodles and broth topped with pork and beef.

$$$ ✕ **Century Riverside Hotel Restaurant.** Perhaps the most upscale dining establishment in Hue, the Century serves a particularly tasty grilled fish in banana leaves as well as superb spring rolls. ✉ *49 Le Loi St.,* ☏ *054/823390. AE, DC, MC, V.*

$$ ✕ **Huong Giang Hotel.** Surprisingly empty, the restaurant serves heaping portions of very solid Vietnamese food and offers what are perhaps the best views in town of the Perfume River. ✉ *51 Le Loi St.,* ☏ *054/822122. AE, DC, MC, V.*

$$ ✕ **Ngoc Anh.** This semi-elegant, open-air restaurant offers hefty portions of high-quality Vietnamese and Chinese food. The sizzling hot clay-pot seafood special is exceptional. ✉ *29 Nguyen Thai Hoc,* ☏ *054/822617. No credit cards.*

$$ ✕ **Ong Tao.** Ong Tao, which literally translates as "God of the Kitchen,"
★ exemplifies Imperial cuisine at its finest. The one located within the citadel serves lunch and dinner in an outdoor setting among trees and ruins. The garlic prawns are delicious, as are the spring rolls. ✉ *Inside Hien Nhou Gate, opposite College of Fine Arts,* ☏ *054/823031; 134 Ngo Duc Ke,* ☏ *054/822037. No credit cards.*

$ ✕ **Am Phu.** This local restaurant serves excellent traditional Vietnamese cuisine. ✉ *35 Nguyen Thai Hoc St.,* ☏ *054/825259. No credit cards.*

$ ✕ **Lac Thanh Restaurant.** Packed with tourists and therefore teeming with postcard and cigarette vendors, this dive and its next-door copycat neighbor serve the tastiest and cheapest meals in Hue. Some notable dishes include shrimp and vegetables over crispy noodles and the Vietnamese tofu or beef and vegetables wrapped in rice paper and dipped in peanut sauce. The delicious coconut ice-cream topped with chocolate sauce and peanuts is the closest thing to a sundae in Vietnam. ✉ *6A Dien Tien Hoang St., no phone. No credit cards.*

$ ✕ **Tong Phuoc Nen.** House specialties include eel soups; try *Lau luon,* a tangy eel-and-vegetable concoction served over noodles. *Chao luon* is a more traditional soup prepared with mushrooms and lotus seed. The upstairs terrace seating has a rustic charm. ✉ *20 Ba Trieu St.,* ☏ *054/825264. No credit cards.*

¢ ✕ **Banh Khoai.** This informal family-run food stall serves the best banh khoai in town. The meat-filled eggy crepe with bean sprouts comes to the table piping hot in a tacolike configuration. Break it up into your small rice bowl, add the greens and the sauce provided, and eat with chopsticks. ⊠ *2 Nguyen Tri Phuong, off Hanoi. No phone. No credit cards.*

¢ ✕ **Bun Bo Hue.** This very low-scale, open-air stand serves some of the best bun bo Hue, a noodle specialty that includes a combination of beef and pork. ⊠ *11b Ly Kiet St. No credit cards.*

Lodging

Most of the hotels are situated on the east bank of the Perfume River. There are a few hotels under construction that look very nice. What was the former budget Hotel Morin (at the corner of Le Loi and Huong Vuong Streets) is being completely rebuilt in the French villa style by Saigon Tourist (☞ Ho Chi Minh City A to Z, *below*), who you can contact for details. It will probably offer the nicest accommodation in town. Most hotels offer travel services, arrange boat tours to tombs and pagodas along the Perfume River, and guided tours in and around Hue. They can also handle car rentals.

$$–$$$ 🏨 **Century Riverside Inn.** This large, riverside, Western-style hotel is slightly more expensive and not as nice as its next-door neighbor, the Huong Giang. Some of the recently renovated rooms are semiluxurious but small for the price. Other rooms are in dire need of repair. In addition to a restaurant that serves a very decadent and tasty dinner banquet and presents live traditional music for busloads of tourists, the Century boasts a refreshing riverfront swimming pool. ⊠ *49 Le Loi St.,* ☎ *054/823390,* ℻ *054/823399. 138 rooms. 2 Restaurants, bar, air-conditioning, minibars, refrigerators, room service, pool, massage, tennis courts, exercise room, laundry service and dry cleaning. AE, DC, MC, V.*

$$–$$$ 🏨 **Huong Giang Hotel.** Fully-equipped riverfront rooms that are bright, ★ airy, and spotless make this the most luxurious accommodation in town. Situated on the northern end of the east bank, the hotel has a very good restaurant and rooftop bar/garden that affords panoramic views of the Perfume River. Unfortunately, the overly heated and heavily chlorinated swimming pool looks more refreshing than it is. ⊠ *51 Loi St.,* ☎ *054/ 822122,* ℻ *054/823102. 102 rooms. 2 restaurants, outdoor café, 2 bars, air-conditioning, pool, massage, tennis court, laundry service and dry cleaning, travel services. AE, DC, MC, V.*

$–$$ 🏨 **Dong Da Hotel.** Somewhere between a minihotel and a Western-style accommodation, the spacious Dong Da offers immaculate, modern rooms with simple Japanese-style decor. ⊠ *15 Ly Thuong Kiet,* ☎ *054/823071,* ℻ *054/823204. 37 rooms. Restaurant, bar, air-conditioning, dance club, laundry service, travel services, car rental. No credit cards.*

$–$$ 🏨 **Hoa Hong Hotel II.** The brand new, slick, U.S.-Vietnamese joint-venture hotel deserves its self-awarded three-star rating. Although it is not on the water, it is tall enough that many of the semiluxurious rooms afford excellent river views. The hotel hosts a variety of traditional live music and dancing performances. ⊠ *1 Pham Ngu Lao St.,* ☎ *054/ 824377,* ℻ *054/826949. 60 rooms. Restaurant, air-conditioning, laundry service and dry cleaning, travel services. No credit cards.*

$ 🏨 **A Dong Hotel 1.** A pleasant, clean, and airy minihotel with proper bathtubs that is scoring big points with daily fresh-fruit-and-flowers offerings. The staff speaks very little English, but is very eager to please. ⊠ *1 Chu Van An St.,* ☎ *054/824148,* ℻ *054/823858. 10 rooms. Restaurant, bar, air-conditioning, minibars, refrigerators, laundry service, travel services, car rental. AE, MC, V.*

$ 🏨 **A Dong Hotel 2.** The cheaper of the A Dong Hotels is a fine example of minihotel efficiency and cleanliness. Proper bathrooms are always a bonus. ⊠ *7 Doi Cung,* ☎ *054/822765,* ℻ *054/828074. 15* *rooms. Restaurant, air-conditioning, laundry service, travel services, car rental. AE, MC, V.*

$ ⊞ **Hoa Hong I.** Despite the fake-flowers finishing touches and cutesy pastel decor, the smaller and less luxurious of the Hoa Hong family of hotels offers cool, comfortable rooms with proper bathrooms with tubs. ⊠ *46 C Le Loi St.,* ☎ *054/824377,* FAX *054/826949. Restaurant, air-conditioning, minibars, refrigerators, laundry service, travel services. No credit cards.*

$ ⊞ **Huan Vu Hotel.** Slightly off the beaten track, the brand-new, bright-white minihotel offers modest rooms at decent though not exceptional prices for what you get. The staff does not speak a word of English. ⊠ *16 Dong Da,* ☎ *054/821560,* FAX *054/821561. 20 rooms. Restaurant, air-conditioning, fans, minibars, refrigerators, laundry service, travel services. No credit cards.*

$ ⊞ **Hue City Tourism Villas.** Rooms in these very quiet but slightly run-down villas are reasonably priced and peaceful. Arrangements can be made through Hue City Tourism. ⊠ *11, 16, and 18 Ly Thuong Kiet St. and 5 Le Loi St.,* ☎ *054/823753,* FAX *054/822470. Air-conditioning, fans, minibars, refrigerators, laundry service. No credit cards.*

$ ⊞ **Huong Giang Tourist Villa.** Just as clean and pleasant as its hotel counterpart (☞ *above*), the villa offers larger rooms and a more intimate environment. Though one does not have the hotel's restaurant and recreational facilites and its proximity to the river, this is a cheaper, homier alternative. ⊠ *3 Hung Vuong,* ☎ *054/826070,* FAX *054/826074. 12 rooms. Restaurant, air-conditioning, fans, minibars, refrigerators, laundry service, travel services, car rental. AE, MC, V.*

$ ⊞ **Kinh Do Hotel.** This no-ambience, white-concrete, '60s structure seems to attract Russian tourists with its fully-equipped clean rooms. ⊠ *1 Nguyen Thai Hoc,* ☎ *054/823566,* FAX *054/821190. 50 rooms. Restaurant, bar, air-conditioning, fans, minibars, refrigerators, massage, shop, laundry service and dry cleaning, travel services, car rental. No credit cards.*

¢–$ ⊞ **Binh Minh.** The Binh Minh offers bright rooms with great balconies and a very helpful staff. ⊠ *12 Nguyen Tri Phuong,* ☎ *054/825526,* FAX *054/828362. 22 rooms, most with bath. Restaurant, air-conditioning, fans, minibars, refrigerators, laundry service, travel services. No credit cards.*

¢–$ ⊞ **Dong Loi Hotel.** Another very reasonably priced, brand-new, roomy, no-frills accommodation with a staff that will arrange city tours and excursions outside of Hue. ⊠ *11A Pham Ngu Lao St.,* ☎ *054/822296,* FAX *054/826234. 30 rooms. Restaurant, air-conditioning, minibars, refrigerators, laundry service, travel services. No credit cards.*

¢–$ ⊞ **Duy Tan Hotel.** Despite its size and semi-grandeur, the once very cheap but recently reworked accommodation functions like a glorified mini-hotel. Bright and spacious rooms with spotty renovation boast new bathrooms with proper tubs. ⊠ *12 Hung Vuong,* ☎ *054/825001,* FAX *054/826477. 58 rooms. Restaurant, air-conditioning, minibars, refrigerators, laundry service, meeting rooms, travel services, car rental. No credit cards.*

¢–$ ⊞ **Hue Hotel.** Run by Thua Thien-Hue Tourism, and adjacent to it, this newly redesigned property offers two types of rooms. The pricier rooms are very clean and sparse, with superb air-conditioning. Cheaper rooms with fans only are not antiseptic like the pricier ones but are clean and utilitarian nonetheless. Oddly enough, the cheaper rooms are situated right on the river, the more expensive ones set back closer Le Loi Street. Like the rest of the government tourist company in Hue, the staff speaks very little English and is not very helpful. ⊠ *15 Le Loi St.,* ☎ *054/822369,* FAX *054/824806. 11 rooms.*

¢–$ ⊞ **Hung Vuong Hotel.** With a range of rooms accommodating backbackers and non-backpackers alike (especially those taking the Sinh Café Travel bus, which drops passengers off here), the Hung Vuong offers clean rooms, an adjoining Thuathien Hue Tourism office, and good central location. ⊠ *2 Hung Vuong St.,* ☎ *054/823866,* FAX *054/825910. 70 rooms, most with bath. Restaurant, air-conditioning, minibars, refrigerators, laundry service, travel services, car rental. No credit cards.*

¢ ⊡ **Le Loi Hue Hotel.** With slightly run-down but passable rooms equipped with minibars, refrigerators, IDD phones and satellite TVs, Le Loi often has vacancies when other places fill up. The hotel is very close to the train station. ⊡ *2 Le Loi,* ☎ *054/824668,* FAX *054/824527. 150 rooms, most with bath. Restaurant, air-conditioning, laundry service, travel services, car rental. No credit cards.*

¢ ⊡ **Saigon Hotel.** Although strangely decorated with a neon backlit cow's head in the restaurant area, the brand-new minihotel offers squeaky clean, sunny rooms and excellent bathrooms with tubs. ⊠ *32 Hung Vuong,* ☎ *054/821007,* FAX *054/821009. 20 rooms. Restaurant, air-conditioning, fans, laundry service, travel services, car rental. No credit cards.*

Hue A to Z

Arriving and Departing

BY BUS

☞ Vietnam A to Z, *below.*

BY CAR

Cars with drivers (but without air-conditioning) start at US$40 at day; minivans, seating up to 8 people, run about US$50 a day to Hoi An, for example. Book at any hotel or goverment-run travel agency.

BY PLANE

Phu Bai Airport is 15 km (9 mi) south of the city center. One-way flights to Ho Chi Minh City are around US$85; to Hanoi, around US$80. International flights are available through Ho Chi Minh City.

Taxis into town are generally 90,000d, but this is negotiable. **Vietnam Airlines** (⊠ 12 Hanoi St., ☎ 054/82249) runs a minibus service to the airport for about 10,000d per person.

BY TRAIN

Hue Railway Station (Ga Hue; ☎ 054/82175) is on the right bank at the southwest end of Le Loi Street. Ticket offices are open 7:30 AM–5 PM. There are four trains into Hue a day—one express, three local— from both Ho Chi Minh and Hanoi. The Hanoi-to-Hue trip (US$38– US$47 soft sleeper) takes about 15 hours, while Ho Chi Minh to Hue (US$57–US$76 soft sleeper) takes 24 hours.

Getting Around

BY CAR

Since Hue is a very walkable town, it's best to use a car only to the beach or to Hoi An (☞ Arriving and Departing, *above*).

BY CYCLO

Grab a cyclo outside of hotels along the right bank. For 5,000d you should get pretty much anywhere, though you will almost always have to talk the price down.

BY TAXI

Taxis to and from the train station are comparable in price to cyclos but cooler and more comfortable, especially if you are traveling with someone else. Call **Hue Taxi ATC** (☎ 054/824500 or 054/833333).

Contacts and Resources

CURRENCY EXCHANGE

Vietcom Bank (ICBV), Thua Thien Hue branch, exchanges currency and may soon offer credit-card cash advances. ⊠ *21 Le Duy Don St.,* ☎ *054/822281.* ⏱ *7–11 AM and 1:30–5 PM.*

DOCTORS AND DENTISTS

Hue General Hospital (Benh Vien Trung Uong Hue; ⊠ 16 Le Loi St., ☎ 054/82325).

GUIDED TOURS

Travel agents and many hotels arrange dragon boat rides on the Perfume River. You have the option of exploring several of the tombs and pagodas along the waterway; the structures are generally a bit of a hike from where your boat docks, so the trip can be rather tiring.

Government travel agencies such as Thua Thien-Hue Tourism or DMZ (☞ *below*) advertise the trips for 35,000d or so. They neglect to inform passengers that they will need to pay an additional 55,000d at each stop. Boats can also be rented privately from a hotel or at the pier across from the train station; these hold up to 10 people can cost anywhere from US$10 to US$35. Tours usually begin at about 8 AM and return at around 3 PM.

PHARMACY

Thuoc Tay. The proprietor here speaks better French than English but is helpful if you write down your request; if she doesn't have what you need, she'll recommend another pharmacy along Hung Vuong. ⊠ *5 Hung Vuong,* ☎ *054/21225.* ⏱ *7:30 AM—10 PM (occasional lunch closure).*

TRAVEL AGENCIES AND VISITOR INFORMATION

DMZ Tour Office offers minibus and car rental, books trains and flights, and conducts guided tours of the city, along the Perfume River, and throughout the surrounding area. ⊠ *26 Le Loi St.,* ☎ *054/825242.*

Hue City Tourism rents villas and arranges traditional theater shows, among other services. ⊠ *18 Le Loi St.,* ☎ *054/83577.*

Thua Thien-Hue Tourism is the government-owned tourism authority. ⊠ *30 Le Loi St.,* ☎ *054/822369 or 054/822288.*

THE CENTRAL COAST

The region south of Hue includes the port city of Danang, famous China Beach, the cave temples known as Marble Mountain, and the delightful town of Hoi An. Because this area held the seat of the Kingdom of Champa from the 2nd to the 10th centuries, it has the greatest concentration of Cham art and architecture in the country. Danang is worth a stop solely for a visit to the impressive Cham Museum; the city's only other attraction, however, is as a convenient transportation hub. Just outside of Danang, en route to Hoi An, are Marble Mountain and China Beach, which could be combined in a single day trip. A pilgrimage to My Son, Vietnam's most significant Cham ruins, merits at least a half-day either from Danang or Hoi An. Plan on spending at least one full day in Hoi An—though more time is recommended.

Danang

108 km (67 mi) from Hue, 30 km (17 mi) from Hoi An, 972 km (603 mi) from Ho Chi Minh City.

At its peak, Danang was second only to Saigon as Vietnam's most cosmopolitan center, known for its restaurants and houses of prostitution.

Today, while ships still call at Danang, the city has little to offer visitors, with the exception of the Cham Museum.

★ The splendid **Cham Museum** certainly merits a visit for those with any interest in Cham sculpture. Artifacts are divided by region, reflecting the changing seats of Cham power—from My Son to Indrapura to Tra Kieu to Khuong My. The highly sensual, innovative, and expressive art from My Son (8th and 9th centuries) and Tra Kieu (7th century), for example, marks periods of prosperity and contact with Indonesian and Indian culture. War with the Vietnamese from the 10th through 14th centuries led to an artistic decline. Cham artists ceased to be so expressive, copying instead motifs like the Chinese dragon and various Khmer designs.

Among the cast of characters to keep in mind when viewing Cham art: Vishnu, god of conservation and life; Garuda, the holy bird; Rama, god of creation and birth; Sarasvati, Rama's wife and goddess of sacred language, whose animal counterpart is a swan; Laksmi, Vishnu's wife, goddess of prosperity; Shiva, god of destruction, represented in phallic (linga) form; Skanda, god of war and son of Shiva and Uma, who is often depicted as a peacock; Ganesha, god of peace. Ganesha was also a son of Shiva and Uma. Shiva found him disobedient and cut off his head. Uma prayed to the gods for forgiveness and a new head for her son. She was granted the head of the first animal she saw, which turned out to be an elephant, hence Ganesha's traditional depiction half man, half elephant.

Although the Buddha is most often portrayed seated cross-legged, the Cham Buddha sits on a throne with his feet flat on the ground. This subtle difference reflects the Cham belief in the spiritual continuum between crown and divinity. The symbol of fertility, Uroja, literally "Woman's Breast," clues viewers into the matriarchial nature of Cham culture. ⊠ *Tran Phu and Le Dinh Duong Sts.* 🎫 *Admission.* ⏱ *Daily 8–11 AM and 1–5 PM.*

Lodging

$$ 🏨 **Marco Polo.** Perhaps the nicest accommodation in town, the Marco Polo is a haven of Western-style efficiency set down in the sleazy streets of Danang. ⊠ *11 Quang Trung St.,* ☎ *051/823295,* FAX *051/827279. 28 rooms. Restaurant, bar, air-conditioning, minibar, refrigerators, room service, laundry services and dry cleaning, business services, travel services, rental cars. AE, MC, V.*

Shopping

If you find yourself stuck in Danang for the day, fabric shops and tailors along Hung Vuong Street make clothes cheaply and quickly.

Danang A to Z

ARRIVING AND DEPARTING

From Danang, planes fly everyday to and from Hanoi (about US$100), Ho Chi Minh (about US$90), and Haiphong (about US$90); Tuesday, Thursday, and Saturday flights arrive from Nha Trang (about US$50). **Vietnam Airlines Danang Booking Office** (⊠ 35 Tran Phu St., ☎ 051/821130, FAX 051/832759) is open 7–11 AM and 1:30–4:30 PM; for Vietnam Airlines flight confirmation and reservations, call ☎ 051/811111. For additional information on transportation to and from Danang, *see* Hoi An A to Z, *below.*

GETTING AROUND

A couple of drivers who hang out at the Cham Museum offer the cheapest rates in town. They also provide transportation outside the city. A regular taxi to the airport should cost no more than 55,000d; call **Airport Taxi** (☎ 051/825555).

CONTACTS AND RESOURCES
Danang Travel Information Center (✉ 3–5 Dong Da St., ☎ 051/823298, 051/824555, or 051/824400, FAX 051/823431), which is part of the Danang Hotel, offers guided tours and transportation in and around Danang and to the airport.

Vietnam Airlines Danang Booking Office (☞ *above*) also has a Vietcom Bank foreign exchange booth.

Marble Mountain

11 km (7 mi) southwest of Danang, 19 km (12 mi) north of Hoi An via the Korean Highway.

Five roughly hewn marble hillocks lie beside the beach southwest of Danang. These mountains are each said to represent one of the five elements: Thuy Son (water), Tho Son (earth), Hoa Son (fire), Moc Son (wood), and Kim So (metal). When the Chams controlled this area, the natural cave temples carved into the hill of Thuy Son were used as Hindu shrines. More recently, Buddhists have adorned, sanctified, and inhabited them. Worthy of note are the Buddhist and Confucian shrines in the guard-flanked Huyen Khong Cave, where touching a stalactite to the right is supposed to bring fertility to the childless. The hole at the top of the cave permits an ethereal light to filter down inside.

The local government has cracked down on solicitation and Marble Mountain now makes a very pleasant day excursion when combined with a trip to China Beach. Polite children in traditional socialist school uniforms will literally take you by the hand, provide guided tours of the various Buddhist cave sanctuaries, and, at the end of a very informative tour, offer their "best price . . . for you only" on marble souvenirs.

China Beach

12 km (7 mi) southwest of Danang, 1 km (½ mi) from Marble Mountain, 20 km (12 mi) from Hoi An.

Famed China Beach is a vast stretch of pristine, quiet sand. The best time to come is from May to July, when the water is placid. Waves can be high at other times—in fact, China Beach held the first international surfing competition in Vietnam in December 1992. The actual stretch of beach once used by U.S. soldiers, as immortalized in the '80s TV show *China Beach,* is located 5 km north of here.

Lodging

$$ 🖾 **China Beach Resort** (Non Nuoc). Situated at the foot of Marble Mountain, this glorified motel next to the sea is unfortunately the only game in town. A '60s concrete structure ripe for the wrecking ball, it's soon to be replaced by an American-Vietnamese joint-venture resort. It does, however, offer reasonably clean, utilitarian rooms with views of the water. ✉ *Non Nuoc, Danang,* ☎ *051/836216, FAX 051/836335. 103 rooms. 2 Restaurants, bar, air-conditioning, fans, tennis courts, beach, laundry service, travel services, car rental.*

China Beach A to Z

ARRIVING AND DEPARTING

Another likely day trip from Hoi An, China Beach is easily accessible by motorbike or by car. Both means of transport can be arranged through most hotels and booking offices in Danang or Hoi An. To get there from Hoi An, take the Korean Highway 19 km (12 mi) north towards Marble Mountain, turn left into the hamlet Nuon Nuc, follow the road past the largest of the marble mountains, and keep going as it curves around to the right. If you rent a car (usually 45,000d per person, per round-trip), specify a pick-up time and place with the driver before you part for your day on the beach.

Hoi An

138 km (86 mi) south of Hue, 30 km (17 mi) south of Danang.

Perhaps the most delightful of all Vietnamese towns, enchanting riverside Hoi An defies the insidious pace of modernization, preserving in pristine condition its 18th century houses, pagodas, and Chinese assembly halls.

Originally called Faifo, Hoi An is a composite of many foreign influences. It emerged as a port town as early as the 2nd century, when the Kingdom of Champa occupied the general area. When the Chams and the Vietnamese fought for control of Hoi An in the 14th and 15th centuries, the disputed turf disappeared from the international trade circuit. Peace in the 16th century once again brought ships from all over Europe, Asia, and the Americas in search of silk, porcelain, lacquerware, Chinese medicines, and other trade goods.

Although untouched by war in this century, Hoi An was severely damaged during the Tay Son Rebellion in the 1770s. After a speedy reconstruction, the town managed to sustain its two-century (17th–18th) tenure as a major international port town for Chinese, Dutch, Japanese, and Portuguese merchants. Colonies of foreigners developed along the riverfront, where seafaring merchants set up shop during the off-season. To this day, ethnic Chinese, having made this their first settlement in Vietnam, make up a significant portion of the population. In addition there is still a major French influence, notably an entire city block of colonnaded French buildings.

Strictly reserved for pedestrians, cyclists, and the occasional motorbike, the Old Town is ideal for a leisurely walking tour. You should be able to pick up a map from your hotel or from one of the local tourist offices at the corner of Nguyen Hue and Phan Chu Trinh. For 50,000d, you can buy a combined entrance ticket for one of three assembly halls, one of four historic houses, the Hoi An Museum of History and Culture, and the Japanese Covered Bridge. However, it is usually possible to enter any of the houses or assembly halls for 5,000d, so the prepaid ticket is not a great bargain.

Head toward the river, down Nguyen Hue. On the left at the corner of Tran Phu is the entrance to the **Hoi An Museum of History and Culture,** a collection of ceramics and photographs in a lovely courtyard adjacent to a small temple. Exiting the museum to the left, make the first left on Tran Phu, where you will see the **Central Market** (⊠ 65 Nguyen Duy Hieu) on the right. Across Tran Phu from the market is the Chinese **Quan Cong Temple** (⊠ 168 Tran Phu St.), founded in 1653. Farther down Tran Phu, at the intersection with the tiny Phan Boi Chau, is the **Assembly Hall** of the Hainan Chinese Congregation, built in 1883, during the reign of Emperor Tu Duc, in memory of 10 merchants mistaken for pirates and killed. Continue on Tran Phu, which becomes Nguyen Duy Hieu. Just after it changes its name, at No. 157, is the **Chaozhou Assembly Hall** (Trieu Chau), built in 1776 and an example of exquisite Chinese wood-carving. The proud white-haired gatekeeper allows visitors in for free.

Cross Hoang Dieu Street, and go back the way you came. Head west on Tran Phu. After the intersection with Nguyen Hue, you will see the **Phuc Kien Assembly Hall** (⊠ 46 Tran Phu) on the right. The **Assembly Hall of the Fujian Chinese Congregation,** built in 1975 as a meeting hall, was then dedicated to the Fujian-born goddess of the sea and protector of fishermen, Thien Hau. Next on the right is the **Chinese All-Community Assembly Hall,** built in 1773 as the meeting place for Cantonese, Chaozhou, Fujian, Hainan, and Hakka. Its entrance is at 31 Phan Chu Trinh. Proceeding west on Tran Phu, the **Diep Dong Nguyen House** is on the right at No. 80. The **Quang Thang House** is on the left at No. 77. Just beyond the intersection with Le Loi Street is **Old House** at No. 103. Return to Le Loi Street and make a right, toward the river, and then an immediate right on Nguyen Thai Hoc. On the right you will see the **Diep Dong Nguyen House** (⊠ 80 Nguyen thai Hoc). On the left in the middle of the block at No. 101 is the 200-year-old **Tan Ky House,** where a tour guide will detail its tasteful blend of Vietnamese, Chinese, and Japanese interior styles.

NEED A BREAK?

In addition to refreshing fruit shakes, **Faifoo** (⊠ 104 Tran Phu, ☎ 051/861548) serves *cao lau,* a special flat noodle dish that can only be found in Hoi An, as the water used in it comes from a special local well. Faifoo also serves another local specialty called "white roses," a shrimp- or vegetable-filled wonton. You might want to avoid the "Pizza Spaghetti-Guacamole."

Follow the road along the river, past the An Hoi Footbridge. At the intersection of Tran Phu on the north side of the street, the **Assembly Hall of the Cantonese Chinese Congregation** (⊠ 176 Tran Phu St.), founded in 1786, appears at the convergence of Nguyen Thai Hoc and Tran Phu. Just west of it, Tran Phu Street, lined with souvenir shops, takes you to the entrance of the beautiful **Japanese Bridge,** past the intersection of Nhi Trung. The bridge was built in 1593 to connect the Japanese and Chinese quarters. It is said that it was constructed atop the body of a legendary monster called Cu, whose unrestrained movement would otherwise incite natural disaster. Perhaps out of guilt or sympathy for the dead beast's soul, the little temple Chua Cau was built in his honor.

After you cross the bridge, you'll see the **Phung Hung House** at No. 4 Nguyen Thi Minh Khai Street—the street name changes at the bridge. Continue along Nguyen Thi Minh and make the first right at Phan Chu Trinh. On the right just past Nhi Trung is the gate from **Ba Mu Pagoda,** all that remains of the structure built in 1628 and leveled in the 1960s to make room for a school. Set back beyond a small garden on the far left corner of Phan Chu Trinh and Le Loi is the **Tran Family Chapel** (⊠ 21 Phan Chu Trinh), built at the end of the 18th century as a place to worship the family ancestors.

If you are motivated, head north on Nguyen Truong To Street for approximately 1 km (½ mi) to the end of the road, turn left, and follow the path until you reach **Chuc Thanh Pagoda.** Built in 1454 by a Chinese Buddhist monk and inhabited by five monks, Chuc Thanh is the oldest pagoda in Hoi An.

Dining

$ ✕ **Café des Amis.** Easily the finest dining experience in Hoi An, the
★ des Amis offers a set-course seafood or vegetarian menu that changes daily and excellent riverfront ambience. After several large, delicious, eclectic courses have been served, the chef, Mr. Nguyen Manh Kim, comes by to chat—his public relations are obviously quite successful, since it's the only restaurant that people talk about. He began his ca-

reer as a cook for the South Vietnamese army during the war. ⊠ *52 Bach Dang St.,* ☎ *051/861616. No credit cards.*

¢ ✕ **Ly Cafeteria 22.** Catering mostly to backpackers, the very friendly Miss Ly serves tasty local specialties such as cao lau and "white roses." She has achieved Lonely Planet fame and has had more international marriage proposals from doting men around the world than Liz Taylor. ⊠ *22 Nguyen Hue St.,* ☎ *051/61603. No credit cards.*

¢ ✕ **My Lac.** This friendly family-run establishment serves excellent traditional Vietnamese and Chinese cuisine. ⊠ *106 Tran Phu St.,* ☎ *051/861591. No credit cards.*

¢ ✕ **Restaurant Thanh.** Restaurant Thanh makes a splendid flounder (or whatever whitefish happens to be fresh that day) cooked in banana leaves as well as a refreshing squid salad prepared with lemon, onions, peanuts, and cucumber and eaten with rice paper. Its open-air, candlelit, riverfront ambience is unfortunately compromised by persistent, bordering on obnoxious, postcard vendors. ⊠ *76 Bach Dang St.,* ☎ *051/861366. No credit cards.*

Lodging

$ ☷ **Cu Dai Hoi An Hotel.** One of the nicest and newest accomodations in town, this plush minihotel offers spotless sunny rooms, and many have their own balconies. Located between the beach and the town center, both attractions are just a short bike ride away. ⊠ *18A Cua Dai,* ☎ *051/861722. 17 rooms. Restaurant, air-conditioning, fans, laundry service, travel services. No credit cards.*

$ ☷ **Hoai Thanh.** Slightly away from the center of town, the Hoai Thanh offers utilitarian rooms when other more centrally located properties fill up. ⊠ *23 Le Hong Phong,* ☎ *051/861242 or 051/861171,* ℻ *051/861135. 43 rooms. Restaurant, air-conditioning, fans, refrigerators, laundry service, travel services, rental cars, free parking. No credit cards.*

$ ☷ **Sea Star (Sao Bien).** Just outside the town center on the way to the beach, the brand new Sea Star offers clean utilitarian rooms. ⊠ *15 Cua Dai,* ☎ *051/861589,* ℻ *051/861858. 11 rooms. Restaurant, air-conditioning, laundry service, travel services, rental cars. No credit cards.*

$ ☷ **Thien Trung.** Very close to the bus station, the Thien Trung is a short bike ride from the Old Town. Rooms are neat and bright. ⊠ *63 Phan Ding Phung,* ☎ *051/861720 or 051/861769. 16 rooms. Restaurant, air-conditioning, fans, laundry service, travel services, car rental. No credit cards.*

¢–$ ☷ **Hoi An Hotel.** By no means luxurious, the Hoi An is just about the only real hotel in all of Hoi An and the only one that takes credit cards or traveler's checks. Comfortable, spacious rooms offer many of the conveniences. The Hoi An tourist office is located in the lobby. ☷ *6 Tran Hung Dao St.,* ☎ *051/861445,* ℻ *051/861636. 130 rooms. Restaurant, air-conditioning, fans, bicycles, laundry services, travel services, car rental. AE, MC, V.*

¢ ☷ **Pho Hoi (Faifoo) Minihotel.** Very close to the river and market, this hotel has a couple of bright and basic rooms with balconies that overlook the tree-lined street. The ones without windows are much less cheerful. ⊠ *73 Phan Boi Chau St.,* ☎ *051/861453. 20 rooms, but adding on. Air-conditioning, fans, bicycles, motorbikes, travel services, rental cars, No credit cards,*

¢ ☷ **Thanh Binh.** This centrally located hotel offers clean, rooms that get plenty of light. ⊠ *1 Le Loi St.,* ☎ *051/861740. 14 rooms. Air-conditioning, fans, laundry service, travel services, car rental, free parking. No credit cards.*

¢ ☷ **Vinh Hung Hotel.** Not too far from the Japanese Bridge, its dramatic Chinese-style lobby with lots of wood-carving opens up to brighter small, efficient rooms. ⊠ *142 Tran Phu St.,* ☎ *051/861621,* ℻ *051/861893.*

Bar, air-conditioning, fans, laundry service, travel services. No credit cards.

Outdoor Activities and Sports

For a low-impact, highly scenic workout, the 20-minute bike ride to Cua Dai Beach (☞ Getting Around *in* Hoi An A to Z, *below*) is a splendid way to catch a breeze. Five km (3 mi) east from the town center, Tran Hung Dao Street/Cua Dai Street take you all the way to the beach. Quotes for bicycle parking are often as much as rental for a day, and are easily negotiable, especially if you are with a group. Short paddle-boat trips along the Thu Bon (Cai River) can be arranged at Huang Van Thu Street or through underage solicitors that hang out at the riverside dock. Hoi An Tourism arranges motorized boat trips, including visits to a ceramic factory and a shipyard. Full-day boat trips to Cham Island, My Son, and Cam Kim Island are also available from the dock.

Shopping

Hoi An is one of the most pleasant places in all of Vietnam to shop for souvenirs and clothing. The quality of goods is generally quite high. Along Tran Phu Street there are numerous shops selling everything from art to ceramics to clothing to opium paraphernalia. Although most ceramic objects are labeled antiques, some are and some are not. Bargaining is advisable, as quoted prices are generally greatly inflated, especially for fine art.

For cheap casual **clothing** and same-day service, the seamstress stalls at Central Market (✉ 65 Nguyen Duy Hieu St.) are filled with Vietnamese, Japanese, and Chinese silks and cottons. The large staff at stall No. 10 Diep will make just about anything in a few hours. Shirts cost as little as 30,000d, pants 50,000d. The tiny Phuong Huy II at 21B Tran Phu, will fill any order for slightly more elaborate articles of clothing, such as fitted jackets and formal attire, in a day.

Hoi An A to Z

ARRIVING AND DEPARTING

The closest airport and railway station are in Danang (☞ Arriving and Departing *in* Danang, *above*). Booking offices in Danang and Hoi An can take care of train and plane reservations.

The only way to get into Hoi An from Danang is by minibus or car, which takes less than an hour and costs anywhere between 50,000d and 100,000d, depending on the number of passengers. It is a winding but highly scenic drive. Cars can be rented from **Danang Travel Information Center** (✉ 3–5 Dong Da St., ☎ 051/823431) or from any travel agency in Hoi An (☞ Contacts and Resources, *below*).

GETTING AROUND

Bicycles (5,000d per day) and motorcycles (50,000d–75,000d per day) are the most enjoyable and most convenient means of transporation. You can rent them from Hoi An Tourism (☞ Contacts and Resources, *below*) and at many hotels and cafés.

CONTACTS AND RESOURCES

There are a number of booking offices along Le Loi and Tran Hung Dao Streets that handle trains, planes, and car rentals, as well as accommodations and excursions from Hoi An. The state-run **Hoi An Tourism** (✉ 6 Tran Hung Dao, ☎ 051/861373 or 051/861362, FAX 861636) offers several intineraries and operates out of the lobby of the Hoi An Hotel.

NHA TRANG

448 km (278 mi) north of Ho Chi Minh City along Highway 1, 541 km (335 mi) south of Danang, and 205 km (127 mi) from Boun Ma Thout.

Despite the shocking buildup of Western-style joint-venture hotels and all the trappings of a seaside tourist community frantic to make up for lost time, Nha Trang retains the beauty of its coconut tree–lined beaches and beachfront cafés. Recreational attractions include scuba diving, snorkeling, and boat trips to neighboring Bamboo (Hon Tre), Mieu (Try Nguyen), Monkey (Dao Khi), and Salangane Island (Hon Yen). Nha Trang's June–September dry season sees many more tourists than the very wet months of October and November.

Exploring Nha Trang

Renting a motorbike, with or without a driver, is probably the best way to see Nha Trang and even more spectacular beaches to the north such as Doc Let, 30 km (18 mi). The equally spectacular Dai Lanh, 83 km (51 mi) north, is perhaps a little far for a motorbike trip.

Sights to See

Long Son Pagoda. While the pagoda itself is very beautiful—and the monks are happy to guide visitors through the main sanctuary—even more impressive is the panoramic view from the statue of the Lady Buddha, which is just a short climb up the stairs behind the pagoda. To reach the pagoda, 2 km (1¼ mi) from town, follow Yerstin Street inland. When you hit 23 Thang 10 Street (called Thai Nguyen Street as you get closer to the water), make a right, and the pagoda is on the right-hand side. Watch out for the persistent women beggars.

Po Nagar Cham Towers (Mother Goddess or Lady of the City). Khan Hoa Province's capital is home to one of the better preserved Cham ruins, located just north of the main beach town, on the other side of the Cai River. Originally a site of Hindu worship dating from the 2nd century AD, the buildings as they exist today were built between the 7th and 12th centuries, and are used by Chinese and Vietamese Buddhists. The North Tower, built under King Harivarman I, originally housed a linga. It was stolen and replaced with the stone statue of Uma that still survives. Of the original eight structures, four remain virtually untouched. Again, beware of importunate beggars. To get here from the center of town, take Quang Trung Street/2 Thang 4 Street and cross the Cai River via the Ha Ra and Xom Bong Bridges—which give you a post-card-perfect view of fishing-boat activity. As you cross the second bridge, you see the impressive towers jutting up from the hill to your left. ✉ *Admission.*

Dining

$$ ✕ **Huong Duong.** In this restaurant, bar, and discotheque complex, Italian chef Marco Russoni serves suprisingly authentic, slightly upscale Italian food. Ideally located on a secluded stretch of sand right on the water, Huong Duong is just south of the Ana Mandara resort construction site, on Tran Phu near the airport. ✉ *Tran Phu,* ☎ *058/823914,* FAX *058/825768. No credit cards.*

$$ ✕ **Ngoc Suong.** In a charming outdoor garden setting, guests watch
★   huge sea creatures plucked from tanks as orders are placed. This local establishment serves easily the best and freshest seafood in town. The rather daunting (if unintelligible) menu also includes suprisingly de-

lightful wild boar. ⊠ *16 Tran Quang Khai St., not far from Tran Phu.* ☎ *058/954516. No credit cards.*

$$ ✕ **Nha Trang Sailing Club.** Perhaps the most charming of all the sea-side café/restaurants, the Sailing Club is very popular with expats, locals, and tourists alike. The restaurant and adjoining bar are run by a charming Aussie named Peter Vidotto, who seems to be the only beach-front proprietor with any musical taste or at least any sense of taste-ful volume (all the other cafés play deafeningly loud music). Try the delicious sweet-and-sour fish soup that comes to your table with its own burner and the fruit shake. Boat trips can be arranged through the office just behind the restaurant. ⊠ *72–74 Tran Phu Blvd.,* ☎ *058/ 826528,* FAX *058/821906. No credit cards.*

$ ✕ **Lac Canh.** Brimming with tourists, locals, and charcoal grills at each table, this smoke-filled space affords cheap and delicious do-it-your-self marinated seafood and meat. ⊠ *11 Hang Ca,* ☎ *058/821391. No credit cards.*

¢ ✕ **Thanh Lich.** This rustic family-run restaurant prepares excellent fresh seafood specials in front of your very eyes. The sublime squid in ginger comes to your table as a raw marinade, is then cooked on a portable charcoal burner at your table and lingers on your breath for the next two days. The marinaded beef in lime juice that comes in a sizzling clay pot is equally delicious. ⊠ *8 Phan Boi Chau St.,* ☎ *058/ 821955. No credit cards.*

¢ ✕ **Thanh The.** Specializing in seafood and traditional Vietnamese fare, Thanh The is packed with local Vietnamese and tourists. ⊠ *3 Phan Chu Trinh St.,* ☎ *058/821931.*

¢ ✕ **Vietnam Restaurant.** This family-run spot serves excellent seafood at low prices. ⊠ *23 Hoang Van Thu St.,* ☎ *058/822933. No credit cards.*

Lodging

A number of ambitious-looking joint-venture hotels are currently under construction. The Hotel Manila or Nga Trang Lodge, with its turquoise-tinted glass, is a towering Philippine joint-venture project close to completion. There is also the Outrigger Canoe Club, an Australian joint-venture to the left of the Duy Tan, a new Saigon Tourist Hotel (⊠ 18 Tran Phu, ☎ 058/825227, FAX 058/825211). Also abuilding is Ana Mandara Nha Trang Resort (Hai Duong Tourism Joint Venture Company, Villa 21, Doan Au Duong ⊠ 26, 86, ☎ 058/827125, FAX 058/823428) at 60 Tran Phu, which will be Nha Trang's only beach-front property (literally on the sand), just south of town on Tran Phu, with rooms/villas starting at US$130/night. As most of the larger prop-erties were built in the '60s or '70s and look like the have hardly been touched since, new efficient minihotels both along the coast and in town are attractive alternatives.

$–$$ 🏨 **Bao Dai Villas.** Though the reworked royal villas could use a little touching up, fine architecture (high ceilings) and a beautiful hilltop lo-cation just a few km south of the town make this an attractive ac-commodation. ⊠ *Cau Da-Vinh Nguyen,* ☎ *058/881471. 48 rooms, most with bath. Restaurant, air-conditioning, fans, room service, ten-nis court, beach, snorkeling, boating, meeting rooms, travel services, No credit cards.*

$–$$ ✕ **Haiyen Hotel.** Catering to large cruise-ship tours, this big waterfront hotel looks like it has not been touched since the '60s. Rooms are pass-able. ⊠ *40 Tran Phu St.,* ☎ *058/822828,* FAX *058/821902. 107 rooms. 2 bars, dining room, outdoor café, lobby lounge, air-conditioning, fans, minibars, refrigerators, room service, pool, beauty salon, mas-*

sage, sauna, dance club, laundry service and dry cleaning, meeting room, travel services, car rental, parking. MC, V.

$–$$ 🏨 **Maritime Hotel.** Screaming for a face-lift, this '60s structure is grossly overpriced. Rooms decorated with dog-eared blue vinyl furniture and stained rugs boast such amenities as satellite TV and IDD phones. ✉ *34 Tran Phu, Vinh Nguyen,* ☎ *058/881135,* FAX *058/881134. 62 rooms. 2 restaurants, bar, air-conditioning, fans, refrigerators, room service, laundry service, travel services, car rental. AE, MC, V.*

$–$$ 🏨 **Vien Dong Hotel.** Another hub of tourist activity, next to the Haiyen Hotel, this popular hotel offers slightly run-down and overpriced accommodations. Still, it takes care of one's needs, handles car rentals, tours, money exchange. It is half a block from the beach and has a pool. ✉ *1 Tran Hung Dao St.,* ☎ *058/821606,* FAX *058/821912. 86 rooms. Restaurant, bar, air-conditioning, fans, minibars, refrigerators, pool, massage, laundry service, travel services. AE, MC, V.*

$ 🏨 **Duy Tan Hotel.** Overlooking the water, the Duy Tan is one of the nicest hotels in Nha Trang, which isn't saying much. Rooms are sparse and efficient, but not depressing. The staff could be friendlier. ✉ *24 Tran Phu St.,* ☎ *058/822671,* FAX *058/825034. 90 rooms. Restaurant, lobby lounge, air-conditioning, fans, minibars. No credit cards.*

$ 🏨 **Matra II.** This fully equipped, bland, '60s-style hotel offers decent, utilitarian rooms. ✉ *34 Tran Phu St., Vinh Nguyen,* ☎ *058/81136,* FAX *058/81134. 60 room with bath. 2 restaurants, 2 bars, air-conditioning, fans, minibars, refrigerators, room service, beach, dance club, laundry service and dry cleaning, meeting rooms, travel services, car rental. No credit cards.*

$ 🏨 **Seaside Hotel.** This posh, brand-new minihotel just south of town
★   on the coast offers some of the nicest and most tastefully decorated rooms in Nha Trang. It is not for those who require a self-contained-universe-style hotel. As it stands on the main seaside drag, many of the rooms have views of the water. ✉ *96 Tran Phu,* ☎ *058/821178,* FAX *058/828038. 15 rooms. Restaurant under construction, air-conditioning, fans, laundry service. No credit cards (credit cards in the future).*

¢–$ 🏨 **Nam Long Hotel.** The Nam Long, located in the center of town not too far from the beach, offers clean, nondescript accommodations. ✉ *7 Le Thanh Ton,* ☎ *058/827714,* FAX *058/824991. 25 rooms. Air-conditioning, fans, minibar, refrigerators, laundry service, travel services. No credit cards.*

¢   🏨 **Thanh Thanh Hotel.** This efficient, brighly lit new minihotel overlooking the water is just south of town. ✉ *98A Tran Phu St.,* ☎ *058/ 824657,* FAX *058/823031. 18 rooms. Restaurant, air-conditioning, minibars, refrigerators, room service, laundry service, travel services. No credit cards.*

Nightlife and the Arts

People tend to congregate on the beach or at such beachfront bar/cafés as the **Coconut Grove** (✉ 40 Tran Phu). **Zippo Bar** (✉ 2 Hung Vuong, ☎ 058/827296) is another popular beachfront bar. The **Nha Trang Sailing Club** (✉ 72–74 Tran Phu, ☎ 058/826528, FAX 058/821906) attracts a lively crowd with its well-equipped bar, pool table, and comfortable, tasteful ambience. It also serves as an exhibition gallery for a brilliant and friendly local photographer by the name of Long Thanh, who works out of his home (✉ 126 Hoang Van Thu St., ☎ 058/824875). Not too far from the airport, the **Huong Duong Center Bar/Discotheque** attracts a dancing crowd (Tran Phu, ☎ 058/823914).

Outdoor Activities and Sports

Like any other seaside resort town, Nha Trang offers snorkeling, jet skiing, scuba diving, and boating. No visit to Nha Trang would be complete without a boat trip to the nearby islands, arranged through any number of hotels and travel agencies (☞ Contacts and Resources *in* Nha Trang A to Z, *below*). **The Blue Diving Club** (✉ 40 Tran Phu, Coconut Cove, ☎ 058/825390, FAX 058/824214), a very well-run P.A.D.I. diving center, offers English- and French-speaking instructors and guided excursions for all diving levels.

Nha Trang A to Z

Arriving and Departing

BY BUS OR CAR

Cars can be rented from hotels and from private and state-run travel agencies (☞ Contacts and Resources, *below*).

BY PLANE

Planes fly between Nha Trang and Ho Chi Minh City (55 minutes, US$60) and Hanoi (2½ hours, US$135) daily; there are flights to Danang three times a week. Tickets are available at **Vietnam Airlines** (✉ 12B Hoang Hoa Tham St., Nha Trang, ☎ 058/823797).

BY TRAIN

Nha Trang is served three times daily by both express and local trains from Hanoi and Ho Chi Minh City. A soft sleeper from Ho Chi Minh costs US$23–US$31; from Hanoi, it's US$80–US$100, depending on which train you take. The ticket office at **Nha Trang Railway Station** (✉ 26 Thai Nguyen St., ☎ 058/822113) is open between 7 AM and 2 PM only.

Getting Around

The best way to get around Nha Trang and the surrounding area is by bicycle or motorbike. You can rent them at any travel agency and most hotels for approximately 65,000d a day for a motorbike or 10,000d a day for a bicycle.

Contacts and Resources

TRAVEL AGENCIES AND VISITOR INFORMATION

The state-run **Khanh Hoa Tourism** (✉ 1 Tran Hung Dao, ☎ 058/822753, FAX 058/824206) can arrange air or train trips and boat excursions, and rents cars, bicycles, and motorbikes. **Nha Trang Tourism** (✉ 3 Tran Hung Dao, Hung Dao Hotel, ☎ 058/821231) is the better of the state-run agencies. The more upscale and efficient **Nam-Viet** (✉ 2 Hung Vung St., ☎ 058/821428, FAX 058/821428) is privately managed by the very helpful Lucien Peeters.

DALAT AND THE CENTRAL HIGHLANDS

The vacation resort of Dalat is somewhat overhyped, but its resort amenities and lovely scenery continues to attract Vietnamese tourists and honeymooners. En route to Dalat is the region known as the Central Highlands, an unspoiled landscape dotted with charming villages and religious complexes.

Central Highlands

Comprising the southern part of the Truong Son mountain range, this region of mountains, streams, lakes and waterfalls includes the provinces of Lam Dong, Dac Lac (Dak Lak), Gia Lai, and Kon Tum. This is one of the few parts of Vietnam where it gets cool enough to wear a sweater. Difficult to access by land, the western part of the Central Highlands is home to a large population of ethnic minority village tribes. Bordering Cambodia and Laos, the strategic Buon Ma Thuot, Pleiku, and Kontum were major battlegrounds during the Vietnam War. Only now has the vegetation, including coffee trees, begun recover from the napalm and defoliants employed by the Americans. What follows are a few of the region's most interesting sights.

Approximately 100 km (62 mi) north of Ho Chi Minh City along Highway 20, **Langa Lake** supports a number of floating fishing villages.

Often inaccessible due to poor road conditions, **Nam Cat Tien National Park,** 240 km (149 mi) northwest of Ho Chi Minh City, close to the Cambodian border, shelters the endangered Javan rhino, as well as monkeys, elephants, and a number of bird species.

About 233 km (149 mi) northwest of Ho Chi Minh City or 75 km (47 mi) soutwest of Dalat, are **Dambri Waterfalls.** Steep slippery steps lead to excellent views of the 300-foot falls. 🎫 *Admission.* 🕐 *Daily 7–6.*

The provinces of Binh Thuan, Ninh Thuan, Khanh Hoa, Phu Yen, Binh Dinh and Quang Ngai, along or around National Highway 1, comprise what is called the **South-Central Coast.** Ninh Thuan and Khanh Hoa provinces are particularly noteworthy for their Cham ruins and beautiful beaches.

West of Dalat on Highway 20, just beyond the semi-arid twin cities Phan Rang-Thap Cham, are the **Po Klong Garai Cham Towers.** The four wonderfully preserved Hindu temples were built under Cham king Jaya Simhavarman III in the 13th century. 🎫 *Admission.* 🕐 *Daily 7–5.*

Dalat

308 km (191 mi) from Ho Chi Minh City.

In the early part of the century, Dalat, the "River of the Lat Tribe" became a vacation spot for Europeans eager to escape the infernal heat of the coastal plains, the big cities, and the Mekong Delta. Discovered by Dr. Alexandre Yersin (1863–1943), a protégé of Louis Pasteur, cool Dalat served as the favorite nonpartisan rest spot for high-ranking North and South Vietnemese officers before the war's end on April 3, 1975.

Dubbed "le petit Paris" and the "City of Eternal Spring," Dalat may be pleasant, but is a far cry from Paris. Furthermore, only a small fraction of its French colonial villas and churches still stand, and it is mostly frequented by Vietnamese tourists and honeymooners. Its panoramic views of majestic mountains and placid lakes are too often sullied by kitschy architecture. Still, its 18-hole golf course is now complete, and the town has become a golfing mecca.

Central Dalat lies to the northwest of **Ho Xuan Huong** (Xuan Huong Lake), named after a 17th-century Vietnemese poet known for her daring attacks on the hypocrisy of social conventions and the foibles of scholars, monks, mandarins, feudal lords, and kings. A path circles the lake and one can rent paddle boats. With the golf course nearby, it is a lovely spot to spend a few hours.

With the exception of the very picturesque **Central Market,** which ranks among Vietnam's best, there is little to see in town. You might consider taking your breakfast there early in the morning, when it is buzzing with activity. The food stalls are on the second floor of the newer structure, which also has a very nice view of the heaps of produce and grains below. The region is famous for its fruit, so you will see lots of candied fruits and preserves.

If you rent a car or motorbike, two rather more far-flung sights are worth a visit. Head north on Tien My Street; after you cross Highway 20, the street name becomes Tran Hung Dao Street. Proceeding west with the lake off in the distance to your left, make a right at Khe Sanh and go about 2 km up the road to **Chua Tao Thien Voung** (Chua Tau, the Chinese Pagoda). The dirt path up to the pagoda is lined with vending stalls that sell candied fruits, and local children push incense—actually not a bad thing to buy, since it provides a way to get spiritually involved. Built in 1958 by the Chaozhou Chinese Congregation, the pagoda is interesting for its majestic mountaintop setting and for its large Hong Kong–made, gilded-sandalwood Buddhas. Located in the third of the three buildings, the three figues represent, from left to right, Dai The Chi Bo Tat (an assistant of A Di Da); Thich Ca Buddha (Sakyamuni, the historical Buddha); and Quan The Am Bo Tat (Avalokiteçvara, the Goddess of Mercy).

Proceed back the way you came to Le Thai To Street or Hung Vuong Street, depending on what sign you are looking at. (In any case, it's the only road you hit walking down the hill.) Make a right, then a left after about 1,500 feet onto Tran Quy Cap, and then a left onto Quang Trung Street, which will lead you up a hill to a picturesque train station. As a point of orientation, Xuan Hong Lake is just about 1,500 feet north of the train station. The only place the train runs is to the neighboring **Trai Mat village** 8 km (5 mi) to the east. Large groups pay as little as 30,000d, small groups or solo travelers (about 5 people) have to pay 150,000d for a train car.

The ride to the village offers a close look at the area's bountiful fields, lush with strawberries, cabbage, flowers, cauliflower, carrots, coffee, avocado trees, durien, rambutan, and more. Upon exiting the train at the impoverished village, make a right and then your second left at the unmarked Tu Phuoc Street (look for a sign that says Bao Duy and Coca Cola on the far left corner storefront). Proceed down the hill towards **Chua Linh Phuoc** (Linh Phuoc Pagoda) at 120 Tu Phuoc. Originally built in 1946, extensive renovations were done from 1990 to 1994. The nine resident monks are often found mingling with the tourists in the garden to the right of the pagoda, which is home to an impressive 157-foot-long dragon sculpture that is adorned with over 13,000 pieces of ceramic and glass bottles.

Dining and Lodging

$ ✗ **Hoang Lan.** With a numerous and friendly wait staff, Hoang Lan serves cheap and tasty traditional Vietnamese fare in a decent enough environment. ⌧ *118 Phan Dinh Phung St.,* ☏ *063/822180. No credit cards.*

$$ ✗⊡ **Thanh Thanh.** For those desperate for white tablecloths and napkins, this decent, though unspectacular, Vietnamese restaurant seems to be the only place recommended to Westerners. The sugar-cane shrimp is quite tasty. ⌧ *4 Tang Bat Ho,* ☏ *063/821836. No credit cards.*

$$$–$$$$ ⊡ **Dalat Sofitel** (Dalat Palace). Ideally set atop a grassy knoll overlooking ★ Xuan Huong Lake, the exquisite Palace/Golf Club was recently renovated to recapture the grandeur and elegance of its original 1922 French design. Spacious rooms tastefully decorated with antiques, original moldings, and unobtrusive modern conveniences combine with impeccable service under the new international management. This is a very peaceful place to stay, especially for golfers. ⌧ *12 Tran Phu St.,* ☏ *063/825444,* FAX *063/825666. 43 rooms. Restaurant, café, lobby lounge, piano bar, pub, in-room safes, minibars, no-smoking rooms, room service, 18-hole golf course, 2 tennis courts, mountain bikes, shops, baby-*

sitting, laundry service and dry cleaning, concierge, business services, meeting rooms, travel services, airport shuttle. AE, MC, V.

$ ⌧ **Anh Dao Hotel.** Overlooking the Central Market, the Anh Dao offers central location and pleasant modern rooms with some of the Western conveniences. ⌧ *50–52 Hoa Binh Square (Nguyen Chi Thanh St.),* ☎ *063/822384. 27 rooms. Restaurant, bar, minibars, room service, laundry service and dry cleaning, travel services. No credit cards.*

Outdoor Activities and Sports

Dalat is a great for cycling and hiking. For more information, contact Dalat Tourist (☞ Guided Tours, *below*). The pristine **Dalat Palace Golf Club** (⌧ Phu Dong Thien Vuong, ☎ 063/821201, ℻ 063/824325) offers an 18-hole course and an ideal setting overlooking Xuan Huong Lake. Hotel guests receive special discounts.

Nightlife and the Arts

Barring a few Bohemian-type cafés like **Stop 'n Go Café** (⌧ Kiosk 6 Hoa Binh Sq., ☎ 063/821512) and **Café Tung** (⌧ 6 Khu Hoa Bin St.), there isn't much going on at night unless you are into karaoke, which is, of course, ubiquitous.

Dalat and Central Highlands A to Z

Arriving and Departing

BY BUS OR CAR

Dalat Tourist offers daily minibus service between offices in Dalat (⌧ 4 Tran Quoc Toan St., ☎ 063/822125) and Ho Chi Minh City (⌧ 21 Nguyen An Ninh, District 1, ☎ 08/823–0227) for around 90,000d. Go to the office one day in advance to reserve a seat. If you decide to rent a car, the inland route via Bao Loc and Di Linh is faster than the coastal route, but if you have the time, take the drive through the Ngoan Muc Pass for its spectacular views.

BY PLANE

Vietnam Airlines has flights to **Lien Khuong Airport,** 30 km (18 mi) south of Dalat, from Hanoi and Ho Chi Minh City on Tuesday, Wednesday, Thursday, and Saturday; flights to Singapore leave on Tuesday and Saturday. For ticket confirmation and reservations go to the **Vietnam Airlines Ticket Office** (⌧ 5 Truong Cong Dinh, ☎ 063/822–895).

Getting Around

The best way to get around is either by bike or motorbike. Mountain bikes are preferable because of the poor road conditions and the hilly roads. Rentals are available through Dalat Tourist (☞ Visitor Information, *below*).

Contacts and Resources

VISITOR INFORMATION

The government-run **Dalat Tourist/Lamdong Tourist Company** (⌧ 4 Tran Quoc Toan, ☎ 063/822125, ℻ 063/822661) offers a number of trips in and around Dalat, as well as excursions to other cities in Vietnam. They also provide car, bike, and motorbike rentals, maps, and general information. It seems that the only person who can answer any questions is Mr. Vo Hoang Xuan. The main office is located near the southwestern end of the lake, not too far from the post office.

HO CHI MINH CITY

The name Ho Chi Minh City is like a matronly shroud that veils the the sensuous "Pearl of the Orient"—or Saigon, as it is still whispered by those who disregard the recent costume change. Despite 20 years under puritanical Hanoi's surveillance, Ho Chi Minh City betrays its penchant for openness and change. Responsible for at least 30% of Vietnam's manufacturing output and 25% of its retail trade, Ho Chi Minh's population of 6 million bristles with its newly discovered *doi moi* (economic liberalization). Still, while the effects of a new-found market economy are omnipresent, political and ideological opinions remain largely unspoken.

Its rapid modernization has created a traffic snarl that could stand as a metaphor for the city as a whole. The trip from the airport to the city center offers a glimpse of a chaotic choreography of motorbikes, cars, cyclos, bicycles, and pedestrians. Crossing the street, whether on foot or on wheels, requires a leap of faith.

Circumscribed by the Thi Nghe Channel to the north, the Ben Nge Channel to the south, and the Saigon River on the east, Ho Chi Minh City is both a natural fortress and commercial thoroughfare. As early as the 14th century, under Cambodian rule, the area attracted Arab, Cham, Chinese, Malaysian, and Indian merchants. Considerably younger than its pedantic northern counterpart, Prey Nokor ("Village in the Forest") as it was originally named, emerged as a Cambodian trading post and gateway to the Kingdom of Champa under the Angkor Empire.

It wasn't until 1674 that the lords of Hue were permitted to establish their own customs service to accommodate the region's growing commercial traffic. Eventually, by de facto law, Prey Nokor (renamed Raigauv) became an increasingly important administrative post. The shift in control from the Angkor empire to Nguyen rule was crystallized with the completion in 1772 of a 6 km (3½ mi) entrenchment on the west; further confirmation came in 1778, with the development of Cholon (also known as Chinatown or, literally, the "big market") as a second commercial hub. The center of corrupt Nguyen power moved from the north to the south, leaving a neglected Central Vietnam vulnerable to the Tay Son rebels. Saigon finally fell in 1783.

The fall of Saigon (it became the capital of Cochin China) to the French in 1859 marked the beginning of an epoch of colonial-style feudalism, indentured servitude, and a "heyday" fondly remembered by those who reaped the benefits of such a structure. Nostalgia for French Saigon's sophisticated conflation of Eastern and Western sensibilities seems almost unavoidable, albeit naive. Saigon's capitulation to North Vietnamese troops capped a 20-year period of political, economic, and ideological isolation with a unified Socialist Republic of Vietnam.

Today the city bustles with an odd blend of Vietnamese traditions. A scrappy, frenetic resilience fuels every makeshift sidewalk establishment and every outward-reaching, joint-venture high-rise. While Vietnam is definitely the most Western of all the cities in Vietnam, with the widest variety of international cuisine and Western-style hotels, it does not have a large number of tourist sights. Still, the bustling Ben Thanh Market and Cholon (Chinatown) offer plenty of diversion as one looks for reminiscences of French Saigon's Rue Catinat, as immortalized in Graham Greene's account in *The Quiet American*.

Exploring Ho Chi Minh City

There are no particular must-sees in Saigon. What is noteworthy is the overall ambience, the juxtapostion of Western style commercial activity with traditional practices, of motorbikes with the sanctity of urban pagodas. On the whole, museums are more interesting as indicators of Vietnam's political and cultural isolation.

Though comprised of 12 districts, most points of interest in Ho Chi Minh City are found in either District 1 (Central Saigon) or District 5 (Cholon). In District 1, major arteries such as Le Loi Boulevard, Ham Nghi Boulevard, and Pham Ngu Lao Street converge at the Ben Thanh Market, an important commercial and transportation hub. Northeast of the central market, at the intersection of Le Loi with Nguyen Hue Boulevard and Dong Khoi Street, is a cluster of French-colonial style public buildings—the Hotel de Ville (or City Hall), Municipal Theater, and such famed hotels as the Rex, the Continental, and the Caravelle. Ho Chi Minh's waterways have traditionally served as its major means of commercial transport, as well as a natural moat; District I is bounded on the east by the Saigon River and on the south by the Ben Nghe Channel. For the visitor, they not only provide alternative ways of getting around, they also serve as convenient orientation landmarks.

The city's rather daunting layout and chaotic traffic situation tend to discourage leisurely walking. The intermittent cyclo or motorbike ride for 10,000d seems an unavoidable and enjoyable alternative. Note that all walks below could also be cyclo rides, an option particularly recommended on hot days.

Numbers in the text correspond to numbers in the margin and on the Ho Chi Minh City map.

District 1 (Central Saigon)

A GOOD WALK

Although slightly away from the center, **War Crimes Museum** ① makes a good starting point. Head northeast on Vo Van Tan Street toward tree-lined Nam Ky Khoi Nghia Street. When you hit Nguyen Thi Minh Khai Street you will see the grounds of **Reunification Palace** ②. Turn left on Le Duan Boulevard, the street that intersects with Nam Ky Khoi Street at the palace entrance. After passing Pasteur Street, you will see the back of **Notre Dame** ③ and it's pink spires. Continuing on Le Duan, just a couple of blocks past Hai Ba Trung Boulevard, you will see the dilapidated former **U.S. Embassy** ④ (1967–75), an architectural monstrosity that has remained virtually untouched since it was evacuated. Proceeding about 1,000 feet down Le Duan, you come to the sprawling grounds of the **Zoo and Botanical Gardens** ⑤ and the **Historical Museum** ⑥.

With your back to the main entrance of the complex, make a left onto Nguyen Binh Khiem and follow it to the intersection with Le Thanh Ton Street. Make a right, then take the first left at Duc Thang, which runs along the Saigon River. Along the riverfront you can admire the newly refurbished turn-of-thecentury Majestic Hotel, at the intersection of Ton Duc Thang and Dong Khoi.

Turn right at Nguyen Hue and make the first left onto Hai Trieu, also known as Whiskey Row. Make a right at Ham Nghi, where you will see a series of international food stores (No. 64 is a good one) jam-packed with Western specialties. Turn right at Ton That Dang, where you can find anything from a live eel to laundry detergent, and walk through the charming market that continues along the intersecting Huynh Thuc Khang Street, a kind of electronics arcade. Continuing a block past Huynh Thuc Khang, you come to Ton That Thiep Street, in what has historically been the Indian quarter.

Make a right onto Ton That Thiep, crossing Ngyuen Hue, turn left on Dong Khoi. Formerly called Rue Catinat, Dong Khoi extends from the river to Notre Dame, and in the French colonial era it was Saigon's Fifth Avenue or Rodeo Drive. Making your way up Dong Khoi Street, you pass the Caravelle Hotel (Doc Lap), once a favorite haunt of "front-line" war correspondents at cocktail hour. Opposite the Caravelle is the newly restored Continental Hotel (Hai Au). Sandwiched between the two at the end of Le Loi Boulevard is the Municipal Theater, recognizable by its coffered dome. Continuing up Dong Khoi, past the Continental, you see Saigon Tourist's main branch office on the left at the corner of Le Thanh Ton Street. Next comes Notre Dame (Na To Due Ba). The Central Post Office (Buu Dien Truing Tam) is housed in the beautiful yellow building on the right side of the square that opens up in front of the cathedral.

With your back to the cathedral, walk toward Nguyen Du Street, make a right, then your first left onto Pasteur, and then the first right on Ly Ty Trong Street. Make a left at Truong Dinh Street. The **Mariamman Hindu temple** ⑦ is in the middle of the block between Ly Tu Trong and Le Thanh Ton on the right-hand side. With your back to the temple, make a left at Le Thanh Ton Street and you will see the activity from the **Ben Thanh Market** ⑧ spilling into the surrounding street. It is best to visit the market first thing in the morning, when stocks of produce are piled high and vendors are hustling.

TIMING

As always in Vietnam, start this tour in the morning, take lots of water breaks in the between. This walking tour could take anywhere between a half day and a whole one, depending on how much time you spend in the museums. You could also split the walk into two parts, with a break after the Historical Museum.

SIGHTS TO SEE

★ ⑧ **Ben Thanh Market** (Cho ben Thanh). Every imaginable product of the Vietnamese economy is sold here—look for a cheap meal, a hat, or live snakes. The structure housing most of the market was built in 1914 by the French, who knew it as Les Halles Centrales. Located at the circular intersection of Le Loi, Pham Ngu Lao, and Ham Nghi Boulevards, the market opens before sunrise and closes at around 7 PM.

⑥ **Historical Museum** (Vien Bao Tang Lich Su). Although the front door leads you right to a statute of the ubiquitous Uncle Ho, this museum is dedicated to the entire span of Vietnamese history, from the earliest inhabitants to 1930, when the Communist Party was established. Half of the museum covers the whole nation's history, while the other half focuses on the art and artifacts of the South; the ethnography section is particularly interesting. The neo-Vietnamese structure was built by the French in 1929, and much of the current collection was compiled by the French Far Eastern Institute. ✉ *2 Nguyen Binh Kiem, District 1,* ☎ *08/829–8146 or 08/829–0268.* ✆ *Admission.* ◷ *Mon.–Sat. 8–11:30 and 1:30–4:30; Sun. 8:30–11:30.*

OFF THE
BEATEN PATH
JADE EMPEROR PAGODA – You'll find the finest Chinese pagoda in Ho Chi Minh north of central Saigon, in District 3. The Jade Emperor Pagoda was built by Cantonese in 1909 and is also known as the "Tortoise Pagoda." A mixture of Taoist, Buddhist, and ethnic myths provide the sources for the pagoda's multitudes of statues and carvings—everything from the King of Hell to a Buddha of the Future. A slow stroll around the interior may be a preferrable viewing strategy to attempting to decifer distinct dieties. Do take a moment to note the main altar, the side panel's depiction of hell, and, in the side room, the miniature women who represent the panorama of human qualities. To get to the Jade Pagoda from the Historical Museum and the zoo, head north on Nguyen Binh Khiem Street to Dien Bien Phu, then jog left to Mai Thi Luu St. ✉ *73 Mai Thi Luu, District 3.* ✆ *Free.*

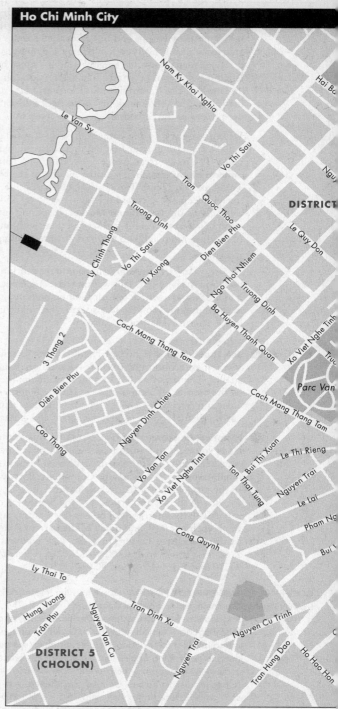

Ho Chi Minh City

DISTRICT

DISTRICT 5
(CHOLON)

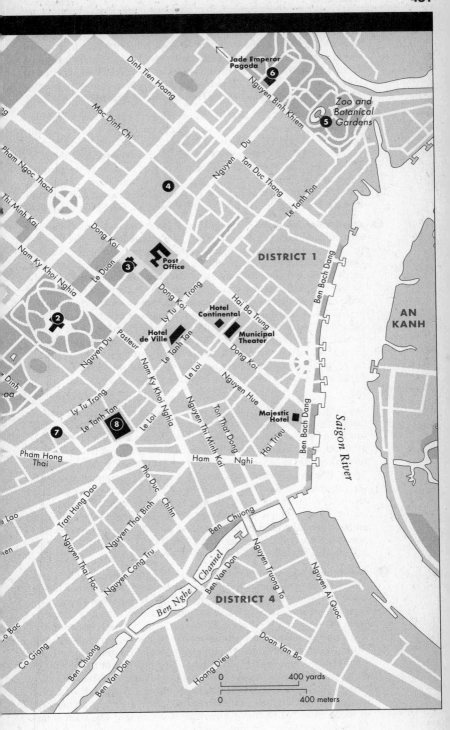

Jade Emperor Pagoda **6**

Nguyen Binh Khien

Dinh Tien Hoang

Zoo and
Botanical
Gardens **5**

Mac Dinh Chi

Nguyen Tan Duc Thang

Du

Pham Ngoc Thach

Le Tanh Ton

Thi Minh Kai

4

Ben Bach Dang

DISTRICT 1

Dong Koi

Nam Ky Khoi Nghia

Le Duan

3 Post
Office

Dong Koi

Ly Tu Trong

Hai Ba Trung

**AN
KANH**

Hotel
Continental

Nguyen Du

Pasteur

2

Nam Ky Khoi Nghia

Le Tanh Tan

Hotel
de Ville

Municipal
Theater

Dong Koi

Dinh
oa

Le Loi

Nguyen Hue

Ly Tu Trong

Le Tanh Tan

7

8

Le Loi

Nguyen Thi Minh Kai

Ton That Dong

Majestic
Hotel

Ben Bach Dang

Saigon River

Pham Hong
Thai

Nguyen Thai Binh

Ham Kai

Nghi

Hai Trieu

Pho Duc Chihn

Lao

Tran Hung Dao

Nguyen Thai Hoc

Nguyen Cong Tru

Ben Chuong

Nguyen Truong To

Nguyen Ai Quoc

Ben Nghe

Channel

Ben Van Don

DISTRICT 4

o Bac

Co Giang

Ben Chuong

Ben Van Don

Hoang Dieu

Doan Van Bo

0   400 yards

0   400 meters

❼ Mariamman Hindu Temple. Lovely statuary and colorful floral offerings at this, the last functioning Hindu temple in the city, create a microcosm of India in the streets of Saigon. Before its recent return to the Hindu community, the temple was used by the government as a factory for joss sticks and dried fish. Today it serves a congregation of a mere 60 Tamil Hindus, but some Vietnamese and Chinese locals also revere it as a holy space. ⊠ *45 Truong Dinh St.* ☉ *Daily 7 AM–7 PM.*

❸ Notre Dame (Nha Tho Duc Ba). A prominent presence on the skyline, this neo-Romanesque cathedral was built by the French in 1880. Catholicism was introduced by Spanish, Portuguese, and French missionaries to Vietnam as early as the 16th century, and is even today a minor religious influence. If it is unpopular, it is in part because of the people's anti-colonial sentiment, and in part owing to the Church's treatment of Buddhists in the 1950s. The mass celebrated at 9:30 AM on Sundays includes short sections in English and French. ⊠ *Top of Dong Khoi St.*

❷ Reunification Palace (Hoi Truong Thong Nhat). This modern architectural attraction was the scene of the Viet Cong's dramatic seizure of Saigon in 1975, with tanks smashing down the gates and a VC flag cascading over the building's balconies—all of it captured by photojournalists. Hundreds of thousands of Vietnamese and tens of thousands of Americans died in the battle that resulted in the seizure of this building, the symbolic center of the South Vietnamese government during the war. The mansion was designed by a European-influenced modernist architect, Ngo Viet Thu, in 1962, when South Vietnamese President Diem decided he had "an image problem" after his own air force bombed his old house in an assassination attempt. They got him a year later, so he never saw the palace finished. The former building on the site was called Norodom Palace and was the home of the French governor general.

If you choose to listen to the informational programming inside the building, be prepared to defer to the protocol of Vietnamese patriotism, including standing during the playing of the national anthem. While tours are free to Vietnamese, foreign visitors pay 40,000d; for another 10,000d, you can sit in the former president's chair and have your picture taken. Yet another 10,000d will get you onto the third-floor heliport. Cheap thrills abound, though, since your entrance fee lets you see the finest of Saigon's modernist architecture, a thorough map room, a bar and game room, elephant's tusks, severed elephant's feet, stuffed tigers, and a whole network of tunnels where the South's government would retreat in sketchy situations. ⊠ *106 Nguyen Du/133 Nam Ky Khoi Nghia, District 1,* ☎ *08/823–3652 or 08/822/3673.* 💷 *Admission.* ☉ *Daily 7:30 AM–10:30 AM and 1–4 PM.*

❶ War Crimes Museum (Nha Trung Bay Toi Ac Chien Tranh Xam). Americans may instinctively shy away from this museum, which is dedicated to the horrors perpetrated by the U.S. during the war, but it's a must-see for any American tourist with a healthy curiosity. Interestingly, the museum offers the government's official perspective on the war, conspicuously omitting mention of the division between South and North Vietnam. While the photographs feature the true horrors and details of war, their presentation ranges from poignant to the dull to the obviously skewed. Along with standard toil-of-war photos, displays feature documentation of the effects of Agent Orange and of actual weaponry. Although the museum has toned down slightly, changing its name from "Museum of American War Crimes," the slant is undoubtedly one-sided, so don't expect to see VC atrocities, the famous self-immolation protest of the Buddhist monk, or the thousands of Americans who protested their government's actions. ⊠ *28 Vo Van Tan St.,*

District 3, ☎ *08/829–0325.* 🖃 *Admission.* ☉ *Daily 7:30–11:45* AM *and 1:30–4:45* PM.

❹ U.S. Embassy. While this historic building allegedly awaits reoccupation by Americans in this new era of diplomacy, the former U.S. embassy in this former capitol of the former South Vietnam remains an echoing shadow of the chaos of a quarter-century past. Nothing to get excited about architecturally, the Americans' symbolic stronghold was attacked in the Tet Offensive of '68 and finally seized with the capture of Saigon in April of '75. It was here, in one of the most memorable images of the war, that the U.S. ambassador, his country's flag clutched to his chest, rushed into a helicopter on the roof, while Marine guards pushed back the mobs of South Vietnamese who had been assured evacuation. 🖃 *Le Duan Blvd. and Mac Din Chi St.*

❺ Zoo and Botanical Gardens (Thao Cam Vien). The fauna here does relatively well, and the flora thrives in its natural subtropical niche. In addition to the array of lackluster live animals, visit the eerie taxidermy-go-round, where stuffed animals can be ridden. As if this were not enough, the gardens have been filled with other carnival-like attractions as well—a rather unfortunate addition, as the gardens were one of the first French building projects in Vietnam and once one of the finest such parks in all of Asia. 🖃 *Nguyen Bien Khiem St. at Le Duan Blvd.*

District 5 (Cholon)

Southwest of central Saigon is Cholon, officially District 5, the city's Chinatown. A bustling market and commercial district, Cholon is of interest to the visitor primarily for its wealth of religious architecture. Negotiate a price of about 55,000d with a cyclo driver to take you on a tour of the pagodas and mosques concentrated around Nguyen Trai Street and Tran Hung Dao Boulevard, the three most memorable of which are detailed below.

SIGHTS TO SEE

Cholon Mosque. Now serving Indonesian and Malaysian Muslims, the mosque was built in 1932 by Tamil Muslims. Observe the discretion in Muslim architecture, in contrast to the exuberant ornamentation that marks the East Asian pagodas. Whereas representations of spirits and dieties are common in the Vietnamese and Chinese traditions, it is strictly sacriligious to portray any animal, human, or God in Islam. Hence decoration takes the form of abstract images and calligraphy. 🖃 *641 Nguyen Trai St., at Ly Thuong Kiet Blvd.*

Ong Bon Pagoda. Featuring representations of many deities, the main attraction here is Ong Bon himself, the beneficent guardian of happiness and virtue. He also serves some financial needs; hence, people bring paper offerings representing their desired wealth to burn in the pagoda's furnace. The centerpiece, an elaborately carved wood-and-gold altar and a statue of Ong Bon, is lovely, but also note the wonderful murals. 🖃 *264 Hai Thuong Lai Ong St. (parallel to Tran Hung Dao St.), at Phung Hung St.* 🖃 *Free.* ☉ *Daily 5* AM–5 PM.

Quan Am Pagoda. Dating from 1816, this pagoda, which shows a strong Chinese influence, portrays a busy array of scenes in lacquer, ceramic, gold, and wood. Many legendary and divine beings are portrayed, some dressed in elaborately embroidered robes. Be prepared for a stiffling cloud of incense upon entry. 🖃 *12 Lao Tu St., (parallel to Huong Vuong Blvd. and Ngyuen Trai St.).*

Dining

Despite the many fine dining options available in Ho Chi Minh City, you will find that what looks and actually tastes best is what the locals eat for breakfast, lunch, and dinner every day, huddled and squatting at the sidewalk eating establishments. Since mealtime is the only time to escape Saigon's oppressive heat or torrential midday downpour, the heavily air-conditioned Vietnamese, French, Thai, or Chinese restaurant is not the most authentic but perhaps the most pleasant.

Foreigners tend to gravitate towards Dong Khoi and the Le Thanh Ton Streets. On the budget end, there are some great cafés with Vietnamese and international food along Pham Ngu Lao Street. Cholon naturally has some of the best Chinese restaurants in town. Most menus have English translations. Some of the more off-the-beaten-track options are for the adventurous eater. You never have to wear jacket, though in some places you might want to look a little hip. What makes a place popular and profitable is if it is frequented by expats or international travelers. You will hear the same recommendations over and over again, because you have to be Vietnamese to feel comfortable going to one of the more local authentic places. Most places are open for lunch and dinner and close in between (unless they are cafés). The whole town virtually shuts down between 11:30 and 1 PM.

District 1

$$$$ ✕ **Camargue.** This is perhaps the most romantic and tasteful setting
★ in all of Saigon. What was once an ambience-driven establishment with decent fare has become Saigon's most exciting culinary forum for the eclectic melding of East and West. Try the pan-roasted sea bass on a bed of wasabi mashed potatoes or the tamarind-glazed crab cake. ⊠ *16 Cao Ba Quat,* ☎ *08/823–3148. Reservations essential. AE, DC, MC, V. No lunch.*

$$$$ ✕ **Le Caprice.** Stodgy but run like a Swiss timepiece, Saigon's expat elite enjoys unoriginal but fine French cuisine, passé but well-maintained hotel decor and a beautiful view of the Saigon River. If you don't actually get around to eating here, it's worth stopping by to have a drink and take in the view. ⊠ *The Landmark Building, 5B Ton Duc Thang St., 15th floor,* ☎ *08/822–8337. AE, DC, MC, V.*

$$$$ ✕ **Sekitei Japanese Restaurant.** The fresh fish flown in daily from Japan accounts for the what is perhaps the best sushi in Vietnam. Chefs Kori and Alex Ny also serve well-executed regional Japanese cuisine, such as a wonderful shiitake-and-chicken custard. Service is excellent and attentive, and the individual dining areas are romantic. ⊠ *188 Nam Ky Nghia, District 3,* ☎ *08/8251110. AE, DC, MC, V.*

$$$ ✕ **Augustin.** Small, intimate and filled with comfortably solo expats reading the newspaper at the bar, Augustin serves tasty French bistro food to a predominantly international crowd. ⊠ *10 Nguyen Thiep,* ☎ *08/829-2941. AE, DC, MC, V. No lunch Sun.*

$$$ ✕ **Blue Ginger.** In an elegant setting with traditional music shows at night, Blue Ginger serves excellent Vietnamese cuisine to its international clientele. ⊠ *37 Ky Khoi Nghia, District 1,* ☎ *08/829–8676. AE, DC, MC, V.*

$$$ ✕ **Lemongrass.** A local expat and tourist favorite, Lemongrass serves
★ excellent Vietnamese food in a French-bistro ambiance. Almost everything on the short menu is delicious, but the spicy mixed-seafood soup deserves special praise. ⊠ *4 Nguyen Thiep,* ☎ *08/822–0496. AE, DC, MC, V. No lunch.*

$$$ ✕ **Liberty.** This spot combines a great Vietnamese menu (though pricier Chinese and Western menus are also available) with a kind of "Star Search" live-entertainment ambience that is definitely worth a visit, if only for the kitsch of it. ✉ *80 Dong Khoi St.,* ☎ *829–9820. AE, DC, MC, V.*

$$$ ✗ **Marine Club Restaurant.** Although more of a happening nightspot than a food mecca, Marine Club boasts the only wood-burning pizza oven in Saigon. Saigon's expat elite gathers here for the great piano bar/nautical paraphernalia ambience and the hip and friendly management. Everyone should feel welcome, however. ✉ *17A4 Le Thanh Ton St.,* ☎ *08/829–2249. AE, DC, MC, V.*

$$$ ✗ **Spices.** This new exotic Malaysian restaurant is getting rave reviews from other fine dining competition in Saigon. The dry chicken curry in banana leaves is excellent, as is a particularly delicate wonton soup. ✉ *Hai Van Nam Hotel, 132 Ham Nghi St., District 1,* ☎ *08/821–1687. No credit cards.*

$$$ ✗ **Vietnam House.** Very popular among travelers and expats, Vietnam House serves a wide selection of hearty noodle dishes and other Vietnamese standards in a glossy Eurasian dining room. It also offers live traditional music performances every night upstairs. ✉ *93–95 Dong Khoi St.,* ☎ *08/829–1623. AE, MC, V.*

$$ ✗ **Café Mogambo.** Run by an American expat and his Vietnamese wife, Mogambo feeds those homesick for a good, inexpensive American meal. ✉ *20 Bis Thi Sach St.,* ☎ *08/825–1311.*

$$ ✗ **Restaurant 13.** This local and expat hangout serves delicious traditional local fare in a no-nonsense setting. ✉ *11–13–15–17 Ngo Duc Ke St.,* ☎ *08/829–1417. No credit cards.*

$$ ✗ **Sapa.** This airy bar/restaurant caters to expats who come for a bacon-and-egg cholesterol fix. The Vietnamese-style chicken curry is also delicious. ✉ *26 Thai Van Lung St.,* ☎ *08/829–5754.*

$ ✗ **Sawaddee.** Very well-run with simple pleasant decor, both Sawaddees serve authentic Thai dishes at very good prices. ✉ *29B Don Dat St., District 1,* ☎ *08/832–2494;* ✉ *252 De Tham, District 1,* ☎ *08/822–1402. No credit cards.*

$ ✗ **Shanti.** With outdoor seating in the heart of Saigon's budget traveler's district, the poor service is forgivable because of the very cheap and tasty Indian fare. ✉ *236 De Tham, District 1,* ☎ *08/8356154. No credit cards.*

¢ ✗ **Bodhi Tree II.** Bodhi serves delectable vegetarian delights in a quaint alley just off Pham Ngu Lao Street, next door to another unrelated vegetarian restaurant. The eggplant sauteed with garlic, the vegetable curry and the braised tofu in a clay pot are superb. Don't miss out on the fresh fruit shakes, which are like meals by themselves. ✉ *175 Pham Ngu Lao, District 1,* ☎ *08/8391545. No credit cards.*

¢ **May Ngan Phuong.** Strictly for the adventurous, this local Vietnamese eatery features delicious hole-in-the-wall dining and traditional live music performances upstairs (☞ Nightlife, *below*). Be prepared to point to whatever looks good at the next table or bring a phrase book, as this place doesn't see many foreigners. ✉ *205 Nguyen Van Gu Si,* ☎ *08/835–7322.*

Other Districts

$$ ✗ **Ngoc Suong Saigon.** Nestled amid what looks like good kindling, ★ this fire hazard on stilts serves some of the best seafood in town. The *cu ra me* (crab with a tamarind sauce) and *gai ca* (fish salad marinated in lime) are both excellent house specialties. ✉ *176/7 Le Van Sy, District 3,* ☎ *08/844–8831. No credit cards.*

$$ ✗ **Vien Hung.** A seafood lovers' pilgrimage, this off-the-beaten-track ★ riverfront establishmen not too far from the Riverside Hotel serves some of the finest and freshest seafood in Saigon. The tamarind crab is exceptional, as are the gigantic grilled prawns that are plucked from the tank when the order is placed. The monkey on a chain in the front driveway is a strange touch. Tell the taxi to take you to Am Phu Street via Cat Lai Street. ✉ *345 Ap Tay A–Xa Binh, Huyen Thu Duc,* ☎ *08/897–6450. No credit cards.*

$　✕ **Bahn Seo Dinh Cong Trang.** The picnic tables at this outdoor establishment are packed with locals who come for the famous house specialty, *ban xeo.* These great seafood pancakes, made with coconut-milk–infused batter, are stuffed with shrimp, pork, vegetables, and herbs. ✉ *46A Ding Cong Trang St. (a tiny street off Hai Ba Trung St., just before and opposite Tan Dinh Market), District 3,* ☎ *08/824–1110. No credit cards.*

$　✕ **Cary Nguyen Kiem.** The *cary ca,* tender braised chicken in an exceptional curry sauce (*cary bo* for beef), is worth the trip from Central Saigon—although it might be worth having the taxi wait. ✉ *452 Nguyen Kiem St., District Phu Nhum,* ☎ *08/845–4021. No credit cards.*

¢　✕ **Pho Hoa.** If you are not quite game for the food-stall sidewalk eating experience, this open air noodle kitchen is perhaps the next-best thing. The homemade noodles and vegetable and meat stocks are fresh and delicious. Just say "chicken," "beef," or "pork," or point to whatever looks good at the next table. ✉ *260C Pasteur, District 3,* ☎ *08/829–7943. No credit cards.*

Lodging

Luxurious and reasonably priced (though not when compared with the per capita income of the Vietnamese people) accommodations with all of the modern amenities abound in Ho Chi Minh City. It seems that at every turn, a new pleasure dome under construction has begun its glorious ascent in anticipation of droves of tourists and businessmen. Saigon Tourist, the government-run behemoth travel bureau, has a bit of a monopoly on the upscale hotels in the city. Many hotels, however, run by joint Vietnamese-foreign ventures are also responsible for Ho Chi Minh's burgeoning skyline. Many of the higher-end hotels in District 1 are on and around Le Loi and Nguyen Hue Boulevards and Dong Khoi Street. Cheap accommodations, though not as cheap as one might expect, are clustered around Pham Ngu Lao, De Tham, and Bui Vien Streets in District 1. All hotels that charge more than US$10 a night have air-conditioning.

Most Westerners prefer to stay in District 1. Although less popular, Districts 3 and 5 offer a wide range of accommodations. Find out if your hotel offers complimentary airport pickup. If you can call ahead or call when you land, it is one less headache. Despite the litany of facilities and conveniences—fax, photocopy, computer centers, health clubs, etc., not to mention cable and minibars and marble bathrooms in almost every room—hotels on the whole seem to be overstaffed with under-qualified management who, although gracious, seem ill-equipped to provide even the most basic information.

$$$$　⊞ **Hotel Continental.** Replete with history, charm, and an ideal location, the Continental is one of the more pleasant places to stay in the
★　city, if you are given to Old World hospitality. Graham Greene's *The Quiet American* was set here. Rooms are spacious, with high ceilings, and the staff is very friendly. The hotel boasts French architecture and a unique outdoor courtyard garden and dining area that date from the late 19th century. The bar, though a little dead, features a very fine cellist who plays Schumann at night. Rooms facing the street are very noisy. ✉ *Dong Khoi 132–134, District 1,* ☎ *8/829–9201,* FAX *8/829–9252. 87 rooms. 2 restaurants, lobby lounge, air-conditioning, in-room safes, minibars, no-smoking rooms, refrigerators, room service, laundry ser-*

vice and dry cleaning, concierge, business services, meeting rooms, travel services. AE, DC, MC, V.

$$$$ ⊞ **Hotel Equatorial.** The brand new four-star hotel with a sprawling lobby and luxurious rooms with all of the conveniences seems like it went up a little too quickly, and the doormen seem to scramble for the sporadic guest arrival through the front entrance. ⊠ 242 Tran Binh Trong, District 5, ☎ 08/8390000, FAX 08/8390011. 2 Restaurants, bar, café, lobby lounge, air-conditioning, minibars, refrigerators, room service, pool, health club, nightclub, piano, laundry service and dry cleaning, business services, meeting rooms, travel services, car rental, free parking. AE, DC, MC, V.

$$$$ ⊞ **New World Hotel Saigon.** A hermetically sealed mini-universe unto itself, this epic five-star hotel caters primarily to overseas businessmen and Chinese-speaking tour groups. The Hong Kong joint venture (Renaissance Hotels) is conveniently located across the street from the Ben Thanh Market. The staff is efficient and helpful and facilities are superb. ⊠ Le Lai St. 76, District 1, ☎ 8/822–8888, FAX 8/823–0710. 541 rooms. 3 restaurants, bar, lounge, air-conditioning, in-room safes, minibars, no-smoking floor, refrigerators, room service, in-room TV, pool, massage, golf-driving range, tennis court, health club, motorbikes, shop, nightclub, piano, baby-sitting, laundry service and dry cleaning, concierge, business services, meeting rooms, travel services, airport shuttle, car rental. AE, DC, MC, V.

$$$$ ⊞ **Omni Saigon Hotel.** An impeccable melding of retro (but tasteful) French elegance with just a hint of Donald Trump glitz, the Omni reeks of finishing touches. Even if you don't stay here and have a hankering for Belgian waffles and omelets, Sunday brunch is a bacchanalian frenzy. ⊠ 251 Nguyen Van Troi St. ☎ 08/844–9222, FAX 08/844–9200. 248 rooms. 3 restaurants, lounge, pub, air-conditioning, in-room safes, minibars, no-smoking rooms, refrigerators, room service, in-room TV, pool, beauty salon, massage, health club, motorbikes, shop, nightclub, piano, baby-sitting, laundry service and dry cleaning, concierge, business services, meeting rooms, travel services, airport shuttle, car rental. AE, DC, MC, V.

$$$$ ⊞ **Saigon Prince Hotel.** Perhaps the most tastefully done of all of Ho ★ Chi Minh's modern Western-style pleasure palaces, the central Prince offers rooms that are more spacious and have higher ceilings and finer finishing touches than at the more extravagant New World. The hotel staff is competent and pleasant. ⊠ 63 Nguyen Hue Boulevard, District 1, ☎ 8/822–2999, FAX 8/824–1888. 203 rooms. Dining room, sushi bar, lobby lounge, air-conditioning, in-room safes, minibars, no-smoking rooms, refrigerators, room service, hot tub, massage, steam room, health club, nightclub, laundry service and dry cleaning, concierge, business services, meeting rooms, travel services. AE, DC, MC, V.

$$$ ⊞ **Kimdo International Hotel.** The very elegant and central Kimdo has recently undergone a Saigon Tourist facelift. Rooms are spacious with high ceilings and exquisite French and Chinese antique reproductions that give it a warmth that is lacking in many of the modern luxury hotels. The staff seems somewhat novice but eager to please. ⊠ Nguyen Hue 133, District 1, ☎ 8/822–5914, FAX 8/822–5913. 135 rooms. Dining room, outdoor café, lobby lounge, air-conditioning, in-room safes, minibars, no-smoking rooms, refrigerators, room service, massage, exercise room, nightclub, laundry service and dry cleaning, concierge, business services, meeting rooms, travel services. AE, DC, MC, V.

$$$ ⊞ **Majestic Hotel.** With exquisite recent renovations of original early-★ 20th-century French architecture, the Majestic has managed to recapture a colonial mood. Rooms with high ceilings and original wooden trimmings strike a delicate balance between airy and intimate. Service standards are high for Ho Chi Minh City and the pool is delightful.

✉ *1 Dong Khoi St., District 1,* ☎ *08/829–5514,* FAX *08/829-5510, 122 rooms. 2 restaurants, outdoor café, 2 bars, lobby lounge, air-conditioning, in-room safes, minibars, no-smoking rooms, refrigerators, room service, pool, massage, health club, piano, laundry service and dry cleaning, concierge, business services, meeting rooms, travel services. AE, DC, MC, V.*

$$$ ☷ **Mercure Hotel.** The hotel's facilities combine warmth and elegance with all of the modern conveniences. Rooms are reasonably sized and neatly decorated in a luxury-utilitarian sense, though nothing original. The hotel is closer to the budget traveler's haven at Pham Ngu Lao Street than to the congregation of upscale hotels and restaurants around Le Loi and Nguyen Hue boulevards. ✉ *Tran Hung Dao 79, District 1,* ☎ *8/824–2555,* FAX *8/824–2602. 104 rooms. 2 restaurants, bar, lobby lounge, air-conditioning, in-room safes, minibars, no-smoking rooms, refrigerators, room service, massage, health club, baby-sitting, laundry service and dry cleaning, business services, meeting rooms, travel services. AE, DC, MC, V.*

$$$ **Rex Hotel.** Ablaze in Vegas-style light at the corner of Le Loi and Nguyen Hue boulevards, the Rex weds Old World luxury with oppressive '60s Chinese decor. The rooftop bar is a nice place to catch a breeze and experience Saigon's sleepless bustle from an aerial perspective. ✉ *141 Nguyen Hue Boulevard, District 1,* ☎ *08/829–2185,* FAX *08/829–1469. 207 rooms. Dining room, lobby lounge, air-conditioning, in-room safes, minibars, no-smoking rooms, refrigerators, room service, pool, beauty salon, massage, sauna, steam room, nightclub, laundry service and dry cleaning, concierge, business services, travel services. AE, DC, MC, V.*

$$$ ☷ **Sol Chancery Saigon.** The brand-new all-suites hotel run by Grupo Sol of Spain has a kind of nouveau-French facade and all the conveniences for businesspeople and tourists. The rooms, though comfortable and neat, are afflicted with low-ceilings and a pastel, no-wood, antiseptic decor typically found in hotels that go up over night. It is not too far from the War Crimes Museum and other points of interest. ✉ *196 Nguyen Thi Minh St., District 3,* ☎ *8/829–9152,* FAX *8/825–1464. 96 suites with bath. Dining room, lobby lounge, air-conditioning, in-room safes, minibars, no-smoking rooms, refrigerators, room service, massage, sauna, exercise room, laundry service and dry cleaning, concierge, business services, meeting rooms, travel services. AE, DC, MC, V.*

$$ ☷ **Arc En Ciel Hotel.** Neon-clad and a mishmash of modern, '60s, and Chinese decor, accommodations are on the higher end of utilitarian and an overall good deal—if you are interested in staying in Cholon. Arc En Ciel takes great pride in its pleasant rooftop garden café. ✉ *52–56 Tan Da, District 5* ☎ *8/855–2550,* FAX *8/855–0332. 91 rooms. Dining room, outdoor café, bars, lobby lounge, air-conditioning, in-room safes, room service, beauty salon, massage, sauna, exercise room, nightclub, laundry service and dry cleaning, concierge, business services, meeting rooms, travel services. AE, DC, MC, V.*

$$ ☷ **Asian Hotel.** In the heart of the Dong Khoi shopping district, the no-frills Asian offers small but tidy rooms. ✉ *Dong Khoi, 146–148–150* ☎ *8/829–6979,* FAX *8/829–7433. 47 rooms. Dining room, bar, lobby lounge, air-conditioning, in-room safes, minibars, room service, laundry service and dry cleaning, business services, travel services. AE, DC, MC, V.*

$$ ☷ **Dong Khanh Hotel.** In the heart of Cholon, the Dong Khanh sees mostly businessmen from Hong Kong and Taiwan. Although very little English is spoken, all are welcome. The Chinese decor is bold but elegant. ✉ *Tran Hung Dao B, 2, District 5* ☎ *8/835–2410,* FAX *8/835–2411. 81 rooms. 2 restaurants, café, bars, lobby lounge, air-conditioning,*

in-room safes, minibars, no-smoking rooms, refrigerators, room service, massage, exercise room, nightclub, laundry service and dry cleaning, business services, meeting rooms, travel services. AE, DC, MC, V.

$$ 🏨 **Hanh Long Hotel.** Located in Cholon, and not too far from District 1, the Hanh Long is another reasonable semiluxurious accommodation. Rooms are spacious and decor is simple and not entirely tasteless. ⊠ *Tran Hung Dao, 1027–1029, District 5* ☎ *8/835–0251,* 🖷 *8/835–0742. 48 rooms. Dining room, bars, lobby lounge, outdoor café, air-conditioning, in-room safes, minibars, room service, laundry service and dry cleaning, travel services. AE, DC, MC, V.*

$$ 🏨 **Mondial Hotel.** Centrally located in Colonial Saigon, the recently renovated Mondial offers small but tidy rooms and a 10%–30% discount for Fodor's travelers. The lobby's interesting decor features various large bas-relief wooden sculptures. The Skyview restaurant offers traditional Vietnamese dancing and music every night. ⊠ *109 Dong Khoi, District 1* ☎ *8/835–2410,* 🖷 *8/835–2411. 40 rooms, most with bath. Restaurant, lobby lounge, air-conditioning, in-room safes, room service, nightclub, laundry service and dry cleaning, travel services. AE, DC, MC, V.*

$$ 🏨 **Norfolk Hotel.** This super-slick establishment conveniently situated between the Ben Tranh Market and the Hotel de Ville landmarks of District 1 has a kind of futuristic white-and-chrome efficiency somewhere between that of a cruise ship and a spaceship. Impeccably neat rooms and facilities cater primarily to businessfolk. They even have a resident interpreter. Discounts of up to 25% depending on length of stay are available to Fodor's travelers. ⊠ *117 Le Thanh Ton St., District 1* ☎ *08/ 829–5368,* 🖷 *08/829–3415. 109 rooms. Restaurants, bars, sports bar, lobby lounge, air-conditioning, in-room safes, minibars, health club, massage, sauna, baby-sitting, laundry service and dry cleaning, business services, meeting rooms, travel services. AE, DC, MC, V.*

$$ 🏨 **Palace Hotel.** With recent tasteful renovations and excellent views, the Palace's facilities are pleasant and utilitarian. The front desk staff is a little unfriendly. Rates include breakfast. ⊠ *56–66 Nguyen Hue Blvd., District 1,* ☎ *8/829–2840,* 🖷 *8/824–4229. 130 rooms. Restaurant, lobby lounge, outdoor café, air-conditioning, in-room safes, minibars, room service, pool, beauty salon, massage, sauna steam room, night club, laundry service and dry cleaning, business services, meeting rooms, travel services, airport shuttle. AE, DC, MC, V.*

$$ 🏨 **Saigon Hotel.** The Saigon offers affordable, clean rooms with decent views of Central Saigon. The establishment betrays a '60s aesthetic despite modern black-lacquer furniture accents. ⊠ *41–47 Dong Du, District 1,* ☎ *8/824–4982,* 🖷 *8/829–1466. 103 rooms. Restaurant, lobby lounge, café, air-conditioning, in-room safes, minibars, room service, night club, laundry service and dry cleaning, business services, meeting rooms, airport shuttle. AE, DC, MC, V.*

$ 🏨 **Cam Mini Hotel.** In a cluster of family-run minihotels in an alley be-
★ tween Pham Ngu Lao and Bu Vien Streets, this particular establishment seems to be handled with incredible care, starting with the mandatory shoe removal at the door and the 24-hour gate post. Simple, spotless new rooms are constantly touched up with fresh coats of paint and general maintenance. The extended family and friends that run it are very friendly and helpful. ⊠ *40/31 Bui Vien St., District 1,* ☎ *08/832–4622. 12 rooms. Air-conditioning, fans, refrigerator. No credit cards.*

$ 🏨 **Prince Hotel.** Not to be confused with the Saigon Prince in District 1, this small-time royalty located in the middle of Chinatown provides cheap charm and efficiency and a very good restaurant. ⊠ *29 Chau Van Liem, District 5,* ☎ *08/855–6765,* 🖷 *08/856–1578. 25 rooms. Dining room, bar, lobby lounge, outdoor café, air-conditioning, in-room* *safes, minibars, refrigerators, room service, travel services. AE, DC, MC, V.*

$ 🏨 **Spring Hotel.** Located in a major dining and nightlife hub in District 1, this cozy new walk-up boasts squeaky-clean rooms with new moldings and fixtures that are made to look old. Some rooms have nice views and the standards have no windows at all. ⊠ *44–46 Le Thanh Ton St., District 1,* ☎ *08/829–7362,* ℻ *08/821–1383. 38 rooms. Dining room, bar, lobby lounge, air-conditioning, in-room safes, room service, travel services. AE, DC, MC, V.*

Nightlife and the Arts

Nightlife

BARS AND LOUNGES

Though it recently got its wrists slapped by local authorities for its notoriously unorthodox practices, the nomadic and ubiquitous **Apocalypse Now** (⊠ 2C Thi Sach St., District 1) is worth a look, wherever it has relocated, if for no other reason than to admire the thematic blood-covered light fixtures.

Café Latin (⊠ 25 Dong Du St., District 1), a multilevel tapas bar, has innovative decor and a fine Australian and French wine list that draws a hip crowd.

Café Mogambo (⊠ 20 Bis Thi Sach St., District 1), run by an American expat and his Vietnamese wife, is a kind of self-parodying Reno roadstop where you can get good draft beer in a kind of kitsch environment.

Frequented by Saigon's expat elite, **Marine Club** (⊠ 17A4 Le Thanh Ton St., District 1) boasts a very nice piano bar, tasteful nautical paraphernalia, and a fine wine list.

The old standby **Q Bar** (⊠ Off Dong Khoi St.), which abuts the Municipal Theater on the Hotel Caravelle side, gets rolling at around 11 PM and serves late-night snacks.

Perhaps a more civilized alternative is to take in a panoramic view of the city from one of many rooftop establishments. Worthy of note are the 5th floor verandah at the **Rex Hotel** (⊠ Khach San Ben Thanh), the **Majestic Hotel** (⊠ 1 Dong Khoi St.), the **Caprice** (⊠ Landmark Building, 513 Le Ton Duch Thang St., District 1), and the piano bar at the Saigon Prince.

NIGHTCLUBS, DANCE CLUBS, AND KARAOKE

It seems that many establishments would offer karaoke before running water. Unfortunately the omnipresent institution has made its way into every nightclub, disco, and lounge. Part of the New World Hotel complex, the upscale **Catwalk** (⊠ 76 Le Lai St., District 1) offers private karaoke dens and a moody dance floor with atmospheric dry ice as a special feature. Hotel Mercure's **Gossip** (⊠ 79 Tran Hung Dao St., District 1) is more or less the same thing.

Outdoor Activities and Sports

In and around Ho Chi Minh's urban bustle are a few spots where you can enjoy the outdoors. **Cong Vien Van Hoa Park,** located on the other side of the Reunification Palace, is a nice place for a stroll. You might be a little put off by the stares from the locals, who rarely see tourists in these parts.

Orchid farms with thousands of plants and varieties abound outside of Ho Chi Minh City. Located 15 km (9 mi) outside of the city on the Korean Highway is the **Artex Saigon Orchid Farm** (✉ 5/81 Xa Lo Vong Dai).

Golf

The 18-hole course at the **Song Be Golf Resort,** just 20 km (12 mi) outside of Ho Chi Minh City, is open, although many of the other facilities, like the hotel and restaurant complex, are still under construction.

Swimming

The **Hotel Majestic** (☞ Lodging, *above*) has a lovely pool that nonguests can use if they order something from the bar.

Shopping

Ho Chi Minh City is a good place to have casual clothes made, or to have designer clothing copied. The city is famous for its laquerware and Chinese woodcarving. Some of the fine local artists display their work at the galleries of Dong Khoi Street. Also worth noting is the availability of inexpensive compact discs, pirated in China.

Continuing its tradition as French Saigon's main shopping thoroughfare, Dong Khoi Street (formerly Rue Catinat), between Le Loi Boulevard and the river, is lined with art galleries and shops that sell jewelry, antique timepieces, lacquerware, wood carvings and other souvenirs. Ready-to-wear Western-style clothes and shoes are available near the Ben Thanh Market on Le Thanh Ton and Ly Tu Trong Streets in District 1.

Department Stores

Tax Department Store (Cua Hang Back Hoa), at the intersection of Nguyen Hue and Le Loi Boulevards, sells everything touristy and also changes traveler's checks. Catering primarily to Chinese tourists, vendors specializing in jewelry, wood carving and lacquerware share space in the enclosed **Nam Hai Yuan Shopping Plaza** (✉ 39 Nguyen Trung Truc St., District 1, ☎ 08/823–1988, ⟨FAX⟩ 08/822–8900). A major Western-style department store is under construction in the Binh Tanh District.

Markets

Local food and clothing staples are available at the **Ben Thanh Market** (Cho Ben Thanh) in the heart of District 1. **Binh Tay Market** (Cho Binh Tay), Cholon's major market, in District 6 (near District 5), also has food and clothing. For dirt-cheap pirated CDs and and assortment of electronic equipment, try **Huynh Thuc Khang Street,** between Nguyen Hue Boulevard and Pasteur Street. There is a charming open air market on **Ton That Dam Street,** between Huynh Thuc Khang Street and Ham Nghi Boulevard, that sells everything from fish and produce to plastic toys and cleaning products. On **Ham Nghi Boulevard,** between Ho Tung mau Street and Ton That Dam, you can find imported cheese, olive oil, and and just about any international food label at tiny jam-packed European-style specialty food shops on the north side of the street.

Specialty Stores

ANTIQUES

Unless you have a very skilled eye, it is very difficult to distinguish between genuine antiques and fakes, especially on Dong Khoi Street, where both abound at comparable prices. Beware of the newly restored antique timepieces that often have the face of the a Rolex from the '50s, for example, and the much cheaper hardware of a Seiko from the '70s.

FINE ART

Paintings and lacquerware by masters Do Xuan Doan, Bui Xuan Phau, Quach Dong Phuong, and Truong dinh Hao are available a wide variety of galleries. Try **Galerie Lotus** (✉ 43 Dong Khoi St., ☎ 08/829–

2695, FAX 829–8947). Fine art is also available at the national art organization **ATC** (Art Tourist Services; ⊠ 172 Nam Ky Khoi Nghia, District 3, ☎ 08/829–6833, FAX 829–8947; ⊠ 29B Dong Khoi, District 1, ☎ 08/829–2695, FAX 08/829–8947; ⊠ 2 Cong Truong Quoc St., District 3, ☎ 08/829–6833, FAX 08/829–8947).

BOOKS

Though definitely lacking in the English literature department, **Xuan Thu** (⊠ 185 Dong Khoi St., District 1), Ho Chi Minh's first foreign-language bookstore, mostly sells international newspapers and periodicals.

Quoc Su (⊠ 20 Ho Huan Nghiep St., District 1) occupies a tiny space off Dong Khoi, and not too far from the river, that is jam-packed with lots of xeroxed bootleg political literature as well as guides to cities in Southeast Asia that date back to the '20s and '30s. French translations abound, whereas English translations are scarcer.

Xunhasaba (⊠ 76E Le Thanh Ton St., District 1), the largest foreign magazine and newspaper distributor in town, doubles as a tailor shop. Nice cheap art books and some novels are also available.

CLOTHING

Linh Phuong Maison de Couture (⊠ 38 Ly Tu Trong, District 1, ☎ 08/824–2985) is very reliable for custom-made clothing for adults and children. Though the English and French-speaking staff specialize in Vietnamese and Japanese silk items, the store carries a wide variety of imported and domestic cottons. Designer clothes are copied cheaply and very well.

LACQUERWARE

In addition to the number of galleries that sell lacquerware on Dong Khoi Street and near the airport in the Phu Nhuan District on Nguyen Van Troi Street (and on its continuation, Cong Hoa Street), there is a large lacquerware distributor called **Tay Son** (⊠ 198 Bo Thi Sau St., District 3, ☎ 08/820–2524, FAX 08/820–2526).

MUSICAL INSTRUMENTS

On Ham Nghi Boulevard, between the circular intersection at the west and Nam Ky Khoi Nghia Street to the east, there are a couple of shops on the north side of the street that sell fake Fender Stratocasters and other cheap acoustic guitars that are actually not all bad.

SHOES

For ready-made, custom-made, embroidered, or leather shoes and sandals, try **Tran Van My** (⊠ 95 Le Thanh Ton St., ☎ 08/822–3041). While the cobblers are quite adept at copying other shoes, some of their own designs are very nice and simple. Quality is very high and prices are low.

WOOD CARVING

Not too far from the airport in the Phu Nhuan District on Nguyen Van Troi Street and on its continuation, Cong Hoa Street (between numbers 72 and 306), there are a number of shops where you can buy wood carvings (as well as lacquerware, rattan, etc.) and actually see the craftsmen at work.

Ho Chi Minh City A to Z

Arriving and Departing

BY BUS

Though buses are definitely the cheapest means of transportation, negotiating Ho Chi Minh's extensive bus service can be a daunting task. Reservations should be made a day in advance by your hotel concièrge or by a travel agent.

BY CAR

That foreigners are prohibited from driving, even with an internationally sanctioned driver's license, is a blessing in disguise, considering traffic conditions in Ho Chi Minh. Cars with a driver can be hired relatively cheaply. Most hotels and such high-end travel agencies as Saigon Tourist and Vietnam Tourism (☞ Travel Agencies *and* Visitor Information, *below*) rent private air-conditioned cars (Mercedes Benzes, Mazdas, Renaults) with driver for US$35 a day (under 100 km). Budget shops like Ann's Tourist provide car rental with an English-speaking driver for US$20–US$30, depending on the season.

BY PLANE

Tan Son Nhat Airport (✉ Hoang van Thu St., Tan Binh District, ☎ 08/844–3179), 7 km (4 mi) from Central Saigon, is small and navigable. Passport-control bureaucracy, depending on the officer behind the counter, is intermittently hassle-free. The airport tax upon arrival is 80,000d.

Between the Airport and Downtown: Take advantage of the complimentary hotel shuttle service provided by many of the middle to high-end hotels. If you don't, you'll be prey to eager taxi drivers. Despite the advent of taxis with meters, negotiate a price of about 75,000d–100,000d, depending on the number of passengers and pieces of luggage, before getting into the cab.

Vietnam Airlines (☎ 08/823–0692 or 08/829–9980), the infamous Vietnemese national carrier, offers direct and indirect flights all over Asia and to various international hubs. The airline offers domestic service from Ho Chin Minh to the following destinations: Buon Ma Thuot, Cantho, Dalat, Danang, Haiphong, Hanoi, Hue, Nha Trang, Phy Quoc, Pleiku. and Qui Nhon. Prices range from US$60 to US$150. It is best to book several days in advance; you can always change the reservation at representative offices all over the city.

Major international airlines with flights to and offices in Ho Chi Minh include: Air France (☎ 08/829–0982), Cathay Pacific Airways (☎ 08/822–3202), China Airlines (☎ 08/825–1387), EVA Air (☎ 08/822–3562), Japan Airlines (☎ 08/842–0601), KLM Royal Dutch Airlines (☎ 08/823–1990), Lufthansa (☎ 08/829–8529), Qantas Airways (☎ 08/829–3249), Singapore Airlines (☎ 08/231–1583), and Thai Airways International (☎ 08/822–3365).

BY TRAIN

Domestic trains connecting Ho Chi Minh City with coastal towns to the north arrive and depart from **Saigon Railway Station** (✉ 1 Nguyen Thong St., District 3, ☎ 08/823–0106), located about 1 km (½ mi) from Central Saigon. (☉ Daily 7:15–11 AM and 1–3 PM). For information and ticketing it is best to ask a travel agent to call, but you could try contacting the **ticketing office** (✉ 275 C Pham Ngu Lao St., District 1, 08/832–3537) directly. Note that Saigon Tourist does not provide any train service information. While local trains abound to places like Nha Trang, Qui Nhon, and Hue, the Reunification Express hits many of the large coastal towns north of Ho Chi Minh City, from Phan Rang-Thap all the way to Hanoi.

Getting Around

BY BOAT

For a tour of the Saigon River, boats (starting at 50,000d an hour) are available at the riverside on Ton Duch Thang Street, between Ham Nghi Street and Me Linh Square.

BY BUS

There are three excellent intercity public bus lines: Saigon–Cholon, the one you are likeliest to use, starts in Me Linh Square at the Tran Hung Dao intersection and ends up at Cholon's Binh Tay Market. Tickets, available aboard, cost 2,000d. The Mien Dong–Mien Tay line offers transportation between these two bus stations for 4,000d. The Van Thanh–Mien Tay line offers transportation between the eastern and western bus stations, respectively.

BY CAR

Renting a car with driver makes the most sense for day trips outside of Ho Chi Minh (☞ Arriving and Departing, *above*).

BY CYCLO

Although cyclos are only supposed to charge 2,000d per km, 5,000d–10,000d is a decent rate for just about any destination within the same district. Cyclo drivers, often former South Vietnamese soldiers, often speak very good English and can provide informative city tours for a small price. Bargaining is advised.

BY MOTORBIKE

Often the quickest way to get around, a ride on the back of a motorbike will usually cost 10,000d. You can also rent motorbikes from any number of cafés, restaurants, and travel agencies for daily rates that start at about 75,000d.

BY TAXI

Taxis are available in front of all the major hotels. Many cluster around the Continental Hotel, the intersection of Le Loi and Nguyen Hue near the Rex Hotel and Hotel Caravelle, along Pham Ngu Lao Street, and outside the New World Hotel, near the Ben Thanh Market intersection. Nowadays, metered taxis are more abundant than non-metered taxis.

Festival Taxi (☎ 08/845–4545) offers the cheapest metered rates. Other services include: **Vina Taxi** (☎ 08/822–2990 or 08/842–2888), **Airport Taxi** (☎ 08/844–6666), **Saigon Taxi** (☎ 08/844–8888), **Cholon Taxi** (☎ 08/842–6666), **Giadinh Taxi** (☎ 08/822–6699), and **Saigon Tourist** (☎ 08/822–2206).

Contacts and Resources

DOCTORS

Medical treatment is available at **Asia Emergency Assistance** (✉ 65 Nguyen Du St., District 1, ☎ 08/829–4740). **Cho Ray Hospital** (✉ 201B Nguyen Chi Thanh St., District 5, ☎ 08/855–8074) offers regular and 24-hour emergency treatment.

EMBASSIES AND CONSULATES

Canada (✉ 203 Dong Khoi St., District 1, ☎ 08/824–2000). **United Kingdom** (✉ 261 Dien Bien Phu St., District 3, ☎ 08/829–8433). At press time, the United States had not yet opened a consular office in Ho Chi Minh.

EMERGENCIES

Ambulance, ☎ 15. **Police,** ☎ 13.

Though American Express does not have an office at the time of writing, **lost credit cards** can be reported to Vietcom Bank (☎ 08/829–3068 or 08/822–5413).

ENGLISH-LANGUAGE BOOKSTORES

For Vietnamese–English phrase books and dictionaries, try **Xuan Thu Bookshop** (✉ 185 Dong Khoi St., District 1, ☎ 08/822–4670), open daily 7:30 AM–9 PM. Many of the traveling street vendors are well equipped with English–Vietnamese phrase books, dictionaries, travel guides, Graham Greene's *The Quiet American,* and other books on Vietnamese culture and history.

GUIDED TOURS

Guided tours of Ho Chi Minh City alone are virtually nonexistent, which is just as well. Because one does not travel to Ho Chi Minh for its sights, but rather for the whole cultural experience, the few half-day, major-sight tours, which cost around US$35–US$50, are ultimately not that worthwhile. Furthermore, though advertised as "English-speaking," guides are often unintelligible. You are better off exploring on your own.

On the other hand, do take advantage of the guided tours outside of the city. For excellent budget guided tours to the Mekong Delta, Cu Chi Tunnels, and various customized trips—some for as little as 45,000d per day with lunch included—check itineraries and schedules at the Saigon Tourist budget office or at any number of cafés and small travel agencies on Pham Ngu Lao Street (☞ Travel Agencies *and* Visitor Information, *below*).

A word about Saigon Tourist: The company operates as virtually two separate agencies for budget and standard or first-class traveling excursions. The only difference seems to be in price and the size of the bus; the main office arranges for large groups to cruise on colossal buses for five times the cost. Whereas many of the budget touring companies will cancel a trip if they have not filled their bus, Saigon Tourist's budget division boasts a no-cancellation policy (just on their end—you are permitted to cancel) whereby a minibus will depart on schedule even if you are the only passenger.

LATE-NIGHT PHARMACIES

My Chau Pharmacy comes recommended by the Travel Medical Consultancy. ✉ *389 Hai BaTrung St., District 1,* ☎ *08/822–2266.* ⊙ *Daily 7:30 AM–10 PM.*

TRAVEL AGENCIES AND VISITOR INFORMATION

Ann's Tourist. This could very well be your only tourist-information stop. The company arranges tours around both Ho Chin Minh City and the entire country; rents cars and makes flight arrangements; does visa extensions; and provides all the historical, cultural, and orientation material you could ever possibly need. Besides offerering a wide array of travel services, Ann's also has a great story behind it: After the fall of Saigon in 1975, Tony and his brother were separated from their mother and moved to the United States. Ann founded Ho Chi Minh's first privately-run travel agency with the intention of finding her sons. Reunited as a family and professional unit, Tony now runs the company full-time. ✉ *58 Ton That Tung St., District 1,* ☎ *08/833–2564,* FAX *08/832–3866.* ⊙ *Mon.–Sat. 8–6, Sun. 9–11 AM.*

Saigon Tourist. This government-run travel service owns an enormous number of luxury hotels, restaurants, and tourist attractions in and around Ho Chi Minh City. It can arrange tours and accomodations in Ho Chi Minh and throughout the country; provide maps, brochures, and basic tourist information; book domestic and international flights on Vietnam Airlines; and arrange car rental. ✉ *Main office: 49 Le Thanh Ton St., District 1,* ☎ *08/823–0100,* FAX *08/822–4987. Budget office (in Café Apricot):* ✉ *187 Pham Ngu Lao St.,* ☎ *08/835–4535.* ⊙ *Daily 7:30–6:30.*

Sinh Café Travel. Specializing in budget travel, this agency offers Vietnam's best travel deal, a US$35 open-ended ticket good for bus travel the length of the country (☞ Getting Around *in* Vietnam A to Z, *below*). ✉ *179 Pham Ngu Lao St., District 1,* ☎ *08/835–5601.*

Other offices and agencies include: **Getra Tour Company** (⊠ 86 Bui Vien St., District 1, ☎ 08/835–3021); **Thanh Thanh Travel Agency** (⊠ 205 Pham Ngu Lao St., District 1, ☎ 08/836–0205; and **Vietnam Tourism** (⊠ 234 Nam Ky Khoi Nghia St., District 3, ☎ 08/829–0776, FAX 08/ 829–0775).

SIDE TRIPS FROM HO CHI MINH CITY

Rather than negotiating Vietnam's overcrowded public transporation, it is easier and cheaper to plan day trips to the famous Cu Chi Tunnels and to the Tay Ninh area—which has one of the most important Cao Dai temples in Vietnam—through tourist cafés along Pham Ngu Lao street or any other travel agency in Ho Chi Minh (☞ Ho Chi Minh City A to Z, *above*). Though you will probably want to spend more than a day along the Mekong Delta, day trips to Mytho are available if you are pressed for time. These same agencies and cafés also organize more extensive excursions that last anywhere from 2 to 8 days.

Cu Chi Tunnels

65 km (40 mi) northwest of Saigon via Highway 22

The Cu Chi Tunnels—a 250-km (155-mi) underground network of field hospitals, command posts, living quarters, eating quarters, and trap doors—stand as a symbol of the Viet Cong's solidarity and ingenuity. First used in the late '40s to combat the French, the repurposed tunnels made it possible for the VC in the '60s to not only communicate with other distant VC enclaves but to command a sizable rural area that was in dangerous proximity (a mere 35 km) to Saigon, South Vietnam's capital.

With the Diem regime's ill-fated "strategic hamlet program" of 1963, disenchanted peasants from Cu Chi were ripe for VC takeover. In fact the stunning Tet Offensive of 1968 was masterminded and launched from the Cu Chi Tunnel nerve center, with weapons crafted by an enthusiastic assembly line of VC-controlled Cu Chi villagers. Despite extensive ground operations and sophisticated chemical warfare—and even after declaring the area a free-fire zone—American troops were incapable of controlling the area until the very end, when gratuitous B-52 bombing reduced the area to a veritable wasteland.

The guided tour of the Cu Chi Tunnels (now enlarged to accommate the droves of gringos) includes a film that documents the handiwork of "American monsters" (with, of course, no mention of South Vietnamese involvement) and an array of booby traps gleefully demonstrated by former VC soldiers/docents. If you are prone to claustrophobia, you might consider skipping the crawl through the hot, stuffy, and tight tunnels. The easiest and best way to visit is to go through one of the budget cafés (☞ Travel Agencies *and* Visitor Information *in* Ho Chi Minh City A to Z, *above*), since every agency—state-run, private, or other—does the same exact tour. A day trip, which will run you about 45,000d per person, will generally combine the tunnels with a visit to the Cao Dai Holy See in neighboring Tay Ninh.

Cao Dai Holy See

95 km (59 mi) from Central Saigon via Highway 22.

Founded in 1926 by a mystic called Ngo Minh Chieu, Caodaism is a religion based on the greatest spiritual and decorative hits of major Eastern and Western religions: Buddhism, Confucianism, Taoism, Vietnamese spiritism, Christianity, and Islam. The goal of basic human goodness is a fusion of a Mahayana Buddist code of ethics with Taoist and Confucian components. Sprinkled into the mix are elements of Roman Catholicism, the cult of ancestors, Vietnamese superstition, and over-the-top interior decoration.

Cao Dai has grown from its original 26,000 members to a present-day membership of 3 million. Meditation, the belief in God, and communicating with spiritual worlds via earthly mediums or seances are among some of its primary practices. Despite its no-holds-barred decorative tendencies, Caodaism emphasizes abstinence from luxury and sensuality, as well as vegetarianism, as a means of escaping the reincarnation cycle. Although the priesthood is strictly nonprofessional, the clergy must remain celibate.

Perhaps most importantly, the Caodaists believe that the divine revelation has undergone three iterations: God's word presented itself first through Lao Tse and other Buddhist, Confucianist, and Taoist players; among the second set of channelers were Jesus, Mohammed, Moses, Confucius, and the Buddha. Whether because of the fallibility of these human agents or because of the changing set of human needs, the Caodaists believe that divine transmission was botched. They see themselves as the third and final expression, the "Third Alliance Between God and Man." Since anyone can take part in this alliance, even Westerners like Joan of Arc, Victor Hugo, and William Shakespeare have been added to the Cao Dai roster.

The noon ceremony (others are held at 6 AM, 6 PM, and midnight) at the Cao Dai Holy See is one of the most fascinating and colorful religious vignettes you will ever be privy to as a tourist. A finely tuned hierarchical procession of men and women of all ages parades through the temple's great hall, where great painted columns, twined with carved dragons, support arched, sky blue vaults; panels of stained glass with a cosmic-eye motif punctuate the walls. Tourists are permitted to watch and take snapshots from the mezzanine. Ignore your feelings of complicity in what appears to be a collective voyeuristic sacrilege: The ceremony goes on as though you were not there.

Mekong Delta

With half of the land under cultivation, conical hats are as much a signature of the regions topography as the lush greenery. They also rank among the Mekong Delta's highest peaks. Vietnam's flat southernmost region—endless fields crisscrossed and navigated by an intricate network of canals—pulsates according to the whims of the mighty Mekong River. This single region generates enough rice to feed the nation, and then some. Considering its current status as the world's third-largest rice exporter, the food shortages that plagued the country until the collectivized farming program ended in 1986 seem unfathomable.

The region is made of sedimentary deposit buildup. A flow that ranges from 1,900 to 38,000 cubic meters per second governs every aspect of life and commerce, which are incidentally one and the same. Picturesque riverside structures built on bamboo stilts accommodate two daily tides, as well as a seasonal flooding that begins at the end of May and peaks in September. The Song Cuu Long, or River of the Nine Dragons, descends from Tibetan plateau, through China, separates Burma from Laos, skirts Thailand, incites territorial warfare as it passes through the much disputed Cambodian and Vietnamese delta regions, and spills into South China Sea. The river divides into two arteries: the Tien Giang (Upper River), which at Vinh Long splinters apart into several seaward capillaries, and Hau Giang (the Lower River), which passes through Chau Doc, Long Xuyen, and Cantho en route to the China Sea.

A historical point of contention, since the region was once a part of the Khmer Kingdom, the Khmer Rouge have attempted to exercise territorial self-entitlement through viscious attacks on civilians. The Vietnamese army responded in 1979 by attacking and overthrowing the murderous regime. Significant ethnic Chinese, Khmer, and Cham populations continue to inhabit the region.

Lodging

$$ ⊞ **Saigon Cantho Hotel.** Saigon Tourist strikes again, with the only Western-style hotel in the Mekong Delta. Whatever is lacking in hotel-management experience is made up for in effort and in comfortable rooms with brand-new facilities. ⊠ *55 Phan Dinh Phung St., Cantho City,* ☎ *071/825831 or 071/822318,* FAX *071/823288. 46 rooms. Restaurant, air-conditioning, room service, massage, sauna, laundry service and dry cleaning, business services, meeting room, travel services, car rental. MC, V.*

Mekong Delta A to Z

ARRIVING AND DEPARTING

Depending on how far into the Mekong Delta you want to travel, motorbikes and buses are the best means of transportation. The easiest way to travel is by bus. And even easier is a tour that inludes tour bus and boat travel.

A number of guided tours that travel via tour bus and boat are available through the Pham Ngu Lao café travel agencies, as well as through such more upscale (though not necessarily better) state-run agencies as Saigon Tourist. Kim's Café and Sinh Café Travel (☞ Travel Agencies *and* Visitor Information *in* Ho Chi Minh City A to Z, *above*) offer a number of tours of various lengths (anywhere from one to eight days) through the Mekong Delta. A day trip can be made to Mytho in Tien Giang Province. Most trips that are more than a day use the regional hub of Cantho as a point of departure for riverboat trips. Vinh Long lies somewhere in between.

GETTING AROUND

The most scenic parts of the Mekong Delta are accessible only by boat. They are either pre-arranged by your tour or are available for hire for as little as 22,000d an hour at every dock in every town.

CONTACTS AND RESOURCES

Tien Giang Tourism (Cong Ty Dy Lich Tien Giang; ☎ 073/872154 or 071/872105) is located on the riverfront at the intersection of Rach Gam and Trung Trac Streets.

Cantho Tourist (Cong Ty Du Lich Can Tho; ⊠ 20 Hai Ba Trung, ☎ 071/821853, FAX 071/822719).

VIETNAM A TO Z

Arriving and Departing

By Bus or Car

The incidents of highway robbery when entering from Cambodia by car are far more frequent than the very sporadic (two, to be exact) but much-talked-about Khmer Rouge attacks on foreigners. Safety in numbers makes travel by bus from the Moc Bai border (Tay Ninh Province) a less risky affair. A bus ride can cost as little as 50,000d. Air travel to and from Cambodia, however, is by far the safest (if not entirely risk-free) of all options.

By Plane

AIRPORTS

International flights into Vietnam typically connect through Bangkok, Hong Kong, and Singapore, and service Ho Chi Minh City or Hanoi. As it stands, there are no direct flights from North American into the country, and all flights require an overnight stay in the connecting city.

CARRIERS

Current International carriers with flights to Vietnam include Air France, Asiana, Cambodia Air, Cathay Pacific, China Airlines, EVA Air, Garuda Indonesia, Japan Airlines, Korean Air, KLM, Lao Aviation, Lufthansa, Malaysian Airline System, Pacific Airlines, Philippine Airlines, Singapore Airlines, Qantas, Thai International Airways, and Vietnam Airlines. The following U.S. carriers are bidding to offer direct service to Vietnam in the very near future: American, Continental, Delta, Northwest, and United.

FLYING TIME

Flight time from Los Angeles to Bangkok is approximately 20 hours. Bangkok to Ho Chi Minh City takes an hour.

By Train

Trains connect Beijing with Hanoi's "B" station (☞ Arriving and Departing *in* Hanoi, *above*) twice weekly; the trip takes 55 hours. The northeastern border crossing is at Dong Dang, located just north of Lang Son. The closest Chinese city to the Vietnamese border crossing is Nanning, the capital of the Guangxi Province.

Getting Around

By Boat

For many riverside or seaside towns in Vietnam, boat rides are naturally the main attraction. Places like the Mekong Delta are only worthwhile if you travel by boat. Even if you do not go through a travel agency or tourist office, cheap boats-for-hire will certainly find you, probably before you even get to the body of water.

By Bus

Though an extensive and dirt-cheap public bus system services every nook and cranny of the country, travel agencies and tourist offices offer more convenient, reliable, and infinitely more comfortable private tour-bus travel for most destinations. Even backpackers opt for the reasonable tourist buses.

The **Sinh Café Travel** (☞ Contacts and Resources *in* Ho Chi Minh City A to Z, *above*) has a monopoly on the private bus transport market with its US$35 open-ended ticket. A 45-seat air-conditioned bus leaves daily from each of the following stops: Ho Chi Minh City, Dalat, Nha Trang, Hoi An, and Hue. Since the service is not a tour but a private means of transportation, travelers have the flexibility to stay (or not) in any of the stops for any number of days. The buses also stop at various points of interest along the way, like the Cham Museum and Marble Mountain between Hue and Hoi An, and the Phan Rang Cham ruins between Nha Trang and Dalat. Although based in Ho Chi Minh City, Sinh Café Travel has representative desks at the affiliated hotels at Sinh Café bus stops.

By Car

Tourists are not permitted to drive in Vietnam. Cars and minibuses, with generally a non-English-speaking driver, are readily available through private and state-run travel agencies, tourist offices, and most hotels. You are charged either by the kilometer or by the day. A daily rate will run anywhere from US$30 to US$50, depending on the city, whether or not the vehicle has air-conditioning, and the make of car. It is advisable to negotiate a price in advance and to see a picture of the car before you agree. The set price should include gas.

Hertz has recently negotiated for exclusive rights for self-drive car rental. It will be a while before this actually gets implemented. As it stands, foreigners are not allowed to drive in Vietnam unless they have some sort of business visa.

By Cyclo

Cyclos (or pedicabs), the bicycle-drawn buggies that are unfortunately on the verge of becoming outlawed, provide the most entertaining and cheapest means of transportation. Although cyclo drivers are supposed to charge 2,000d a km, they definitely deserve more, since many double as informed English-speaking tour guides. Plan to pay 10,000d–25,000d per hour. While bargaining is advised, since quoted prices are often inflated, give the guys a break.

By Plane

Major transportation hubs for domestic air travel are Ho Chi Minh City, Hanoi, and Danang, but there is service to Ban Me Thuot, Dalat, Dien Bien, Haiphong, Hue, Nha Trang, Pleiku, Quy Nhon, and Vinh. Vietnam Airlines, the only state-run service, has the monopoly on most domestic air travel in Vietnam, although Pacific Airlines covers offers service to some of the same routes at comparable prices. Domestic air travel will cost you anywhere from US$60 to US$150.

By Train

Provided you can get a soft sleeper or at least a soft chair, train travel through Vietnam can be an enjoyable experience, not to mention a time-saver if you take overnight trips. Much safer, more relaxing, and more comfortable than car or bus travel, the 2,600-km railway system services coastal towns between Ho Chi Minh and Hanoi. The only drawback is that trains are rather slow. The quickest trains from Ho Chi Minh to Hanoi will take about 36 hours. Train travel is better for the 12–14 hour hops between Ho Chi Minh City and Nha Trang or Hanoi and Hue (approximately US$45 for a soft berth), for example.

Contacts and Resources

Customs and Duties

Do not attempt to bring any weapons or pornographic materials into Vietnam, as you may be detained and receive a hefty fine. It is illegal to export antique furniture and ceramics.

Dining

MEALTIMES

Lunch time is anywhere between 11:30 AM and 2 PM, and dinner is any-time after 5 PM. The Vietnamese, an industrious people, keep restaurants open all day and well into the night, even after they are supposed to close.

Guided Tours

Agencies provide English-speaking guides for US$15 a day. You will often be approached on the street by former interpreters or by cyclo drivers who want to make 50,000d for a full day's work. While this is just as viable an option as any, make sure you understand their English and conduct an informal interview before agreeing on an amount.

Health and Safety

CRIME

Pickpocketing and bag-snatching is becoming a problem in Ho Chi Minh City, and even Hanoi and Danang are beginning to see more petty crime.

For the most part, however, the greater menace to travelers comes from doggedly persistent beggars and cyclo drivers.

MEDICAL CARE

Vietnam's medical infrastructure is not up to Western standards. Hospitals and pharmacies are often undersupplied and out-of-date. Foreign insurance is very rarely accepted, and travelers should expect to pay cash immediately upon having been treated.

Language

A blend of Mon-Khmer, Tai, and Chinese, Vietnamese or *kinh* is written in a Roman-based *quoc ngu* script created by a French Jesuit scholar in the 17th century. Before that, the Vietnamese created their own system, called *nom*, which drew on the Chinese system of characters. While pronunciation of individual letters is similar to French, the language is tonally based and therefore totally foreign to the Western ear. The word *pho*, for example, pronounced one way means noodles and another way means street. A phrase book is best used as a point-and-show device.

Mail

Note that the Vietnamese government reserves the right to censor or even confiscate incoming and outgoing mail, should its contents be deemed subversive.

POSTAL RATES

Postage is based on weight. On average, postage for a postcard to the United States will cost about 5,000d, while a letter should be under 10,000d. In addition to post offices (which are generally open 6 AM–8 PM daily), many hotels and shops sell stamps.

RECEIVING MAIL

Like everything else in Vietnam, receiving mail is alternately easy and a bureaucratic nightmare. You can receive letters most efficiently at the poste-restante windows at post offices in Hanoi and Ho Chi Minh City. Bring your passport and be prepared to pay a small fee (no more than 1,000d). Picking up packages can be a little trickier; you may often be required to fill out paperwork, and sometimes you will be charged a small tax.

Money and Expenses

CURRENCY

The unit of currency is the dong, which comes in 200d, 500d, 700d, 1,000d, 2,000d, 5,000d, 10,000d, 20,000d and 50,000d notes. Since a 50,000d note is just worth less than US$5, you have to lug around quite a few notes. It's a good idea to keep plenty of 5,000d, 10,000d, and 20,000d notes handy for cyclos, cabs, and snacks. Pulling out a 50,000d note for a bowl of noodles is like paying with gold bouillon. Be careful to familiarize yourself with the 5,000d and 20,000d notes, as they are the same color. The multiple zero epidemic sometimes makes it difficult to distinguish between 5,000d and 50,000d notes.

EXCHANGING MONEY

The exchange rate at press time was around 8,300d to the Canadian dollar, 11,000d to the U.S. dollar, and 18,000d to the pound sterling. Hotels offer convenience but lousy exchange rates. VietcomBank has numerous branches nationwide and offers a decent rate. The best place to change money is in gold or jewelry shops, where American dollars are at a premium. With the exchange rate hovering just above 10,000d to the American dollar, it is better to carry dong, since vendors and taxi drivers will tend not to round in your favor.

Traveler's checks in U.S. dollars can be exchanged at banks for dollar bills or dong. Credit cards are now widely accepted at more upscale establishments, and cash advances are available at some banks.

Though not as much of a bargain as other Southeast Asian countries, Vietnam is still a relatively inexpensive destination. Upscale Western-style hotels in Ho Chi Minh City and in Hanoi command international prices, perhaps a little less. Reasonably priced minihotels are abundant in and outside of the major cities. Food is very cheap, especially it the south. Dollars and dong are accepted everywhere except in certain train stations, where they will only take dong.

Sample Costs. Unless you are at a five-star hotel, a cup of coffee in a street café will cost you as little as 2,000d; a cyclo ride will generally cost 5,000d; 2,000d for a liter of *bia hoi* (home-brewed beer); 10,000d for a bottled beer; 5,000d for a bowl of noodles from a food stall.

National Holidays
The traditional New Year, or Tet, falls in January or February depending on the lunar calendar. Although it is very picturesque, accommodations are scarce, and museums, offices, and shops tend to close for indefinite periods of time. Other national holidays include the Anniversary of the Vietnamese Communist Party (February 3); Liberation Day (April 30), commemorating the taking of Saigon by the North Vietnamese Army; Ho Chi Minh's Birthday (May 19); and National Day (September 2).

Opening and Closing Times
Small family-run shops seem to stay open indefinitely, often since living and working quarters are one and the same. Many offices, museums, and governement-run agencies are open weekdays and Saturdays in the morning from 7:30 or 8 AM until 11:30 AM and 1–5 PM in the afternoon; they are generally closed on Sundays. Cafés and restaurants are open all day and all night as are many shops. Towns tend to shut down during lunch, between 11:30 AM and 2 PM.

Passports and Visas
Tourist visas must be obtained from the **Vietnamese Embassy** (✉ 1233 20th St., Suite 501, NW, Washington, DC 20036, ☎ 202/861–0694, FAX 202/861–1297). The standard processing fee is US$65 for two-week turn-around, US$80 for a four- or five-day rush turn-around. Although the embassy is officially only supposed to grant 30-day visas (that can be extended once you are in Vietnam), persistent callers have been known to receive two-month visas.

Since the trade embargo was only recently lifted and relations are a still a little tenuous, you are still subject to the arbitrary bureaucracy, whimsy, or ignorance of passport control. There seems to be no standard procedural paperwork for visa extension or for re-entry visas. Some passport-control officers have been said to refuse to honor legitimate stamps issued in another province.

Telephones
To call Vietnam from overseas, dial the country code, 84, and then the area code, omitting the first 0.

You can make local calls for free from most hotels. Even if your hotel room doesn't have a phone, you can usually make calls from the downstairs phone. Once in a while you will be charged something like 1,000d–2,000d.

INTERNATIONAL CALLS

International phone calls cost a small fortune and require a phone that has international direct-dial, which many hotels advertise as a selling point. You can buy phone cards at the telephone companies that are usually located in or near the post offices that are to be used on special phones located in the actual phone companies themselves or in hotel lobbies. Cards are available in the following denominations: 30,000d, 60,000d, 150,000d and 300,000d. Card calls to the United States, Europe, and Canada cost about US$4 for the first minute and about US$3 for each additional minute.

When calling the States, you can dial the following **access numbers** to reach a U.S. long-distance operator: AT&T (☎ 1/201–0288); MCI (☎ 1/201–9999).

Tipping

Many cyclo drivers will ask for a "souvenir" after you have paid the agreed amount, to which you might feel compelled to answer "but I'm the tourist." What he is asking for is a tip. In some of the more upscale establishments, 10% gratuity is added to the bill. If not, and the service is good, you might consider 5%–10%. As you go further north, however, some goverment-run hotel employes will not even accept tips.

Visitor Information

There is no official source of tourist info abroad, but you might try calling the embassy. Or, to get the latest tips on where to eat, dance, drink, and tour in Vietnam, pick up a copy of *Destination Vietnam* before you leave the States. There are also a couple of business magazines available internationally, such as *The Vietnam Business Journal,* that make recommendations on places to eat, etc. The local papers provide slanted news coverage with little emphasis on the arts or on leisure.

In Vietnam, privately owned travel agencies and budget tourist offices run out of café generally offer the best information and the lowest prices. Most every city and/or province also has a state-run tourist office that does everthing from booking trains, planes and cars to operating guided tours to extending visas. These state-run agencies are often pricey, slow, and not that helpful, but in some smaller provinces, they are often the only game in town. Hotels, big and small, are often affiliated with a state-run or private agency or operate their own excursions and travel services.

When to Go

In the north (above the 18th parallel), the chilly, wet winter starts in November and continues through April; sweltering heat is common from May to October. The Central Highlands are cool year round and dry from December to March. Along the central coast, the northeast monsoon brings rain from December to February; dry heat is the norm from June to October. In the subequatorial south, the wet season brings sporadic showers, usually during lunchtime, and lasts from May to November; the dry season lasts from December to April.

CLIMATE

The following are average high and low temperatures in Hanoi.

Jan.	66F	19C	May	84F	29C	Sept.	82F	28C
	54	12		72	22		68	20
Feb.	66F	19C	June	88F	31C	Oct.	81F	27C
	55	13		73	23		68	20
Mar.	70F	21C	July	86F	30C	Nov.	75F	24C
	59	15		73	23		63	17
Apr.	77F	25C	Aug.	84F	29C	Dec.	70F	21C
	66	19		73	23		59	15

The following are average highs and lows in Ho Chi Minh City.

Jan.	84F	29C	**May**	88F	31C	**Sept.**	82F	28C
	68	20		75	24		73	23
Feb.	86F	30C	**June**	84F	29C	**Oct.**	82F	28C
	70	21		73	23		72	22
Mar.	88F	31C	**July**	82F	28C	**Nov.**	82F	28C
	72	22		73	23		70	21
Apr.	90F	32C	**Aug.**	82F	28C	**Dec.**	82F	28C
	75	24		73	23		68	20

8 Other Destinations

Pagodas in Burma, Khymer sanctuaries in Cambodia, ancient Buddhist temples in Laos, and tropical forests in Brunei are begging to be rediscovered. Closed to visitors for decades, these countries are now opening their frontiers. Untainted, as yet, by mass tourism, their peoples greet outsiders with a natural warmth and hospitality.

By Nigel Fisher

THIS CHAPTER COVERS FOUR COUNTRIES that are, as yet, secondary destinations on most Southeast Asian itineraries. Brunei is a small nation tucked between the two provinces of Malaysia on the island of Borneo. Because the country doesn't need foreigners' hard currency and generally disdains foreign values and customs, tourism is not a highly developed industry, although recently Brunei has been promoting ecotourism with trips to the interior.

Cambodia, Laos, and Burma (now officially called Myanmar) are opening themselves up to international trade and tourism. Many tour companies offer trips covering these countries singly or in combination, but you can also travel independently. It's much easier than you would think, and so long as you travel within secure areas, reasonably safe. (Ongoing banditry and guerrilla warfare make some towns and provinces dangerous, however.) Locals are not yet inured to countless visiting foreigners and, hence, volunteer assistance. Moreover, because these countries have yet to have their hospitality commercialized and caught up in the techno-consumerism of the late 20th century, you have the chance to experience the best of Southeast Asia's traditions and cultures. The easiest way into any of these countries is through Bangkok.

Dining

Price categories throughout the chapter are based on the following ranges (as a number of the countries covered have instable currencies, prices are quoted in dollars):

CATEGORY	BRUNEI	BURMA, CAMBODIA, LAOS*
$$$$	over US$30	over US$20
$$$	US$20–US$30	US$10–US$20
$$	US$8–US$20	US$4–US$10
$	under US$8	under US$4

*per person for a three-course dinner, excluding tax, service, and drinks.

Lodging

Price categories throughout the chapter are based on the following ranges (as a number of the countries covered have instable currencies, prices are quoted in dollars):

CATEGORY	BRUNEI	BURMA, CAMBODIA, LAOS*
$$$$	over US$115	over US$160
$$$	US$90–US$115	US$100–US$160
$$	US$60–US$90	US$60–US$100
$	US$20–US$60	US$20–US$160
¢	under US$20	under US$20

*for a standard double room in high season, excluding service charge and tax.

BRUNEI

Nestled between Sabah and Sarawak on the island of Borneo is a tiny nation different from any other in Southeast Asia. Since 1929, when oil was discovered off its shores, the sultanate of Brunei Darussalam—no larger than the state of Delaware and with a population of only 245,000—has developed into one of the richest countries in the world. While Brunei shares with its neighbors a blend of Malay and Muslim traditions, a tropical climate, and a jungle terrain, its people enjoy a standard of living unmatched except by that in pre-invasion Kuwait.

In the 16th century, Brunei dominated an empire reaching as far north as Manila, but the nobility was cruel and unpopular, and its power was gradually eroded by internal politics and revolts. Partly to protect the primitive tribes of the interior—and partly to exploit the weakness of the Brunei throne—the first British White Rajah, James Brooke, took over the region in 1839. Brunei became a British protectorate in 1888, and the money started flowing when the oil did, about 40 years later. Britain helped quell a rebellion against the sultanate in 1962; political stability followed, and Brunei was granted full independence in 1984.

Brunei's 29th sultan has ruled since 1967, when his father abdicated. Like his predecessors, he takes seriously his role as a guardian of Islamic values. For instance, he mandated whippings for criminals convicted of crimes ranging from vandalism to rape. His fabulous personal fortune (estimated at $40 billion and compounding rapidly) also makes him a major player in global politics: His US$10 million contribution to the Nicaraguan rebels linked his name with the Iran-Contra arms scandal. Bragging about his extravagance—his passion for polo ponies, Italian sports cars, and London fashions—is a national pastime. His extravagent 50th birthday celebrations included hiring Michael Jackson to perform; Whitney Houston did the singing honors at the wedding of his daughter. He is famous also for his beneficence. His government uses oil revenues to finance free public education, health care, and cultural programs. And his business and real-estate investments abroad have ensured that Brunei's prosperity will continue long after its oil and gas are exhausted.

Great Itinerary

A quick overview of Brunei may be gleaned with a full day in **Bandar Seri Begawan** (BSB), a modern capital where visitors can be comfortably accommodated. The city, situated on a wide, lovely river, and the Kampung Ayer (water village), where many of its citizens dwell in houses built on stilts, are well worth a stop.

The nation's interior may also be of interest to those looking for adventure and undisturbed wilderness. More than 80% of the country is forest, mostly primary rain forest dominated by giant dipterocarp trees, with eagles, ospreys, bears, wildcats, bats, and monkeys of all kinds—plus ants, snakes, and some of the other less attractive jungle dwellers. For trips into the interior, you should plan on at least another three days.

Bandar Seri Begawan

Unlike most Asian cities, where imposing modern offices and hotels dominate the skyline, Brunei's capital city has a traditional look. Its buildings are appealing and well landscaped, but few are more than six stories tall. This low profile makes the mosque's stately minarets and huge golden dome—the first thing you see as you drive into Bandar Seri Begawan—all the more impressive. You can easily walk to the main attractions of this clean little city in a day: most are near the mosque in the central district. The sultan's palace and several fine museums are short distances from the central district.

★ The **Sultan Omar Ali Saifuddin Mosque** may be the most beautiful in Southeast Asia. This superb example of modern Islamic architecture was built in 1959 of imported white marble, gold mosaic, and stained glass—all made possible by petrodollars. The exterior is constructed of granite from Hong Kong, the interior is covered with marble from Italy, the chandeliers come from England, and prayer rugs were brought from Persia. Be sure to take the elevator up the 145-foot minaret for the best view of the city. The mosque's beauty is further enhanced by being partly surrounded by a lagoon, where a religious stone boat called the **Mahaligal** floats year-round, as elegant and ornate as the mosque itself. ⊠ *Jln. Elizabeth II and Jln. Stoney.* ☉ *Public viewing: Sat.–Wed. 8–noon and 1:30–4:30, Fri. 4:30–5:30.*

Across from the mosque on Jalan Elizabeth II, note the mosaic mural on the facade of the **Language and Literature Bureau,** depicting scenes from village life. Walk away from the mosque to Jalan Sultan, where a left turn will take you past **Parliament House,** a gilted and tiled building now used mainly for ceremonial purposes, and a new mosque.

Backtrack from Parliament House on Jalan Sultan and turn left toward the river on Jalan Cator. Along the riverbank here is the town market, where women come daily to buy and sell fresh produce and other necessities. Merchandise is spread on mats on the ground, and everybody bargains. Walking along the riverfront, you'll come to Jalan Residency and the **Brunei Arts and Handicrafts Centre.** The eight-story building, shaped like the scabbard of a kris, contains workshops for silversmithing, brassmaking, weaving, and basketware. The silver goods—including such oddities as miniature cannons and boats—are exquisitely made. Crafts are for sale in the showroom, but prices are steep. ☎ *02/ 440676.* ☉ *Sat.–Thurs. 7:45–12:15 and 1:30–4:30.*

On the river near the Brunei Hotel, you can hop on a local water bus for B$1 or board a boat for a tour (☞ *Getting Around, below*) of the **Kampung Ayer,** the water communities on the far side of the river. More than a third of the city's population lives in modern homes built on stilts in these river communities, actually 28 separate kampungs linked by concrete-and-wood bridges and by systems for water, electricity, and sewage. Schools, clinics, and small mosques stand among the houses, all of which all bristle with TV antennae. Such artisans as boatbuilders, weavers, and brassworkers earn their living in these communities, but most residents commute by water taxi or private boat to work on terra firma. And while most women shop at the market across the river, you'll still see the older generation in paddleboats on the water selling food and household goods.

The **Sultan's Palace** (called Istana Nurul Iman, or "Palace of Righteous Light") is about 3 km (2 mi) west on Jalan Tutong. Although the palace is officially closed to the public, impromptu tours are sometimes given if you ask, and there's a three-day open house during the Hari Raya Puasa festival in late spring. Built in the shape of a Borneo longhouse at a cost of US$500 million, this is the largest and most opulent home in the world. The sultan, his first wife, and their children actually inhabit the palace, which numbers 1,788 rooms and a throne room that seats 2,000. If you can't visit the interior, drive by just to glimpse the massive arched roofs, gold domes, and expanses of imported marble. Near the palace wall is a sculpture garden, a permanent ASEAN exhibit that features modern works from neighboring countries, all based on the theme "Harmony in Diversity." Several other palaces have been newly constructed by members of the royal family, including one built by the sultan for his second wife. Be sure to ask your guide/driver to show you some of these magnificent buildings; they stand in rich contrast to the houses of Kampung Ayer.

About 6 km (4 mi) from town is the **Brunei Museum,** set on 120 acres near the river. The brassware, silver, Chinese bronzes, ivory, and gold collections are magnificent. A natural history gallery displays stuffed animals and mounted insects; another exhibit showcases ancient ceramics, traditional tools and weapons, and other artifacts of Borneo life. The museum has an entire section, sponsored by Shell Petroleum, devoted to the local oil industry. ⊠ *Kota Batu Rd.* ☉ *Sat.–Thur. 10–5.*

Adjacent to the Brunei Muesum is the relocated **Churchill Memorial.** The late sultan, educated at Sandhurst in Britain, revered Winston Churchill and built this memorial to instill the statesman's values in the children of Brunei. The museum here houses the largest collection of Churchilliana outside Britain, including a series of hats symbolizing his many roles: soldier, patriot, scholar, and polo player. Other exhibits are memorabilia from the last days of Britain's Far Eastern empire, displays and videos commemorating Brunei's independence, and documents tracing the history of its constitution. ⊠ *Kota Batu Rd.* ☉ *Sat.–Thur. 10–5.*

A building near the Churchill Museum houses the **Museum of Malay Technology,** which emphasizes native ingenuity in coppersmithing, loom weaving, hunting, fishing, and extracting juice from sugarcane. This and the Churchill Memorial are the two most interesting museums in Bandar Seri Begawan. ⊠ *Jln. Subok,* ☎ *02/444545.* ▨ *Free.* ☉ *Tues.–Sun. 9:30–5.*

Dining and Lodging

Bandar Seri Begawan is not a great place for eating out, although it has a few noteworthy restaurants. Hotel coffee shops are popular with locals as well as visitors. Restaurants close at 10:30 PM. If you enjoy low-cost hawker food, visit the open-air stalls near the Edinburgh Bridge and along the river on Jalan Kianggeh, near Jalan Pemancha.

Because Brunei is ambivalent toward tourists, accommodations are not plentiful and advance reservations are advised. Apart from the Sheraton, most hotels are plain, but clean and comfortable. All listed below have a private bath, air-conditioning, and a TV in each room.

$$$ ✕ **Deal's.** The Sheraton's formal dining room offers the only respectable European fare beyond the coffee-shop variety. In a small, personable room with Regency-style decor, the German chef serves Dover sole, U.S. prime beef, and New Zealand lamb, as well as local seafood. Recipes are simple but professionally executed. ⊠ *Sheraton Utama, Jln. Tasek,* ☎ *02/444272. AE, DC, MC, V.*

$$ ✕ **Lucky Restaurant.** In a shopping complex close to the Supreme Court, this second-floor restaurant is popular with local Chinese and expatriates. White tablecloths, lazy Susans, and bare, wood-panel walls are the extent of the decor. The cuisine is Cantonese and, for Western tastes, uses too much corn starch, but offers an array of dishes. The best choices are those made with duck—very crisp yet succulent. ⊠ *107–110 H.H. Princess Amal Shophouses, Jln. Tutong,* ☎ *02/ 220181. AE, DC, MC, V.*

$$ ✕ **Rasa Sayang.** On the fifth floor of a Central Business District office/shopping complex, the Rasa Sayang has excellent dim sum at lunchtime. The Malaysian waitresses are happy to help you select a variety of dishes, from steamed buns to barbecued ribs. For something more substantial, the fish dishes (particularly pomfret with onions and a soy-based sauce) are better than the beef. ⊠ *Top floor, Bangunan Guru 2 Melayu,* ☎ *02/223600. AE, DC, V.*

$$$$ ▦ **Sheraton Utama.** Despite the opening of the **Riverview Inn** (☎ 02/ 221900) under the sponsorship of the sultan's family, the Sheraton Utama in the Central Business District is the smartest and most professionally managed hotel in Brunei. The light fabrics and furnishings help overcome the limited sunlight from the small windows. Superior rooms, with two queen-size beds or a large king, are worth the extra B$20.

Two- and three-room suites are available; rooms overlooking the pool have the best view. Bathrooms are functional rather than luxurious, though toiletries and bathrobes are supplied. Deal's (☞ *above*) serves European cuisine. The more casual Café Melati serves a buffet breakfast, lunch, and dinner from 7 AM to 10:30 PM. On most evenings, there is a barbecue or fondue dinner served poolside. The bar is a friendly meeting place. ⊠ *Box 2203, Jln. Tasek, 1922 BSB,* ☎ *02/244272,* FAX *02/221579; U.S.,* ☎ *800/325–3535; U.K.,* ☎ *0800/353535. 166 rooms. 2 restaurants, bar, pool, exercise room, business services. AE, DC, MC, V.*

$$$ 🏨 **Ang's Hotel.** Ang's offers modest air-conditioned rooms with queen-size beds, color televisions, and en suite bathrooms. At half the room rates of the Sheraton, this hotel does not have the smartness, professionalism, or the amenities of its neighbor. The staff is polite but abrupt. The bar is a favorite watering hole for expats under contract in Brunei. ⊠ *Jln. Taser Lama, Box 49, 1900 BSB,* ☎ *02/243553,* FAX *02/227302. 80 rooms. Bar, coffee shop, dining room, pool, beauty salon. AE, DC, MC, V.*

$$$ 🏨 **Brunei Hotel.** In the heart of the central business district, this hotel has neat, clean, minimally furnished but pleasant rooms with oak trim. The Coffee Garden restaurant serves local and Western food (seafood is the best thing to order); there's usually a theme buffet in the evening. The VIP Room offers classic Cantonese fare. ⊠ *Box 50, 95 Jln. Pemancha, 1900 BSB,* ☎ *02/242372,* FAX *02/226196. 75 rooms. Restaurant. AE, DC, V.*

Shopping

The showroom at the **Brunei Arts and Handicrafts Centre** (☞ *above*) has the best selection of local work, but its prices—especially for finely worked silver—are high. Popular items include *karis* (ornamental daggers) and *kain songket,* a cloth containing gold or silver thread.

Gold jewelry (24 karat) is popular among Brunei's citizens, so goldsmiths offer a wide selection. Look through the selection at **Chin Chin Goldsmith** (⊠ 33 Jln. Sultan, ☎ 02/222893). At **Million Goldsmith and Jewelry** (⊠ Mile 1, Teck Guan Plaza, Jln. Sultan, ☎ 02/429546), you'll find interesting designs of gold necklaces, brooches, and bracelets.

The **Plaza Abdul Razak** (⊠ Jln. Tutong, ☎ 41536) shopping complex is anchored by the Yaohan department store. Less than half a mile from the city center, the high-rise structure includes office units, apartments, a music center, restaurants, and shops. Stores close at 9:30 PM. The most fun place to browse for an assortment of inexpensive goods is at the **open market** alongside the Kianggeh River.

Outdoor Activities and Sports

The Sheraton Utama publishes a jogger's guide, which features a 20-minute run up to Tasek Park to see the waterfall, or a 35-minute hilly route through Kampung Kianggeh. Joggers are urged to run early in the morning to avoid the heat and traffic. Also at the Sheraton is a fitness center with aerobics classes.

Brunei A to Z

Arriving and Departing

BY BOAT

You can get to Brunei from Limbang in northern Sarawak via a riverboat that takes half an hour and costs about B$14. A ferry also runs between Bandar Seri Begawan and the island of Labuan in Sabah in two hours; fare is B$20.

BY BUS

A paved road links Kuala Belait, 112 km (70 mi) southwest of Bandar Seri Begawan, with the Malaysian town of Miri in Sarawak. It's slow going and involves two river crossings by ferry and two immigration-control stops. Shared taxis charge about B$35 for the ride. Brunei's **Sharikat Berlima Belait** runs daily buses on this route; the fare is B$16.

BY PLANE

Brunei International Airport, near Bandar Seri Begawan, is sleek, modern, and efficient. Departing passengers pay an airport tax of B$12 on international flights, B$5 to Singapore or Malaysia.

Between the Airport and City Center. The only way to get downtown from the airport is by taxi. Taxis are unmetered, but the fare is fixed at B$20. If you have a flight arriving after 8 PM, be sure to order your taxi beforehand. Taxis are never plentiful even during the day, and many stop working early in the evening.

The national carrier, **Royal Brunei Airlines** (☎ 02/242222), has routes throughout Southeast Asia. Malaysia Airlines flies from Kuching in Sarawak and Kota Kinabalu in Sabah, though not daily. Singapore Airlines, Cathay Pacific, and Thai Airways International also serve Brunei.

Getting Around

BY BOAT

Water taxis—small, open boats—to the Kampung Ayer areas are available near the market off Jalan Sungai Kianggeh. Bargain with drivers for fares; a complete hour tour should cost between B$20 and B$25.

BY BUS

Bus service in Bandar Seri Begawan is erratic. Buses leave only when full, so there may be a long wait. The central bus terminal is behind the Brunei Hotel on Jalan Pemancha—also where you catch the bus to Seria.

BY CAR

Two rental agencies have counters at the airport: **Avis** (☎ 02/242284); **National** (☎ 02/224921).

BY TAXI

You can hire a private taxi for sightseeing, but drivers often speak little English. Hotels will arrange such service for B$45 an hour, often with a minimum of three hours.

Contacts and Resources

EMERGENCIES

Ambulance, ☎ 02/222366. **Fire,** ☎ 02/222555. **Police,** ☎ 02/222333.

GUIDED TOURS

Sunshine Borneo Tours and Travel (✉ Box 2612, No. 205, 1st floor, Bangunan Awang Mohd Yussuf Shopping Complex, 2682 Jln. Tutong, ☎ 02/441790) organizes tours of the capital, as well as river trips and tours to Iban longhouses both in Brunei and across the border in Sarawak. The enthusiastic owner, Cany, will customize a tour to meet your interests.

LANGUAGE

The official language is Bahasa Malaysia, but English and the Hokkien Chinese dialect are widely spoken.

MONEY AND EXPENSES

Currency. Brunei dollars are issued in notes of B$1, B$5, B$10, B$50, B$100, B$500, and B$1,000. Coins come in denominations of 1, 5, 10, 20, and 50 cents.

Exchanging Money. The Brunei dollar is at par with the Singapore dollar, which also circulates in Brunei. At press time the exchange rate was B$1.50 to the U.S. dollar, B$2.25 to the pound sterling.

What It Will Cost. Breakfast of toast, eggs, and coffee, B$10–B$15; taxi ride, B$4 for first mile, B$2 per mile thereafter; double room, B$230 expensive, B$100–B$145 moderate.

PASSPORTS AND VISAS

Canadian, U.K., and U.S. citizens require a visa only for stays of more than two weeks. Note that visas cannot be obtained in Sabah or Sarawak. To apply, contact the **Embassy of Brunei Darussalam** (✉ Consular Section, Watergate, Suite 300, 2600 Virginia Ave. NW, Washington, DC 20037, ☎ 202/342–0159; ✉ 49 Cromwell Rd., London SW7 ZED, ☎ 0171/581–0521). The **Brunei Permanent Mission to the United Nations** (✉ 866 UN Plaza, Room 248, New York, NY 10017, ☎ 212/838–1600) can also process requests.

TELEPHONES

To call Brunei from overseas, dial the country code, 673, and then the area code, omitting the first 0. The area code for Bandar Seri Begawan is 02.

Pay phones use phone cards in values of B$10, B$20, B$50, and B$100, on sale at Telecom offices and post offices. You can direct-dial international calls from the major hotels or from the Central Telegraph Office on Jalan Sultan.

TIPPING

Hotel porters should be given B$1 per bag. The driver of a hired car appreciates a B$10 for a morning's work, but there is no need to tip the taxi driver.

VISITOR INFORMATION

Brunei has no official agency to handle visitors. Your best bet is to inquire at the local offices of Brunei's national airline, Royal Brunei Airlines. In Brunei, the **Economic Development Board** (✉ State Secretariat Office, BSB, ☎ 02/231794) can provide general information, and a booth at the airport distributes city maps and hotel brochures.

WHEN TO GO

Brunei lies between 4° and 6° north of the equator, and temperatures don't vary much from one season to the next: it is hot and humid year-round, and the equatorial sun is fierce. (The annual mean temperature is 80°F.) Though sudden, brief rainstorms are prevalent throughout the year (particularly November–May), the wettest months are December and January. Even during the monsoon season, be prepared for blasts of heat between downpours. There is no peak tourist season.

Festivals and Seasonal Events. The widely observed Muslim religious holidays vary according to the Islamic calendar. Chinese, Hindu, and Christian holidays are also observed, some on fixed dates. *See* Festivals and Seasonal Events *in* Malaysia A to Z for common celebrations; in addition, Brunei celebrates National Day (Feb. 23), the anniversary of the Royal Brunei Army (May 31), and the sultan's birthday (July 15).

BURMA (MYANMAR)

The tale of modern Burma is a sad one. When it achieved independence from Great Britain in 1948, it was the rice bowl of Asia and potentially the richest country in the region. But the only person who had the strength of leadership and nobility of purpose to unite the independent-minded ethnic groups and establish a democracy was Aung

San, and he was assassinated a few months before Burma was granted full sovereignty. Political squabbling, ethnic fighting, and communist terrorism became the rule, and in 1962 a military coup was engineered by General Ne Win, who has since presided over flagrant abuses of human rights and the disintegration of the country's economy; although he resigned as president in 1982, his influence is still felt.

Popular resolve against the one-party rule of the Burmese Socialist Programme Party (BSPP), chaired by Ne Win, boiled over in 1988, and democratic demonstrations swept through the country. The government butchered the demonstrators—approximately 12,000 people were killed or disappeared—and the military seized absolute power on September 18, 1988. Since then the State Law and Order Restoration Council (SLORC), a 19-man military junta, has ruled by terror. Surprisingly, SLORC permitted elections in 1990, expecting that their party would win. They totally miscalculated. Despite the fact that the two leaders of the National League for Democracy (NLD), Aung San Suu Kyi and U Tin U, had been under detention since July 1989, the NLD won 82% of the 13 million votes cast. As many expected, SLORC refused to hand over the reigns of power. SLORC tightened its grip, imprisoning any opposition, many of whom "just disappear." Charles Humana, who produces a widely accepted index of human rights, has given Burma the lowest human-rights index of any country in the world.

In an attempt to rescue the failing economy, SLORC has embarked on a program to open the country to foreign investment and tourism. Visas have become easier to obtain, travelers no longer have to exchange a daily minimum amount of money on arrival, and foreigners are no longer required to stay at government-run hotels. Better yet, independent travel is now possible, though most travelers arrange transport and accommodation through a tour operator. In 1996, 40,000 tourists are estimated to have entered the country. The government hopes to increase that figure to half a million in the next five years.

Herein lies your dilemma: By visiting Burma (now officially renamed Myanmar), are you contributing to the coffers of SLORC and their oppression of the people, or are you helping to create social and political change? Aung San Suu Kyi, who won the Nobel Peace Prize for her fight to win her people's freedom and is the most loved person in Burma, argues that foreign money (and that includes tourist dollars) should not be spent in Burma while SLORC denies freedom and human rights to the people. Others argue that so long as tourists purchase goods and services from the people and not from government-owned facilities, tourism may assist the Burmese in eventually overthrowing the SLORC dictatorship.

Pleasures and Pastimes

ARCHITECTURE

Burma is a land of pagodas—although "pagoda" is actually an English term and slightly misleading. The generic Burmese term for a Buddhist holy structure is *paya,* of which there are two types, the *zedi* and the *pahto.*

Pahto is usually translated into English as temple or shrine. Temple is the word most frequently used, but shrine is a better description: monks are not necessarily in attendance, nor, more importantly, do Buddhist believers *worship* in the Western sense. Rather, they go to a shrine to contemplate and meditate, seeking inspiration from the Buddha as a spiritual mentor.

The other form of pagoda is the zedi (also known as a chedi or a stupa), a solid, bell-shaped structure raised on a series of terraces and crowned by a golden shape called a *hti*. These commemorative structures house important Buddhist relics, either objects taken from the Buddha or such holy materials as Buddhist images or prayer tablets.

Bear in mind that a paya can have both pahtos and zedis, such as Rangoon's Schwedagon Pagoda, where the famous mon zedi has numerous pahtos off to the side as places for the devout to seek sanctuary.

Most Buddhist structures are open from dawn to dusk and free. In a few instances, such as the Shwedagon in Rangoon, foreigners are required to make a donation. An entrance fee to Bagan Historical area is mandatory.

DINING

Burmese food is disappointing. It has none of the intrigue and subtleties of Thai cuisine. Rice and rice noodles are the staples. Curries—chicken, meat, or fish—fried in peanut oil are the usual substantive dishes. Unfortunately, these do not use all the herbs and spices found in Indian curries. At best, Burmese curries limit themselves to garlic, onions, tomatoes, tumeric, ginger, and chili peppers. Offsetting the oiliness of the curries, every meal comes with a bowl of clear soup. If you don't like curries, seafood or simple fried chicken are your best, if not only, bets.

In Rangoon and Mandalay, Western food is served in hotel dining rooms; in the smarter restaurants, Chinese recipes and perhaps a few Western dishes will be on the menu. In the larger provincial capitals and resorts, your only alternative to Burmese cooking is Chinese; in smaller towns, you won't have that choice.

LODGING

Only in the last couple of years has the nation opened its doors to tourists. Consequently, hotels are few and far between, and what accommodation is available is limited and often ugly. The former Soviet Union built the Inle Lake in Rangoon and the Novotel in Mandalay. Both were disasters—dreary inside and prison-like on the outside; both have revamped their interiors, but the exteriors remain eyesores. The only first-class hotel in the entire country is the Strand in Rangoon—and it costs a bundle—and the only hotel of old colonial charm is Candacraig (Thirimyaing) in Maymyo, 67 km (41 mi) east of Mandalay.

In Rangoon, a few hotels have recently been built and more are under construction. Mandalay and Pagan are also slated to have new hotels by 2000. In other areas, you'll find hotels of a very bare-bones nature, with not much more than a bed, ceiling fan, and basic plumbing, including private bathrooms. Surprisingly, perhaps because they are limited in number, these basic hotels are expensive for what you get—about $35 a night. Even the cheapest accommodation in Rangoon, where the bathroom is shared, runs $20 a night; in the country, a room with a cot, mosquito net, and a washbasin can run $15.

THE PEOPLE

The greatest pleasure in Burma is meeting the people—excluding the military, of course. The Burmese are exceedingly congenial, polite, and generous in a way reminiscent of the Thai attitude toward visitors the 1950s. They are eager to talk, to help, and to welcome you to their country. They give unstintingly of their warm sincerity—often all that they have to give, considering the average per capita income of around $100 a year. Most are devout Buddhists who take their religion seriously by practicing good thoughts and deeds every day.

SHOPPING

One would suspect that Burma would offer much for the shopper, but the range of goods is limited. While crafts are least expensive at the place where they are made, in Rangoon you can find lacquerware, tables, trays, and chests from Pagan; Shan shoulder bags, many from the Inle Lake region; and wooden chests made throughout Burma. Precious gems, for which Burma is known, are really no cheaper than what you can find in Thailand, and unless you are a gemologist, the risk of being taken is equally as great.

Great Itinerary

Moving swiftly, you can cover the major sights in Rangoon, Mandalay, Pagan, and Inle Lake in little over a week. This certainly does not do justice to all the sights or give much of a chance to take in the depth of Burma's fascination, but it will be sufficient to whet your appetite. Our coverage of Burma includes only these most popular destinations, all of which have a tourist infrastructure sufficient to satisfy the demands of the international traveler. For those willing to rough it a bit, Burma has a lot more to offer, from beaches at Ngapali and Chaung Tha to the architectural wonders of Mrauk U.

IF YOU HAVE 10 DAYS

On day one, fly into **Rangoon** from Thailand in the morning; in the afternoon, stroll around downtown, visit the National Museum, and shop at Bogyoke Aung San Market. Take dinner at a restaurant on Kandawgyi Lake and catch a "cultural show." Start the next day at the Shwedagon Pagoda, and in the afternoon, take a tour of the outer townships to get a sense of the expanding city and to visit small pagodas.

On the morning of the third day, fly to **Pagan.** Spend that afternoon, all of the next day, and the following morning visiting a few of the 2,000 monuments in the Pagan Architectural Zone. In the afternoon of the fifth day, fly or go by road to **Mandalay.** For the sixth day, visit the pagodas at the foot of Mandalay Hill and then tour the hills in **Sagaing,** visiting the monasteries and taking in the breathtaking views. On the way back, stop at U Bien Bridge in **Amarapura.** For the seventh day take the ferry up the Ayeyarwady (Irrawaddy) to **Mingun** for its monuments and the world's largest uncracked bell. Return to Mandalay for the afternoon; pay homage to the Buddha at the Mahamuni Pagoda, and visit Shwe Kyaung palace.

If you have two more days in Burma, fly out of Mandalay to **Inle Lake** to relax and enjoy the serenity of the mountains, the lake, and the people. Leave on the morning of the 10th day for Bangkok, changing planes in Rangoon.

Rangoon (Yangon)

Only some 4 million people live in the Burmese capital, Rangoon (in Burmese, Yangon, meaning "end of strife," a title given to the city in 1755 by King Alaungpaya after defeating enemy forces in the south), and yet it spreads over a wide expanse that includes teak forests, gardens, wide boulevards, lakes, parks, and pagodas. The result is an open city, a complete contrast to crowded and congested Bangkok. Turn a blind eye toward the SLORC soldiers, the economic despair, and the crumbling buildings, and Rangoon could be an attractive place to live.

Rangoon is relatively new as a capital. The British chose it in 1885 for its proximity to the sea, just 32 km (20 mi) away, and its natural defensive position: the Rangoon River encases the city on its west and south side, and the Pazundaung Canal, which flows south into the Rangoon River, flanks the east side. The heart of the city clusters close to the banks of the river. Here colonial architecture is being dwarfed by the recent building boom created by foreign investment. Since 1992, when the capitalist-minded General Than Shwe became the head of

SLORC, foreign investment and imports have been flooding into the city. People still move at a slow pace, but the traffic is building. One wonders if Rangoon is to go the same way as other Asian cities, bounding into the 21st century with neon lights, traffic jams, and concrete high-rises.

Downtown is built on a grid system: minor north–south streets are numbered, while the other streets often have both a pre- and post-independence name. Expect to be confused. The city is divided into townships. Aside from the downtown area, the most important townships are Dagon (with the Shwedagon Pagoda, several embassies, and a couple of hotels) and, slightly farther out, Bahan (with more hotels).

Your downtown landmark should be the **Golden Sule Pagoda** (Sule Paya). Its octagonal shape rises 150 feet above the surrounding shops, and the central stupa is said to contain a hair of the Buddha. The complex has been rebuilt so often that no one truly knows when it was begun, but some suggest it may have been as long as 2,000 years ago. ▨ *Free.* ☉ *Dawn–dusk.*

★ The best-known and most venerated of all the country's pagodas is the **Shwedagon Pagoda.** It was first erected 2,500 years ago to house eight sacred hairs of the Buddha, so legend claims. Situated northwest of the city center on Singuttara Hill, the golden stupa rises to 320 feet to dominate the city's skyline. Its spiritual power reaches out to all of Burma; tens of thousands of pilgrims come to pay homage each year.

When the pagoda was first built it was only 30 feet high, but successive monarchs have added to it, committing their empire's coffers to its restoration and elaboration. The dome is now covered with about 70 tons of gold, and the gilded hti on top is studded with rubies, sapphires, and topaz. The gold-and-silver weather vane is decorated with 1,100 diamonds; on it is an orb encrusted with 4,350 small diamonds and crowned with a 76-carat diamond.

Entry to Shwedagon Pagoda is up one of the four stairways. Foreigners are only allowed entry from the southern entrance from Pagoda Road. (If you don't feel like walking up the stairs, elevators are available). The stairway enters the pagoda at the **Temple of the Konagama Buddha,** one of the four Buddhas that the Burmese believe preceded Guatama. From there, circle to the left around the golden stupa and pass by a religious fairyland of pavilions and shrines, sculpted images, and small stupas. Plan on at least two hours at Shwedagon, which will only allow enough time to duck in and out of the two dozen or more small shrines. A guide is strongly recommended, as otherwise you will miss many of the fascinating details and intricacies of Burmese Buddhism. ▨ *Admission.* ☉ *Daily 6 AM–10 PM.*

Just five-minutes' walk from the historic Strand Hotel, the **National Museum** contains the Mandalay regalia from Burma's last royal court and other artifacts from Burma's past. The showpiece is King Thibaw's 26-foot-high Lion's Throne, which was originally in the Royal Palace at Mandalay. Once displayed in London's Victoria and Albert Museum, it was returned to Rangoon in 1964. ✉ *Pansodan St.* ▨ *Admission.* ☉ *Mon.–Fri. 10–3.*

Rangoon's largest and liveliest market, **Bogyoke Aung San Market** (formerly known as and still often called Scott's Market) throbs with activity, and more than anywhere else in Rangoon, it is where the depressed economy and oppressive rule of SLORC can be forgotten. In its maze of covered alleys, you'll find a huge collection of crafts from all over Burma, including the Shan states and Upper Burma. There are numerous jewelry stalls: Search for **Su Yadana** (⊠ 58 West D Hall), whose owners are honest, fair, extremely helpful, and speak some English. Locals come to Bogyoke Market for dry goods, black-market items, gold, and clothes. Some stalls will change dollars at the black-market rate.

Dining and Lodging

$$ ✕ **Lone Ma Lay Restaurant.** One of several restaurants known more for its "cultural show" than its cuisine, Lone Ma Lay usually has a good repertoire of both traditional regional dances and contemporary acts. Food here is better than at most dinner-show establishments, perhaps because it has a number of Chinese dishes to supplement the Burmese. The restaurant is just up the bank from Kandawgyi Lake, so the lights dance prettily on the water and a cool breeze wafts through the open-sided dining room. ⊠ *Natmauk Rd., Kandawgyi Lake,* ☎ *01/50357. Reservations essential. No credit cards. Breakfast served. Dinner show starts about 8 PM.*

$ ✕ **Nan Yu.** Local businessmen come for lunch at this spot in the center of Rangoon. The hybrid Burmese-Chinese cooking is quite good; hot-and-sour fried prawns and fried chicken with green chili are good bets. A meal for two runs about $10, including a Mandalay beer. The decor is relatively plain, but the tables are draped in white cloths and a few photographs decorate the walls. ⊠ *81 Pansodan St.,* ☎ *01/577796. No credit cards.*

$ ✕ **Schwe Ba.** This neigborhood spot on the north side of Shwedagon Pagoda is known throughout Rangoon for good local cooking. Sit at one of the long tables (where other diners may pull up a bench and join you), and an assortment of plates will be brought by—you pay only for those dishes that you accept. Try the hingho (clear soup), fried chicken, and *hin* (curries zesty with garlic, coriander, chili peppers, and onions, and fried in peanut oil). This homey spot is recommended for intrepid travelers; tables and plates may look a little grubby, but no stomach problems have been reported. ⊠ *U Wizara Rd., Dagon Township. No phone. No credit cards.*

$$$$ ▦ **Strand Hotel.** Not only is this the best hotel in Rangoon, it is also
★ one of the best in Asia. The cost of a room for one night is exorbitant—three times the nation's annual per-capita income—but if you do treat yourself, you'll find the experience well worth the tab. The hotel was founded in 1901 by the Sarkies brothers, and it reached its international zenith in the 1920s. After Burmese independence, however, the Strand deteriorated into little more than a boardinghouse. It wasn't until the early '90s, when the property was purchased from the government and completely renovated, that the Strand returned to (or perhaps even surpassed) its former glory. One only wishes that the Sarkies' other hotel, Singapore's Raffles, had been so tastefully refurbished. You'll find all the conveniences of the late 20th century, wrapped in impeccable Edwardian sensibilities. A tie and jacket at dinner are de rigeur, and sipping a pink gin in the wood-paneled bar seems entirely appropriate. Throughout, 20-foot celings, potted palms, lazy overhead fans, and elegant wicker funishings suggest the height of colonial elegance. In the huge guest rooms—located on two floors, each with a valet on duty at all times—king-size beds rest on highly polished teak floors; spacious tile baths have separate shower and tub. The dining room is pleasantly formal, and the food is the best that you will eat in Burma. Much of the produce is imported, and there is a reasonable wine selection—choose an Australian, as that wine seems to travel better than French. The attentive staff is eager to assist you in negotiating Burma, whether you are on business or a tourist. ⊠ *92 Strand Rd.,*

☎ 01/81532, ℻ 01/89880; U.S., ☎ 800/447–7462 or 212/223–2848; U.K., ☎ 0800/282684. 32 suites. 2 restaurants, bar, room service, laundry, business services, travel services. AE, DC. MC, V.

$$$ ☎ **Inle Lake.** The Soviets built this hotel—that may acoount for its ugly facade—but the interior has been revamped. A private management team has taken over from the government, and the service, the accommodation, and the food have greatly improved. Its big drawback is its location, isolated on 38 acres near the airport and a good 9 km (6 mi) from downtown. Nonetheless, book ahead, as many tour groups stay here and the government hosts gem auctions here each year, pocketing the revenue of Burma's rich mineral resources. ⊠ 37 Kaba Aye Pagado Rd., ☎ 01/662826, ℻ 01/665537. 239 rooms. 4 restaurants, pool, 2 tennis courts, business services, meeting rooms. AE, DC, MC, V.

$$$ ☎ **Summit Parkview.** For a strictly utilitarian hotel 3 km (2 mi) from town, the Summit Parkview functions well. Its concrete curved building is a bit of an eyesore, but all is new and designed efficiently for the business traveler. The box-shaped rooms are large and everything works. Equally important, the staff is really friendly and speaks good English. ⊠ 350 Ahlone Rd., Dagon Township, ☎ 01/27966, ℻ 01/27993. 152 rooms. Restaurant, business services. AE, MC, V.

$$$ ☎ **Traders Hotel.** Under construction at press time, this is likely to be the best reasonably priced hotel in downtown Rangoon when it opens in 1997. The Traders hotels, a division of the Shangri-la group, are geared toward providing top-quality accommodation without the frills (and concommitant price tag) of a five-star hotel. This 22-story property will have all the modern facilities, including 24-hour medical services, a travel desk, and in-house movies. Four restaurants will provide Burmese, Japanese, international, Cantonese, and Italian cuisines. ⊠ Bogyoke Aung San Rd., ☎ 01/27757, ℻ 01/28226. 500 rooms. 4 restaurants, pool, health club, business services, travel services, meeting rooms. AE, MC, V.

Inle Lake

Nyaung Shwe, the main lake town, is 23 km (14 mi) southwest of Taunggyi, the capital of the Shan state. Taunggyi is 350 km (217 mi) northeast of Rangoon, a 14-hour bus trip, and 150 km (93 mi) southeast of Mandalay, an eight-hour trip.

Surrounded by mountains, Inle Lake is the most beautiful lake in Asia. Located in the Shan state, which borders Thailand, Laos, and China, it's magical and serene and often spoken of in the same breath as Kashmiri Lake. If beauty isn't attraction enough, the inhabitants add human interest. This narrow body of water—30 km (18 mi) north to south and only 8 km (5 mi) wide—supports nearly 200 villages with a total population of 150,000.

Although the lake is in the Shan state, those that live on its shores are not Shan, but a Mon people known as the **Intha** (Sons of the Lake). The Intha have developed an ingenious way of farming the lake: they weave the rubbery tubes of hyacinths and rushes into gigantic mats, then dredge fertile mud from the lake's bottom and lay on a layer of humus. This floating garden is then staked in the water near a family's home. They also fish, with a unique style that involves rowing and using a large conical net simultaneously. With one leg wrapped around the oar, an Intha fisherman is able to move through the hyacinths cluttering the lake while leaving one hand free to control the net. When the fisherman spots a shoal of fish, down goes the net, allowing him to spear dinner at his leisure.

Boats depart at about 8 AM for a five-hour tour past floating gardens, one-leg rowers, and small lakeshore communities. Most tour boats make for the village of Ywama, where once every five days there is a colorful floating market. This is the ideal day to take the tour, but you'll have to be persistent to find out which day the market is being held—the guides often claim that there is a market every day. Purchase tickets (✉ 200 kyats per person) in advance, which can be done with a private boatman or at the tourist office at the pier in Yaunghwe.

Pagan (Bagan)

450 km (279 mi) north of Rangoon. 193 km (120 mi) south of Mandalay, a four-hour drive by car or six-hour trip by local bus.

On the banks of the Ayeyarwady river at Pagan (also called Bagan) once stood the mighty Myanmar kingdom, established by King Anawrahta (1044–77), the 42nd ruler of the Pagan dynasty. Pagan was probably founded around 849, but it its Golden Age began when Anawrahta defeated his rivals, primarily the Mons from the south, and expanded his borders to include most of present day Burma. Wealth poured in. At the same time, Anawrahta introduced Theravada Buddhism with the help of Shin Arahan, a missionary monk from Thaton, the Mon capital. The king was wise enough to incorporate into the cosmic whole of Buddhism the worship of *nats* (guardians of the spirit world that were part of the traditional animistic Burmese religion).

After about two centuries of dominance, however, the Pagan dynasty began to be eaten away by corruption. The final blow came when Kublai Khan demanded that Pagan pay tribute to the great Mongol lord. Pagan's ruler, the pompous King Narathihapati (1256–87), refused, and executed the Khan's messenger. Kublai Khan's army attacked, and the Pagan royal family fled.

★ Today more than 2,000 stupas, shrines, and monasteries still remain from the 6,000 built during the Pagan dynasty, covering an immense area of 10,000 acres (or about 16 square miles) now known as the **Pagan Archeological Zone.** With so many architectural wonders, you can quickly tire of seeing yet another stupa or shrine. Limit yourself to a few of the more famous and better preserved, three of which we detail below. Admission to the Pagan Archeological Zone is US$10. Transport is either by hired car, rented bicycle, or bullock cart. The latter is romantic, but even well padded bones begin to crunch after four hours.

The most famous monument in Pagan is the **Ananda Temple.** Erected in 1091, it was reconstructed after the devastating earthquake in 1979. The shrine represents the endless wisdom of Buddha. The central square has 175-foot sides and rises in terraces to 168 feet. In the center of the cube are four vestibules, each with a standing Buddha 31 feet high. These statues represent the four Buddhas who attained Nirvana prior to Guatama Buddha. Only the images facing north and south are original; the east- and west-facing images are replacements for figures destroyed by fires. The base and the terraces are decorated with a great number of glazed tiles showing scenes from the Jataka, as tales of Guatama Buddha's prior lives are called. In the western sanctum, there are life-size statues of the shrine's founder, Kyannzittha.

Tradition has it that a holy tooth, collar bone, and frontlet relics of the Buddha are enshrined in the **Shwezigon Pagoda.** The chronicles relate that the tooth was presented by the King of Ceylon, and that King Anawrahta placed the bone relic on a jeweled white elephant and, making a solemn vow, said, "Let the white elephant kneel in the place where the holy relic is fated to rest!" It was at Shwezigon that the elephant knelt, and that is where Anawrahta built the pagoda. Anawrahta used this shrine to assimilate the old worship of nats into the new faith of Buddhism. Notice inside the building the murals of nats riding mythical animals, while outside on the terraces are plaques depicting scenes from the Jataka.

The highest shrine in Pagan is the 200-foot-tall **Thatbyinnyut Temple,** built in the mid-12th century and repaired in 1979 after the earthquake. To give some idea of the enormous undertaking of building this temple, note the small shrine to the northeast. Known as the "tally pagoda," it was built with one brick for every 10,000 used in the main shrine and is, in theory, one ten-thousandth its big brother's size.

Dining and Lodging

Dining options in Pagan are limited; the River View is your best bet for dinner. Several hotels are under construction, including one under the auspices of Bangkok's Oriental Hotel, but currently the choice is limited. For now the Kumadara is the top spot.

$$ ✕ **River View.** The tables here are outside, along the banks of the Ayeyarwady, and candles provide the light (it's a bit hard to see what you are eating, but go with the mood and have faith). The Burmese curries and fish dishes are nicely prepared—not as oily as you often find—although service can be slow. ☎ 062/70099. *Reservations essential. No credit cards.*

$$ 🏠 **Kumadara.** Scattered around the small garden behind the main building of this 1996 property are three long structures that house the guest rooms. These accommodations are quite basic, but each has cheerful drapes and bed covers and a small balcony. The bathroom has a good shower, which usually streams hot water. The restaurant—located in the main house with the bar and reception—has quite good food. ✉ *Dawna St., Pyu Saw Hte Quarter, Pagan,* ☎ *062/70080; in Rangoon,* FAX *01/97486. 42 rooms. Restaurant, bar. No credit cards.*

$ 🏠 **Queen Saw Guest House.** This small guest house in the village of New Pagan is owned by very a friendly, if rather shy, Burmese couple. The fan-cooled rooms are clean—choose one with a terrace—and the bathrooms have lukewarm showers. ✉ *Shwe Laung Kyan Sittya, New Pagan, Nyaung U,* ☎ *062/70032. 8 rooms. Breakfast room. No credit cards.*

Mandalay

193 km (120 mi) north of Pagan, 580 km (360 mi) north of Rangoon. Bus routes radiate out of Mandalay, including a long-distance bus to Rangoon that takes about 13 hours. The train between Mandalay and Rangoon takes approximately 14 hours.

In 1857 King Mindon decided to fulfil a sacred prophecy that a great city would be built at the foot of Mandalay Hill on the eastern bank of the Ayeyarwady River. All signs were auspicious for a great capital, and the time seemed right: It was the 2,400th anniversary of the founding of the Buddhist faith. King Mindon designed his new capital as a fortified city in a form of a square, each side of which was ten furlongs (2,200 yards) in length. Following tradition, it is said that the king had 52 people buried alive beneath the four corners of the site to become guardians of the city. More prosaic protection was afforded by a moat, 225 feet wide and 11 feet deep. The battlements were made of brick and mud and rose to a height of 25 feet. Entrance was through 12 gates, three on each side and equidistant from each other. In the center was the king's palace. Four years after the foundations were laid, King Mindon moved his capital and his court, plus 15,000 of his subjects, from Amarapura to Mandalay.

The city's guardians, however, did not do their job: The British attacked the city 25 years later and annexed all of Upper Burma. Mindon's palace, renamed Fort Dufferin, became the British colonial barracks. Later, the Japanese made the palace their command headquarters, which prompted the British to drop bombs on it, and the ensuing fire destroyed a third of the city. For the next 40 years, the grounds and moat became not much more than a garbage dump. It wasn't until 1996 that the moat was cleaned out, largely in an effort to promote tourism and the "Visit Myanmar Year" campaign; the labor was provided by conscripted locals and chained convicts.

Part of the **Royal Palace,** in the center of the city, is also being partially reconstructed in cement at great expense and should offer an idea of what the original looked like. An sense of the aesthetic beauty of the old palace can be gleamed from the scale model, made in 1952, kept in an iron cage to the west of the old palace. The Lion Throne, which consists of several tons of regal regalia, is in the National Museum in Rangoon.

The **Shwe Nandaw Kyaung** (Golden Palace Monastery) was the only palace of King Mindon that escaped bombing in World War II. It had been moved from the fortified city's grounds after King Mindon had inauspiciously died in it. This spectacular building is made of carved teak and mosaics. Inside it is held up by pillars, each a single trunk of teak. The original lacquering and gilding can still be seen on the pillars and walls. ⊠ *62nd St., south of Mandalay Hill and due west of Fort Mandalay.* 🎫 *Admission.* ⊙ *Daily 8–4.*

Near the foot of Mandalay Hill is the **Kyauktawgyi Pagoda,** famous for its huge Buddha statue carved from a single block of marble. Near the Kyauktawgyi Pagoda is the **Kuthodaw Pagoda,** built in 1857. King Mindon wanted to make Mandalay the world center of Buddhism, and built the complex to house the entire Tripitaka, the Buddhist scriptures. These are inscribed on marble slabs and enshrined in 729 miniature pagodas. For this reason, Kuthadaw is often referred to as the world's largest book.

The religious heart of Mandalay is the **Mahamuni Pagoda,** on the south side of town, which houses Mandalay's most venerated image of the Buddha. According to the Burmese, the image is one of only five that were molded to the actual likeness of Guatama Buddha. However, so much gold leaf has been affixed to the statue by the thousands of devotees who pay their respects each day that the shape of the body is now distorted. Only the gleaming, polished face remains untouched. The approach to the shrine is lined with stalls and astrologers' booths. Follow the lines of pilgrims to the small room where the venerated image of Mahamumi sits. Only men are permitted in this room; women must go off to the side and look upon the Buddha from a balcony. Pick up some gold leaf before you enter, and as you walk around the image, apply it to the surface. ⊠ *84th St., 5 km (3mi) south of Fort Mandalay.* 🎫 *Admission.* ⊙ *Daily 8–5.*

Lodging

$$$ 🏨 **Novotel.** This arc-shaped building gets a thumbs down for its Soviet-designed architecture, but the interior has been revamped and it's now one of Burma's better modern hotels. Large, functional guest rooms have modern bathrooms and picture windows that face the hotel's gardens or Mandalay Hill (those at the back have the best view, with

a pagoda or two in the distance). The "superior" rooms are even larger and worth the extra price. The hotel's best feature is a restaurant where the influence of the French management prevails. It's the only place in Mandalay to eat good European food; you may also want to try the Burmese buffet at lunch, where an array of dishes offers a crash course in the nation's cuisine. ✉ *Oo Boke Taw Quarter, Aung Myea Township,* ☎ *02/35638,* 🖷 *02/35639. 215 rooms. 2 restaurants, business services. AE, MC, V.*

Amarapura

19 km (12 mi) south of Mandalay.

Until King Mindon moved his court to Mandalay, Amarapura (the City of Immortals) was the capital of Upper Burma. Not much is left of the old town—a new township has taken its place. Most of important buildings were dismantled and reassembled in Mandalay.

It's worth spending a couple of hours at the **U Bien Bridge.** The two-century-old footbridge, made from teak planks salvaged from yet another former capital, Ava, crosses the Taung Thaman lake. If you make the 1.2 km (¾ mi) hike, your reward will be the charming **Kyauk-tawgyi Pagoda,** with its immense jade Buddha inside. If you are lazy, you can hang around the beginning of the bridge, where Burmese families come for afternoon picnics or eat at one of the several outdoor restaurants.

Ava

22 km (13 mi) southeast of Mandalay.

A few miles downriver from Mandalay stands what remains of Ava, one of the three cities around Mandalay that formerly served as capitals. In 1364, sometime after the fall of Pagan, Ava became the capital and remained the most important town in Upper Burma for the next four centuries. The city was largely demolished by an 1838 earthquake, and what did remain was dismantled and taken to Amarapura. Still discernable are the Namyin Watch Tower and some city walls. Only the **Maha Aungmye Bonzan monastery,** built of brick and stucco, remains intact.

Sagaing

25 km (15 mi) east of Mandalay, across the Ayeyarwady River.

With a dozen monasteries and nunneries and 600 pagodas, Sagaing is regarded as the religious center of Burma. To reach the city, you'll travel across the 2,400-foot Ava Bridge, built by the British in 1934 and still the only bridge to cross the Ayeyarwady. (A new bridge is being built between Rangoon and Mandalay at Pyay.) Sagaing is a township, once the capital of an independent Shan state, and the area around it is known as the Sagaing Hills. On the tops and crests of these hills are the religious centers, some of which have tremendous views overlooking the Ayeyarwady. One of the best views is from **Soon U Ponya Pagoda** on Shin Bin Man Kai hill.

The largest of the pagodas is **Kaungmudaw,** built in 1636 by King Thalun and said to contain a tooth and strands of hair from the Buddha. Its perfectly hemispherical dome rises 150 feet; some government guides claim that it was modeled after the Mahaceti Stupa in Sri Lanka, although the more pragmatic of them suggest it represents the perfect and ample breast of King Thalun's favorite queen. Around the base of the stupa are 812 stone pillars, each of which has a small hollow for an oil lamp. At one time these lights illuminated the huge dome. Also around the base are 120 niches containing the images of nats, animistic spirit guardians. Over the last nine centuries, Buddhist kings and governments have tried to downplay the role of nats, but nat worship is so embedded in Burmese culture that appeasing the nats is still part of everyday life.

The **Hsinmyashin Pagoda,** known as the Elephant Pagoda, is between the town of Sagaing and Kaungmudaw. Twenty-foot-high elephants stand guard at the gates of the temple, built in 1429 to house religious relics brought from Sri Lanka. They fell down on the job in 1985, when they failed to prevent the wrath of an earthquake. Much of the pagoda has since been restored, and it's one of the few where you can enter the relic chamber to see the display of votive tablets and images.

Mingun

13 km (8 mi) north of Mandalay by boat.

A popular day trip out of Mandalay is the hour-long boat ride up the Ayeyarwady to Mingun. Boats leave from Mandalay's Ma Yan Chan jetty from 8 AM on. You can either hire your own boat for about 1,000 kyat or take a public boat for 100 kyat. The hour on the river goes quickly as you pass by fishing communities on the river banks and bamboo rafts floating downriver to destinations as far off as Rangoon.

King Bodawpaya, the predecessor to King Mindon, was rather pleased with himself. He had expanded his kingdom by conquering Arakan. To celebrate, he had 20,000 Arakanese slaves construct what was to be the biggest pagoda in the world, the **Mingun Pagoda.** Out of cash by 1819, the builders abandoned the project, with a long way to go before reaching its projected 500-foot height. Nevertheless, with each of its four sides measuring 450 feet, it was and still is the largest brick-base structure in the world. You can climb the 150 feet to the unfinished top for the views, but its really just the sheer mass of this vanity that's impressive.

As part of his grandiose aspirations, King Bodawpaya commissioned a **bell** for his pagoda. Finished in 1790 and hung on teak uprights, the bell weighted approximately 100 tons. It proved too much for the teak supports, and the 1838 earthquake brought it to the ground. Now, hung on chains and housed in a small shed, it remains the largest uncracked bell in the world. (One larger, flawed bell is in Moscow.) Give the bell a tap and hear its superb resonance.

The most charming structure in Mingun is the **Hsinbyame Pagoda,** built in 1816 by Bagyidaw, King Bodawpaya's grandson, in memory of his wife. He loved her beyond all else and was terribly upset by her death. It's a long way up the covered staircase to the shrine, a climb you should think of as climbing Mount Meru, the center of the earth in Buddhist cosmology. Your earthly reward will be breathtaking views of the village below and the timeless flow of the Ayeyarwady.

Burma A to Z

Arriving and Departing

AIRPORT

The only way into Burma, other than by stepping off the occasional cruise ship or visiting a border town over the Thai frontier, is by plane. **Rangoon Airport** is on the northern edge of town, a 500 kyat ($4) taxi ride from downtown.

CARRIERS

Thai International Airways has two daily flights from Bangkok to Rangoon; round-trip fare is around US$230. Myanma Airways also flies between Bangkok and Rangoon. Malaysia Airways, in partnership with Myanma Airways, offers three flights a week from Kuala Lumpur; a round-trip ticket costs about US$180. A new route between Chiang Mai and Mandalay is operated by Air Mandalay, which makes the flight three times a week; fares are around US$220, round trip.

At press time, there were no nonstop flights to Burma from North America or Britain, although several major airlines (among them British Airways, Lufthansa, and JAL) were in negotiations.

Getting Around

BY BUS OR CAR

Regularly scheduled buses run between Burma's towns and cities. Self-drive rental cars are not available, but you can hire cars with a driver. Travel agencies and tour operators can make the arrangements. The cost is about $40 to $50 a day, depending on the distance covered; the driver will appreciate a gratuity of $5 a day.

Roads are generally paved between the major destinations covered in this chapter. Off the main roads and in the Pagan Historical Area, expect gravel and potholes.

BY PLANE

Myanma Airways and Air Mandalay connect Burma's tourist destinations. There are direct flights from both Mandalay and Rangoon to Pagan and to Heho, the airport nearest Inle Lake, 40 km (24 mi) from Taunggyi and 18 km (11 mi) from Nyaung Shwe.

BY TRAIN

Tickets need to be purchased in advance. There is no first class on the train. Seats recline slightly in second class.

Contacts and Resources

EMERGENCIES

Always use your hotel or tour operator for assistance in the case of medical and police emergencies. Provincial towns have clinics, but major medical emergencies are best attended to in Mandalay or Rangoon. Better yet, get back to Thailand for hospital treatment. In the case of theft, such as of your passport, notify your embassy immediately.

GUIDED TOURS AND TRAVEL AGENCIES

Abercrombie & Kent (⊠ 4th floor, Silom Plaza, 491/29-30 Silom Rd., Bangkok 10500, ☎ 02/266-7660, FAX 02/266-7854) are well set up to arrange custom trips through Burma, or you can arrange trips with them out of their U.S. office, ⊠ *1520 Kensington Rd., Suite 212, Oak Brook, IL 60521,* ☎ *708/954-2944 or 800/323-7308.*

Journeys International (⊠ 4011 Jackson Rd., Ann Arbor, MI 48103, ☎ 313/255-8735 or 800/255-8735) has 8- and 15-day tours as well as group packages for five to 28 people. Unlike many U.S. tour operators they do not use government guides, vehicles, and hotels—a plus in my book.

A very special, albeit expensive, way to visit the sights of Pagan and Mandalay is by taking the river cruise ship, *The Road to Mandalay,* operated and owned by the **Orient-Express Hotels, Trains, & Cruises** (U.S., ☎ 800/5242420; U.K. ☎ 0171/620-0003, FAX 0171/620-1210), the same company that operates the luxury train between Singapore and Bangkok. The ship, originally used on the Rhine, accommodates 138 passengers in 72 cabins. Each cabin has its own en-suite shower and toilet, as well as air-conditioning and personal safe. On board there is a dining room (dress for dinner, please), swimming pool, and bar. The ship makes the day-and-a-half run on the Ayerarwady between Mandalay and Pagan; you sleep on board for the two days that it is berthed in Mandalay and two in Pagan. All sightseeing tours with guides are in the package.

LANGUAGE

The national language, Burmese, uses a non-Roman phonetic alphabet that is exceedingly difficult to comprehend, let alone write. Speaking Burmese is equally difficult, since it is tonal; in that regard it is similar to Thai. However, an amazing number of educated Burmese, particularly those in the travel industry, speak English.

MONEY AND EXPENSES

Currency. Burmese currency comes in kyats (pronounced chi-ats). Notes include the following denominations: five, 10, 15, 20, 45, 50, 90, 10, and 500. (The 45 and 90 banknotes were the inspiration of Ne Win, who considered those numbers to be lucky.)

Exchanging Money. The official rate of exchange is nine kyats to the U.S. dollar, the only western currency in common circulation. However, tourists may use cash or traveler's checks to purchase Foreign Trading Certificates (FTC), on a one-dollar-to-one-FTC basis. These certificates may then be cashed at international hotels for about 105 kyats each. Most international hotels require guests to pay their bills in dollars or FTCs. Airline tickets also must be paid in U.S. dollars or FTCs.

Independent travelers are required to change US$300 into FTCs immediately upon on arrival. Those traveling on pre-paid package tour are exempt from this requirement. (The type of Burmese visa in your passport informs immigration whether you are on a tour or not.)

Then there's the black market (really more of a gray market), where you can get an exchange rate of about 123 kyats to the U.S. dollar. (Other currencies and travelers checks are almost never accepted.) You cannot change kyats back into dollars. Most travelers to Burma change the minimum required amount into FTCs and use the black market to convert dollars into kyats for any remaining needs.

Forms of Payment. Credit cards are rarely accepted, except at international hotels. ATMs are *not* linked to such networks as Cirrus and Plus; it is possible to obtain cash from a bank with a Mastercard or Visa, but the rate of exchange is poor, the commission fees are high, and the paperwork is time consuming.

Taxes. Government tax is 10% on hotels and restaurants. A service charge of 10% is added to the bill in tourist hotels.

What It Will Cost. Burma can be surprisingly expensive. International-style hotels charge $150 and up for a double room, and even budget hotels with not much more than a cot and a shared bathroom charge as much as $30 in Rangoon. Air travel within Burma is expensive for foreigners; fares between Rangoon and Mandalay are approximately $100. However, bus and rail travel is very inexpensive—and uncomfortable. Taxis run about 100 kyats per kilometer. Local beer (Mandalay is the best) is 180 kyats in a local café. At a hotel, an imported beer will cost about $4.

PASSPORTS AND VISAS

All foreign nationals require a visa. Visitors from North America, Britian, Australia, and New Zealand can obtain a 30-day tourist visa within 48 hours from most embassies and consulates. Cost is approximately $10. Contact the **Embassy of the Union of Myanmar** (✉ 2300 S Street NW, Washington, DC 20008, 202/332–9044; ✉ 10 E. 77th St., New York, NY 10021, ☎ 212/535–1310).

TELEPHONES

To call Burma from overseas, dial the country code, 95, and then the area code, omitting the first 0. Telephoning Burma is expensive— about $7 a minute from the U.S.

Telephoning out of Burma is exceeding expensive and time consuming as there are not sufficient international lines available. Many of the international hotels have access to international lines, but, as they warn you, expect to pay through the nose. Burmese citizens must book overseas calls and are limited to five minutes per call.

TIPPING

Tipping is not a wide-spread custom in Burma, but there are times when a gratuity is expected: A bell boy would like 100 kyats to take your luggage to your room, and the driver of your car may expect 500 kyats per day.

VISITOR INFORMATION

If asked, the embassies of the Union of Myanmar (☞ Passports and Visas, *above*) will forward basic tourist information along with your visa application. The Burmese ministry of tourism is an arm of the SLORC and is not set up to assist the traveler.

WHEN TO GO

The cool season is from late November through February, with temperatures ranging from 70°F. to 85°F. The hot season is March and April when the mercury can peak out at 110°F. May to October is the rainy season, often making the upcountry roads impassable for a day or two.

The best festival to experience is Thingyan, or Water Festival, which celebrates the Burmese new year in April. The Burmese become carried away in dousing and being doused with water and for three days the country comes practically to a stand still.

CAMBODIA

As the seat of the Khmer empire from the 9th to the 13th century, Cambodia developed a complex society based first on Hinduism and then Buddhism. After the decline of the Khmers and the ascendency of the Siamese, Cambodia was colonized by the French in the 19th century and become part of Indochina. Shortly after the end of World War II, during which the Japanese had occupied Cambodia, independence became the rallying cry for all of Indochina. Cambodia became a sovereign power with a monarchy and an elected government.

In the early '70s, the destabilizing consequences of the Vietnam War led Cambodia's political factions to take up arms. A very bloody civil war ensued, with the barbaric Khmer Rouge, under the French-educated Pol Pot, emerging as victors. A regime of terror followed. Under a program of Mao Tse Tsung–inspired re-education centered around forced agricultural collectives, hundreds of thousands of Cambodians died through torture and execution or from malnutrition and exhaustion in the camps.

Vietnam, unified now under the Hanoi government, eventually intervened, partially defeated the Khmer Rouge, and brought back Prince Sihanouk as head of state. The United Nations was brought in as a peace-keeping forc, and in 1996 a government was formed though democratic elections. However, the Khmer Rouge still exist as a military force and control the northwestern part of the country. Their presence is a continued threat to the country's stability and has limited foreign investment and the development of tourism.

Great Itinerary

Though four days in **Siem Reap** would give the opportunity for a leisurely appreciation of the Khmer complexes at **Angkor,** most people limit their stay to two days and one night. One day and night in **Phnom Penh** may be enough time to give a brief view of the city, but flight connections may be such to require one night in Phnom Penh on the way to Siem Reap and one night on your return.

Phnom Penh

As the capital of the Kingdom of Cambodia, Phnom Penh is strategically positioned in the center of the country at the confluence of four branches of the Mekong River. Though it was founded in 1434, Phnom Penh is a small city with only a million inhabitants. There are only a few notable sights, whivh you can easily cover in a morning.

According to legend, a wealthy woman named Penh found four statues of the Buddha washed up on the banks of the Mekong, and in 1372 she comissioned a sanctuary to house them in. **Wat Phnom,** Penh's temple, stands on a 90-foot-high knoll that's visible from all parts of the city to which it gave a name—Phnom Penh means "Hill of Pehn."

The **Royal Palace,** now the home to Prince Sihanouk, is a 1913 reconstruction of the one built in 1886. Though the royal palace itself is closed to the public, **Wat Phra Keo** (Temple of the Emerald Buddha), in the southern courtyard of the palace grounds, is open. The temple is often referred to as the Silver Pagoda because of the 5,000 silver blocks (six tons of pure silver) that make up the floor. At the back of the temple is the venerated **Emerald Buddha**—some say it's carved from jade, while others hold that it's Baccarat crystal. Nearby is a 200-pound, solid-gold Buddha studded with 10,000 diamonds. Along the wall of the courtyard enclosing the temple complex are murals depicting scenes from the *Ramayana.* ⊙ *Tue.–Sun. 7–11 and 2–5.*

If the Silver Pagoda is a tribute to Cambodia and its civilization, the **Toul Sleng Holocaust Museum** is a horrific reminder of the what cruelty humans are capable of wreaking on each other. Once a neighborhood school, the building was seized in 1975 by Pol Pot's Khmer Rouge and turned into a prison; during its four years of operation as an interrogation center, some 20,000 Cambodians were tortured here. Fewer than 10 prisoners survived. The bodies of those that died under torture were tossed into the school's garden and playing fields; those that survived the torture went to the extermination camp outside of town called **Choeung Ek,** now known as the Killing Fields. A memorial stupa stands at Choeung Ek, 14 km (9 mi) southwest of Phnom Penh, filled with the skulls of the Cambodians exhumed from the mass graves. ⊙ *Daily 8–11 and 2–5.*

The **National Museum,** a red building constructed in 1917 in the Khmer style, contains the nation's treasure of archeological finds, from the pre-Angkor periods of Funan and Chenia (5th–9th centuries), the Indravarman period (9th–10 centuries), the classical Angkor period (10th–13th centuries), and the post-Angkor period up to the present. ⊙ *Tues.–Sun. 8–11 and 2–5.*

Lodging

Since most of the United Nation's security forces have left Cambodia, accommodation at hotels in Phnom Penh has become easier to find.

The Sofitel-managed **Cambodiana** (✉ 313 Sisowath Quay, ☎ 023/26288, FAX 023/855–26290; U.S. ☎ 800/221–4542) is the best property.

Shopping

While in Phnom Penh, find some time to visit a market or two. The largest is the **Central Market,** an art deco–style structure in the center of the city that sells foodstuffs, household goods, fake antiques, and some silver and gold jewelry; it's most active in the morning. **O Russel Market** has lots of food stalls and small shops selling jewelry. For serious shopping, go to **Tuol Tom Pong Market,** which has real and fake antiques, carved-wood furniture, and small Buddha statues.

Siem Reap

314 km (196 mi) north of Phnom Penh.

Siem Reap, meaning "Siam Defeated," is a small market town that has become a base for visits to the Khmer monuments at Angkor. During the Khmer Rouge era of the late 1970s, Siem Reap was largely destroyed and abandoned. With the Khmer Rouge's retreat into the jungles, hotels have reopened to provide modest accommodation for visitors.

Angkor Temple Complex

★ *8 km (5 mi) north of Siem Reap.*

If Angkor been discovered before the late 19th century, it certainly would have been classified as one of the Seven Wonders of the World. The Khmer Empire reached the zenith of its power, influence, and creativity from the 9th to 13th centuries, and Angkor, the seat of the Khmer kings, was one of the largest capitals in Southeast Asia. In all there are some 300 monuments scattered in all directions through the surrounding jungle. Only the largest and best preserved are mentioned here.

If you are very energetic, only have one day, and want to cover as much as possible, then visit Angkor Thom and its two vast temple complexes, Bayon and Baphuon, in the early morning hours. Visit Ta Prohm, a wonderful 12th-century temple that has receded back into the jungle, by midday, and by midafternoon be at Angkor Wat, which faces west and is best seen and photographed as the sun sinks.

To get around, you need to hire transport and a guide. It's best to link up with a group traveling in a minivan, but you can rent a car and driver in Siem Reap for about $50 a day. Bicycles may be rented, but make sure that you know where you are going and that there are no bands of Khmer Rouge roaming in the vicinity. *Never* stray off the beaten paths—live land mines still dot the area.

Angkor Thom

Angkor Thom was the last great Khmer City before the empire began to fall apart in the 13th century. The **Bayon** is the mystical and focal heart of the former capital, built by King Jayavarman VII (reigned 1181–1200). The central tower has 53 secondary towers, on each of which are four strangely smiling faces of Bhodisattava Avalokitecvara in the likeness of Jayavarman. On the outer walls of the central santuary and on the inner walls of the laterite enclosure are marvelous bas-reliefs—three-quarters of a mile of them in all. On the outer walls, the depictions are of common man pursuing his mundane life; on the inner walls, the gods do legendary deeds.

The **Baphuon** was built in the 12th century, shortly before Bayon, by King Udayadityavarman II (reigned 1050-66). This is a fine example of poor planning: inferior architects erected the monument on a hill without the proper supports. When the earth shifted, the eventual collapse was inevitable. Much of what is there today is collapsed stone forming a chaotic ruin in the form of a pyramid with remarkable stone reliefs. Walk out past the moats and through the southeastern gate and you'll enter the Royal Enclosure. This vast rectangular yard was the epicenter of the Angkor empire. At the northeastern corner is what was perhaps a cremation tower, but is now known as the Terrace of Leper King. The 23-foot-high platform is richly carved with dancing apsaras and mythological animals known to have inhabited the upper slopes of Mt. Meru, the Hindu and Buddhist center of the cosmos. To the north is the Terrace of the Elephants, which was used as a reviewing stand. The walls, measuring 1150 feet long with a height of 10 feet, are sculpted with scenes showing hunting elephants, water buffaloes, and lions.

Ta Prohm

Ta Prohm, between Baphuon and Angkor, has been kept more or less as it was when French explorers rediscovered Angkor at the end of the 19th century. Vines twist through pillars and trees black out the sun. It is here that you can very easily be transported back 800 years to the time when King Jatavarman VII had this structure built to honor his mother. Though you would not know it today, this complex had 566 stone dwellings, 39 major sanctuaries, 18 chief abbots, 2,740 priests, 2,202 assistants, and 615 dancing girls to assist the priests. With all of the sounds of the jungle around you and knotted trees contending for space, you can easily become lost and bewildered. Don't stray away too far!

Angkor Wat

In the typical architectural art of the Khmers, the plan of Angkor Wat is simple and audacious. The five towers dominate the complex, forming a bud of lotus flowers (the emblem of the Cambodian flag). The reliefs of the lower gallery show scenes of daily life and war. The Apsaras, celebrated dancers, surround the monument.

Angkor Wat was founded at the beginning of the 12th century and is the best preserved of the Khmer temples. It was erected by King Suryavarman II (reigned 1112–52) and dedicated to the Hindu god Vishnu. Like all the major monuments at Angkor, the buildings form a complex representing the Hindu (and Buddhist) universe. The central shrines symbolize Mt. Meru, while the gates and cloisters depict the successive outer reaches of cosmic reality. Moats represent the seven oceans that surround Mt. Meru.

Angkor Wat is reached by an impressive avenue lined with balustrades in the form of serpents. The complex itself rises in three concentric enclosures and you must wander around the terraces marveling at the Hindu deities and Buddha images, many of which lost their heads thanks to wanton destruction on the part of the Khmer Rouge. The other amazing collection of images is sculpted on the half-mile-long open colonnaded gallery. This collection tells the Hindu epics and Suryavarman's earthly deeds, both of which are celebrated by dancing apsaras.

Architecture and the fine reliefs symbolize the richness, the power and prosperity of the Khmer empire during this period, but such was the tremendous outlay required to build Angkor Wat that it nearly bankrupted the Empire. It took 30 years to recover and it was King Jayavarman VII who had the energy to revitalize the kingdom. Breaking with the established Hindu gods, he adopted Buddhism.

Banteay Srei

If you have the time, Banteay Srei (Citadel of Women), northeast of Angkor Wat, is a magnificent temple from the 10th century dedicated to Shiva. The fine sculptures of rose-colored sandstone are surprising.

Cambodia A to Z

Arriving and Departing

BY BUS OR CAR

Road travel from Phnom Penh to Ho Chi Minh City, Vietnam, either by hired car or by bus, poses no problem, it is only a matter of time and rough, bumpy travel. The bus fare is certainly cheap—approximately $10. Access to Siem Reap by land from Thailand is not likely to be possible until at least 1998.

BY PLANE

Daily flights on Thai Airways International between Bangkok and Phnom Penh are quite heavily subscribed, so try to book in advance. Bangkok Airways and Royal Cambodian also fly this route.

Getting Around

The road to Siem Reap from Phnom Penh is open, but most travelers find it more comfortable to fly.

Contacts and Resources

EMERGENCIES

For medical and police emergencies, use the services of your hotel. In the case of a lost passport, immediately notify your embassy.

GUIDED TOURS

You can make tour arrangements (round-trip flight from Bangkok, Phnom Penh hotel, day trip to Angkor Wat, and visas) through a travel agency in Bangkok for approximately US$530. Strongly recommended is **Abercrombie & Kent** (⊠ 4th floor, Silom Plaza, 491/29-30 Silom Rd., Bangkok 10500, ☎ 02/266–7660, ⅻAX 02/266–7854).

HEALTH AND SAFETY

About a quarter of a million people enter Cambodia every year, either as tourists or on business. Although travel in parts of Cambodia is not advised—the killings and kidnappings of a number of Western tourists in recent years attest that the Khmer Rouge are not to be taken lightly—neither Phnom Penh nor the Khmer ruins at Angkor are considered particularly dangerous.

LANGUAGE

The Cambodian language is based on the Khmer phonetic alphabet and is tonal. Within the tourist industry, English is spoken and, to a lesser degree, French. Many in Phnom Penh speak some English from their dealings with the U.N. forces. Many of the older Cambodians know some French. If you take a guide around Angkor, which is advisable, be certain to ascertain that he speaks clearly in a language that you understand.

MONEY AND EXPENSES

Currency. The monetary unit in Cambodia is the rial, but dollars are in demand and it is best to take lots of low-denomination bills. Payment in dollars is required by hotels and airlines. At press time, the exchange rate was approximately 2,500 rials to the U.S. dollar.

What It Will Cost. Hotel prices in Phnom Penh are quite high, around $180 a night, for very average accommodation. Western-style restaurants are also fairly expensive for very ordinary fare; expect to pay $20 a head. Local food is inexpensive. With the U.N. presence diminishing, prices are declining and Cambodia should be a less expensive place to visit in 1997.

PASSPORTS AND VISAS

U.S. citizens are required to have a passport and a one-month visa, obtainable from the **Embassy of Cambodia** (✉ 4500 16th Street, NW, Washington, DC 20001, ☎ 202/726–7742). The **Cambodian Permanent Mission to the U.N.** (✉ 866 U.N. Plaza, Room 420, New York, NY 10017, ☎ 212/421–7626) can also issue visas.

Visas are also available at travel agencies in Bangkok for around $90. Allow five days. You can also fly from Bangkok to Phnom Penh and collect a visa when you arrive; although this is not recommended since you could theoretically be denied entry. Nine times out ten there is no problem.

TELEPHONES

To call Cambodia from overseas, dial the country code, 855, and then the area code, omitting the first 0.

Calling overseas is very expensive, and you cannot do it from public telephones. If you have to make a call, either go to main post office or, more conveniently, use your hotel's switchboard.

TIPPING

A bell boy would like a dollar for carrying your luggage. Guides may expect $5 for a day's sightseeing. At tourist hotels, gratuities are included in the cost of meals and accommodation.

VISITOR INFORMATION

A good travel agent is your best bet for assistance with travel in Cambodia.

WHEN TO GO

The dry season runs from November through March, with temperatures ranging between 65°F and 80°F. The monsoon season, with heavy downpours of rain for an hour or two on most days, lasts from April to October. During this season temperatures range from 80°F to 95°F.

LAOS

Of all the peoples in Southeast Asia, Laotians seem the most gentle and peace loving, but this tiny landlocked nation, not much larger than Great Britain, has for centuries been a strategic battleground. Most recently, during the Vietnam War, the U.S. Air Force engaged in a vain attempt to disrupt the Ho Chi Minh Trail and dropped more bomb tonnage on Laos than was dropped on Germany during World War II. Since the end of the Vietnam War, the People's Democratic Party has ruled the country, first on Marxist-Leninist lines and now on the basis of limited pro-market reforms. Overtures are being made to the outside world, particularly to Thailand and China, to assist in developing the country—not an easy task.

Some changes are taking place. Blue jeans, motor cycles, and radios are creeping into the capital, Vientiane, and the road north to Luang Prabang, Laos's ancient capital, has just been paved. New hotels are opening, and the Friendship Bridge over the Mekong from Thailand's northern town of Nong Khai has made Vientiane accessible to trade from the south. Even so, with an average annual income of $170 and a rugged landscape that makes transportation and communications extremely difficult, Laos is likely to remain a sleepy backwater for a while longer.

Great Itinerary

If you limit your visit to the sights of Vientiane and Luang Prabang, a minimum of three days is required: one in Vientiane and two in Luang Prabang.

Vientiane

Vientiane is the quietest Southeast Asian capital. It's modern and small, with none of the imposing sights that you find in Bangkok. Notwithstanding the imports slipped in from Thailand and the occasional burst of pop music coming from newly acquired stereos, Vientiane's pace is as slow as the Mekong, which flows through town.

To immerse yourself in Vientiane, visit the morning **market** (Talat Sao) in the center of town, less than 1,000 yards northeast of the Presidential Palace and the bank of the Mekong.

The one temple worth finding is **Wat Phra Keo,** a name that has good reason for being similar to one in Bangkok's Royal Palace: The original Wat Phra Keo temple was built in 1565 to house the Emerald Buddha taken from the Thais by the Lao; the Buddha was recaptured by the Thai army in 1778 and taken to Bangkok. The present temple dates from 1936 and has become a national museum. On display are Lao wood sculptures and a vast array of Buddhas in different styles, including a Laotian interpretation of the walking Buddha first developed in Thailand's Sukhothai. There are also wonderful images of Khmer deities and a 16th-century door carved with Hindu images. ✆ *Tue.–Sun. 8–11:30 and 2–4:30.*

Luang Prabang

230 km (144 mi) north of Vientiane.

Most visitors to Laos go to the country not to visit the present-day capital of Vientiane but to see the ancient capital of Luang Prabang, a sleepy town of about 21,000 inhabitants that also sits on the banks of the Mekong. It is still, at least unofficially, the historic, religious, and artistic capital. Some 30 temples remain intact, making it a pleasant place to tour on a rented bicycle for a couple of days.

Start your Luang Prabang experience with a visit to the **Royal Palace Museum,** the former palace of the Savang family. (King Savang Vattana and his family were exiled to northern Laos in 1975 and have not been heard from since.) The most prized exhibit is the **Pha Bang,** a gold Buddha standing a few inches under three feet tall and weighing more than 100 pounds. Its history goes back to the first century, when it was cast in Sri Lanka; it was brought to Luang Prabang in 1353 as a gift to King Fa Bang. This event is celebrated as the introduction of Buddhism to Laos, and Fa Bang is venerated as the protector of the faith. Also on display are excellent friezes removed from local temples, Khmer bong drums, elephant tusks with carved images of the Buddha, and a Luang Prabang–style standing Buddha. The eclectic assortment of items also includes, in the Queen's reception room, teacups presented by Mao Tse Tung and medals from Lyndon Johnson. In the king's reception room, the walls are covered with murals painted in the 1930s, depicting scenes of traditional Lao life.

Luang Prabang's most awesome temple is **Wat Xieng Thong.** Constructed in 1559, it is one of the few structures to have survived centuries of marauding Chinese and Thais. Low sweeping roofs overlap to make complex patterns and create a feeling of harmony and peace. There are marvelous interior mosaics, and decorated wooden columns support the ceiling, which is covered with dharma-wheels, suggesting the timelessness of life.

Several small **chapels** at the sides of the main hall contain images of the Buddha; the bronze 16th-century reclining Buddha was displayed in the 1931 Paris Exhibition. On the back wall of this chapel is a mosaic, an unusual creation that commemorates the 2,500th anniversary of Buddha's birth with a depiction of Lao village life. Another chapel, near the compound's east gate, contains the royal family's funeral statuary, including funeral urns and a 40-foot wooden chariot used as a hearse; the peculiarity of this chapel are the walls, which have gilt panels etched with erotic scenes from the *Ramayana*.

Pak Ou Caves

25 km (15 mi) up the Mekong from Luang Prabang.

In high limestone cliffs are two sacred caves stuffed with Buddha statues. The lower cave, **Tham Thing,** is accessible from the river by a stairway and has enough daylight to allow you to find your way around. The stairway continues to the upper cave, **Tham Phum,** for which you will need a flashlight.

It takes about two hours by boat to reach the caves. Along the way you pass small villages, and you will probably stop at **Xang Hai** for refreshment. Be forewarned: the village makes *Lao Lao,* a fermented rice drink of great potency. Try it, but don't try to water it down it with unfiltered water—better a temporarily swimming head than stomach troubles.

Laos A to Z

Arriving and Departing

BY BUS, CAR, OR TAXI

Entry into Laos from Northern Thailand is also permitted by crossing the Friendship bridge at Nong Khai. Buses and taxis wait on the Laotian side to make the run into Vientiane, 12 mi away. However, you will need a visa and at press time these cannot be obtained in Nong Khai.

BY PLANE

Vientiane may be reached by plane from Bangkok on Thai International Airways. There are also three flights a week from Hanoi, Vietnam.

Getting Around

Though an assortment of buses and trucks can take you by road from Vientiane to Luang Prabang, it is a rough ride requiring two days. Most people fly on Air Lao Aviation, which has daily flights that leave Vientiane early in the morning. Cost: approximately $50. River ferries also ply the waters between Vientiane and Luang Prabang. It takes three nights upstream and two nights coming down the Mekong. The fare is about $10 and you must bring your own food. You are also supposed to have a pass, but it is rarely requested.

Contacts and Resources

EMERGENCIES

For medical and police emergencies, use the services of your hotel. In the case of a lost passport, immediately notify your embassy.

GUIDED TOURS

You can make tour arrangements (round-trip flight from Bangkok to Vientiane and Luang Prabang, hotels, guides, and visas) through a travel agency in Bangkok for approximately U.S.$600. Strongly recommended is **Abercrombie & Kent** (⊠ 4th floor, Silom Plaza, 491/29-30

Silom Rd., Bangkok 10500, ☎ 02/266–7660, FAX 02/266–7854; in the U.S, ✉ 1520 Kensington Rd., Suite 212, Oak Brook, IL 60521, ☎ 708/954–2944 or 800/323–7308). **Journeys International** (✉ 4011 Jackson Rd., Ann Arbor, MI 48103, ☎ 313/255–8735 or 800/255–8735) also organizes tours to Laos.

LANGUAGE

In the tourist hotels, staff speak some English. You will also find a smattering of English speakers in the shops and restaurants. A few old-timers know some French. The national language, Lao, is tonal; although a few words are similar to Thai, most are not, and the alphabet differs.

MONEY AND EXPENSES

Currency. The local currency is the kip. It suffers inflationary pressure and continually drops against the dollar. Hence, dollars are preferred and always used to pay hotel and airline bills. The Thai baht is accepted in Vientiane; it's better to use baht than kip, as any excess kip cannot be exchanged back into a hard currency. At press time the exchange rate was 950 kip to the U.S. dollar.

What It Will Cost. Anticipate spending $150 for a double room in a Western-style hotel that has private bathrooms. Dinner with Western food costs $18; in a local restaurant, a meal will cost under $4. A local beer runs $1.50.

PASSPORTS AND VISAS

A passport and visa are required for visits to Laos. Tourist visas are good for 15 days and extendable for another 15; you must provide proof of cholera immunization to receive this visa. Contact the **Embassy of the Lao Peoples' Democratic Republic** (✉ Consular Section, 2222 S. St. NW, Washington, DC 20008, ☎ 202/667–0076) for the most recent entry requirements.

Visas (approximately $90) can also be applied for through a travel agency in Bangkok; allow a week for processing. In Rangoon, you can deal directly with the Laotian embassy and get a visa in about two days for about $20. Many travelers heading for Thailand from Hanoi prefer the cheaper five-day transit visa (which is, in any case, the only type issued from Hanoi), because with it they can fly cheaply from Hanoi to Vientiane and take the new Friendship Bridge across the Mekong to Nong Khai, Thailand—as opposed to paying US$180 for a flight from Hanoi to Bangkok. However, visitors on transit visas are officially not supposed to step foot outside Vientiane.

TELEPHONES

To call Laos from overseas, dial the country code, 856, and then the area code, omitting the first 0. If you have to make an international call from Laos, use your hotel's switchboard.

TIPPING

Give bell boys a dollar. Guides expext $5 for a day's sightseeing. At tourist hotels, gratuities are included in the cost of meals and accommodation.

VISITOR INFORMATION

A good travel agency in Bangkok is your best source of information on Laos.

WHEN TO GO

The dry season is from December through May and is much cooler, even chilly at night, than the rainy season. Sudden downpours occur from June through November.

9 Portraits of Southeast Asia

Southeast Asia at a Glance:
A Chronology

Religion in Southeast Asia

Further Reading

SOUTHEAST ASIA AT A GLANCE: A CHRONOLOGY

20,000 BC   First evidence of human settlement in the Philippines.

6000   Rice cultivation begins in Southeast Asia.

3000   Use of bronze begins in Thailand.

c. AD 150   Coastal Indonesians establish direct trade with South India. Early Malayan rulers adopt Indian Sanskrit.

c. 400   Chinese inscriptions from Province Wellesley (along the coast of Malay Peninsula) indicate presence of Mahayana Buddhism.

638–700s   Empire of Srivijaya emerges on Sumatra and power extends to Malay Peninsula and small archipelagoes to the south; West Java and southwest Borneo are influenced. Eighth-century inscriptions attest to "Old Malay," earliest-known use of national language in Southeast Asia.

c. 775–856   Under Sailendra dynasty the Central Java region prospers; great monuments are built in devotion to Mahayana Buddhism.

1000–1100   Suryavarman I of Angkor conquers area that is now Thailand and Laos. Old Javanese literature flourishes.

1100–1200   Singapore Island becomes prosperous trading center, while Kediri is chief political center in East Java. Khmer temples are built at Lopburi (the region now occupied by Thailand and Laos).

1230   Theravada Buddhist becomes ruler of Ligor (now Malaysia).

1291   Marco Polo arrives in Pasai, in northern Sumatra.

1292–93   Mongols attack Java. Northern Sumatran states adopt Islam.

1293   Majapahit, near present-day town of Modjokerto, is founded as capital of eastern Javanese kingdom.

1350–78   Siamese kingdom of Ayutthaya is founded and shortly thereafter conquers state of Sukhothai.

1364   Nagarajertagama (Old Javanese survey of Indonesian culture) is completed.

1402–1500   Malacca, located along southwestern coast of Malay Peninsula, becomes greatest international trading center in eastern world and is greatest diffusion center of Islam; Islam spreads throughout Sumatra and eastward. Buddhist reforms begin in Burma region.

1431   Brahman political advisors are brought to Ayutthaya (capital of Siam), and king becomes divine monarch; Siamese sack Angkor.

1511   The Portuguese conquer Malacca.

1521   Ferdinand Magellan, on the first voyage to circumnavigate the globe, reaches what is now the Philippines; he is slain in battle by a local chieftain, Lapu-Lapu.

1525–36   Spanish expeditions, under Charles V, claim Philippines.

1596   The Dutch arrive in Indonesia.

1600–1700   Ayutthaya becomes principal port of Far East. The French, under Louis XIV, exchange embassies with Siam; European influence on Southeast Asia increases.

1633 The Dutch blockade Malacca, but do not gain control until 1641, when the Portuguese surrender the city.

1688 Siam enters a period of comparative isolation, not to be broken until the 19th century.

1767 The Burmese destroy Ayutthaya, and Sino-Siamese, Phy Tak Sin, becomes monarch; Siam's capital moves to Thonburi.

1781 The Philippines enter time of prosperity as the state holds monopoly on cultivation, manufacture, and tobacco sales.

1782 The Chakri dynasty is established in Siam.

1795 Great Britain takes over Malacca.

1807 Organized by Herman Willem Daendels (governor general), Indonesian highway is constructed across the length of northern coast of Java.

1811 British troops occupy Java.

1819 Under East India Company, Singapore becomes new British port south of Malacca.

1824 Britain returns Indonesia to the Dutch.

1826–32 Singapore joins with Penang and Malacca (both in present-day Malaysia) to form Straits Settlements; the territory then becomes seat of government.

1834 After years of clandestinely trading sugar, abaca, and other tropical produce with Europe, Manila enters the world trade market.

1839 At outbreak of Opium War, British merchants withdraw from Canton to Hong Kong.

1842 Hong Kong's cession to Britain is confirmed by Treaty of Nanking.

1851 Siam's King Rama IV begins to reestablish previously severed diplomatic relations with Western powers.

1896–1901 The Philippines experience a countrywide revolt led by Katipunan Society; General Emilio Aguinaldo declares the Philippines independent of Spain; instead of independence, sovereignty changes hands and United States takes control. Though Aguinaldo's troops refuse to recognize transfer, United States forces collapse of Filipino resistance.

1907–9 Siam cedes Laos and Cambodia to France, and recognizes British control over Kedan, Kelantan, Perlis, and Trengganu.

1916 The Philippines adopt bicameral legislature.

1922 Singapore chosen as principal base for defense of British interests in Far East.

1932 Western-educated minority stages revolution in Siam, sparking what will be years of change in political power but little change in policy.

1935 Primary education is made compulsory throughout Thailand.

1941–42 Japan occupies most of Southeast Asia (Malaya, the Philippines, Hong Kong, Singapore, Taiwan, Burma, Indochina).

1945–49 Indonesia stages resistance against Dutch and declares independence. Singapore liberated from Japanese by Great Britain. Great Britain regains possession of Hong Kong.

1946 Straits Settlements are disbanded and Singapore becomes separate colony; Malacca and Penang are incorporated into Malaya. Republic of the Philippines becomes independent. U.S. economic assistance to Thailand begins. (More than $2 billion of aid sent between 1950 and 1975.)

1947–57 Thailand enters time of political unrest and flux of government policy until finally, in 1957, a state of national emergency is declared; Field Marshal Phibun is ousted and new elections are held.

1947–66 Indonesia's Communist Party becomes increasingly powerful, with several coup attempts; in 1965, political tension climaxes with coup that leads to more than 100,000 deaths. Sukarno replaced by Suharto (present-day leader), and Indonesia's Communist Party is banned.

1948–60 Federation of Malaya is proclaimed; Malaya enters 12-year state of emergency as Malayan Communist Party begins widespread terrorist campaign and attacks police stations, plantations, communication facilities; thousands murdered, including High Commissioner Sir Henry Gurney in 1951.

1953–57 Ramon Magsaysay elected President of Philippines; defeats Communist insurgents, the Huks.

1954 In hope of presenting a united front to forestall Communist aggression, Southeast Asia Treaty Organization (SEATO) is formed. Singapore's People's Action Party (PAP) is established under leadership of Lee Kuan Yew.

1958–63 Despite dissension among leading politicians, Thailand's economy grows under generals Sarit Thanarat and Thanom Kittikachorn.

1959 Lee Kuan Yew wins general elections (agreed upon by Great Britain in 1957) and becomes Singapore's first prime minister.

1963 Malaysia established, joining together the Federation of Malaya, Singapore, Sabah, and Sarawak. Association of Southeast Asian Nations (ASEAN) is formed.

1963–65 The people of Singapore vote heavily in favor of becoming part of Malaysia; after two years Singapore secedes.

1965 Ferdinand Marcos takes office as president of the Philippines. Singapore leaves the Federation of Malaysia and becomes independent sovereign state.

1972 Martial law, imposed by Philippine president Marcos, stifles dissent but increases armed insurgency. The country prospers for a while but by the 1980s falls into deep recession.

1973–76 Continual student demonstrations, strikes, and political assassinations occur in Thailand.

1974 Unrest erupts in Indonesia when students stage street demonstrations against the visit of Japan's premier.

1977 SEATO is disbanded.

1978 Vietnam invades Cambodia, ousting Pol Pot and Khmer Rouge.

1979 Elections for lower house of bicameral legislature are held in Thailand.

1983 Benigno Aquino, Jr., Philippines' opposition leader, is assassinated when he returns from exile; Marcos's downfall begins.

1984 Great Britain agrees that Hong Kong will revert to China in 1997.

1986 In a bloodless, four-day February Manila uprising known as "People Power," the Marcoses are forced into exile. The popular Corazon Aquino, widow of Benigno Aquino, Jr., wins victory as president, and democratic rule is restored.

1989 Burma changes name to Myanmar.

1990 Powerful earthquake causes major destruction in Philippines.

1991 Military coup d'état in Thailand. Aung San Suu Kyi of Burma is awarded the Nobel Peace Prize.

1992 Thais take to the streets in bloody demonstrations against military junta, forcing the junta out of power and the return of democratic elections.

In the first freely held presidential elections since 1969, Fidel V. Ramos succeeds Corazon Aquino as president of the Philippines.

1994 United States lifts its embargo on Vietnam.

1995 Burma's Aung San Suu Kyi is realsed from house arrest for the first time since 1989. Thailand holds general elections. The U.S. establishes full diplomatic relations with Vietnam.

1996 U.N.-sponsored elections take place in Cambodia. Two activists from the Indonesian island of Timor are awarded the Nobel Peace Prize.

RELIGION IN SOUTHEAST ASIA

LIKE THE SHIFTING PATTERNS in a kaleidoscope, the rituals, ceremonies, prayers, and customs of all the world's major religions meet the eye of a visitor to Southeast Asia. Intrepid tourists will spend many hours "doing temples," and their weary feet will them carry up hundreds of steps and through miles of courtyards. Their cameras will click unceasingly, recording images of Buddha, of Jesus, of Rama, and the pantheon of Hindu and Chinese gods. They will take pictures of mosques with golden domes and of minarets festooned with loudspeakers. At night, if they are in Malaysia or Indonesia, they may turn on the TV and listen to a Koran-reading competition.

A quick glance at the calendar in Singapore demonstrates the impact of multiple faiths on a modern society. The government of multiracial Singapore is basically Chinese. The only holiday when these hardworking people close up shop altogether is the Chinese new year. Nevertheless, the government recognizes holidays sacred to four religions. Important Buddhist, Islamic, and Hindu occasions are public holidays as well.

After all, the fact that it is nearly 2,000 years since the birth of Christ is not particularly meaningful for most Asians. Muslims date the era from the year of Muhammad's hegira in AD 622. The Buddhist year goes back to 563 BC. Christian dating, like the English language, is used for business, banking, and all international transactions. Many Asian calendars are bilingual, with Arabic numerals and Christian dates on one side and Chinese, Buddhist, or Islamic dates on the other. In Thailand, the cornerstones of important buildings usually carry two dates.

The calendar plays an important part in the lives of the people, because elements of astrology (both Hindu and Chinese) are taken into consideration when making important decisions. Statesmen, kings, and peasants refer to astrologers or *bomohs* or *dukuns* for help. The Chinese and Thais, for example, attach great importance to the year of a person's birth within a 12-year cycle, each year represented by an animal.

In most of Asia, time is regarded as cyclical, whereas for most Occidentals it is linear. For people in the Judeo-Christian tradition (and in Islam, which evolved from that tradition), each individual life is an entity—a unit—created at a specific moment in time. Death is considered the termination of the physical life of that individual, while the soul may continue to exist through eternity. The conditions of the afterlife, according to Christian and Muslim belief, depend in large part on the behavior of the individual during his or her earthly sojourn. Christians, according to most dogmas, believe in resurrection, but nowhere do you find any reference to the idea of reincarnation. And here is where the great schism between Eastern and Western thought begins. Hindus and Buddhists assume that life, as well as time, follows a cycle. The soul may endure over the course of many lives. Often the conditions of the new life depend on the behavior of the soul in its previous body. A Christian seeks eternal life through the teaching of Christ. A Buddhist seeks *nirvana*, or eternal nothingness, and follows the teachings of Buddha as set forth in his sermon "Setting in Motion the Wheel of Righteousness."

Buddhism

Buddhism, being a nontheistic religion, is tolerant of other faiths and beliefs. Thus elements of older religions turn up in the practices and customs of Buddhists. The cyclical notion of time and the idea of reincarnation were taken over by Buddhists from older Hindu and Vedic beliefs. Indeed, the Buddha was born a Hindu prince, and much of his teaching was aimed at a reform of the structure and complexities of Hinduism. For example, the Buddha, like another great Indian religious reformer, Gandhi, deplored the Hindu caste system.

The "historical Buddha" (the term "buddha" actually refers to an awakened or enlightened being) was born **Siddhartha Gautama** about 563 BC, near the border of Nepal. A wealthy prince, he lived in luxury, married happily, and had a son. Like many people of his class, he had been protected from viewing the harsher aspects of life. Legend has it that one day he went out from the palace and for the first time saw poverty, sickness, and death. Overwhelmed by these realities, he renounced his worldly position and became a wandering mendicant, seeking the meaning of life. After years of fasting, begging, and traveling, he sat down under a bodhi tree and sank into a deep meditation lasting 49 days. At last he achieved enlightenment, and Siddhartha became a buddha.

The answer he found after his contemplation was that to escape from suffering and misery, human beings must eliminate desire and attachment. In this world, he maintained, evil is caused by desire, which grows from ignorance caused by wrong thought and misdirected action. Thus, in order to achieve nirvana, an individual must extinguish desire by renouncing evil action and atoning for wrongs already done, either in this or in a previous life. Each life an individual passes through is another chance to escape the wheel. If he or she ignores opportunities for thinking and right action, in the next incarnation he or she will have to pay for past mistakes. The **Five Precepts** in Buddhist teaching resemble the Ten Commandments and prescribe guidelines for right living. They are: not to kill, steal, do sexual wrong, lie, or use any intoxicants. Thus, a devout Buddhist should be both a pacifist and a vegetarian.

Forms of Buddhism

As it spread from northern India throughout Asia, Buddhism branched into many schools and sects. The basic divisions are Theravada Buddhism (sometimes called Hinayana, or "Lesser Vehicle"), Mahayana ("Greater Vehicle"), and Tantric Buddhism. **Theraveda Buddhism** is closest to the original Buddhism of Gautama. It emphasizes that each person must seek salvation through enlightenment, attained by prayer, fasting, and the rigorous avoidance of temptation and evil. Theravada is a monastic religion, and people enter religious communities (the *sangha*) for mutual guidance and support.

Myanmar (formerly called Burma) and Thailand are both Buddhist countries where religion forms an integral part of life. In Thailand, for example, it is customary for every young man who can to spend at least three months of his youth as a monk, when he will eat only the food he has received as "merit" offerings by the people early in the morning. The remainder of the day is spent in study, prayer, and meditation. Buddhist monks appear at every official function, whether it be the opening of a village school or the inauguration of a military airfield.

Mahayana Buddhism originated in India but developed most fully in China, Korea, and Japan. The Greater Vehicle is so called because it acknowledges that most people do not have the fortitude to achieve enlightenment on their own. Believers in Mahayana sects such as the Pure Land School call upon the aid of saints to help them to salvation. These saints, called bodhisattvas, are fully enlightened beings who have voluntarily postponed their own entry into nirvana to help others along the way. In Southeast Asia, most Mahayana temples, such as the famous Ayer Hitam Temple in Penang (Malaysia), were founded by Chinese immigrants. These temples are filled with images of Kuan Yin, the Goddess of Mercy, and other bodhisattvas, which have become objects of devotion among the faithful.

Tantric Buddhism is a subsect of Mahayana Buddhism; it in turn has divided into various sects that are found most prominently in Tibet, but also in northern Burma as well as in China and Japan. Tantric Buddhism is also centered on monasteries, and emphasizes secret rituals designed to combat demons and overcome evil.

Hinduism

Hindu belief in reincarnation forms the basis of religious practice and faith. Unlike the Buddhist concept of nirvana, the Hindu notion is one of attained deliverance. Hindu dogma teaches that the soul can be released from the wheel of life only by the observance of dharma—doing one's duty according to one's position in life. The aim of each existence is to perform the dharma of that life so correctly that the soul will be rewarded with a higher station in the next life.

Hindu Deities

The Hindu godhead consists of a holy trinity: Brahma the Creator, Vishnu the Preserver, and Shiva the Destroyer. Each god appears in a number of different forms, or incarnations, and has a consort and many minor deities attached to his worship. Brahma is usually depicted with four heads to indicate his creativity and intellect. Vishnu is usually pictured with four arms, stressing his versatility and strength. His consort is the popular goddess of wealth and fortune, Lakshmi. Shiva is probably the most popular of the three, and the most widely worshiped. As he is the god of both destruction and regeneration, he is thought to be sympathetic to the human condition. In his incarnation as Shiva Nataraja, Lord of the Dance, he dances continuously to keep the world in existence. His consort, who is known by many names and is worshiped in several forms, is a source of comfort and inspiration. Her more familiar names are Kali, Parvati, or Dewi. Shiva has two sons: Ganesha, the elephant-headed god of knowledge and "remover of obstacles," and Subramaniam, god of war. Worship of the deities takes place daily in the home and in the temple on festival days. Thaipusam, which pays homage to Subramaniam, is celebrated widely in Singapore and Kuala Lumpur. The other major Hindu holiday is Deepavali, the autumn festival of lights.

Hinduism in Southeast Asia

Hindu-Brahmanic influence, which can be seen throughout Southeast Asia from Burma to the island of Java in Indonesia, is a relic of historical kingdoms that came under Indian influence in the 6th to 10th centuries. In Thailand some of these Hindu traditions came from the great Khmer kingdom that flourished in the 9th to 12th centuries. (The most spectacular example of the Khmer glories, of course, is the Angkor Wat complex of temples in Cambodia.) Thai royalty retains several court Brahman priests as a holdover from the times when they advised the king on heavenly omens so that he might rule more wisely. In modern times, these priest-astrologers advise only on special matters affecting the royal family and in connection with public ceremonies such as the annual opening of the plowing season, celebrated in Bangkok on the Pramane Ground.

The Hindu influence in Indonesia dates back to the powerful Srivijaya kingdom, which controlled much of Sumatra and the Malay Peninsula in the 10th century. In Java, a succession of empires combined several aspects of Hindu and Buddhist traditions so that in some instances Shiva, the Hindu god of destruction and regeneration, became merged with the Buddha—as can be seen in the temple at Prambanan near Yogyakarta.

The grounds of the Prambanan temple provide the setting for performances of a modern dance-drama based on the *Ramayana* and held during the summer months. One of two great Sanskrit epics (the other being the *Mahabharata*), the *Ramayana* narrates the life and adventures of Rama, an incarnation of Vishnu descended to earth in human form to subdue the demon Ravanna. The *Ramayana* story is narrated in dance, painting, and sculpture throughout Southeast Asia.

Hinduism on Bali

The advent of Islam in the 16th century, and its rapid spread thereafter, extinguished Hinduism in Indonesia except on the island of Bali. Balinese religion, which encompasses all aspects of life from work to play, from birth to death, is a rich mixture of Hindu mythology, animist beliefs, and an underlying awe of nature and God as manifest in the great volcano Gunung Agung. The Balinese, who accept the Hindu concept of Kali Yug—the last of the four great epochs before the end of the world—believe that in such times as these it is imperative to maintain a proper reverence for all the gods and spirits who dwell on the island, for their anger can be very destructive. Many Balinese believe that both the eruption of the volcano in 1963 and the wave of killings during the civil unrest in 1965 occurred because of religious improprieties.

Balinese Hinduism has absorbed so many local island deities as well as mystic practices from Java that it has very little in common with Hinduism as observed by other communities in Southeast Asia.

The two most famous local deities of Balinese Hinduism are the witch Rangda and her adversary, the lionlike beast called Barong. The Barong Kris dance performed daily at Batubulan is a modern, secular version of the very sacred *calonerang* exorcistic dance-drama that is used by the Balinese to protect their villages from evil; calonerang is rarely seen by outsiders, because it is performed at midnight at village crossroads and in graveyards. Both versions depict a struggle between Rangda, the personification of darkness and evil, and the protective Barong; the struggle always ends in a draw, because in the mortal world neither good nor evil can completely triumph.

Islam

Despite its long cultural and historical role, Hinduism is a minority religion in Southeast Asia today. The reason for this was the great Islamic expansion during the 15th and 16th centuries, when part of the Malay Peninsula (including the four southernmost provinces of Thailand), all of the Indonesian archipelago (with the exception of Bali), and the southern islands of what is today the Philippines became Muslim.

Islam, which is monotheistic (believing in one god), exclusive, and highly moralistic, came as quite a contrast to the pantheism of the Hindu and Buddhist religions it replaced. With the advent of Islam, the way of life in these areas changed. Some of the more obvious changes were in the calendar, the status of women, and the role of the state in regulating citizens' behavior.

The Islamic Calendar
The Islamic calendar is divided into 12 lunar months, as is the Chinese, so that all festivals move forward every year. Unlike the Chinese calendar, however, the Muslim lunar calendar does not attempt to make any accommodation to the solar year by adding "leap months" (7 months during the course of every 19 years). Muslim holidays, therefore, move forward 11 days each year, which explains why Muslims do not celebrate a fixed New Year's Day. Coincidentally, this system ensures that the month of fasting, Ramadan, rotates through the seasons and therefore is never confused with local planting or harvest festivities, which hark back to pagan customs and would be considered taboo for orthodox Muslims.

Islam and Women
Islam is often seen in the West as a religion that oppresses women. Muslims, however, contend that men and women are treated differently but equally. In Islam's Arabian homeland, the laws of the Koran regarding women were designed mainly to protect their personal dignity and legal rights. Women were expected to cover their hair (but *not* necessarily to wear a veil; that is a later development that varies widely in the Islamic world according to local custom) and to be modest in their dealings with outsiders. They were also given the legal right to own property, and protection from arbitrary divorce. Muslim men may have up to four wives, if they can afford them and treat them all equally. A man may divorce his wife by saying "I divorce thee" three times, but both law and custom require a waiting period for the divorce to become final, and a woman who has borne a son may not be divorced except for grave, and legally specified, causes.

On the other hand, Islamic law clearly also makes women both separate and inferior. The Koran says: "Men have authority over women because God has made the one superior to the other . . . so good women are obedient." Among some orthodox groups in Southeast Asia, unmarried women are strictly segregated from men in schools and social organizations, and married women are expected to avoid any dealings with men outside their own families. But other groups have adapted Islamic law to local custom; among the Minangkabau of Sumatra and Malaysia, for example, women own most of the property and have a strong voice in community affairs. In other cases, women have received some protection from the strictness of Islamic law through parliamentary women's-rights legislation.

Islam and the State
In Southeast Asia, Malaysia and Brunei are avowedly Islamic nations; Indonesia has no official religion, but the population is overwhelmingly Muslim. Government departments include a bureau of religious affairs. Indonesia's constitution requires that every citizen must profess belief in a single deity. This law is inconvenient for the Chinese and Balinese, who have been forced rather artificially to add a "supreme deity" to their elaborate pantheons. In recent years many Chinese have become Christian to avoid harassment.

The Koran
Islam, like Christianity, is based on a specific holy scripture: the Koran, or Qu'ran, which is a collection of the words of God as revealed to his prophet, Muhammad.

To a devout Muslim the book is the holy of holies, and much time is spent reading and studying it. The book must be treated with reverence, never handled carelessly, and should never be placed beneath any other books. One should never drink or smoke while the Koran is being read aloud, and it should be heard in respectful silence. In many villages children are taught to memorize great numbers of verses, and Koran competitions are annual events.

The Five Pillars of Islam

The Koran and Muslim tradition set forth the Five Pillars of Islam: the Profession of Faith, the Five Daily Prayers, the obligation to fast, the obligation to make the pilgrimage, and the obligation to give alms. The **Profession of Faith** is the familiar doctrine of the Unity of God, which is heard in every mosque and from every minaret: There is no God but God; Muhammad is the messenger of God.

The **Five Daily Prayers** are made at specific times of day: at dawn, at noon, in the afternoon, at sunset, and at night. The Muslim tradition gives specific instructions on how to say prayers: kneeling and bowing in the direction of Mecca (of course, in this part of the world to "face Mecca" means to turn west, not east). Because the Koran demands cleanliness before prayer (preferably a total bath, but if this is not possible then a ritual cleansing of face, hands, and feet), you will see tanks and basins of water outside all mosques.

The third Pillar of Islam is **fasting.** The ninth month of the year, Ramadan, is set aside for ritual fasting. For 30 days all adult Muslims are enjoined against taking any food, drink, or cigarettes from dawn to dusk. During this month, as one would expect, work efficiency tends to drop, because in addition to being hungry and thirsty, many Muslims are also sleepy because they have stayed up much of the night eating. Adherence to the tradition is quite strict, and in some villages special police prowl the streets looking for secret munchers. The Koran does, however, give dispensation to the sick and to those who must take a meal in the course of their work. The end of Ramadan is the great feast, Hari Raya Puasa. After a morning visit to the mosque, the family returns home for a memorable feast that more than makes up for the month of deprivation.

The fourth Pillar is the duty to make a **pilgrimage to Mecca.** Obviously for many Muslims in Southeast Asia this is an expensive and long journey, and therefore the pilgrimage is obligatory only for those who can afford it. Nevertheless, because of the honor and prestige accorded to those who have made the journey and because the pious regard it as a religious duty, every year thousands of men and women, many of them old, board pilgrim ships and planes for the long, arduous journey westward. Those who return are addressed as Haji (or Hijah for women), indicating that they have fulfilled their obligation. The last Pillar is **almsgiving,** similar to the Christian custom of tithing. In Malaysia this money is collected by the Department of Religious Affairs and is used for welfare projects for the poor.

Christianity

Because of its claims to universal validity and the simplicity of its faith, Islam swept through the islands of Southeast Asia up to the Philippines, where it ran head-on into the Spanish Catholic Church. With the establishment of Spanish authority in Manila on June 3, 1571, Islam encountered a nearly impenetrable barrier to further expansion.

The Filipinos often pride themselves on having the only Christian country in Asia, as well as the most westernized. Before the 16th century, the myriad islands that make up the Philippines had never reached the advanced stage of civilization of their western neighbors. The Filipinos accepted the Catholic teaching eagerly for a variety of reasons. In the first place, Catholicism did not have to contend with an organized, established religion because most of the indigenous beliefs involved ancestral spirits and nature gods; they offered neither a systematic theology nor a firm promise of salvation. So for the Filipino, acceptance of the new religion did not involve any deeply traumatic rejection of old ways. In fact, many of the older customs were absorbed into Catholic ritual. The second factor was the language problem. The islands were a hodgepodge of languages and dialects. Catholic schools, which taught Spanish as well as the catechism, gave the Spanish colonial authorities a means of unifying the country both religiously and linguistically. Furthermore, the church offered protection from marauding pirates and outlaw gangs—one of the terms for new Christians was "those who live under the bells."

As you travel through the Philippine countryside, you will come across some huge, stark, very un-Roman-looking cathedrals. These are the churches of an indigenous Christian faith, the Iglesia ni Kristo, which incorporates nationalistic feelings into a Protestant liturgy. It is estimated to have almost a million members.

Elsewhere in Southeast Asia, Christian missionaries, both Catholic and Protestant, followed the colonizing European powers. The lovely churches in Macau, Malacca, and parts of Indonesia and along the coastal regions of Sri Lanka, where nearly all the fisherfolk are Catholic, are remnants of the Portuguese presence.

Missionary work in Southeast Asia did not disappear with the departure of the colonial powers. Indeed, in certain areas proselytizing church groups are now more active than ever. Much current missionary effort is directed toward the tribal peoples living in remote mountains and jungles, where pagan practices still prevail. Though Islam is Malaysia's national religion, the East Malaysian states are predominantly Christian.

Changing Times

Religion no longer plays the role in Southeast Asia that it once did, when personal identity was established by an individual's spiritual tenets. Educational, national, and professional ties have superseded the bonds that rituals in the home and ceremonies in the community once forged. Overcrowding in the cities has pushed people closer together, sometimes with unfortunate results, when vastly different customs clash with one another. The Call to Prayer, when amplified over a loudspeaker, becomes noise pollution to some ears; the clanging cymbals accompanying a Chinese funeral are equally unwelcome to the ears of others.

But just as people in the West have become aware of the value of tradition, so in the East old customs and rituals are undergoing a reassessment, both with regard to their importance for one's cultural identity and the spiritual sustenance they provide. During these transitional times a visitor to Southeast Asia has a unique opportunity to observe and participate in the customs, rituals, and ceremonies of many different religions. Nevertheless, sensitivity and good manners are essential. Do not persist in trying to enter a religious building if the people within ask you not to. Do not intrude on or photograph people at prayer. Remove your shoes when entering a mosque, and wear a waist sash when entering a Balinese temple. Dress modestly, as you would want strangers to dress if they visited your own church or synagogue.

Throughout Southeast Asia, religion has remained a more important feature of day-to-day social activity than it has in most of the West. Although the forms and nature of this religious feeling vary widely within the region, a large proportion of the population is actively involved in it. There is still a strong sense of traditional values, reflected in fundamental social attitudes.

FURTHER READING

Southeast Asia

The Travelers' Guide to Asian Customs and Manners, by Kevin Chambers, advises on how to dine, tip, dress, make friends, do business, bargain, and do just about everything else in Asia, Australia, and New Zealand. *Shopping in Exotic Places,* by Ronald L. Krannich, Jo Reimer, and Carl Rae Krannich, discusses all major shopping districts and tells how to pick a tailor, how to bargain, and how to pack.

For full reservation information with detailed descriptions of lodgings in 16 countries, read Jerome E. Klein's *Best Places to Stay in Asia.*

Video Night in Kathmandu, by Pico Iyer, is a delightful collection of essays on the *Time* correspondent's travels through Southeast Asia.

Three highly recommended works on Southeast Asian history are *Southeast Asia,* 3rd edition, by M. Osborne; *Southeast Asia: A History* by Lea E. Williams; and *In Search of Southeast Asia: A Modern History,* edited by David J. Steinberg.

Southeast Asia was the inspiration for much of Joseph Conrad's work, including the novels *An Outcast of the Islands, Lord Jim, The Shadow-Line, Victory, Almayer's Folly,* and *The Rescue,* and the short stories "Karain," "The Lagoon," "Youth," "The End of the Tether," "Typhoon," "Flak," "The Secret Sharer," and "Freya of the Seven Isles."

Indonesia

Anthology of Modern Indonesian Poetry, edited by B. Raffle, provides insight into Indonesian society. Christopher Koch's *The Year of Living Dangerously* is a historical novel of the chaotic state of Indonesia in 1965. *The Religion of Java,* by Clifford Geertz, is a modern classic that describes the religious and social life of the Javanese.

Malaysia

Denis Walls and Stella Martin's *In Malaysia* is a dramatic novel set in Malaysia. Somerset Maugham's *Ah King and Other Stories* and *The Casuarina Tree* are two volumes of short stories that capture the essence of colonial life in Malaya.

Philippines

In Our Image, by S. Karnow, and *The Philippines,* by Onofre D. Corpuz, are good standard texts on the history of the nation. An excellent book dealing with the 1986 People Power revolution is *Endgame,* by Ninotchka Rosca, while José Ma. Sison's *The Philippine Revolution* places the People Power phenomenon in the context of earlier history. *Waltzing with a Dictator,* by R. Bonner, is an in-depth study of the relationship between the United States and the Philippines. Also try Bryan Johnson's *The Four Days of Courage: The Untold Story of the People Who Brought Marcos Down.* D. Schirmer's *Philippine Reader* is a good collection of left-wing essays. *Playing with Water: Love and Passion on a Philippine Island,* by James Hamilton Patterson, is a fascinating account of a year's stay on a small island.

Singapore

Maurice Collis's *Raffles* is a rich biographical account of the founder of Singapore. *Singapore Malay Society,* by T. Li, is a solid historical reference. *Saint Jack* is a novel by Paul Theroux set in Singapore.

Thailand

Monsoon Country is a contemporary novel by Pira Sudham, who portrays life in the northeast of Thailand. For insights into Thai culture and everyday life, read Denis Segaller's *Thai Ways* and *More Thai Ways.* For a humorous account of an expatriate's life in Thailand in the 1950s, read *Mai Pen Rai,* by Carol Iollinger. An excellent account of life in northern Thailand is provided by Gordon Young in *The Hill Tribes of Northern Thailand.*

VOCABULARY

To properly experience the culture of a foreign country, one must feast on its cuisine, learn the history of its monuments, and speak its native tongue. Southeast Asian languages, like its history, are as diverse as its people and customs.

To simplify communications, Fodor's has compiled a vocabulary chart of six languages you may encounter throughout your travels in the region. This easy-reference listing includes important words and significant phrases in English, Cantonese, Malay (which is usually similar to Indonesian), Mandarin, Tagalog, and Thai. Use the phonetical chart to assist you in getting around, asking directions, and dining out.

	English	Cantonese	Malay
Basics			
	Yes/No	hai/mm'hai	ya/**tee'** -dak
	Please	m'goy	**see**-la/**min**-ta
	Thank you (very much).	doy-jeh/fehseng doh jeh	**tree**-ma **ka**-say (**ban**-yak)
	You're welcome.	foon ying	**sa**-ma **sa**-ma
	Excuse me.	dai'm jee	ma-fkan sa-ya
	Hello	wa´	apa khabar or "hello"
	Goodbye	joy geen	se-**la**-mat **ja**lan/ se-**la**-mat **ting**-gal
Numbers			
	One	yaht	sa-too
	Two	eee	doo-a
	Three	som	tee-ga
	Four	say	em-pat
	Five	m'	lee-ma
	Six	look	e-nam
	Seven	chut	tu-juh
	Eight	baht	la-pan
	Nine	gou	sem-bee-lan
	Ten	sup	se-pu-luh
Days and Time			
	Today	gäm-yät	**ha**-ree ee-nee
	Tomorrow	ting-yat	**ay**-sok (also **bay**-sok)
	Yesterday	chum-yät	kel-**mar**-in
	Morning	joo-joh	**pa**-gee
	Afternoon	ahn-joh	**pe**-tang
	Night	man-hak	**ma**-lam
	Monday	lye bye **yaht**	**ha**-ree **iss**-nin
	Tuesday	lye bye **ee**	**ha**-ree se-**la**-sa
	Wednesday	lye bye **som**	**ha**-ree **ra**-boo
	Thursday	lye bye **say**	**ha**-ree **ka**-mees
	Friday	lye bye m	**ha**-ree **ju**-ma-at
	Saturday	lye bye **look**	**ha**-ree **sab**-too
	Sunday	lye bye **yaht'**	**ha**-ree **a**-had (also **ha**-ree **ming**-gu)

Mandarin	Tagalog	Thai	English
shee/pu shee	oh-oh/hin-deé	khrap/mai khrap (M)/kha/mai kha(F)	Yes/No
ching	pah-keé	dai prōd	Please
sy-eh sy-eh nee	(mah-rah́-ming) sah-lah-maht	khob khun khrap	Thank you (very much).
boo sy-eh	wah-lahńg ah-noo-mahń	mai pen rai	You're welcome.
too-eh pu-shee	pah-oó-manh-hiń po	kaw-tōd	Excuse me.
way	kuh-moos-tah́/heh-ló	sa-wat dee khrap (M)/sa-wat dee kha (F)	Hello
tsay jen	pah-ah-lam nah pó	sa-wat dee khrap (M)/sa-wat dee kha (F)	Goodbye
ee	ee-sah́	nung	One
err	dah-lah-wah́	song	Two
san	taht-loh́	sam	Three
soo	ah́-paht	see	Four
woo	lee-mah	hah	Five
lee-oo	ah́-neem	hōk	Six
chee	pee-toh́	jet	Seven
bah	wah-ló	paat	Eight
joo	see-yahm´	kaw	Nine
shur	sahm-poó	sip	Ten
chin tien	nga-yohń	wun nee	Today
ming tien	boó-kahss	proong nee	Tomorrow
tso tien	kah-há-pon	moo-ah-wan-nee	Yesterday
shang wu	oo-mah́-gah	toan-chao	Morning
sha wu	hah́-pon	toan-klang-wun	Afternoon
wan shang	gah-beh́	toan-klang-koon	Night
lee-pa-ee	loó-ness	wun-chan	Monday
lee-pa-ayr	mahr-tesś	wun-ung-khan	Tuesday
lee-pa-san	moo-yehŕ-koh-less	wun-poot	Wednesday
lee-pa-soo	hoo-whé-bess	wun-pru-roo-hud	Thursday
lee-pa-wu	bee-yehŕ-ness	wun-sook	Friday
lee-pa-ee-oo	sah́-bah-doh	wun-sao	Saturday
lee-pa-tien	leeng-goh́	wun-ar-teet	Sunday

English	Cantonese	Malay

Useful Phrases

English	Cantonese	Malay
Do you speak English?	nay gäng m' gäng ying män	**ta**-hoo-kah ber-ba-**ha**-sa **Ing**-gris?
I don't speak . . .	ah m' woiy gäng gäng doong wah.	**sa**-ya **tee**-dak ber-**cha**-kap ba-**ha**-sa
I don't understand.	äh m' sic	**sa**-ya **tee**-dak **fa**-ham
I don't know.	äh m' jee	**sa**-ya **tee**-dak **ta**-hoo
I am American/British.	ä hay may gäc yan/ying gäk yan	**sa**-ya **o**-rang Amerika/**Ing**-gris
I am sick.	ä beng **jah**	**sa**-ya **sa**-kit
Please call a doctor.	m goy nay gew yee sung	**see**-la ta-**lee**-pon **dok**-ter
Have you any rooms?	nay yaw mohfäng	**bi**-lik **a**-da
How much does it cost?	gay′ däh chien	**har**-ga-nya ber-**a**-pa
Too expensive	gai′ gway	ter-**la**-loo **ma**-hal
It's beautiful.	hoh leng	**chan**-tik
Help!	bong jô	**to**-long
Stop!	ting jee	ber-**hen**-ti

Getting Around

English	Cantonese	Malay
How do I get to . . .	deem yerng huy . . .	ba-gai-ma-ner boh-lee per-gee-ku . . .
. . . the train station?	fäw ché jäm	**stay**-shen **kray**-ta a-pee dee **ma**-na
. . . the post office?	yaw jing gook	pe-**ja**-bat pos dee **ma**-na
. . . the tourist office?	le hang se′	ja-bat-ban pe-**lan**-chong des **ma**-na
. . . the hospital?	yee′ yuen	**roo**-mah **sa**-kit dee **ma**-na
Does this bus go to . . . ?	ga ba se′ huy m huy . . .	a-da-kah bas ee-nee per-gee ke . . .
Where is the W.C.?	say soh gahn herng been doh	**tan**-das **a**-da dee **ma**-na
Left	jäh	**kee**-ree
Right	yäw	**ka**-nan
Straight ahead	chiem mein	troos

Mandarin	Tagalog	Thai	English
nee fweh sho yung yoo má	mah-roo-nohng hoh kay-yohng mahg-Ing-glehs?	khun pood pas-sa ung-grid dai-mai	Do you speak English?
wo pu fweh sho (thai kway yoo)	hin-deé a-koh mah-roo-nohng mahg-tah-gah-lohg	phom mai pood (Thai)	I don't speak . . .
wo pu lee-oo chee-ay	hin-deé koh nah-ee-een-tin-deé-hahn	phom mai kao chai	I don't understand.
wo pu tung	hin-deé koh ah-lahm	phom mai rue	I don't know.
wo sher may kwo jen/ing kwo jen	ah-ko ay Ah-meh-ree-kah-noh/Ing-glehs	phom pen (American/ ung-grid)	I am American/British.
wo sheng ping ler	ah-ko ay may sah-kit	phom mai sa-bai	I am sick.
ching chow ee sung lin	pah-kee-tah-wahg ang dook-tohr	dai-prod re-ak moa mai	Please call a doctor.
nee hay yoo fwang chien ma	may-roh-ohn kah-yong mang-ah kuh-wahr-toh	khun-mee hong-mai	Have you any rooms?
to shaw chien	mahg-kah-noh?	ra-ka tao rye	How much does it cost?
tao kwa la	mah-hal mah-shah-doh	pa-eng goo-pai	Too expensive
chen pee-ow lee-ang	mah-gahn-dah	soo-ay ma	It's beautiful.
choo-ming	sahk-loh-loh	choo-ay doo-ay	Help!
ting	hin-toh	yoot	Stop!
wo tsen yang tao . . .	pah-pah-no pah-poon-tah sah . . .	phom ja pai . . . dai yang-rye	How do I get to . . .
. . . fwa chu chan	ee-stah-syon nahng tren	sa-tai-nee rod-fai	. . . the train station?
. . . yu choo	post oh-pis/tahn-gah-pahn nahng koh-reo	pai-sa-nee	. . . the post office?
. . . kuan kuang choo	oh-pee-see-nah nahng too-ris-moh	sam-nak-ngan tóng-tee-oh	the tourist office?
. . . ee-yuen	oh-spee-tal	rung-pa-ya-bal	. . . the hospital?
chu pu pa shur tao . . . ma	poo-moo-poon-tah bah ee-tohngboos sah . . .	rod-mai-nee pai-nai . . . chai mai	Does this bus go to . . . ?
chaw soo tsai na lee	sah-ahn ahng bahn-noih	hong-nam yoo tee-nai	Where is the W.C.?
tso	kah-lee-wah	sai	Left
yoo	kah-nahn	kuah	Right
ching sung chien tson	dee-reh-tsoh	trong-pai	Straight ahead

INDEX